RxPrep®

THE REVIEW PROGRAM TRUSTED BY TOP EMPLOYERS AND SCHOOLS

NOT SURE HOW TO LEARN IT ALL?

The RxPrep Videos Match to Each Chapter in this Course Book.

Calculations simply done, step-by-step. Common (tested) devices are demonstrated. Watch and learn as a compounding pharmacist explains each step. Includes all the drug knowledge needed. Matched to the new NAPLEX competencies.

The RxPrep Test Bank Assessments

The test assessment sections match to the chapters in ... ponding video. The questions cover must-know basic competer ... ld be known prior to testing. Find out what you know and what you ... e the exam. Watch videos and take test assessments on your phone or tablet, ... tra cost.

Available at www.rxprep.com

RXPREP COURSE BOOK

2017 EDITION

KAREN SHAPIRO, PHARMD, BCPS

STEPHANIE D. GARRETT, PHARMD, BCPS

With JENNIFER S. SCHMITZ, PHARMD, BCPS

CONTRIBUTORS

JENNIFER BEAN
PHARMD, BCPS, BCPP

PAUL BERINGER
PHARMD, BCPS, FASHP

HEATHER R. BREAM-ROUWENHORST
PHARMD, BCPS

JEANNINE CONWAY
PHARMD, BCPS

GEORGE DEMAAGD
PHARMD, BCPS

PAULINA DEMING
PHARMD

CATRINA DERDERIAN
BS, PHARMD, BCACP

ANN SNYDER FRANKLIN
PHARMD, MED, BCPS

JEFFREY FUDIN
BS, PHARMD, DAAPM, FCCP, FASHP

MUOI GI
PHARMD, BCPS, BCOP

TAYLOR K. GILL
PHARMD, BCPS, AAHIVP

JEFF GOAD
PHARMD, MPH, FAPHA, FCSHP, FCPHA

SUSAN E. GORMAN
PHARMD, MS, DABAT, FAACT

MEGAN HEIM
PHARMD, BCACP, TTS

DARREN HEIN
PHARMD

JAN D. HIRSCH
BSPHARM, PHD

DARREL W. HUGHES
PHARMD, BCPS

KIM M. JONES
PHARMD, BCPS

JEFF LEE
PHARMD, FCCP

JOEL C. MARRS
PHARMD, FCCP, FASHP, FNLA, BCPS-AQ CARDIOLOGY, BCACP, CLS

BETH A. MARTIN
PHD, MS, RPH

EMI MINEJIMA
PHARMD

CYNTHIA L. MORRIS-KUKOSKI
PHARMD, DABAT, FAACT

BETHANY L. MURPHY
PHARMD, BCACP, BC-ADM

TIEN M. H. NG
PHARMD, FHFSA, FCCP, BCPS (AQ-CARDIOLOGY)

SUZANNE PARKER
PHARMD

ELIZABETH POGGE
PHARMD, MPH, BCPS, FASCP

DOREEN PON
PHARMD, BCOP, BCPS

ALLISON PROVINE
PHARMD, BCPS, BCPPS

SALLY RAFIE
PHARMD, BCPS

MARY SOLIMAN
PHARMD, BCPPS, CPH

CHRISTINE TRAHMS
BA, MS

PAMELA TU
PHARMD

ANGIE VEVERKA
PHARMD, BCPS

ROBIN WACKERNAH
PHARMD, BCPP

D. RAYMOND WEBER
PHARMD, BSPHARM, BCOP, BCPS, RPH

ANNIE WONG-BERINGER
PHARMD, FCCP, FIDSA

© 2017 RXPREP, Inc.

All rights reserved. Material contained in this book cannot be distributed or reproduced without permission.

The authors in good faith have made every attempt to ensure that the information included in this book is accurate and up to date. However, the content is intended for instructional purposes only, therefore the authors make no guarantees, offer no warranties or representations, nor accept any liabilities with respect to the accuracy of the content contained within.

The RxPrep test bank assessments and video lectures for NAPLEX, and the MPJE and CPJE law review courses can be found on the RxPrep website at www.rxprep.com. Click on "Products".

Book production and cover design by midnightbookfactory.com

TABLE OF CONTENTS

EXAM OVERVIEW

INTRODUCTION

This section includes four topics:

- NAPLEX® Overview
- Format of the Exam
- How to Use this Book
- CPJE Pointers for CA Exam Takers

NAPLEX® OVERVIEW

The NAPLEX® Competency Statements are available on the National Association of Boards of Pharmacy (NABP) website at www.nabp.net. These provide a blueprint (or outline) of topics that are tested. The Competency Statements last changed in November of 2015. These are the Competency Statements currently being tested. Please visit the NABP website to stay up-to-date on the exam and any upcoming changes.

The exam is made up of two sections:

Area #1: Ensure Safe and Effective Pharmacotherapy and Health Outcomes (67% of the exam)

- This section includes drug mechanism of action, indications, side effects, contraindications and drug interactions. Trade/generics are tested, along with common dosage forms.
- Questions are largely asked in a patient-case format. It will be important to quickly identify pertinent information from the case (e.g., abnormal labs, past medical history, medication use history, etc.) and recognize appropriate or inappropriate treatments. Refer to the following chapters: Lab Values & Drug Monitoring and Patient Charts and Assessment & Healthcare Provider Education.
- The ability to monitor patient outcomes is assessed. This includes the patient's response to treatment and safety/efficacy of the chosen treatment. Improving medication adherence, recommending better treatment options and providing information to patients and healthcare providers are tested as well.
- Pharmacoeconomic factors may be important: if a patient cannot afford a drug and a less-expensive, but valid option is available, the pharmacist should recommend the preferable drug. It will be important to be able to read study summaries and interpret the data. Refer to the Biostatistics & Pharmacoeconomics chapter.
- Be able to apply pharmacokinetic and pharmacogenomic parameters to individualize drug treatment. Refer to the following chapters: Pharmacokinetics and Pharmacogenomics.

- Be familiar with drug reference sources, how to administer and counsel on emergency care and vaccinations, and be able to make recommendations regarding common dietary supplements.
- Review self-care products and self-monitoring of health status by the patient.
- Medication safety concepts are tested in this section including quality improvement, evaluation of medication errors and the role of automated systems/technology. Refer to the Medication Safety & Quality Improvement chapter.

Area #2: Safe and Accurate Preparation, Compounding, Dispensing, and Administration of Medications and Provision of Health Care Products (33% of the exam)

- This section includes calculations. It covers nutritional requirements and basic PN calculations. Flow rates for drugs administered by IV infusion are essential, along with drug concentrations, and the other general calculations in the section. Many of the math problems will require identifying necessary information from a patient case (dose, patient weight, IV flow rate, etc.) in order to perform the calculation. A math mistake in pharmacy is a dosing mistake. Accuracy in calculations is an important skill to demonstrate on the exam. Calculations are included throughout the RxPrep Course Book, but specifically in the following chapters: Calculations, Pharmacokinetics and Biostatistics & Pharmacoeconomics.
- Techniques, procedures and equipment for sterile and nonsterile compounding are assessed. Refer to the Sterile and Nonsterile Compounding chapters.
- Be familiar with storage, packaging, handling and medication disposal.
- Instructions and techniques for medication administration are tested in this section.

FORMAT OF THE EXAM

NAPLEX® is a fixed-form exam consisting of 250 questions. Of these, 200 questions are used to calculate the score. The other 50 questions are pre-test questions that are being evaluated for inclusion on future exams. Pre-test questions are interspersed throughout the exam, so it will be impossible to identify which questions they are. The total test time is 6 hours. The computer screen will display a prompt for an optional 10-minute break. Any other necessary breaks will be subtracted from the total testing time.

- There are 5 question types on NAPLEX®. Each of the 5 types are represented in the RxPrep Test Bank:
    - Multiple-Choice: Select the one correct answer.
    - Multiple-Response: Select all of the correct responses and no incorrect response(s) for credit.
    - Constructed-Response: Enter the answer using the computer keyboard (usually for math problems).
    - Ordered-Response: Put the items in a specified order.
    - Hot Spot: Select the correct area on a diagram or picture by clicking on it.
- The majority of the questions (including calculations) are asked in a scenario-based format (such as patient profiles with accompanying questions). There are also stand alone questions.
- All questions must be answered in the order in which they are presented. It is not possible to skip questions, or to go back at a later time.
- Personal calculators may not be used during the exam. The Pearson VUE testing center console uses an on-screen calculator which looks similar to the Texas Instruments TI-30XS Multiview and other similar hand-held calculators. The on-screen calculator can be opened in a pop-up window during the exam at any time (a similar on-screen calculator is available in the RxPrep Test Bank for practice). A candidate requesting a handheld calculator will be supplied a five function calculator by Pearson VUE. Some of the calculations may require advanced functions only available on the on-screen calculator. Refer to the Calculations chapters for math tips.

- On the day of the exam, arrive at least 30 minutes prior to your appointment to get signed in (fingerprints will be taken, you will need 2 forms of ID, and do not bring prohibited items into the exam room). Acceptable forms of ID and the list of prohibited items is in the exam registration booklet.
- If you arrive 30 minutes or later than your scheduled appointment, and are refused admission to sit for the exam, you will be required to forfeit your appointment.

HOW TO USE THE RXPREP MATERIALS

This book is designed as a companion to our live or online courses and test bank. You can review these options on our website at www.rxprep.com. Select the online course without the text if you have the current version; this reduces the course cost by the price of the text and prevents another text from being sent.

- RxPrep's Roadmap to Passing begins with the free assessment tests at www.rxprep.com. These are online assessment tests that cover basic math and basic drug information. Your scores on the assessment tests will direct you to start the NAPLEX exam preparation or focus on remediation preparation to "brush up" on the basics first.
- Once you have passed the basic assessment tests, follow the study method in the free YouTube video "RxPrep's High Score Pass on the NAPLEX".
- This course book is complete; you do not need to have a myriad of additional resources. If you are testing through most of 2017, this book is sufficient. However, if testing towards the latter part of the year, you should check for key updates. We often post these as they come along on our website. Only reputable resources should be used for NAPLEX preparation.
- If a drug is bolded it is a MUST KNOW drug and if information is underlined it is essential.
  - Not all essential information is designated. You can be tested on drugs that are not top sellers, but have important safety considerations. Hospital drugs that are essential are noted in the text. Use the top seller list in the Appendix as a guide to must-know drugs.
- Study Tip and Key Drug boxes (at right) highlight must know information and methods to approach complex concepts.

STUDY TIP

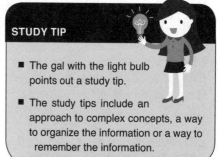

- The gal with the light bulb points out a study tip.
- The study tips include an approach to complex concepts, a way to organize the information or a way to remember the information.

- At the end of many of the core chapters are patient cases with practice questions. These are designed to be somewhat similar to cases you might see on the exam – either in a written format, or the profile you might see on a pharmacy computer. The cases are designed to review key drug points and should not be missed. They do not overlap with the test bank questions.

KEY DRUGS

KEY DRUGS

These are the MUST KNOW drugs for testing purposes

The guy with the key points out key drugs.

This part of the box includes a list of drugs that cause something (like hypoglycemia or hypertension)

- The questions in the RxPrep test banks match to the chapters in this text. The questions are designed to test the most basic drug competency knowledge. The knowledge in these questions, including calculations, should be at 100%. If you get something wrong do not skip it! Follow the study method outlined on the YouTube video "RxPrep's High Score Pass on NAPLEX". Adult learners do not learn well passively, by sitting in front of a text or computer screen; this video includes our best experience on how an adult learner can learn all this information, The exam is not complex; rather, there is much information to pack inside your brain, and the math must be done with good speed and accuracy.
- Take RxPrep's NAPLEX-Style assessment exam (available with test bank access) to know when you are ready to do well.

STUDY TIPS

- Be sure to review the Lab Values & Drug Monitoring and Patient Charts, Assessment and Healthcare Provider Communication chapters which discuss how to interpret charts (medical records); this is required in order to answer case-based questions. Common case formats are included in this course book at the end of most of the clinical chapters. Interpreting medical records requires an understanding of lab values (what the value is used for and the interpretation of common measurements).
- It is advisable to start with the beginning chapters in this course book, which represent the "foundation" material. Math should be done at the beginning of study and repeated (over and over) throughout the study period. Other foundation topics (such as drug interactions) will help make the clinical chapters easier to manage. For example, if you are familiar with the big inducers or big inhibitors you will have familiarity when reviewing them in the specific topic chapters in which they are used. It will make the process go smoother if the study is done in a logical fashion.
- Counseling is critical; pharmacists must make sure that patients can use drugs safely. In this text, counseling for key drugs is presented after the drug tables in each chapter. It is essential to be able to counsel on formulations that come in novel delivery vehicles, such as dry powder inhalers, self-injectables, patches and other formulations. These are each demonstrated in the online course videos, and are tested in the correlating test bank section. Counseling on healthy-living and disease-monitoring is also important when "lifestyle" plays an important role (e.g., diabetes, heart failure).
- Pharmacoeconomics (with the necessary biostatistics equations) is a required competency; this area, similar to calculations, must be known well prior to sitting for licensure. Pharmacokinetic calculations must be known. The calculations in this area can be mastered through repetition; you must do the math repeatedly until you can do the math in all the sections with decent speed, and with accuracy. If you cannot manage to make this happen, please consider getting help with the RxPrep Online Course. The instructors explain each calculation in the simplest manner, step by step. The course also includes our assistance, as-needed.
- Dosing? What is important to know? Trade/generics? Use the underlining (for key information) and bolding (for key drugs) that is present throughout this text as our "best guess" on material that should be known prior to testing. Use your own judgement as well. When we decide, for example, that a dose is important, it is because our team here agrees that the drug is used commonly or is particularly toxic, and an unsafe dosing level would be dangerous. For example, if a patient begins a dopamine agonist at too high a dose the patient could get hurt, or could cause harm to others. Dopamine agonists cause excessive sedation, with onset that can be sudden. They must be started low and titrated carefully.

CPJE POINTERS – FOR CA EXAM TAKERS

This text includes the topics that overlap with the CPJE (Medication Safety, ID, Immunizations, HIV, others). The clinical topics not covered on the NAPLEX that are tested on the CPJE are included in the separate CPJE course (therapeutic interchange, formulary, others). The California law is covered completely. The CPJE course is available at www.rxprep.com. We recommend, in addition, reading through Fred Weissman's book on California community law; this is a standard resource in California for community pharmacy law.

Best wishes for your exam preparation.

CALCULATIONS I

BASICS FOR NAPLEX MATH SUCCESS

BASICS FOR NAPLEX MATH SUCCESS

When the basic techniques and conversions in this section are mastered, proceed to Calculations II.

Formulas and Math Calculations

Math calculations and important formulas in the RxPrep Course Book are shown in two types of shaded boxes with different fonts for easy identification:

Math Calculation

$$\frac{0.5\text{ mg}}{2\text{ mL}} = \frac{0.2\text{ mg}}{X\text{ mL}} \qquad X = 0.8\text{ mL}$$

Formula

$$\text{mmols} = \frac{\text{mg}}{\text{MW}}$$

MATH IS READY FOR NAPLEX WHEN:

- The formula(s) can be quickly recalled in response to a problem ("automatic recall") [exclude the Basal Energy Expenditure (BEE) and Body-Surface Area (BSA) calculations, which may be provided].
- Math mistakes have become a thing of the past.

Make a score sheet like this. Keep going until the math is flawless. Math mistakes cause a cliff-dive in the exam score—a math mistake in pharmacy means the patient got the wrong dose.

Track Your Scores	
Calculations #1	48, 78, 96, 100 Yeah!
Calculations #2	55, 82, 92, 100 Yeah!
Calculations #3	60, 77 keep going...
Calculations #4	66, 74 keep going...
Biostats math	48, 59 keep going...
PK math	76 keep going...

Rounding Numbers

The majority of problems that require rounding will specify to round to the nearest whole number. It may be necessary to round differently, such as rounding to the nearest tenth, or to the nearest ten milligrams.

- 37.3333333 rounded to the nearest whole number is 37.
- 0.45 rounded to the nearest tenth is 0.5. This is the same as rounding to the nearest one decimal place.
- 458.68 mg rounded to the nearest 10 mg is 460 mg.

ROUNDING

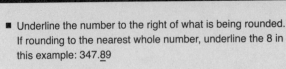

- Underline the number to the right of what is being rounded. If rounding to the nearest whole number, underline the 8 in this example: 347.89
- Look at the number that is underlined and apply one of these rules:
  - If the underlined number is 5, 6, 7, 8, or 9, round up.
  - If the underlined number is 0, 1, 2, 3, or 4, round down.
- 347.89 rounded to the nearest whole number is 348

Never round until the last step in the calculation.

In the Calculations II chapter, some intermediate steps (that do not affect the final answer) may have been rounded for simplicity and space. The exam may also provide approximations without stating to do so; for example, if the answer to a problem is 13.567 and the answer choices on the exam are 2, 5, 14 and 32, it would be best to select 14.

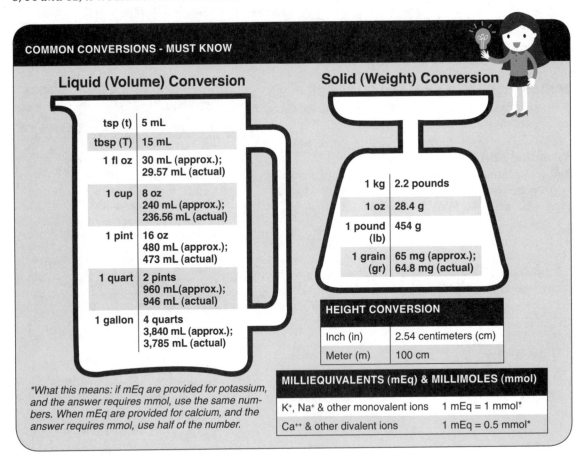

COMMON CONVERSIONS - MUST KNOW

Liquid (Volume) Conversion

tsp (t)	5 mL
tbsp (T)	15 mL
1 fl oz	30 mL (approx.); 29.57 mL (actual)
1 cup	8 oz 240 mL (approx.); 236.56 mL (actual)
1 pint	16 oz 480 mL (approx.); 473 mL (actual)
1 quart	2 pints 960 mL(approx.); 946 mL (actual)
1 gallon	4 quarts 3,840 mL (approx.); 3,785 mL (actual)

Solid (Weight) Conversion

1 kg	2.2 pounds
1 oz	28.4 g
1 pound (lb)	454 g
1 grain (gr)	65 mg (approx.); 64.8 mg (actual)

HEIGHT CONVERSION	
Inch (in)	2.54 centimeters (cm)
Meter (m)	100 cm

MILLIEQUIVALENTS (mEq) & MILLIMOLES (mmol)	
K^+, Na^+ & other monovalent ions	1 mEq = 1 mmol*
Ca^{++} & other divalent ions	1 mEq = 0.5 mmol*

**What this means: if mEq are provided for potassium, and the answer requires mmol, use the same numbers. When mEq are provided for calcium, and the answer requires mmol, use half of the number.*

Equivalent Measurements

Drugs can be measured in different ways:

- As weights [grams (g), milligrams (mg), micrograms (mcg), nanograms (ng)].
- As liquid volumes [liters (L), milliliters (mL)].
- As percentage strengths (g in 100 mL, g in 100 g, or mL in 100 mL).
- As concentrations of a given amount of a drug in a given volume of liquid (mcg/mL or mg/L). Very small amounts are measured in ng/mL. BUN and serum creatinine concentrations are measured in mg/dL (one liter is 10 dL).
- As concentrations using milliequivalents (mEq) per liter (mEq/L) (e.g., lithium, and common electrolytes).

The common conversions in the Study Tip on the previous page must be known for the exam; they may or may not be provided. Measurements can be approximations (e.g., 30 mL for a liquid ounce). The rounding instructions provided on the exam questions will generally account for any differences in using actual vs approximate conversions. If a specific conversion is provided on an exam question, use it.

Proportions and Dimensional Analysis

These methods are important for most of the math that pharmacists do routinely.

Proportions

Proportions are two fractions that are set equal to each other. One variable is unknown and labeled "X". When setting up proportions, make sure that the numerators match to each other and the denominators match to each other in every item except the value (the number) or make sure the items in the left fraction match and the items in the right fraction match (see problem #1 for an example).

Dimensional Analysis

Dimensional analysis allows multiple proportion calculations to be completed quickly. Diagonal units that are the same can be crossed out ("canceled out"), leaving the desired units. The numbers can be plugged into the calculator exactly as written. Pharmacists tend to either love dimensional analysis, or they prefer to do individual proportion calculations. When done correctly, both methods provide the same answer.

> **SETTING UP PROPORTIONS**
>
> 
>
> **Two methods of matching:**
>
> **Match both numerators and both denominators:** Every item in the left numerator must match to every item in the right numerator (except the values of the numbers).
>
> Every item in the left denominator must match to every item in the right denominator (except the values of the numbers).
>
> **Match numerator and denominator of each fraction:** Items in the left fraction (numerator and denominator) must match and items in the right fraction (numerator and denominator) must match (except the value of the numbers).
>
> Carefully review Problem #1 to see how both methods provide the same answer.

Converting from one common unit of measure to another (e.g., pounds to kilograms) is a simple way to illustrate both methods.

---

1. A patient weighs 176 pounds. What is the patient's weight in kilograms?

Method 1: Proportion. Solve for X by multiplying diagonally and then dividing.

$$\frac{176 \text{ lbs}}{X \text{ kg}} = \frac{2.2 \text{ lbs}}{1 \text{ kg}} \quad X = 80 \text{ kg}$$

$$\frac{176 \text{ lbs}}{2.2 \text{ lbs}} = \frac{X \text{ kg}}{1 \text{ kg}} \quad X = 80 \text{ kg}$$

Method 2: Dimensional analysis. Cancel out the same units diagonally, leaving the desired units.

$$\frac{176\ \text{lbs}}{} \times \frac{1\ \text{kg}}{2.2\ \text{lbs}} = 80\ \text{kg}$$

Notice that there is an equal sign (=) between the fractions in a proportion and a multiplication symbol (x) between the fractions in dimensional analysis.

Converting Common Units

Larger → Smaller Volume

Liters (L) → milliliters (mL)

2. How many milliliters are in 5 liters?

Method 1: Proportion

$$\frac{5\ \text{L}}{X\ \text{mL}} = \frac{1\ \text{L}}{1{,}000\ \text{mL}} \quad X = 5{,}000\ \text{mL}$$

Method 2: Dimensional analysis

$$5\ \text{L} \times \frac{1{,}000\ \text{mL}}{1\ \text{L}} = 5{,}000\ \text{mL}$$

Pick the method that works best for you.

Smaller → Larger Volume

Milliliters (mL) → liters (L)

3. Convert 5,000 mL to liters.

$$5{,}000\ \text{mL} \times \frac{1\ \text{L}}{1{,}000\ \text{mL}} = 5\ \text{L}$$

Larger → Smaller Weight

Kilogram (kg) → grams (g) → milligrams (mg) → micrograms (mcg) → nanograms (ng)

4. How many nanograms are equal to 5 kg?

This example requires 4 separate proportions or dimensional analysis (shown).

$$5\ \text{kg} \times \frac{1{,}000\ \text{g}}{1\ \text{kg}} \times \frac{1{,}000\ \text{mg}}{1\ \text{g}} \times \frac{1{,}000\ \text{mcg}}{1\ \text{mg}} \times \frac{1{,}000\ \text{ng}}{1\ \text{mcg}} = 5\ \text{trillion ng (or } 5 \times 10^{12}\ \text{ng)}$$

Smaller → Larger Weight

Nanograms (ng) → micrograms (mcg) → milligrams (mg) → grams (g) → kilograms (kg)

5. How many grams are equal to 50,000,000 nanograms?

$$50{,}000{,}000\ \text{ng} \times \frac{1\ \text{mcg}}{1{,}000\ \text{ng}} \times \frac{1\ \text{mg}}{1{,}000\ \text{mcg}} \times \frac{1\ \text{g}}{1{,}000\ \text{mg}} = 0.05\ \text{g}$$

Complex Proportions and Multi-Step Problems

Another common application for proportions is converting one drug and dose to another drug and dose. Practical conversions that pharmacists should be prepared to perform include opioids (see example) and loop diuretics. Most problems on NAPLEX will require more than one step. Some of the following examples illustrate this.

6. A patient received 4 mg of IV morphine. What is an equivalent dose of oral hydromorphone? (10 mg of IV morphine = 7.5 mg of oral hydromorphone)

$$\frac{\text{4 mg IV morphine}}{\text{X mg oral hydromorphone}} = \frac{\text{10 mg IV morphine}}{\text{7.5 mg oral hydromorphone}} \quad \text{X = 3 mg oral hydromorphone}$$

Notice that the numerators match each other (drug name, units and route) and the denominators match each other.

---

7. How many grams of bacitracin and nystatin are required to prepare 150 g of a 2:3 topical bacitracin:nystatin ointment?

Parts are another way to express the ratio of ingredients in a mixture. For every 2 parts of bacitracin in the ointment, there are 3 parts of nystatin. The pharmacist needs to know the weight of one part in order to calculate the weight of the two drugs. Since the total weight is given (150 g) and the total number of parts can be calculated (2 parts + 3 parts = 5 total parts), the value of 1 part can be determined using a proportion.

$$\frac{\text{5 total parts}}{\text{150 g}} = \frac{\text{1 part}}{\text{X g}} \quad \text{X = 30 g per 1 part}$$

$$\text{2 parts bacitracin} \times \frac{\text{30 grams}}{\text{1 part}} = \text{60 g bacitracin}$$

$$\text{3 parts nystatin} \times \frac{\text{30 grams}}{\text{1 part}} = \text{90 g nystatin}$$

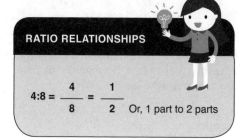

RATIO RELATIONSHIPS

$$4{:}8 = \frac{4}{8} = \frac{1}{2}$$ Or, 1 part to 2 parts

Add the weights to confirm that they match the total weight:

60 g bacitracin + 90 g nystatin = 150 g of 2:3 bacitracin:nystatin ointment

---

8. Digoxin injection is supplied in ampules of 500 mcg per 2 mL. How many milliliters must a nurse administer to provide a dose of 0.2 mg?

Method 1: Two steps using a proportion.

First, convert micrograms to milligrams by dividing 500 micrograms by 1000.

$$\text{500 mcg} \times \frac{\text{1 mg}}{\text{1,000 mcg}} = \text{0.5 mg}$$

Then use a proportion to calculate the number of mL for a 0.2 mg dose.

$$\frac{\text{0.5 mg digoxin}}{\text{2 mL}} = \frac{\text{0.2 mg digoxin}}{\text{X mL}} \quad \text{X = 0.8 mL}$$

Method 2: Dimensional analysis.

$$0.2\,\cancel{\text{mg}} \times \frac{1{,}000\,\cancel{\text{mcg}}}{1\,\cancel{\text{mg}}} \times \frac{\text{2 mL}}{500\,\cancel{\text{mcg}}} = 0.8\,\text{mL}$$

9. If one 10 mL vial contains 0.05 g of diltiazem, how many milliliters should be administered to provide a 25 mg dose of diltiazem?

Method 1: Two steps using a proportion.

First, convert grams to milligrams. It is usually best practice to convert to the units required for the answer when beginning the problem.

$$\text{0.05 g diltiazem} \times \frac{1{,}000\ \text{mg}}{1\ \text{g}} = 50\ \text{mg}$$

Next, calculate the number of milliliters for a 25 mg dose.

$$\frac{50\ \text{mg}}{10\ \text{mL}} = \frac{25\ \text{mg}}{X\ \text{mL}} \qquad X = 5\ \text{mL}$$

Method 2: Dimensional analysis.

$$\text{25 mg dose} \times \frac{1\ \text{g}}{1{,}000\ \text{mg}} \times \frac{10\ \text{mL}}{0.05\ \text{g}} = 5\ \text{mL}$$

---

10. A patient will receive 400 mg of a drug that has been put in a 250 mL IV bag. The rate of drug administration is 375 mcg per minute. Calculate the flow rate in milliliters per hour. Round to the nearest whole number.

Sometimes the total dose of a drug (e.g., 400 mg) is delivered by continuous infusion. The rate of administration, or flow rate, is the amount of drug given in a set period of time. This can be ordered as the amount of drug per unit of time (e.g., infuse 375 mcg/min), but many infusion pumps are set to deliver a certain volume of fluid per unit of time (e.g., mL/hr). This requires a conversion.

Dimensional analysis works well for flow rate problems. Here is a breakdown of the steps:

1. The 1st fraction is the drug concentration. Since you are solving for mL/hr, milliliters needs to be in the numerator.

2. The 2nd converts the drug weight from mg to micrograms.

3. The 3rd is the rate of drug administration.

4. The 4th converts minutes to hours.

$$\frac{250\ \text{mL}}{400\ \cancel{\text{mg}}} \times \frac{1\ \cancel{\text{mg}}}{1000\ \cancel{\text{mcg}}} \times \frac{375\ \cancel{\text{mcg}}}{\cancel{\text{min}}} \times \frac{60\ \cancel{\text{min}}}{1\ \text{hr}} = 14\ \text{mL/hr}$$

Decimals and Percentage Conversion

To convert a decimal to a percentage, multiply the decimal by 100.

To convert a percentage to a decimal, divide the percentage by 100.

---

11. JJ is a 16 year old female who complains of weakness, fatigue and heavy menstrual periods. She is diagnosed with anemia. JJ takes ferrous sulfate 220 mg once daily. What is the daily amount of elemental iron (in milligrams) that JJ receives from the supplement? Ferrous sulfate is 20% elemental iron.

Divide the percentage by 100: 20%/100 = 0.2

Multiply the total amount of ferrous sulfate by 0.2 to determine the amount of elemental iron in mg:

220 mg x 0.2 = 44 mg elemental iron

Squaring a Number

Required for calculating the Body Surface Area (BSA) with the Mosteller formula.

12. Calculate 3.5^2.

Either method will provide the answer:

Multiply the number by itself:

3.5 x 3.5 = 12.25

Use the x^2 key on the calculator:

1. Enter the number to square on the calculator: 3.5
2. Hit the x^2 key
3. This will provide the same answer: 12.25

Exponents

This will work with squaring as well, but has an extra step.

13. Calculate 2^4.

1. Enter the first number (in this example, enter 2)
2. Hit the x^y key
3. Enter the exponent (in this example, enter 4)
4. This will provide the answer; in this example, the answer is 16

Calculating the Log of a Number

Required for acid-base calculations.

14. Calculate log (1/0.5). Round to the nearest tenth.

$$\log\left[\frac{1}{0.5}\right]$$

1. If there is a division, solve the division first. 1/0.5 = 2
2. The number 2 will be on the calculator screen. Solve for log[2] by hitting the $\log_{10}$ or log key.

Some hand-held and on-screen calculators may require you to press the log key first, followed by "2" to solve this problem.

3. This will provide the answer, in this example, the answer is 0.3 (rounded to the nearest tenth).

Some calculators have parenthesis that allow you to enter the calculation as written in the problem, rather than performing each step separately.

Order of Operations

Math calculations that involve more than one function need to e completed in a specified order. The order is brackets (first), then parenthesis, then exponents, then multiplication and division (left to right), then addition and subtraction (left to right). See Study Tip. In fractions, the fraction bar is a grouping symbol; the entire numerator and the entire denominator are calculated before dividing the denominator into the numerator.

> **ORDER OF OPERATIONS**
>
> Brackets → Parenthesis (and other grouping symbols) → Exponents → Multiplication and Division → Addition and Subtraction
>
> Mnemonic: **B-PEMDAS**
>
> Billy, Please Eat Mom's Delicious Apple Strudel

Phenytoin and valproate require a specific formula to calculate the corrected drug level when the albumin is low (< 3.5 g/dL). Refer to the Epilepsy/Seizures chapter for additional discussion. The order of operations must be followed in order to get the correct result.

---

15. SJ is a female patient in the internal medicine unit receiving treatment following a motor vehicle accident. Her medications include lorazepam, morphine and phenytoin. Using the lab values provided, calculate SJ's corrected phenytoin level. Round to the nearest one decimal place.

$$\text{Corrected Phenytoin} = \frac{\text{Measured Phenytoin}}{(0.2 \times \text{Albumin}) + 0.1}$$

Reported Lab Values:
Phenytoin 9.6 mg/L
Albumin 1.8 mg/dL

$$\text{Corrected Phenytoin} = \frac{9.6}{(0.2 \times 1.8) + 0.1} = 20.9 \text{ mg/L}$$

1. Math inside parenthesis: 0.2 x 1.8 = 0.36
2. Add 0.1 to the answer: 0.36 + 0.1 = 0.46
3. Divide 9.6 by the answer: 9.6 divided by 0.46 = 20.9 (per rounding instructions provided)

Solving Case-Based Math Problems

- Most of the math problems on the exam will be in a case-based format. This chapter contains several cases, and other chapters include practice cases. There are more cases in the video lectures and test banks.
- It will be necessary to locate information in a case. For example, if the problem requires a creatinine clearance calculation, the patient's weight, sex and creatinine may need to be determined from the case. The flow rate for IV medications may need to be gathered from a patient profile. Once the information is located, the math is the same.
- Since finding the information takes time, each calculation should be able to be completed with reasonable speed and accuracy. For example, if the

> **READY TO SUBMIT YOUR ANSWER?**
>
> **Not so fast. Do a double check first!**
>
> **Ask yourself these questions to avoid common mistakes:**
>
> - Does the answer match the question?
>   - Re-read the question. Did you solve for the right thing? Remember many problems on the exam require more than one step.
> - Is the answer in the correct units? This is a common mistake. The problem may have been done correctly, but one more step is required to convert the answer to the specified units.
> - Is the answer rounded correctly?
> - Does the answer make sense?
>   - If the problem asks how many liters of fluid a patient will receive in one day, 20,000 liters is unlikely to be the right answer. It doesn't make sense.

case states that 10 units of regular insulin was added to the fluid bag on 3/11 and the fluid bag ordered on 3/9 is chosen instead, the fluid may be a different volume and the answer will be incorrect. Or, if a patient weight is needed to calculate a dose, such as mg/kg, and several of the patient's weights are provided in the case, be careful to select the weight from the correct date.

PRACTICE CASE

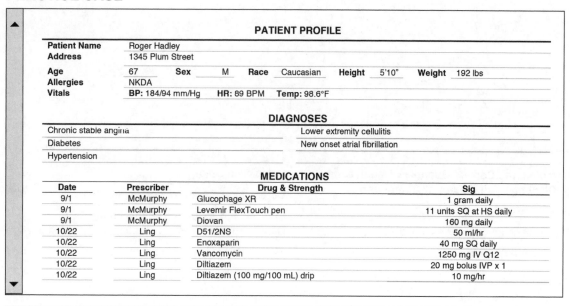

PATIENT PROFILE

Patient Name	Roger Hadley
Address	1345 Plum Street
Age	67 **Sex** M **Race** Caucasian **Height** 5'10" **Weight** 192 lbs
Allergies	NKDA
Vitals	**BP:** 184/94 mm/Hg **HR:** 89 BPM **Temp:** 98.6°F

DIAGNOSES

Chronic stable angina	Lower extremity cellulitis
Diabetes	New onset atrial fibrillation
Hypertension	

MEDICATIONS

Date	Prescriber	Drug & Strength	Sig
9/1	McMurphy	Glucophage XR	1 gram daily
9/1	McMurphy	Levemir FlexTouch pen	11 units SQ at HS daily
9/1	McMurphy	Diovan	160 mg daily
10/22	Ling	D51/2NS	50 ml/hr
10/22	Ling	Enoxaparin	40 mg SQ daily
10/22	Ling	Vancomycin	1250 mg IV Q12
10/22	Ling	Diltiazem	20 mg bolus IVP x 1
10/22	Ling	Diltiazem (100 mg/100 mL) drip	10 mg/hr

16. Use the case provided to answer the following question. At what rate (mL/hr) should Mr. Hadley's diltiazem drip be set at to provide the prescribed dose?

$$\frac{10\text{ mg}}{\text{hr}} \times \frac{100\text{ mL}}{100\text{ mg}} = 10\text{ mL/hr}$$

17. Use the case provided to answer the following question. Premixed bags of D5½NS (1 liter) are available on the floor. Mr. Hadley's infusion is started at 1300 on the day it was ordered. On what date and time will the premixed bag run out?

a. 10/22 at 0100
b. 10/22 at 1300
c. 10/22 at 2000
d. 10/23 at 1300
e. 10/23 at 0900

The correct answer is (e).

$$1000\text{ mL} \times \frac{\text{hr}}{50\text{ mL}} = 20\text{ hours}$$

The 1 liter bag will last 20 hours at the prescribed rate of 50 mL/hr. If the bag is started at 1300 (1 pm) on 10/22, it will run out 20 hours later, at 0900 on 10/23. Refer to the Patient Charts, Assessment & Healthcare Provider Communication chapter for a discussion of military time.

3

CALCULATIONS II

CALCULATIONS II – LEARN AND PRACTICE

Start Calculations II after you have mastered the basic math concepts in Calculations I. It is important to master all of the concepts in Calculations II before testing. Review the Study Tip "Math is Ready for NAPLEX When..." at the beginning of Calculations I to assess your preparedness.

CALCULATE THE CORRECT QUANTITY OF MEDICATION TO DISPENSE, ADMINISTER OR COMPOUND

Proportions

1. If 200 capsules contain 500 mg of an active ingredient, how many milligrams of the active ingredient will 76 capsules contain?

$$\frac{200 \text{ caps}}{500 \text{ mg}} = \frac{76 \text{ caps}}{X \text{ mg}} \quad X = 190 \text{ mg}$$

---

2. If phenobarbital elixir contains 18.2 mg of phenobarbital per 5 mL, how many grams of phenobarbital would be used in preparing a pint of the elixir? Round to the nearest tenth.

First, convert milligrams to grams.

$$18.2 \text{ mg} \times \frac{1 \text{ g}}{1{,}000 \text{ mg}} = 0.0182 \text{ g}$$

Use a proportion to calculate the grams needed for 1 pint.

$$\frac{0.0182 \text{ g}}{5 \text{ mL}} = \frac{X \text{ g}}{473 \text{ mL}} \quad X = 1.7 \text{ g}$$

Because of the rounding specifications in the question, the answer is the same regardless of the pint conversion used. Expect the same on the exam.

---

3. A penicillin V 250 mg tablet equals 400,000 units of penicillin activity. A patient is taking penicillin V 500 mg tablets QID for 7 days. How much penicillin activity, in units, will this patient receive in the total prescription?

If 250 mg contains 400,000 units, then 500 mg contains 800,000 units. The patient is taking 4 tablets daily, for 7 days (or 28 total tablets), at 800,000 units each.

$$\frac{800{,}000 \text{ units}}{1 \text{ tab}} = \frac{X \text{ units}}{28 \text{ tabs}} \quad X = 22{,}400{,}000 \text{ units}$$

---

4. A cough syrup contains 4 grams of brompheniramine maleate per liter. How many milligrams are contained in a teaspoonful dose of the elixir?

First, convert grams to milligrams.

$$4 \text{ g} \times \frac{1000 \text{ mg}}{1 \text{ g}} = 4{,}000 \text{ mg per 1 liter}$$

- 1 L = 1,000 mL
- 1 teaspoonful = 5 mL

Next, solve using a proportion.

$$\frac{4{,}000\text{ mg}}{1{,}000\text{ mL}} = \frac{X\text{ mg}}{5\text{ mL}} \qquad X = 20\text{ mg}$$

---

5. A patient is to receive acyclovir 5 mg/kg every 8 hours for an acute outbreak of herpes zoster. What daily dose, in milligrams, should a 110 pound female receive?

Begin by converting the patient's weight in pounds (lbs) to kilograms (kg).

$$110\text{ pounds} \times \frac{1\text{ kg}}{2.2\text{ pounds}} = 50\text{ kg}$$

$$\frac{5\text{ mg}}{1\text{ kg}} = \frac{X\text{ mg}}{50\text{ kg}} \qquad X = 250\text{ mg/dose} \times 3\text{ doses/day} = 750\text{ mg/day}$$

---

6. MH is a 72 year old male patient hospitalized with decompensated heart failure and fever. Cultures are positive for aspergillosis. MH weighs 110 kg and will receive 0.25 mg/kg per day of amphotericin B (reconstituted and diluted to 0.1 mg/mL) by IV infusion. How many milliliters of amphotericin solution is required to deliver the daily dose?

Begin by calculating the total daily dose (mg) for this patient.

$$\frac{0.25\text{ mg}}{1\text{ kg}} = \frac{X\text{ mg}}{110\text{ kg}} \qquad X = 27.5\text{ mg daily}$$

Calculate the volume of reconstituted amphotericin B solution needed per day.

$$\frac{27.5\text{ mg}}{X\text{ mL}} = \frac{0.1\text{ mg}}{1\text{ mL}} \qquad X = 275\text{ mL}$$

---

7. Oral potassium chloride 20% solution contains 40 mEq of potassium per 15 milliliters of solution. A patient needs 25 mEq of potassium daily. What is the amount, in milliliters, of 20% potassium chloride that the patient should take? Round to the nearest tenth.

$$\frac{40\text{ mEq K}}{15\text{ mL}} = \frac{25\text{ mEq K}}{X\text{ mL}} \qquad X = 9.375\text{, or } 9.4\text{ mL}$$

Calculations Involving Prescriptions

8. A pharmacist receives this prescription for *Vicodin.* How many tablets should be dispensed?

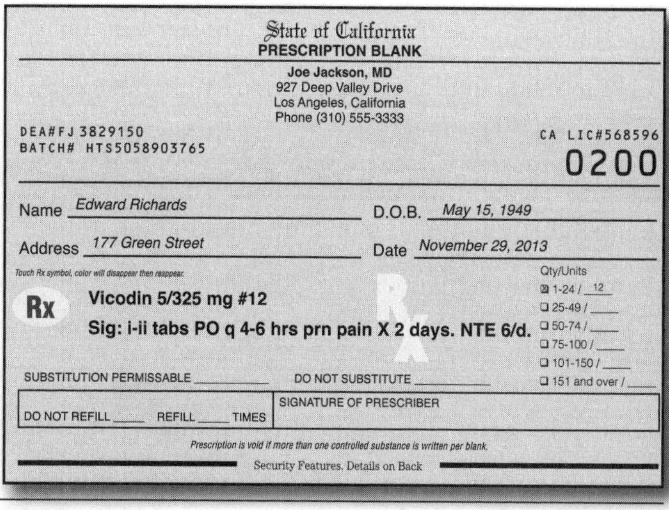
State of California
PRESCRIPTION BLANK
Joe Jackson, MD
927 Deep Valley Drive
Los Angeles, California
Phone (310) 555-3333
DEA#FJ 3829150
BATCH# HTS5058903765
CA LIC#568596
0200
Name Edward Richards D.O.B. May 15, 1949
Address 177 Green Street Date November 29, 2013
Touch Rx symbol, color will disappear then reappear.
Qty/Units
☒ 1-24 / 12
☐ 25-49 / ___
☐ 50-74 / ___
☐ 75-100 / ___
☐ 101-150 / ___
☐ 151 and over / ___
Rx Vicodin 5/325 mg #12
Sig: i-ii tabs PO q 4-6 hrs prn pain X 2 days. NTE 6/d.
SUBSTITUTION PERMISSABLE ___ DO NOT SUBSTITUTE ___
DO NOT REFILL ___ REFILL ___ TIMES
SIGNATURE OF PRESCRIBER
Prescription is void if more than one controlled substance is written per blank.
Security Features. Details on Back

a. 6 tablets
b. 8 tablets
c. 12 tablets
d. 16 tablets
e. 24 tablets

The correct answer is (c). The dispense quantity is indicated and consistent with the "not to exceed" instructions. Generally, the acetaminophen component has the higher risk of toxicity (liver toxicity).

---

9. A pharmacist receives a prescription for *"Vigamox* 0.5%. Dispense 3 mL. 1 gtt tid ou x 7d". How many drops will the patient use per day?

a. 1 drop
b. 2 drops
c. 3 drops
d. 6 drops
e. 21 drops

The correct answer is (d). Refer to the Appendix for common abbreviations used in prescriptions and medical charts. It is important to properly counsel patients on the correct technique for instilling eye drops. Refer to the Glaucoma, Ophthalmics & Otics chapter.

---

10. A 7 year old male child (3 feet, 4 inches and 48 pounds) presents to the urgent care clinic with a fever of 102°F, and nausea/vomiting that began the previous day. He will receive an acetaminophen 5 grain suppository for the fever. A pharmacist receives a prescription for the suppository with the instructions: Use 1 PR Q4-6H PRN temperature > 102 degrees. How many milligrams per kilogram (mg/kg) will the child receive per dose? Round to the nearest whole number.

a. 3 mg/kg
b. 15 mg/kg
c. 89 mg/kg
d. 60 mg/kg
e. 325 mg/kg

The correct answer is (b). Five grains is 325 milligrams (65 mg/grain x 5 grains). The recommended weight-based acetaminophen dosing for children under 12 years of age is 10-15 mg/kg Q4-6H.

11. Which of the following are correct regarding the *Keflex* prescription? (Select ALL that apply.)

a. If taken correctly, this prescription will last 14 days.

b. The patient should be counseled to take the medication after meals and at bedtime.

c. The patient should be counseled to finish all of the medication even if she starts to feel better.

d. The patient should be counseled to take the medication every 6 hours around the clock.

e. The pharmacist should verify whether the patient has any allergies.

JOE JACKSON, MD
927 DEEP VALLEY DRIVE
LOS ANGELES, CALIFORNIA

PHONE (310) 555-3333 DEA NO. FJ3829150

NAME *Melissa Atkins* DATE *October 29, 2013*

ADDRESS *18469 Lotus Circle* AGE *57*

℞

Keflex 500 mg PO QID: ac and hs. #28

☐ LABEL

REFILL *0* TIMES

______, M.D. DO NOT SUBSTITUTE

______, M.D. SUBSTITUTION PERMISSIBLE

The correct answers are (c) and (e). The patient should be counseled to finish all of the medication even if they start to feel better. Cephalexin *(Keflex)* is a first generation cephalosporin antibiotic that comes as tablets, capsules and powder for suspension. Allergies must be verified before dispensing any prescription.

---

12. How many milliliters (mL) of *Mylanta* suspension are contained in each dose of the prescription below? Round to the nearest whole number.

PRESCRIPTION	QUANTITY
Belladonna Tincture	10 mL
Phenobarbital	60 mL
Mylanta susp. qs. ad	120 mL
Sig. 5 mL BID	

The total prescription is 120 mL; 10 mL belladonna, 60 mL of phenobarbital, and that leaves 50 mL for the *Mylanta*.

$$\frac{50 \text{ mL } Mylanta}{120 \text{ mL total Rx}} = \frac{X \text{ mL } Mylanta}{5 \text{ mL total Rx dose}} \quad X = 2.08, \text{ or } 2 \text{ mL } Mylanta \text{ per dose}$$

After solving the problem, read the question again to be certain it was answered with the correct units (mL of *Mylanta* per dose).

13. A pharmacist received this sulfamethoxazole/trimethoprim prescription and dispensed 3 oz to Ms. Brooks. How many days of therapy will Ms. Brooks be short? Use 30 mL for 1 fluid ounce and round to the nearest whole number.

Gene Tran, MD
5445 Grand Ave.
Fallbrook, California
Phone (760) 555-2112

005-1015
CA LIC. #A19666
D.E.A. #SK456789

Name *Angelina Brooks* Date *January 22, 2014*
Address *33 Walden Rd. N Falls* D.O.B. *May 5, 1951*

℞

TMP/SMX 40-200 mg/5 mL
Sig: 1 tsp PO BID x 10 days, until all taken.

❑ Do Not Substitute Refill ______ Times

Quantity	Units
❑ 1-24	____
❑ 25-49	____
❑ 50-74	____
❑ 75-100	____
❑ 101-150	____
❑ 151 and over	____

Physician Signature

Prescription is void if more than one controlled substance is written per blank.

a. 10 mL
b. 90 mL
c. 1 day
d. 3 days
e. 9 days

The correct answer is (c). Use caution with calculations like this where one step of the calculation is included as an answer choice. Always go back and read the question prior to selecting an answer.

5 mL (per dose) x 2 times/day x 10 days = 100 mL

Quantity dispensed: 3 oz x 30 mL/oz = 90 mL dispensed

Difference: 100 mL - 90 mL = 10 mL

Each tsp (t) is 5 mL. The patient must take 2 tsp (t) daily (10 mL), so she is 1 day short for her prescribed course of therapy.

---

14. A pharmacist has tablets that contain 0.25 mg of levothyroxine per tablet. The tablets will be crushed and mixed with glycerol and water to prepare a prescription for a 36 pound child. How many levothyroxine tablets will be needed to compound the following prescription?

PRESCRIPTION	QUANTITY
Levothyroxine Liq.	0.1 mg/mL
Disp.	60 mL
Sig. 0.01 mg per kg PO BID	

$$60 \text{ mL total Rx} \times \frac{0.1 \text{ mg levo}}{\text{mL}} = 6 \text{ mg of levothyroxine needed}$$

$$6 \text{ mg levo} \times \frac{1 \text{ tab}}{0.25 \text{ mg levo}} = 24 \text{ tabs of levothyroxine needed}$$

The first step can also be performed as a proportion. <u>If the proportion is set up correctly, the answers will be the same</u>.

$$\frac{0.1 \text{ mg levo}}{1 \text{ mL}} = \frac{X \text{ mg levo}}{60 \text{ mL}} \quad X = 6 \text{ mg of levothyroxine needed}$$

$$6 \text{ mg levo} \times \frac{1 \text{ tab}}{0.25 \text{ mg levo}} = 24 \text{ tabs of levothyroxine needed}$$

Or, it can be solved by dimensional analysis:

$$\frac{1 \text{ tab levo}}{0.25 \text{ mg levo}} \times \frac{0.1 \text{ mg levo}}{\text{mL}} \times 60 \text{ mL total Rx} = 24 \text{ tabs of levothyroxine needed}$$

After solving the problem, read the question again to be certain the question was answered with the correct units (tablets). Refer to Calculations I for a review of proportions and dimensional analysis.

---

15. A pharmacist will prepare an *Amoxil* suspension to provide a 1600 mg daily dose for a child with an otitis media infection. The dose will be divided BID. To prepare an *Amoxil* suspension containing 200 mg/5 mL the pharmacist should add 76 mL of water to the powder for a final volume of 100 mL. The pharmacist should add approximately 1/3 of the water first, shake vigorously, add the remaining water, and shake again to form the suspension. The pharmacist mistakenly adds too much water and finds that the final volume is 110 mL. The pharmacy has no other bottles of *Amoxil,* so the pharmacist will dispense the bottle with the extra water added. How many mL should the patient take twice daily to receive the correct dose? Round to the nearest whole number.

Two methods to solve this calculation are shown:

$$\frac{200 \text{ mg}}{5 \text{ mL}} = \frac{X \text{ mg}}{100 \text{ mL}} \quad X = 4{,}000 \text{ mg}$$

$$\frac{4{,}000 \text{ mg}}{110 \text{ mL}} = \frac{800 \text{ mg}}{X \text{ mL}} \quad X = 22 \text{ mL}$$

$$\frac{4{,}000 \text{ mg}}{110 \text{ mL}} = \frac{X \text{ mg}}{\text{mL}} \quad X = 36.36 \text{ mg/mL}$$

$$\frac{36.36 \text{ mg}}{1 \text{ mL}} = \frac{800 \text{ mg}}{X \text{ mL}} \quad X = 22 \text{ mL}$$

---

16. How many milligrams of codeine will be contained in each capsule?

PRESCRIPTION	QUANTITY
Codeine Sulfate	0.6 g
Guaifenesin	1.2 g
Caffeine	0.15 g
M. ft. caps. no. 24	
Sig. One capsule TID PRN cough	

Begin by converting to the units requested in the answer (mg).

$$0.6 \text{ g codeine} \times \frac{1{,}000 \text{ mg}}{1 \text{ g}} = 600 \text{ mg of codeine for the total prescription}$$

The prescription order is for 24 capsules.

$$\frac{600 \text{ mg codeine total}}{24 \text{ caps}} = 25 \text{ mg of codeine/capsule}$$

After solving the problem, read the question again to be certain the question was answered with the correct units (mg of codeine per capsule).

17. A physician writes an order for aminophylline 500 mg IV, dosed at 0.5 mg per kg per hour for a patient weighing 165 pounds. There is only theophylline in stock. How many milligrams (mg) of theophylline will the patient receive per hour? Round to the nearest whole number.

$$\frac{0.5\text{ mg Amino}}{\text{kg/hr}} \times \frac{1\text{ kg}}{2.2\text{ pounds}} \times 165\text{ pounds} = 37.5\text{ mg/hr aminophylline}$$

The aminophylline dose must now be converted to theophylline.

- Aminophylline to theophylline; multiply by 0.8
- Theophylline to aminophylline; divide by 0.8

37.5 mg/hr aminophylline x 0.8 = 30 mg/hr of theophylline

After solving the problem, read the question again to be certain the question was answered with the correct units (mg per hour of theophylline).

---

18. How many grains of aspirin will be contained in each capsule? Round to the nearest tenth.

PRESCRIPTION	QUANTITY
Aspirin	6 g
Phenacetin	3.2 g
Caffeine	0.48 g
M. ft. no. 20 caps	
Sig. One capsule Q6H PRN pain	

$$6\text{ g ASA} \times \frac{1{,}000\text{ mg}}{1\text{ g}} \times \frac{1\text{ grain}}{65\text{ mg}} = 92.3\text{ grains}$$

We have 92.3 grains of aspirin that will be divided into 20 capsules.

$$\frac{92.3\text{ grains}}{20\text{ capsules}} = 4.6\text{ grains/capsule}$$

After solving the problem, read the question again to be certain the question was answered with the correct units (grains per capsule).

---

19. A 45 milliliter nasal spray delivers 20 sprays per milliliter of solution. Each spray contains 1.5 mg of active drug. How many milligrams of drug are contained in the 45 mL package?

First calculate the amount of drug per mL.

$$\frac{1.5\text{ mg drug}}{\text{spray}} \times \frac{20\text{ sprays}}{\text{mL}} = 30\text{ mg/mL}$$

Then solve for milligrams of drug in 45 mL.

$$\frac{30\text{ mg}}{\text{mL}} = \frac{X\text{ mg}}{45\text{ mL}} \quad X = 1{,}350\text{ mg}$$

20. A metered dose inhaler provides 90 micrograms of albuterol sulfate with each inhalation. The canister provides 200 inhalations. If the patient uses the entire canister, how many total milligrams will the patient have received?

$$200 \text{ inhalations} \times \frac{90 \text{ mcg}}{\text{inhalation}} = 18{,}000 \text{ mcg}$$

$$18{,}000 \text{ mcg} \times \frac{1 \text{ mg}}{1{,}000 \text{ mcg}} = 18 \text{ mg}$$

Percentage Strength

A percentage is a number or ratio as a fraction of 100. Expressions of concentration describe the amount of solute that will be contained in the total preparation. The percentage concentrations are defined as follows:

- Percent weight-in-volume (% w/v) is expressed as g/100 mL (a solid mixed into a liquid)
- Percent volume-in-volume (% v/v) is expressed as mL/100 mL (a liquid mixed into a liquid)
- Percent weight-in-weight (% w/w) is expressed as g/100 g (a solid mixed into a solid)

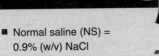

STUDY TIP: COMMON IV FLUIDS

- Normal saline (NS) = 0.9% (w/v) NaCl
  - 1/2 NS (called "half normal saline") = 0.45% (w/v) NaCl
  - 1/4 NS (called "quarter normal saline") = 0.225% (w/v) NaCl
- D5W (called "D-5-W") = 5% (w/v) dextrose in water
- D20W = 20% (w/v) dextrose in water
- Combination fluid examples
  - D5NS (called "D-5-N-S") = 5% dextrose and 0.9% NaCl in water
  - D51/2NS (called "D-5-Half-N-S") = 5% dextrose and 0.45% NaCl in water

21. How many grams of NaCl are in 1 liter of normal saline (NS)?

Refer to Study Tip for percentage strengths of common IV fluids. Remember (w/v) is always expressed as grams per 100 mL, therefore, NS contains 0.9 g NaCl per 100 mL of solution.

$$\frac{0.9 \text{ g}}{100 \text{ mL}} = \frac{X \text{ g}}{1{,}000 \text{ mL}} \quad X = 9 \text{ g}$$

22. How many grams of NaCl are in 500 mL of ½NS? Round to the nearest hundredth.

Since NS is 0.9% NaCl, 1/2NS is 1/2 the percentage strength or 0.45%.

$$\frac{0.45 \text{ g}}{100 \text{ mL}} = \frac{X \text{ g}}{500 \text{ mL}} \quad X = 2.25 \text{ g}$$

23. How many grams of dextrose are in 250 mL of D5W? Round to the nearest tenth.

$$\frac{5 \text{ g}}{100 \text{ mL}} = \frac{X \text{ g}}{250 \text{ mL}} \quad X = 12.5 \text{ g}$$

24. How many milligrams of triamcinolone should be used in preparing the following prescription? Round to the nearest whole number.

PRESCRIPTION	QUANTITY
Triamcinolone (w/v)	5%
Glycerin qs	60 mL
Sig. Two drops in right ear	

$$\frac{5\text{ g}}{100\text{ mL}} = \frac{X\text{ g}}{60\text{ mL}} \quad X = 3\text{ g, or }3{,}000\text{ mg}$$

---

25. A prescription reads as follows: "Prepare a 3% w/w coal tar preparation qs with petrolatum to 150 grams". How many grams of petrolatum are required to compound the prescription? Round to the nearest tenth.

$$\frac{3\text{ g coal tar}}{100\text{ g preparation}} = \frac{X\text{ g coal tar}}{150\text{ g preparation}} \quad X = 4.5\text{ g coal tar}$$

150 g (total weight of preparation) − 4.5 g (coal tar) = 145.5 g petrolatum

---

26. JL has mucositis secondary to methotrexate chemotherapy. His oncologist ordered lidocaine HCl 2% w/v solution; qs with pure water to 120 mL. How much lidocaine, in grams, is required to make the prescription? Round to the nearest tenth.

$$\frac{2\text{ g}}{100\text{ mL}} = \frac{X\text{ g}}{120\text{ mL}} \quad X = 2.4\text{ g}$$

---

27. SS is a 79 year old female with dry mouth and dry eyes from Sjögren's syndrome. She is picking up the prescription below. What is the maximum milligrams of pilocarpine she will receive per day?

PRESCRIPTION	QUANTITY
Pilocarpine	1% (w/v)
Sodium Chloride qs ad	15 mL
Sig: 2 gtts (0.05 mL/gtt) po TID prn up to 5 days for dry mouth	

First, calculate the amount of pilocarpine in the prescription.

$$\frac{1\text{ g}}{100\text{ mL}} = \frac{X\text{ g}}{15\text{ mL}} \quad X = 0.15\text{ g}$$

Then, convert to mg since the problem asks for mg of pilocarpine.

$$0.15\text{ g} \times \frac{1{,}000\text{ mg}}{1\text{ g}} = 150\text{ mg of pilocarpine}$$

The patient will receive up to 3 doses per day (0.1 mL x 3 = 0.3 mL). Calculate the amount of pilocarpine in 0.3 mL.

$$\frac{150 \text{ mg pilocarpine}}{15 \text{ mL}} = \frac{X \text{ mg}}{0.3 \text{ mL}} \quad X = 3 \text{ mg pilocarpine}$$

---

28. If 1,250 grams of a mixture contains 80 grams of drug, what is the percentage strength (w/w) of the mixture? Round to the nearest tenth.

$$\frac{80 \text{ g}}{1{,}250 \text{ g}} = \frac{X \text{ g}}{100 \text{ g}} \quad X = 6.4 \text{ g, which is } 6.4\%$$

---

29. A mouth rinse contains $^1/_{12}$% (w/v) of chlorhexidine gluconate. How many grams of chlorhexidine gluconate should be used to prepare 18 liters of mouth rinse? Round to the nearest whole number.

- $^1/_{12}$% = 0.083 g per 100 mL (w/v)
- 18 L x 1,000 mL/L = 18,000 mL

$$\frac{0.083 \text{ g}}{100 \text{ mL}} = \frac{X \text{ g}}{18{,}000 \text{ mL}} \quad X = 14.94 \text{ g, rounded to } 15 \text{ g}$$

---

30. If 12 grams of lanolin are combined with 2 grams of white wax and 36 grams of petrolatum to make an ointment, what is the percentage strength (w/w) of lanolin in the ointment?

$$\frac{12 \text{ g lanolin}}{50 \text{ g ointment}} = \frac{X \text{ g}}{100 \text{ g}} \quad X = 24\% \text{ w/w}$$

---

31. A pharmacist dissolves 6 tablets. Each tablet contains 250 mg of metronidazole. The pharmacist will put the drug into a liquid base to prepare 60 mL of a topical solution. What is the percentage strength (w/v) of metronidazole in the prescription? Round to the nearest tenth.

$$6 \text{ tablets} \times \frac{250 \text{ mg}}{1 \text{ tab}} = 1{,}500 \text{ mg, or } 1.5 \text{ g}$$

$$\frac{1.5 \text{ g}}{60 \text{ mL}} = \frac{X \text{ g}}{100 \text{ mL}} \quad X = 2.5 \text{ g, which is } 2.5\% \text{ w/v}$$

---

32. A pharmacist adds 5.3 grams of hydrocortisone to 150 grams of a 2.5% hydrocortisone ointment. What is the percentage (w/w) of hydrocortisone in the finished product? Round to the nearest whole number.

First, determine the amount of hydrocortisone (HC) in the current product.

$$\frac{2.5 \text{ g HC}}{100 \text{ g ointment}} = \frac{X \text{ g HC}}{150 \text{ g ointment}} \quad X = 3.75 \text{ g HC}$$

5.3 grams of hydrocortisone is being added to the existing product which contains 3.75 g of hydrocortisone: 5.3 g + 3.75 g = 9.05 g.

Next, find the percent concentration of the final product (5.3 g + 150 g = 155.3 g).

$$\frac{9.05 \text{ g HC}}{155.3 \text{ g ointment}} = \frac{X \text{ g HC}}{100 \text{ g ointment}} \quad X = 5.8274 \text{ g, rounded to } 6\%$$

---

33. How many milliliters of hydrocortisone liquid (40 mg/mL) will be needed to prepare 30 grams of a 0.25% cream (w/w)? Round to the nearest hundredth.

First, calculate the amount of hydrocortisone needed in the final product.

$$\frac{0.25 \text{ g}}{100 \text{ g}} = \frac{X \text{ g}}{30 \text{ g}} \quad X = 0.075 \text{ g or } 75 \text{ mg}$$

Then, solve for mL of hydrocortisone liquid needed.

$$\frac{40 \text{ mg}}{\text{mL}} = \frac{75 \text{ mg}}{X \text{ mL}} \quad X = 1.875 \text{ mL, rounded to } 1.88 \text{ mL}$$

After solving the problem, read the question again to be certain the question was answered with the correct units (mL).

---

34. What is the percentage strength of imiquimod in the following prescription? Round to the nearest hundredth.

PRESCRIPTION	QUANTITY
Imiquimod 5% cream	15 g
Xylocaine	20 g
Hydrophilic ointment	25 g

First, calculate the amount of imiquimod (5%) in the prescription.

$$\frac{5 \text{ g}}{100 \text{ g}} \times 15 \text{ g} = 0.75 \text{ grams of imiquimod}$$

The total weight of the prescription is 60 g (15 g + 20 g + 25 g).

$$\frac{0.75 \text{ g}}{60 \text{ g}} = \frac{X \text{ g}}{100 \text{ g}} \quad X = 1.25 \text{ g, which is } 1.25\%$$

Ratio Strength

The concentration of weak solutions can be expressed in terms of ratio strength. Ratio strength describes the drug concentration in terms of a ratio (as the name suggests). It is denoted as one unit of solute contained in the total amount of the solution or mixture (e.g., 1:500). Ratio strength is another way of presenting a percentage strength. This makes sense because percentages are ratios of parts per hundred.

STUDY TIP: RATIO STRENGTH

Most multi-step calculations will require converting ratio strength to percentage strength. If a ratio strength is presented in a problem, convert it to a percentage strength and convert it back if needed.

- Ratio strength → Percentage strength
  - % strength = 100 / ratio strength
- Percentage strength → Ratio strength
  - Ratio strength = 100 / % strength

35. Express 0.04% as a ratio strength.

$$\frac{0.04}{100} = \frac{1\ \text{part}}{X\ \text{parts}} \quad X = 2{,}500.\ \text{Ratio strength is } 1{:}2{,}500$$

Convert back to 0.04% by taking 1/2,500 x 100 or simply 100/2,500. Try it.

---

36. Express 1:4,000 as a percentage strength.

$$\frac{1\ \text{part}}{4{,}000\ \text{part}} = \frac{X}{100} \quad X = 0.025,\ \text{which is } 0.025\%$$

Problem #53 can be done using the shortcut above for converting between ratio and percentage strength:

Percentage strength = 100 / 4,000 = 0.025%

---

37. There are 50 mg of drug in 50 mL of solution. Express the concentration as a ratio strength (% w/v).

First, convert 50 mg to grams. 50 mg x 1 g/1,000 mg = 0.05 g

Then, calculate grams per 100 mL.

$$\frac{0.05\ \text{g}}{50\ \text{mL}} = \frac{X\ \text{g}}{100\ \text{mL}} \quad X = 0.1\ \text{g}$$

Now solve for ratio strength.

$$\frac{0.1\ \text{g}}{100\ \text{mL}} = \frac{1\ \text{part}}{X\ \text{parts}} \quad X = 1{,}000,\ \text{or } 1{:}1{,}000$$

---

38. How many milligrams of iodine should be used in compounding the following prescription?

ITEM	QUANTITY
Iodine	1:400
Hydrophilic ointment ad	10 g
Sig. Apply as directed.	

First, convert the ratio strength to a percentage strength.

$$\frac{1\ \text{part}}{400\ \text{parts}} = \frac{X\ \text{g}}{100\ \text{g}} \quad X = 0.25\%$$

Then, determine how much iodine will be needed for the prescription.

$$\frac{0.25\ \text{g}}{100\ \text{g}} = \frac{X\ \text{g}}{10\ \text{g}} \quad X = 0.025\ \text{g, or } 25\ \text{mg}$$

Or, solve another way:

1:400 means 1 g in 400 g of ointment.

$$\frac{1\ \text{g}}{400\ \text{g}} = \frac{X\ \text{g}}{10\ \text{g}} \quad X = 0.025\ \text{g, or } 25\ \text{mg}$$

39. A 10 mL mixture contains 0.25 mL of active drug. Express the concentration as a percentage strength (% v/v) and a ratio strength.

First, find out how much drug is in 100 mL.

$$\frac{0.25 \text{ mL drug}}{10 \text{ mL}} = \frac{\text{X mL drug}}{100 \text{ mL}} \quad \text{X} = 2.5 \text{ mL, or } 2.5\% \text{ (v/v)}$$

Now solve for ratio strength.

$$\frac{2.5 \text{ mL drug}}{100 \text{ mL}} = \frac{1 \text{ part}}{\text{X parts}} \quad \text{X} = 40\text{; or } 1{:}40$$

---

40. What is the concentration, in ratio strength, of a trituration made by combining 150 mg of albuterol sulfate and 4.05 grams of lactose?

First, add up the total weight of the prescription.

$$0.150 \text{ g} + 4.05 \text{ g} = 4.2 \text{ g}$$

Now solve for ratio strength.

$$\frac{0.150 \text{ g}}{4.2 \text{ g}} = \frac{1 \text{ part}}{\text{X parts}} \quad \text{X} = 28\text{, or } 1{:}28$$

Parts Per Million

Parts indicate amount proportions. Parts per million (PPM) and parts per billion (PPB) are used to quantify strengths of very dilute solutions. It is defined as the number of parts of the drug per 1 million (or 1 billion) parts of the whole. The same default units are followed as for percentage systems (% w/w, % w/v and % v/v).

STUDY TIP: PARTS PER MILLION

- PPM → Percentage strength
  - Move the decimal left 4 places
- Percentage strength → PPM
  - Move the decimal right 4 places

---

41. Express 0.00022% w/v as PPM. Round to the nearest tenth.

$$\frac{0.00022 \text{ g}}{100 \text{ mL}} = \frac{\text{X parts}}{1{,}000{,}000} \quad \text{X} = 2.2 \text{ PPM}$$

---

42. Express 30 PPM of copper in solution as a percentage.

$$\frac{30 \text{ parts}}{1{,}000{,}000} = \frac{\text{X g}}{100 \text{ mL}} \quad \text{X} = 0.003\%$$

---

43. Express 5 PPM of iron in water as a percentage.

$$\frac{5 \text{ parts}}{1{,}000{,}000} = \frac{\text{X g}}{100 \text{ mL}} \quad \text{X} = 0.0005\%$$

44. A patient's blood contains 0.085 PPM of selenium. How many micrograms of selenium does the patient's blood contain if the blood volume is 6 liters?

$$\frac{0.085 \text{ parts}}{1{,}000{,}000} = \frac{X \text{ g}}{6{,}000 \text{ mL}} \quad X = 0.00051 \text{ g, or } 510 \text{ mcg}$$

45. A sample of an intravenous solution is found to contain 0.4 PPM of DEHP. How much of the solution, in milliliters, will contain 50 micrograms of DEHP?

$$\frac{0.4 \text{ parts}}{1{,}000{,}000} = \frac{0.00005 \text{ g}}{X \text{ mL}} \quad X = 125 \text{ mL}$$

If asked to express something in PPB (parts per billion), divide by 1,000,000,000 (9 zeros).

Specific Gravity

Specific gravity (SG) is the ratio of the density of a substance to the density of water. SG can be important for calculating doses of IV medications, in compounding, and in interpreting a urinalysis. Water has a specific gravity of 1 where 1 g water = 1 mL water. Substances with a SG < 1 are lighter than water and those with SG > 1 are heavier than water.

$$SG = \frac{\text{weight of substance (g)}}{\text{weight of equal volume of water (g)}} \quad \text{or more simply:} \quad SG = \frac{g}{mL}$$

46. What is the specific gravity of 150 mL of glycerin weighing 165 grams? Round to the nearest tenth.

$$SG = \frac{165 \text{ g}}{150 \text{ mL}} \quad SG = 1.1$$

Check the answer: 150 mL x 1.1 = 165 g

47. What is the weight of 750 mL of concentrated acetic acid (SG = 1.2)?

$$1.2 = \frac{X \text{ g}}{750 \text{ mL}} \quad X = 900 \text{ g}$$

Check the answer: 900 g/750 mL = 1.2

48. How many mL of polysorbate 80 (SG = 1.08) are needed to prepare a prescription that includes 48 grams of the surfactant/emulsifier (polysorbate)? Round to the nearest hundredth.

$$1.08 = \frac{48 \text{ g}}{X \text{ mL}} \quad X = 44.44 \text{ mL}$$

Check the answer: 48 g/44.44 mL = 1.08

49. What is the specific gravity of 30 mL of a liquid weighing 23,400 milligrams? Round to the nearest hundredth.

$$SG = \frac{23.4\ g}{30\ mL} \qquad SG = 0.78$$

---

50. What is the weight of 0.5 L of polyethylene glycol 400 (SG = 1.13).

$$1.13 = \frac{X\ g}{500\ mL} \qquad X = 565\ grams$$

---

51. Nitroglycerin has a specific gravity of 1.59. How much would 1 quart weigh in grams? Use 1 quart = 946 mL. Round to the nearest whole number.

$$1.59 = \frac{X\ g}{946\ mL} \qquad X = 1{,}504\ g$$

Check the answer: 1,504 g/946 mL = 1.59

Note that the SG is equivalent to the density in g/mL (with units). If asked for the density in the above problem, the answer would be 1.59 g/mL.

Calculation Practice

The following problem integrates multiple calculation concepts.

---

52. A pharmacist receives a prescription for a 1.5% (w/w) hydrocortisone cream using cold cream as the base. She will use hydrocortisone injection (100 mg/mL, SG 1.5) to prepare the prescription because she has no hydrocortisone powder in stock. How many grams of cold cream are required to compound 60 grams of the preparation?

First, calculate the grams of hydrocortisone required for the prescription.

$$\frac{1.5\ g}{100\ g} = \frac{X\ g}{60\ g} \qquad X = 0.9\ \text{grams of hydrocortisone required}$$

Calculate the volume of hydrocortisone injection required.

$$\frac{100\ mg}{1\ mL} = \frac{900\ mg}{X\ mL} \qquad X = 9\ mL$$

Calculate the weight of 9 mL of hydrocortisone injection using the SG provided.

$$1.5 = \frac{X\ g}{9\ mL} \qquad X = 13.5\ \text{grams (weight of hydrocortisone injection)}$$

Calculate the grams of cold cream required.

60 g final product - 13.5 g (weight of hydrocortisone) = 46.5 g of cold cream

Dilution and Concentration

Often the strength of a product must be increased or decreased, or a new quantity is required. This formula can be used to change the strength or quantity. Be careful: the units on each side must match and one or more may need to be changed, such as mg to gram, or vice-versa.

Q1 x C1 = Q2 x C2	
Q1 = old quantity	Q2 = new quantity
C1 = old concentration	C2 = new concentration

53. A pharmacist has an order for parenteral nutrition that includes 550 mL of D70%. The pharmacist checks the supplies and finds the closest strength he has available is D50%. How many mL of D50% will provide an equivalent energy requirement?

550 mL x 70% = Q2 mL x 50%

Q2 = 770 mL of D50%

54. How many grams of petrolatum (diluent) should be added to 250 grams of a 20% ichthammol ointment to make a 7% ichthammol ointment? Round to the nearest tenth.

Note the difference from the previous problem. In this example, the problem asks how much diluent should be added to make the final weight.

250 g x 20% = Q2 x 7%

Q2 = 714.3 g of 7% ichthammol ointment

Read the question again to be certain about what is being asked. Since the question did not ask how much of the 7% ointment can be prepared, but rather how much diluent is required, an additional step is needed:

714.3 g total weight - 250 g (already present) = 464.3 g petrolatum required

55. Using 20 grams of a 9% boric acid ointment base, the pharmacist will manufacture a 5% ointment. How much diluent is required?

20 g x 9% = Q2 x 5%

Q2 = 36 g of the 5% ointment can be prepared

36 g total weight - 20 g (already present) = 16 g diluent required

56. If 1 gallon of a 20% (w/v) solution is evaporated to a solution with a 50% (w/v) strength, what will be the new volume (in mL)? Round to the nearest 100 mL.

3,785 mL x 20% = Q2 x 50%

Q2 = 1,514 mL, rounded to the nearest 100 mL = 1500 mL

This answer will be the same regardless of which conversion is used for gallon to mL.

57. A patient has been receiving 200 mL of an enteral mixture that contains 432 mOsm/L. The pharmacist will reduce the contents to 278 mOsm/L. How many mL of bacteriostatic water should be added to the bag? Round to the nearest mL.

200 mL x 432 mOsm/L = Q2 x 278 mOsm/L X = 311 mL

Q2 = 311 mL of the 278 mOsm/L enteral mixture can be prepared

There are 200 mL in the original bag. The final volume will be 311 mL.

311 mL - 200 mL = 111 mL of bacteriostatic water

Calculation Practice

The following problems integrate multiple calculation concepts.

---

58. How many mL of a 1:2,500 (w/v) solution of aluminum acetate can be made from 100 mL of a 0.2% solution?

Both concentrations must be in the same units to use the Q1C1 = Q2C2 formula. So, 1:2,500 must be converted to a percentage strength first.

$$\frac{1 \text{ part}}{2{,}500 \text{ parts}} = \frac{X \text{ g}}{100 \text{ mL}} \qquad X = 0.04 \text{ g, or } 0.04\%$$

Now use the formula.

100 mL x 0.2% = Q2 x 0.04%

Q2 = 500 mL

---

59. What is the ratio strength (w/v) of 50 mL containing a 1:20 (w/v) ammonia solution diluted to 1 liter?

First, convert 1:20 to a percentage strength.

$$\frac{1 \text{ part}}{20 \text{ parts}} = \frac{X \text{ g}}{100 \text{ mL}} \qquad X = 5 \text{ g, or } 5\%$$

50 mL x 5% = 1,000 mL x C2

C2 = 0.25%

Convert 0.25% to ratio strength = 1:400

Alligation

Alligation is used to obtain a new strength (percentage) that is between two strengths the pharmacist has in stock. Occasionally, no math is required to solve this type of problem if the new strength needed is exactly in the middle of the 2 strengths that are given. If the prescription calls for an ingredient that is pure, the concentration is 100%. If given a diluent, such as petrolatum, lanolin, alcohol, "ointment base", etc., the concentration of the diluent is 0%.

60. A pharmacist must prepare 100 grams of a 50% hydrocortisone powder using the 25% and 75% powders that she has in stock. How much of each is required?

Since the desired strength is exactly in the middle of the strengths available, divide the desired quantity in half (100 g / 2 = 50 grams). Use 50 g of the 75% and 50 g of the 25% to prepare 100 g of a 50% powder.

---

61. A pharmacist is asked to prepare 80 grams of a 12.5% ichthammol ointment with 16% and 12% ichthammol ointments in stock.

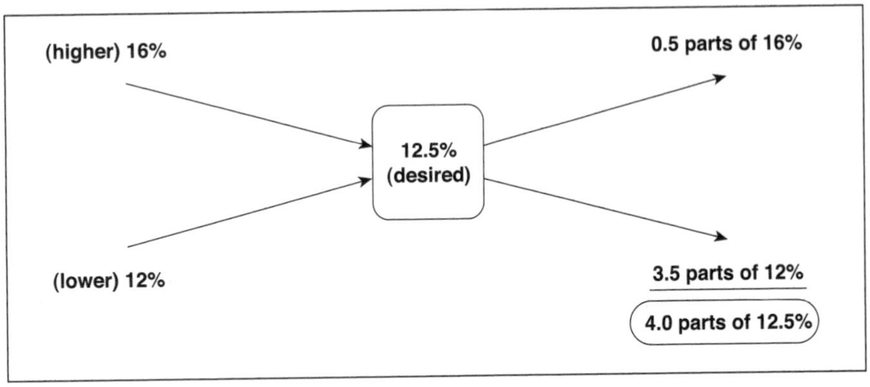

- To set up the X method:
  - Put the more concentrated product at the top left (high goes high)
  - Put the less concentrated product at the bottom left (low goes low)
  - Place the desired concentration in the middle of the X
- Subtract along the "X" lines to obtain the number of parts on the right (16% – 12.5% = 3.5 parts; 12% – 12.5% = 0.5 parts).
- Add the number of parts on the right to find the total number of parts (4 parts).
- Divide the total weight (80 g) by the number of parts to obtain the weight per part.

$$\frac{80\text{ g}}{4\text{ parts}} = 20 \text{ grams per part}$$

- Take the amount per part (20 g) and multiply it by the parts from each of the concentrations (from the high, and from the low).

$$0.5 \text{ parts of } 16\% \times \frac{20\text{ g}}{\text{part}} = 10 \text{ g of the } 16\% \text{ ichthammol ointment}$$

$$3.5 \text{ parts of } 12\% \times \frac{20\text{ g}}{\text{part}} = 70 \text{ g of the } 12\% \text{ ichthammol ointment}$$

Mix together; the end product provides 80 g of a 12.5% ichthammol ointment.

62. A pharmacist is asked to prepare 1 gallon of tincture containing 5.5% iodine. The pharmacy has 3% iodine tincture and 8.5% iodine tincture in stock. How many mL of the 3% and 8.5% iodine tincture should be used? (Use 1 gallon = 3,785 mL)

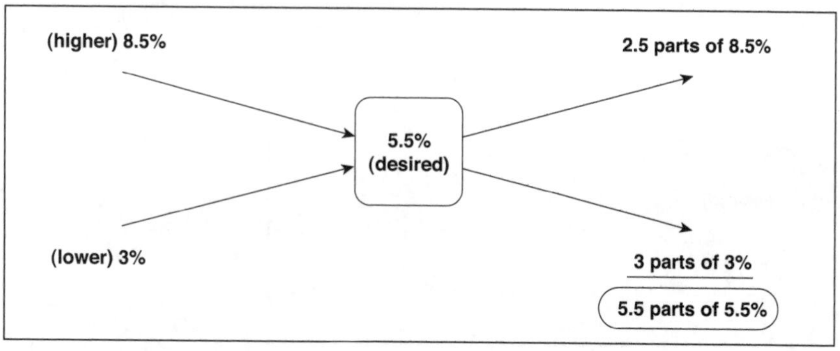

- To set up the X method:
  - Put the more concentrated product at the top left (high goes high)
  - Put the less concentrated product at the bottom left (low goes low)
  - Place the desired concentration in the middle of the X
- Subtract along the "X" lines to obtain the number of parts on the right (e.g., 8.5% – 5.5% = 3 parts; 3% – 5.5% = 2.5 parts for this problem).
- Add the number of parts on the right to find the total number of parts (5.5 parts in this problem).

Divide the total volume (3,785 mL) by the number of parts to obtain the volume per part.

$$\frac{3{,}785 \text{ mL}}{5.5 \text{ parts}} = 688.2 \text{ mL per part}$$

$$2.5 \text{ parts} \times \frac{688.2 \text{ mL}}{\text{part}} = 1{,}720 \text{ mL of the 8.5\% iodine tincture}$$

$$3 \text{ parts} \times \frac{688.2 \text{ mL}}{\text{part}} = 2{,}065 \text{ mL of the 3\% iodine tincture}$$

The end product provides 3,785 mL of a 5.5% iodine tincture. Alligation can also be used when the final volume is not known.

---

63. A hospice pharmacist receives a prescription for 1% morphine sulfate oral solution. She has a 120 mL bottle of morphine sulfate labeled 20 mg/5 mL and a 240 mL bottle of morphine sulfate labeled 100 mg/5 mL. How much of the 100 mg/5 mL product must be mixed with the contents of the 20 mg/5 mL morphine sulfate bottle to prepare the desired percentage strength for the patient?

First determine the percentage strengths of the two available products.

$$\frac{0.02 \text{ g}}{5 \text{ mL}} = \frac{\text{X g}}{100 \text{ mL}} \quad X = 0.4\%$$

$$\frac{0.1 \text{ g}}{5 \text{ mL}} = \frac{\text{X g}}{100 \text{ mL}} \quad X = 2\%$$

Since you are asked to prepare a strength in between two available strengths, this problem will require alligation.

Set up the X method in the same way:

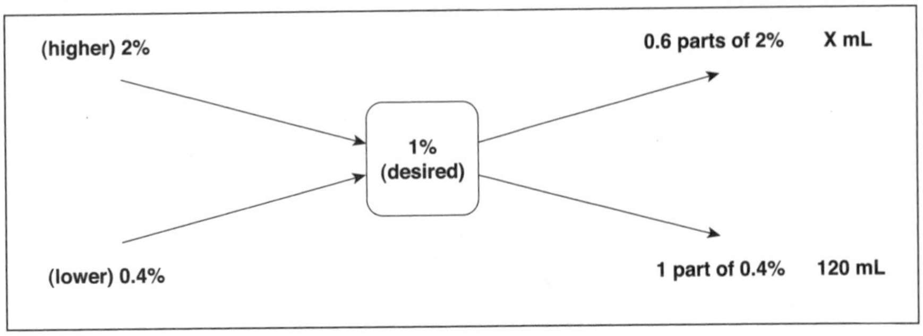

In this case, we do not know the final volume of the product, but we know the proper ratio of the parts is 0.6 parts of 2% to 1 part of 0.4%.

$$\frac{\text{1 part of 0.4\% morphine}}{\text{0.6 parts of 2\% morphine}} = \frac{\text{120 mL of 0.4\% morphine}}{\text{X mL of 2\% morphine}} \qquad \text{X = 72 mL of 2\% morphine sulfate}$$

Therefore, 72 mL of 2% (100 mg/5 mL) morphine sulfate must be added to the 120 mL of 0.4% (20 mg/5 mL) morphine sulfate to get a 1% solution. Ultimately, 192 mL of 1% product can be prepared, but the alligation had to be solved to determine that.

Osmolarity

The total number of particles in a given solution is directly proportional to its osmotic pressure. The particles are usually measured in milliosmoles. Osmolarity is the measure of total number of particles (or solutes) per liter (L) of solution, defined as osmoles/Liter (Osmol/L) or, more commonly as milliosmoles/Liter (mOsmol/L). Solutes can be either ionic (such as NaCl, which dissociates into 2 solutes in solution, Na^+ and Cl^-) or non-ionic, which do not dissociate (such as glucose and urea). The term for osmolarity when used to refer to the solute concentration of body fluids is tonicity, and solutions are thus isotonic (osmolarity is the same as blood, which is ~300 mOsmol/L), or is lower (hypotonic) or higher (hypertonic).

If the osmolarity is higher in one cellular compartment, it will cause water to move from the lower to the higher concentration of solutes. If a PN solution is injected with a higher osmolarity than blood, fluid will flow into the vein, resulting in edema, inflammation, phlebitis and possible thrombosis.

COMPOUND	# OF DISSOCIATION PARTICLES
Dextrose	1
Mannitol	1
Potassium chloride (KCl)	2
Sodium chloride (NaCl)	2
Sodium acetate ($NaC_2H_3O_2$)	2
Calcium chloride ($CaCl_2$)	3
Sodium citrate ($Na_3C_6H_5O_7$)	4

Milliosmole calculation problems differ from osmolarity calculation problems in that osmolarity will always need to be normalized to a volume of 1 liter. Some compounds for which it may be useful to know dissociations are listed in the table.

Osmolarity Calculations

Use this formula to find the mOsmol/L.

$$\text{mOsmol/L} = \frac{\text{Wt of substance (g/L)}}{\text{MW (g/mole)}} \times (\text{\# of particles}) \times 1{,}000$$

- Add up the number of particles into which the compound dissociates.
- Calculate the number of grams of the compound present in 1 L.
- Use the molecular weight (M.W.) to solve the problem.

Milliosmole calculations do not normalize to 1 liter.

---

64. What is the osmolarity, in mOsmol/L, of normal saline (0.9% NaCl)? M.W. = 58.5. Round to the nearest whole number.

NaCl dissociates into 2 particles; Na^+ and Cl^-.

Calculate the number of grams of the compound (NaCl) present in 1 L.

$$\frac{0.9\text{ g}}{100\text{ mL}} = \frac{X\text{ g}}{1{,}000\text{ mL}} \qquad X = 9\text{ g}$$

Use the molecular weight to solve for mOsmol/L.

$$\text{mOsmol/L} = \frac{9\text{ g/L}}{58.5\text{ g/mole}} \times 2 \times 1{,}000 = 308\text{ mOsmol/L}$$

---

65. What is the osmolarity, in mOsmol/L, of D5W? M.W. = 198. Round to the nearest tenth.

Dextrose does not dissociate and is counted as 1 particle.

$$\frac{5\text{ g}}{100\text{ mL}} = \frac{X\text{ g}}{1{,}000\text{ mL}} \qquad X = 50\text{ g}$$

Use the molecular weight to solve for mOsmol/L.

$$\text{mOsmol/L} = \frac{50\text{ g/L}}{198\text{ g/mole}} \times 1 \times 1{,}000 = 252.5\text{ mOsmol/L}$$

---

66. A solution contains 373 mg Na ions per liter. How many milliosmoles are represented in the solution? M.W. = 23. Round to the nearest tenth.

First, convert the units to match the formula.

$$\frac{373\text{ mg Na}}{\text{L}} \times \frac{1\text{ g}}{1{,}000\text{ mg}} = 0.373\text{ g/L}$$

$$\text{mOsmol} = \frac{0.373\text{ g/L}}{23\text{ g/mole}} \times 1 \times 1{,}000 = 16.2\text{ mOsmol}$$

The problem asks for milliosmoles and not osmolarity. Since the problem provides the amount of Na ions in 1 liter, the numerical answer is the same (mOsmol or mOsmol/L).

---

67. Calculate the osmolar concentration, in milliosmoles, represented by 1 liter of a 10% (w/v) solution of anhydrous dextrose (M.W. = 180) in water. Round to the nearest one decimal place.

$$\frac{10\text{ g}}{100\text{ mL}} = \frac{X\text{ g}}{1{,}000\text{ mL}} \qquad X = 100\text{ g}$$

$$\text{mOsmol} = \frac{100\text{ g/L}}{180\text{ g/mole}} \times 1 \times 1{,}000 = 555.6\text{ mOsmol}$$

The problem asks for milliosmoles and not osmolarity. Since the problem asks for mOsmol of dextrose in 1 liter, the numerical answer is the same (mOsmol or mOsmol/L).

---

68. How many milliosmoles of $CaCl_2$ (M.W.= 147) are represented in 150 mL of a 10% (w/v) calcium chloride solution? Round to the nearest whole number.

$$\frac{10\text{ g}}{100\text{ mL}} = \frac{X\text{ g}}{150\text{ mL}} \qquad X = 15\text{ g}$$

$$\text{mOsmol} = \frac{15\text{ g}}{147\text{ g/mol}} \times 3 \times 1{,}000 = 306\text{ mOsmol}$$

Note that the problem is asking for milliosmoles and not osmolarity. Therefore, the answer is in milliosmoles and not mOsmol/L. It is not normalized to 1 liter.

---

69. A solution contains 200 mg Ca ions per liter. How many milliosmoles are represented in the solution? M.W = 40

$$\text{mOsmol} = \frac{0.2\text{ g/L}}{40\text{ g/mole}} \times 1 \times 1{,}000 = 5\text{ mOsmol}$$

The problem is asking for milliosmoles and not osmolarity. Therefore, the answer is in milliosmoles and not mOsmol/L. It is not normalized to 1 liter.

---

70. How many grams of potassium chloride are needed to make 200 mL of a solution containing 250 mOsmol/L? Round to the nearest hundredth. (M.W. K = 39, M.W. Cl = 35.5)

First calculate the M.W. of KCl.

$$\text{M.W. of KCl} = \text{M.W. of K} + \text{M.W. of Cl} = 39 + 35.5 = 74.5$$

$$250\text{ mOsmol/L} = \frac{X}{74.5} \times 2 \times 1{,}000 \qquad X = 9.31\text{ g/L}$$

$$\frac{9.31\text{ g}}{1{,}000\text{ mL}} = \frac{X\text{ g}}{200\text{ mL}} \qquad X = 1.86\text{ g}$$

You may be provided with the molecular weight on the exam or asked to calculate it.

Isotonicity

Osmolarity is the measure of total number of particles (or solutes) per liter (L) of solution. Tonicity is the term used to describe osmolarity used in the context of body fluids. When solutions are prepared, they need to match the tonicity of the body fluid as closely as possible. Solutions that are not isotonic with the body fluid produce pain upon administration, and cause fluid transfer. In pharmacy, the terms hypotonic rather than hypo-osmotic, hypertonic rather than hyperosmotic, and isotonic rather than iso-osmotic, are used. Isotonicity is commonly used when preparing eye drops and nasal solutions.

Since isotonicity is related to the number of particles in solution, the dissociation factor (or ionization), symbolized by the letter *i*, is determined for the compound (drug). Non-ionic compounds do not dissociate and will have a dissociation factor, *i*, of 1. The table shows the dissociation factors (*i*) based on the percentage that dissociates into ions; for example, a dissociation factor of 1.8 means that 80% of the compound will dissociate in a weak solution.

NUMBER OF DISSOCIATED IONS	DISSOCIATION FACTOR (OR IONIZATION) *i*
1	1
2	1.8
3	2.6
4	3.4
5	4.2

As mentioned above, body fluids are isotonic, having an osmotic pressure equivalent to 0.9% sodium chloride. When making a medication to place into a body fluid, the drug provides solutes to the solvent and needs to be accounted for in the prescription in order to avoid making the prescription hypertonic. The relationship between the amount of drug that produces a particular osmolarity and the amount of sodium chloride that produces the same osmolarity is called the sodium chloride equivalent, or "E value" for short. This is the formula for calculating the E value of a compound:

$$E = \frac{(58.5)(i)}{(\text{MW of drug})(1.8)}$$

The "E value" formula takes into account the molecular weight of NaCl (58.5) and the dissociation factor of 1.8 since normal saline is around 80% ionized; adding 0.8 for each additional ion beyond 1 into which the drug dissociates. The reason the compound is compared to NaCl is because NaCl is the major determinant of the isotonicity of body fluid.

Once the "E value" is determined, the following steps outline the process of doing isotonicity problems:

1. Calculate the total amount of NaCl needed to make the final product/prescription isotonic. This is done by multiplying 0.9% NS by the desired volume of the prescription.
2. Multiply the total drug amount, in grams, by the "E value".
3. Subtract step 2 from step 1 to determine the total amount of NaCl needed to prepare an isotonic prescription.

---

71. Calculate the E value for mannitol (M.W. = 182). Round to the nearest hundredth.

$$\frac{(58.5)(i)}{(\text{MW of drug})(1.8)} = \frac{58.5\ (1)}{182\ (1.8)} = 0.18$$

---

72. Calculate the E value for potassium iodide, which dissociates into 2 particles (M.W. = 166). Round to two decimal places.

$$\frac{(58.5)(i)}{(\text{MW of drug})(1.8)} = \frac{58.5\ (1.8)}{166\ (1.8)} = 0.35$$

73. Physostigmine salicylate (M.W. = 413) is a 2- ion electrolyte, dissociating 80% in a given concentration (therefore, use a dissociation factor of 1.8). Calculate its sodium chloride equivalent. Round to two decimal places.

$$\frac{(58.5)(i)}{(\text{MW of drug})(1.8)} = \frac{58.5\ (1.8)}{413\ (1.8)} = 0.14$$

---

74. The E-value for ephedrine sulfate is 0.23. How many grams of sodium chloride are needed to compound the following prescription? Round to 3 decimal places.

PRESCRIPTION	QUANTITY
Ephedrine sulfate	0.4 g
Sodium chloride	q.s.
Purified water qs	30 mL
Make isotonic soln.	
Sig. For the nose.	

Step 1. Determine how much NaCl would make the product isotonic.

$$\frac{0.9\text{ g}}{100\text{ mL}} = \frac{X}{30\text{ mL}} \quad X = 0.27\text{ g}$$

Step 2. Determine amount of sodium chloride represented from ephedrine sulfate.

0.4 g x 0.23 ("E value") = 0.092 g of sodium chloride

Step 3. Subtract step 2 from step 1.

0.27 g - 0.092 g = 0.178 g of NaCl are needed to make an isotonic solution

---

75. The pharmacist receives an order for 10 mL of tobramycin 1% ophthalmic solution. He has tobramycin 40 mg/mL solution. Tobramycin does not dissociate and has a M.W. of 468. Find the E value for tobramycin and determine the amount of NaCl needed to make the solution isotonic. Round to two decimal places.

$$\frac{(58.5)(i)}{(\text{MW of drug})(1.8)} = \frac{58.5\ (1)}{468\ (1.8)} = 0.07\text{, which is the "E value" for tobramycin}$$

The "E value" for tobramycin is 0.07. The prescription asks for 10 mL of 1% solution.

Step 1. Determine how much NaCl would make the product isotonic (if that is all you were using).

$$\frac{0.9\text{ g}}{100\text{ mL}} = \frac{X}{10\text{ mL}} \quad X = 0.09\text{ g, or 90 mg}$$

Step 2. Determine amount of sodium chloride represented from tobramycin.

$$\frac{1\ g}{100\ mL} = \frac{X}{10\ mL} \quad X = 0.1\ g,\ \text{or}\ 100\ mg$$

100 mg x 0.07 ("E value") = 7 mg of sodium chloride

Step 3. Subtract step 2 from step 1.

You are using tobramycin, so you do not need all the NaCl. Subtract out the equivalent amount of tonicity provided by the tobramycin, which is 7 mg.

90 mg - 7 mg = 83 mg (83 mg additional sodium chloride is needed to make an isotonic solution)

To calculate how much of the original stock solution is required, use the stock solution that is 40 mg/mL. The prescription is written for 10 mL of a 1% solution. In the previous steps it was found that 100 mg of tobramycin is needed to provide 10 mL of a 1% solution.

$$\frac{40\ mg}{1\ mL} = \frac{100\ mg}{X\ mL} \quad X = 2.5\ mL\ \text{of the original stock solution.}$$

Moles and Millimoles

A mole (mol) is the molecular weight of a substance in grams, or g/mole. A millimole (mmol) is 1/1,000 of the molecular weight in grams, or 1/1,000 of a mole. For monovalent species, the numeric value of the milliequivalent and millimole are identical.

$$\text{mols} = \frac{g}{MW} \quad \text{or} \quad \text{mmols} = \frac{mg}{MW}$$

---

76. How many moles of anhydrous magnesium sulfate (M.W. = 120.4) are present in 250 grams of the substance? Round to the nearest hundredth.

$$\text{mols} = \frac{g}{MW}$$

$$\text{mols} = \frac{250\ g}{120.4} = 2.076,\ \text{or}\ 2.08\ \text{mols}$$

---

77. How many moles are equivalent to 875 milligrams of aluminum acetate (M.W. = 204)? Round to 3 decimal places.

First, convert 875 mg to grams.

$$875\ mg \times \frac{1\ g}{1{,}000\ mg} = 0.875\ g$$

Next, solve for mols.

$$\text{mols} = \frac{g}{MW} = \frac{0.875\ g}{204} = 0.004\ \text{mols}$$

78. How many millimoles of sodium phosphate (M.W. = 138) are present in 90 g of the substance? Round to the nearest whole number.

$$\frac{90{,}000 \text{ mg}}{138} = 652 \text{ mmols}$$

Or, solve another way:

$$\frac{90 \text{ g}}{138} = 0.652 \text{ mols, which is } 652 \text{ mmols}$$

---

79. How many moles are equivalent to 45 grams of potassium carbonate (M.W. = 138)? Round to the nearest thousandth.

$$\text{mols} = \frac{\text{g}}{\text{MW}}$$

$$\text{mols} = \frac{45 \text{ g}}{138} = 0.326 \text{ mols}$$

---

80. How many millimoles of calcium chloride (M.W. = 147) are represented in 147 mL of a 10% (w/v) calcium chloride solution?

Step 1: Calculate the amount (g) of $CaCl_2$ in 147 mL of 10% $CaCl_2$ solution.

$$\frac{10 \text{ g}}{100 \text{ mL}} = \frac{X \text{ g}}{147 \text{ mL}} \qquad X = 14.7 \text{ g}$$

Step 2: Calculate the mols of $CaCl_2$ in 147 mL of 10% $CaCl_2$ solution.

$$\text{mols} = \frac{14.7 \text{ g}}{147} \qquad X = 0.1 \text{ mol}$$

Step 3: Solve the problem by converting moles to millimoles; 0.1 mol x 1,000 = 100 mmols

---

81. How many milligrams of sodium chloride (MW = 58.5) represent 0.25 mmol? Do not round the answer.

$$0.25 \text{ mmols} = \frac{X \text{ mg}}{58.5} \qquad X = 14.625 \text{ mg}$$

---

82. How many grams of sodium chloride (M.W. = 58.5) should be used to prepare this solution? Do not round the answer.

PRESCRIPTION	QUANTITY
Methylprednisolone	0.5 g
NaCl solution	60 mL
Each 5 mL should contain 0.6 mmols of NaCl	

$$\frac{0.6 \text{ mmols}}{5 \text{ mL}} = \frac{X \text{ mmols}}{60 \text{ mL}} \quad X = 7.2 \text{ mmols}$$

$$7.2 \text{ mmols} = \frac{X \text{ mg}}{58.5} \quad X = 421.2 \text{ mg or } 0.4212 \text{ g}$$

Milliequivalents

Drugs can be expressed in solution in different ways:

- Milliosmoles refers to the number of particles in solution.
- Millimoles refers to the molecular weight (MW).
- Milliequivalents (mEq) represent the amount, in milligrams (mg), of a solute equal to 1/1,000 of its gram equivalent weight, taking into account the valence of the ions. Like osmolarity, the quantity of particles is important – but so is the electrical charge. Milliequivalents refers to the chemical activity of an electrolyte and is related to the total number of ionic charges in solution and considers the valence (charge) of each ion.

To count the valence, divide the compound into its positive and negative components, and then count the number of either the positive or the negative charges. For a given compound, the milliequivalents of cations equals that of anions. Some common compounds and their valences are listed in the table.

COMPOUND	VALENCE
ammonium chloride (NH_4Cl)	1
potassium chloride (KCl^-)	1
potassium gluconate ($KC_6H_{11}O_7$)	1
sodium acetate ($NaC_2H_3O_2$)	1
sodium bicarbonate ($NaHCO_3$)	1
sodium chloride	1
calcium carbonate ($CaCO_3$)	2
calcium chloride ($CaCl_2$)	2
ferrous sulfate ($FeSO_4^{2-}$)	2
magnesium sulfate ($MgSO_4^{2-}$)	2

$$\text{mEq} = \frac{\text{mg x valence}}{\text{MW}} \quad \text{or} \quad \text{mEq} = \text{mmols x valence}$$

---

83. A 20 mL vial is labeled potassium chloride (2 mEq/mL). How many grams of potassium chloride (M.W. = 74.5) are present? Round to the nearest hundredth.

$$20 \text{ mL} \times \frac{2 \text{ mEq}}{\text{mL}} = 40 \text{ mEq KCl total}$$

$$\text{mEq} = \frac{\text{mg x valence}}{\text{MW}}$$

$$40 \text{ mEq} = \frac{\text{mg} \times 1}{74.5} = 2{,}980 \text{ mg, which is } 2.98 \text{ g}$$

If asked to convert KCl liquid to tablets, use simple proportion since KCl 10% = 20 mEq/15 mL. For example, if someone is using Klor-Con 20 mEq BID, the total daily dose is 40 mEq. Convert to KCl 10%, by solving the following equation:

$$\frac{40 \text{ mEq}}{X \text{ mL}} = \frac{20 \text{ mEq}}{15 \text{ mL}} \quad X = 30 \text{ mL}$$

84. How many milliequivalents of potassium chloride are present in a 12 mL dose of a 10% (w/v) potassium chloride (M.W. = 74.5) elixir? Round to 1 decimal place.

$$\frac{10\ g}{100\ mL} = \frac{X\ g}{12\ mL} \qquad X = 1.2\ g,\ or\ 1{,}200\ mg$$

$$mEq = \frac{1{,}200\ mg \times 1}{74.5} = 16.1\ mEq$$

---

85. Calculate the milliequivalents of a standard ammonium chloride (M.W. = 53.5) 21.4 mg/mL sterile solution in a 500 mL container.

$$\frac{21.4\ mg}{mL} \times 500\ mL = 10{,}700\ mg$$

$$mEq = \frac{10{,}700\ mg \times 1}{53.5} = 200\ mEq$$

---

86. How many milliequivalents of $MgSO_4$ (M.W. = 120.4) are represented in 1 gram of anhydrous magnesium sulfate? Round to the nearest tenth.

$$mEq = \frac{1{,}000\ mg \times 2}{120.4} = 16.6\ mEq$$

---

87. How many milliequivalents of sodium are in a 50 mL vial of sodium bicarbonate (M.W. = 84) 8.4%?

$$\frac{8.4\ g}{100\ mL} = \frac{X\ g}{50\ mL} \qquad X = 4.2\ g,\ or\ 4{,}200\ mg$$

$$mEq = \frac{4{,}200\ mg \times 1}{84} = 50\ mEq$$

Calculation Practice

The following problem integrates multiple calculation concepts.

---

88. A pharmacist receives an order for sodium chloride 4 mEq/kg/day for a patient who weighs 165 pounds. Using ½NS, how many liters will the patient require per day? Round to the nearest tenth. (M.W. of Na = 23, M.W. of Cl = 35.5)

$$\frac{4\ mEq}{kg} \times 75\ kg = 300\ mEq/day$$

$$300\ \text{mEq} = \frac{X\ \text{mg} \times 1}{58.5} = 17{,}550\ \text{mg, or } 17.55\ \text{g}$$

$$\frac{0.45\ \text{g}}{100\ \text{mL}} = \frac{17.55\ \text{g}}{X\ \text{mL}} \quad X = 3{,}900\ \text{mL or } 3.9\ \text{L}$$

Body Mass Index

Overweight and obesity is a health problem associated with increased morbidity from hypertension, dyslipidemia, diabetes, coronary heart disease, stroke, gallbladder disease, osteoarthritis and some other conditions. Higher body weights are also associated with increases in all-cause mortality. Body mass index (BMI) is a measure of body fat based on height and weight that applies to adult men and women. BMI is a useful measure of body fat, but the BMI can over-estimate body fat in persons who are muscular, and can under-estimate body fat in frail elderly persons and others who have lost muscle mass. Waist circumference is used concurrently with BMI. If most of the fat is around the waist, there is higher disease risk. High risk is defined as a waist size > 35 inches for women or > 40 inches for men. Underweight can be a problem if a person is fighting a disease such as a frail, hospitalized patient with an infection.

BMI should be calculated as follows:

$$\text{BMI (kg/m}^2\text{)} = \frac{\text{weight (kg)}}{[\text{height (m)}]^2}$$

Alternatively, BMI can be calculated with weight in pounds and height in inches using a conversion factor to convert to units of kg/m^2:

$$\text{BMI (kg/m}^2\text{)} = \frac{\text{weight (pounds)}}{[\text{height (in)}]^2} \times 703 \text{ (to convert to kg/m}^2\text{)}$$

BMI Classifications

BMI (kg/m^2)	CLASSIFICATION
< 18.5	Underweight
18.5 - 24.9	Normal weight
25 - 29.9	Overweight
≥ 30	Obese

89. A male comes to the pharmacy and tells the pharmacist he is 6′7″ tall and 250 pounds. His waist circumference is 43 inches. Calculate his BMI. Round to the nearest whole number. Is the patient underweight, normal weight, overweight, or obese?

- Convert weight to kg: 250 pounds x 1 kg/2.2 lbs = 113.6363 kg
- Convert height to cm: 6′7″ = 79 inches x 2.54 cm/inch = 200.66 cm

$$200.66 \text{ cm} \times \frac{\text{m}}{100 \text{ cm}} = 2.0066 \text{ m}$$

$$\text{BMI (kg/m}^2\text{)} = \frac{113.6363 \text{ kg}}{(2.0066 \text{ m})^2} = 28.2 \text{ kg/m}^2\text{, rounded to 28, overweight}$$

Because of the rounding specifications in the question, the answer is the same regardless of the formula used. Expect the same on the exam.

---

90. Calculate the BMI for a male who is 6′ tall and weighs 198 lbs. Round to the nearest tenth. Is the patient underweight, normal weight, overweight, or obese?

$$\text{BMI (kg/m}^2\text{)} = \frac{198 \text{ pounds}}{(72 \text{ in})^2} \times 703 = 26.9 \text{ kg/m}^2 \text{ overweight}$$

Because of the rounding specifications in the question, the answer is the same regardless of the formula used. Expect the same on the exam.

Body Weight

Actual Body Weight or Total Body Weight

Actual body weight or total body weight (TBW) is the weight of the patient when weighed on a scale.

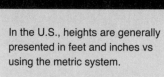

STUDY TIP: HEIGHT IN INCHES

In the U.S., heights are generally presented in feet and inches vs using the metric system.

- Example 1:
  A patient is 5 feet 6 inches tall (often written 5′6″). How many inches tall is the patient?
  - ❑ 1 ft = 12 inches, so 5 ft = 60 inches
  - ❑ Next, add the additional 6 inches
  - ❑ 5′6″ = 66 inches
  - ❑ For IBW calculation: patient is 6 inches over 5 feet
- Example 2:
  A patient is 6′3″. How many inches tall is this patient?
  - ❑ 6 ft x 12 inches/ft = 72 inches
  - ❑ Next, add the additional 3 inches
  - ❑ 6′3″ = 75 inches
  - ❑ For IBW calculation: patient is 15 inches over 5 feet

Ideal Body Weight

Ideal body weight (IBW) is the healthy (ideal) weight for a person. The IBW formula must be memorized:

IBW (males) = 50 kg + (2.3 kg)(number of inches over 5 feet)

IBW (females) = 45.5 kg + (2.3 kg)(number of inches over 5 feet)

There are alternate methods of calculating IBW in children and adults < 5 feet.

Adjusted Body Weight

Adjusted body weight is calculated when patients are obese or overweight. The adjusted body weight formula must be memorized:

$$AdjBW_{0.4} = IBW + 0.4(TBW - IBW)$$

Adult doses are generally the same for all patients (e.g., lisinopril 10 mg daily, memantine 5 mg BID). Weight-based (mg/kg) dosing is common in pediatrics and is recommended for some medications in adult patients (see table). Total body weight is used for weight-based dosing of most drugs in adults, but there are some exceptions. Some drugs with a narrow therapeutic index (e.g., aminophylline, theophylline) are best dosed based on IBW to avoid toxicity. Dosing drugs in obese and overweight patients can be complicated; these patients are often excluded from clinical trials, leading to a lack of data about this patient population. Some drugs (e.g., enoxaparin, vancomycin, others) are dosed based on actual body weight (even if a patient is obese) because that has been determined in clinical trials to be the best weight to use. In clinical practice, it may be necessary to consult primary literature for the best dosing strategy in obese patients. For the exam, the following table can be used.

WHICH WEIGHT TO USE FOR DRUG DOSING (mg/kg)?		
Underweight: TBW < IBW	**Normal Weight: TBW ≅ IBW***	**Obese**: TBW >> IBW**
Use TBW to dose all medications (to avoid overdosing)	Use TBW to dose most medications	Use TBW for: LMWHs, UFH, vancomycin
	Use IBW for: Aminophylline, theophylline, acyclovir	Use IBW for: Aminophylline, theophylline, acyclovir
		Use $AdjBW_{0.4}$ for: Aminoglycosides#

If a question specifies what weight to use, even if different from above, use it. Follow all instructions on the exam.

**Very few patients weigh exactly their IBW. If TBW is < 120% of IBW, use the middle column recommendations above.*

***Definition of obesity for drug dosing can differ, but is generally considered to be ≥ 120 – 130% of IBW.*

#Aminoglycosides are dosed based on total body weight or IBW, unless the patient is considered obese, then adjusted body weight is used.

Renal Function and Creatinine Clearance Estimation

The normal range for serum creatinine is approximately 0.6 to 1.2 mg/dL. A serum creatinine above this range usually indicates that the kidneys are not functioning properly. However, the values can appear normal even when renal function is compromised. Refer to the Lab Values & Drug Monitoring and Renal Disease Chapter.

Creatinine is a break-down product produced when muscle tissue makes energy. If kidney function declines and creatinine cannot be cleared (excreted), the creatinine level will increase in the blood and the creatinine clearance (CrCl) will decrease. This tells us that the concentration of drugs that are renally cleared will also increase and a dose reduction may be required.

Patients should be assessed for dehydration when the serum creatinine value is elevated. Dehydration can cause both the serum creatinine (SCr) and the blood urea nitrogen (BUN) values to increase. Generally, a BUN:SCr ratio > 20:1 indicates dehydration. Correcting the dehydration will reduce both BUN and SCr, and can prevent or treat acute renal failure. Signs of dehydration should also be assessed and these can include decreased urine output, tachycardia, tachypnea, dry skin/mouth/mucous membranes, skin tenting (skin does not bounce back when pinched into a fold) and possibly fever. Dehydration is usually caused by diarrhea, vomiting, and/or a lack of adequate fluid intake.

EXAM SCENARIO

A patient profile is provided for a 72 year old female (5'5" and 198 lbs).

- Without doing any calculations, most pharmacists know that a female who is 5'5" and 198 lbs would be obese per BMI.
  - TBW = 90 kg, IBW = 57 kg
  - 90 kg/57 kg = 1.58 or 158% of IBW
- If asked to recommend heparin (UFH) dosing to treat an acute VTE for this patient, use the table above to decide which weight to use:
  - UFH bolus: 80 units/kg x TBW = 7200 units
  - UFH drip: 18 units/kg/hr x TBW = 1620 units/hr

Refer to the Anticoagulation chapter for UFH heparin dosing.

91. Looking at the laboratory values below, make an assessment of the patient's hydration status.

	PATIENT'S VALUE	REFERENCE RANGE
BUN	54 mg/dL	7–25 mg/dL
Creatinine	1.8 mg/dL	0.6–1.2 mg/dL

a. The patient appears to be well hydrated.

b. The patient appears to be too hydrated.

c. The patient is not experiencing dehydration.

d. The patient is experiencing dehydration and may need to be started on fluids.

e. The patient has subjective information indicating dehydration but the patient needs to be assessed objectively as well.

The correct answer is (d). The patient's BUN:SCr ratio is 54/1.8 = 30:1. Since 30:1 > 20:1, the BUN is disproportionately elevated relative to the creatinine, indicating that the patient is dehydrated.

---

92. Nancy is receiving a furosemide infusion at 5 mg/hr. The nurse notices her urine output has decreased in the last hour. Laboratory values are drawn and the patient has a SCr of 1.5 mg/dL and a BUN of 26 mg/dL. The nurse wants to know if she should stop the furosemide infusion due to the patient becoming dehydrated. What is the correct assessment of the patient's hydration status?

a. The patient appears to be too hydrated given the laboratory results.

b. The patient is not experiencing dehydration given the laboratory results.

c. The patient is experiencing dehydration and may need to be started on fluids.

d. The patient has objective information indicating dehydration but the patient needs to be assessed subjectively as well.

e. None of the above are correct.

The correct answer is (b). The BUN:SCr ratio is 26/1.5 = 17.3:1, which is < 20:1. Continue to monitor the patient.

The Cockcroft-Gault Equation

This formula is used by pharmacists to estimate renal function. However, it is not commonly used in very young children, ESRD patients or when renal function is fluctuating rapidly. There are different methods used to estimate renal function in these circumstances. The Cockcroft-Gault equation should be known, as it is commonly used in practice.

$$\text{CrCl (mL/min)} = \frac{140 - (\text{age of patient})}{72 \times \text{SCr}} \times \text{weight in kg (x 0.85 if female)}$$

Use age in years, weight in kg and SCr in mg/dL (same as mmol/L) in the Cockcroft-Gault equation

WHICH WEIGHT TO USE FOR CALCULATING CrCl?		
Underweight: TBW < IBW	**Normal Weight*: TBW ≅ IBW**	**Overweight or Obese**: TBW > IBW**
Use TBW in CrCl calculation	Use IBW in CrCl calculation	Use $AdjBW_{0.4}$ in CrCl calculation

**Very few patients weigh exactly their IBW. If TBW > IBW and BMI < 25, use the middle column recommendations above*
***Overweight/obese determined by BMI ≥ 25*

Once the CrCl has been calculated, it is used to renally adjust all necessary medications (unless serum creatinine changes). The proper weight to use in the Cockcroft-Gault equation will not always be the same weight used to calculate a weight-based (mg/kg) dose. The following examples illustrate this point.

Calculation Practice

The following problems integrate multiple calculation concepts. Refer to other chapters if you are unfamiliar with the dosing of the medications in the following questions.

93. A female patient is to receive 5 mg/kg/day of theophylline. The patient is 5'7" and weighs 243 pounds. Calculate the daily theophylline dose the patient should receive.

Theophylline and aminophylline should be dosed on IBW unless a different weight is specified in the problem. Check for instructions in the problem regarding rounding or which weight to use.

IBW (female) = 45.5 kg + (2.3 x 7 in) = 61.6 kg

Theophylline 5 mg/kg x 61.6 kg = 308 mg

STUDY TIP: CrCl

Use the information in the previous table and follow these steps to calculate CrCl on the exam. Do not do more math than necessary.

- Step #1: Calculate the patient's IBW and TBW in kg.
  - ❑ Is TBW < IBW? If yes, you are finished. Use TBW for CrCl calculation. If no, continue.
- Step #2: Is TBW approximately equal to IBW?
  - ❑ If yes, you are finished. Use IBW for CrCl calculation. If no, continue.
- Step #3: Is TBW > IBW? If yes, calculate BMI.
  - ❑ Is BMI ≥ 25? If yes, use $AdjBW_{0.4}$ for CrCl calculation.
  - ❑ If no, use IBW for CrCl calculation.

94. A 64 year old female patient (height 5'5", weight 205 pounds) is hospitalized with a nosocomial pneumonia which is responding to treatment. Her current antibiotic medications include ciprofloxacin, *Primaxin* and vancomycin. Her morning laboratory values include: K 4 mEq/L, BUN 60 mg/dL, SCr 2.7 mg/dL and glucose 222 mg/dL. Based on the renal dosage recommendations from the package labeling below, what is the correct dose of *Primaxin* for this patient?

CrCl	≥ 71 mL/min	41–70 mL/min	21–40 mL/min	6–20 mL/min
Primaxin Dose	500 mg IV Q6H	500 mg IV Q8H	250 mg IV Q6H	250 mg IV Q12H

First determine which weight to use to calculate CrCl:

$$\text{Total Body Weight} = 93.1818 \text{ kg}$$

$$\text{IBW} = 45.5 \text{ kg} + (2.3 \times 5 \text{ in}) = 57 \text{ kg}$$

$$\text{BMI} = \frac{205 \text{ lbs}}{65^2} \times 703 = 34.1, \text{ obese}$$

Now calculate her adjusted body weight:

$$\text{AdjBW}_{0.4} = 57 + 0.4\,(93.1818 - 57) = 71.47 \text{ kg}$$

Then, solve using the Cockcroft-Gault equation:

$$\text{CrCl} = \frac{140 - 64}{72 \times 2.7} \times 71.47\,(0.85) = 23.75 \text{ mL/min.}$$

The correct dose of *Primaxin* is 250 mg IV Q6H.

---

95. A 34 year old male (height 6'7", weight 287 pounds) is hospitalized after a motor vehicle accident. He develops a *Pseudomonas aeruginosa* infection. The physician orders tobramycin 2 mg/kg IV Q8H. Calculate the tobramycin dose. Round to the nearest 10 milligrams.

$$\text{Total Body Weight} = 287 \text{ lb} \times \frac{1 \text{ kg}}{2.2 \text{ lbs}} = 130.4545 \text{ kg}$$

$$\text{IBW (male)} = 50 \text{ kg} + (2.3 \times 19 \text{ in}) = 93.7 \text{ kg}$$

$$\text{\% above IBW} = \frac{130.4545 \text{ kg}}{93.7 \text{ kg}} = 1.39, \text{ he is} \sim 39\% \text{ above his IBW}$$

Aminoglycosides are dosed on adjusted body weight in obese patients.

$AdjBW_{0.4}$ = 93.7 + 0.4 (103.4545 − 93.7) = 108.4 kg

Tobramycin 2 mg/kg x 108.4 kg = 216.8 mg, round to 220 mg IV Q8H

---

96. Levofloxacin, dosing per pharmacy, is ordered for an 87 year old female patient (height 5'4", weight 103 pounds). Her labs include BUN 22 mg/dL and SCr 1 mg/dL. Choose the correct dosing regimen based on the renal dosage adjustments from the package labeling below.

CrCl	≥ 50 mL/min	20–49 mL/min	< 20 mL/min
Levofloxacin Dose	500 mg Q24 hours	250 mg Q24 hours	250 mg Q48 hours

First, determine which weight to use in calculating the CrCl.

Total Body Weight = 46.8181 kg

IBW = 45.5 kg + (2.3 x 4 in) = 54.7 kg

Use total body weight for calculating CrCl since the patient's total body weight is less than her IBW.

$$CrCl = \frac{140 - 87}{72 \times 1} \times 46.8181 \text{ kg} (\times 0.85) = 29 \text{ mL/min}$$

The correct dose of levofloxacin is 250 mg Q24H.

---

97. A 50 year old male (height 6'1", weight 177 pounds) has HIV and is being started on tenofovir, emtricitabine and efavirenz therapy. His laboratory values include K 4.4 mEq/L, BUN 40 mg/dL, SCr 1.8 mg/dL, and CD4 count of 455 cells/mm³. Using the renal dosage recommendations from the package labeling below, what is the correct dose of tenofovir for this patient?

CrCl	≥ 50 mL/min	30–49 mL/min	10–29 mL/min	< 10 mL/min
Tenofovir Dose	300 mg daily	300 mg Q48 hours	300 mg Q72-96 hours	300 mg weekly

First, determine which weight to use in calculating the CrCl.

Total Body Weight = 80.4545 kg

IBW = 50 kg + (2.3 x 13 in) = 79.9, or 80 kg

The IBW is almost the same as the actual weight. Either weight will yield a similar CrCl.

Next, calculate the CrCl.

$$CrCl = \frac{140 - 50}{72 \times 1.8} \times 80 \text{ kg} = 55 \text{ mL/min}$$

The dose of tenofovir should be 300 mg daily.

98. The pharmacist reviews Ms. Hoydt's *Lovenox* order and labs in the profile. At this hospital, pharmacists have the authority to make renal dosage adjustments per package labeling when necessary. What is the correct *Lovenox* dose for Ms. Hoydt?

PATIENT PROFILE

Patient Name	Carolyn Hoydt								
Address	13 Windgate Road								
Age:	37	**Sex:**	F	**Race:**	Caucasian	**Height:**	5'6"	**Weight:**	175 pounds
Allergies	NKDA								

DIAGNOSES

DVT confirmed by ultrasound

MEDICATIONS

Date	Rx #	Prescriber	Drug/Strength/Sig
7/5	98732	Langston	*Ortho Tri-Cyclen* 1 PO Daily
7/5	98733	Langston	Centrum 1 PO Daily
11/15	102345	Mason	*Lovenox* 1 mg/kg SC Q12H
11/15	102347	Mason	D51/2NS @ 70 ml/hr

LAB/DIAGNOSTIC TESTS

Test	Normal Value	Results		
		Date: 7/5	**Date:** 11/15	**Date:**
Na	135-146 mEq/L	136	142	
K	3.5-5.3 mEq/L	3.5	5.2	
Cl	98-110 mEq/L	109	105	
HCO3	22-28 mEq/L	25	26	
BUN	7-25 mg/dL	10	22	
Creatinine	0.6-1.2 mg/dL	0.7	1.4	
Glu	65-99 mg/dL	100	120	
Hgb	12-16 g/dL	12	13.6	
Hct	36-46%	37	41	

a. 175 mg SC Q12H
b. 175 mg SC once daily
c. 80 mg SC once daily
d. 80 mg SC Q12H
e. 60 mg SC Q12H

The correct answer is (d). Total body weight is used to determine the weight-based dose of LMWHs. Since the patient's BMI is 28.3 kg/m^2 (overweight), her adjusted body weight is used in the Cockcroft-Gault equation to calculate CrCl. Her CrCl is 58.5 ml/min (well above the threshold of 30 ml/min, for changing the dosing interval of *Lovenox* to once daily).

99. The pharmacist reviews the order for IV *Bactrim* and the labs for Mr. Ross in the profile. What dose should Mr. Ross receive given the renal dosage recommendations below?

CrCl	> 30 mL/min	15–30 mL/min	< 15 mL/min
Sulfamethoxazole/ trimethoprim (SMX/TMP)	No dosage adjustment required	Administer 50% of the recommended dose	Use is not recommended

PATIENT PROFILE

Patient Name	Jeremy Ross
Address	22 Harris Lane
Age:	41 **Sex:** M **Race:** Hispanic **Height:** 6'1" **Weight:** 70 kg
Allergies	NKDA

DIAGNOSES

Depression	Dyslipidemia
HIV	

MEDICATIONS

Date	Prescriber	Drug/Strength/Sig
5/5	Sangler	Nicotine patch 21 mg/day – apply 1 patch daily
5/5	Sangler	*Stribild* 1 tablet daily
6/15	Sangler	*Celexa* 20 mg 1 tablet daily
11/15	Mason	*Lipitor* 10 mg 1 tablet daily
12/1	Hern	*Bactrim* 20 mg TMP/kg/day IV divided Q6H

LAB/DIAGNOSTIC TESTS

Test	Normal Value	Results		
		Date: 12/1	**Date:** 5/5	**Date:**
WBC	4,000-11,000 cells/mm^3	10.7	9.5	
CD4	800-1,100 cells/mm^3	187	226	
Na	135-146 mEq/L	139	142	
K	3.5-5.3 mEq/L	3.7	4.1	
Cl	98-110 mEq/L	109	105	
HCO3	22-28 mEq/L	24	26	
BUN	7-25 mg/dL	7	9	
Creatinine	0.6-1.2 mg/dL	0.6	0.8	
Glu	65-99 mg/dL	120	136	

a. 1400 mg TMP IV Q6H
b. 700 mg TMP IV Q6H
c. 400 mg TMP IV Q12H
d. 350 mg TMP IV Q6H
e. Mr. Ross should not receive *Bactrim*

The correct answer is (d). Mr. Ross is of normal weight per BMI (BMI = 20.4 kg/m^2). His *Bactrim* dose will be calculated with his total body weight (20 mg TMP/kg/day x 70 kg = 1400 mg TMP/day or 350 mg TMP Q6H for normal renal function). His TBW is less than his IBW, so his CrCl should be calculated with his TBW and is ~160 ml/min. Renal dose adjustments will not be needed for any medications at this level of CrCl.

100. How many milligrams of aminophylline will Mike receive per day based on the order in the profile? Round to the nearest whole number.

PATIENT PROFILE

Patient Name	Mike Kelly
Address	65 Laney Road
Age:	22 **Sex:** M **Race:** Caucasian
Allergies	NKDA

DIAGNOSES

Asthma
Allergies

MEDICATIONS

Date	Prescriber	Drug/Strength/Sig
8/23	Sanchez	*Singulair* 10 mg 1 tablet in the evening daily
8/23	Sanchez	*Qvar* 1 puff (40 mcg) BID
9/29	Williams	Methylprednisolone 40 mg IV Q12H
9/29	Williams	Aminophylline 0.5 mg/kg/hr
9/29	Williams	D5$^1/_2$NS at 80 ml/hr
9/29	Williams	Albuterol nebulization 2.5 mg Q6H

LAB/DIAGNOSTIC TESTS

Test	Normal Value	Results		
		Date: 9/1	**Date:** 1/7	**Date:** 9/29
Weight		125 pounds	141 pounds	160 pounds
Height		5'9"		5'9"
WBC	4,000-11,000 cells/mm^3	12,000		11,225
K	3.5-5 mEq/L	3.7	4.1	3.6
Glu	65-99 mg/dL	101		142

The aminophylline dose will be calculated based on Mike's IBW.

IBW (male) = 50 kg + (2.3 x 9 in) = 70.7 kg

Aminophylline 0.5 mg/kg/hr x 70.7 kg x 24 hrs = 848.4 mg/day, round to 848 mg/day

CALCULATE PATIENTS' NUTRITIONAL NEEDS

Calorie Sources

A calorie is a measurement of the energy, or heat, it takes to raise the temperature of 1 gram of water by 1° C. Calories are associated with nutrition because humans obtain energy from the food they consume, or from enteral nutrition (EN) formulas delivered by "feeding" tubes into the stomach or intestine, or from parenteral nutrition (PN), which is delivered peripherally through a vein, or centrally through an artery. Calories from any of these nutrition sources are provided by these 3 components: carbohydrates, fat and protein.

A calorie is a very small unit, and these are therefore measured in kilocalories, or kcals, where 1,000 calories = 1 kcal. It is common to find the term "calories" used interchangeably for kcals. For example, the "Nutrition Facts" box on the side of a container of Honey Nut Cheerios® states that a serving of ¾ cup of the cereal provides 110 Calories. Precisely, this is 110 kcals. Looking at the box, the word "Calories" is written with a capital "C" which is sometimes used to indicate kcals, versus a lower case "c". For pharmacy calculations, "calories" or "Calories" are meant to refer to kilocalories, or kcals.

Carbohydrates

Glucose is the primary energy source. Unless a patient purchases glucose tablets or gel, carbohydrates are consumed as simple sugars, such as fruit juice, or complex "starchy" sugars, such as legumes and grains. These are hydrolyzed by the gut into the monosaccharides fructose, galactose and glucose, which are absorbed. The liver converts the first two into glucose, and excess glucose is stored as glycogen.

Carbohydrates from food or in enternal nutrition formulas provide 4 kcal/gram. In PN, dextrose monohydrate provides the carbohydrate source. This is the isomer of glucose (D-glucose) which can be metabolized for energy. The dextrose in PN provides 3.4 kcal/gram. Occasionally, glycerol is used as an alternative to dextrose in patients with impaired insulin secretion. Glycerol provides 4.3 kcal/gram and comes pre-mixed with amino acids.

Fat

Fats, or lipids, are used by the body for energy or for various critical functions, including being an essential component of cell membranes, a solvent for fat soluble vitamins, in hormone production and activity, in cell signaling, and other functions. In food or from EN formulas, fat is provided as four types: saturated, *trans*, monounsaturated and polyunsaturated. Each of these provides 9 kcal/gram. In PN, lipids are not measured in grams but in kcal/mL due to the caloric contribution provided by the egg phospholipid and glycerol components in the intravenous fat emulsion (IVFE). 10% IVFE provides 1.1 kcal/mL, 20% provides 2 kcal/mL and 30% provides 3 kcal/mL.

Protein

Protein is used either to repair or build muscle cells, or as a source of energy. Protein in enteral intake is present in various forms, and in PN as the constituent amino acids. If adequate energy is provided by carbohydrates and fat, the protein may be "spared" and can be used by muscle (although the protein calories may not end up in the intended location). If "protein sparing" is used, the energy required by the patient will come from only the dextrose and lipids, which are the "non-protein calories" (NPC).

Protein calories from food, enteral nutrition formulas or as parenteral amino acid solutions each provide 4 kcal/gram. The kcal amounts in the chart below should be known:

USUAL DIET*			EN FORMULAS*		PN FORMULAS	
Carbs	Bread, Rice....	4 kcal/g	Corn syrup solids, cornstarch, sucrose....	The components contribute the same as from the diet, but are measured (together) as kcal/mL	Dextrose Monohydrate	3.4 kcal/gram
					Glycerol/ Glycerin**	4.3 kcal/gram
Fat	Butter, Oil....	9 kcal/g	Borage oil, canola oil, corn oil....		IV Fat Emulsion (IVFE) 10%	1.1 kcal/mL
					IVFE 20%	2 kcal/mL
					IVFE 30%	3 kcal/mL
Protein	Fish, Meat....	4 kcal/g	Casein, soy, whey....		Amino Acid Solutions *(Aminosyn, Freamine....)*	4 kcal/gram

**The diet and enteral formula components are common examples; there are others.*

***Glycerol may be used to decrease hyperglycemia; more commonly, the dextrose load is decreased or the insulin dose is increased.*

Parenteral Nutrition

It is preferable to use the least invasive and most physiologic method of feeding. Parenteral nutrition (PN) is neither and has a higher risk of complications, including infection and thrombosis. It may be indicated when the patient is not able to absorb adequate nutrition via the GI tract for > 5 days. Usual conditions that may require PN include bowel obstruction, ileus, severe diarrhea, radiation enteritis and untreatable malabsorption.

There are 2 types of PN admixtures. Mixtures that contain dextrose, amino acids, sterile water for injection, electrolytes, vitamins and minerals are referred to as 2-in-1 formulations, while the intravenous fat emulsion (IVFE) is infused separately. When the IVFE is contained in the same bag, it is referred to as a total nutrient admixture (TNA), or 3-in-1, or all-in-one formulation.

If the PN is expected to be short-term (< 1 week), peripheral administration may be possible, but has a high risk of phlebitis and vein damage. Central line placement allows for a higher osmolarity and a wider variation in pH. Common types of central lines include peripherally-inserted central catheters ("PICC" lines), Hickman, Broviac, Groshong and others.

The fluid, kcal, protein and lipid requirements, plus the initial electrolyte, vitamin and trace element requirements will be determined. Additional additives may be needed, such as insulin and histamine-2 receptor antagonists (H2RAs). PN requires monitoring, including assessing the need, the degree of glucose intolerance and the risk of refeeding syndrome, which is an intracellular loss of electrolytes, particularly phosphate, which causes serious complications. The calculations for PN that follow are basic and should be known by pharmacists who work in the hospital setting. Nutrition pharmacy itself is more complex and is a specialty area.

Determining Fluid Needs

Fluid requirements are often calculated first when designing a PN regimen. Enough (but not too much) fluid needs to be given to maintain adequate hydration. Daily fluid needs can be calculated using this formula:

When weight > 20 kg: 1,500 mL + (20 mL)(Wt in kg – 20)

Alternatively, some institutions estimate adult fluid requirements using a general guideline of 30 – 40 mL/kg/day. The PN and fluid volume should be tailored to the patient. If the patient has problems with fluid accumulation (such as heart failure, renal dysfunction, etc.), the amount of fluid provided will be reduced. Fluid volume from medications (including IVPBs) should be included in the calculation of the overall volume the patient is receiving.

---

101. GG is a 57 year old female admitted to the hospital with bowel obstruction. She will be NPO for the next 5 – 7 days. The decision was made to start PN therapy. She weighs 65 kg and is 5'6". The SCr is 1.3 mg/dL. Calculate GG's daily fluid requirements.

1,500 mL + (20 mL)(65 - 20) = 2,400 mL/day

---

102. A 76 year old, 154 lbs (IBW) patient is NPO and needs hydration. She is afebrile and does not have HF, renal disease, or ascites. What volume of fluid should the patient receive per day?

1,500 mL + (20 mL)(70 - 20) = 2,500 mL/day

Determining Caloric Needs: Basal Energy Expenditure and Total Energy Expenditure

The basal energy expenditure (BEE), otherwise referred to as the basal metabolic rate (BMR), is the energy expenditure in the resting state, exclusive of eating and activity. It is estimated differently in male and female patients using the Harris-Benedict equations below:

BEE (males): 66.47 + 13.75 (weight in kg) + 5 (height in cm) – 6.76 (age in years)

BEE (females): 655.1 + 9.6 (weight in kg) + 1.85 (height in cm) – 4.68 (age in years)

Total energy expenditure (TEE; or total daily expenditure, TDE) is a measure of basal energy expenditure plus excess metabolic demands as a result of stress, the thermal effects of feeding, and energy expenditure for activity. Once the BEE is calculated, calculate the TEE by taking the BEE calories and multiplying by the appropriate activity factor and stress factor. This will increase the calories required. Energy requirements are increased 12% with each degree of fever over 37° C.

TEE = BEE x activity factor x stress factor

The activity factor is either 1.2 if confined to bed (non-ambulatory), or 1.3 if out of bed (ambulatory). Commonly used stress factors are listed in the table. These are likely to be specified if needed on the exam.

STATE OF STRESS	STRESS FACTOR
Minor surgery	1.2
Infection	1.4
Major trauma, sepsis, burns up to 30% BSA	1.5
Burns over 30% BSA	1.5–2

103. Using the Harris-Benedict equation, calculate the basal energy expenditure for a major trauma patient (stress factor 1.5) who is a 66 year old male, 174 pounds and 5'10" in height. Activity factor is 1.2. Round to the nearest whole number.

Height = 70 inches x 2.54 cm/inch = 177.8 cm. Weight 174 pounds x 1 kg/2.2 pounds = 79.0909 kg.

BEE (males): 66.47 + 13.75 (weight in kg) + 5 (height in cm) – 6.76 (age in years)

BEE = 66.47 + (13.75 x 79.0909) + (5 x 177.8) - (6.76 x 66)

BEE = 66.47 + 1,087.5 + 889 - 446.16 = 1,596.81, or 1,597 kcal/day

The stress factor is not needed in this calculation, because you were asked to calculate BEE only. The BEE can be estimated using 15 – 25 kcal/kg (adults). It may be helpful to check the calculation with this estimate and see if the numbers are close. In this case, an estimation using 20 kcal/kg/day would provide 1,582 kcal/day (very close to 1,597 kcal/day as above).

104. Calculate the total energy expenditure for a major trauma patient (stress factor is 1.5, activity factor is 1.2) who is a 66 year old male, weighing 174 pounds and measuring 5'10" in height. (Use the BEE calculated from the patient in the previous problem.) Round to the nearest whole number.

TEE = BEE x activity factor x stress factor. BEE was calculated above.

TEE = 1,597 kcal/day x 1.2 x 1.5 = 2,875 kcal/day

105. A 25 year old female major trauma patient survives surgery and is recovering in the surgical intensive care unit. The medical team wants to start PN therapy. She is 122 pounds, 5'7" with some mild renal impairment. Calculate her BEE using the Harris-Benedict equation and her TEE (stress factor = 1.7 and activity factor =1.2). Round each to the nearest whole number.

Height = 67 inches x 2.54 cm/inch = 170.18 cm. Weight 122 pounds x 1 kg/2.2 pounds = 55.4545 kg.

BEE (females): 655.1 + 9.6 (weight in kg) + 1.85 (height in cm) – 4.68 (age in years)

BEE = 655.1 + (9.6 x 55.4545) + (1.85 x 170.18) - (4.68 x 25)

BEE = 655.1 + 532.3636 + 314.833 - 117 = 1,385.2966, or 1,385 kcal/day

TEE = BEE x activity factor x stress factor

TEE = 1,385 kcal/day x 1.2 x 1.7 = 2,825 kcal/day

Calculating Protein Calories

The typical protein requirement for a non-stressed, ambulatory patient is 0.8 – 1 g/kg/day. Protein requirements increase if the patient is placed under stress, which is defined as illness severity. The more severely ill, the greater the protein requirements will be. In patients with a high degree of metabolic stress the protein requirements can be as high as 1.8 – 2 g/kg/day. Which weight to use (TBW, IBW or adjusted) in calculating protein requirements is somewhat controversial in clinical practice; the desired weight is likely to be specified (if needed) in an exam scenario.

CONDITION	PROTEIN REQUIREMENTS
Ambulatory, non-hospitalized (non-stressed)	0.8–1 g/kg/day
Hospitalized, or malnourished	1.2–2 g/kg/day

---

106. MK is a 62 year old female who has been admitted with enteritis and pneumonia. She has a history of Crohn's disease and COPD. She is 158 pounds, 5'4". The staff gastroenterologist has ordered PN therapy with 1.5 g/kg IBW/day of protein. How many grams of protein will MK receive per day. Round to the nearest whole number.

First, calculate IBW: 45.5 + (2.3)(4) = 54.7 kg

Then, calculate the protein requirement: 54.7 kg x 1.5 g/kg IBW/day = 82 g protein/day

---

107. PP is a 46 year old male (207 pounds, 5'11") who has been admitted for bowel resection surgery. Post surgery, he is to be started on PN therapy. The physician wants the patient to receive 1.3 g/kg/day of protein. Calculate his protein requirements using his actual weight. Round to the nearest whole number.

First, convert pounds to kg: 207 pounds x 1 kg/2.2 pounds = 94.1 kg

Then, calculate the protein requirement: 94.1 kg x 1.3 g/kg/day = 122 g protein/day

Calculating Amino Acids

Amino acids are the source of proteins in PN. Amino acids are used to build muscle mass. Because critically ill patients are catabolic (protein breakdown occurs faster than synthesis), many clinicians prefer to use "protein sparing" techniques in this population. This means that most or all of the TEE calories are provided by dextrose and fat (protein is spared for protein synthesis and healing). Overall, whether to include the calories from protein in the total calories provided by a PN regimen is controversial. Amino acids come in stock preparations of 5%, 8.5%, 10%, 15%, and others. Amino acids provide 4 kcal/gram.

---

108. If the pharmacy stocks *Aminosyn* 8.5%, how many mL will be needed to provide 108 grams of protein? Round to the nearest whole number.

$$\frac{8.5\text{ g}}{100\text{ mL}} = \frac{108\text{ g}}{X\text{ mL}} \qquad X = 1{,}270.58\text{, or } 1{,}271\text{ mL}$$

---

109. How many calories are provided by 108 grams of protein?

$$\frac{4\text{ kcal}}{\text{g}} \times 108\text{ g} = 432\text{ kcal of protein}$$

---

110. The pharmacy stocks *FreAmine* 10%. A patient requires 122 grams of protein per day. How many milliliters of *FreAmine* will the patient need?

$$\frac{10\text{ g}}{100\text{ mL}} = \frac{122\text{ g}}{X\text{ mL}} \qquad X = 1{,}220\text{ mL}$$

---

111. JR requires 1.4 g/kg/day of protein and the pharmacy stocks *Aminosyn* 8.5%. JR is a 55 year old male (weight 189 pounds) who is confined to bed (activity factor 1.2) due to his current infection (stress factor 1.5). Calculate the amount of *Aminosyn*, in milliliters, JR should receive. Round to the nearest whole number.

First, convert weight to kg: 189 pounds x 1 kg/2.2 pounds = 85.90 kg

Next, calculate protein requirement: 1.4 g/kg/day x 85.9090 kg = 120.27 g/day

Then, calculate the amount of *Aminosyn* (mL) needed. Note that the activity factor and stress factor are not required to calculate the protein requirement.

$$\frac{8.5\text{ g}}{100\text{ mL}} = \frac{120.27\text{ g}}{X\text{ mL}} \qquad X = 1{,}414.97\text{, or } 1{,}415\text{ mL}$$

---

112. JR is receiving 97 grams of protein in an *Aminosyn* 8.5% solution on day 8 of his hospitalization. How many calories are provided by this amount of protein?

$$\frac{4\text{ kcal}}{\text{g}} \times 97\text{ g} = 388\text{ kcal of protein}$$

---

113. A PN order is written to add 800 mL of 10% amino acid solution. The pharmacy only has 15% amino acid solution in stock. Using the 15% amino acid solution instead, how many mL should be added to the PN bag? Round to the nearest whole number.

First, calculate the grams of protein that would be provided with the 10% solution.

$$\frac{10\ g}{100\ mL} = \frac{X\ g}{800\ mL} \quad X = 80\ g$$

Next, calculate how much of the 15% amino acid solution will supply 80 grams of protein.

$$\frac{15\ g}{100\ mL} = \frac{80\ g}{X\ mL} \quad X = 533\ mL$$

Nitrogen Balance

Determining The Grams Of Nitrogen From Protein

Nitrogen is released during protein catabolism and is mainly excreted as urea in the urine. Nitrogen balance is the difference between the body's nitrogen gains and losses. While grams of protein are calculated in a nutritional plan, grams of nitrogen are used as an expression of the amount of protein received by the patient. There is 1 g of nitrogen (N) for each 6.25 g of protein. To calculate the grams of nitrogen in a certain weight of protein, divide the protein grams by 6.25.

$$\text{Nitrogen intake} = \frac{\text{grams of protein intake}}{6.25}$$

---

114. A patient is receiving PN containing 540 mL of 12.5% amino acids per day. How many grams of nitrogen is the patient receiving? Round to the nearest tenth.

$$\frac{12.5\ g}{100\ mL} = \frac{X\ g}{540\ mL} \quad X = 67.5\ g\text{ of protein}$$

$$\frac{67.5\ g\text{ of protein}}{6.25} = 10.8\ g\text{ of nitrogen}$$

Calculating the Non-Protein Calories to Nitrogen Ratio

The non-protein calorie to nitrogen ratio (NPC:N) is calculated as follows:

- First, calculate the grams of nitrogen supplied per day (1 g N = 6.25 g of protein).
- Then, divide the total non-protein calories (dextrose + lipids) by the grams of nitrogen.

Desirable NPC:N ratios are:

- 80:1 the most severely stressed patients
- 100:1 severely stressed patients
- 150:1 unstressed patient

---

115. A patient is receiving PN containing 480 mL of dextrose 50% and 50 grams of amino acids plus electrolytes. Calculate the non-protein calories to nitrogen ratio for this patient.

First, calculate the nitrogen intake.

$$\text{Nitrogen} = \frac{50\ g\text{ of protein}}{6.25} = 8\ g$$

Next, calculate the non-protein calories.

$$\frac{50\ g\text{ dextrose}}{100\ mL} = \frac{X\ g}{480\ mL} \quad X = 240\ g\text{ dextrose}$$

$$240 \text{ g dextrose} \times \frac{3.4 \text{ kcal dextrose}}{1 \text{ g}} = 816 \text{ kcal of dextrose}$$

Then, set up the NPC:N ratio.

NPC:N ratio is 816:8, or 102:1

Calculating Dextrose

Dextrose is the carbohydrate source in PN. The usual distribution of non-protein calories is 70 – 85% as carbohydrate (dextrose) and 15 – 30% as fat (lipids). Dextrose comes in concentrations of 5%, 10%, 20%, 30%, 50%, 70% and others. The higher concentrations are used for PN. When calculating the dextrose, do not exceed 4 mg/kg/min (some use 7 g/kg/day). These are conservative estimates of the maximum amount of dextrose that the liver can handle.

---

116. Using 50% dextrose in water, how many mL are required to fulfill a PN order for 405 grams of dextrose?

$$\frac{50 \text{ g}}{100 \text{ mL}} = \frac{405 \text{ g}}{X \text{ mL}} = 810 \text{ mL}$$

---

117. DF, a 44 year old male, is receiving 1,235 mL of D30W, 1,010 mL of *FreAmine* 8.5%, 200 mL of *Intralipid* 20% and 50 mL of electrolytes/minerals in his PN. How many calories from dextrose is DF receiving from the PN? Round to the nearest whole number.

$$\frac{30 \text{ g}}{100 \text{ mL}} \times \frac{1{,}235 \text{ mL}}{\text{day}} \times \frac{3.4 \text{ kcal}}{\text{g}} = 1{,}260 \text{ kcal/day}$$

---

118. A pharmacist has mixed 200 mL of D20% with 100 mL of D5%. What is the final concentration in the bag?

The 200 mL bag has 40 g of dextrose (20 g/100 mL x 2).

The 100 mL bag has 5 g of dextrose. There are a total of 45 g of dextrose in the bag.

$$\frac{45 \text{ g}}{300 \text{ mL}} = \frac{X \text{ g}}{100 \text{ mL}} \quad X = 15 \text{ g; the percentage is } 15\%$$

---

119. If a 50% dextrose injection provides 170 kcal in each 100 mL, how many milliliters of a 70% dextrose injection would provide the same caloric value? Round to the nearest tenth.

$$\frac{70 \text{ g}}{100 \text{ mL}} = \frac{50 \text{ g}}{X \text{ mL}} = 71.4 \text{ mL}$$

$$\frac{100 \text{ mL}}{70 \text{ g}} \times \frac{1 \text{ g}}{3.4 \text{ kcal}} \times 170 \text{ kcal} = 71.4 \text{ mL}$$

Or, since the calories are from 50% dextrose, and the pharmacist is using 70% dextrose:

$$100 \text{ mL} \times 50\% = Q2 \times 70\%$$

$$Q2 = 71.4 \text{ mL}$$

120. AH is receiving 640 mL of D50W in her PN. How many calories does this provide?

$$\frac{50\text{ g}}{100\text{ mL}} \times \frac{640\text{ mL}}{\text{day}} \times \frac{3.4\text{ kcal}}{\text{g}} = 1{,}088\text{ kcal}$$

---

121. A PN order is written for 500 mL of 50% dextrose. The pharmacy only has D70W in stock. How many mL of D70W should be added to the PN bag? Round to the nearest whole number.

First, calculate the grams of dextrose needed for the PN as written.

$$\frac{50\text{ g}}{100\text{ mL}} = \frac{X\text{ g}}{500\text{ mL}} \quad X = 250\text{ g}$$

Next, calculate how much of the 70% dextrose solution provides 250 grams of dextrose.

$$\frac{70\text{ g}}{100\text{ mL}} = \frac{250\text{ g}}{X\text{ mL}} \quad X = 357\text{ mL of D70W}$$

Calculating Lipids

Lipids are the source of fat in PN. The standard distribution of non-protein calories is 70 – 85% as carbohydrate (dextrose) and 15 – 30% as fat (lipids). Lipids are available as 10%, 20% or 30% emulsions. Do not exceed 2.5 g/kg/day of lipids. Lipids do not need to be given daily, especially if triglycerides are high. Due to the risk of infection, the recommended hang time limit for IV fat emulsions (IVFE) is 12 hours when infused alone. However, an admixture containing IVFE, such as a TNA, may be administered over 24 hours. Patients receiving lipids should have their triglycerides monitored. If lipids are given once weekly, then divide the total calories by 7 to determine the daily amount of fat the patient receives. Lipid emulsions cannot be filtered through 0.22 micron filters; 1.2 micron filters are commonly used for lipids. PN requires a filter itself due to the risk of a precipitate.

---

122. A patient is receiving 500 mL of 10% lipids. How many calories is the patient receiving from the lipids? Round to the nearest whole number.

$$\frac{1.1\text{ kcal}}{\text{mL}} = \frac{X\text{ kcal}}{500\text{ mL}} \quad X = 550\text{ kcal}$$

---

123. The total energy expenditure (TEE) for a critically ill patient is 2,435 kcal/day. The patient is receiving 1,446 kcal from dextrose and 810 kcal from protein. In this critical care unit, clinicians do not include protein calories in the TEE estimation. How many kcal should be provided by the lipids?

As stated in the problem, at this institution TEE refers to the non-protein calories.

2,435 kcal (total non-protein) – 1,446 kcal (dextrose) = 989 kcal remaining from lipids

---

124. Using a 20% lipid emulsion, how many mL are required to meet 989 calories? Round to the nearest whole number.

$$\frac{2\text{ kcal}}{\text{mL}} = \frac{989\text{ kcal}}{X\text{ mL}} \quad X = 495\text{ mL}$$

125. A patient is receiving 660 mL of 10% *Intralipid* on Saturdays along with his normal daily PN therapy of 1,420 mL of D20W, 450 mL *Aminosyn* 15%, and 30 mL of electrolytes. What is the daily amount of calories provided by the lipids? Round to the nearest whole number.

$$\frac{1.1 \text{ kcal}}{\text{mL}} = \frac{X \text{ kcal}}{660 \text{ mL}} \quad X = 726 \text{ kcal/week. Divide by 7 to get kcal/day} = 104 \text{ kcal/day}$$

---

126. A patient is receiving 180 mL of 30% lipids. How many calories is the patient receiving from the lipids?

$$\frac{3 \text{ kcal}}{\text{mL}} = \frac{X \text{ kcal}}{180 \text{ mL}} \quad X = 540 \text{ kcal}$$

---

127. A PN order calls for 475 calories to be provided by lipids. The pharmacy has 10% lipid emulsion in stock. How many mL should be administered to the patient? Round to the nearest whole number.

$$\frac{1.1 \text{ kcal}}{\text{mL}} = \frac{475 \text{ kcal}}{X \text{ mL}} \quad X = 432 \text{ mL}$$

---

128. TE is a 35 year old female who is receiving 325 grams of dextrose, 85 grams of amino acids, and 300 mL of 10% lipids via her PN therapy. What percentage of total calories is provided by the protein content? Round to the nearest whole number.

First, calculate the calories from all sources; dextrose, amino acids, and lipids.

Dextrose

$$\frac{3.4 \text{ kcal}}{\text{g}} \times 325 \text{ g} = 1{,}105 \text{ kcal of dextrose}$$

Protein

$$\frac{4 \text{ kcal}}{\text{g}} \times 85 \text{ g} = 340 \text{ kcal of protein}$$

Lipids

$$\frac{1.1 \text{ kcal}}{\text{mL}} \times 300 \text{ mL} = 330 \text{ kcal of fat}$$

Then, add up the total calories from all the sources. 1,105 + 340 + 330 = 1,775 kcal
Finally, calculate the percent of calories from protein.

$$\frac{340 \text{ kcal}}{1{,}775 \text{ kcal}} \times 100 = 19\%$$

129. WC, a 57 year old male, is receiving 1,145 mL of D30W, 850 mL of *FreAmine* 8.5%, and 350 mL of *Intralipid* 10% in his PN therapy. What percentage of the non-protein calories are represented by dextrose? Round to the nearest whole number.

First, calculate the non-protein calories (dextrose and lipids).

Dextrose

$$\frac{3.4 \text{ kcal}}{\text{g}} \times \frac{30 \text{ g}}{100 \text{ mL}} \times 1{,}145 \text{ mL} = 1{,}168 \text{ kcal}$$

Lipids

$$\frac{1.1 \text{ kcal}}{\text{mL}} \times 350 \text{ mL} = 385 \text{ kcal}$$

Then, add up the calories from the non-protein sources. 1,168 + 385 = 1,553 kcal

Finally, calculate the percent of non-protein calories from dextrose.

$$\frac{1{,}168 \text{ kcal from dextrose}}{1{,}553 \text{ kcal non-protein}} \times 100 = 75\%$$

---

130. A 46 year old female with radiation enteritis is receiving 1,800 kcal from her parenteral nutrition. The solution contains amino acids, dextrose and electrolytes. There are 84.5 grams of protein in the PN and it is running at 85 mL/hour over 24 hours. What is the final concentration of dextrose in the PN solution? Round to the nearest whole number.

First, calculate the amount of dextrose the patient is receiving by subtracting out the protein component.

$$84.5 \text{ g} \times \frac{4 \text{ kcal}}{\text{g}} = 338 \text{ kcal}$$

$$1{,}800 \text{ kcal} - 338 \text{ kcal of protein} = 1{,}462 \text{ kcal from dextrose}$$

Next, calculate the grams of dextrose in this PN.

$$1{,}462 \text{ kcal} \times \frac{1 \text{ g}}{3.4 \text{ kcal}} = 430 \text{ grams of dextrose}$$

Then, calculate the final concentration. This requires calculating the total volume the patient is receiving.

$$\frac{85 \text{ mL}}{\text{hr}} \times 24 \text{ hours} = 2{,}040 \text{ mL or } 2.04 \text{ L}$$

$$\frac{430 \text{ g dextrose}}{2{,}040 \text{ mL}} = \frac{X \text{ g}}{100 \text{ mL}} \quad X = 21\%$$

Determining the Amount of Electrolytes

Sodium Considerations

Sodium is the principal extracellular cation. Sodium may need to be reduced in renal dysfunction or cardiovascular disease, including hypertension. Sodium chloride comes in many concentrations, such as 0.9% (NS), 0.45% (1/2 NS) and others. Sodium chloride 23.4% is used for PN preparation and contains 4 mEq/mL.

Sodium can be added to PN as either sodium chloride or sodium acetate. If a patient is acidotic, sodium acetate should be added. Sodium acetate is converted to sodium bicarbonate and may help correct the acidosis. A patient may require a certain quantity from each formulation or they may get sodium chloride alone. Hypertonic saline (greater than 0.9%) is dangerous if used incorrectly and is discussed in the Medication Safety & Quality Improvement chapter.

---

131. The pharmacist is going to add 80 mEq of sodium to the PN; half will be given as sodium acetate (2 mEq/mL) and half as sodium chloride (4 mEq/mL). How many mL of sodium chloride will be needed?

40 mEq will be provided by the NaCl.

$$\frac{4 \text{ mEq}}{\text{mL}} = \frac{40 \text{ mEq}}{X \text{ mL}} \qquad X = 10 \text{ mL}$$

---

132. The pharmacist is making PN that needs to contain 80 mEq of sodium and 45 mEq of acetate. The available pharmacy stock solutions contain 4 mEq/mL sodium as sodium chloride and 2 mEq/mL sodium as sodium acetate. The final volume of the PN will be 2.5 liters to be given at 100 mL/hr. What quantity, in milliliters, of each stock solution should be added to the PN to meet the requirements? Round to the nearest hundredth.

First, calculate the acetate component as this contributes sodium as well.

$$\frac{2 \text{ mEq}}{\text{mL}} = \frac{45 \text{ mEq}}{X \text{ mL}} \qquad X = 22.5 \text{ mL of sodium acetate}$$

Next, determine how many mEq of sodium are supplied by 22.5 mL sodium acetate.

$$\frac{2 \text{ mEq}}{\text{mL}} \times 22.5 \text{ mL sodium acetate} = 45 \text{ mEq of sodium}$$

So, 45 mEq of sodium acetate also supplies 45 mEq of sodium. How many mEq of sodium are left to be provided from sodium chloride?

$$80 \text{ mEq Na total} - 45 \text{ mEq Na from Na Acetate} = 35 \text{ mEq of sodium still needed from NaCl}$$

Calculate how much sodium chloride will supply the remaining sodium (35 mEq).

$$\frac{4 \text{ mEq}}{\text{mL}} = \frac{35 \text{ mEq}}{X \text{ mL}} \qquad X = 8.75 \text{ mL of sodium chloride}$$

---

133. A 2 liter PN solution is to contain 60 mEq of sodium and 30 mEq of acetate. The pharmacy has in stock sodium chloride (4 mEq/mL) and sodium acetate (2 mEq/mL). What quantity, in milliliters, of each solution should be added to the PN? Round to the nearest tenth.

First, calculate the amount of sodium acetate needed.

$$\frac{2 \text{ mEq}}{\text{mL}} = \frac{30 \text{ mEq}}{X \text{ mL}} \qquad X = 15 \text{ mL of sodium acetate}$$

This amount (15 mL of sodium acetate) supplies 30 mEq of sodium (15 mL x 2 mEq/mL = 30 mEq). The additional amount of sodium required is 30 mEq from NaCl (60 mEq – 30 mEq).

Calculate the amount of sodium chloride needed.

$$\frac{4 \text{ mEq}}{\text{mL}} = \frac{30 \text{ mEq}}{\text{X mL}} \quad X = 7.5 \text{ mL of NaCl}$$

Potassium, Calcium and Phosphate Considerations

Potassium

Potassium is the principal intracellular cation. Potassium may need to be reduced in renal or cardiovascular disease. Potassium can be provided by potassium chloride (KCl), potassium phosphate (K Phos) or potassium acetate. The normal range for serum potassium is 3.5 – 5 mEq/L.

Calcium

Calcium is important for many functions including cardiac conduction, muscle contraction, and bone homeostasis. The normal serum calcium level is 8.5 – 10.5 mg/dL. Almost half of serum calcium is bound to albumin. Low albumin will lead to a falsely low serum calcium concentration. If albumin is low (< 3.5 g/dL), the calcium level must be corrected with this equation prior to the addition of calcium into the PN or providing calcium replacement in any manner:

$$Ca_{corrected} \text{ (mg/dL)} = calcium_{reported(serum)} + [(4.0 - albumin) \times (0.8)]$$

Use serum calcium in mg/dL and albumin in g/dL (standard units in the U.S.) in the corrected calcium formula

---

134. Calculate the corrected calcium value for a patient with the following lab values:

LAB	VALUE
Calcium	7.6 mg/dL (reference range 8.5–10.5 mg/dL)
Albumin	1.5 g/dL (reference range 3.5–5 g/dL)

$$Ca_{corrected} = 7.6 + [(4.0 - 1.5) \times (0.8)] = 9.6 \text{ mg/dL}$$

The corrected calcium provides an estimate of what the patient's serum calcium would be if the albumin was normal. In this example, the patient's corrected calcium is within the reference range for the lab.

Calcium and Phosphate Solubility

Phosphorus (or phosphate, PO4) is present in DNA, cell membranes, ATP, acts as an acid-base buffer, and is vital in bone metabolism. Phosphate and calcium need to be added to the PN carefully, or they can bind together and precipitate which can cause a pulmonary embolus. This can be fatal. The following considerations can help reduce the risk of a calcium-phosphate precipitate:

- Choose calcium gluconate over calcium chloride ($CaCl_2$) because it is less reactive and has a lower risk of precipitation with phosphates. Calcium gluconate has a lower dissociation constant compared to calcium chloride, leaving less free calcium available in solution to bind phosphates.
- Add phosphate first (after the dextrose and amino acids), followed by other PN components, agitate the solution, then calcium should be added near the end to take advantage of the maximum volume of the PN formulation.

- The calcium and phosphate added together (units must be the same to do this) should not exceed 45 mEq/L.
- Maintain a proper pH (lower pH; less risk of precipitation) to eliminate binding and refrigerate the bag once prepared (PNs are kept in the refrigerator until they are needed). When temperature increases, more calcium and phosphate dissociate in solution and precipitation risk increases.

An additional safety consideration involves ordering the correct dose of phosphate. Phosphate can be ordered as potassium or sodium salts. The two forms do not provide equivalent amounts of phosphate. The order should be written in mmol (of phosphate), followed by the type of salt form (potassium or sodium).

---

135. The pharmacist has calculated that a patient requires 30 mmol of phosphate and 80 mEq of potassium. The pharmacy has stock solutions of potassium phosphate (3 mmol of phosphate with 4.4 mEq of potassium/mL) and potassium chloride (2 mEq K/mL). How much potassium phosphate and how much potassium chloride will be required to meet the patient's needs?

First, calculate the phosphate required (since phosphate can only be provided by KPO4 and potassium will also be provided by this solution).

$$\frac{\text{3 mmol phosphate}}{\text{mL}} = \frac{\text{30 mmol phosphate}}{\text{X mL}} \quad \text{X = 10 mL KPO4}$$

Each mL of the potassium phosphate (KPO4) supplies 4.4 mEq of potassium. Calculate the amount of potassium the patient will receive from the 10 mL of KPO4.

$$\text{10 mL} \times \text{4.4 mEq/mL} = \text{44 mEq potassium from KPO4}$$

The remaining potassium will be provided by KCl.

$$\text{80 mEq K required} - \text{44 mEq potassium (from KPO4)} = \text{36 mEq to be obtained from KCl}$$

$$\frac{\text{2 mEq K}}{\text{mL}} = \frac{\text{36 mEq K}}{\text{X mL}} \quad \text{X = 18 mL KCl}$$

The patient requires 10 mL of potassium phosphate and 18 mL of potassium chloride.

---

136. A patient is to receive 8 mEq of calcium. The pharmacy has calcium gluconate 10% in stock which provides 0.465 mEq/mL. How many mL of calcium gluconate should be added to the PN? Round to the nearest whole number.

$$\text{8 mEq Ca} \times \frac{\text{1 mL}}{\text{0.465 mEq Ca}} = \text{17.2, or 17 mL calcium gluconate}$$

---

137. A patient is receiving 30 mmol of phosphate and 8 mEq of calcium. The volume of the PN is 2,000 mL. There are 2 mEq PO4/mmol. Confirm that the sum of the calcium and phosphorus does not exceed 45 mEq/L.

First, calculate mEq from the phosphate.

$$\frac{\text{2 mEq PO4}}{\text{mmol}} \times \text{30 mmol PO4} = \text{60 mEq phosphate}$$

Then, add the phosphate and calcium. 60 mEq phosphate + 8 mEq calcium = 68 mEq.

Read the question again. Has it been answered?

The volume of the PN is 2,000 mL, or 2 L. Calculate the mEq per liter.

68 mEq/2 L = 34 mEq/L, which is less than 45 mEq/L.

Calculation Practice

The following problems integrate multiple calculation concepts.

---

138. A pharmacy receives the following PN order. Calculate the amount, in mL, of dextrose 70% that should be added to the PN. Round to the nearest whole number.

ITEM	QUANTITY
Dextrose 70%	250 g
Amino acids	50 g
Sodium chloride (M.W. 58.5)	44 mEq
Sodium acetate (M.W. 82)	20 mEq
Potassium	40 mEq
Magnesium sulfate	12 mEq
Phosphate	18 mmol

ITEM	QUANTITY
Calcium	4.65 mEq
MVI-12	5 mL
Trace elements-5	1 mL
Vitamin K-1	0.5 mg
Famotidine	10 mg
Regular insulin	20 units
Sterile water qs ad	960 mL

$$\frac{70\text{ g}}{100\text{ mL}} = \frac{250\text{ g}}{X\text{ mL}} \quad X = 357\text{ mL of dextrose }70\%$$

---

139. Using amino acids 10%, calculate the amount of amino acids that should be added to the PN.

$$\frac{10\text{ g}}{100\text{ mL}} = \frac{50\text{ g}}{X\text{ mL}} \quad X = 500\text{ mL of }10\%\text{ amino acids}$$

---

140. How many milliliters of 23.4% sodium chloride should be added to the PN.

$$44\text{ mEq} = \frac{X\text{ mg} \times 1}{58.5} \quad X = 2{,}574\text{ mg, or }2.574\text{ g}$$

$$\frac{23.4\text{ g}}{100\text{ mL}} = \frac{2.574\text{ g}}{X\text{ mL}} \quad X = 11\text{ mL of }23.4\%\text{ NaCl}$$

This concentration of NaCl is hypertonic and is a high-alert drug due to heightened risk of patient harm when dosed incorrectly. Refer to the Medication Safety & Quality Improvement chapter.

---

141. Calculate the amount of 16.4% sodium acetate that should be added to the PN.

$$20\text{ mEq} = \frac{X\text{ mg} \times 1}{82} \quad X = 1{,}640\text{ mg, or }1.64\text{ g}$$

$$\frac{16.4\text{ g}}{100\text{ mL}} = \frac{1.64\text{ g}}{X\text{ mL}} \quad X = 10\text{ mL of } 16.4\%\text{ sodium acetate}$$

---

142. Using the potassium phosphate (3 mmol of phosphate and 4.4 mEq of potassium/mL) vials in stock, calculate the amount of potassium phosphate that should be added to the PN to meet the needs of the phosphate requirements.

$$\frac{3\text{ mmol phosphate}}{\text{mL}} = \frac{18\text{ mmol phosphate}}{X\text{ mL}} \quad X = 6\text{ mL potassium phosphate}$$

---

143. The PN contains 6 mL of potassium phosphate (3 mmol of phosphate and 4.4 mEq of potassium/mL). The daily potassium requirement from the PN order is 40 mEq. How much potassium chloride (2 mEq/mL), in milliliters, should be added to the PN? Round to the nearest tenth.

First, calculate the amount of K already required in the PN from potassium phosphate.

$$\frac{4.4\text{ mEq K}}{\text{mL}} \times 6\text{ mL} = 26.4\text{ mEq K}$$

Total K needed is 40 mEq. 40 mEq – 26.4 mEq = 13.6 mEq still needed from KCl

$$\frac{2\text{ mEq K}}{\text{mL}} = \frac{13.6\text{ mEq K}}{X\text{ mL}} \quad X = 6.8\text{ mL KCl}$$

---

144. The PN order calls for 4.65 mEq of calcium. The pharmacy has calcium gluconate 10% (0.465 mEq/mL) in stock. How many mL of calcium gluconate 10% should be added to the PN?

$$\frac{0.465\text{ mEq Ca}}{\text{mL}} = \frac{4.65\text{ mEq Ca}}{X\text{ mL}} \quad X = 10\text{ mL calcium gluconate } 10\%$$

---

145. The PN calls for 18 mmol of phosphate and 4.65 mEq of calcium (provided by 10 mL of calcium gluconate 10%, as calculated in the previous problem) in a volume of 960 mL. There are 2 mEq PO4/mmol. Confirm that the sum of the calcium and phosphorus do not exceed 45 mEq/L.

First, calculate mEq from the phosphate.

$$\frac{2\text{ mEq PO4}}{\text{mmol}} \times 18\text{ mmol PO4} = 36\text{ mEq phosphate}$$

Then, add the phosphate to the calcium. 36 mEq phosphate + 4.65 mEq calcium = 40.65 mEq.

The volume of the PN is 960 mL, or 0.96 L. Calculate the mEq per liter

40.65 mEq/0.96 L = 42.3 mEq/L, which is less than 45 mEq/L

---

146. Calculate the amount of magnesium sulfate (4 mEq/mL) that should be added to the PN.

$$\frac{4\text{ mEq}}{\text{mL}} = \frac{12\text{ mEq}}{X\text{ mL}} \quad X = 3\text{ mL magnesium sulfate}$$

147. What percentage of the total calories from the above PN are represented by the protein component? Round to the nearest whole number.

First, calculate the total calories.

Dextrose

$$\frac{3.4 \text{ kcal dextrose}}{\text{g}} \times 250 \text{ g dextrose} = 850 \text{ kcal of dextrose}$$

Protein

$$\frac{4 \text{ kcal protein}}{\text{g}} \times 50 \text{ g protein} = 200 \text{ kcal of protein}$$

Total calories = 850 + 200 = 1,050 kcal. Now, calculate the percent of calories from protein.

$$\frac{200 \text{ kcal}}{1{,}050 \text{ kcal}} \times 100 = 19\%$$

Multivitamins, Trace Elements, and Insulin

Multivitamins

There are 4 fat-soluble vitamins (A, D, E and K) and 9 water-soluble vitamins (thiamine, riboflavin, niacin, pantothenic acid, pyridoxine, ascorbic acid, folic acid, cyanocobalamin, biotin) in the standard MVI-13 mixture. The MVI-12 mixture does not contain vitamin K since certain patients may need less or more of this vitamin. If patients on PN therapy are using warfarin, the INR will need to be monitored.

Trace Elements

The standard mix includes zinc, copper, chromium and manganese (and may include selenium). Manganese and copper should be withheld in severe liver disease. Chromium, molybdenum and selenium should be withheld in severe renal disease. Iron is not routinely given in a PN.

Insulin

PNs may contain insulin, usually ≤ 50% of what the person is expected to require per day, supplemented by a sliding scale. A minimum dose to add is 10 units, and is usually increased in 10 unit increments. It is important to avoid adding too much insulin. Half the previous day's sliding scale or less can be used as a safe amount. PN formulas are often titrated on and off (e.g., started at less than the goal rate and not abruptly stopped) to facilitate physiologic glucose regulation.

Enteral Nutrition

Enteral nutrition (EN) is the provision of nutrients via the gastrointestinal (GI) tract through a feeding tube. Nasogastric (NG) tubes are often used, primarily for short-term administration. For longer-term, or if the stomach cannot be used, tubes are placed further down the GI tract. EN is the preferred route for patients who cannot meet their nutrition needs through voluntary oral intake. Tube feedings can range from providing adjunctive support to providing complete nutrition support. Several advantages of EN over PN include lower cost, using the gut which prevents atrophy and other problems, and a lower risk of complications (less infections, less hyperglycemia, reduced risk of cholelithiasis and cholestasis). The most common risk associated with enteral feeding is aspiration which can lead to pneumonia. Enteral feedings can cause drug interactions. The general rule for preventing drug/enteral feeding interactions is to hold the feedings one hour before or two hours after the drug is administered. Some drugs may require further separation.

Tube feeds do not, by themselves, provide enough water. Water is given in addition to the tube feeds. If fluid intake is inadequate, it will be uncomfortable for the patient and put them at risk for complications, including hypernatremia.

Drug-Nutrient interactions with enteral feedings (most common problems):

- Warfarin: many enteral products bind warfarin, resulting in low INRs and the need for dose adjustments. Hold tube feeds one hour before and one hour after warfarin administration. EN formulas contain varying amounts of vitamin K, which can complicate warfarin dosing in some patients.
- Tetracycline: will chelate with metals, including calcium, magnesium, and iron, which reduces drug availability; separate from tube feeds.
- Ciprofloxacin: the oral suspension is not used with tube feeds because the oil-based suspension adheres to the tube. The immediate-release tablets are used instead; crush and mix with water, flush line with water before and after administration.
- Phenytoin *(Dilantin* suspension): levels are reduced when the drug binds to the feeding solution, leading to less free drug availability and sub-therapeutic levels. Separate tube feeds by 2 hours.

Tube Names

- A tube in the nose to the stomach is called a nasogastric (NG), or nasoenteral, tube.
- A tube that goes through the skin into the stomach is called a gastrostomy, or percutaneous endoscopic gastrostomy (PEG, or G) tube.
- A tube into the small intestine is called a jejunostomy, or percutaneous endoscopic jejunostomy (PEJ, or J) tube.

Patient Case (For Questions 148 – 150)

Wilma is a patient starting enteral nutrition therapy. Wilma has a past medical history significant for type 2 diabetes. She will be started on *Glucerna* Ready-to-Drink Vanilla shakes. See the nutrient label provided.

---

148. According to the case above, what percent of calories will Wilma receive from the protein component? Round to the nearest whole number.

First, calculate the amount of calories provided by the protein component.

$$19.6 \text{ g protein} \times \frac{4 \text{ kcal}}{\text{g}} = 78.4 \text{ kcal}$$

Next, find the percentage of protein calories.

$$\frac{78.4 \text{ kcal}}{356 \text{ kcal}} \times 100 = 22\%$$

Nutrition Facts

Serving Size: 8 fl oz (237 mL)

Amount Per Serving	
Calories	356 kcal
Total Fat	17.8 g
Protein	19.6 g
Total Carbohydrate	31.5 g
Dietary Fiber	3.8 g
L-Carnitine	51 mg
Taurine	40 mg
m-Inositol	205 mg
Vitamin A	
Vitamin C	
Iron	

© RxPrep

149. How many calories will Wilma receive from the fat component of 1 (8 fl oz.) shake? Round to the nearest whole number.

$$17.8 \text{ g} \times \frac{9 \text{ kcal}}{\text{g}} = 160.2, \text{ or } 160 \text{ kcal}$$

---

150. What percent of calories are derived from the fat component? Round to the nearest whole number.

$$\frac{160.2 \text{ kcal}}{356 \text{ kcal}} \times 100 = 45\%$$

Patient Case (For Questions 151 – 153)

Jonathan is a patient receiving *Osmolite* (a high-protein, low-residue formula) enteral nutrition through a PEG tube. See the nutrient label provided.

---

151. According to the case above, how many calories will Jonathan receive from the carbohydrate component in 4 fl oz? Round to the nearest whole number.

First, calculate the total calories from carbohydrates per 1 can (8 fl oz).

$$37.4 \text{ g carbohydrate} \times \frac{4 \text{ kcal}}{\text{g}} = 149.6 \text{ kcal from 8 fl oz}$$

The question asks about calories in 4 fl oz (1/2 can).

$$\frac{149.6 \text{ kcal}}{2} = 74.8, \text{ or } 75 \text{ kcal from 4 fl oz}$$

Nutrition Facts

Serving Size: 8 fl oz (237 mL)

Amount Per Serving	
Calories	285 kcal
Total Fat	9.2 g
Protein	13.2 g
Total Carbohydrate	37.4 g
L-Carnitine	36 mg
Taurine	36 mg
Vitamin A	
Vitamin C	
Iron	

© RxPrep

---

152. What percent of calories will Jonathan receive from the carbohydrate component? Round to the nearest whole number.

First, calculate the amount of calories from the carbohydrate component.

$$37.4 \text{ g carbohydrate} \times \frac{4 \text{ kcal}}{\text{g}} = 149.6 \text{ kcal}$$

Next, find the percentage of carbohydrate calories.

$$\frac{149.6 \text{ kcal}}{285 \text{ kcal}} \times 100 = 52.49, \text{ or } 52\%$$

---

153. The nurse was administering 1 can (8 fl oz.) of *Osmolite* to Jonathan when she accidentally spilled 2 fl oz. onto the floor. The remaining amount in the can was accurately delivered to Jonathan. How many calories did he actually receive? Do not round the answer.

$$\frac{8 \text{ fl oz}}{285 \text{ kcal}} = \frac{6 \text{ fl oz}}{X \text{ kcal}} \quad X = 213.75 \text{ kcal}$$

CALCULATE RATES OF ADMINISTRATION

Flow Rates

Intravenous (IV) infusions or continuous infusions are commonly used to deliver medications in different settings, including hospitals. Flow rates are used to calculate the volume or amount of drug a patient will receive over a given period of time. An order can specify the rate of flow of continuous intravenous fluids in milliliters per minute, drops per minute, milligrams per hour, or as the total time to administer the entire volume of the infusion (e.g., give over 8 hours). IV tubing is set to deliver a certain number of drops per minute (gtts/min). There are various types of IV tubing and each has a hollow plastic chamber called a drip chamber. One can count the number of drops per minute by looking at the drip chamber. Also, it is important to know how big the drops are to calibrate the tubing in terms of drops/mL. This is called the drop factor. Calculating flow rates from a drop factor is not as common with the prevalence of programmable "smart" pumps. It is a good skill to know in the event a programmable pump is not available, fails, or simply as a double check.

---

154. The pharmacist has an order for heparin 25,000 units in 250 mL D5W to infuse at 1,000 units/hour. The pharmacy has the following premixed heparin bags in stock: 25,000 units in 500 mL ½ NS, 10,000 units in 250 mL D5W, and 25,000 units in 250 mL D5W. What should the infusion rate be set at in mL/hour?

The pharmacy has the heparin product that was ordered. First, calculate units per mL.

$$\frac{25{,}000 \text{ units}}{250 \text{ mL}} = 100 \text{ units/mL}$$

Next calculate the infusion rate.

$$\frac{1{,}000 \text{ units}}{1 \text{ hr}} \times \frac{1 \text{ mL}}{100 \text{ units}} = 10 \text{ mL/hr}$$

Since 1,000 units/hour must be delivered to the patient and there are 100 units in each mL, the pump should be programmed for an infusion rate of 10 mL/hr.

A second way to solve flow rate problems is using dimensional analysis, which combines individual steps into one calculation. If using dimensional analysis, make sure that all units cancel out to leave the correct units for the answer:

$$\frac{250 \text{ mL}}{25{,}000 \text{ units}} \times \frac{1{,}000 \text{ units}}{1 \text{ hr}} = 10 \text{ mL/hr}$$

Another way to solve these problems is to use a ratio:

$$\frac{25{,}000 \text{ units}}{250 \text{ mL}} = \frac{1{,}000 \text{ units}}{X \text{ mL}} \quad X = 10 \text{ mL (10 mL/hr since we need to administered 1,000 units in 1 hour)}$$

Try solving the problems in this section both ways and decide which you prefer.

---

155. If 50 mg of drug are added to a 500 mL bag, what rate of flow, in milliliters per hour, will deliver 5 mg of drug per hour?

$$\frac{500 \text{ mL}}{50 \text{ mg}} \times \frac{5 \text{ mg}}{\text{hr}} = 50 \text{ mL/hour}$$

156. If 200 mg of drug are added to a 500 mL bag, what rate of flow, in milliliters per hour, will deliver 500 mcg of drug per hour? Round to the nearest hundredth.

$$200\ \text{mg} \times \frac{1{,}000\ \text{mcg}}{1\ \text{mg}} = 200{,}000\ \text{mcg}$$

$$\frac{200{,}000\ \text{mcg}}{500\ \text{mL}} = \frac{500\ \text{mcg}}{X} \qquad X = 1.25\ \text{mL/hour}$$

---

157. A 68 kg patient is receiving a drug in standard concentration of 400 mg/250 mL of 1/2 NS running at 15 mL/hr. Calculate the dose in mcg/kg/min. Round to the nearest hundredth.

$$\frac{15\ \text{mL}}{\text{hr}} \times \frac{400\ \text{mg drug}}{250\ \text{mL}} = 24\ \text{mg drug/hr}$$

$$\frac{24\ \text{mg drug}}{\text{hr}} \times \frac{1{,}000\ \text{mcg}}{1\ \text{mg}} = 24{,}000\ \text{mcg/hr}$$

$$\frac{24{,}000\ \text{mcg}}{\text{hr}} \times \frac{1\ \text{hr}}{60\ \text{min}} = 400\ \text{mcg/min}$$

$$\frac{400\ \text{mcg/min}}{68\ \text{kg}} = 5.88\ \text{mcg/kg/min}$$

---

158. The pharmacist has an order for heparin 25,000 units in 250 mL D5W to infuse at 1,000 units/hour. How many hours will it take to infuse the entire bag?

$$25{,}000\ \text{units} \times \frac{1\ \text{hr}}{1{,}000\ \text{units}} = 25\ \text{hrs}$$

The problem could ask how many drops will be administered per minute (or per hour). The problem would state the number of drops/mL, which depends on the infusion set used.

---

159. A physician orders an IV infusion of D5W 1 liter to be delivered over 8 hours. The IV infusion set delivers 15 drops/mL. How many drops/min will the patient receive? Round to the nearest whole number.

$$\frac{15\ \text{drops}}{1\ \text{mL}} \times \frac{1{,}000\ \text{mL}}{8\ \text{hr}} \times \frac{1\ \text{hr}}{60\ \text{min}} = 31.25\ \text{drops/min, rounded to 31 drops/min}$$

---

160. A nurse is hanging a 4% lidocaine drip for a patient. If the dose ordered is 6 mg/min, how many hours will a 250 mL bag last? Round to the nearest tenth.

$$\frac{4\ \text{g}}{100\ \text{mL}} = \frac{X\ \text{g}}{250\ \text{mL}} \qquad X = 10\ \text{g or } 10{,}000\ \text{mg}$$

$$\frac{6\ \text{mg}}{\text{min}} = \frac{10{,}000\ \text{mg}}{X\ \text{min}} \qquad X = 1{,}666.67\ \text{minutes}$$

Convert to hours = 27.777 hrs, or 27.8 hrs

Or, solve another way:

$$\frac{1\ \text{hr}}{60\ \text{min}} \times \frac{1\ \text{min}}{6\ \text{mg}} \times \frac{1{,}000\ \text{mg}}{1\ \text{g}} \times \frac{4\ \text{g}}{100\ \text{mL}} \times 250\ \text{mL} = 27.8\ \text{hours}$$

---

161. A patient is to receive *Keppra* at a rate of 5 mg/min. The pharmacy has a 5 mL *Keppra* vial (100 mg/mL) which will be diluted in 100 mL of NS. What is the *Keppra* infusion rate, in mL/min? Do not include the volume of the 5 mL additive.

First, calculate the amount of *Keppra* in the vial.

$$\frac{100\ \text{mg}}{\text{mL}} = \frac{X\ \text{mg}}{5\ \text{mL}} \qquad X = 500\ \text{mg}$$

Then, solve for the answer in mL/min.

$$\frac{100\ \text{mL}}{500\ \text{mg}} \times \frac{5\ \text{mg}}{\text{min}} = 1\ \text{mL/min}$$

---

162. A physician orders 15 units of regular insulin to be added to a liter of D5W to be given over 10 hours. What is the infusion rate, in drops/minute, if the IV set delivers 15 drops/mL? Do not round the answer.

$$\frac{15\ \text{drops}}{\text{mL}} \times \frac{1{,}000\ \text{mL}}{10\ \text{hrs}} \times \frac{1\ \text{hr}}{60\ \text{min}} = 25\ \text{drops/min}$$

---

163. The pharmacy has insulin vials containing 100 units of insulin/mL. A physician orders 15 units of regular insulin to be added to a liter of D5W to be given over 10 hours. How many units of insulin will the patient receive each hour if the IV set delivers 15 drops/mL? Do not round the answer.

$$\frac{15\ \text{units}}{10\ \text{hrs}} = \frac{X\ \text{units}}{1\ \text{hr}} \qquad X = 1.5\ \text{units/hr}$$

STUDY TIP: FINAL VOLUME OF COMPOUNDED IV SOLUTIONS

Why does problem #161 include the instructions "do not include the volume of the 5 mL additive"? Because the answer might be different (depending on the rounding instructions) if you used 100 mL vs 105 mL for the final volume.

- Exam scenarios:
  - Explicit instructions (e.g., #161).
  - Language stating that a specific volume is "added to" some volume of a fluid (e.g., #164).
  - Rounding instructions are such that either method will yield the correct answer.
  - Language stating that a specific volume is added "to make 1 liter" or "for a final volume of 1 L" (e.g., #195).

This can be handled in many ways in clinical practice, but institutions should have clear policies to avoid medication errors.

---

164. An order is written for 10 mL of a 10% calcium chloride injection and 10 mL of multivitamin injection (MVI) to be added to 500 mL of D5W. The infusion is to be administered over 6 hours. The IV set delivers 15 drops/mL. What should be the rate of flow in drops/minute to deliver this infusion? Round to the nearest whole number.

Total volume of the infusion = 500 mL (D5W) + 10 mL ($CaCl_2$) + 10 mL (MVI) = 520 mL

$$\frac{15\ \text{drops}}{\text{mL}} \times \frac{520\ \text{mL}}{6\ \text{hr}} \times \frac{1\ \text{hr}}{60\ \text{min}} = 22\ \text{drops/min}$$

165. RS is a 45 year old male, 5'5", 168 pounds, hospitalized with a diabetic foot infection. The pharmacist prepared a 500 mL bag of D5W containing 1 gram of vancomycin to be infused over 4 hours using a 20 gtts/mL IV tubing set. How many mg of vancomycin will the patient receive each minute? Round to the nearest tenth.

$$\frac{1{,}000 \text{ mg vanco}}{4 \text{ hrs}} \times \frac{1 \text{ hr}}{60 \text{ min}} = 4.16 \text{ mg/min, rounded to } 4.2 \text{ mg/min}$$

---

166. A patient is to receive 600,000 units of penicillin G potassium in 100 mL D5W. A vial of penicillin G potassium 1,000,000 units is available. The manufacture states that when 4.6 mL of diluent is added, a 200,000 units/mL solution will result. How many milliliters of reconstituted solution should be withdrawn and added to the bag of D5W?

$$\frac{200{,}000 \text{ units}}{\text{mL}} = \frac{600{,}000 \text{ units}}{X \text{ mL}} \quad X = 3 \text{ mL}$$

---

167. A patient is to receive 1.5 liters of NS running at 45 gtts/min using a 15 gtts/mL IV tubing set. Calculate the total infusion time in hours. Round to the nearest tenth.

$$\frac{15 \text{ gtts}}{1 \text{ mL}} = \frac{45 \text{ gtts}}{X \text{ mL}} \quad X = 3 \text{ mL}$$

$$\frac{3 \text{ mL}}{\text{min}} = \frac{1{,}500 \text{ mL}}{X \text{ min}} \quad X = 500 \text{ min}$$

$$500 \text{ min} \times \frac{1 \text{ hr}}{60 \text{ min}} = 8.3 \text{ hrs}$$

---

168. An intravenous infusion contains 2 mL of a 1:1,000 (w/v) solution of epinephrine and 250 mL of D5W. At what flow rate, in mL/min, should the infusion be administered to provide 0.3 mcg/kg/min of epinephrine to an 80 kg patient? Round to the nearest whole number.

- 1:1,000 ratio strength = 0.1% (w/v)

$$\frac{0.1 \text{ g}}{100 \text{ mL}} = \frac{X \text{ g}}{2 \text{ mL}} \quad X = 0.002 \text{ g, or } 2 \text{ mg}$$

The patient is 80 kg x 0.3 mcg/kg/min = 24 mcg/min

$$\frac{252 \text{ mL}}{2 \text{ mg}} \times \frac{1 \text{ mg}}{1{,}000 \text{ mcg}} \times \frac{24 \text{ mcg}}{\text{min}} = 3 \text{ mL/min}$$

---

169. A patient is to receive *Flagyl* at a rate of 12.5 mg/min. The pharmacy has a 5 mL (100 mg/mL) *Flagyl* injection vial to be diluted in 100 mL of NS. How much drug in milligrams will the patient receive over 20 minutes?

$$\frac{12.5 \text{ mg}}{\text{min}} \times 20 \text{ minutes} = 250 \text{ mg}$$

170. A physician has ordered 2 grams of cefotetan to be added to 100 mL NS for a 56 year old female with an anaerobic infection. Using a reconstituted injection containing 154 mg/mL, how many milliliters should be added to prepare the order? Round to the nearest whole number.

$$2{,}000 \text{ mg} \times \frac{1 \text{ mL}}{154 \text{ mg}} = 13 \text{ mL}$$

---

171. JY is a 58 year old male hospitalized for a total knee replacement. He was given unfractionated heparin and developed heparin-induced thrombocytopenia (HIT). Argatroban was ordered at a dose of 2 mcg/kg/min. The pharmacy mixes a concentration of 100 mg argatroban in 250 mL of D5W. JY weighs 187 lbs. At what rate (mL/hour) should the nurse infuse argatroban to provide the desired dose? Round to the nearest whole number.

First, determine the amount of drug needed based on body weight.

$$2 \text{ mcg/kg/min} \times 85 \text{ kg} = 170 \text{ mcg/min}$$

Then, calculate mL/hr.

$$\frac{250 \text{ mL}}{100 \text{ mg}} \times \frac{1 \text{ mg}}{1{,}000 \text{ mcg}} \times \frac{170 \text{ mcg}}{\text{min}} \times \frac{60 \text{ min}}{\text{hr}} = 25.5 \text{ mL/hr, rounded to } 26 \text{ mL/hr}$$

---

172. The 8 a.m. medications scheduled for a patient include *Tygacil* dosed at 6 mg/kg. The patient weighs 142 pounds. The nurse has *Tygacil* labeled 500 mg/50 mL NS. The dose will be administered over thirty minutes. The IV tubing in the unit delivers 15 drops per milliliter. What is the correct rate of flow in drops per minute? Round to the nearest drop.

$$\frac{142 \text{ pounds}}{2.2 \text{ pounds/kg}} \times \frac{6 \text{ mg}}{\text{kg}} = 387.27 \text{ mg required dose}$$

$$387.27 \text{ mg} \times \frac{50 \text{ mL}}{500 \text{ mg}} = 38.727 \text{ mL}$$

$$\frac{38.727 \text{ mL}}{30 \text{ min}} \times \frac{15 \text{ drops}}{\text{mL}} = 19.36 \text{ drops/min, rounded to } 19 \text{ drops/min for } 30 \text{ minuntes}$$

---

173. A 165 pound patient is to receive 250 mL of a dopamine drip at a rate of 17 mcg/kg/min. The pharmacy has dopamine premixed in concentration of 3.2 mg/mL in D5W. Calculate the infusion rate in mL/minute. Round to the nearest tenth.

Step 1: Calculate amount of drug in the 250 mL bag.

$$\frac{3.2 \text{ mg}}{\text{mL}} \times 250 \text{ mL} = 800 \text{ mg}$$

Step 2: Calculate amount of drug the patient needs per minute.

$$\frac{17 \text{ mcg}}{\text{kg/min}} \times \frac{1 \text{ kg}}{2.2 \text{ lbs}} \times 165 \text{ lbs} = 1{,}275 \text{ mcg/min or } 1.275 \text{ mg/min}$$

Step 3: Solve for milliliters per minute.

$$\frac{250 \text{ mL}}{800 \text{ mg}} \times \frac{1.275 \text{ mg}}{\text{min}} = 0.4 \text{ mL/min}$$

---

174. An order is written for phenytoin IV. A loading dose of 15 mg/kg is to be infused at 0.5 mg/kg/min for a 33 pound child. The pharmacy has phenytoin injection solution 50 mg/mL in a 5 mL vial in stock. The pharmacist will put the dose into 50 mL NS. Over how many minutes should the dose be administered? Round to the nearest whole number.

First, calculate the child's body weight in kg.

$$33 \text{ lbs} \times \frac{1 \text{ kg}}{2.2 \text{ lbs}} = 15 \text{ kg}$$

Next, find the dose the child will receive.

$$\frac{15 \text{ mg}}{\text{kg}} \times 15 \text{ kg} = 225 \text{ mg}$$

Then, calculate the time it will take to infuse this amount of drug at the given rate.

$$0.5\text{mg/kg/min} \times 15 \text{ kg} = 7.5 \text{ mg/min}$$

$$\frac{1 \text{ min}}{7.5 \text{ mg}} \times 225 \text{ mg} = 30 \text{ minutes}$$

ADDITIONAL CALCULATION TYPES

pH, Arterial Blood Gas (ABG), Anion Gap, Buffer Systems and Ionization

pH

The pH refers to the acidity or basicity of the solution. As a solution becomes more acidic (the concentration of protons increases), the pH decreases. Conversely, when the pH increases, protons decrease, and the solution is more basic, or alkaline. Pure water is neutral at a pH of 7, and blood, with a pH of 7.4, is slightly alkaline. Stomach acid has a pH of ~2, is therefore acidic, with many protons in solution.

Arterial Blood Gas

The acid-base status of a patient can be determined by an arterial blood gas (ABG). The primary buffering system of the body is the bicarbonate/carbonic acid system. The kidneys help to maintain a neutral pH by controlling bicarbonate (HCO_3) resorption and elimination. Bicarbonate acts as a buffer and a base. The lungs help maintain a neutral pH by controlling carbonic acid (which is directly proportional to the partial pressure of carbon dioxide or pCO_2) retained or released from the body. Carbon dioxide acts as a buffer and an acid. Alterations from the normal values lead to acid-base disorders. Diet and cellular metabolism lead to a large production of H^+ ions that need to be excreted to maintain acid-base balance. See Lab Values & Drug Monitoring chapter for ABG component reference ranges. ABGs are presented as follows in a written chart note:

ABG: pH/pCO2/pO2/HCO3/O2 Sat

An acid-base disorder that leads to a pH < 7.35 is called an acidosis. If the disorder leads to a pH > 7.45, it is called an alkalosis. These disorders are further classified as either metabolic or respiratory in origin. The primary disturbance in a metabolic acid-base disorder is the plasma HCO3 (bicarbonate) concentration. A metabolic acidosis is characterized primarily by a decrease in plasma HCO3 concentration. In a metabolic alkalosis, the plasma HCO3 concentration is increased. Metabolic acidosis may be associated with an increase in the anion gap (see below). In respiratory acidosis, the pCO2 is primarily elevated and in respiratory alkalosis, the pCO2 is decreased. Each disturbance has a compensatory (secondary) response that attempts to correct the imbalance toward normal and keep the pH neutral.

STUDY TIP: INTERPRETING ABGs

- Step #1: Is it an acidosis or alkalosis?
  - $\downarrow$ pH = acidosis
  - $\uparrow$ pH = alkalosis
- Step #2: What other value(s) are abnormal?
  - Respiratory: $\downarrow$ CO2 = alkalosis $\uparrow$ CO2 = acidosis
  - Metabolic: $\uparrow$ HCO3 = alkalosis $\downarrow$ HCO3 = acidosis
- Step #3: Which of the abnormal values in Step #2 matches with the pH in Step #1?
  - Example: $\downarrow$ pH, $\uparrow$ CO2 and normal HCO3
  - pH = acidosis and $\uparrow$ CO2 = acidosis; this is a respiratory acidosis
- Step #4: What if both CO2 and HCO3 are abnormal?
  - Usually only one of the values will match the pH, the other will go in the opposite direction from the pH. This is called compensation.
  - Example: $\downarrow$ pH, $\downarrow$ CO2 and $\downarrow$ HCO3
  - pH = acidosis, $\downarrow$ HCO3 = acidosis and $\downarrow$ CO2 = alkalosis; this is a metabolic acidosis with some degree of respiratory compensation

---

175. A babysitter brings a 7 year old boy to the Emergency Department. He is unarousable. Labs are ordered and an ABG is drawn. The ABG results are as follows: 6.72/40/89/12/94%. What acid base disorder does the child have?

Based on the pH, this is an acidosis. The pCO2 is normal and the HCO3 is decreased (low bicarbonate indicates acidosis). This is a metabolic acidosis.

---

176. An elderly female is admitted to the hospital after a motor vehicle accident. She suffered a head injury and is in the ICU. An ABG is obtained and the results are as follows: 8.25/29/97/26/98%. What acid base disorder does the patient have?

Based on the pH, this is an alkalosis. The pCO2 is decreased (low pCO2 indicates alkalosis) and the HCO3 is normal. This is a respiratory alkalosis.

Calculating Anion Gap

When a patient is experiencing metabolic acidosis, it is common to calculate an anion gap. The anion gap is the difference in the measured cations and the measured anions in the blood. An anion gap assists in determining the cause of the acidosis. A mnemonic to remember the causes of a gap acidosis is CUTE DIMPLES [cyanide, uremia, toluene, ethanol (alcoholic ketoacidosis), diabetic ketoacidosis, isoniazid, methanol, propylene glycol, lactic acidosis, ethylene glycol, salicylates]. The anion gap is considered high if it is > 12 mEq/L (meaning the patient has a gap acidosis). The anion gap can also be low, which is less common. A non-gap acidosis is caused by other factors, mainly hyperchloremic acidosis. Anion gap is calculated with this formula:

$$\text{Anion gap (AG)} = Na - Cl - HCO_3$$

177. A patient in the ICU has recently developed an acidosis. Using the laboratory parameters below, calculate the patient's anion gap.

Na	139
Cl	101
K	4.6
HCO_3	19
SCr	1.6
BUN	38

Anion Gap = 139 - 101 - 19 = 19; therefore, the patient has a positive anion gap acidosis

---

178. SJ was recently admitted to the ICU with a pH of 7.27. Below is her laboratory data. Calculate SJ's anion gap.

144	95	68	414
3.22	21	2.1	

Anion Gap = 144 - 95 - 21 = 28; therefore, SJ has a positive anion gap acidosis

Buffer Systems and Ionization

Buffer systems help to reduce the impact of too few or too many hydrogen ions in body fluids. These hydrogen ions could cause harm including degrading some drugs, destabilizing proteins, inhibiting cellular functions, and with too much of a change outside of the narrow range, cells die and death can occur. Therefore, buffers minimize fluctuations in pH so that harm is avoided. Buffer systems are common in the body and are composed of either a weak acid and salt of the acid (e.g., acetic acid and sodium acetate), or weak base and salt of the base (e.g., ammonium hydroxide and ammonium chloride). An acid is a compound that dissociates, releasing (donating) protons into solution. Once the proton is released, the compound is now a conjugate base, or its salt form. For example, HCl in solution is an acid and dissociates (giving up the proton) into H^+ and Cl^-. A base picks up, or binds, the proton. For example, NH_3 is a base that can pick up a proton and become NH_4^+.

Acid-base reactions are equilibrium reactions; there is drug moving back and forth between the acid and base state. The pH and the pKa are used to determine if the drug is acting as an acid or a base. When the pH = pKa, the molar concentration of the salt form and the molar concentration of the acid form of the buffer acid-base pair will be equal: 50% of the buffer will be in salt form and 50% in acid form. Notice that the percentage of buffer in the acid form when added to the percentage of buffer in the salt form will equal 100%. When the pH = pKa, this is the point at which half the compound is protonated (ionized), and half is not protonated (un-ionized).

A 'strong' acid or base means 100% dissociation and a 'weak' acid or base means very limited dissociation. Any time a pKa is provided, it refers to the acid form losing protons to give to the base, or salt, form.

If the 'pKb' is provided, think 'base' simply because of the definitions of the two terms.

If the pH > pKa, more of the acid is ionized, and more of the conjugate base is un-ionized.

If the pH = pKa, the ionized and un-ionized forms are equal.

If the pH < pKa, more of the acid is un-ionized, and more of the conjugate base is ionized.

The percentage of drug in the ionized versus un-ionized state is important because an ionized drug is soluble but cannot easily cross lipid membranes. An un-ionized drug is not soluble but can cross the membranes and reach the proper receptor site. Most drugs are weak acids. They are soluble, and can pick up a proton to cross the lipid layer.

Most drug molecules are weak acids (or weak bases). These molecules can exist in either the un-ionized or the ionized state, and the degree of ionization depends on the dissociation constant (Ka) of the drug and the pH of the environment. This leads to the Henderson-Hasselbalch equation, also known as the buffer equation, which is used to solve for the pH.

Weak acid formula

$$pH = pK_a + \log\left[\frac{salt}{acid}\right]$$

Weak base formulas

$$pH = (pK_w^* - pK_b) + \log\left[\frac{base}{salt}\right] \quad \text{or} \quad pH = pK_a + \log\left[\frac{base}{salt}\right]$$

**where pKw = 14*

---

179. What is the pH of a solution prepared to be 0.5 M sodium citrate and 0.05 M citric acid (pKa for citric acid = 3.13)? Round to the nearest hundredth.

$$pH = pK_a + \log\left[\frac{salt}{acid}\right]$$

$$pH = 3.13 + \log\left[\frac{0.5M}{0.05M}\right]$$

$$pH = 3.13 + \log[10]$$

$$pH = 3.13 + 1$$

$$pH = 4.13$$

---

180. What is the pH of a solution prepared to be 0.4 M ammonia and 0.04 M ammonium chloride (pKb for ammonia = 4.76)? Round to the nearest hundredth.

$$pH = (pK_w - pK_b) + \log\left[\frac{base}{salt}\right]$$

$$pH = (14 - 4.76) + \log\left[\frac{0.4}{0.04}\right]$$

$$pH = 9.24 + \log(10)$$

$$pH = 9.24 + 1$$

$$pH = 10.24$$

181. What is the pH of a buffer solution containing 0.5 M acetic acid and 1 M sodium acetate in 1 liter of solution (pKa for acetic acid = 4.76)? Round to the nearest hundredth.

$$pH = pK_a + \log\left[\frac{salt}{acid}\right]$$

$$pH = 4.76 + \log\left[\frac{1}{0.5}\right]$$

$$pH = 4.76 + \log(2)$$

$$pH = 4.76 + 0.301$$

$$pH = 5.06$$

---

182. What is the pH of a solution containing 0.2 mole of a weakly basic drug and 0.02 mole of its salt per liter of solution (pKa of the drug = 9.36)? Round to the nearest hundredth.

$$pH = pK_a + \log\left[\frac{base}{salt}\right]$$

$$pH = 9.36 + \log\left[\frac{0.2}{0.02}\right]$$

$$pH = 9.36 + 1$$

$$pH = 10.36$$

---

183. A buffer solution is prepared using 0.3 mole of a weakly basic drug and an unknown quantity of its salt (pKa of the drug = 10.1). The final solution has a pH of 8.99. How much of the salt was used? Round to the nearest hundredth.

$$pH = pK_a + \log\left[\frac{base}{salt}\right]$$

$$8.99 = 10.1 + \log\left[\frac{0.3}{X}\right]$$

$$8.99 - 10.1 = \log\left[\frac{0.3}{X}\right]$$

$$10^{-1.11} = \frac{0.3}{X}$$

$$X = 3.86 \text{ mole of the salt}$$

Percent of Ionization

The Henderson-Hasselbalch equation can be modified to calculate the percent of ionization of a drug.

To calculate the % ionization of a weak acid:

$$\% \text{ ionization} = \frac{100}{1+10^{(pKa-pH)}}$$

To calculate % ionization of a weak base:

$$\% \text{ ionization} = \frac{100}{1+10^{(pH-pKa)}}$$

---

184. What is the % ionization of amitriptyline, a weak base with a pKa = 9.4, at a physiologic pH of 7.4?

Use the weak base formula:

$$\% \text{ ionization} = \frac{100}{1+10^{(pH-pKa)}}$$

$$\% \text{ ionization} = \frac{100}{1+10^{(7.4-9.4)}}$$

$$\% \text{ ionization} = \frac{100}{1+10^{(-2)}}$$

$$\% \text{ ionization} = \frac{100}{1.01}$$

$$\% \text{ ionization} = 99\%$$

---

185. What is the % ionization of naproxen, a weak acid with a pKa of 4.2, in the stomach at a pH of 3? Round to the nearest whole number.

Use the weak acid formula:

$$\% \text{ ionization} = \frac{100}{1+10^{(pKa-pH)}}$$

$$\% \text{ ionization} = \frac{100}{16.85}$$

$$\% \text{ ionization} = 6\%$$

Calcium Formulations and Conversions

Calcium carbonate (*Oscal, Tums*, etc) has acid-dependent absorption and should be taken with meals. Calcium carbonate is a dense form of calcium and contains 40% elemental calcium. A tablet that advertises 500 mg of elemental calcium weighs 1,250 mg. If 1,250 mg is multiplied by 0.40 (which is 40%), it will yield 500 mg elemental calcium.

Calcium citrate (*Citracal*, etc) has acid-independent absorption and can be taken with or without food. Calcium citrate is less dense and contains 21% elemental calcium. A tablet that advertises 315 mg calcium weighs 1,500 mg. If 1,500 mg is multiplied by 0.21 (or 21%), it will yield 315 mg elemental calcium. This is why the larger calcium citrate tablets provide less elemental calcium per tablet. They may be preferred if the gut fluid is basic, rather than acidic.

Calcium acetate (*PhosLo*, etc) is used as a phosphate binder and not for calcium replacement. Though the capsules contain 25% elemental calcium, absorption from this formulation is poor. Calcium carbonate and citrate are most commonly used for calcium replacement.

---

186. A patient is taking 3 calcium citrate tablets daily (one tablet, TID). Each weighs 1,500 mg total (non-elemental) weight. She wishes to trade her calcium tablets for the carbonate form. If she is going to use 1,250 mg carbonate tablets (by weight), how many tablets will she need to take to provide the same total daily dose?

1,500 mg/tablet x 3 tablets/day x 0.21= 945 mg elemental calcium daily

Each of the carbonate tablets (1,250 mg x 0.4) has 500 mg elemental calcium per tablet.

$$\frac{945 \text{ mg elemental calcium}}{X \text{ tablets}} = \frac{500 \text{ mg elemental calcium}}{1 \text{ tablet}} \qquad X = 1.89 \text{ tablets}$$

She would need to take 2 tablets daily to provide a similar dose. Calcium absorption increases with lower doses, so this patient should be instructed to take one tablet with the morning meal and one with the evening meal.

Absolute Neutrophil Count

Neutrophils are our body's main defense against infection. The lower a patient's neutrophil count, the more susceptible that patient is to infection. The normal range for the absolute neutrophil count (ANC) is 2,200 – 8,000 cells/microliter. The microliter may be written as mm^3, or μL, but it is preferable to avoid the latter designation for safety reasons. Definitions vary, but an ANC < 1,000 cells/mm^3 would predispose a patient to infection; an ANC < 500 cells/mm^3 indicates very high risk for developing an infection. The Clozapine REMS Program is designed to reduce the risk of severe clozapine-induced neutropenia; clozapine cannot be refilled if the ANC is < 1,000 cells/mm^3. A neutropenic patient should be monitored for signs of infection, including fever, shaking, general weakness or flu-like symptoms. Precautions to reduce infection risk, such as proper hand-washing and avoiding others with infection, should be followed. Further information is in the Lab Values & Drug Monitoring chapter.

Calculating the ANC

Multiply the WBC (in total cells/mm^3) by the percentage of neutrophils (the segs plus the bands) and divide by 100.

ANC (cells/mm^3) = WBC x [(% segs + % bands)/100]

---

187. A patient is being seen at the oncology clinic today after her first round of chemotherapy one week ago. A CBC with differential is ordered and reported back as WBC = 14.8 x 10^3 cells/mm^3, segs 10% and bands 11%. Calculate this patient's ANC.

WBC = 14,800 cells/mm^3, Segs = 10% Bands = 11%

ANC = 14,800 x [(10% + 11%)/100] = 14,800 x 0.21 = 3,108 cells/mm^3

188. A patient is taking clozapine and is at the clinic for a routine visit. Today's labs include WBC = 4,300 cells/mm³ with 48% segs and 2% bands. Calculate this patient's ANC.

WBC = 4,300 cells/mm^3, Segs = 48% Bands = 2%

$$ANC = 4{,}300 \times [(48\% + 2\%)/100] = 4{,}300 \times 0.5 = 2{,}150 \text{ cells/mm}^3$$

Calculation Practice

The following problems integrate multiple calculation concepts.

---

189. A patient is receiving D5½NS with potassium chloride at 20 drops/min. After 10 hours, the patient has received a total of 40 mEq of potassium chloride using tubing that delivers 15 drops/mL. What is the percentage concentration of potassium chloride in the patient's IV fluid? Round to 2 decimal places. (M.W. of K = 39, M.W. of Cl = 36)

$$40 \text{ mEq} = \frac{X \text{ mg} \times 1}{75} = 3{,}000 \text{ mg, or } 3 \text{ g of KCl have been given in 10 hours}$$

$$\frac{20 \text{ drops}}{\text{min}} \times \frac{60 \text{ min}}{1 \text{ hr}} \times 10 \text{ hrs} = 12{,}000 \text{ drops infused in 10 hours}$$

$$\frac{15 \text{ drops}}{\text{mL}} = \frac{12{,}000 \text{ drops}}{X \text{ mL}} \quad X = 800 \text{ mL have infused in 10 hours}$$

$$\frac{3 \text{ g KCl}}{800 \text{ mL}} = \frac{X \text{ g}}{100 \text{ mL}} \quad X = 0.375 \text{ g, or } 0.38\%$$

---

190. An order is written for a dopamine drip in the ICU. The order reads: "Start dopamine drip at 3 mcg/kg/min, titrate by 5 mcg/kg/min Q5 minutes to achieve SBP > 100 mmHg. Page the critical care resident for additional orders if maximum dose of 20 mcg/kg/min is reached". The patient weighs 165 pounds and the ICU stocks premixed dopamine drips (400 mg/250 mL) in the automated dispensing cabinet (ADC). What rate (mL/hr) should the dopamine drip be started at? Round to the nearest whole number.

$$3 \text{ mcg/kg/min} \times 75 \text{ kg} = 225 \text{ mcg/min}$$

$$\frac{250 \text{ mL}}{400 \text{ mg}} \times \frac{1 \text{ mg}}{1000 \text{ mcg}} \times \frac{225 \text{ mcg}}{\text{min}} \times \frac{60 \text{ min}}{1 \text{ hr}} = 8.4 \text{ mL/hr, or } 8 \text{ mL/hr}$$

---

191. The patient in the previous problem is started on the dopamine drip as ordered. Later that day, the pharmacist checks on the patient and notes that the dopamine drip is running at 70 mL/hr and the patient's SBP is still < 100 mmHg. According to the original order, should the resident be paged?

$$20 \text{ mcg/kg/min} \times 75 \text{ kg} = 1500 \text{ mcg/min}$$

$$\frac{250 \text{ mL}}{400 \text{ mg}} \times \frac{1 \text{ mg}}{1000 \text{ mcg}} \times \frac{1500 \text{ mcg} \quad 60 \text{ min}}{\text{min} \quad 1 \text{ hr}} = 56.25 \text{ mL/hr – max rate per order}$$

The drip is running at 70 mL/hr and the maximum rate on the order was 56.25 mL/hr. According to the original order, the resident should be paged.

---

192. A pharmacist in an oncology clinic receives the following prescription for a patient with Hodgkin lymphoma: "Prednisone 40 mg/m²/day PO on days 1-14." The patient is 5'1" and weighs 116 pounds. The hospital uses the following formula for BSA (m²) = 0.007184 x height(cm)$^{0.725}$ x weight(kg)$^{0.425}$. How many 20 mg prednisone tablets should be dispensed to the patient?

$$\text{BSA } (m^2) = 0.007184 \times (154.94)^{0.725} \times (52.7272)^{0.425} = 1.5 \text{ m}^2$$

$$40 \text{ mg/m}^2\text{/day} \times 1.5 \text{ m}^2 = 60 \text{ mg/day}$$

Refer to Oncology II chapter for discussion of BSA.

The patient will take 60 mg of prednisone (three 20 mg tablets) per day for 14 days. The pharmacist should dispense 42 of the 20 mg prednisone tablets.

---

193. A nephrologist is treating a patient with hyponatremia. She estimates the patient's sodium deficit to be 210 mEq. How many mL of normal saline (M.W. Na = 23, M.W. Cl = 35.5) will be required to replace the deficit?

$$210 \text{ mEq} = \frac{\text{mg} \times 1}{58.5} \qquad 12{,}285 \text{ mg or } 12.285 \text{ g}$$

$$\frac{0.9 \text{ g}}{100 \text{ mL}} = \frac{12.285 \text{ g}}{X \text{ mL}} \qquad X = 1{,}365 \text{ mL of NS are required}$$

---

194. A pharmacy technician is asked to compound three 500 mL doses of 5% albumin. How many 50 mL vials of 25% albumin will be required?

$$\frac{5 \text{ g}}{100 \text{ mL}} = \frac{X \text{ g}}{500 \text{ mL}} \qquad X = 25 \text{ g, or } 75 \text{ g for the three required doses}$$

$$\frac{25 \text{ g}}{100 \text{ mL}} = \frac{X \text{ g}}{50 \text{ mL}} \qquad X = 12.5 \text{ g per } 50 \text{ mL vial}$$

$$75 \text{ g required} \times \frac{1 \text{ vial}}{12.5 \text{ g}} \qquad X = 6 \text{ vials of } 25\% \text{ albumin required}$$

195. A patient is to receive a potassium acetate infusion prepared by adding 9 mL of 39.2% potassium acetate ($KC_2H_3O_2$) to 0.45%NS to make 1 liter. The patient is to receive the potassium acetate at 5 mEq/hr. What rate in mL/hr will provide this dose? Round to the nearest whole number. (M.W. of K = 39, M.W of $C_2H_3O_2$ = 59)

$$\frac{39.2\ g}{100\ mL} = \frac{X\ g}{9\ mL} \quad X = 3.528\ g \text{ or } 3{,}528\ mg$$

$$X\ mEq = \frac{3{,}528\ mg \times 1}{98} = 36\ mEq$$

$$\frac{1{,}000\ mL}{36\ mEq} \times \frac{5\ mEq}{hr} = 138.88\ mL/hr, \text{ or } 139\ mL/hr$$

196. Mrs. Gudot uses the following regular insulin sliding scale: "take 1 unit of insulin SQ for every 20 mg/dL of blood sugar > 160 mg/dL". How many units of sliding scale insulin should have been administered on December 12th?

PATIENT PROFILE

Patient Name	Helene Gudot
Address	1365 Stephens Avenue
Age:	64 **Sex:** F **Race:** African American **Height:** 5'5" **Weight:** 135 pounds
Allergies	Bactrim

DIAGNOSES

Type 2 Diabetes	Dyslipidemia
Hypertension	Heart Failure

MEDICATIONS

Date	Prescriber	Drug/Strength/Sig
12/10	Marks	Metformin 1 gram BID
12/10	Marks	Regular insulin sliding scale per protocol
12/11	Marks	*Lantus* 10 units at HS
12/12	Ventrakhan	D51/4NS + 20 mEq KCL at 75 mL/hr
12/12	King	*Coreg* 6.25 mg BID
12/13	Marks	D51/2NS + 10 mEq KCL at 60 mL/hr
12/13	Marks	Lasix 40 mg IV Q12H
12/13	Ventrakhan	*Altace* 5 mg BID

LAB/DIAGNOSTIC TESTS

Test	Normal Value	Results		
		Date: 12/13	**Date:** 12/12	**Date:** 12/11
WBC	4,000-11,000 cells/mm³	10.7	10.1	12.2
Na	135-146 mEq/L	139	142	145
K	3.5-5.3 mEq/L	4.3	4.1	3.3
Cl	98-110 mEq/L	104	105	101
HCO3	22-28 mEq/L	26	26	25
BUN	7-25 mg/dL	23	26	28
Creatinine	0.6-1.2 mg/dL	1.1	1.3	1.4
Glu	65-99 mg/dL	180 @ 0700	140 @ 0700	260 @ 0700
Glu	65-99 mg/dL	280 @ 1100	280 @ 1100	320 @ 1100
Glu	65-99 mg/dL	220 @ 1700	300 @ 1700	280 @ 1700
Glu	65-99 mg/dL	100 @ 2100	220 @ 2100	220 @ 2100

140 mg/dL = no insulin

280 mg/dL – 160 mg/dL = 120 mg/dL; 120 mg/dL / 20 mg/dL = 6 units

300 mg/dL – 160 mg/dL = 140 mg/dL / 20 mg/dL = 7 units

220 mg/dL – 160 mg/dL = 60 mg/dL / 20 mg/dL = 3 units

Total sliding scale units for December 12th = 6 + 7 + 3 = 16 units

---

197. The pharmacist is asked to convert several of Mrs. Gudot's labs to different units so her case can be compared to a published case report. Convert her serum potassium level on December 13th to mg/dL. (M.W. of potassium = 39)

$$4.3 \text{ mEq} = \frac{X \text{ mg} \times 1}{39} \qquad X = 167.7 \text{ mg}$$

4.3 mEq = 167.7 mg. The patient's serum potassium is reported as 4.3 mEq/L, which equals 167.7 mg/L.

$$\frac{167.7 \text{ mg}}{1 \text{ L}} \times \frac{1 \text{ L}}{10 \text{ dL}} = 16.77 \text{ mg/dL}$$

198. Convert Mrs. Gudot's serum sodium level on December 11th to mmol/L. (M.W. of Na = 23)

$$145 \text{ mEq} = \frac{X \text{ mg} \times 1}{23} \qquad X = 3{,}335 \text{ mg}$$

$$X \text{ mmols} = \frac{3{,}335 \text{ mg}}{23} \qquad X = 145 \text{ mmols, therefore } 145 \text{ mEq/L} = 145 \text{ mmol/L for sodium}$$

Note that mmols = mEq in this problem. For Na and K, the mmol and mEq are the same; 1 mmol = 1 mEq.

NON-STERILE COMPOUNDING

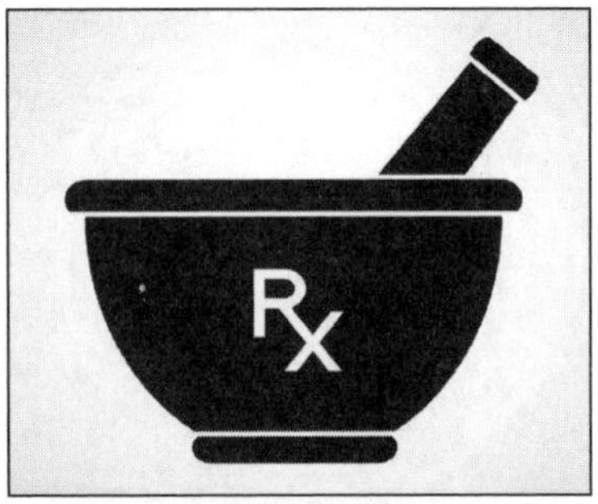

NON-STERILE COMPOUNDING HOW-TO'S

GUIDELINES/REFERENCES

USP Chapter 795, Pharmaceutical Compounding, Non-Sterile Preparations.

BACKGROUND

Traditional compounding is when drugs are combined, mixed or altered to create a drug tailored to the unique needs of an individual patient, and based on a prescription received for that patient. Compounding can be performed in a non-sterile environment or in a sterile environment (see the Sterile Compounding chapter).

The compounded drug is prepared to address the patient's need for a dose or formulation that is not commercially available. If the same product is available commercially, or if it was withdrawn from the market for safety reasons, then the compounded product should not be made. Purposes of preparing a compounded product could include a child who needs a liquid form of a drug that is only available in capsules, a middle-aged female who requires a topical hormone cream to address hormone deficiency, or an elderly male with severe hand arthritis who requires a unique combination of topical analgesics.

TRADITIONAL COMPOUNDING MEETS PATIENT NEEDS

Changing the form of a medication from a solid tablet to a liquid to help a patient who cannot use the solid formulation.

Avoiding a non-essential ingredient that a patient cannot tolerate.

Formulating a dose that is not commercially available.

Adding a flavor to a medication to make it more palatable.

Yummy. Chicken-flavored thyroid medicine for a dog.

Best practices for sterile and non-sterile compounding are set by the U.S. Pharmacopeia (USP). Compounding is exempt from the FDA's drug approval process and Current Good Manufacturing Practices (CGMPs).

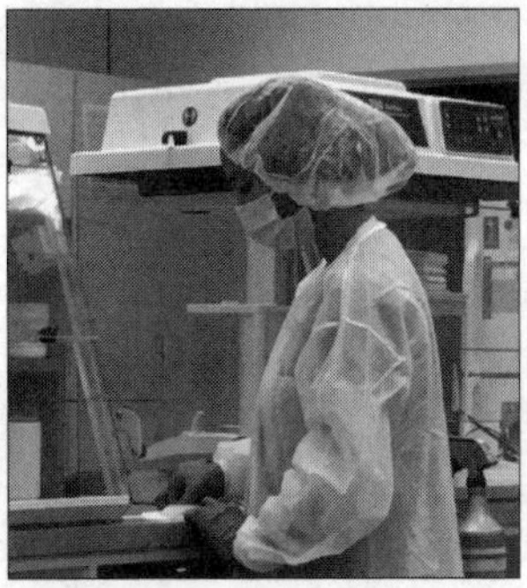

Garb protects the compounder from the drugs, and protects the drugs from the compounder.

Simple compounding involves reconstituting ("manipulating") a commercial product by adding one or more ingredients (such as water or alcohol), as directed by the manufacturer. An example would be adding water to amoxicillin powder to make a suspension, according to the instructions on the container. Reconstituting according to the manufacturer's instructions may not be considered compounding in all states. Moderate compounding requires calculations or procedures to determine the quantities of components needed for each dose. Complex compounding requires special training, environment, facilities, equipment and procedures.

COMPOUNDING IS DONE BY PHARMACIES, NOT BIG PHARMA

Manufactured drugs are prepared in bulk (large) quantities. They are not made for a specific patient.

Manufactured drugs must be FDA-approved. The manufacturing process must follow Current Good Manufacturing Practices (CGMPs).

Outsourcing facilities combine elements of traditional compounding and manufacturing. Outsourcing is reviewed in RxPrep's MPJE and CPJE courses.

PERSONNEL TRAINING/GARBING

Personnel, commonly referred to as staff, who are involved in compounding must have proper training for the types of compounding they perform, and the training must be documented. Staff must follow recommendations for hand hygiene (cleaning) and garb attire.

Garb attire includes hair covers (bonnets), beard covers, special shoes or shoe covers, gowns, gloves, face masks, eye shields and aprons. The garb attire required depends on the type of compounding performed. The staff have to be protected from chemical exposure (some drugs are more toxic than others), and the drug needs to be protected from contamination. Hand hygiene and garbing is more detailed for sterile compounding, and is reviewed in the following chapter.

SPACE

Compounding space must be separate from the rest of the pharmacy. The sterile compounding area (which has very specific requirements) must be separate from the non-sterile compounding area. All areas require adequate heating, air conditioning and ventilation, and facilities for hand and equipment washing.

For non-sterile compounding, washing facilities for cleaning hands and equipment must minimally include a sink with hot and cold water, soap/detergent, and an air-dryer or single-use towels.

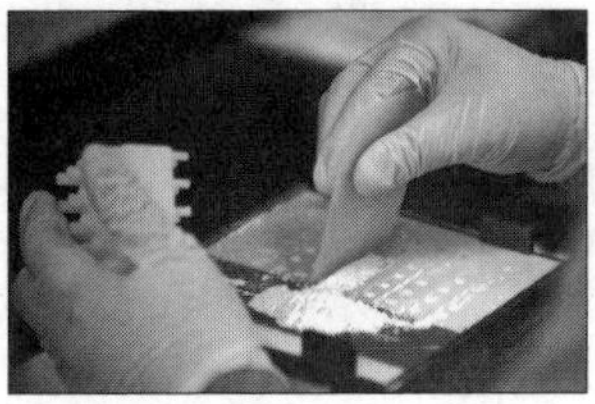

The compounding space is separate from the dispensing space.

EQUIPMENT

Equipment must be calibrated regularly, to confirm the accuracy. It should be made of material that does not react with the compounding ingredients.

If possible, there should be dedicated equipment for handling specific drugs (e.g., chemotherapeutics). If the equipment is used with other drugs, it must be cleaned prior to the next preparation to prevent cross-contamination.

Types of equipment used for non-sterile compounding are reviewed on the next few pages.

Measuring Equipment

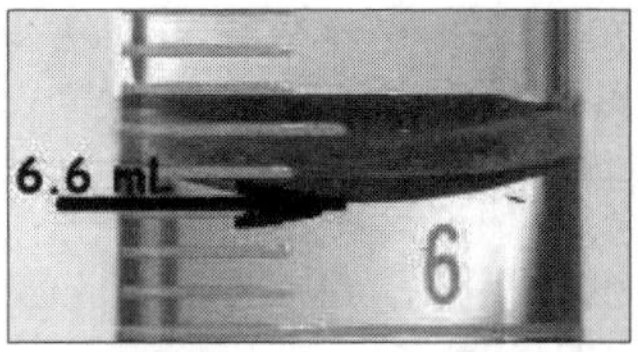

Liquids measured in a graduated cylinder can form a curve called a meniscus. Measure the level at the bottom (center) of the meniscus, at eye level.

Pharmacists use various equipment to measure ingredients, and patients use some of the same equipment (such as oral syringes and pipettes) to self-administer the dose.

When measuring, select a device that has a measuring capacity equal to or slightly larger than the amount in order to get the most accurate measurement.

A graduate is a measuring equipment with lines on the glass that are used to measure the volume. A graduated cylinder (see first figure below) has the same diameter from the top to the bottom of the container and provides more accurate measurements than conical graduates. To read the volume, place the graduated cylinder on a flat surface and view the height of the liquid in the cylinder at eye-level. The liquid will tend to curve downward from both sides. This curve is called the meniscus. The bottom of the meniscus, at the center, is where the liquid measurement is read (see figure at top of page). A conical (cone-shaped) graduate has a wide mouth (see second figure below) so that the compounder can stir the components using a glass stirring rod. The wider the mouth, the lower the measuring accuracy.

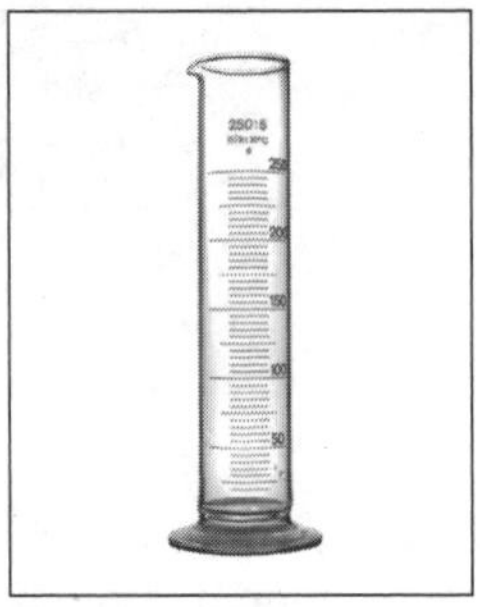
Graduated cylinder

Conical graduate

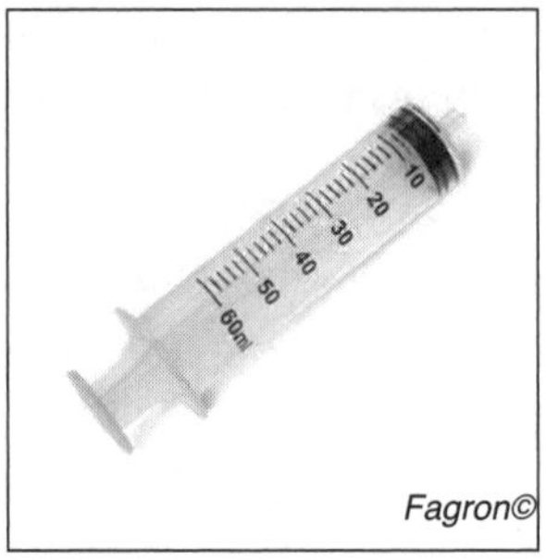

Syringes come as hypodermic & oral

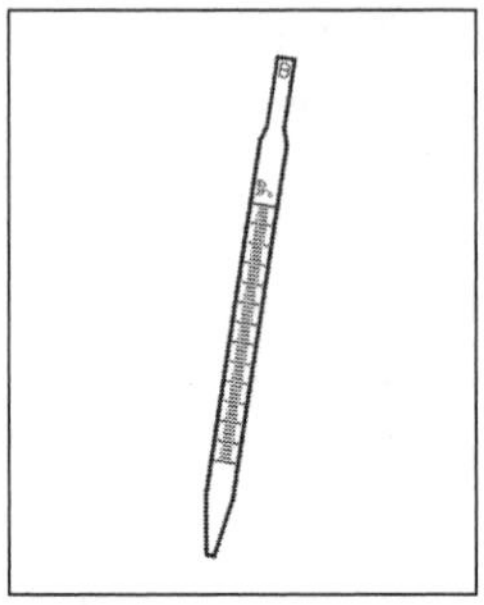
Mohr Pipette (graduated)

A compounding pharmacist can measure with an oral syringe or a hypodermic syringe [without the cannula (needle) if it's too narrow]. Syringes are most accurate for measuring small volumes. They are especially useful for measuring viscous (thick) liquids, such as glycerin. Patients who require a very accurate dose should use an oral syringe for measurement rather than a small dosing cup. Oral syringes are useful for squirting the medication into the side of the mouth (as are small pipettes or droppers).

Pipettes are thin tubes used for very small volumes. A volumetric pipette draws up a set volume only, which is the volume of the pipette. A Mohr pipette is graduated and is used to measure small (different) volumes. Mohr pipettes are commonly used in compounding. Pipettes can be used to deliver medication to the patient because they are easy to use to draw up a dose.

Weighing Equipment

There are two types of balances used to weigh ingredients: the common electronic balance (also called an analytical balance) and a class III torsion balance (also called a class A balance). A top-loading electronic balance is simple to use, has higher sensitivity than a torsion balance, and can weigh small amounts accurately.

YE OLD TORSION BALANCE

Class III (Class A) torsion balances have internal weights, which are used to weigh quantities ≤ 1 gram. When weighing > 1 gram, external weights (see picture) are placed on 1 pan and the substance to be weighed is placed on the other.

The balance weights must be handled with a forceps (pincers) to avoid damaging the weights.

Torsion balances have a sensitivity requirement (SR) of 6 mg, which means 6 mg can be added or removed before the dial moves 1 division.

The minimum weighable quantity (the minimum amount that can be weighed) is 120 mg, which is calculated by dividing the SR (6 mg) by 0.05, which is 5%, the acceptable error rate.

The material to be weighed, such as a powder, will be placed on a plastic weigh boat (a shallow dish) or on glassine weighing paper, which is coated to reduce moisture penetration. When using an electronic scale, the compounder must "zero out" the scale after placing the weigh boat or paper on it; this ensures that only the ingredient is weighed (not the weighing paper or boat).

Electronic balance

Torsion balance

Weigh boats

Mixing Equipment

Mortars and Pestles

A compounding pharmacy needs at least one glass and one Wedgwood or porcelain mortar and pestle. Glass mortars are used for liquids, such as suspensions and solutions, and for mixing compounds that are oily or can stain. Wedgwood mortars have a rougher surface than porcelain, and are preferred for grinding dry crystals and hard powders. Porcelain mortars have a smoother surface, and are preferred for blending powders and pulverizing gummy consistencies.

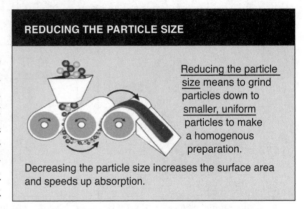

REDUCING THE PARTICLE SIZE

Reducing the particle size means to grind particles down to smaller, uniform particles to make a homogenous preparation.

Decreasing the particle size increases the surface area and speeds up absorption.

Glass mortar and pestle

Wedgwood mortar and pestle

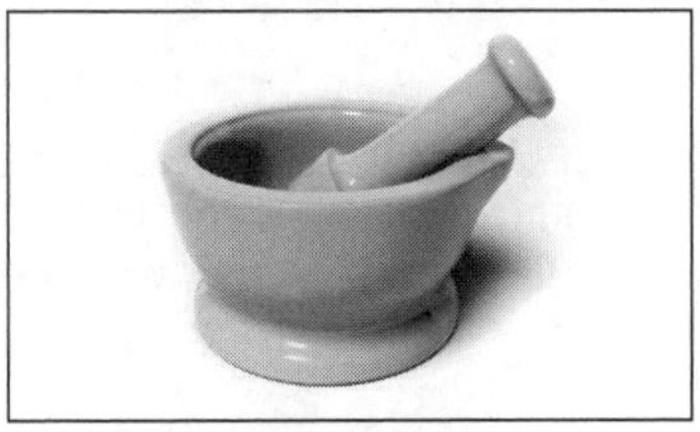

Porcelain mortar and pestle

Spatulas

Spatulas are used to mix and transfer (move) ingredients. Spatulas are made of stainless steel, plastic or hard rubber. Stainless steel and disposable plastic spatulas are used commonly. The type of spatula to use depends on what ingredients are being transferred or mixed. A steel (metal) spatula would not be used if making a mixture that contains metallic ions. A rubber spatula is used to handle corrosive material.

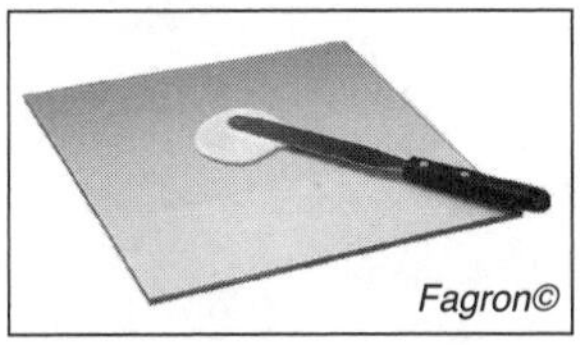

Slab and spatula

Ointment Slabs and Pill Tiles

Ingredients are mixed into ointments on a compounding (or ointment) slab, which is a flat board made of porcelain or glass. Pill tiles are slabs of porcelain or glass, similar to ointment slabs, and are designed to roll out pills. Pill tiles can be used as ointment slabs. Alternatively, disposable parchment ointment pads can be used if the water content of the mixture will not cause the paper to tear. Mixtures that have a higher water content than an ointment, such as a cream, can be mixed on an ointment slab if the mixture will hold its shape (and not flow off the slab). Otherwise different equipment is used, such as homogenizers.

Electric Mixing Equipment Saves Time

Electric mixing equipment speeds up the mixing process and helps make a uniform mixture.

An ointment mill draws the ointment (or another semi-solid preparation) between rollers that grind and homogenize the ingredients. This will make the ointment smoother and remove the grittiness of the compounded product.

A homogenizer (also called an electric mortar and pestle) can be used to mix ointments, creams, or other semi-solid preparations. The homogenizer is like a smoothie blender. A popular brand of homogenizer is called the *Unguator*.

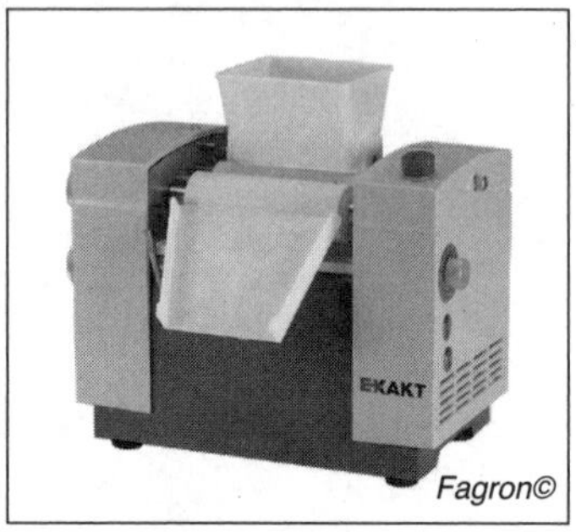

Ointment mill; see roller box above.

Homogenizer (also called an electric mortar & pestle)

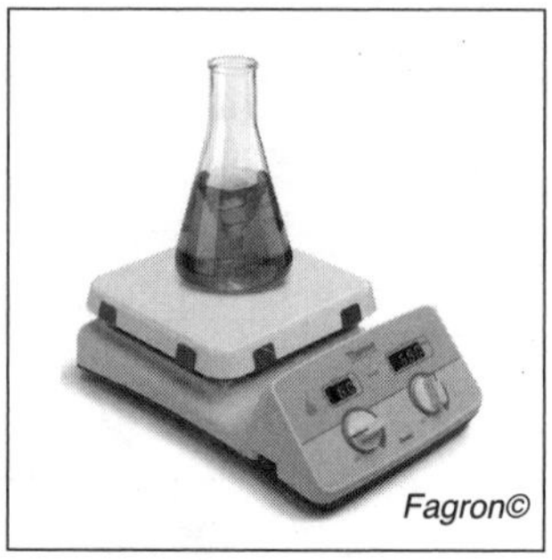

Hot plate with a stir bar in the glass. A magnet inside the hot plate moves the stir bar.

A hot plate and magnetic stirrer can save time by continuously stirring the mixture, in order to dissolve and mix the ingredients. The stirrer has a rotating magnet which causes the stir bar (placed inside the glass) to spin, which stirs the components.

Molds, Presses and Packaging Equipment

Reusable or disposable molds are used to prepare tablets, lozenges/troches (orally-dissolving tablets), and suppositories. With soft delivery forms, such as suppositories and lozenges, the medication is often dispensed in the disposable mold. This helps keep the shape. A tablet press is two plastic or metal plates used to compress powder into tablets. Similar to forcing *Play-Doh* into a mold to form a shape, the compounder takes the pasty mass and uses the tablet press to form tablet shapes. A capsule-filling machine can be used to prepare a large number of capsules. Tube-sealers heat/squeeze the ends of tubes shut; the end will look similar to the crimped end of a toothpaste tube. In the picture below, a filled tube is being sealed shut.

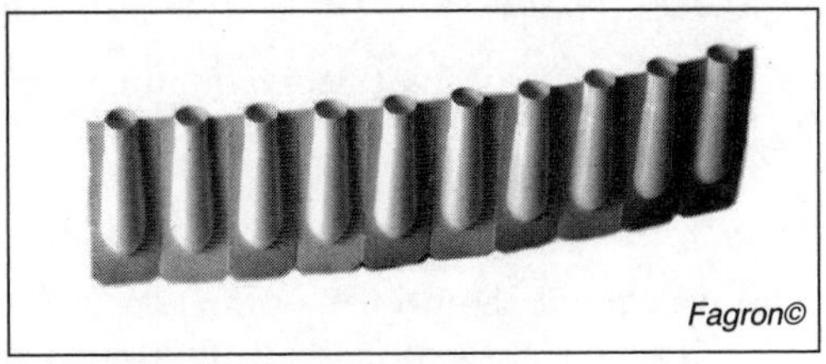

Suppository mold

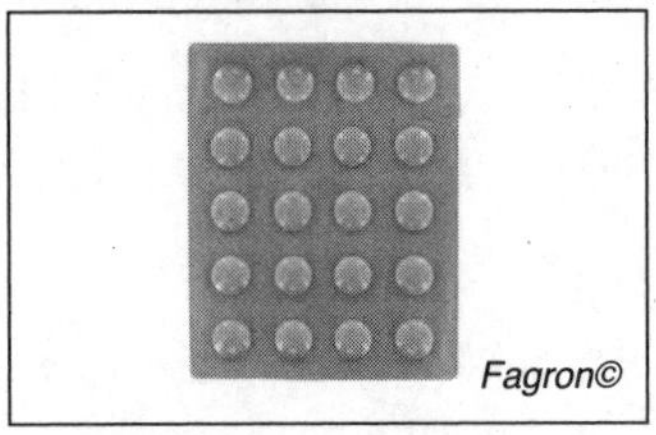

Lozenge mold

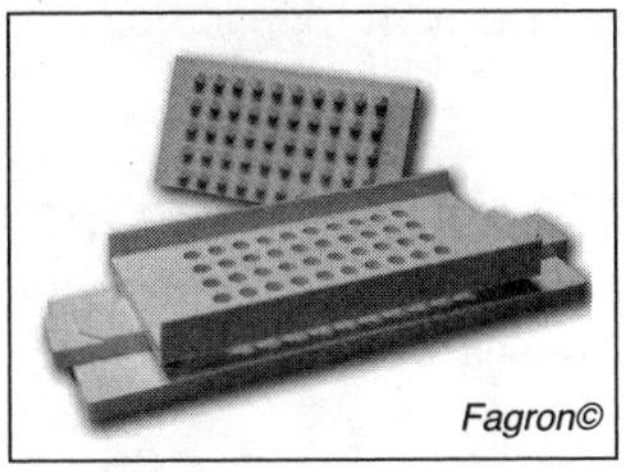

Tablet press

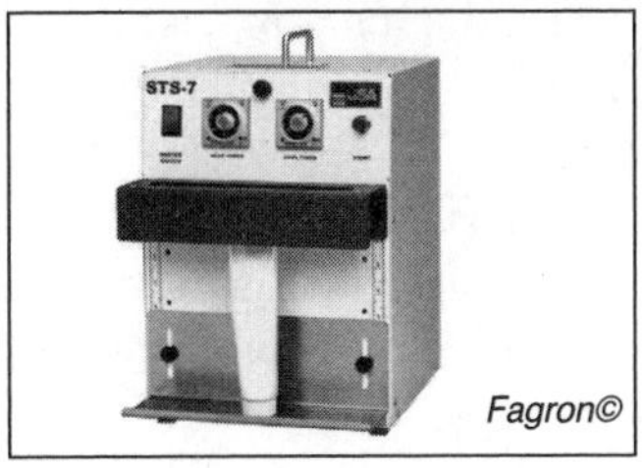

Tube sealer (sealed at bottom)

DOCUMENTATION

Two very important records that each compounded product must have are the master formulation record and the compounding record.

A master formulation record is the "recipe" that provides the ingredients and instructions on how to prepare the compounded product. It includes the compound's official or assigned name, strength, dosage form, calculations/doses and the ingredients and quantities, stability and compatibility data (with references), equipment needed, the mixing instructions, labeling information, packaging and storage requirements, a description of the final product, and quality control procedures and results.

The compounding log is the log book of all products made at the pharmacy, and includes the compound's official or assigned name, the strength and dosage form, the reference for the master formula (a number or page in the master formulation record), the components with their source, lot numbers and expiration dates, the compounder, the person who did the quality control, the pharmacist who approved the preparation with the date, the control or prescription number, the beyond-use date, a duplicate prescription label and a description of the final preparation.

Documentation must be detailed enough so that another trained person can replicate the steps involved in the preparation, evaluate if the procedure was correct, and trace the origin of all components.

The pharmacy must also keep records of steps and processes that relate to the compounded product. These include the equipment cleaning, calibration and maintenance, temperature logs for the refrigerator, freezer and room (ambient) air and records of chemicals, bulk drugs, drug products, and any other component.

QUALITY ASSURANCE

A quality assurance (QA) plan outlines the steps and actions that ensure the maintenance of proper standards for the compounded preparations. The QA plan includes the Standard Operating Procedures (SOPs), which are itemized steps on how to perform routine and expected tasks in the pharmacy.

The QA plan must be reviewed and updated regularly. Properly maintained and implemented SOPs result in quality preparations and less errors.

The QA program should include periodic testing of the finished compounded preparations. A pharmacy may do some QA testing in-house (such as confirming weight and consistency) and outsource others (such as sending some of the compounded products to an outside company to conduct sterility testing).

QA records need to include the names of the staff that are involved with compounding, including their orientation and training records.

PATIENT COUNSELING

The pharmacist must counsel the patient or caregiver about the proper use of a compounded product, with similar information as required for prescription drugs. ADRs resulting from a compounded product should be reported to the pharmacy, and the pharmacist will need to record the ADR in the compounding record. The patient's profile should include the ADR. Depending on the reaction, further action may be necessary.

PREPARATION BASICS: PREPARATION, COMPOUNDING & COMPLETION

Whether the pharmacist is compounding a topical ointment or a suppository, there are similar steps at the beginning (to prepare to compound) and similar steps at the end (packaging, documentation, QA and patient counseling).

Preparation

1. Calculate the quantities needed for each component. Gather all the components and the equipment needed. Check to see if the equipment needs to be washed or calibrated.
2. Garb and wash hands, which is detailed in the following chapter on sterile compounding. For non-sterile compounding, the garb required depends on the components, including the drug's toxicity, whether it can splash (may need eye shield/face mask) or release powder or fumes (may need a mask). Minimally, most compounders wear a lab coat and gloves.

Compounding

3. The product is made according to the Master Formulation Record. Most formulations will require common techniques, such as trituration, levigation, and geometric dilution. Other steps are unique to the formulation type, such as calculating the density factor to make suppositories.

Completion

4. Package the product and apply the label for the patient and auxiliary labels. Enter the required information into the compounding record (the "log book" of what was made).
5. Perform Quality Analysis (QA): validate the weight, check the product for mixing adequacy, color, clarity, odor, consistency and pH. Enter the measurements and observations in the compounding record.
6. Counsel the patient, and if any subsequent ADRs are reported, add them to the compounding record.

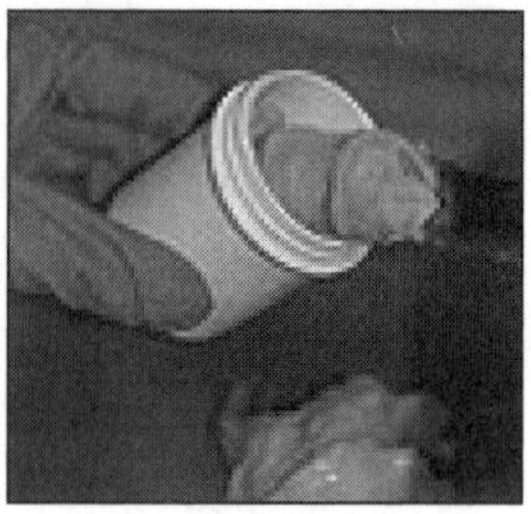

Packing an ointment

STUDY TIPS: TRITURATION, LEVIGATION, GEOMETRIC DILUTION & CAKE BAKING

A baker wishes to make a smooth, uniform cake, without any lumps. Steps:

1. Select finely-ground cake flour.
2. Mix a small amount of ingredients with a mixing spoon until the mixture is smooth and uniform. Add in more ingredients, repeat. This process makes the ingredients uniformly distributed and prevents a lumpy cake.

A compounding pharmacist uses similar steps to prepare fine powders:

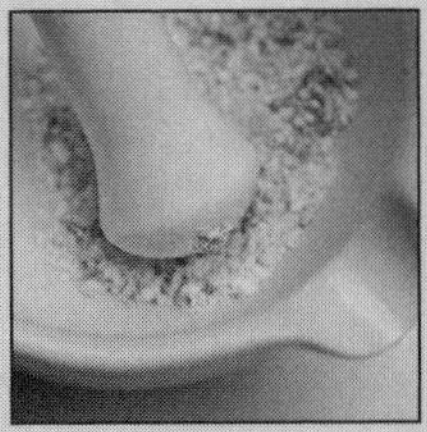

The pharmacist needs a fine powder, too, or the end product will be lumpy and gritty with an uneven drug distribution. The pharmacist usually starts with either tablets or coarse powder. There are important terms to describe what the pharmacist needs to do:

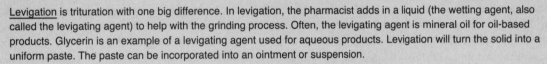

Comminution means to reduce solids from an average particle size to a smaller average particle size, by crushing, grinding or a similar process. Triturition and levigation are two very common ways in which communition is done:

Trituration means grinding the powder into smaller, finer particles. This can be done with a mortar and pestle.

Levigation is trituration with one big difference. In levigation, the pharmacist adds in a liquid (the wetting agent, also called the levigating agent) to help with the grinding process. Often, the levigating agent is mineral oil for oil-based products. Glycerin is an example of a levigating agent used for aqueous products. Levigation will turn the solid into a uniform paste. The paste can be incorporated into an ointment or suspension.

Spatulation means that a spatula is used (instead of a pestle used in a mortar).

When the grittiness is gone, geometric dilution is used to make a smooth and uniform mixture: a small amount of the drug powder is mixed into an equal amount of other ingredients. The drug powder could be mixed with other powders (such as lactose as a filler for a capsule) or with a delivery vehicle (such as petrolatum for a topical ointment) or another preparation. After the initial small amount is thoroughly mixed, another equal amount of the remaining ingredients is mixed in. This is repeated until all the ingredients are mixed together.

Capsules, tablets, ointments, creams—and cakes—come out smooth and uniform.

Compounding Ingredients

All medications, whether compounded or not, include the drug/s (called the active pharmaceutical ingredients, or APIs) and the excipients, which are all the other ingredients.

High-quality ingredients ensure the purity and safety of the formulations. The recommended compounding ingredients are listed in the USP National Formulary (USP-NF), or in the list of Food Chemicals Codex (FCC) substances. Preferably, the approved substances should be manufactured at an FDA-registered facility. If any substance comes from a non-FDA registered facility, a Certificate of Analysis (CoA) should be obtained that confirms the specification and quality requirements. If any component is moved to a different container, the new container should be labeled with the component name, original supplier, lot or control number, transfer date and expiration date. Ingredients deteriorate, and expiration dates are important. If there is a component without an expiration date, the pharmacist will assign a conservative (cautious) date that is no more than 3 years from the date of receipt (the day the pharmacy received the item). The label should contain both the date of receipt and the assigned expiration date.

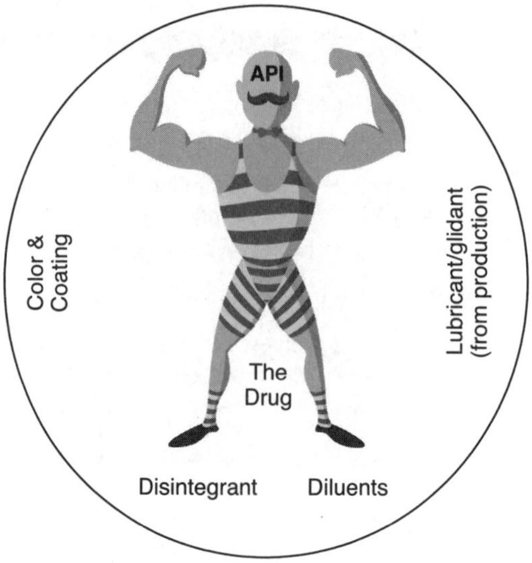

Powders

Powders are fine particles of a solid. A dose of medication can be given as the dry powder (put into liquid or a small amount of soft food) for someone who could not swallow capsules or tablets, such as a small child or elderly person with a feeding tube. Powders can also be used to prepare tablets, capsules, inhalations, suspensions or creams and other topical treatments. Powders can consist of only the active drug, or include excipients. The excipients listed here are specific to powders. The specific excipient examples are commonly used for this purpose:

- Glidant/lubricant to improve the flowability of a powder: magnesium stearate.
- Surfactant to neutralize the static charge and keep the powder from floating away: sodium lauryl sulfate.

Powders are finely ground and particle size is measured in microns. Initially, the compounder likely has coarse granules or broken tablet pieces. A fine powder is prepared by trituration.

Caution is required with eutectic mixtures. This means that two components, when mixed, will melt at a lower temperature than the melting temperature of the individual components. When powders start to melt, they become sticky. An adsorbent powder (magnesium oxide, magnesium carbonate or kaolin) can be used to keep the powder dry.

How to Prepare Powders

Reduce the size of the powder. This may require breaking down tablets with a grinder, followed by trituration or levigation.

If the amount of powder per dose is very small, it will be necessary to add an inert filler (diluent). A filler could also be needed to provide a minimum weighable quantity if using a torsion balance (see previous description). A common diluent is lactose. Add the filler and other excipients using geometric dilution. See the Study Tip for levigation and geometric dilution.

Capsules

Capsules are soluble shells of gelatin (an animal product) or hypromellose (a vegetable product), which are filled with the active drug, diluents (fillers) and any other excipients. Hard-shell capsules are used most commonly in compounding, and are filled with powders. Soft-shell capsules are used mostly for oils. Glycerol and sorbitol are used as plasticizers to make the capsules less brittle and more flexible.

Common capsule sizes range from largest (size 000, ~1 inch long) to smallest (size 5, ~0.4 inches long).

How to Prepare Capsules

Capsules are made by first triturating the dry ingredients and geometrically mixing with the fillers/other excipients (see Study Tip). The powder is put into the capsules by either hand filling (also known as the "punch method") or by using a capsule-filling machine (see the Molds, Presses and Packaging Equipment section).

Hand filling: To begin, the powder is placed on powder paper or on an ointment slab. The pile of powder is smoothed with a spatula to a height about a third of the length of the capsule. The open end of the capsule is repeatedly "punched" into the pile of powder until the capsule is filled. When the base is filled, it is fitted with the cap.

Manual capsule-filling machine: These are small devices that help the pharmacist quickly load 50, 100 or 300 capsules. Plates sort the capsule bodies to stand upright and hold them in place. The powder is put above the capsules on to a plastic sheet where a plastic spreader and comb is used to brush the powder into the capsules. The comb and spreader are used repeatedly until the powder is packed into the capsules. Then, the caps are put over the capsule bodies.

Tablets

There are many types of tablets, including molded tablets, sublingual tablets, buccal tablets, orally disintegrating tablets, chewable tablets, effervescent tablets, and compressed tablets. The molded tablet is the most common tablet type made in compounding, and the compressed tablet is the most common type made in manufacturing.

Tablets contain the active drug and excipients, including diluents, binders, disintegrants, lubricants, coloring agents, and flavoring agents.

How to Prepare Molded Tablets

The first step to compound a molded tablet is to triturate the dry ingredients and mix by geometric dilution (see Study Tip). Alcohol and/or water is added to moisten the powder. The powder mixture should have a pasty consistency, which can be molded into tablets (using tablet molds), and allowed to dry. If the tablet is a lozenge (see next), flavoring can be added. Coloring and coating may be added.

Lozenges/Troches

Lozenges (also referred to as troches) are hard, soft or chewable oral tablets that slowly dissolve in the mouth or are easily chewed and swallowed. This dosage form is generally used to deliver a medication that acts locally in the mouth. A commercially available example is a clotrimazole troche for treatment of oral thrush.

A lozenge contains the active drug in a base of sucrose or syrup for hard lozenges, PEG for soft lozenges, and glycerin or gelatin for chewable lozenges. Flavoring agents and coloring agents are added. The base is melted, mixed with the API and excipients, placed into a mold, and allowed to cool back into a solid.

Lotions

Lotions contain the most water, are more fluid than creams, and can be poured. They absorb quickly and are easy to spread on the skin. Since lotions contain a lot of water, they can be delivered in pumps.

Creams

Creams contain more than 20% water and less than 50% oil. They spread easily and are reasonably hydrating. Creams are packaged in tubes, and sometimes in tubs.

Ointments

Ointments usually contain less than 20% water and more than 50% oil. Ointments contain the least water, which makes them useful for several purposes: they do not soak quickly into the skin, they make a good delivery vehicle to evenly deliver medication over a period of time, they provide a barrier to exposure (from organisms, sun, moisture etc.) and they prevent moisture loss to foster burn and scar healing. Ointments are packaged in tubes or tubs.

Ointments are classified into five types depending on the base: oleaginous (oily/greasy) bases, absorption bases, water-in-oil (w/o) emulsion bases, oil-in-water (o/w) emulsion bases and water-soluble bases.

How to Prepare Ointments

Powders should be triturated well, using a levigating agent. The levigating agent must be miscible with the base, which means they can mix together well. The powder will be mixed into the ointment base, using geometric dilution (see Study Tip).

Certain ointments will require heat in order to mix components together well. This is called the fusion method. Always use the lowest temperature possible. First, melt the ingredients with the highest melting point, then add the others, according to their decreasing melting points. Otherwise, undesired chemical reactions could occur. A water bath used to heat the ointment components will help prevent over-heating.

Pastes

Pastes are the thickest ointments and are also used as protective barriers.

Gels

Gels are semisolids interpenetrated by a liquid. The active ingredient and other excipients are added to the gel. Pluronic lecithin organogel ("PLO gel") is commonly used for transdermal drug delivery. It has an organic (lipophilic) base in a water and alcohol vehicle. Drugs are dissolved or suspended in the gel.

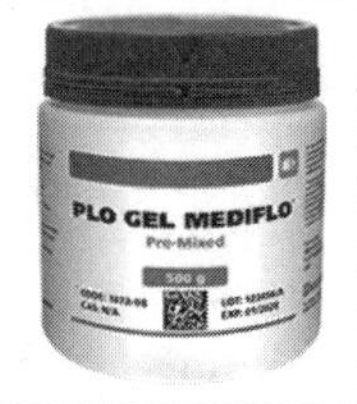

PLO gel

Suppositories

A suppository base is either oil-soluble (oleaginous) or water-soluble. Oil-soluble bases include cocoa butter (also called theobroma oil) and hydrogenated vegetable oils (palm, palm kernel, and coconut oils). Water-soluble bases include polyethylene glycol (PEG) polymers and glycerinated gelatin. If a drug powder is added to a base, the powder should be triturated to a fine consistency (see Study Tip on trituration).

STUDY TIPS: SUPPOSITORIES

Vaginal suppositories are used to treat conditions inside the vagina or a condition related to the female reproductive system.

Vaginal suppositories can be used to treat *Candida* infections (including OTC suppositories), dryness or vaginal pain, menopausal symptoms (including local pain, dryness and hot flashes), and for contraception (spermicides come in OTC suppositories). Compounding pharmacies make hormone replacement suppositories that are tailored to a woman's individual requirements.

Rectal suppositories are used either to treat a local condition (such as a hemorrhoid, local infection, rectal pain, distal ulcerative colitis) where the condition is close to the end of the GI tract, or to treat a systemic condition, such as pain and fever in a patient who cannot take oral medication (e.g., acetaminophen suppository). Suppositories bypass the oral route and avoid first-pass metabolism.

Suppository bases must be hard enough to be briefly handled, but soft enough to melt easily once inserted. Suppositories are kept refrigerated.

The API (the drug) will displace part of the base. If the drug has the same density as the base, it will displace an equal amount of volume. If the density is greater, it will displace less, and if lower, it will displace more. To calculate the amount of base displaced, the density factor of the drug is needed. The density factor can be found in compounding references, or calculated with the Paddock Method:

$$\text{Density Factor} = \frac{B}{A - C + B}$$

A = weight of the suppository blank, B = weight of medication per suppository, and C = weight of medicated suppository

How to Prepare Suppositories

There are three methods to prepare a suppository:

Hand molding can be used when only a few suppositories are to be prepared, using a cocoa butter base. The cocoa butter is not melted. It is grated and then mixed with the drug(s) in a mortar and pestle or on a pill tile with a spatula. The mass is rolled into a cylinder, which is cut into suppository-size pieces. A tip is formed on one end to make insertion easier.

In the fusion molding method, the base is gently heated, the ingredients are added, and the mixture is poured into molds, and cooled. Disposable plastic molds can be used for molding. Often, the suppositories are dispensed in the mold; suppositories are soft, and easily damaged. They are stored in the mold until needed.

In the compression molding method, the pharmacist will need to know the weight of each mold, and the drug's density factor (see above). The amount of base required to fill each mold is calculated, the base is grated, mixed with the drug, and put into a cold compression mold.

Lubricants applied to the mold make it easier to remove the suppositories. Glycerin or propylene glycol are good lubricants for oil-soluble bases, and mineral oil or vegetable oil spray are good lubricants for water-soluble bases.

Emulsions, Suspensions, Solutions, & Surfactants

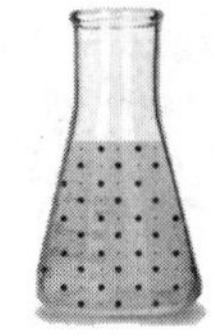

An **EMULSION** is a liquid dispersed in a liquid. It's a two-phase heterogeneous mixture*. Emulsions can be oil-in-water (oil droplets in an aqueous vehicle) or water-in-oil. Water and oil normally do not mix.

An emulsifier is a type of surfactant that is used to reduce the surface tension between oil and water. The emulsifier allows the two phases to come closer together.

To make the emulsion, the emulsifier will need to be carefully chosen, according to the hydrophilic-lipophilic balance (HLB) number.

EMULSIFIERS
Acacia, agar, carbomers, glyceryl monostearate, pectin, PEG (see PEG box that follows), sodium laurel sulfate, sorbitan lipophilic esters *(Arlacel, Span)*, sorbitan hydrophilic esters *(Myri, Tween)*

**Emulsions and suspensions have two phases, and are thus heterogenous because the two phases do not mix. This is the opposite of homogenous, which means a uniform, consistent mixture throughout.*

A **SUSPENSION** is a solid dispersed in a liquid. It's a two-phase heterogeneous mixture.

A wetting agent/levigating agent is a type of surfactant used to incorporate an insoluble drug into a liquid, which makes a suspension.

LEVIGATING AGENTS
Glycerin
Mineral oil
Polyethylene glycol
Propylene glycol

Emulsions, Suspensions, Solutions, & Surfactants, continued

A **SOLUTION** is a solute dissolved in a solvent (such as NaCl, dissolved in water).

Solutions are homogenous (consistent, uniform throughout).

Solutions include syrups, elixirs, tinctures and spirits.

PRECIPITATION/SEDIMENTATION is when the dispersed phase settles (clumps) together. This can happen with suspensions and emulsions. The process of a solid settling on the bottom of a container is sedimentation. Shake or gently roll to re-disperse.

This happens less commonly with solutions, but with some, such as insulin, the solid can settle to the bottom and must be re-dispersed prior to use.

Surfactants and the HLB Number

Surfactants are used to help two compounds that resist each other to move closer together by reducing the surface tension between them. Surfactants help to put a hydrophobic compound (which will interact with the surfactant's lipophilic ends) into a hydrophilic vehicle (which will interact with the hydrophilic ends), or vice-versa.

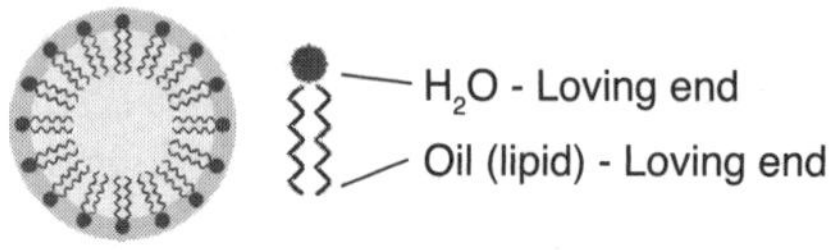

Surfactants work by forming a micelle structure (see figure), which can reverse (turn inside-out). Amphiphilic refers to surfactants and other compounds that are both hydrophilic and hydrophobic. If oil and water are mixed, the oil will interact with the hydrophobic (lipid-loving) end of the surfactant, and the water will interact with the hydrophilic (water-loving) end of the surfactant.

When a surfactant is used to reduce the surface tension between a solid particle (an insoluble drug) and a liquid, it is referred to as a wetting agent or levigating agent. An emulsifier is a surfactant that reduces the surface tension between oil and water. Detergents are also surfactants. The oil-end of the detergent picks up the oily-dirt on the clothing that is being washed in water.

The hydrophilic-lipophilic balance (HLB) number is used to describe how hydrophilic or lipophilic a surfactant is, and is used to choose the right surfactant for a preparation. The HLB scale range is 0-20. The midpoint is 10. Agents with a low HLB number (< 10) are more oil-soluble and are used for water-in-oil (w/o) emulsions. Agents with a high HLB number (> 10) are more water-soluble and are used for oil-in-water (o/w) emulsions.

Examples of Surfactants (Commercial Name, Chemical Name) and their HLB Values

COMMERCIAL NAME	CHEMICAL NAME	HLB VALUE
Glyceryl monostearate	Glyceryl monostearate	3.8
PEG 400 monooleate	Polyoxyethylene monooleate	11.4
Span 65	Sorbitan tristearate	2.1
Tween 81	Polyoxyethylene sorbitan monooleate	10
Tween 85	Polyoxyethylene sorbitan trioleate	11

How to Prepare Emulsions

The Continental Gum Method (Dry Gum Method): 4 parts oil, 2 parts water, 1 part emulsifier.

The preparation contains oil, water, and an emulsifier in a 4:2:1 mixture. Acacia, or another gum-type emulsifier is used.

Levigate the gum with oil, then add water all at once and shake mixture to triturate until a cracking sound is heard and the mixture looks creamy white. Add other ingredients by dissolving them first in solution, and add a quantity of water sufficient to make the final volume (this is called QS). Homogenize to make the emulsion uniform.

The English Gum Method (Wet Gum Method): 4 parts oil, 2 parts water, 1 part emulsifier.

The preparation contains the same 4:2:1 oil, water and emulsifier mixture, with different preparation steps. Triturate the gum and water to form a mucilage, then add the oil slowly, while triturating to form the emulsion. Finish the same as in the previous method.

EXCIPIENTS

There are many reasons to add excipients when compounding. Excipients can be used as a thickener, to increase viscosity, to increase stability and prevent degradation, to add flavoring, to add color, to apply a protective coating, and to help with disintegration and absorption. There are hundreds of excipients. This section reviews commonly used excipients for testing purposes. Several questions at the end of the chapter require selecting the use of an excipient.

Selected Excipients

INGREDIENT	PURPOSE AND NOTES	EXAMPLES
Adsorbents	To keep powders dry.	Magnesium oxide/carbonate, kaolin
Anti-adherent	Prevents tablet ingredients from sticking to punches and dyes during production.	Magnesium stearate
Anti-foaming agent	Breaks up and inhibits the formation of foams.	Simethicone, dimethicone
Antioxidants	Prevents oxidation.	Ascorbic acid, ascorbyl palmitate Sodium ascorbate/bisulfate/sulfoxylate/thiosulfate
Buffers	Buffers maintain the formulation within the acceptable pH range.	Potassium phosphate/metaphosphate, sodium acetate/citrate
Coatings (regular)	Prevent degradation due to oxygen, light, moisture, mask unpalatable taste.	Shellac, gelatin, gluten (food grade)
Coloring agent	Provides color to the compounded product. The color sometimes correlates with the flavor (cherry-flavored syrup with red coloring).	FD&C Red No. 3, Yellow No. 6, etc. Caramel, ferric oxide (red)
Diluents (fillers)	To add size to very small dosages. In liquids, the diluent also helps suspend the drug, and can help it disintegrate. White lactose is commonly used as a filler in tablets and capsules. The quantity is small enough to not cause GI distress with lactose intolerance in most cases, but it may need to be avoided. Sorbitol can cause GI distress with IBS. Starches come from many plants, including corn, rice and wheat. Avoid wheat with gluten sensitivity. Cellulose is used for many other purposes in compounding, including as an adsorbent and as a suspending agent. Powdered cellulose is used as a thickener.	Liquids: fillers include water or glycerin, alcohol is used less commonly Dry products, like tablets and capsules: fillers include starches, calcium salts, lactose (and other sugars, including mannitol and sorbitol), cellulose, in various forms, gelatin, bentonite In topical products like creams and ointments: fillers include mineral oil, petrolatum, lanolin and various waxes

Excipients continued

INGREDIENT	PURPOSE AND NOTES	EXAMPLES
Disintegrant	Oral products have to dissolve in order to be absorbed. Alginates absorb water, causing the tablet to swell and burst. Cellulose is from plants, or is synthetic, and absorbs water well.	Alginic acid, polacrilin potassium (e.g., *Amberlite*), various cellulose products, starches, compressible sugar (e.g., *Nu-Tab*)
Emollient	Softens and soothes the skin or mucous membranes, provides a barrier, acts as a vehicle for drug delivery. Emollient bases are either oleaginous (oil-containing), aqueous (water-containing), absorbent or water-in-oil or oil-in-water (emulsions). Oleaginous bases do not release medication as well as bases that contain water. They are good as emollients and are occlusive (barrier; keeps air, water from skin/wounds).	*Aquaphor* *Aquabase* *Vaseline* Petroleum jelly *Polybase* *Eucerin* *Cetaphil*
Enteric-coating	Most drugs dissolve in the stomach and are absorbed in the small intestine. Some drugs would be destroyed by stomach acid and require an acid-resistant (enteric-coated) protective layer to prevent dissolution in the stomach. The coating can also be used to mask poor taste.	Cellulose acetate phthalate Shellac (a natural polymer resin, from insects)
Flavoring agent, sweetener	Gives sweetness to a preparation (e.g., chewable tablets). Salty or sweet tastes mask a bitter flavor. Mint and spices mask poor flavor. Acids (such as citric acid) enhance fruit flavors. Do not use phenylalanine with phenylketonuria (PKU); common sweetener in manufactured chewables.	Syrups, oils Sugar-coating for tablets: sucrose, glucose Artificial, sugar-free: aspartame and saccharin Glycerin, dextrose, lactose, mannitol, sorbitol, phenylalanine
Gelling (thickening) agent, stabilizer	Increases the viscosity of a substance; can stabilize the mixture. Gelatin and bentonite are used commonly; both swell well when mixed with water. Cetyl alcohol is not water-soluble.	Agar, alginates, guar gums, acacia (a natural gum), gelatins, tragacanth, bentonite (a type of clay), *Carbomer*, cellulose, starches, acrylates, cetyl alcohol
Glidant	Improves flow of properties of the powder mixture in tablet and capsule formulations.	Colloidal silica, cornstarch, talc
Humectant	Prevents preparations from becoming dry and brittle.	Glycerin, sorbitol, propylene glycol
Hydrophilic solvent	Liquid with high miscibility with water, used to dissolve solutes.	PEG, alcohols, caprylic or lauric acid, lemoxene, terpenes
Hydrophobic solvent	Liquid with low or no miscibility with water, used to dissolve solutes.	Oils: borage, canola, coconut, etc.) Fats: Omega-3 (alpha-linolenic fatty acids, DHA/EPA) Omega-6 (gamma-linoleic fatty acids)
Levigating (wetting) agent	See Study Tip.	Mineral oil, glycerin, glycols, PEG, propylene glycol
Lubricant	Lubricants help in the manufacturing: they keep ingredients from sticking to each other and the equipment, reduce static charge This makes tablet molding and capsule filling easier.	Calcium and magnesium stearate PEG Stearic acid, talc
Preservatives	To prevent growth of bacteria or other pathogens. Eye drops will include a preservative if they are multi-dose containers. Single-dose containers may not have a preservative since they will not be used more than once. Chlorhexidine is used as a preservative, and is also used as an alcohol-based antiseptic for surgical scrubs and as a dental rinse *(Hibiclens, Biotene).*	Oral: parabens, sodium benzoate, benzoic acid Topical/nasal: various alcohols, acids, chlorhexidine Opthalmics: EDTA, sodium benzoate, benzoic acid, benzalkonium chloride, thimerosal (contains a small amount of mercury, used in some vaccines)

Excipients continued

INGREDIENT	PURPOSE AND NOTES	EXAMPLES
Suppository base	Suppository bases have to stay intact for insertion, but melt once inserted.	Cocoa butter (theobroma oil), hydrogenated vegetable oils (palm, palm kernel, and coconut oils), PEG polymers, glycerinated gelatin
Water	Purified Water is used as an excipient for non-sterile compounding and for cleaning non-sterile equipment. Potable water (tap/drinking water) is safe to drink and is used for non-sterile compounding, unless higher purity is required. Potable water is used for hand washing and initial equipment cleaning.	Water, most pure to less pure: Sterile water for injection > Purified > Potable (Tap). Sterile water is required in sterile compounding. Bacteriostatic water is sterile water with a preservative (usually benzyl alcohol).

STUDY TIP: POLYETHYLENE GLYCOL (PEG) IN PHARMACY, IT'S EVERYWHERE

$H{-}(O{-}CH_2{-}CH_2)_n{-}OH$

PEG is a common excipient: it's a long, synthetic polymer useful for many purposes. It has low toxicity and low systemic absorption. *Carbowax*, a similar product, is methoxy-polyethylene glycol (MPEG).

PEG is used as a surfactant, solvent, plasticizer, suppository base, ointment base and lubricant. It's water-soluble and water-miscible (mixes well with water into a homogenous mixture). *Polybase* is a PEG mixture that is commonly used as a suppository base—it's a good delivery vehicle and slides out of molds without the need for a lubricant. It is also a good emulsifier.

PEG-400 is a popular lubricant used in OTC eye drops (*Liquifilm*, others). Larger molecular weights (PEG-3350) such as *Miralax* and *Golytely*, are used as osmotics to treat constipation or clear the gut (bowel prep) before a colorectal procedure. PEG linked to a protein drug (pegylated), such as PEG-filgrastim, increases the half-life by helping the drug escape the immune system and decreasing the renal clearance.

STORAGE AND HANDLING

TEMPERATURE DEFINITIONS	F°	C°
Room	68° to 77°	20° to 25°
Refrigerator	36° to 46°	2° to 8°
Freezer	-13° to 14°	-25° to -10°

The bulk products and ingredients used for compounding should be stored and handled according to the manufacturer's storage requirements, or per the USP-NF, or the FCC monograph. This includes following recommended ranges for temperature and humidity. Products used in compounding should be visibly labeled, stored off the floor (on shelves) and rotated so that the stock that is oldest (with the closest expiration date) is placed in front of the others, and will be used first.

Hazardous drug storage and handling is managed according to USP 800. A hazardous classification means that the drug is hazardous to the healthcare professionals handling it, including pharmacists and pharmacy technicians. This includes chemotherapeutics (antineoplastics), hormones and other toxic compounds. Hazardous drugs must be compounded in a separate area with negative air pressure. Only personnel trained in hazardous drugs can compound or handle in any manner, including the janitorial (custodial) staff, who must be trained in safe disposal.

Compounding Kits

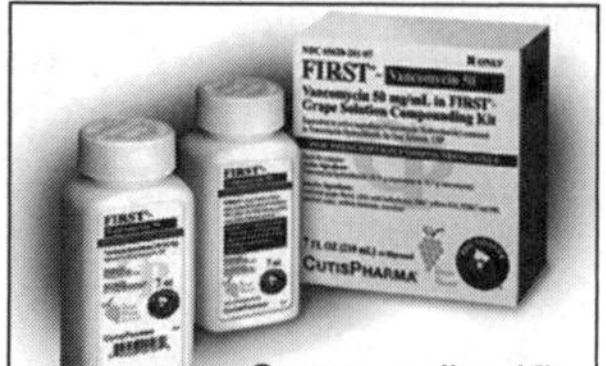

Compounding Kit

There are some companies that package pre-measured ingredients for a compounded product into "compounding kits". If the pharmacy does not receive many prescriptions for a certain product, it can be cost-effective for the pharmacy to purchase compounding kits (as needed) instead of purchasing the bulk ingredients. See the practice questions for kit examples.

Selecting the Beyond Use Date

The table provides the default beyond use dates (BUDs) for non-sterile compounded preparations that are packaged in tight, light-resistant containers and stored at room temperature or refrigerated.

FORMULATION	BEYOND USE DATE
Nonaqueous Formulations (such as a drug in petrolatum)	Not later than the time remaining until the earliest expiration date of any API or 6 months, whichever is earlier.
Water-Containing Oral Formulations (such as an oral suspension)	Not later than 14 days when stored at controlled cold temperatures (refrigerator temperature).
Water-Containing Topical/Dermal and Mucosal Liquid and Semisolid Formulations (such as a cream or lotion)	Not later than 30 days.

In some cases, the default BUD is not used. Here are the exceptions:

1. If any ingredients decompose easily, select a shorter BUD.
2. If any ingredient expires before the BUD, use the earlier expiration date.
3. BUDs may be extended if stability data is obtained that determines the drug is stable for a longer period.

Applying Product and Auxiliary Labels

The labeling of all compounded products must include the BUD and storage and handling information.

There should be a label indicating that it is a compounded product:

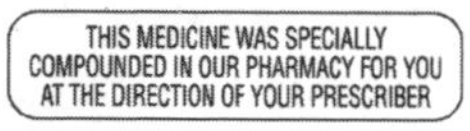

THIS MEDICINE WAS SPECIALLY
COMPOUNDED IN OUR PHARMACY FOR YOU
AT THE DIRECTION OF YOUR PRESCRIBER

All hazardous drugs should be labeled appropriately:

HD
CAUTION: HAZARDOUS DRUG
OBSERVE SPECIAL HANDLING, ADMINISTRATION AND DISPOSAL REQUIREMENTS

Certain formulations may need additional auxiliary labels (see below).

Topical products:

Emulsions, suspensions:

Suppositories, some troches, some suspensions:

Questions

Compounding is an important area to know well in order to perform well on the exam. Additional practice questions are included in the non-sterile compounding test banks.

A compounding pharmacist will prepare a 3.5% hydrocortisone ointment. The master formula includes these ingredients:

Hydrocortisone powder
Mineral oil
Petrolatum
Dimethicone

1. The mineral oil will be added to the powder, prior to mixing into the base. What is the purpose of the mineral oil?

   a. Prevent oxidative damage
   b. To aid in trituration.
   c. To assist disintegration in the gut pH.
   d. To act as a preservative during the preparation process.
   e. To add lubrication

2. The earliest expiration date of the ingredients in the compounded hydrocodone ointment is March 2021. What beyond-use-date should be applied to the container for the compounded hydrocodone ointment?

   a. 14 days
   b. 30 days
   c. 6 months
   d. March 1, 2021
   e. March, 31, 2021

3. A pharmacist will prepare a hydrocortisone ointment. Put the following preparation steps in order:

   1. Levigate the powder on an ointment slab.
   2. Place the powder on an ointment slab.
   3. Add powder to petrolatum using geo metric dilution.
   4. Weigh the hydrocortisone powder.
   5. Add a small amount of mineral oil to the powder.

Questions 4 – 6 do not apply to the above case.

4. A pharmacist has received an order to compound 200 mg progesterone suppositories. She will use a white, amorphous progesterone powder which has a low density, and aerosolizes easily.

   The master formula requires the following ingredients:

   Theobroma oil
   Progesterone powder
   Sodium lauryl sulfate

   What is the purpose of the theobroma oil?

   a. Suppository base
   b. Active Pharmaceutical Ingredient (API)
   c. Surfactant
   d. Enteric-coating, stability agent
   e. Preservative

5. A pharmacist will prepare an oil-in-water emulsion. She can choose from the stock surfactants at the pharmacy.

   ❑ Tween 80, HLB 10.5
   ❑ Span 80, HLB 1.3
   ❑ Jojoba oil, HLB 6.5
   ❑ Glycerol monostearate, HLB 3.8
   ❑ Cottonseed oil, HLB 6

   Which surfactant should be chosen?

   a. Tween 80
   b. Span 80
   c. Jojoba oil
   d. Glycerol monostearate
   e. Cottonseed oil

6. A pharmacist is preparing lansoprazole suspension from a compounding kit for a patient using a nasogastric feeding tube. The lansoprazole suspension compounding kit contains:

   0.9 g lansoprazole powder

   300 mL suspension vehicle

   Suspension ingredients: artificial strawberry flavor, FD&C Red #40, *Magnasweet* 100 (ammonium glycyrrhizate), poloxamer 188, propylene glycol, purified water, simethicone emulsion, sodium bicarbonate, sodium citrate (dihydrate), sucralose, benzoic acid and xanthan gum.

   In the compounding kit above, what is the purpose of the xanthan gum?

   a. Thickening agent
   b. Levigating agent
   c. Coating
   d. Emollient base
   e. Antioxidant

Answers

1-b, 2-c, 3- 4, 2, 5, 1, 3, 4-a, 5-a, 6-a

5

STERILE COMPOUNDING

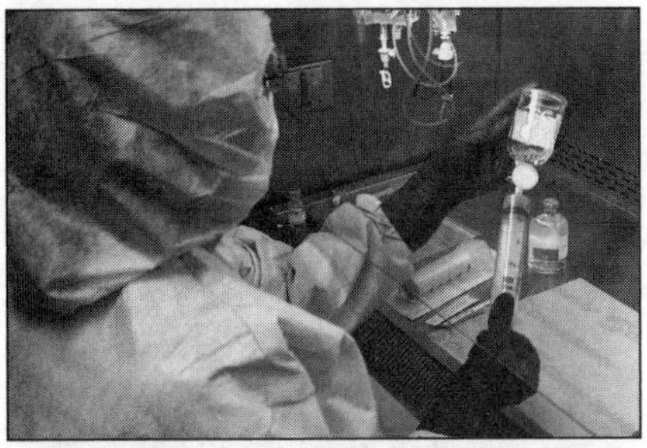

GUIDELINES/REFERENCES

USP Chapter 797, Pharmaceutical Compounding, Sterile Preparations.

USP Chapter 800, Hazardous Drugs, Handling in Healthcare Settings.

ASHP Guidelines on Compounding Sterile Preparations – *Am J Health Syst Pharm.* 2014:71(2):145-166.

ISMP. The "Dirty Dozen" 12 persistent safety gaffes that we need to resolve! ISMP Medication Safety Alert! 2014;19(20):1-5.

STERILE COMPOUNDING HOW-TO'S

BACKGROUND

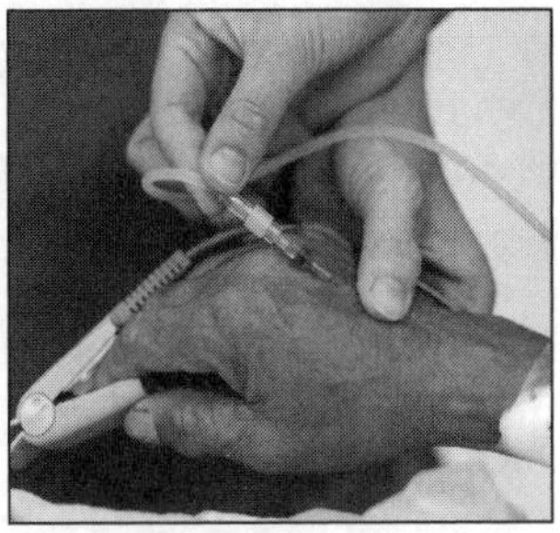

Fluids and IV drugs bypass the protection of the skin, and must be sterile.

Preparing compounded sterile preparations (CSPs) is a fundamental part of hospital pharmacy practice. Medications that must be prepared in a sterile manner include ophthalmics, inhalations, irrigations and intravenous (IV) medications.

Most of the sterile products prepared by pharmacists are IV medications. An injection given directly into a vein bypasses the protection provided by the skin and GI tract (see above figure). Blood is sterile, which means it is free from microorganisms and other contaminants. If the medication is not sterile, it will carry contaminants into the blood, which can cause severe illness.

Risk levels are classified by how likely it is for the drug to become contaminated. If a pharmacist is working in a sterile hood and injects 1 – 2 sterile products (such as a drug or electrolytes) into an IV bag that contains sterile fluid inside, the risk for contamination would be considered low. High-risk is the opposite extreme, and involves using non-sterile components. Risk levels are important because they are used to assign the beyond use date (BUD) to the sterile drug (see figure on the next page). BUDs are described further in this chapter.

Hazardous Drugs

Hazardous drugs (HDs) are handled by healthcare workers, including pharmacy staff. Depending on the toxicity of the drug and the amount handled at a facility, the staff who handle these drugs are put at risk. HDs are drugs that can damage genes, cause cancer, harm organs or have developmental or reproductive toxicity. Protection is provided by engineering controls (the room design and the equipment, including negative pressure hoods that keep drug particles and fumes away from the staff), and proper protective equipment (the garb, including face masks and double-gloving). HDs are reviewed in the Medication Safety & Quality Improvement chapter and the Oncology I chapter.

STUDY TIP

BUDs are determined by the risk of contamination.

The lower the risk, the longer the BUD.

Drawing up a sterile drug with a sterile syringe, and putting the drug into an IV bag of sterile fluid (in a sterile hood), is all low risk. If refrigerated, the BUD is 14 days.

ISO AIR QUALITY

Clean air is important in the compounding area in order to reduce the risk of contamination. The International Standards Organization (ISO) sets the standards for air quality, which is determined by the number of particles per volume of air of a specified particle size. The lower the count, the cleaner the air.

In critical areas that are closest to exposed sterile drugs and containers, such as inside the sterile hood, the air must be at least ISO 5. This means that there are no more than 3,520 particles per cubic meter. Particles are included in this count if they are 0.5 micrometers in size or larger.

COMPOUNDING AREA	ISO RATING	PARTICLES/M^3
Primary engineering control (hood, isolator)	5	3,520
Not applicable*	6	35,200
Buffer area	7	352,000
Ante area, if it opens into a negative pressure room		
Ante area, if it opens into a positive pressure room	8	3,520,000

**No compounding area has a minimum requirement of ISO 6*

The farther away from the primary engineering control (PEC), the dirtier the air: the PEC must be at least ISO 5, the buffer area (the air in the room around the PEC) must be at least ISO 7, the ante area (adjacent to the buffer area, where hand washing and garbing is done) must be at least ISO 8 if it opens into a positive pressure buffer area, or must be at least ISO 7 if it opens into a negative pressure buffer area. Regular room air is called "unclassified air" because it does not have an ISO rating.

High-efficiency particulate air (HEPA) filters are used to maintain the clean air in the compounding areas. HEPA filters are > 99.97% efficient in removing particles as small as 0.3 microns (μm). The air flow moves in one direction (unidirectional) to move particles away from CSPs.

ISO AIR QUALITY IN THE PEC

Compounded sterile products (CSPs) are made inside a hood or isolator, which is the primary engineering control (PEC). The air quality in the PEC is ISO 5, which is very clean air.

To keep it that way, the staff regularly cleans the PEC, before each shift, before and after a batch of drugs, every 30 minutes and whenever it needs it, including after a spill.

Clean with sterile IPA 70% and sterile lint-free wipes.

DEFINITIONS

Ante area (ante room): refers to the space directly adjacent to the buffer area where non-sterile activities related to sterile compounding are performed, such as reviewing orders, storing sterile drug stock and equipment, garbing and hand washing. Once the staff member has garbed and washed their hands, they enter the buffer area. The ante area must be at least ISO 8 if it opens only into a positive pressure cleanroom (for non-hazardous CSPs), or must be ISO 7 if it opens into a negative pressure cleanroom (for hazardous CSPs).

Aseptic technique: aseptic means free of microorganisms and other contaminants.

Beyond use date (BUD): the date or time after which the CSP should not be used. The BUD depends on CSP risk level and storage temperature.

Buffer area (buffer room/cleanroom/IV room): the area where the PEC is located. It is sometimes called the IV room since most hospital pharmacies make only IV CSPs. The buffer area must be at least ISO 7.

Biological safety cabinet (BSC, chemo hood): a negative pressure hood that is used to prepare hazardous CSPs.

Coring: after a needle is inserted through the rubber stopper of a medication vial, a small piece of the stopper is sometimes sheared off and gets pushed by the syringe into the solution.

Compounded sterile preparations (CSPs): the sterile drugs prepared by the pharmacy staff.

Garb: specialized clothing and protective gear that is part of the PPE. Garb is required when entering the cleanroom. "Garbing" or "donning" means to put on the garb prior to entering the cleanroom.

Hazardous drugs (HDs): drugs that pose danger to the staff (can cause cancer, reproductive, genomic or developmental toxicity). Most are chemotherapy drugs (antineoplastics).

High-efficiency particulate air (HEPA) filters: HEPA filters are unidirectional (air flows in one direction). The filter removes particles from the compounding area. HEPA filters remove at least 99.97% of airborne particles as small as 0.3 microns (μm).

ISO classification: classification of how clean the air is depending on the number of particles present per volume of air. The smaller the number, the cleaner the air.

Isolators (glove boxes): a type of PEC that is completely enclosed. A compounder can put their hands through the glove ports in the front of the isolator to prepare CSPs. Compounding aseptic isolators (CAIs) and compounding aseptic containment isolators (CACIs) are two types of isolators.

Laminar airflow workbench (LAFW) or laminar airflow hood: a common PEC used to prepare non-hazardous CSPs. Laminar flow is described on the following page.

Line of demarcation: a line that separates the ante area and buffer area.

Negative pressure: the net airflow is flowing inward (e.g., into the hood/room) in order to protect the staff from toxic drug fumes. The air is vented to the outside. Required for preparing HDs.

Personal protective equipment (PPE): specialized clothing or equipment worn by an employee for protection against infectious or toxic materials, such as garb and respirator masks. Most PPE used in sterile compounding is disposable. Some masks, gowns and shoes can be reused after proper cleaning.

Positive pressure: the net airflow is flowing outward (e.g., out of the hood/room) to prevent contamination of the CSPs. Positive pressure is used for preparing non-HD CSPs.

Primary engineering control (PEC): the isolator or hood that provides the ISO Class 5 space.

Secondary engineering control (SEC): the ante area and buffer area.

Segregated compounding area (SCA): a space designated for compounding that has unclassified (room) air. CSPs made in a SCA have < 12-hr BUDs.

Unclassified air: air without ISO classification, such as regular room air.

FACILITIES AND EQUIPMENT

CSPs can be prepared in a primary engineering control (PEC) with a buffer area and an ante area. Alternatively, CSPs can be prepared in an ISO 5 PEC in a segregated compounding area.

Primary Engineering Controls

The primary engineering controls are the hood or isolator that provides the ISO Class 5 environment for preparing CSPs. PECs are referred to as ventilation devices since the airflow design is essential to keep the CSPs free of contaminants. Examples of PECs include laminar airflow workbenches (LAFW), compounding aseptic isolators (CAI), biological safety cabinets (BSC), and compounding aseptic containment isolators (CACI). PECs all rely on HEPA filters to maintain the clean air. The air sweeps away particles. The air pressure inside the hood is either positive (for non-hazardous drugs) or negative (for hazardous drugs).

Laminar Airflow Workbench

The laminar airflow workbench (LAFW) is the most common PEC used for preparing non-hazardous CSPs. It is also referred to as the "sterile hood". The hood should be stainless steel with smooth surfaces that are easy to clean. Otherwise, spores might accumulate and contaminate the CSPs.

Laminar Airflow Workbench

Laminar airflow is air that moves at the same speed, in the same direction, in parallel lines. The smooth airflow keeps the particles from hitting each other and landing on surfaces, where they can cause contamination. In contrast, if the airflow is turbulent, the particles will hit each other and randomly settle on surfaces.

The direction of the airflow can be either horizontal (the airflow moves forward from the HEPA filter located at the back of the hood) or vertical (the airflow moves downward from a filter positioned above the work surface).

The hood is designed to keep the air moving from the cleanest air to the dirtiest air, which then exits the hood. Compounding is done in the cleanest part of the hood, which is ~6 inches from the front and not right against the inside front edge, where the air from the buffer area mixes with the filtered air in the hood.

In a horizontal LAFW, nothing should be behind a sterile object. In a vertical LAFW, nothing should be above the sterile object. This ensures that the sterile items receive the first air that comes out of the HEPA filter.

Biological Safety Cabinets

Biological safety cabinets (BSCs), which are used for chemotherapy and some other hazardous drugs, are negative pressure, vertical laminar hoods.

Negative pressure airflow keeps hazardous drugs away from the staff. This air is vented outside the building. Negative pressure is required with BSCs since they are used to compound hazardous drugs, and the staff exposure to toxic drugs needs to be limited.

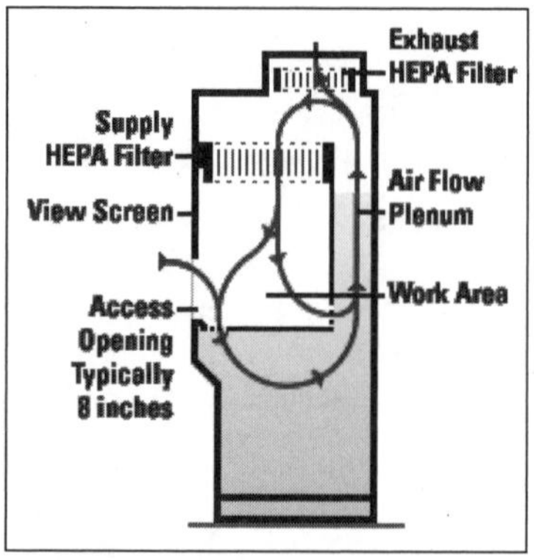

Diagram showing negative pressure (flows into the hood), vertical (flows upward) laminar (flows in parallel, non-turbulent streams) airflow.

Isolators

These isolators are often referred to as "glove boxes". They are ISO 5 inside the isolator, which permits sterile drugs to be made despite the air quality around the isolator. The compounder's hands reach into the isolator through the glove box (glove ports) to prepare the CSPs. They can be located in unclassified air, such as a satellite pharmacy that does not have a cleanroom. Isolators can be used for hazardous or non-hazardous drugs:

Isolator

- Hazardous drugs: use compounding aseptic containment isolators (CACIs), which have negative pressure.
- Non-hazardous drugs: use compounding aseptic isolators (CAIs), which have positive pressure.

Segregated Compounding Area

Another option for pharmacies that do not have enough physical space or resources for an IV room is to place the PEC in a segregated compounding area (SCA). The SCA has unclassified air. CSPs prepared in a SCA have a relatively shorter BUD of 12 hours. The SCA cannot be located next to unsealed windows or doors that connect to the outdoors or near high traffic flow, such as next to the cafeteria or a construction zone. Sinks should not be located next to the PEC. The staff preparing the product in a SCA still have to perform proper hand hygiene, garbing, cleaning and disinfecting, and environmental sampling. See the How to Determine Risk Levels section in this chapter for a discussion on which CSPs can be prepared in a SCA.

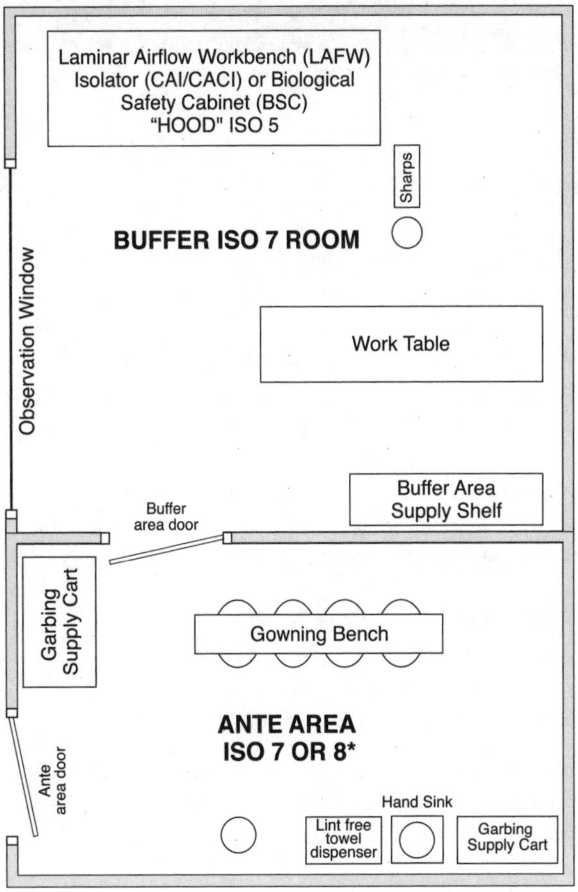

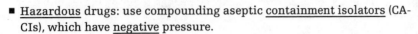

**The ante area is at least ISO 8 if it opens into a positive P° area, or ISO 7 if it opens into a negative P° buffer room.*

PERSONNEL TRAINING

All compounding personnel require proper training in hand hygiene, garbing technique, gloving technique, cleaning and disinfecting procedures, and aseptic technique.

The glove fingertip test is used to evaluate gloving and garbing technique. Passing requires 3 consecutive gloved fingertip samples with zero CFUs for both hands. This is required at initial training and on an ongoing basis (annually for personnel who compound low- and medium-risk CSPs and semi-annually for those who compound high-risk CSPs). Immediately after the personnel completes the hand hygiene and garbing procedure, the evaluator will collect a gloved fingertip sample from both hands of the personnel onto agar plates by lightly pressing each fingertip onto the agar. One agar plate is used per hand. These plates are incubated and then investigated for microbial growth.

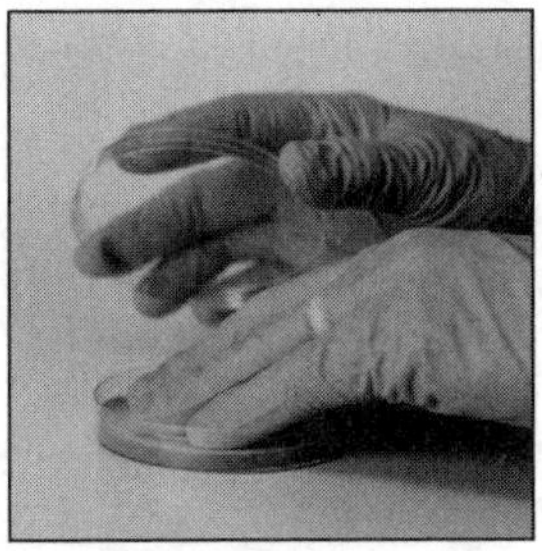

Glove fingertip test

The media-fill test is used to evaluate the aseptic technique of compounding personnel. A sterile fluid culture media (e.g., soybean–casein digest medium) that is able to promote colonization of bacteria is commonly used. If any of the media-fill units appear turbid on or before 14 days, then the personnel did not pass.

When preparing CSPs, no eating, drinking, coughing or talking is permitted. No distractions or interruptions should be present.

CLEANING AND DISINFECTING

Surfaces should be cleaned with sterile water and disinfected with 70% isopropyl alcohol (IPA). Allow the disinfectant to dry before compounding. Clean from the cleanest to dirtiest areas (opposite of garbing procedure). First clean the buffer area, then the ante area, and then the general supply area, with non-shedding dedicated mops and cleaners for each area. Hazardous drugs require decontamination, which involves additional steps.

The compounding areas must be cleaned according to the following schedule:

COMPOUNDING AREA	CLEANING SCHEDULE
Primary engineering control	At the beginning of each shift Before and after each batch After spills Every 30 minutes of continuous use Anytime contamination is suspected
Counters, work surfaces, and floors	Daily
Walls, ceiling, and storage shelves	Monthly

PHYSIOCHEMICAL CONSIDERATIONS

IV solutions should be isotonic (osmotic pressure matches to human blood by having the same number of particles in solution), measured in milliosmoles (mOsm) per liter (L). Human blood has an osmolarity of 285 mOsm/L. This prevents fluid transfer across the biological semipermeable membranes. The pH should be close to neutral (pH of 7); blood is slightly alkaline at a pH of 7.35 – 7.45. Non-PVC bags should be used for medications that have leaching or sorption issues (refer to the IV Drug Compatibility, Administration & Degradation chapter). The IV set must be sterile and nonpyrogenic.

TERMINAL STERILIZATION

Terminal sterilization is required for some high-risk CSPs. Terminalization methods include steam sterilization, dry-heat sterilization (depyrogenation), gas sterilization, sterilization by ionizing radiation, and unidirectional aseptic processing.

CSPs that are heat-labile (e.g., hormones, other proteins) can be sterilized with filtration using a 0.22 micron filter. If filtering is used, the bubble-point test must be performed. This test uses pressure to force liquid to "bubble" out of the filter to test the filter integrity.

LABEL REQUIREMENTS

The labels of CSPs must have the names and amounts or concentrations of ingredients, the total volume, the BUD, the route of administration, the storage requirements, and other information for safe use.

All chemotherapy preparations must have a label that reads "Chemotherapy – dispose of properly" or something similar.

Auxiliary labels should be placed on CSPs that are not refrigerated, if a filter is required and if light protection is required.

High-alert medications are drugs that have a heightened risk of causing significant patient harm when used incorrectly. High-alert medications should have auxiliary labels such as "Contains Potassium" or "Warning: Paralyzing drug."

DOCUMENTATION

Master formulation records and compounding log requirements are discussed in the Non-Sterile Compounding chapter.

STERILITY TESTING

Certain high-risk level CSPs and CSPs intended for use beyond the recommended BUD must have sterility testing. The sterility testing should use either tryptic soy broth (TSB) or fluid thioglycollate medium (FTM), and include bacterial endotoxin (pyrogen) testing prior to use.

PYROGEN (BACTERIAL ENDOTOXIN) TESTING

Endotoxins are produced by both Gram-positive and Gram-negative bacteria and fungi. Endotoxins from Gram-negative bacteria are more potent and represent a serious threat to patient safety. Pyrogens can come from using equipment (such as glassware and utensils) that has been washed with tap water. To avoid this issue, glassware and utensils should be rinsed with sterile water and depyrogenated using dry-heat oven sterilization or autoclave.

Certain CSPs must be tested for endotoxins. The reagent for the bacterial endotoxins test (BET) is called the Limulus Amebocyte Lysate (LAL).

ENVIRONMENTAL MONITORING

The environment of the compounding area is important to monitor and control in order to minimize the risk of contamination. The following table lists various environmental parameters along with how often it should be monitored.

ENVIRONMENTAL PARAMETER	MONITORING INTERVAL	NOTES
Temperature	Daily (at a minimum)	
Air sampling	At least every 6 months	Performed by a compounding personnel or qualified certifier.
Surface sampling	Periodically	Use plates containing tryptic soy agar with polysorbate 80 and lecithin. Use sample surfaces at the end of the day to simulate the dirtiest condition. After the plates have been incubated, the results should indicate zero CFUs (preferred); action must be taken if > 3 CFUs in the ISO Class 5 area.
Air pressure	Each shift (preferably) or daily (minimally)	

QUALITY ASSURANCE

Every facility that prepares CSPs must have a quality assurance (QA) plan that evaluates, corrects and improves the quality processes. The plan should minimally include:

- Personnel training and assessment
- Environmental monitoring
- Equipment calibration and maintenance

Every process must be documented and follow-up actions identified that have assigned personnel responsible for each item, with expected dates of completion. If a problem has been identified or a medication error or safety issue has occurred, the analysis should be started as soon as possible with a root cause analysis, discussed in the Medication Safety chapter. A failure mode and effects analysis of new techniques can help to identify problems with new procedures in advance.

RECALLS

When high-risk level CSPs are dispensed before receiving the results of their sterility tests, there must be a written procedure requiring daily observation of the incubating test specimens and immediate recall of the dispensed CSPs if there is evidence of microbial growth. All patient and physicians who received the recalled CSPs are notified of the potential risk.

If sterility test results come back positive, there should be an investigation of aseptic technique, environmental control, and other sterility assurance controls to determine the source of contamination and improve the methods or processes.

Recalls are discussed further in the MPJE law course.

CLASS	DESCRIPTION
Class I Recall	A situation in which there is a reasonable probability that the use or exposure will cause serious adverse health consequences or death. For example, microbial growth is observed in an intrathecal injection.
Class II Recall	A situation in which use or exposure can cause temporary or reversible adverse health consequences or where the probability of harm is remote. For example, ketorolac injections have been recalled in 2010 and 2015 due to the possibility of particles in the vials.
Class III Recall	A situation in which use or exposure is not likely to cause adverse health consequences. For example, the coloring on tablets may have been applied inconsistently.

COMMERCIALLY AVAILABLE STERILE PRODUCTS USED FOR IV ADMIXTURES

BY TYPE

Ampules: ampules are small, sealed glass containers that contain medication. The neck is long. The ampule is broken by snapping the neck. This will introduce glass particles into the drug solution. A filter needle or straw will be required to filter out the glass. In the figure, the score mark is where the ampule is broken. The glass is weaker at that area and will snap off.

Vials that contain liquids: a volume of drug is drawn up in a syringe, which can then be added to an IV bag.

The compounder usually injects a volume of air equal to the volume of non-hazardous drug that is withdrawn. This is not done for hazardous drugs, such as chemotherapeutic drugs.

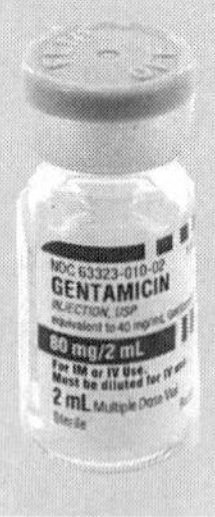

Vials that contain lyophilized or freeze-dried powder: the powder needs to be reconstituted by adding sterile water for injection, bacteriostatic water for injection, or a diluent supplied by the manufacturer. Drugs may be commercially available as powders because they are unstable as a solution.

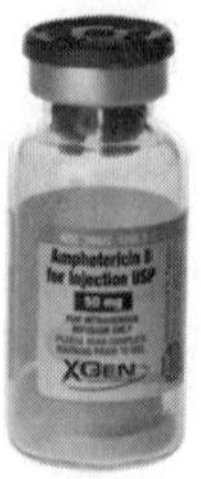

BY VOLUME

Small volume parenteral (SVP): SVPs are IV containers (IV bags) that are usually 50 or 100 mL of normal saline (NS) or 5% dextrose in water (D5W). These are the two smaller bags in the front of the figure. Another common SVP is prefilled syringes. Bags and syringes can be sent to the floor for floor stock or labeled for a specific patient.

The SVPs are often "piggybacked" off the LVP. These are called IVPB; see figure. This reduces the need to have multiple lines running into the patient. The drugs will mix together in the line; the drugs must be compatible in the line.

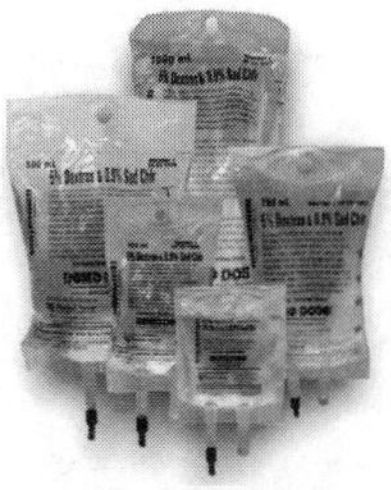

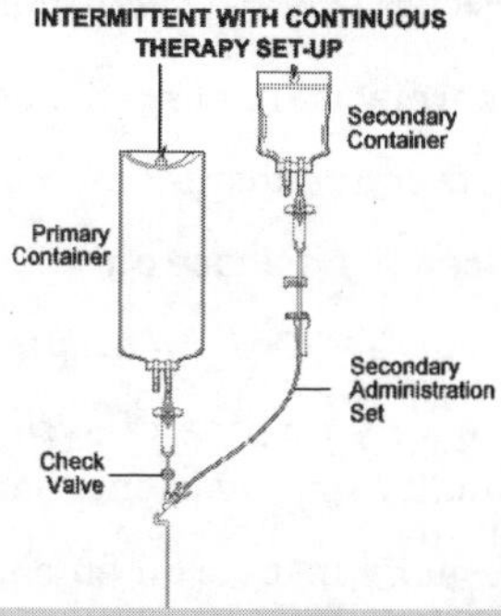

Syringes: SVPs that are used for IV <u>and</u> oral medications.

Caution: oral syringes must be labeled (preferably over the opening to avoid being missed) if they are for oral use or they can be mistakenly injected into an IV line, which can be fatal.

IV Syringes

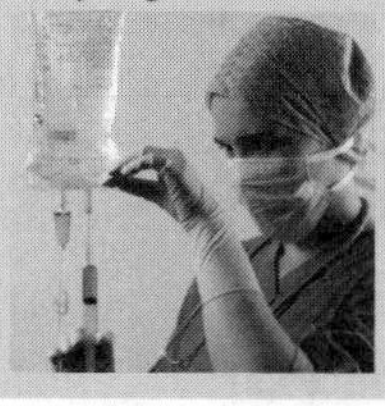

Large volume parenteral (LVP): IV containers that are larger; see figure.

1 liter bags are commonly used for fluids, which are given in a variety of forms: NS, 1/2NS, D5W, D51/2NS, lactated ringers (LR), etc.

Parenteral nutrition (PN) for adults is prepared in a LVP.

The yellow "banana" bag contains multivitamins, which causes the yellow color. The creamy colored bag contains lipids.

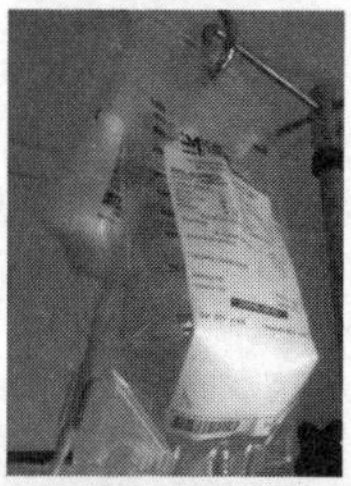

READY-TO-USE STERILE MEDICATIONS

Ready-to-use (RTUs): are available as prepared IV bags or prefilled syringes. The pharmacy staff opens the outer container and applies the patient label. These do not have a CSP risk level, as they are not compounded. The BUD is provided by the manufacturer, and is on the packaging.

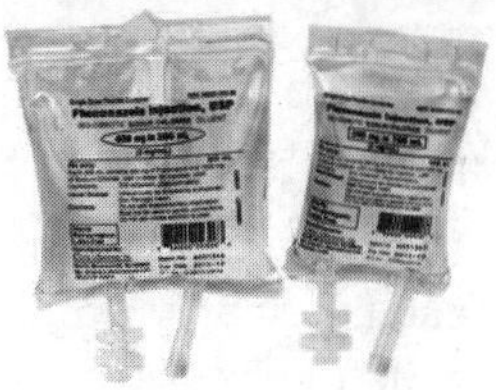

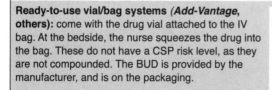

Ready-to-use vial/bag systems *(Add-Vantage*, others): come with the drug vial attached to the IV bag. At the bedside, the nurse squeezes the drug into the bag. These do not have a CSP risk level, as they are not compounded. The BUD is provided by the manufacturer, and is on the packaging.

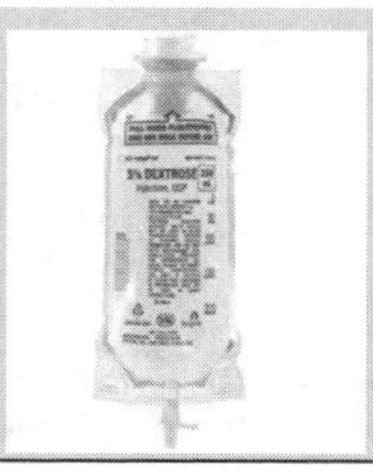

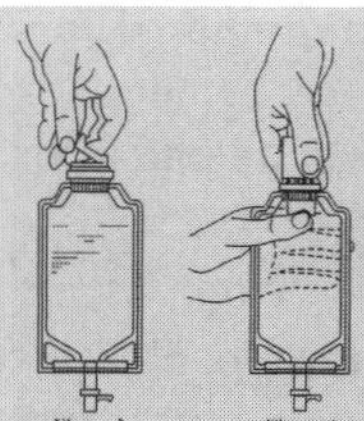

Figure 3 Figure 4

STERILE COMPOUNDING HOW-TO'S

How to Prepare CSPs

These are overview steps for the general process:

- Pharmacist reviews the order.
- Gather and inspect all materials.
- Clean hood. Place only needed items in the hood.
- Prepare CSPs with aseptic technique.
- Properly dispose of syringes and needles into the sharps container. See the Medication Safety & Quality Improvement chapter.
- Visually inspect all finished CSPs.

How to Garb

Garb is the protective clothing and protective gear that is worn for compounding. Garbing is donned in the ante area. The order in which the garb should be donned is from dirtiest to cleanest.

1. Remove coats, rings, watches, bracelets and makeup. Artificial or long nails are not permitted.
2. Don dedicated shoes or shoe covers, head and facial hair covers, and face masks. A second pair of shoe covers are needed for compounding hazardous drugs (HDs). The ante area should have a mirror that is used to check that the hair is completely covered. An eye shield is optional, except if disinfecting or preparing a hazardous drug.
3. Perform hand hygiene with soap and warm water for 30 seconds (see side bar). Most contamination of CSPs comes from the touch.
4. Dry hands and forearms with lint-free disposable towels (preferred) or an electronic hand dryer.
5. Don a non-shedding gown that fits snugly around the wrists and has an enclosure at the neck. Disposable gowns are required for HD compounding and preferred for non-HD compounding. If gowns are reusable, they must be laundered prior to reuse.
6. Enter the buffer area (IV room).
7. Apply an alcohol-based surgical hand scrub (e.g., chlorhexidine gluconate, povidone-iodine) with persistent antimicrobial activity for the recommended amount of time (per manufacturer) and allow to dry.
8. Don sterile, powder-free gloves. Two pairs of gloves are required for compounding HDs. Tuck one pair under the cuffs of the gown. The second pair goes over the cuffs.

HAND HYGIENE

- Vigorously and thoroughly wash hands and forearms up to the elbows for at least 30 seconds.
- Use either microbial or non-microbial soap and warm water.
- Do not use scrub brushes on the skin; they can damage the skin and cause shedding.
- Clean dirt from nails with nail cleaner.

HANDLING HAZARDOUS DRUGS REQUIRES EXTRA PRECAUTION

- Use two pairs of shoe covers.
- Use two pairs of chemotherapy gloves. These are resistant to the penetration of chemotherapy drugs. The chemotherapy gloves are used anytime hazardous drugs are handled (e.g., unpacking, compounding, administering, disposing). The first pair should be tucked under the cuffs of the gown and the second pair should go over the cuffs.
- Use eye shields when necessary (e.g., cleaning HD spills).

9. Sanitize the gloves with 70% IPA routinely during compounding and whenever the gloves touch non-sterile surfaces. Do not resume compounding until the alcohol has dried. Continually inspect gloves for tears.

All garb must be used when compounding with an isolator (glove box) unless the isolator's manufacturer provides written documentation, that garb is not required.

When the compounding is completed and the compounding personnel leaves the clean room/compounding area, all garb except for the gown is disposed of. If the gown is not visibly soiled, it can be taken off and kept in the compounding area in order to be re-worn for the current work shift. The gown cannot leave the ante area if it is going to be re-worn. Hand hygiene is repeated and all other garb is replaced when re-entering the compounding area.

How to Clean the Hood

Lint-free sterile wipes are used to clean the hood. First clean the hood with sterile water, then clean with 70% IPA. There are commercially available wipes that are pre-soaked with 70% IPA. Alternatively, a 70% IPA spray bottle can be used to wet a dry wipe. Never spray inside the hood and never spray onto the HEPA filter. This is how you would clean a horizontal airflow hood:

1. Clean the side walls starting from back to front, wiping up and down in a long sweeping motion. Do not start-stop-start-stop. Use a new side of the wipe when cleaning the next area.

2. Clean the bottom surface (the work area) starting from back to front, with a side to side motion.

The hood can either remain on at all times or turned on for at least 30 minutes before use.

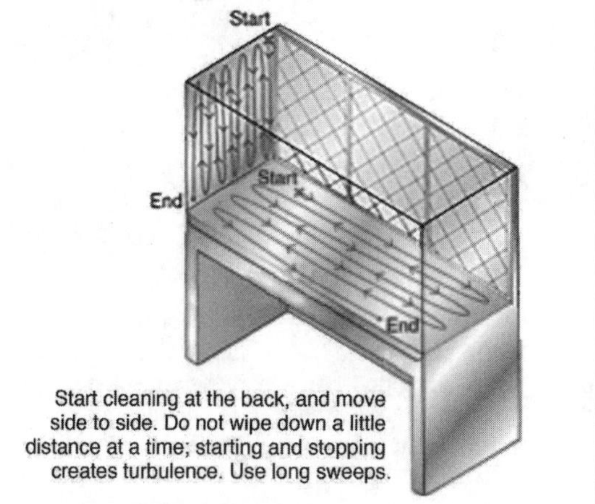

Start cleaning at the back, and move side to side. Do not wipe down a little distance at a time; starting and stopping creates turbulence. Use long sweeps.

At the start of each shift
Before every batch
Every 30 minutes of continuous work
If there's a spill or contamination is suspected.

Hood Cleaning Schedule—each hood needs a checklist to document cleanings.

How to Set Up Items in the Hood

- Only required items can be placed in the hood. No paper, pens, labels, calculators or trays.
- All work must be done at least six inches within the hood, not near the front of the hood where the hood air and room air mingle. Work in the center and place critical items reasonably close to the air source.
- Place all items in the hood side-by-side. Occasionally, items may be placed behind each other (e.g., IV bags for batch preparation). If so, place the smaller items closest to the air filter. Items should not be closer than six inches from the back of the hood.
- Nothing should be between the sterile object and the HEPA filter in a horizontal airflow hood or above a sterile object in a vertical airflow hood. Hazardous drugs must be prepared in a vertical hood.
- Do not tear open components. Open along the seal within the hood. Do not touch the syringe tip or plunger, even with gloved hands.

How to Transfer Solutions and Inject into IV Bags

- For greatest accuracy, use the smallest syringe that can hold the desired amount of solution. The syringe should not be larger than twice the volume to be measured.
- Powders are reconstituted by introducing a diluent such as sterile water for injection, bacteriostatic water for injection (which is sterile) or a diluent provided by the manufacturer. In some cases, dilution is done with saline or dextrose solution.
- Swab the rubber top (or ampule neck) with 70% IPA, and wait for it to air-dry; do not blow on or wave over it to dry faster.
- Prior to withdrawing any liquid from a vial, first inject a volume of air equal to the volume of fluid removed. Exception: do not inject air prior to removing cytotoxic drugs from vials.
- Puncture the rubber top of the vial with the needle bevel up. Then bring the syringe and needle straight up, penetrate the stopper, and depress the plunger of the syringe, emptying the air into the vial. Invert the vial with the attached syringe. Draw up from the vial the amount of liquid required. Withdraw the needle from the vial. In the case of a multi-dose vial, the rubber cap will close, sealing the contents of the vial.
- The volume of solution drawn into a syringe is measured at the point of contact between the rubber piston and the side of the syringe barrel.
- Coring occurs when a small piece of rubber from the stopper is aspirated into the needle, and is put into the solution in the vial. The rubber piece can get injected into a patient. Look for small cored pieces floating near the top of the solution during the visual inspection of the CSP.

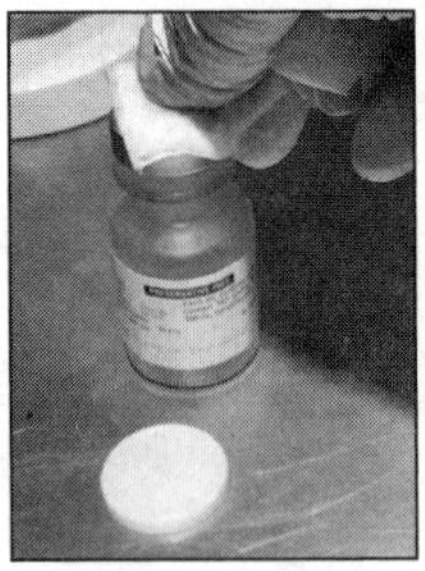

Snap off the plastic top, swab the rubber stopper and injection port on the IV bag with 70% IPA.

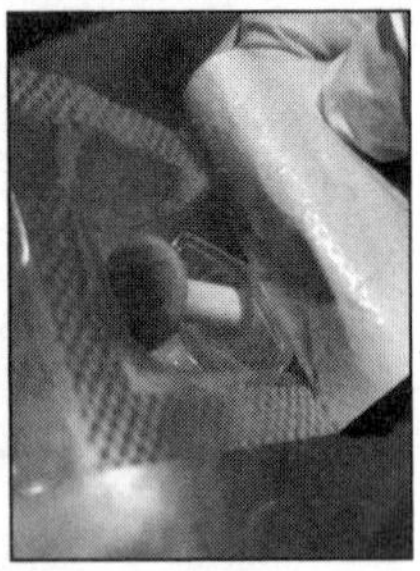

Open syringes, sterile gloves, and other packages along the rip line. Do not tear open; tearing makes particle dust.

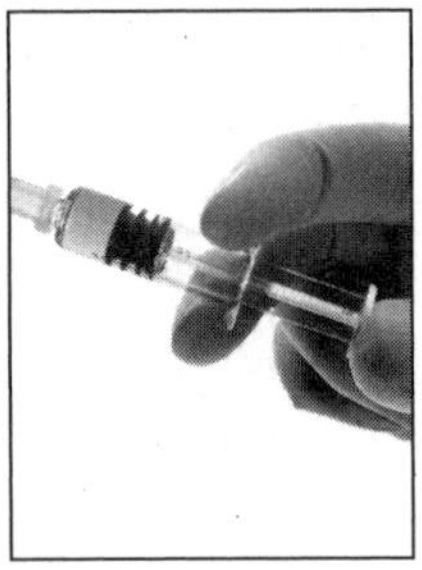

Never touch the barrel of the syringe (between the pointer finger and thumb).

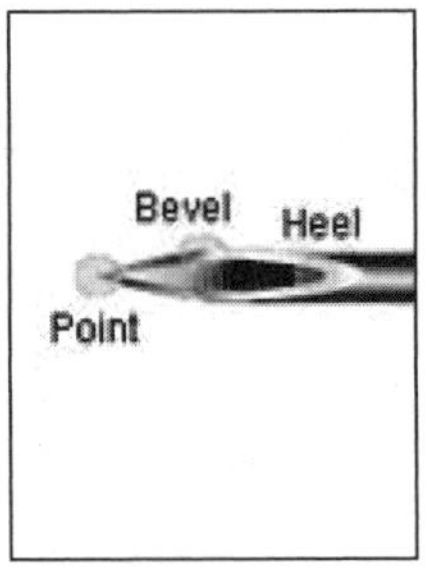

To avoid coring, the bevel should be facing up when inserting through the rubber stopper.

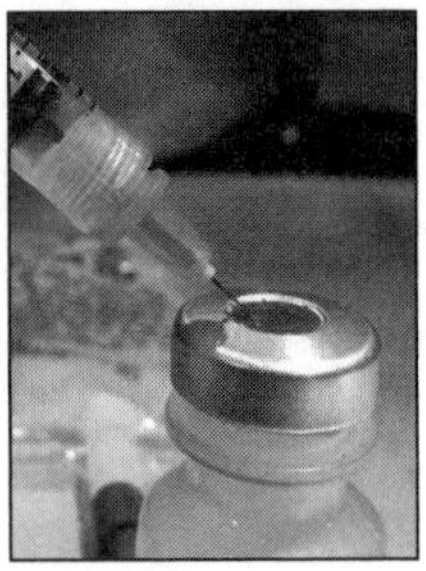

Position the needle tip at a 45-60° angle. When pushing the needle, move the syringe to be positioned upright (90° angle to surface) as it passes through the stopper.

- If the medication is in a glass ampule, open the ampule by forcefully snapping the neck away from you, then tilt the ampule, place the needle bevel of a filter needle or tip of a filter straw in the corner near the opening, and withdraw the medication. Use a needle equipped with a filter for filtering out any tiny glass particles, fibers, or paint chips that may have fallen into the ampule. Before injecting the contents of a syringe into an IV, the needle must be changed to avoid introducing glass or particles into the admixture. A standard needle could be used to withdraw the drug from the ampule; it is then replaced with a filter device before the drug is pushed out of the syringe.

Visual Inspection

- The supervising pharmacist should verify that the correct volume of product is in the syringe before the compounding personnel continues compounding. This is the preferred method because the pharmacist can see the actual volume in the syringe. The "syringe pull-back method" is a common method to verify IV admixtures, but not recommended by ISMP nor addressed by USP. This is when the pharmacist would verify that the correct volumes were added after the compounding is done; the compounding personnel would "pull-back" the plunger of the syringe to the volume of product he/she believes was added into the IV admixture and place the empty syringe next to the corresponding vial. The latter method is not recommended because it solely relies on the compounding personnel's memory and the pharmacist would be verifying an empty syringe.
- Finished CSPs are individually inspected immediately after preparation, against a dark background, for particulates, cored pieces and other foreign matter, precipitates and cloudiness. The container should be lightly squeezed to check for leakage.

How to Determine Risk Levels

USP categorizes CSPs by the risk of contamination, which is based on the compounding area, the ingredients, the equipment, and the complexity of the preparation. The risk levels are low, medium, and high. Low-risk and medium-risk CSPs are commonly prepared by pharmacy staff. There are two other special categories: low with less than 12-hour BUD and immediate use. The risk levels are used to determine an appropriate BUD.

CSP RISK LEVEL	COMPOUNDING AREA	CHARACTERISTICS	EXAMPLES
Low	ISO 5 PEC ISO 7 buffer area ISO 8 ante area (non-HD) ISO 7 ante area (HD)	■ Use only sterile ingredients ■ Use only sterile equipment ■ No more than 3 ingredients ■ No more than 2 entries into any 1 sterile container or device ■ Use only closed or sealed systems ■ Limited to transferring, measuring, and mixing manipulations	Reconstituting a single-dose vial of antibiotic with sterile water and transferring it to a normal saline IV bag.
Low, non-HD Low & medium HD, < 12-hr BUD	ISO 5 PEC in a SCA	■ Non-hazardous, low-risk ■ Hazardous, low- and medium-risk	See examples for low-risk and medium-risk.
Medium	ISO 5 PEC ISO 7 buffer area ISO 8 ante area (non-HD) ISO 7 ante area (HD)	■ Multiple individual or small doses of sterile products combined to prepare a CSP for multiple patients or for one patient on multiple occasions ■ More than 3 ingredients ■ Complex aseptic manipulations	Using a multi-dose vial of antibiotic and transferring single-doses to several normal saline IV bags for multiple patients. This process is called batch preparation. Preparing total parenteral nutrition.
High	ISO 5 PEC ISO 7 buffer room ISO 8 ante area (non-HD) ISO 7 ante area (HD)	■ Non-sterile ingredients ■ Non-sterile equipment	CSPs from bulk drug containers, preparations that require sterilization, and products made with non-sterile components.
Immediate-use	Clean, uncluttered, functionally separate area	■ Only intended for emergency administration. ■ Must be for administration within 1 hour.	Providing stat IV administration in a medical setting or ambulance

Commercially available IV medications that are prepared according to manufacturer's directions are not considered CSPs. Therefore, these IV medications do not have CSP risk levels. These include ready-to-use IVs and vial/bag systems.

How to Choose a Beyond Use Date

The BUD is the date or time after which the CSP should not be used. The BUD is determined by USP 797 standards and the stability/expiration date of the individual ingredients, whichever is shorter. A sterility test can be performed to determine if a longer BUD is possible.

USP 797 determines the BUD by the CSP risk level and the storage temperature.

USP Guidelines for Assigning BUD

CSP RISK LEVEL	BUD ROOM TEMP	BUD FRIDGE TEMP	BUD FREEZER TEMP
Low	48 hours	14 days	45 days
Low non-HD Low/medium HD < 12-hr BUD	12 hours	12 hours	N/A
Medium	30 hours	9 days	45 days
High	24 hours	3 days	45 days
Immediate-use	1 hour	N/A	N/A

6

MEDICATION SAFETY & QUALITY IMPROVEMENT

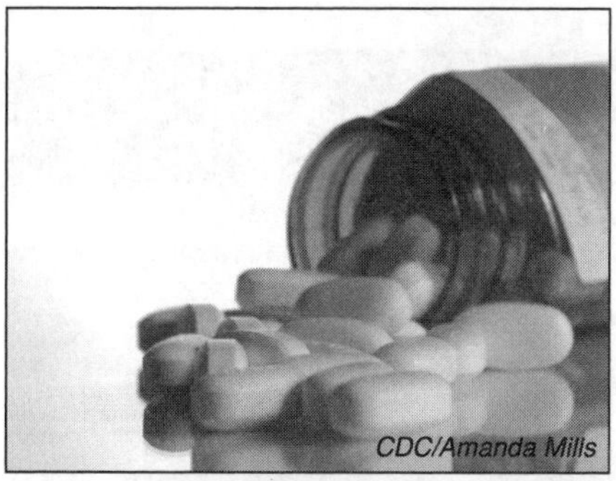

GUIDELINES/REFERENCES

Institute for Safe Medication Practices. www.ismp.org (accessed 2016 Nov 2).

The Joint Commission. www.jointcommission.org (accessed 2016 Nov 2).

MMWR Guideline for Hand Hygiene in Health-Care Settings October 25, 2002, 51(RR16);1-44.

Additional guidelines included with the online course.

BACKGROUND

Awareness of the prevalence of medical errors increased after the release of a study from the Institute of Medicine (IOM), *To Err is Human* (1999), which found that up to 98,000 Americans die each year in U.S. hospitals due to preventable medical errors, 7,000 from medication errors alone. These numbers understated the problem because they did not include preventable deaths due to medical treatments outside of hospitals. Since the release of the IOM study, there has been a greater focus on the quality of healthcare provided in the U.S. The Joint Commission (TJC) and the Institute for Safe Medication Practices (ISMP) are two organizations actively involved in improving medication safety.

MEDICATION ERRORS

The formal definition of a medication error developed by the National Coordinating Council for Medication Error Reporting and Prevention (NCC MERP) is "any preventable event that may cause or lead to inappropriate medication use or patient harm while the medication is in the control of the healthcare professional, patient, or consumer". This can include errors made in prescribing, order communication, product labeling and packaging, compounding, dispensing, administration, education and monitoring.

Do not confuse medication errors with adverse drug reactions (ADRs). ADRs are generally not avoidable, although they may be more likely to occur if the drug is given to a patient at high risk for certain complications. Refer to the Drug Allergies & Adverse Reactions chapter for a discussion of ADRs.

A sentinel event is an unexpected occurrence involving death or serious physical or psychological injury, or risk thereof. When a sentinel event occurs, it is important to find out what went wrong and implement measures to prevent it from happening again.

System-Based Causes of Medication Errors

Experts in medication safety concur that the most common cause of medication errors is not individual error but problems with the design of the medical system itself. Instead of blaming the "new pharmacist" or the "lazy technician" (or the prescriber), healthcare professionals should find ways to improve the system. Errors will always occur, but the goal is to design systems to prevent medication errors from reaching the patient. Some "at risk" behaviors that can compromise patient safety are included on the following page.

EXAMPLE OF AN ADR (NOT A MEDICATION ERROR)

A 55 year old female has a history of herpes zoster. She has no other known medical conditions. The patient reports considerable "shingles pain" that "runs from my back through my left breast". She received a prescription for pregabalin. The patient returned to the clinic with complaints of ankle swelling, which required drug discontinuation.

This problem would not be attributable to a medication error made by the prescriber of pregabalin or by the pharmacist who dispensed it. Rather, this is a side effect that can occur with the use of this drug.

Response to Medication Errors

Institutions should have a plan in place for responding to medication errors. The plan should address the following:

- Internal notification: Who should be notified within the institution and within what time frame?
- External reporting: Who should be notified outside of the institution? See below.
- Disclosure: What information should be shared with the patient/family? Who will be present when this occurs?
- Investigation: What is the process for immediate and long-term internal investigation of an error?
- Improvement: What process will ensure that immediate and long-term preventative actions are taken?

ERRORS OF OMISSION AND COMMISSION

Error of Omission	Error of Commission
Something was left out that is needed for safety	Something was done incorrectly
Example: Failing to warn a patient about an important side effect with a new medication	Example: Prescribing bupropion to a patient with a history of seizures

Reporting

Medication errors, preventable adverse drug reactions, hazardous conditions and "close calls" or "near misses" should be reported. Medication errors are reported so that changes can be made to the system to prevent similar errors in the future. Without reporting, these events may go unrecognized and will likely happen again because others will not learn from the incident.

In a community pharmacy, the staff member who discovers the error should immediately report it (using the established reporting structure) to the corporate office or in the case of an independently owned pharmacy, the owner, who is involved with the quality assurance program. These are mandated by many state boards of pharmacy and have the purpose (in the words of the California Board) "to develop pharmacy systems and workflow processes designed to prevent medication errors." Error investigations need to take place quickly (often as soon as within 48 hours of the incident) so that the sequence of events remains clear to those involved. Many states mandate the ethical requirement that errors be reported to the patient and the prescriber as soon as possible.

In a hospital setting, the staff member should report a medication error through the hospital's specific medication event reporting system. Many medication error reporting systems within hospitals are electronic; however, some hospitals still maintain a paper reporting system. The hospital's Pharmacy and Therapeutics (P&T) committee and Medication Safety Committee (or similar entity) should be informed of the error.

Reporting to Organizations that Specialize in Error Prevention

The Patient Safety and Quality Improvement Act of 2005 (Patient Safety Act) authorized the creation of Patient Safety Organizations (PSOs) to improve the quality and safety of health care delivery in the United States. The Patient Safety Act encourages clinicians and healthcare organizations to voluntarily report and share quality and patient safety information without fear of the information being used in legal proceedings. The Agency for Healthcare Research and Quality (AHRQ) administers the provisions of the Patient Safety Act and the Patient Safety Rule dealing with PSO operations.

AT-RISK BEHAVIORS THAT CAN COMPROMISE PATIENT SAFETY

Drug and Patient-Related
- Failure to check/reconcile home medications and doses
- Dispensing medications without complete knowledge of the medication
- Not questioning unusual doses
- Not checking/verifying allergies

Communication
- Not addressing questions/concerns
- Rushed communication

Technology
- Overriding computer alerts without proper consideration
- Not using available technology

Work Environment
- Trying to do multiple things vs focusing on a single complex task
- Inadequate supervision and orientation

Organizations that specialize in error prevention can analyze the system-based causes of errors and make recommendations. The ISMP National Medication Errors Reporting Program (MERP) is a confidential national voluntary reporting program that provides expert analysis of the system causes of medication errors and disseminates recommendations for prevention.

On the ISMP website (www.ismp.org), medication errors and close calls can be reported. Click on "Report Errors." Professionals and consumers should be encouraged to report medication errors using this site even if the error was reported internally. When there are many reports of a particular error, the manufacturer may take measures to increase safety (e.g., REMS program, name change, packaging change, etc.).

Every pharmacist should make it a practice to read medication error reports and use the information to improve their own practice setting.

Evaluating Medication Errors and Quality Improvement

A root cause analysis (RCA) is a retrospective investigation of an event that has already occurred which includes reviewing the sequence of events that led to the error. The information obtained in the analysis is used to design changes that will hopefully prevent future errors. Findings from the RCA can be applied proactively to analyze and improve processes and systems before they fail again.

The RCA can be of great value in capturing both the big picture perspective and the details of the error. Targeting corrective measures at the identified root causes is the best way to prevent similar problems from occurring in the future. However, it is recognized that complete prevention of recurrence by a single intervention is not always possible. Thus, RCA is often considered to be a repetitive process, and is frequently viewed as an important continuous quality improvement (CQI) tool.

An analysis can also be done prospectively to identify pathways that could lead to errors and to identify ways to reduce the error risk. Failure mode and effects analysis (FMEA) is a proactive method used to reduce the frequency and consequences of errors. FMEA is used to analyze the design of the system in order to evaluate the potential for failures, and to determine what potential effects could occur when the medication delivery system changes in any substantial way or if a potentially dangerous new drug will be added to the formulary.

THE JOINT COMMISSION ON ACCREDITATION OF HEALTHCARE ORGANIZATIONS (JOINT COMMISSION)

The Joint Commission (TJC) is an independent, not-for-profit organization that accredits and certifies more than 17,000 healthcare organizations and programs in the U.S., including hospitals, healthcare networks, longterm care facilities, homecare organizations, office-based surgery centers and independent laboratories. TJC focuses on the highest quality and safety of care and sets standards that institutions must meet to be accredited. An accredited organization must undergo an on-site survey at least every three years and surveys can be unannounced.

National patient safety goals (NPSGs) are set annually by TJC for different types of healthcare settings (ambulatory care, behavioral health, hospital etc.) in order to improve patient safety. Each goal includes defined measures called "Elements of Performance" that must be met. These will be included in the institution's protocol. There are other NPSGs not discussed here, such as a goal related to identifying patients at risk of suicide. The Study Tip and text describe some of the most important 2017 hospital NPSGs related to medication safety.

NPSG 03.05.01: Reduce the likelihood of harm associated with anticoagulant therapy. There are many important elements to this goal, including the requirement to use standardized dosing protocols, to use programmable pumps for heparin and to provide education to patients and families. Protocols should include starting dose ranges, alternate dosing strategies to address drug-drug interactions and communication with the dietary department to address drug-food interactions. The protocol must also include requirements for a baseline INR, frequency of INR monitoring and monitoring for bleeding and HIT.

NPSG 03.06.01: Maintain and communicate accurate patient medication information. This includes medication reconciliation, providing written information to the patient and conducting discharge counseling. In conducting the reconciliation, the medication name, dose, frequency, route, and purpose (at the minimum) should be confirmed. Refer to Medication Reconciliation later in this chapter.

SELECT NATIONAL PATIENT SAFETY GOALS

NPSG 01.01.01: Use at least two patient identifiers when providing care, treatment and services.

- ❑ Appropriate patient identifiers include name, medical record number and date of birth; non-patient specific identifiers (e.g., zip code, physician name, or room number should not be used). Even date of birth can be the same for more than one patient.

NPSG 02.03.01: Report critical results of tests and diagnostic procedures on a timely basis.

- ❑ Includes lab and blood culture results; protocols must stipulate acceptable length of time for reporting.

NPSG 03.04.01: Label all medications, medication containers and other solutions on and off the sterile field in perioperative and other procedural settings.

- ❑ Numerous errors have been associated with removing medications from their original containers and placing them into unlabeled containers.

NPSG 03.05.01: Reduce the likelihood of harm associated with anticoagulant therapy (see text).

NPSG 03.06.01: Maintain and communicate accurate patient medication information (see text).

NPSG 07.01.01: Comply with the Centers for Disease Control (CDC) hand hygiene guidelines.

NPSG 07.03.01; 07.04.01; 07.05.01; 07.06.01: Implement evidence-based practices to reduce healthcare associated infections. These include recommendations to prevent healthcare-associated infections with multidrug-resistant organisms (e.g., MRSA, CDI, VRE and multidrug-resistant gram-negative bacteria). The elements of performance address care of central lines, bloodstream infections and post-surgical infections.

NPSG 7.06.01 has been revised for 2017 and addresses catheter-associated urinary tract infections (CAUTIs). Some of the elements of performance include education for staff and patients regarding the risks and importance of infection prevention, development of criteria for placement of indwelling urinary catheters and written procedures for inserting and maintaining the catheters. Procedures should address limiting use and duration, hand hygiene, sterility of the system and replacement (as needed).

COMMON METHODS USED TO REDUCE MEDICATION ERRORS

Avoid "Do Not Use" Abbreviations, Symbols, and Dosage Designations

Abbreviations are unsafe and contribute to many medical errors. TJC standards include recommendations against the use of unsafe abbreviations. The minimum list of "Do Not Use" abbreviations per TJC is shown in the table. ISMP also publishes a list of error-prone abbreviations, symbols, and dosage designations which includes those on TJC's list and many others. All institutions accredited by TJC are required to have a list of abbreviations that may not be used in the facility. This list must include all of the abbreviations from the TJC "Do Not Use" list, and any additional abbreviations selected by the institution (e.g., those that have resulted in significant errors at the site in the past). The unapproved abbreviation list should be readily accessible in the institution (e.g., wall charts, pocket cards, etc.). It is best to try to avoid abbreviations entirely.

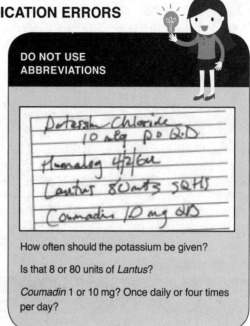

DO NOT USE ABBREVIATIONS

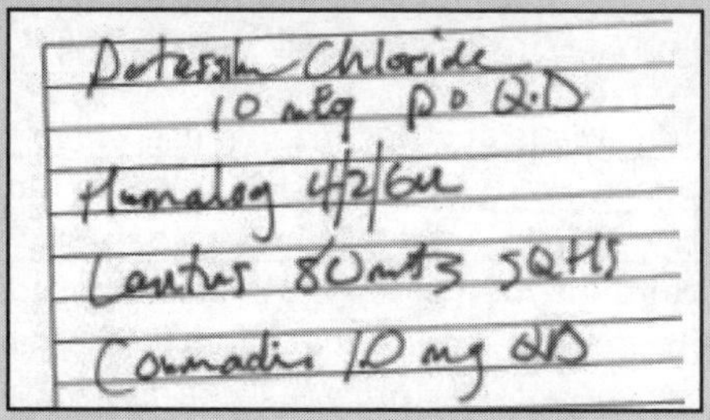

How often should the potassium be given?

Is that 8 or 80 units of *Lantus*?

Coumadin 1 or 10 mg? Once daily or four times per day?

Electronic prescribing can virtually eliminate errors associated with poor handwriting. Despite this, handwritten prescriptions and progress notes are still used in many settings.

DO NOT USE	POTENTIAL PROBLEM	USE INSTEAD
U, u (unit)	Mistaken for "0" (zero), the number "4"(four) or "cc"	Write "unit"
IU (International Unit)	Mistaken for IV (intravenous) or the number 10 (ten)	Write "International Unit"
Q.D., QD, q.d., qd (daily)	Mistaken for each other	Write "daily"
Q.O.D., QOD, q.o.d., qod (every other day)	Period after the Q mistaken for "I" and the "O" mistaken for "I"	Write "every other day"
Trailing zero (X.0 mg)	Decimal point is missed	Write X mg
Lack of leading zero (.X mg)		Write 0.X mg
MS	Can mean morphine sulfate or magnesium sulfate	Write "morphine sulfate" Write "magnesium sulfate"
MSO_4 and $MgSO_4$	Confused with one another	

Tall Man Lettering

Look-alike, sound-alike (LASA) medications are a common cause of medication errors. Poor handwriting and similar product labeling aggravate the problem. Drugs that are easily mixed up should be labeled with tall man letters (e.g., CeleXA, CeleBREX). Using tall man letters, which mix upper and lower case letters, draws attention to the dissimilarities in the drug names. The letters that are upper cases are the ones that are different between the two look-alike, sound-alike drugs. ISMP, FDA, TJC, and other safety-conscious organizations have promoted the use of tall man letters as one means of reducing confusion between similar drug names. The FDA's and ISMP's approved tall man lettering information is available at: http://www.ismp.org/tools/tallmanletters.pdf

Drug dictionaries within computer systems and automated dispensing cabinets (ADCs) often have alerts that prompt the provider to confirm that the correct medication is being ordered or withdrawn. For example a warning may appear on the screen of the ADC which will state: "This is DILAUDID. Did you want hydroMORPHONE?" to avoid confusion with morphine.

High-Alert Drugs

Drugs that bear a heightened risk of causing significant patient harm when used in error should be designated as "High-Alert". Some examples include: insulin and oral hypoglycemics, anticoagulants, concentrated electrolytes (e.g., injectable potassium chloride, phosphate, magnesium and hypertonic saline), antiarrhythmics, anesthetics, chemotherapeutics, opioids, inotropic medications and epidural/intrathecal medications. The ISMP "high-alert" list is available at: http://www.ismp.org/Tools/highAlertMedicationLists.asp. ISMP's list represents the most common agents that are high risk, but an institution's list may include additional drugs based on experience in that setting.

High-alert medications can be used more safely by developing protocols or order sets for use, using premixed products whenever possible, limiting concentrations available in the institution, stocking high-alert products only in the pharmacy (not in ADCs or on nursing units). See example of safe use precautions for insulin and potassium chloride below. Protocols for high-risk drugs increase the rate of appropriate prescribing and reduce the chance of errors from inappropriate prescribing. The NPSG for anticoagulants has previously been discussed.

Example Safe-Use Precautions

DRUG	PRECAUTIONS
Insulin	If U-500 is stocked, specify conditions under which it is to be used Standardize all insulin infusions to one concentration Develop protocols for insulin infusions, transition from infusion to SC and sliding scale orders; use standard orders for management of hypoglycemia Do not use "U" for units; always label with "units" or "units = mL", but never just "mL" Do not place insulin in ADCs; all insulin orders should be reviewed by a pharmacist prior to dispensing
Potassium Chloride	Remove all KCl vials from floor stock; centralize KCl infusion preparation in the pharmacy Use premixed containers Use protocols for KCl delivery which include indications for IV administration, maximum rate of infusion, maximum allowable concentration, guidelines for when cardiac monitoring is required, stipulation that all KCl infusions must be given via a pump, prohibition of multiple simultaneous KCl solutions (e.g., no IV KCl while KCl is being infused in another IV) Allow for automatic substitution of oral KCl for IV KCl, when appropriate Label all fluids containing potassium with a "Potassium Added" sticker

Any drug that is high risk for significant harm if dispensed incorrectly can be placed in a medication bin that provides a visual alert to the person pulling the medication. The bin can be labeled with warnings and include materials (placed inside the bin) that should be dispensed with the drug (such as oral syringes or MedGuides). In the hospital setting, certain drugs are classified as "high-alert" and these can be placed in bins labeled with dispensing requirements.

Medication Therapy Management

Errors may be discovered during a comprehensive medication review (CMR), through the process of medication therapy management (MTM). A personal medication record (PMR) is prepared, and a medication-related action plan (MAP) is developed, preferably by a pharmacist-led team. The next steps involve interventions, referrals, documentation and plans for follow-up. Patients targeted for MTM include those with multiple chronic conditions who are taking multiple drugs and are likely to incur annual costs for covered drugs that exceed a predetermined level. Computer databases are used to identify patients with certain high-risk conditions (such as heart failure or uncontrolled diabetes) who are generally using many medications (some systems tag patients taking many chronic medications daily) and assign a pharmacist (preferably) to review profiles for proper use.

The pharmacist can form a partnership with the patient and prescriber to remedy any issues or lapses. Often, these reviews identify missed therapy such as lack of an ACE inhibitor or ARB in patients with diabetes, missing beta blocker therapy post-MI, missing bisphosphonate therapy with high-dose chronic steroids, and others, since these are easily searchable in databases. A popular MTM initiative is to improve nonadherence in heart failure patients due to the high-rate of ED visits due to decompensated heart failure. MTM is also used to identify cost-savings, by promoting switches to generics or more affordable brands, or by suggesting patient assistance programs or low income subsidies for eligible members.

Medication Reconciliation

According to TJC, "medication reconciliation is the process of comparing a patient's medication orders to all of the medications that the patient has been taking." This reconciliation is done to avoid medication errors such as omissions, duplications, dosing errors, or drug interactions. The NPSG that incorporates medication reconciliation was previously discussed.

Medication reconciliation ("med rec") was previously done on paper forms, but it is now usually performed within the electronic health record (EHR). Prescribers can view side-by-side lists of home medications and ordered medications and address any discrepancies. This process is most effective when complete and accurate information is entered into the patient's medical record (PMR). For this reason, pharmacy departments are often actively involved in documenting home medication use and performing medication reconciliation. In many hospitals, admission orders for a patient cannot be entered into the electronic system until medication reconciliation is completed by a physician, pharmacist or nurse.

Medication reconciliation should be done at every transition of care in which new medications are ordered or existing orders are rewritten. Transitions of care include changes in setting, service, practitioner or level of care. This process comprises five steps:

1. Develop a list of current medications;
2. Develop a list of medications to be prescribed;
3. Compare the medications on the two lists;
4. Note discrepancies and make clinical decisions based on the comparison; and
5. Communicate the new list to appropriate caregivers and to the patient

At discharge, medication reconciliation will occur again. This is an opportunity for the prescriber to address any of the patient's home medications that were "on hold" during the hospitalization and which medications used during the hospitalization should be continued when the patient goes home. Discrepancies are addressed and the patient is educated. Though most often discussed in the hospital context, medication reconciliation can be equally important in ambulatory care, as many patients receive prescriptions from more than one outpatient provider and may go to several pharmacies.

EXAMPLE OF THE BENEFIT OF MEDICATION RECONCILIATION

Ann is an 82 year old female. Her only medication for the previous ten years has been atenolol 25 mg daily. Ann recently developed influenza. She began to have trouble breathing and was taken to the hospital. It was discovered that Ann had pneumonia and heart failure. She was prescribed lisinopril, carvedilol and furosemide. Ann was discharged to transitional care and received the new medications plus her home medication (atenolol). The consultant pharmacist conducted a medication review to reconcile the medications and, after discussion with the physician, the pharmacist wrote an order to discontinue the atenolol.

Include Indications for Use and Proper Instructions on Prescriptions

An indication for use that is written on the prescription (such as lisinopril 10 mg once daily for hypertension) helps pharmacists ensure appropriate prescribing and drug selection. If the pharmacist does not know the indication for the prescribed medication, the prescriber should be contacted.

Using the term "as directed" is not acceptable on prescriptions because the patient often has no idea what this means and the pharmacist cannot verify a proper dosing regimen. Occasionally, this term is used on the bottle along with a separate dosing calendar, such as with warfarin. It would be preferable to write "use per instructions on the dosing calendar" since the patient may not understand how to take the medication and may not be aware that a separate dosing calendar exists.

Use of the Metric System

Measurements should be recorded in the metric system only. Prescribers should use the metric system to express all weights, volumes and units. Computer systems generally have a drop-down menu for selecting the correct units (lb vs kg, for example) and easily converting between units. It is critical to record the correct units, since many calculations (CrCl or eGFR) and dosing checks are performed automatically by the EHR system based on the height and/or weight recorded for the patient. With the increasing prevalence of overweight and obesity in the U.S., it is not uncommon to care for patients weighing 100 kg (or more); but serious errors can occur if this weight was intended to be 100 pounds. Unfortunately, these types of errors do occur in healthcare facilities.

Do Not Rely on Medication Packaging for Identification Purposes

Look-alike packaging can contribute to errors. If unavoidable, separate look-alike drugs in the pharmacy and patient care units, or repackage. Never rely on the package to identify the right drug product. Pharmacies frequently have to purchase products from different manufacturers (and these may look vastly different).

Avoid Multiple-Dose Vials, If Possible

These pose risk for cross-contamination (infection) and over-dosing. If used, they should be (ideally) designated for a single patient and labeled appropriately. Discard the remainder when the patient is done with the medication, or is discharged.

EXAMPLE OF AN ERROR DUE TO MISIDENTIFICATION OF A CONCENTRATION BASED ON THE PACKAGING

The intravenous catheters of three neonates in a NICU unit in Los Angeles were flushed with the adult therapeutic dose of heparin (10,000 units/mL) rather than the heparin flush dose of 10 units/mL. This accident did not result in fatalities although two of the babies required the reversal agent protamine. Three babies died from a similar incident the previous year at a different hospital. The overdose was administered because the nurse thought she was using a lower concentration of heparin.

Due to the high risk associated with heparin overdose, high concentration heparin vials should not be present in patient care areas. Instead, therapeutic doses should be sent by the pharmacy department.

Use Safe Practices for Emergency Medications/Crash Carts

Staff must be properly trained to handle emergencies and use crash cart medications. The medications should be unit dose and age-specific, including pediatric-specific doses. A weight-based dosing chart can be placed in the trays used in the pediatric units. If a unit dose medication is not available, it is best to have prefilled syringes and drips in the cart (to the extent possible) because it is easy to make a mistake under the stress of a code. The emergency medications should be stored in sealed or locked containers in a locked room and replaced as soon as possible after use (through a cart exchange so that the area is not left without required medications). Monitor the drug expiration dates. Trained pharmacists should be present at codes when possible.

CODE BLUE

A code blue refers to a patient requiring emergency medical care, typically for cardiac or respiratory arrest. The overhead announcement will provide the patient's location. The code team (often including a pharmacist) will rush to the room and begin immediate resuscitative efforts.

Dedicate Pharmacists to the ICU, Pediatric Units and Emergency Departments

These are units with a high incidence of preventable medication errors, and pharmacists working in these units can assist in identifying and preventing medication errors by developing process improvements designed to reduce errors.

Monitor for Drug-Food Interactions

Check for drug-food interactions routinely and have the nutrition department (also called "dietary") involved with this effort when drugs with a high rate of food interactions (such as warfarin) are ordered.

Education

Staff education programs such as "in-services" should be provided whenever new high-alert drugs are being used in the facility, to introduce new procedural changes aimed at preventing medication errors and to introduce any new guidelines. The information provided in these "in-services" should be unbiased and should not be provided in a skewed manner by drug company representatives. Many hospitals now limit access of pharmaceutical companies and representatives due to the inherent bias.

Patients can play a vital role in preventing medication errors when they have been encouraged to ask questions and seek satisfactory answers about their medications before drugs are dispensed at a pharmacy. If a patient questions any part of the medication dispensing process, whether it is about the drug's appearance, or dose, or something else, the pharmacist must be receptive and responsive (not defensive). All patient inquiries should be thoroughly investigated before the medication is dispensed. The written information about the medications should be at a reading level that is comprehensible for the patient.

It may be necessary to provide pictograms or other means of instruction to patients who do not speak English or are unable to read English. Attempts must be made to communicate to the patient in their language, using on-site staff or dial-in services. Refer to the Patient Charts, Assessment & Healthcare Provider Communication chapter.

USE OF TECHNOLOGY AND AUTOMATED SYSTEMS

Computerized Prescriber Order Entry and Clinical Decision Support

Computerized physician/provider order entry (CPOE) is a computerized process that allows direct entry of medical orders by prescribers. Directly entering orders into a computer has the benefit of reducing errors by minimizing the ambiguity resulting from handwritten orders. A much greater benefit is seen with the combination of CPOE and clinical decision support (CDS) tools. Clinical guidelines and patient labs can be built into the CPOE system and alerts can notify a prescriber if the drug is inappropriate, or if labs indicate that the drug could be unsafe (such as a high potassium level and a new order for a potassium-sparing agent). CPOE can include standard order sets and protocols. In addition to medication orders, CPOE is used for laboratory orders and procedures. An example of an on-screen alert from a CDS system is shown. The alert in this example pops up when a prescriber attempts to order citalopram with a dose greater than 40 mg/day. In most hospitals, pharmacists are actively involved in creating, updating and monitoring the CDS tools. One aspect of QI is monitoring, reporting trends and addressing alert overrides.

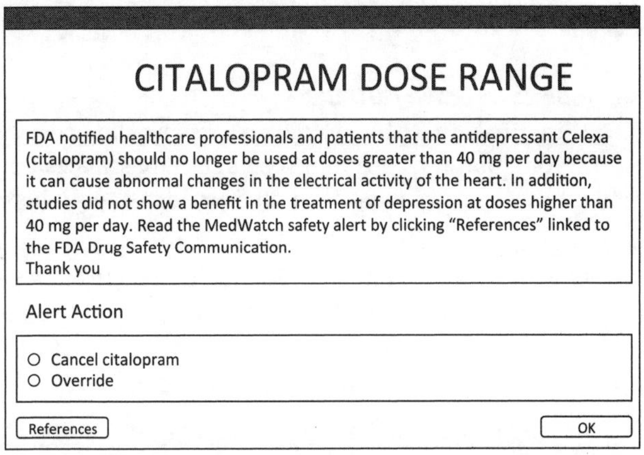

CITALOPRAM DOSE RANGE
FDA notified healthcare professionals and patients that the antidepressant Celexa (citalopram) should no longer be used at doses greater than 40 mg per day because it can cause abnormal changes in the electrical activity of the heart. In addition, studies did not show a benefit in the treatment of depression at doses higher than 40 mg per day. Read the MedWatch safety alert by clicking "References" linked to the FDA Drug Safety Communication.
Thank you
Alert Action
Cancel citalopram
Override
References
OK

Barcoding

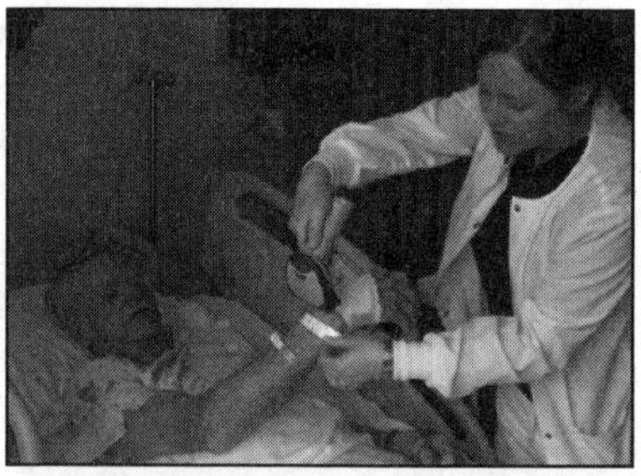

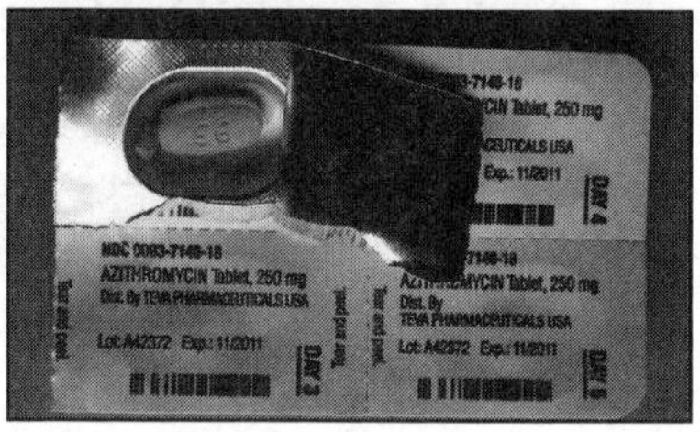

Barcoding may be the most important medication error reduction tool available right now. The barcode follows the drug through the medication use process to make sure it is being properly stocked (such as in the right space in the pharmacy or in the right pocket in the dispensing cabinet), through compounding (if required), and to the patient. The barcode is used at the bedside to identify that the correct drug (by scanning the barcode on the drug's packaging) is going to the right patient (by scanning the barcode on the patient's wristband) and confirms that the dose is being given at the right time. The nurse may have a badge barcode to track who administered the dose. Barcodes are now on many pumps and can prevent errors involving medications being given IV that are not meant to be administered in this manner. When a medication is scanned and administered using barcode technology, the administration can automatically populate on the medication administration record (MAR), thus avoiding the time associated with manual charting of medication administration.

Automated Dispensing Cabinet Overview and Safety Concerns

Most pharmacy interns will have seen automated dispensing cabinets (ADCs) while on clinical rotations. Common names are *Pyxis, Omnicell, ScriptPro* and *AccuDose.* Over half of the hospitals in the U.S. now use ADCs. In many hospitals, the ADCs have replaced patient cassettes that had to be filled at least once daily and exchanged.

Practical Benefits of ADCs

The drug inventory and medication can be automated when drugs are placed into the cabinet and removed. Controlled drug security can be improved (versus the previous method of keeping the controlled drugs locked in a metal cabinet or in a drawer in the nurses' station). The drugs are easily available at the unit and do not require individual delivery from the pharmacy. ADCs provide alerts, usage reports and work well with barcoding.

Methods to Improve ADC Safety

- TJC requires that the pharmacist review the order before the medication can be removed from the ADC for a patient, except in special circumstances (an override). The override function should be limited to true emergencies and all overrides should be investigated.
- The most common error associated with ADC use is giving the wrong drug or dose to a patient. The patient's MAR should be accessible to practitioners while they are removing medications from the ADC. Barcode scanning improves ADC safety. The drug can be scanned to make sure it is going into the right place in the cabinet and can ensure that the right drug is being pulled. Prior to administration, the patient's wristband can be scanned to make sure the drug is going to the right patient.
- Look-alike and sound-alike medications should be stored in different locations within the ADC. Using computerized alerts, ideally pop-ups that require a confirmation when medications with high potential for mix-up in a given setting are selected, can help reduce error risk.
- Certain medications should not be put into the ADCs, including insulin, warfarin and high-dose narcotics (such as hydromorphone 10 mg/mL and morphine 20 mg/mL).
- Nurses should not be permitted to put medications back into the medication compartment because it might be placed in the wrong area; it is best to have a separate drawer for all "returned" medications.
- If the machine is in a busy, noisy environment, or in one with poor lighting, errors increase.

Patient Controlled Analgesia Device Overview and Safety Concerns

Opioids are effective agents used for moderate to severe post-surgical pain and are the mainstay of treatment. These may be administered with patient controlled analgesia (PCA) devices. PCAs allow the patient to treat pain quickly (there is no need to call the nurse and wait for the dose to arrive) and allow the administration of small doses, which helps reduce side effects (particularly over-sedation). PCA drug delivery can mimic the pain pattern more closely and provide good pain control. Increasingly, the PCA is administered with anesthetics for a synergistic benefit in pain relief.

PCA Safety Considerations

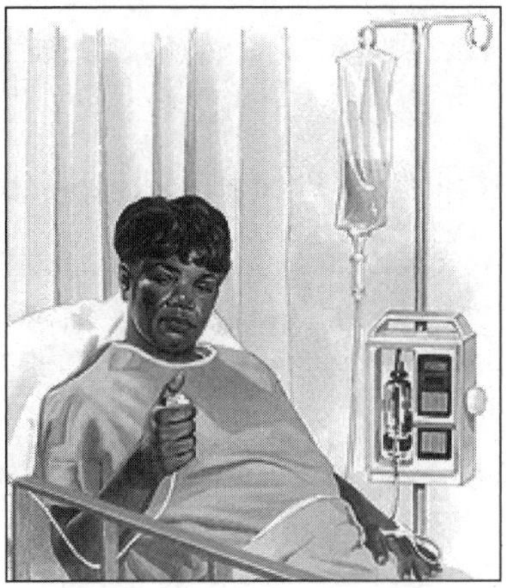

- The devices can be complex and require set-up and programming. This is a significant cause of preventable medication errors. PCAs should be used only by well-coordinated healthcare teams.
- Patients may not be appropriate candidates for PCA treatment. They should be cooperative and should have a cognitive assessment prior to using the PCA to ensure that they can follow instructions.
- Friends and family members should not administer PCA doses. This is a TJC requirement.
- PCAs do not frequently cause respiratory depression, but the risk is present. Advanced age, obesity and concurrent use of CNS depressants (in addition to higher opioid doses) increases risk.

PCA Safety Steps

- Limit the opioids available in floor stock. Use standard order sets (set drug dosages, especially for opioid-naïve patients) so that drugs are not over-dosed.
- Educate staff about HYDROmorphone and morphine mix-ups.
- Implement PCA protocols that include independent double-checking of the drug, pump setting, and dosage. The concentration on the Medication Administration Record (MAR) should match the PCA label.
- Use barcoding technology. Some infusion pumps incorporate barcoding technology. Scanning the barcode on the PCA bag would help ensure the correct concentration is entered during PCA programming. It will also ensure that the right patient is getting the medication.
- Assess the patient's pain, sedation and respiratory rate on a scheduled basis.

INFECTION CONTROL IN HOSPITALS

Nearly two million infections occur in hospitals annually – about one infection for every twenty patients. Hospital infections cause avoidable illness and death and add enormous financial costs. The worst part is that many of these infections are preventable if proper techniques are followed. Many states now require hospitals to report infection rates and Medicare has begun to refuse reimbursement for hospital-acquired infections that are largely avoidable.

It is important to properly clean surfaces, including bed rails, eating trays, and other room surfaces. Healthcare professionals should be careful not to be sources of infection from contaminated clothing (including white coats and ties). Organisms that spread via surface contact include VRE, *C. difficile*, noroviruses and other intestinal tract pathogens.

Common Types of Hospital (Nosocomial) Acquired Infections

- Urinary tract infections, from indwelling catheters (very common), remove the catheter as soon as possible) – preventing catheter associated infections is one of TJC's National Patient Safety Goals (NPSG).
- Blood stream infections from IV lines (central lines have the highest risk) and catheters
- Surgical site infections (see Surgical Prophylaxis in the Infectious Diseases II chapter)
- Decubitus ulcers
- Hepatitis
- *Clostridium difficile,* other GI infections
- Pneumonia (mostly due to ventilator use), bronchitis

Universal Precautions to Prevent the Transmission of Infectious Agents in the Healthcare Setting

Universal precautions is an approach to infection control that treats human blood and body fluids as if they are known to be infectious for HIV, HBV and other bloodborne pathogens. Contact with bodily fluids should be avoided through the use of good hand hygiene and, in select cases, the use of gowns, masks, or patient isolation.

There are 3 categories of transmission-based precautions defined by the CDC:

Contact Precautions

- Intended to prevent transmission of infectious agents which are spread by direct and indirect contact with the patient and the patient's environment.
- Single patient rooms are preferred. If not available, keep ≥ 3 feet spatial separation between beds to prevent inadvertent sharing of items between patients.
- Healthcare personnel caring for these patients wear a gown and gloves for all interactions that may involve contact with the patient or contaminated areas in the patient's room.
- Contact precautions are recommended for patients colonized with MRSA and VRE.

Droplet Precautions

- Intended to prevent transmission of pathogens spread through close respiratory contact with respiratory secretions.
- Single patient rooms are preferred. If not available, keeping ≥ 3 feet spatial separation and drawing a curtain between beds is especially important for diseases transmitted via droplets.
- Healthcare personnel wear a mask (a respirator is not necessary) for close contact with the patient. The mask is donned upon entry to the patient's room.
- Droplet precautions are recommended for patients with active *B. pertussis*, influenza virus, adenovirus, rhinovirus, *N. meningitides*, and group A streptococcus (for the first 24 hours of antimicrobial therapy).

Airborne Precautions

- Intended to prevent transmission of infectious agents that remain infectious over long distances when suspended in the air.
- Patient should be placed in an airborne infection isolation room (AIIR). An AIIR is a single-patient room that is equipped with special air and ventilation handling pressure rooms. The air is exhausted directly to the outside or re-circulated through HEPA filtration before return.

- Healthcare personnel wear a mask or respirator (N95 level or higher), depending on the disease, which is donned prior to room entry.
- Airborne precautions are recommended for patients with rubella virus (measles), varicella virus (chickenpox), or *M. tuberculosis*.

Prevention Of Catheter-Related Bloodstream Infections

- The most important and most cost-effective strategy to minimize catheter-related bloodstream infections (CRBSI) is through aseptic technique during catheter insertion, including proper handwashing and utilization of standard protocols/catheter insertion checklist.
- It is also important to minimize use of intravascular catheters, if possible, through intravenous to oral route protocols and setting appropriate time limits for catheter use. For example, peripheral catheters should be removed/replaced every 2 – 3 days to minimize risk for infection.
- Other strategies shown to reduce the risk of CRBSI, include the use of skin antiseptics (2% chlorhexidine), antibiotic impregnated central venous catheters, and antibiotic/ethanol lock therapy, but must be weighed against the potential risk for increased rates of resistance.

Hand Hygiene

Numerous studies show that proper hand hygiene by those working in healthcare settings reduces the spread of nosocomial infection. Alcohol-based hand rubs (gel, rinse or foam) are considered more effective in the healthcare setting than plain soap or antimicrobial soap and water, but soap and water are preferable in some situation. Fingernails should be clipped short and no jewelry should be worn under gloves (this can harbor bacteria and tear the gloves).

Antimicrobial hand soaps that contain chlorhexidine (*Hibiclens,* others) may be preferable to soap and water to reduce infections in healthcare facilities. Triclosan may also be better but this compound gets into the water supply and has environmental concerns.

When to Wash Hands

- Before entering and after leaving patient rooms.
- Between patient contacts if there is more than one patient per room.
- Before and after removing gloves (new gloves with each patient).
- Before handling invasive devices, including injections.
- After coughing or sneezing.
- Before handling food and oral medications.

CDC/Amanda Mills

Use Soap and Water (not Alcohol-Based Rubs) in These Situations

- Before eating.
- After using the restroom.
- Anytime there is visible soil (anything noticeable on the hands).
- After caring for a patient with diarrhea or known *C. difficile* or spore forming organisms; alcohol-based hand rubs have poor activity against spores.
- Before caring for patients with food allergies.

Soap and Water Technique

- Wet both sides of hands, apply soap, rub together for at least 15 (slow) seconds.
- Rinse thoroughly.
- Dry with paper towel and use the towel to turn off the water.

Alcohol-Based Hand Rubs Technique

- Use enough gel (2 – 5 mL or about the size of a quarter).
- Rub hands together until the rub dries (15 – 25 seconds).
- Hands should be completely dry before putting on gloves.

Hand-Hygiene for Sterile Compounding

- Refer to the Sterile Compounding chapter.

SAFE INJECTION PRACTICES

Outbreaks involving the transmission of blood borne pathogens (e.g., HIV, hepatitis B or C) or other microbial pathogens to patients (and occasionally to healthcare workers) continue to occur due to unsafe injection technique. The majority of safety breaches involve the reuse of syringes in multiple patients, contamination of IV bags with used syringes, failure to follow basic injection safety when administering IV medications and inappropriate care or maintenance of glucometer equipment that is used on multiple patients.

If someone is stuck with a used needle, contact the proper department at a healthcare facility immediately. If post exposure prophylaxis (PEP) is required (for HIV and/or hepatitis), acting quickly is important. In the outpatient setting, instruct the patient to wash the area right away with soap and water, and contact their healthcare provider.

Sharps Disposal

SAFE INJECTION PRACTICES FOR HEALTHCARE FACILITIES

- Never administer an oral solution/suspension intravenously; fatal errors have occurred. Use oral syringes (which are difficult or impossible to attach to a needle for IV injection) and label oral syringes "for oral use only".
- Never reinsert used needles into a multiple-dose vial or solution container. Single-dose vials are preferred over multiple-dose vials, especially when medications will be administered to multiple patients.
- Needles used for withdrawing blood or any other body fluid, or used for administering medications or other fluids should preferably have "engineered sharps protection" which reduces the risk of an exposure incident by a mechanism such as drawing the needle into the syringe barrel after use.
- Never touch the tip or plunger of a syringe.
- Disposable needles that are contaminated (e.g., with drugs, chemicals or blood products) should never be removed from their original syringes, unless no other option is available. Throw the entire needle/syringe assembly (needle attached to the syringe) into the red plastic sharps container.
- Immediately discard used disposable needles or sharps into a sharps container without recapping.
- Sharps containers should be easily accessible and not allowed to overfill; they should be routinely replaced.

Patients who use injectable medications should have a disposal container and be instructed to put needles and other sharps in the container immediately after use. Sharps should be disposed of in an FDA-cleared sharps container, which is puncture resistant, labeled or color-coded appropriately, closeable, and leak-proof. They come marked with a line that indicates when the container should be considered full (about ¾ full). Never compress or "push down" on the contents of any sharps container.

If an FDA-cleared container is not available, some community guidelines recommend using a heavy-duty plastic household container as an alternative (e.g., a plastic laundry detergent container). The container must be leak and puncture-resistant, with a tight-fitting lid.

The entire needle/syringe assembly is discarded. Do not instruct patients to remove the needle or attempt to cut it. The only time that recapping a needle is permitted is when the sharps container is not immediately available; in that case, use the one-hand method to recap until the sharps container can be reached: (1)

Place the cap on a table or counter next to something firm to push the cap against; (2) Hold the syringe with the needle attached and slip the needle into the cap without using the other hand. Push the capped needle on the firm surface to "seat" the cap onto the needle using only the one hand. Sharps disposal guidelines and programs vary. The local trash removal services or health department should have the available service(s), and the pharmacy can provide this information to patients. Services include drop boxes or supervised collection sites (such as in a hospital, pharmacy, police or fire station), household hazardous waste collection sites, mail-back programs and residential special waste services pick-up.

HAZARDOUS DRUGS

The National Institute for Occupational Safety and Health (NIOSH) issues a list of hazardous drugs that require special precautions in order to prevent work-related injury and illness. Drugs that are hazardous are included in the Key Drugs box. The requirements for handling drugs on the NIOSH list are set by the U.S. Pharmacopeia (USP), in chapter 800. Minimally, a pharmacy or other setting handling hazardous drugs must have the following:

- Engineering controls, such as closed system transfer devices and biological safety cabinets (BSCs). BSCs are negative pressure hoods that vent the drug's toxic fumes to the outside (away from the staff standing at the hood).
- Personal protective equipment (e.g., protective gown, respiratory protection, goggles, gloves). Drugs will require either single or double gloves during handling.
- Spill kits, safe work practices and disposal requirements.

Healthcare personnel should avoid manipulating hazardous drugs (e.g., crushing tablets, opening capsules). Liquid formulations are preferred if solid oral dosage forms are not appropriate for the patient. There should be dedicated equipment for hazardous drugs, such as a dedicated counting tray. Refer to the Oncology I and Compounding chapters for further discussion on handling hazardous drugs.

If the drug will be administered to a patient by a nurse, hazardous drug labeling is required to caution the nurse to use safe handling practices. If a nurse or caregiver is providing a hazardous drug to a patient, such as a tablet of raloxifene, single gloves are acceptable.

HAZARDOUS DRUGS THAT REQUIRE SPECIAL HANDLING TO AVOID TOXICITY TO WORKERS

KEY DRUGS

Hazardous drugs are:

Teratogenic

Carcinogenic

Genotoxic (damage the DNA and can cause cancer)

Have reproductive toxicity

Cause organ toxicity at low doses

Others

All Pregnancy Category X drugs, many Category D's and a few C's.

Chemotherapy drugs

5-alpha reductase inhibitors (dutasteride, finasteride)

Hormones (contraceptives, estradiol, testosterone)

Transplant drugs (mycophenolate, tacrolimus, cyclosporine, everolimus, sirolimus)

Others (colchicine, dronedarone, fluconazole, methotrexate, misoprostol, mifepristone, paroxetine, spironolactone, ribavirin, risperidone, raloxifene, rasagiline, ziprasidone)

Auxiliary Labels

When a hazardous drug is placed into a pill container, no further action is required unless an auxiliary label about a specific toxicity is required. High-alert drugs, including chemotherapy, require "high-alert" labels when used in a hospital setting for patient administration. Drugs put into containers may require labels such as "Do not use if pregnant or planning to become pregnant" for finasteride or dutasteride, or "cytotoxic drug – dispose of properly" for chemotherapy drugs.

DRUG ALLERGIES AND ADVERSE DRUG REACTIONS

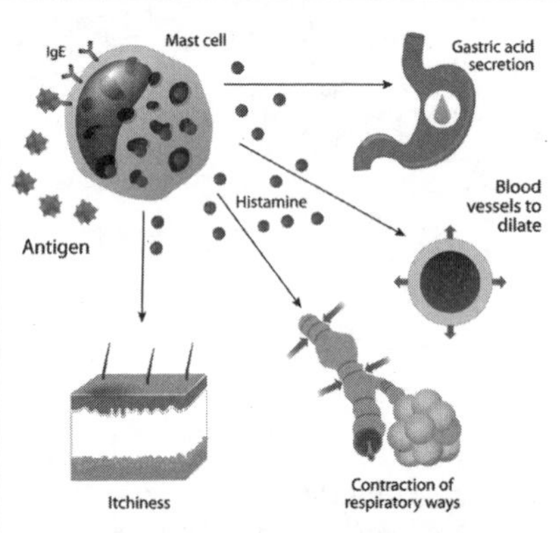

designua © 123RF.com

GUIDELINES/REFERENCES

Food and Drug Administration MedWatch program http://www.fda.gov/Safety/MedWatch/ (accessed 2016 September 8)

Drug Allergy: An Updated Practice Parameter. *Ann Allergy Asthma Immunol.* 2010 Oct;105:259-273.

BACKGROUND

Adverse drug reaction (ADR) is a term that encompasses all unintended pharmacologic effects of a drug when it is administered correctly and used at recommended doses. ADRs should not be confused with medication errors, which can include overdose and administration mistakes, and are discussed in the Medication Safety and Quality Improvement chapter. ADRs result in substantial morbidity and mortality and reports are increasing; 807,270 reports with serious outcomes were logged with the FDA in 2014 (including 123,927 deaths).

Although side effects or adverse effects can occur in anyone, some patients are more susceptible than others. For example, some degree of renal damage can occur with use of an aminoglycoside for longer than 7 days. However, in patients with underlying renal impairment, nephrotoxicity may be more likely to occur and may happen after a shorter duration.

ADVERSE DRUG REACTIONS

ADRs are categorized into predictable (Type A) and unpredictable (Type B) reactions.

Type A Reactions

Type A reactions are dose-dependent, related to the known pharmacologic actions of the drug, can occur in any patient, and range from mild to severe. Type A reactions are the most common and account for an estimated 80% of ADRs. An example of a Type A reaction is orthostatic hypotension with doxazosin. If a patient starts doxazosin at 1 mg QHS, they will have much less orthostatic hypotension and dizziness than if the medication is started at a 4 mg dose. Because of this, the drug should be slowly titrated upward to reduce the severity of the side effect.

Type B Reactions

Type B reactions are generally not dose-dependent, are unrelated to the pharmacologic actions of the drug, and can be influenced by patient-specific susceptibility factors (e.g., rash with abacavir). Type B reactions include drug allergies, and pseudoallergic reactions (itching after opioid administration or redman syndrome with rapid vancomycin infusion), drug intolerances (e.g., nausea with codeine), and idiosyncratic reactions (Stevens-Johnson syndrome).

Drug allergy is one category of adverse drug reactions that refers to an immune-mediated response to a medication or excipient (inactive ingredient). True drug allergies, or hypersensitivity reactions, are classified into four types. Type I reactions are immediate (within 15 – 30 minutes of exposure) and involve an IgE-mediated immune response. Reactions can include urticaria (hives), angioedema, bronchospasm and anaphylaxis. Severity can range from minor inconvenience to death. Type II reactions occur minutes to hours after exposure. Examples include hemolytic anemia and thrombocytopenia. Type III describes immune-complex reactions, which have an onset of 3 – 10 hours after exposure. Examples include drug-induced lupus and serum sickness. Type IV reactions are delayed hypersensitivity reactions. They can occur anywhere from 48 hours to several weeks after exposure. A classic example of a type IV reaction is the PPD skin test for tuberculosis; if positive, the intradermal response peaks at 48 – 72 hours.

FDA TOOLS TO REDUCE ADVERSE DRUG REACTIONS

Boxed Warnings

Boxed warnings are one of the FDA's strictest warning about a drug's safety risks and are issued for some prescription drugs that can cause serious injury or death. The boxed warning is designed to inform healthcare prescribers about the risk, and is displayed prominently in a black box at the beginning of the package labeling. Drugs that increase risk of mortality may still be used in select patients or under certain conditions. For example, long-acting beta agonists have a boxed warning for asthma-related death if they are used as monotherapy; thus, the boxed warning is to avoid using them alone (without a steroid) in asthma. In other cases, the drug should not be used if there are other options available (e.g., tigecycline). Other boxed warnings are designed to avoid mishaps due to prescribing or dispensing errors. Traditional amphotericin B carries a boxed warning to verify doses > 1.5 mg/kg. This is an effort to avoid confusion with lipid amphotericin formulations (typically dosed at 3 – 6 mg/kg) that could lead to dosing errors and severe renal damage. If a boxed warning concerns an adverse effect that the patient could experience (e.g., suicide risk in adolescents using antidepressants), the patient or caregiver must be informed of the risk and counseled on methods to use the drug in the safest manner possible (such as monitoring for changes in mood).

Risk Evaluation and Mitigation Strategies

Risk Evaluation and Mitigation Strategies (REMS) are risk management plans required by the FDA for some drugs. They are developed by the manufacturer and approved by the FDA to ensure the benefits of a drug outweigh the risks. REMS can include a variety of approaches. For example, the REMS for a drug could require physicians or pharmacies to have special certification to prescribe or dispense the drug, or that patients enroll in a registry so that ADRs can be tracked, or that lab testing is completed before dispensing. Examples include the clozapine REMS, the APPRISE program for erythropoietin use in oncology, the iPLEDGE program for isotretinoin, and others. In 2011 the FDA began new REMS to reduce the misuse of long-acting opioids due to the inherent danger with these drugs. The list of REMS drugs continues grow. When studying from this book, note the many drugs that have REMS requirements.

Medication Guides

Medication Guides (or MedGuides) present important adverse events that can occur with over 300 medications. MedGuides are FDA-approved patient handouts that are written in non-technical language and are considered part of the drug's labeling. If a medication has a MedGuide, it should be dispensed with the original prescription and with each refill. Some medications dispensed while inpatient require MedGuides and these should be available to the patient or family upon request. It is not necessary to dispense them to inpatients routinely because the patient is being monitored. MedGuides are required for many individual agents and some entire classes of medications (including anticonvulsants, antidepressants, long-acting opioids, NSAIDs and the ADHD stimulants and atomoxetine).

ASSESSING CAUSALITY OF AN ADVERSE DRUG REACTION

When an adverse reaction occurs, the Naranjo Scale (a validated causality assessment scale) can help determine the likelihood that a drug caused an adverse reaction. Based on the questionnaire, a probability score is calculated. A score > 9 = definite ADR; 5 – 8 = probable ADR; 1 – 4 = possible ADR; 0 = doubtful ADR.

QUESTION	YES	NO	DO NOT KNOW
Are there previous conclusive reports on this reaction?	+1	0	0
Did the adverse event appear after the suspected drug was given?	+2	-1	0
Did the adverse reaction improve when the drug was discontinued or a specific antagonist was given?	+1	0	0
Did the adverse reaction appear when the drug was readministered?	+2	-1	0
Are there alternative causes that could (on their own) have caused the reaction?	-1	+2	0
Did the reaction reappear when a placebo was given?	-1	+1	0
Was the drug detected in any body fluid in toxic concentrations?	+1	0	0
Was the reaction more severe when the dose was increased or less severe when the dose was decreased?	+1	0	0
Did the patient have a similar reaction to the same or similar drugs in any previous exposure?	+1	0	0
Was the adverse event confirmed by any objective evidence?	+1	0	0

Characterizing an Adverse Drug Reaction

When patients report an adverse drug reaction, pharmacists must ask the right questions in order to determine whether an adverse reaction is an intolerance or drug allergy:

- What reaction occurred (a mild rash, a severe rash with blisters, trouble breathing)?
- When did it occur? About how old were you?
- Can you use similar drugs in the same class? For example, if a penicillin allergy is reported, ask if the patient has ever used *Keflex*.
- Do you have any food allergies or a latex allergy?

Some food allergies (e.g., soy, peanut) have implications for certain drugs or formulations. Latex allergies should be collected because some drugs require tubing, have latex vial stoppers, or require gloves for administration. All allergies should be noted in the patients record.

ADR REPORTING

Side effects, adverse events and allergies should be reported to the FDA's MedWatch program, which is called the FDA Adverse Event Reporting System (FAERS), that provides a central collection point for problems caused by drugs. Vaccines are an exception and are reported under a different program called VAERS. See Immunizations chapter for more information.

The FDA can require Phase IV (post-marketing safety surveillance programs) for approved drugs and biologics and collects and analyzes the reports to better understand the drug safety profile in a real world

EXAMPLE: ADR INCIDENCE IN REAL LIFE VS. CLINICAL TRIAL

When spironolactone was studied in heart failure patients during the RALES trial, patients with renal insufficiency or elevated potassium levels were excluded due to the known risk of additional hyperkalemia from the use of spironolactone. The drug was found to have benefit in advanced heart failure patients and doctors in the community began to use it in their heart failure patients. In this real life setting, patients with renal insufficiency or elevated potassium were occasionally prescribed spironolactone, and arrhythmias and sudden death due to hyperkalemia were reported.

setting. When drugs are studied in trials, high-risk patients are typically excluded. Yet in real life settings, some high risk patients will receive the medication. Post-marketing reports also help identify side effects that occur less frequently. If a drug causes a reaction in 1 out of every 3,000 people, the problem may not be apparent in a smaller clinical trial. For this reason, community-based adverse event reporting is critical.

- Reporting is voluntary but has important implications for safe medication use. Healthcare professionals and patients may also report adverse events to the drug manufacturer, who is required by law to send the report to the FDA. The MedWatch form used for reporting can be found online via the link provided in the references at the beginning of this chapter. Reports can also be made by calling the FDA directly. MedWatch is also used for reporting problems with biologics, medical devices, some dietary supplements and cosmetics.
- If the FDA receives enough reports that a drug is linked to a particular problem, the manufacturer can required to update the labeling (e.g., package insert). In especially risky cases, a drug safety alert is issued to prescribers, usually before the labeling is changed.

EXAMPLE: ADR REPORTS LEAD TO FDA REQUIREMENT FOR SAFETY LABELING CHANGES

Oseltamivir *(Tamiflu)* was initially released without any warning of unusual behavior in children. The FDA received enough reports that they issued a warning to prescribers in 2006. After many more reports, in 2008, the FDA required the manufacturer to update the prescribing information to include a precaution about hallucinations, confusion and other strange behavior in children.

EXAMPLE: INTOLERANCE REPORTED INCORRECTLY AS A DRUG ALLERGY

CG received acetaminophen 300 mg-codeine 30 mg *(Tylenol #3)* for pain relief after a dental extraction. She got very nauseated from the medicine. When she was admitted to the hospital several years later for a left hip replacement, she reported to the intake coordinator that she was "allergic" to codeine. The intake coordinator did not attempt to clarify the reaction. The hospital's pain management protocol calls for hydromorphone in a patient-controlled analgesic device for postoperative pain control. The physician used a less desirable option for pain control due to the reported allergy.

Example of a Posting on the FDA Website of a Drug that is Being Monitored Under Phase IV

DRUG	USAGE	ADVERSE EVENT REPORTS	NOTES
Fluconazole *(Diflucan)*	Treatment of yeast infections of the vaginal area, mouth, and esophagus, Cryptococccal meningitis and prevention of yeast infections in patients with a weakened immune system.	A Danish study identified possible increased risk of miscarriage with use of oral fluconazole for yeast infections.	FDA is evaluating this study and additional data and will communicate conclusions and recommendations when the review is complete.

INTOLERANCES, SENSITIVITIES AND IDIOSYNCRATIC REACTIONS

Stomach Upset/Nausea

Stomach upset or nausea is often incorrectly reported as an allergy. It should be listed on the patient profile because the drug bothered the patient and, if possible, should be avoided in the future; but this is not an allergy and should not prevent drugs in the same class from being used. This is more accurately categorized as an intolerance. Modern electronic medical records often allow for documentation of intolerances separately from allergies. An example of an intolerance is the patient who has stomach upset with codeine (but not hydrocodone or other drugs in the morphine class) or from erythromycin (but not azithromycin or other macrolides).

Mild Rash

Opioids cause a non-allergic release of histamine from mast cells in the skin, causing itching and hives in some patients. This is particularly problematic in the inpatient setting after surgery, when opioid-naïve patients receive the medication or when non-naïve patients receive higher-than-normal doses. Pruritus due to this or other causes, if not severe, can be reduced or avoided if the patient is pre-medicated with an antihistamine, such as diphenhydramine.

Photosensitivity

Photosensitivity can occur when sunlight reacts with a drug in the skin and causes tissue damage that looks like a severe sunburn on sun-exposed areas; this occurs within hours of sun exposure. A type IV (delayed hypersensitivity) reaction can also occur with sun exposure and some medications. It appears as a red, itchy rash that can spread to areas that were not exposed to sun and occurs within days of sun exposure.

When dispensing medications that can cause photosensitivity, it is important to advise the patient and/or their caregivers to limit sun exposure and to use sunscreens that block both UVA and UVB radiation (these are labeled broad spectrum).

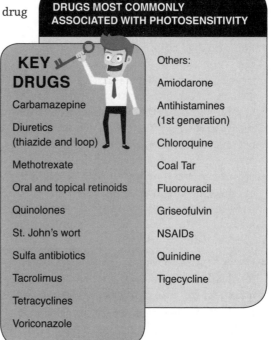

DRUGS MOST COMMONLY ASSOCIATED WITH PHOTOSENSITIVITY

KEY DRUGS

- Carbamazepine
- Diuretics (thiazide and loop)
- Methotrexate
- Oral and topical retinoids
- Quinolones
- St. John's wort
- Sulfa antibiotics
- Tacrolimus
- Tetracyclines
- Voriconazole

Others:

- Amiodarone
- Antihistamines (1st generation)
- Chloroquine
- Coal Tar
- Fluorouracil
- Griseofulvin
- NSAIDs
- Quinidine
- Tigecycline

Thrombotic Thrombocytopenic Purpura

TTP is a blood disorder in which clots form throughout the body. This process consumes platelets and leads to bleeding under the skin and the formation of purpura (bruises) and petechiae (dots) on the skin. TTP can be fatal and should be treated immediately with plasma exchange.

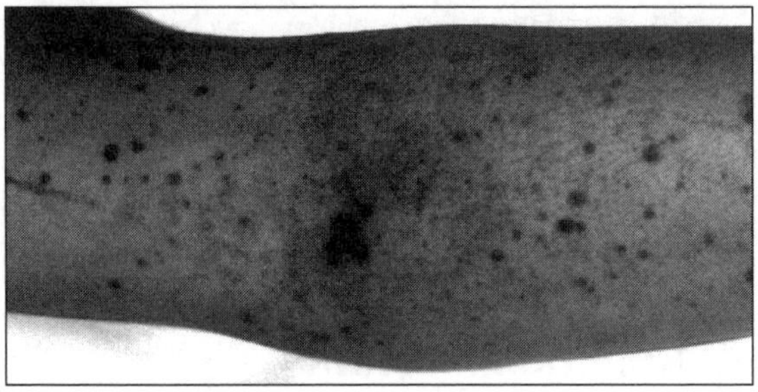

Patient with Thrombotic Thrombocytopenic Purpura

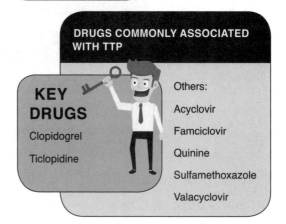

DRUGS COMMONLY ASSOCIATED WITH TTP

KEY DRUGS

- Clopidogrel
- Ticlopidine

Others:

- Acyclovir
- Famciclovir
- Quinine
- Sulfamethoxazole
- Valacyclovir

Severe Skin Reactions

There are several severe skin reactions that can be caused by drugs, including Stevens-Johnson syndrome (SJS), toxic epidermal necrolysis (TEN), and drug reaction with eosinophilia and systemic symptoms (DRESS). All of these can be life-threatening and require prompt treatment. A table listing the drugs most commonly associated with severe skin reactions is included. Cases of severe reaction have also been associated with the use of the OTC analgesics acetaminophen and ibuprofen, which are generally considered to be safe medications.

DRUGS COMMONLY ASSOCIATED WITH SEVERE SKIN REACTIONS

SJS/TEN		DRESS
Abacavir	Fosphenytoin	Carbamazepine
Carbamazepine	Hydroxychloroquine	Celecoxib
Caspofungin	Isavuconazonium	Doxycycline
Clindamycin	Letrozole	Ethosuximide
Clopidogrel	Minocycline	Fosphenytoin
Deferasirox	Nevirapine	Gabapentin
Ethosuximide	Oseltamivir	Ibuprofen
	Oxcarbazepine	Lacosamide
	Peramivir	Minocycline
	Phenobarbital	Oxcarbazepine
	Quinine	Sulfasalazine
	Terbinafine	Terbinafine
	Ticlopidine	Valproate
	Tiagabine	Vancomycin
	Varenicline	
	Voriconazole	
	Zonisamide	

KEY DRUGS

- Allopurinol
- Lamotrigine
- Penicillins
- Phenytoin
- Piroxicam
- Sulfamethoxazole

Stevens-Johnson Syndrom and Toxic Epidermal Necrolysis

SJS and TEN involve epidermal detachment and skin loss that is equivalent to 3rd degree burns. SJS and TEN generally occur 1 – 3 weeks after drug administration, and almost always more than 72 hours after administration. These reactions can result in severe mucosal erosions, a high body temperature and organ damage (eyes, liver, kidney, lungs). SJS and TEN are commonly classified by the percent of skin detachment. The key to treating both is to stop the offending agent as soon as possible. In addition, patients will receive fluid and electrolyte replacement, wound care and pain medications. Systemic steroids are contraindicated in TEN, but may be used in SJS, though benefit is controversial. Due to the severity of the mucosal involvement, antibiotics are often necessary to prevent or treat an infection.

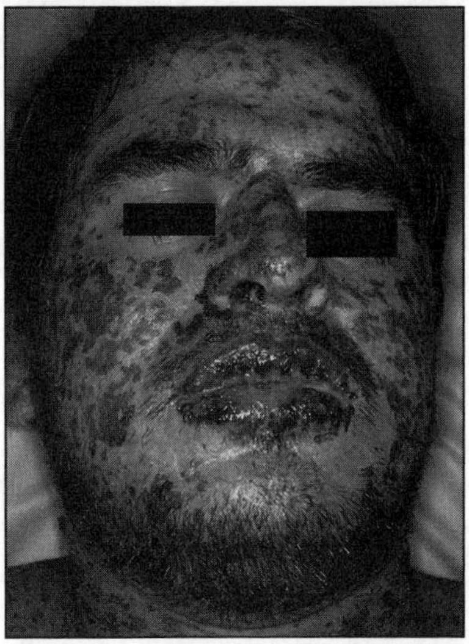

Patient with Stevens-Johnson Syndrome

Drug Reaction with Eosinophilia and Systemic Symptoms

DRESS can include a variety of skin eruptions accompanied by systemic symptoms such as fever, hepatic dysfunction, renal dysfunction and lymphadenopathy, but rarely involves mucosal surfaces. Treatment consists of stopping the offending agent, although symptoms may continue to worsen for a period of time after the agent has been discontinued.

DRUG ALLERGIES

Some drugs are more commonly associated with drug allergies than others. Penicillins and sulfonamides are two classes that cause the most drug allergies. For a true drug allergy to occur, the person must have taken the drug previously. Initial exposure will cause a Type I hypersensitivity reaction, resulting in IgE production, which primes the body to release excessive histamine at the next drug exposure. This section describes drug allergy reactions and treatment, but keep in mind that similar treatment may be used for non-drug allergies. A pharmacist who is dispensing an epinephrine auto-injector for other types of allergies will provide the same instructions.

Some medications (e.g., phytonadione, contrast media) are associated with a pseudoallergic reaction, sometimes called an anaphylactoid reaction. It is not IgE-mediated, but the clinical appearance and treatment are similar to that of anaphylaxis.

A reaction without breathing difficulty can sometimes be treated by simply stopping the offending drug. Antihistamines can be used to counteract the histamine release that causes itching, swelling and rash. Systemic steroids, and sometimes NSAIDs, can be used to decrease swelling. Severe swelling may necessitate a steroid injection. Epinephrine is used to reverse bronchoconstriction if the patient is wheezing or has other signs of trouble breathing.

Anaphylaxis

Anaphylaxis is a severe, life-threatening allergic reaction that occurs within seconds to minutes of drug exposure. Anaphylaxis can occur after an initial exposure and subsequent immune response, but some drugs can cause anaphylaxis with the first exposure. A patient experiencing anaphylaxis may have generalized urticaria (hives), swelling of the mouth and throat, difficulty breathing or wheezing sounds, abdominal cramping and hypotension (which can cause dizziness or lightheadedness). The patient can become unconscious or go into shock. Symptoms can develop quickly, within seconds or minutes; treatment must be administered immediately.

Anyone with serious allergies to food, drugs or serious medical conditions (including hypoglycemia that may require glucagon) should wear a medical ID bracelet. This will alert emergency responders and many can be linked to the patient's health profile that is accessible through a 24-hour information center.

Anaphylaxis Treatment

An anaphylactic reaction requires immediate emergency medical care. The patient or family should be instructed to call 911 if anaphylaxis occurs. Treatment includes epinephrine injection ± diphenhydramine ± steroids ± IV fluids. To avoid blocking the airway, nothing should be placed under the head or in the mouth. Swollen airways can be quickly fatal; patients who have had such a reaction should carry injectable single-use epinephrine (*EpiPen, EpiPen Jr, Adrenaclick, Auvi-Q,* or generic equivalent) if they may be at future risk. These are available in dosages of 0.3 mg or 0.15 mg of epinephrine. The patient's emergency kit should also include diphenhydramine tablets (25 mg x 2) and emergency contact information.

Patient Counseling for Epinephrine Auto-Injectors

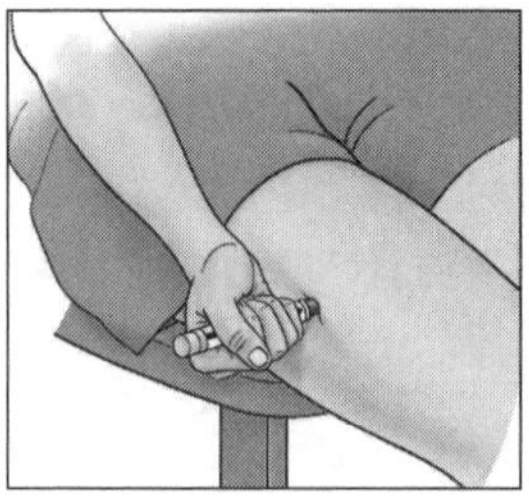

- Tell your family, caregivers and others where you keep your epinephrine auto-injector and how to use it, as you may not be able to speak in an allergic emergency.
- For *EpiPen*:
    - Flip open the cap and remove the auto-injector from the carrying case.
    - Grasp the epinephrine auto-injector in one fist with the orange tip pointing down. Keep thumb, fingers and hand away from the orange tip.
    - Remove the safety release by pulling it straight up.
    - Hold the orange tip close to the middle of your outer thigh. Swing away from leg, then push the auto-injector against the thigh until it "clicks" (through clothing if necessary). The injector should be at a 90-degree angle to your thigh.
    - Hold the injector firmly in place in your outer thigh while slowly counting to 3.

  - Remove the injector and massage the area where the medicine entered your skin for 10 seconds.
  - The orange tip will extend to cover the needle. If the needle is visible, it should not be reused.
  - If you have two pens, you may need to use the second (in the opposite thigh) to maintain breathing prior to the arrival of medical help.
- For *Adrenaclick:*
  - Two gray end caps must be removed and the thumb, fingers and hand must be kept away from the red tip.
  - After injection in the thigh, the injector should remain against the thigh while slowly counting to 10.
  - Examine the red tip: if the needle is visible, the dose has been received. If the needle is not visible, repeat the injection step.
- For *Auvi-Q:* pull off the outer case, then follow the voice instructions to administer.
- When injecting an uncooperative child, hold leg firmly to avoid bending or breaking the needle.
- Skin infections can occur after injection. Report any prolonged redness, swelling, warmth or tenderness at the injection site.
- Take the antihistamine tablets (2 x 25 mg) in your allergy kit (only if there is no tongue/lip swelling).
- Seek emergency medical care (call 911) because additional care may be needed.

DRUGS COMMONLY ASSOCIATED WITH ALLERGIC REACTIONS

While any drug can lead to an allergic reaction, some are known to do so more than others. These are discussed below. Often the drug that caused a reaction can be replaced with another drug. Patch testing by an allergist is the most reliable way to determine if a person is truly allergic to a drug, but it does not provide any information regarding certain types of rashes (e.g., SJS or TEN).

Beta-Lactams

Penicillin is a beta-lactam antibiotic and there are many related compounds in this family, including nafcillin, oxacillin, ampicillin, amoxicillin, piperacillin and others. Anyone who is allergic to one of the penicillins should be presumed to be allergic to all penicillins and should avoid the entire group, unless they have been specifically evaluated for this problem.

Cephalosporins are structurally related to penicillin. People with a history of penicillin allergy have a small risk of also having an allergic reaction to a cephalosporin or carbapenem. Risk of cross-reactivity is low; however, it is prudent on the exam to avoid any beta-lactam with a stated allergy to another, unless there is no acceptable alternative agent. A notable exception is in acute otitis media (AOM); the American Academy of Pediatrics recommends use of 2nd or 3rd generation cephalosporins in patients with a non-severe penicillin allergy, due to toxicities and decreased efficacy of alternative AOM therapies in children.

Sulfa Drugs

Reactions are most commonly reported with sulfamethoxazole (in *Bactrim, Septra),* and the patient should avoid using sulfasalazine, sulfadiazine and sulfisoxazole. "Non-arylamine" sulfonamides (thiazide diuretics, loop diuretics, sulfonylureas, acetazolamide, zonisamide and celecoxib) contain warnings or contraindications, although they usually do not cross react with a sulfamethoxazole allergy. On the exam you should recognize the possible interaction. The risk of cross-reactivity with sulfamethoxazole, thiazides and loops is very low, and in clinical practice the reaction is usually not considered significant when these drugs are needed. Even so, the patient should be aware to watch for a possible reaction. Some other sulfa-type groups also have low risk of cross-reactivity. Sulfite or sulfate allergies do not cross react with sulfonamides. The rotigotine patch, orphenadrine injection, the *Rowasa* mesalamine enema, some dobutamine formulations and some eye drops contain sulfites.

Opioids

Opioid intolerance due to histamine release is common; however, true opioid allergy is uncommon. See Pain chapter for information on opioid allergy and treatment options.

Heparin

See Anticoagulation chapter for information on heparin-induced thrombocytopenia (HIT).

Biologics

Biologics (e.g., rituximab and others) can cause hypersensitivity reactions, among other ADRs. Desensitization is possible for some agents in patients who need a biologic but have had a prior poor reaction. See the following page for more information regarding desensitization processes.

NSAIDs

Reactions to NSAIDS, including aspirin, can either be a drug sensitivity or a true allergic reaction. A drug sensitivity can cause rhinitis, mild asthmatic-type reactions, or skin reactions. If a true allergy is present, the patient will experience urticaria, angioedema, and occasionally anaphylaxis. COX-2 selective NSAIDs may be used in practice, but on licensing exams it is prudent to avoid all NSAIDs.

Contrast Media

Contrast media (used in CT scans, etc.) can cause anaphylactoid reactions and delayed skin reactions. Systemic steroids and antihistamines are sometimes used to prevent reactions if contrast media is needed in a patient who has had a prior reaction.

Peanuts and Soy

It is important for the pharmacist to be aware if a patient has a peanut allergy. Peanuts and soy are in the same family and can have cross-reactivity. Soy is used in some medications. Parents of children with peanut allergies should be CPR-trained and an epinephrine auto-injector may need to be kept within close reach. Most likely, a reaction will be due to consuming peanuts or soy unknowingly in food products. Drugs to avoid with peanut or soy allergy: clevidipine *(Cleviprex)*, propofol *(Diprivan)*, progesterone in *Prometrium* capsules.

Eggs

If a patient has a true allergy to eggs, they cannot use clevidipine *(Cleviprex)*, propofol *(Diprivan)* or Yellow Fever vaccine (chicken eggs are used in vaccine production). For influenza vaccine (chicken eggs are used in vaccine production), ACIP states that people who have experienced only hives from consuming eggs can receive any indicated inactivated vaccine (the injection). Patients who have had more severe symptoms (such as wheezing, requiring epinephrine, hypotension, or cardiovascular changes) can receive any indicated inactivated vaccine. Administration should be supervised by a healthcare provider who is able to recognize and treat severe allergic reactions. *Flublok* is the only seasonal influenza vaccine made using recombinant techniques and does not use eggs at all in its production. *Flublok* is one option in patients with severe reactions to consuming eggs, but is not preferentially recommended by ACIP. A patient who has a severe reaction to an influenza vaccine, regardless of which ingredient is suspected, should not receive further doses of any formulation.

SKIN TESTING AND DESENSITIZATION

Penicillin Skin Testing

A penicillin allergy is the most common drug allergy in the U.S., reported in about 10% of the general population. A true penicillin allergy has been found to be present in only about 10% of those that are reported. Some patients report a penicillin "allergy" when their reaction was more properly categorized as an intolerance (e.g., nausea or diarrhea). In other cases, patients may have had a true allergic reaction to penicillin in the past, but over time, the antibodies can wane and the patient may be able to safely receive penicillins. Due to concerns of cross-reactivity with cephalosporins and carbapenems, a penicillin allergy can severely limit the selection of antibiotics available to treat infectious diseases. Patients who report a penicillin allergy have been shown to more often receive broad-spectrum antibiotics that cause more collateral damage, such as quinolones, and antibiotics with greater toxicity potential, such as vancomycin. The goal of penicillin skin testing is to identify patients who are at the greatest risk of a Type I hypersensitivity reaction if exposed to a systemic penicillin.

The penicillin skin test uses the components of penicillin that most often cause an immune (allergic) response. *Pre-Pen* (benzylpenicilloyl polylysine injection) contains the major determinants of penicillin allergy and is used with very dilute solutions of penicillin G. A step-wise skin test is done: a skin prick test followed by intradermal testing. A localized reaction around the *Pre-Pen* or penicillin G test site indicates a high risk of a reaction to systemic penicillin and the patient should not receive it. A patient with a negative skin test, (no reaction to the test solutions) can be considered to be at the same risk as a patient in the general population who does not report a penicillin allergy. Skin testing only predicts an IgE-mediated reaction. Regardless of skin test results, a patient should never be re-challenged with an agent that caused SJS or TEN.

Induction of Drug Tolerance (Desensitization)

In many cases when a drug allergy is present, an alternative medication can be chosen. When no acceptable alternative is available, induction of drug tolerance (often referred to as desensitization) may be recommended. For example, if a pregnant patient has syphylis and a penicillin allergy, the CDC recommends desensitization and penicillin treatment, rather than using second-line agents. Desensitization is a step-wise process that begins by administering a very small dose of the medication and then incrementally increasing the dose at regular time intervals up to the target dose. This modifies the patient's response to the medication and temporarily allows safe treatment. The desensitization procedure must take place in a medical setting where emergency care can be provided if a serious reaction occurs. Treatment with the agent must start immediately following the desensitization procedure and must not be interrupted. If doses are missed, the drug-free period allows the immune system to re-sensitize to the drug and serious hypersensitivity reactions (including anaphylaxis) could occur with subsequent doses. Induction of drug tolerance is a more accurate term than desensitization, because the process does not "cure" the patient of an allergy, and the reaction should not be removed from the patient's medical record. If the drug is required on a separate occasion, the process must be repeated. Desensitization protocols exist for a number of antimicrobial agents, some biologics and a few others medications (such as aspirin). Desensitization should never be attempted if an agent has previously caused SJS or TEN.

8

PHARMACOKINETICS

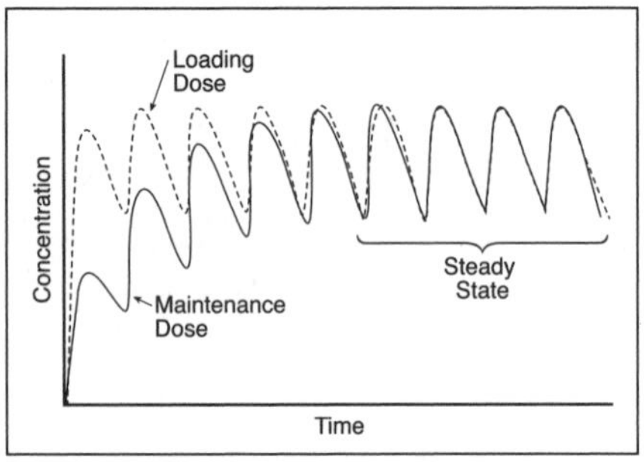

We gratefully acknowledge the assistance of Paul Beringer, PharmD, BCPS, FASHP, Associate Professor of Clinical Pharmacy and Clinical Medicine, University of Southern California, in preparing this chapter.

BACKGROUND

Pharmacokinetics is what the human body does to a drug and pharmacodynamics is what the drug does to the human body. Pharmacokinetics involves the study of the time course of drug absorption, distribution, metabolism and excretion. Mathematical relationships are used to describe these processes. Clinicians use pharmacokinetics to assess drug levels and optimize drug therapy. Pharmacodynamics refers to the relationship between the drug concentration at the site of action and both therapeutic and adverse effects.

ABSORPTION

When a drug is administered intravascularly, it directly enters the blood either intravenously or intra-arterially. The drug directly enters the systemic circulation (bloodstream) and absorption is not necessary. If a drug is administered extravascularly, drug absorption occurs as the drug moves from the site of administration to the systemic circulation. Some examples of extravascular administration include oral, sublingual, buccal, intramuscular, subcutaneous, transdermal, inhaled, topical, ocular, intraocular, intrathecal and rectal.

Absorption of oral drugs occurs via two primary processes: passive diffusion across the gut wall or active transport. Passive diffusion occurs when a high concentration of drug in the gut lumen moves across the gut wall to equalize drug concentration (or reach an equilibrium). Drug particles move through the gut wall into the portal vein, unassisted by cellular machinery. Active transport occurs when drugs are moved across the gut wall via transporter proteins that are normally used to absorb nutrients from food.

Extravascular Administration

Drugs administered extravascularly can be divided into two categories: drugs intended for local effects and drugs intended for systemic effects. Drugs intended for local effects are often applied topically where the drug effect is needed. Examples of this include eye drops for glaucoma (e.g., latanoprost), dermal preparations for psoriasis (e.g., coal tar preparations), and nasal sprays for allergies (e.g., fluticasone nasal spray). Topical administration of a drug can produce therapeutic effects while minimizing systemic toxicity due to lower systemic exposure, but some topical formulations are designed to deliver a systemic dose (e.g., *Duragesic* patch). The extent of topical absorption is affected by many factors, including presence of open wounds on the skin (increased absorption) and the amount of drug applied.

Drugs intended for systemic effects are generally administered to facilitate absorption to the circulatory system. Examples of drugs intended for systemic effects are oral tablets for seasonal allergies (e.g., loratadine), suppositories for fever (e.g., acetaminophen) and sublingual tablets for angina (nitroglycerin SL). Some percentage of a drug intended for systemic effect will move from the site of administration into the systemic circulation.

Dosage Form Dissolution and Drug Solubility

When an oral dosage form is ingested, it begins to dissolve in the gastrointestinal (GI) tract and the active ingredient is released from the dosage form (typically a compressed tablet or a capsule). This is called dissolution. Dissolution is a function of the inactive matrix that is used to formulate the drug dosage form. Many pharmaceutical companies utilize biocompatible polymers to develop controlled release drug products with a predefined dissolution process. This can provide less variability in drug concentrations and reduce the dosing frequency. Most immediate release formulations dissolve and get absorbed rapidly, but some can be destroyed in the gut (primarily by hydrolysis, or lysis with water) making them less available for absorption. Drug formulations have been developed with protective coatings to limit drug degradation in the acidic medium of the stomach but permit dissolution in the basic medium of the intestine. Examples of drugs with these protective coatings include enteric coated formulations such as *Dulcolax* and *Entocort EC*.

If a drug has poor absorption, one of the methods used to increase the dissolution rate is to reduce particle diameter, which increases surface area. Drugs with very small particle diameters are referred to as micronized, which means the diameter was measured in micrometers, but may now refer to even smaller particle sizes measured in nanometers. Drugs with poor absorption that are micronized include progesterone and fenofibrate formulations. Without micronization, these drugs would be poorly absorbed. The rate of dissolution is described by the Noyes-Whitney equation.

Following dissolution, the drug that is released from the dosage form can be dissolved in GI fluids. The rate and extent to which the drug dissolves depends on the drug's solubility. Poorly soluble drugs are generally lipophilic, or lipid-loving. Freely soluble drugs are generally hydrophilic, or water-loving. As a drug moves through the GI tract, only dissolved drug is absorbed into the bloodstream. Thus poorly soluble drugs generally have poor systemic absorption, and highly soluble drugs often have good systemic absorption.

Bioavailability

The extent to which a drug is absorbed into the systemic circulation is called bioavailability. Bioavailability is the percentage of drug absorbed from extravascular (e.g., oral) relative to intravascular administration (e.g., IV). It is affected by absorption, dissolution, route of administration and other factors. Bioavailability is reported as a percentage from 0 to 100%. A drug with good absorption characteristics will generally have high bioavailability (> 70%), while a drug with poor absorption will have low bioavailability (< 10%). Levofloxacin and linezolid have high bioavailability. With these two drugs, nearly 100% of the oral dose is absorbed, and the oral and IV doses are the same. In many hospitals, these drugs are automatically converted from IV to oral in the same dose under the hospital's therapeutic interchange or IV to PO protocol. Bisphosphonates, like ibandronate, have low oral bioavailability, so the oral dose (150 mg PO monthly) must be much higher than the IV dose (3 mg IV every 3 months) to produce the therapeutic effect.

Bioavailability can be calculated using the area under the plasma concentration time curve, or AUC. The AUC represents the total exposure of drug following administration.

Absolute bioavailability, represented by F, is calculated using the following equation:

$$F(\%) = 100 \times \frac{AUC_{extravascular}}{AUC_{intravenous}} \times \frac{Dose_{intravenous}}{Dose_{extravascular}}$$

---

1. A pharmacokinetic study of an investigational drug was conducted in healthy volunteers. Following an IV bolus dose of 15 mg, the AUC was determined to be 4.2 $^{mg \times hr}/_{L}$. Subjects were later given an oral dose of 50 mg and the AUC was determined to be 8 $^{mg \times hr}/_{L}$. Calculate the absolute bioavailability of the investigational drug. Round to the nearest whole number.

$$F(\%) = 100 \times \frac{\frac{8\ mg \times hr}{L}}{\frac{4.2\ mg \times hr}{L}} \times \frac{15\ mg}{50\ mg} = 57\%$$

Different dosage forms of the same drug (e.g., tablet vs solution) may have different bioavailabilities. The formula below can be used to calculate an equivalent dose of a drug when the dosage form is changed:

$$\text{Dose of New Dosage Form} = \frac{\text{Amount Absorbed from Current Dosage Form}}{\text{F of New Dosage Form}}$$

DISTRIBUTION

Distribution is the process by which drug molecules move from the systemic circulation to the various tissues and organs of the body. Distribution occurs for intravascular and extravascular routes of administration and depends on the physical and chemical properties of the drug molecule and interactions with membranes and tissues throughout the body. In general, drugs distribute throughout the body based on the drug's lipophilicity, molecular weight, solubility, ionization status and the extent of protein binding. Factors that favor passage across membranes and greater drug distribution to the tissues include high lipophilicity, low molecular weight, unionized status and low protein binding. Human plasma contains many proteins, and albumin is the primary protein responsible for drug binding. If a drug is highly protein-bound (> 90%) and serum albumin is low (< 3.5 g/dL), then a higher percentage of the drug will be in the unbound form. Only the unbound (free) form can interact with receptors, exert therapeutic or toxic effects and be cleared from the body.

Though the unbound form of the drug is responsible for the therapeutic effect, many drug assays cannot differentiate between bound and unbound (active) drug. When assessing levels of highly protein bound compounds (e.g., phenytoin, calcium), a patient with low serum albumin will have more of the unbound (active) compound in the serum, and may experience therapeutic or even adverse effects at what appears to be a normal or subtherapeutic drug level. This issue can be overcome by obtaining a "free" phenytoin level or ionized calcium level. Free phenytoin and ionized calcium only measure the unbound portion, so no adjustment is required for hypoalbuminemia. Otherwise, adjustment of the total level is required. The adjustment formulas allow us to determine what the concentration would be if albumin was normal. With hypoalbuminemia, the corrected level will be higher than the total level reported by the lab. The formulas to adjust these levels for low albumin are in the Calculations chapter (calcium) and Epilepsy/Seizures chapter (phenytoin).

2. A pharmacist receives a call from a provider asking for assistance with two patients in the clinic. Both patients have a seizure disorder and are taking phenytoin. Patient A is seizure free, but is experiencing symptoms of toxicity. Patient B has a higher phenytoin level and is doing fine. Both patients have normal renal function. Which of the following statements are true of this scenario? (Select ALL that apply.)

LAB	REFERENCE RANGE	PATIENT A	PATIENT B
Phenytoin level (total)	10-20 mcg/mL	14.3	17.8
Albumin	3.5-5 g/dL	2.1	4.2

a. Patient B's corrected phenytoin level will be lower than the total level reported.
b. Patient A's corrected phenytoin level will be lower than the total level reported.
c. Patient A's corrected phenytoin level will be higher than the total level reported.
d. Patient A has a greater percentage of bound phenytoin.
e. Patient A has a greater percentage of unbound phenytoin.

The correct answers are (c and e). The corrected phenytoin level for Patient A (using the formula found in the Epilepsy/Seizures chapter) is 27.5 mcg/mL. Increased unbound phenytoin is contributing to the patient's side effects.

Volume of Distribution

The volume of distribution (V or Vd) is how large an area in the patient's body the drug has distributed into, and is based on the properties of that drug (discussed previously). The volume of distribution relates the amount of drug in the body to the concentration of drug measured in plasma (or serum). When a dose of drug is administered (e.g., 1,000 mg), a concentration (e.g., 12 mcg/mL) from a sample of biological fluid can be measured and reported. To convert between amounts and concentrations, a volume is needed. The equation for volume of distribution is:

SUBSCRIPTS IN FORMULAS

Vd can be written as V_d and ke can be written as k_e. In this chapter the subscripts are not used for Vd and ke for simplicity.

$$Vd = \frac{\text{Amount of drug in body}}{\text{Concentration of drug in plasma}}$$

The Vd is determined from the amount of drug in the body after the dose has been given.

---

3. A 500 mg dose of gentamicin is administered to a patient, and a blood sample is drawn. The concentration of gentamicin is measured as 25 mcg/mL (which is the same as 25 mg/L). What is the volume of distribution of gentamicin in this patient?

$$Vd = \frac{500 \text{ mg}}{25 \text{ mg/L}} = 20 \text{ L}$$

Vd is a theoretical value, which is why it is sometimes called the "apparent" volume of distribution. Vd is not an exact physical volume that has been measured, but is a helpful parameter because it is used to make inferences regarding how widely a drug distributes throughout the body. Drugs with a small Vd tend to remain in the intravascular space (blood compartment) and those with a very large Vd distribute to most tissues in the body.

METABOLISM

Metabolism is the process by which a drug is converted from its original chemical structure into other forms to facilitate elimination from the body. The original chemical form is called the parent drug and the additional forms are called metabolites. Metabolism can occur throughout the body; however, the gut and liver are primary sites for drug metabolism due to high levels of metabolic enzymes in these tissues.

Enzyme metabolism involves Phase I reactions (oxidation, reduction and hydrolysis), followed by Phase II (conjugation) reactions. Phase I reactions, which can terminate the activity of the drug or convert a prodrug into its active form, provide a reactive functional group on the compound that permits the drug to be attacked by Phase II enzymes. For example, breaking carbon bonds or adding a hydroxyl group to a drug will make the drug more hydrophilic – this means more of the drug will stay in the blood, the blood then passes through the kidneys, and the drug can be renally excreted. Glucuronidation and other Phase II reactions create compounds that are more readily excreted in the urine and bile. Cytochrome P450 (CYP450) enzymes, located mainly in the liver and intestines, metabolize the majority of drugs. Metabolism is described in detail in the Drug Interactions chapter.

Blood from the gut travels to the liver before it reaches the rest of the body. Some drugs are partially or extensively metabolized by the liver before they reach the systemic circulation. This is called first-pass metabolism. First-pass metabolism reduces the bioavailability of an oral formulation. For a drug with extensive first-pass metabolism (e.g., propranolol), the IV dose will be much lower than the equivalent oral dose even if the oral formulation is well absorbed.

EXCRETION

Excretion is the process of irreversible removal of drugs from the body. Excretion can occur through the kidney (urine), liver (bile), gut (feces), lungs (exhaled air) and skin (sweat). The primary route of excretion for most drugs is the kidney (renal excretion). P-glycoprotein (P-gp) efflux pumps play a role in absorption and excretion of many drugs. Drugs affected by P-gp are discussed in the Drug Interactions chapter. Renal excretion is described in detail in the Renal Disease and Calculations chapters.

Clearance and Area Under the Curve

Clearance (Cl) describes the rate of drug removal in a certain volume of plasma over a certain amount of time. Since the liver and kidneys clear most of the drug (and these organs do not usually speed up or slow down), most drug elimination occurs at a steady rate (called the rate of elimination). This is true of drugs that follow first-order kinetics (discussed later in the chapter). The term clearance is used to describe the efficiency of drug removal from the body. Clearance is generally described by the following equation:

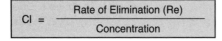

$$Cl = \frac{\text{Rate of Elimination (Re)}}{\text{Concentration}}$$

4. A dose of gentamicin is given to a patient and urine is collected from the patient for 4 hours after drug administration. It is determined that 300 mg of gentamicin was eliminated during that time period, and the measured plasma concentration at the midpoint of the collection was 12.5 mg/L. Calculate the patient's gentamicin clearance.

$$Cl = \frac{300 \text{ mg of gentamicin } / \text{ 4 hours}}{12.5 \text{ mg/L}} = 6 \text{ L/hr}$$

or

$$Cl = \frac{300 \text{ mg of gentamicin}}{4 \text{ hours}} \times \frac{L}{12.5 \text{ mg}} = 6 \text{ L/hr}$$

The rate of elimination (Re) has units of mass per time (e.g., mg/hr), and drug concentration has units of amount per volume (e.g., mg/L); units of mass (mg) cancel out and clearance has units of volume per time (e.g., L/hr). Because the rate of elimination is difficult to assess clinically, another method is used to calculate the clearance of a drug from the body:

$$F \times Dose = Cl \times AUC$$

The area under the curve (AUC) is the most reliable measurement of a drug's bioavailability because it directly represents the amount of the drug that has reached the systemic circulation. The clearance for extravascular administration is calculated with this formula:

$$Cl = \frac{F \times Dose}{AUC}$$

Following IV administration, F = 1, which can be inserted into the previous equation to determine clearance for a drug given intravenously:

$$Cl = \frac{Dose}{AUC}$$

---

5. A patient is currently receiving 400 mg of gentamicin IV once daily and, based on measured serum concentrations, the AUC is determined to be 80 $^{mg \times hr}/_{L}$. Calculate the patient's gentamicin clearance.

$$Cl = \frac{400 \text{ mg}}{\frac{80 \text{ mg} \times \text{hr}}{L}} = 5 \text{ L/hr}$$

ZERO-ORDER AND FIRST-ORDER PHARMACOKINETICS

Most drugs follow first-order elimination or "first-order kinetics", where a constant percent of drug is removed per unit of time. For example, a 325 mg dose of acetaminophen is eliminated at the same rate as a 650 mg dose. With zero-order elimination, a constant amount of drug (mg) is removed per unit of time no matter how much drug is in the body. The following table provides an example of zero-order and first-order elimination of a 2 gram dose of a drug.

Zero-Order vs First-Order Pharmacokinetics

	ZERO-ORDER			FIRST-ORDER		
Hour	Amount of Drug (mg)	Percent Removed in Previous Hour	Amount (mg) Removed in Previous Hour	Amount of Drug (mg)	Percent Removed in Previous Hour	Amount (mg) Removed in Previous Hour
0	2,000			2,000		
1	1,700	15	300	1,600	20	400
2	1,400	17.65	300	1,280	20	320
3	1,100	21.43	300	1,024	20	256

Michaelis-Menten Kinetics

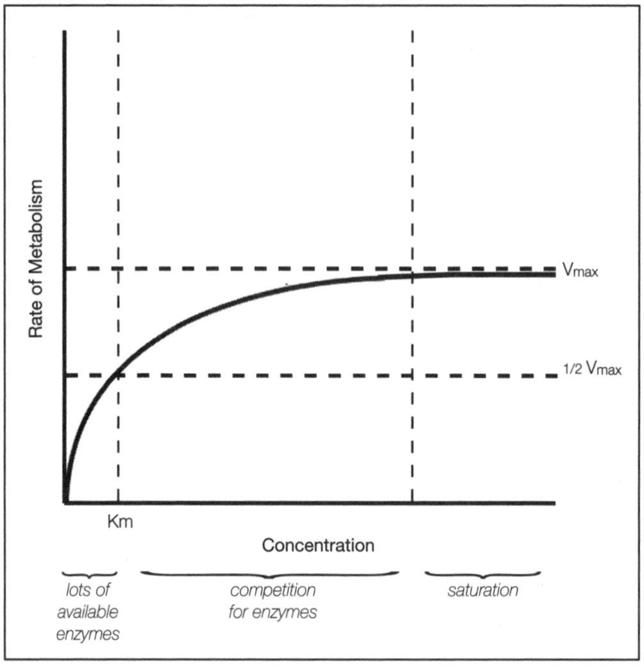

Michaelis-Menten kinetics, or saturable kinetics, begin as first-order, but at higher concentrations the rate of metabolism approaches maximum capacity. At this point, any increase in dose leads to a disproportionate increase in drug concentration at steady state. The maximum rate of metabolism is defined as the Vmax (see figure). The concentration at which the rate of metabolism is half maximal is defined as the Michaelis-Menten constant (Km). At concentrations less than the Km, the rate of metabolism is first-order. At concentrations above the Km, the rate of metabolism becomes mixed (first-order and zero order) and at even higher concentrations relative to the Km, the rate of metabolism becomes zero order (e.g., Vmax). Phenytoin, theophylline and voriconazole have this type of saturable kinetics. Phenytoin experiences saturable kinetics even at drug concentrations within the accepted therapeutic range. Because of this, phenytoin dose adjustments should be made in small increments (30 - 50 mg) when the serum concentration is > 7 mg/L.

---

6. A patient has been using phenytoin 100 mg three times daily. The phenytoin level was drawn and found to be 8.8 mcg/mL (reference range 10 - 20 mcg/mL). The prescriber doubled the dose to 200 mg three times daily. The patient started to slur her words, felt fatigued and returned to the clinic. The level was repeated and found to be 23.7 mcg/mL. Which of the following statements is accurate regarding the most likely reason for the change in phenytoin level?

a. Phenytoin half-life is reduced at higher doses.
b. Phenytoin volume of distribution increases at higher doses.
c. The patient's serum albumin level likely increased.
d. Phenytoin bioavailability can decrease at higher doses.
e. Phenytoin metabolism can become saturated at higher doses.

The correct answer is (e). The most likely explanation for the increase in phenytoin level is that when the dose was doubled, the metabolism became partially or completely saturated, and the steady-state level increased dramatically.

ELIMINATION RATE CONSTANT

The elimination rate constant (ke) is the fraction of the drug that is eliminated (cleared) per unit of time. It is calculated from the Vd and the clearance:

$$ke = \frac{Cl}{Vd}$$

---

7. A drug has the following pharmacokinetic parameters: Vd = 50 liters and Cl = 5,000 mL/hour. Calculate the elimination rate constant of the drug.

$$ke = \frac{5\ L/hr}{50\ L} = 0.1\ hr^{-1}$$

Be certain that the values have been converted to units that will properly cancel out in the equation. The ke is 0.1 hr^{-1} (meaning that 10% of the drug remaining is cleared per hour).

HALF-LIFE AND STEADY STATE

The time required for the drug concentration (and drug amount) to decrease by 50% is called the elimination half-life ($t_{½}$). For example, it takes 5 hours for theophylline concentrations to fall from 16 to 8 mg/L. Thus the half-life of theophylline is 5 hours. It would take 5 more hours for the drug concentration to fall from 8 mg/L to 4 mg/L. It is important to note that the half-life is independent of the drug concentration (for drugs exhibiting first-order kinetics).

Half-life is more clinically meaningful than ke. The half-life of a drug can be calculated from the ke:

$$t_{½} = \frac{0.693}{ke}$$

The half-life of a drug can be used to calculate the time required for drug washout or the time required to achieve steady-state (refer to table). The most clinically useful information is obtained from drug levels collected at steady state. When a fixed dose is administered at regular intervals, the drug accumulates until it reaches steady state where the rate of drug intake equals the rate of drug elimination. The time required to reach steady state depends on the elimination half-life of the drug. If the drug follows first-order kinetics (described previously) in a one-compartment distribution model (the drug is rapidly and evenly distributed throughout the body) and if a loading dose has not been given, it takes ~5 half-lives to reach steady state. Similarly, 5 half-lives are required to eliminate more than 95% of the drug if no additional doses are given.

# OF HALF-LIVES	ELIMINATION % OF DRUG REMAINING IN THE BODY	ACCUMULATION % OF STEADY-STATE ACHIEVED
1	50	50
2	25	75
3	12.5	87.5
4	6.25	93.8
5	3.13	96.9

8. Tetracycline has a clearance of 7.014 L/hr and a volume of distribution of 105 L. Calculate the half-life of tetracycline (round to the nearest tenth) and the time required for elimination of greater than 95% of the drug from the body.

$$ke = \frac{Cl}{Vd} = \frac{7.014 \text{ L/hr}}{105 \text{ L}} = 0.0668 \text{ hr}^{-1}$$

$$t_{1/2} = \frac{0.693}{ke} = \frac{0.693}{0.0668 \text{ hr}^{-1}} = 10.4 \text{ hours}$$

The time required is 10.4 hours x 5 half-lives = 52 hours.

---

9. A patient receives 200 mg of a drug with a half-life of 5 hours. How much of the drug still remains in the patient after 10 hours?

- 10 hours = 2 half-lives
- 50 mg of drug remains after 10 hours

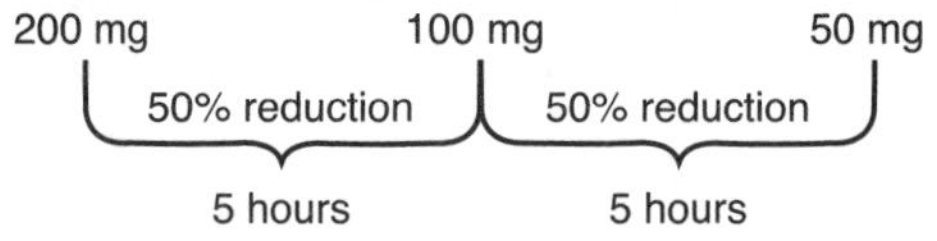

---

10. The serum concentration of Drug A over time is plotted in the figure. What is the half-life of Drug A?

Choose two times (in hours) where the drug concentration has decreased by half to find the half-life.

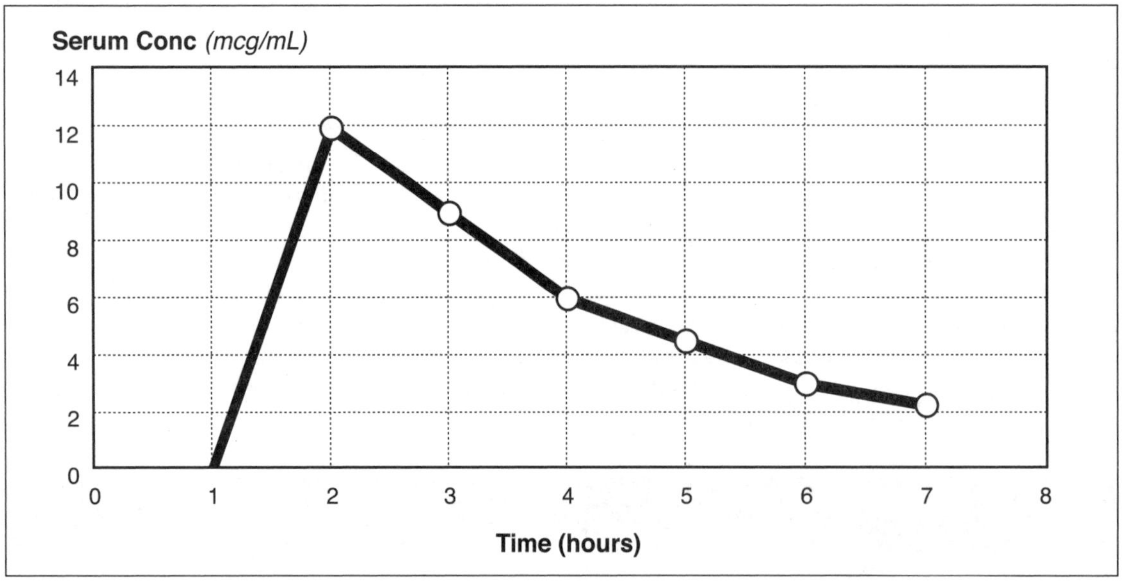

- At 2 hours the concentration is 12 mcg/mL and at 4 hours the concentration is 6 mcg/mL.
- It takes 2 hours for the concentration to decrease by 50%, so the half-life is 2 hours.

LOADING DOSE

Administration of a loading dose may be necessary to rapidly achieve therapeutic concentrations of a drug. When the half-life of a drug is long relative to the frequency of administration, it will take several doses before steady state is achieved.

---

11. A patient will be started on daily oral digoxin for management of atrial fibrillation. The following pharmacokinetic parameters for oral digoxin are known: F = 0.6, Vd = 500 L and Cl = 120 L/day. When would steady state be reached? Round to the nearest day.

$$ke = \frac{Cl}{Vd} = \frac{120\ L/day}{500\ L} = 0.24\ days^{-1}$$

$$t_{1/2} = \frac{0.693}{ke} = \frac{0.693}{0.24\ days^{-1}} = \sim 2.89\ days$$

Steady Sate = 5 half-lives x 2.89 days = ~14 days

Therefore, it is beneficial to administer a loading dose to achieve the targeted levels more quickly in this case. The loading dose can be determined with the following equation:

$$\text{Loading Dose} = \frac{\text{Desired Concentration x Vd}}{F}$$

---

12. Using the pharmacokinetic parameters provided in the previous question, what oral loading dose of digoxin is appropriate to rapidly achieve a peak concentration of 1.5 mcg/L?

$$\text{Loading Dose} = \frac{\text{Desired Concentration x Vd}}{F} = \frac{1.5\ mcg/L \times 500\ L}{0.6} = 1{,}250\ mcg \text{ or } 1.25\ mg$$

Questions

1. A patient is currently receiving ciprofloxacin 400 mg IV Q12H. The pharmacist recommends a conversion to oral therapy in preparation for hospital discharge. Ciprofloxacin tablets are available in 250, 500 and 750 mg strengths. If the bioavailability of ciprofloxacin is 70%, which of the following is the closest equivalent oral dose?

   a. 250 mg PO once daily
   b. 250 mg PO BID
   c. 500 mg PO BID
   d. 750 mg PO BID
   e. 250 mg PO Q8H

2. A patient will be started on gentamicin for an infection. The patient weighs 176 pounds and the volume of distribution of gentamicin is 0.25 L/kg. What is an appropriate IV loading dose to achieve a peak concentration of 10 mcg/mL?

   a. 2.5 mg IV
   b. 200 mg IV
   c. 440 mg IV
   d. 2,000 mg IV
   e. 2,500 mg IV

3. The AUC of an IV drug is 600 $^{mg \times hr}/_{L}$. When the same dose is given orally, the AUC is 240 $^{mg \times hr}/_{L}$. What is the drug's oral bioavailability?

   a. 2.5%
   b. 4%
   c. 40%
   d. 50%
   e. 250%

4. A patient is to be initiated on intravenous vancomycin for treatment of a bloodstream infection. Based on the patient's renal function the estimated clearance is 5 L/hr. What is an appropriate dose to achieve a 24 hour AUC of 400 $^{mg \times hr}/_{L}$?

   a. 1 gram IV Q24H
   b. 2 grams IV Q12H
   c. 1 gram IV Q8H
   d. 500 mg IV Q12H
   e. 1 gram IV Q12H

5. A patient has been receiving phenytoin 300 mg PO QHS for one month for treatment of a seizure disorder. A plasma sample is obtained and measures 10 mg/L. If the goal is to achieve a steady-state concentration of 15 mg/L, which recommendation is most appropriate?

   a. Increase dose to 450 mg PO QHS.
   b. Increase dose to 330 mg PO QHS.
   c. Increase dose to 500 mg PO QHS.
   d. Decrease dose to 250 mg PO QHS.
   e. Maintain current dose.

6. A patient is currently receiving an intravenous infusion of theophylline at a rate of 40 mg/hr. The patient begins to experience nausea/vomiting and agitation and the decision is made to stop the infusion. If the estimated elimination rate constant is 0.17 hr^{-1}, approximately how long will it take for the medication to be completely removed (> 95%) from the body?

   a. 4 hours
   b. 7 hours
   c. 20 hours
   d. 48 hours
   e. 235 hours

Answers

1-c, 2-b, 3-c, 4-e, 5-b, 6-c

9

DRUG INTERACTIONS

BACKGROUND

Drug effects (therapeutic or adverse) result from the concentration present at the site of action. The principles of absorption, distribution, metabolism and excretion (ADME) determine what concentration is present and where. Two of the primary organs involved in the processes of metabolism and excretion are the liver and the kidneys. The effects of the cytochrome P450 (CYP450) enzyme system on drug metabolism have been extensively studied; however, the role of other processes on drug exposure must also be considered. More information is becoming available on transporter interactions, which include P-glycoprotein (P-gp), as well as others that will be discussed in this chapter.

Drug interactions can lead to changes in the systemic exposure due to alterations in metabolism and excretion. This can result in loss of efficacy, adverse drug reactions or toxicity. Elimination of a drug or its metabolites (breakdown products) occurs either by metabolism, usually by the liver or intestinal lining, or by excretion, usually by the kidneys and liver. Drug interactions can be complex and may involve more than one mechanism of interaction. Examples include:

- Induction and inhibition of the same enzyme or transporter (often dose-dependent)
- Additive effects when multiple inhibitors or inducers are used concurrently
- Use of inhibitors in patients with liver or kidney impairment, which can result in excessive levels

When these are considered, along with the genetic variation in enzyme activity among patients, it is clear that understanding the impact of drug interactions is vital in order to safely and effectively use medications and while avoiding excessive risk of potentially lethal effects.

CYTOCHROME P450 ENZYMES

Cytochrome P450 (CYP450) enzymes are found in many cells, but are primarily located in the liver and intestines. The majority of medications (75%) are metabolized by CYP450 enzymes, and of these, greater than 80% are metabolized by CYP450 3A4 alone, or 3A4 and other enzymes.

The CYP450 enzymes include many types, but about a dozen of them are involved in the metabolism of most drugs. This discussion begins with the most common isoenzymes that are well known to pharmacists. Enzyme metabolism involves Phase I reactions (oxidation, reduction and hydrolysis), followed by Phase II, which normally terminates the activity of the drug. Phase I provides a reactive functional group on the compound that permits the drug to be attacked by the Phase II enzymes. Drugs are considered by the body to be a foreign substance, similar to a toxin, to be eliminated. Elimination occurs through a pump that pushes the drug back into the gut (for elimination in the feces via the P-gp efflux pumps (efflux means "to flow out"), or in the bile (which eliminates through the gallbladder) or through the kidney (in the urine). For most drugs to be excreted renally, they must be first converted (metabolized) into a more hydrophilic form, which occurs by the process of enzyme metabolism, described here.

All enzymes in the body work using an enzyme-substrate system. The enzyme is a protein that performs some action. The substrate is a chemical that is acted upon. Drug molecules, foods, and toxins are substrates for CYP enzymes. In the following figure, warfarin (the substrate) is joined with the CYP 2C9 enzyme in a manner similar to puzzle pieces. The enzyme converts the warfarin into an inactive metabolite. This is generally the case; however, sometimes the conversion produces a toxic metabolite or an active or beneficial metabolite. The metabolite is generally more water-soluble than the parent compound, which facilitates excretion (exit from the body) via filtration through the kidneys. Warfarin causes an increase in the INR (a pharmacologic action), but warfarin metabolites do not. Thus each time warfarin molecules pass through the liver, some are captured by the CYP 2C9 enzyme and converted into inactive metabolites, leaving less warfarin to elicit its beneficial effects of increasing the INR. Much of this reaction occurs during the "first pass" when the drug (substrate) passes through the gut wall and liver prior to reaching the systemic circulation.

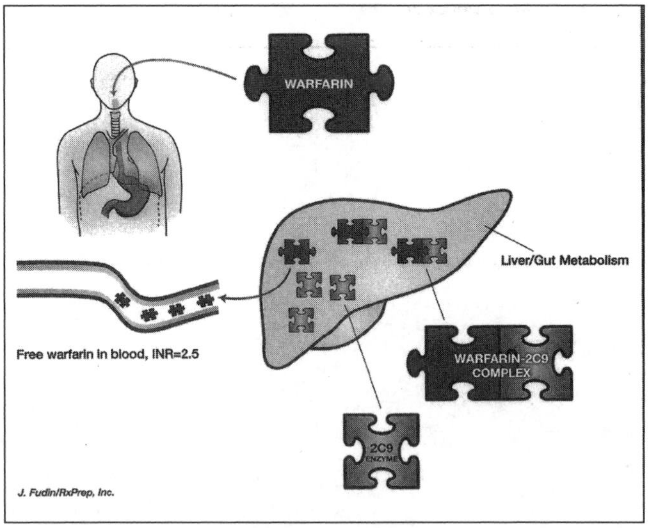

FDA DEFINITIONS

TERM	INDUCERS	INHIBITORS
Strong	≥ 80% ↓ in AUC	≥ 5-fold ↑ in AUC
Moderate	50-80% ↓ in AUC	≥ 2 but < 5-fold ↑ in AUC
Weak	20-50% ↓ in AUC	≥ 1.25 but < 2-fold ↑ in AUC

CYP Inducers

Inducers are compounds (many are drugs) that either increase the production of the enzyme (by increasing the expression of the gene sequence that codes for the enzyme), or, increase the activity of the enzyme. The net effect of inducers is to increase the degree of drug metabolism, which results in lower blood levels of the substrate. In the following figure, rifampin has caused induction of the enzyme 2C9, which causes more of the enzyme to be present, resulting in more drug metabolism. The warfarin metabolism increases, less warfarin is available systemically, and the INR will decrease. Rifampin is used as an example here because it is one of the strongest inducers and induces many enzymes [1A2, 2C8, 2C9, 2C19, 3A4 and the P-glycoprotein (P-gp) pump]. If

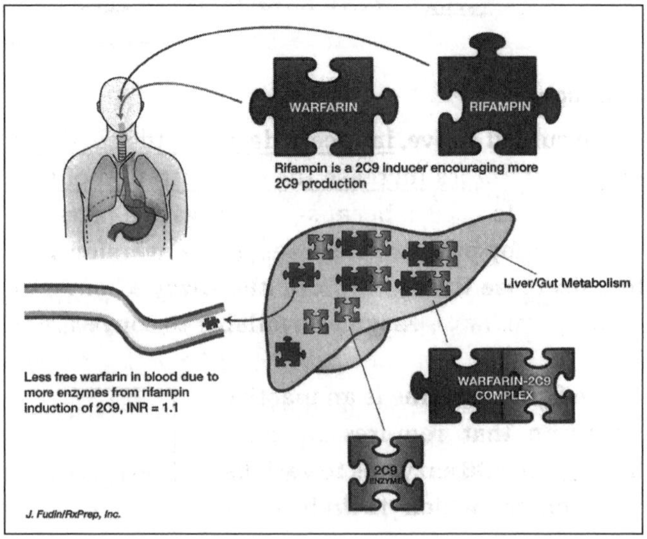

rifampin is given to a patient on warfarin the warfarin dose will need to be increased between 100-300% to keep the INR therapeutic.

With prodrugs, the inducer can increase an enzyme that is responsible for converting the substrate into a more active form (instead of a less active or inactive form). Prodrug conversion is technically referred to as bioactivation. Giving an inducer with a prodrug will result in more active drug and increased drug effects.

CYP Inhibitors

Inhibitors are compounds (many are drugs) that inhibit the activity of the enzyme. Enzyme inhibition results in decreased drug metabolism. The drug serum level (and therapeutic effect) will increase. This can result in drug toxicity. In the next figure, amiodarone, a 2C9 inhibitor is given to a patient using warfarin. Amiodarone inhibits the metabolism of warfarin. The warfarin level in the serum will increase and there will be a corresponding increase in the INR. This interaction would cause a supratherapeutic INR with risk of bleeding. This reaction is well known to pharmacists; when amiodarone is given to a patient who has been using warfarin (commonly combined) the reaction is anticipated and the warfarin dose is decreased 30-50%. If they are started concurrently, a lower dose of warfarin will be given.

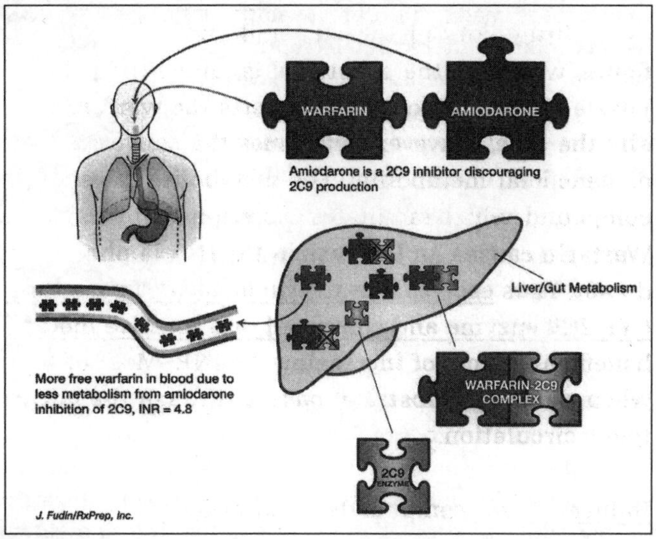

In the case of a prodrug, an inhibitor of the enzyme involved in bioactivation would block the production of the active form of the drug. Inhibitors decrease the levels of the prodrug's active form.

As a practical consideration, discontinuation of an inhibitor or inducer can have dangerous consequences. If a patient is using methadone and the dose has been increased to compensate for induction and the inducer is stopped, the methadone level could become lethal. In the warfarin and rifampin example, if the rifampin is stopped the warfarin levels and INR would become supratherapeutic, and potentially very dangerous.

Prodrugs

Prodrugs are taken by the patient in an inactive form and are converted by bioactivation (enzyme conversion) into the active form. For this reason, the effects of enzyme inhibitors and inducers on prodrugs are opposite. Inhibitors decrease enzyme available for bioactivation resulting in decreased concentrations of active drug. Inducers cause an increase in bioactivation enzymes and result increased levels of active drug.

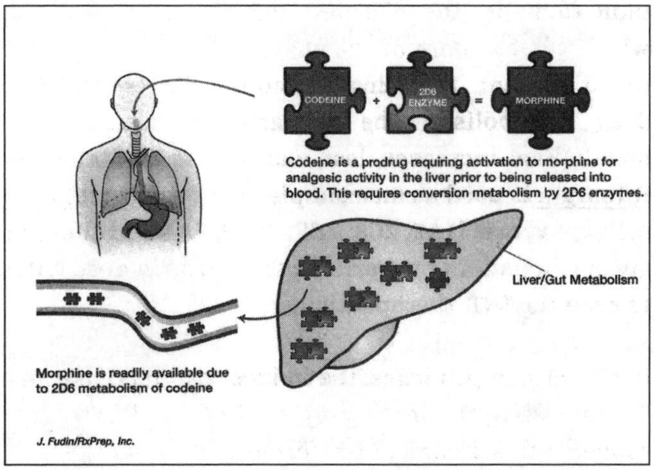

In the figure, codeine is an inactive substrate that requires metabolism by the 2D6 enzymes to various metabolites, which include morphine. Much of the analgesic efficacy of codeine is due to the morphine metabolite. When codeine is dispensed to a patient who has not had a pharmacogenomic analysis there is no way to predict how a dose will affect the patient. The 2D6 enzyme is not inducible but is subject to a wide variability in 2D6 expression due primarily to ethnic variations in gene expression. Patients could be 2D6 ultrarapid metabolizers (UM), producing a lot of the enzyme, extensive metabolizers (EM), producing a lot of the enzyme but less than the UMs, intermediate metabolizers (IM) or poor metabolizers (PM). A PM is a person with low or no 2D6 activity (~10% of patients overall, but varies by race). Gene expression varies widely even within ethnic groups. About 25% of drugs go through the 2D6 system, including many pain and psychiatric drugs. These two conditions, more than most others, typically involve multiple medications given concurrently for the same condition, which makes drug interaction analysis essential. Although diminished analgesic efficacy is a clinical concern, tragedies have occurred repeatedly because of the use of codeine in an UM, resulting in death from morphine overdose. In one case, a breastfeeding mother had taken codeine and (unknown to anyone) she was an UM of 2D6. Morphine passes readily into breast milk and the infant suffered fatal respiratory depression. Several children have received morphine overdoses after receiving codeine for post-tonsillectomy pain, which led to a safety alert in 2016.

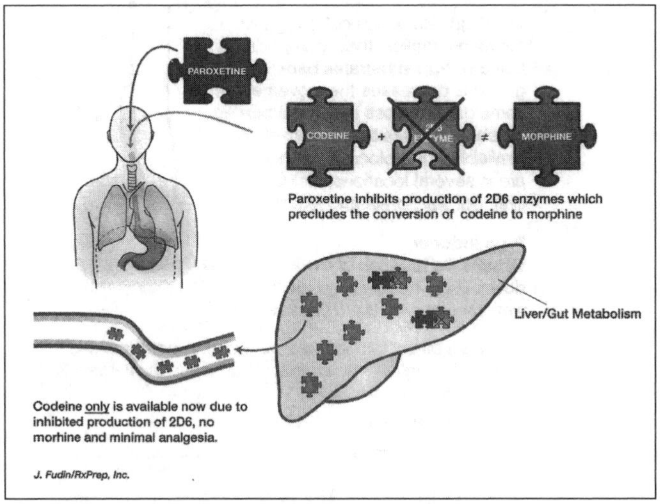
PAROXETINE
CODEINE
MORPHINE
Paroxetine inhibits production of 2D6 enzymes which precludes the conversion of codeine to morphine
Liver/Gut Metabolism
Codeine only is available now due to inhibited production of 2D6, no morhine and minimal analgesia.
J. Fudin/RxPrep, Inc.

In this figure the 2D6 inhibitor paroxetine blocks the conversion of codeine to morphine, resulting in suboptimal analgesia.

Note that not all prodrugs involve CYP enzymes. For example, phenytoin was formulated as the prodrug fosphenytoin to improve the solubility. Phenytoin has tolerability issues; it is irritating to the vein, which affects the ability to administer it quickly in an emergency situation like status epilepticus. Fosphenytoin is hydrolyzed by alkaline phosphatases in the liver and gut, and then spontaneously breaks down into the active entity: phenytoin. In this case, the amount of active drug would not be affected by CYP inducers or inhibitors.

"Lag" Time for Inhibition and Induction

Inhibition of an enzyme is fast; effects are seen within a few days and will end quickly when the inhibitor is discontinued. Induction most often requires additional enzyme production, which takes time. The full effect may not be present for up to two weeks. When the inducer is stopped it could take 2-4 weeks for the induction to disappear completely; the excess enzymes will degrade based on their half-lives.

Cytochrome P450 Substrates, Inducers and Inhibitors (Partial List)

The list of clinically significant drug interactions involving CYP450 (and other enzymes and transporters) is extensive. While memorizing every interaction is likely out of reach, there are some helpful ways to think about drug interactions that might help identify pertinent interactions (see Study Tip).

STUDY TIP: IDENTIFYING SIGNIFICANT DRUG INTERACTIONS

Group similar drugs (see the following table)

- When you see certain drugs or drug classes, it should prompt you to assess for drug interactions
- Think of which classes have similar properties of inhibition (e.g., azole antifungals) or induction (e.g., many anticonvulsants)

Know the consequences

- Think of what would occur if drug concentrations decreased (reduced efficacy of vital drugs, such as HIV meds) or increased (dose-related side effects such as sedation)
- Use extra caution with narrow therapeutic index drugs, since small changes in drug concentrations can impact efficacy or toxicity potential

CYP	SUBSTRATES	INDUCERS	INHIBITORS
3A4	**Analgesics** (buprenorphine, diclofenac, fentanyl, hydrocodone, meloxicam, methadone, oxycodone, tramadol); **Anticoagulants** (apixaban, rivaroxaban, R-warfarin); **Antidiabetic drugs** (nateglinide, pioglitazone, repaglinide, saxagliptin, sitagliptin); **Antiplatelet drugs** (cilostazol, prasugrel, ticagrelor); **Cardiovascular drugs** (amiodarone, diltiazem, eplerenone, ivabradine, nifedipine, quinidine, ranolazine, tolvaptan, verapamil); **Immunosuppressants** (cyclosporine, tacrolimus, sirolimus); **Statins** (atorvastatin, lovastatin, simvastatin); **Key HIV drugs** (atazanavir, efavirenz, ritonavir, tipranavir); **PDE-5 inhibitors** (avanafil, sildenafil, tadalafil, vardenafil); **Others** (alfuzosin, aprepitant, aripiprazole, benzodiazepines, brexpiprazole, buspirone, carbamazepine, citalopram, clarithromycin, colchicine, dapsone, dutasteride, erythromycin, escitalopram, ethinyl estradiol, felbamate, haloperidol, ketoconazole, levonorgestrel, mirtazapine, modafinil, ondansetron, paritaprevir, progesterone, quetiapine, simeprevir, tamoxifen, trazodone, venlafaxine, zolpidem)	carbamazepine, oxcarbazepine, phenytoin, phenobarbital, primidone, rifabutin, rifampin, rifapentine, simeprevir, smoking, St. John's wort	**Anti-infectives** (clarithromycin, erythromycin, fluconazole, isoniazid, itraconazole, ketoconazole, posaconazole, voriconazole); **Cardiovascular drugs** (amiodarone, diltiazem, dronedarone, quinidine, ranolazine, verapamil); **Key HIV drugs** (atazanavir, cobicistat, efavirenz, darunavir, ritonavir); **Other HIV drugs** (delavirdine, efavirenz, fosamprenavir, indinavir, nelfinavir, nevirapine, saquinavir); **Others** (aprepitant, bosentan, cimetidine, cyclosporine, fluvoxamine, grapefruit juice, haloperidol, nefazodone, sertraline)
1A2	alosetron, aprepitant, clozapine, cyclobenzaprine, duloxetine, ethinyl estradiol, methadone, mirtazapine, olanzapine, ondansetron, pimozide, propranolol, rasagiline, ropinirole, theophylline, R-warfarin	carbamazepine, phenobarbital, phenytoin, primidone, rifampin, ritonavir, smoking, St. John's wort	atazanavir, cimetidine, ciprofloxacin, fluvoxamine, zileuton
2C8	amiodarone, dasabuvir, pioglitazone, repaglinide, rosiglitazone	phenytoin, rifampin	amiodarone, atazanavir, clopidogrel, gemfibrozil, ketoconazole, trimethoprim/ sulfamethoxazole, ritonavir
2C9	alosetron, carvedilol, celecoxib, diazepam, diclofenac, fluvastatin, glyburide, glipizide, glimepiride, meloxicam, netaglinide, phenytoin, ramelteon, S-warfarin, tamoxifen, zolpidem	aprepitant, carbamazepine, phenobarbital, phenytoin, primidone, rifampin, rifapentine, St. John's wort	amiodarone, atazanavir, capecitabine, cimetidine, efavirenz, etravirine, gemfibrozil fluconazole, fluvoxamine, fluorouracil, isoniazid, ketoconazole, metronidazole, oritavancin, tamoxifen, trimethoprim/sulfamethoxazole, valproic acid, voriconazole, zafirlukast
2C19	clopidogrel, phenytoin, thioridazine, voriconazole	carbamazepine, phenobarbital, phenytoin, rifampin	cimetidine, esomeprazole, etravirine, efavirenz, fluoxetine, fluvoxamine, isoniazid, ketoconazole, modafinil, omeprazole, topiramate, voriconazole
2D6	aripiprazole, atomoxetine, brexpiprazole, carvedilol, codeine, dextromethorphan, doxepin, flecainide, fluoxetine, haloperidol, hydrocodone, meperidine, methadone, methamphetamine, metoprolol, mirtazapine, oxycodone, propafenone, propranolol, risperidone, thioridazine, tamoxifen, tramadol, trazodone, tricyclic antidepressants, venlafaxine		amiodarone, bupropion, cimetidine, cobicistat, darifenacin, dronedarone, duloxetine, fluoxetine, mirabegron, paroxetine, propafenone, quinidine, ritonavir, sertraline

STUDY TIP: CYP INDUCERS

PS PORCS (BIG INDUCERS)

Phenytoin

Smoking

Phenobarbital

Oxcarbazepine (and eslicarbazepine)

Rifampin (and rifabutin, rifapentine)

Carbamazepine (and is an auto-inducer)

St. John's wort

Effects

- Increased metabolism of substrates
- Decreased serum concentrations and decreased clinical effect of substrates
- InDucers = Decreased levels/effects of substrates
- Effect on prodrugs: inducers ↑ levels of active drug form

Recognizing the Problem

- Review labs for therapeutic drug monitoring
- Monitor for therapeutic effect

Possible Actions

Increase dose of substrate (unless a prodrug), use alternate agent to avoid combination

STUDY TIP: CYP INHIBITORS

G ♥ PACMAN (BIG INHIBITORS)

Grapefruit

♥

PIs Protease Inhibitors (don't miss ritonavir) but check all PIs since many are potent inhibitors

Azole antifungals (fluconazole, itraconazole, ketoconazole, posaconazole, voriconazole and isavuconazonium)

C – cyclosporine, cimetidine, cobicistat

Macrolides (clarithromycin and erythromycin, but not azithromycin)

Amiodarone (and dronedarone)

Non-DHP CCBs (diltiazem and verapamil)

Effects

- Decreased metabolism of substrates
- Increased serum concentrations and increased clinical effect of substrates
- INhibitors = INcreased effects/levels/ADR/toxicities of substrates
- Effect on prodrugs: inhibitors ↓ levels of active drug form

Recognizing the Problem

- Review labs for therapeutic drug monitoring
- Monitor for therapeutic effect, ADR, toxicity

Possible Actions

Decrease dose of substrate (unless a prodrug), use alternate agent to avoid combination

CLINICAL CASE EXAMPLE

Upon profile review, the pharmacist notices that a patient who takes warfarin for Afib was started on rifampin as part of a regimen for endocarditis.

Recognizing the Problem

Review rifampin start date and labs to see if INR has decreased since rifampin was initiated. Look for any evidence of a thrombotic event (e.g., stroke, DVT, PE) secondary to a subtherapeutic INR.

Possible Pharmacist Actions

Increase warfarin dose and monitor INR more frequently.

CLINICAL CASE EXAMPLE

A 76 year old male presents to the pharmacy with a voriconazole prescription from the infectious diseases specialist for aspergillosis.

Recognizing the Problem

Voriconazole is a strong 3A4 inhibitor, so it should trigger a detailed interaction assessment. Review the profile: meloxicam 7.5 mg PO QAM, betaxolol 1 drop OU BID, simvastatin 40 mg PO QHS, hydrochlorothiazide 25 mg PO QAM. Voriconazole use in this patient will result in elevated simvastatin concentrations, increasing the risk of muscle toxicity, including rhabdomyolysis.

Possible Pharmacist Actions

The combination of voriconazole and simvastatin is contraindicated. The pharmacist should intervene to ensure that the drugs are not given concurrently. Consider rosuvastatin.

OTHER ENZYMES

CYP450 enzymes are common Phase I enzymes. Other enzymes, including Phase II enzymes can impact drug concentrations. One example is UDP-glucuronosyltransferases (UGT), most commonly UGT1A1. UGT functions to conjugate substances to glucuronide (glucuronidation). Glucuronidation is typically only one part of the metabolism process, often along with CYP450 enzymes, so the impact is not as substantial (rarely more than a 2-fold change in drug levels). With some drugs UGT1A1 is a major part of the metabolic pathway, interactions can require intervention. A clinical example is raltegravir, which is metabolized by the UGT1A1-mediated glucuronidation pathway. Rifampin, a strong inducer of UGT1A1, will ↓ levels of raltegravir. When given concurrently with rifampin, the dose of raltegravir must be increased to 800 mg BID.

TRANSPORTERS

P-glycoproteins

P-glycoproteins (P-gp) are efflux transporters found in the gut and other organs. They pump drugs back into the gut (to exit out of the body). If a drug is subject to efflux, and the transporter is inhibited by a different drug, the substrate drug concentration will increase in the plasma. If an inducer is given that causes the production of more pumps, the blood levels of the substrate will decrease. See figure for a schematic representation of this activity.

Selected Drugs Affected by P-gp Efflux Pump

The following table provides a list of P-glycoprotein efflux pump substrates, inhibitors and inducers. This is not a complete list, but includes many clinically important drugs.

SUBSTRATES	STRONG INDUCERS	STRONG INHIBITORS
Anticoagulants (apixaban, edoxaban, rivaroxaban, dabigatran) **Cardiovascular drugs** (carvedilol, digoxin, ranolazine) **Immunosuppressants** (cyclosporine, sirolimus, tacrolimus) **HCV drugs** (dasabuvir, paritaprevir, ombitasvir, simeprevir, sofosbuvir) **Others** (atazanavir, colchicine, dolutegravir, fexofenadine, posaconazole, raltegravir, saxagliptin)	Carbamazepine, dexamethasone, phenobarbital, phenytoin, rifampin, St. John's wort, tipranavir	**Anti-infectives** (clarithromycin, itraconazole, posaconazole) **Cardiovascular drugs** (amiodarone, carvedilol, dronedarone, conivaptan, diltiazem, quinidine, verapamil) **HIV drugs** (cobicistat, ritonavir) **HCV drugs** (daclatasvir, ledipasvir, paritaprevir, simeprevir) **Others** (cyclosporine, flibanserin, ticagrelor)

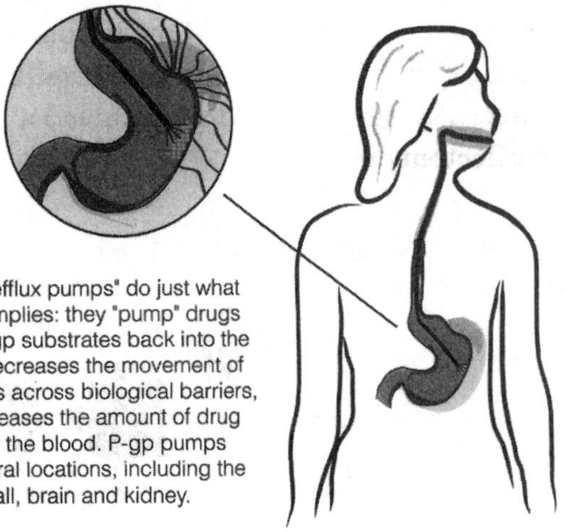

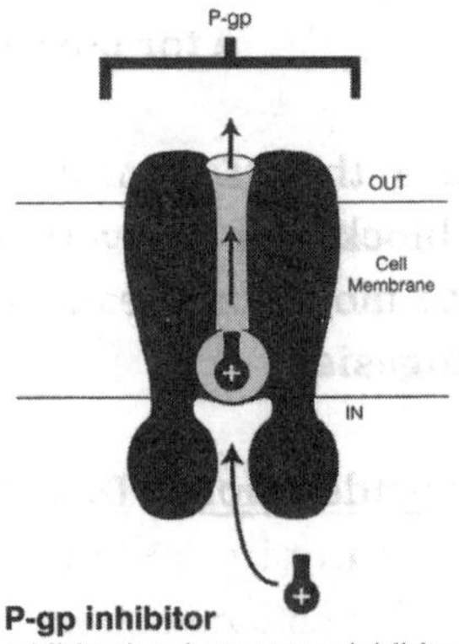

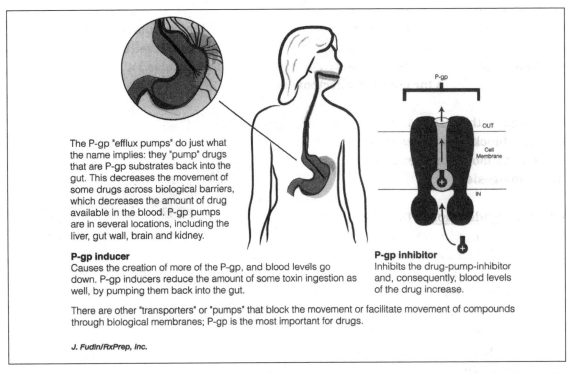

The P-gp "efflux pumps" do just what the name implies: they "pump" drugs that are P-gp substrates back into the gut. This decreases the movement of some drugs across biological barriers, which decreases the amount of drug available in the blood. P-gp pumps are in several locations, including the liver, gut wall, brain and kidney.

P-gp inducer
Causes the creation of more of the P-gp, and blood levels go down. P-gp inducers reduce the amount of some toxin ingestion as well, by pumping them back into the gut.

P-gp inhibitor
Inhibits the drug-pump-inhibitor and, consequently, blood levels of the drug increase.

There are other "transporters" or "pumps" that block the movement or facilitate movement of compounds through biological membranes; P-gp is the most important for drugs.

J. Fudin/RxPrep, Inc.

Other Transporters

In addition to P-gp, other transporters are increasingly being examined in the pre-approval drug studies. Some examples include the following:

- Breast cancer resistance protein (BCRP) – it is an efflux pump that works to prevent drugs from penetrating tissues such as brain, intestines, liver and kidney. An example of a drug interaction: tedizolid inhibits BCRP in the intestine. Avoid use with substrates that have a narrow therapeutic index (e.g., methotrexate) and monitor for adverse effects of other substrates, such as rosuvastatin.
- Organic anion transporting polypeptide (OATP) – its function is uptake in liver. A drug interaction example: *Zepatier*, the direct acting antiviral for HCV, is contraindicated with strong inhibitors of OATP1B1/3, including darunavir and atazanavir, as this can increase levels of one component, grazoprevir.
- Organic anion transporter (OAT) and organic cation transporter (OCT) – these are present in the gut, the liver and the kidneys and functions include uptake of substances. Some substrates and inhibitors have been identified, but clinical interactions have not been well-studied for most drugs that are currently on the market.

SIGNIFICANT DRUG INTERACTION EXAMPLES

Example 1 – Use of phenytoin (3A4 inducer) with tacrolimus (a 3A4 substrate) could cause decreased tacrolimus levels. This could result in transplant rejection if not recognized and monitored.

Example 2 – The anticoagulant rivaroxaban is a substrate of both 3A4 and P-gp. Increased rivaroxaban levels could result in bleeding. When given with a drug that inhibits both 3A4 and P-gp (e.g., amiodarone), risk is compounded.

SELECT DRUGS WITH SIGNIFICANT INTERACTIONS TO WATCH

This section includes some, but not all of the common drug interactions – refer to the individual chapters.

Amiodarone

The following medications must have the doses decreased 30 – 50% when starting amiodarone: digoxin, warfarin, quinidine and procainamide. Use lower doses of simvastatin, lovastatin and atorvastatin. Digoxin and warfarin are likely drugs to be given with amiodarone (for heart failure, and for arrhythmia). If the drugs are started concurrently a lower dose of digoxin or warfarin is used. If warfarin or digoxin is on board first, the pharmacist must recognize the interaction and decrease the dose when amiodarone is started. The drug interaction between warfarin and amiodarone generally peaks in 2 weeks, but can take up to 6 weeks.

Digoxin

Increases in digoxin levels are most often due to a decline in renal function. Digoxin toxicity is more likely to occur when hypokalemia is present, regardless of the digoxin level. The interaction with amiodarone is described previously. Digoxin is a P-gp substrate and interactions are important because digoxin is kept in a narrow therapeutic range. Concurrent use or addition of drugs that can decrease the heart rate (HR < 60) must be considered, primarily beta blockers and the non-DHP calcium channel blockers (diltiazem and verapamil). Other drugs that lower heart rate are amiodarone, dexmedetomidine *(Precedex)*, clonidine and opioids.

Grapefruit Juice/Fruit Interactions

Grapefruit and grapefruit juice have been shown to inhibit 3A4, which can result in increased concentrations of 3A4 substrates. The precise amount of grapefruit/juice that must be consumed to have a clinical effect is not well studied for many drugs, but for others, effects were demonstrated with substantial amounts (> 1.2 liters in one case). Some drug labels, including simvastatin, lovastatin, nifedipine and tacrolimus, recommend that patients avoid grapefruit/juice. For other drugs, it has not been studied, but could be clinically relevant. For example, with ticagrelor higher concentrations could cause increased bleeding risk and with QT prolonging agents there could be risk of torsades (lurasidone, quinidine, many others). On the exam, it is likely best to avoid grapefruit/juice if asked about a 3A4 substrate.

Lamotrigine & Valproate

This combination of drugs has high risk for severe rash and requires a careful titration and self monitoring. The interaction should not be missed by pharmacists because the rash may occur in children and the parents must be counseled that this is an emergency if it occurs. Dosing recommendations for lamotrigine are specific based on drug interactions; this is in order to avoid severe rash while maintaining seizure control.

Monoamine Oxidase Inhibitors, Opioids and Serotonin Syndrome

Monoamines are neurotransmitters, which include dopamine, epinephrine, norepinephrine and serotonin. Monoamine oxidase (MAO) is the enzyme that metabolizes monoamines. Drugs that block MAO are called MAO inhibitors and should not be used with serotonergic drugs, as it can lead to an excess of serotonin and other monoamines resulting in serotonin syndrome and/or hypertensive crisis, which are potentially fatal. There is some degree of risk with the drugs for Parkinson's Disease; refer to the chapter for specifics. Symptoms of serotonin syndrome include agitation, hallucinations, rapid heart rate, fever, excessive sweating, shivering or shaking, muscle twitching or stiffness, trouble with coordination and/or nausea, vomiting, or diarrhea. MAO inhibitors must be stopped for a period of time (a wash-out period) before starting other serotonergic drugs (specified as 2 weeks in some drug labels).

Tyramine metabolism is also decreased. Patients taking non-selective MAO inhibitors, the selegiline patch (at the two higher doses) or rasagiline should be counseled to avoid foods high in tyramine, which include aged cheeses, air-dried meats, certain wines and beers and other foods which have been aged, fermented, pickled or smoked.

In 2016, the FDA issued a Drug Safety Communication and warnings were added to the labels of all opioid medications to raise awareness of the risk of additive serotonergic effects and serotonin syndrome when opioids are used with other serotonergic medications. Patients should be counseled on the symptoms of serotonin syndrome and to seek immediate care if they experience these effects.

- Serotonergic drugs: ephedrine and analogs (pseudoephedrine, etc.), bupropion, buspirone, linezolid, lithium, meperidine, SSRIs, SNRIs, TCAs, tramadol, levodopa, mirtazapine, dextromethorphan, cyclobenzaprine (and other skeletal muscle relaxants), 5HT3-RA, some of the triptans, St. John's wort, procarbazine, lorcaserin, and some others.

Tramadol

Tramadol is metabolized by 2D6 to its active (analgesic) metabolite. Poor metabolizers or those on 2D6 inhibitors (fluoxetine, paroxetine, others) can have diminished analgesic effects of tramadol, due to the inability to convert tramadol to its active metabolite.

Codeine

Codeine is a partial prodrug for morphine and undergoes conversion by the 2D6 enzyme. Ultrarapid metabolizers or extensive metabolizers of 2D6 will produce morphine rapidly, which could be fatal to the patient, or to an infant if the mother is using codeine and is breastfeeding. Patients who lack 2D6 or those on 2D6 inhibitors would have a lack of analgesic efficacy from the drug.

Fentanyl, Hydrocodone, Oxycodone, Methadone

These opioids are primarily metabolized by 3A4; patients on 3A4 inhibitors could suffer fatal respiratory depression. Oxycodone bears a boxed warning and methadone carries a warning to avoid use with 3A4 inhibitors. Using 3A4 inducers could cause a subtherapeutic response.

PDE5-Inhibitors

These are approved for erectile dysfunction, pulmonary arterial hypertension, benign prostatic hypertrophy. They are contraindicated with nitrates due to severe hypotension. The nitrate most commonly used in the outpatient setting is the sublingual formulations, which are not dosed on a regular basis; it may be necessary to review further back in the dispensing history to find if the patient has the drug. Increasingly, patients use more than one pharmacy and the pharmacy computer will not contain the complete history unless it is collected at intake and entered manually.

PDE5-inhibitors drugs can cause orthostasis with headache and dizziness. They are used commonly in older men, who may also be taking alpha blockers for prostate enlargement, which have similar side effects. The additive effect could be dangerous. Due to additive side effects, when using alpha blockers and PDE5-inhibitors together, initial doses should be lower and should be carefully increased. PDE5-inhibitors are 3A4 substrates and the product labeling warns against using higher doses with 3A4 inhibitors as it would result in more dizziness, orthostasis, flushing and headache. These side effects are related to the action of the drug; blood is moving outward, towards the periphery. Patients should be counseled on dizziness, lightheadedness, and increase risk for falls. It is important to get up slowly from lying down or from sitting, and to hold onto the bed rail or a strong table top until you feel steady.

Chelation Risk – Quinolones, Tetracyclines

Antacids, didanosine, sucralfate, bile acid resins, magnesium, aluminum, calcium, iron, zinc, multivitamins, phosphate binders or any product containing these multivalent cations can chelate and inhibit absorption; the quinolone separation times vary. The tetracycline class (including doxycycline and minocycline) have the chelation interaction and require separation. See Infectious Diseases I chapter for details.

Statins

When statin levels are increased, the risk is higher for muscle toxicity: muscle aches, soreness, weakness, or worse, including a rapid breakdown of muscle tissue (rhabdomyolysis), which can cause renal failure as the muscle breakdown products enter the blood and travel to the kidneys, causing damage. Atorvastatin, simvastatin and lovastatin undergo the greatest degree of 3A4 metabolism and have higher risk of drug interactions that can cause increased serum levels and adverse effects. 3A4 inhibitors and other drugs can increase the likelihood of muscle toxicity. See Dyslipidemia chapter.

Calcineurin Inhibitors – Tacrolimus, Sirolimus & Cyclosporine

To prevent rejection, the serum levels of transplant drugs must remain consistent. The calcineurin inhibitors (CNIs) are used chronically for immunosuppression after transplant and they are subject to many drug interactions. Transplant patients are immune-suppressed and at higher risk of some infections. Fungal infections may be treated with systemic azoles (which are inhibitors), bacterial infections may be treated with macrolides (most are inhibitors) or with rifampin (a strong inducer) or with aminoglycosides or other nephrotoxic drugs – and the calcineurin inhibitors themselves are nephrotoxic. Depression is common post-transplant; many of the SSRIs are inhibitors.

ADDITIVE DRUG INTERACTIONS

These involve classes of drugs which may or may not pose a problem individually, but can become dangerous when used with other drugs that cause similar side effects. The MAO inhibitors discussed previously could be placed in this section since the toxic effect is generally additive. For example, a patient using fluoxetine 60 mg daily, bupropion 150 mg BID and, due to a recent infection, is given linezolid 600 mg PO Q12H (which is a weak MAO inhibitor). Consider the additive effect. Patients at risk should be told to seek urgent medical care if you have symptoms of toxicity: severe nausea, dizziness and headache, diarrhea, feeling agitated, tremors (shakiness), a racing heartbeat or hallucinations.

Bleeding Risk

Anticoagulants (warfarin, dabigatran, rivaroxaban, heparin and others) and antiplatelets (aspirin, dipyridamole, clopidogrel, prasugrel, ticagrelor) and other agents that increase bleeding risk have an additive effect: a patient has a higher risk for bleeding depending on dose, age and number of drugs are being used that carry a risk for bleeding.

In some high-risk cases (such as a patient on warfarin who had a stroke) there may be intentional use of an anticoagulant with an antiplatelet (such as warfarin plus aspirin). However, the use of this combination may be inadvertent; the cardiologist may have prescribed the warfarin (or other anticoagulant) and the patient is using the aspirin OTC on their own – or is using it based on an old recommendation. Patients taking the agents above or who are at high risk of bleeding for other reasons (including a history of bleeding(should avoid these drugs:

- NSAIDs, SSRIs (and some SSRIs are inhibitors that will increase warfarin levels) and SNRIs, natural products, including ginkgo biloba (a commonly used agent that inhibits platelet activating factor and must be stopped in advance of surgery).

Ginkgo biloba increases bleeding risk with no effect on the INR. Ginkgo is one of the "5 Gs" that can raise bleeding risk: ginkgo biloba, garlic, ginger, glucosamine and ginseng. Other natural products with known risk for bleeding include fish oils (at higher doses), vitamin E and willow bark. Others included in the warfarin package insert are listed in the Anticoagulation chapter.

Hyperkalemia Risk

Potassium is renally cleared; severe renal disease causes hyperkalemia by itself. The largest increases among the drugs listed here would be expected from the aldosterone blockers (spironolactone and eplerenone). Aldosterone regulates potassium excretion; blocking aldosterone poses significant risk of hyperkalemia. The American Heart Association has issued recommendations to minimize the risk of hyperkalemia in patients treated with these agents, which include to avoid use if the potassium is high at baseline (> 5 mEq/L), monitoring renal function and avoiding the use of concurrent NSAIDs. This is discussed further in the Heart Failure chapter.

- Additive potassium accumulation: ACE inhibitors, ARBs, aliskiren, amiloride, triamterene, eplerenone, spironolactone, salt substitutes (KCl), and the drospirenone-containing oral contraceptives.
- Other drugs that can cause or worsen hyperkalemia include the calcineurin inhibitors (tacrolimus and cyclosporine), canagliflozin, pentamidine and sulfamethoxazole/trimethoprim.

CNS Depression

CNS side effects are caused by drugs that enter the CNS (lipophilic) and primarily involve sedation (somnolence), dizziness, confusion (↓ cognitive function) and altered consciousness. CNS side effects can be activating (such as with the use of stimulants), but are primarily sedating. CNS side effects are serious and can lead to automobile accidents. CNS side effects are additive, and are increased with higher doses and when combined with alcohol or other drugs (prescription or illicit) that have CNS side effects.

- Additive CNS effects: alcohol, most pain medications (all of the opioids, some of the NSAIDs, other pain drugs), skeletal muscle relaxants, anticonvulsants, benzodiazepines, barbiturates, hypnotics, mirtazapine, trazodone, dronabinol, nabilone, propranolol, clonidine, sedating antihistamines, cough suppressants, and others, along with many illicit substances.

QT Prolongation & Torsade De Pointes (TdP)

QT risk drugs and QT risk conditions are listed in the Arrhythmia chapter. The risk of drug-induced TdP is low relative to other drug-induced effects, but the lethality is high. TdP is always preceded by QT prolongation; yet it is only within the last ten years that the FDA set a requirement that new drugs had to be tested for the effect on the QT interval. In some cases, the drug (alone) has high QT risk (such as with dofetilide and sotalol). With many others with lower risk the danger develops when the risk is additive. A normal QT interval is less than 440 ms while QT intervals exceeding 500 ms are higher risk for developing arrhythmias. Patients with an underlying cardiac disease or long QT syndrome are at high risk for for additive effects even with lower risk drugs.

Ototoxicity

Ototoxicity is disturbing to patients: hearing loss can cause social isolation and impair relationships. Tinnitus can become chronic and cause a large decrease in the quality of life. A loss of equilibrium and dizziness, including increased falls, can decrease confidence and lead to injury, including falls. The risk increases with concurrent ototoxic drugs, higher drug levels and the duration of exposure. Drugs with known ototoxic risk include:

- Salicylates, vancomycin, aminoglycosides, cisplatin and loop diuretics. If mefloquine (anti-malarial agent) causes tinnitus, it will be present with other symptoms of neurotoxicity.

Additive ototoxic drugs are given inpatient and audiology should be consulted to conduct a baseline hearing exam and throughout treatment on a scheduled basis. With some drugs an audiology consult is ordered after a certain period of time when damage would be expected.

Questions

1. Drug A is a substrate of enzyme X. Drug B is an inducer of enzyme X. A patient has been using Drug A with good results. The patient has now started therapy with Drug B. What will happen to the concentration of Drug A?
   a. Increase
   b. Decrease
   c. Stay the Same
   d. There is not enough information given
   e. None of the above

2. Drug A is a substrate of enzyme X. Drug B is an inhibitor of enzyme X. A patient has been using Drug A with good results. The patient has now started therapy with Drug B. What will happen to the concentration of Drug A?
   a. Increase
   b. Decrease
   c. Stay the Same
   d. This is not enough information given
   e. None of the above

3. Drug A is a substrate of enzyme X. Drug A is also an inducer of enzyme Y. Drug B is a substrate of enzyme Y. Drug B is also an inhibitor of enzyme X. When these drugs are both administered, what will happen to the concentrations of Drug A and Drug B?
   a. Levels of both Drug A and Drug B will increase
   b. Levels of Drug A will increase and levels of Drug B will decrease
   c. Levels of Drug A will decrease and levels of Drug B will increase
   d. Levels of Drug A will increase and levels of Drug B will stay the same
   e. There is not enough information given

4. A patient with heart failure is using many medications, including digoxin, warfarin and pravastatin. She is started on amiodarone therapy. Which statement is correct?
   a. The INR will increase; the warfarin dose will need to be reduced
   b. The digoxin will increase; the digoxin dose will need to be reduced
   c. The pravastatin level will increase; the pravastatin dose will need to be reduced
   d. A and B
   e. All of the above

5. A patient has been using warfarin for DVT treatment. She was hospitalized for afibrillation and started on amiodarone therapy. While hospitalized, she developed an infection and was prescribed trimethoprim/sulfamethoxazole and ketoconazole. Which of the following agents will increase the INR and could result in bleeding?
   a. Amiodarone
   b. Trimethoprim/Sulfamethoxazole
   c. Ketoconazole
   d. A and B
   e. All of the above

6. The pharmacist is dispensing a prescription for ciprofloxacin. The only medication the patient is using is a daily multivitamin, which she takes with breakfast and an iron supplement, which she takes with dinner. She has yogurt or cheese every day with lunch. Which counseling statement is correct?
   a. She will need to separate the ciprofloxacin from the multivitamin
   b. She will need to separate the ciprofloxacin from the iron supplement
   c. She will need to separate the ciprofloxacin from the yogurt and cheese
   d. A and B
   e. All of the above

7. A major drug interaction can occur with the use of grapefruit juice and which of the following medications?
   a. Atorvastatin and amiodarone
   b. Celecoxib and felodipine
   c. Lovastatin and lithium
   d. Levetiracetam and topiramate
   e. Duloxetine and mirtazapine

Answers

1-b, 2-a, 3-b, 4-d, 5-e, 6-e, 7-a

10

PHARMACOGENOMICS

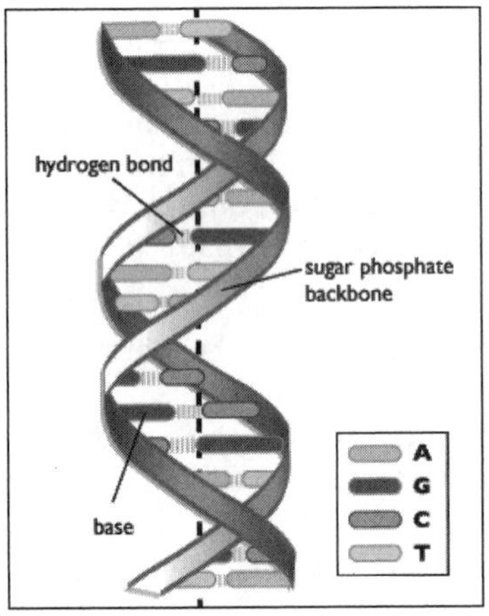

BACKGROUND

Pharmacogenomics is the science which examines inherited variations in genes that determine a patient's response to a drug. It is estimated that genetic factors contribute 20 – 40% of the differences in drug metabolism and response between patients. The goal of pharmacogenomics is to identify these factors and design treatments with improved efficacy and reduced adverse reactions. Pharmacogenomics is called "personalized medicine" because drugs are tailored for a person's unique genotype. Since pharmacogenomic information and testing recommendations can change, reputable references are required. Two resources to locate current pharmacogenomic recommendations include the FDA's Table of Pharmacogenomic Biomarkers in Drug Labeling and information provided by the Clinical Pharmacogenetics Implementation Consortium (CPIC).

Definitions

The table lists commonly used pharmacogenomic terms.

TERM	DEFINITION
Deoxyribonucleic acid (DNA)	The genetic information that is inherited from both parents that is present in two long chains of nucleotides, joined together by hydrogen bonds and twisted into a double helix (see above figure). The strands of DNA are very long. DNA is the main component of chromosomes.
Chromosomes	Tightly packed structures called chromosomes. Human cells contain 23 pairs of chromosomes.
Nucleotides	Subunits of the nucleic acids DNA and RNA. Each nucleotide contains a nitrogen base, a five-carbon sugar (deoxyribose in DNA, and ribose in RNA), and a phosphate group. In DNA, the bases consist of two purines (adenine and guanine) and two pyrimidines (thymine and cytosine). In RNA, uracil is used instead of thymine.
Gene	Specific sequences of nucleotides that code (provide instructions) for a single protein. A gene is similar to a recipe, or a set of instructions, on how to make a protein. Since proteins make up the entire life form, genes are referred to as the "blueprint" of life.

Definitions continued

TERM	DEFINITION
Allele	The specific form of a gene. Alleles are either wild-type or variants. Wild-type is usually the most commonly occurring allele. Two identical alleles make up a homozygous genotype, and two different alleles make up a heterozygous genotype.
Genotype	The set of unique genes that determine a specific trait in an individual.
Phenotype	An observable trait (outward expression) of the genotype, such as hair color, or an inherited trait that is not outwardly visible, such as sickle cell disease.
Haplotype	A group of genes or DNA variations inherited from a single parent that exist on the same chromosome and are likely to be inherited together.
Single nucleotide polymorphism (SNP)	A change in a single nucleotide in a genetic sequence (e.g., C replaced by G). SNPs are the most common genetic polymorphism in DNA. A SNP can be harmless, or result in a disease, such as with cystic fibrosis, in which a SNP results in defective coding for a protein involved in sweat and mucus production. SNPs are responsible for the majority of individual variability in response to a drug.
Structural variation (SV)	SVs are polymorphisms, like SNPs, except that they are longer. They involve a large portion of DNA. SVs, like SNPs, can be harmless or associated with a certain risk or disease.
Polymorphism	An inherited variation in the DNA sequence (such as a SNP or SV).

SELECT DRUGS WITH REQUIRED/STRONGLY RECOMMENDED GENETIC TESTING

The table includes drugs where genetic testing is routinely done and/or required according to the product labeling.

DRUG	INDICATIONS	TESTING AND/OR RECOMMENDATIONS	CLINICAL SIGNIFICANCE
Abacavir *(Ziagen)* **Abacavir + lamivudine *(Epzicom)*** Abacavir + zidovudine + lamivudine *(Trizivir)* **Abacavir + dolutegravir + lamivudine *(Triumeq)***	HIV	HLA-B*5701 If positive or severe reaction in past, do not use abacavir.	Serious and fatal hypersensitivity reactions have occurred. Test for HLA-B*5701 prior to starting abacavir. Patients who are HLA-B*5701 positive are at ↑ risk for a hypersensitivity reaction. Discontinue as soon as a hypersensitivity reaction is suspected.
Carbamazepine *(Tegretol*, others)	Seizures, neuralgia	HLA-B*1502; test all Asian patients. If positive, do not use carbamazepine unless benefit clearly outweighs risk.	Serious skin reactions, including Stevens-Johnson syndrome (SJS) and toxic epidermal necrolysis (TEN), have occurred. Patients with the HLA-B*1502 allele are at an ↑ risk of serious skin reactions; this allele is more common in Asian populations. Testing for HLA-B*1502 should be done in Asian patients prior to starting carbamazepine.

Select Drugs With Required/Strongly Recommended Genetic Testing continued

DRUG	INDICATIONS	TESTING AND/OR RECOMMENDATIONS	CLINICAL SIGNIFICANCE
Trastuzumab *(Herceptin)*, ado-trastuzumab emtansine *(Kadcyla)*, lapatinib *(Tykerb)*, pertuzumab *(Perjeta)*	Breast and gastric cancer	HER2 protein overexpression If negative, do not use drug.	HER2 overexpression is required for use. The test must be 2+ or 3+ positive on immunohistochemical (IHC) testing. HER2 negative status and those with weakly positive (1+) tumors do not respond well to therapy.
Cetuximab *(Erbitux)*, panitumumab *(Vectibix)*	Colorectal cancer	KRAS If positive for a KRAS mutation, do not use drug.	These agents are not effective in patients with colorectal cancer who have a KRAS mutation (~40% of patients). Therefore, only patients who are KRAS mutation-negative (wild-type) should receive these medications.
Azathioprine,	Solid organ cancers, leukemia, Crohn's disease, ulcerative colitis	Thiopurine methyltransferase (TPMT) If TPMT function low/absent, start at a very low dose or use an alternative treatment.	Low/absent TPMT activity ↑ risk of severe, life threatening myelosuppression (↓ WBCs, ↓ RBCs, ↓ platelets); patients with intermediate TPMT activity are also at ↑ risk for myelosuppression with lower severity.

SELECT DRUGS WHERE GENETIC TESTING SHOULD BE CONSIDERED

The table lists drugs that are known to have genetic risk factors for which standardized testing is not yet routine.

DRUG	INDICATIONS	TESTING AND/OR RECOMMENDATIONS	CLINICAL SIGNIFICANCE
Allopurinol *(Aloprim, Zyloprim)*	Gout	HLA-B*5801 If positive, do not use drug. Consider testing prior to starting therapy in high-risk individuals (Korean patients with significant renal impairment or those of Han Chinese or Thai ancestry).	Increased risk of SJS in patients testing positive for HLA-B*5801. Discontinue at first s/sx of allergic reaction, including skin rash.
Clopidogrel *(Plavix)*	Acute coronary syndromes, PAD, stroke	CYP450 2C19 genotype Consider alternative treatment in patients identified as 2C19 poor metabolizers (have 2C19*2 or *3 alleles).	The 2C19*1 allele is fully functional (able to convert clopidogrel to the active metabolite) whereas *2 and *3 alleles are reduced/loss of function of alleles, a 2C19 poor metabolizer will have a loss of function of the allele. Poor metabolizers exhibit higher cardiovascular event rates than patients with normal 2C19 function.

Select Drugs Where Genetic Testing Should Be Considered continued

DRUG	INDICATIONS	TESTING AND/OR RECOMMENDATIONS	CLINICAL SIGNIFICANCE
Codeine	Pain, cough	CYP450 2D6 If 2D6 ultra-rapid metabolizer, do not use due to toxicity risk. In 2D6 poor metabolizers, do not use due to lack of efficacy.	Codeine (a prodrug) is metabolized to morphine via 2D6. Ultra-rapid metabolizers may have exaggerated response due to extensive conversion to morphine metabolite. Over-production of morphine can result in ↑ CNS effects, including ↑ risk of respiratory depression. Case reports exist of infant deaths due to nursing mothers who are ultra-rapid metabolizers taking codeine for pain. Excessive amounts of morphine were present in breast milk and passed on to the infant, resulting in respiratory depression and death. Use extreme caution in women who are breastfeeding and in children.
Warfarin *(Coumadin, Jantoven)*	Clot prevention	CYP450 2C9 *2 and*3, VKORC1 If allele variations, start with a safer, lower dose.	Increased bleeding risk due to decreased function of alleles and haplotypes (2C9*2 and 2C9*3) and VKORC1 G > A variant.
Capecitabine *(Xeloda),* fluorouracil *(Adrucil, Carac)*	Breast, colon, pancreatic cancers	Dihydropyrimidine dehydrogenase (DPD) deficiency If DPD deficiency, do not use drug.	A deficiency in DPD can ↑ toxicity (diarrhea, neutropenia, neurotoxicity).
Phenytoin *(Dilantin),* fosphenytoin *(Cerebyx)*	Seizures	HLA-B*1502 (all Asian patients) If positive, do not use unless benefit clearly outweighs risk.	Association between developing SJS and TEN and the presence of the HLA-B*1502 allele.

Questions

1. A 15 year old female of Asian ancestry presents with a seizure disorder. The physician plans to initiate carbamazepine therapy, but first orders genetic testing in order to determine if she is at an increased risk for the following adverse drug reaction:
   a. Gastrointestinal bleeding
   b. Hemorrhage
   c. Serious skin reactions
   d. Neuropathy
   e. Tendon rupture

2. When initiating carbamazepine in a patient of Asian descent, which is the appropriate allele and/or polymorphism to test for?
   a. HLA-B *5701
   b. HLA-B *1502
   c. CYP 2C9
   d. HER2
   e. TPMT activity

3. Trastuzumab is indicated in cancers with an overexpression of this gene:
   a. ALK
   b. BCR ABL+
   c. BRAF
   d. HER2
   e. KRAS

4. A patient was started on warfarin 5 mg once daily. She presents to the clinic 4 days later and is found to have an INR of 4.7 with excessive gum bleeding when she brushes her teeth. Which of the following most likely describes the patient's genotype?
   a. CYP 2C9 *1/*1
   b. CYP 2C9 *3/*3
   c. CYP 3A4 *1/*1
   d. CYP 2D6 *1/*1
   e. CYP 2D6 *1/*2

5. CG is a 38 year old male that has been prescribed abacavir therapy. The physician has ordered a genotype test for HLA-B*5701. If the patient is positive for HLA-B*5701, what is the risk when starting therapy?
   a. Ototoxicity
   b. Increased risk of bleeding
   c. Syndrome of inappropriate antidiuretic syndrome (SIADH)
   d. Serious hypersensitivity reaction
   e. Intracranial hemorrhage

Questions 6-7 apply to the following case.

A 33 year old mother gave birth to a full term, healthy male infant, delivered vaginally. The mother was prescribed acetaminophen with codeine for episiotomy pain and took the medication for 2 weeks. Her infant had intermittent periods of breastfeeding. On Day 7, her infant was noted to be lethargic; on Day 10, her infant had grey colored skin, decreased milk intake; on Day 11, her infant was non-responsive. A postmortem analysis revealed no anatomical abnormalities. Morphine blood concentrations postmortem in the infant were 70 ng/mL (average concentrations in breast fed neonates are 0 to 2.2 ng/mL).

6. Which CYP enzyme metabolizes codeine into morphine?
   a. CYP 2D6
   b. CYP 2C9
   c. CYP 2C19
   d. CYP 3A4
   e. CYP 1A2

7. Which metabolizer phenotype of the mother best correlates with the symptoms experienced by her infant?
   a. Poor metabolizer
   b. Intermediate metabolizer
   c. Extensive metabolizer
   d. Ultra-rapid metabolizer
   e. The mother lacked CYP 2D6 enzymes

Answers

1-c, 2-b, 3-d, 4-b, 5-d, 6-a, 7-d

11

BIOSTATISTICS & PHARMACOECONOMICS

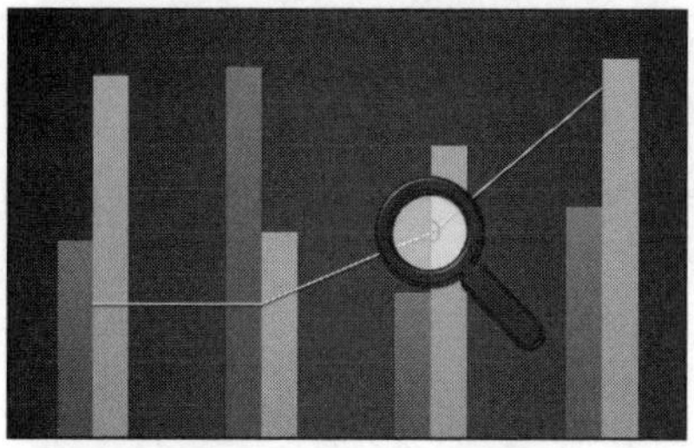

We gratefully acknowledge the assistance of Jeff Lee, PharmD, FCCP, Associate Professor, Lipscomb University College of Pharmacy, and Jan D. Hirsch, BSPharm, PhD, Associate Professor at the University of California San Diego, Skaggs School of Pharmacy and Pharmaceutical Sciences, in preparing this chapter.

BIOSTATISTICS

Background

Health care is evolving at an exponential rate. The development of new technologies and care delivery strategies has contributed to an explosion in the sheer quantity of evidence being created and published in the health care field. As pharmacists, the "drug experts," it is our responsibility to review and evaluate biomedical literature assessing safety, efficacy and value of new drugs and innovative uses of current drugs. Biomedical literature presents clinical data, and uses statistical methods and tools to answer research questions and aid in the development of clinical guidelines and consensus statements on the optimal treatment of various medical conditions. While there are a few types of studies that do not require statistical analysis (e.g., case studies, case series), most robust studies include statistical analyses and pharmacists should acquire the basic knowledge of statistical methods to best interpret available data. Descriptive statistics are use to characterize a set of information (data). Inferential statistics can be used to take the data from a sample of the whole population to test a hypothesis.

Descriptive Statistics

Descriptive statistics are designed to describe the basic features of the data and provide simple summaries in a meaningful way. Measures of central tendency estimate the "center" of a distribution of values. There are three ways of estimating central tendency: the mean, the median and the mode. Although they all estimate the "center" of a group of data, the values obtained can be quite different.

Mean

The mean is the average value of a data set. It is calculated by adding up the values in a list, and dividing by the number of values present. The mean is affected by outlying (extreme) values, either large or small. Mean can be used properly when the data are not skewed (see discussion of skewness that follows). The mean is used for continuous data.

$$\text{Mean} = \frac{\text{Sum of all values}}{\text{Number of values}}$$

Median

The median is the value in the middle of a ranked list. To calculate the median:

1. Arrange all the numbers/values in numerical order (lowest to highest).
2. Pick the middle number/value. Half of the values will be above the median, and half will be below.
3. If the list contains an even number of values, then select the 2 values in the middle of the ranked list, add them together and divide by 2 to get the median.

Unlike the mean, the median is less influenced by outliers. Another term for the median is the 50th percentile, where 50% of the values are below the median and the other 50% are above the median. The median should be used when data are skewed. When the mean and the median values are very different, the data set is skewed. Median values can be used with both continuous and ordinal, or ranked, data.

Mode

The mode is the value that occurs most frequently in a set of data. A data set can have zero, one or multiple modes.

Range

The range is the difference between the highest and the lowest values. It is found by subtracting the highest and lowest values.

---

1. From the given data set, calculate the mean, median, mode and range. Data = 4, 3, 7, 8, 1, 11, 6, 12, 15, 8

$$\text{Mean} = \frac{4+3+7+8+1+11+6+12+15+8}{10} = 7.5$$

Median: arrange the values in order (1, 3, 4, 6, 7, 8, 8, 11, 12, 15).
Since it is an even number of values, use the middle two:

$$\text{Median} = \frac{(7+8)}{2} = 7.5$$

Mode: 1, 3, 4, 6, 7, 8, 8, 11, 12, 15 Mode = 8 (value that occurs most frequently)

Range = 15 − 1 = 14

Normal Distribution

A "normal" distribution is also known as a bell-shaped curve or Gaussian curve. Generally, clinical studies rely on "sample" populations that appear to be representative of the population since the entire population cannot be studied and, therefore, an approximation has to be made. When the sample group with continuous data is large, the distribution approximates a normal, bell shaped curve (see picture) where μ is the mean, and σ is the standard deviation (SD). In a Gaussian or normal distribution, the mean, mode and median would all have the same (or similar) value and would look like the figure. Notice the curve is symmetric around the mean.

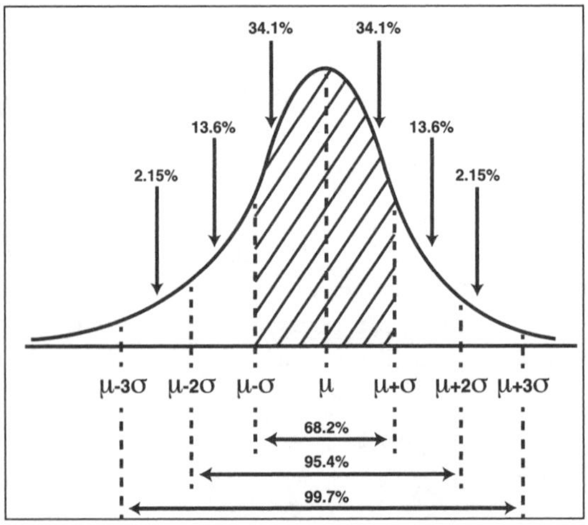

Standard Deviation

The standard deviation (SD) shows how much variation, or dispersion, there is from the mean. The closer the numbers cluster around the mean, the smaller the standard deviation. If the SD is small, one would conclude that the drug being studied had a similar effect on most subjects. SD is a positive number expressed in the same units as the data and it is used for continuous data that is normally distributed. In a normal distribution, roughly 68% of the values are within 1 standard deviation from the mean and 95% of the values are within 2 standard deviations.

Skewness

Data that do not have a normal distribution are skewed and have an asymmetric curve (see curves A and C below). This means the data has extremes, or outliers. Data that are skewed to the right have a positive skew (curve C below) and data that are skewed to the left have a negative skew (curve A below). The direction of the skew refers to the direction of the longer tail, not to the bulk of the data or curve hump. Notice that in curve B, the right and left are perfect mirrors of one another indicating symmetrical data.

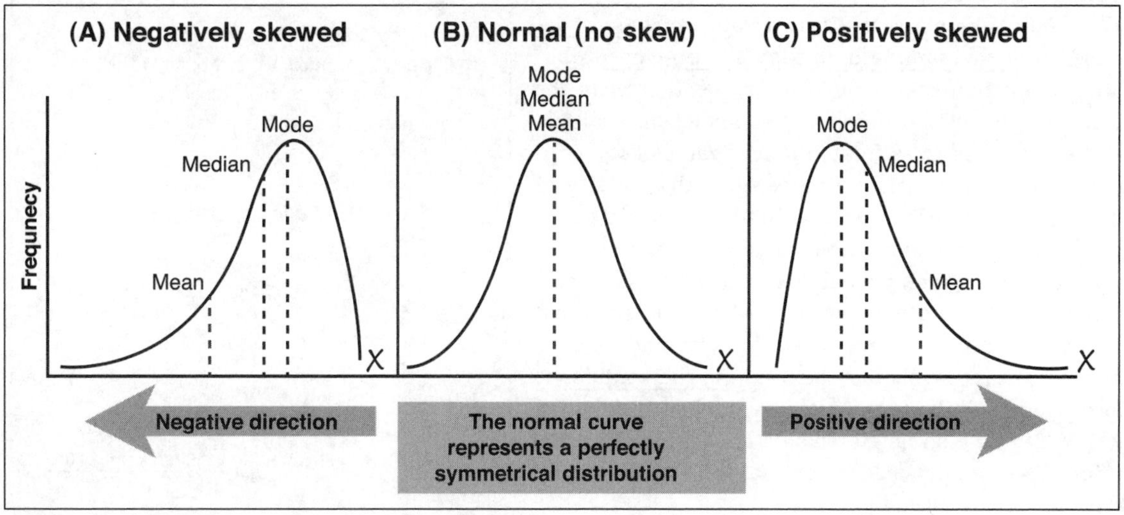

Statistical Inference and Error

Null Hypothesis (H_0)

The null hypothesis of a clinical trial states that there is no difference (or relationship) between groups (i.e., Drug A = Drug B). A study is designed to disprove this assertion by testing for a statistically significant difference between Drug A and Drug B (this is called the alternative hypothesis or H_A). If the study data concluded that there was a statistically significant difference between Drug A and Drug B, then the null hypothesis would fail to be accepted (therefore, it would be rejected).

Alternative Hypothesis (H_A)

The alternative hypothesis states that there is a treatment difference (or a relationship between the intervention and the outcome or endpoint) between groups in the trial (i.e., the effects of Drug A ≠ Drug B). When we accept the H_A (i.e., when statistical significance of the primary endpoint is met), we must fail to accept (that is, reject) the H_0.

P-value

The p-value is the likelihood (or probability) of finding a difference as large or larger than the one found in the study, if the null hypothesis is true (i.e., there is no difference between groups). Generally, a p-value of < 0.05 (and sometimes < 0.01 or other values, depending on the trial design) indicates statistical significance. If the p-value is < 0.05, there is < 5% probability that the result occurred by chance. In other words, the p-value is the probability of a random difference, given that the null hypothesis is true.

If there is a low probability the result was obtained by chance (e.g., p-value < 0.05) we can state that the conclusion is "statistically significant" (i.e., unlikely to have occurred randomly). The study would reject the H_0 when the p-value is less than the chosen significance level (also called an alpha level), indicating that the observed result would have been unlikely to occur if H_0 were true. The p-value provides no information about the size of the observed effect or its clinical significance, only statistical significance.

Confidence Interval

The confidence interval (CI) is a range of values derived from the sample data that has a given probability of encompassing the "true" value. It reflects the margin of error that inherently exists when a sample statistic is used to estimate the true value of the population. Therefore, CIs help determine the validity of the sample statistic by attempting to capture the true population parameter. The confidence interval states that there is a given probability that the population's true value is contained within this interval. The most common confidence level used in medicine is 95%; however, other levels may be used. As the confidence level increases, the confidence interval becomes wider. A 95% CI can also be stated as a 5% degree of uncertainty. The confidence level is equal to 1 – alpha (type I error), or CI = 1 – type I error.

RULES FOR INTERPRETING CONFIDENCE INTERVALS

Comparing difference data

- The result is statistically significant if the CI does not include (or cross) zero
- Example:
  - CI (0.05-3.76) does not cross zero, because 0.05 is > 0

Comparing ratio data (e.g., risk ratio, odds ratio, hazard ratio)

- The result is statistically significant if the CI does not include (or cross) one
- Examples:
  - CI (0.05-3.76) does cross 1, because 0.05 is < 1
  - CI (1.13-4.23) does not cross 1, because 1.13 is > 1

Note

If a 95% CI is used, and the conditions above are met, the result is said to be significant at the 0.05 level.

The use of p-values and confidence intervals is complementary. P-values allow a quick decision about whether a result is statistically significant or not. Confidence intervals provide information on statistical significance, plus it estimates the effect size as well as the variability of the estimate. See examples of inferential use of CIs and p-values using the difference and RR in the tables below.

LUNG FUNCTION	ROFLUMILAST (N = 745)	PLACEBO (N = 745)	DIFFERENCE (95% CI)	P-VALUE
Change in pre-bronchodilator FEV1 (mL)	46	8	38 (18 – 58)	p = 0.0003
Change in pre-bronchodilator FEV1/FVC (%)	0.314	0.001	0.313 (-0.26 – 0.89)	p = 0.2858

EXACERBATIONS	ROFLUMILAST	PLACEBO	RELATIVE RISK (95% CI)	P-VALUE
Severe (mean rate, per patient per year)	0.11 (n = 69)	0.12 (n = 81)	RR 0.92 (0.61 – 1.29)	p = 0.5275
Moderate (mean rate, per patient per year)	0.94 (n = 299)	1.11 (n = 343)	RR 0.85 (0.72 – 0.99)	p = 0.0325

Clinical Significance

A measure of statistical significance is not the same as "clinical significance". Statistical significance reflects the influence of chance on the outcome; clinical significance reflects the clinical value of the outcome. For example, a blood pressure drug that is shown to lower SBP by 3 mmHg may demonstrate statistical significance (with a p-value < 0.05) versus placebo. However, since other drugs lower BP to a greater degree, the drug is unlikely to be used; the difference in BP is not clinically significant. It would not be "clinically significant" because it does not measure up to other available drugs and would not have an clinical advantage.

Correlation

Correlation describes the relationship between two or more variables which is then plotted on a linear scale. The direction and magnitude of the linear correlation can be quantified with a correlation coefficient. The most widely-used type of correlation coefficient is the Pearson Correlation Coefficient, abbreviated r. Values of the correlation coefficient vary from -1 to 1. If the coefficient is 0, then the two variables have no relationship or correlation. If the coefficient is positive, the 2 variables tend to increase or decrease together. If the coefficient is negative, the 2 variables are inversely related, that is, as one variable decreases, the other variable increases. If the coefficient is 1 or -1, the two variables have perfect correlation and the data points form a straight line.

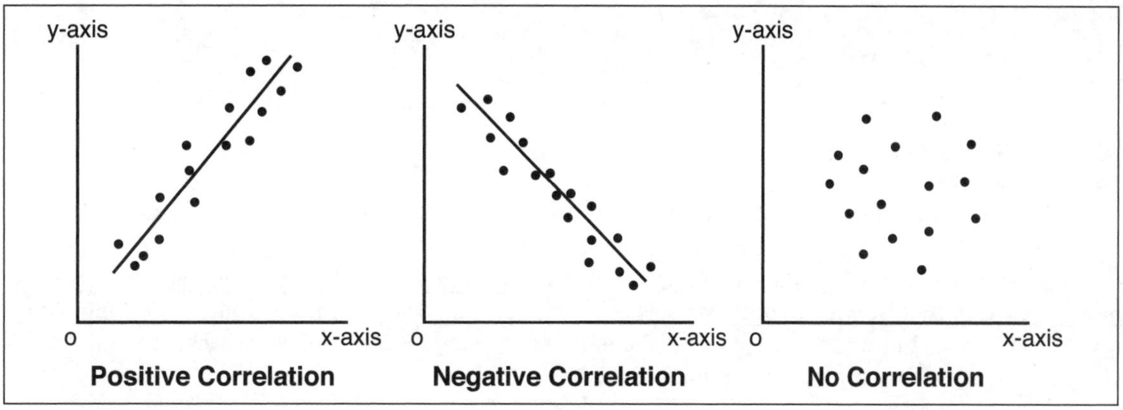

Type I error

The Greek letter, alpha (α) is the probability of a type I error. The alpha value is chosen by the researcher before the study starts, to be the acceptable threshold of statistical significance. Commonly, α is set to equal 0.05, which means < 5% of the time the null hypothesis will be rejected in error. A type I error occurs when the null hypothesis is true, yet it is rejected in error. Said another way, it was concluded that there was a difference between two groups when, in fact, there was not. When a researcher chooses the p-value of < 0.05 for statistical significance, the researcher accepts the fact that this error will occur < 5% of the time. A type I error is also known as a false positive (e.g., a drug is concluded to be better than placebo when it is not). Confidence interval is related to type I error: CI = 1 – type I error (alpha).

Type II error

The Greek letter, beta (β) is the probability of a type II error. Beta is generally set at 0.1 or 0.2, indicating a willingness to accept a type II error 10 or 20 times in 100 comparisons. A type II error occurs when the null hypothesis is false, yet it is accepted in error. Said another way, it was concluded that there was no difference between two groups when, in fact, there was. A type II error is also known as a false negative (e.g., a drug is concluded not to have benefit over placebo when it actually has benefit). Beta is usually expressed in terms of statistical power, which is calculated as 1 – beta. See discussion of statistical power that follows.

The Importance of Type I and Type II Errors is Dependent on the Situation

Consider a screening test for a biological marker known to give a good estimate of whether or not a particular disease will develop within the next 5 years. There is a prophylactic medication that can be given if the patient is at risk, but the medication is very expensive and can have serious side effects. The null hypothesis (H_0) is that the patient does not have the biological marker.

A false positive test (type I error – testing positive for the marker of the disease when indeed the patient does not have the biological marker) may make the patient anxious and seek unnecessary treatments and/or surgery. A false negative (type II error – testing negative for the marker of the disease when indeed the patient has the biological marker) may be more serious since the patient may not seek further treatment that could have prevented or halted the disease.

	UNDERLYING "TRUTH" IS BIOLOGICAL MARKER PRESENT?	
DECISION BASED ON SCREENING TEST	H_0 TRUE – DO NOT HAVE THE MARKER	H_0 FALSE – DO HAVE THE MARKER
Accept (fail to reject) H_0 No biological marker, therefore, no disease	No error (No unnecessary treatment given)	Type II error "false negative" (Necessary treatment not given)
Reject H_0 Have biological marker and will develop disease	Type I error "false positive" (Unnecessary treatment given)	No error (Necessary treatment given)

Statistical Power

Power of a statistical test is the probability that the test will reject the null hypothesis when the null hypothesis is false (avoiding a type II error). As the power increases, the chance of a type II error occurring decreases. Therefore, power is equal to 1 – beta. A higher statistical power means that we can be more certain that the null hypothesis was correctly rejected. The power of a study is determined by several factors including the sample size, the number of events (MIs, strokes, deaths, etc.), the effect size and the statistical significance criterion used.

Variables and Data Types

Dependent & Independent Variables

A dependent variable is the outcome of interest, which should change in response to some intervention. An independent variable is the intervention, or what is being manipulated. For example, aspirin is compared to placebo to see if it leads to a reduction in coronary events. The dependent variable (or outcome of interest) is the number of coronary events, while the independent variable (the intervention) is aspirin.

Discrete & Continuous Data

NAME	DESCRIPTION

Discrete Data – can have only a limited, or finite, set of values (i.e., not continuous) and can assume only whole numbers. There are 2 types of discrete data:

Nominal	Consists of categories, where the order of the categories is arbitrary (e.g., marital status, gender, ethnicity). The numbers do not have a true numerical, or quantitative, value (e.g., 0 = male, 1 = female).
Ordinal	Consists of ranked categories, where the order of the ranking is important. However, the difference between categories cannot be considered to be equal. These are usually scoring systems that are ranked by severity (e.g., Apgar score, Likert scales, NYHA functional class) but cannot be measured/quantified. There is no consistent correlation between the rank and the degree of severity. For example, a trauma score of 4 does not necessarily mean you are twice as ill as a trauma score of 2.

Continuous Data – can take an infinite number of possible values (such as height, weight, A1C, blood pressure) within a defined range. Continuous data can include fractional data (e.g., A1C of 7.3%). Types of continuous data include:

Interval	Interval data is used to measure continuous data that have legitimate mathematical values. The difference between 2 consecutive values is consistent along any point of the scale, but the zero point is arbitrary and does not mean "none" of the variable (e.g., Celsius temperature scale).
Ratio	Ratio data has equal intervals between values and a meaningful zero point; meaning there is none of the variable (e.g., height, weight, time, length).

Determining the appropriate statistical test depends on many factors, including the type of data, the number of groups being compared, whether the samples are independent or paired and the assumptions within a specific test. Below is a chart outlining some of the statistical tests commonly used in clinical trials.

Comparison of Statistical Tests*

NUMBER OF GROUPS COMPARED	INDEPENDENT SAMPLES	PAIRED SAMPLES	CORRELATION
Nominal Data			
2	Chi-squared test or Fisher's Exact test	McNemar test	Phi
3 or more	Chi-squared test	Cochran Q	
Ordinal Data			
2	Wilcoxon rank sum test or Mann-Whitney U test‡	Wilcoxon signed-rank test‡	Spearman's
3 or more	Kruskal-Wallis test‡	Friedman test‡	
Continuous Data			
2	Student's t-test**	Paired Student's t-test** or Wilcoxon signed-rank test‡	Pearson's
3 or more	Analysis of variance (ANOVA)** or Kruskal-Wallis test‡	ANOVA**	

* *Other tests may also apply. Specific test utilized also depends on distribution of data.*
** *Parametric test*
‡ *Nonparametric test*

Risk

Relative Risk/Risk Ratio (RR)

The relative risk (or risk ratio) is the probability of an unfavorable event occurring in the treatment group versus the control group. First, the risk of developing the event must be calculated for both groups. Risk is defined as the probability of an unfavorable event occurring by the end of a clinical trial. Once the risk for each arm is determined, the relative risk can be calculated by comparing the risk calculated for the treatment group (numerator) to the risk calculated for the control group (denominator). The RR is generally expressed as a decimal but can also appear as a percentage. RR is simply the ratio of risks in the 2 groups.

$$\text{Risk} = \frac{\text{Number of subjects with unfavorable event in that arm}}{\text{Total number of subjects in that arm}}$$

$$\text{RR} = \frac{\text{Risk in treatment group}}{\text{Risk in control group}}$$

Interpreting RR

- RR = 1: no difference in risk between the 2 groups
- RR < 1: fewer events are occurring in the treatment group compared to the control group
- RR > 1: more events are occurring in the treatment group compared to the control group

By reporting only the relative risk (as opposed to absolute risk), the value of the treatment may be overstated (as is often done in the lay press).

---

2. A randomized, double-blind placebo-controlled study was performed to evaluate whether metoprolol reduced disease progression in heart failure (HF) patients. A total of 10,111 patients were enrolled and followed for over 12 months. Using the results below, calculate the relative risk of HF progression.

RESULTS	METOPROLOL (N = 5,123)	PLACEBO (N = 4,988)
Incidence of HF progression	16%	28%
Death rate	1.9%	3.3%

Heart failure progression occurred in 28% of placebo-treated patients and in 16% of metoprolol-treated patients

$$\text{RR} = \frac{0.16}{0.28} = 0.57 \text{ or } 57\%$$

Therefore, subjects treated with metoprolol were only 57% as likely as placebo-treated patients to have heart failure progression.

3. A pilot study was conducted to evaluate a new drug, Drug A, for the prevention of chemotherapy-induced nausea and vomiting (CINV) in patients receiving a doxorubicin-containing regimen. The study included a total of 245 patients. Using the results below, calculate the risk ratio of CINV.

RESULTS	DRUG A (N = 120)	PLACEBO (N = 125)
Diarrhea (# of patients)	8	11
CINV (# of patients)	6	20

First, calculate the risk of CINV in the Drug A arm.

$$\text{Risk} = \frac{6}{120} = 0.05 \times 100 = 5\%$$

Then calculate the risk of CINV in the placebo arm.

$$\text{Risk} = \frac{20}{125} = 0.16 \times 100 = 16\%$$

Then the risk ratio can be calculated.

$$\text{RR} = \frac{0.05}{0.16} = 0.3125 \text{ or } 31\%$$

Therefore, subjects treated with Drug A were only 31% as likely as placebo-treated patients to have CINV.

Another formula for calculating RR

$$\text{RR} = \frac{a/(a + b)}{c/(c + d)}$$

	DISEASE	
EXPOSURE OR TREATMENT	PRESENT	ABSENT
Present (Drug group)	a	b
Absent (Placebo group)	c	d

---

4. A prospective, cohort study was initiated to evaluate the risk of developing lung cancer (CA) in heavy smokers (> 2 packs of cigarettes/day). The study enrolled 200 patients and the duration of follow up was 15 years. Using the results below, calculate the relative risk of developing lung CA from smoking.

RESULTS	LUNG CA PRESENT	LUNG CA ABSENT
Smokers (n = 100)	40	60
Non-smokers (n = 100)	10	90

$$\text{RR} = \frac{40/(40 + 60)}{10/(10 + 90)} = 4$$

The RR of 4 means that smokers are 4 times as likely to develop lung CA than non-smokers.

Relative Risk Reduction (RRR)

Relative risk reduction measures how much the risk is reduced in the treatment group compared to the control group. It can be calculated by either dividing the absolute risk reduction by the control group risk rate or by subtracting the relative risk (expressed as a decimal) from 1.

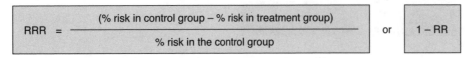

$$\text{RRR} = \frac{(\text{\% risk in control group} - \text{\% risk in treatment group})}{\text{\% risk in the control group}} \quad \text{or} \quad 1 - \text{RR}$$

---

5. Using the study from problem 1: a randomized, double-blind placebo-controlled study was performed to evaluate whether metoprolol reduced disease progression in heart failure (HF) patients. A total of 10,111 patients were enrolled and followed for over 12 months. Using the results below, calculate the relative risk reduction of HF progression.

RESULTS	METOPROLOL (N = 5,123)	PLACEBO (N = 4,988)
Incidence of HF progression	16%	28%
Death rate	1.9%	3.3%

$$\text{RRR} = \frac{(28\% - 16\%)}{28\%} = 0.43$$

or

$$\text{RRR} = 1 - 0.57 = 0.43 \text{ or } 43\%$$

There is a 43% relative risk reduction of heart failure progression in patients being treated with metoprolol. This means patients taking metoprolol are 43% less likely to experience heart failure progression.

---

6. Using the study from problem 3: a pilot study was conducted to evaluate a new drug, Drug A, for the prevention of chemotherapy-induced nausea and vomiting (CINV) in patients receiving a doxorubicin-containing regimen. The study included a total of 245 patients. Using the results below, calculate the relative risk reduction of CINV.

RESULTS	DRUG A (N = 120)	PLACEBO (N = 125)
Diarrhea (# of patients)	8	11
CINV (# of patients)	6	20

$$\text{RRR} = \frac{(16\% - 5\%)}{16\%} = 0.69$$

or

$$\text{RRR} = 1 - 0.31 = 0.69 \text{ or } 69\%$$

There is a 69% relative risk reduction of CINV in patients being treated with Drug A. This means patients taking Drug A are 69% less likely to experience CINV.

Expressing the result as a relative risk reduction is more intuitively understandable. RR and RRR are limited in that these data do not reflect how important, or large, the treatment effect is in the population at-large. They only provide a measure of what the risk of an event is in one group (treatment or exposed) compared to the risk of that event in a comparison (or control) group.

Absolute Risk Reduction (ARR)

Absolute risk reduction, or attributable risk, is the difference between the control group's event rate and the treatment group's event rate.

ARR = (% risk in control group) – (% risk in treatment group)

---

7. Using the study from problem 2: a randomized, double-blind placebo-controlled study was performed to evaluate whether metoprolol reduced disease progression in heart failure (HF) patients. A total of 10,111 patients were enrolled and followed for over 12 months. Using the results below, calculate the attributable risk of HF progression.

RESULTS	METOPROLOL (N = 5,123)	PLACEBO (N = 4,988)
Incidence of HF progression	16%	28%
Death rate	1.9%	3.3%

ARR = 28% - 16% = 12%

This is the difference in risk that can be attributed to the intervention (drug). Meaning, for every 100 patients treated with metoprolol, 12 fewer patients experience heart failure progression.

---

8. Using the study from problem 3: a pilot study was conducted to evaluate a new drug, Drug A, for the prevention of chemotherapy-induced nausea and vomiting (CINV) in patients receiving a doxorubicin-containing regimen. The study included a total of 245 patients. Using the results below, calculate the absolute risk reduction of CINV.

RESULTS	DRUG A (N = 120)	PLACEBO (N = 125)
Diarrhea (# of patients)	8	11
CINV (# of patients)	6	20

ARR = 16% - 5% = 11%

The ARR is 11%. This means, for every 100 patients treated with Drug A, 11 fewer patients experience CINV.

Number Needed to Treat (NNT)

The number needed to treat represents the number of people who would need to be treated with the intervention (drug) for a certain period of time (e.g., one year) in order to achieve the desired outcome (e.g., prevent adverse event) in one patient.

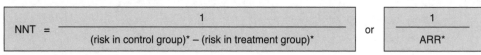

$$NNT = \frac{1}{\text{(risk in control group)}^* - \text{(risk in treatment group)}^*} \quad \text{or} \quad \frac{1}{ARR^*}$$

**expressed as a decimal*

9. Using the study from problem 7, calculate the number needed to treat.

$$NNT = \frac{1}{0.12} = 8.3\text{, rounded up to } 9$$

Anything greater than a whole number must always be rounded up because you cannot divide a person into fractions. Thus, for every 9 patients who received metoprolol for 1 year, heart failure progression is prevented in one patient.

---

10. Using the study from problem 8, calculate the number needed to treat.

$$NNT = \frac{1}{0.11} = 9.09\text{, rounded up to } 10$$

Again, it must be rounded up. Treating 10 patients with Drug A will prevent CINV in 1 patient. The NNT puts the results of a trial in a clinically relevant context.

When the treatment or exposure causes harm (e.g., cigarette smoking, *Vioxx*, etc.), the term NNT does not work and it is more accurate to report the results as the number needed to harm (NNH) which is calculated the same way as NNT. However, the NNH, is always rounded down.

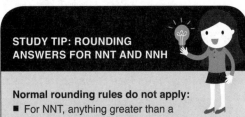

STUDY TIP: ROUNDING ANSWERS FOR NNT AND NNH

Normal rounding rules do not apply:

- For NNT, anything greater than a whole number must be rounded up to the next whole number. This avoids over-stating the potential benefit of an intervention.
  - Example: NNT of 52.1 → round up to 53
- For NNH, anything greater than a whole number must be rounded down to the whole number. This avoids understating the potential harm of an intervention.
  - Example: NNH of 41.9 → round down to 41

Odds

Odds are not the same as risk. Risk is the probability that a person who has not developed the event will develop the event whereas odds represent the probability of the event occurring compared with the probability that it will not occur. Using the example of 100 smokers, if 40 smokers developed lung cancer and 60 smokers did not develop lung cancer, the risk would be 40/100, or 40%, and the odds would be 40:60, 40/60 or 67%.

Odds Ratio (OR)

The odds ratio is the ratio of two odds, or the ratio of the odds of an event occurring in the treatment group to the odds of an event occurring in the control group. It is a measure of association between an exposure and an outcome. Odds ratios are used mostly in case-control studies, but they are the unit of outcome provided by logistic regression analysis which is a valuable statistical tool.

$$\text{Odds Ratio (OR)} = \frac{ad}{bc}$$

	DISEASE	
EXPOSURE OR TREATMENT	PRESENT	ABSENT
Present (Drug group)	a	b
Absent (Placebo group)	c	d

11. Using the study from problem 4: a prospective, cohort study was initiated to evaluate the risk of developing lung cancer (CA) in heavy smokers (> 2 packs of cigarettes/day). The study enrolled 200 patients and the duration of follow up was 15 years. Using the results below, calculate the odds ratio of developing lung CA from smoking.

RESULTS	LUNG CA PRESENT	LUNG CA ABSENT
Smokers (n = 100)	40	60
Non-smokers (n = 100)	10	90

$$\text{Odds of a smoker developing cancer} = \frac{40}{60} = 0.67$$

$$\text{Odds of a non-smoker developing cancer} = \frac{10}{90} = 0.11$$

$$OR = \frac{0.67}{0.11} = 6$$

The odds ration of 6 means that smokers are 6 times as likely to develop lung cancer than non-smokers. If an odds ratio is 1, this indicates no difference between groups (ratio is 1:1). The smaller the event rate, the closer the odds ratio is to the relative risk.

Hazard Ratio (HR)

Hazard ratios are often used when clinical trials present data related to the time survived to an event (e.g., mortality, cure, specified level of symptom reduction).

A hazard rate is the chance of an unfavorable event occurring by a given point in time. A hazard ratio is the hazard or chance of an event occurring at any given time during the study in the treatment group as compared to a comparator group. Hazard ratios are used in clinical trials with time-to-event (or survival) analysis. Hazard ratios assume that the ratio is constant over time. Hazard ratios are a specific type of RR with the distinction that HR ratios are the relative likelihood of an event in the treated vs. comparator group at any given point in time during the trial and the RR is the likelihood of an event in the treated vs. comparator group at the end of the trial.

$$HR = \frac{\text{Hazard rate in the treatment group}}{\text{Hazard rate in the control group}}$$

Interpreting HR

- HR = 1: event rates are the same in both arms over time
- HR < 1: at any given time, relatively fewer patients in the treatment group have had an event compared to the control group
- HR > 1: at any given time, relatively more patients in the treatment group have had an event compared to the control group

For example, in a clinical trial assessing the cure rate provided by Drug A vs. placebo the hazard ratio (HR) is reported to be 4. This means that a treated patient who has not been cured by a certain time point has four times the chance of being cured by the next time point compared to someone in the placebo group.

Sensitivity and Specificity

Sensitivity and specificity are concepts often applied to diagnostic testing for diseases. Sensitivity is the proportion of time a test is positive in patients who have the disease; also stated as the ability of the test to correctly identify patients who are known to have the disease in question. If a test has high sensitivity, it will pick up nearly everyone with the disease. A test with 100% sensitivity will recognize all patients with the disease by testing positive. Therefore, a negative test would definitely rule out the presence of the disease. Sensitivity is the percentage of "true-positive" results and is equal to 1 – type II error.

Specificity is the proportion of time a test is negative in patients who do not have the disease; also stated as the ability of the test to correctly identify patients who are known to not have the disease. If a test has high specificity, it will not mistakenly give a positive result to many people without the disease. A test with 100% specificity will read negative and accurately exclude disease in all healthy patients. Specificity is the percentage of "true-negative" results and is equal to 1 – type I error. Sensitivity and specificity can be described using a simple 2x2 table:

	PATIENTS WITH DISEASE	PATIENTS WITHOUT DISEASE
Test is positive	a (True +)	b (False +)
Test is negative	c (False -)	d (True -)
	a + c	b + d

Using this table, sensitivity may be calculated using the following formula:

$$\text{Sensitivity} = \frac{a}{(a + c)}$$

Specificity, then, can be calculated using the following formula:

$$\text{Specificity} = \frac{d}{(b + d)}$$

Overview of Study Designs

There are many types of study designs used in evidence-based medicine. Each trial design has certain strengths and weaknesses. Clinical study designs include observational designs (such as case reports, case series, cross-sectional, case-control, cohort) and experimental designs (such as a randomized, controlled trial). A placebo, or an inert compound indistinguishable from the active drug, may be used in experimental trials to minimize bias. This practice is called "blinding" or "masking" the treatment allocation in a clinical trial. In a single-blind trial, generally the subject (the patient) is unaware of the treatment allocation, whereas the investigator is aware of the treatment the patient is receiving. In a double-blind trial, neither the subjects nor the researchers know who is receiving active drug or placebo. The hierarchy presented in the following figure is indicative of the confidence in results that is generally attributed to each type of study.

Observational Studies

An observational study is a type of trial in which individuals are enrolled and observed and/or certain outcomes are measured under precisely defined conditions in a systematic and objective manner. No attempt is made to affect the outcome (no intervention). Observational studies follow subjects with a certain condition or those who receive a particular treatment over time. They may be compared to another group who are not affected by the condition or are not taking the particular treatment. Large observational studies can clarify the tolerability profile of marketed medications. An example of an observational study is the Women's Health Initiative trial. Types of observational studies are listed below.

Case Report or Case Series

A simple descriptive account of observations of a single patient (case report) or series of patients (case series) can be useful from a clinical perspective for unusual or rarely observed events. Based on observed clinical aspects of a patient(s) and intervention, the possibility of an association between treatment and effect may be proposed. However, no conclusion can be drawn from these small studies. They may generate hypotheses that can then be studied in larger trials with more robust study designs (e.g., prospective cohort or randomized controlled trial).

Case-Control Study

Case-control studies compare patients who have a disease or outcome of interest (the cases) to patients who do not have the disease or outcome (the controls), and look back retrospectively to compare exposure to a risk factor. Risk factor exposure is compared in each group to determine if a relationship between the risk factor and the disease exists. Case-control studies are observational because no intervention is implemented and no attempt is made to alter the course of the disease. For example, did subjects exposed to statins have a higher incidence of liver damage? Case-control studies are good for studying rare diseases or outcomes, can be conducted in less time since the condition has already occurred, and are useful to establish an association. They are often used to generate hypotheses that can then be studied via a prospective cohort or other studies.

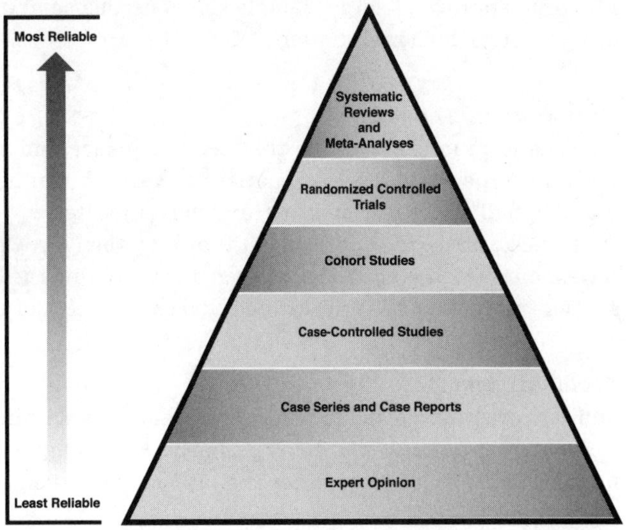

© RxPrep

Cohort Study

A cohort is a group of people who share a common characteristic(s) or experience within a defined period of time (e.g., year born, exposure to pollutant/drug/vaccine, or having undergone a certain procedure). This study type follows the cohort over time (longitudinal) and the outcomes are compared to a subset of the group who were not exposed to the intervention, such as a drug (e.g., the Framingham studies). Cohort members must be at risk of experiencing the event and they must not have had the outcome of interest at the start of the study. A cohort study is a good trial design when conducting a randomized trial would be considered unethical. Cohort studies may be prospective in design (carried out into the future) but can be done retrospectively as well (e.g., by reviewing patient medical charts).

Cross-Sectional Study

Cross-sectional studies are descriptive, observational trials and are used to estimate the relationship between an outcome of interest and population variables as they exist at a cross-section (one point in time). Cross-sectional studies are used to determine prevalence of disease. By identifying associations between exposures and outcomes, they can be used to generate hypotheses about causation that can be tested with other study designs.

Experimental Studies

Randomized Controlled Trial (RCT)

This experimental trial design involves randomization, which minimizes bias and increases internal validity, thereby increasing the overall strength of the study conclusions. These are generally designed as superiority trials, which aim to determine if one treatment is better than another. RCTs are always prospective and are considered the gold standard trial design in evaluating safety and efficacy of an intervention (e.g., drug). The clinical trial setting can be controlled in many ways.

Within a RCT, there are different study designs and a few are listed below:

Parallel study design
Subjects are randomized to either the treatment group or the placebo group only and stay in that group for the duration of the study. This is the most common design used in Phase III comparative trials for FDA drug approval. A larger sample size is needed compared to the crossover design; however, this trial design can be done in a shorter period of time.

Crossover study design
Subjects are randomized to a treatment sequence and each subject receives all of the interventions. With this type of design, every patient serves as his or her own control. For example, comparing drugs A and B, half of the subjects are randomly allocated to receive them in the order A then B, and half of the subjects are to receive them in the order B then A. A washout period between treatments is required. A washout period is the time between discontinuing the first treatment and before the initiation of the second treatment and is needed to reduce the effects of the 1st drug taken in the 2nd phase of the trial.

Factorial design
Subjects are randomized to multiple assignments within the study and it is designed to evaluate multiple interventions in a single experiment. For example, in a simple 2x2 factorial design, patients can be assigned to 1 of 2 drug doses (e.g., 100 mg or 200 mg) and 1 of 2 drugs (Drug A or Drug B).

Intention-To-Treat (ITT) vs. Per Protocol (PP) Analyses
Data from clinical trials can be analyzed in two different ways; intention-to-treat or per protocol. Intention-to-treat analysis includes data for all patients originally allocated to each treatment group (active and control) even if the patient did not complete the trial according to the study protocol (e.g., due to non-compliance, protocol deviations or study withdrawal). This method provides a conservative estimate of the treatment effect. A per protocol analysis is conducted for the subset of the trial population who completed the study according to the protocol (or at least without any major protocol violations). This method may provide an optimistic estimate of treatment effect since it is limited to the subset of patients who were adherent to the protocol. In practice, both methods are often used to analyze the results of a clinical trial.

Composite Endpoints
A composite endpoint is a single measure of effect, comprised of multiple individual endpoints or outcomes being collected in a trial. Composite endpoints are common in reporting clinical trial results. They can be helpful in instances where there is no single primary outcome variable that adequately portrays efficacy. A more common rationale for using composite endpoints is to reduce the sample size needed to show an effect by increasing the event rate in the control group.

Despite these potential advantages, the use of composite endpoints may complicate the interpretation of the results, as it blends individual endpoint results into a single endpoint. When assessing the appropriateness of a composite endpoint in a clinical trial, the

STUDY TIP: ENDPOINT INTERPRETATION

Focus on:

- The population specified in the question (e.g., intention-to-treat or per protocol).
- The endpoint specified in the question (data may be presented for multiple endpoints, sometimes in a table).

Composite endpoints:

- Do not focus on the individual endpoints that make up a composite endpoint unless specifically asked.
- The individual endpoints cannot simply be added up to make the composite.

reader should ensure that the individual endpoints comprising the composite endpoint are similar in importance to patients, they occur with similar frequency, and are affected to a similar degree by the intervention.

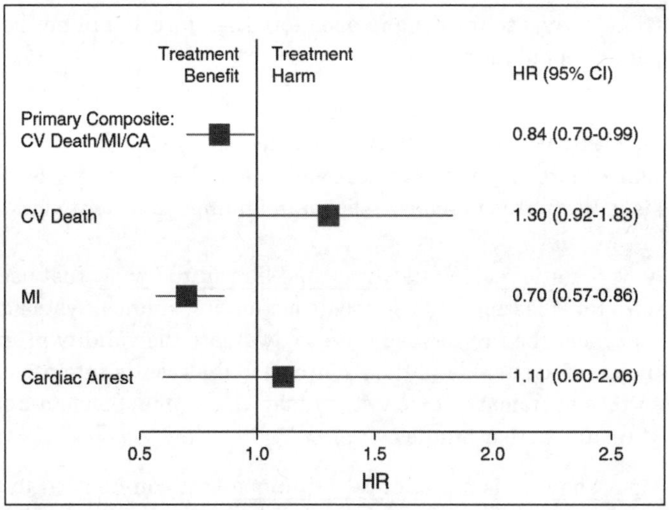

Pogue, et al. PLoS One 2012; 7(4): e34785.

In this example, the primary composite endpoint encompasses the endpoints of cardiovascular death (CV death), myocardial infarction (MI), and cardiac arrest (CA) and is statistically significant, although only one of the individual components (MI) shows a statistically significant treatment benefit.

When the primary endpoint is designated as a composite endpoint, then the primary analysis for statistical significance will focus on the combined endpoint, not on the individual endpoints that make up the composite. However, by reporting both the composite and individual endpoints, the reader can evaluate the relative contribution of each component to the composite result.

Noninferiority and Equivalence Trial Designs

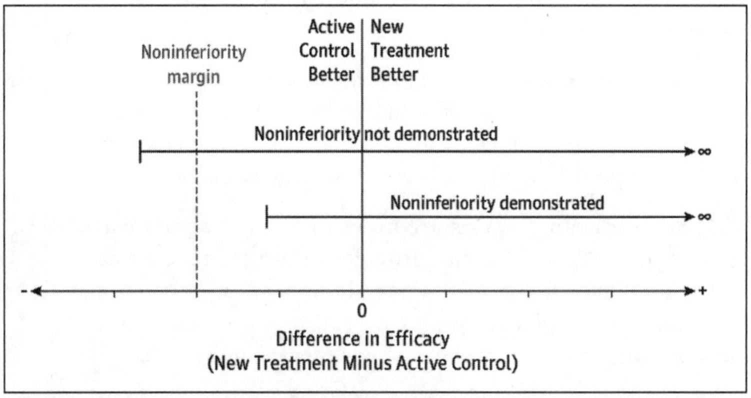

Kaji and Lewis. JAMA, 2015; 313(23): 2371-2372.

The terms "noninferiority" and "equivalence" are often used interchangeably (incorrectly) in describing trial designs where the objective is to demonstrate that a new treatment is similar to the standard treatment. In reality, these two terms define different trial designs. An equivalence trial represents a study designed to demonstrate that two interventions do not differ in either direction (more or less effective) by more than a prespecified equivalence margin (two-way margin). A noninferiority trial, in contrast, seeks to determine whether a new treatment is not worse than a reference treatment by more than a prespecified noninferiority margin (one-way margin). Noninferiority trials are much more common than equivalence trials.

In this example, the prespecified noninferiority margin is between 0 and the dashed line. In the top example, the lower limit of the confidence interval falls to the left of the noninferiority margin, so noninferiority is not demonstrated. In the lower example, the lower limit of the confidence interval does not cross the noninferiority margin, thus noninferiority is demonstrated.

Clinical trials may not provide "real life" comparisons

Patients in clinical trials may not be reflective of those treated in everyday clinical practice. Patients in clinical trials tend to be younger, more compliant with therapy, more likely to reach target doses of the drug, and do so more quickly than in everyday practice. They are not as likely to have as complex a presentation as real-life patients. For example, practitioners use a drug that is cleared renally in patients with moderate to severe renal impairment, when this subgroup of patients was excluded from clinical trials related to the drug in question. Therefore, it will not be known how to use the drug safely in this patient population.

Systematic Reviews and Meta-Analyses

When there are many studies available in the literature, a systematic review and possible meta-analysis is useful to summarize the main findings in order to guide evidence-based medical decisions.

A systematic review is a structured literature review that uses a step-by-step protocol with preset criteria for selecting and rigorously evaluating studies. Systematic reviews attempt to identify all studies that meet the pre-defined criteria, evaluate the validity of findings (considering possible bias within the study design), and then synthesize the results into a meaningful, transparent presentation of results. A systematic review study may also conduct a meta-analysis to present a quantitative synthesis of results across studies.

Meta-analysis is a statistical technique that can be used to combine results from multiple studies to develop a single conclusion that has greater statistical power than is possible in the individual smaller studies. The validity and usefulness of a meta-analysis is largely dependent on the quality of the systematic review that identified which studies to include. A meta-analysis considers the differing sizes and quality of trials for a treatment, giving more weight to the findings from larger, more rigorous studies. The technique also considers how the studies differ and the possible contribution of differing factors to driving treatment outcomes.

Although there are many potential flaws in this type of pooled data analysis, if the studies included in the meta-analysis are rigorous, randomized, controlled trials, the results could provide the highest level of evidence for medical decisions.

Results of a meta-analysis are presented in a diagram called a forest plot. The forest plot provides information about each study included in the meta-analysis as well as a combined summary effect of the results overall. Several columns are used to summarize the meta-analysis results in the forest plot.

META-ANALYSIS CAN BE USED:

- To establish statistical significance with studies that have conflicting results
- To develop a more correct estimate of effect magnitude
- To provide a more complex analysis of harms, safety data, and/or benefits
- To examine subgroups from multiple studies with individual numbers that are not statistically significant

Looking at the figure below, a forest plot from Larsson et al that compared the risk of atrial fibrillation between groups of subjects with the highest vs. lowest category of coffee consumption.

The first three columns are:

1. List of studies, by author name, included in the meta-analysis.
2. Year of each study was published.
3. Population studied (i.e., men, women or both).

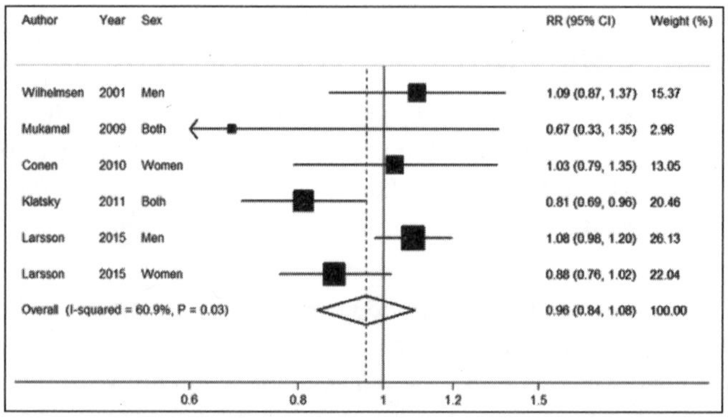

Results of each study are plotted to the right.

- The values on the x-axis are the study outcomes (relative risk in this study) and the solid vertical line at 1.0 is the "line of no effect". This line would be at 1.0 if study outcomes were expressed as odds ratios but at zero if expressed as weighted mean differences.

- The point estimate of the result in each study is plotted as a square. The size of the square represents the weight given to the study in the summary result. Larger studies with smaller confidence intervals will be given more weight and have a larger square. The confidence interval for each study is expressed as a horizontal line running through the box; longer lines indicate wider confidence intervals, thus less precision and if the line crosses the "line of no effect" it is possible the intervention had no effect.

The meta-analysis combined summary effect is presented as a diamond, with a dotted vertical line running through the center representing the point estimate of the combined summary effect.

- The width of the diamond indicates the confidence interval for the combined effect.
- If the diamond does not cross the "line of no effect" then the differences between groups can be interpreted as statistically significant. Note, in this study the diamond does cross the "line of no effect" thus the authors conclude no overall association between coffee consumption and atrial fibrillation risk.

The two columns to the right of the plotted data contain the numeric results of each study (same as graphed) and then the weight given to the study in the overall analysis.

PHARMACOECONOMICS

Background

Health care costs in the United States rank among the highest of all industrialized countries. In 2015, total health care expenditures reached 3.2 trillion dollars, which translates to an average of $9,990 per person, or about 17.8% of the nation's gross domestic product. The increasing costs have highlighted the need to understand how our limited resources can be used most effectively and efficiently in the care of our patients and society as a whole. Therefore, it is necessary to scientifically evaluate the value (e.g., costs vs. outcomes) of interventions such as drug therapy.

Definitions

Pharmacoeconomics is a collection of descriptive and analytic techniques for evaluating pharmaceutical interventions (drugs, devices, procedures, etc.) in the health care system. Pharmacoeconomic research identifies, measures, and compares the costs (direct, indirect and intangible) and consequences (clinical, economic and humanistic) of pharmaceutical products and services. Various research methods can be used to determine the impact of the pharmaceutical product or service. These methods include: cost-effectiveness analysis, cost-minimization analysis, cost-utility analysis, and cost-benefit analysis. Although the term "pharmacoeconomics" is frequently referred to as "outcomes research", they are not the same thing. Pharmacoeconomic methods are specific to assessing the costs and consequences of pharmaceutical products and services, whereas outcomes research represents a broader research discipline that attempts to identify, measure, and evaluate the end result of health care services generally.

Health care providers, payers and other decision makers use these methods to evaluate and compare the total costs and consequences of pharmaceutical products and services. As the results of pharmacoeconomic analyses can vary significantly based on the point of view of the analyst, a critical consideration in evaluating pharmacoeconomic analyses is to clearly identify the study perspective. What may be viewed as good value for society or for the patient may not be deemed as such from an institutional or provider perspective (e.g., the importance of assessing the costs of lost productivity due to illness may be critically important to a patient or employer, but perhaps less so to a health plan).

Pharmacoeconomic analyses can provide useful supplemental evidence to traditional efficacy and safety endpoints. They help translate important clinical benefits into economic and patient-centered terms, and can assist providers and payers in determining where, if at all, a drug fits into the treatment paradigm for a specific condition. Pharmacoeconomic studies serve to guide optimal healthcare resource allocation, in a standardized and evidence-based manner.

The ECHO model (Economic, Clinical and Humanistic Outcomes) provides a broad evaluative framework to assess the outcomes associated with disease and its treatment.

- Economic outcomes: Include direct, indirect and intangible costs of the drug compared to a medical intervention.
- Clinical outcomes: Include medical events that occur as a result of the treatment or intervention.
- Humanistic Outcomes: Include consequences of the disease or treatment as reported by the patient or caregiver (e.g., patient satisfaction, quality of life).

COSTS

Direct Medical Costs
Costs associated with the detection, prevention, or treatment of a disease or illness. Direct cost examples include medications, medication administration, hospitalizations, clinic visits, emergency room visits, and nursing services.

Direct Non-Medical Costs
Costs for non-medical services associated with disease and treatment. Direct non-medical costs include travel costs (gas, bus, hotel stays for family), child care services (for children of patients), or costs for other household services required due to illness.

Indirect Costs
Costs that result from the effects of morbidity or mortality on production capacity, including costs of time lost from work, or working at a lower productivity level due to disease or treatment. Indirect costs can occur at both the patient and caregiver level.

Intangible Costs
Costs incurred that represent the nonfinancial outcomes of disease and treatment, including pain and suffering, anxiety, and fatigue.

Average and Incremental Cost Effectiveness Ratios

Commonly, the results of a pharmacoeconomic analysis will be expressed in terms of a cost ratio, representing the costs incurred to achieve a particular outcome [e.g., cost per case cured, cost per treatment success, cost per quality-adjusted life year (QALY) gained]. Two fundamental cost ratios are commonly used to communicate results of a pharmacoeconomic analysis.

Average Cost Effectiveness Ratios

Average cost ratios reflect the cost per outcome of one treatment alternative independent of other alternatives. For example, if a treatment costs $50 to generate two successful outcomes, the average cost ratio is $25/treatment success ($50/2 successfully treated).

Incremental Cost Effectiveness Ratios

Incremental cost ratios represent the change in costs and outcomes when two treatment alternatives are compared. An incremental cost ratio is calculated when evaluating costs and outcomes between competing alternatives, and represents the additional costs required to produce an additional unit of effect. Mathematically, it is calculated as follows where C is for costs and E is for effects:

$$\text{Incremental Cost Ratio} = \frac{(C_2 - C_1)}{(E_2 - E_1)}$$

12. If spending $200 on Drug A results in 5 treatment successes while spending $300 on Drug B results in 7 treatment successes, what is the incremental cost ratio?

$$\text{Incremental Cost Ratio} = \frac{(\$300 - \$200)}{(7 - 5)} = \frac{\$100}{2} = \$50$$

Drug B costs $50 more relative to Drug A for each additional treatment success.

Pharmacoeconomic Methodologies

Cost-Minimization Analysis

Cost-minimization analysis (CMA) is used when two or more interventions have already demonstrated equivalency in outcomes and the costs of each intervention are being compared. CMA measures and compares the input costs of treatment alternatives that have been deemed as equivalent from an outcomes perspective. This determination of equivalence is a key consideration in adopting this methodology. Ideally, evidence will exist to support the clinical equivalence of the alternatives. In some instances, assumptions will be made in the absence of relevant evidence. For example, two ACE-inhibitors, captopril and lisinopril, are considered therapeutically equivalent in the literature, but the acquisition cost (the price paid for the drug) and administrative costs may be different (captopril is administered TID and lisinopril is administered once daily). A CMA would look at "minimizing costs" when multiple drugs have equal efficacy and tolerability. Another example of CMA is looking at the same drug regimen given in two different settings (e.g., hospital versus home health care). CMA is considered the easiest analysis to perform. However, the use of this method is limited given its ability to compare only alternatives with demonstrated equivalent outcomes.

Cost-Benefit Analysis

Cost-benefit analysis (CBA) is a systematic process for calculating and comparing benefits and costs of an intervention in terms of monetary units. CBA consists of identifying all the benefits from an intervention and converting them into dollars in the year that they will occur. Also, the costs associated with the intervention are identified and are allocated to the year when they occur. All costs are then discounted back to their present day value. Given that all other factors remain constant, the program with the largest present day value of benefits minus costs is the best economic value. In CBA, both benefits and costs are expressed in terms of dollars and are adjusted to their present value. This can be difficult when required to measure the benefits and then assign a dollar amount to that benefit (e.g., measuring the benefit of patient quality of life, which is difficult to quantify, and assigning a dollar value to it). One advantage to using CBA is the ability to determine if the benefits of the intervention exceed the costs of implementation. CBA can also be used to compare multiple programs for similar or unrelated outcomes, as long as the outcome measures can be converted to dollars.

Cost-Effectiveness Analysis

Cost-effectiveness analysis (CEA) is defined as a series of analytical and mathematical procedures that aid in the selection of a course of action from various alternative approaches. Inputs are usually measured in dollars and outputs are usually measured in natural units (e.g., LDL values in mg/dL, % clinical cures, length of stay). The main advantage of this method is that the outcomes are easier to quantify when compared to other analyses, and clinicians and decision makers are familiar with these types of outcomes since they are similar to outcomes seen in clinical trials and practice. Therefore, CEA is the most common pharmacoeconomic methodology seen in the literature today. A disadvantage of CEA is the inability to directly compare different types of outcomes. For example, one cannot compare the cost effectiveness of implementing a diabetes program with implementing an asthma program where the outcome units are different (e.g., blood glucose values versus asthma exacerbations). It is also difficult to combine two or more outcomes into one value of measurement (e.g., comparing one chemotherapeutic agent that prolongs survival but has significant side effects to another chemotherapeutic agent that has less effect on prolonging survival and has fewer side effects).

Cost-Utility Analysis

Cost-utility analysis (CUA) is a specialized form of CEA that includes a quality-of-life component associated with morbidity using common health indices such as quality-adjusted life years (QALYs) and disability-adjusted life years (DALYs). With CEA, you can measure the quantity of life (years gained) but not the "quality" or "utility" of those years. In a CUA, the intervention outcome is measured in terms QALY gained. QALY takes into account both the quality (morbidity) and the quantity (mortality) of life gained. CUA measures outcomes based on years of life that are adjusted by utility weights, which range from 1 for "perfect health" to 0 for "dead". These weights can take into account patient and society preferences for specific health states; however, there is no consensus on the measurement, since both patient and society preferences may vary based on culture. An advantage of CUA is that different types of outcomes and diseases with multiple outcomes of interest can be compared (unlike CEA) using one common unit, like QALY. In addition, CUA combines morbidity and mortality into one unit without having to assign a dollar value to it (unlike CBA).

Four Basic Pharmacoeconomic Methodologies

METHODOLOGY	COST MEASUREMENT UNIT	OUTCOME UNIT
Cost-minimization analysis	Dollars	Demonstrated or assumed to be equivalent in comparative groups
Cost-benefit analysis	Dollars	Dollars
Cost-effectiveness analysis	Dollars	Natural units (e.g., life-years gained, mmHg blood pressure, % at treatment goal)
Cost-utility analysis	Dollars	Quality-adjusted-life-year (QALY) or other utilities

Health-Related Quality of Life

Health-related quality of life (HRQOL) refers to the effects of a disease and its treatment on an individual's functioning and well being as perceived by that individual. It is commonly included under a broad umbrella of assessments known as patient-reported outcomes (PROs). HRQOL is comprised of several important domains, including physical and mental functioning, role functioning, vitality, social functioning, and general health perceptions, among others.

HRQOL assessments can provide important patient-centered information related to the effects of a disease or treatment on patient functioning and well-being. These assessments are typically developed as either general (or generic) health status instruments that can be used across a number of disease areas (e.g., SF-36 Health Survey can be used for asthma and diabetes, among others) or disease-specific measures applicable to a limited disease population (e.g., Asthma Quality of Life Questionnaire). Prior to their use in practice, it is critical that the reliability and validity of HRQOL assessments in specific patient populations has been documented.

PRACTICE CASE

The NEW ENGLAND JOURNAL of MEDICINE

ESTABLISHED IN 1812 NOVEMBER 15, 2007 VOL. 357 NO. 20

Prasugrel versus Clopidogrel in Patients with Acute Coronary Syndromes

Stephen D. Wiviott, M.D., Eugene Braunwald, M.D., Carolyn H. McCabe, B.S., Gilles Montalescot, M.D., Ph.D., Witold Ruzyllo, M.D., Shmuel Gottlieb, M.D., Franz-Joseph Neumann, M.D., Diego Ardissino, M.D., Stefano De Servi, M.D., Sabina A. Murphy, M.P.H., Jeffrey Riesmeyer, M.D., Govinda Weerakkody, Ph.D., C. Michael Gibson, M.D., and Elliott M. Antman, M.D., for the TRITON–TIMI 38 Investigators*

ABSTRACT

BACKGROUND

Dual-antiplatelet therapy with aspirin and a thienopyridine is a cornerstone of treatment to prevent thrombotic complications of acute coronary syndromes and percutaneous coronary intervention.

METHODS

To compare prasugrel, a new thienopyridine, with clopidogrel, we randomly assigned 13,608 patients with moderate-to-high-risk acute coronary syndromes with scheduled percutaneous coronary intervention to receive prasugrel (a 60-mg loading dose and a 10-mg daily maintenance dose) or clopidogrel (a 300-mg loading dose and a 75-mg daily maintenance dose), for 6 to 15 months. The primary efficacy end point was death from cardiovascular causes, nonfatal myocardial infarction, or nonfatal stroke. The key safety end point was major bleeding.

RESULTS

The primary efficacy end point occurred in 12.1% of patients receiving clopidogrel and 9.9% of patients receiving prasugrel (hazard ratio for prasugrel vs. clopidogrel, 0.81; 95% confidence interval [CI], 0.73 to 0.90; P<0.001). We also found significant reductions in the prasugrel group in the rates of myocardial infarction (9.7% for clopidogrel vs. 7.4% for prasugrel; P<0.001), urgent target-vessel revascularization (3.7% vs. 2.5%; P<0.001), and stent thrombosis (2.4% vs. 1.1%; P<0.001). Major bleeding was observed in 2.4% of patients receiving prasugrel and in 1.8% of patients receiving clopidogrel (hazard ratio, 1.32; 95% CI, 1.03 to 1.68; P=0.03). Also greater in the prasugrel group was the rate of life-threatening bleeding (1.4% vs. 0.9%; P=0.01), including nonfatal bleeding (1.1% vs. 0.9%; hazard ratio, 1.25; P=0.23) and fatal bleeding (0.4% vs. 0.1%; P=0.002).

CONCLUSIONS

In patients with acute coronary syndromes with scheduled percutaneous coronary intervention, prasugrel therapy was associated with significantly reduced rates of ischemic events, including stent thrombosis, but with an increased risk of major bleeding, including fatal bleeding. Overall mortality did not differ significantly between treatment groups. (ClinicalTrials.gov number, NCT00097591.)

Questions

1. Looking at the results of the trial above, which of the following statements is correct?

   a. Clopidogrel has demonstrated a statistically significant benefit over prasugrel in reducing the primary efficacy endpoint.
   b. Prasugrel has demonstrated a statistically significant benefit over clopidogrel in reducing the primary efficacy endpoint.
   c. Prasugrel has demonstrated a statistically significant benefit over clopidogrel in preventing major bleeding.
   d. Clopidogrel has demonstrated a statistically significant benefit over prasugrel in reducing the primary efficacy endpoint and preventing major bleeding.
   e. There is no statistical difference between clopidogrel and prasugrel in the primary efficacy endpoint.

2. In the trial above, what is the absolute risk reduction in the primary efficacy endpoint?

   a. 22%
   b. 2.2%
   c. 9.9%
   d. 200%
   e. 28%

3. In the trial above, what is the relative risk reduction of experiencing the primary efficacy endpoint?

   a. 81.8%
   b. 50%
   c. 18.2%
   d. 122%
   e. 69%

4. In the trial above, how many people need to be treated with prasugrel to achieve the primary efficacy measure in one patient?

   a. 40
   b. 45
   c. 4.5
   d. 46
   e. 14

5. In the trial above, the hazard ratio for nonfatal bleeding of 1.25 can be interpreted as:

   a. At any time a patient in the prasugrel group was 1.25 times as likely to experience nonfatal bleeding as a patient in the clopidogrel group.
   b. At any time a patient in the prasugrel group was 75% more likely to experience nonfatal bleeding as a patient in the clopidogrel group.
   c. At any time a patient in the clopidogrel group was 1.25 times as likely to experience nonfatal bleeding as a patient in the prasugrel group.
   d. At any time a patient in the clopidogrel group was 75% more likely to experience nonfatal bleeding as a patient in the prasugrel group.
   e. At only this point in time a patient in the prasugrel group was 1.25 times more likely to experience nonfatal bleeding as a patient in the clopidogrel group.

Questions 6-14 do not relate to the case.

6. A trial is conducted between 2 different beta blockers, referred to as Drug A and Drug B. The null hypothesis is that both drugs will be equal in their effects on lowering BP. In the study, Drug A demonstrated greater BP lowering effects than Drug B (p-value < 0.01). Which of the following statements is correct?

   a. We can accept the null hypothesis.
   b. We can fail to accept the null hypothesis.
   c. There is a 10% chance that Drug A is superior.
   d. There is a 0.1% chance that Drug B is superior.
   e. This trial did not reach statistical significance.

7. Correlation in a clinical trial describes:

   a. The ability of 1 or more variables to predict another
   b. The relationship between 2 variables
   c. Nominal data
   d. Confounding variables
   e. A cause and effect relationship

8. Which of the following statements concerning a Type I error is correct?

   a. A type I error means that the null hypothesis is accepted in error.
   b. A type I error means that the null hypothesis is rejected in error.
   c. A type I error means failing to reject the null hypothesis in error.
   d. A type I error means that the null hypothesis is accepted.
   e. A type I error is a beta error.

9. Which of the following statements concerning case-control studies is correct? (Select **ALL** that apply.)

   a. They are retrospective.
   b. The patient serves as their own control.
   c. The researcher analyzes individual patient cases.
   d. They include cases without the intervention.
   e. They provide conclusive evidence of cause and effect.

10. Which of the following statements regarding the median is correct? (Select **ALL** that apply.)

    a. It is the value in the middle of a ranked list.
    b. It is not appropriate to use with skewed data.
    c. It is not sensitive to outliers.
    d. It is a measure of dispersion.
    e. In a normal distribution, it is the same as the mean.

11. Choose the example(s) that represent direct medical cost. (Select **ALL** that apply.)

    a. Lost productivity
    b. Quality of life
    c. Clinic visit
    d. Nursing services
    e. Cost of taking the bus to the hospital

12. Choose the best description of the purpose of a pharmacoeconomic analysis:

    a. To measure and compare the costs and outcomes of drug therapy and other medical interventions.
    b. To reduce health care expenditures by limiting medication use to only those who need it most.
    c. To get the best treatments available to as many people as possible.
    d. To examine the indirect costs of medical care in each medical specialty within hospitals, clinics, and outpatient surgery centers.
    e. To reduce the pharmacy drug budget within a hospital setting as a way to control health care costs.

13. Which of the following statements regarding average and incremental cost ratios is correct? (Select **ALL** that apply.)

    a. Average cost ratios represent the average cost per outcome between competing alternatives.
    b. Incremental cost ratios represent the cost per additional unit of outcome between competing alternatives.
    c. Average cost ratios represent the average cost per outcome within a single alternative.
    d. Incremental cost ratios represent the cost per additional unit of outcome within a single alternative.In most instances, incremental and average cost ratios are equal.
    e. In most instances, incremental and average cost ratios are equal.

14. A pharmacist is conducting an analysis to determine the best way to manage patients with diabetes based on A1C values. Three treatment regimens will be evaluated based on cost and effects on A1C reduction. Choose the type of analysis the pharmacist should perform:

    a. A cost-utility analysis
    b. A cost-minimization analysis
    c. A cost-optimization analysis
    d. A cost-benefit analysis
    e. A cost-effectiveness analysis

Answers

1-b, 2-b, 3-c, 4-d, 5-a, 6-b, 7-b, 8-b, 9-a,c,d, 10-a,c,e, 11-c,d, 12-a, 13-b,c, 14-e

12

DRUG MECHANISMS, CLASSES & STRUCTURES

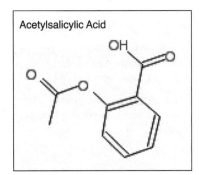

Acetylsalicylic Acid

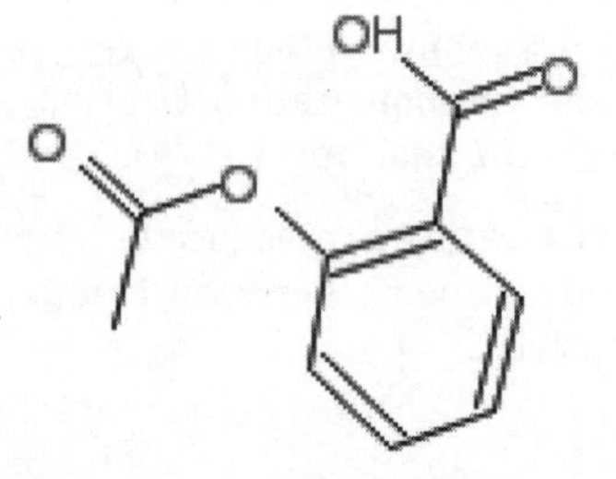

BACKGROUND

Medications can be referred to by their mechanism of action (beta adrenergic blockers or phosphodiesterase-5 inhibitors) or by their main purpose (antihypertensives or decongestants). The expected effect of a drug can be predicted from its mechanism of action and chemical structure. The relationship between the structure of a compound and its activity is referred to as structure activity relationship.

Drugs that Interact with Receptors

An agonist refers to a drug that behaves in a similar manner to a naturally occurring endogenous (produced by the body) ligand; the ligand (or substrate) is the compound that would normally bind to the receptor. An agonist will generally activate a receptor that starts a chain reaction that produces an effect, such as altering a second messenger system. For example, theophylline blocks phosphodiesterase (PDE), which increases the second messenger cyclic adenine monophosphate (cAMP), which in turn induces the release of epinephrine (which causes the bronchioles to open).

A drug that blocks the endogenous substrate is an antagonist (or blocker), such as beta blockers which block beta adrenergic transmitters such as epinephrine, which normally increases heart rate and blood pressure. Drugs can activate or inhibit enzymes, such as heparin which binds to antithrombin, an enzyme that inactivates thrombin. The interaction of the enzyme with the drug can be competitive or non-competitive. Competitive interaction occurs when a drug binds to the receptor which blocks the active site where the substrate would normally bind, preventing the activity (such as aspirin binding to cyclo-oxygenase in platelets which blocks thromboxane synthesis). In non-competitive interaction the drug binds to the enzyme at a site other than the active site, and reduces the activity of the substrate.

Except for the drugs that affect GABA, most seizure drugs bind to a receptor to alter ion entry or departure from a cell, which (in this case) reduces the excessive electrical activity (seizures). Antiarrhythmics work by a similar mechanism.

Many drugs interfere with normal cell duplication by binding to the DNA or some type of protein (such as ribosomes) or intercalating (inserting) itself into the DNA to prevent replication. Antibodies and hormones can amplify or provide a normal cellular process, such as erythropoietin injection to stimulate RBC production or testosterone gel to provide a substitute for low endogenous testosterone. Monoclonal antibodies are identical clones to a parent cell, and are used to interact with a cell receptor and block the receptor [such as infliximab, which inhibits tumor necrosis factor (TNF)-alpha] or as an agonist (such as immune globulin).

This chapter describes some common mechanisms with graphic representations of select pathways and common neurotransmitters (NT). Important mechanisms are also reviewed in the disease state chapters.

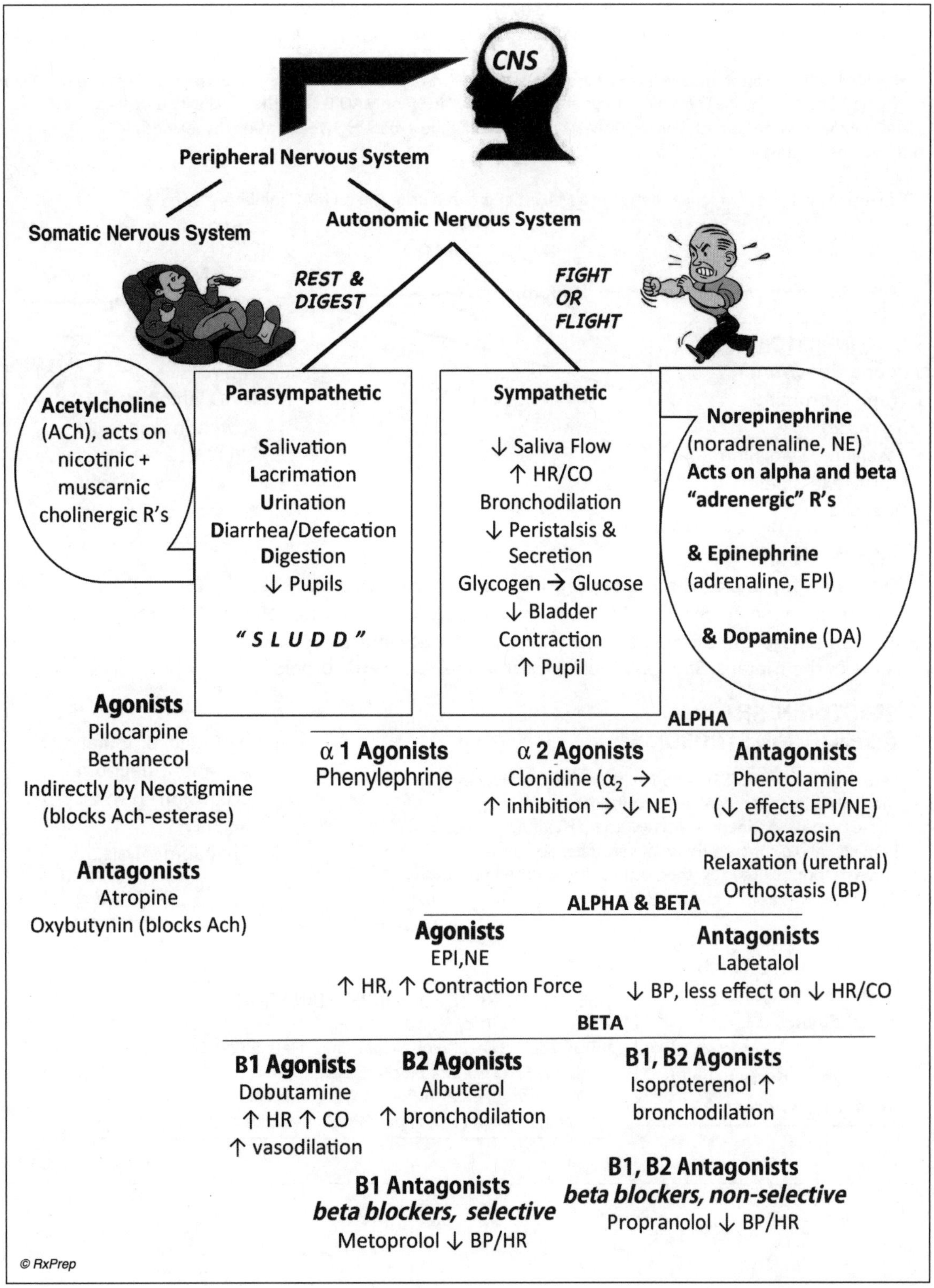

EPI, NE, DA (CATECHOLAMINES) & HYPERTENSIVE CRISIS

These NTs are monoamines and are metabolized by monoamine oxidase (MAO) or catechol-o-methyl transferase (COMT).

The older MAO inhibitor antidepressants are non-selective (MAO A and B), and they bind irreversibly to the MAO enzyme—and destroy it.. The newer drugs are specific for MAO A or MAO B...but the specificity is dose-related. MAO inhibitors & drugs metabolized by MAO → catecholamine excess → hypertension, hyperthermia, tachycardia, agitation...coma, death.

Remedy: Wait 14 days or longer between a MAO-metabolized drug and an MAO inhibitor.

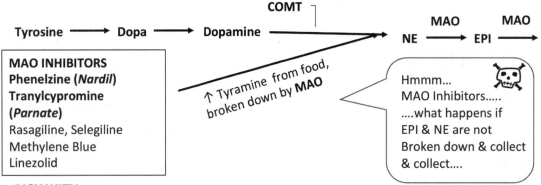

Tyrosine → Dopa → Dopamine → (COMT) NE → (MAO) EPI → (MAO)

↑ Tyramine from food, broken down by **MAO**

MAO INHIBITORS
Phenelzine (*Nardil*)
Tranylcypromine (*Parnate*)
Rasagiline, Selegiline
Methylene Blue
Linezolid

Hmmm...
MAO Inhibitors.....
....what happens if EPI & NE are not Broken down & collect & collect....

RISK WITH

Ephedrine and analogs (pseudoephedrine, etc.), bupropion, buspirone, lithium, meperidine, SSRIs, SNRIs, TCAs, tramadol, levodopa, mirtazapine, dextromethorphan, cyclobenzaprine (and other skeletal muscle relaxants), some of the triptans, St. John's wort, procarbazine, lorcaserin, others.

SEROTONIN: 5HT & SEROTONIN SYNDROME

Serotonin syndrome (SS) can be mild....or lethal (depending on how high).
More 5HT-drugs in recent years ↑ incidence.
Cause of most: Antidepressants + other 5HT-drugs
Remedy: Avoid concurrent use of serotonergic
Some cannot be used together, others can be dosed cautiously.
Caution: 5HT is also metabolized by MAO.

↑ 5HT mild, or lethal
Agitation...delirium
Confusion...tremor...
Rigidity....
Rhabdomyolysis....
...Coma

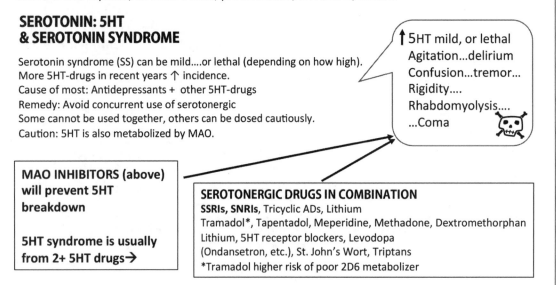

MAO INHIBITORS (above) will prevent 5HT breakdown

5HT syndrome is usually from 2+ 5HT drugs→

SEROTONERGIC DRUGS IN COMBINATION
SSRIs, SNRIs, Tricyclic ADs, Lithium
Tramadol*, Tapentadol, Meperidine, Methadone, Dextromethorphan
Lithium, 5HT receptor blockers, Levodopa
(Ondansetron, etc.), St. John's Wort, Triptans
*Tramadol higher risk of poor 2D6 metabolizer

© RxPrep

GABA is the primary INHIBITORY NT.
GABA ↓Brain Stimulation, Fear & Anxiety.

CNS DEPRESSANT EFFECTS
Common & cause of many auto accidents & injuries
Often additive...some drugs on their own can knock a person out, including GABA drugs:

GABA Agonists or ↑ GABA Effect
Barbiturates
Benzodiazepines...both cause physical dependence, tolerance can occur and addiction/abuse (especially with benzodiazepines) is common.

AND THESE cause CNS Depression:
Most pain medications (all of the opioids, some of the NSAIDs, other pain drugs), skeletal muscle relaxants, anticonvulsants, benzodiazepines, barbiturates, hypnotics, mirtazapine, trazodone, dronabinol, nabilone, propranolol, clonidine, others, many illicit substances and alcohol.

© RxPrep

INSULIN

Insulin works primarily on 3 areas: the liver (makes the liver convert glucose into glycogen, to store for later use, and also prevents the glycogen from breaking back down into glucose after a person eats and the glucose in the blood increases), the muscle cells (which need a lot of insulin; insulin brings glucose into the cells for energy) and adipose (fat) cells (insulin causes excess glucose to be converted into fat, which is stored in adipose cells). To supply cells with energy, insulin activates glucose transporters on the cells so glucose can get in; this reduces hyperglycemia.

Normally, the pancreas releases the right amount of insulin that the body requires. When the beta cells in the pancreas have been destroyed (type 1) the patient must take insulin. In type 2, there is less insulin over time, and there can be resistance to insulin in the cells, which means more insulin is required in order to open up the glucose transporters and let glucose get into the cells.

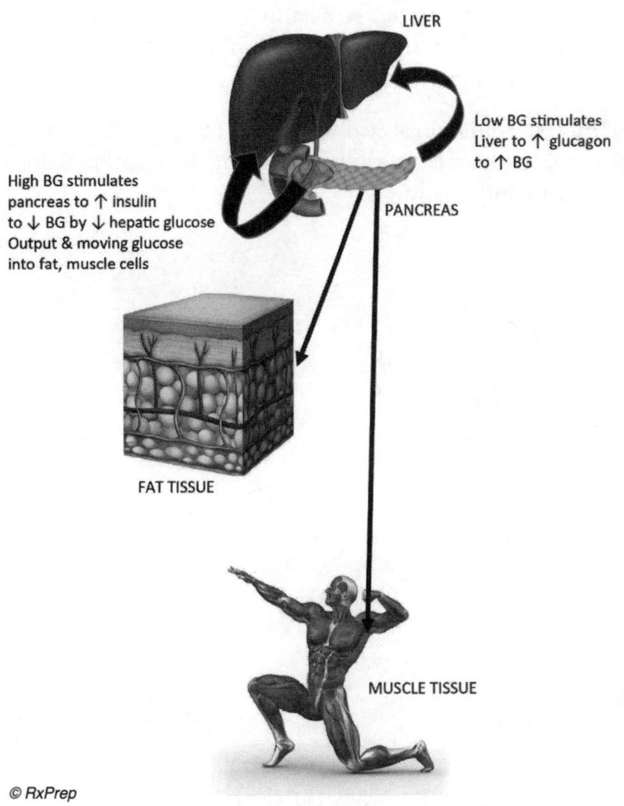
LIVER
Low BG stimulates
Liver to ↑ glucagon
to ↑ BG
High BG stimulates
pancreas to ↑ insulin
to ↓ BG by ↓ hepatic glucose
Output & moving glucose
into fat, muscle cells
PANCREAS
FAT TISSUE
MUSCLE TISSUE

© RxPrep

THYROID

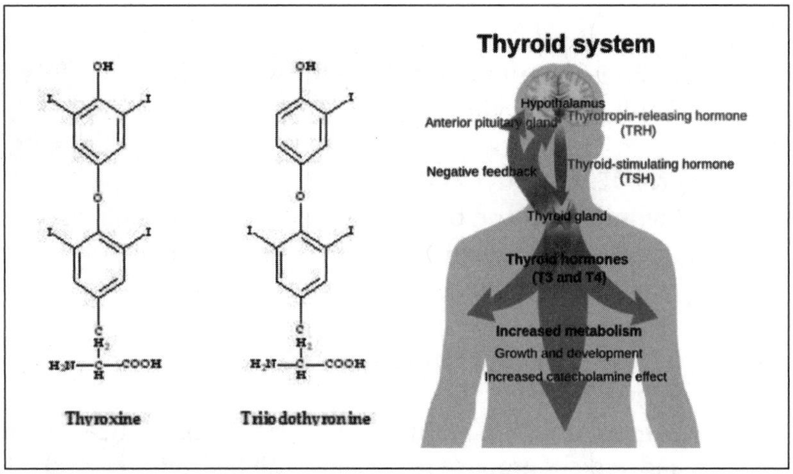

The thyroid gland produces triiodothyronine (T3) and thyroxine (T4). Both require iodine; if iodine is low, the thyroid will increase in size in an attempt to overcome the deficiency, producing a goiter. Propylthioruracil and methimazole block iodine oxidation to block production of thyroid hormones (to treat hyperthyroidism).

The thyroid gland is controlled by the hypothalamus and the pituitary gland. The hypothalamus produces thyrotropin-releasing hormone (TRH), which stimulates the production of TSH, which increases production of T3 and T4. Over-production of thyroid hormones has the reverse effect by decreasing production through "feedback inhibition," in which the end product (thyroid hormone) is high, and the thyroid hormone reduces it's own synthesis.

CORTISOL

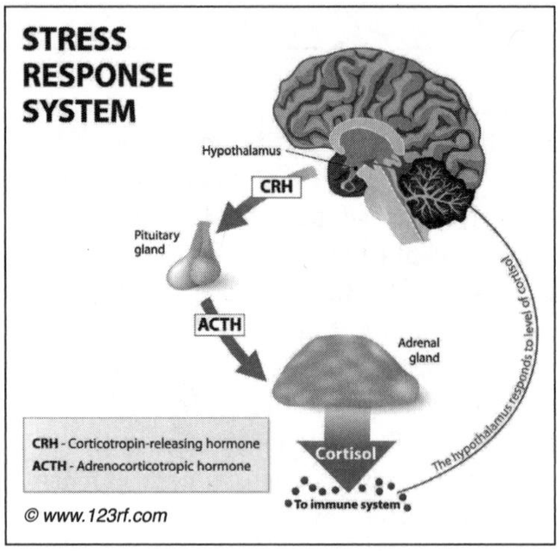

Hypothalamus--> anterior pituitary--> ACTH--> adrenal gland--> cortisol. Physical and emotional stress increases cortisol production, with effects shown in the diagram. Notice that endogenous steroids cause the same effects, but dysregulated.

Giving steroids chronically has the reverse effect, and shuts down cortisol production through negative feedback, causing Cushing's.

ESTROGEN, PROGESTERONE AND THE FEMALE MENSTRUAL CYCLE

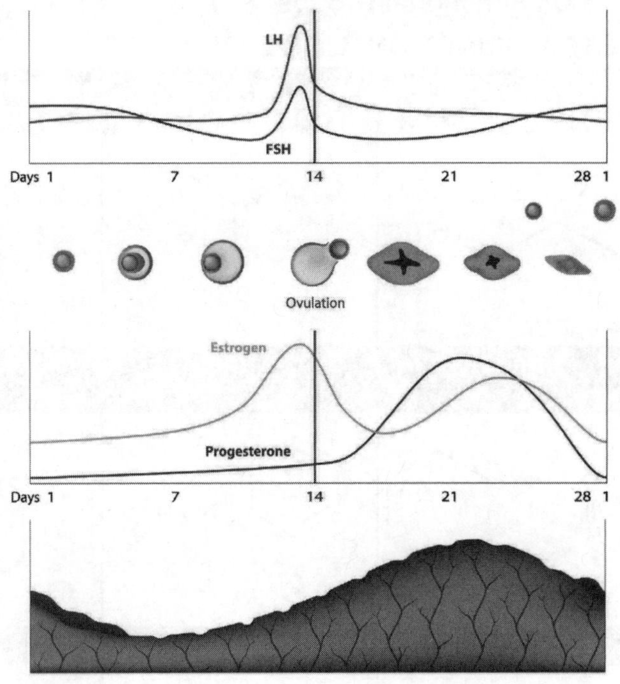

© www.123rf.com

The menstrual cycle has 3 phases. 1st: The follicular phase begins on the 1st day bleeding (the start of the period). Follicle stimulating hormone (FSH) stimulates egg (follicle) development, and increases estrogen. 2nd: The ovulatory phase, which is a short phase. It begins when the luteinizing hormone (LH) level surges, which triggers ovulation 24-36 hours later (release of the egg from the ovary), and the end of the phase. 3rd: The luteal phase, which begins with ovulation and lasts about 14 days.

Notice in phase 1 that estrogen (E) and progesterone (P) are low, and this triggers bleeding. E and P causes the endometrium to thicken, and when low, the lining drips off. Estrogen increases, which causes LH to surge and trigger ovulation. Estrogen and Progesterone cause the endometrium (the lining of the uterus) to thicken to prepare for an embryo, and P causes the cervical mucus to thicken and increases body temperature.

FUNCTIONAL GROUPS

Some of the common functional groups are depicted. Knowledge of these functional groups allows a pharmacist to predict certain effects of drugs. For example, identification of the sulfonamide functional group on the celecoxib compound explains why the product labeling for celecoxib states that it is contraindicated in patients with allergic-type reactions to sulfonamides.

Celecoxib *(Celebrex)*

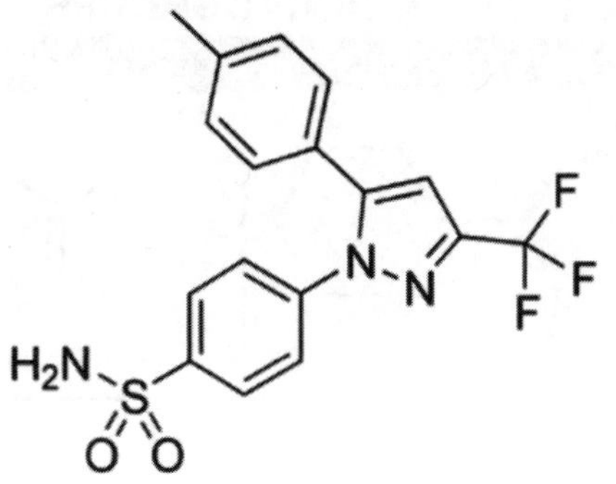

Common Functional Groups

NEUTRAL FUNCTIONAL GROUPS

HYDROXYL OR ALCOHOL (PRIMARY)	KETONE	ALDEHYDE	AMIDE
	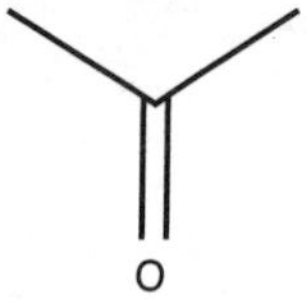	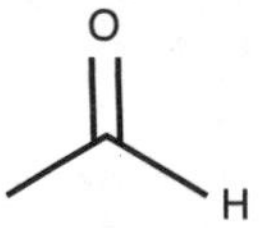	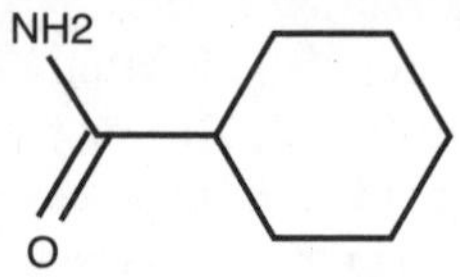
NITRATE	**NITRO**	**AROMATIC (BENZENE) RING**	**UREA**
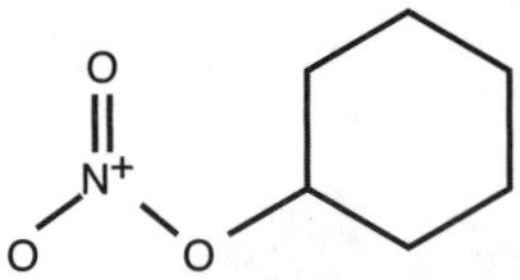	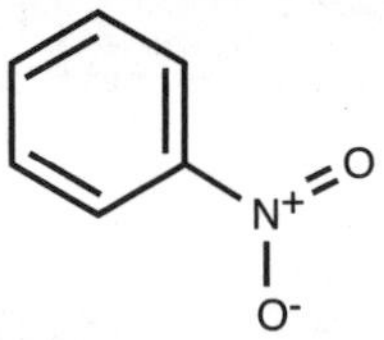		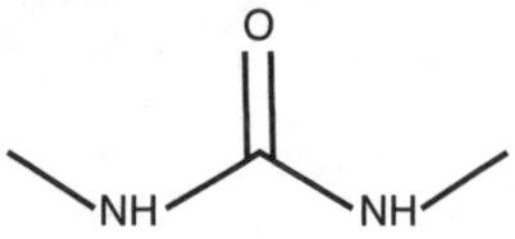
CARBONATE	**CARBAMATE**	**ETHER**	**THIOETHER**
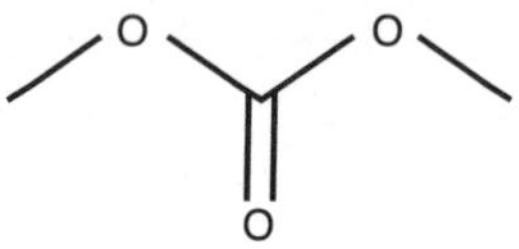	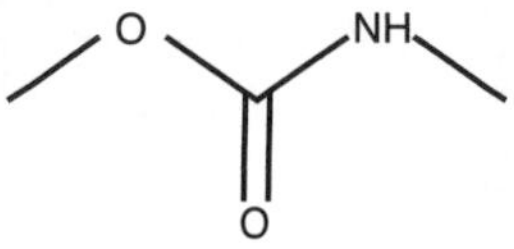		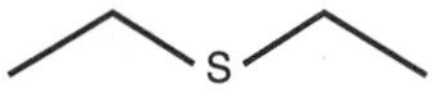

ACIDIC FUNCTIONAL GROUPS

CARBOXYL	PHENOL	IMIDE	SULFONAMIDE
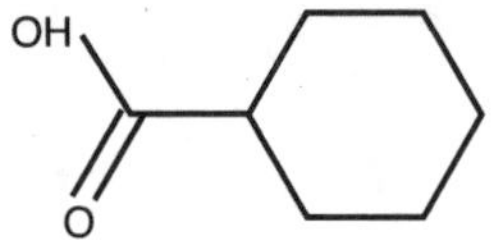	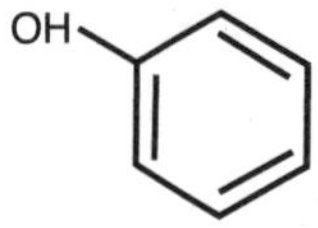	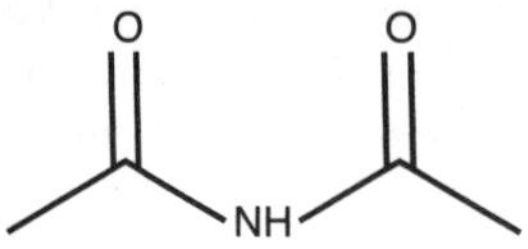	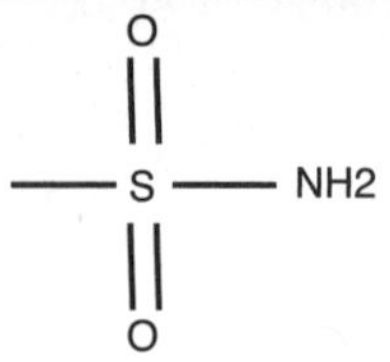

BASIC FUNCTIONAL GROUPS

AMINE (PRIMARY)	AMINE (TERTIARY)	IMINE	AMIDINE
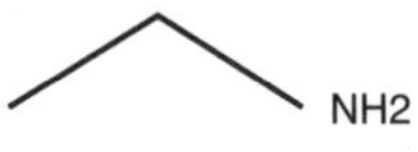	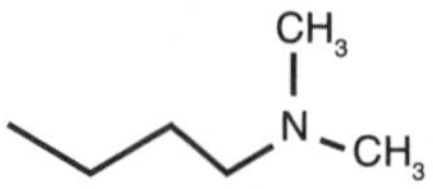	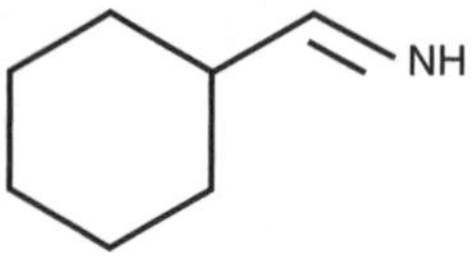	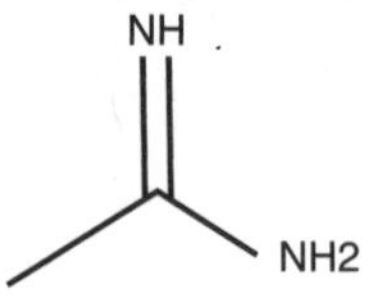

DRUG FORMULATIONS

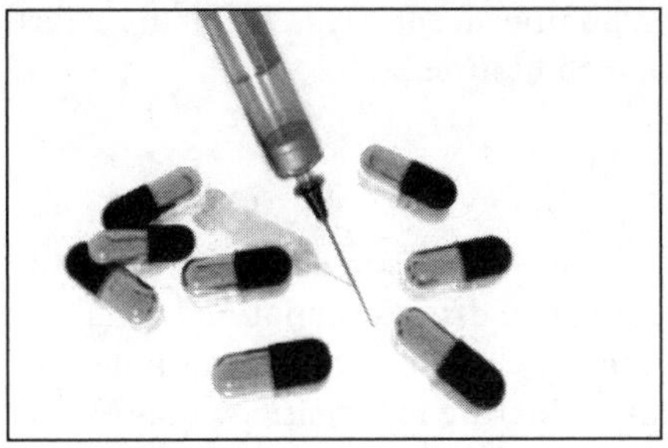

DRUG FORMULATION CONSIDERATIONS

Compressed tablets are the least expensive drug formulation to manufacture and the most common formulation type. Capsules are also relatively inexpensive to make. If a pharmaceutical company develops a drug in any other formulation the cost will be higher – and a patient group that would benefit from the new formulation would be required. Prednisolone 10 mg tablets cost < 25¢ per tablet. A similar steroid in an oral disintegrating formulation (ODT), *Orapred ODT,* is branded and is ~$16 per tablet. The higher-priced formulation might be beneficial in a child with facial swelling who might choke on a hard tablet or who cannot yet swallow tablets.

It is helpful to recall a drug's formulation types by asking two questions:

1) Who typically uses this drug?

2) Would there be a reason to have this type of formulation for this patient population?

This can be useful on the exam if unsure if the formulation exists.

Examples

Olanzapine

Olanzapine is an antipsychotic with various formulations available: immediate-release (IR) tablet, oral disintegrating tablet, short-acting injection, and long-acting injection.

Who uses this drug? People with schizophrenia, bipolar disorder or some type of psychosis.

What types of formulations would be beneficial? The majority of patients with schizophrenia discontinue antipsychotics. It is useful to deliver the drug in a long-acting injection to improve adherence. A few of the antipsychotics come as orally disintegrating tablets (ODTs) – these are useful to block the patient from hiding the medication in the mouth ("cheeking") and then spitting it out when no one is watching. The ODT formulations dissolve in the mouth quickly which prevents cheeking. The fast-acting injection works quickly and is useful for acute agitation.

Ondansetron

Ondansetron, a $5\text{-}HT_3$-receptor antagonist used to prevent or treat nausea is available in with various formulations available: IR tablet, short-acting injection, oral solution, ODT and oral film.

Who uses this drug? Patients receiving emetogenic chemotherapy or any other emetogenic drug, post-surgical patients, opioid-naïve patients using opioids acutely or with any condition that causes nausea/vomiting.

What types of formulations would be beneficial? If vomiting is an issue, oral medications would be useless and the injection would be used instead. If there is nausea alone, the ODT or the film or the injection can be given. ODTs are preferred if there is dysphagia, which could be present due to age and/or a medical condition, including cancer. It would be difficult to swallow tablets with painful esophageal ulcers, strictures or tumors. Films can be placed on or under the tongue or along the inside of the cheek and provide similar benefit to ODTs. With some film formulations the loss to first-pass metabolism is reduced. The oral solution would be preferable if the patient has an NG-tube or any dysphagia or pain from solid oral formulations. The solution can be swallowed directly and is sweetened with sorbitol to mask the bitter taste of the medicine. One of the 5-HT_3-receptor antagonists comes in a long-acting patch (*Sancuso*) that reduces nausea for up to seven days; this would be useful for a patient with nausea from chemotherapy that lasts awhile. The patch is put on prior to chemo (not useful for nausea happening when the patch is first applied) since, like most patches, it takes time for drug absorption through the skin. Aprepitant *(Emend)* comes in a solution to meet similar needs. This summary chart contains select medications and the reasoning behind the unique formulation.

Warning: Sweeteners Are Not Sweet For All

Formulations that are exposed to taste buds often contain sweeteners, which are generally well-tolerated, with exceptions. Lactose is the most commonly used excipient in drug formulations. It is tolerated by some, but not all, patients with lactose-intolerance. Sensitivity to lactose is variable and changes with age. Sorbitol metabolism produces gas, cramping and bloating in sensitive patients, including those with IBS. Phenylalanine is a dangerous sweetener for those with phenylketonuria (PKU), a genetic defect in which the enzyme that degrades phenylalanine is absent.

Select Medications in Unique Formulations

FORMULATION	EXAMPLES	REASONS FOR USE
ODTs – placed on the tongue and disintegrate rapidly in saliva	*Abilify Discmelt* – aripiprazole *Parcopa* – carbidopa/levodopa *Zyrtec Allergy Children* – cetirizine *FazaClo* – clozapine *Aricept ODT* – Donepezil *Prevacid SoluTab* – lansoprazole *Lamictal ODT* – lamotrigine *Metozolv ODT* – metoclopramide *Remeron SolTab* – mirtazapine *Zyprexa Zydis* – olanzapine *Zofran ODT* – ondansetron *Orapred ODT* – prednisone *Risperdal M-TAB* – risperidone *Maxalt-MLT* – rizatriptan *Zelapar* – selegiline *Staxyn* – vardenafil *Zomig-ZMT* – zolmitriptan	Dysphagia – trouble swallowing due to a variety of reasons: Stroke is the #1 cause of dysphagia due to paralysis of the throat muscles. Dysphagia can be due to esophagitis, esophageal tumors, ↓ LES pressure/reflux, facial swelling from an allergic reaction, or with other conditions that worsen motor function, including multiple sclerosis and Parkinson disease. Children are often too young to swallow tablets or capsules. Nausea can make it difficult to tolerate anything orally, however, ODTs cause less nausea than oral formulations swallowed whole. If vomiting is present or is likely a non-oral route should be used. Non-adherence – ODTs prevent holding the drug in the corner of the mouth to spit out shortly afterward – the tablet would dissolve quickly and the caregiver could follow with a drink of water.

Common (Select) Medications Given in Unique Formulations continued

FORMULATION	EXAMPLES	REASONS FOR USE
Films that use gut absorption	*Zuplenz* – ondansetron Many OTC products used for children come as films, and films are used for some adult OTC drugs and for breath fresheners.	Films have similar benefits to ODTs; they dissolve in the mouth easily and do not have issues associated with swallowing.
Lozenges for oral mucosa drug administration	*Mycelex* – clotrimazole troche, compounded formulations	Used to treat a condition in the oral mucosa – the drug is held in the mouth while the troche slowly dissolves.
Sublingual (SL) or buccal delivery with tablets, film, or sprays	*Saphris* – asenapine SL tablet *Edluar* – zolpidem SL tablet *Intermezzo* – zolpidem SL tablet *Nitrostat* – nitroglycerin SL tablet *Nitrolingual, NitroMist* – nitroglycerin SL spray *Bunavail* – buprenorphine/naloxone buccal film *Subsys, Actiq, Fentora, Abstral*– fentanyl	SL and buccal absorption has a faster onset than a tablet or capsule that is swallowed; the drug is readily absorbed into the venous circulation right under the absorption site (e.g., under the tongue). Less of the drug is lost to gut degradation and first-pass metabolism.
Nasal sprays (NS)	*Lazanda* – fentanyl NS *Miacalcin* – calcitonin NS *Nascobal* – cyanocobalamin (vitamin B12) NS *Sprix* – ketorolac NS *Imitrex* – sumatriptan NS *Zomig* – zolmitriptan NS *Afrin* – oxymetazoline NS *Flonase* – fluticasone NS	Nasal sprays such as *Afrin* and *Flonase* are used primarily to treat localized nasal symptoms. The nasal route has a faster onset than the GI route, and is useful for acute conditions that should be treated quickly, including pain. Nasal sprays bypass gut absorption; proteins that would get destroyed in the gut (calcitonin) can be given nasally. A compound that requires a gut factor for absorption can also be given nasally (vitamin B12).
Creams, ointments, gels, solutions for topical conditions	*Voltaren* – diclofenac gel *Latisse* – bimatoprost gel *Bactroban* – mupirocin ointment Many others, including topical retinoids and benzoyl peroxide or salicylic acid products for acne, psoriasis treatments, first aid products, steroids, antifungals, many compounded formulations	Topical treatments used for topical conditions have a decreased incidence of systemic side effects and generally provide faster relief. Common conditions treated topically include muscle/joint painold sores, acne, eczema, inflammation, mild infections, hair loss, rash, fungal infections, viral sores, hypotrichosis.
Topicals for systemic conditions	*AndroGel, others* – testosterone Compounded formulations, including hormonal products	

Common (Select) Medications Given in Unique Formulations continued

FORMULATION	EXAMPLES	REASONS FOR USE
Injections that patients can self-administer (mostly SC)	*Imitrex* – sumatriptan *Arixtra* – fondaparinux *Lovenox* – enoxaparin *Humira* – adalimumab *EpiPen* – epinephrine *Enbrel* – etanercept *Evzio* – naloxone *Simponi* – golimumab *Copaxone* – glatiramer *Peg-Intron, Rebif* – and other interferons *Aranesp* – darbepoetin alfa *Epogen/Procrit* – epoetin alfa	SC administration is used for acute relief (such as pain, with triptans) or for stat treatment of a severe condition (such as opioid overdose with *Evzio* or bronchoconstriction with the *EpiPen*) or, for drugs that would get destroyed or not absorbed if given by oral administration (enoxaparin). The erythropoiesis stimulating agents (ESAs) are given SC by patients with impaired renal function, and if in ESRD, are given IV at the dialysis center.
Chewable Tablets	Many OTCs *(Pepto-Bismol, Immodium, Claritin)* *Augmentin* – amoxicillin/clavulanate *Suprax* – cefixime *Amoxil* – amoxicillin *Dilantin Infatabs* – phenytoin *Fosrenol* – lanthanum (must chew for drug to bind gut phosphate) *Singulair* – montelukast *Lamictal CD* – lamotrigine *Quillichew ER, Methylin* – methyphenidate	These are primarily used for children who are unable to swallow tablets. A few are for adults; calcium citrate tablets are large, and chewable calcium products are easier to tolerate. Note that *Pepto-Bismol* and *Immodium* are used for diarrhea; with a gut infection, nausea could be present.
Long-Acting Oral Tablets/Capsules Some capsules can be opened and the beads put in a small amount of soft food-instruct the patient to swallow without chewing. Note the danger if long-acting formulations are crushed: a fatal dose could be released. This includes ER opioids. Be sure to look for the suffix and counsel. There are a few long-acting formulations that can be cut at the score line – but still NOT crushed, such as *Toprol XL* and *Sinemet CR.*	*Concerta* *Detrol LA* Do not crush or chew any drug that has the following suffix that indicates it is a long-acting formulation: XR, ER, LA, SR, CR, CRT, SA, TR, TD, or have 24 in the name, or the ending –cont (for controlled release), or timecaps or sprinkles. *Concerta, Covera HS* and about a dozen other long-acting medications use the OROS formulation to provide fast drug delivery, followed by an extended-release in one drug. Water from the gut is absorbed into the delivery system by osmosis, which increases the pressure inside and forces the drug out through a small opening.	Certain drugs are designed as slow release or are enteric-coated to avoid irritation to the GI lining or are designed to dissolve in the small intestine. Or, the drug may be designed to release drug slowly to avoid nausea or to provide a long-duration of action to avoid repeated day-time dosing. Providing a smooth level of drug release over time reduces high "peaks" which reduces side effects due to too much drug hitting the "wrong" receptor and provides a safe level of drug over the dosing interval. This is required for conditions that require steady drug levels such as with epilepsy, hypertension, and with many others.

Common (Select) Medications Given in Unique Formulations continued

FORMULATION	EXAMPLES	REASONS FOR USE
Granules, powders or capsules that can be opened and sprinkled into soft food or water Typically these are long-acting beads - if they sit in soft food the liquid will ruin the slow release. The food must not be warm or the beads will dissolve. Instruct patients to consume right after they sprinkle or stir; do not chew if long-acting or an irritant. To swallow without chewing requires that the drug be placed in a small amount of soft food.	*Avinza* – morphine, on applesauce or soft food *Kadian* – morphine, on applesauce or soft food *Micro-K* – potassium, on applesauce or pudding *Coreg CR* – carvedilol, on applesauce *Creon, Lip-Prot-Amyl, Pancreaze, Pertzye, Ultresa, Viokace, Zenpep* – pancrelipase, on soft food with low pH (applesauce, pureed pears or banana) *Depakote Sprinkle* – valproic acid, on soft food *Namenda XR* – memantine, on applesauce *Ritalin LA, Metadate CD* – methylphenidate, on applesauce *Focalin XR* – dexmethylphenidate, on applesauce *Adderall XR* – dextroamphetamine/amphetamine ER, on applesauce *Vyvanse* – lisdexamfetamine, in water, yogurt or orange juice *Singulair* – montelukast granules, in 5 mL baby formula or breast milk or in a spoonful of applesauce, carrots, rice or ice cream *Topamax Sprinkle* – topiramate, on soft food *Dexilant* – dexlansoprazole, in applesauce or acidic juice *Prevacid* – lansoprazole, in applesauce or acidic juice Nexium – esomeprazole, in applesauce or acidic juice *Prilosec* – omeprazole, in applesauce or water *Welchol* – colesevelam, in 4-8 oz water, fruit juice or diet soda *Questran, Questran Light* – cholestyramine, in 2-6 oz water or non-carbonated liquid	These are used primarily for geriatric and pediatric patients who have some type of swallowing issue. Sometimes the capsule or tablet is too large to swallow. Instruct patient not to chew any long-acting pellets or beads that are emptied out from a capsule, not to let the mixture sit too long (take within the time directed) and not to add to anything warm or hot (the contents will dissolve too quickly).
Patches	See chart of common patches later in this chapter; a few examples are listed here: *Exelon* – rivastigmine *Duragesic* – fentanyl *Sancuso* – granisetron	Provides drug for a longer period of time (up to 1 week), Less side effects (↓ nausea, ↓ GI irritation) and ↓ side effects from high peak levels with frequent oral dosing. Useful option if vomiting. Helps with adherence if family member can apply patch.
Intravenous (IV) Infusion	Many, acute care drugs	Fast response, achieves high concentrations and/or avoid poor absorption with critical illness, bypasses the oral route, avoids loss of drug due to N/V.
Long-Acting Intramuscular (IM) Injections	*Haldol* – haloperidol decanoate *Zyprexa Relprevv* – olanzapine *Risperdal Consta* – risperidone *Abilify Maintena* – aripiprazole *Invega Sustenna* – paliperidone *Lupron Depot* – leuprolide	Various drugs come as long-acting injections to improve adherence (such as antipsychotics) or to ↓ the need for more frequent (painful) injections.

Common (Select) Medications Given in Unique Formulations continued

FORMULATION	EXAMPLES	REASONS FOR USE
Suppositories/ Enemas	*Rowasa* – mesalamine enema *Canasa* – mesalamine suppository *Babylax* – glycerin suppository *Dulcolax* – bisacodyl suppository *Fleet Enema* – sodium phosphates enema *Preparation H* – phenylephrine/cocoa butter suppository *FeverAll* – acetaminophen suppository	Used either for localized treatment (treating constipation, hemorrhoids) or for systemic treatment (such as mesalamine rectal forms for distal ulcerative colitis. Suppositories can be used when the patient is NPO and systemic treatment is needed (such as acetaminophen for treating pain or fever in an infant).

PATCHES

Medications are increasingly being delivered via transdermal delivery systems. Common concerns with their use includes non-adhesion (patches falling off the skin), patients inappropriately cutting patches, improper disposal, MRI burns, heat exposure leading to toxicity, and lag-time to effect. This list contains the more commonly used patches and how to address common issues concerning patches.

Common Patches, Application Sites

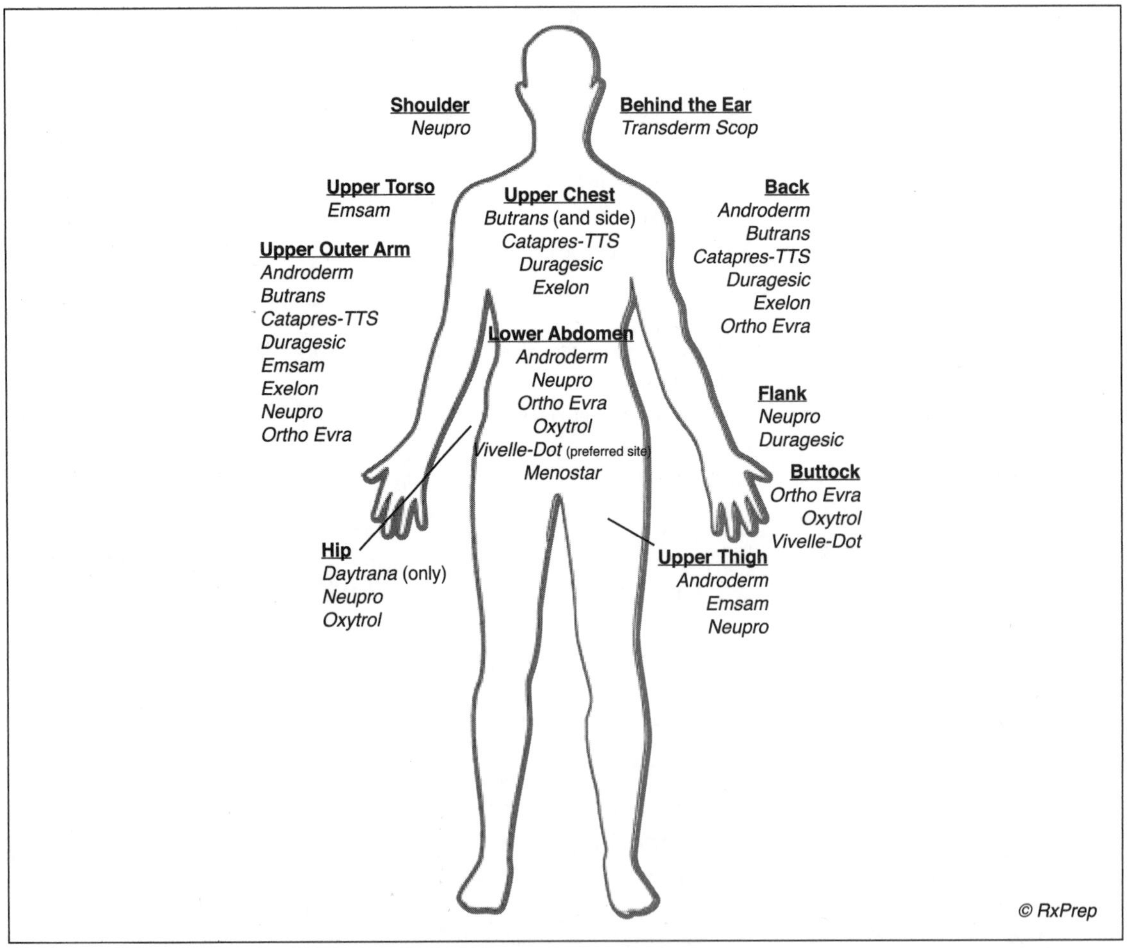

Common Concerns with Patches

QUESTION	RESPONSE	
Can I cut the patch into pieces?	■ Usually no, except *Lidoderm*, which is designed to be cut and applied over the painful regions. ■ Some patients are instructed by their healthcare providers to cut matrix patches, such as fentanyl. This is not advisable since prescribed doses can change and medication errors can happen. Fentanyl patches are available in five different doses and as less expensive generics, which should make cutting unnecessary.	
Can the patch be exposed to heat from an electric blanket, heating pad, or body temperature > 38 °C (> 100.4 °F)?	In almost all cases no heat exposure; this causes the drug to pour out of the patch, resulting in toxicity. With fentanyl and buprenorphine this can be quickly toxic (fatal).	
The patch is bothering my skin. What can I do?	■ Check if the patient is alternating the application site. An alternative site (if permitted) may be beneficial. ■ The skin should not be shaved shortly before applying; shaving is irritating to the skin. ■ In some cases a topical steroid, such as hydrocortisone (OTC) can be applied after the patch is removed; if applied before application it will prevent the patch from sticking well.	
Which patches need to be removed prior to an MRI?	Patches containing metal, such as aluminum, need to be removed prior to an MRI or else it will burn the skin. Clonidine *(Catapres-TTS)* Diclofenac *(Flector)* Estrogen (some, including *Alora)* Rotigotine *(Neupro)* Scopolamine *(Transderm-Scop)* Testosterone *(Androderm)* Check package insert; this can change.	

Common Concerns with Patches continued

QUESTION	RESPONSE
The patch does not stick (it falls or peels off). Can the patch be covered with tape if it will not stick?	With most patches, if it comes off, a new patch is reapplied to the same or a different site. ■ Most patches cannot be covered with tape. A few patches permit tape around the edges. If patches are placed on lubricated skin they will not stick. Place on dry, non-lubricated skin. No moisturizer or bath oils beforehand. Press down for the right amount of time, with palm over the patch. Some require a rather long time, such as the fentanyl patch which takes 30 seconds of pressure to adhere to the skin. ■ Hairy skin will block some of the drug from touching the skin, and can prevent the patch from sticking well. Although patches are not placed on hairy skin, do not shave right before the patch application. This can cause little bumps on delicate skin, and patches cannot be placed on irritated or broken skin. Cut hair close to the skin or shave in advance. Or, use a permitted site that is not hairy. ■ Try not to touch the sticky-side of the patch. ■ Warning: Do not cover patches with the exception of fentanyl (*Duragesic*) or buprenorphine (*Butrans*), which can be covered only with the permitted adhesive film dressings *Bioclusive* or *Tegaderm.* ■ *Catapres-TTS* comes with its own adhesive cover, which goes over the patch to hold it in place.  
How often do I need to apply my patch?	Clonidine *(Catapres-TTS)*: Weekly Estradiol *(Climara, Menostar)*: Weekly Estradiol *(Alora, Vivelle-Dot)*: Twice weekly Estradiol/levonorgestrel *(ClimaraPro)*: Weekly Fentanyl *(Duragesic)*: Q72H, if it wears off after 48 hours, change to Q48H Diclofenac *(Flector)*: Twice daily Lidocaine *(Lidoderm):* 1-3 patches on for 12 hours, then off 12 hours Methylphenidate *(Daytrana)*: Q AM, 2 hours prior to school, alternate hips daily Nicotine *(NicoDerm CQ)*: Daily Nitroglycerin *(Minitran, Nitro-Dur)*: On 12-14 hours/day, off 10-12 hours/day Ethinyl estradiol/norelgestromin *(Ortho Evra)*: Weekly for 3 weeks, off for the 4th week Oxybutynin *(Oxytrol)*: Twice weekly Rivastigmine *(Exelon)*: Daily Rotigotine *(Neupro)*: Daily Scopolamine *(Transderm-Scop)*: Q72H, if needed Selegiline *(Emsam)*: Daily Testosterone *(Androderm)*: Nightly, not on scrotum

Common Concerns with Patches continued

QUESTION	RESPONSE
Where is the patch applied?	Check individual agent. Common application sites include upper chest or upper/sides of back (below the neck), upper thigh, upper outer arm. Most require alternating sites to reduce skin irritation. ■ *Daytrana* is on hip, alternating right and left hips daily. ■ *Transderm Scop* is behind the ear, alternating ears Q 72H. ■ Estrogen patches are mostly lower abdomen; some can be applied to upper buttock. Never to breasts. ■ Testosterone patch is never to scrotum (testicles and surrounding sac). ■ Topical pain patches, such as *Flector, Lidoderm* and *Salonpas* are over the painful area(s). ■ Systemic pain patches, such as *Duragesic*, are applied to the chest, back, flank, or upper arm.
How do I dispose of used patches?	■ In most cases, remove and fold patch to press adhesive surfaces together, then discard, but not in the toilet for most patches. Some should be placed in a childproof container prior to disposal. The DEA requires flushing of highly potent narcotic patches (*Duragesic, Butrans*), since these are dangerous and a child or animal could ingest a fatal amount. ■ Some patches that are dangerous (but less dangerous than a narcotic patch) can be flushed or placed in a trash container only if it is lidded to prevent easy access. *(Daytrana).* 

14

DIETARY SUPPLEMENTS, NATURAL & COMPLEMENTARY MEDICINE

GUIDELINES/REFERENCES

National Center for Complementary and Integrative Health (NCCIH). Use of complementary health approaches in the U.S. National Health Interview Survey. https://nccih.nih.gov/research/statistics/NHIS/2012/natural-products (accessed 2016 Oct 11).

Baker RD, Greer FR. Diagnosis and prevention of iron deficiency and iron-deficiency anemia in infants and young children (0-3 years of age). *Pediatrics.* 2010;126(5):1040-50.

Additional guidelines included with the video files (RxPrep Online).

We gratefully acknowledge the assistance of Darren Hein, PharmD, Center for Drug Information & Evidence-Based Practice, Creighton University School of Pharmacy, in preparing this chapter.

BACKGROUND

Complementary medicine refers to a non-mainstream practice that is used together with conventional medicine (such as physician visits, lab work, diagnostic and surgical procedures, and prescription medications). For example, most Americans with cancer will use conventional chemotherapy, and many of these will also use complementary medicine approaches to manage side effects and promote healing. These could include the use of melatonin or valerian to help with sleep, or marijuana to help reduce nausea and improve appetite. Some of the cancer treatment centers offer complementary approaches that include popular "mind-body" practices to help the patient develop strength and handle the stressors of treatment, such as yoga, meditation and massage.

The term *alternative* medicine is used when conventional medicine is not used. Most Americans practice complementary medicine, which commonly includes natural medicines.

NATURAL MEDICINE

'Natural medicine' is a general umbrella term that includes herbals (plant products), vitamins, minerals, and many substances that are not plant-derived but exist in nature, such as glucosamine from shellfish. The FDA uses the term "dietary supplements."

Dietary supplements are regulated by the *Dietary Supplement Health and Education Act* (DSHEA) of 1994. By this law, the dietary supplement manufacturer is responsible for ensuring that their products are safe before they are marketed. In contrast, drugs must be proven safe and effective for the intended use before they can be sold. Under DSHEA, once the product is marketed, the FDA has the responsibility for showing that a dietary supplement is "unsafe," before it can take action to restrict the product's use or remove it from the marketplace. The company selling or distributing the product is required to record, investigate, and forward to the FDA reports they receive of any serious adverse events. Patients and healthcare providers can also submit reports about adverse events from dietary supplements via the FDA's MedWatch program (see the Drug Allergies chapter for information on MedWatch).

Since dietary supplements do not need to be proven effective before they are marketed, the manufacturers cannot make claims that the product treats or cures a condition. Manufacturers are only allowed to make claims about the nutrient content, the relationship to health, and the impact on normal body structure or function, such as "calcium builds strong bones," "fiber maintains bowel regularity," or "antioxidants maintain cell integrity." Products that make structure/function claims are required to include the warning: "This statement has not been evaluated by the FDA. This product is not intended to diagnose, treat, cure, or prevent any disease."

Although dietary supplement manufacturers are required by law to follow current good manufacturing practices (CGMPs), many do not adequately comply with this requirement. There have been many reports of dietary supplements that are adulterated with incorrect ingredients, including prescription drugs. Pharmacists can help consumers choose a reputable product. The United States Pharmacopeia (USP) establishes standards for dietary supplements. Products that are awarded the USP Verified mark have met requirements for CGMPs. In recent years, other third party organizations have put in place programs that will issue a grade or put a seal of approval on products made by a company following CGMPs.

Some natural medicines themselves can pose safety risks in certain patients. Four areas of particular safety concern are natural medicines that increase bleeding risk, those that interact with prescription drugs, and those that cause cardiotoxicity or hepatotoxicity.

Increased Bleeding Risk

Several natural medicines have the potential to increase bleeding risk, especially in those with other risk factors. Some of the most prominent are known as the "5 Gs:" garlic, ginger, ginkgo, ginseng, and glucosamine. Other natural products with known risk for bleeding include fish oils (at higher doses), vitamin E and willow bark. [Willow bark is a salicylate and is occasionally used for pain. As a salicylate, it should not be taken with anticoagulants due to bleeding risk.] Other natural medicines that may pose a risk with warfarin are discussed in the Anticoagulation chapter.

Interactions with Drugs

Natural medicines interact with prescription medications through pharmacokinetic and pharmacodynamic interactions. Pharmacokinetic interactions are most often due to induction or inhibition of metabolic enzymes and drug transporters. St. John's wort, which is used as an antidepressant, is a good example of a dietary supplement that has both pharmacokinetic and pharmacodynamic interactions. This herbal is a "broad-spectrum" inducer and should be avoided or used cautiously with oral contraceptives, transplant drugs, warfarin, and many other drugs. St. John's wort induces the major CYP enzyme (CYP 3A4) and p-glycoprotein (P-gp). It is also an inducer of other CYP enzymes: CYP 2C19 >> 2C9 > 1A2. St. John's wort has pharmacodynamic interactions due to serotonergic effects, and can cause serotonin syndrome when taken with MAO inhibitors (including linezolid), SSRIs, SNRIs, triptans, and others. St. John's wort causes photosensitivity, and requires counseling on sun protection and avoidance. It would not be an acceptable agent in someone using other photosensitizing drugs. It can lower the seizure threshold and should be avoided in anyone with a seizure history.

Liver Toxicity

Natural products can be hepatotoxic, including black cohosh (used for menopausal symptoms), chaparral, comfrey and kava (used for stress/anxiety). Kava should not be recommended due to hepatotoxic risk. If liver enzymes are elevated, check with the patient – sometimes the use of "tea blends" or mixtures can be contributory. The liver toxicity may be due to an additive in the mixture.

Cardiac Toxicity

Some natural medicines can cause cardiotoxicity. Ephedra was removed from the market due to reports of cardiac toxicity related to its stimulant effects. Bitter orange (also known as *Citrus aurantium* or synephrine) replaced ephedra in many products promoted for weight loss. Bitter orange has stimulant effects and there are case reports of cardiac toxicity, including myocardial infarction, stroke and arrhythmias. Other products promoted for weight loss or those used as "pre-workout" supplements often contain stimulants (e.g., dimethylamylamine) that can raise the risk of cardiac toxicity.

VITAMIN SUPPLEMENTATION

People who consume an adequate diet typically do not require vitamin supplementation. Many people have poor diets that are low in nutritional value, and may require a vitamin supplement to prevent nutrient deficiencies. It is concerning to healthcare professionals that calcium and vitamin D intake remains insufficient for the majority of adults and children. Folate intake among women of child-bearing age can be insufficient. If thiamine (vitamin B1) is insufficient, it can cause Wernicke's encephalopathy. Symptoms of Wernicke's include mental confusion, ataxia, tremor and vision changes. A lack of thiamine is common in alcoholism, and can be due to malabsorption, including from Crohn's, and can occur after obesity surgery, with advanced HIV, and from a few other conditions. As the symptoms of Wernicke's fade, Korsakoff syndrome tends to develop (also called Korsakoff psychosis), which is permanent neurologic (mental) damage. Pharmacists are part of the solution to problems associated with vitamin deficiencies. Anticonvulsants can contribute to calcium deficiency and may require calcium and vitamin D supplementation. There are other individual drugs that deplete nutrients, require a supplement to work properly or require a supplement to reduce toxicity (see table at end of chapter).

VITAMINS	NAMES
Vitamin A	Retinol
Vitamin B1	Thiamine
Vitamin B2	Cobalamin
Vitamin B3	Riboflavin
Vitamin B6	Niacin
Vitamin B9	Pyridoxine
Vitamin B12	Folic Acid
Vitamin C	Ascorbic Acid

Calcium & Vitamin D Supplementation

All prescription medications for low bone density (osteopenia or osteoporosis) recommend adequate calcium and vitamin D supplementation taken concurrently, if dietary intake is inadequate. Low levels of vitamin D impairs calcium absorption. Patients who do not receive enough vitamin D from the sun or diet can benefit from supplementation with both calcium and vitamin D. Calcium and vitamin D supplementation is an essential topic for pharmacists since they are often recommending OTC products, which are required with many prescription drugs; product type and selection is discussed in the Osteoporosis and Hormone Therapy chapter.

Folic Acid (Folate)

Any woman planning to conceive (and all women of child-bearing age) should be taking a folate supplement (400 – 800 mcg/daily, which is 0.4-0.8 mg/daily) to help prevent birth defects of the brain and spinal cord (neural tube defects). Folate needs to be taken at least one month before pregnancy and continued for the first 2-3 months of pregnancy. Once pregnant, the woman is likely taking a prescription prenatal vitamin and this is continued throughout since it also contains calcium (not enough, about 200 mg) and some iron. Folate is in many healthy foods, including fortified cereals (some of which are not healthy), dried beans, leafy green vegetables and orange juice. Multivitamins usually contain an amount in the recommended range. Prescription prenatal vitamins usually contain 1000 mcg, or 1 mg, of folate. The newer birth control pills *Beyaz* and *Safyral* contain folate, however it is less expensive to use a different birth control pill with a supplement. *Beyaz* and *Saryral* contain the potassium-sparing progestin drospirenone, with ethinyl estradiol and levomefolate.

Vitamin E

It is unusual to have a vitamin E deficiency, since it is present in many foods. Vitamin E in foods is considered healthy, but excess intake in supplements is considered a health risk (particularly CVD risk); patients should not be exceeding 400 IU daily.

Vitamin Requirements For Infants & Children

Most children do not need vitamins, except as listed per the American Academy of Pediatrics (AAP); see table below.

- Exclusively breastfed infants or babies drinking less than 1 liter of baby formula need 400 IU of vitamin D daily (can use *Poly-Vi-Sol* or generic).
- Older children who do not drink at least 4 cups of Vitamin D fortified milk also need Vitamin D supplements.

Iron Requirements For Infants & Children

AGE	TREATMENT
0 – 4 months	Supplemental iron not required.
4 – 6 months	Formulas contain adequate iron; supplementation not required. Breast-fed babies need 1 mg/kg/day from 4-6 months old and until consuming iron-rich foods. At about 6 months most breast-fed babies get about half their calories from other foods, which may be adequate.
6 – 12 months	Need 11 mg/day of iron. Food sources are preferred; supplement as-needed.
1 – 3 years	Need 7 mg/day of iron. Food sources are preferred; supplement as-needed.

Pre-term infants

- Preterm (< 37 weeks) breast-fed infants should receive 2 mg/kg/day of elemental iron supplementation from age 1 to 12 months. Most preterm formula-fed infants receive enough iron from formula, but some may still require supplementation.

Adolescent girls

- At risk of anemia once they begin menstruating. During this time, females should consume a diet high in iron-rich foods such as beans, eggs, fortified-cereals, and meats. Some will need an oral iron supplement.

Iron-only supplements (generics available) – check label on iron drops because the mg of iron provided by the dropper ranges from 10-15 mg

- *Fer-In-Sol* Iron Supplement Drops
- *Feosol* Tablets and Caplets

Vitamin supplements with iron

- *Poly-Vi-Sol* Vitamin Drops With Iron: use if they need both vitamin D and iron
- Or others, such as: *Flintstones* Children's Chewable Multivitamin plus Iron, *Pokemon* Children's Multiple Vitamin with Iron, and store brands

Drugs that Cause Clinically Significant Nutrient Depletion

DRUG	DEPLETED NUTRIENT	CHAPTER
Acetazolamide	Calcium, potassium	Travelers' Medicine, Glaucoma
Amphotericin B	Magnesium, potassium	Infectious Disease
Carbamazepine	Calcium*	Epilepsy, Bipolar
Isoniazid	Vitamin B6	Infectious Disease (for neuropathy prevention)
Lamotrigine	Calcium*	Epilepsy, Bipolar
Loop diuretics	Potassium	Hypertension, CHF
Methotrexate	Folate	Autoimmune Conditions, Oncology
Orlistat	Beta-carotene, fat-soluble vitamins	Weight Loss
Oxcarbazepine	Calcium*	Epilepsy
Phenobarbital/Primidone	Calcium*	Epilepsy
Phenytoin	Calcium*	Epilepsy
PPIs	Magnesium, vitamin B12 (> 2 yrs tx)	GERD
Sulfamethoxazole	Folate	Infectious Disease
Topiramate	Calcium*	Epilepsy, Weight Loss
Valproic Acid/Divalproex	Calcium*	Epilepsy, Bipolar
Zonisamide	Calcium*	Epilepsy

*A supplement is needed for most patients using these drugs. Calcium should be given with vitamin D, if needed.

Conditions with Recommended Supplements

CONDITION	RECOMMENDED SUPPLEMENT	CHAPTER
Alcoholism	Vitamin B1, folate	Hepatitis
Microcytic Anemia	Ferrous sulfate	Anemia
Macrocytic Anemia	Vitamin B12 and/or folate	Anemia
Pregnancy	Folate, calcium, vitamin D, pyridoxine (for nausea)	Pregnancy
Osteopenia/Osteoporosis	Calcium, vitamin D	Osteoporosis, Pregnancy
Osteomalacia (Rickets)	Calcium, vitamin D	Vitamin deficiency
Chronic Kidney Disease	Vitamin D	Renal Disease, Bipolar Disorder (for Lithium side effect)
Scurvy	Vitamin C	Vitamin deficiency
Crohn's Disease (and possibly ulcerative colitis)	Patient specific-depends on levels; can require iron, zinc, folate, calcium, vitamin D, B vitamins	IBD
Bariatric Surgery	Various; patient-specific, refer to chapter	Weight Loss

Safety Comments on Homeopathic Products and Medical Foods

Homeopathic Products: Homeopathy is based on "the law of similars" or the concept that "like is cured by like." This is the belief that giving very small amounts of a substance, which in its undiluted form causes similar symptoms of the illness, will protect the patient or cure them of the illness. The quantity of homeopathic substances in a product are reported in X or C dilution scales. X represents a 1:10 dilution and C represents a 1:100 dilution of solute:solvent. The number in front of the X or C is the number of subsequent dilutions. The more dilute a substance is, the more "potent" it is considered.

Most evidence does not support the validity of homeopathy; however, many adherents (including the Queen of England) are advocates. The remedies may be providing a placebo benefit or may be labeled as homeopathic but actually contain measurable concentrations of drugs, nutrients or dietary supplements. In 2010, *Hyland's Teething Tablets* were recalled due to cases of belladonna toxicity. The amount of belladonna could be measured and was unsafe. It is tempting to use the term "homeopathic" on a label. It sounds nice, and if a manufacturer labels a product "homeopathic", they are permitted to make health claims, while dietary supplements are not allowed by law to claim benefit for particular conditions. There have been other recent examples of products labeled as homeopathic which actually were not. Always check the quantity of ingredients.

Medical Foods: These are products that are supposed to meet a nutritional need for certain patient groups for a specific condition. In a medical food, all ingredients must be Generally Recognized as Safe (G.R.A.S.) or be approved food additives. Most of the medical foods have *Rx-only* on the label and have NDC numbers.

A recent medical food that many pharmacists will have seen is a formulation of folate called *Deplin* that is being marketed for help in treating depression. The advertisement for this product states that "*Deplin* is a medical food containing L-methylfolate, the active form of the vitamin, folate. It is the only folate that can be taken up by the brain where it helps balance the chemical messengers that affect mood (serotonin, norepinephrine and dopamine)." It is less expensive to use OTC folate supplements and there is no evidence that this supplement would provide more benefit. The manufacturer can make this claim since it is a medical food.

15

DRUG REFERENCES

We gratefully acknowledge the assistance of Darren Hein, PharmD, Center for Drug Information & Evidence-Based Practice, Creighton University School of Pharmacy, in preparing this chapter.

BACKGROUND

Providing drug information to patients as well as other healthcare professionals is one of the critical functions of pharmacists, regardless of the practice setting. In order to perform this function effectively and efficiently, it is important to be able to choose the most appropriate and specific resources based on the type of information needed. The following section is intended to highlight some of the key resources based on the type of information needed. It is not intended to be a comprehensive review of drug information resources available, but should provide a basic understanding for licensure.

It is important to continually evaluate new drug information resources and technology, and incorporate them into your practice to ensure the resources being reviewed are current and are reflecting the most current information available.

It is also important to recognize that patients also have access to many of the same drug information resources. As healthcare providers, pharmacists need to be aware of what patients are reading in order to provide appropriate answers.

The following list useful resources for answering a variety of drug information questions. Today, most of these resources are available online and as mobile applications. The Centers for Disease Control and Prevention (CDC), U.S. Food and Drug Administration (FDA), and U.S. National Library of Medicine provide many free, helpful resources on various topics.

STUDY TIP: "COLOR" DRUG REFERENCES

Orange Book (FDA)
Provides a list of approved drug products and indicates which drugs can be interchanged (e.g., *Zocor* can be substituted with simvastatin).

Pink Book (CDC)
Provides information on epidemiology and vaccine-preventable diseases.

Purple Book (FDA)
Provides list of biological drug products and indicates which biological products can be interchanged (e.g., *Neupogen* can be substituted with *Zarxio*).

Red Book (Micromedex)
Provides drug pricing information.

Yellow Book (CDC)
Provides health information for healthcare professionals who advise international travelers of health risks.

SOURCES, BY CATEGORY

Regulatory and Business Development

FDA Center for Drug Evaluation and Research (CDER)

US Pharmacopoeia National Formulary (USP-NF)

- USP sets standards for quality, purity, identity, and strength of medicines, food ingredients and dietary supplements

The Pink Sheet: biopharma regulatory, legislative, legal & business developments

Package Insert Database/Compilation

NLM: DailyMed

Physician's Desk Reference (PDR)

See drug manufacturer's website for most current package insert

General Drug Information

Most general drug information resources include information on drug identification, drug interactions, adverse drug reactions, toxicology, drug pricing, compatibility and stability, and use in special populations.

Lexicomp Clinical Drug Information

Facts & Comparisons

Clinical Pharmacology

Micromedex

American Hospital Formulary Service (AHFS) Clinical Drug Information

Food and Drug Administration (FDA):

- FDA Drugs Homepage
- Drugs@FDA: FDA Approved Drug Products
- National Drug Code (NDC) Directory

National Library of Medicine (NLM): Drug Information Portal

Pharmacist's Letter

Drugs of Choice from the Medical Letter

International Drug Information

Lexicomp Clinical Drug Information (international version)

Martindale: The Complete Drug Reference

International Drug Directory (Index Nominum)

Diccionario de Especialidades Farmacéuticas (Spanish)

USP Dictionary of United States Adopted Names (USAN) and International Drug Names

General Medical Information (Professional)

CDC: Diseases & Conditions

Harrison's Principles of Internal Medicine

The Merck Manual

Washington Manual of Medical Therapeutics

General Medical/Drug Information (Consumer)

CDC: Diseases & Conditions

FDA: Consumer pages

NIH: MedlinePlus

Therapeutic Equivalence

FDA's Orange Book: Approved Drug Products with Therapeutic Equivalence Evaluations

FDA's Purple Book: Lists of Licensed Biological Products with Reference Product Exclusivity and Biosimilarity or Interchangeability Evaluations

Drug Identification

Lexicomp: Lexi-Drug ID

Facts & Comparisons Drug Identifier

Therapeutic Research Center's Ident-A-Drug

Micromedex: IDENTIDEX

NLM: Pillbox

Drug Interactions

Hansten and Horn's Drug Interactions Analysis and Management

Individual product package inserts and general drug information resources

SOURCES, BY CATEGORY *Continued*

Adverse Drug Reactions
American Society of Health-System Pharmacists (ASHP): Drug-Induced Diseases: Prevention, Detection, and Management

Individual product package inserts and general drug information resources

Reporting Adverse Drug Reactions
Drugs/Devices: FDA's MedWatch Adverse Event Reporting System (FAERS)

Compounded products: reported to the compounding pharmacy

Vaccines: CDC's/FDA's Vaccine Adverse Event Reporting System (VAERS)

Reporting Medical Errors
In any setting

- ISMP Medication Errors Reporting Program (MERP)
- FDA MedWatch
- MedMARx program

In hospital

- To the P&T Committee, at staff meetings (as defined by facility), to the Medication Safety Committee

Overdoses, Poisoning and Toxicology
The American Association of Poison Control Centers

State Poison Control Center

Micromedex: POISINDEX

Lexicomp: Lexi-Tox

NLM: TOXNET, Toxicology Data Network

Medication Safety
FDA:

- Drug Safety Communications
- Medication Guides
- MedWatch

Institute for Safe Medication Practices (ISMP)

See Medication Safety chapter

Geriatrics
FDA: Medicines and You: A Guide for Older Adults

Lexicomp: Geriatric Dosage Handbook and Geriatric Lexi-Drugs online

NIH: Senior Health at nihseniorhealth.gov

The American Geriatrics Society (AGS) Guidelines & Recommendations including the Beers Criteria

Individual product package inserts and general drug information resources

Pediatrics
AHFS Drug Information

CDC: Vaccines & Immunizations

Harriet Lane Handbook

Micromedex

Nelson: Textbook of Pediatrics

Neofax

Lexicomp's Pediatric & Neonatal Dosage Handbook

ASHP: Pediatric Injectable Drugs

Individual product package inserts and general drug information resources

Pregnancy and Lactation
Breastfeeding: A Guide for the Medical Profession

Briggs' Drugs in Pregnancy and Lactation

CDC: Medications and Pregnancy

Hale's Medications and Mothers' Milk

NLM: LactMed

Individual product package inserts and general drug information resources

Women's Health (Consumer)
CDC: Women's Health

Department of Health and Human Services (DHHS) Women's Health

FDA: For Women

NLM: Women's Health

World Health Organization (WHO): Women's Health

SOURCES, BY CATEGORY *Continued*

Drug Pricing
Micromedex: The Red Book

Drug and Biologic Recalls
FDA: Drug Recalls

FDA: Biologic Recalls

Note: manufacturers issue drug recalls, the FDA can request the recall.

Drug Shortages
ASHP: Drug Shortages

FDA: Drug Shortages

CDC: Vaccines and Immunizations – Current Vaccine Shortages & Delays

Compounding
USP Compounding Compendium:

- USP 795: Non-Sterile Preparations
- USP 797: Sterile Preparations
- USP 800: Hazardous Drugs - Handling in Healthcare Settings

Allen's The Art, Science, and Technology of Pharmaceutical Compounding

International Journal of Pharmaceutical Compounding

Extemporaneous Formulations for Pediatric, Geriatric, and Special Needs Patients

Pediatric Drug Formulations

Remington: The Science and Practice of Pharmacy

- Includes a chapter on extemporaneous prescription compounding

ASHP Guidelines on Compounding Sterile Preparations

Trissel's Stability of Compounded Formulations

IV Drug Compatibility and Stability
Trissel's Handbook on Injectable Drugs

ASHP Handbook on Injectable Drugs

King Guide to Parenteral Admixtures

Individual package inserts and other general drug information resources

Immunizations
CDC Pink Book: Epidemiology and Prevention of Vaccine Preventable Disease

CDC Advisory Committee on Immunization Practices (ACIP). Updates are published in the Morbidity and Mortality Weekly Report (MMWR).

American Pharmacists Association (APhA) Immunization Resources

Immunization Action Coalition

Travel Medicine
CDC: Travelers' Health

CDC Yellow Book: Health Information for International Travel

- Reference book for healthcare professionals who advise international travelers about health risks

International Society of Travel Medicine (ISTM)

International Association For Medical Assistance To Travelers (IAMAT)

Psychiatry
Clinical Handbook of Psychotropic Drugs

Diagnostic and Statistical Manual of Mental Disorders: Fifth edition (DSM-5)

Infectious Disease
Johns Hopkins ABX Guide

Sanford Guide to Antimicrobial Therapy

Sanford Guide to HIV/AIDS Therapy

U.S. Dept. of Health and Human Services AIDS*info*

Oncology
National Cancer Institute (NCI)

Natural Products/Alternative Medicine
Natural Medicines

PDR for Herbal Medicines

US Pharmacopoeia

Micromedex

SOURCES, BY CATEGORY *Continued*

Pharmacology/Pharmacotherapy Textbooks
DiPiro's Pharmacotherapy: A Pathophysiologic Approach

Koda-Kimble's Applied Therapeutics: The Clinical Use of Drugs

Handbook of Nonprescription Drugs (OTC)

Goodman and Gilman's: The Pharmacological Basis of Therapeutics

Pharmaceutics
Handbook of Pharmaceutical Excipients

Merck Index

Remington: The Science and Practice of Pharmacy

Clinical Guidelines
National Guideline Clearinghouse

Select Key Guidelines

- ACC/AHA Guideline on the Treatment of Blood Cholesterol to Reduce Atherosclerotic Cardiovascular Risk in Adults (2013)
- 2014 Evidence-based guideline for the management of high blood pressure in adults. Report from the panel members appointed to the Eighth Joint National Committee (JNC 8)
- American Diabetes Assoc (ADA) Clinical Practice Recommendations and American Association of Clinical Endocrinologists/American College of Endocrinology Consensus Statement (AACE), both for diabetes
- CHEST guidelines for antithrombotic therapy

Refer to the professional organization websites (e.g., AACE, ACG, ACOG, others)

Clinical Trials
NIH: ClinicalTrials.gov

Professional Organizations
American Academy of Pediatrics (AAP)

American Cancer Society (ACS)

American Diabetes Association (ADA)

American Heart Association (AHA)

American Society of Clinical Oncology (ASCO)

Infectious Diseases Society of America (IDSA)

Go to NLM for a comprehensive directory of professional organizations

Pharmacy Organizations
Academy of Managed Care Pharmacy (AMCP)

American College of Clinical Pharmacy (ACCP)

American Pharmacists Association (APhA)

American Society of Health-System Pharmacists (ASHP)

National Community Pharmacists Association

Literature Search
Cochrane Library

Excerpta Medica dataBASE (EMBASE)

International Pharmaceutical Abstracts (IPA)

NLM: PubMed

16

LAB VALUES & DRUG MONITORING

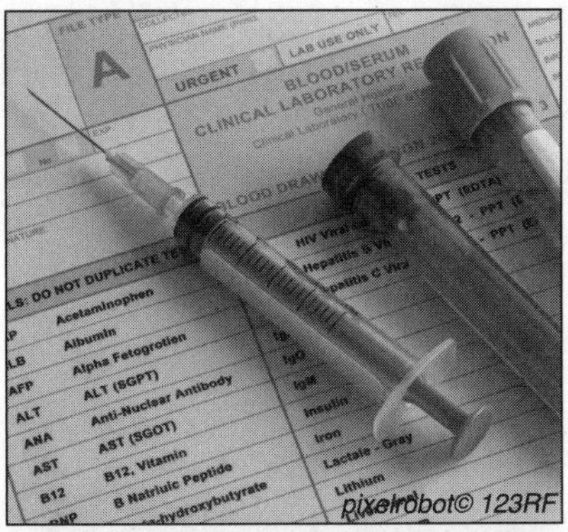

BACKGROUND

Laboratory values assist healthcare providers in diagnosing and monitoring diseases and drug therapies. Blood or other samples can be sent to a hospital or outside laboratory, but there are newer methods. Point-of-care (POC) testing provides quick results at the site of patient care. There are many POC tests including tests for cardiac enzymes, A1C, INR, various infections and others. Home testing kits provide convenience and privacy and are available to test for pregnancy, ovulation, HIV infection, herpes, fecal occult blood and presence of illicit substances or opioids. Many are available OTC.

Therapeutic drug monitoring (TDM) involves obtaining a drug level or related labs to monitor for efficacy and safety. For example, if a patient is receiving traditional dosing of gentamicin, the healthcare team will monitor both the gentamicin trough level and the patient's renal function since aminoglycosides can cause nephrotoxicity. Pharmacists in many states can order and interpret lab tests for a variety of purposes, including tests to screen for and diagnose disease, to check for medication adherence or to screen for drugs of abuse. Prescribing privilege is advancing in many states.

GUIDELINES/REFERENCES

Lab Tests Online. www.labtestsonline.org (accessed 2016 Sept 21).

Lee M. Basic Skills in Interpreting Laboratory Data. 5th ed. Betheseda, MD: ASHP; 2013.

Schmidt J, Wieczorkiewicz J. Interpreting Laboratory Data: A Point-of-Care Guide. Betheseda, MD: ASHP; 2012.

DEFINITIONS

Complete Blood Cell Count

The complete blood count (CBC) is a commonly ordered lab panel that analyzes the white blood cells (WBCs), or neutrophils, the red blood cells (RBCs), and the platelets (PLTs). The CBC includes the hemoglobin (oxygen-carrying protein in RBCs) and the hematocrit (the level of RBCs in the fluid component of the blood, or plasma). When a CBC with differential is ordered, the types of neutrophils are analyzed. RBCs have an average life span of 120 days. Anemia occurs if there is decreased production, loss (bleeding), or destruction (hemolysis) of RBCs. Platelets have an average life span of 7 – 10 days.

Basic Metabolic Panel / Comprehensive Metabolic Panel

The basic metabolic panel (BMP) includes seven or eight tests that analyze electrolytes and glucose, acid/base (with the HCO3, or bicarbonate) and renal function. Some labs calculate and report the anion gap along with the BMP (see Calculations chapter).

A comprehensive metabolic panel (CMP) includes the tests in the BMP plus albumin, alanine aminotransferase (ALT), aspartate aminotransferase (AST), total bilirubin and total protein. The additional tests are used primarily to assess liver function. The BMP and CMP are groups of labs that are ordered together for convenience.

The stick diagrams below are used in practice when writing a paper chart note to denote the primary components of the CBC or BMP.

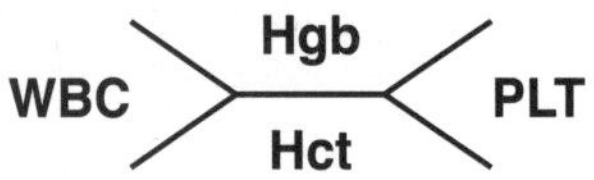

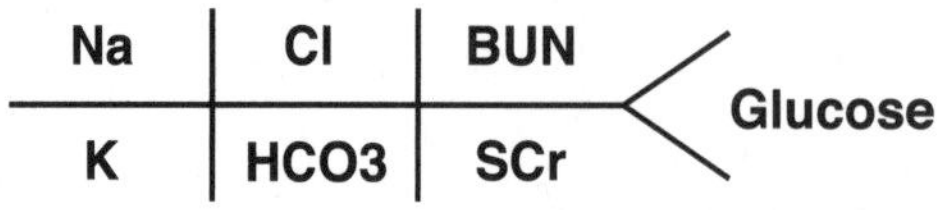

LAB RESULTS

Lab results are usually reported as a numerical value (e.g., sodium = 139 mEq/L). Some are reported as "positive" or "negative" or indicate a specific item, such as "Gram-positive cocci". Reference ranges can vary slightly from one facility to another (due to slight variances in products and techniques) and between pediatric and adult populations. A patient's lab results may be within the reference ranges or outside of the reference ranges (which can indicate a serious condition that needs to be addressed rapidly). A value that is termed critical can be life-threatening unless a corrective action is taken quickly. The Joint Commission requires that all accredited facilities create and follow a protocol to identify and report critical values to the responsible healthcare provider, who has an established time frame to manage the result. This applies to critical lab values and diagnostic procedure results.

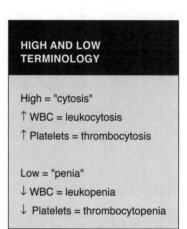

HIGH AND LOW TERMINOLOGY

High = "cytosis"

↑ WBC = leukocytosis

↑ Platelets = thrombocytosis

Low = "penia"

↓ WBC = leukopenia

↓ Platelets = thrombocytopenia

COMMON LABORATORY REFERENCE RANGES - ADULT

The reference range for a healthy adult is provided, unless otherwise noted.
Drugs specifically indicated to treat a lab abnormality (e.g., urate lowering therapies) are not included in Notes.

ITEM	COMMON REFERENCE RANGE	NOTES
BMP and Electrolytes		
Calcium, total Calcium, ionized **(Ca)**	8.5–10.5 mg/dL 4.5–5.1 mg/dL	Calculate corrected calcium if albumin is low (see Calculations chapter for formula). Correction is not needed for ionized calcium. ↑ due to calcium supplementation, vitamin D, thiazide diuretics. ↓ due to systemic steroids, long-term heparin, loop diuretics, bisphosphonates, cinacalcet, calcitonin, foscarnet, topiramate. Supplement in pregnancy, other conditions and with certain drugs (see Osteoporosis & Hormone Therapy, Dietary Supplements & Natural and Complementary Medicine and Epilepsy/Seizures chapters).
Chloride **(Cl)**	95–106 mEq/L	Used with other labs to assess acid-base status and fluid balance.

Common Adult Laboratory Reference Ranges Continued

ITEM	COMMON REFERENCE RANGE	NOTES
Magnesium (Mg)	1.3–2.1 mEq/L	↑ due to magnesium-containing antacids and laxatives with renal impairment. ↓ due to PPIs, diuretics, amphotericin, foscarnet, echinocandins, diarrhea, chronic alcohol intake.
Phosphate (PO_4)	2.3–4.7 mg/dL	↑ in renal failure. ↓ due to phosphate binders, foscarnet, oral calcium intake.
Potassium (K)	3.5–5 mEq/L	↑ due to ACE inhibitors, ARBs, aldosterone receptor antagonists (ARAs), aliskiren, NSAIDs, cyclosporine, tacrolimus, mycophenolate, potassium supplements, drospirenone-containing oral contraceptives, sulfamethoxazole/trimethoprim, chronic heparin use, canagliflozin, pentamidine. ↓ due to steroids, beta-2 agonists, conivaptan, diuretics, insulin, mycophenolate (both ↑ and ↓ reported).
Sodium (Na)	135–145 mEq/L	↑ due to hypertonic saline. ↓ due to carbamazepine, oxcarbazepine, SSRIs, diuretics, desmopressin.
Bicarbonate (HCO_3 or "bicarb")	Venous: 24–30 mEq/L Arterial: 22–26 mEq/L (varies by method)	Used to assess acid-base status. ↑ due to loop diuretics, systemic steroids. ↓ due to topiramate, zonisamide, salicylate overdose.
Blood Urea Nitrogen (BUN)	7–20 mg/dL	↑ in renal impairment and dehydration. Used with SCr (e.g., BUN:SCr ratio) to assess fluid status and renal function.
Serum Creatinine (SCr)	0.6–1.3 mg/dL	↑ due to many drugs that impair renal function (e.g., aminoglycosides, amphotericin B, cisplatin, colistimethate, cyclosporine, loop diuretics, NSAIDs, radiocontrast dye, tacrolimus and vancomycin). False ↑ due to sulfamethoxazole/trimethoprim, H2RAs. ↓ with low muscle mass, amputation, hemodilution.
Anion Gap (AG)	5–12 mEq/L	A calculated value, but often reported on the BMP (see Calculations chapter). Presence of ↑ anion gap suggests metabolic acidosis.

WBC and Differential

Many drugs (including chemotherapy, immunosuppressants and antivirals) have the potential to affect WBC, Hgb and PLTs.

White Blood Cells (WBC)	4,000–11,000 cells/mm^3	Used to diagnose and monitor infection/inflammation. Can ↑ as an acute phase reactant, indicating a systemic reaction to inflammation or stress (e.g., surgery). ↑ due to systemic steroids, colony stimulating factors, epinephrine. ↓ due to clozapine, chemotherapy that targets the bone marrow, carbamazepine, cephalosporins, immunosuppressants (e.g., DMARDs, biologics, etc.), procainamide, vancomycin.
Neutrophils	45–73%	Neutrophils and bands are used with clinical s/sx to assess likelihood of acute infection and with WBC in absolute neutrophil count (ANC) calculation (see Calculations chapter). Neutrophils are also called polymorphonuclear cells (PMNs or polys) and segmented neutrophils (segs). Bands are immature neutrophils released from bone marrow to fight infection (called a "left shift").
Bands	3–5%	

Common Adult Laboratory Reference Ranges Continued

ITEM	COMMON REFERENCE RANGE	NOTES
Eosinophils	0–5%	↑ in drug allergy, asthma, inflammation, parasitic infection.
Basophils	0–1%	↑ in inflammation, hypersensitivity reaction, leukemia.
Lymphocytes	20–40%	↑ in viral infections, lymphoma. ↓ in bone marrow suppression, HIV, or due to systemic steroids.
Monocytes	2–8%	↑ in chronic infections, inflammation, stress.

Anemia

Red Blood Cells (RBC)	Males: 4.5–5.5 x 10^6 cells/μL Females: 4.1–4.9 x 10^6 cells/μL	↑ due to erythropoiesis-stimulating agents (ESAs), smoking, and in polycythemia (a condition that causes high RBCs). ↓ due to chemotherapy that targets the bone marrow, low production, blood loss, deficiency anemias (e.g., B12, folate), hemolytic anemia, sickle cell anemia.
Hemoglobin **(Hgb, Hb)** Hematocrit (Hct)	Males: 13.5–18 g/dL Females: 12–16 g/dL Males: 38–50% Females: 36–46%	Hgb is the iron-containing protein that carries oxygen in the RBCs. The Hct mirrors the Hgb result (providing the same clinical information). ↑ due to ESAs (see Anemia chapter). ↓ in anemias and bleeding (risk with anticoagulants, antiplatelets, P2Y12 inhibitors and fibrinolytics). See Coombs Test and G6PD for drug-induced anemias.
Mean Corpuscular Volume **(MCV)**	80–100 mm³	↑ due to B12 or folate deficiency. ↓ due to iron deficiency.
Mean Corpuscular Hemoglobin (MCH)	26–34 pg/cell	Additional tests used in an anemia workup. Together MCV, MCHC and RDW are called "RBC indices".
Mean Corpuscular Hgb Concentration (MCHC)	31 - 37 g/dL	
RBC Distribution Width (RDW)	11.5–14.5%	RDW measures the variability in the RBC size.
Iron	65–150 mcg/dL	↑ due to iron supplementation. ↓ due to blood loss or poor nutritional intake.
Total Iron Binding Capacity (TIBC)	250–400 mcg/dL	Monitored as part of the workup and treatment for iron deficiency anemia, anemia of chronic disease or anemia of chronic kidney disease (CKD). Often parenteral iron is required in conjunction with an ESA for patients on dialysis (see Anemia chapter).
Transferrin	> 200 mg/dL	
Transferrin Saturation (TSAT)	Males: 15–50% Females: 12–45%	
Ferritin	11–300 ng/mL	
Erythropoietin	2–25 mIU/mL	

Common Adult Laboratory Reference Ranges Continued

ITEM	COMMON REFERENCE RANGE	NOTES
Folic acid (folate)	5–25 mcg/L	B12 and folate are ordered for further workup of macrocytic anemia. ↓ due to phenytoin/fosphenytoin, phenobarbital, primidone, methotrexate, sulfasalazine, sulfamethoxazole/trimethoprim. Supplement folate in women of childbearing age and alcoholism (see Dietary Supplements & Natural and Complementary Medicine chapter).
Vitamin B12	> 200 pg/mL	↓ due to PPIs, metformin, colchicine, chloramphenicol.
Methylmalonate (MMA)	Varies	Used for further workup of macrocytic anemia when B12 deficiency is suspected. Schilling test has also been used.
Reticulocyte count	0.5–2.5%	Measures the amount of reticulocytes (immature red blood cells) being made by the bone marrow; reticulocyte count is ↑ in blood loss and ↓ in bone marrow suppression.
Coombs Test, Direct Also known as: Direct Antiglobulin Test (DAT)	Negative	Used to determine cause of hemolytic anemia (autoimmune vs. drug-induced) and in assessment of transfusion compatibility (see Anemia chapter). Positive in drug-induced hemolysis caused by penicillins and cephalosporins (prolonged use/high concentrations), isoniazid, levodopa, methyldopa, nitrofurantoin, quinidine, quinine, rifampin and sulfonamides. If positive, discontinue offending drug.
Glucose-6-phosphate dehydrogenase **(G6PD)**	5–14 units/gram	Used to determine if hemolytic anemia is due to G6PD deficiency (the result will be low). The RBC destruction with G6PD deficiency is triggered by stress, foods (fava beans) or these drugs: chloroquine, dapsone, methylene blue, nitrofurantoin, primaquine, probenecid, quinidine, quinine, rasburicase and sulfonamides (see Anemia chapter).

Anticoagulation

These tests monitor different aspects of clotting and are used to monitor specific drugs.

Antifactor Xa Activity **(Anti-Xa)**	Obtain a peak anti-Xa 4 hours after LMWH dose for proper interpretation. Refer to Therapeutic Drug Levels table at end of chapter.	Used to monitor low molecular weight heparins (LMWHs). Monitoring is recommended in pregnancy and possibly in obesity, low body weight, pediatrics, elderly, or renal insufficiency (see Anticoagulation chapter). ↑ due to heparin, LMWHs and fondaparinux.
Prothrombin Time/ International Normalized Ratio **(PT / INR)**	PT: 10–13 seconds (varies) INR: < 1.2 (for those not on warfarin)	Used to monitor warfarin. INR ↑ (without warfarin) due to liver disease. False ↑ from daptomycin, oritavancin, telavancin. Many drugs ↑ or ↓ INR (see Anticoagulation chapter).
Activated Partial Thromboplastin Time **(aPTT or PTT)**	22–38 seconds (varies, this is called the "control") Treatment goal (on UFH): 1.5–2.5x control	Used to monitor unfractionated heparin (UFH) and direct thrombin inhibitors (e.g., argatroban). False ↑ from oritavancin, telavancin.
Activated Clotting Time (ACT)	70–180 seconds (varies)	Used to monitor anticoagulation in the cardiac catheterization lab during percutaneous coronary intervention (PCI) and in surgery.

Common Adult Laboratory Reference Ranges Continued

ITEM	COMMON REFERENCE RANGE	NOTES
Platelets **(PLTs)**	150,000–450,000/mm^3	Platelets are required for clot formation. Spontaneous bleeding can occur when platelets are < 20,000/mm^3. ↓ due to heparin, LMWHs, fondaparinux, glycoprotein IIb/IIIa receptor antagonists, linezolid, valproic acid, chemotherapy that targets the bone marrow, rarely other drugs.
Heparin-induced platelet antibodies: 1st ELISA test, then 2nd Serotonin release assay (SRA)	Negative	To confirm diagnosis of heparin-induced thrombocytopenia (HIT). If the ELISA test is positive, a positive SRA is confirmatory.

Liver and Gastroenterology

Albumin	3.5–5 g/dL	↓ due to cirrhosis and malnutrition. Highly protein bound drugs (e.g., warfarin) are impacted by changes in albumin; phenytoin, valproic acid and calcium serum concentrations require correction for low albumin (see Epilepsy/Seizures and Calculations chapters).
Alkaline Phosphatase (Alk Phos or ALP)	33–131 IU/L	Used with other labs to assess liver, biliary tract (cholestatic) and bone disease.
Aspartate Aminotransferase **(AST)**	10–40 units/L	AST and ALT are enzymes released from injured hepatocytes (liver cells). Numerous medications and herbals can ↑ AST and ALT (see Hepatitis & Liver Disease chapter).
Alanine Aminotransferase **(ALT)**	10–40 units/L	
Gamma-Glutamyl Transpeptidase (GGT)	9–58 units/L	Used with other labs to assess liver, biliary tract (cholestatic) and pancreas.
Bilirubin, total (T Bili)	0.1–1.2 mg/dL	Used along with other liver tests to monitor drug toxicity, determine other cause of liver damage and detect bile duct blockage.
Ammonia	19–60 mcg/dL	Though not diagnostic, often measured in suspected hepatic encephalopathy (HE). ↑ due to valproic acid, topiramate. ↓ due to lactulose.

Pancreatitis

Amylase	60–180 units/L	↑ in pancreatitis which can be caused by didanosine, stavudine, GLP-1 agonists, valproic acid and hypertriglyceridemia.
Lipase	5–160 units/L	

Cardiovascular

Creatine Kinase or **Creatine Phosphokinase** **(CK** or **CPK)**	Males: 55–170 IU/L Females: 30–135 IU/L	To assess muscle inflammation (myositis) or more serious muscle damage and to diagnose cardiac conditions. ↑ due to daptomycin, quinupristin/dalfopristin, statins, fibrates (especially if given with a statin), emtricitabine, tenofovir, tipranavir, raltegravir, dolutegravir, telbivudine.

Common Adult Laboratory Reference Ranges Continued

ITEM	COMMON REFERENCE RANGE	NOTES
CK-MB isoenzymes, total	≤ 6.0 ng/mL	As a group, these are called "cardiac enzymes" and are used in the diagnosis of MI. The troponins can be elevated with a few other conditions (sepsis, PE, CKD). BNP and NT-proBNP are both markers of cardiac stress. They are not HF nor heart disease-specific, but higher values indicate higher likelihood of HF when consistent with HF symptoms. Renal failure is the second most common cause of ↑ in BNP and NT-proBNP. Myoglobin and CK-MB are not interchangeable; they are 2 separate markers. Myoglobin is a sensitive marker for muscle injury but has relatively low specificity for acute MI and therefore is not routinely used for diagnosis (see Acute Coronary Syndrome chapter).
Troponin T (TnT)	0–0.1 ng/mL (assay dependent)	
Troponin I (TnI)	0–0.5 ng/mL (assay dependent)	
B-Type Natriuretic Peptide **(BNP)**	< 100 pg/mL or ng/L	
N-Terminal-ProBNP **(NT-proBNP)**	Males: < 61 pg/mL Females: 12–151 pg/mL	

Lipids and Cardiovascular Risk

Total Cholesterol **(TC)**	< 200 mg/dL	For complete discussion, see Dyslipidemia chapter. Fasting begins 9-12 hours prior to lipid blood draw. Guidelines do not support specific TC, HDL or TG goals; they support a statin intensity level for LDL-C reductions based on those most likely to benefit.
High Density Lipoprotein **(HDL)**	< 40 mg/dL, low ≥ 60 mg/dL, desirable	
Low Density Lipoprotein **(LDL)**	LDL: 70–189, depending on risk factors	
Triglycerides **(TG)**	< 150 mg/dL	
Lipoprotein-a, Lp(a) Apoliprotein-B, Apo B	< 10 mg/dL < 130 mg/dL	↑ Lp(a) and ↑ ApoB are being used more commonly; these are associated with ↑ coagulation and ↑ risk of CVD.
C-reactive Protein **(CRP)**	0–0.5 mg/dL	↑ CRP indicates inflammation, which could be due to many conditions (infection, trauma, malignancy). Higher levels indicate ↑ risk. High-sensitivity CRP (hs-CRP) is more sensitive for CVD.
Coronary Artery Calcium score	< 300 Agatston units or < 75 percentile for age, sex and ethnicity; higher is at risk	The coronary artery calcium score measures calcium build-up in the coronary arteries.
Ankle Brachial Index (ABI)	1–1.4	The ankle brachial index measures the ratio of the BP in the lower legs to the BP in the arms. It is used to assess severity of peripheral artery disease (PAD). An ABI < 1 indicates some degree of PAD.

Common Adult Laboratory Reference Ranges Continued

ITEM	COMMON REFERENCE RANGE	NOTES

Diabetes

Fasting Plasma Glucose (FPG)	≥ 126 mg/dL is positive for diabetes 100–125 mg/dL is positive for pre-diabetes	Fasting is 8+ hours. See Diabetes chapter for complete information and medications that can cause hyper and hypoglycemia.
Hemoglobin A1C **(A1C)**	< 7% (ADA), ≤ 6.5% (AACE)	Average blood glucose over the past 3 months; based on attachment of glucose to hemoglobin; ↑ glucose = ↑ BG attached to Hgb = ↑ A1C.
Estimated Average Glucose (eAG)	< 154 mg/dL (ADA)	Used to correlate a finger stick glucose with an A1C; an eAG of 154 mg/dL corresponds to an A1C of 7%.
Preprandial blood glucose	70–130 mg/dL (ADA), < 110 mg/dL (AACE)	Blood glucose measurement taken before a meal.
Postprandial blood glucose	< 180 mg/dL (ADA), < 140 mg/dL (AACE)	Blood glucose measurement taken after a meal (1-2 hours after the start of eating).
C-peptide (fasting)	0.78–1.89 ng/mL	Insulin breakdown product used to evaluate beta-cell function (distinguish type 1 from type 2 diabetes).
Urine Albumin to Creatinine Ratio or Albumin to Creatinine Ratio (UACR or ACR) or Urinary Albumin Excretion (UAE)	Males: < 17 mg/gram Females: < 25 mg/gram < 30 mg/24 hours	See Diabetes and Renal Disease chapters.

Thyroid Function

Thyroid Stimulating Hormone **(TSH)**	0.3–3 mIU/L	TSH is used with FT4 to diagnose hypothyroidism and is used alone (sometimes with FT4) to monitor patients being treated. Low iodine intake is a cause of hypothyroidism; this is rare in the U.S. because iodine is added to table salt (NaCl). ↑ or ↓ due to amiodarone, interferons. ↑ (hypothyroidism) due to lithium, carbamazepine, oxcarbazepine.
Total thyroxine (T4)	4.5–10.9 mcg/dL	T4 and FT4 are two of several tests used for a detailed assessment of thyroid function (see Thyroid chapter for additional interacting drugs).
Free thyroxine (FT4)	0.9–2.3 ng/dL	

Uric Acid/Gout

Uric acid	Males: 3.5–7.2 mg/dL Females: 2–6.5 mg/dL	Used in diagnosis/treatment of gout. ↑ due to diuretics, niacin, high doses of aspirin, pyrazinamide, cyclosporine, tacrolimus, ribavirin, some pancreatic enzyme products.

Common Adult Laboratory Reference Ranges Continued

ITEM	COMMON REFERENCE RANGE	NOTES

Inflammation/Autoimmune Disease

C-Reactive Protein (CRP)	Normal: 0–0.5 mg/dL High risk: > 3 mg/dL	Nonspecific tests used in autoimmune disorders, inflammation and infections. Drug-induced lupus erythematosus (DILE) can be caused by many drugs. More likely with anti-TNF agents, hydralazine, isoniazid, methimazole, methyldopa, minocycline, procainamide, propylthiouracil, quinidine and terbinafine. If ANA is positive, histone antibody and anti-dsDNA tests will be help establish diagnosis. The causative drug must be discontinued (see Systemic Steroids & Autoimmune Conditions chapter).
Rheumatoid Factor, serum (RF)	< 40 IU/mL	
Erythrocyte Sedimentation Rate (ESR)	Males: ≤ 20 mm/hr Females: ≤ 30 mm/hr	
Antinuclear Antibodies (ANA)	Negative (titers may be provided)	
Antihistone Antibodies (Detected by ELISA)	Negative	

HIV

CD4+ T Lymphocyte Count	800–1,100 cells/mm^3	Used to assess HIV and monitor treatment (see HIV chapter).
HIV RNA Concentration (Viral Load)	Undetectable Measured in copies/mL	
HIV Antibody	Negative (non-reactive)	Detects infection with the virus; may not become positive until several weeks after exposure.
HIV DNA PCR	Negative	Useful for early detection.
HIV p24 Antigen	Undetectable	

Acid-Base (arterial sample)

pH	7.35–7.45	Together these values are called an arterial blood gas (ABG) sample. Often written in chart notes with a stick diagram: pH/pCO2/pO2/HCO3/O2 Sat (see Calculations chapter for ABG interpretation). Bicarbonate on the ABG is a calculated value and reference range may differ from venous samples.
pCO2	35–45 mmHg	
pO2	80–100 mmHg	
HCO3	22–26 mEq/L	
O2 Sat	> 95%	

Common Adult Laboratory Reference Ranges Continued

ITEM	COMMON REFERENCE RANGE	NOTES

Hormonal

Testosterone total, free	Males: 300–950 ng/dL	↑ with testosterone supplementation.
Prostate-Specific Antigen (PSA)	< 4 ng/mL	Can ↑ with testosterone supplementation.
Human Chorionic Gonadotropin (hCG)	Varies by test	Tested in blood or urine to determine pregnancy. A positive test means woman is likely pregnant.
Luteinizing Hormone (LH)	Varies during cycle	Rises mid-cycle, causing egg release from the ovaries. Tested in urine with ovulation predictor kits for women attempting pregnancy.
Parathyroid Hormone (PTH)	Varies	Used in evaluation of parathyroid disorders, hypercalcemia and chronic kidney disease (CKD) (see Renal Disease chapter).

Other

Cosyntropin Stimulation Test	Baseline and timed increase are measured	Used to test for adrenal suppression; medications that affect baseline cortisol or suppress adrenal response will impact test and may need to be held prior (e.g., steroids).
Lactic acid (lactate)	0.5–2.2 mEq/L	Lactic acidosis indicates anaerobic metabolism, which occurs in long distance running and in certain medical conditions (e.g., sepsis). ↑ due to NRTIs (see HIV chapter), metformin (low risk/mostly with renal disease and heart failure), alcohol, cyanide.
Procalcitonin	≤ 0.15 ng/mL	↑ due to systemic bacterial infections or severe localized infections.
Prolactin	1–25 ng/mL	Secretion is regulated by dopamine; can ↑ with haloperidol, risperidone, paliperidone, methyldopa. Can ↓ with bromocriptine.
Purified Protein Derivative or Mantoux test **(PPD)**	No induration; induration is measured for diagnosis of TB exposure.	TB skin test (TST) administered by intradermal injection. Not used alone for diagnosis of active TB. Response is measured by diameter (mm) of induration at 48-72 hours (see ID II chapter for interpretation of the PPD).
Rapid Plasma Reagin **(RPR)**	Negative	Antibody test used to screen for syphilis. If the RPR is positive, confirmatory testing is performed. Titers may be reported and are used to monitor response to therapy.
Serum osmolality	275–290 mOsm/kg H2O	Used with Na, BUN/SCr, and clinical volume status to evaluate hypo/hypernatremia. ↑ due to mannitol, toxicities (e.g., ethylene glycol, methanol, propylene glycol, others).
Thiopurine Methyltransferase (TPMT)	≥ 15 units/mL	Those with genetic deficiency of TPMT are at ↑ risk for myelosuppression (bone marrow suppression) and may require lower doses with azathioprine and mercaptopurine.
Vitamin D, serum 25(OH)	> 30 ng/mL	↓ levels increase risk of osteoporosis, osteomalacia (rickets), CVD, diabetes, hypertension, infectious diseases & other conditions. Supplement vitamin D with various conditions and drugs (see Osteoporosis & Hormone Therapy, Renal Disease and Dietary Supplements & Natural and Complementary Medicine chapters).

RECOGNIZING LAB PATTERNS

Reference ranges for labs are generally provided on NAPLEX, but may not be provided on the California law exam (CPJE). Patient cases can be assessed more quickly by recognizing lab patterns and signs and symptoms that provide a clue to the patient's diagnosis. Additional information can be found in the chapters on these disease states.

STUDY TIP: ASSESSING PATIENT CASES QUICKLY

Cases on the exam are like cases in real life – not all of the information is needed and it may be presented differently from one case to the next.

- Maximize your time by looking for patterns in lab results.
- Watch for drug-induced s/sx and lab abnormalities.
- Scan labs for contraindications to drugs (e.g., +hCG, ↑ K, etc.).
- Use the information in the table to match s/sx, lab values and diagnosis.

ABNORMAL LAB OR PATTERN	S/SX TO LOOK FOR IN PATIENT CASE	LIKELY DIAGNOSIS
↑ BNP / NT-proBNP	Edema, shortness of breath, cough, fatigue	Heart Failure
↓ Hgb / Hct / RBC. Abnormal RBC indices will indicate type of anemia.	Shortness of breath, fatigue, weakness, dizziness, pallor, exercise intolerance	Anemia
↓ Hgb / Hct / RBC (sometimes ↓ is dramatic). RBC indices should be normal. ↑ Reticulocyte count if bone marrow is normal.	General s/sx of anemia listed above and possibly chest pain, tachycardia	Blood Loss
↑ AST / ALT (released from injured hepatocytes)	Nausea, vomiting, abdominal pain, jaundice	Liver Injury (acute)
↑ INR, ↓ albumin, ↓ platelets (all reflect ↓ functional capacity of the liver)	General s/sx of liver injury listed above and ascites, edema, drowsiness, confusion	Liver Disease (chronic)
↑ AST > ↑ ALT / ↑ GGT	Jaundice, nausea, vomiting, weakness, abdominal tenderness, loss of appetite	Alcoholic Hepatitis
↑ Alk Phos / T Bili / GGT with normal or slightly ↑ AST / ALT	Pruritus, light colored stools, dark urine, jaundice, nausea, vomiting (symptoms depend on cause)	Cholestasis (biliary)
↑ Amylase and lipase	Abdominal pain (feels worse after eating and can radiate to back), nausea, vomiting	Pancreatitis
↑ BUN / SCr, possibly ↑ K Dehydration: BUN:SCr ratio > 20:1 Other causes: BUN:SCr ratio < 20:1	Often asymptomatic. If caused by dehydration: dry mouth, dry skin, headache	Acute Kidney Injury
↑ BUN / SCr / K / PO4 / PTH with ↓ Hgb / Hct / Ca	Edema, nausea, pruritus, weight loss, fatigue, loss of appetite	Chronic Kidney Disease, untreated
↑ WBC with ↑ neutrophils and/or bands (often ↑ lactate / ESR / CRP / procalcitonin depending on severity)	↑ temperature, other s/sx depending on type of infection (e.g., coughing, burning on urination, etc.)	Infection, bacterial
↑ or normal WBC without ↑ neutrophils and/or bands	Variable	Infection, viral
↑ Eosinophils	Variable	Infection, parasitic
↑ ESR / CRP / ANA	Systemic lupus erythematosus (SLE): achy joints, butterfly rash, fatigue Rheumatoid arthritis: joint stiffness, swollen joints	Autoimmune
↑ CPK (and ↑ SCr in rhabdomyolysis)	Rhabdomyolysis: muscle pain or weakness, nausea, vomiting, dark urine, ↓ urine output	Muscle Damage / Rhabdomyolysis
↑ Lactic acid, ↑ AG and metabolic acidosis by ABGs	↓ blood pressure, deep/sighing respirations, confusion	Lactic Acidosis

THERAPEUTIC DRUG MONITORING

Drug levels or other values (such as anti-Xa levels for LMWHs) are used to reach dosing goals and to avoid toxicity. Therapeutic drug monitoring (TDM) is increasingly common due to the need to target highly resistant organisms and dose medications properly in overweight and obese patients. The peak level is the highest concentration in the blood the drug will reach and requires time for the drug to distribute in the body's tissues. The trough level is the lowest concentration the drug will reach in the blood and is drawn right before the next dose or some short period of time before the next dose (30 minutes is common). This allows time for assessment of the level before another dose is given and time to hold the next dose if the level is high. The time that drug levels are drawn is critical for accurate interpretation. For example, a tobramycin level of 6 mcg/mL would be interpreted differently if the level was a trough versus a peak. Obtaining drug levels at steady state is often (but not always) preferred. See Pharmacokinetics chapter for further discussion.

Narrow therapeutic index (NTI) drugs have a narrow separation between the subtherapeutic (low), therapeutic (desired), and supratherapeutic (high) drug levels. Supratherapeutic drug levels can be toxic.

TDM is commonly performed by pharmacists. The following table lists drugs that are routinely monitored. These drugs and usual therapeutic ranges are felt to be essential for NAPLEX.

Therapeutic Drug Levels

DRUG	USUAL THERAPEUTIC RANGE
Amikacin (traditional dosing)	Peak: 20–30 mcg/mL Trough: < 5 mcg/mL
Carbamazepine	4–12 mcg/mL
Digoxin	0.8–2 ng/mL (AFib) 0.5–0.9 ng/mL (HF)
Gentamicin (traditional dosing)	Peak: 5–10 mcg/mL Trough: < 2 mcg/mL
Lithium	0.6–1.2 mEq/L (up to 1.5 mEq/L for acute symptoms)
Enoxaparin	VTE treatment with daily therapy. Anti-Xa: 1–2 anti-Xa units/mL VTE treatment with Q12H therapy. Anti-Xa: 0.6–1 anti-Xa units/mL Recurrent VTE prophylaxis in pregnancy. Anti-Xa: 0.2–0.6 anti-Xa units/mL
Phenobarbital/Primidone	20–40 mcg/mL (adults)
Phenytoin/Fosphenytoin Free Phenytoin	10–20 mcg/mL; if albumin is low, correct serum level; see Epilepsy/Seizures chapter. 1–2.5 mcg/mL
Procainamide NAPA Combined	4–10 mcg/mL 15–25 mcg/mL 10–30 mcg/mL
Theophylline	5–15 mcg/mL 5–10 mcg/mL (neonates)
Tobramycin (traditional dosing)	Peak: 5–10 mcg/mL Trough: < 2 mcg/mL
Valproic acid	50–100 mcg/mL (up to 150 mcg/mL in some patients); if albumin is low, correct serum level; see Epilepsy/Seizures chapter.
Vancomycin	Trough: 15–20 mcg/mL for most serious infections (pneumonia, endocarditis, osteomyelitis, meningitis, and bacteremia) Trough: 10–15 mcg/mL for others
Warfarin	Goal INR is 2–3 for most indications, use higher range (2.5–3.5) with mechanical mitral valves

17

PATIENT CHARTS, ASSESSMENT & HEALTHCARE PROVIDER COMMUNICATION

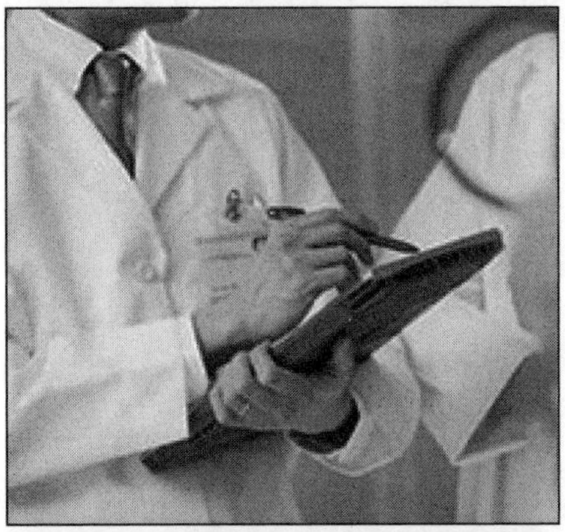

GUIDELINES/REFERENCES

American Society of Health-System Pharmacists. ASHP Guidelines on Pharmacist-Conducted Patient Education and Counseling. *Am J Health-Syst Pharm.* 1997;54:431-4.

Office of Disease Prevention and Health Promotion. Health Literacy and Communication at http://health.gov/communication/ (accessed 2016 Dec 2).

Agency for Healthcare Research and Quality (AHRQ). Pharmacy Health Literacy Center at http://www.ahrq.gov/ (accessed 2015 Dec 2).

Additional guidelines included with the online course.

BACKGROUND

The increased use of electronic health records (EHRs) has provided pharmacists with greater access to patient-specific information, including labs, test results and notes from other healthcare providers. Pharmacists must be prepared to effectively use all of this information to make decisions about drug therapy.

This is welcome news to the profession. It helps pharmacists be more involved in improving patient outcomes, and in assisting patients with health literacy and empowerment in improving their health.

THE PATIENT MEDICAL RECORD

Electronic Health Records

The patient medical record (PMR) provides complete documentation of a patient's medical history at a particular institution. The PMR can be referred to using older terminology such as the medical record or the patient chart. These terms are from the era of paper records, when all records of the patient's medical care were gathered into ring binders. Paper charts remain in some healthcare settings, but are being phased out and replaced by EHRs. Once implemented, EHRs improve accuracy and efficiency. EHRs are not without drawbacks; they can be subject to hacking and confidentiality breaches, discussed further.

The EHR is expedient and simpler to review: if, for example, a patient is admitted to the hospital with an elevated SCr, the EHR provides current and previous lab results (by selecting a date range that can go back years in time) which are used to determine if this is a new or an old finding, and what recent work-up has been completed. With a paper chart, time is required to look back and compile this history. With paper charts, papers can be missing (sometimes the entire chart can be lost) and time is required to transport the chart to wherever the patient is going next or to gather history with calls and faxes. Labs and tests are often duplicated because it may be easier to reorder them rather than locating them in the paper records. Procedures with results recorded on paper can be quickly scanned into the EHR. EHRs allow providers to have immediate access to information when they are off-site.

The Health Insurance Portability and Accountability Act of 1996 (HIPAA) security protections for paper records remain the same with electronic records. Access is limited with PINs and passwords, information is encrypted so unauthorized users cannot read it, and an "audit trail" is used to track access. Security can still be violated. Individuals can access medical records for patients they are not involved with, an employee can forget to log out, or the system can be hacked from the outside. All personnel using the EHR are responsible for security, education on security must be continual, and the software must be evaluated for breaches. As part of the HIPAA requirements, patients have a right to access their own medical records that are kept in either paper or electronic formats.

HIPAA & PHI

The HIPAA Privacy Rule covers all individually identifiable health information, which is called "protected health information" (PHI).

PHI includes the patient's address (anything more specific than the state they live in), the patient's physical and psychological conditions, the care received or planned, and information that could be used to identify that patient, including name, address, date of birth, medical record number, social security number, phone, fax and email.

It is acceptable to use PHI for treatment decisions, payment (insurance purposes) and for the specific facility operations (such as QI, infection control, etc.) and, if legally warranted (such as with an abuse case) or if required for public health.

Patient's can request to see their own PHI. If the PHI is used for other purposes (e.g., research), an authorization by the patient is required and identifiers are removed.

When the EHR is linked to Computerized Prescriber Order Entry (CPOE) and electronic prescribing (e-prescribing), the problem of illegible handwriting is eliminated. The CPOE system can be designed to present only formulary drugs with proper dosing as options. As a result, pharmacists spend less time clarifying orders or changing to a formulary drug. Clinical decision support (CDS) tools can be built into the order entry process. Examples include order sets, pathways, limited drop-down menus that reflect the preferred drug(s), drug interaction and dose checking alerts, and others. The alerts can appear to the prescriber and/or the pharmacist. Alerts can be constructed that require the user to take action to respond to the alert. An example is checking a box stating that the user is aware of a potential drug interaction and wishes to proceed with the order anyway. Critical results (e.g., aPTT ≥ 150 secs., platelets < 50,000/mm³) can be linked to alert systems, including automatic texts to providers. Electronic information is easier to pool together to measure clinical outcomes and perform quality improvement (QI) activities. EHR implementation at a facility does not occur without complaints; a few primary issues have involved safeguards for patient privacy, the increased time required for training and charting, and the implementation costs for the facility. A common complaint in all practice settings is "alert fatigue" or reduced sensitivity to the alerts. This can cause users to bypass important alerts and compromise patient safety. Refer to the Medication Safety & Quality Improvement chapter for additional information.

Sections of the Patient Medical Record

The first additions to the PMR (paper or EHR) are the patient's demographic data (including insurance information), admission sheet, a service agreement form ("this is what I am having done at this facility"), a page describing the patient's rights (a Joint Commission requirement), and an advanced directive to document the patient's wishes concerning medical treatment if he or she is unable to make decisions on their own behalf.

Certain religious groups will request a refusal form for blood transfusions and blood products. Blood products primarily involve albumin and immune globulins, but some patients will refuse drugs buffered in blood *(Epogen/Procrit, Kogenate* – used for hemophilia), natural clotting factors/tissue adhesives/interferons and a few other uncommon agents. A few vaccines contain porcine-derived gelatin as a stabilizer. The major religious groups consider this use acceptable, but a specific patient may not.

Other forms in the PMR include progress notes, the vital signs record, clinical pathway sheets used for some conditions, medication records used for some medications (such as warfarin to track the INR history), medication administration records and procedure records, including the diagnostic and operating room (OR) records. The list of "Do Not Use" abbreviations should be easily available. It is important to avoid abbreviations that could be interpreted to mean something else (refer to the Medication Safety & Quality Improvement chapter for further discussion). At the end of the hospital stay the planning and discharge forms are added to the EHR.

Requirements for Reimbursement: Documentation and Quality of Care

Pharmacists are involved with many patient care activities and frequently make verbal recommendations concerning patient care. While verbal recommendations may be effective, they are not part of the PMR and do not allow the information to be shared with other healthcare providers involved in the patient's care who are not present at that time. Interventions require documentation for reimbursement since the quality of the care is (increasingly) tied to the payment. Departments of pharmacy should have policies in place that describe the authority of pharmacists to document in the PMR, what activities will be documented, and the proper format for documentation. Some activities that pharmacists document in the PMR include patient counseling, medication histories, consultations (e.g., pharmacokinetics, anticoagulation) and dosage adjustments. Documenting in the PMR is critical to establishing pharmacists as central members of the healthcare team.

The federal health insurance program is currently called the Affordable Care Act (ACA) (or "Obamacare"). The ACA includes a "National Quality Strategy" which assesses the improvement in quality of care by determining if the members are healthier and if the costs are lower. Since the Centers for Medicare and Medicaid Services (CMS) provides health insurance to many Americans, CMS is directly involved with quality measurements and cost control. CMS has penalties for poor care and incentives for quality care. Two areas in which the penalties are steep are the rate of hospital-acquired infections and the hospital's readmission rate. These measures are chosen because they are expensive and are often, but not always, avoidable.

The Joint Commission, the Pharmacy Quality Alliance (PQA) and the Agency for Healthcare Research and Quality (AHRQ) are also involved in setting the criteria to measure the quality of care. The PQA quality measurements focus on medications. Specific goals that involve medications include increasing adherence, avoiding unnecessary or unsafe medications (such as high-risk medications in the elderly) and increasing the use of medications indicated for certain conditions.

MEDICARE & MEDICAID

Medicare is the federal health insurance program for people ≥ 65 years old, < 65 with disability and all ages with end stage renal disease (ESRD).

The prescription drug benefit under Medicare is called Part D.

Part A covers the hospital visit and Part B covers medical costs, such as doctor visits, and some vaccines.

Medicaid provides health insurance for all ages with very low income (< 133% of the federal poverty level). Medicaid is a federal and state program. A senior who qualifies for both Medicare and Medicaid has "dual coverage."

THE SOAP FORMAT FOR PROGRESS NOTES

A progress note records a patient encounter. The SOAP note format is organized into four parts: Subjective, Objective, Assessment and Plan (SOAP). Paper charts and EHRs often use this format. Prior to the use of SOAP notes it was difficult to understand patient chart entries, because the format was not standardized. The SOAP note was developed to provide a standard structure for recording the patient encounter. Pharmacists may write SOAP notes to document their activities and read the SOAP notes of others while providing patient care. An example SOAP note from an EHR is included at the end of this chapter.

Subjective

The 1st section in a SOAP note is the subjective information recorded from the patient. It is the patient's own narrative of their symptoms. Only the relevant information is recorded. The person conducting the interview should use only open-ended and direct questions while avoiding closed-ending and leading questions. For example, the leading question: "You always take your blood pressure pills, right?" is not likely to get a useful response. Phrasing the question in a direct manner that is worded to avoid a yes or no response will elicit a more useful response: "In a typical week, about how many mornings do you forget to take the blood pressure pills?"

The subjective section begins with a one-line Chief Complaint (CC), the specific reason the patient is being seen today, such as "I've had a stabbing pain in my right hip for three days" or "I feel like I need to go all the time but nothing much comes out." The subjective section includes the history of the present illness (HPI): the onset and duration of the specific complaint, the quality and severity (for example, with a pain complaint, descriptive words should be used to identify the type of pain, with a numerical pain rating), any modifying factors (what reduces or aggravates the condition), and treatment that has been tried to resolve the condition and the effect of the treatment, if any.

SIGNS AND SYMPTOMS (S/Sx)

A symptom is subjective information, described by the patient, such as "My lower back hurts."

A sign is generally objective (described by the clinician), such as recording the patient's vital signs.

Occasionally objective evidence (such as a skin rash), can be seen by either the patient or family members or the clinician.

This section includes the past medical history (PMH), social history (alcohol, tobacco and illicit drug use), family history (first-degree relatives only – parents and siblings), allergies and medication use. Medication use includes prescriptions, samples, and OTCs, including vitamins and natural products. Information on start date and last refill is important when recording medication information.

Objective

The 2nd section in a SOAP note is the objective information obtained by the clinician, either through observation or analysis. This includes the vital signs (respiration rate, heart rate, blood pressure, temperature). Note that on the top of the sample EHR at the end of this chapter the vitals are recorded at the top of the page, but they are part of the objective section. Any other measurements (for example, height and weight, spirometry), physical findings, tests performed (e.g., ECG, chest x-ray, urinalysis) and laboratory results go into this section. If medications are obtained from a source other than the patient (recording information from prescription bottles, calling another pharmacy, etc.) they are occasionally recorded in the objective section of the SOAP because they were objectively verified.

CRITICAL RESULTS

Critical results are levels significantly outside the normal range and can indicate a life-threatening situation.

They need to be reported to a healthcare provider right away and must be responded to quickly.

This is a Joint Commission National Patient Safety Goal.

Units of Measure

It is important to document measurements according to the policies of the institution. Documentation is generally done in metric system units (kg, cm, etc.). Recording weights and heights with incorrect units (150 pounds vs 150 kg) can have fatal consequences in terms of dosing medications. Refer to the Calculations I chapter for common height and weight conversions. In the U.S., temperatures are still frequently recorded in degrees Fahrenheit and may need to be converted to degrees Celsius.

Temperature Conversions

$^{\circ}C = (^{\circ}F - 32)/1.8$

$^{\circ}F = (^{\circ}C \times 1.8) + 32$

Assessment

The 3rd section is the assessment. This is the provider's thought process of possible causes of the current situation. Many conditions present with similar signs and symptoms; the assessment will often include multiple possible diagnoses. The differential diagnosis is a list of possible diagnoses that could explain the patient's current signs and symptoms. Each diagnosis on the list will be investigated.

Plan

The 4th section is the plan. This is how the problem(s) will be addressed. The plan should be as specific as possible. Labs might be ordered, the patient might require diagnostic exams, referrals may be requested, or the patient may require education. Education could be required for a variety of reasons (e.g., suspected nonadherence, poor device technique, nutritional education or smoking cessation support). If there is a differential diagnosis there will be multiple steps in the plan to eliminate ("rule out") some of the possible conditions. Patients often have many medical problems that must be addressed, and they may be vastly different from the complaint that prompted the patient to seek medical attention.

Military Time

In all medical records, including the SOAP note, time is recorded with a 24-hour clock, rather than splitting the day into two 12-hour segments (AM/PM). The 24-hour clock is called "military time." The day begins at midnight, which is called 24:00 (pronounced "twenty-four hundred"). This is actually the start of the day and is sometimes referred to as 00:00. One minute past midnight is 00:01, thirty minutes is 00:30, one hour is 01:00, and so on. After 12:00 noon the time continues on the same number scale for the rest of the day: 1:00 PM is 13:00, 2:00 PM is 14:00, and so on. The last minute of the day is 23:59, then 24:00 (midnight), and then the next day begins.

MILITARY TIME

12-Hr Clock	24-Hr Clock
12:00 midnight	24:00
1:00 am	01:00
...(continuing)	(pronounced "Oh-100")
7:00 pm	19:00
8:00 pm	20:00
9:00 pm	21:00
10:00 pm	22:00
11:00 pm	23:00
12:00 midnight	24:00

ASSESSMENT OF TREATMENT PLANS

Pharmacists caring for patients are often faced with complex medication regimens. In order to provide the best care possible, a systematic approach to assessment of the treatment plan and medication regimen is warranted. Pharmacists should assess for medication therapy problems (see Study Tip and example), intervene when appropriate, and document the intervention(s) in the PMR as policy permits. Cases on the exam will require the same type of systematic assessment to identify risks to the patient and potential solutions to problems.

STUDY TIP: HOW TO LOOK FOR MEDICATION PROBLEMS IN A PATIENT CASE

Review the case for the following medication problems:

Untreated medical condition	Drug allergy
Medications used without an indication	Drug interaction
Improper drug selection	Improper use of medication
Dose that is too low or high	Failure to receive medication
Therapeutic duplication	Adverse drug reaction
Lack of understanding about medication	Nonadherence

Practice reviewing cases until it becomes routine to check for each of these problems, every time. This is essential for a pharmacist.

Case Scenario

A new patient transfers the following prescriptions to a community pharmacy on December 15th: *Benicar* 20 mg daily, *Zocor* 20 mg daily, *Stribild* 1 daily (last refilled November 1st) and *Avapro* 150 mg TID. All are written for a 30-day supply.

Identify the potential problems:

- Therapeutic duplication: two ARBs
- Drug interaction: cobicistat is contraindicated with simvastatin
- Dose too high: *Avapro* should be dosed once daily
- Potential nonadherence: *Stribild* should be refilled every 30 days

Exam Scenario

A case is provided regarding a patient with a past medical history of type 2 diabetes who is currently taking no medications. The question is "Which of the following medications is best to recommend at this time?" The answer choices are *Glucophage XR, Actos, Invokana, Victoza* and regular insulin IV infusion.

Correct approach to the case:

Metformin is recommended as the first-line medication along with lifestyle modifications for type 2 diabetes. It could be the right answer, but the cases on an exam may be tesing something more advanced than simple recall of the recommended first-line medication. Before selecting metformin, make sure it is a safe choice in this specific patient and that nothing was missed in the case that would make another choice better:

- Insulin is one of the answer choices. Could this patient have hyperglycemia hyperosmolar state (HHS) or diabetic ketoacidosis (DKA), which would require an insulin infusion? Read the HPI. Look for signs, symptoms and labs that help (e.g., very high blood glucose, altered mental status, extreme dehydration; refer to the Diabetes chapter).
- Metformin should not be started if eGFR is < 45 mL/min/1.73 m^2. If eGFR is not provided, calculate the patient's CrCl and use this as an eGFR estimate.
- Check the progress notes and other information provided. Metformin should not be used within 48 hours of receiving IV iodinated contrast media.

If the patient does not require an insulin infusion to treat DKA or HHS, and there are no contraindications or allergy to metformin, select it as the correct answer choice. If metformin is not a safe choice, go through the same steps to determine which of the other choices is best for this patient.

HEALTHCARE PROVIDER COMMUNICATION

Health Literacy

Good communication skills are essential for pharmacists and are linked to patient satisfaction and trust. Despite providing valuable information to patients, much of the information that pharmacists provide may not be understood. Only about 12% of adults have proficient health literacy, an example of this is being able to correctly interpret a prescription label. Health literacy is the degree to which individuals are able to obtain, process and understand basic health and medication information to make appropriate health decisions. Health literacy is different than simply being able to read or being well educated; many educated people have difficulty understanding medical information. Low health literacy is common in the elderly, minority populations, those with lower income, poor health, and limited English proficiency but can be an issue for any patient. A person's health literacy is dependent on age, communication skills, knowledge, experience and culture. Low health literacy is linked to poor health outcomes.

Effective Communication and Education Strategies

- Approach all patients as if they may not understand the health information presented. Do not assume that it is easy to tell who has low health literacy.
- Use everyday, non-medical language that patients can understand.
  Example: Say "high blood pressure" instead of "hypertension" or "tired" instead of "fatigued".
- Ask open-ended questions that require more than a "yes" or "no" answer.
  Example: Ask "what questions can I answer about your new medication today?" instead of "do you have any questions?"
- Avoid leading questions.
  Example: Ask "what about your high blood pressure concerns you?" instead of "are you most concerned about the side effects from the high blood pressure medication?"
- Confirm understanding. Ask the patient to repeat the information or ask what they would tell their spouse or friend about the new medication.

- Use different communication strategies (verbal, written, visual aids) to enhance understanding. Ask the patient how he/she prefers to receive the information.
- Use active listening. Clarifying or summarizing what the patient has said is helpful and gives the patient an opportunity to offer correction.
- Speak clearly, make eye contact, introduce yourself and refer to patients by their name. Avoid "sweet-ie", "dear" and other similar terms.

Communication Challenges

Communicating medical information to patients with language/cultural differences and disabilities presents additional challenges. Be creative to ensure that all patients receive the education they need. Use interpreters or interpreter services (computer or phone services) when needed. Family members and friends (especially children) should not be used to interpret, if this can be avoided. They might edit or incorrectly relay the information. Strategies to enhance communication with certain patient types are included in the table.

PATIENT TYPE OR DISABILITY	STRATEGIES TO ENHANCE COMMUNICATION
Blindness or visual impairment	Provide information electronically when possible (some technology can "read" this aloud or convert to Braille). Use large text in written information. Speak normally.
Hearing impairment	Conduct counseling in a quiet, well-lit area. Speak directly to the patient; avoid explaining and demonstrating at the same time (many patients read lips and have difficulty focusing on two things at the same time).
Older adults	Issues above with visual and hearing impairment may apply. Older adults may not trust young healthcare providers. Earn their trust by being professional, competent and caring. Older adults may have difficulty with child-resistant caps and complicated devices. Recommend alternatives as needed.
Different cultures	Some cultures rely heavily on complementary and alternative medicine. Be sure to ask patients about this.

EXAMPLE ELECTRONIC HEALTH RECORD SOAP NOTE

Juanita Burrows (PRN: JB747114): SOAP Note for 09/25
Age on DOS: 40 yrs, DOB: 03/13/1974

San Diego Medical Group
35 La Jolla Drive Suite 100 San Diego, CA 92130
(444) 444-4444

seen by: Alison James
seen on: Thursday 25 September

VS

Height:	Weight:	BMI:	Blood Pressure:	Temp:	Pulse:	Resp Rate:
67.0 in	195.0 lb	30.5	154 / 92 mmHg	97.9 F	80 bpm	12 rpm

CC "I feel limp"

S JB is a 40 y/o female who presents with a 3 month history of increasing fatigue. She first noticed that she felt tired when she was working long hours to get a job done at work, but has been working her usual 8 hours a day for the past 2 months and has not regained her energy. She describes her fatigue as "feeling limp". It is present throughout the day, but worse with significant exertion (e.g., walking > 3-4 blocks or going up stairs). She has tried to go to bed earlier, but even sleeping up to 10 hours/night (increased from 8 hours/night) has not helped. She is concerned that there is something seriously wrong, as she is usually full of energy and her family and friends are starting to ask if she is sick. She has also not been able to exercise, which she usually enjoys. She denies chest pain, SOB, abdominal pain, N/V/D, or changes in her stool. She has no alopecia or skin changes. She has had no fever, chills or night sweats. She has gained about 6-7 lbs in the last few months, which she attributes to inactivity due to fatigue. She denies depressed mood, sadness, or anhedonia. She states that she goes to bed at 10pm and wakes feeling tired at 6am on weekdays and 8am on weekends. Her husband states that she has "always" snored quite loudly. Her menses are regular in timing, heavy flow for 1-2 days, then lighter for another 2-3 days. This pattern is unchanged from prior to the onset of her fatigue. Her last menstrual period was one week ago. When asked about compliance with her medications, she states that she takes everything regularly "except the one for her blood pressure because she doesn't feel like her pressure is high".

She reports a history of GERD, HTN, and depression.
Her medications include: Zantac 150 mg PO QHS, Chlorthalidone 25 mg PO Daily,
Zoloft 100 mg Daily, and Caltrate + D 600 mg BID.

O Well-appearing black female in no acute distress.
SKIN: not pale, no rashes
NECK: no thyromegaly or thyroid nodules
NODES: no cervical, axillary or inguinal lymphadenopathy
CHEST: clear to auscultation and percussion bilaterally
CV: RRR, 2/6 systolic ejection murmur heard best at the LLSB that radiates to the apex, no S3 or S4
ABD: normal active bowel sounds, no hepatosplenomegaly by palpation or percussion, no abdominal tenderness
EXT: no edema, pulses normal

A Recent onset of fatigue with no obvious inciting event. Hypothyroidism is possible especially given her weight gain, though this also may have occurred from her inactivity. It is possible that she is anemic though her menstrual periods have not lengthened or increased and there is no other obvious source of blood loss. A recent menses makes pregnancy unlikely. Given her history of snoring, sleep apnea is possible, but her history of snoring over many years is not entirely consistent with her more recent onset of fatigue. She does not seem to have a recurrence of her depression since she has no new symptoms. She does not have symptoms of infection, nor has her murmur changed, so subacute bacterial endocarditis is possible but unlikely. BP is elevated and she has been noncompliant with prescribed therapy for HTN.

P #1. Check TSH to rule out hypothyroidism
#2. Check CBC to rule out anemia
#3. If the above are unremarkable, consider a sleep study to rule out sleep apnea
#4. Consider blood cultures to rule out subacute bacterial endocarditis
#5. Pharmacy consult for medication adherence
#6. Follow-up visit in 1 week to discuss test results and further work-up

26 September 5:23 PM
page 1 of 1

PRACTICE CASE

PATIENT PROFILE

Patient Name	Celene Molina
Address	456 Washington Drive
Age:	58 **Sex:** F **Race:** Hispanic **Height:** 5'2" **Weight:** 146 pounds
Allergies	NKDA

Date	Prescriber	Drug/Strength/Sig/Quantity
12/11	Williams	Captopril 25 mg 1 tab PO TID #90
12/11	Williams	Furosemide 40 mg 1 tab with breakfast and lunch #60
12/11	Williams	*Klor-Con* 20 mEq 1 tab PO QAM #30
12/11	Williams	Metoprolol tartrate 50 mg 1 tab BID #60
12/11	Williams	Sertraline 50 mg 1 tab PO BID #60
12/11	Williams	Metformin 500 mg 1 tab PO TID #90
12/11	Williams	Simvastatin 20 mg 1 tab PO QHS #30
12/11	Williams	Albuterol inhaler 1 puff QID PRN #1 inhaler
12/11	Williams	*Advair Diskus* 1 puff BID #1 inhaler

ADDITIONAL INFORMATION

Date: 12/11	**Notes:** Patient out of medications. Provided refills for all medications. Follow-up in one month. Instructed patient to bring medication bottles to next clinic appointment.
Date: 1/15	**Notes:** Follow-up visit. Patient accompanied by daughter. Each bottle has 10-20 tabs remaining. Daughter states that her mother does not know how to use the inhalers. Vital signs today: BP 158/98, HR 82, Glucose (not fasting) 258 mg/dL

Questions

1. Celene speaks very little English and has limited health literacy. According to her daughter, she does not understand how to use her prescribed inhalers. All of the following methods are helpful to assist patients with limited English language proficiency EXCEPT:

   a. Use a translator or translator service.

   b. Reinforce the counseling with Celene's daughter.

   c. Talk loudly with exaggerated speech when explaining key points.

   d. Provide written information in the patient's language.

   e. Use pictures and diagrams, or pictograms, as aids during counseling.

2. The patient's daughter explained that the person who helped them in the clinic in December was not very friendly and "scared" her mom. The pharmacist and nursing team leader will work together to prepare an educational program to help the staff improve relationships with the patients. Each of the following strategies can improve relationships between healthcare professionals and patients EXCEPT:

   a. Use short words and sentences.

   b. Adopt a friendly rather than a business-like attitude.

   c. Use medical terminology when educating patients (e.g., use "hypertension" instead of "high blood pressure").

   d. Repeat instructions to patients if they look confused.

   e. Have patients repeat back the instructions.

3. Which of the following techniques would be most helpful to assist with Celene's medication adherence at this time?

   a. Switch the *Advair Diskus* to *Flovent HFA*.
   b. Simplify the medication regimen.
   c. Instruct the patient to move the simvastatin dose to the morning.
   d. Have the patient repeat back how to take each medication.
   e. Change the albuterol to oral tablets to reduce inhaler use.

4. Celene has reviewed her medications with the pharmacist and will leave for home shortly. The pharmacist would like to verify that Celene has received proper instruction on how to use her inhalers. Which of the following is the best method?

   a. Have the patient use pictures or pictograms to explain the technique to the pharmacist.
   b. The pharmacist should follow-up the visit with a telephone call.
   c. Celene's daughter should explain back the technique that her mother will use.
   d. Celene should demonstrate to the pharmacist how the inhaler is used.
   e. Have Celene watch video instructions before she goes home.

Answers

1-c, 2-c, 3-b, 4-d

DRUG DISPOSAL

Courtesy of Appalachian Voices

GUIDELINES/REFERENCES

Drug Enforcement Administration. Drug Disposal Information. http://www.deadiversion.usdoj.gov/drug_disposal/ (accessed 2015 October 12)

Food and Drug Administration. How to Dispose of Unused Medicines. http://www.fda.gov/forconsumers/consumerupdates/ucm101653.htm (accessed 2015 October 12)

U.S. Environmental Protection Agency. How to Dispose of Medicines Properly. http://water.epa.gov/scitech/swguidance/ppcp/upload/ppcpflyer.pdf (accessed 2015 October 12)

BACKGROUND

It is important to dispose of drugs properly to avoid accidental ingestion, environmental pollution and limit drug abuse. More Americans currently abuse prescription drugs than the number of those using cocaine, hallucinogens, heroin, and inhalants combined. Children and pets can accidently ingest drugs. Drugs that are flushed down the toilet can be found in the waterways, from the east to west coast.

There are safe and responsible ways to dispose of drugs through law enforcement-sponsored take-back events, collection receptacles and mail-back packages.

If the above disposal options are not available, patients can be instructed to follow local guidelines for Home Hazardous Waste (HHW) collection. HHW is any waste, produced in the home, which contains hazardous substances that can harm the environment, wildlife, and human health, and includes unwanted drugs. Cities and/or states have regulations on how to dispose of home hazardous waste, including prescription drugs.

If programs are not available, it is sometimes possible to dispose of unwanted drugs in the household trash if certain precautions are taken. Some drugs cannot be discarded in household trash due to higher risk, and these drugs can be flushed down the toilet instead. The complete list of drugs that should be flushed is at the end of this chapter. Drug disposal instructions are included in the package labeling.

NATIONAL AND LOCAL DRUG TAKE-BACK EVENTS

Courtesy of Penn State.

In 2010, the DEA implemented the National Prescription Drug Take-Back Day program at over 3,000 collection sites nationwide, which provided consumers a safe way to dispose of unused controlled substances. Take-Back events are a significant part of the government's effort to reduce prescription drug diversion and abuse by removing unwanted or expired medications from America's home medicine cabinets. Pharmacists volunteer at these events to help collect unwanted medications. The first four years of the program collected over 2,400 tons of unused drugs. The National Prescription Drug Take-Back Days were temporarily discontinued but are now reinstated.

Local law enforcement can host community take-back events. If these are available, the information should be known to local law enforcement and waste management services.

COLLECTION RECEPTACLES

Until recently, federal law did not provide a legal method for controlled drug disposal, except to return them to law enforcement. This caused unwanted drugs to be flushed or otherwise discarded or kept at home and subject to diversion. Currently, the Secure and Responsible Drug Disposal Act allows manufacturers, distributors, reverse distributors, narcotic treatment programs, hospitals/clinics with an on-site pharmacy, and retail pharmacies to voluntarily register with the DEA to collect controlled drugs (and non-controlled drugs) from patients for destruction. This is a welcome change since patients will have more disposal options and do not need to wait for a specific Take-Back Day to dispose of their unused medications. These DEA-authorized collection receptacles are to collect unused/unwanted drugs from patients only. Pharmacies and hospitals cannot dispose of unused/unwanted controlled substances from their inventory into the collection receptacle.

Courtesy of Sharps Compliance, Inc.©

The drugs collected should not be individually counted or inventoried. The patient or patient's agent should place the drugs directly into the collection receptacle themselves.

MAIL-BACK PROGRAMS

Courtesy of Sharps Compliance, Inc.©

Pharmacies and other DEA-authorized collectors can provide envelopes for patients to return drugs to a mail-back program. The medications are placed into the envelope and dropped off in the mail. The package is plain and does not have markings or other information that indicates what is inside the envelope.

The package should be pre-addressed with the collector's registered address or the participating law enforcement's address. The cost of shipping the package is postage paid.

DISPOSING DRUGS IN THE HOUSEHOLD TRASH

If no disposal instructions are given on the prescription drug labeling, and if there are no local disposal options or take-back programs in the local area, the U.S. Environmental Protection Agency and the FDA recommend throwing away drugs in the household trash by following these steps:

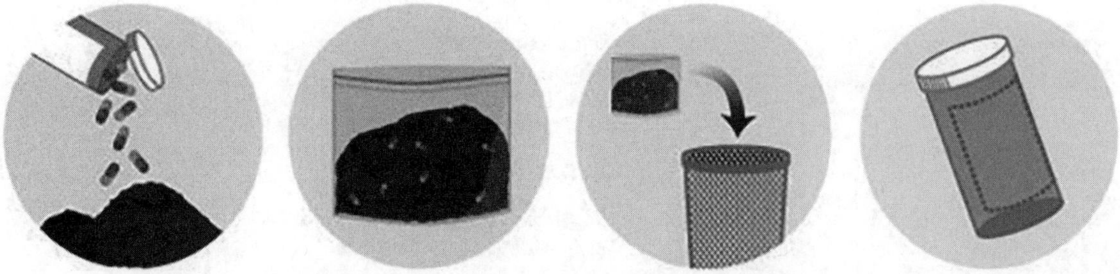

Courtesy of the Substance Abuse and Mental Health Services Administration

1. Remove the drugs from their original containers and mix them with an undesirable substance, such as used coffee grounds, dirt or kitty litter. This makes the drug less appealing to children and pets, and not easily recognizable to people who may intentionally go through the trash to look for drugs.
2. Scratch out all identifying information on the prescription label to make it unreadable if the container is being discarded. This will help protect the patient's identity.
3. Place the mixture in a sealable bag, empty can or other container to prevent the drug from leaking or breaking out of a garbage bag.
4. Place in trash can.

FLUSHING DRUGS DOWN THE TOILET OR SINK

In most cases, drugs should not be disposed of by flushing them down the sink or toilet because this will contaminate the water supply or soil. However, some medications can be particularly fatal if accidently ingested by others (especially children and pets), causing respiratory depression, and possibly death. The FDA recommends flushing specific drugs down the sink or toilet so the risk can be immediately and permanently removed from the home only when it is not possible for the drugs to be disposed of through a take-back program, collection receptacle, or mail-back program. With these drugs only the health risks from accidental ingestion will outweigh the environmental risks.

The FDA list of unwanted medicines that should be flushed down the sink or toilet (as of September 2015):

ACTIVE INGREDIENT	DRUG
Buprenorphine	*Belbuca,* soluble film (buccal) *Butrans*, transdermal patch (extended-release) Buprenorphine, tablet (sublingual)*
Buprenorphine/Naloxone	*Bunavail*, buccal film *Suboxone*, film (sublingual) *Zubsolv*, tablet (sublingual) Buprenorphine/Naloxone, tablet (sublingual)*
Diazepam	*Diastat/Diastat AcuDial*, rectal gel
Fentanyl	*Abstral*, tablet (sublingual) *Actiq*, oral transmucosal lozenge* *Duragesic*, patch (extended-release)* *Fentora*, tablet (buccal) *Onsolis*, soluble film (buccal)
Hydromorphone	*Dilaudid*, tablet* *Dilaudid*, oral liquid* *Exalgo*, tablets (extended-release)
Hydrocodone	*Hysingla ER*, tablet (extended-release) *Zohydro ER*, capsule (extended-release)
Meperidine	*Demerol*, tablet* *Demerol*, oral solution*
Methadone	*Dolophine*, tablet* *Methadose*, tablet* *Methadose,* oral solution*
Methylphenidate	*Daytrana*, transdermal patch system
Morphine	*Avinza*, capsule (extended-release) *Kadian*, capsule (extended-release) *Morphabond*, tablet (extended-release) *MS Contin*, tablet (extended-release)* Morphine, tablet (immediate-release)* Morphine, oral solution*
Morphine/Naltrexone	*Embeda*, capsule (extended-release)
Oxycodone	*Oxaydo*, tablet (immediate-release) *Oxycontin*, tablet (extended-release) Oxycodone, capsule Oxycodone, oral solution
Oxycodone/Acetaminophen	*Percocet*, tablet* *Xartemis XR*, tablet
Oxycodone/Aspirin	*Percodan*, tablet*
Oxycodone/Naloxone	*Targiniq ER*, tablets (extended-release)
Oxymorphone	*Opana*, tablet (immediate-release) *Opana ER*, tablet (extended-release)
Sodium Oxybate	*Xyrem*, oral solution
Tapentadol	*Nucynta ER*, tablet (extended-release)

** These medicines have generic versions available or are only available in generic formulations.*

SHARPS DISPOSAL

Used needles and other sharps cause injuries and spread infections, including hepatitis B and C, and HIV. Sharps should be disposed of in an FDA-cleared sharps container, which are puncture resistant, labeled or color-coded appropriately, closeable, and leak-proof. They come marked with a line that indicates when the container should be considered full (about ¾ full); never overfill or press down to fit in more waste. Patients who use sharps should have a disposal container and be instructed to put needles and other sharps in the container immediately after use.

The entire assembly is discarded (needle plus syringe). Do not instruct patients to remove the needle or attempt to cut it. The only time that recapping a needle is permitted is when the sharps container is not immediately available; in that case, use the one-hand method to recap until the sharps container can be reached: Place the cap on a table or counter next to something firm to push the cap against; 2. Hold the syringe with the needle attached and slip the needle into the cap without using the other hand. Push the capped needle on the firm surface to "seat" the cap onto the needle using only the one hand.

Anyone using syringes should be instructed not to contaminate the injection by touching the tip or plunger, and not to share needles with others. Needles are not meant to be reused. Sharps disposal guidelines and programs vary. The local trash removal services or health department should have the available service/s, and the pharmacy can relate this information to patients. These include drop boxes or supervised collection sites (such as in a hospital, pharmacy, police or fire station), household hazardous waste collection sites, mail-back programs and residential special waste services pick-up. If someone is stuck with a used needle, the proper department at a healthcare facility, and may require post exposure prophylaxis (PEP) for HIV and hepatitis B. In the outpatient setting, instruct the patient to wash the area right away with soap and water, and contact their healthcare provider.

19

IV DRUG COMPATIBILITY, STABILITY, ADMINISTRATION & DEGRADATION

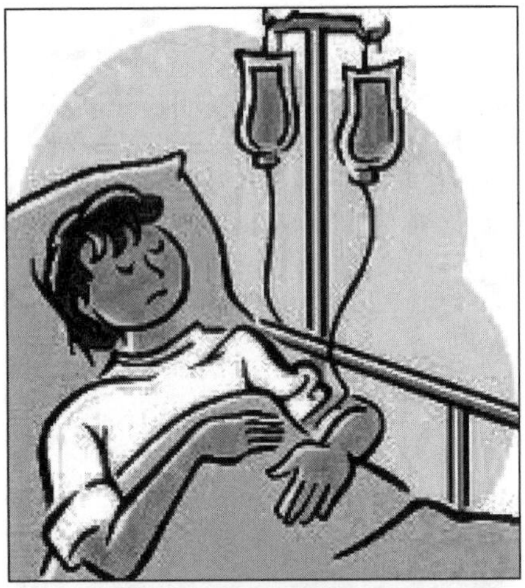

GUIDELINES/REFERENCES

Handbook on Injectable Drugs. 18th Ed. American Society of Health-System Pharmacists. 2014.

King Guide to Parenteral Admixtures. https://www.kingguide.com/online.html (accessed 2016 September 27).

Package inserts, various (accessed 2016 September 28).

BACKGROUND

When possible, medications are administered by the oral or enteral route. Parenteral administration (outside the GI tract) is used when the oral or enteral route is not feasible. This can be related to patient issues which make the enteral route unavailable, such as GI surgery, or to properties of the drug (e.g., poor oral bioavailability) or to the clinical situation and the need for a quick onset of action (e.g., vasopressors). Common parenteral routes of administration include intravenous (IV), intramuscular, subcutaneous and transdermal. This chapter focuses on the aspects of intravenous administration that are important to the pharmacist, including venous access (IV lines), compatibility issues, special administration requirements and drug stability.

VENOUS CATHETERS

A variety of IV access types are available to meet patient needs. Two of the most common are discussed here. A venous catheter is often called a "line."

Peripheral Lines

A peripheral line is inserted into a smaller vein, often in the hand or arm (sometimes in the foot for pediatric patients). Peripheral lines are simple and inexpensive to insert, but have some notable limitations. Peripheral lines are only for short-term use, as they are associated with phlebitis (irritation of the vein that can lead to blockage) and infiltration (the catheter becomes dislodged from the vein and the infusion enters the tissue instead of the bloodstream).

Central Lines

Central lines include catheters that are placed into a large vein. They can be placed directly through the skin into a large vessel, such as the superior vena cava, jugular or femoral vein. Another type of central line is called a peripherally inserted central catheter (PICC). This catheter is inserted into a vein in the upper arm and then the tip is advanced through the vein until it rests in the superior vena cava (which empties into the right atrium). Since it enters a large vessel larger volumes and higher infusion rates can be used. Because it empties into the right atrium, anything that is infused is rapidly diluted into a larger volume of blood, which enables the infusion of solutions with higher osmolality (e.g., TPN solutions) and vesicant solutions that can damage the vein or tissues due to pH or other issues (e.g., potassium, some chemotherapy). A central line is less likely to become dislodged from the vessel, so use is preferred when infusing vasopressors that could cause tissue damage if they were to escape the bloodstream and infuse into the tissues.

For drugs where the use of a certain type of line is important, this information is underlined throughout the book.

INCOMPATIBILITIES

The pharmacist is the primary resource for questions concerning the compatibility and stability of parenteral medications. There are many drugs and the information changes; reputable resources are required. The *Handbook on Injectable Drugs* (formerly called *Trissel's*) or the *King Guide to Parenteral Admixtures* (commonly called *King's*) are the primary compatibility and stability resources, along with the drug's package insert. Some drug information databases, including *Micromedex*, *Clinical Pharmacology* and *Lexicomp*, have an IV compatibility database that can be used in the clinical setting. A reputable group of pharmacists prepares lists of compatibility issues on a periodic basis that are published in *Pharmacy Practice News* and in *Hospital Pharmacy*. These lists are used for handy reference purposes; however, the pharmacist must verify the information as it may have changed. Chemical incompatibility causes drug degradation or toxicity due to a hydrolysis, oxidation or decomposition reaction. Physical incompatibility is commonly due to compounds binding together and forming a precipitate, which may or may not be visible, but can be quickly fatal if the precipitate travels to the lungs.

Physical incompatibilities can occur between a drug and the following:

- The container (e.g., polyvinyl chloride containers)
- The solution or diluent (e.g., dextrose or saline)
- Other drugs (e.g., phenytoin binding to dextrose or calcium binding to phosphate). Drug-drug incompatibility can occur when drugs are mixed in the same syringe or container, or during Y-site administration.

Container Compatibility (Polyvinyl Chloride)

The majority of polyvinyl chloride (PVC) containers use diethylhexyl phthalate (DEHP) as a "plasticizer" to make the plastic flexible. The DEHP compound is of concern, as it may affect male fertility. The two primary concerns with the use of PVC containers are leaching (DEHP moves from the PVC container into the solution) and sorption. Absorption occurs when drug moves into the PVC container and adsorption ocucurs when drug adheres (or "sticks") to the container. Drugs that are incompatible with PVC containers can be placed in polyolefin, polypropylene or glass containers (although glass is heavy and can break).

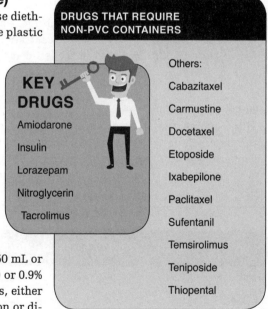

DRUGS THAT REQUIRE NON-PVC CONTAINERS

KEY DRUGS

Amiodarone

Insulin

Lorazepam

Nitroglycerin

Tacrolimus

Others:

Cabazitaxel

Carmustine

Docetaxel

Etoposide

Ixabepilone

Paclitaxel

Sufentanil

Temsirolimus

Teniposide

Thiopental

Diluent Compatibility

When drugs are put into solution for IV administration in the pharmacy they are commonly placed into 50 mL or larger IV "piggybacks" that contain 5% dextrose (D5W) or 0.9% sodium chloride (normals saline, NS). For many drugs, either solution is acceptable, but others have specific solution or diluent requirements for dextrose or for saline.

Incompatibility During Y-Site Administration

When a patient is receiving medication through an IV line, sometimes another medication needs to be given at the same time. If another IV line is not available, more than one medication can often be given through a single IV line using "Y-site" administration (see figure). The maintenance bag is the primary bag. The second container is sometimes called an IV piggyback. Since the drugs mix together briefly in the common portion of the IV tubing, it is important that the drugs and solutions are compatible. Nursing staff (who hang the infusion bags) commonly consult with the pharmacist to check for compatibility issues.

When a pharmacist references a resource to check whether drugs can be co-administered, several types of compatibility listings are available. "Additive compatibility" (drugs are mixed in the same container) and "syringe compatibility" (drugs are mixed in a syringe) are listed separately from Y-site compatibility. Y-site incompatibilities are important in pharmacy because this type of administration is common and many drugs that cannot be mixed in the same container are compatible to mix in the line.

In the following examples, the reference drug is listed above the table (cefepime) with the manufacturer and concentration listed directly below. The drug tested with it is listed in the left column (gentamicin). References are cited for each compatibility listing.

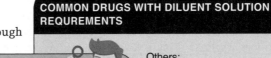

COMMON DRUGS WITH DILUENT SOLUTION REQUREMENTS

KEY DRUGS

Saline (No Dextrose)
Ampicillin

Ampicillin/ Sulbactam *(Unasyn)*

Caspofungin *(Cancidas)*

Daptomycin *(Cubicin)*

Phenytoin

Ertapenem *(Invanz)*

Infliximab *(Remicade)*

Dextrose (No Saline)
Amphotericin B (all formulations)

Quinupristin/Dalfopristin *(Synercid)*

Sulfamethoxazole/ Trimethoprim *(Bactrim)*

Others:

Saline (No Dextrose)
Abatacept *(Orencia)*

Azacitidine *(Vidaza)* NS

Belimumab *(Benlysta)*

Bevacizumab *(Avastin)*

Idarucizumab *(Praxbind)*

Iron Sucrose *(Venofer)*

Sodium Ferric Gluconate Complex *(Ferrlecit)*

Natalizumab *(Tysabri)*

Trastuzumab *(Herceptin)*

Dextrose (No Saline)
Carfilzomib *(Kyprolis)*

Mycophenolate *(CellCept IV)*

Pentamidine

INTERMITTENT WITH CONTINUOUS THERAPY SET-UP

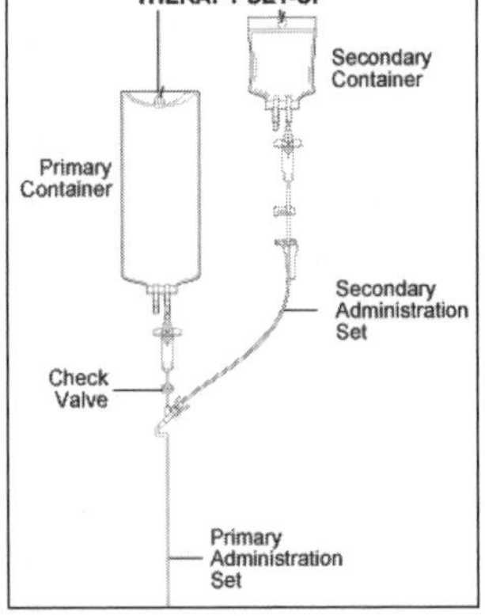

Additive Compatibility

In this example, the pharmacist looks to see if cefepime can be mixed with gentamicin in the same container. Based on the information below, cefepime and gentamicin are incompatible when mixed together in either D5W or NS at the concentrations listed. This is indicated by an "I" in the final column and the remarks, which indicate that a precipitate formed.

			Cefepime					
DRUG	**MFR**	**CONC/L**	**MFR**	**CONC/L**	**TEST SOLN**	**REMARKS**	**REF**	**C/I**
Gentamicin	ES	1.2 g	BR	40 g	D5W, NS	Cloudiness forms in 18 hr at room temp	588	I

C = compatible; I = incompatible

Y-Site Injection Compatibility (1:1 Mixture)

In this example, a nurse called to ask the pharmacist whether cefepime can be given in the same line while gentamicin is infusing. The pharmacist finds that cefepime and gentamicin are compatible for Y-site administration at the concentrations listed, indicated by the "C" in the far right column and by the remarks.

Cefepime							
DRUG	**MFR**	**CONC**	**MFR**	**CONC**	**REMARKS**	**REF**	**C/I**
Gentamicin	ES	6 mg/mL	BMS	120 mg/mL	Physically compatible with less than 10% cefepime loss. Gentamicin was not tested.	2212	C

C = compatible; I = incompatible

Information is extensive for incompatibilities; this is a discussion of a select few. Amphotericin B is incompatible with the majority of IV drugs with any type of IV administration. The common hospital drug piperacillin/tazobactam (discussed further below) forms a precipitate when it mixes with acyclovir, amphotericin B and many other IV drugs.

Heparin is incompatible when administered with many drugs, including those which are often given concurrently in a patient requiring heparin (e.g., nitroglycerin, alteplase and hydromorphone). Caspofungin, another common hospital drug for treating *Candida* infections, has many Y-site incompatibilities. All of the IV quinolones are incompatible with Y-site infusion of many drugs. When incompatibilities exist, particularly with long or continuous infusions, additional IV sites may be required.

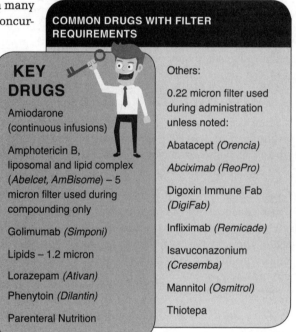

COMMON DRUGS WITH FILTER REQUIREMENTS

KEY DRUGS

Amiodarone (continuous infusions)

Amphotericin B, liposomal and lipid complex (*Abelcet, AmBisome*) – 5 micron filter used during compounding only

Golimumab *(Simponi)*

Lipids – 1.2 micron

Lorazepam *(Ativan)*

Phenytoin *(Dilantin)*

Parenteral Nutrition

Others:

0.22 micron filter used during administration unless noted:

Abatacept *(Orencia)*

Abciximab (ReoPro)

Digoxin Immune Fab *(DigiFab)*

Infliximab *(Remicade)*

Isavuconazonium *(Cresemba)*

Mannitol *(Osmitrol)*

Thiotepa

Filters

In-line filters (attached to the IV tubing) are used with drugs that have a risk of particulates, precipitates, crystals, contaminants or entrapped air in the final solution. The size of the filter required is determined by the size of the particles to be removed. The majority of drugs in which filters are necessary use a <u>0.22 micron filter</u> (1 micron = 1/1,000 mm);

another common filter size is 1.2 microns which is used for lipids. Some drugs come packaged with the required filter. If compounding IV medications packaged in glass ampules, filter needles or filter straws are used to prevent particulates from entering the IV bag and a filter may be required in the line.

DO NOT REFRIGERATE

KEY DRUGS

- Dexmedetomidine (*Precedex*)
- Enoxaparin (*Lovenox*)
- Furosemide – Crystallizes
- Metronidazole
- Moxifloxacin (*Avelox*)
- Phenytoin – Crystallizes
- Sulfamethoxazole/Trimethoprim (*Bactrim*)

Others:

- Acetaminophen (*Ofirmev*)
- Acyclovir – Crystallizes
- Deferoxamine (*Desferal*) – Precipitates
- Levetiracetam (*Keppra*)
- Pentamidine – Crystallizes
- Valproate

STABILITY AND THE EFFECTS OF TIME, TEMPERATURE, LIGHT, AGITATION

A drug that is "stable" at room temperature will be stable only for a certain time, at a certain temperature, with a certain degree of light exposure, and sometimes varies based on the concentration. Compounded sterile products (CSPs) have variable storage requirements due to sterility concerns. See Sterile Compounding chapter.

Drugs in solution decompose faster than other formulations. As a drug remains in solution longer the likelihood of a chemical reaction occurring increases. Compatibility concerns due to longer infusion times have become an important issue in recent years with piperacillin/tazobactam (*Zosyn*) extended infusions. *Zosyn* is also commonly used with shorter, intermittent infusions (which cause fewer compatibility issues). The longer infusion period is used to increase time above the minimum inhibitory concentration (T > MIC) in order to counter drug resistance with some of the common nosocomial pathogens, including *Pseudomonas*, *Enterobacter* and *Acinetobacter*. The higher T > MIC is beneficial, but the longer infusion times result in more significant compatibility issues with some of the other drugs that the hospitalized patient receives. Interactions with piperacillin/tazobactam, azithromycin, ciprofloxacin, tobramycin, vancomycin, other antibiotics, insulin and some vasopressors occur more commonly when given as a longer infusion.

Higher temperatures promote chemical reactions, which is why the majority of compounded IV drugs are kept cold (refrigerated) in order to extend the time that the drug is stable. There are exceptions; for example, furosemide crystallizes if kept cold and is stored at room temperature. See the table of IV drugs that do not require refrigeration.

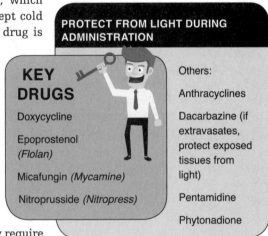

PROTECT FROM LIGHT DURING ADMINISTRATION

KEY DRUGS

- Doxycycline
- Epoprostenol (*Flolan*)
- Micafungin (*Mycamine*)
- Nitroprusside (*Nitropress*)

Others:

- Anthracyclines
- Dacarbazine (if extravasates, protect exposed tissues from light)
- Pentamidine
- Phytonadione

Light exposure causes photo-degradation that can destroy the drug and in some cases will increase the toxicity. Many medications should be protected from light during storage to avoid degradation. Some medications are supplied in amber vials, while others should be kept in their original packaging (foil overwrap or box) until administration. A small number of drugs are so light-sensitive that they require protection from light during administration. Pharmacy staff dispense these medications in a light-protective cover. Additionally, in some cases, light-protective tubing (generally amber colored) is required. See the table for a list of "photosensitive" drugs that require light-protection during administration.

Agitation destroys some drugs, particularly hormones and other proteins. Drugs that are easily destroyed include alteplase, immune globulins, insulins, rasburicase and some vaccines, including zoster. Quinupristin/dalfopristin *(Synercid)* and etanercept *(Enbrel)* are some of the drugs that form a foam and should only be swirled when reconstituting. Do not shake; wait for the foam to dissolve.

IV DRUG DISCOLORATION

Most intravenous medications are clear and colorless. In some cases discoloration can be of little or no consequence. However, in most cases, discoloration indicates oxidation or another type of decomposition. Some examples include:

- Nitroprusside – Light causes decomposition, which is visible as an orange, dark brown or blue liquid. A blue color indicates nearly complete decomposition. If discolored, do not use.
- Chlorpromazine – A slightly yellowed color is acceptable. Do not use if darker than light yellow.
- Dacarbazine – Turns pink if drug has decomposed; do not use.
- Dobutamine – Oxidation turns the liquid slightly pink, but potency is not lost.
- Dopamine – A slightly yellowed color is acceptable. Do not use if darker than light yellow.
- Norepinephrine – Oxidation turns the liquid brown. If discolored, do not use.
- Epinephrine – Oxidation turns the liquid pink, then brown. If discolored, do not use.
- Isoproterenol – Exposure to air, light or ↑ temperature turns the liquid pink or darker. If discolored, do not use.
- Morphine – If the solution is dark, do not use.
- Tigecycline – Reconstituted solution is yellow/orange, do not use if green/black.
- The antidote *Cyanokit* – Discard if solution is not dark red.

PARTICULATE MATTER

The clinician (or the patient if using a self-injectable) should be instructed to check for particulate matter. If particulates are present, the product should not be used.

20

EMERGENCY PREPAREDNESS, TOXICOLOGY & ANTIDOTES

KEEP CALM
AND
ASK A PHARMACIST
AT THE
POISON CONTROL CENTER

GUIDELINES/REFERENCES

National Library of Medicine TOXNET. http://toxnet.nlm.nih.gov (accessed 2016 Oct 4).

Lexi-Comp Toxicology Online. http://online.lexi.com/lco/action/home/tox (accessed 2016 Oct 4).

CDC, Emergency Preparedness. http://emergency.cdc.gov (accessed 2016 Oct 4).

ASHP Best Practices, ASHP Statement on the Role of Health-System Pharmacists in Emergency Preparedness. 2015-2016 Ed., Bethesda, MD: ASHP; 2015.

We gratefully acknowledge the assistance of Susan E. Gorman, PharmD, MS, DABAT, FAACT, Former Past-President, American Board of Applied Toxicology, and Cynthia L. Morris-Kukoski, PharmD, DABAT, FAACT, Former Past-President, American Board of Applied Toxicology, in preparing this chapter.

EMERGENCY PREPAREDNESS

Pharmacy staff can be involved in the response to a disaster, which can include natural disasters (e.g., floods), industrial accidents, terrorist attacks that involve the release of biological and chemical agents, and disasters from radioactive, nuclear, or explosive devices.

Pharmacists should be primarily involved in the areas in which they have expertise: drug management required for the specific disaster (e.g., antidotes) and in the usual drug management of patients during and after a disaster. Legal issues regarding dispensing a drug during an emergency (such as with the Emergency Prescription Assistance Program), are discussed in RxPrep's MPJE Course.

It is most important for the pharmacy staff involved in preparing for an emergency to be well-informed about likely threats in their locality and to coordinate the drug components that will be included in the emergency response plans with the federal, regional/state and local agencies responsible for the plan development and maintenance. The pharmacists involved with these efforts should ensure that any drug stockpiling efforts are in agreement with these plans. Pharmacists should discourage inappropriate stockpiling by individual institutions that are not involved with the emergency response plans. Pharmacists should be familiar with emergency protocols for their institution or workplace, including those for evacuation, disaster preparedness, mass dispensing (if required), and poisoning emergencies.

Communications concerning emergency planning and response requires an electronic network that should include the hospital pharmacy department directors, and local pharmacies that can serve the needs of the community. The network should be used to transmit urgent information related to emergency preparedness and to circulate important new information related to pharmacist involvement on disaster response teams, such as a new biological threat, or a heightened state of emergency. Pharmacists involved from a hospital setting should be familiar with the recommendations of the American Society of Health-System Pharmacists (ASHP), which is referenced on the first page of this chapter. The CDC pages on Emergency Preparedness (also referenced) include recommendations for the treatment of likely biological agents, information on current disease outbreaks, and treatment for chemical and radiation exposure. One of the antidotes for exposure to radioactive iodine (KI, potassium iodide) is reviewed in the Thyroid Disorders chapter because it is used for other purposes.

TOXICOLOGY AND ANTIDOTES

Toxic means poisonous, and toxicology is the study of poisonous chemicals, which includes drugs at unsafe doses. Antidotes are substances that stop the harmful effects of the poison (or overdosed drug). Many are used off-label in the management of poisonings. Children are the most common victims of accidental poisoning in the United States. The top categories of substances in accidental pediatric exposures are cosmetics/personal care products, analgesics and cleaning substances. Accidental poisoning is common among the elderly and is primarily due to mental or physical impairment, the use of multiple drugs, and reduced elimination of the drug from the body. Poisoning can be due to illicit drug use, including FDA approved and non-approved (illegal) opioids, taken alone or in combination with other drugs. Poisoning can be intentional, such as with attempted suicide or as an act of revenge, or in situations such as drug-facilitated sexual assault.

Prevention of Accidental Poisoning

To reduce accidental poisoning in children, child-resistant (C-R) containers are helpful, but are not foolproof. These are required for prescription drugs unless waived by the patient (or by the provider for a single exception), or with specific substances that are excluded from this requirement, such as nitroglycerin sublingual tablets. Non-prescription drugs that require C-R containers include anything containing iron, diphenhydramine, acetaminophen, salicylates, NSAIDs, "imidazoline" vasoconstrictors such as naphazoline and oxymetazoline and drugs that have been switched from Rx to OTC status. Non-drug compounds that are dangerous if swallowed require C-R packaging, such as turpentine. A complete list of drugs that must have C-R packaging (and those that do not need to have this type of packaging) is provided in the RxPrep MPJE Course, since this is a federal legal requirement. Common C-R packaging includes screw caps that require more than a simple turn to open (such as having the user press down with the palm when turning to open), unit-dose packaging and the card adherence and safety packaging that require the user to press on one side while pulling the medication card out of the other side. The picture demonstrates the *Optilock* packaging, which, additionally, can help with adherence since each dose is labeled with the day it should be taken.

Early Suspicion, Actions and Decontamination

Anyone can contact the national poison control line (phone # 800-222-1222) for a questionable exposure. With topical exposure, remove any contaminated clothing and run water over the skin for 10 minutes, then wash with soap and rinse. For ocular exposure, remove contact lenses and rinse eye/s with water from a tap or hose with a gentle stream for at least 15 minutes. With oral ingestion, remove anything in the mouth and collect any suspect containers to bring to the emergency department. If unconscious, place the patient on the left side to more easily clear vomit if emesis (vomiting) occurs. Ipecac syrup was used previously to induce emesis for certain exposures, but is no longer commercially available, and is no longer recommended. Instruct others not to give ipecac syrup; it remains in many home medicine cabinets. Do not use any other mechanism to induce vomiting.

If the patient is unconscious, having difficulty breathing, appears agitated or is having a seizure, emergency help should be contacted (call 911). If the patient is not breathing and/or has no pulse, CPR should be initiated. Initially, in an emergency situation, the ABC's (Airway, Breathing and Circulation) must be addressed, in order. The airway is required for breathing, which is required for circulation. Breathing support, including assisted ventilation, may be required. Maintenance of the ABC's is commonly referred to as supportive care. Cardiac monitoring with an ECG will be needed with drugs that affect heart rate or rhythm or with any cardiac abnormality present. With some substances, specific antidotes or dialysis may be used.

Multiple Drug Overdose

In many cases of overdose, more than one drug is involved. Opioids, whether legal (such as hydrocodone) or illegal (such as heroin) are often mixed with benzodiazepines, alcohol and other drugs. People can overdose on fixed-dose combination drugs (e.g., an acetaminophen-opioid combination). In multiple-drug overdose, more than one antidote may be required. If symptoms of opioid overdose are present (pinpoint pupils, difficult to arouse/unconsciousness, respiratory depression), naloxone must be given quickly to reverse respiratory depression and prevent death.

Caution: Asymptomatic or Non-Specific Presentation

Several of the most dangerous compounds do not cause immediate symptoms when toxic. To identify whether a patient is at risk, the clinician should determine the time/s of ingestion, the quantity, and the formulation ingested. For example, in an acetaminophen overdose the patient can remain asymptomatic or have non-specific symptoms (such as nausea, abdominal pain, fatigue) until end organ toxicity (liver failure) becomes apparent. Early administration of N-acetylcysteine (NAC) after suspected acetaminophen overdose is essential to prevent hepatotoxicity. When the acetaminophen level is available and the exposure has occurred within the past 24 hours, it is used as the basis for treatment.

Decontamination with Activated Charcoal

Activated charcoal is used in the emergency treatment of specific types of orally ingested drugs and is an early step in some overdose protocols. The idea is to stop the absorption of as much of the drug as possible while it is still in the gut. The charcoal adsorbs the drug, which prevents GI absorption and systemic toxicity. Activated charcoal needs to be given quickly and is most effective when used within one hour of ingestion. Some activated charcoal products contain sorbitol, which is a sweetener and laxative. Sorbitol should be avoided because it can induce vomiting and cause electrolyte depletion. Vomiting can cause aspiration of the stomach contents, including the toxin, and injure the esophagus. Prior to using activated charcoal, the airway should be protected in any patient who is unconscious or likely to become unconscious. This will prevent vomiting and aspiration. Activated charcoal is contraindicated when the airway is unprotected, or if the ingested compound can increase the risk of aspiration (such as with hydrocarbons). Drugs will bind to the activated charcoal and should be separated by at least two hours. Alcohols, heavy metals (iron, lead, lithium, mercury) and corrosives (alkalis, acids) do not bind to charcoal. The dose of activated charcoal is 1 g/kg.

Antidotes for Common Drug and Non-Drug Poisonings

DRUG/TOXIN	ANTIDOTE	COMMENTS
Acetaminophen	**N-acetylcysteine** (oral, or *Cetylev* effervescent tablets for oral solution, or *Acetadote* IV)	N-acetylcysteine restores hepatic glutathione (acts as a glutathione substrate). It should be initiated immediately if overdose is suspected, regardless of symptoms. Oral: 140 mg/kg x 1, followed by 70 mg/kg every 4 hours x 17 additional doses. Repeat the dose if emesis occurs within 1 hour of administration. Intravenous: 150 mg/kg IV over 60 minutes, followed by 50 mg/kg IV over 4 hours, followed by 100 mg/kg IV over 16 hours.
Animal bites	Rabies vaccine ***(RabAvert****, Imovax)* with Human rabies immune globulin ***(HyperRAB S/D****, Imogam Rabies HT)*	High-risk animal bites or exposure (no previous rabies vaccination): give vaccine and human rabies immune globulin (HRIG). Vaccine given 1 mL IM in the deltoid (adults) or thigh (children, infants) on days 0, 3, 7, 14 and immune globulin is given 20 units/kg on day 0, infiltrated around wound site and a location separate from vaccine site. HRIG is not useful after day 7 of vaccine or in previously immunized individuals. Clean wound with soap and water. Tetanus shot is required if it has been at least 10 years since the last booster shot.
Anthrax	Anthrax immune globulin *(Anthrasil)*, raxibacumab *(Abthrax)*, obiltoxaximab *(Anthim)*	For adults and pediatric patients for treatment of inhalation anthrax due to *Bacillus antharacis,* in combination with antibiotics.
Organophosphates (OPs), include industrial insecticides (malathion, others) and nerve (warfare) gases (sarin, others)	**Atropine** and **pralidoxime** or in combination *(DuoDote, ATNAA)*	OPs block acetylcholinesterase, which increases acetylcholine (Ach) levels. Atropine is an anticholinergic and blocks the effects of Ach to reduce the cholinergic SLUDGE symptoms: salivation, lacrimation, urination, diarrhea, gastrointestinal distress and emesis. Pralidoxime treats the muscle weakness and relieves paralysis of respiratory muscles secondary to the toxicity.
Botulinum toxin (BTX)	Botulism antitoxin heptavalent *(BAT)*, botulism immune globulin *(BabyBIG)*, supportive care (ventilator for respiratory support)	Botulinum toxin causes botulism/neuroparalysis; respiratory support is central. Heptavalent botulism antitoxin is only available through the CDC. *BabyBIG* (botulism immune globulin) is used for infant botulism (different than foodborne botulism) and is available through the California Department of Public Health.
Black Widow spider bites	**Antivenin** for *Latrodectus mactans*, supportive care	Predominantly found in southern and western states. Children and frail elderly at highest risk for severe injury. The spiders are non-aggressive if left alone. Supportive care is the mainstay of therapy (opioids for pain management and benzodiazepines for muscle spasms).
Carbon monoxide (CO)	Oxygen, possibly hyperbaric	Accidental exposure from gas heaters, wood or charcoal stoves, CO-emitting kerosene heaters (colorless, odorless) or automobile exhaust.
Ethanol (alcoholic drinks)	Supportive care, correct hypoglycemia, vitamin B1 with chronic ingestion	If any question if chronic alcohol user, administer thiamine (vitamin B1) to prevent Wernicke encephalopathy (neurological damage).

Antidotes for Common Drug and Non-Drug Poisonings Continued

DRUG/TOXIN	ANTIDOTE	COMMENTS
Ethylene glycol (antifreeze), diethylene glycol, methanol	Fomepizole *(Antizol)* is preferred Ethanol (2nd line)	Fomepizole and ethanol inhibit alcohol dehydrogenase (ADH). Caution: children are very prone to hypoglycemia. Methanol or ethylene glycol toxicity should be suspected with anion-gap metabolic acidosis along with an osmolar gap.
Anticholinergics: atropine, diphenhydramine, dimenhydrinate, *Atropa belladonna* (deadly nightshade), jimson weed, scopolamine	Supportive care, rarely physostigmine	Physostigmine inhibits acetylcholinesterase, which breaks down acetylcholine. Increased acetylcholine reduces the anticholinergic toxicity, but physostigmine is not routinely recommended. It may be used in severe cases of delirium if no contraindications are present (cardiac conduction defects, seizures). Benzodiazepines/anticonvulsants if seizures present. Anticholinergic overdose symptoms can be remembered with the mnemonic "red as a beet, dry as a bone, blind as a bat, mad as a hatter, and hot as a hare" for the symptoms of flushing, dry skin and mucous membranes, mydriasis with double or blurry vision, altered mental status and fever. Severe symptoms include tachycardia, hypertension, psychosis, seizures, respiratory and cardiovascular collapse.
Benzodiazepines	**Flumazenil** *(Romazicon)*	Flumazenil is also used off-label for non-benzodiazepine hypnotic overdose (e.g., zolpidem), but is not routinely recommended. Flumazenil can precipitate seizures when used in benzodiazepine-dependent patients.
Beta blockers	Supportive care, possibly glucagon and/or high dose insulin with glucose, and/or lipid emulsion therapy	Treat bradycardia, hypotension and seizures. Glucagon may be used if unresponsive to standard supportive care. High dose insulin with glucose may be used in patients refractory to glucagon therapy. Enhanced elimination of some lipophilic drugs using 20% lipid emulsion bolus, followed by continuous infusion.
Calcium channel blockers	Supportive care (see beta blockers above), Calcium (chloride or gluconate), possibly glucagon and/ or high dose insulin with glucose, and/or lipid emulsion therapy	Administer calcium IV only, avoid fast infusion, monitor ECG, do not infuse calcium in same line as phosphate-containing solutions. Glucagon may be used if unresponsive to standard care. High dose insulin with glucose may be used in patients refractory to glucagon therapy. Enhanced elimination of some lipophilic drugs using 20% lipid emulsion bolus, followed by continuous infusion.
Cyanide	2 IV antidotes: Hydroxocobalamin *(Cyanokit)* Sodium thiosulfate + sodium nitrite *(Nithiodote)*	Cyanide toxicity may be due to treatment with nitroprusside when used in high dose, long duration, or with renal impairment, or from ingestion of amygdalin, a synthetic form of laetrile (used as an ineffective cancer treatment), or most commonly, due to smoke inhalation. Do not use *Cyanokit* if solution is not dark red.
Dabigatran	Idarucizumab *(Praxbind)*	Idarucizumab is a reversal agent for dabigatran *(Pradaxa)*. Use if urgent surgery is required or with life-threatening/uncontrolled bleeding. Dose is 5 mg IV (2.5 mg vial x 2).

Antidotes for Common Drug and Non-Drug Poisonings Continued

DRUG/TOXIN	ANTIDOTE	COMMENTS
Digoxin, oleander, foxglove	**Digoxin Immune Fab *(DigiFab)***	*DigiFab* 40 mg vial binds ~0.5 mg digoxin. Interferes with digoxin levels drawn after it has been given. When the amount ingested or digoxin level is unknown, the adult dose is 20 vials.
5-fluorouracil (5-FU), capecitabine	Uridine triacetate *(Vistogard, Xuriden)*	For emergency treatment following overdose, beginning as soon as possible after overdose or early-onset toxicity within 96 hours after the end of fluorouracil or capecitabine administration.
Heavy metals, including arsenic, copper, gold, lead, mercury, thallium	**Dimercaprol**: arsenic, gold, mercury (or lead in conjunction with calcium disodium edetate ($CaNa_2$ EDTA)) Penicillamine: copper **Succimer** *(Chemet)*, dimercaptosuccinic acid *(DMSA)*: lead Ferric hexacyanoferrate, also referred to as "Prussian blue" *(Radiogardase)*: thallium	Succimer is a water-soluble, oral chelating agent that is used in asymptomatic children with serum lead levels > 45 mcg/dL. EDTA is a parenteral chelating agent. It does not cross the blood-brain barrier and can exacerbate encephalopathy; dimercaprol, which does cross the blood-brain barrier, is given first. Do not use disodium EDTA; use $CaNa_2$ EDTA. Lead poisoning is initially asymptomatic; toxicity results in cognitive deficits, highest risk in children with exposure to lead-containing paint chips.
Heparin, Low Molecular Weight Heparin (LMWH)	**Protamine**	1 mg will reverse ~100 units of heparin. See Anticoagulation chapter.
Insulin or other hypoglycemics, severe low blood glucose	**Dextrose** Glucagon (when IV or oral dextrose cannot be administered)	Dextrose injection or infusion (drip): do not exceed 12.5% peripherally or 25% IV due to risk of thrombosis or phlebitis, may require co-administration of potassium (IV dextrose will result in hypokalemia). Sulfonylurea induced-hypoglycemia: octreotide *(SandoSTATIN)* may be given with dextrose.
Isoniazid	**Pyridoxine (vitamin B6),** benzodiazepines and/or barbiturates	For acute neurotoxicity (seizure, coma), administer IV pyridoxine in a gram-per-gram amount (max 5g), along with benzodiazepines and/or barbiturates. If ingested amount is unknown, 70mg/kg (max 5g) is recommended. May repeat if seizures persist/recur. Oral pyridoxine 10 – 50 mg is used daily with isoniazid to prevent neuropathies.
Iron Aluminum	**Deferoxamine *(Desferal)***, deferiprone *(Ferriprox)* and deferasirox *(Exjade, Jadenu)* – for iron overload from blood transfusions	Overdose can be due to accidental ingestion or secondary to multiple blood transfusions. Common childhood overdose because iron tablets look like candy. Most lethal iron overdoses are from prenatal multivitamins and OTC iron tablets. Deferoxamine is used for iron and aluminum toxicity and can cause reddish brown discoloration of urine. Deferoxamine is contraindicated in severe renal disease.
Local anesthetics (bupivacaine, mepivacaine, ropivacaine) and other lipophilic drugs (bupropion, TCAs, CCBs, beta blockers)	Lipid emulsion 20%, supportive care, benzodiazepines if seizures present	IV infusion of lipid emulsion reverses the cardiac and neurologic effects of local anesthetic toxicity.
Methotrexate	Leucovorin (folinic acid), levoleucovorin *(Fusilev)*, glucarpidase *(Voraxaze)*	Leucovorin/levoleucovorin: for rescue after high-dose methotrexate treatment (in cancer treatment), or after an accidental overdose, to diminish the toxicity and counteract the effects of impaired methotrexate elimination.

Antidotes for Common Drug and Non-Drug Poisonings Continued

DRUG/TOXIN	ANTIDOTE	COMMENTS
Methemoglobinemia	Methylene blue *(ProvayBlue)*	Drugs that cause methemoglobinemia (an altered form of hemoglobin) include anesthetics, dapsone, phenytoin, chloroquine and silver sulfadiazine; this condition is rare, and is more likely to occur if multiple drugs listed are used together or can be due to a congenital condition. Chemicals that can cause methemoglobinemia include amyl nitrite and other nitrites, including illicit "poppers". Methylene blue is contraindicated in patients with G6PD deficiency.
Amatoxin-containing mushrooms	Supportive care, silibinin *(Legalon SIL)* +/- atropine	There are various types of mushrooms; some are poisonous, many are not. Treatment is guided by symptoms, such as hallucinations. Atropine if severe muscarinic symptoms (bradycardia). Silibinin is the flavonoid in milk thistle, sometimes used for hepatoprotection.
Naphthalene, from mothballs	Supportive care, methylene blue	Methylene blue is also indicated for drug-induced methemoglobinemia.
Neostigmine, pyridostigmine	Pralidoxime *(Protopam)*	Pralidoxime counteracts the muscle weakness and/or respiratory depression secondary to overdose of anticholinesterase medications used to treat myasthenia gravis.
Nicotine, including e-cigarettes	Supportive care, **atropine**	Atropine is a nicotinic receptor antagonist and should be given to treat symptomatic bradycardia. Benzodiazepines should be given to treat seizures.
Opioids, legal and illicit (e.g., heroin)	**Naloxone *(Narcan,*** *Evzio)*	*Evzio* is a naloxone auto-injector for emergency treatment outside of the hospital. See Pain chapter.
Petroleum distillates (gasoline, kerosene, mineral oil, paint thinners)	Oxygen, supportive care	Do not induce vomiting. Keep patient NPO due to aspiration risk.
Plants: castor beans, jequirity beans, oleander and foxglove, hemlock	Supportive care, *DigiFab* if oleander or foxglove	Castor beans contain ricin. Jequirity beans contain abrin; structurally has the same two-subunit configuration as ricin. Oleander and foxglove contain digitalis glycosides.
Rocuronium bromide, vecuronium bromide, pancuronium bromide	**Neostigmine methylsulfate *(Bloxiverz)*** for rocuronium bromide, vecuronium bromide, and pancuronium bromide **Sugammadex *(Bridion)*** for rocuronium bromide and vecuronium bromide	For reversal of the effects of neuromuscular blockade induced in adults undergoing surgery. Administer an anticholinergic agent such as atropine or glycopyrrolate prior to or with neostigmine to prevent bradycardia.
Salicylates	**Sodium bicarbonate**	Salicylates may cause metabolic acidosis; sodium bicarbonate is an alkalinizing agent and is given to alkalinize the urine. This will decrease the drug reabsorption and increase the excretion of the salicylates and other weak acids.
Scorpion stings	Antivenin immune FAB *Centruroides (Anascorp)*, supportive care.	Scorpions with venom potent enough to cause clinically severe symptoms are found mainly in the southwest.

Antidotes for Common Drug and Non-Drug Poisonings Continued

DRUG/TOXIN	ANTIDOTE	COMMENTS
Snake bites: eastern coral snake, Texas coral snake, copperhead snake, rattlesnake	Crotalidae polyvalent immune FAB *(CroFab)* for copperhead and rattlesnake bites Antivenin *Micrurus fulvius* for coral snake bites Crotalidae Immune F(ab')2 *(Anavip)* for rattlesnake bites	Do not use ice; do not cut/suck out venom; transport patient to healthcare facility.
Stimulant overdose from amphetamines, including ADHD and weight loss drugs, cocaine, ephedrine, caffeine, theophylline, MDMA (ecstasy), alcohol withdrawal	Supportive care, possibly benzodiazepines	Symptoms of overdose include tachycardia, hypertension, mydriasis, agitation, possible seizures, hyperthermia and psychosis. Benzodiazepines (e.g., lorazepam) if agitation or seizures.
Tricyclic antidepressants	Supportive care, sodium bicarbonate	Overdose can cause several conditions that must be managed, including arrhythmias, seizures and respiratory depression. IV hypertonic sodium bicarbonate can be given to decrease a widened QRS complex. Benzodiazepines can be used if agitation or seizures are present. Vasopressors may be needed for hypotension.
Valproate or topiramate-induced hyperammonemia	Levocarnitine *(Carnitor)*	Treat if symptomatic (changes in mental status, elevated ammonia level).
Warfarin, rat poison (rodenticides)	**Phytonadione (vitamin K) *(Mephyton)***	This is given as vitamin K1 (the precursor of other vitamin K forms). Refer to the Anticoagulation chapter.

21

CRITICAL CARE & FLUIDS/ ELECTROLYTES

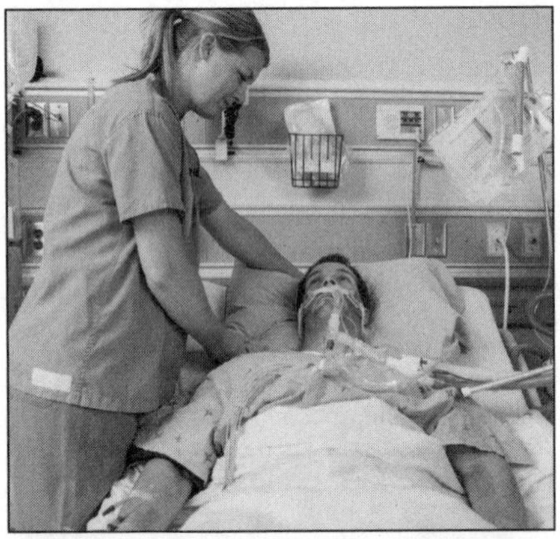

GUIDELINES/REFERENCES

Singer M, Deutschman CS, Seymour CW, et al. The Third International Consensus Definitions for Sepsis and Septic Shock (Sepsis-3). *JAMA.* 2016; 315(8):801-10.

Dellinger RP, Levy MM, Rhodes A, et al. Surviving Sepsis Campaign: International Guidelines for Management of Severe Sepsis and Septic Shock: 2012. *Crit Care Med.* 2013; 41(2):580-637.

Barr J, Fraser GL, Puntillo K, et al. Clinical Practice Guidelines for the Management of Pain, Agitation, and Delirium in Adult Patients in the Intensive Care Unit. *Crit Care Med.* 2013; 41(1):263-306.

We gratefully acknowledge the assistance of Darrel W. Hughes, PharmD, BCPS, Clinical Specialist, Emergency Medicine at University Health System and University of Texas Health Science Center San Antonio, in preparing this chapter.

BACKGROUND

Patients with life-threatening injuries or illnesses require specialized care that is often initiated pre-hospital or in an emergency department and continued in the intensive care unit (ICU). Large hospitals have specialized ICUs for different types of patients: medical, surgical, cardiovascular, trauma, pediatric, neonatal, etc. Patients in the ICU receive most of their medications intravenously (IV), with an infusion pump, ideally through a central line. This route provides rapid onset of effect and easy titration, avoids gut/absorption issues, and permits administration when the patient is sedated. Although patients in the ICU are very sick, many recover and eventually go home. The ICU mortality rate in the U.S. is ~15%. Conditions that are common in the ICU are addressed in this chapter.

SHOCK

Shock is a medical emergency characterized by hypoperfusion usually in the setting of hypotension, defined as systolic blood pressure (SBP) < 90 mmHg or mean arterial pressure (MAP) < 70 mmHg. There are four main types of shock: (1) hypovolemic (e.g., hemorrhagic), (2) distributive (e.g., septic), (3) cardiogenic (e.g., post-myocardial infarction), and (4) obstructive (e.g., massive pulmonary embolism). Diagnosis of shock is based on hemodynamic parameters. Patients may experience more than one type of shock at a time. Drugs used for shock may also be used for advanced cardiac life support (ACLS)/cardiac arrest, hypotension during surgery/anesthesia, acute decompensated heart failure (ADHF), and other critical conditions.

Hypovolemic Shock

Treatment of hypovolemic shock requires restoring intravascular volume (with crystalloids) and improving oxygen-carrying capacity with blood transfusion when indicated. Fluid resuscitation with crystalloids is generally recommended as first-line therapy in patients with hypovolemic shock that is not caused by hemorrhage. Blood products (packed red blood cells and fresh frozen plasma) should be administered in hypovolemic shock for patients with hemoglobin < 7 g/dL (< 10 g/dL in patients with cardiovascular disease) or patients who have a significant active bleed. If the patient does not respond to the initial crystalloid therapy ("fluid challenge"), then vasopressors may be indicated. Vasopressors will not be effective unless intravascular volume is adequate (at least 30 mL/kg of crystalloid or CVP ≥ 8 mmHg).

STUDY TIP: GENERAL PRINCIPLES FOR TREATING SHOCK

Fill the Tank
Optimize preload with 30 mL/kg of crystalloid bolus (as needed) to a central venous pressure (CVP) ≥ 8 mmHg

Squeeze the Pipes
Peripheral vasoconstrictor to ↑ systemic vascular resistance (SVR)

Kick the Pump
Beta-1 agonist to ↑ myocardial contractility and cardiac output (CO)

Crystalloids vs Colloids

Hospitalized patients frequently receive IV fluids to replace patient losses and treat various conditions. IV fluids are categorized as crystalloids or colloids. Crystalloids contain various concentrations of sodium and/or dextrose that pass freely between semipermeable membranes. Most of the administered volume does not remain in the intravascular space (inside the blood vessels), but moves into the extravascular space or interstitial space. Crystalloids are less costly and generally have fewer adverse reactions than colloids. Some data suggest that balanced solutions (chloride-restrictive) may be preferred in certain disease states like sepsis. The chloride load provided to ICU patients can be high enough to contribute to cell injury, including renal damage. Colloids are large molecules (typically protein or starch) dispersed in solutions that primarily remain in the intravascular space and ↑ oncotic pressure. Colloids provide greater intravascular volume expansion than equal volumes of crystalloids, but are more expensive and have not shown clear clinical benefit over crystalloids.

FLUID	COMMENTS
CRYSTALLOIDS	
Dextrose 5% (D5W)*	Slightly hypotonic, equivalent to "free water" (crosses membranes easily), useful in dehydration, avoid in head injury (can ↑ intracranial pressure)
NaCl 0.9% (normal saline, NS)*	Isotonic, useful for fluid resuscitation, risk of hypernatremia and hyperchloremic metabolic acidosis
Lactated Ringer's (LR) Chloride-restrictive	Isotonic, contains NaCl, KCl, CaCl, Na-lactate (lactate is converted to bicarbonate to help correct acidosis), risk for hyperkalemia, equally effective to NS
Multiple electrolyte injection (*Plasma-Lyte A*, others) Chloride-restrictive	Isotonic, *Plasma-Lyte A* contains electrolytes and acetate (acetate is converted to bicarbonate to help correct acidosis), risk for hyperkalemia

Crystalloids vs Colloids Continued

FLUID	COMMENTS
COLLOIDS	
Albumin 5%, 25% ***(Albuked, Albuminar, Albutein, AlbuRx, Flexbumin,*** *others)*	Natural colloid, more expensive than crystalloids with no evidence of superiority Remains in the intravascular space; useful with significant edema (cirrhosis). Albumin 5% and 25% are isotonic; 25% albumin pulls water into the intravascular space; not effective for nutritional supplementation Albumin 5% can be prepared by diluting 25% albumin with NS or D5W, not sterile water (sterile water may cause hemolysis/renal damage due to hypotonicity), do not use if sediment present, do not begin administration > 4 hours after puncturing the container
Dextran *(Dextran 40, Dextran 70)*	Used infrequently. High risk for ADRs (urticaria, acute renal failure, increased bleeding time), can cause anaphylaxis, impairs hemostasis (sometimes used as an anticoagulant)
Hydroxyethyl starch *(Hespan, Hextend)*	Used infrequently. Semi-synthetic colloid, can cause anaphylaxis, impairs hemostasis. Boxed Warning: avoid use in critically ill patients (including sepsis) due to mortality and renal injury

**There are various crystalloid concentrations and combinations including: D50, D5NS, D5½NS, ½NS*

Distributive Shock

Distributive shock is characterized by low systemic vascular resistance (SVR), and initially high CO followed by low or normal CO. Septic, anaphylactic, and neurogenic shock are examples of distributive shock.

Sepsis and Septic Shock

Sepsis is now defined as life-threatening organ dysfunction caused by dysregulated host response to infection. Organ dysfunction can be identified by an acute change in the total Sequential Organ Failure Assessment (SOFA) score ≥ 2 points due to infection. The quickSOFA (qSOFA) is a simplified version that uses only three criteria: altered mental status, systolic blood pressure ≤ 100 mmHg and respiratory rate ≥ 22 breaths per min. SOFA and/or qSOFA have replaced the systemic inflammatory response syndrome (SIRS) criteria for screening patients likely to have sepsis. Septic shock is sepsis in the presence of persistent hypotension requiring a vasopressor to maintain MAP ≥ 65 mmHg and having a serum lactate level ≥ 2 mEq/L despite adequate fluid resuscitation. The Surviving Sepsis Campaign is an initiative that prompts the use of selected evidence-based interventions (called "bundles") to reduce mortality from sepsis and septic shock. The use of early goal-directed therapy, administration of broad-spectrum antibiotics, 30 mL/kg of crystalloid, CVP ≥ 8 mmHg and MAP ≥ 65 mmHg were associated with lower overall mortality than standard of care.

Vasopressors work by vasoconstriction (think "pressing down on the vasculature") and therefore they ↑ SVR, which ↑ blood pressure. Phenylephrine is a pure alpha agonist that ↑ SVR without increasing heart rate. Epinephrine and norepinephrine are mixed alpha and beta agonists. Norepinephrine is considered the vasopressor of choice in septic shock, while epinephrine is a mainstay in advanced cardiac life support and anaphylactic shock states. Dopamine is a natural precursor of norepinephrine that stimulates different receptors depending on the dose (see table on next page). High doses of dopamine are required to stimulate alpha receptors and exert vasopressor effects. Medium doses stimulate beta-1 receptors and produce positive inotropic effect, along with other actions. Low doses stimulate dopaminergic (D-1) receptors in the kidney, causing vasodilation. Refer to the Drug Mechanisms, Classes & Structures chapter for a review of sympathetic nervous system receptors.

Vasopressors

DRUG	DOSING/MOA	SAFETY/SIDE EFFECTS/MONITORING
DOPamine	**Low dose: D-1 agonist** 1-4 mcg/kg/min **Med dose: Beta-1 agonist** 5-10 mcg/kg/min **High dose: Alpha-1 agonist** 10-20 mcg/kg/min	**BOXED WARNING** Dopamine and norepinephrine have a boxed warning regarding extravasation; all vasopressors are vesicants when administered IV, treat extravasation with phentolamine **WARNINGS** Use extreme caution in patients taking an MAO inhibitor; prolonged hypertension may result (dopamine, epinephrine and norepinephrine)
EPINEPHrine *(Adrenalin)* *EpiPen*, others for anaphylaxis	**Alpha-1, beta-1, beta-2 agonist** 0.1-2 mcg/kg/min IV ACLS: 1 mg IV Q3-5 min	**SIDE EFFECTS** Arrhythmias, tachycardia (especially with dopamine, epinephrine, vasopressin), bradycardia (with phenylephrine), tachyphylaxis, peripheral/gut ischemia, necrosis (gangrene), hyperglycemia (with epinephrine), hyponatremia (with vasopressin)
Norepinephrine *(Levophed)*	**Alpha-1 agonist > beta-1 agonist** 0.1-3 mcg/kg/min	**MONITORING** Continuous BP monitoring (with continuous infusions), HR, MAP, ECG, urine output, infusion site for extravasation, serum and urine sodium (vasopressin)
Phenylephrine (*Vazculep)* *Vazculep* approved for hypotension during anesthesia	**Alpha-1 agonist** 0.5-9 mcg/kg/min	**NOTES** No clear evidence that low dose dopamine (renal dosing) provides benefit. Solutions should not be used if they are discolored or contain a precipitate. **Epinephrine** Epinephrine used for IV route is 1:10,000 ratio strength or 0.1 mg/mL, epinephrine used for IM route is 1:1,000 ratio strength or 1 mg/mL.
Vasopressin *(Vasostrict)* Known as arginine vasopressin (AVP) and antidiuretic hormone (ADH)	**Vasoconstrictor, no inotropic or chronotropic effects** Shock: 0.01-0.03 units/min	As of 2016, ratio expressions are no longer permitted on single entity drug products. Only the mg/mL concentration will be displayed. Lidocaine with epinephrine is discussed with Anesthetics in this chapter. **Vasopressin** Taper dose to avoid rebound hypotension/maintain target blood pressure. Removed from 2016 ACLS guidelines (no advantage over epinephrine alone and simplified ACLS algorithm).

Treatment of Extravasation

Vasopressors are vesicants that cause severe tissue damage/necrosis with extravasation. This is a medical emergency. To reduce the risk, every attempt should be made to infuse vasopressors through a central line. Treat vasopressor extravasations with phentolamine, an alpha-adrenergic blocker that antagonizes the effects of the vasopressor. If extravasation occurs with norepinephrine, epinephrine or phenylephrine, stop the infusion but do not disconnect the needle/canula and do not flush the line. Gently aspirate out the drug. Nitroglycerin ointment is sometimes used topically (off-label) as an alternative if phentolamine is unavailable.

Acute Decompensated Heart Failure and Cardiogenic Shock

Heart failure patients may experience episodes of worsening symptoms such as sudden weight gain, inability to lie flat without becoming short of breath, decreasing functionality (unable to perform their daily routine), increasing shortness of breath and fatigue. This is called acute decompensated heart failure (ADHF), and when hypotension and hypoperfusion are also present, it is called cardiogenic shock.

Clinical Presentation and Assessment

ADHF is caused by worsening HF, a cardiac event (MI, arrhythmia, valvular disease, uncontrolled hypertension) or a non-cardiac cause (e.g., non-adherence with medications or dietary restrictions, worsening renal function, infection, illicit drug use). Use of drugs that can worsen cardiac function (e.g., negative inotropes, NSAIDs/COX-2 inhibitors, drugs which cause fluid retention and direct cardiotoxic drugs) can also cause/exacerbate HF. Beta blockers should only be stopped in an ADHF episode if hypotension or hypoperfusion is present.

Patients with ADHF present with congestion, hypoperfusion, or both. Some patients with ADHF require invasive monitoring with a catheter that is guided through the right side of the heart into the pulmonary artery, called a Swan-Ganz or pulmonary artery (PA) catheter. The catheter provides hemodynamic measurements of congestion (pulmonary capillary wedge pressure or PCWP), hypoperfusion (cardiac output) and other measurements (SVR, CVP) useful for guiding treatment. Treatment of ADHF generally consists of diuretics, inotropes and vasodilators in various combinations depending on the patient's signs/symptoms (see Study Tip).

Treating Congestion

The majority of patients with ADHF present with congestion. Congestion is treated with diuretics and possibly IV vasodilators. Loop diuretics are initially given IV since congestion also affects the vessels of the gut and can decrease their oral absorption. If diuretic resistance develops, the dose can be increased or a thiazide-type diuretic (e.g., metolazone, chlorothiazide) can be added to the loop.

IV vasodilators include nitroglycerin (NTG), nitroprusside and nesiritide. Frequent or continuous blood pressure monitoring is required when using vasodilators and the dose must be decreased if hypotension or worsening of renal function is noted. Nitroglycerin is a venous vasodilator (at low doses), but an effective arterial vasodilator at high doses. NTG is often used when there is active myocardial ischemia or uncontrolled hypertension, but effectiveness may be limited after 24 – 48 hours due to tachyphylaxis.

STUDY TIP: TREATING ADHF

Patients with edema (pulmonary or lower extremity), jugular venous distention (JVD) and/or ascites are **CONGESTED**, treatment options are:

- Loop diuretics
- Vasodilators (NTG, nitroprusside, nesiritide)

Patients with hypotension, ↓ renal function, altered mental status and/or cool extremities have **HYPOPERFUSION**, treatment options are:

- Vasopressors (dopamine, norepinephrine, phenylephrine)

*Avoid vasodilators; these can ↓ BP and worsen hypoperfusion

Some patients experience **CONGESTION** and **HYPOPERFUSION**, treatment options are:

- A combination of agents above or
- Inotropes with vasodilatory properties (dobutamine, milrinone)

Nitroprusside is a mixed (equal) arterial and venous vasodilator at all doses. It has greater effect on BP than NTG, but it should not be used in active myocardial ischemia because it can cause blood to be diverted away from the diseased coronary arteries ("coronary steal"). Metabolism of nitroprusside results in formation of thiocyanate and cyanide, both of which can cause toxicity (especially in renal and hepatic insufficiency, respectively). Hydroxocobalamin can be administered to reduce risk of thiocyanate toxicity and sodium thiosulfate is used for cyanide toxicity (see Emergency Preparedness, Toxicology & Antidotes chapter).

Nesiritide (*Natrecor*) is a recombinant B-type natriuretic peptide that binds to vascular smooth muscle, increases cGMP, resulting in smooth muscle relaxation which causes vasodilation. Nesiritide produces both arterial and venous vasodilation. It has not been found to reduce mortality or hospitalizations compared to other treatments and is not commonly used.

Vasodilators

DRUG	DOSING	SAFETY/SIDE EFFECTS/MONITORING
Nitroglycerin See Ischemic Heart Disease chapter for other formulations	Initial: 5 mcg/min Max: 400 mcg/min Continuous IV infusion due to short t½ Titrate to effect	**CONTRAINDICATIONS** SBP < 90 mmHg, concurrent use with PDE-5 inhibitors or riociguat **WARNINGS** Severe hypotension and ↑ intracranial pressure **SIDE EFFECTS** Hypotension, headache, lightheadedness, tachycardia, tachyphylaxis (within 24-48 hours of continuous administration) **MONITORING** BP, HR **NOTES** Requires non-PVC container (e.g., glass, polyolefin). Use administration sets (tubing) intended for NTG.
Nitroprusside *(Nitropress, Nipride)*	Initial dose varies by indication ADHF: 5-10 mcg/min Titrate to effect Requires light protection during administration. Use only clear solutions, a blue color indicates degradation to cyanide – do not use	**BOXED WARNINGS** Metabolism produces cyanide (use the lowest dose for the shortest duration necessary), excessive hypotension (continuous BP monitoring required), not for direct injection (must be further diluted; D5W preferred). **WARNINGS** ↑ intracranial pressure **SIDE EFFECTS** Hypotension, headache, tachycardia, thiocyanate/cyanide toxicity (especially in renal and hepatic impairment) **MONITORING** BP (continuous), HR, renal/hepatic function, urine output, thiocyanate/cyanide toxicity, acid-base status, venous oxygen concentration
Nesiritide *(Natrecor)*	Bolus: 2 mcg/kg; draw bolus only from prepared (reconstituted) IV bag Infusion: 0.01 mcg/kg/min; max 0.03 mcg/kg/min	**CONTRAINDICATIONS** Persistent SBP < 100 mmHg prior to treatment, cardiogenic shock (if used as the primary treatment) **SIDE EFFECTS** Hypotension, ↑ SCr **MONITORING** BP, renal function, urine output **NOTES** Limited experience with infusions lasting longer than 96 hours

Treating Hypoperfusion

The most common cause of cardiogenic shock (or ADHF with hypoperfusion) is myocardial infarction (MI) with resulting failure of the left ventricle. Cardiogenic shock requires treatment with vasopressors (discussed previously) and/or inotropes.

Inotropes increase contractility of the heart. Dobutamine is a beta-1 agonist; it ↑ heart rate and force of contraction, which ↑ cardiac output. It has weak beta-2 (vasodilation) and alpha-1 agonist activity. Milrinone is a selective phosphodiesterase-3 inhibitor in cardiac and vascular tissue. It produces inotropic effects with significant vasodilation. Because both dobutamine and milrinone produce vasodilation, they should only be used when BP is adequate. The vasodilatory + inotropic properties of dobutamine and milrinone make them uniquely suited to treating ADHF in patients with both congestion and hypoperfusion when BP is adequate. Dopamine in medium doses is the inotrope of choice in heart failure when SBP < 90 mmHg. Inotropes are associated with worse outcomes in heart failure and should be stopped as soon as the patient is stabilized.

Inotropes with Vasodilatory Effects

<table>
<tr><th>DRUG</th><th>DOSING</th><th>SAFETY/SIDE EFFECTS/MONITORING</th></tr>
<tr><td>DOBUTamine</td><td>Beta-1 agonist with some beta-2 and alpha-1 agonism (both weak)
Initial: 0.5-1 mcg/kg/min
Maintenance: 2-20 mcg/kg/min</td><td rowspan="2">SIDE EFFECTS
Dobutamine: hyper and hypotension, ventricular arrhythmias, tachycardia, angina
Milrinone: ventricular arrhythmias, hypotension

MONITORING
Continuous BP and ECG monitoring, HR, CVP, MAP, urine output, LFTs and renal function (with milrinone)

NOTES
Milrinone: dose must be reduced for renal impairment.
Dobutamine may turn slightly pink due to oxidation, but potency is not lost.
Dobutamine and milrinone often referred to as "inodilators".
Because of risk of hypotension, dobutamine may be used for inotropic effect only after adequate perfusion is achieved.</td></tr>
<tr><td>Milrinone</td><td>Phosphodiesterase-3 (PDE-3) inhibitor
Maintenance: 0.125-0.75 mcg/kg/min; may consider a 50 mcg/kg loading dose (often omitted due to propensity to cause hypotension)</td></tr>
</table>

PAIN, AGITATION AND DELIRIUM

Pain

Opioids given IV (such as morphine and fentanyl) are first-line for analgesia (to reduce pain) in the ICU, but the principles of pain management are the same for all patients (see Pain chapter for a full discussion of the opioids). The pharmacokinetic properties of the drug and the renal/hepatic function of the patient will dictate the choice of agent, because all IV opioids exhibit similar analgesic efficacy when used correctly. Adjuvants (acetaminophen, NSAIDs, others) may be appropriate depending on the type of pain. Assessment of pain (with a validated pain scale) should be performed as frequently as every 2 – 4 hours in the ICU, and all ICU patients should be evaluated for pain at rest. Analgesia-based sedation or "analgosedation" is a sedation strategy that uses analgesia first to relieve pain and discomfort, which are primary causes of agitation. Analgosedation is associated with less time on the ventilator and shorter ICU length of stay.

Agitation

Sedation (to reduce distress, fear and anxiety) is necessary in most ICU patients to maintain synchronized breathing if on a ventilator (prevent "bucking" the ventilator), and to limit suffering in the harsh ICU environment. Agitation is managed with benzodiazepines (lorazepam, midazolam) and/or hypnotics (propofol, dexmedetomidine). Nonbenzodiazepines (propofol and dexmedetomidine) are associated with improved ICU outcomes, shorter duration of mechanical ventilation, and ↓ length of stay (LOS), though they are more expensive than benzodiazepines. Dexmedetomidine *(Precedex)* is the only sedative approved for use in non-intubated patients. Benzodiazepines will always have an important role in sedation of the ICU patient with seizures or alcohol/benzodiazepine withdrawal. Benzodiazepines are discussed in the Anxiety chapter.

RICHMOND AGITATION AND SEDATION SCALE (RASS)

SCORE	TERM	DESCRIPTION
+4	Combative	Overtly combative, violent, immediate danger to staff
+3	Very agitated	Pulls or removes tube(s) or catheter(s); aggressive
+2	Agitated	Frequent non-purposeful movement, fights ventilator
+1	Restless	Anxious, but movements not aggressive or vigorous
0	Alert and calm	
-1	Drowsy	Not fully alert, but has sustained awakening (eye opening/eye contact) to voice (≥ 10 seconds)
-2	Light sedation	Briefly awakens with eye contact to voice (< 10 seconds)
-3	Moderate sedation	Movement or eye opening to voice (but no eye contact)
-4	Deep sedation	No response to voice, but movement or eye opening to physical stimulation
-5	Unarousable	No response to voice or physical stimulation

Sedatives are used with validated sedation scales that allow for titration to light or deep sedation. Light sedation (unless contraindicated) is associated with improved outcomes. Some commonly used sedation scales include the Richmond Agitation Sedation Scale (RASS – see table), the Ramsay Agitation Scale (RAS), and the Riker Sedation-Agitation Scale (SAS). Patients should be monitored every 2 – 3 hours while receiving a sedation protocol to make sure they are receiving the minimal amount of drug(s) to keep them calm and pain-free. Daily interruptions of continuous infusions of sedative drugs ("sedation vacations") are used to assess the readiness to wean off/stop the sedative as soon as medically feasible.

Delirium

Delirium affects up to 80% of ventilated ICU patients and is associated with ↑ mortality and ↑ LOS. Delirium assessment is required. Early mobilization and control of the patient's environment (light, noise, stimuli) is recommended to ↓ incidence of delirium, but no medications are recommended for prevention. Providing sedation with non-benzodiazepines may ↓ the incidence of delirium and/or shorten the duration in patients who already have it. There is little evidence to support the use of haloperidol for treatment of ICU delirium, although this practice is commonplace. Atypical antipsychotics (primarily quetiapine, which is mildly sedating and has little risk for movement disorders) can be useful. Antipsychotics are discussed in the Schizophrenia/Psychosis chapter.

Agents for Pain, Agitation, and Delirium in the ICU

DRUG	DOSING	SAFETY/SIDE EFFECTS/MONITORING
PAIN/ANALGESIA		
Morphine	LD: 2-4 mg IV push MD: 2-30 mg/hr	See Pain chapter for additional information. In critical care patients, monitor BP, HR, respiration, pain and sedation. Fentanyl: less hypotension (no histamine release) than morphine (preferred for hemodynamically unstable patients), 100x more potent than morphine; rapid onset and short duration of action (half-life increases with duration of infusion), can accumulate in hepatic impairment; 3A4 substrate and potential for numerous drug interactions. Hydromorphone: very potent, dose carefully.
FentaNYL	LD: 0.35-0.5 mcg/kg slow IV push Q30-60 min (25-35 mcg for ~70 kg patient) MD: 0.7-10 mcg/kg/hr	
HYDROmorphone *(Dilaudid)*	LD: 0.2-0.6 mg IV push MD: 0.5-3 mg/hr	
Remifentanil *(Ultiva)*	LD: 1.5 mcg/kg over 1 min MD: 0.5-15 mcg/kg/hr	
SEDATION/AGITATION		
LORazepam (***Ativan,*** *LORazepam Intensol)* Benzodiazepine	LD: 0.02-0.04 mg/kg IV push (max 2 mg) MD: 0.02-0.06 mg/kg IV Q2-6H PRN or an infusion 0.01-0.1 mg/kg/hr (max 10 mg/hr) Dose varies by indication; often used off-label	Injection is formulated in propylene glycol. Total daily dose as low as 1 mg/kg/day can cause propylene glycol toxicity (acute renal failure and metabolic acidosis). In critical care patients, monitor BP, HR, RR, sedation scale, s/sx of propylene glycol toxicity (BUN, SCr, lactate, anion gap) if receiving continuous infusion. Limit use for delirium. See Anxiety chapter for additional information.
Midazolam *(Versed)* Benzodiazepine used specifically in acute care settings; injection only	LD: 0.01-0.05 mg/kg IV push MD: 0.02-0.1 mg/kg/hr IV Dose varies per indication Shorter acting than lorazepam if patient has normal organ function (no hepatic or renal impairment or HF) Highly lipophilic, can accumulate in obese patients Active metabolite that accumulates in renal impairment (caution with continuous infusion) Major 3A4 substrate; caution/use lower dose if used with 3A4 inhibitors	**BOXED WARNINGS** Respiratory depression, respiratory arrest, or apnea; start at lower end of dosing range in debilitated patients and geriatric population, do not administer by rapid IV injection in neonates **CONTRAINDICATIONS** Intrathecal or epidural administration due to benzoyl alcohol in the formulation, acute narrow angle glaucoma, use of potent CYP 3A4 inhibitors **SIDE EFFECTS** Respiratory depression, apnea, oversedation, hypotension **MONITORING** BP, HR, RR, sedation scale

LD = loading dose, MD = maintenance dose

Agents for Pain, Agitation, and Delirium in the ICU Continued

DRUG	DOSING	SAFETY/SIDE EFFECTS/MONITORING
Propofol *(Diprivan)* Short-acting general anesthetic	Initial Infusion: 5 mcg/kg/min IV, ↑ by 5-10 mcg/kg/min until desired level of sedation achieved MD: 5-50 mcg/kg/min IV Oil-in-water emulsion (opaque, white solution); provides 1.1 kcal/mL	**CONTRAINDICATIONS** Hypersensitivity to egg, egg product, soy and soy product **SIDE EFFECTS** Hypotension, apnea, hypertriglyceridemia, green urine/hair/nail beds, propofol-related infusion syndrome (PRIS – rare but can be fatal), myoclonus, pancreatitis, pain on injection (particularly peripheral vein), QT prolongation **MONITORING** BP, HR, RR, sedation scale, triglycerides (if administered longer than 2 days), signs and symptoms of pancreatitis **NOTES** Shake well before use. Do not use if there is separation of phases in the emulsion. Use strict aseptic technique due to potential for bacterial growth. Discard vial and tubing within 12 hours of use. If transferred to a syringe prior to administration, must discard syringe within 6 hours. Do not use a filter < 5 micron for administration. Does not require refrigeration.
Dexmedetomidine *(Precedex)* Alpha-2 adrenergic agonist Used for sedation in intubated and non-intubated patients; patients are arousable and alert when stimulated (less respiratory depression than other sedatives)	LD: 0.5-1 mcg/kg IV over 10 minutes (may be omitted) MD: 0.2-1.5 mcg/kg/hr IV (rate can be adjusted until desired level of sedation achieved) Duration of infusion should not exceed 24 hours	**WARNINGS** Use with caution in patients with hepatic impairment, diabetes, heart block, bradycardia, severe ventricular dysfunction, hypovolemia or chronic hypertension **SIDE EFFECTS** Hypo and hypertension, bradycardia, dry mouth, nausea, constipation **MONITORING** BP, HR, sedation scale **NOTES** Does not require refrigeration
Etomidate *(Amidate)* Nonbarbiturate hypnotic Ultra short-acting; used as an induction agent for anesthesia Minimal cardiovascular effects	Sedation: 0.1-0.2 mg/kg IV followed by 0.05 mg/kg every 3-5 minutes	**WARNING** Inhibits 11-B-hydroxylase which can lead to ↓ cortisol production for up to 24 hours **MONITORING** Monitor for adrenal insufficiency (hypotension, hyperkalemia), respiratory status, BP, HR, infusion site, sedation scale
Ketamine *(Ketalar)* NMDA receptor antagonist Used as an induction agent for anesthesia	Sedation: 0.2-0.8 mg/kg IV (may follow with continuous infusion) Pretreatment with benzodiazepine can ↓ incidence of emergence reactions (see warnings) by 50%	**WARNINGS** Emergence reactions (vivid dreams, hallucinations, delirium), cerebrospinal fluid (CSF) pressure elevation, respiratory depression/apnea, may cause dependence/tolerance **MONITORING** BP, HR, respiratory status, emergence reactions, sedation scale

LD = loading dose, MD = maintenance dose

Agents for Pain, Agitation, and Delirium in the ICU Continued

DRUG	DOSING	SAFETY/SIDE EFFECTS/MONITORING
DELIRIUM		
Haloperidol *(Haldol)*	0.5-10 mg IV push at 5 mg/minute; may repeat Q15-30 minutes until calm, then administer 25% of last dose Q6H	See Schizophrenia/Psychosis chapter. Commonly used, but not recommended for treatment of delirium in current guidelines.
QUEtiapine *(SEROquel)*	50 mg PO Q12H; may increase by 50-100 mg/day every 24 hours up to 200 mg Q12H	See Schizophrenia/Psychosis chapter. May decrease duration of delirium.

STRESS ULCER PROPHYLAXIS

Stress ulcers can result from the metabolic stress experienced by a patient in an ICU. Patients with critical illness have reduced blood flow to the gut as blood flow is diverted to the major organs of the body. This results in a breakdown of gastric mucosal defense mechanisms, including prostaglandin synthesis, bicarbonate production and cell turnover.

Histamine-2 receptor antagonists (H2RAs) and proton pump inhibitors (PPIs) are the recommended agents for prevention of stress-related mucosal damage. H2RAs can cause thrombocytopenia and mental status changes in the elderly or those with renal/hepatic impairment. Tachyphylaxis (tolerance) has also been reported. PPIs have been associated with an increased risk of GI infections *(C. difficile)*, fractures and nosocomial pneumonia. These agents are discussed in the GERD and PUD chapter. Patients without risk factors for stress ulcers should not receive stress ulcer prophylaxis (see risk factors in table).

RISK FACTORS FOR THE DEVELOPMENT OF STRESS ULCERS
Mechanical ventilation
Coagulopathy
Sepsis
Traumatic brain injury
Burn patients
Acute renal failure
High dose systemic steroids

ADDITIONAL DRUGS USED IN THE ICU AND OPERATING ROOM

Anesthetics

Anesthetics are used for a variety of effects including numbing of an area (local anesthesia), to block pain (regional anesthesia), or to cause a reversible loss of consciousness and sleepiness during surgery (general anesthesia). Anesthetics can be given via several routes of administration: topical, inhaled, intravenous, epidural or spinal. Increasingly, anesthetics are being used with opioids to reduce the opioid requirement for pain control. They work by blocking the initiation and conduction of nerve impulses by decreasing the neuronal permeability to sodium ions. Most patients receiving anesthetics must be continuously monitored (vital signs and respiration). The main side effects of anesthetics include hypotension, bradycardia, nausea and vomiting and a mild drop in body temperature that can cause shivering. Overdose can cause respiratory depression. Allergic reactions are possible. Inhaled anesthetics can rarely cause malignant hyperthermia (MH). See side bar for some commonly used anesthetics.

COMMONLY USED ANESTHETICS
Local – lidocaine *(Xylocaine)*, benzocaine, liposomal bupivacaine *(Exparel)*
Inhaled – desflurane *(Suprane)*, sevoflurane *(Ultane)*, isoflurane *(Forane)*, nitrous oxide, others
Injectable – bupivacaine *(Marcaine, Sensorcaine)*, lidocaine *(Xylocaine)*, ropivacaine *(Naropin)*, others

Bupivacaine, commonly used in epidurals, can be fatal if administered intravenously. Lidocaine should not be given by dual routes of administration (IV and topical). Lidocaine/epinephrine combination products are used for some local procedures that require an anesthetic, such as inserting an IV line. The epinephrine is added for vasoconstriction, which keeps the lidocaine localized to the area where the numbing is needed. Deaths have occurred due to mix-ups with epinephrine products and lidocaine/epinephrine products. Be careful to use the proper product, concentration and route of administration.

Neuromuscular Blocking Agents

These agents cause paralysis of the skeletal muscle, including those used for respiration. Patients can require the use of a paralytic agent in surgery conducted under general anesthesia, to facilitate mechanical intubation, to manage increased intracranial pressure, to treat muscle spasms (tetany) or to prevent shivering in patients undergoing therapeutic hypothermia after cardiac arrest. The use of neuromuscular blocking agents (NMBAs) is typically recommended when other methods have proven ineffective; they are not routinely used in all critically ill patients. These agents have no effect on pain or sedation. Therefore, patients should receive adequate sedation and analgesia prior to starting a NMBA. Patients must be mechanically ventilated as these agents paralyze the diaphragm. These are considered high risk medications by ISMP. All NMBAs should be labeled with a bright red auxiliary label stating "WARNING, PARALYZING AGENT".

There are 2 types of NMBAs: depolarizing and non-depolarizing. Succinylcholine is the only available depolarizing agent and is typically reserved for intubation. It is not used for continuous neuromuscular blockade. Succinylcholine has been rarely associated with causing malignant hyperthermia (particularly when used with inhaled anesthetics). Resembling acetylcholine, succinylcholine binds to and activates the acetylcholine receptors and desensitizes them. The non-depolarizing NMBAs work by binding to the acetylcholine receptor and blocking the actions of endogenous acetylcholine.

DRUG	SAFETY/SIDE EFFECTS/MONITORING
DEPOLARIZING NMBA	
Succinylcholine *(Anectine, **Quelicin**)*	Short-acting, fast onset (30-60 seconds)
NON-DEPOLARIZING NMBAs	
For all non-depolarizing NMBAs	**SIDE EFFECTS** Flushing, bradycardia, hypotension, tachyphylaxis, acute quadriplegic myopathy syndrome (AQMS) with long-term use **MONITORING** Peripheral nerve stimulator to assess depth of paralysis during continuous infusions [also called train-of-four (TOF)], vital signs (BP, HR, RR)
Atracurium	Short t½; intermediate-acting; metabolized by Hofmann elimination (independent of renal and hepatic function)
Cisatracurium *(Nimbex)*	Short t½; intermediate-acting; metabolized by Hofmann elimination (independent of renal and hepatic function)
Pancuronium	Long-acting agent, can accumulate in renal or hepatic dysfunction, ↑ HR
Rocuronium *(Zemuron)*	Intermediate-acting agent
Vecuronium	Intermediate-acting agent; can accumulate in renal or hepatic dysfunction

Patients receiving paralytics are unable to breath, move, blink, or cough. Special care must be taken to protect the skin, lubricate the eyes, and suction the airway frequently to clear secretions while NMBAs are being used. Glycopyrrolate *(Robinul)* is an anticholinergic agent that can be used to reduce secretions. Numerous medications can enhance the neuromuscular blocking activity of the NMBAs, leading to toxicity (aminoglycosides, calcium channel blockers, colistimethate, cyclosporine, inhaled anesthetics, lithium, quinidine, vancomycin, others). Monitoring for the appropriate depth of paralysis is recommended.

Neostigmine methylsulfate *(Bloxiverz)* and sugammadex *(Bridion)* are used to reverse the effects of NMBAs. Neostigmine is an acetylcholinesterase inhibitor. Sugammadex was approved in 2016 for reversal of rocuronium or vecuronium (non-deplorarizing NMBAs only). It works by forming a complex with the NMBA and reducing the amount of the NMBA available for binding. Refer to the Emergency Preparedness, Toxicology & Antidotes chapter.

Hemostatic Agents

The term hemostasis means causing bleeding to stop. A variety of hemostatic methods can be used, ranging from simple manual pressure with one finger to electrical tissue cauterization, or the systemic administration of blood products (transfusions) or hemostatic agents. The systemic hemostatic drugs work by inhibiting fibrinolysis or enhancing coagulation. Several factor products are available to treat hemorrhage in patients with hemophilia or rare factor deficiencies *(FEIBA, Coagadex)*. Newer hemostatic drugs (*Kcentra* and *Praxbind*) have been approved as reversal agents for specific anticoagulants. See Anticoagulation chapter.

SYSTEMIC HEMOSTATIC AGENTS

DRUG	SAFETY/SIDE EFFECTS/MONITORING
Aminocaproic acid *(Amicar)* Tablet, solution, injection	**CONTRAINDICATIONS** Disseminated intravascular coagulation (without heparin); active intravascular clotting process **SIDE EFFECTS** Injection-site reactions, thrombosis **NOTES** FDA-approved for excessive bleeding associated with cardiac surgery, liver cirrhosis, and urinary fibrinolysis. Do not use in patients with active clots, do not give with factor IX complex concentrates due to ↑ risk for thrombosis.
Tranexamic acid *(Cyklokapron,* injection) *(Lysteda,* tablet)	**CONTRAINDICATIONS** IV: acquired defective color vision, active intravascular clotting, subarachnoid hemorrhage Oral: previous or current thromboembolic disease, current use of combination hormonal contraception **SIDE EFFECTS** Injection: vascular occlusion, thrombosis Oral: retinal clotting **NOTES** *Lysteda* (oral) is approved for heavy menstrual bleeding (menorrhagia). The injection is approved for bleeding with hemophilia and is often used off-label to control surgical bleeding.
Recombinant Factor VIIa *(NovoSeven RT)* Injection	**BOXED WARNING** Risk of thrombotic events, particularly when used off-label **NOTES** FDA-approved for hemophilia and factor VII deficiency; has been used successfully off-label for patients with hemorrhage from trauma and warfarin-related bleeding events.

There are many topical hemostatic agents and most are used surgically. These include thrombin in bandages, liquids and spray forms, fibrin sealants, acrylates and a few others (names often include "throm": *Recothrom, Evithrom)*. A few topical hemostatics are OTC.

Intravenous Immunoglobulin

Intravenous immune globulin (IVIG or IGIV) contains pooled immunoglobulin (IgG), administered intravenously. The IgG is extracted from the plasma of a thousand or more blood donors (this is the FDA's minimum; typically the IVIG is derived from between 3,000 – 10,000 donors). IVIG is given as plasma protein replacement therapy (IgG) for immune deficient patients who have decreased or abolished antibody production capabilities. Initially, IVIG was used only for immunodeficiency conditions. Currently, IVIG has several FDA-approved indications and is used for a variety of off-label indications (multiple sclerosis, myasthenia gravis, Guillaine-Barré, others) with varying results. Treatment with IVIG can impair response to vaccination. Refer to the Immunizations chapter.

DRUG	DOSING	SAFETY/SIDE EFFECTS/MONITORING
Intravenous immunoglobulin *(Bivigam,* ***Carimune NF,*** *Flebogamma,* ***Flebogamma DIF, Gammagard,*** *Gammagard S/D, Gammaked, Gammaplex,* ***Gamunex-C,*** *Hizentra, Hyqvia,* ***Octagam, Privigen)***	Indication and product specific Use IBW to calculate dose Use slower infusion rate in renal and cardiovascular disease Do not freeze, shake or heat	**BOXED WARNINGS** Acute renal dysfunction can rarely occur and has been associated with fatalities; usually within 7 days of use (more likely with products stabilized with sucrose). Use with caution in the elderly, patients with renal disease, diabetes mellitus, volume depletion, sepsis, paraproteinemia, and nephrotoxic medications due to risk of renal dysfunction. Thrombosis may occur with IVIG products even in the absence of risk factors. For patients at risk, administer at the minimum dose. Monitor all patients. **CONTRAINDICATIONS** IgA deficiency (can use product with lowest amount of IgA) **WARNINGS** Use with caution in patients with cardiovascular disease (use isotonic products and low infusion rate) **SIDE EFFECTS** Headache, nausea, diarrhea, injection site reaction, infusion reaction (facial flushing, chest tightness, fever, chills, hypotension – slow/stop infusion), renal failure or blood dyscrasias (both rare) **MONITORING** Renal function, urine output, volume status, Hgb **NOTES** Patients should be asked about past IVIG infusions, including product used and any reactions that occurred. The lot numbers of IVIG products administered to a patient must be tracked, as IVIG is a blood product.

ELECTROLYTE DISORDERS

Any patient (including outpatients) can experience electrolyte abnormalities, but these are common in critically ill patients. Some drugs deplete electrolytes and cause acute deficiency. Some electrolyte abnormalities can be fatal when severe (seizures, cardiac arrhythmias, coma). Protocols to replace electrolytes should be followed in order to avoid toxicity. Electrolytes and their reference ranges are discussed in the Lab Values & Drug Monitoring chapter.

Sodium

Hyponatremia

Hyponatremia (Na < 135 mEq/L) may develop from many causes and is usually not symptomatic until < 120 mEq/L, unless the serum level falls rapidly. Hyponatremia is classified first according to serum osmolality and then by clinical volume status:

- Hypotonic hypovolemic hyponatremia is caused by diuretic use, salt-wasting syndromes, adrenal insufficiency, blood loss, vomiting/diarrhea. The treatment is typically to correct the underlying cause and to administer sodium chloride-containing solutions.
- Hypotonic hypervolemic hyponatremia is caused by fluid overload, usually with cirrhosis, heart failure, or renal failure. Diuresis with fluid restriction is the preferred treatment.
- Hypotonic isovolemic (euvolemic) hyponatremia is usually caused by the syndrome of inappropriate antidiuretic hormone (SIADH). It is treated with fluid restriction or diuresis. Demeclocycline is frequently used off-label for hyponatremia associated with SIADH.

The arginine vasopressin (AVP) receptor antagonists (conivaptan or tolvaptan) may be used to treat SIADH and hypervolemic hyponatremia. They increase excretion of free water while maintaining sodium. The role for these agents is still being determined, as they are more expensive than 3% saline and use beyond 30 days with the oral product, tolvaptan *(Samsca)*, is not recommended. Caution should be taken in treating patients with hyponatremia to prevent correcting too quickly. Correcting sodium more rapidly than 12 mEq/L over 24 hours can cause osmotic demyelination syndrome (ODS) or central pontine myelinolysis (CPM), which can cause paralysis, seizures and death. Conservative correction goals are advised as accidental overcorrection is common. Administration of desmopressin reduces water diuresis and may help avoid overcorrection.

DRUG	DOSE	SAFETY/SIDE EFFECTS/MONITORING
Conivaptan *(Vaprisol)* Injection Dual AVP antagonist [vasopressin 1A (V1A) and vasopressin 2 (V2)]	LD: 20 mg IV over 30 minutes MD: 20 mg continuous IV infusion over 24 hours. May increase to 40 mg IV daily if Na does not ↑ at desired rate. Do not use longer than 4 days CrCl < 30 mL/min: avoid ↓ dose in moderateand severe hepatic impairment	**CONTRAINDICATIONS** Hypovolemic hyponatremia, concurrent use with strong 3A4 inhibitors, anuria **WARNING** Overly rapid correction of hyponatremia (> 12 mEq/L/24 hours) associated with osmotic demyelination syndrome (life-threatening) **SIDE EFFECTS** Orthostatic hypotension, fever, hypokalemia, infusion site reactions (> 60%) **MONITORING** Rate of Na increase, BP, volume status, urine output

LD = loading dose, MD = maintenance dose

DRUG	DOSE	SAFETY/SIDE EFFECTS/MONITORING
Tolvaptan *(Samsca)* Tablet Selective AVP antagonist [vasopressin 2 (V2) only]	15 mg PO daily; max 60 mg PO daily; limited to ≤ 30 days due to hepatotoxicity Not recommended if CrCl < 10 mL/min Avoid fluid restriction in first 24 hours of therapy	**BOXED WARNINGS** Should be initiated and re-initiated in a hospital under close monitoring of serum Na Overly rapid correction of hyponatremia (> 12 mEq/L/24 hours) associated with osmotic demyelination syndrome (life-threatening) **CONTRAINDICATIONS** Patients who are unable to sense or respond appropriately to thirst, urgent need to raise Na, hypovolemic hyponatremia, concurrent use with strong 3A4 inhibitors, anuria **WARNINGS** Hepatotoxicity (avoid use > 30 days and in liver disease/cirrhosis) **SIDE EFFECTS** Thirst, nausea, dry mouth, polyuria, weakness, hyperglycemia, hypernatremia **MONITORING** Rate of Na increase, BP, volume status, urine output; signs of drug-induced hepatotoxicity

Hypernatremia

Hypernatremia (Na > 145 mEq/L) is associated with a water deficit and hypertonicity.

- Hypovolemic hypernatremia is caused by dehydration, vomiting, diarrhea and is treated with fluids.
- Hypervolemic hypernatremia is caused by intake of hypertonic fluids and is treated with diuresis.
- Isovolemic (euvolemic) hypernatremia is frequently caused by diabetes insipidus (DI), which can ↓ antidiuretic hormone (ADH). It is treated with desmopressin.

Potassium

Treatment of hyperkalemia is discussed in the Renal Disease chapter. Hypokalemia (K < 3.5 mEq/L) is a common occurrence in hospitalized patients. Management includes treating the underlying cause [e.g., metabolic alkalosis, overdiuresis, some medications (amphotericin, insulin)] and administering oral or IV potassium. The oral route is preferred for replacement when feasible. Oral potassium salt formulations are reviewed in the Chronic Heart Failure chapter. In general, a drop of 1 mEq/L in serum K below 3.5 mEq/L represents a total body deficit of 100 – 400 mEq. Hospitals use K sliding scales that allow a healthcare provider (usually a nurse) to administer a certain dose of potassium based on the serum potassium level (e.g., for K 3.5 – 3.7 mEq/L, give 20 mEq KCl PO x 2 doses; for K 3.3 – 3.4 mEq/L, give 20 mEq KCl PO x 3 doses, etc.). Potassium chloride premixed IVs are generally used for IV replacement. Safe recommendations for IV potassium replacement through a peripheral line include an infusion rate ≤ 10 mEq/hr and maximum concentration of 10 mEq/100 mL. More rapid infusions and higher concentrations may be warranted in severe or symptomatic hypokalemia; these require a central line and cardiac monitoring. IV potassium can be fatal if administered undiluted or IV push. When hypokalemia is resistant to treatment, serum magnesium should be checked and replaced as needed. Magnesium is necessary for potassium uptake.

Magnesium

Hypomagnesemia (Mg < 1.3 mEq/L) is more common than hypermagnesemia. Common causes of hypomagnesemia include chronic alcohol use, diuretics, vomiting, and diarrhea. Hypermagnesemia is most commonly due to renal insufficiency. When serum Mg is < 1 mEq/L with life-threatening symptoms (seizures or arrhythmias), IV replacement is recommended. Magnesium sulfate is used for IV replacement. When serum Mg is < 1 mEq/L without life-threatening symptoms, therapy can be administered IV or IM. When serum Mg is > 1 mEq/L and < 1.5 mEq/L, there are many options including oral replacement. Magnesium replacement regimens should continue for 5 days to fully replace body stores.

Phosphorous

Treatment of hyperphosphatemia is discussed in the Renal Disease chapter. Hypophosphatemia is considered severe and usually symptomatic when serum PO4 is < 1 mg/dL. Hypophosphatemia can be associated with phosphate-binding drugs (calcium, sevelamer, antacids), chronic alcohol intake, and hyperparathyroidism. When serum PO4 is < 1 mg/dL, IV phosphorus is used for replacement. Many regimens can be used, but 0.08 – 0.16 mmol/kg in 500 mL of NS over 6 hours is common. Patients must be carefully monitored and additional doses may be necessary. Patients with hypophosphatemia often have hypokalemia and hypomagnesemia that will require correction. Less severe hypophosphatemia can be treated orally and full replacement often takes one week or longer.

PRACTICE CASE

JL is a 65 y/o female in the ER with pneumonia. Over the past hour, she has had increasing difficulty breathing and oxygen saturation is not markedly improving with nasal administration of O_2. ER staff believes she will require admission to the ICU for intubation and mechanical ventilation. Past medical history includes COPD, chronic kidney disease, and diabetes.

Home Medications:
Lantus 30 units SC at HS
Novolog 5 units SQ TID with meals
Lisinopril 10 mg PO daily
Symbicort 2 inhalations BID
Albuterol nebulizer PRN
Oxygen at 1 liter (delivered via home health company)

Labs: Na (mEq/L) = 138 (135-145)
K (mEq/L) = 5.1 (3.5-5)
Cl (mEq/L) = 100 (95-103)
HCO_3 (mEq/L) = 33 (24-30)
BUN (mg/dL) = 24 (7-20)
SCr (mg/dL) = 1.7 (0.6-1.3)
Glucose (mg/dL) = 202 (100-125)
WBC (mm^3) = 14.6 (4,000-11,000)
Hgb (g/dL) = 11.2 (13.5-18 male, 12-16 female)
Hct (%) = 33.5 (38-50 male, 36-46 female)
Plt (mm^3) = 227,000 (150,000-450,000)
PMN (%) = 85 (45-73)
Bands (%) = 1 (3-5)
MCV (mm^3) = 78 (80-96)
RDW (%) = 15 (11.5-14.5)

Vitals and Tests:
BP: 138/87 HR: 98 RR: 25 Temp: 101.2°F O_2 Saturation on 1 liter = 92%
CXR: RML infiltrate

Questions

1. Based on this patient's past medical history and labs, which of the following medications may accumulate and cause side effects? (Select **ALL** that apply.)
   - *a.* Dexmedetomidine
   - *b.* Lorazepam
   - *c.* Midazolam
   - *d.* Propofol
   - *e.* Remifentanil

2. Propofol and fentanyl continuous IV infusions were started for this patient. What general principle is correct regarding management of these medications for this patient?
   - *a.* Heavier sedation is preferred to minimize risk to staff.
   - *b.* Pain and sedation should be monitored with validated scales at least weekly.
   - *c.* Daily sedation vacations are recommended to reduce the duration of mechanical ventilation.
   - *d.* Propofol may be sufficient as a single agent since it also has analgesic properties.
   - *e.* Benzodiazepines are preferred over propofol or dexmedetomidine because they cause less delirium.

3. The patient's respiratory status worsened and she is now requiring cisatracurium to maintain adequate oxygenation. Which of the following is correct regarding the propofol and fentanyl?
   - *a.* Propofol may be discontinued since the patient should not be agitated while receiving a neuromuscular blocking drug.
   - *b.* Fentanyl may be discontinued since pain should be well controlled while receiving a neuromuscular blocking drug.
   - *c.* Haloperidol should be added to propofol and fentanyl since cisatracurium will cause delirium.
   - *d.* Propofol and fentanyl should be continued and sedation and analgesia assessed prior and during cisatracurium therapy.
   - *e.* Propofol and fentanyl should be continued, but succinylcholine is a better choice of neuromuscular blocking drug for this patient.

Questions 4-15 do not apply to the case.

4. Which of the following statements about colloids is/are true? (Select **ALL** that apply.)
   - *a.* Sodium chloride 0.9% is a colloid
   - *b.* Approximately 25% of the volume of a colloid remains intravascularly after administration
   - *c.* Colloids are significantly more expensive than crystalloids
   - *d.* Patients receiving colloids have a higher risk of developing pulmonary edema compared to patients receiving crystalloids.
   - *e.* Albumin 25% is a colloid

5. Which of the following vasopressors is considered first-line in treating patients with sepsis?
   - *a.* Norepinephrine
   - *b.* Vasopressin
   - *c.* Epinephrine
   - *d.* Phenylephrine
   - *e.* Ephedrine

6. Which of the following is an antidote for morphine overdose?
   - *a.* Naloxone
   - *b.* Sodium thiosulfate
   - *c.* Flumazenil
   - *d.* Protamine
   - *e.* Deferoxamine

7. Which of the following statements is true regarding neuromuscular blocking agents (NMBAs)?
   - *a.* Cisatracurium is a non-depolarizing agent.
   - *b.* Patients receiving these drugs do not require sedation/analgesia.
   - *c.* These drugs should be used routinely in critically ill patients.
   - *d.* NMBAs are not associated with significant adverse effects.
   - *e.* NMBAs are monitored using the Ramsay agitation scale.

8. Which of the following is true of *Precedex*?

   a. It is a benzodiazepine.
   b. It can only be used in intubated patients.
   c. It is an oil-in-water emulsion.
   d. It is an alpha-2 antagonist.
   e. It can be used in both intubated and non-intubated patients.

9. What effect can be expected from dopamine at medium doses (5 – 10 mcg/kg/min)?

   a. Alpha-1 antagonist, vasoconstriction
   b. Alpha-1 agonist, vasoconstriction
   c. Beta-1 agonist, positive inotropic effect
   d. Beta-2 agonist, positive inotropic effect
   e. D-1 agonist, vasodilation

10. Which of the following electrolyte disorders is conivaptan approved to treat?

    a. Hypovolemic hypotonic hyponatremia
    b. Euvolemic hyponatremia
    c. Hypervolemic hypernatremia
    d. Diabetes insipidus
    e. Euvolemic hypernatremia

11. How much of a change in sodium should be avoided in patients with sodium imbalances?

    a. > 6 mEq/L/day
    b. > 10 mEq/L/day
    c. > 12 mEq/L/day
    d. > 12 mEq/L/hr
    e. > 20 mEq/L/hr

12. The medical team will start a dobutamine drip at 10 mcg/kg/min for a patient weighing 60 kg. The standard concentration of dobutamine in the pharmacy is 250 mg/250 mL bag. Calculate how many hours the bag will last at the prescribed rate?

    a. 3 hours
    b. 5 hours
    c. 7 hours
    d. 10 hours
    e. 15 hours

13. Which of the following medications used for ICU sedation has a high concentration of propylene glycol, which may lead to metabolic acidosis?

    a. *Diprivan*
    b. *Precedex*
    c. *Ativan*
    d. *Haldol*
    e. Midazolam

14. Which of the following is important to monitor before and during haloperidol administration for ICU delirium?

    a. Blood glucose
    b. Potassium
    c. Cortisol
    d. QT interval
    e. Lactate

15. A 75 year-old is admitted with ADHF. He presents with congestion, altered mental status and poor urine output. His vital signs are BP 80/57, HR 112, RR 24 and oxygen saturation 93%. He is started on bumetanide 1 mg IV Q12H. Which of the following medications is most appropriate to start at this time?

    a. Dopamine
    b. Nitroprusside
    c. Nitroglycerin
    d. Milrinone
    e. Clevidipine

Answers

1-b,c, 2-c, 3-d, 4-c,e, 5-a, 6-a, 7-a, 8-e, 9-c, 10-b, 11-c, 12-c, 13-c, 14-d, 15-a

22

DRUG USE IN PREGNANCY AND LACTATION

© Artisticco, LLC

GUIDELINES/REFERENCES

American College of Obstetricians and Gynecologists (ACOG) Practice Guidelines, available at www.acog.org (accessed 2016 Nov 28).

CDC Recommendations for STI/STD, available at www.cdc.gov (accessed 2016 Nov 28).

We gratefully acknowledge the assistance of Mary Soliman, PharmD, BCPPS, CPh, Assistant Professor, University of South Florida, in preparing this chapter.

PREGNANCY

BACKGROUND

Pregnancy typically lasts 36 – 40 weeks and is divided into 3 trimesters. A positive human chorionic gonadotropin (hCG+) lab result confirms pregnancy. The first trimester is when the embryo is most susceptible to birth defects caused by teratogens. Birth defects due to the use of teratogens can also occur in the second and third trimesters. For drugs to be teratogenic, the drug has to cross the placenta into fetal circulation. Teratogenic drugs should be discontinued prior to pregnancy, if possible. Pharmacokinetic changes during pregnancy may require dose and regimen changes. For example, in women being treated for hypothyroidism, an increased dose of levothyroxine will be required in order to keep thyroid hormones within normal ranges.

LIFESTYLE MANAGEMENT

Lifestyle modifications should always be considered first when treating pregnant patients. This includes encouragement to stop the use of illicit drugs, alcohol and tobacco, each of which is teratogenic. Behavioral intervention is a safe and sometimes effective strategy for prenatal smoking cessation. Refer to the Tobacco Cessation chapter.

Folic Acid Supplements in Women of Childbearing Age

Folate deficiency causes birth defects of the brain and spinal cord (neural tube defects). All women of childbearing age should obtain 400 mcg/day of folic acid (folate) from dietary supplements and/or fortified foods, in addition to the folate received from the diet. During pregnancy, folate requirements increase to 600 mcg/day. Folate is in many healthy foods, including fortified flour and cereals, dried beans, green leafy vegetables and orange juice.

The baby's skeleton requires adequate calcium and vitamin D. If deficient in calcium, the mother's bone health will be sacrificed to provide for the baby. Pregnant women from 19 - 50 years old require 1,000 mg/day of calcium, and 600 IU/day of vitamin D. Prescription prenatal vitamins contain adequate folate and vitamin D for most women, but contain ~200 mg calcium, which is insufficient with low dietary intake. Calcium is bulky and the prenatal vitamin would be quite large if it contained larger amounts. If the woman's dietary intake is insufficient, she may need a separate calcium supplement.

VACCINATION DURING PREGNANCY

- Inactivated influenza vaccine is recommended in pregnancy, regardless of the trimester.
- Tdap is recommended between weeks 27 – 36 of each pregnancy. Vaccination protects the baby and mother from pertussis (whooping cough), which is severe in infants.
- No live vaccines (e.g., MMR, varicella, live influenza nasal) one month before and during pregnancy.
- Other vaccines may be needed in unusual circumstances (e.g., foreign travel); refer to the CDC guidelines.

DRUG TREATMENT

Drug selection during pregnancy should consider the following:

- The use of lifestyle measures first.
- Selecting drugs carefully, and only when necessary if lifestyle alone is not sufficient.

FDA Pregnancy Categories: Older Safety Rating, Remains in Use

The old pregnancy categories were viewed as confusing and overly simplistic. In some cases, ratings were applied incorrectly due to inadequate information on the safety risks.

PREGNANT? HOW IN THE WORLD DID THAT HAPPEN?

Preferably, teratogens should be discontinued prior to pregnancy, but about half of pregnancies are not planned.

There are conditions that occur in women of child-bearing age that are treated with teratogens. If the pregnancy is not planned, and the woman is taking a drug that poses a danger, the risk/benefit must be considered. If possible, the drug should be discontinued.

- Psychiatric (lithium, paroxetine, benzodiazepines)
- Hyperparathyroidism (methimazole, propylthiouracil)
- Hypertension (ACE Inhibitors, ARBS)
- Migraines (DHE)
- Rheumatoid Arthritis (methotrexate)
- Seizure disorders (valproate, carbamazepine, topiramate, others)
- Infections, acne (tetracyclines, quinolones)

New labeling requirements for pregnancy and lactation (described in the next section) apply to prescription drugs approved since the law went into effect on June 30, 2015. The FDA is giving the manufacturers 5 years to add the information to drugs approved since June 30, 2001 to the start of the new requirements in 2015. The new requirements do not apply to drugs approved before June 30, 2001 except that the Pregnancy Category will need to be removed within three years. Currently, except for drugs recently approved (which have the 2015 requirements), the package labeling for a prescription drug can include:

- The old pregnancy category for the drug (A, B, C, D or X).
- The old pregnancy category removed, and nothing else added.
- The new requirements.
- The old pregnancy category and the new requirements.

Drugs with known risk from the old categories should be considered to have the same risk unless known otherwise. If a drug is Pregnancy Category X, it's contraindicated in pregnancy, which means it cannot be used in pregnancy for any reason. If a drug is Category D, it should only be used if the benefit outweighs the risk. This is true for all drugs, and especially for drugs with risk for more severe effects.

Previous Pregnancy Categories & Interpretation

A	Controlled studies in animals & women show **no risk in the first trimester**. Risk of fetal harm is remote.
B	Animal studies have not demonstrated a fetal risk, but no controlled studies in pregnant women, or animal studies show an adverse effect that was not confirmed in studies in women in 1st trimester.
C	No controlled studies in humans & animal studies show adverse events, or studies in humans and animals are not available; give only if potential benefit outweighs the risk.
D	Positive evidence of fetal risk is available, but the benefits may outweigh the risk with life-threatening or serious disease.
X	Studies in animals or humans show fetal abnormalities; use in pregnancy is contraindicated.

New Pregnancy, Lactation & Reproduction Labeling Requirements

The FDA approved new pregnancy, lactation and reproduction labeling requirements that apply to new prescription drugs/biologics. The new labeling is intended to provide patients and clinicians with more detailed benefit/risk data in order to make informed decisions. Refer to the previous section for dates when package labeling should reflect changes.

New Pregnancy Sections in Package Inserts

8.1 Pregnancy	A pregnancy risk summary is required for all medications that includes the risk of adverse developmental outcomes based on human and animal data and the drug's pharmacology. Includes any dose adjustments, maternal/fetal adverse reactions and disease risks. Includes pregnancy exposure registry information. Pregnant women should be encouraged to participate in registries, which exist for select disease states and drugs. The registries collect health information from women who take prescription drugs and vaccines when pregnant and breastfeeding. Information is also collected on the newborn baby.
8.2 Lactation	Includes whether the drug/metabolites go into human milk, the effects on the breastfed infant, and the effects on milk production. If applicable, ways to minimize exposure and monitor for adverse reactions are included.
8.3 Females & Males of Reproductive Potential	Includes any effects on fertility and requirements for pregnancy testing and contraception.

Common Teratogens

The teratogens in the Key Drugs table could be present in a patient case. The disease state chapters in this book state "Safety issue - see Pregnancy chapter" in the drug table where these drugs are listed. Teratogenic drugs should be discontinued in pregnancy (and preferably prior to pregnancy), whenever possible. With any medication, the drug's potential harm must be weighed against the risk of the condition not being adequately treated. For example, the use of lamotrigine in pregnancy carries a risk of congenital malformations, but seizures cause damage to both the mother and child. In some cases, a switch to a safer drug is possible, or, the woman may have had a history of poor seizure control prior to the use of lamotrigine.

Teratogens are hazardous drugs according to USP Chapter 800, and require special handling to avoid risk to healthcare workers; see hazardous drug section in the Medication Safety chapter.

TERATOGENS: DANGER IN PREGNANCY

KEY DRUGS

Brand names included if the drug is generally referred to by the brand

- Dihydroergotamine, ergotamine (*DHE 45, Migranal*)
- Isotretinoin, and topical retinoids, including tazarotene
- Hormones, including estradiol, progesterone [including megestrol *(Megace)]*, raloxifene, *Duavee*, testosterone, contraceptives
- Hydroxyurea
- Lithium
- Methotrexate
- Misoprostol
- Paroxetine
- Quinolones
- RAAS Inhibitors [ACE Inhibitors, ARBs, aliskiren, *Entresto)]*
- Statins
- Tetracyclines
- Thalidomide
- Topiramate
- Valproic Acid/Divalproex
- Warfarin
- Weight Loss Drugs (detail in Weight Loss chapter)

Others:

- Amiodarone, Dronedarone
- Atenolol
- Benzodiazepines
- Carbamazepine
- Dutasteride, Finasteride
- Fluconazole, Voriconazole
- ERAs (e.g., bosentan)
- Griseofulvin
- Lenalidomide, Leflunomide
- Lomitapide
- Methimazole, Propylthiouracil (detail in this chapter)
- Nafarelin
- NRTIs
- NSAIDs
- Phenobarbital
- Ribavirin
- Tobramycin
- Phenytoin
- Radioactive iodine
- Ribavirin

**Metronidazole, Nitrofurantoin, Sulfamethoxazole/Trimethoprim and Televancin--see ID I chapter.*

Select Conditions and Preferred Management during Pregnancy

CONDITION	PREFERRED MANAGEMENT	NOTES
Morning Sickness, Nausea, Vomiting	Lifestyle first: eat smaller, more frequent meals, avoid spicy or odorous foods, take more frequent naps, and reduce stress, including working long hours. If lifestyle measures fail, ACOG recommends pyridoxine (vitamin B6) +/- doxylamine first line. Rx: doxylamine/pyridoxine *(Bonjesta)*	Ginger is rated "possibly effective" for treating morning sickness. Hyperemesis gravidarum is severe N/V, causing weight loss, dehydration and electrolyte imbalance. It will be treated under the care of an obstetrician and may require hospitalization.
GERD/Heartburn	Lifestyle first: eat smaller, more frequent meals, avoid foods that worsen GERD. If symptoms occur while sleeping, recommend elevating the head of the bed and not eating 3 hours prior to sleep. If lifestyle measures fail, recommend antacids. Calcium antacids, such as calcium carbonate in *Tums*, are a good choice since calcium intake is often deficient.	
Flatulence	Simethicone (*Gas-X, Mylicon*).	
Constipation	Lifestyle first: ↑ fluid intake, ↑ dietary fiber intake, ↑ physical activity If lifestyle measures fail, fiber (psyllium, calcium polycarbophil, methylcellulose), with adequate amounts of fluids, is first line.	
Cough, Cold, Allergies	First line: first-generation antihistamines. Chlorpheniramine (drug of choice) and diphenhydramine are Pregnancy Category B. The non-sedating 2nd generation agents loratadine and cetirizine are often recommended by obstetricians during the second and third trimesters. If nasal steroids are needed for chronic allergy symptoms, budesonide *(Rhinocort)* and beclomethasone *(Beconase AQ)* are considered safest (hint: b's for babies).	The oral decongestants should not be recommended during first trimester. The cough-suppressant dextromethorphan and the mucolytic guaifenesin have limited safety data in pregnancy/lactation, but are sometimes used. Avoid liquid formulations that contain alcohol.
Pain	Non-drug options such as hot/cold packs, light massage or physical therapy can help limit or avoid the use of analgesics. ACOG continues to recommend acetaminophen first-line for mild pain during pregnancy because the perceived risk with acetaminophen may be less than the known risk with NSAIDs and opioids. There is a possible link between acetaminophen use during pregnancy and ADHD/autism in the child; the FDA is investigating the risk.	Avoid NSAIDs, including aspirin. Opioid metabolism can affect safety risk (see Drug Interactions and Pain chapters). If codeine is given to a breastfeeding mother who is a CYP 2D6 rapid metabolizer, the infant could suffer fatality. To reduce risk, avoid codeine, use a short-acting opioid at the lowest effective dose, and take after feedings.

Select Conditions and Preferred Management during Pregnancy continued

CONDITION	PREFERRED MANAGEMENT	NOTES
Infection	Generally considered safe to use: penicillins (including amoxicillin and ampicillin), cephalosporins, erythromycin and azithromycin. **VAGINAL FUNGAL INFECTIONS** Topical antifungals (creams, suppositories) x 7 days. **URINARY TRACT INFECTIONS** Cephalexin 500 mg PO Q6H x 7 days Ampicillin 500 mg PO Q6H x 7 days Nitrofurantoin and SMX/TMP should be considered last line during the 1st trimester, and should not be used in the last 2 weeks of pregnancy. Must treat bacteriuria, even if asymptomatic with negative urinalysis. Untreated bacteriuria can lead to premature birth, pyelonephritis, and neonatal meningitis.	Do not use: quinolones (due to cartilage damage) and tetracyclines (due to teeth discoloration). **VAGINAL FUNGAL INFECTIONS** Avoid fluconazole. **URINARY TRACT INFECTION** SMX/TMP has mixed data for use in pregnancy; per ACOG, use in pregnancy (if necessary) may be acceptable. See Infectious Disease II chapters for STI/STD management in pregnancy.
Asthma	Maintenance therapy (steroid): inhaled budesonide Rescue therapy (short-acting beta agonist): inhaled albuterol	Budesonide is also the preferred steroid for infants in the *Respules*, which are put in a nebulizer.
Venous Thromboembolism/ Mechanical Valves	Use pneumatic compression devices prior to delivery in women with thrombosis if they are getting a C-section.	The newer anticoagulants are not currently recommended in the guidelines.
Hypothyroidism	Levothyroxine Will require a 30-50% dose increase during pregnancy.	Hypothyroidism must be treated during pregnancy; if left untreated, severe consequences could include miscarriage or stillbirth, preeclampsia, low birth weight, cognitive impairment and growth retardation.
Hyperthyroidism	Mild hyperthyroid cases will not require treatment. Preferable to normalize the mother's thyroid function prior to pregnancy. Contraception should be used until the condition is controlled. If drugs are necessary (i.e., Graves' disease): propylthiouracil is preferred if trying to conceive and in the 1st trimester, methimazole is preferred during the 2nd and 3rd trimester.	Both drugs are high risk for liver damage, readily cross the placenta, and can cause congenital defects. Uncontrolled maternal hyperthyroidism can cause premature delivery and low birth weight. Radioactive iodine is teratogenic and not used in pregnancy.
Iron Deficiency Anemia	Supplemental iron, prenatal vitamins with iron.	
Hypertension	Labetalol, methyldopa, nifedipine.	ACE inhibitors, ARBs, aliskiren, *Entresto* are contraindicated in pregnancy.
Diabetes	Insulin is preferred if not controlled with lifestyle. Metformin and glyburide are commonly used.	

Managing hypertension, diabetes, HIV and bipolar disorder during pregnancy are discussed further in the respective chapters.

LACTATION

The American Academy of Pediatrics (AAP) recommends that babies be exclusively breastfed for the first 6 months of life, as long as it is mutually desired by the mother and baby and if safety risks are not present. Babies receiving breast milk partially or exclusively should receive 400 IU of vitamin D daily until they are consuming at least 1 liter of vitamin D-fortified formula/day. Breastfed babies require 1 mg/kg daily of iron during 4 – 6 months. See Dietary Supplements, Natural & Complementary Medicine chapter.

Excretion into breast milk is higher with drugs that are non-ionized, have a small molecular weight, a low volume of distribution, and high lipid solubility. The majority of medications have low excretion into breast milk, and can be taken safely while breastfeeding. Additionally, breastfeeding can continue when the mother has a cold, influenza and with the majority of other infections. *LactMed* can be used to check for drug safety during breastfeeding (http://toxnet.nlm.nih.gov).

Select Exceptions: If the mother is HIV-positive, the baby should receive formula, unless the baby is also HIV-positive. An HIV-positive mother can breastfeed an HIV-negative baby only in quite unusual circumstances, such as a lack of safe water or formula.

Amphetamines, ergotamines, lamotrigine, lithium and statins should not be used during breastfeeding.

Metronidazole should be avoided, or the milk should be pumped and discarded for 12 – 24 hours after a single dose. Phenobarbital is excreted in breast milk, and can result in acute withdrawal effects when breastfeeding is abruptly stopped.

Particularly in newborns, even small doses of opioids taken by the mother can cause CNS depression, including excessive sedation and possible fatality to the breastfed infant. Codeine is well-studied in pregnancy and is known to be unsafe, especially if the mother is a CYP 2D6 ultra-rapid metabolizer. *LactMed* should be checked prior to the use of other opioids, and other drugs.

Mothers who are breastfeeding should increase their diet by 450 – 500 kcal/day and continue prenatal vitamins and omega-3 supplements.

23

PEDIATRIC CONDITIONS

GUIDELINES/REFERENCES

Zoorob R, Sidani M, Murray J. Croup: an overview. *Am Fam Physician.* 2011; 83:1067-1073.

Vande Walle J, Rittig S, Bauer S, et al. Practical consensus guidelines for the management of enuresis. *Eur J Pediatr.* 2012; 171(6):971-983.

Additional guidelines included with the video files (RxPrep Online).

We gratefully acknowledge the assistance of Allison Provine, PharmD, BCPS, BCPPS, Lipscomb University College of Pharmacy, in preparing this chapter.

BACKGROUND

Pediatric patients have unique and important differences in pharmacokinetic and pharmacodynamic properties that change as they mature. Several conditions common in younger patients are covered in this chapter. Additional pediatric topics are covered elsewhere in this course book.

PEDIATRIC TOPIC	CHAPTER
Iron and vitamin D recommendations	Dietary Supplements, Natural & Complementary Medicine
Infections	Infectious Diseases
Vaccines	Immunizations
Asthma	Asthma
Cough and cold	Allergic Rhinitis, Cough & Cold
Head lice and diaper rash	Common Skin Conditions
Sickle cell anemia	Sickle Cell Disease

Infants can become seriously ill very quickly. See the following box that indicates conditions in which a child should be referred for urgent care.

Safe Medication Administration

Studies have demonstrated that when parents measure liquid doses, the dose is often incorrect. Household spoons should not be used for measuring medication. All liquid medications should be dispensed with an oral dosing syringe or dosing cup, although oral syringes can decrease measuring errors and are preferred over cups. The parent (or caregiver) should be able to read the markings on the device when it contains medication. Instruct the parents on how to draw up the correct dose. When dispensing liquid medications that carry high risk, follow safe practice recommendations:

- Stock only one strength if a dangerous drug comes in a variety of strengths. Place the container into a high-risk bin with instructions attached to the container.

AGE CLASSIFICATIONS	
Neonate	0 – 28 days
Infant	1 month – 12 months
Child	1 – 12 years
Adolescent	13 – 18 years

- The dose should be written in terms of total mg and in mg/kg per dose.
- The pharmacist should check that the dose is appropriate for the child's weight. Ask the parent for the child's weight if it is not available.
- The container label should include the dose (mg) and the volume (mL). Dispense with a measuring device.

With some high-risk drugs, it is preferable to administer at a medical facility, where help is available if needed.

REFER FOR URGENT CARE WITH ANY OF THE FOLLOWING SIGNS OR SYMPTOMS
Age < 3 months old with a temperature of 100.4°F (rectal)
Age 3 – 6 months with a temperature of 101°F (rectal)
Age > 6 months with a temperature of 103°F (rectal)
Any cough/cold that worsens or does not improve in several days
Unusual, severe, or persistent pain that does not go away after several hours
Blood in the urine or stool
Inability to sleep or drink
Rash that looks severe or any rash with fever
Abrasions that are dirty or deep (requiring sutures)
Limping or unable to move an extremity
Seizure

BACTERIAL MENINGITIS

This topic is included in the Infectious Diseases II chapter, but is emphasized here because of the unique aspects of neonatal meningitis. The fatality rate if untreated is close to 100% and the treatment recommendations are different. This is because the common pathogens differ and there are safety issues with use of ceftriaxone in neonates.

The classic signs of meningitis are uncommon in neonates (age 0 – 28 days). Bulging fontanelles (swelling between the bones of the skull) and nuchal rigidity (inability to bend the neck) will be present in < 25% of cases; otherwise, the symptoms are non-specific and a definite diagnosis in a suspected case can be made with a lumbar puncture.

The likely pathogens causing bacterial meningitis in a neonate differ from other age groups due to the vertical transmission of organisms from the mother to the baby in the birth canal. The predominant pathogens are Group B *Streptococcus* (GBS), *Escherichia coli, Listeria and Klebsiella*. Empiric treatment of meningitis in neonates consists of ampicillin plus either cefotaxime or gentamicin. Ceftriaxone, which is used in adults, is generally avoided in neonates. Ceftriaxone displaces bilirubin from albumin, which can cause bilirubin-induced brain damage (kernicterus). Ceftriaxone and calcium-containing solutions can precipitate, causing an embolus and death. Therefore, concurrent use in neonates is contraindicated. See Infectious Diseases II chapter for more information on empiric treatment of bacterial meningitis.

AGE	COMMON BACTERIAL PATHOGENS	EMPIRIC TREATMENT
< 1 month	*Streptococcus agalactiae (Group B strep), Escherichia coli, Listeria monocytogenes, Klebsiella*	Ampicillin + Cefotaxime or Ampicillin + Aminoglycoside (Gentamicin)
1 – 23 months	*Streptococcus pneumoniae, Neisseria meningitidis, S. agalactiae, Haemophilus influenzae, E. coli*	Vancomycin + 3rd generation cephalosporin (Ceftriaxone or Cefotaxime)
2+ years	*N. meningitidis, S. pneumoniae*	Vancomycin + 3rd generation cephalosporin (Ceftriaxone or Cefotaxime)

RESPIRATORY SYNCYTIAL VIRUS

Respiratory Syncytial Virus (RSV) infection occurs commonly and nearly all children have been infected by the age of two years. In older, healthy children, the symptoms mimic the common cold, but in premature babies and neonates, RSV can be deadly. RSV is a common cause of bronchiolitis (swelling and mucus build up in the bronchioles). Symptoms include low-grade fever, cough, dyspnea and cyanosis (bluish skin due to lack of oxygen). Similar to other viral infections, the treatment is primarily supportive (supplemental oxygen, IV fluids, suction of secretions).

RSV Prophylaxis

No vaccine is available for RSV and no lasting immunity develops after infection, therefore risk remains high. Palivizumab *(Synagis)* is a humanized monoclonal antibody indicated for the prevention of serious lower respiratory tract disease caused by RSV in children at high risk of the disease.

RSV prophylaxis is recommended by the American Academy of Pediatrics (AAP) during RSV season (late fall, early winter, early spring). In addition to premature infants, palivizumab is used for certain infants and children < 24 months with select medical conditions that affect respiration.

Palivizumab is dosed monthly at 15 mg/kg per dose by intramuscular (IM) injection. In neonates and infants, the IM injection site is the anterolateral thigh muscle. The deltoid can be used in children once the muscle mass is adequate, which usually does not occur until at least 3 years of age. Infants should not receive more than 5 monthly doses during the RSV season. If the baby becomes infected with RSV, no further doses of palivizumab should be given.

WHO SHOULD RECEIVE PALIVIZUMAB *(SYNAGIS)*?

In the first year of life:

- Premature infants born at < 29 weeks gestation
- Premature infants born < 32 weeks gestation with chronic lung disease (CLD) and are < 12 months of age
- Infants < 12 months of age with certain heart conditions

CROUP

Croup, or laryngotracheobronchitis, is usually due to a viral infection which causes inflammation of the upper airway, larynx, trachea and bronchi. Bacterial infections are less common and are often associated with severe symptoms. The inflammation results in the hallmark signs of inspiratory stridor (high pitched breathing sound), barking cough, and hoarseness. Croup is most common in children < 6 years old and is often worse at night. The illness is classified and treated by the severity of the symptoms.

Non-Drug Treatment

In mild cases, a child may present with only a croupy cough, which can be managed at home and should resolve within a few days. Cool mist or steam (avoid spilling hot water on infants) and adequate hydration may help alleviate symptoms, although evidence of benefit is lacking.

Drug Treatment for Mild, Moderate or Severe Illness

A systemic steroid (usually dexamethasone 0.6 mg/kg) is used in mild, moderate, and severe cases of croup. In more moderate to severe cases, nebulized racemic epinephrine may be used. Some severe symptoms (e.g., stridor at rest, respiratory distress, severe retractions, mental status changes) can require respiratory support such as intubation.

In a typical croup case presenting to an acute care setting with moderate to severe symptoms, a patient having difficulty breathing will be given a steroid (oral if tolerated, or by injection) and then nebulized racemic epinephrine, if needed. Nebulized racemic epinephrine is a 1:1 mixture of dextro (D) isomers and levo (L) isomers (the L-isomer is the active component). If racemic epinephrine is not available, L-epinephrine is used; this is ½ of the drug (one of the isomers) and the dose is, consequently, ½ of the racemic formulation.

Epinephrine is an adrenergic agonist that will relax the bronchial smooth muscle and cause bronchodilation. When given with a nebulizer (or as an injection – these are used occasionally in an outpatient self-administered device for other conditions) the onset of action is fast but lasts at most up to 2 hours; a child receiving epinephrine should be monitored for up to 4 hours for recurrence of symptoms. The child should not be discharged until breathing is easy with no stridor at rest and after receiving steroids to reduce the inflammation. Antibiotics are used only if there a bacterial infection.

DRUG	DOSING	SAFETY/SIDE EFFECTS/MONITORING
Dexamethasone Oral solution, injection (other forms not used in infants)	0.6 mg/kg x 1 PO/IM/IV, max 16 mg/dose	See Asthma chapter for steroid safety issues. This refers to acute use only.
Nebulized: Racemic epinephrine 2.25% solution or L-epinephrine 1 mg/mL solution 10 mg racemic epinephrine = 5 mg L-epinephrine	Racemic epinephrine dose: 0.05-0.1 mL/kg (max 0.5 mL) diluted in 2 mL NS, can repeat Q20 min PRN L-epinephrine dose: 0.5 mL/kg of 1 mg/mL solution (maximum dose: 5 mL) diluted in NS, can repeat Q20 min PRN	**WARNINGS** Caution with cardiovascular disease, cerebrovascular disease, thyroid disease, diabetes (can ↑ blood glucose) **SIDE EFFECTS** ↑ BP, HR, anxiety, arrhythmia **NOTES** Monitor for recurrent bronchospasm

NOCTURNAL ENURESIS

Nocturnal enuresis, or bed-wetting, is a normal part of a child's development and is not generally treated before age 5. Boys (more often than girls) can still be developing nighttime bladder control until 7 years old.

Non-Drug Treatment

Behavioral approaches should be used first. Practices that can be effective include positive reinforcement, establishing a normal daytime voiding pattern and a normal bowel pattern, and establishing a normal hydration pattern. Fluid intake should be limited prior to bedtime. Bladder training exercises (such as attempting to hold the urine during the day for a set time period) are not recommended. Embarrassment should be minimized. Behavioral approaches are effective in many children and should be tried for up to 3 months. If behavioral methods do not result in dryness, either alarm therapy or alarm therapy with drug treatment (desmopressin) can be tried. There are numerous alarms available that attach to the underwear or pajamas and sound an alarm when wet. The child may sleep through the alarm but will generally stop voiding. When the alarm sounds a parent should wake the child and escort him or her to the bathroom.

Alarm therapy can be useful and should be considered for a minimum of three consecutive months. If unsuccessful initially, alarm therapy might work when the child is older and more motivated. Alarm therapy is effective in about two out of three children initially; many will relapse and require the intervention repeated.

Drug Treatment

Desmopressin (oral tablet) is the only preferred medication for enuresis. Desmopressin is a synthetic analogue of antidiuretic hormone (ADH); simulating ADH will ↓ nocturnal urine production. Desmopressin can be used in combination with alarm therapy.

DRUG	DOSING	SAFETY/SIDE EFFECTS/MONITORING
Desmopressin *(DDAVP)* Tablets used for enuresis Tablets, nasal spray or injection used for diabetes insipidus and hemophilia A (to control bleeding)	Start 0.2 mg PO QHS, can titrate to 0.6 mg max	**CONTRAINDICATIONS** Hyponatremia or history of hyponatremia CrCl < 50 mL/min **WARNINGS** Hyponatremia, water intoxication **SIDE EFFECTS** Headache, fatigue, possible ↓ Na due to water retention **NOTES** Limit fluid intake starting 1 hour before dose and until the next morning

OVER THE COUNTER PRODUCTS FOR CHILDREN < 12 MONTHS OLD

If the condition does not require urgent care, there are several over the counter (OTC) products approved that are deemed generally safe for use in infants.

Intestinal Gas

Intestinal gas is a common condition with infants and causes distress post-feedings. Simethicone drops can offer mild, if any, benefit. The drug is not absorbed and is safe to use. Typically, as the child's digestive tract grows, the crying and fussiness will resolve. Parents can be comforted that symptoms will generally dissipate when the child is around 6 – 8 months old.

Nasal Congestion

Nasal congestion is very common in babies and is generally not serious. Children < 2 years old breathe mostly through their nose; they have not yet learned to breathe through their mouths. Smoke, including that from e-cigarettes, will cause irritation; do not permit anyone to smoke near children. Using a car seat indoors to sit the child upright may help. A cool mist humidifier near the bedside may reduce congestion – especially in the winter months when the home is heated. A steamy bathroom may help relieve congestion. A parent can sit with the child outside the shower, while hot water runs. Care should be taken to avoid hot water or steam getting near the child's skin, as burns could result.

According to FDA recommendations, OTC cough and cold medications should not be used in children age < 2 years old. Manufacturers labels state, "do not use" in children under age 4, and the American Academy of Pediatrics has recommended against their use in patients under age 6, due to inadequate data on efficacy and the potential for errors and adverse effects. Gentle suction with saline drops or spray to loosen the mucus can provide relief. Suction bulbs are sold in pharmacies.

Mild Pain and Fever

Aspirin and other salicylate-containing products (bismuth subsalicylate, others) have been associated with Reye's syndrome when used in patients recovering from viral infections (especially influenza and chickenpox). These should not be recommended in anyone < 16 years old because it may not be clear that the child is recovering from a virus. Acetaminophen infant drops and children's suspension are the same concentration to help reduce dosing errors in older children; previously, the infant drops were more concentrated. Acetaminophen is the most common cause of liver failure when used in doses above the safe amount. Accidental acetaminophen overdose can be due to the parent's inadvertent use of acetaminophen in multiple products. Take the time to counsel parents about this danger and the various names under which acetaminophen is packaged. This is discussed further in the Allergic Rhinitis, Cough & Cold chapter. Ibuprofen comes in different dosage strengths for infants and children and should be avoided in infants < 6 months old for pain/fever due to the risk of nephrotoxicity. With either acetaminophen or ibuprofen infant drops, the medicine can be squirted into the child's mouth. It is acceptable to mix with a small amount of formula, but if the child does not drink the entire dose, it will be difficult to know how much of the dose was taken. The branded acetaminophen and ibuprofen are more expensive than the store's own formulations, which contain the same active ingredients, and are less costly.

Constipation

In 2014, guideline recommendations were published on the evaluation and treatment of functional constipation in infants and children. Oral polyethylene glycol 3350 *(MiraLax)* is recommended for intermittent constipation treatment. This use is off-label and assumes the child will be able to swallow the medication. Polyethylene glycol 3350 is dosed at 0.2 – 0.8 g/kg/day. Dietary measures (prunes or pears, either the fruit or juice) are helpful. OTC pediatric-size glycerin suppositories are commonly used for quick relief of constipation in an uncomfortable baby, although the FDA indication is for children age 2 years and older. Any child with continuing issues with constipation should be seen by the pediatrician.

Select OTC Products for Infants

DRUG	DOSING	SAFETY/SIDE EFFECTS/MONITORING
Intestinal Gas		
Simethicone *(Mylicon Infants' Gas Relief Drops, Baby Gas-X Infant Drops)*	20 mg, 1-4 times/day PRN	Take after meals for mild gas pains. Shake drops before using. Can mix with water, formula, or other liquids.
Nasal dryness/congestion		
NaCl 0.9% intranasal saline solution *(Little Remedies Saline Nasal Drops, Ocean for Kids)*	2-6 drops per nostril PRN	See Allergic Rhinitis, Cough & Cold chapter; saline can be used with a suction bulb.
Fever		
Acetaminophen *(Children's Tylenol, PediaCare Infants' Fever Reducer/Pain Reliever,* others)	10-15 mg/kg/dose every 4-6 hours (max 75 mg/kg/day) All acetaminophen oral liquid formulations (infants and children) are the same concentration: 160 mg/5 mL	For simplicity, age and weight-based dosing for infants is on the side of the dropper container. Caution for incorrect dosing or overdose from use of a multiple products.
Ibuprofen (*Motrin Infant Drops, Infants' Advil Drops, Motrin* or *Advil* children's suspension, others)	5-10 mg/kg/dose every 6-8 hours (max 40 mg/kg/day) Infant drop strength: 50 mg/1.25 mL	Indicated for infants > 6 months old. Caution for nausea.
Constipation		
Polyethylene glycol *(MiraLax)*	Age ≥ 6 months, starting dose: 0.4 gram/kg. Dose range: 0.2-0.8 gram/kg/day (max 17 grams). Dissolve in at least 4 oz water or other beverage. The capful (filled to the indicated line) contains ~17 grams.	Instruct parent to discuss with the pediatrician if using more than occasionally.
Glycerin suppositories *(Babylax, Pedia-Lax)*	1 pediatric suppository. Insert high into the rectum. Retain for ~15 minutes.	Instruct parent to discuss with the pediatrician if using more than occasionally.

Systemic Drugs Not Generally Recommended in Pediatrics

- Quinolones are not routinely recommended in pediatric patients due to the possibility of adverse musculoskeletal adverse effects. In special cases, such as anthrax treatment, cystic fibrosis or in the treatment of multidrug-resistant organisms, they are used on a case-by-case basis.
- Tetracyclines are not generally recommended in children < 8 years of age due to permanent discoloration of teeth and retardation of skeletal development and bone growth. One notable exception is in tick-borne Rickettsial diseases (Rocky Mountain spotted fever, ehrlichiosis and anaplasmosis). Doxycycline is the most effective treatment and is recommended by AAP and the CDC for this indication in pediatric patients, as the risk of severe illness or death outweighs the risk of tooth discoloration. See the Infectious Diseases II chapter.
- Promethazine is contraindicated in children < 2 years of age due to the potential for severe and potentially fatal respiratory depression.
- Codeine is metabolized to morphine by the CYP450 2D6 enzyme; certain children over-express this enzyme and consequently, would produce a higher than expected amount of morphine. This can result in toxicity and a possible lethal overdose. Codeine has a boxed warning to avoid use with two common childhood surgeries (tonsillectomy, adenoidectomy); codeine is dangerous if used for any condition if the child over-expresses this enzyme. The FDA is currently reviewing safety data on the use of codeine-containing cough and cold products.
- Several OTC products are not safe in young children; even OTC diphenhydramine can quickly become toxic if used in ages < 6 years. Consult drug information sources prior to recommending OTC or prescription drugs for use in children.

Primary Toxicities From Accidental Overdose in Children

Iron and acetaminophen are two common culprits of accidental overdose in children. Toddlers put anything in their mouths, especially if it looks like it could be candy. One tablet of several drug classes, including sulfonylureas, can be fatal to an infant. It is important to counsel older patients about the safe storage of medications to prevent accidental overdoses. If the child has ingested anything that could be toxic (even if the ingestion is suspected only) the poison control center should be contacted immediately for advice. Review the Emergency Preparedness, Toxicology & Antidotes chapter for further information on pediatric poisoning.

Vaccine-Preventable Childhood Diseases

Vaccine-preventable illness occurs more commonly than in previous years due to a lower immunization rates in some areas. Recent immigrants who have not received vaccination in their home countries can also introduce disease. Vaccine information is found in the Immunizations chapter. The symptoms of the more common vaccine-preventable illnesses are listed so that the pharmacist can recognize the illness if it presents in a child. Each of the conditions below can lead to severe, permanent damage. Chickenpox generally dissipates without long-term consequences for most of the person's life. Anyone who has had chickenpox is at risk for developing shingles later in life, a painful condition that occurs most commonly in patients > 50 years of age and can lead to postherpetic neuralgia and chronic pain. Shingles only occurs in patients who have had chickenpox. For additional information, see Infectious Diseases II chapter.

Vaccine-Preventable Childhood Diseases

ILLNESS	EMBLEMATIC SYMPTOMS	SYMPTOM DESCRIPTION
Measles	Koplik spots are small white spots on the inside of the cheeks (inside the mouth) that appear 2-5 days prior to the rash seen below. 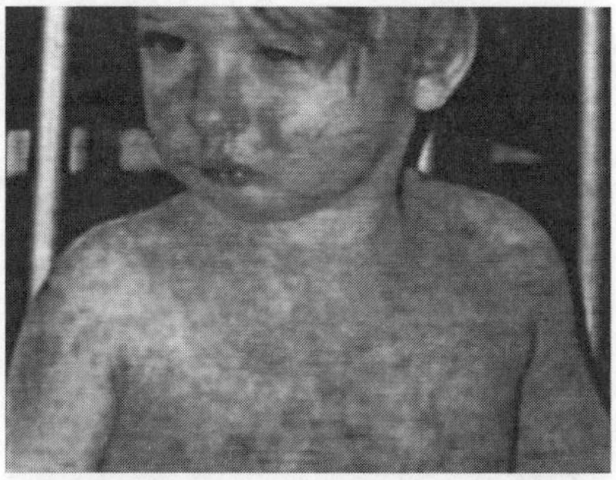	Koplik spots in mouth, maculopapular rash, fever, malaise, cough, rhinitis, conjunctivitis. Transmission is airborne and measles are highly contagious. If not immune, 90% of people who are in contact with an infected person will also become infected.
Mumps	Swollen and tender salivary glands under the ears (parotitis) 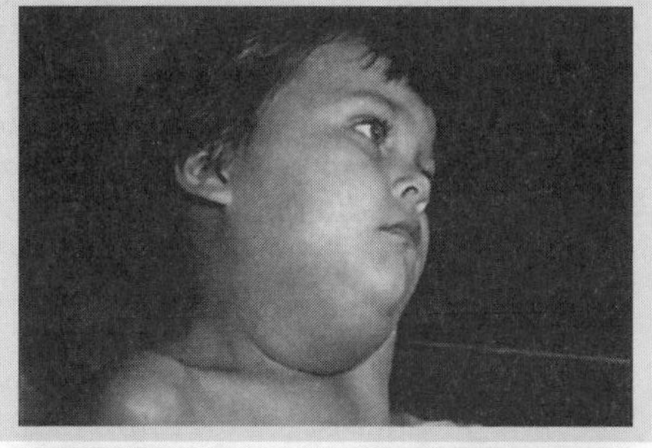	Swollen salivary glands, fever, headache, myalgia, fatigue, loss of appetite; up to 50% of patients have mild or no symptoms.
Rubella	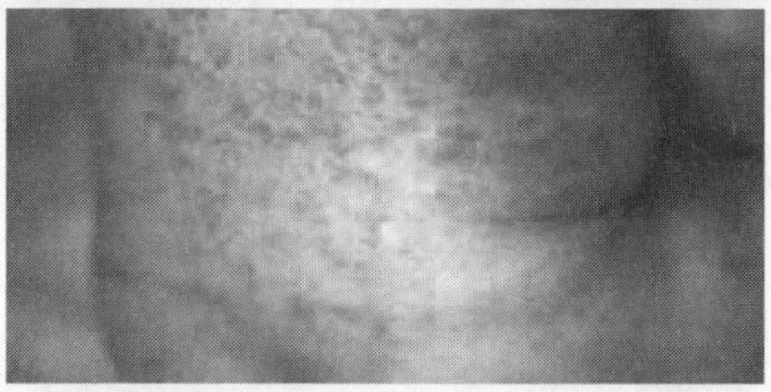	Fever, rash, swollen glands, cold-like symptoms, aching joints; up to 50% of patients have mild or no symptoms. Can cause birth defects if contracted by a pregnant woman.
Polio	Child with poliomyelitis 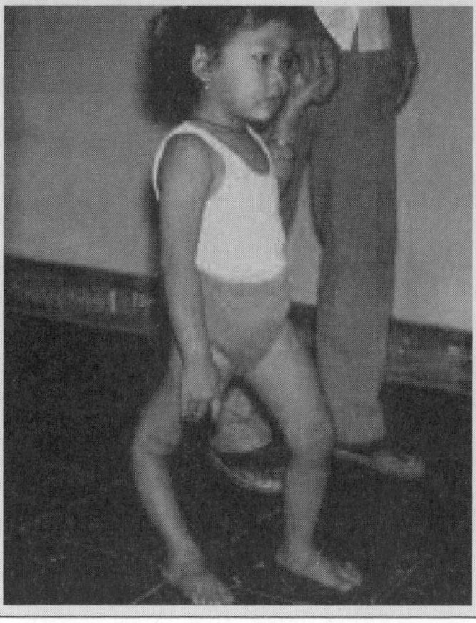	Fever, sore throat, fatigue, nausea, headache, abdominal pain; the majority have no symptoms and never know they were infected – others get severe nerve damage (paralytic polio) and later in life, post-polio syndrome, which causes progressive weakness and cognitive issues.

Vaccine-Preventable Childhood Diseases Continued

ILLNESS	EMBLEMATIC SYMPTOMS	SYMPTOM DESCRIPTION
Pertussis	"WHOOP" Listen to a child making whooping sounds on YouTube; several parents have posted videos.	Sudden cough outbursts, fever, rhinitis, bluish skin (cyanosis), vomiting, fatigue. Can cause respiratory failure and death, especially in infants.
Chickenpox (Varicella)	Chicken pox rash (spots) 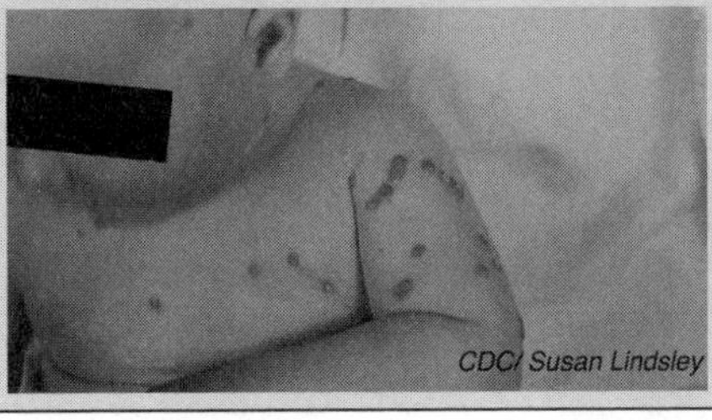	Itchy rash, fever, malaise. The rash appears as crops of sores (head, then trunk, then arms & legs), that turn into blisters, burst, then form crusts. Long-term implications include shingles (herpes zoster) with risk of ophthalmic involvement and post-herpetic neuralgia (severe pain after the infection).

Questions

1. An 8 year old male weighs 55 pounds. Select an appropriate acetaminophen dose to recommend for this child:

   a. 1000 mg PO Q6 hours PRN pain
   b. 650 mg PO Q6 hours PRN pain
   c. 325 mg PO Q6 hours PRN pain
   d. 120 mg PO Q6 hours PRN pain
   e. 80 mg PO Q6 hours PRN pain

2. HY is a 2 year old female who presents to the emergency department with a frequent barking cough, prominent inspiratory stridor, marked sternal retractions, and agitation. She is afebrile with some rhinorrhea. Which of the following drug treatments is most likely warranted for her severe condition, based on the presentation?

   a. Dexamethasone and nebulized racemic epinephrine
   b. Dexamethasone only
   c. Nebulized budesonide and dextromethorphan
   d. Dexamethasone, pseudoephedrine, and nebulized racemic epinephrine
   e. Nebulized racemic epinephrine

3. MS is a 6 year old female (37.4 pounds) who presents to your pharmacy with a prescription for cefpodoxime written by her pediatrician for presumed bacterial pneumonia. She has a history of rash with penicillin. The pediatrician chose to use a cephalosporin. The dose of cefpodoxime recommended in the drug information reference is 10 mg/kg/day divided every 12 hours. The pharmacist should counsel the parent/caregiver to give the following milligrams for each dose:

   a. 15 mg
   b. 25 mg
   c. 55 mg
   d. 85 mg
   e. 115 mg

4. A 4 day old male presents to the hospital with increased lethargy, poor feeding, and hypothermia. Blood and urine cultures are obtained along with a lumbar puncture to evaluate his cerebrospinal fluid. The most appropriate empiric regimen for suspected meningitis would be:

   a. Vancomycin and ampicillin
   b. Ampicillin and ceftriaxone
   c. Vancomycin and ceftriaxone
   d. Ampicillin and gentamicin
   e. Ceftriaxone and gentamicin

5. Which of the following statements concerning respiratory syncytial virus (RSV) are correct? (Select **ALL** that apply.)

   a. A patient presenting with RSV should be given nebulized corticosteroids early in the course to improve respiratory function.
   b. All patients requiring hospital admission due to RSV should be given nebulized ribavirin.
   c. An 11 month old infant born at 31 weeks gestation with chronic lung disease on home oxygen should receive prophylaxis against RSV with palivizumab (*Synagis*).
   d. Palivizumab (*Synagis*) should be given once a week for the duration of RSV season for patients who meet criteria for prophylaxis.
   e. The treatment for RSV infection is primarily supportive and does not routinely require drug treatment.

6. Which of the following statements concerning croup are correct? (Select **ALL** that apply.)

   a. Clinical manifestations are caused by inflammation of the upper airway leading to narrowing of the trachea.
   b. Croup is most common in children 6-10 years of age.
   c. Croup is most commonly caused by a fungal infection.
   d. Mild cases are treated with supportive care and inhaled corticosteroids.
   e. Antibiotics should generally be given in children presenting with croup in order to prevent severe consequences.

7. A 14 year old male who weighs 132 lbs is diagnosed with a deep vein thrombosis and started on a heparin continuous infusion at 20 units/kg/hour. The heparin concentration in the IV bag is 25,000 units in 250 mL. How many milliliters of heparin should this patient receive each hour?

   a. 12 mL
   b. 22 mL
   c. 32.5 mL
   d. 55 mL
   e. 111.5 mL

8. A father brings his 2 month old daughter to the pharmacy. The girl weighs 14 pounds. The father states she has a rectal temperature of 100.6°F (38.1°C) and wants advice on an over-the-counter medication to treat her fever. The most appropriate recommendation is:

   a. Recommend ibuprofen 5-10 mg/kg/dose every 6-8 hours as needed until her fever subsides.
   b. Recommend putting his daughter in a cold bath to lower her temperature.
   c. Recommend acetaminophen 10-15 mg/kg/dose every 4-6 hours as needed until her fever subsides.
   d. Recommend he seek immediate medical care for his daughter.
   e. Recommend he continue monitoring her and seek medical care only if her temperature rises to 103°F (39.4°C).

9. Which of the following would be an appropriate over-the-counter recommendation for an infant?

   a. Simethicone drops for gas
   b. Dextromethorphan for a dry cough
   c. Bisacodyl suppository for constipation
   d. Fexofenadine (*Allegra Allergy Children's*) for runny nose/sneezing
   e. Loperamide for diarrhea

Answers

1-c, 2-a, 3-d, 4-d, 5-c, e, 6-a, 7-a, 8-d, 9-a

IMMUNIZATIONS

© Tamara Radavanavich

BACKGROUND

Immunizations in the United States over the past century are one of public health's greatest achievements. Since vaccines are medications, pharmacists should review immunization histories with patients. Vaccines prevent patients from acquiring serious or potentially fatal diseases. Many formerly prevalent childhood diseases (diphtheria, measles, meningitis, polio, tetanus) are now rare because many children are vaccinated to prevent the illness, and others are protected by herd immunity (people around them are protected – thus the unvaccinated are less likely to become infected). If immunization rates drop below 85% to 95%, vaccine-preventable diseases may once again become common threats, as recent scattered pertussis outbreaks in the United States demonstrate.

The CDC Advisory Committee on Immunization Practices (ACIP) develops written recommendations for the routine administration of vaccines to children and adults in the civilian population. The Immunization Action Coalition's (IAC) website has useful information for clinicians, such as vaccine records and clinic tools.

GUIDELINES/REFERENCES

Immunization recommendations are written by the CDC Advisory Committee on Immunization Practices (ACIP) and the Committee on Infectious Diseases of the American Academy of Pediatrics (AAP). The pediatric and adult schedules are updated annually and published in January. Updates are published in the Morbidity and Mortality Weekly Report (MMWR).

The CDC's Pink Book, Epidemiology and Prevention of Vaccine Preventable Disease is published every 2 years and is available at www.cdc.gov.

Helpful resources for immunizing pharmacists are available on the following websites:

- American Pharmacists Association www.pharmacist.com/immunization-center (Accessed 2016 Nov 17)
- Centers for Disease Control and Prevention/Vaccines and Immunizations www.cdc.gov/vaccines and www.cdc.gov/travel (Accessed 2016 Nov 17)
- Immunization Action Coalition www.immunize.org (Accessed 2016 Nov 17)

Read through the background information before reviewing the individual vaccines. Immunization has become standard pharmacy practice in many settings, especially in the community pharmacy. Principles of immunization should be well understood.

Safety Concerns

Some parents withhold vaccines due to misconceptions about the risk of autism, a developmental disorder. There is no evidence that vaccines cause autism. Thimerosal, a mercury-containing preservative used in vaccines, was alleged to be a possible cause since mercury has been linked to some brain disorders. Evidence does not suggest that thimerosal poses a risk for or is linked to autism. Thimerosal has been removed from most childhood vaccines. Andrew Wakefield, a one time British researcher, falsified research concluding that MMR caused autism. This led to a decrease in MMR vaccination in the UK and a resurgence in measles in that country and around the world. It is important for pharmacists to provide patients with credible sources of information to counter erroneous information found on the internet and in the media. Promoting vaccination requires open communication and education.

Usually, vaccine adverse effects are minor and include mild fever, soreness or swelling at the injection site. Some vaccines may cause headache, loss of appetite and dizziness – but these quickly dissipate. Very rarely, anaphylaxis can occur. Anyone giving vaccines must screen for previous reactions and be prepared to treat a severe reaction. Some vaccines have specific contraindications to use, such as a true egg allergy with some of the influenza vaccines (this has been modified in recent years; see allergy discussion in this chapter), and with yellow fever and in one brand of the rabies vaccine.

Federal law requires that patients receive the most up-to-date version of the Vaccine Information Statement (VIS) before each vaccine is administered. The VIS standardized forms describe the risk and benefit of the vaccines, purpose of the vaccine, who should receive it and who should not, and what the patient can expect for both mild and serious adverse effects. VISs are created by the CDC and updated versions are available on the CDC and IAC websites.

Gelatin in Vaccines

Gelatin, which is porcine-derived, is used in some vaccines as a stabilizer. For observant Muslims, Jews and Seventh Day Adventists who follow dietary rules that prohibit pork products, most religious leaders permit the use of gelatin-containing vaccines because the gelatin is injected, not ingested, and the end-product has been rendered pure.

Pharmacist's Role in Immunization

Pharmacists in the community setting have increased immunization rates, particularly by providing influenza, meningococcal, pneumococcal, pertussis (in Tdap) and herpes zoster (shingles) vaccinations. The pharmacist's role is expanding to include more vaccines and management of immunization clinics in healthcare settings. Pharmacists have become increasingly involved in pre-travel health services, providing travel advice, medications and immunizations per protocol for international travel. During comprehensive medication therapy management (MTM) sessions and in many inpatient and community pharmacy settings, pharmacists routinely screen and order vaccines under protocols.

PRINCIPLES OF IMMUNITY

Immunity is the ability of the human body to tolerate the presence of material indigenous to the body ("self"), and to recognize and eliminate foreign ("nonself") material. This discriminatory ability provides protection from infectious diseases, since most microbes are identified as foreign by the immune system. Immunity to a microbe is usually indicated by the presence of antibody to that organism. There are two basic mechanisms for acquiring immunity, active and passive.

Active and Passive Immunity

Active immunity is protection that is produced by the person's own immune system. This type of immunity is usually permanent. One way to acquire active immunity is to survive an infection. Another way to produce active immunity is by vaccination. Passive immunity is protection by antibody containing products produced by an animal or human and transferred to a human, usually by injection. Passive immunity is useful when quick protection is required, such as providing rabies immune globulin to a patient who has been bitten by a rabid animal. This will be administered concurrently with the rabies vaccine, which takes time to offer protection. Protection from passive immunity wanes with time, usually within a few weeks or months. Common forms of passive immunity are immune globulin injections and the antibodies an infant receives from the mother shortly before birth. The mother's antibodies provide passive protection from illness while the child is building its own immunity.

Live Attenuated and Inactivated Vaccines

Live attenuated (weakened) vaccines are produced by modifying a disease-producing ("wild") virus or bacterium in a laboratory; they retain the ability to replicate (grow) and produce immunity, but usually do not cause illness. Administering live vaccines to immunocompromised patients may be contraindicated since uncontrolled replication of the pathogen could take place (see other chapters for immunization recommendations in specific populations, such as patients with diabetes, HIV/AIDS, others). Live attenuated vaccines are most similar to the actual disease and produce a strong immune response to the vaccine.

Inactivated vaccines can be composed of either a whole virus or bacterium, or fractions of either. Immunity can diminish with time. As a result, some inactivated vaccines may require supplemental doses to increase, or "boost" immunity.

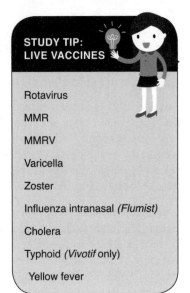

STUDY TIP: LIVE VACCINES

- Rotavirus
- MMR
- MMRV
- Varicella
- Zoster
- Influenza intranasal *(Flumist)*
- Cholera
- Typhoid *(Vivotif* only)
- Yellow fever

Polysaccharide and Conjugate Vaccines

Inactivated vaccines are available in polysaccharide or conjugate formulations or, for some of the vaccines, in both forms (such as pneumococcal and meningococcal vaccines). Because the immune system in infants and young children is not completely developed, polysaccharide vaccines do not consistently produce an effective immune response (via the antibody production) in children under 2 years of age, and the antibodies that are made are less effective. For this reason, polysaccharide vaccines are not given to infants and young children. When the polysaccharide is chemically combined (conjugated) with a protein molecule, the antibody response improves and the vaccine is viable for this patient population. This is why infants and young children receive the pneumococcal conjugate vaccine (*Prevnar 13*) as infants, and may receive the pneumococcal polysaccharide vaccine (*Pneumovax*) when older than 2 years old, if indicated.

TIMING AND SPACING OF VACCINES

Simultaneous Administration

According to ACIP, most common live or inactivated vaccines can be administered simultaneously (on the same day or at the same visit) without decreasing antibody response or increasing the risk of adverse reactions (see Study Tip). Simultaneous administration of all vaccines for which a child is eligible is very important in childhood vaccination; every effort should be made to provide all necessary vaccinations at one visit to improve compliance and increases the probability that a child will be fully immunized at the appropriate age.

Intervals Between Doses for Vaccines Given in Series

Increasing the interval between doses of a multidose vaccine does not diminish the effectiveness of the vaccine after completion of all doses. It may, however, delay more complete protection. Decreasing the interval between doses of a multidose vaccine may interfere with antibody response and protection.

Vaccines and Antibody

Vaccines and antibody products may require a separation period. The presence of circulating antibody to a vaccine antigen may reduce or completely eliminate the immune response to the vaccine. The amount of interference produced by circulating antibody generally depends on the type of vaccine and the amount of antibody administered. Products that contain antibody against vaccine antigens may interfere with live vaccine replication, which is necessary to cause an immune response.

The necessary interval between an antibody-containing blood product and MMR or varicella-containing vaccine (except zoster vaccine – this is not affected by circulating antibody) is a minimum of 3 months and may be up to 11 months. The specific blood product and dose administered determines the time interval. Consult "The Pink Book" to determine the specific recommended interval. During pregnancy, maternal antibodies are passed from the mother to the baby and may reduce the subsequent live vaccine response in the baby. This is why live vaccines are withheld until the child is 12 months. Inactivated vaccines may be started at the age of 2 months, with the exception of hepatitis B vaccine which should be started at birth.

Inactivated antigens are generally not affected by circulating antibody, so they can be administered before, after, or at the same time as the antibody.

Interval for Administration of Live Vaccines and TB Skin Test

The tuberculin skin test (TST) is used to determine if a person is infected with *Mycobacterium tuberculosis*. The test is performed by intradermally injecting 0.1 ml of tuberculin purified protein derivative (PPD) into the inner surface of the forearm. Live vaccines can cause a false negative results, posing a significant risk to the patient and to public health. To reduce interference, administer the live vaccine on the same day as the skin test. If a live vaccine has been given recently (but not on the same day) as the PPD, wait 4 weeks before placing the PPD in order to avoid a false negative TB test result. Alternatively, administer the PPD test first, then wait 48-72 hours and determine the PPD results before administering the live vaccine. The interferon-gamma release assay (IGRA) is a blood test which can also be used to detect TB infection. Live vaccines may theoretically affect IGRA results, therefore live vaccines should be done on the same day or the IGRA drawn before administration of a live vaccine.

VACCINES AND ANTIBODY

- MMR and varicella-containing vaccines (not zoster) require separation from antibody-containing products (e.g., blood transfusions, IVIG)
  - ❑ Vaccine → 2 weeks → antibody-containing product
  - ❑ Antibody-containing product → 3 months or longer → vaccine
- Simultaneous administration of antibody (in the form of immune globulin) and vaccine is recommended for postexposure prophylaxis of certain diseases, such as hepatitis A and B, rabies and tetanus.

STUDY TIP: VACCINE ADMINISTRATION & SPACING

- Vaccines can generally be given at the same time (same visit or same day)*
- Multiple live vaccines must be given on the same day or they must be spaced 4 weeks apart**
- If a vaccine series requires > 1 dose, the intervals between doses can be extended without restarting the series, but cannot be shortened
- Some products are supplied as powder vaccine + diluent; others consist of 2 vaccine components, one powder and one liquid (e.g., *Menveo, Pentacel*)
- Vaccines should not be mixed in the same syringe
- It is not recommended to routinely administer acetaminophen before vaccination to prevent adverse effects. It can be given if symptoms occur

**Exception: Prevnar and Menactra in patients with asplenia should be separated by 4 weeks*

***Exception: no separation required for oral rotavirus vaccines*

VACCINE ADVERSE REACTIONS

Vaccine adverse reactions fall into three general categories: local, systemic, and allergic. Local reactions are generally the least severe and most frequent. Allergic reactions can be the most severe, but are the least frequent.

Local reactions occur commonly (with up to 80% of vaccine doses, depending on the vaccine type) and include pain, swelling and redness at the site of injection. Local reactions are most common with inactivated vaccines, particularly those, such as DTaP, that contain an adjuvant. These reactions generally occur within a few hours of the injection and are usually mild and self-limited. Rarely, local reactions may be very exaggerated or severe.

Systemic adverse reactions are more generalized events and include fever, malaise, myalgias (muscle pain), headache, loss of appetite, and mild manifestations similar to the actual disease being prevented (such as a few chickenpox vesicles after receiving the varicella vaccine). These symptoms are common and may be nonspecific. Systemic adverse reactions following live vaccines are usually mild, and often occur 3 – 21 days after the vaccine was given (i.e., after an incubation period of the vaccine virus). Intranasal LAIV is cold adapted, meaning it can replicate in the cooler temperatures of upper airways (nose and throat) but not in the higher temperatures of the lower airways and the lungs. Mild cold-like symptoms such as a runny nose can occur.

A third type of vaccine adverse reaction is an allergic reaction. The allergic reaction may be caused by the vaccine antigen itself or some other component of the vaccine, such as cell culture material, stabilizer, preservative, or antibiotic used to inhibit bacterial growth. Minor allergic reactions are self-limited and can be treated with diphenhydramine. Minor allergic reactions are not a contraindication to subsequent vaccination. Severe allergic reactions, like anaphylaxis, may be life-threatening if not managed correctly. Fortunately, they are rare, occurring at a rate of less than one in half a million doses. The risk of an allergic reaction can be minimized by good screening prior to vaccination. A severe, anaphylactic allergic reaction following a dose of vaccine is a contraindication to a subsequent dose of that vaccine. Anaphylactic allergies are those that are mediated by IgE, and usually occur within minutes of receiving the vaccine, and require immediate medical attention. Examples of symptoms and signs typical of an anaphylactic reaction can include generalized urticaria (hives), swelling of the mouth and throat, difficulty breathing, wheezing, abdominal cramping, hypotension, or shock. In the event of an anaphylactic reaction, the appropriate emergency protocols should be followed and epinephrine should be immediately accessible. Immunizations should never be administered if epinephrine is not available.

All patients should be monitored for at least 15 minutes after vaccination. Providers should report clinically significant adverse events to the FDA's Vaccine Adverse Event Reporting System (VAERS) even if they are unsure whether a vaccine caused the event.

All providers who administer vaccines must have emergency protocols and supplies to treat anaphylaxis. If symptoms are generalized, a second person should activate the emergency medical system (EMS), by calling 911 and notifying the on-call physician. The primary healthcare provider should remain with the patient, assessing the airway, breathing, circulation, and level of consciousness.

- Administer aqueous epinephrine 1:1,000 (1 mg/mL) dilution intramuscularly, 0.01 mL per kg of body weight per dose, up to a 0.5 mL maximum per dose.
- Most pharmacies use prefilled epinephrine auto-injection devices. At least three adult (0.3 mg) auto-injectors should be available. While patients taking beta blockers may need higher or more frequent doses of epinephrine, emergency guidelines for use of epinephrine do not vary. Most adults will require 1 to 3 doses spaced every 5-15 minutes until paramedics arrive.
- In addition, for systemic anaphylaxis such as generalized urticaria, diphenhydramine may be administered either orally or by injection after the epinephrine has been administered. Due to the risk of choking, no drug should be administered orally if the patient is exhibiting signs of mouth, throat or lip swelling or difficulty breathing.
- Monitor the patient closely until EMS arrives. Perform cardiopulmonary resuscitation (CPR), if necessary, and maintain the airway. Keep the patient in a supine position (flat on back) unless he or she is having breathing difficulty. If breathing is difficult, the patient's head may be elevated, provided blood pressure is adequate to prevent loss of consciousness. If blood pressure is low, elevate legs. Monitor blood pressure and pulse every 5 minutes.

- If EMS has not arrived and symptoms are still present, repeat dose of epinephrine.
- Record all vital signs, medications administered to the patient, including the time, dosage, response, the name of the medical personnel who administered the medication and other relevant clinical information.
- Notify the patient's primary care physician.
- Report reaction to VAERS.
- Immunizing pharmacists should always maintain a current basic life support (BLS or CPR) certification.

CONTRAINDICATIONS AND PRECAUTIONS

Contraindications and precautions to vaccination generally specify circumstances when vaccines should not be given. Most precautions are temporary, and the vaccine can be given at a later time.

A contraindication is a condition that greatly increases a potential vaccine recipient's chance of a serious adverse reaction. It is a condition related to the recipient, not with the vaccine per se. In general, vaccines should not be administered when a contraindicated condition is present. Two important contraindications to vaccination with live vaccines are pregnancy and immunosuppression. A severe, anaphylactic allergic reaction following a dose of vaccine is a contraindication to a subsequent dose of that vaccine. Two conditions are temporary precautions to vaccination: moderate or severe acute illness (all vaccines), and having recently received an antibody-containing blood product (live vaccines only).

INVALID CONTRAINDICATIONS TO VACCINATION

VACCINATIONS MAY BE GIVEN, IF REQUIRED & INDICATED

- Mild acute illness (slight fever, mild diarrhea)
- Antimicrobial treatment (some exceptions: see varicella, zoster and oral typhoid vaccines)
- Previous local skin reaction (mild/moderate)
- Allergies: bird feathers, penicillin, allergies to products not in the vaccine
- Pregnancy, breastfeeding, preterm birth
- Tuberculin skin test (see text for timing and spacing with live vaccines only)
- Immunosuppressed person in the household, recent exposure to the disease, or convalescence
- Family history of adverse events to the vaccine

Altered Immunocompetence

Altered immunocompetence refers to patients who are immunosuppressed (e.g., due to drugs), immunocompromised (decreased immune function due to an underlying condition, such as HIV/AIDS). Altered immunocompetence affects a patient's risk for disease and impacts the vaccines they can receive. Live vaccines may be contraindicated (depending on the condition), due to the potential for uncontrolled replication of the vaccine virus (which can cause disease that can be fatal in some). Inactivated vaccines can be administered, but efficacy may be reduced.

Examples of immunosuppressed patients include those who are receiving most cancer chemotherapy or biologics. Live vaccines can be given after chemotherapy has been discontinued for at least 3 months. Anyone receiving large doses of systemic steroids should not receive live vaccines

STUDY TIP: STEROIDS & IMMUNOSUPPRESSION

- Systemic steroids for 14 days or longer at a daily dose ≥ 2 mg/kg or 20 mg prednisone or prednisone equivalent*
- Systemic steroids only, NOT intra-articular injections, metered-dose inhalers, topical, alternate day or short treatment courses (< 14 days)

**See Systemic Steroids and Autoimmune Diseases chapter for equivalent doses* (see Study Tip). MMR and varicella, both of which are live vaccines, are contraindicated for HIV patients with CD4+ T lymphocyte counts < 200 cells/mm^3. Patients with asplenia are considered to have altered immunocompetence; specific recommendations are discussed in the following section.

VACCINATIONS FOR SPECIFIC CONDITIONS/POPULATIONS

Pregnancy

In general inactivated vaccines may be administered to pregnant women, if indicated (except HPV). Live vaccines should not be administered to women within 1 month before or during pregnancy.

An inactivated influenza vaccine is recommended for all pregnant patients, due to the risk of poor outcomes from influenza infection in pregnancy. Pertussis can be deadly for infants and children. In order to provide protection from pertussis (whooping cough) before the child is old enough to be fully vaccinated, one dose of Tdap is recommended with each pregnancy. The optimal time for Tdap vaccination is between weeks 27 and 36 of the pregnancy. If the woman has not been vaccinated or her vaccination history is unclear, a 3-dose series is needed; one Tdap then two Td doses at 1 – 2 months and 6 months. If the woman delivers and has not received vaccination, she should receive it post-delivery. In addition to the mother, other family members and close caregivers should receive pertussis vaccination.

STUDY TIP: SPECIFIC CONDITIONS

Pregnancy

- Influenza vaccine, inactivated (in season)
- Tdap x1 with each pregnancy*
- Live vaccines are contraindicated during pregnancy

Asplenia

- *H. influenzae* type B (HiB) vaccine
- Pneumococcal vaccines (*Prevnar* and *Pneumovax 23*)
- Meningococcal vaccines (*Menactra*, *Menveo*, or *Menomune* and *Bexsero* or *Trumenba*)

**All who will have close contact with an infant should receive a 1x dose of Tdap (e.g., fathers, grandparents, child-care providers)*

Asplenia

The spleen carries out significant immune functions for certain pathogens. Asplenia refers to conditions where the spleen has been removed (splenectomy) or is severely damaged (e.g., patients with sickle cell disease). Patients with asplenia are at higher risk of infections and are considered to have altered immunocompetence. In addition to routine vaccinations based on age and other comorbidities, additional vaccines are recommended. Live vaccines, when indicated, may be administered to asplenic patients. It is important to assess the patient's vaccination history, particularly adults. Many vaccines that are part of the current childhood vaccination schedule were not available during the childhood of today's adult patients.

Healthcare Professionals

- Hepatitis B: if there is no documented evidence of a complete hepatitis B vaccine series or no serologic evidence of immunity then the healthcare professional should receive the 3 dose series. Some employers require testing for antibody to hepatitis B surface (HBsAb) 1 – 2 months after completion.
- Influenza: receive vaccine annually.
- MMR (measles, mumps, & rubella): if born in 1957 or later and have not had the MMR vaccine or if lacking an up-to-date blood test showing immunity to measles, mumps, and rubella, receive 2 doses of MMR, 4 weeks apart.
- Varicella (chickenpox): if no varicella vaccine received, or without positive serology to varicella, receive 2 doses of varicella vaccine, 4 weeks apart.

- Tdap (tetanus, diphtheria, pertussis): receive a one-time dose of Tdap as soon as possible if no Tdap previously (regardless of when previous dose of Td was received). Get Td boosters every 10 years thereafter.

SCREENING PRIOR TO VACCINE ADMINISTRATION

Use a screening form to rule out specific contraindications and precautions to the vaccine in adults. Note that a "yes" response to some of these questions will indicate a type of vaccine to use, rather than a contraindication to all (e.g., if a person has diabetes and selects "yes" to question #4, they should receive the inactivated influenza vaccine rather than the live influenza vaccine).

1. Are you sick today?
2. Do you have allergies to medications, food, a vaccine component, or latex?
3. Have you ever had a serious reaction after receiving a vaccination?
4. Do you have a long-term health problem with heart disease, lung disease, asthma, kidney disease, metabolic disease (e.g., diabetes), anemia, or other blood disorder?
5. Do you have cancer, leukemia, AIDS, or any other immune system problem?
6. Do you take cortisone, prednisone, other steroids, or anticancer drugs, or have you had radiation treatments?
7. Have you had a seizure or nervous system problem?
8. During the past year, have you received a transfusion of blood or blood products, or been given immune (gamma) globulin or an antiviral drug?
9. For women: Are you pregnant or could you become pregnant during the next month?
10. Have you received any vaccinations in the past 4 weeks?

IMMUNIZATION REGISTRIES

Immunization registries are computerized information systems that collect vaccination histories and help ensure correct and timely immunizations, especially for children. They are useful for healthcare providers, who can use the registries to obtain the patient's history, produce vaccine records, manage vaccine inventories, among other benefits. It helps the community at-large to identify groups who are not receiving vaccines in order to target outreach efforts. Some systems are able to notify parents if vaccines are needed. Where allowed, pharmacists should strive to report all vaccines administrated to their state or local registry.

VACCINES

VACCINE	ADMINISTER TO	STORAGE/ADMINISTRATION
Diphtheria Toxoid-, Tetanus Toxoid- and acellular Pertussis-Containing Vaccines The pediatric formulations (with the upper-case D, as in DTaP) have 3-5 times as much of the diphtheria component than the adult formulation. The adult formulations have a lower case d (Tdap, or Td).		
DTaP: *Daptacel, Infanrix* DTaP-IPV: *Kinrix, Quadracel* DTaP-HepB-IPV: *Pediarix* DTaP-IPV/Hib: *Pentacel*	Children get 5 doses of DTaP at age 2, 4, 6, 12-18 months and 4-6 years, then the Tdap x 1 at age 11-12 years. (see Tdap section). DTaP series given to children younger than 7 years of age.	Store in refrigerator. Do not freeze. Shake the prefilled syringe or vial before use. Give IM.

Vaccines Continued

VACCINE	ADMINISTER TO	STORAGE/ADMINISTRATION

Haemophilus influenzae **type b (Hib)-Containing Vaccines**

Hib: *ActHIB, Hiberix, PedvaxHIB* DTaP-IPV/Hib: *Pentacel* MenCY-Hib: *Menhibrix* (Meningococcal serogroups C and Y, Hib)	Hib: Given to children. Given to adults after splenectomy. *Menhibrix* is only for high risk infants ages 6 weeks-18 months.	Store in refrigerator. Do not freeze. Shake the prefilled syringe or vial before use. Give IM.

Hepatitis-Containing Vaccines

Hepatitis A: *Havrix, Vaqta* **Hepatitis B: *Engerix-B, Recombivax HB*** High-dose (40 mcg/mL) is indicated for dialysis patients. **Hepatitis A and B: *Twinrix*** DTaP-HepB-IPV: *Pediarix*	**Hepatitis A** Children: routine vaccination at age 1 year (2 doses) Adults: men who have sex with men, illicit drug users, chronic liver disease, clotting factor disorders, travelers to countries with high Hep A incidence, or anyone else who asks for it **Hepatitis B** Children: routinely given shortly after birth (3 doses) Adults: healthcare workers; patients with ESRD, chronic liver disease, HIV, diabetes (age 19-59 yrs); IV drug users, men who have sex with men, anyone who has sex with multiple partners, some travelers 3-dose series given at months 0, 1 and 6 (can be completed in 4 months total if necessary) **Hepatitis A and B** 3-dose series given at months 0, 1 and 6	Store in refrigerator. Do not freeze. Shake the vial or prefilled syringe before use. Give IM.

Human Papillomavirus Vaccines: Prevents ~90% of cervical cancers, as well as vulvar, vaginal, oropharyngeal and anal cancers (depends on formulation)

HPV2: *Cervarix* Bivalent vaccine. Provides immunity against the 2 primary HPV strains that cause cancer. For females only. **HPV4: *Gardasil*** Quadrivalent vaccine. Provides immunity against HPV strains responsible for causing certain cancers and genital warts. **HPV9: *Gardasil 9*** (9-valent) Either vaccine recommended for females. Only *Gardasil* 4 or 9 is indicated for males.	**Females age 9-26 years*, ideally before sexual activity** Recommended: age 11-12 years (may be started at age 9) **Males 9-26 years*** Recommended: age 11-21 and up to age 26 in immunocompromised (including HIV) and men who have sex with men Optional: age 22-26 who are not described above **Regimens** Age 9-14 years → <u>2 doses</u> (month 0 and 6-12) Age 15-26 years, or immunocompromised → <u>3 doses</u> (month 0, 1-2, 6) *Start at age 9 years in anyone with history of sexual abuse *Gardasil 9* (9-valent) will replace *Gardasil* (quadrivalent); both will be available initially	Store in refrigerator. Do not freeze. Shake the prefilled syringe or vial before use. Give IM. Caution for fainting (incidence is similar to other vaccines); administer to seated patient and monitor after vaccination.

Influenza Vaccines

Influenza (the flu) is the most common vaccine preventable illness in the U.S. Most illness occurs in children age 2 – 17 years. Complications, hospitalization and death are typically greatest in people < 5 years, ≥ 65 years or those with comorbid conditions. Patients should be informed:

- Everyone 6 months and older should be vaccinated annually – patients at highest risk will get vaccinated first if there is a vaccine shortage; check the CDC vaccination website if a shortage is present.
- Pregnant women are at risk for severe disease and should be vaccinated.
- Individuals can and should be vaccinated for influenza even if it is late in the season.
- The influenza vaccine cannot cause the flu. It can cause a sore arm, or mild systemic reactions that will resolve in 1 to 2 days.
- Chronic diseases are a precaution to receiving the intranasal live-attenuated influenza vaccine (LAIV).

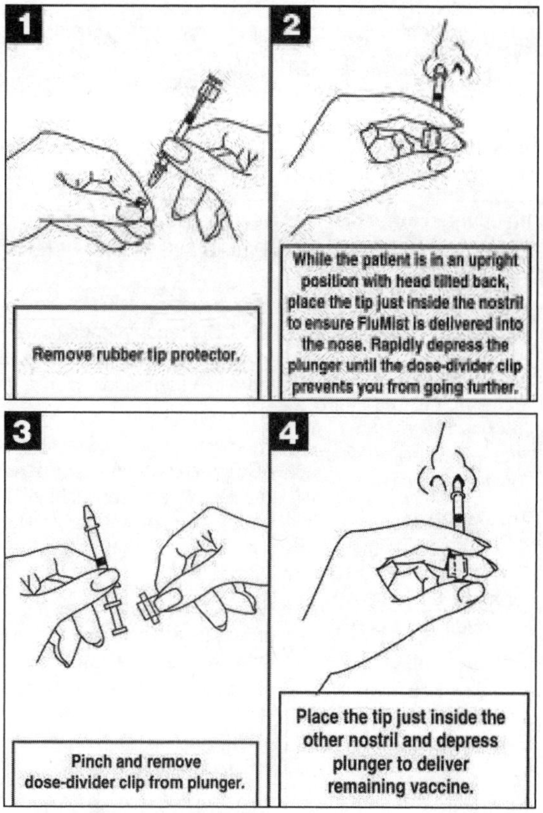
1
Remove rubber tip protector.
2
While the patient is in an upright position with head tilted back, place the tip just inside the nostril to ensure FluMist is delivered into the nose. Rapidly depress the plunger until the dose-divider clip prevents you from going further.
3
Pinch and remove dose-divider clip from plunger.
4
Place the tip just inside the other nostril and depress plunger to deliver remaining vaccine.

Influenza – live nasal vaccine, annually, each fall, if healthy, ages 2-49 years

Influenza A and B are the two types of influenza viruses that cause epidemic human disease. Influenza A viruses are further categorized into subtypes on the basis of two surface antigens: hemagglutinin and neuraminidase. Immunity to the surface antigens, particularly the hemagglutinin, reduces the likelihood of infection and severity of disease if infection occurs. Frequent development of antigenic variants through antigenic drift is the virologic basis for seasonal epidemics and is the reason the influenza vaccine generally changes from year to year. It is given annually. More dramatic antigenic changes, or shifts, occur approximately every 30 years and can result in the emergence of a novel influenza virus with the potential to cause a pandemic.

The virus spreads from person to person, primarily through respiratory droplet transmission. This can happen when an infected person coughs or sneezes in close proximity to an uninfected person. If someone sneezes in their hands and touches something it is possible to spread illness. Influenza illness is characterized by the abrupt onset of these symptoms: fever, myalgia, headache, malaise, nonproductive cough, sore throat, and rhinitis. Among children, otitis media, nausea, and vomiting also are commonly reported with influenza illness.

Uncomplicated influenza illness typically resolves after 3 – 7 days for the majority of persons, although cough and malaise can persist for more than 2 weeks. However, for certain people, influenza can exacerbate underlying medical conditions (e.g., pulmonary or cardiac disease), lead to secondary bacterial pneumonia or primary influenza viral pneumonia (older and immunocompromised), and ultimately hospitalization and death. See the Infectious Diseases III chapter for antiviral medications in influenza.

Vaccines Continued

Influenza Vaccines: Many formulations. Key differences include number of strains (3-trivalent or 4-quadrivalent), inactivated or live-attenuated (LAIV), route of administration (IM, intradermal, intranasal), dose, presence of adjuvant.

VACCINE	ADMINISTER TO	STORAGE/ADMINISTRATION
Inactivated Influenza Vaccine (IIV); given IM Quadrivalent, grown in eggs (IIV4): various ages ***Fluarix, Fluzone,*** *Afluria, Flulaval* Trivalent, grown in eggs (IIV3): various ages *Afluria, Fluarix, Flulaval, Fluvirin, Fluzone* Trivalent, high-dose, grown in eggs (IIV3): approved for age ≥ 65 years *Fluzone High-Dose* Quadrivalent, grown in cell culture (ccIIV4): approved for ≥ 4 years *Flucelvax* **Recombinant Inactivated Vaccine (RIV) egg-free; given IM** Trivalent or quadrivalent: approved for ≥ 18 years *Flublok,* *Flublok Quadrivalent* **Inactivated Influenza Vaccine (IIV4); given intradermally** Quadrivalent, grown in eggs: approved for ages 18-64 years *Fluzone Intradermal* **Adjuvanted Inactivated Influenza Vaccine (aIIV3); given IM** Trivalent, grown in eggs: approved for ages ≥ 65 years ***Fluad*** **Live Attenuated Influenza Virus (LAIV4) given intranasally** Quadrivalent: approved for healthy people ages 2-49 years *FluMist* Live vaccine	Seasonal vaccine recommendations are updated annually and can be found at www.cdc.gov. **Who should get vaccinated?** The CDC recommends that everyone 6 months of age and older get a seasonal flu vaccine each year, unless there is a contraindication. **Which vaccine should be used?** ACIP does not have a preference for any particular flu vaccine, when used within FDA indications (exception: LAIV4 is not recommended for use in 2016-17). **Vaccine timing** Give vaccine as soon as it is available, even if it arrives in late summer and preferably before October. Offer throughout the influenza season; outbreaks usually peak by February, but can be later. **Who needs 2 doses?** Children aged 6 months through 8 years who have never received the vaccine or who have not previously received a total of ≥ 2 doses of influenza vaccine before July 1, 2016 require 2 doses for 2016–17 given 4 weeks apart. **Live-attenuated vaccine** LAIV4 is not recommended for use in the 2016-2017 season. Chronic, non-immunocompromising illnesses are a precaution, not a contraindication to the use of LAIV4, and LAIV4 has specific indications when it can be used: healthy (no underlying medical conditions that predisposes them to influenza complications), in ages 2-49 years. **Trivalent vs. quadrivalent** Trivalent flu vaccines protect against three influenza viruses: two influenza A's (an H1N1 and an H3N2) and one influenza B. The quadrivalent flu vaccines protect against two influenza A's and two influenza B's. **PRECAUTIONS:** 1. Defer if patient has a moderate-severe acute illness. 2. Refer to physician if patient had Guillain-Barré within 6 weeks of a prior dose of flu vaccine. 3. Those who can eat lightly cooked eggs without reactions or if they experience only hives after eating eggs can receive any inactivated vaccine. No additional observation period is recommended (it is recommended to observe all patients for 15 minutes). See "Allergy to Vaccine Components" for details. *Flublok* is completely egg-free (recombinant vaccine).	Store in the refrigerator. Do not freeze. *Fluzone Intradermal* uses smaller needle (30 gauge, 1.5 mm vs 22 to 25 gauge, 15.8-38.1 mm), but causes more redness, swelling, itching. *Afluria*: Note the product is labeled for children > 5 years old, but ACIP recommends giving it after age 9 years or older due to reports of febrile seizure in young children. If vaccine shortage occurs, discuss risks/benefits of using *Afluria* in younger children with parents. Can be given with a needle-free jet injector. *FluMist Quadrivalent* is given as 0.2 mL, divided between the two nostrils; see diagram later in chapter. *Fluad* contains an oil-in-water emulsion of MF59 (an adjuvant), to improve antibody response.

Vaccines Continued

VACCINE	ADMINISTER TO	STORAGE/ADMINISTRATION
Measles, Mumps and Rubella-Containing Vaccines		
MMR: ***M-M-R II*** MMRV: ***ProQuad*** Live vaccine	Given to children and non-immune adults. *ProQuad*: 12 months-12 years. Adults born before 1957 generally are considered immune to measles and mumps. Healthcare providers born before 1957 must prove immunity or receive 2 doses MMR vaccine at least 4 weeks apart.	MMR: Store in refrigerator or freezer. MMRV: Store vaccine in freezer only due to varicella component. Store diluents at room temperature or in refrigerator. Give SC.
Meningococcal Vaccines: Quadrivalent vaccines include meningococcal conjugate vaccine (MCV4), meningococcal polysaccharide vaccine (MPSV4). There are separate vaccines for serogroup B (MenB).		
MCV4 (conjugate vaccines) ***Menactra:*** use in age 9 months-55 years ***Menveo:*** use in age 2 months-55 years MPSV4 (polysaccharide vaccine) ***Menomune:*** use in age ≥ 2 years	Age 2 months and older with high risk: HIV, asplenia/ sickle cell disease, complement component deficiencies. MCV4 *(Menactra or Menveo)* preferred. Age 2-55 years old if at high risk (see above). Also, travelers to certain countries like the meningitis belt in Sub-Saharan Africa, lab workers with *N. meningitidis* exposure Age 11-12 years (1 dose), one booster dose at age 16-18 years People with continued risk of meningococcal disease should be revaccinated every 5 years	Store in refrigerator. MCV give IM, MPSV give SC. *Menveo*– both vials (the powder and the liquid) contain vaccine; use only the supplied liquid for reconstitution. *Menomune* – powder vaccine, sterile water diluent ACWY vaccine is required by Saudi Arabia for travel to the Hajj and Umrah pilgrimages; must have proof of vaccination.
MenB ***Bexsero:*** use in age 10-25 years ***Trumenba:*** use in age 10-25 years	Patients age ≥ 10 years with high risk (see above) or in outbreaks Optional in patients age 16-23 years who are not high risk (if given, preferred at age 16-18) *Bexsero:* 2 doses (month 0 and month 1) *Trumenba:* 2 doses (month 0 and month 6). If high risk of meningococcal disease or during outbreak: 3 doses (months 0, 1-2 and 6)	*Bexsero* or *Trumenba* cover the serogroup B strain and are used in addition to one of the other meningococcal vaccines.

Pneumococcal Vaccines

The bacteria *S. pneumoniae* is also called pneumococcus. It is the most common cause of otitis media, pneumonia, meningitis and bloodstream infections in children. Adults age 65 years and older and those with altered immunocompetence are also at increased risk of pneumococcal disease. As you learn the complex pneumococcal vaccine recommendations, keep in mind the following concepts:

STUDY TIP:
PNEUMOCOCCAL CONJUGATE VACCINE (PCV13)

- PCV13 is currently a routine childhood vaccine. Once it has been given, the patient is considered to be protected; no further doses are recommended, even if a patient later develops a condition for which it would be indicated (e.g., malignancy).
- If receiving for the first time at age ≥ 6, only 1 dose of PCV13 is required for protection.
- If PCV13 and PPSV23 are both required, PCV13 is given first.
- PCV13 was approved in 2010. If a case does not state that the patient received PCV13 previously (particularly in an elderly patient), it cannot be presumed.

- Children age < 2 years receive PCV13 (*Prevnar*) because they do not produce an adequate antibody response to polysaccharide vaccines such as *Pneumovax 23* (PPSV23).
- Adults age 65 years and older, who have had no previous pneumococcal vaccines, receive PCV13, then PPSV23 12 months later. This allows vaccines to be coordinated with annual check-ups.
- Some patients age 2 – 64 years should receive PCV13 ± PPSV23. The recommended vaccine(s) and spacing varies based on patient characteristics. A shorter interval is used between PCV13 and PPSV23 in immunocompromised patients, to provide protection more quickly.

VACCINE	ADMINISTER TO	STORAGE/ ADMINISTRATION
Pneumococcal Vaccines		
13-valent conjugate vaccine (PCV13) ***Prevnar 13*** **23-valent polysaccharide vaccine (PPSV23)** ***Pneumovax 23***	**PCV13** All children < 5 years, some age 6 years and older if risk factors, and all adults > 64 years (1 dose) If received childhood series, no further doses of PCV13 are needed for any indication Minimum age at immunization: 6 weeks **PPSV23** All adults > 64 years and some children and adults age 2-64 years Minimum age at immunization: 2 years	Store in refrigerator. Do not freeze. Shake the vial or prefilled syringe prior to use. **PCV13** Give IM **PPSV23** Give IM or SC

Recommendations below are abridged. For complete recommendations, see table in MMWR Weekly (June 28, 2013/ 62(25);521-524) www.cdc.gov/mmwr/preview/mmwrhtml/mm6225a3.htm. Complete adult recommendations available at: http://www.cdc.gov/vaccines/vpd-vac/pneumo/downloads/adult-vax-clinician-aid.pdf

<table>
<tr><th>WHO SHOULD RECEIVE PCV13 (PREVNAR 13)?</th><th colspan="2">WHO SHOULD RECEIVE PPSV23 (PNEUMOVAX 23)?</th></tr>
<tr><td rowspan="3">All patients age < 5 years (it is part of the routine childhood vaccine series). The series is 4 doses if started as an infant. If not completed on this schedule, check CDC website for catch-up regimens.

If never received, give a 1x dose to:

Patients age 6-18 years with certain conditions: diabetes, heart disease or lung disease (including asthma if treated with high dose oral steroids)

Immunocompromised patients age 6-64 (e.g., sickle cell disease, asplenia, HIV, chronic renal failure, malignancy, transplant, or immunosuppressive drugs, including steroids)

All patients age 65 and older</td><td>Who should receive 1 dose before age 65?</td><td>Immunocompetent patients age 2-64 with diabetes, heart, lung or liver disease, alcohol abuse, and those who smoke</td></tr>
<tr><td>Who should receive 2 doses before age 65?</td><td>Immunocompromised patients age 2-64 (e.g., sickle cell disease, asplenia, HIV, chronic renal failure, malignancy, transplant, or immunosuppressive drug use, including steroids)</td></tr>
<tr><td>Who should receive 1 dose after age 65?</td><td>Everyone
Note: Some patients will receive 3 doses in their lifetime.</td></tr>
</table>

VACCINE SPACING
If both vaccines are indicated, PCV13 is given before PPSV23 (PCV13 → PPSV23)
In immunocompromised patients, PPSV23 is given 8 weeks after PCV13 (PCV13 → 8 weeks → PPSV23)
If PPSV23 is given first, must wait 1 year to give PCV13 (PPSV23 → 1 year → PCV13)
In immunocompetent patients, PPSV23 is given 1 year after PCV13 (PCV13 → 1year → PPSV23)
Doses of PPSV23 should be separated by at least 5 years (PPSV23 → 5 years → PPSV23)

Vaccines Continued

CLINICAL SCENARIOS – CURRENT PNEUMOCOCCAL VACCINE RECOMMENDATIONS

Patient 1: A 50 year old male newly diagnosed with diabetes should receive PPSV23 x1 today → at age 65 → PCV13 → 1 year → PPSV23

Patient 2: A 3 year old female with sickle cell disease who just finished the PCV13 series today should wait 8 weeks then receive PPSV23 → 5 years → PPSV23 → at age 65 → PPSV23

Patient 3: A 43 year old patient newly diagnosed with HIV should receive PCV13 today → 8 weeks → PPSV23 → 5 years → PPSV23 → at age 65 → PPSV23

Patient 4: A 65 year old patient with no past medical history should receive PCV13 today → 1 year → PPSV23

VACCINE	ADMINISTER TO	STORAGE/ ADMINISTRATION
Poliovirus-Containing Vaccines: Inactivated poliovirus vaccines (IPV)		
IPV: *IPOL* DTaP-HepB-IPV: *Pediarix* DTaP-IPV: *Kinrix, Quadracel* DTaP-IPV/Hib: *Pentacel*	Vaccine series to all children.	Store in refrigerator. Do not freeze. Shake the prefilled syringe or vial before use. Give IM or SC.
Rotavirus Vaccines		
RV1: *Rotarix* RV5: ***RotaTeq*** Live vaccines	Oral vaccine series given to all infants. Do not initiate the series after age 15 weeks.	Store in refrigerator. Do not freeze.
Tetanus Toxoid- and Diphtheria Toxoid-Containing Vaccines The pediatric formulations (with the upper-case D, as in DTaP) have 3-5 times as much of the diphtheria component than the adult formulation. The adult formulations have a lower case d (Tdap, or Td).		
DT: **Diphtheria and Tetanus Toxoid** Td: *Tenivac* **Tdap: *Adacel, Boostrix*** See previous table for DTaP series, indicated for children 6 weeks to 6 years of age. See right for children who did not receive the complete DTaP series.	DT is used for primary vaccination series in infants and children < 7 years old who have a contraindication to the acellular pertussis antigen. Tdap: give 1x booster for ages 11 years and up with no previous record of Tdap. Routine booster: in patients age $\geq$ 7 years give Td every 10 years. Wound prophylaxis: if a deep or dirty wound, revaccinate with Td if more than 5 years since the last dose. Tetanus immunoglobulin (TIG) may also be required if no previous tetanus vaccines. Can use Tdap x 1 if never received. Tdap is recommended in: 1) pregnant or postpartum women (see study tip on Special Populations), 2) close contacts of infants younger than age 12 months (e.g., father, grandparents and child-care providers), and 3) healthcare personnel with direct patient contact. Since DTaP is only for children < 7, if a child age 7-10 years does not get fully vaccinated with the DTaP series, a single Tdap dose is given instead of DTaP.	Store in refrigerator. Do not freeze. Shake the prefilled syringe or vial before use. Give IM.

Vaccines Continued

VACCINE	ADMINISTER TO	STORAGE/ ADMINISTRATION
Varicella-Containing Vaccines		
VAR: ***Varivax*** **(chickenpox)** **ZOS:** ***Zostavax*** **(herpes zoster/shingles)** MMRV: *ProQuad* Live vaccines	Children get varicella vaccine at 12-15 months & again at 4-6 years. All without evidence of immunity to varicella should receive 2 doses of varicella vaccine. Varicella vaccines are live vaccines; do not use in pregnancy or if immunocompromised. Herpes zoster vaccine potency is 14 times greater than varicella in order to elicit needed immune response. The FDA indication for zoster vaccine is for adults 50+ years. ACIP recommends use in 60+ years. *Zostavax* is indicated for prevention of shingles and not for treatment of active case. Also reduces complications such as severity of postherpetic neuralgia following infections. Vaccinate even if the patient has a history of zoster infection, since recurrence is possible. Some antivirals (e.g., acyclovir, valacyclovir, famciclovir) can interfere with this live vaccine. Stop 24 hours before vaccine and do not administer for 14 days after vaccination.	Varicella-containing vaccines have 2 components: vaccine & diluent. Store vaccine in freezer. Store diluent in refrigerator or room temp. Do not give if hypersensitivity to gelatin or neomycin. Give SC. Reconstituted; reconstitute immediately upon removal from freezer and inject; short stability. SC injection in adults for vaccines is in the fatty tissue at triceps; see diagram at end of chapter.

NON-ROUTINE VACCINES

DRUG	ADMINISTER TO	STORAGE/ADMINISTRATION
Rabies *Imovax, RabAvert*	May be given preventively if high risk exposure (animal handlers, traveling to high risk area, etc.) or given with rabies exposure. Prevention: 3 vaccine doses Exposure, without previous vaccination: Rabies Ig with vaccine x 1, then 3 more vaccine doses Exposure, with previous vaccination: 2 vaccine doses	Refrigerate. Reconstitute with provided diluent. Give IM.
Typhoid *Vivotif* (capsules) Live vaccine, oral *Typhim Vi* (Injection) Polysaccharide (inactivated)	To prevent Typhoid fever caused by *Salmonella typhi*. See Travelers chapter for disease information. Oral: complete at least 1 week prior to possible exposure. Give every 5 years if continued risk. Infection: give at least 2 weeks prior to jpossible exposure. Give every 2 years if continued risk.	Oral capsules: Store in refrigerator. Injection: store in refrigerator. Do not freeze. Oral: 1 capsule PO on alternate days (day 0, 2, 4 & 6); take on an empty stomach (1 hour before a meal) with cold or lukewarm water. Injection: give IM x1
Japanese Encephalitis *Ixiaro*	May be given if spending 1 month+ in endemic areas during transmission season, especially if travel will include rural areas.	Store in refrigerator. Do not freeze. Give 2 doses IM, 28 days apart. Complete at least 1 week prior to potential exposure. See Travelers chapter for disease information.

Non-Routine Vaccines Continued

DRUG	ADMINISTER TO	STORAGE/ADMINISTRATION
Tuberculosis bacille Calmette-Guerin (BCG) Live vaccine	Not used often in U.S. Given to infants and small children in countries with higher TB incidence. Provides weak protection for pulmonary TB.	Can cause a positive reaction to TB skin test.
Yellow Fever *(YF-VAX)* Live vaccine	Those who travel to or live in areas of risk and in travelers to countries that require vaccination. Contraindicated with a severe (life-threatening) allergy to eggs or gelatin, immunosuppression, age < 6 months, or breastfeeding. Avoid donating blood for 2 weeks after receiving vaccine.	Store in refrigerator. Reconstitute with provided diluent; swirl, do not shake. Give SC. After vaccination, provide International Certificate of Vaccination (yellow card) valid for 10 years, starting 10 days after vaccination. May be required to enter endemic areas.
Cholera ***(Vaxchora)*** Packet for reconstitution Live vaccine, oral	Ages 18-64 who are traveling to an area of active toxigenic *Vibrio cholerae* transmission and have increased risk for exposure or poor clinical outcome if infected. 1x oral dose, ≥ 10 days prior to exposure	Store in the freezer. Remove no more than 15 minutes prior to reconstitution. Dissolve buffer packet in 100 mL of cold or room temperature water, then add active component packet; stir for 30 seconds and drink within 15 minutes.

STORAGE

Store refrigerated vaccines immediately upon arrival. Vaccines are stored in refrigerator and freezer units designed for storing biologics, including vaccines, or in separate, free-standing freezer and refrigerator units. A household-style unit can be used if there is a separate exterior door for the freezer and separate thermostats for the freezer and refrigerator. Dormitory-style refrigerators should not be used. The CDC recommends a calibrated thermometer or a digital data logger connected to a buffered temperature probe in the refrigerator and freezer. A probe can be buffered by immersing it in a vial of liquid (e.g., glycol) that prevents false readings due to the rapid changes in air temperature that occur when refrigerator doors are opened. Maintain a consistent power source. Store vaccines on the shelves away from the walls; never place in the door of the freezer or refrigerator as the temperature there is unstable. Read and document refrigerator and freezer temperatures at least twice each workday: in the morning and before the end of the workday. Keep temperature logs for at least 3 years (or longer, as required by individual states). Rotate stock so vaccine and diluent with the earliest expiration date is used first. Place vaccine with the longest expiration date behind the vaccine that will expire the soonest.

Staff can easily confuse the vaccines within the storage unit. Use labels & separate containers.

Store refrigerated vaccines between 36°F and 46°F (2°C and 8°C). Store frozen vaccines between -58°F and +5°F (-50°C and -15°C); check specific vaccines for freezer temperature requirements, as some vary. Keep vaccines in the original packaging (box) until use, as some vaccines require protection from light.

ADMINISTRATION

In adults, intramuscular (IM) injections are given in the deltoid muscle at the central and thickest portion above the level of the armpit and below the acromion. Emerging evidence suggests providers may be giving IM vaccines too high on the deltoid; make sure to give in the thickest, most central part of the deltoid. Adults require a 1″ needle (or a 1½″ needle for women greater than 200 lbs or men greater than 260 pounds). Use a 22-25 gauge needle inserted at a 90 degree angle. The higher the gauge, the thinner the needle. Subcutaneous (SC) vaccinations are given in the fatty tissue over the triceps with a 5/8″, 23-25 gauge needle at a 45 degree angle.

Administering Vaccines to Adults: Dose, Route, Site, and Needle Size

VACCINE	DOSE	ROUTE
Hepatitis A (HepA)	≤18 yrs: 0.5 mL ≥19 yrs: 1.0 mL	IM
Hepatitis B (HepB)	≤19 yrs: 0.5 mL ≥20 yrs: 1.0 mL	IM
HepA-HepB (Twinrix)	≥18 yrs: 1.0 mL	IM
Human papillomavirus (HPV)	0.5 mL	IM
Influenza, live attenuated (LAIV)	0.2 mL (0.1 mL into each nostril)	NAS (Intranasal spray)
Influenza, inactivated (IIV) **and recombinant** (RIV)	0.5 mL	IM
Influenza (IIV) **Fluzone Intradermal, for ages 18 through 64 years**	0.1 mL	ID (Intradermal)
Measles, Mumps, Rubella (MMR)	0.5 mL	SubCut
Meningococcal conjugate (MenACWY)	0.5 mL	IM
Meningococcal protein (MenB)	0.5 mL	IM
Meningococcal serogroup B (MenB)	0.5 mL	IM
Meningococcal polysaccharide (MPSV)	0.5 mL	SubCut
Pneumococcal conjugate (PCV13)	0.5 mL	IM
Pneumococcal polysaccharide (PPSV)	0.5 mL	IM or SubCut
Tetanus, Diphtheria (Td) **with Pertussis** (Tdap)	0.5 mL	IM
Varicella (VAR)	0.5 mL	SubCut
Zoster (HZV)	0.65 mL	SubCut

Intramuscular (IM) injection

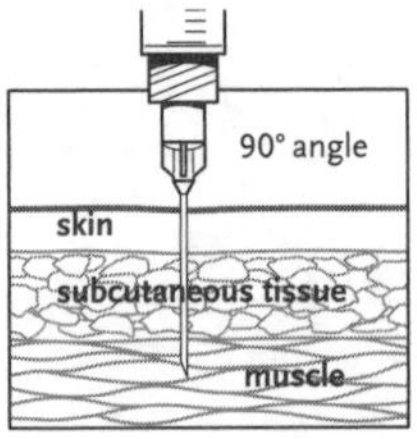

Subcutaneous (SubCut) injection

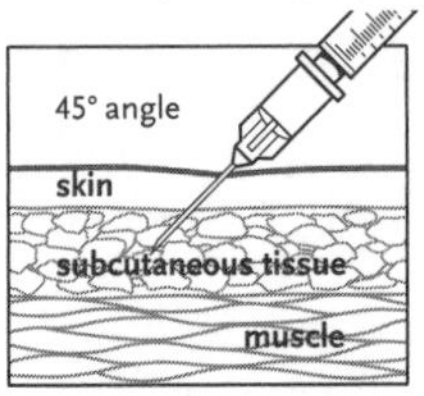

Intradermal (ID) administration of Fluzone ID vaccine

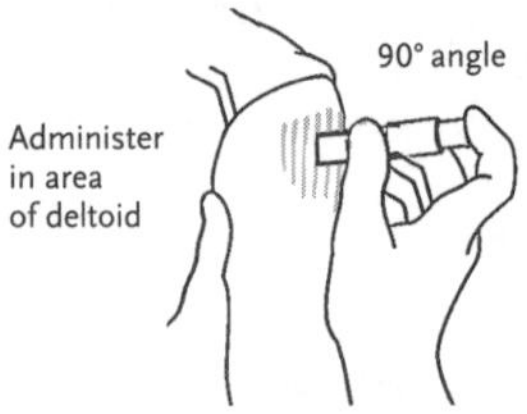

Intranasal (NAS) administration of Flumist (LAIV) vaccine

NOTE: Always refer to the package insert included with each biologic for complete vaccine administration information. CDC's Advisory Committee on Immunization Practices (ACIP) recommendations for the particular vaccine should be reviewed as well. Access the ACIP recommendations at www.immunize.org/acip.

Injection Site and Needle Size

Subcutaneous (SubCut) injection – Use a 23–25 gauge, 5/8" needle. Inject in fatty tissue over triceps.

Intramuscular (IM) injection – Use a 22–25 gauge needle. Inject in deltoid muscle of arm. Choose the needle length as indicated below:

Gender/Weight	Needle Length
Female or male less than 130 lbs	5/8"*–1"
Female or male 130–152 lbs	1"
Female 153–200 lbs	1–1½"
Male 153–260 lbs	1–1½"
Female 200+ lbs	1½"
Male 260+ lbs	1½"

* A 5/8" needle may be used for patients weighing less than 130 lbs (<60 kg) for IM injection in the deltoid muscle **only** if the subcutaneous tissue is not bunched and the injection is made at a 90-degree angle.

http://www.immunize.org/catg.d/p3084.pdf

TRAVELERS

GUIDELINES/REFERENCES

Centers for Disease Control (CDC) Center on Travelers Health. Available at http://wwwnc.cdc.gov/travel (accessed 2016 Oct 10).

International Society of Travel Medicine (ISTM), Pharmacist Professional Group of the ISTM, Available at www.istm.org (accessed 2016 Oct 10).

Riddle MS, DuPont HL, Connor BA. ACG Clinical Guideline: Diagnosis, treatment, and prevention of acute diarrheal infections in adults. *Am J Gastroenterol* 2016; 111:602–622.

We gratefully acknowledge the assistance of Catrina Derderian, BS, PharmD, BCACP, Clinical Pharmacist, Cambridge Health Alliance, in preparing this chapter.

BACKGROUND

In 2014, over 44 million U.S. residents traveled abroad to non-Canadian and non-European destinations. Reasons for travel are diverse and include tourism, business, research, study abroad, and visiting family. Each of these distinct travel purposes predisposes the traveler to certain diseases. Travelers often do not recognize the health risks associated with certain areas of the world and may not seek consultation with an appropriate healthcare professional prior to travel. Pharmacists can provide formal advice to the traveling public, administer travel vaccines, and provide malaria prophylaxis and other medications prior to travel. Consultative services provided by pharmacists can include educational awareness of country-specific risks, and ways to prevent and address them.

Travelers should bring a list of all medical conditions and medications (prescription and OTC). Prescriptions medications should be stored in the original prescription containers. Patients should be advised to pack medications and medical supplies in carry-on luggage. Travel health information, including travel health insurance recommendations, is available on the CDC's travel website where the "Yellow Book" (the CDC's standard resource on travel information) is located. Travel advisories and visa requirements can be checked on the U.S. State Department website. This chapter addresses prevention and treatment of common complications that can be encountered by travelers. See Immunizations chapter for more detailed information on available vaccines.

When preparing a patient for travel, healthcare professionals should routinely consider: 1) diseases spread through food and water, 2) diseases spread through blood and bodily fluids, and 3) diseases transmitted by insects. A traveler's risk for contracting disease should be assessed based upon travel duration, destination-specific risks, itinerary, and patient-specific health concerns.

DISEASES TRANSMITTED THROUGH CONTAMINATED FOOD AND WATER

Contaminated food and water represent a common route for transmission of some travel-related illnesses. Many international travel destinations (especially developing countries) vary in the availability of clean water, plumbing and refrigeration. These factors can lead to unsafe food handling practices and the contamination of food and water with fecal matter, leading to increased risk of illness.

Traveler's Diarrhea

Of the 44 million international travelers from the U.S. in 2014, reports of traveler's diarrhea (TD) ranged from 4 to 17 million. Areas of highest risk include most of Asia, the Middle East, Africa, Mexico, and Central and South America. TD usually presents as the passage of three or more unformed stools per day plus one or more associated symptoms, such as abdominal cramping, nausea or vomiting. Symptoms usually occur within 6 – 72 hours if caused by a bacterial or viral pathogen. More than 80% of TD cases are bacterial and *E. coli* is the primary pathogen.

TD Prevention

Safe food and water habits can reduce, but do not eliminate, risk. The rule "cook it, peel it, or forget it" is helpful when discussing food consumption. These food and water precautions can be recommended:

- Eat only food that is cooked and served hot. Avoid food that has been sitting on a buffet.
- Eat raw fruits and vegetables only if washed in clean water or peeled (e.g., oranges).
- Use bottled water or boil for ~ 1 minute before drinking or using to brush teeth. Avoid ice.
- Eating at well-known restaurants can help reduce risk. Poor hygiene practice in small, local restaurants or food stands can increase risk of contracting TD.
- Keep hands clean and out of the mouth. Wash hands often with soap and water, especially after using the bathroom and before eating. If soap and water are not available, use an alcohol-based hand sanitizer.

Prophylaxis with bismuth subsalicylate (BSS), the active ingredient of *Pepto-Bismol*, can reduce the incidence of TD by 60%. Antibiotic prophylaxis is not routinely recommended, but may be considered in patients who are at high risk of developing TD and are susceptible to health risks if they develop it.

TD Treatment

Hydration (with increased fluid and salt intake) is essential for all TD cases. In an elderly patient with severe diarrhea or in any traveler with prolonged watery (cholera-like) diarrhea or vomiting, oral rehydration solution is preferred for fluid replacement. The packets are available in pharmacies throughout the world. They are easy to prepare: mix 1 packet with 1 liter of boiled purified water.

Medical treatment is not required in patients with non-severe, non-cholera-like diarrhea. OTC anti-diarrheal drugs have been shown to reduce the number of stools passed in cases of diarrhea, allowing travelers to continue their planned itinerary. See Constipation and Diarrhea chapter for more information on the drugs discussed here.

The primary antimotility drug used for treatment of acute diarrhea is loperamide *(Imodium A-D)*. By decreasing the frequency and urgency of bowel movements, loperamide makes it easier for a person with diarrhea to ride on a bus or airplane while waiting for an antibiotic to take effect. The dosage is 4 mg after the first loose stool and 2 mg after each subsequent loose stool up to a maximum dose of 8 mg/day for traveler's diarrhea (it is 16 mg/day for general use). Loperamide may be used for up to 2 days.

BSS is another treatment option. The salicylate portion of BSS has antisecretory, anti-diarrheal properties and it can reduce stools passed by 40%. The Constipation and Diarrhea chapter provides specific information on contraindications and side effects, such as black tongue/stools, risk of Reye's syndrome in pediatric patients and salicylate toxicity.

Compared with BSS, loperamide reduced the number of diarrheal stools passed and has been shown to shorten the duration of acute diarrhea in both children and adults.

TD caused by a bacterial infection can be treated with quinolones, macrolides, or other antibiotics depending on antibiotic resistance patterns. Antibiotics shorten the duration of moderate-to-severe TD to a little over 24 hours. Untreated bacterial diarrhea can last 3 – 7 days. See the Infectious Diseases II chapter.

Typhoid Fever

Typhoid fever is caused by strains of the bacterium *Salmonella typhi*. The disease can be severe and life-threatening. The highest areas of risk for contracting typhoid fever include East and Southeast Asia, Africa, the Caribbean, and Central and South America.

Humans are the only source for this bacteria and disease is spread through food or water contaminated by the feces of someone with either an acute infection or from a chronic, asymptomatic carrier. The incubation period of typhoid fever and paratyphoid fever (a similar illness) is 6 – 30 days. Patients present with fatigue and increasing fever over 3 – 4 days. Headache, malaise and anorexia, along with enlargement of the liver and spleen are common, and transient rash can occur. Intestinal hemorrhage or perforation can occur 2 – 3 weeks later and can be fatal.

Vaccines include *Vivotif,* an oral, live, attenuated vaccine and *Typhim Vi,* an inactivated, intramuscular injection. The oral vaccine should not be used if a patient is on antibiotics or has an extremely sensitive stomach. The regimen should be completed 1 week prior to travel and is not used in children < 6 years. Revaccination is recommended every 5 years *Vivotif* and every 2 years for *Typhim Vi* in patients who remain at risk. The intramuscular vaccine must be given ≥ 2 weeks before the expected exposure. The injectable vaccination is not recommended for children < 2 years.

Typhoid vaccines are recommended but are only 50 – 80% effective; therefore, even vaccinated travelers should follow safe food and water precautions and wash hands frequently. These precautions are the only prevention method for paratyphoid fever, for which there is no vaccine.

Cholera

Cholera is a bacterial infection caused by *Vibrio cholerae.* Although very rare in the U.S., the disease still occurs in many places including Africa, Southeast Asia, and Haiti. The infection is often mild or asymptomatic, but it can be severe and life threatening, with profuse diarrhea and vomiting, and eventual dehydration. The most common symptom includes watery diarrhea, which is referred to as "rice-water stools."

In addition to food and water precautions, a vaccine (approved in 2016) is available for cholera prevention. The cholera vaccine *(Vaxchora)* is a live, attenuated vaccine administered as a single, oral liquid dose at least 10 days before travel to a cholera-affected region. It is approved for use in adults age 18 through 64 years.

Hepatitis A

Hepatitis A is one of the most common vaccine-preventable infections among international travelers. Persons from developed countries who travel to developing countries are at highest risk. The infected patient may be asymptomatic or can have symptoms that include fever, malaise, jaundice, nausea and abdominal discomfort that can last for up to 7 weeks. Vaccination should be considered for travelers to most parts of the world, except Canada, western Europe and Scandinavia, Japan, New Zealand, and Australia.

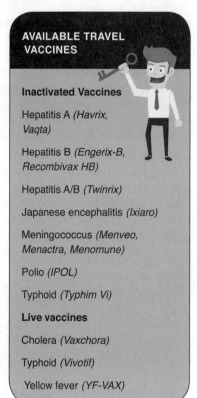

AVAILABLE TRAVEL VACCINES

Inactivated Vaccines

Hepatitis A *(Havrix, Vaqta)*

Hepatitis B *(Engerix-B, Recombivax HB)*

Hepatitis A/B *(Twinrix)*

Japanese encephalitis *(Ixiaro)*

Meningococcus *(Menveo, Menactra, Menomune)*

Polio *(IPOL)*

Typhoid *(Typhim Vi)*

Live vaccines

Cholera *(Vaxchora)*

Typhoid *(Vivotif)*

Yellow fever *(YF-VAX)*

DISEASES TRANSMITTED THROUGH BLOOD AND BODILY FLUIDS

Hepatitis B

Hepatitis B is transmitted through contact with contaminated blood or other body fluids. The risk for travelers who do not participate in high risk behaviors is low. Hepatitis B has an incubation period of about 90 days. Infection may present as malaise, jaundice, nausea and abdominal discomfort. Chronic infection with Hepatitis B can result in chronic liver disease and liver cancer.

Hepatitis B vaccination is extremely important for travelers who plan to have sexual encounters with new partners, are traveling to receive medical care, or who are volunteering to provide medical work. Piercings and tattoos can also transmit the virus and should be avoided. The 3-dose vaccine series takes 6 months to complete. If a traveler is unable to receive all three doses before departure, administer as many doses as possible before departure and complete the series upon return. In instances of high risk, an accelerated series may be administered.

Meningococcal Meningitis

Bacterial meningitis involving *N. menigitidis* has a high mortality rate and is a medical emergency. Patients with symptoms of fever, severe and unrelenting headache, nausea, stiff neck and mental status changes require urgent treatment to avoid the risk of permanent neurological damage and death.

Meningitis is spread by respiratory secretions and is widespread in many parts of the world. Vaccination is recommended by the CDC for people who travel to or reside in countries where *N. meningitidis* is hyperendemic or epidemic, particularly if contact with the local population will be prolonged. Hyperendemic regions include the meningitis belt of Africa during the dry season (December – June). Additionally, the meningococcal vaccine is required by the government of Saudi Arabia for travel during the period of the annual Hajj and Umrah pilgrimages. Current recommendations include only the quadrivalent vaccine (containing four bacterial types: ACWY). There are no recommendations to use either serogroup B meningococcal vaccine for travelers.

Polio

Most people in the U.S. received the polio vaccine in childhood; unfortunately, the virus has not been eradicated worldwide. Many countries remain endemic and have had active spread of poliovirus in the recent past. These include Afghanistan, Burma (Myanmar), Guinea, Laos, Nigeria, Madagascar, Pakistan and Ukraine. For adults spending $\geq$ 4 weeks in regions with wild poliovirus, the CDC recommends receive a single lifetime booster dose at least 4 weeks prior to travel. As of May 2015, travelers to polio-infected countries may be required to show proof of polio vaccination when leaving a polio-infected country. Vaccination should be documented on an International Certificate of Vaccination or Prophylaxis (ICVP), which is commonly used for Yellow Fever vaccine.

DISEASES TRANSMITTED BY INSECT BITES

Insects that transmit disease are vectors; a vector carries an organism to an individual, causing infection. A reservoir is any place (such as an animal, insect, soil or plant) in which the disease lives and can multiply. The primary insects that transmit infections to travelers are mosquitos, which transmit Japanese encephalitis, yellow fever, dengue, malaria and Zika virus. Insect bites should be avoided as much as possible, using the following strategies:

- Stay and sleep in screened or air-conditioned rooms and use a bed net, which can be pre-treated with mosquito repellent.
- Cover exposed skin by wearing long-sleeved shirts, long pants and hats.
- Use proper application of mosquito repellents containing 20% to 50% DEET as the active ingredient on exposed skin. DEET also provides protection against ticks. Other insect repellents that can be used topically for mosquitos (but not for ticks) are picaridin, oil of lemon, eucalyptus or IR3535.
- Use permethrin to treat clothing, gear and bed nets but do not apply directly to the skin.

Dengue

Dengue is transmitted between people by the *Aedes aegypti* and *Aedes albopictus* mosquitoes. In many parts of the tropics and subtropics, dengue is endemic; it occurs every year, usually during a season when mosquito populations are high and rainfall is optimal for breeding. Sequential infections put people at greater risk for dengue hemorrhagic fever and dengue shock syndrome, both of which can be fatal. No vaccine is available and treatment is supportive, as there are no specific medications to treat dengue infection. Protection from mosquito bites is essential.

Malaria

About 1,500 cases of malaria are diagnosed in the U.S. annually, mostly in returned travelers. Malaria is transmitted by the *Anopheles* mosquito. It is endemic in Asia, Latin America, North Africa, Eastern Europe and the South Pacific. *Plasmodium vivax* is the most common of four human malaria species (*P. falciparum, P. malariae, P. ovale,* and *P. vivax*). *P. vivax* causes 50% of malaria cases in India and is becoming increasingly resistant to malaria drugs. By contrast, *P. falciparum* is the most deadly species and the subject of most malaria-related research. The CDC website features maps of malaria presence by country, the species of malaria, and resistance patterns. All of this information is incorporated into the CDC's region-specific prophylaxis medication recommendations. Recommendations may change year-to-year.

Drugs for Malaria Prophylaxis

DRUG	DOSING	SAFETY/SIDE EFFECTS/MONITORING
Atovaquone/Proguanil *(Malarone)* Advantages: Well tolerated Start right before travel Short treatment Disadvantages: Daily dosing Not used in pregnancy High cost	250/100 mg PO daily with food or milk Start: 1-2 days pre-travel Stop: 7 days post-travel	**CONTRAINDICATIONS** Do not use for prophylaxis with CrCl < 30 mL/min **SIDE EFFECTS** Abdominal pain, N/V, headache, ↑ LFTs **NOTES** Consider monitoring LFTs and renal function Per CDC, not recommended in pregnancy
Primaquine Advantages: Start right before travel—once G6PD deficiency ruled out Short treatment Disadvantages: Daily dosing Not used in pregnancy	30 mg PO daily Take with food to ↓ nausea CDC requires screening for G6PD deficiency prior to use Start: 1 day pre-travel Stop: 7 days post-travel	**CONTRAINDICATIONS** Severe G6PD deficiency, concurrent drugs that can cause hemolytic anemia or bone marrow suppression/agranulocytosis, current or recent use of quinacrine, acute illness **WARNINGS** Hemolytic anemia, other hematologic effects, arrhythmias/QT prolongation **SIDE EFFECTS** N/V **NOTES** Per CDC, not recommended in pregnancy

Malaria Drugs Continued

DRUG	DOSING	SAFETY/SIDE EFFECTS/MONITORING
Mefloquine *(Lariam)* Advantages: Once weekly dosing (more convenient for long trips) Used in pregnancy Disadvantages: Start 2-3 weeks prior to travel Long treatment (for short trip) Side effects	250 mg PO weekly with food and water Start: 2-3 weeks pre-travel Stop: 4 weeks post-travel	**BOXED WARNING** Do not use in patients with neuropsychiatric disorders; discontinue if symptoms occur during treatment **WARNINGS** Arrhythmias, QT prolongation, agranulocytosis/aplastic anemia, caution with liver impairment **CONTRAINDICATIONS** Seizure history, psychiatric disorders **SIDE EFFECTS** Chills, dizziness, fatigue, nausea **MONITORING** Psychiatric symptoms: anxiety, depression, hallucinations Neurologic symptoms: dizziness, tinnitus, loss of balance, seizures
Chloroquine *(Aralen)* Advantages: Once weekly dosing (more convenient for long trips) Some may already take for rheumatoid arthritis Used in pregnancy Disadvantages: Start 1-2 weeks prior to travel Long treatment (for short trip)	500 mg PO weekly with food CrCl < 10 mL/min: 50% dose Start: 1-2 weeks pre-travel Stop: 4 weeks post-travel	**CONTRAINDICATIONS** Retinal or visual field changes **WARNINGS** Retinal toxicity Arrhythmias, QT prolongation Skeletal muscle myopathy/weakness, extrapyramidal effects, hematologic effects (agranulocytosis, others) **SIDE EFFECTS** Nausea, exacerbation of psoriasis, anxiety, visual changes/damage, hearing loss/tinnitus, alopecia, blue-gray skin pigmentation, serious skin reactions (SJS/TEN/DRESS) **MONITORING** CBC and neuromuscular function with long-term use, ophthalmologic exam at baseline **NOTES** Avoid use with hypersensitivity to quinine compounds, G6PD deficiency (risk hemolytic anemia, bleeding) Chloroquine-resistance is common in some regions
Doxycycline *(Vibramycin)* Advantages: Start right before travel Inexpensive for long trips Some may already take for acne Disadvantages: Long treatment (for short trip) Side effects (GI, photosensitivity) Not used in pregnancy	100 mg daily for prophylaxis Take with food to ↓ nausea Start: 1-2 days pre-travel Stop: 4 weeks post-travel	**WARNINGS** Use in pregnancy, children < 8 years can affect tooth development and cause permanent discoloration **SIDE EFFECTS** Nausea, photosensitivity Use alternate agent in children < 8 years old See Infectious Diseases I chapter for further information

Japanese Encephalitis

The Japanese Encephalitis (JE) virus is transmitted by mosquitos. Infection can be asymptomatic, or can develop into encephalitis, with rigors and risk of seizures, coma and death. Travelers are most likely to become infected when visiting rural agricultural areas. The best prevention is to reduce exposure to mosquitos. The JE vaccination is sometimes recommended with travel to Asia and parts of the western Pacific. The vaccine (*Ixiaro*) is recommended for travelers older than 2 months of age who plan to spend at least 1 month in endemic areas during the JE virus transmission season or for those with extended exposure to the outdoors (e.g., campers).

Yellow Fever

Yellow fever is caused by a virus found in tropical and subtropical areas in South America and Africa. Reducing mosquito exposure is essential. Most infections are asymptomatic. If symptoms develop, the initial illness presents with influenza-like symptoms. Most patients will improve, but ~15% progress to a more toxic form of the disease with risk of shock and organ failure. There is no specific treatment for acute infection except symptomatic relief with fluids, analgesics and antipyretics. Aspirin and other NSAIDs cannot be used due to increased risk for bleeding.

A vaccine is available for prevention of yellow fever transmission. In 2015, the CDC Advisory Committee on Immunization Practices (ACIP) approved a new recommendation that a single dose of yellow fever vaccine provides life-long protection and is adequate for most travelers. Healthcare providers should review the entry requirements for destination countries, as some countries continue to require a booster vaccine dose every 10 years (as previous guidelines recommended).

Vaccination is recommended only in travelers who are at a high risk of exposure or who require proof of vaccination to enter a country. This is due to the high risk of serious adverse effects after vaccination, including low grade fever, headache, and in rare cases, yellow fever vaccine-associated neurologic disease. After vaccination, the patient is provided an "International Certificate of Vaccination or Prophylaxis" (ICVP), which is sometimes called the "yellow card." The card is valid only if the vaccination is completed 10 days before arrival. The vaccine is live and is contraindicated patients with hypersensitivity to eggs.

Zika Virus

The Zika virus is transmitted primarily by the *Aedes* species mosquito. Sexual and possible blood transfusion-associated transmission have been reported. Most Zika virus infections are asymptomatic. Symptomatic infections are generally mild with symptoms consisting of fever, maculopapular rash, arthralgia (joint pain), and conjunctivitis (red eyes).

The most pressing concern with Zika virus arose in 2015 when Brazil observed a marked increase in the number of infants born with microcephaly, a birth defect that can cause significant disability and can be life-threatening in severe cases. Zika virus RNA was subsequently identified in tissues from infants with microcephaly and from fetal losses in women who were infected during pregnancy. Zika infection during pregnancy can cause birth defects of the brain, eye, hearing deficits, and impaired growth. Reports of Guillain-Barré syndrome, an uncommon sickness of the nervous system, have also increased in areas affected by Zika.

No vaccine is available at this time for the Zika virus. Avoiding mosquito bites and using condoms during sexual contact with people with possible Zika virus infection may reduce transmission risk.

The CDC recommends against pregnant women traveling to any area with ongoing local transmission of Zika virus. Women who are trying to become pregnant should consult with their healthcare provider prior to travel. Men who have a pregnant partner and have traveled to an area with Zika should use condoms or should avoid sex during the pregnancy. These recommendations may change as more data about the Zika virus during the periconceptional period become available.

ADDITIONAL CONCERNS FOR TRAVELING INDIVIDUALS

Venous Thromboembolism Prevention

Travelers are at increased risk for deep vein thrombosis (DVT) and pulmonary embolism (PE) due to limited movement with intercontinental air travel. Wearing compression stockings during long trips reduces risk; these are sold in pharmacies. Travelers should be instructed to get up and walk (choosing an aisle seat is helpful) and to perform lower leg exercises when sitting. Patients should know the symptoms of a DVT and PE and be instructed to seek immediate medical care if suspected. DVT risk factors, symptoms and treatment are discussed in the Anticoagulation chapter.

Motion Sickness, Altitude Sickness and Jet Lag

Motion sickness is common among travelers and is discussed in the Motion Sickness chapter. Acute mountain sickness (AMS) occurs when people climb rapidly to a high altitude. It occurs commonly above 8,000 feet and is more likely in individuals who live close to sea level and those who have had the condition previously. Primary symptoms are dizziness, headache, tachycardia and shortness of breath. The primary prophylactic medication is acetazolamide *(Diamox)* 125 mg twice daily, started the day before (preferred) or on the day of ascent. Higher doses are used for treatment. This can improve breathing, but is not without side effects (polyuria, taste alteration, risk of dehydration, photosensitivity, urticaria and a possibility of severe skin rashes). Acetazolamide is contraindicated with a sulfa allergy. Sun protection and hydration are recommended. In acute cases of altitude sickness, oxygen, inhaled beta-agonists and dexamethasone are given to reduce cerebral edema.

For treatment of jet lag, see the Dietary Supplements, Natural & Complementary Medicine chapter.

THE RETURNED TRAVELER

It is imperative that travelers who are ill upon returning home see a healthcare provider. It is important for patients to communicate travel specifics to the healthcare provider, including the travel itinerary, the trip duration, accommodations (where they stayed), travel activities and any precautions that were taken to reduce infection risk, including vaccination history prior to leaving the U.S.

Some diseases have longer incubations periods and symptoms may not appear for weeks or months. Travelers often return home before their symptoms begin. This can lead to epidemics and the spread of disease from country to country. An example of this is the 2014 outbreak of Ebola virus in West Africa, the largest Ebola outbreak in history. Ebola is transmitted by direct contact with blood or bodily fluids of a symptomatic person. Symptoms (fever, headache, diarrhea, and hemorrhaging) can appear from 2 – 21 days after exposure. Due to the potentially long incubation, an infected person could be asymptomatic when returning to the U.S. and could spread the disease before a diagnosis is made. Isolation upon return can reduce transmission.

Another example of this is illustrated by the more recent Zika outbreak, discussed previously in this chapter. In 2015, the Zika virus was identified for the first time in the Western hemisphere with large outbreaks reported in Brazil. Since then, the virus spread throughout much of the Americas and is still a concern for travelers, especially for those who are pregnant or are planning pregnancy in the near future.

RENAL DISEASE

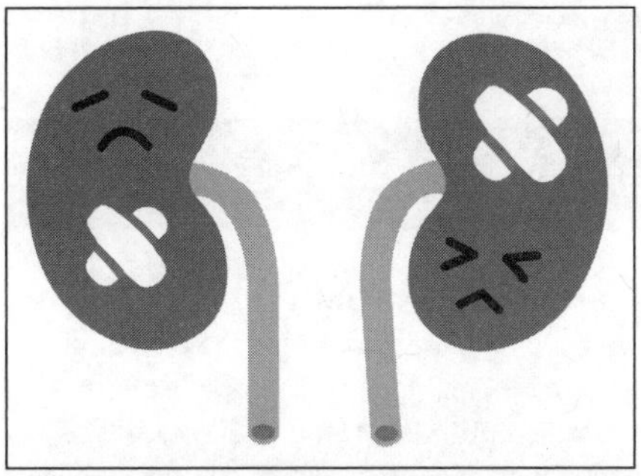

GUIDELINES/REFERENCES

Kidney Disease: Improving Global Outcomes (KDIGO) CKD Work Group. KDIGO 2012 Clinical Practice Guideline for the Evaluation and Management of Chronic Kidney Disease. *Kidney Inter.*, Suppl. 2013;3:1-150.

Additional guidelines included with the video files (RxPrep Online).

BACKGROUND

More than 20 million adults have chronic kidney disease (CKD). American Indians, Asians, African-Americans and Hispanics are at highest risk for developing CKD. The most common causes of CKD are diabetes and hypertension. Controlling blood glucose and blood pressure can prevent or reduce further renal damage. There are other less common causes of CKD, including polycystic kidney disease, some types of infections, renal artery stenosis (a blocked artery that prevents blood flow to the kidney), and drug-induced kidney disease (DIKD, occurring with the use of nephrotoxic medications).

One in two adults ages 30 – 64 will develop some degree of CKD. Although the majority will not reach end-stage renal disease, the need for medication dosage adjustments is common. Pharmacists are involved in ensuring safe and effective medication dosing based on kidney function and in treatment of related disorders caused by renal impairment. These include anemia, bone and mineral metabolism disorder (management of parathyroid hormone, phosphate, calcium and vitamin D levels), hypertension, and acid-base and electrolyte disturbances.

RENAL PHYSIOLOGY

The nephron is the functional unit of the kidney and there are roughly one million nephrons in each kidney. A primary function of the nephron is to control the concentration of water and sodium. The nephrons reabsorb what is needed (to go back into the circulation) and the remainder is excreted as urine. This regulates the blood volume, and in turn, the blood pressure. The parts of the nephron include Bowman's capsule, the glomerulus, the proximal tubule, the loop of Henle, the distal convoluted tubule and the collecting duct (see figure on the following page).

Glomerulus

Blood is delivered into the glomerulus, a large filtering unit that is located within Bowman's capsule. Substances with a molecular weight < 40,000 daltons, including most drugs, can pass through the glomerular capillaries into the filtrate and are excreted in the urine. If the glomerulus is healthy, larger substances (e.g., proteins and protein-bound drugs) are not filtered and stay in the blood. If the glomerulus is damaged, some albumin passes into the urine. The amount of albumin in the urine is used along with the glomerular filtration rate (GFR) to assess the severity of kidney damage in patients with kidney disease (also called nephropathy).

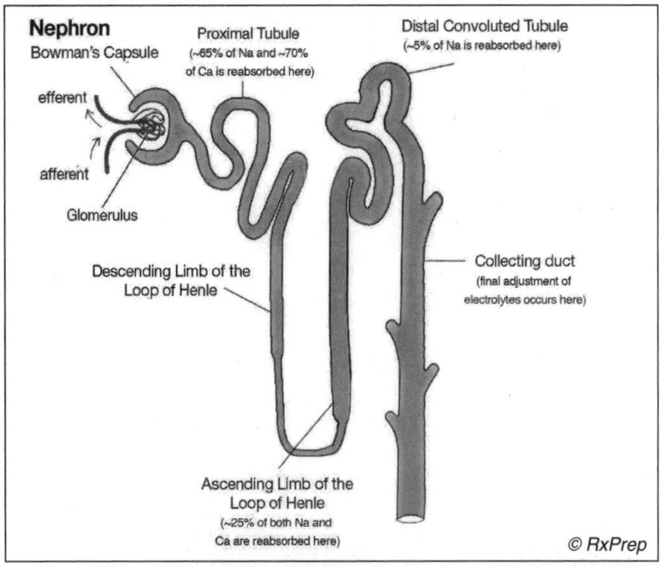

Proximal Tubule

Proximal means "close to", and the proximal tubule is the part of the nephron closest to Bowman's capsule (the entry point into the nephron). Much of the sodium (Na), chloride (Cl), calcium (Ca) and water that are initially filtered out are reabsorbed into the bloodstream here. The pH is regulated by the exchange of hydrogen ions and bicarbonate ions. Water, Na and Cl reabsorption continues further along the nephron.

Loop of Henle

As filtrate moves down the loop of Henle (the descending limb), water is reabsorbed into the blood, but Na and Cl ions are not; this increases the concentration of Na and Cl in the lumen (the inside of the nephron "tube"). As the filtrate moves up the loop of Henle (the ascending limb), Na and Cl ions are reabsorbed back into the blood, but water is not. If antidiuretic hormone (ADH, also called vasopressin) is present, water will pass through the walls of the duct and will not be eliminated. When ADH increases, more water is reabsorbed back into the blood (anti-diuresis).

Normally, about 25% of sodium is reabsorbed into the blood in the ascending loop of Henle. Loop diuretics inhibit the Na-K pump in the ascending limb of the loop of Henle, which leads to a significant increase in the tubular concentration of Na, and less water is reabsorbed (more is excreted as urine). By blocking the pump, loop diuretics cause decreased Ca reabsorption, leading to Ca depletion. Long-term use has a harmful effect on bone density.

DEFINITIONS

Acute Kidney Injury (AKI)
A sudden, temporary loss of kidney function due to another condition. Damage is often reversible, but AKI can lead to a total loss of kidney function if the precipitating condition is not corrected.

Chronic Kidney Disease (CKD)
A progressive loss of kidney function over months or years. The degree of kidney function is measured by the GFR (or the CrCl) and how much albumin is present in the urine.

End-Stage Renal Disease (ESRD)
Total and permanent kidney failure. Fluid is retained and waste accumulates. Dialysis (or transplant) is required to take over the functions of the kidneys.

Distal Convoluted Tubule

Distal means "farther away" and the distal convoluted tubule is the farthest away from the entry point to the nephron. The distal tubule is also involved in regulating K, Na, Ca and pH. Thiazide diuretics inhibit the Na-Cl pump in the distal tubule. Only about 5% of sodium is reabsorbed at this point, which makes thiazides weaker diuretics than loops. Thiazides increase Ca reabsorption by affecting the Ca pump in the distal convoluted tubule. Consequently, the long-term use of thiazide diuretics has a protective effect on bone.

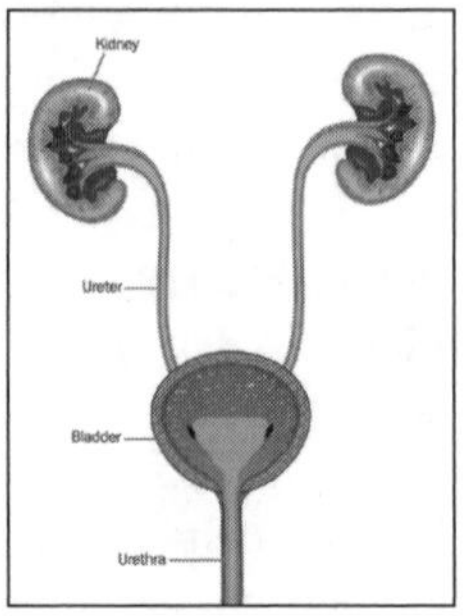

Collecting Duct

The collecting duct is a network of tubules and ducts that connect the nephrons in each kidney to a ureter. Urine passes from the ureters into the bladder, and from there out of the body via the urethra (see figure). The collecting duct is involved with water and electrolyte balance and is affected by levels of ADH and aldosterone. Aldosterone works in the distal tubule and collecting duct to increase Na and water retention and decrease K. By blocking aldosterone (with antagonists like spironolactone or eplerenone), serum K increases.

DRUG-INDUCED KIDNEY DISEASE

Drug-induced kidney disease (DIKD) is linked to numerous medications; it may be acute and reversible if the medication is stopped, but DIKD can be irreversible and progress to CKD. DIKD is especially common in the hospital setting and contributes to morbidity and mortality. Risk factors for DIKD include underlying reduction in renal blood flow (e.g., due to preexisting kidney disease, chronic or acute heart failure, dehydration, or hypotension), increased age, use of multiple nephrotoxic medications, large doses or frequent use of nephrotoxic medications, and others. Recently, warnings were strengthened about the risk of acute kidney injury with the SGLT2 inhibitors (such as canagliflozin and dapagliflozin), which are used to treat diabetes.

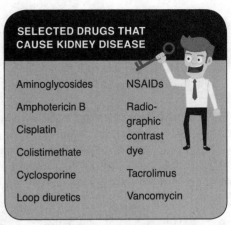

SELECTED DRUGS THAT CAUSE KIDNEY DISEASE

Aminoglycosides	NSAIDs
Amphotericin B	Radiographic contrast dye
Cisplatin	
Colistimethate	
Cyclosporine	Tacrolimus
Loop diuretics	Vancomycin

ESTIMATING KIDNEY FUNCTION

Two common laboratory markers used to estimate kidney function are blood urea nitrogen (BUN) and serum creatinine (SCr). BUN measures the amount of nitrogen that comes from urea, a waste product of protein metabolism. As kidney function declines, BUN increases. BUN is not used alone to estimate kidney function because other factors besides renal impairment can increase BUN (primarily dehydration).

Creatinine, a waste product of muscle metabolism, is mostly filtered by the kidneys and is easily measured. The concentration correlates inversely with kidney function; as kidney function decreases, creatinine increases (similar to BUN). The normal range of serum creatinine (SCr) is approximately 0.6 to 1.3 mg/dL.

While other compounds, such as inulin, can provide a more accurate estimate of the GFR, their use in the clinical setting is not practical.

STUDY TIP: CrCl vs. GFR

CrCl

- Cockcroft-Gault equation

$$CrCl = \frac{140 - (\text{patient age})}{72 \times SCr} \times \text{weight in kg } (\times 0.85 \text{ if female})$$

- For CrCl calculation, use actual body weight if patient is < IBW, use IBW if normal weight (by BMI)*
- Dosing adjustments and contraindications are generally based on CrCl calculated with Cockcroft-Gault

GFR

- CKD-EPI or MDRD equation
- Used for staging kidney disease and for dosing select drugs
- Not commonly calculated in the clinical setting, but may be reported by some laboratories
- For the exam, if GFR is not provided, CrCl provides a close estimate for dosing and contraindications purposes

*See Calculations II chapter for more information on CrCl

Creatinine Clearance

The Cockcroft-Gault equation for calculating creatinine clearance (CrCl) is the most commonly used equation to estimate kidney function for medication dosing. The accuracy of creatinine-based estimation equations is decreased when a patient has very low muscle mass, which is often the case in frail elderly patients (little muscle mass = low SCr). This can lead to overestimation of CrCl and inappropriate drug dosing for the patient's true kidney function.

The presence of obesity, liver disease, pregnancy, high muscle mass or other conditions that cause abnormal muscle turnover can also affect the accuracy of kidney function measured using SCr.

In addition, although creatinine is mostly filtered, it is partially secreted. The contribution of tubular secretion increases with reduced renal function. The Cockcroft-Gault formula may not be preferable in very young children, in end-stage renal disease (ESRD) or in unstable renal function. Drug dosing recommendations are generally based on CrCl (calculated with Cockcroft-Gault). Exception: a few medication package inserts, including the SGLT2 inhibitors and metformin, use GFR for dosing purposes.

GFR and Albuminuria for Staging Kidney Disease

While the Cockroft-Gault equation is used to calculate CrCl, GFR is calculated using other equations, including the Modification of Diet in Renal Disease (MDRD) and Chronic Kidney Disease Epidemiololgy Collaboration (CKD-EPI). Although it is not the only protein present in the urine, albumin is the primary protein that is measured to assess kidney disease and proteinuria is often used to refer to albuminuria.

The guidelines recommend using both the GFR and degree of albuminuria (level of albumin present in the urine), along with the cause of CKD, to determine the degree/stage of renal impairment in order to make treatment decisions. The goal of these two tables is not to memorize the values, but to understand how the GFR and degree of albuminuria are used to stage the severity of kidney disease.

In the first table, the GFR value in the 1st column is used to determine the severity of renal impairment. The two guidelines (KDIGO and KDOQI) have different names for each category/stage. The degree of albuminuria is classified according to the second table. The 1st and 2nd columns are both measurements of albumin (in different units) and the 3rd column contains an interpretation of these measurements.

GFR Categories

GFR (mL/min/1.73m^2)	TERMS	GFR CATEGORY (KDIGO 2012)	CKD STAGE (KDOQI 2002)
≥ 90 + kidney damage*	Normal or high	G1	Stage 1
60-89 + kidney damage*	Mild decrease	G2	Stage 2
45-59	Mild to moderate decrease	G3a	Stage 3
30-44	Moderate to severe decrease	G3b	
15-29	Severe decrease	G4	Stage 4
< 15 or dialysis dependent	Kidney failure	G5	Stage 5

** Markers of kidney damage include history of kidney transplant, structural abnormalities on imaging, albuminuria and others*

ACR (mg/g) OR AER (mg/24hr)	ACR (mg/mmol)	TERMS	ALBUMINURIA CATEGORY (KDIGO 2012)
< 30	< 3	Normal to mild increase (previously called normoalbuminuria)	A1
30-300	3-30	Moderate increase (previously called microalbuminuria)	A2
> 300	> 30	Severe increase (previously called macroalbuminuria)	A3

ACR: albumin to creatinine ratio; AER: albumin excretion rate

ACE INHIBITORS AND ARBs FOR PROTEINURIA, BLOOD PRESSURE CONTROL

Uncontrolled blood pressure, diabetes and proteinuria are all risk factors for the progression of CKD. Renal function decreases (and proteinuria increases) if blood glucose or blood pressure remains elevated; both must be well-controlled.

ACE inhibitors and ARBs are used for renal protection and, if hypertension is present, for blood pressure control. The BP goal in CKD is < 140/90 mmHg (with no proteinuria) or < 130/80 mmHg (with proteinuria). When starting treatment with either drug class, the SCr can increase by up to 30%. This is expected, and treatment should not be stopped. If the SCr increase is > 30%, the treatment should be discontinued and the patient will generally be referred to a nephrologist. ACE inhibitors or ARBs increase potassium which can result in hyperkalemia. It is important to maximize the dose of the ACE inhibitor or ARB for renal protection. Patients should be counseled to avoid potassium supplements and salt substitutes (KCl) to decrease the risk of hyperkalemia with ACE inhibitors or ARBs. The serum creatinine and potassium should be monitored 1 – 2 weeks after initiating ACE inhibitors or ARBs in patients with CKD. Use of ACE inhibitors and ARBs is discussed in more detail in the Hypertension and Chronic Heart Failure chapters.

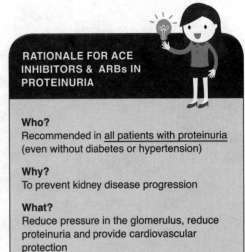

RATIONALE FOR ACE INHIBITORS & ARBs IN PROTEINURIA

Who?
Recommended in all patients with proteinuria (even without diabetes or hypertension)

Why?
To prevent kidney disease progression

What?
Reduce pressure in the glomerulus, reduce proteinuria and provide cardiovascular protection

How?
Inhibit renin-angiotensin-aldosterone system (RAAS), causing efferent arteriolar dilation

MODIFYING DRUG THERAPY

Some drug regimens will require modification (by a dose reduction and/or extending the dosing interval) in patients with impaired kidney function since some medications can accumulate and cause side effects/toxicity. Medications can directly cause or worsen kidney disease and, in some cases, become less effective as kidney function worsens (e.g., diuretics). Dose reductions reduce peak concentrations but maintain trough concentrations. This strategy is effective for drugs that must maintain effective trough concentrations. For example, beta-lactam antibiotics must maintain a specific time above the minimum inhibitory concentration (MIC) for optimal bacterial killing. This is called time-dependent killing. Extending the interval of a regimen maintains peak concentrations and reduces the trough concentration. This strategy is most useful for drugs that rely on achieving a specific peak concentration, such as quinolones and aminoglycosides, which exhibit concentration-dependent bacterial killing. For some drugs, a combination of lower doses and longer intervals is required in renal impairment.

Other drugs are contraindicated at different levels of kidney impairment for a variety of reasons. Drug accumulation could be dangerous (e.g., increased bleeding risk with some anticoagulants), the drug could cause kidney damage (as with NSAIDs), or the drug may cause harmful effects for the patient when kidney function is reduced (e.g., hyperkalemia with aldosterone receptor antagonists).

As illustrated in the graphic, it is helpful to remember that dose adjustments may be necessary at a CrCl of 50 – 60 mL/min (about half of normal kidney function). When CrCl ≤ 20 – 30 mL/min (about 25% of normal kidney function), additional adjustments may be needed, and some drugs may be contraindicated.

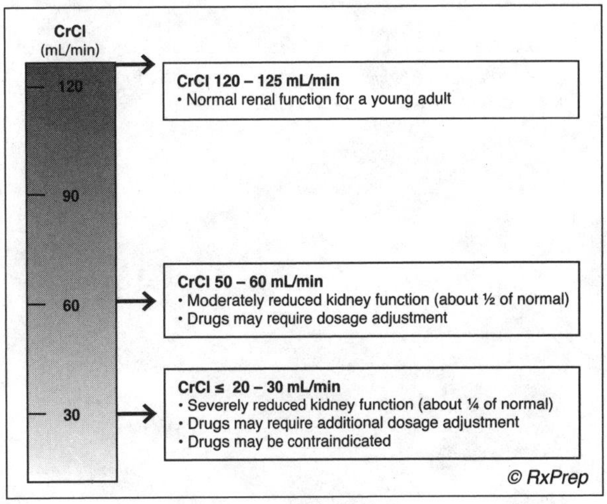

CrCl
(mL/min)
120
90
60
30
CrCl 120 – 125 mL/min
• Normal renal function for a young adult
CrCl 50 – 60 mL/min
• Moderately reduced kidney function (about ½ of normal)
• Drugs may require dosage adjustment
CrCl ≤ 20 – 30 mL/min
• Severely reduced kidney function (about ¼ of normal)
• Drugs may require additional dosage adjustment
• Drugs may be contraindicated
© RxPrep

SELECT DRUGS THAT REQUIRE ↓ DOSE OR ↑ INTERVAL WITH IMPAIRED KIDNEY FUNCTION

Anti-infectives

Aminoglycosides (↑ dosing interval)

Aztreonam

Beta-lactam antibiotics (most)

Polymyxins

Quinolones (except moxifloxacin)

Sulfamethoxazole/trimethoprim

Vancomycin

Anti-tuberculosis medications (ethambutol, pyrazinamide)

Antivirals (acyclovir, valacyclovir, ganciclovir, valganciclovir, oseltamivir)

Amphotericin B

Fluconazole

NRTIs, including tenofovir

Cardiovascular

Antiarrhythmics (digoxin, disopyramide, dofetilide, procainamide, sotalol*)

Dabigatran* (for AFib)

LMWHs (enoxaparin)

Rivaroxaban* (for AFib)

Statins (most)

Pain/Gout

Allopurinol

Colchicine

Gabapentin, pregabalin

Morphine and codeine

Tramadol ER

Gastrointestinal

Famotidine, ranitidine

Metoclopramide

Other

Bisphosphonates*

Cyclosporine

Lithium

Topiramate

**Medication has indication-specific recommendations*

SELECT DRUGS THAT ARE CONTRAINDICATED IN KIDNEY IMPAIRMENT

CrCl < 50

Elvitegravir/cobicistat/emtricitabine/tenofovir disoproxil fumarate *(Stribild)*

Voriconazole IV

CrCl < 30

Avanafil

Bisphosphonates*

Dabigatran*

Duloxetine

Fondaparinux

NSAIDs

Potassium-sparing diuretics

Rivaroxaban*

Tadalafil*

Tramadol ER

GFR < 30

SGLT2 inhibitors (canagliflozin, dapagliflozin, empagliflozin)

Metformin

Other**

Dofetilide

Edoxaban

Glyburide

Meperidine

Nitrofurantoin

Sotalol* *(Betapace AF)*

**Medication has indication-specific recommendations*
***Not specified or another CrCl cut-off is used*

COMPLICATIONS OF CHRONIC KIDNEY DISEASE

See the figure illustrating some common complications of chronic kidney disease (study focus should be on the treatments).

CKD Mineral and Bone Disorder

CKD mineral and bone disorder (CKD-MBD) is common in patients with renal impairment and affects almost all patients receiving dialysis. CKD-MBD is associated with fractures, cardiovascular disease and increased mortality. Patients with advanced kidney disease require monitoring of parathyroid hormone (PTH), phosphorus (phosphate, PO4), calcium and vitamin D levels.

Hyperphosphatemia

Chronically elevated PTH levels (secondary hyperparathyroidism) must be treated in order to avoid bone disease and fractures. Treatment is initially focused on controlling serum phosphorus by restricting dietary phosphate (such as avoiding dairy products, cola, chocolate and nuts). As CKD progresses, phosphate binders are often required. Phosphate binders block the absorption of dietary PO4 by binding to it in the intestine. If a dose is missed (and the food is absorbed), the phosphate binder should be skipped, and the patient should resume normal dosing at the next meal or snack. There are three types of phosphate binders: 1) aluminum-based, 2) calcium-based and 3) aluminum-free, calcium-free agents.

COMPLICATIONS OF CHRONIC KIDNEY DISEASE

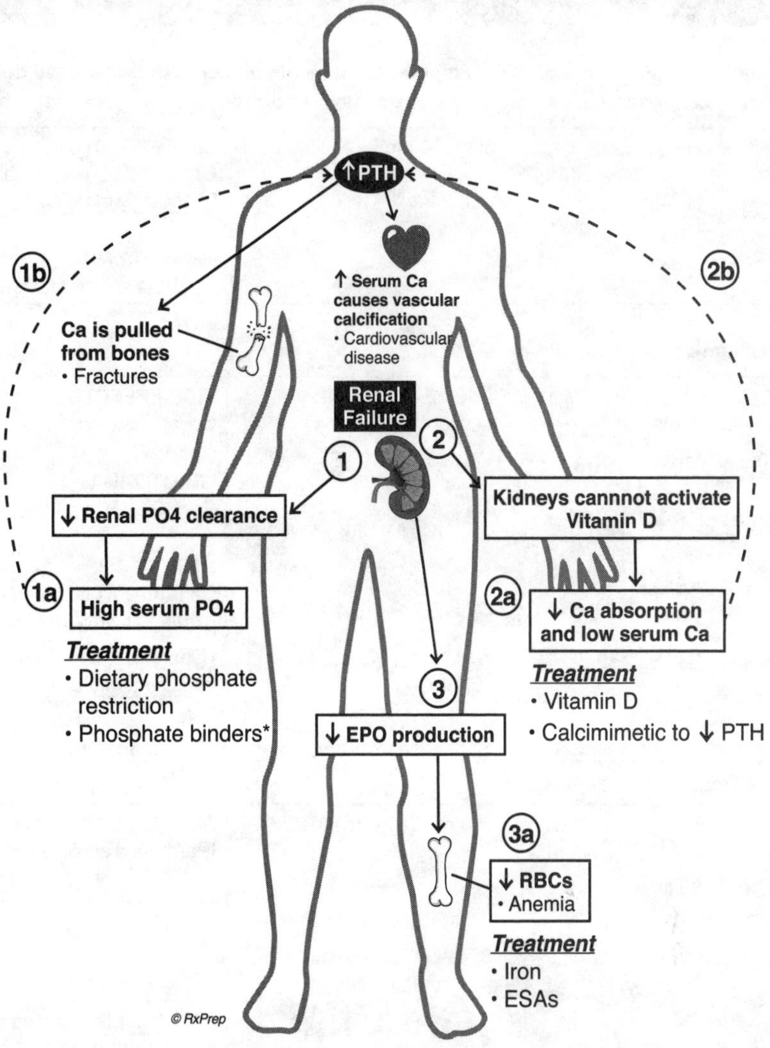

* Caution: Hypercalcemia can result when calcium-based phosphate binders are given with vitamin D due to ↑ Ca absorption.

The interactions of Ca, PO4 and vitamin D in CKD are complex. **1)** PO4 levels increase (because the kidneys cannot clear excess PO4 absorbed from the diet) **2)** Vitamin D cannot be activated, causing dietary calcium absorption to decrease. Both high PO4 (**1a**) and low Ca (**2a**) cause increased release of PTH. Under normal circumstances, PTH would cause the kidneys to increase Ca reabsorption, but in CKD this is no longer possible and Ca is pulled from the bones, leading to bone demineralization and increased fractures. Normally, when Ca levels return to normal, PTH release is shut down, but in renal disease the chronically high PO4 levels continue to stimulate PTH release, and hypercalcemia can persist, causing calcification and cardiovascular disease. **3)** In CKD, the kidneys produce less erythropoietin (EPO), resulting in decreased RBC production in the bone marrow and anemia.

Phosphate Binders

DRUG	DOSE	SAFETY/SIDE EFFECTS/MONITORING

Aluminum-based: One of the most potent phosphate binders but rarely used due to risk of aluminum accumulation (and subsequent nervous system and bone toxicity). Treatment duration is limited to 4 weeks.

DRUG	DOSE	SAFETY/SIDE EFFECTS/MONITORING
Aluminum hydroxide (*ALternaGEL*, others) Suspension	300-600 mg TID with meals	**SIDE EFFECTS** Constipation, poor taste, nausea, aluminum intoxication, "dialysis dementia" and osteomalacia **MONITORING** Ca, PO4 serum aluminum concentrations, PTH

Calcium-based: First line.

DRUG	DOSE	SAFETY/SIDE EFFECTS/MONITORING
Calcium acetate (*PhosLo*, *Phoslyra*, others) Tablet, capsule, solution	2,001-2,668 mg TID with meals	**SIDE EFFECTS** Constipation, nausea, hypercalcemia **MONITORING** Ca, PO4, PTH **NOTES** Calcium acetate binds more dietary phosphorus on an elemental calcium basis compared to calcium carbonate. Hypercalcemia is especially problematic with concomitant use of vitamin D (due to increased calcium absorption).
Calcium carbonate (*Tums*, others) Tablet, chewable tablet	500 mg TID with meals	

Aluminum-free, calcium-free: Some are iron-based. No aluminum accumulation, less hypercalcemia, but more expensive.

DRUG	DOSE	SAFETY/SIDE EFFECTS/MONITORING
Sucroferric oxyhydroxide (*Velphoro*) Chewable tablet	500 mg TID with meals	**SIDE EFFECTS** Diarrhea, discolored (black) feces **MONITORING** Iron, ferritin, TSAT (only with ferric citrate), PO4, PTH **NOTES** Iron absorption occurs with ferric citrate; dosage reduction of IV iron may be necessary. Absorption is minimal with sucroferric oxyhydroxide.
Ferric citrate (*Auryxia*) Tablet	2 grams TID with meals, up to 12 grams per day	
Lanthanum carbonate (*Fosrenol*) Chewable tablet, powder	500-1,000 mg TID with meals. Must chew tablet thoroughly to reduce risk of severe GI adverse effects Use powder if unable to chew tablets	**CONTRAINDICATIONS** GI obstruction, fecal impaction, ileus **WARNINGS** GI perforation **SIDE EFFECTS** N/V/D, constipation, abdominal pain **MONITORING** Ca, PO4, PTH **NOTES** MedGuide required

Phosphate Binders Continued

DRUG	DOSE	SAFETY/SIDE EFFECTS/MONITORING

Sevelamer: A non-calcium, non-aluminum based phosphate binder that is not systemically absorbed. Also, has the benefit of lowering total cholesterol and LDL by 15-30%. Sevelamer carbonate may have an advantage over sevelamer hydrochloride in maintaining bicarbonate concentrations.

DRUG	DOSE	SAFETY/SIDE EFFECTS/MONITORING
Sevelamer carbonate ***(Renvela)*** Tablet, powder Sevelamer hydrochloride (*Renagel*) Tablet	800-1,600 mg TID with meals	**CONTRAINDICATIONS** Bowel obstruction **SIDE EFFECTS** N/V/D (all > 20%), dyspepsia, constipation, abdominal pain, flatulence **MONITORING** Ca, PO4, HCO3, Cl, PTH

Phosphate Binder Drug Interactions

Phosphate binders are designed to "bind" and have many drug interactions. Levothyroxine and antibiotics that chelate (quinolones, tetracyclines) are common interactions. Administration should be separated.

- Calcium-based binders (calcium acetate and calcium carbonate) have many drug interactions. Common interactions include quinolones, tetracyclines, oral bisphosphonates, and thyroid products.
- Sucroferric oxyhydroxide and ferric citrate are iron-based products. Doxycycline should be taken 1 hour before sucroferric oxyhydroxide or ferric citrate. Ciprofloxacin should be separated by 2 hours from ferric citrate. Levothyroxine should not be used with sucroferric oxyhydroxide.
- Lanthanum can interact with drugs that bind to aluminum-, calcium- or magnesium-containing antacids and these should be spaced 2 hours from the lanthanum dose. Quinolone antibiotics should be given 1 hour before or 4 hours after lanthanum. Separate levothyroxine by at least 2 hours.
- Sevelamer can decrease the absorption of some medications. Quinolone antibiotics should be given 2 hours before or 6 hours after the sevelamer dose. Mycophenolate, tacrolimus and levothyroxine serum concentrations can also be affected and doses should be given several hours before sevelamer.

Vitamin D Deficiency & Secondary Hyperparathyroidism

After controlling hyperphosphatemia, elevations in PTH are treated primarily with vitamin D. Vitamin D deficiency occurs when the kidney is unable to hydroxylate vitamin D to its final active form, 1,25-dihydroxy vitamin D. Vitamin D deficiency exacerbates bone disease, impairs immunity and increases cardiovascular disease.

Vitamin D occurs in two primary forms: vitamin D3 or cholecalciferol, which is synthesized in the skin after exposure to ultraviolet light, and vitamin D2 or ergocalciferol, which is produced from plant sterols and is the primary dietary source of vitamin D. Supplementation with oral ergocalciferol or cholecalciferol may be necessary (especially in patients with CKD Stage 3 and 4).

Calcitriol *(Rocaltrol)* is the active form of vitamin D3 and is used in patients with CKD to increase calcium absorption from the gut, raise serum calcium concentrations and inhibit PTH secretion. Newer active vitamin D analogs, such as paricalcitol and doxercalciferol, cause less hypercalcemia than calcitriol.

Treatment of vitamin D deficiency can result in hypercalcemia or hyperphosphatemia. These values must be monitored during treatment. Further information on vitamin D is contained in the Dietary Supplements, Natural and Complementary Medicine and Osteoporosis chapters.

The vitamin D analogs increase Ca levels. Calcium, in turn, inhibits PTH release. Another method to inhibit PTH release is to increase the sensitivity of the calcium receptor on the parathyroid gland. Cinacalcet *(Sensipar)* is used for this purpose in dialysis patients. It is a "calcimimetic" which mimics the actions of calcium on the parathyroid and causes a further reduction in PTH.

Agents for the Treatment of Secondary Hyperparathyroidism

DRUG	DOSING	SAFETY/SIDE EFFECTS/MONITORING
Vitamin D analogs: ↑ intestinal absorption of Ca and provide a negative feedback to the parathyroid gland.		
Calcitriol *(Rocaltrol)* Capsule, solution, injection	CKD: 0.25-0.5 mcg PO daily Dialysis: 0.5-1 mcg PO daily or 0.5-4 mcg IV 3x weekly	**CONTRAINDICATIONS** Hypercalcemia, vitamin D toxicity **WARNINGS** Digitalis toxicity potentiated by hypercalcemia **SIDE EFFECTS** N/V/D (> 10%), hypercalcemia, hyperphosphatemia **MONITORING** Ca, PO4, PTH, 25-hydroxyvitamin D (cacifediol) **NOTES** Take with food or shortly after a meal to ↓ GI upset (calcitriol). Caldifediol is a prodrug of calcitriol.
Calcifediol *(Rayaldee)* ER capsule	CKD Stage 3 or 4: 30 mcg QHS	
Doxercalciferol *(Hectorol)* Capsule, injection	CKD: 1-3.5 mcg PO daily Dialysis: 10-20 mcg PO 3x weekly or 4-18 mcg IV 3x weekly	
Paricalcitol *(Zemplar)* Capsule, injection	CKD: 1-2 mcg PO daily or 2-4 mcg 3x weekly Dialysis: 2.8-7 mcg IV 3x weekly	
Calcimimetic: ↑ sensitivity of calcium-sensing receptor on the parathyroid gland, thereby ↓ PTH, ↓ Ca, ↓ PO4		
Cinacalcet *(Sensipar)* Tablet	Dialysis: 30-180 mg PO daily with food	**CONTRAINDICATIONS** Hypocalcemia **WARNING** Caution in patients with history of seizure **SIDE EFFECTS** Hypocalcemia, N/V/D, paresthesia, HA, fatigue, depression, anorexia, constipation, bone fracture, weakness, arthralgia, myalgia, limb pain, URTIs **MONITORING** Ca, PO4, PTH **NOTES** Take tablet whole, do not crush or chew.

Anemia of CKD

Anemia is defined as a hemoglobin level < 13 g/dL. Anemia is common in CKD and is typically due to a combination of factors.

- The primary problem is a lack of erythropoietin (EPO), which is normally produced by the kidneys and travels to the bone marrow to stimulate the production of red blood cells (RBCs). RBCs are released into the blood where they transport oxygen. As kidney function declines, EPO production decreases.

- CKD causes an inflammatory state, which causes a different type of anemia called anemia of chronic disease. This type of anemia also decreases EPO production.
- Eventually, erythropoiesis stimulating agents (ESAs) are required to prevent the need for transfusions. ESAs include epoetin *(Procrit, Epogen)* and the longer-lasting formulation darbepoetin alfa *(Aranesp)*.
    - ESA treatment carries risk, including elevated blood pressure and clotting risk. Careful monitoring is required. In CKD, ESAs are used only when a patient's hemoglobin level is < 10 g/dL and the dose should be held or discontinued if the Hgb exceeds 11 g/dL, as increased risk for thromboembolic disease (DVT, PE, MI, CVA) is seen with higher levels.
- ESAs can only be effective if adequate iron is available to make hemoglobin. It is important to assess iron status properly, which requires levels of iron, ferritin and TSAT. In ESRD, iron levels are low because of reduced GI absorption and blood loss from dialysis treatments. Intravenous (IV) iron is given at the dialysis center. See the Anemia chapter for more information on identifying anemia and ESA use.
- Folate and vitamin B12 can be low due to poor dietary intake or some other factor, such as a lack of intrinsic factor. Supplementation may be necessary.

Hyperkalemia

A normal potassium level is 3.5 – 5 mEq/L. Hyperkalemia can be defined as a potassium level > 5.3 or > 5.5 mEq/L (ranges vary), although clinicians will be concerned with any level > 5 mEq/L.

Potassium is the most abundant intracellular cation and is essential for life. Humans obtain potassium through the diet from many foods, including meats, beans and fruits. Daily intake through the GI tract is about 1 mEq/kg/day. Excess intake is excreted primarily via the kidneys and partially via the gut. Renal potassium excretion is increased by aldosterone, diuretics (loop > thiazide), by a high urine flow (via osmotic diuresis), and by negatively charged ions in the distal tubule (via bicarbonate).

High dietary potassium intake does not typically cause hyperkalemia unless there is significant renal damage. In normal kidney function, the acute rise in potassium from a meal would be offset by the release of insulin, which causes potassium to shift into the cells. The most common cause of hyperkalemia is decreased renal excretion due to kidney failure. This can be in combination with a high potassium intake or can be partially due to the use of drugs that interfere with potassium excretion.

Patients with diabetes often have a diet high in sodium and low in potassium, and are taking ACE inhibitors or ARBs. The insulin deficiency reduces the ability to shift potassium into the cells. These factors put patients with diabetes at higher risk for hyperkalemia. Hospitalized patients, primarily due to the use of drugs, are at higher risk of hyperkalemia than outpatients. Rarely, acute hyperkalemia can be due to tumor lysis, rhabdomyolysis or succinylcholine administration.

A patient with elevated potassium, depending on the level, may be asymptomatic or symptomatic. Symptoms include muscle weakness and bradycardia. Fatal arrhyth-

SELECTED DRUGS THAT RAISE POTASSIUM LEVELS

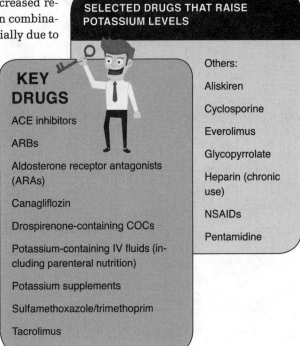

KEY DRUGS

ACE inhibitors
ARBs
Aldosterone receptor antagonists (ARAs)
Canagliflozin
Drospirenone-containing COCs
Potassium-containing IV fluids (including parenteral nutrition)
Potassium supplements
Sulfamethoxazole/trimethoprim
Tacrolimus

Others:
Aliskiren
Cyclosporine
Everolimus
Glycopyrrolate
Heparin (chronic use)
NSAIDs
Pentamidine

mias can develop. If the potassium is high or the heart rate/rhythm is abnormal, the patient will generally be monitored with an ECG. The risk for severe, negative outcomes increases as the potassium level increases.

Treatment of Hyperkalemia

All potassium sources must be discontinued. If hyperkalemia is severe, the urgent clinical need is to stabilize the myocardial cells (to prevent arrhythmias) and to rapidly shift potassium intracellularly. Several medications move potassium from the extracellular compartment to the intracellular compartment. One or more of these methods should be used in severe hyperkalemia. These agents work quickly, but they do not lower total body potassium. Interventions to enhance potassium elimination may be initiated, though these methods generally take longer to reduce potassium. They are commonly used in conjunction with the methods described above in severe hyperkalemia or alone in less severe situations. In addition to the treatments listed below, fludrocortisone (*Florinef*) may be used, particularly in a patient with hypoaldosteronism.

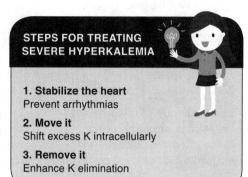

STEPS FOR TREATING SEVERE HYPERKALEMIA

1. Stabilize the heart
Prevent arrhythmias

2. Move it
Shift excess K intracellularly

3. Remove it
Enhance K elimination

MECHANISM OF BENEFIT	INTERVENTION	ROUTE OF ADMINISTRATION	ONSET	NOTES
Stabilize the heart	Calcium gluconate	IV	1-2 minutes	Does not decrease potassium. Stabilizes myocardial cells to prevent arrhythmias.
Move it: Shift K intracellularly	Regular insulin	IV	30 minutes	Co-administered with glucose or dextrose to prevent hypoglycemia.
	Dextrose	IV	30 minutes	Stimulates insulin secretion, but does not shift K intracellularly on its own.
	Sodium bicarbonate	IV	30 minutes	Used when metabolic acidosis is present.
	Albuterol	Nebulized	30 minutes	Monitor for tachycardia and chest pain.
Remove it: Eliminate K from the body	Furosemide	IV	5 minutes	Clears K in the urine. Monitor volume status.
	Sodium polystyrene sulfonate	Oral or rectal	1 hour; oral not for acute emergency	Binds K in the GI tract. Oral may take hours to days to work. Rectal route has faster onset and can be used in acute (emergency) treatment.
	Patiromer	Oral	~7 hours	Binds K in the GI tract. Not for acute or emergency use due to onset.
	Hemodialysis		Immediate, once started	Removes K from the blood. Other methods are generally used in conjunction. It may take several hours to set up/complete dialysis. Hyperkalemia can be fatal in patients with kidney failure.

Agents for Treatment of Hyperkalemia

DRUG	DOSE	SAFETY/SIDE EFFECTS/MONITORING
Sodium polystyrene sulfonate *(SPS, Kayexalate,* *Kalexate, Kionex)* Powder, suspension Non-absorbed cation exchange resin	Oral: 15 grams 1-4 times/day Rectal: 30-50 grams Q6H	**WARNINGS** Electrolyte disturbances including hypokalemia, fecal impaction; do not mix oral products with sorbitol (↑ risk of GI necrosis) **SIDE EFFECTS** Hypernatremia, hypocalcemia, hypokalemia, hypomagnesemia, N/V, constipation or diarrhea **MONITORING** K, Mg, Na, Ca **NOTES** Do not mix oral products with fruit juices containing K
Patiromer *(Veltassa)* Powder for oral suspension Non-absorbed cation exchange polymer	8.4 grams PO once daily with food. Max 25.2 grams once daily. Adjust by 8.4 grams per day PRN at ≥ one week intervals to obtain desired K Instructions: pour 1/3 cup of water into an empty cup, empty *Veltassa* packet contents into water and stir well, add an additional the remaining water to the mixture and stir well (mixture will be cloudy), drink right away. If powder remains in cup, add additional water and drink. Repeat as needed.	**WARNINGS** Binds to many oral drugs; give other drugs at least 6 hours before or 6 hours after. If ≥ 6 hr separation is not possible, choose only one drug to administer. Can worsen GI motility and cause hypomagnesemia. **SIDE EFFECTS** Constipation, hypomagnesemia, hypokalemia, N/D **MONITORING** K, Mg **NOTES** Delayed onset of action (~7 hrs); not for emergency use Store powder in refrigerator. If stored at room temperature, use within 3 months. Primarily studied in CKD patients taking an ACE inhibitor, ARB or ARA

Metabolic Acidosis

The ability of the kidney to generate bicarbonate decreases as CKD progresses and may result in the development of metabolic acidosis. In the ambulatory care setting, treatment of metabolic acidosis is initiated when the serum bicarbonate concentration is < 22 mEq/L. Agents to replace bicarbonate include:

- Sodium bicarbonate *(Neut)*
  - Sodium load can cause fluid retention.
  - Monitor sodium level and use caution in patients with HTN, cardiovascular disease.
- Sodium citrate/citric acid solution *(Bicitra, Cytra-2, Oracit, Shohl's solution)*
  - Monitor sodium level.
  - Metabolized to bicarbonate by the liver, may not be effective in concomitant liver failure.

DIALYSIS

If chronic kidney disease progresses to failure (stage 5 disease), dialysis will be required in all patients who do not receive a kidney transplant. The two primary types of dialysis are hemodialysis (HD) and peritoneal dialysis (PD). In hemodialysis, the patient's blood is pumped to the dialyzer (dialysis machine) and runs through a semipermeable dialysis filter which, using a concentration gradient, removes waste products, electrolytes and excess fluid. HD is typically a 3 – 4 hour process, done several times per week (usually three times). Some patients are able to do HD at home, which can be done more frequently (typically 5 – 6 times per week).

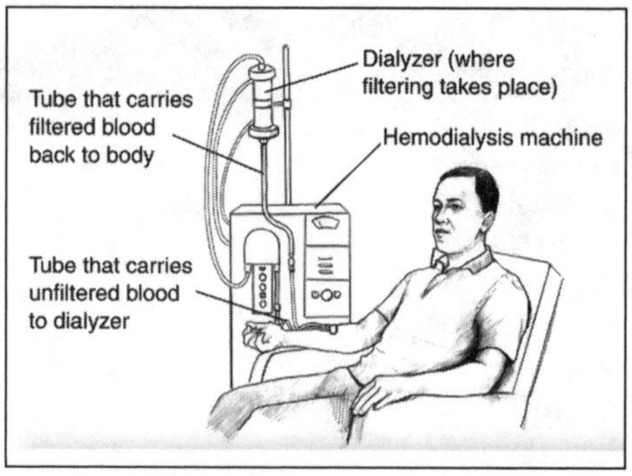

In PD, a dialysis solution (usually containing glucose) is pumped into the peritoneal cavity (the abdominal cavity surrounding the internal organs), and the peritoneal membrane acts as the semipermeable membrane (i.e., as the dialyzer). The solution is left in the abdomen to "dwell" for a period of time, then is drained. This cycle is repeated throughout the day, every day. PD is performed by the patient at home.

Factors Affecting Drug Removal During Dialysis

When a patient is on dialysis, the pharmacist must consider the amount of medication cleared during dialysis in order to recommend the correct dose and interval. Medications that are removed during dialysis (including many antibiotics) must be given after dialysis or may require a supplemental dose following dialysis. Drug removal during dialysis depends primarily on the factors below.

FACTOR	EFFECT
Drug Characteristics	
Molecular weight/size	Smaller molecules tend to be more readily removed by dialysis
Volume of distribution	Drugs with large Vd are less likely to be significantly removed by dialysis
Protein-binding	Highly protein-bound drugs are less likely to be removed by dialysis
Dialysis Factors	
Membrane	High-flux (large pore size) and high-efficiency (large surface area) HD filters remove substances more than conventional/low-flux filters
Blood flow rate	Higher dialysis blood flow rates increase drug removal during dialysis over a given time interval

HEPATITIS & LIVER DISEASE

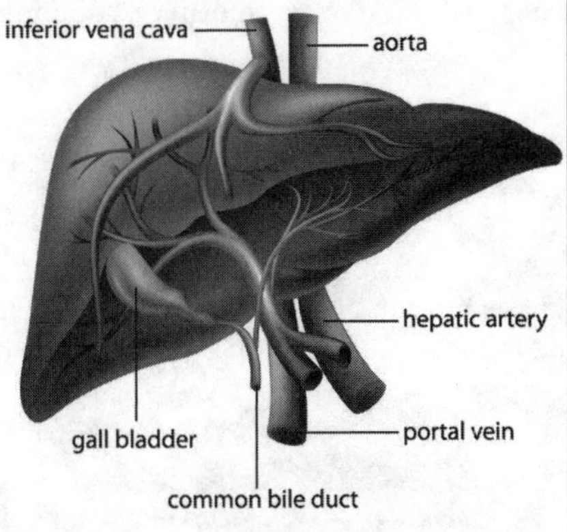

pblueringmedia © 123RF

GUIDELINES/REFERENCES

AASLD-IDSA. Recommendations for Testing, Managing, and Treating Hepatitis C. http://www.hcvguidelines.org (accessed 2016 Oct 18).

We gratefully acknowledge the assistance of Paulina Deming, PharmD, Associate Professor at the University of New Mexico College of Pharmacy, in preparing this chapter.

HEPATITIS

Background

The term hepatitis means inflammation of the liver. Hepatitis viruses are the most common cause, but alcohol, certain drugs, autoimmune diseases and other viruses/infections can also cause hepatitis. Viruses that damage the liver include hepatitis A through E (most cases of viral hepatitis are caused by hepatitis A, B and C), along with herpesvirus, CMV, Epstein-Barr virus, and adenoviruses. Symptoms and treatment differ depending on the cause of hepatitis and extent of liver damage (see discussion of cirrhosis in this chapter). Many patients with hepatitis B and C do not know they are infected.

Hepatitis A, B and C

Hepatitis A virus (HAV) causes an acute, self-limiting illness in most patients. Transmission is primarily via the fecal-oral route through improper hand washing after exposure to an infected person or via contaminated food/water. Symptoms are generally mild and non-specific.

Hepatitis B virus (HBV) and hepatitis C virus (HCV) can cause acute illness and can lead to chronic infection, cirrhosis of the liver, liver cancer, liver failure, and death. Transmission requires contact with infectious blood, semen, or other body fluids by having sex with an infected person, sharing contaminated needles to inject drugs, or from an infected mother to her newborn (perinatal transmission). Oral direct acting antivirals (DAAs) are the cornerstone of current treatment for HCV.

Comparison of Hepatitis Viruses

	HEPATITIS A	HEPATITIS B	HEPATITIS C
Acute vs Chronic	Acute	Both	Both
Transmission	Fecal-oral	Blood, body fluid	Blood, body fluid
Vaccine	Yes*	Yes*	No
First-Line Treatment	Supportive	PEG-INF or NRTI (tenofovir or entecavir)	No cirrhosis / treatment naive: DAA combination
Other Treatments for Select Patients			DAA combination + RBV

**See Immunizations chapter*

PEG-INF = pegylated interferon, RBV = ribavirin

NON-DRUG TREATMENT

Counseling patients with HBV and HCV is essential to prevent disease transmission to others. Alcohol cessation is recommended.

DRUG TREATMENT

Direct Acting Antiviral Agents

DAAs have revolutionized the treatment of HCV, almost entirely eliminating older, poorly tolerated treatments (e.g., interferon and ribavirin) and offering a cure for most patients. Treatment of HCV is currently approached much like HIV, with regimens consisting of combinations of drugs that target different phases of the HCV life cycle. DAAs include NS3/4A protease inhibitors, NS5A replication complex inhibitors and NS5B polymerase inhibitors. Many DAAs are available only in combination products. Preferred HCV regimens currently consist of 2 – 3 DAAs with different mechanisms (+ ribavirin in some cases), usually for 12 weeks (see Study Tip).

There are 6 different HCV genotypes (1 – 6) and various subtypes (e.g., 1a or 1b). Treatment options and duration of therapy depend on the genotype and presence of cirrhosis. Some combinations include ritonavir, which is not active for HCV, but is used to boost (increase) levels of HCV protease inhibitors used with it. Because treatment of HCV is rapidly changing, healthcare providers should consult the AASLD website for the most up-to-date recommendations (www.hcvguidelines.org).

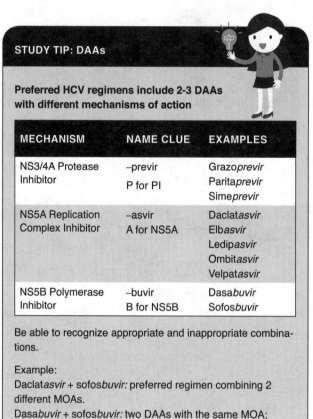

STUDY TIP: DAAs

Preferred HCV regimens include 2-3 DAAs with different mechanisms of action

MECHANISM	NAME CLUE	EXAMPLES
NS3/4A Protease Inhibitor	–previr P for PI	Grazo*previr* Parita*previr* Sime*previr*
NS5A Replication Complex Inhibitor	–asvir A for NS5A	Daclat*asvir* Elb*asvir* Ledip*asvir* Ombit*asvir* Velpat*asvir*
NS5B Polymerase Inhibitor	–buvir B for NS5B	Dasa*buvir* Sofos*buvir*

Be able to recognize appropriate and inappropriate combinations.

Example:
Daclat*asvir* + sofos*buvir:* preferred regimen combining 2 different MOAs.
Dasa*buvir* + sofos*buvir:* two DAAs with the same MOA; should not be used together in a combination regimen.

In October 2016, a boxed warning was added to the labeling of all DAAs regarding the risk of reactivating HBV. Patients should be tested for HBV before starting a DAA and monitored for reactivation during and after DAA treatment.

DRUG	DOSING	SAFETY/SIDE EFFECTS/MONITORING
Sofosbuvir *(Sovaldi)* Tablet **+ ledipasvir *(Harvoni)*** **+ velpatasvir *(Epclusa)***	400 mg daily with or without food	**WARNINGS** Serious symptomatic bradycardia in patients taking amiodarone + sofosbuvir + another DAA (especially in those also taking beta blockers, with cardiac comorbidities or advanced liver disease). Co-administration of amiodarone, sofosbuvir and another DAA is not recommended. Potentially serious drug interactions (see drug interactions). **SIDE EFFECTS** Fatigue, HA, weakness **MONITORING** LFTs (including bilirubin), HCV-RNA **NOTES** Sofosbuvir monotherapy is not effective and not recommended *Epclusa* is the first DAA approved for all HCV genotypes ***Harvoni* and *Epclusa*** Acid suppressive therapy should be avoided or minimized during therapy (see drug interactions)
Sofosbuvir + ledipasvir *(Harvoni)* Tablet	1 tablet daily with or without food	
Sofosbuvir + velpatasvir *(Epclusa)* Tablet	1 tablet daily with or without food	
Simeprevir *(Olysio)* Capsule	150 mg daily with food Screening for NS3 Q80K polymorphism may be performed at baseline for certain patients receiving simeprevir; if positive, consider alternate therapy	**CONTRAINDICATIONS** When used in combination with ribavirin or interferon, the contraindications to those agents are applicable to combination treatment regimens with simeprevir **WARNINGS** Serious symptomatic bradycardia in patients taking amiodarone + sofosbuvir + another DAA (especially in those also taking beta blockers, with cardiac comorbidities or advanced liver disease). Co-administration of amiodarone, sofosbuvir and another DAA is not recommended; photosensitivity, rash **SIDE EFFECTS** HA, fatigue, nausea, rash (photosensitivity), diarrhea, dizziness **MONITORING** LFTs, HCV-RNA levels **NOTES** Simeprevir monotherapy is not effective and not recommended.

Direct Acting Antiviral Agents continued

DRUG	DOSING	SAFETY/SIDE EFFECTS/MONITORING
Daclatasvir (*Daklinza*) Tablet	60 mg daily with or without food in combination with sofosbuvir 30 mg daily with strong 3A4 inhibitors 90 mg daily with moderate 3A4 inducers	**CONTRAINDICATIONS** Use with strong 3A4 inducers **SIDE EFFECTS** Fatigue, HA **MONITORING** LFTs (including bilirubin), HCV-RNA **NOTES** Daclatasvir monotherapy is not effective and not recommended Consider screening for NS5A polymorphism if treating patient with HCV genotype 1a with cirrhosis
Paritaprevir/ritonavir/ombitasvir (*Technivie*) Tablet	2 tablets once daily in the morning with a meal	**CONTRAINDICATIONS** Moderate-severe hepatic impairment (Child Pugh B or C), concomitant use with drugs highly dependent on 3A4 for elimination (if ↑ levels can cause serious events) and moderate-strong inducers of 3A4, all contraindications to ribavirin apply when used in combination regimens *Viekira Pak* and *Viekira XR*: above contraindications apply; also contraindicated with strong inducers or inhibitors of 2C8 **WARNINGS** Hepatic decompensation and hepatic failure in patients with cirrhosis, risk of ↑ LFTs (> 5 x ULN) within 4 wks of treatment (female patients taking ethinyl estradiol products are at ↑ risk), significant drug interaction potential, risk of HIV protease inhibitor resistance **SIDE EFFECTS** Fatigue, nausea, insomnia, pruritus **MONITORING** LFTs (including bilirubin), HCV-RNA **NOTES** MedGuide required
Paritaprevir/ritonavir/ombitasvir + dasabuvir (*Viekira Pak, Viekira XR*) Tablet *Viekira Pak:* paritaprevir + ritonavir + ombitasvir fixed dose combination tablet copackaged with dasabuvir (250 mg) tablets	*Viekira Pak:* 2 tablets of paritaprevir/ritonavir/ombitasvir once daily in the morning and 1 dasabuvir tablet twice daily with meals *Viekira XR:* 3 tablets once daily with a meal	
Elbasvir/grazoprevir (*Zepatier*) Tablet	1 tablet daily with or without food	**CONTRAINDICATIONS** Moderate-severe hepatic impairment (Child Pugh B or C); use with strong inducers of 3A4, OATP1B1/3 inhibitors and efavirenz; all contraindications to ribavirin apply when used in combination regimens **WARNINGS** Risk of ↑ LFTs (> 5 x ULN) within 4 wks of treatment, significant drug interaction potential **SIDE EFFECTS** Fatigue, HA, nausea **MONITORING** LFTs (including bilirubin), HCV-RNA **NOTES** Screening for NS5A polymorphism is recommended when treating HCV genotype 1a

DAA Drug Interactions

All DAAs are contraindicated with strong inducers of 3A4 (e.g., carbamazepine, oxcarbazepine, phenobarbital, phenytoin, rifampin, rifabutin and St. John's wort). Additional product-specific drug interactions are highlighted below.

Sofosbuvir and daclatasvir

- Can ↑ bradycardic effect of amiodarone.
- Can ↑ risk of myopathy with statins (most data with rosuvastatin).
- Avoid tipranavir/ritonavir with sofosbuvir.

Harvoni and *Epclusa*

Interactions for sofosbuvir apply to these medications and:

- Antacids, H2RAs and PPIs can ↓ concentrations of ledipasvir and velpatasvir.
    - Separate *Harvoni* and *Epclusa* from antacids by 4 hrs. Take H2RAs at the same time or 12 hrs apart and use ≤ famotidine 40 mg BID or equivalent.
    - Take PPIs at the same time as *Harvoni* on an empty stomach; avoid PPIs at doses ≥ omeprazole 20 mg/day or equivalent. Using PPIs with *Epclusa* is not recommended.

Technivie and *Viekira*

- Monitoring is required because of the potential for numerous drug-drug interactions (consult the product labeling for a complete list). See HIV chapter for additional ritonavir drug interactions.
- *Technivie* and *Viekira Pak* are substrates (major) and inhibitors (strong) of 3A4 and P-gp; avoid use with drugs highly dependent on 3A4 for elimination (if ↑ levels can cause serious events) and avoid moderate-strong 3A4 inducers due to ↓ efficacy of HCV therapy.
    - Drugs contraindicated with *Technivie* and *Viekira* include: strong inducers of 3A4 (above) and alfuzosin, colchicine, ranolazine, dronedarone, lurasidone, pimozide, ergotamine derivatives, ethinyl estradiol-containing products, cisapride, lovastatin, simvastatin, efavirenz, sildenafil (dosed for PAH), triazolam, and oral midazolam.
- Dasabuvir (component of *Viekira)* is a substrate (major) of 2C8; avoid strong inducers or inhibitors of 2C8 (e.g., gemfibrozil)

Zepatier

- Contraindicated with efavirenz, HIV protease inhibitors (specifically atazanavir, darunavir, lopinavir, saquinavir, tipranavir) and cyclosporine. *Zepatier* is not recommended with nafcillin, ketoconazole, bosentan, tacrolimus, etravirine, *Stribild*, *Genvoya* and modafinil.
- Can ↑ risk of myopathy with statins (see product labeling for maximum statin doses when used with *Zepatier)*.

Simeprevir

- Simeprevir is a 3A4 substrate (major); do not administer with moderate or strong inducers or inhibitors of 3A4.
    - Drugs not recommended with simeprevir include: strong inducers of 3A4 (above) and erythromycin, clarithromycin, azole antifungals, calcium channel blockers, numerous HIV medications, cisapride, cyclosporine, sirolimus, PDE-5 inhibitors for PAH, triazolam, and oral midazolam.
    - Can ↑ risk of myopathy with statins (see product labeling for management).
- Simeprevir inhibits P-gp; can ↑ concentrations of P-gp substrates.
- Can ↑ bradycardic effect of amiodarone.

Technivie and *Viekira* Counseling

- Read the MedGuide that has been given to you. This medication can cause increases in liver function blood tests. Get immediate medical help if you develop any of the following: yellowing of the white part of your eyes or yellowing of your skin, dark-colored urine, light colored stool, or bad stomach pain with severe nausea.
- *Technivie* and *Viekira (Pak* or *XR):* certain medications cannot be used with this medication. Ethinyl estradiol-containing medicines must be stopped before starting it. Use another method of birth control during treatment and for ~2 weeks after. Examples of ethinyl estradiol products include:
    - Combination oral contraceptive pills or patches like *Lo Loestrin FE, Norinyl, Ortho Tri-Cyclen Lo, Ortho Evra*
    - Hormonal vaginal rings like *NuvaRing*
    - Hormone replacement therapy like *femhrt*
- *Viekira Pak* contains 2 different types of tablets. You must take both types of tablets exactly as prescribed to treat your chronic hepatitis C virus (HCV) infection.
    - The pink tablet contains the medicines ombitasvir, paritaprevir, and ritonavir (taken once daily)
    - The beige tablet contains the medicine dasabuvir (taken twice daily)
- *Viekira XR:* swallow the tablets whole and do not consume alcohol within 4 hours of taking *Viekira XR*.

Ribavirin

Ribavirin (RBV) is an oral antiviral agent that inhibits replication of RNA and DNA viruses. It is indicated for HCV in combination with other agents and never as monotherapy. Aerosolized ribavirin has been used for respiratory syncytial virus (RSV).

DRUG	DOSING	SAFETY/SIDE EFFECTS/MONITORING
Ribavirin *(Copegus, Moderiba, Rebetol, Ribasphere, Ribasphere RibaPak)* Capsule, tablet, solution (oral) ***Virazole*** for RSV	400-600 mg BID, varies based on indication, patient weight and genotype ↑ tolerability if given with food When Hgb < 10 g/dL, ↓ dose (avoid if Hgb < 8.5 g/dL) Capsule should not be crushed, chewed, open, or broken	**BOXED WARNINGS** Significant teratogenic effects (avoid in pregnancy or women wishing to become pregnant) Monotherapy is not effective for HCV Hemolytic anemia (primary toxicity of oral therapy mostly occurring within 4 weeks of therapy) Caution with inhalation formulation in patients on a ventilator (precipitation of drug may interfere with ventilation) **CONTRAINDICATIONS** Pregnancy, women of childbearing age who will not use contraception reliably, male partners of pregnant women, hemoglobinopathies, CrCl < 50 mL/min *(Ribasphere, Rebetrol)*, autoimmune hepatitis, concomitant use with didanosine **SIDE EFFECTS** Hemolytic anemia (can worsen cardiac disease and lead to MIs; do not use in unstable cardiac disease), fatigue, HA, insomnia, N/V/D, anorexia, myalgias, hyperuricemia **MONITORING** CBC with differential and PLTs, electrolytes, uric acid, LFTs (including bilirubin), HCV-RNA, TSH, monthly pregnancy tests **NOTES** Safety issue - see Pregnancy chapter Can stay in body for as long as 6 months. Avoid pregnancy in female patients and female partners of male patients during therapy and for 6 months after completing therapy. At least two reliable forms of effective contraception must be utilized during treatment and during the 6-month post-treatment follow-up period MedGuide required

Ribavirin Drug Interactions

- Do not use with didanosine due to cases of fatal hepatic failure, peripheral neuropathy and pancreatitis.
- Ribavirin can ↑ hepatotoxic effects of all NRTIs; lactic acidosis can occur.
- Zidovudine can ↑ risk and severity of anemia from ribavirin.

Ribavirin Counseling

- Read the MedGuide that has been given to you. Ribavirin can cause birth defects or death of an unborn child.
  - Female patients: do not take ribavirin if you are pregnant or plan to become pregnant. You must not become pregnant during therapy and for 6 months after you have stopped therapy. During this time, you must use 2 forms of birth control and have pregnancy tests that show that you are not pregnant.

- Male patients: do not take ribavirin if your partner is pregnant or plans to become pregnant. Your female sexual partner must not become pregnant during treatment and for 6 months after treatment has stopped. Two forms of birth control must be used during this time.

- If you or a female sexual partner becomes pregnant, tell your healthcare provider immediately. There is a Ribavirin Pregnancy Registry that collects confidential information about pregnancy outcomes in female patients and female partners of male patients exposed to ribavirin.
- If using the oral solution, wash the measuring cup or spoon to avoid swallowing of the medicine by someone other than the person to whom it was prescribed.
- This medicine can cause a dangerous drop in your red blood cell count, called anemia. Your healthcare provider should check your red blood cell count before you start therapy and often during the first 4 weeks of therapy. Your red blood cell count may be checked more often if you have any heart or breathing problems.
- Do not take ribavirin alone to treat hepatitis C infection. It is used in combination with other medications.

Interferon Alfa

Interferon alfa (INF-alfa) is indicated for treatment of HBV and HCV. Interferons are naturally-produced cytokines that have antiviral, antiproliferative, and immunomodulatory effects. The pegylated forms (PEG-INF-alfa) have polyethylene glycol added to the interferon via pegylation, which prolongs the half-life, reducing the dosing frequency to once weekly. The interferons cause substantial toxicities and laboratory abnormalities that limit their use. As better-tolerated treatments for HCV are approved, use of interferon continues to decline.

DRUG	DOSING	SAFETY/SIDE EFFECTS/MONITORING
Interferon-alfa-2b (*Intron A*) – for HBV, HCV, many cancers Pegylated interferon-alfa-2a *(Pegasys)* – for HBV and HCV Pegylated interferon-alfa-2b *(PegIntron, Sylatron)* – for HCV Interferon-beta is used for Multiple Sclerosis; see Systemic Steroids & Autoimmune Conditions chapter	Dosing varies based on indication. **HCV dosing example** *Intron A:* 3 million units SC 3 times weekly *PegIntron:* 1.5 mcg/kg SC weekly *Pegasys:* 180 mcg SC weekly + ribavirin (different doses depending on interferon type used)	**BOXED WARNINGS** May cause or exacerbate neuropsychiatric, autoimmune, ischemic or infectious disorders; combination treatment with ribavirin may cause birth defects and/or fetal mortality and/or hemolytic anemia **CONTRAINDICATIONS** Autoimmune hepatitis, decompensated liver disease in cirrhotic patients, infants and neonates *(Pegasys)* **WARNINGS** Neuropsychiatric and cardiovascular events, endocrine disorders (hypo/hyperthyroidism, hypo/hyperglycemia), ophthalmologic disorders (retinopathy, decrease in vision), pancreatitis, myelosuppression, serious skin reactions **SIDE EFFECTS** CNS effects (fatigue, depression, anxiety, weakness), GI upset (N/V, anorexia, weight loss), ↑ LFTs (5-10x ULN during treatment), myelosuppression, mild alopecia Flu-like syndrome (fever, chills, HA, malaise); pre-treat with acetaminophen and an antihistamine **MONITORING** CBC with differential and platelets, LFTs, uric acid, SCr, electrolytes, TGs, thyroid function tests, serum HBV-DNA or HCV-RNA levels **NOTES** MedGuide required

Nucleoside/Tide Reverse Transcriptase Inhibitors (NRTIs)

These agents inhibit HBV replication by inhibiting HBV polymerase resulting in DNA chain termination. Prior to starting HBV therapy, all patients should be tested for HIV. Antivirals used for HBV can have activity against HIV and if a patient is co-infected with both HIV and HBV, it is important that the chosen therapy is appropriate for both viruses to minimize risk of HIV antiviral resistance.

DRUG	DOSING	SAFETY/SIDE EFFECTS/MONITORING
All NRTIs	CrCl < 50 mL/min: ↓ dose or frequency	**BOXED WARNINGS (FOR ENTIRE CLASS)** Lactic acidosis and severe hepatomegaly with steatosis, which may be fatal. Exacerbations of HBV may occur upon discontinuation, monitor closely. See HIV chapter for further information.
Tenofovir disoproxil fumarate (TDF) ***(Viread)*** Tablet, powder (oral) 1st line agent	300 mg daily	**WARNINGS** Renal toxicity including acute renal failure and/or Fanconi syndrome, osteomalacia and ↓ bone mineral density **SIDE EFFECTS** TDF: N/V/D, HA, depression, renal impairment, ↓ bone mineral density, ↑ LFTs, ↑ CPK *Vemlidy:* HA, abdominal pain, fatigue, cough, nausea, ↓ bone mineral density, ↑ LFTs **NOTES** Tenofovir alafenamide (TAF) is associated with ↓ renal and bone toxicity compared to TDF. *Vemlidy* alone is not recommended for treating HIV; see HIV chapter for tenofovir combination products used for HIV.
Tenofovir alafenamide (TAF) ***(Vemlidy)*** Tablet	25 mg daily with food	
Entecavir *(Baraclude)* Tablet, oral solution 1st line agent	Nucleoside-treatment naïve: 0.5 mg daily Lamivudine-resistant: 1 mg daily Take on empty stomach	**BOXED WARNING** May cause HIV resistance in patients with unrecognized or untreated HIV infection. **SIDE EFFECTS** Peripheral edema, pyrexia, ascites, ↑ LFTs, hematuria, nephrotoxicity, ↑ SCr **NOTES** Food reduces AUC by 18-20%; take on an empty stomach (2 hours before or after a meal).
Adefovir *(Hepsera)* Tablet	10 mg daily	**BOXED WARNING** May cause HIV resistance in patients with unrecognized or untreated HIV infection. Use caution in patients with renal impairment or those at risk of renal toxicity (including concurrent nephrotoxic agents or NSAIDs). **SIDE EFFECTS** HA, weakness, abdominal pain, hematuria, rash, nephrotoxicity
LamiVUDine *(Epivir HBV)* Tablet, oral solution	100 mg daily 150 mg BID or 300 mg daily if co-infected with HIV	**BOXED WARNING** Do not use *Epivir HBV* for treatment of HIV (contains lower dose of lamivudine); can result in HIV resistance. **SIDE EFFECTS** HA, N/V/D, fatigue, insomnia, myalgias, ↑ LFTs
Telbivudine *(Tyzeka)* Tablet	600 mg daily	**SIDE EFFECTS** ↑ CPK, fatigue, HA, ↑ LFTs

NRTI Drug Interactions

- Ribavirin can ↑ hepatotoxic effects of all NRTIs; lactic acidosis can occur.
- Lamivudine: SMX/TMP can ↑ lamivudine levels due to ↓ excretion.
- Tenofovir disoproxil fumarate: avoid concomitant treatment with didanosine or adefovir due to ↑ risk of virologic failure and potential for ↑ side effects.
- Tenofovir alafenamide is a P-gp substrate; avoid use with oxcarbazepine, phenytoin, phenobarbital, rifampin and St. John's wort.
- Telbivudine: avoid concomitant interferon alpha treatment due to ↑ risk of peripheral neuropathy.

NRTI Counseling

- *Epivir HBV* tablets and oral solution are not interchangeable with *Epivir* tablets and solution (which have higher doses).
- Entecavir: food ↓ the absorption of this drug; take on an empty stomach (take 2 hours before or after a meal).
- Some people (rarely) have developed a serious condition called lactic acidosis (a buildup of an acid in the blood). Lactic acidosis is a medical emergency and must be treated in the hospital. See your healthcare provider right away if you feel very weak or tired, have unusual muscle pain, have trouble breathing, have stomach pain with nausea and vomiting, and/or feel dizzy or lightheaded.
- Lamivudine: some people (rarely) have developed pancreatitis, which is a medical emergency and must be treated in the hospital. See your healthcare provider right away if you have upper abdominal pain that radiates to your back, or abdominal pain that feels worse after eating with or without nausea or vomiting.

LIVER DISEASE AND CIRRHOSIS

Background

Cirrhosis is advanced, frequently irreversible fibrosis (scarring) of the liver. There are many causes, but the most common in the U.S. are hepatitis C and alcohol consumption. As scar tissue replaces the healthy liver tissue, blood flow through the liver is impaired, leading to numerous complications including portal hypertension, varices, ascites, hepatic encephalopathy and others.

Clinical Presentation

Symptoms can include nausea, loss of appetite, vomiting, diarrhea, malaise, pain in the upper right quadrant of the abdomen, yellowed skin and yellowed whites of the eyes (jaundice), darkened urine and/or lightened color (white or clay-colored) stool caused by low bile in the stool due to decreased production or a blocked bile duct.

Objective Criteria

Cirrhosis is definitively diagnosed with a liver biopsy, but certain labs can suggest cirrhosis or liver damage. Aspartate aminotransferase (AST) and alanine aminotransferase (ALT) are liver enzymes. The normal range for both AST and ALT is 10 – 40 units/L. There is some slight variance in these ranges on different lab reports. In general, the higher the values, the more active (acute) the liver disease. Clinical signs of liver disease, in addition to ↑ ALT and ↑ AST, include ↓ albumin (protein produced by the liver; normal range 3.5 – 5.5 g/dL), ↑ alkaline phosphatase (Alk Phos or ALP), ↑ total bilirubin (Tbili), ↑ lactate dehydrogenase (LDH), and ↑ in prothrombin time (PT). Albumin and PT/INR are markers of synthetic (production ability) liver function and are likely to be altered in chronic liver disease (particularly cirrhosis). Liver disease can be classified as hepatocellular (↑ ALT and ↑ AST), cholestatic (↑ Alk Phos and ↑ Tbili), or mixed (↑ AST, ALT, Alk Phos and Tbili). See Lab Values & Drug Monitoring chapter for additional information.

Assessing Severity of Liver Disease

It is important to assess the severity of the liver disease as it serves as a predictor of patient survival, surgical outcomes, and the risk of complications such as variceal bleeding. The Child-Turcotte-Pugh (CPT) or Child-Pugh classification system is widely used and online calculators are available. The score ranges from 0 – 15. Class A (mild disease) is defined as a score < 7; Class B (moderate disease) is a score of 7 – 9, and Class C (severe disease) is a score of 10 – 15. The model for end-stage liver disease (MELD) is another scoring system that ranges from 0 – 40, with higher numbers indicating a greater risk of death within three months. Noninvasive tests are increasingly used to predict fibrosis and cirrhosis.

Unlike drug dosing in renal failure, little data are available to guide drug dosing of hepatically cleared agents in patients with liver failure. It is becoming more common to see package labeling for medications make specific recommendations based on Child-Pugh class. In general, caution is advised when using hepatically cleared agents in severe liver disease (Class C) and, in select cases, dose adjustment may be necessary. In general, for drugs that are extensively hepatically metabolized, it is best to start at lower doses and titrate to clinical effect.

Natural Products

Milk thistle, an extract derived from a member of the daisy family, is sometimes used by patients with liver disease. Although there are limited data to demonstrate efficacy of milk thistle for alcoholic liver disease, hepatitis B or C, milk thistle does not appear to be harmful. A possible side effect is mild diarrhea and there are concerns for possible drug interactions with milk thistle and antiviral hepatitis C medications. Kava, comfrey, flavocoxid (*Limbrel,* a medical food) are known hepatotoxins.

Drug-Induced Liver Injury

Many drugs can cause liver damage. If this occurs, the primary treatment (in most cases) is to stop the drug. Hepatotoxic drugs are typically discontinued when the LFTs are > 3 times the upper limit of normal (> 150 units/L of ALT or AST), however clinical judgment is warranted. Rechallenging with the potential agent can be considered if clinically necessary. An excellent reference for drug-induced liver injury (DILI) is http://livertox.nih.gov.

Acetaminophen is a known hepatotoxic agent and can cause severe injury. Acetaminophen may be used by patients with cirrhosis, for limited periods of time and at lower dosages. Patients with alcoholic cirrhosis who are actively drinking and/or malnourished may be more susceptible to further liver damage. NSAIDs should be avoided in patients with cirrhosis because these agents can lead to decompensation, including bleeding.

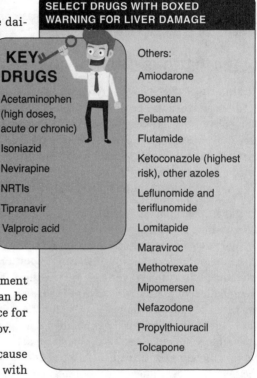

SELECT DRUGS WITH BOXED WARNING FOR LIVER DAMAGE

KEY DRUGS

- Acetaminophen (high doses, acute or chronic)
- Isoniazid
- Nevirapine
- NRTIs
- Tipranavir
- Valproic acid

Others:

- Amiodarone
- Bosentan
- Felbamate
- Flutamide
- Ketoconazole (highest risk), other azoles
- Leflunomide and teriflunomide
- Lomitapide
- Maraviroc
- Methotrexate
- Mipomersen
- Nefazodone
- Propylthiouracil
- Tolcapone

ALCOHOLIC LIVER DISEASE

Alcohol-induced liver disease is the most common type of drug-induced liver disease. Risk increases with the amount of alcohol consumed and duration. Women have higher risk than men. Alcoholic liver disease can include fatty liver, alcoholic hepatitis, and chronic hepatitis with hepatic fibrosis or cirrhosis. Chronic alcohol ingestion over a long period of time causes "steatosis" or fatty liver, due to fat deposition in the hepatocytes. This can be reversible and self-limited (if drinking is stopped) or can lead to fibrosis and cirrhosis. Some patients develop alcoholic hepatitis, an acute process with poor short-term survival. Of all chronic heavy drinkers, only 15 – 20% develop hepatitis or cirrhosis, which can occur simultaneously or in succession.

Chronic consumption of alcohol results in the secretion of pro-inflammatory cytokines (TNF-alpha, IL-6 and IL-8), oxidative stress, lipid peroxidation, and acetaldehyde toxicity. These factors cause inflammation, apoptosis (cell death) and eventually fibrosis of liver cells. Drinking habits of patients need to be assessed routinely. If alcohol consumption is ceased, the liver can possibly regenerate to some extent.

Treatment

The most important part of treatment is alcohol cessation. Maintenance of abstinence is essential to improving outcomes and should include the use of drug treatment to control cravings. Treatment programs use mainly benzodiazepines for alcohol withdrawal in inpatients whereas anticonvulsants are used for outpatients. Naltrexone *(ReVia)*, acamprosate *(Campral)* and disulfiram *(Antabuse)* are used to prevent relapses. There are a few off-label treatments. An alcohol rehabilitation program and a support group whose members share common experiences and problems are extremely helpful in breaking the addiction to alcohol. Proper nutrition is essential to help the liver recover. Vitamins and trace minerals, including vitamin A, vitamin D, thiamine (vitamin B1), folate, pyridoxine (vitamin B6) and zinc can help reverse malnutrition. Thiamine is used to prevent and treat Wernicke-Korsakoff syndrome. Wernicke's encephalopathy and Korsakoff syndrome are different conditions that are both due to brain damage caused by a lack of vitamin B1. Lastly, hepatotoxic drugs should be avoided if possible or doses should be adjusted as appropriate.

COMPLICATIONS OF LIVER DISEASE AND CIRRHOSIS

Portal Hypertension and Variceal Bleeding

Portal hypertension, or increased blood pressure in the portal vein, can cause further complications including the development and bleeding of esophageal varices. Varices are enlarged veins in the lower part of the esophagus. When blood flow through the liver is blocked by scar tissue, it backs up and flows into smaller blood vessels. These vessels can balloon out and bleed if they break open (see figure).

Esophageal Varices

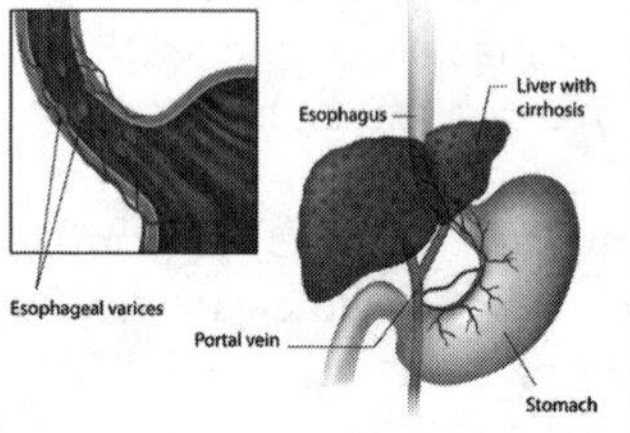

alila © 123RF

Acute variceal bleeding can be fatal. Patients should be stabilized by providing supportive therapy such as blood volume resuscitation/blood products, mechanical ventilation, correction of coagulopathy, and attempts to stop the bleeding and preventing rebleeding. Band ligation (putting a band around the vessel) or sclerotherapy (injecting a solution into the vessel to make it collapse and close) are recommended first-line treatments for bleeding varices. These procedures are performed by a physician using endoscopy. Medications that vasoconstrict the splanchnic (GI) circulation can stop or minimize the bleeding. Octreotide is selective for the splanchnic vessels whereas vasopressin is non-selective. Surgical interventions may be considered if the patient is not responding to treatment or to prevent future rebleeding episodes. Common surgical procedures include balloon tamponade (may help control current bleeding) or transjugular intrahepatic portosystemic shunt (TIPS), in which a stent is placed in the liver to allow blood to flow directly from the portal vein to the hepatic vein (bypassing the scarred liver tissue). Short-term antibiotic prophylaxis (ceftriaxone or quinolone for up to 7 days) should be provided to cirrhotic patients with a variceal bleed to reduce bacterial infections and mortality. Non-selective beta-blockers should be added after resolution of variceal bleeding for secondary prevention of variceal bleeding recurrence.

DRUG	DOSING	SAFETY/SIDE EFFECTS/MONITORING
Octreotide *(SandoSTATIN)* Analog of somatostatin with greater potency and longer duration of action	Bolus: 25-100 mcg IV (usual 50 mcg), may repeat in 1 hr if hemorrhage not controlled Infusion: followed by 25-50 mcg/hr continuous IV infusion x 2-5 days	**SIDE EFFECTS** Bradycardia, chest pain, fatigue, HA, pruritus, hyperglycemia, hypoglycemia (highest risk in type 1 diabetes), N/V/D, hypothyroidism, abdominal pain, malaise, fever, dizziness, flatulence, cholelithiasis, biliary sludge, constipation, injection site pain, arthropathy, myalgias, URTIs **MONITORING** Blood glucose, HR, ECG
Vasopressin *(Vasostrict)* Antidiuretic hormone analog Not 1st line (usually used with nitroglycerin IV to prevent myocardial ischemia)	Infusion: 0.2-0.4 units/min IV (max 0.8 units/min), max duration 24 hours	**SIDE EFFECTS** Arrhythmias, chest pain, MI, ↓ cardiac output, ↑ BP, N/V **MONITORING** BP, HR, ECG, fluid balance

Non-selective beta blockers (such as nadolol and propranolol) or endoscopic variceal ligation (EVL) are used for primary prevention of variceal bleeding. Beta blockers reduce portal pressure by reducing portal venous inflow by two mechanisms: 1) decreased cardiac output (via beta-1 blockade), and 2) decreased splanchnic blood flow by vasoconstriction (via beta-2 blockade and unopposed alpha activity). The beta blocker should be titrated to the maximal tolerated dose (target HR 55 – 60 BPM) and continued indefinitely.

DRUG	DOSING	SAFETY/SIDE EFFECTS/MONITORING
Nadolol *(Corgard)*	Initial: 40 mg PO daily	Refer to Hypertension chapter for a complete review of beta blockers. **BOXED WARNING** Do not withdraw beta blockers abruptly (particularly in patients with CAD), gradually taper over 1-2 weeks to avoid acute tachycardia, HTN, and/or ischemia. **CONTRAINDICATIONS** Sinus bradycardia, 2nd or 3rd degree heart block, sick sinus syndrome (unless patient has a functioning artificial pacemaker) or cardiogenic shock. Do not initiate in patients with active asthma exacerbation. Non-selective agents are used for portal hypertension; use extreme caution with asthma or severe COPD or peripheral vascular disease and Raynaud's disease. May mask signs of hyperthyroidism; may aggravate psychiatric conditions, and use caution in patients with diabetes particularly with recurrent hypoglycemia. Monitor HR and BP.
Propranolol *(Inderal LA, Inderal XL, InnoPran XL)*	Initial: 20 mg PO BID	

Hepatic Encephalopathy

Hepatic encephalopathy (HE) is a syndrome of neuropsychiatric abnormalities caused by acute or chronic hepatic insufficiency. Symptoms include musty odor of the breath and/or urine, changes in thinking, confusion, forgetfulness, mood changes, poor concentration, drowsiness, disorientation, worsening handwriting and hand tremor (asterixis), sluggish movements, and many others, including risk of coma. The symptoms of HE result from an accumulation of gut-derived nitrogenous substances in the blood (such as ammonia, glutamate, others). These substances would normally be cleared by the liver, but when the liver is not functioning properly, blood is shunted through collateral vessels that empty directly into the circulation instead. Treatment includes identifying and treating precipitating factors and reducing blood ammonia levels through diet (limiting the amount of animal protein) and drug therapy.

Patients should have a daily protein intake of 1 – 1.5 g/kg. Vegetable and dairy sources of protein are preferred to animal sources due to the lower calorie to nitrogen ratio. Branched-chain amino acids (BCAAs) (e.g., leucine, isoleucine, valine) are favored over aromatic amino acids (AAAs); they interfere with AAAs ability to cross the blood-brain barrier and increase hepatocyte growth factor synthesis.

Drug therapy consists of nonabsorbable disaccharides (such as lactulose) and antibiotics (rifaximin, neomycin, others) for acute and chronic therapy. Lactulose is first line therapy for both acute and chronic (prevention) therapy, followed by rifaximin. Lactulose works by converting ammonia produced by intestinal bacteria to ammonium, which is polar and therefore cannot readily diffuse into the blood. Lactulose also enhances diffusion of ammonia into the colon for excretion. Antibiotics work by inhibiting the activity of urease-producing bacteria, which decreases the ammonia production. Zinc (220 mg PO BID) may be used; it can serve as a cofactor for enzymes of the urea cycle and further decrease ammonia concentrations and correct a zinc deficiency.

DRUG	DOSING	SAFETY/SIDE EFFECTS/MONITORING
Lactulose *(Constulose, Enulose, Generlac, Kristalose)* Oral solution and packet	Treatment: 30-45 mL (or 20-30 grams) PO every hour until evacuation; then 30-45 mL (20-30 grams) PO 3-4 times/day titrated to produce 2-3 soft bowel movements daily Enema: Q4-6H PRN Prevention: 30-45 mL (or 20-30 grams) PO 3-4 times/day titrated to produce 2-3 soft bowel movements daily	**SIDE EFFECTS** Flatulence, diarrhea, dyspepsia, abdominal discomfort, dehydration, hypernatremia, hypokalemia **MONITORING** Mental status, bowel movements, ammonia, fluid status, electrolytes
RifAXIMin ***(Xifaxan)*** Tablet	Treatment (off-label): 400 mg PO Q8H x 5-10 days Prevention: 550 mg PO BID	**SIDE EFFECTS** Peripheral edema, dizziness, fatigue, nausea, ascites, flatulence, headache **MONITORING** Mental status, ammonia
Neomycin	4-12 g daily divided Q4-6H x 5-6 days	**BOXED WARNINGS** Neurotoxicity, (hearing loss, vertigo, ataxia); nephrotoxicity (particularly in renal impairment or with concurrent use of other nephrotoxic drugs); may cause neuromuscular blockade and respiratory paralysis especially when given soon after anesthesia or with muscle relaxants **SIDE EFFECTS** GI upset, ototoxicity, nephrotoxicity, irritation/soreness of mouth/rectal area **MONITORING** Mental status, renal function, hearing, ammonia
MetroNIDAZOLE *(Flagyl, Flagyl ER, Metro)*	250 mg PO Q6-12H	**NOTES** Do not use long term due to peripheral neuropathies See Infectious Diseases I for additional information

Ascites

Ascites is fluid accumulation within the peritoneal space that can lead to the development of spontaneous bacterial peritonitis (SBP) and hepatorenal syndrome (HRS). Ascites is a common occurrence when the portal hypertension leads to an increase in systemic and splanchnic vasodilation, which results in increased arterial pressure, sodium and water retention, and renal vasoconstriction.

There are many treatment approaches to managing ascites, which are chosen based on the severity. Patients with ascites due to portal hypertension should restrict dietary sodium intake to < 2 grams/day, avoid sodium-retaining medications (including NSAIDs), and use diuretics to increase fluid loss. Restriction of fluid is recommended only in patients with symptomatic severe hyponatremia (serum Na < 120 mEq/L).

Diuretic therapy for ascites can be initiated with either spironolactone monotherapy or with a combination of furosemide and spironolactone. Spironolactone is initiated at a single daily dose of 50 – 100 mg and increased to a maximum of 400 mg per day. When used in combination, the drugs should be titrated to a maximal weight loss of 0.5 kg/day with a ratio of 40 mg furosemide to 100 mg spironolactone to maintain potassium balance, if possible. Furosemide by itself is ineffective. All patients with cirrhosis and ascites should be considered for liver transplantation. In severe cases abdominal paracentesis may be needed to directly remove ascitic fluid. Large volume paracentesis (removal of > 5 L) has been associated with significant fluid shifts and the addition of albumin (6 – 8 grams per liter of fluid removed) is recommended to prevent paracentesis-induced circulatory dysfunction and progression to hepatorenal syndrome.

Spontaneous Bacterial Peritonitis

Spontaneous bacterial peritonitis (SBP) is an acute infection of the ascitic fluid. Diagnosis is guided by cell and microbiologic analysis. In general, targeting *Streptococci* and enteric Gram-negative pathogens with ceftriaxone (or equivalent) for 5 – 7 days is recommended. The addition of albumin (1.5 grams/kg of body weight on day 1 and 1 gram/kg on day 3) can improve survival in some patients. Patients who have survived an episode of SBP should receive secondary prophylaxis with oral norfloxacin or sulfamethoxazole/trimethoprim.

Hepatorenal Syndrome

Hepatorenal syndrome (HRS) is the development of renal failure in patients with advanced cirrhosis. HRS is the result of renal vasoconstriction, mediated by activation of the renin-angiotensin-aldosterone system (RAAS) and the sympathetic nervous system (SNS) through a feedback mechanism known as hepatorenal reflex. Appropriately treating the various stages and complications of cirrhosis, and avoiding nephrotoxins and renal hypoperfusion help prevent progression to HRS. HRS can be directly treated with albumin, octreotide, and midodrine, but prevention is critical given the difficulty in managing HRS in this patient population.

PRACTICE CASE

PM is a 44 y/o male patient being seen in the gastroenterology clinic for follow-up. He was recently diagnosed with HCV and expected to started treatment this week with Harvoni. His past medical history is significant for depression and GERD. PM stopped using alcohol and IV drugs 5 years ago. He has repeatedly tested negative for HIV over many years.

Allergies: NKDA

Medications:
Celexa 40 mg daily
Pepcid 20 mg daily
Tums 1-2 tabs PRN heartburn

Vitals:
Height: 5'9" Weight: 196 pounds
BP: 131/82 mmHg HR: 75 BPM RR: 13 BPM Temp: 98.°F Pain: 3/10

Labs:

Na (mEq/L) = 140 (135 - 145)	WBC (cells/mm^3) = 6.1 (4 - 11 x 10^3)
K (mEq/L) = 4.1 (3.5 - 5)	Hgb (g/dL) = 14.1 (13.5 - 18 male, 12 - 16 female)
Cl (mEq/L) = 101 (95 - 103)	Hct (%) = 42.3 (38 - 50 male, 36 - 46 female)
HCO_3 (mEq/L) = 29 (24 - 30)	Plt (cells/mm^3) = 187 (150 - 450 x 10^3)
BUN (mg/dL) = 17 (7 - 20)	AST (IU/L) = 87 (1 - 40)
SCr (mg/dL) = 1.1 (0.6 - 1.3)	ALT (IU/L) = 75 (1 - 40)
Glucose (mg/dL) = 132 (100 - 125)	Albumin (g/dL) = 3.7 (3.5 - 5)
Ca (mg/dL) = 10.1 (8.5 - 10.5)	T Bili (mg/dL) = 1.1 (0.1 - 1.2)
Mg (mEq/L) = 1.5 (1.3 - 2.1)	TSH (mIU/L) = 1.9 (0.3 - 3)
PO_4 (mg/dL) = 4.2 (2.3 - 4.7)	

Refer to the clinical pharmacist for review of medication side effects and additional counseling.

Questions

1. PM is starting *Harvoni*. What are the components of *Harvoni*?
   a. Ledipasvir + sofosbuvir
   b. Elbasvir + grazoprevir
   c. Paritaprevir + ritonavir + ombitasvir + dasabuvir
   d. Simeprevir + sofosbuvir
   e. Sofosbuvir + daclatasvir

2. Upon review of PM's medication list, which medication/s pose a potential drug-drug interaction risk with *Harvoni*?
   a. *Celexa*
   b. *Tums*
   c. *Pepcid*
   d. *Celexa* and *Pepcid*
   e. *Tums* and *Pepcid*

Questions 3 – 7 do not apply to the above case.

3. Which of the following is the most serious and primary toxicity of ribavirin?

   a. Hemolytic anemia
   b. Hemorrhagic cystitis
   c. Pancreatitis
   d. Agranulocytosis
   e. Gastrointestinal hemorrhage

4. A patient is scheduled to start immunosuppressive therapy for chronic inflammatory bowel disease. Testing for which of the following is indicated? (Select **ALL** that apply.)

   a. Latent Hepatitis A virus infection
   b. Latent Hepatitis B virus infection
   c. Latent Hepatitis C virus infection
   d. HIV
   e. Herpes Simplex Virus

5. A patient with liver failure presents with acute hepatic encephalopathy. Which of the following is considered first-line treatment for acute hepatic encephalopathy?

   a. Decreasing protein intake to < 1 gram/kg/day
   b. Lactulose
   c. Furosemide
   d. Neomycin
   e. Metronidazole

6. Which of the following is/are correct regarding *Zepatier*? (Select **ALL** that apply.)

   a. Administration with *Dilantin* is contraindicated.
   b. Avoid acid suppressive therapy while on treatment.
   c. It is used in combination with daclatasvir.
   d. The components are elbasvir and grazoprevir.
   e. It is indicated for treatment of acute variceal bleeding.

7. Which of the following medications can lead to renal insufficiency and osteomalacia?

   a. Adefovir
   b. Tenofovir
   c. Daclatasvir
   d. Lamivudine
   e. Entecavir

Answers

1-a, 2-e, 3-a, 4-b, 5-b, 6-a,d, 7-b

28

INFECTIOUS DISEASES I: BACKGROUND & ANTIBACTERIALS BY DRUG CLASS

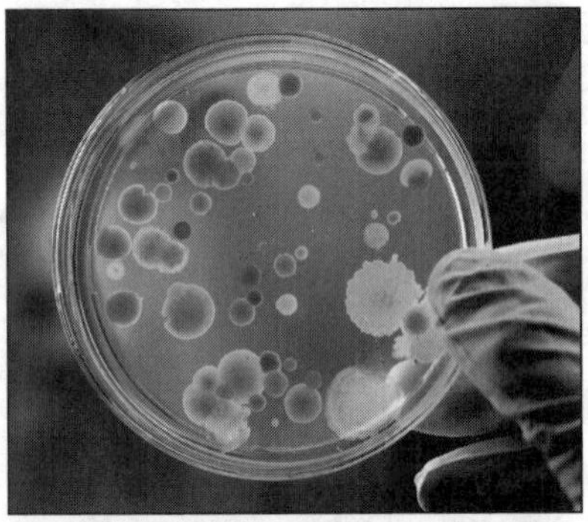

GUIDELINES/REFERENCES

Barlett JG, Auwaerter PG, Pham PA. Johns Hopkins Antibiotic Guide: Diagnosis & Treatment of Infectious Diseases 3rd Ed. Massachusetts: Jones and Bartlett Learning; 2012.

Additional guidelines (by disease state) included with online course.

We gratefully acknowledge the assistance of Emi Minejima, PharmD, Assistant Professor and Annie Wong-Beringer, PharmD, FCCP, FIDSA, Associate Dean and Professor, University of Southern California School of Pharmacy, in preparing this chapter.

HOW TO APPROACH INFECTIOUS DISEASES

Infectious diseases (ID) can be a challenging area for many to master. In most disease states, the two factors to consider are the patient and the drug. In ID, three factors impact decision-making: the <u>patient</u> (host), the <u>drug</u> (anti-infective), and the <u>bug</u> (pathogen). Important patient-specific information for ID includes medication allergies, immune function, and chronic diseases that put a patient at risk for certain types of infections or which can change the treatment approach (e.g., the presence of renal failure may require a change in the drug or the dose).

HOW DO I START?

- Recognize common organisms and groups of organisms
- Focus on resistant organisms and the drugs that treat them
- Use bolded drugs, underlined information and study tips to identify important points and think of how to assess a patient profile

EXAM SCENARIO

When studying the carbapenems, think of how you would approach a case on the exam in which one of the answer choices is *Invanz* 1 gram IV Q24H. How can you decide if this is a the best answer choice? Assess the following, using the underlined information in the carbapenems drug table:

- Allergies: if the patient has a penicillin allergy, there is likely a better answer choice because of the possibility of cross-reactivity.
- Culture and susceptibility: if it is growing ESBL-positive *E. coli*, ertapenem may be a good choice. If *Pseudomonas* is growing, you can rule out this answer choice, based on ertapenem's coverage.
- Past medical history and medication profile: if the patient has a history of seizures or takes a seizure drug, such as phenytoin, there is likely a better choice than a carbapenem, due to the risk of seizures.

Infectious diseases are organized into four chapters: ID-I covers the principles of infectious diseases and pharmacology of antibacterial drugs; ID-II discusses treatment of specific bacterial infections; ID-III reviews antifungals, antivirals and selected diseases; and ID-IV examines prophylaxis and treatment of opportunistic infections in immunocompromised patients.

Do not be tempted to think of bugs, drugs and infectious diseases as separate sections to simply memorize. Instead, try to tie in the infection, the typical pathogens involved and the antimicrobial spectrum of coverage together as you progress through the chapters.

BACKGROUND

An infectious disease is caused by one or more pathogens [disease-causing viruses, bacteria, fungi, protozoa, parasites, and/or infectious proteins (prions)]. Infectious diseases are transmitted through various mechanisms, including physical contact with an infected individual or their body fluids, consuming contaminated food or water, or by touching contaminated objects. Some conditions are transmitted by airborne inhalation and others are spread by a vector (carrier). Transmissible diseases that are spread from person to person are referred to as communicable or contagious, and can be highly infective; these involve the patient and the facility taking specific steps to stop the infection from spreading.

Bacterial Organism Identification

One of the first steps in bacterial identification is the Gram stain. Bacteria stain differently based on the composition of their cell wall. Gram-positive organisms have a thick cell wall and stain dark purple, or bluish in color from the crystal violet stain. Gram-negative organisms have a thin cell wall and take up the safranin counterstain, resulting in a pink or reddish color. In addition to revealing the cell wall composition, the Gram stain outlines the organism, so it can be categorized by shape (or morphology). Gram stain results can help determine the appropriate empiric antibiotic regimen, which is based on a best-guess of the likely organism(s) causing the infection. Empiric treatment is usually broad-spectrum, which means it covers several different types of bacteria. After identification, antibiotic streamlining occurs, the process of converting from a broad-spectrum regimen to a treatment that is targeted to the organism (narrow spectrum).

This table is designed to provide a framework to classify the organisms, and can serve as a reference, especially as you review the coverage of specific antibiotics.

Selected Bacterial Organisms

GRAM-POSITIVE ORGANISMS	
COCCI	
Clusters	**Pairs/Chains**
Staphylococcus aureus (MSSA, MRSA, CA-MRSA) *Staphylococcus epidermidis* (Coagulase-negative staphylococci) 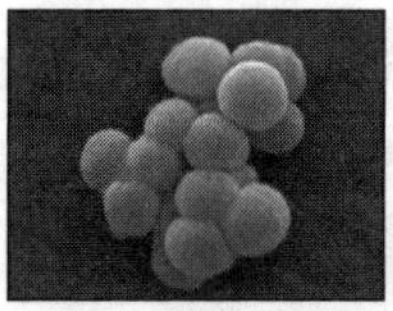	*Streptococcus pneumoniae* *Streptococcus pyogenes* (Group A) *Streptococcus agalactiae* (Group B) *Viridans* group *Streptococcus* *Enterococcus faecalis* (including VRE) *Enterococcus faecium* (including VRE)
RODS	**ANAEROBES**
Bacillus anthracis *Corynebacterium* species *Listeria monocytogenes* *Nocardia asteroides* (branched appearance)	*Peptostreptococcus* *Actinomyces israelii* (branched appearance) *Clostridium difficile* *Clostridium perfringens* *Lactobacillus* species *Propionibacterium acnes*

Selected Bacterial Organisms continued

GRAM-NEGATIVE ORGANISMS	
COCCI	**COCCOBACILLI**
Neisseria gonorrhoeae *Neisseria meningitidis*	*Acinetobacter baumannii* *Bordetella pertussis* *Pasteurella multocida* *Moraxella catarrhalis* 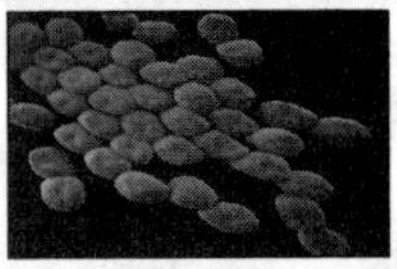
RODS	
Enterobacteriaceae (colonize the gut)	**Non-Enterobacteriaceae (do not colonize the gut)**
Escherichia coli *Klebsiella* species *Enterobacter cloacae* *Proteus mirabilis* *Serratia* species *Citrobacter* species *Morganella morganii* *Salmonella* species *Shigella* species 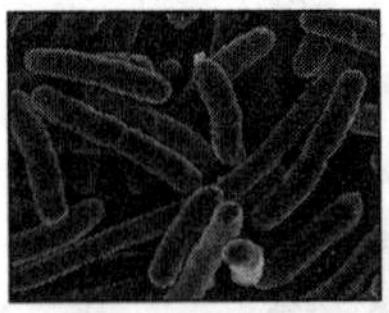	*Pseudomonas aeruginosa* *Burkholderia cepacia* *Stenotrophomonas maltophilia* *Legionella pneumophila* *Haemophilus influenzae* *Eikenella corrodens* *Providencia* species *Campylobacter jejuni* (curved rod) *Helicobacter pylori* (curved rod) *Vibrio cholerae* *Yersinia pestis*
ANAEROBES	**ATYPICAL ORGANISMS**
Bacteroides fragilis *Prevotella* species *Fusobacterium* species	*Chlamydia/Chlamydophila pneumoniae* *Mycoplasma pneumoniae* *Mycobacterium tuberculosis* (acid-fast bacillus)

MSSA = Methicillin-susceptible Staphylococcus aureus; MRSA = Methicillin-resistant Staphylococcus aureus; CA-MRSA = Community-associated methicillin-resistant Staphyolcoccus aureus; VRE = Vancomycin-resistant Enterococcus

Common groups of organisms: PEK = Proteus, E. coli, Klebsiella; HNPEK = Haemophilus, Neisseria, Proteus, E. coli, Klebsiella; CAPES = Citrobacter, Acinetobacter, Providencia, Enterobacter, Serratia; Mouth flora (anaerobes) = Peptostreptococcus, Actinomyces

ANTIBIOTIC RESISTANCE

Antibiotic resistance is the ability of an organism to multiply in the presence of a drug that would normally limit its growth or kill it. The CDC estimates that there are ~2,000,000 infections a year where the causative organism is resistant to the usual treatment. These infections are difficult to treat and often require drugs that are costly and/or toxic.

There are a variety of mechanisms that cause resistance. It can be intrinsic (natural) to the organism. For example, *E. coli* is resistant to vancomycin because this antibiotic is too large to penetrate the bacterial cell wall. It can be due to selection pressure; antibiotics kill off the susceptible bacteria, leaving behind the more resistant strains to multiply. For example, normal GI flora includes *Enterococcus*, some of which is vancomycin-resistant *Enterococcus* (VRE), which can become predominant after the use of antibiotics that have eliminated susceptible organisms. Enzyme inactivation is another mechanism of resistance. For example, beta-lactamases are enzymes produced by some bacteria, which break down beta-lactams before they can bind to the site of activity. This is a primary resistance mechanism to beta-lactam antibiotics. Beta-lactamase inhibitors (clavulanate, sulbactam, tazobactam, avibactam) are combined with some penicillins and cephalosporins to preserve or increase their spectrum of activity. Extended-spectrum beta-lactamases (ESBLs) are beta-lactamases that can break down all penicillins and most cephalosporins. Organisms that produce ESBLs are a therapeutic challenge, and serious infections involving these organisms are treated with carbapenems, or newer cephalosporin/beta-lactamase inhibitors.

COMMON RESISTANT PATHOGENS
S. aureus (MRSA)
E. faecalis, E. faecium (VRE)
E. coli, extended-spectrum beta-lactamase producing (ESBL, CRE)
K. pneumoniae (ESBL, CRE)
Acinetobacter baumannii
Pseudomonas aeruginosa

Carbapenem-resistant *Enterobacteriaceae* (CRE) are a group of multidrug-resistant (MDR) Gram-negative organisms that are becoming more common. CRE produce enzymes that break down penicillins, most cephalosporins, and carbapenems and are most commonly found in *Klebsiella* spp. (present in normal GI flora). Infections with *Klebsiella* are normally treatable with older, safer drugs. Carbapenem-resistant *Klebsiella pneumoniae* infections typically require treatment with a combination of antibiotics that can include a polymyxin, an older drug class which was not used for many years because less toxic drugs became available. The emergence of CRE and some other resistant Gram-negative infections (including *Acinetobacter baumannii* and *Pseudomonas aeruginosa*), pulled polymyxins back into use, with the need to manage the toxicity that came with them. Another treatment option is a newer, costly drug [the combination of ceftazidime/avibactam *(Avycaz)*], which is active against some carbapenemase-producing organisms.

ANTIBIOTICS AND COLLATERAL DAMAGE

Collateral damage refers to the unintended consequences of antibiotic use, including altered GI flora, which can lead to antibiotic resistance and can cause superinfections such as *C. difficile* infections (CDI). Antibiotics kill the pathogens and normal, healthy GI flora, resulting in overgrowth of organisms that are resistant to the drug. *C. difficile* spores are normally present as part of the flora in the inactive form. When an antibiotic kills off the normal flora, the *C. difficile* spores can become activated and infectious. Activated spores produce toxins that inflame the GI mucosa. Symptoms depend on the degree of inflammation, which can be mild (loose stools and abdominal cramping) to severe (pseudomembranous colitis that can require colonectomy and can be fatal). Older, sicker patients are at a higher risk of developing a *C. difficile* infection. They are also more likely to do poorly once the infection is contracted. In recent years, *C. difficile* infections have become more common, more severe, and more difficult to treat. All antibiotics are associated with risk for CDI, and include a warning of risk of superinfection. Certain antibiotic classes are associated with high risk for CDI, such as clindamycin, which has a boxed warning. When appropriate, antibiotic treatment should be streamlined, or discontinued to reduce risk of CDI.

INFECTIOUS DISEASES CONCEPTS

- Minimum inhibitory concentration (MIC): lowest drug concentration that prevents visible microbial growth after a 24 hour incubation. The MIC is usually reported on the culture and susceptibility report, with the susceptibility interpretation (S, I, or R, described below).
- Breakpoint: the MIC at which an organism is deemed either susceptible or resistant to an antibiotic. Breakpoints vary for different antibiotic classes. Breakpoints are established by the FDA and Clinical and Laboratory Standards Institute (CLSI), not by individual hospitals.
- Synergy: when two or more drugs combine to produce a greater effect than the sum of their individual effects (in contrast to an additive effect, which is the sum of the effect of the individual drugs). Synergy is important for treating certain types of infections.

Culture and Susceptibility

Culture and Susceptibility (C&S) reports are provided by the microbiology laboratory. Patient specimens (lung secretions, urine, blood, tissue from a wound or fluid from an abscess) are sent to the lab, where bacteria are Gram-stained (to reveal the cell wall type and shape). Once an organism has grown in culture, it is identified, and tested against different concentrations of antibiotics to determine the MIC. In the report, each antibiotic has a susceptibility interpretation: S (susceptible or sensitive), I (intermediate) or R (resistant), and the MIC in mg/L (or µg/mL). Refer to the sample C&S.

Susceptible (S) means that the drug inhibits the organism and is likely a good treatment option. Drugs listed as intermediate (I) may be effective under specific circumstances (e.g., higher doses, extended infusions). A drug rated as intermediate would not be expected to achieve as good a result as a drug rated as susceptible. Resistant (R) means the drug is unlikely to be effective and is not a treatment option. MICs are specific to each antibiotic and organism and should not be compared among different classes of antibiotics. In addition to the susceptibility interpretation and the MIC, the choice of antibiotic will depend upon the site of infection, plus patient-specific characteristics and cost.

Sample Culture and Susceptibility Report

URINE CULTURE > 100,000 CFU/mL *E. coli*		
DRUG	**MIC INTERPRETATION**	**MIC (mg/L)**
Ampicillin	R	> 32
Ampicillin/Sulbactam	S	< 2
Cefazolin-UTI	S	< 16
Cefepime	S	< 1
Ceftriaxone	S	< 1
Ciprofloxacin	S	1
Gentamicin	S	< 1
Piperacillin/Tazobactam	S	< 4
Meropenem	S	< 0.25
Nitrofurantoin	S	< 32
Tobramycin	S	< 1
Sulfamethoxazole/ Trimethoprim	R	> 76/4

CFU = colony-forming units; S = susceptible; I = intermediate; R = resistant

Antibiogram

An antibiogram combines the C & S data from individual patients at an institution into one chart (such as all Gram-positive organisms cultured at that hospital). This provides the susceptibility patterns at the hospital over a specific time period (generally 1 year). On the left side, the bacteria are listed. Along the top, the drugs are listed, and below are the percentage of each organism that are susceptible to that drug. Antibiograms aid in selecting empiric treatment (for example, if a patient has a Gram-positive cocci lung infection, a drug that covers a high percentage of the likely organism can be chosen from the antibiogram). They are also used to monitor resistance trends over time.

Antibiogram Example (abridged)

HOSPITAL ANTIBIOGRAM JANUARY-DECEMBER REPORTED AS % SUSCEPTIBLE	# OF ISOLATES	PENICILLIN	OXACILLIN	AMPICILLIN	CEFOTAXIME	CEFTRIAXONE	CLINDAMYCIN	ERYTHROMYCIN	GENTAMICIN	LEVOFLOXACIN	LINEZOLID	TETRACYCLINE	SMX/TMP	VANCOMYCIN
GRAM-POSITIVE ORGANISMS ALL ISOLATES														
Staphylococcus aureus	1360													
MSSA	830	–	100	–	–	–	88	78	98§	87	100	93	98	100
MRSA	530	–	–	–	–	–	78	10	92§	15	100	93	92	100
Streptococcus pneumoniae	42	91* 83**	–	–	100* 92**	100* 92**	–	79	–	97	–	85	80	100
Enterococcus spp.	663	–	–	93	–	–	–	–	69§	–	99	–	–	100
Enterococcus faecalis	99	–	–	98	92	–	–	–	62§	–	99	–	–	87
Enterococcus faecium	164	–	–	10	100	–	–	–	90§	100	99	–	–	15
URINE ISOLATES														
Enterococcus spp.	153	–	–	79	–	–	–	–	–	61	100	–	–	81

**Non-meningitis; **Meningitis; §Synergy only*

ANTIMICROBIAL STEWARDSHIP PROGRAMS

Antimicrobial stewardship programs (ASPs) involve efforts to 1) improve patient safety and outcomes, 2) curb resistance, 3) reduce adverse effects and 4) promote cost-effectiveness.

ASPs are a team effort among ID physicians, ID pharmacists, microbiology lab personnel, infection prevention and control, information technology and prescribers. Teams work to coordinate interventions to improve and measure optimal antibiotic selection, dosage, route of administration and duration.

ASPs use national guidelines with local antibiogram data to establish antibiotic guidance for their hospital. Most ASPs conduct audits of prescribing habits and provide feedback or education to change suboptimal prescribing habits and improve care.

Other examples of ASP interventions are 1) management of aminoglycosides and vancomycin, using pharmacokinetic monitoring to optimize doses and minimize toxicities, 2) use of data from rapid diagnostic tests along with specialized computer software (e.g., clinical decision support programs) that integrate patient information to identify pathogens and shorten the time to starting effective treatment, 3) preauthorization of select antimicrobials and 4) ensuring a timely transition from IV to PO antibiotics.

CLINICAL CASE EXAMPLE

A 77 year old female presents to the hospital from home with confusion and cough. The patient's temperature is 101.9°F, respiratory rate is 32 breaths per minute and oxygen saturation is 88% on room air. The patient's CXR is consistent with pneumonia, the sputum Gram stain shows Gram-positive cocci in pairs and she is being admitted to the ICU. The pharmacist is asked to choose a beta-lactam (in addition to azithromycin) for the empiric antibiotic regimen. After reviewing the institutional antibiogram (see example), the pharmacist recommends ceftriaxone. Local susceptibility patterns are consistent with national guidelines, showing that third generation cephalosporins are highly active against the likely pathogen in this patient *(S. pneumoniae)*.

Antibiotic Mechanisms of Action

Knowledge of the mechanism of action (MOA) can help distinguish what types of organisms can be treated by a given antibiotic. The major targets of antibacterials are outlined in the following diagram.

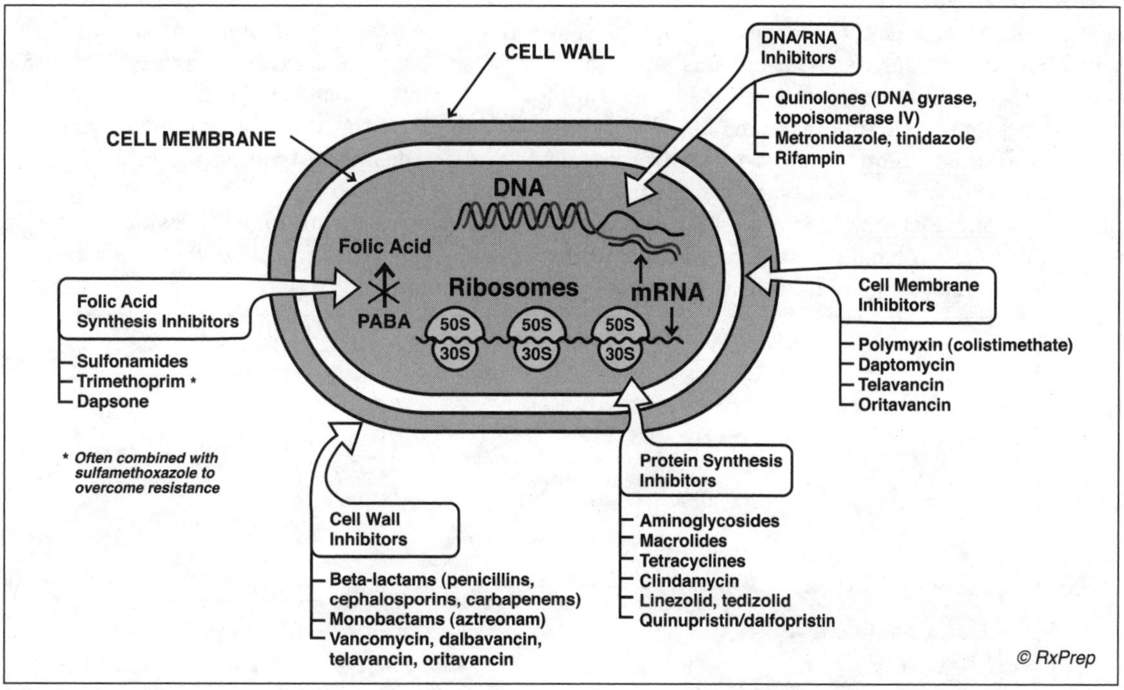

ANTIBIOTIC PHARMACOKINETICS AND PHARMACODYNAMICS

The appropriate selection of an antibiotic regimen requires an understanding of pharmacokinetic (PK) principles (absorption, distribution, metabolism and excretion) and pharmacodynamic principles (concentration-dependent or time-dependent killing). Refer to the Pharmacokinetics chapter.

Hydrophilic or Lipophilic Drugs

Hydrophilicity or lipophilicity of the antibiotic can be used to predict a number of PK parameters (see following figure). Lipophilic drugs generally have enhanced penetration of bone, lung and brain tissues.

Hydrophilic agents Beta-lactams Aminoglycosides Glycopeptides Daptomycin Colistimethate	1) Small volume of distribution 2) Renal elimination 3) Does not achieve intracellular concentrations 4) Increased clearance and/or distribution in sepsis 5) Poor-moderate bioavailability	1) Poor tissue penetration 2) Nephrotoxicity 3) Not active against atypical (intracellular) pathogens 4) Consider loading doses and aggressive dosing in sepsis 5) PO to IV ratio is < 1:1
Lipophilic agents Quinolones Macrolides Rifampin Linezolid Tetracyclines Chloramphenicol	1) Large volume of distribution 2) Hepatic metabolism 3) Achieves intracellular concentrations 4) Clearance/distribution has minimal change in sepsis 5) Excellent bioavailability	1) Excellent tissue penetration 2) Hepatotoxicity and DDI 3) Active against atypical (intracellular) pathogens 4) Dose adjustment generally not needed in sepsis 5) PO to IV ratio often is 1:1

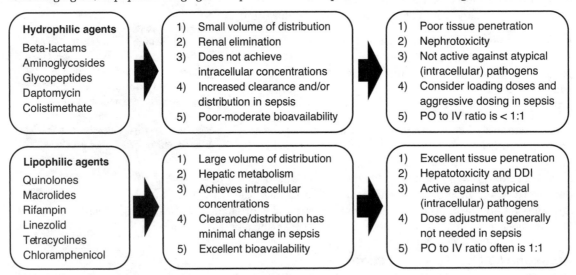

PO = oral, IV = intravenous, DDI = drug-drug interaction

Dose Optimization

Pharmacodynamics of selected drugs are displayed in the following figure. Drugs that exhibit time-dependent killing (such as beta-lactams) are generally dosed more frequently to maximize the time above the MIC, while concentration-dependent drugs (such as aminoglycosides) are generally dosed less frequently and in higher doses to maximize the concentration above the MIC. The pharmacodynamics of beta-lactam antibiotics can be maximized by more frequent dosing, extending the infusion time (e.g. from 30 minutes to 4 hours) or administering as a continuous infusion, which can lead to greater time spent above the MIC. Studies have documented that extended/continuous infusions of beta-lactams can reduce length of stay, mortality and costs particularly when treating pneumonia caused by multidrug-resistant Gram-negative pathogens like *Pseudomonas*.

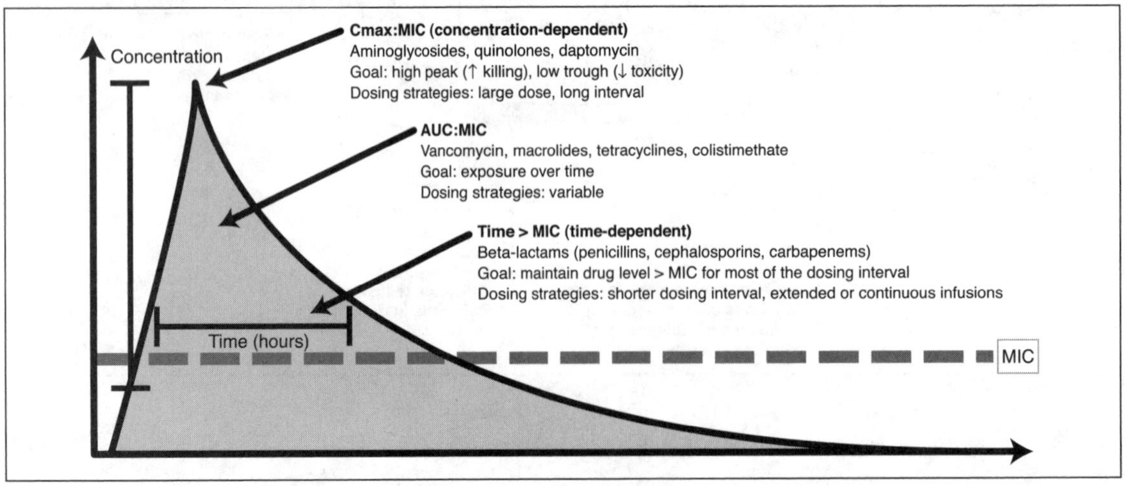

AUC = Area under the concentration-time curve, Cmax = Maximum plasma concentration, MIC = Minimum inhibitory concentration

BETA-LACTAM ANTIBIOTICS

Penicillins, cephalosporins and carbapenems are beta-lactam antibiotics, whose chemical structure is characterized by a beta-lactam ring. They inhibit bacterial cell wall synthesis by binding to penicillin-binding proteins (PBPs), which prevents the final transpeptidation step of peptidoglycan synthesis in bacterial cell walls. Beta-lactams exhibit time-dependent antibacterial activity.

Drug interactions that are common to the beta-lactam antibiotics include:

- Probenecid can ↑ levels of beta-lactams by interfering with renal excretion. This combination is sometimes used intentionally in severe infections to ↑ antibiotic levels.
- Beta-lactams (except nafcillin and dicloxacillin) may enhance the anticoagulant effect of warfarin by inhibiting the production of vitamin K-dependent clotting factors.

Penicillins

- Coverage:
  - Natural penicillins are mainly active against Gram-positive cocci, including *Enterococcus* and anaerobes (mouth flora), with little Gram-negative activity.
  - Addition of the amino group to form the aminopenicillins expands coverage to include the Gram-negative bacilli *Haemophilus, Neisseria, Proteus, E. coli, Klebsiella* (HNPEK).
  - The beta-lactamase inhibitors, clavulanate, sulbactam and tazobactam, add activity against MSSA, increase Gram-negative coverage (cover more resistant strains of HNPEK) and add Gram-negative anaerobes (*B. fragilis).*
  - The extended-spectrum penicillin plus beta-lactamase inhibitor, piperacillin/tazobactam, has very broad coverage with expanded Gram-negative coverage including *Citrobacter, Acinetobacter, Providencia, Enterobacter, Serratia* (CAPES), *Pseudomonas aeruginosa* and Gram-negative anaerobes.
  - Nafcillin, oxacillin and dicloxacillin have enhanced activity against methicillin-susceptible *Staphylococcus aureus* (MSSA), but lack *Enterococcus* activity.

Select Penicillins

DRUG	DOSING	SAFETY/SIDE EFFECTS/MONITORING
Natural Penicillins – *Streptococci* (↑ resistance with *S. pneumoniae*), *Enterococci*, Gram-positive anaerobes (mouth flora)		**BOXED WARNING** Penicillin G benzathine: not for intravenous (IV) use, can cause cardiorespiratory arrest and death. **CONTRAINDICATIONS** *Augmentin/Unasyn*: history of cholestatic jaundice or hepatic dysfunction associated with previous use; severe renal impairment (CrCl < 30 mL/min) **SIDE EFFECTS** GI upset, diarrhea, rash/allergic reactions/ anaphylaxis, hemolytic anemia, renal failure, myelosuppression with prolonged use, ↑ LFTs, seizures with accumulation **MONITORING** Renal function, symptoms of anaphylaxis with 1st dose, CBC and LFTs with prolonged courses **NOTES** When CrCl < 30 mL/min, avoid amoxicillin 875 mg and 775 mg XR formulations. For Amoxicillin/Clavulanate, use a 14:1 ratio to ↓ diarrhea due to the clavulanate component. Ampicillin PO is rarely used orally due to poor bioavailability. Amoxicillin is preferred. Ticarcillin/clavulanate *(Timentin)* is no longer available. Antistaphylococcal penicillins used for soft tissue, bone and joint infections, endocarditis and bloodstream infections. Nafcillin is a vesicant – if extravasation occurs, use cold packs and hyaluronidase injections. Administration through a central line is preferred.
Penicillin *(Pen VK)* Tablet, suspension	125-500 mg PO Q6-12H on an empty stomach	
Penicillin G Benzathine *(Bicillin L-A)* Pen G Benzathine and Pen G Procaine *(Bicillin C-R)*	1.2-2.4 million units IM x 1 (frequency varies)	
Penicillin G Aqueous *(Pfizerpen-G)*	2-4 million units IV Q4-6H	
Aminopenicillins – *Streptococci, Enterococci*, HNPEK and Gram-positive anaerobes (mouth flora). Beta-lactamase inhibitor combos are active against MSSA, more resistant strains of HNPEK plus Gram-negative anaerobes (*B. fragilis*)		
Amoxicillin *(Amoxil, Moxatag)* Tablet, capsule, chewable, suspension **+ Clavulanate *(Augmentin,*** *Augmentin ES-600, Augmentin XR)* Tablet, chewable, suspension	Amoxicillin: 250-500 mg PO Q8H or 500-875 mg PO Q12H or 775 mg XR *(Moxatag)* PO daily Amox/clav: 500 mg PO TID, 875 mg PO BID, or 2,000 XR PO BID with food	
Ampicillin Injection, capsule, suspension **+ Sulbactam** *(Unasyn)* Injection *Unasyn* 3 g = 2 g ampicillin/1 g sulbactam *Unasyn* 1.5 g = 1 g ampicillin/0.5 g sulbactam	Ampicillin: 250-500 mg PO Q6H on an empty stomach 1 hr before or 2 hrs after meals or 1-2 grams IV/IM Q4-6H Ampicillin/Sulbactam: 1.5-3 grams IV Q6H Ampicillin and ampicillin/sulbactam must be diluted in NS only	
Extended-Spectrum Penicillins – *Streptococci*, MSSA, *Enterococci*, more resistant strains of HNPEK, CAPES, Gram-positive anaerobes (mouth flora) and Gram-negative anaerobes (*B. fragilis*), *Pseudomonas*		
Piperacillin **+ Tazobactam *(Zosyn)*** Contains 65 mg Na/1 gram piperacillin	3.375 grams IV Q6H or 4.5 grams IV Q6-8H Prolonged or extended infusions: 3.375-4.5 grams IV Q8H (each dose infused over 4 hours)	
Antistaphylococcal Penicillins – *Streptococci, Staphylococci* (MSSA only); no coverage of *Enterococcus* or Gram-negatives		
Nafcillin	1-2 grams IV/IM Q4-6H	
Oxacillin	250-2,000 mg IV Q4-6H	
Dicloxacillin	125-500 mg PO Q6H	

See lab interactions, storage requirements, renal dosage information near the end of this chapter.

Penicillin Drug Interactions

- Tetracyclines can ↓ effectiveness of penicillins by slowing bacterial growth (penicillins work best against actively growing bacteria).
- Penicillins can ↑ the serum concentration of methotrexate.
- Penicillins can ↓ serum concentrations of the active metabolites of mycophenolate due to impaired enterohepatic recirculation.
- Nafcillin is a moderate CYP3A4 inducer.
- Dicloxacillin and nafcillin can ↓ INR through ↑ metabolism of warfarin; other PCNs may ↑ warfarin effects.

STUDY TIPS: PENICILLINS

Penicillin G benzathine *(Bicillin L-A)*

- Drug of choice for syphilis* (2.4 million units IM x1)
- Not for IV use; can cause death

Amoxicillin *(Amoxil)*

- First-line treatment for otitis media* (80-90 mg/kg/day)
- Drug of choice for endocarditis prophylaxis before dental procedures* (2 grams PO x1)
- *H. pylori* treatment**

Amoxicillin/clavulanate *(Augmentin)*

- First-line treatment for otitis media* (90 mg/kg/day)
- Choosing a product: use the lowest dose of clavulanate to ↓ diarrhea

Piperacillin/tazobactam *(Zosyn)*

- Dosage strength is the sum of the ingredients
  3.375 grams = 3 grams piperacillin + 0.375 grams tazobactam
  4.5 grams = 4 grams piperacillin + 0.5 grams tazobactam)
- Active against *Pseudomonas*
- Extended infusions (4 hours) can be used to maximize T > MIC

Nafcillin, oxacillin and dicloxacillin

- Cover MSSA only (no MRSA)
- No renal dose adjustment needed

*See ID-II chapter **See GERD/PUD chapter

Cephalosporins

- Coverage: the spectrum of activity is variable by cephalosporin generation. The spectrum summary is contained in the drug table.
  - First generation cephalosporins excel against Gram-positive cocci (in most cases 1st generation is preferred if a cephalosporin is used for MSSA infection), with activity against some Gram-negative rods: *Proteus, E. coli, Klebsiella* (PEK).
  - Second generation cephalosporins are split into two groups. Drugs such as cefuroxime cover more resistant *S. pneumoniae* and *Haemophilus, Neisseria, Proteus, E. coli, Klebsiella* (HNPEK), where the cephamycin second generation drugs (cefotetan and cefoxitin) have added anaerobic coverage (*B. fragilis*).
  - Third generation cephalosporins are also best thought of in two groups: ceftriaxone, cefotaxime and oral drugs cover more resistant *Streptococci*, and have enhanced Gram-negative coverage, plus *Citrobacter, Acinetobacter, Providencia, Enterobacter, Serratia* (CAPES). The second group of 3rd generation drugs includes ceftazidime, which lacks Gram-positive activity but covers *Pseudomonas*, and the newer beta-lactamase inhibitor combinations ceftazidime/avibactam and ceftolozane/tazobactam, which have added activity against MDR *Pseudomonas* and other Gram-negative rods.
  - The fourth generation drug, cefepime, has broad Gram-negative activity including *Pseudomonas*, and Gram-positive activity similar to ceftriaxone.
  - The fifth generation agent, ceftaroline, is similar to ceftriaxone, but is the only beta-lactam with MRSA activity.
  - Class trends: cephalosporins are not active against *Enterococcus* spp. or atypicals.

DRUG	DOSING
1st Generation – *Streptococci, Staphylococci* (MSSA), PEK, Gram-positive anaerobes (mouth flora). Overall, $\uparrow$ Staphylococci, $\downarrow$ Gram-negative activity compared to $2^{nd}/3^{rd}/4^{th}$ generations. Generally, 1st generation is preferred for MSSA.	
Cefadroxil	1-2 grams PO Q12-24H
CeFAZolin *(Ancef, Kefzol)*	1-1.5 grams IV/IM Q8H
Cephalexin *(Keflex)*	250-2,000 mg PO Q6-12H
2nd Generation – Same as 1st generation plus: *Haemophilus, Neisseria* (HNPEK). Cephamycin group (cefotetan and cefoxitin) have additional activity against Gram-negative anaerobic bacteria (*Bacteroides fragilis*).	
Cefaclor *(Ceclor)*	250-500 mg PO Q8H
Cefprozil *(Cefzil)*	250-500 mg PO Q12-24H
Cefuroxime *(Ceftin, Zinacef)*	250-1,500 mg PO/IV/IM Q8-12H, take suspension with food
CefoTEtan *(Cefotan)*	1-2 grams IV/IM Q12H
CefOXitin *(Mefoxin)*	1-2 grams IV/IM Q6-8H
3rd Generation Group 1 – *Streptococci* (covers more resistant *S. pneumoniae* and Viridans group *Strep.*), *Staphylococci* (MSSA), more resistant strains of HNPEK, Gram-positive anaerobes (mouth flora).	
Cefdinir *(Omnicef)*	300 mg PO Q12H or 600 mg PO daily
Cefditoren *(Spectracef)*	200-400 mg PO Q12H with food
Cefixime *(Suprax)*	400 mg PO divided Q12-24H
Cefpodoxime *(Vantin)*	100-400 mg PO Q12H
Ceftibuten *(Cedax)*	400 mg PO daily on empty stomach
CefTRIAXone *(Rocephin)*	1-2 grams IV/IM Q12-24H
Cefotaxime *(Claforan)*	1-2 grams IV/IM Q4-12H
3rd Generation Group 2 – Ceftazidime has very little Gram-positive activity, $\uparrow$ Gram-negative activity, including *Pseudomonas*. Beta-lactamase inhibitor combos ceftazidime/avibactam and ceftolozane/tazobactam have extended coverage of MDR Gram-negative rods, including *Pseudomonas*.	
CefTAZidime *(Fortaz, Tazicef)*	1-2 grams IV/IM Q8-12H
+ Avibactam *(Avycaz)* *Avycaz* 2.5 grams = 2 g ceftazidime/0.5 g avibactam	Ceftazidime/avibactam: 2.5 grams IV Q8H
Ceftolozane/Tazobactam *(Zerbaxa)* *Zerbaxa* 1.5 g = 1 g ceftolozane/0.5 g tazobactam	1.5 gram IV Q8H

SAFETY/SIDE EFFECTS/ MONITORING

CONTRAINDICATIONS

Ceftriaxone: hyperbilirubinemic neonates (causes biliary sludging), concurrent use with calcium-containing IV products in neonates ≤ 28 days old

WARNINGS

Anaphylaxis/hypersensitivity reactions.

Some drugs may $\uparrow$ INR in patients taking warfarin.

Cross sensitivity (< 10%) with PCN allergy – do not use in patients who have a type 1 PCN allergy (swelling, angioedema, anaphylaxis).

Cefotetan contains a N-methylthiotetrazole (NMTT or 1-MTT) side chain, which can $\uparrow$ risk of hypoprothrombinemia (bleeding) and a disulfiram-like reaction with alcohol ingestion.

SIDE EFFECTS

GI upset, diarrhea, rash/allergic reactions/anaphylaxis, acute interstitial nephritis, myelosuppression with prolonged use, $\uparrow$ LFTs, seizures with accumulation, drug fever

MONITORING

Renal function, signs of anaphylaxis with 1st dose, CBC, LFTs

NOTES

Ceftriaxone–no renal adjustment

Cefixime available in chewable tablet

Ceftazidime/avibactam covers some carbapenem-resistant *Enterobacteriaceae* (CRE)

Cephalosporins continued

DRUG	DOSING	SAFETY/SIDE EFFECTS/MONITORING
4th Generation – Gram-negative activity includes HNPEK, *Citrobacter, Acinetobacter, Providencia, Enterobacter* and *Serratia* species (CAPES) and *Pseudomonas*. Gram-positive activity similar to 3rd generation.		See previous page
Cefepime *(Maxipime)*	1-2 grams IV/IM Q8-12H	
5th Generation – Broadest Gram-positive activity; *Staphylococci* (covers MRSA), Gram-negative activity similar to ceftriaxone (no *Pseudomonas* coverage).		
Ceftaroline fosamil ***(Teflaro)***	600 mg IV Q12H	

See lab interactions, storage requirements, renal dosage information near the end of this chapter.

Cephalosporin Drug Interactions

- Drugs that ↓ stomach acid can ↓ the bioavailability of some cephalosporins. Cefuroxime, cefpodoxime, cefdinir and cefditoren should be separated by 2 hours from short-acting antacids. H2RAs and PPIs should be avoided.

STUDY TIPS: CEPHALOSPORINS

Common to the class: due to small risk (< 10%) of cross-reactivity, on the exam do not choose a cephalosporin if the patient case lists a penicillin allergy. Exceptions: syphilis in a pregnant patient, otitis media*

Cefazolin

- Common use: surgical prophylaxis

Cephalexin

- Common use: skin infections

Cefotetan and cefoxitin

- Anaerobe coverage *(B. fragilis)*
- Common use: surgical prophylaxis (colorectal procedures)
- Cefotetan can cause disulfiram-like reaction with alcohol ingestion

Cefdinir

- Common use: community-acquired pneumonia (CAP)

**See ID-II chapter*

Ceftriaxone

- Common uses: CAP, meningitis, spontaneous bacterial peritonitis, pyelonephritis
- No renal dose adjustment
- Do not use in neonates

Cefotaxime

- Common uses: see ceftriaxone
- Can be used in neonates

Ceftazidime and cefepime

- Active against *Pseudomonas*

Ceftolozane/tazobactam and ceftazidime/avibactam

- Used in cases of MDR Gram-negative organisms (including *Pseudomonas*)

Ceftaroline

- The only beta-lactam that is active against MRSA

Carbapenems

Carbapenems are beta-lactams that inhibit bacterial cell wall synthesis by binding to one or more penicillin-binding proteins (PBPs), which in turn prevents the final transpeptidation step of peptidoglycan synthesis in bacterial cell walls. Carbapenems exhibit time-dependent antibacterial activity.

- Coverage: Very broad spectrum ("big gun") generally reserved for MDR Gram-negative infections. Activity against most Gram-positive, Gram-negative (including ESBL producing bacteria) and anaerobic pathogens. No coverage of atypical pathogens, MRSA, VRE, *C. difficile* and *Stenotrophomonas*. Ertapenem is different from other carbapenems; it has no activity against *Pseudomonas, Acinetobacter* or *Enterococcus*.

DRUG	DOSING	SAFETY/SIDE EFFECTS/MONITORING
Doripenem *(Doribax)* Injection	500 mg IV Q8H CrCl ≤ 50 mL/min: adjustment required	**CONTRAINDICATIONS** Anaphylactic reactions to beta-lactam antibiotics **WARNINGS** Carbapenems have been associated with CNS adverse effects, including confusional states and seizures Doripenem: do not use for the treatment of pneumonia including healthcare-associated pneumonia (HAP) and ventilator-associated pneumonia (VAP) Do not use in patients with PCN allergy; cross-reactivity has been reported to be as high as 50%, but newer studies show rates < 10% **SIDE EFFECTS** Diarrhea, rash/severe skin reaction (DRESS), seizures with higher doses and in patients with impaired renal function (mainly imipenem), bone marrow suppression with prolonged use, ↑ LFTs **MONITORING** Renal function, symptoms of anaphylaxis with 1st dose, CBC, LFTs **NOTES** Imipenem is combined with cilastatin to prevent drug degradation by renal tubular dehydropeptidase Common uses: ESBL-producing bacteria, *Pseudomonas* infections, broad-spectrum empiric coverage
Imipenem/Cilastatin *(Primaxin)* Injection	250-1,000 mg IV Q6-8H CrCl ≤ 70 mL/min: adjustment required	
Meropenem *(Merrem)* Injection	500-1,000 mg IV Q8H CrCl ≤ 50 mL/min: adjustment required	
Ertapenem *(INVanz)* Injection	1 gram IV/IM daily CrCl ≤ 30 mL/min: adjustment required Stable in NS only	See above **NOTES** No coverage of *Pseudomonas, Acinetobacter* or *Enterococcus* Common uses: ESBL-producing bacteria, diabetic foot infections

See lab interactions, storage requirements, renal dosage information near the end of this chapter.

Carbapenem Drug Interactions

- Carbapenems can ↓ serum concentrations of valproic acid leading to a loss of seizure control.
- Use with caution in patients at risk for seizures or with other drugs known to lower seizure threshold (e.g., ganciclovir, quinolones, bupropion, tramadol). See Epilepsy/Seizures chapter for a complete list.

MONOBACTAM

Aztreonam

Inhibits bacterial cell wall synthesis by binding to penicillin-binding proteins (PBPs), which prevents the final transpeptidation step of peptidoglycan synthesis in bacterial cell walls. The monobactam structure makes cross-reactivity with beta-lactam allergy unlikely. Primarily used when beta-lactam allergy is present.

- Coverage: similar to ceftazidime, encompassing many Gram-negative organisms including *Pseudomonas*. It has no Gram-positive activity.

DRUG	DOSING	SAFETY/SIDE EFFECTS/MONITORING
Aztreonam *(Azactam)* Injection *Cayston* – inhaled for CF	500-2,000 mg IV Q6-12H CrCl < 30 mL/min: adjustment required	**SIDE EFFECTS** Similar to penicillins, including rash, N/V/D, ↑ LFTs **NOTES** Can be used with penicillin allergy

See lab interactions, storage requirements, renal dosage information near the end of this chapter.

Spectrum of Activity

This chart provides a visual representation of the spectrum of beta-lactams and aztreonam. It can be used to identify common coverage gaps, see which drugs have unique coverage (ceftaroline is the only agent that covers MRSA) or where coverage is lacking (cephalosporins do not cover *Enterococcus*) or which beta-lactams are active against *Pseudomonas*.

<table>
<tr><th>MRSA</th><th>S. aureus (MSSA)</th><th>S. pneumoniae</th><th>Viridans Group Streptococcus</th><th>Enterococcus</th><th>PEK</th><th>HNPEK</th><th>CAPES</th><th>Pseudomonas</th><th>Gram-positive anaerobes (mouth flora)</th><th>Bacteroides fragilis</th><th>Atypical organisms</th></tr>
<tr><td></td><td></td><td colspan="3">Penicillin</td><td></td><td></td><td></td><td></td><td>Penicillin</td><td></td><td></td></tr>
<tr><td></td><td></td><td colspan="5">Amoxicillin</td><td></td><td></td><td>Amoxicillin</td><td></td><td></td></tr>
<tr><td></td><td colspan="3">Oxacillin
Nafcillin</td><td></td><td></td><td></td><td></td><td></td><td></td><td></td><td></td></tr>
<tr><td></td><td colspan="6">Amoxicillin/Clavulanate
Ampicillin/Sulbactam</td><td></td><td></td><td colspan="2">Amoxicillin/Clavulanate
Ampicillin/Sulbactam</td><td></td></tr>
<tr><td></td><td colspan="10">Piperacillin/Tazobactam</td><td></td></tr>
<tr><td></td><td colspan="3">Cefazolin
Cephalexin</td><td></td><td>Cefazolin
Cephalexin</td><td></td><td></td><td></td><td>Cefazolin
Cephalexin</td><td></td><td></td></tr>
<tr><td></td><td colspan="3">Cefuroxime
Cefotetan
Cefoxitin</td><td></td><td colspan="2">Cefuroxime
Cefotetan
Cefoxitin</td><td></td><td></td><td colspan="2">Cefotetan
Cefoxitin</td><td></td></tr>
<tr><td></td><td colspan="3">Cefotaxime
Ceftriaxone</td><td></td><td colspan="3">Cefotaxime
Ceftriaxone</td><td></td><td>Cefotaxime
Ceftriaxone</td><td></td><td></td></tr>
<tr><td></td><td></td><td></td><td></td><td></td><td colspan="4">Ceftazidime
Aztreonam</td><td></td><td></td><td></td></tr>
<tr><td></td><td colspan="3">Cefepime</td><td></td><td colspan="5">Cefepime</td><td></td><td></td></tr>
<tr><td colspan="4">Ceftaroline</td><td></td><td colspan="3">Ceftaroline</td><td></td><td>Ceftaroline</td><td></td><td></td></tr>
<tr><td></td><td colspan="3">Ceftazidime/Avibactam
Ceftolozane/Tazobactam</td><td></td><td colspan="6">Ceftazidime/Avibactam*
Ceftolozane/Tazobactam*</td><td></td></tr>
<tr><td></td><td colspan="10">Imipenem/Cilastatin**
Meropenem**
Doripenem**</td><td></td></tr>
<tr><td></td><td colspan="3">Ertapenem</td><td></td><td colspan="3">Ertapenem***</td><td></td><td colspan="2">Ertapenem</td><td></td></tr>
</table>

Must be given with metronidazole for adequate anaerobic coverage **E. faecalis only * No Acinetobacter coverage*

AMINOGLYCOSIDES

Aminoglycosides (AMGs) interfere with bacterial protein synthesis by binding to the ribosome, resulting in a defective bacterial cell membrane. AMGs exhibit concentration-dependent antibacterial activity and demonstrate a post-antibiotic effect (PAE). The PAE is defined as the continued suppression of bacterial growth when antibiotic levels fall below the MIC of the organism. Extended interval dosing of AMGs allows use of higher doses that reliably achieve the desired peak (≥ 10x the MIC) for Gram-negative organisms, while preventing accumulation, which can lead to toxicity. Extended interval dosing has been shown to ↓ nephrotoxicity and ↓ cost, but has not been shown to be clinically superior in efficacy relative to traditional dosing. In extended interval dosing nomograms, a random level is drawn after the first dose and the result is used to determine the appropriate dosing interval. If it falls on the line, the dosing interval is always rounded up, to avoid potential toxicity.

- Coverage: mainly Gram-negative bacteria (including *Pseudomonas*); gentamicin and streptomycin are used for synergy when treating Gram-positive cocci (e.g., *Streptococcus* and *Enterococcus*, in the setting of endocarditis) in combination with a beta-lactam or vancomycin. Streptomycin and amikacin are used as second line therapy for *Mycobacterial* infections.

DRUG	DOSING	SAFETY/SIDE EFFECTS/MONITORING
Gentamicin IV, IM, ophthalmic, topical **Tobramycin** IV, IM, ophthalmic, inhaled Tobramycin inhalation for CF *(TOBI, TOBI Podhaler, Bethkis, Kitabis Pak)* **Amikacin** IV, IM Streptomycin IM	If underweight, use actual body weight for dosing If not obese, ideal body weight or actual body weight can be used for dosing (follow hospital's protocol) If obese, use adjusted body weight for dosing (see notes) **Traditional Dosing** Gent/tobra: 1-2.5 mg/kg/dose (lower doses for Gram-positive infections; higher doses for Gram-negative infections) Amikacin: 5-7.5 mg/kg/dose **Renal Adjustments:** CrCl ≥ 60 mL/min: Q8H CrCl 40-60 mL/min: Q12H CrCl 20-40 mL/min: Q24H CrCl < 20 mL/min: 1x dose, then dose per levels **Extended Interval Dosing** Gent/tobra: 4-7 mg/kg/dose (commonly 7 mg/kg) Frequency determined by nomogram (example on next page) Do not use extended interval dosing nomograms with these conditions: Pregnancy, ascites, burns, cystic fibrosis, CrCl < 30 mL/min (including end-stage renal disease on dialysis), or when using for synergy in Gram-positive infections	**BOXED WARNINGS** Nephrotoxicity, ototoxicity, (hearing loss, vertigo, ataxia), neuromuscular blockade and respiratory paralysis, fetal harm if given in pregnancy (tobramycin). Avoid use with other neurotoxic/nephrotoxic drugs. **WARNINGS** Use with caution in patients with impaired renal function, in the elderly, and those on other nephrotoxic drugs (amphotericin B, cisplatin, colistimethate, cyclosporine, loop diuretics, NSAIDs, radiocontrast dye, tacrolimus and vancomycin). **SIDE EFFECTS** Nephrotoxicity (acute tubular necrosis), hearing loss (early toxicity associated with high-pitched sounds), vestibular toxicity (resulting in balance deficits) **MONITORING** Renal function, urine output, hearing tests, drug levels Traditional dosing: draw trough level right before the 4th dose, draw peak level ½ hour after the end of drug infusion of the 4th dose (follow hospital's protocol). Extended interval dosing: draw random level per timing on the nomogram (example of nomogram follows). **NOTES** Safety issue – see Pregnancy chapter. Amikacin has the broadest spectrum of activity. The clinical definition of obesity varies. For exam purposes, obesity will be obvious, and may be stated in the question, indicating that adjusted body weight should be used for weight-based dosing.

See lab interactions, storage requirements, renal dosage information near the end of this chapter.

Traditional Dosing Target Drug Concentrations

DRUG	PEAK	TROUGH
Gentamicin		
Gram-negative infection:	5-10 mcg/mL	< 2 mcg/mL
Gram-positive infection (synergy):	3-4 mcg/mL	< 1 mcg/mL
Tobramycin	5-10 mcg/mL	< 2 mcg/mL
Amikacin	20-30 mcg/mL	< 5 mcg/mL

Organism-specific peak goals are typically ≥10 times the MIC of the bacteria causing the infection.

Example of Extended Interval Dosing Nomogram

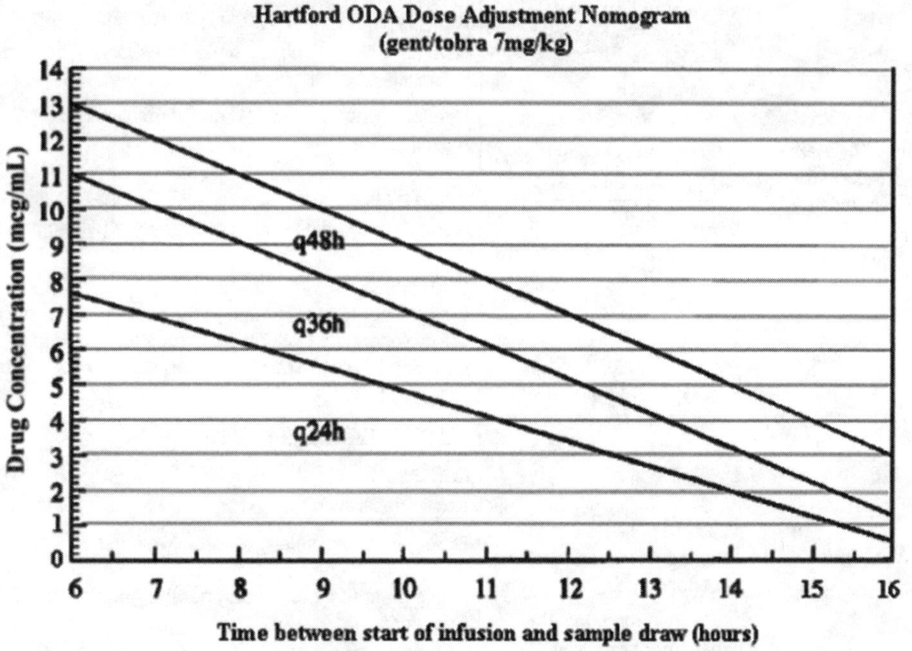

Nicolau DP, Freeman CD, et al. *Antimicrob Agents and Chemother* 1995;39:650-655

QUINOLONES

Quinolones inhibit bacterial DNA topoisomerase IV and inhibit DNA gyrase (topoisomerase II) inside the bacteria, preventing supercoiling of DNA and promoting breakage of double-stranded DNA. Quinolones exhibit concentration-dependent antibacterial activity.

- Coverage: broad spectrum drugs with activity against a variety of Gram-negative, Gram-positive, and atypical pathogens. Gemifloxacin, levofloxacin and moxifloxacin are often referred to as respiratory quinolones due to enhanced coverage of *S. pneumoniae* and atypical coverage. Ciprofloxacin and levofloxacin have enhanced Gram-negative activity, including *Pseudomonas*, but are typically used in combination with another agent empirically (e.g., a beta-lactam) when treating *Pseudomonas* infections. Moxifloxacin has enhanced Gram-positive and anaerobic activity and can be used alone for mixed infections (intra-abdominal infections). Quinolones are noted in some resources to have activity against *Staphylococcus* species, including MRSA; however, because of high rates of resistance, quinolones should generally be avoided for treatment of MRSA.

DRUG	DOSING	SAFETY/SIDE EFFECTS/MONITORING
Ciprofloxacin *(Cipro,* *Cipro XR, Ciloxin* eye drops, *Cetraxal* ear drops) Tablet, suspension, injection, ointment, ophthalmic, otic + dexamethasone *(Ciprodex* ear drops) + fluocinolone *(Otovel* ear drops)	250-750 mg PO or 200-400 mg IV Q8-12H CrCl 30-50 mL/min: Q12H CrCl < 30 mL/min: Q18-24H	**BOXED WARNINGS** Tendon inflammation and/or rupture (most often in Achilles tendon); ↑ risk with concurrent systemic steroid use, organ transplant patients, > 60 years of age. Peripheral neuropathy (with systemic formulations) – can last months to years after the drug has been discontinued. In some cases, it may become permanent. If symptoms, discontinue the drug. CNS effects [tremor, restlessness, confusion, and hallucinations, ↑ intracranial pressure (including pseudotumor cerebri) or seizures]; use with caution in patients with known or suspected CNS disorder. May exacerbate muscle weakness related to myasthenia gravis. Avoid use in patients with myasthenia gravis. Use for bacterial sinusitis or acute exacerbation of chronic bronchitis only if there is no alternative treatment option. Use for uncomplicated UTI only if no alternative (all except moxifloxacin). **CONTRAINDICATIONS** Concurrent administration of tizanidine (with ciprofloxacin) **WARNINGS** QT prolongation; avoid use in patients at risk for or with known QT prolongation. Caution with drugs that prolong QT interval including Class Ia and Class III antiarrhythmics (highest risk with moxifloxacin). Hypoglycemia/hyperglycemia Hepatotoxicity Photosensitivity/phototoxicity Risk of musculoskeletal toxicity. Avoid use of systemic quinolones in children. Can use if benefit outweighs the risk (e.g., anthrax exposure) per the American Academy of Pediatrics Crystalluria (patients must stay hydrated) **SIDE EFFECTS** Nausea/diarrhea, headache, dizziness, insomnia, acute renal failure, serious skin reactions (SJS/TEN), hemolytic anemia, bone marrow suppression **NOTES** *Cipro* oral suspension should not be given through a NG or other feeding tube (the oil-based suspension adheres to the tubing). Shake vigorously for 15 seconds each time before use. *Cipro* – can crush immediate-release tablets, mix with water and give via feeding tube. Hold tube feedings at least 1 hour before and 2 hours after dose. Moxifloxacin does not reach adequate concentrations in the urine and should not be used for UTIs. MedGuide required.
LevoFLOXacin *(Levaquin,* *Quixin* eye drops) Tablet, solution, injection, ophthalmic	250-750 mg IV/PO daily CrCl < 50 mL/min: Extend dosing interval (Q48H) and/or ↓ dose. Adjustment varies based on indication and renal function.	
Moxifloxacin *(Avelox,* *Avelox ABC Pack, Moxeza* eye drops, *Vigamox* eye drops) Tablet, injection, ophthalmic	400 mg IV/PO Q24H No adjustment needed in renal impairment.	
Gemifloxacin *(Factive)* Tablet	320 mg PO daily CrCl ≤ 40 mL/min: adjustment required	
Norfloxacin *(Noroxin)* Tablet	400 mg PO BID or 800 mg PO daily CrCl ≤ 30 mL/min: adjustment required	
Ofloxacin Tablet, ophthalmic, otic	200-400 mg PO Q12H CrCl < 30 mL/min: adjustment required	
Gatifloxacin *(Zymaxid* eye drops)	No oral formulation	

See lab interactions, storage requirements, renal dosage information near the end of this chapter.

Quinolone Drug Interactions

- Antacids, didanosine, sucralfate, bile acid resins, magnesium, aluminum, calcium, iron, zinc, multivitamins or any product containing these multivalent cations can chelate and inhibit absorption. See patient counseling for specific administration information.
- Lanthanum *(Fosrenol)* can ↓ the serum concentration of quinolones; take oral quinolones at least 2 hours before or after lanthanum.
- Sevelamer *(Renagel)* can ↓ the serum concentration of quinolones; take oral quinolones at least 2 hours before or 6 hours after sevelamer.
- Can ↑ the effects of warfarin, sulfonylureas/insulin and QT-prolonging drugs (moxifloxacin prolongs the QT interval the most).
- Probenecid and NSAIDs can ↑ quinolone levels.
- Ciprofloxacin is a P-glycoprotein substrate, strong 1A2 inhibitor and weak 3A4 inhibitor; ciprofloxacin can ↑ the levels of caffeine and theophylline by reducing metabolism.

STUDY TIPS: QUINOLONES

Respiratory quinolones
- Moxifloxacin, gemifloxacin, levofloxacin

Antipseudomonal quinolones
- Ciprofloxacin, levofloxacin

IV to PO ratio = 1:1
- Levofloxacin and moxifloxacin

Profile review tips
- Watch for other drugs with QT prolongation (e.g., azole antifungals, antipsychotics, methadone)
- Avoid use in patients with a history of seizures
- Avoid systemic quinolones in children (see drug table for rare exceptions)
- Renal dose adjustment is required for all except moxifloxacin

MACROLIDES

Macrolides bind to the 50S ribosomal subunit, resulting in inhibition of RNA-dependent protein synthesis; antibacterial activity is related to total exposure of the drug (AUC/MIC).

- Coverage: good <u>atypical</u> coverage (*Legionella, Chlamydia, Mycoplasma* and *Mycobacterium avium* complex) and *Haemophilus*. Macrolides are treatment options for community-acquired upper and lower respiratory tract infections and certain sexually transmitted infections, but utility against *S. pneumoniae, Haemophilus, Neisseria* and *Moraxella* is limited due to increasing resistance.

DRUG	DOSING	SAFETY/SIDE EFFECTS/MONITORING
Azithromycin *(Zithromax,* ***Z-Pak,*** *Zmax, Zithromax Tri-Pak, AzaSite* ophthalmic) Tablet, suspension, injection, ophthalmic Better Gram-negative coverage compared to erythromycin	Oral treatment: 500 mg PO on day 1, then 250 mg on days 2-5 *(Z-Pak)* or 500 mg daily x 3 days or 1-2 grams x 1 (*Zmax*) or 600 mg daily See ID-IV chapter for opportunistic infection information IV: 250-500 mg daily No adjustment in renal impairment	**CONTRAINDICATIONS** History of cholestatic jaundice/hepatic dysfunction with prior use Clarithromycin and erythromycin: Concomitant use with pimozide, ergotamine or dihydroergotamine, lovastatin or simvastatin Clarithromycin: Concurrent use with colchicine in patients with renal or hepatic impairment, history of QT prolongation or ventricular arrhythmia **WARNINGS** QT prolongation; use with caution in patients at risk of prolonged cardiac repolarization; avoid use in patients with uncorrected hypokalemia or hypomagnesemia, clinically significant bradycardia, and patients receiving Class Ia or Class III antiarrhythmic drugs (highest risk with erythromycin) Hepatotoxicity; use caution in patients with liver disease Exacerbation of myasthenia gravis **SIDE EFFECTS** GI upset (diarrhea, abdominal pain and cramping especially with erythromycin), taste perversion, ↑ LFTs, ototoxicity (reversible and rare), severe skin reactions (SJS/TEN/DRESS with azithromycin) **NOTES** *AzaSite* – viscous solution is for ophthalmic use. Store at room temp once dispensed (cold makes solution more viscous). Azithromycin ER suspension (*Zmax*) is not bioequivalent with *Zithromax* and should not be interchanged.
Clarithromycin ***(Biaxin, Biaxin XL,*** *Biaxin XL Pac)* Tablet, suspension Better Gram-positive coverage	250-500 mg PO Q12H or 1 gram (*Biaxin XL*) PO daily CrCl < 30 mL/minute: adjustment required	
Erythromycin ***(E.E.S., Ery-Tab, EryPed, Erythrocin, PCE)*** Capsule, tablet, suspension, injection, ophthalmic, topical	E.E.S.: 400-800 mg PO Q6-12H Erythromycin base/stearate: 250-500 mg PO Q6-12H Erythromycin lactobionate: 15-20 mg/kg/day IV Q6H (max 4 grams/day) 400 mg E.E.S. = 250 mg base or stearate No adjustment in renal impairment	

See lab interactions, storage requirements, renal dosage information near the end of this chapter.

Macrolide Drug Interactions

- Erythromycin and clarithromycin are substrates of 3A4 (major) and 3A4 inhibitors (moderate/strong); use caution or avoid with many medications metabolized by 3A4 including apixaban, colchicine, conivaptan, cyclosporine, dabigatran, digoxin, quetiapine, quinidine, rifabutin, rivaroxaban, theophylline, warfarin and others. See Drug Interactions chapter for more information.
- Azithromycin is a substrate of 3A4 (minor) and inhibitor of 1A2 (weak) and P-gp; it has fewer clinically significant drug interactions.
- All macrolides: Do not use concurrently with drugs that can prolong the QT interval.

TETRACYCLINES

Tetracyclines inhibit bacterial protein synthesis by reversibly binding to the 30S ribosomal subunit. Antibacterial activity is related to the total exposure of the drug (AUC/MIC). Doxycycline is used more often in practice due to improved tolerability and broader indications, including for respiratory tract infections, tick-borne/rickettsial diseases, spirochetes and *Chlamydia* infections. Doxycycline is also an option for the treatment of CA-MRSA in mild skin infections and VRE in urinary tract infections. Minocycline has enhanced Gram-positive coverage and is often preferred for skin infections, including acne. Tetracycline is rarely used in practice, but is used as part of *H. pylori* regimens.

- Coverage: many Gram-positive bacteria, including *Staphylococci, Streptococci, Enterococci, Nocardia, Bacillus* and *Propionibacterium* spp., Gram-negative bacteria, including respiratory flora *(Haemophilus, Moraxella,* atypicals) and other unique pathogens (spirochetes, *Rickettsiae, Bacillus anthracis, Treponema pallidum*, etc.).

DRUG	DOSING	SAFETY/SIDE EFFECTS/MONITORING
Doxycycline *(Acticlate, Adoxa, Doryx, Monodox, Oracea, Vibramycin,* others) Capsule, tablet, suspension, syrup, injection	100-200 mg PO/IV in 1-2 divided doses Take *Oracea* 40 mg on an empty stomach (1 hr before or 2 hrs after meals). Take other forms with food to ↓ GI irritation No adjustment in renal impairment	**WARNINGS** Children < 8 years of age, pregnancy and breastfeeding (suppresses bone growth and skeletal development, permanently discolors teeth), photosensitivity, tissue hyperpigmentation, severe skin reactions (DRESS), exfoliative dermatitis, ↑ BUN, gastrointestinal inflammation/ulceration, intracranial hypertension Drug-induced lupus erythematosus DILE (minocycline) **SIDE EFFECTS** N/V/D, rash/severe skin reactions (SJS/TEN) **MONITORING** LFTs, renal function, CBC **NOTES** Safety issue – see Pregnancy chapter IV:PO is 1:1 (doxycycline, minocycline)
Minocycline *(Minocin, Solodyn)* Capsule, tablet, injection	200 mg PO/IV x 1, then 50-100 mg Q12H CrCl < 80 mL/min: maximum 200 mg/day	
Tetracycline Capsule	250-500 mg PO Q6H on an empty stomach CrCl ≤ 50 mL/min: adjustment required	

See lab interactions, storage requirements, renal dosage information near the end of this chapter.

Tetracycline Drug Interactions

- Tetracycline absorption is impaired by antacids containing magnesium, aluminum, calcium or medications that contain divalent cations such as iron-containing preparations, sucralfate, bile acid resins or bismuth subsalicylate – separate doses (take 1 – 2 hours before or 4 hours after). Dairy products should be avoided within 1 hour before or 2 hours after tetracycline.
- Doxycycline and minocycline can be taken with food to reduce GI upset. Patients are frequently advised not take with dairy products (calcium), although the concern is less than with tetracycline.
- Lanthanum *(Fosrenol)* can ↓ the concentration of tetracycline derivatives; take at least 2 hours before or after lanthanum.
- Tetracycline is a substrate of 3A4 (major) and 3A4 (moderate) inhibitor. Caution with the use of 3A4 inhibitors, which ↑ levels, and 3A4 inducers, which ↓ levels.
- Doxycycline is a weak 3A4 inhibitor.
- Tetracyclines can enhance the anticoagulant effects in patients taking warfarin.
- Tetracycline derivatives can enhance the effects of neuromuscular blocking drugs.
- Avoid concomitant use with retinoic acid derivatives due to the risk of intracranial hypertension.

- Tetracyclines can ↓ the effectiveness of penicillins by slowing bacterial growth (penicillins work best against actively growing bacteria).

SULFONAMIDES

Sulfamethoxazole (SMX) interfering with bacterial folic acid synthesis by inhibition of dihydrofolic acid formation from para-aminobenzoic acid. Trimethoprim (TMP) inhibits dihydrofolic acid reduction to tetrahydrofolate resulting in inhibition of the folic acid pathway.

- Coverage: Gram-positive bacteria, including *Staphylococci*/MRSA (including CA-MRSA). *S. pneumoniae* and Group A Strep coverage is unreliable. Active against many Gram-negative bacteria, including *Haemophilus, Proteus, E. coli, Klebsiella, Enterobacter, Shigella, Salmonella,* and *Stenotrophomonas*. Coverage also includes some opportunistic pathogens *(Nocardia, Pneumocystis, Toxoplasmosis)*, but lacks *Pseudomonas, Enterococci*, atypical or anaerobic coverage.

DRUG	DOSING	SAFETY/SIDE EFFECTS/MONITORING
Sulfamethoxazole/Tri methoprim *(Bactrim, Bactrim DS, Septra DS, Sulfatrim,* others) **Single Strength (SS)** 400 mg SMX/80 mg TMP **Double Strength (DS)** 800 mg SMX/160 mg TMP Sulfamethoxazole: Trimethoprim dose is always a 5:1 ratio	Dose (including weight-based dosing) is based on the TMP component **Severe Infections** 10-20 mg/kg/day TMP divided Q6-8H (2 DS tabs BID-TID) **Uncomplicated UTI** 1 DS tab BID x 3 days ***Pneumocystis* Pneumonia (PCP) Prophylaxis** 1 DS or SS tab daily **PCP Treatment** 15-20 mg/kg/day TMP IV/PO divided Q6H CrCl 15-30 mL/min: adjustment required CrCl < 15 mL/min: Not recommended	**CONTRAINDICATIONS** Sulfa allergy, pregnancy (at term), breastfeeding, anemia due to folate deficiency, marked renal or hepatic disease, infants < 2 months of age **WARNINGS** Blood dyscrasias including agranulocytosis and aplastic anemia SJS/TEN, thrombotic thrombocytopenic purpura (TTP), and other dermatologic reactions G6PD deficiency; use caution and discontinue drug if hemolysis occurs Embryofetal toxicity **SIDE EFFECTS** N/V/D, anorexia, skin reactions (rash, urticaria, SJS/TEN), crystalluria (take with 8 oz of water), photosensitivity, ↑ K, hypoglycemia, ↓ folate, positive Coombs test, myelosuppression with prolonged use, false elevations in SCr due to inhibition of tubular secretion of creatinine (pseudoazotemia), renal failure, CNS (confusion, drug fever, seizures), ↑ LFTs **MONITORING** Renal function, LFTs, electrolytes, CBC, folate **NOTES** Safety issue – see Pregnancy chapter

See lab interactions, storage requirements, renal dosage information near the end of this chapter.

Sulfonamide Drug Interactions

- Sulfonamides are inhibitors of 2C8/9 (moderate/strong). Can cause significantly ↑ INR, caution with concurrent use of warfarin. See Drug Interactions chapter for more 2C8/9 substrates.
- Can ↑ levels/effects of sulfonylureas, metformin, fosphenytoin/phenytoin, dofetilide, azathioprine, methotrexate and mercaptopurine.
- Levels of SMX/TMP can be ↓ by 2C8/9 inducers and the therapeutic effects may be diminished by the use of leucovorin/levoleucovorin.
- ACE inhibitors, ARBs, aliskiren, aldosterone receptor antagonists (ARAs), potassium-sparing diuretics, NSAIDs, cyclosporine, tacrolimus, drospirenone-containing oral contraceptives and canagliflozin will ↑ risk for hyperkalemia when used concurrently; monitor.

ANTIBIOTICS FOR GRAM-POSITIVE INFECTIONS

Vancomycin

Glycopeptide: inhibits bacterial cell wall synthesis by binding to the D-alanyl-D-alanine portion of cell wall precursor and blocking peptidoglycan polymerization.

- Coverage: Gram-positive bacteria, including *Staphylococcus* (MRSA), *Streptococci, Enterococci* (not VRE) and *C. difficile* (PO route only).

DRUG	DOSING	SAFETY/SIDE EFFECTS/MONITORING
Vancomycin *(Vancocin)* Injection, capsule, solution kit	**Systemic infections** 15-20 mg/kg IV Q8-12H Dose based on actual body weight CrCl 20-49 mL/min: Q24H CrCl < 20 mL/min: Give x1 dose, then dose per levels Infuse peripheral IV at a concentration not to exceed 5 mg/mL ***C. difficile*-associated diarrhea** 125-500 mg PO QID x 10-14 days (upper end used for recurrent or severe, complicated disease) PO: no adjustment in renal impairment	**WARNINGS** Ototoxicity and nephrotoxicity. Caution with the use of other nephrotoxic or ototoxic drugs or with prolonged high serum concentration) Dose adjustment required in renal impairment PO is used only for *C. difficile* colitis and enterocolitis, not for systemic infections Infusion reaction/red man syndrome (maculopapular rash from too rapid of an infusion rate, hypotension, flushing, chills – every 500 mg of drug should be infused over a minimum of 30 minutes) **SIDE EFFECTS** Abdominal pain, nausea (oral route), phlebitis (irritation to vein), myelosuppression (neutropenia/thrombocytopenia), drug fever, severe skin reactions (SJS/TEN) **MONITORING** Renal function, WBC, trough concentration at steady state (generally before the 4th dose) Goal trough: 15-20 mcg/mL – pneumonia, endocarditis, osteomyelitis, meningitis, bacteremia Goal trough: 10-15 mcg/mL – other infections **NOTES** First-line treatment for MRSA infections Consider alternative agent when MRSA MIC ≥ 2 mcg/mL

See lab interactions, storage requirements, renal dosage information near the end of this chapter.

Vancomycin Drug Interactions

- Nephrotoxicity ↑ when used with other nephrotoxic drugs (e.g., aminoglycosides, amphotericin B, cisplatin, colistimethate, cyclosporine, loop diuretics, NSAIDs, radiographic contrast dye and tacrolimus). Vancomycin can ↑ toxicity of other ototoxic drugs (e.g., aminoglycosides, cisplatin, loop diuretics and others).

Lipoglycopeptides

Inhibit bacterial cell wall synthesis by 1) blocking polymerization and cross-linking of peptidoglycan by binding to the D-Ala-D-Ala portion of the cell wall and 2) disrupting bacterial membrane potential and changing cell permeability due to the presence of a lipophilic side chain moiety. They exhibit concentration-dependent antibacterial activity.

- Coverage: similar to vancomycin.
- Note that all of these drugs are IV only and cannot be used to treat *C. difficile* infection.

DRUG	DOSING	SAFETY/SIDE EFFECTS/MONITORING
Telavancin *(Vibativ)* Injection Approved for complicated skin and soft-tissue infections (SSTI) and hospital-acquired and ventilator-associated pneumonia REMS – warning of ↑ mortality in patients with pre-existing renal dysfunction and risk of fetal developmental toxicity	10 mg/kg IV daily CrCl ≤ 50 mL/min: adjustment required Infuse over 60 minutes to prevent infusion reaction	**BOXED WARNINGS** Fetal risk – obtain pregnancy test prior to starting therapy; nephrotoxicity; ↑ mortality versus vancomycin in some patients treated for pneumonia with pre-existing moderate-to-severe renal impairment (CrCl ≤ 50 mL/minute) **CONTRAINDICATIONS** Concomitant use of IV unfractionated heparin (UFH) **WARNINGS** Can falsely ↑ PT/INR results but the drug does not ↑ bleeding risk. Does not interfere with anti-Xa monitoring. Red man syndrome with rapid IV administration (give over ≥ 60 minutes). QT prolongation. **SIDE EFFECTS** Metallic taste, N/V, ↑ SCr, foamy urine **MONITORING** Renal function, pregnancy status **NOTES** Safety issue – see Pregnancy chapter MedGuide required
Oritavancin *(Orbactiv)* Injection Approved for SSTI	Single-dose regimen: 1,200 mg IV x 1 Infuse over 3 hours CrCl < 30 mL/min: has not been studied, use with caution	**CONTRAINDICATIONS** Oritavancin: use of intravenous unfractionated heparin for 120 hours (5 days) hours after oritavancin administration due to interference with aPTT laboratory results. **WARNINGS** Oritavancin: may ↑ risk of bleeding in patients on warfarin due to weak 2C9 inhibition. Enhanced monitoring is recommended. Can cause falsely ↑ PT/INR for up to 12 hours and aPTT for up to 120 hours after a dose. Use a different antibiotic if osteomyelitis confirmed or suspected. Dalbavancin: infusion reactions-red man syndrome with rapid IV administration, infuse over 30 minutes; ↑ ALT > 3x upper limit of normal. **SIDE EFFECTS** N/V/D, headache, rash, infusion reaction (red man syndrome) **MONITORING** Signs of osteomyelitis (oritavancin), LFTs, renal function **NOTES** Extremely long half-life, allows a single-dose regimen for both
Dalbavancin *(Dalvance)* Injection Approved for SSTI	Single-dose regimen: 1,500 mg IV x 1 Two-dose regimen: 1,000 mg IV x 1, then 500 mg IV one week later Infused over 30 minutes CrCl < 30 mL/min (not on dialysis): adjustment required	

See lab interactions, storage requirements, renal dosage information near the end of this chapter.

Telavancin/Oritavancin Drug Interactions

- Avoid telavancin in patients with congenital long QT syndrome, known QT prolongation or uncompensated heart failure. Caution with the use of other medications known to prolong the QT interval (see Arrhythmias chapter).
- Oritavancin is a weak inhibitor of 2C9 and 2C19 and weak inducer of 3A4 and 2D6. Use caution when coadministered with drugs metabolized by these enzymes (including warfarin).

Daptomycin

Daptomycin is a cyclic lipopeptide. It binds to cell membrane components, causing rapid depolarization, which inhibits all intracellular replication processes, including protein synthesis, causing cell death. Daptomycin exhibits concentration-dependent antibacterial activity.

- Coverage: most Gram-positive bacteria, including *Staphylococci* (MRSA) and *Enterococci,* including VRE *(E. faecium* and *E. faecalis).*

DRUG	DOSING	SAFETY/SIDE EFFECTS/MONITORING
DAPTOmycin ***(Cubicin, Cubicin RF)*** Injection Approved for complicated skin and soft-tissue infections (SSTI) and *S. aureus* (MRSA) bloodstream infections, including right-sided endocarditis	SSTI: 4 mg/kg IV daily Bacteremia/right-sided endocarditis: 6 mg/kg IV daily CrCl < 30 mL/min: adjustment required	**WARNINGS** Eosinophilic pneumonia – generally develops 2-4 weeks after therapy initiation Myopathy and rhabdomyolysis – discontinue in patients with signs and symptoms and CPK > 1,000 units/L (5x ULN) or in asymptomatic patients with a CPK ≥ 2,000 units/L (10x ULN); consider temporarily withholding other drugs that can cause muscle damage (e.g., statins) during treatment Can falsely ↑ PT/INR readings but no ↑ bleeding risk Peripheral neuropathy ↓ efficacy when CrCl < 50 mL/min **SIDE EFFECTS** ↑ CPK, abdominal pain, pruritus, chest pain, edema, hypertension, acute kidney injury, ↑ PO4, ↑ LFTs **MONITORING** CPK level weekly (more frequently if on a statin or with renal impairment); muscle pain/weakness, s/sx of neuropathy, dyspnea **NOTES** Compatible with NS (no dextrose) Do not use to treat pneumonia; drug is inactivated in the lungs by surfactant

See lab interactions, storage requirements, renal dosage information near the end of this chapter.

Daptomycin Drug Interactions

- Daptomycin can have additive risk of muscle toxicity when used in conjunction with statins.

Oxazolidinones

Bind to the 50S subunit of the bacterial ribosome inhibiting translation and protein synthesis.

- Coverage: similar to vancomycin, but also cover VRE (*E. faecium* and *E. faecalis*).

DRUG	DOSING	SAFETY/SIDE EFFECTS/MONITORING
Linezolid *(Zyvox)* Tablet, suspension, injection	600 mg PO/IV Q12H No adjustment in renal impairment IV:PO is 1:1	**CONTRAINDICATIONS** Do not use with or within 2 weeks of MAO inhibitors **WARNINGS** Duration-related myelosuppression (thrombocytopenia, anemia, leukopenia), peripheral and optic neuropathy when used > 28 days, serotonin syndrome, hypoglycemia – caution in patients on insulin or hypoglycemic drugs, seizures, lactic acidosis, hypertension when used with adrenergic drugs (e.g., pseudoephedrine), closely monitor BP in patients with untreated hyperthyroidism **SIDE EFFECTS** ↓ platelets , ↓ Hgb, ↓ WBC, HA, nausea, diarrhea, ↑ pancreatic enzymes, ↑ LFTs, neuropathy **MONITORING** HR, BP, BG, weekly CBC, visual function **NOTES** Do not shake linezolid suspension
Tedizolid *(Sivextro)* Tablet, injection Approved for SSTI	200 mg IV/PO daily for 6 days Infuse over 1 hour, stable in NS No adjustment in renal impairment IV:PO is 1:1	**WARNINGS** Consider alternative therapy in patients with neutropenia. **SIDE EFFECTS** Nausea, diarrhea, paresthesias, hypertension, visual impairment, blurred vision **MONITORING** Visual function **NOTES** Less GI and myelotoxicity expected with tedizolid compared to linezolid

See lab interactions, storage requirements, renal dosage information near the end of this chapter.

Linezolid/Tedizolid Drug Interactions

- Linezolid is a reversible monoamine oxidase inhibitor. Use with caution when used with serotonergic or adrenergic drugs. Avoid tyramine-containing foods and serotonergic drugs. See Drug Interactions chapter.
- Linezolid can exacerbate hypoglycemic episodes, caution in patients receiving insulin or oral hypoglycemic drugs.
- Tedizolid is a reversible monoamine oxidase inhibitor. Patients taking MAO inhibitors or serotonergic drugs were excluded from the clinical studies. There are no recommendations to avoid tyramine-containing food.
- Tedizolid (PO) is a BCRP inhibitor in the intestine. Consider interrupting treatment with BCRP substrates with a narrow therapeutic index (e.g., methotrexate) during tedizolid treatment. If coadministration cannot be avoided, monitor for adverse reactions related to concomitantly administered BCRP substrates, including rosuvastatin.

Quinupristin/Dalfopristin

Streptogramin class – binds to the 50S ribosomal subunit inhibiting protein synthesis.

- Coverage: most Gram-positive bacteria, including *Staphylococci* (MRSA), *Enterococcus faecium* (VRE, but not active against *E. faecalis*). Approved for complicated skin and soft-tissue infections, but is not well-tolerated and use is typically limited to vancomycin-resistant *E. faecium* infections.

DRUG	DOSING	SAFETY/SIDE EFFECTS/MONITORING
Quinupristin/Dalfopristin *(Synercid)* Injection	7.5 mg/kg IV Q8-12H No adjustment in renal impairment	**SIDE EFFECTS** Arthralgias/myalgias (up to 47%), infusion reactions, including edema and pain at infusion site (up to 44%), phlebitis (40%), hyperbilirubinemia (up to 35%), CPK elevations, GI upset, ↑ LFTs **NOTES** Dilute in D5W only

See lab interactions, storage requirements, renal dosage information near the end of this chapter.

Quinupristin/Dalfopristin Drug Interactions

- Quinupristin/Dalfopristin is a weak 3A4 inhibitor; can ↑ levels of CCBs, cyclosporine, dofetilide and others.

Tigecycline

Glycylcycline class – binds to the 30S ribosomal subunit inhibiting protein synthesis; structurally related to the tetracyclines.

- Coverage: Very broad spectrum activity against Gram-positive bacteria including *Staphylococci* (MRSA), *Enterococci* (including VRE), Gram-negative, anaerobic and atypical organisms. Among the Gram-negatives, no activity against the "3 P's": *Pseudomonas, Proteus, Providencia* species. Approved for complicated skin and soft-tissue infections, intra-abdominal infections and community-acquired pneumonia; however, use should be limited (see boxed warning).

DRUG	DOSING	SAFETY/SIDE EFFECTS/MONITORING
Tigecycline *(Tygacil)* Injection Derivative of minocycline	100 mg IV x 1 dose, then 50 mg IV Q12H Severe hepatic impairment: adjustment required No adjustment in renal impairment	**BOXED WARNING** ↑ risk of death, use only when alternative treatments are not suitable. **WARNINGS** Hepatotoxicity, pancreatitis, photosensitivity, teeth discoloration in children < 8 years old (avoid use) Lower cure rates in ventilator-associated pneumonia **SIDE EFFECTS** N/V/D, headache, dizziness, ↑ LFTs, rash/severe skin reactions (SJS) **NOTES** Safety issue – see Pregnancy chapter. Avoid use in bloodstream infections. It does not achieve adequate concentrations in the blood since it is lipophilic (drug distributes quickly out of blood into tissues). Reconstituted solution should be yellow-orange; discard if not this color.

See lab interactions, storage requirements, renal dosage information near the end of this chapter.

Tigecycline Drug Interactions

- Tigecycline can ↑ INR in patients taking warfarin.

ADDITIONAL BROAD SPECTRUM DRUGS

Polymyxins

The polymyxin class consists of two main drugs, colistimethate (also called colistin) and polymyxin B. Colistimethate is an inactive prodrug that is hydrolyzed to colistin, which acts as a cationic detergent and damages the bacterial cytoplasmic membrane causing leaking of intracellular substances and cell death. This is thought to be the mechanism of nephrotoxicity as well. These antibiotics exhibit concentration-dependent antibacterial activity.

- Coverage: Gram-negative bacteria such as *Enterobacter* spp., *E. coli, Klebsiella pneumoniae*, and *Pseudomonas aeruginosa*; used primarily in setting of MDR Gram-negative pathogens. These do not cover *Proteus* spp.
- Polymyxins should be used in combination with another antibiotic due to emergence of resistance.

DRUG	DOSING	SAFETY/SIDE EFFECTS/MONITORING
Colistimethate sodium or colistin *(Coly-Mycin M)* Injection (also used for inhalation)	2.5-5 mg/kg/day IV/IM in 2-4 divided doses Dose is expressed in terms of colistin base activity CrCl < 80 mL/min: adjustment required Solutions for inhalation must be mixed immediately prior to administration.	**WARNING** Dose-dependent nephrotoxicity (monitor renal function and electrolytes), neurotoxicity **SIDE EFFECTS** Nephrotoxicity (proteinuria, ↑ SCr, ↓ urine output), neurologic disturbances (dizziness, headache, tingling, oral paresthesia, vertigo), rash (pruritus) **NOTES** Assess dose carefully, as dosage can be represented in units of colistimethate sodium, mg of colistimethate sodium, or mg of colistin base activity. Avoid use with other nephrotoxic medications. The neurotoxicity of colistimethate can result in respiratory paralysis from neuromuscular blockade.
Polymyxin B Sulfate Injection (IM/IV, intrathecal)	15,000-25,000 units/kg/day IV divided every 12 hours CrCl < 80 mL/min: adjustment required	**BOXED WARNINGS** Nephrotoxicity (dose-dependent) Neurotoxicity Safety in pregnancy is not established. Intramuscular/intrathecal administration only to hospitalized patients Avoid concurrent or sequential use of other neurotoxic or nephrotoxic drugs The neurotoxicity of polymyxin B sulfate can result in respiratory paralysis from neuromuscular blockade. **SIDE EFFECTS** Nephrotoxicity (proteinuria, ↑ BUN, ↓ urine output), neurologic disturbances (dizziness, tingling, numbness, paresthesia, vertigo), fever, urticaria **MONITORING** Renal function **NOTES** 1 mg = 10,000 units polymyxin B

See lab interactions, storage requirements, renal dosage information near the end of this chapter.

Polymyxin Drug Interactions

- Other nephrotoxic drugs can enhance the nephrotoxic effect.

Chloramphenicol

Reversibly binds to the 50S subunit of the bacterial ribosome inhibiting protein synthesis.

- Coverage: Activity against Gram-positives, Gram-negatives, anaerobes, and atypicals.

DRUG	DOSING	SAFETY/SIDE EFFECTS/MONITORING
Chloramphenicol Injection Rarely used due to side effects	50-100 mg/kg/day IV in divided doses Q6H (max 4 g/day) No adjustment in renal impairment but use with caution	**BOXED WARNING** Serious and fatal blood dyscrasias (aplastic anemia, thrombocytopenia, granulocytopenia) **WARNINGS** Gray syndrome – characterized by circulatory collapse, cyanosis, acidosis, abdominal distention, myocardial depression, coma, and death; associated with high serum levels G6PD deficiency **SIDE EFFECTS** Myelosuppression (pancytopenia, which may be irreversible), aplastic anemia, dermatologic (angioedema, rash, urticaria) **MONITORING** CBC at baseline and every 2 days during therapy, LFTs and renal function, serum drug concentrations

See lab interactions, storage requirements, renal dosage information near the end of this chapter.

MISCELLANEOUS ANTIBIOTICS

Clindamycin

Lincosamide class – reversibly binds to the 50S subunit of the bacterial ribosome inhibiting protein synthesis.

- Coverage: most aerobic and anaerobic Gram-positive bacteria (including some community-associated MRSA). It does not cover *Enterococcus*.

DRUG	DOSING	SAFETY/SIDE EFFECTS/MONITORING
Clindamycin *(Cleocin)* Injection, capsule, suspension Topical: Foam, gel, lotion, kit, solution, swab (*Cleocin-T, Clindagel, ClindaMax, Clindacin ETZ, Clindacin Pac, Clindacin-P, Evoclin)* Vaginal: Cream, suppository *(Clindesse, Cleocin* ovule*)*	150-450 mg PO Q6H 600-900 mg IV Q8H No adjustment in renal impairment	**BOXED WARNING** Colitis *(C. difficile)* **WARNING** Severe or fatal skin reactions (SJS/TEN/DRESS) **SIDE EFFECTS** N/V/D, rash, urticaria, ↑ LFTs (rare) **NOTES** An induction test (D-test) should be performed on *S. aureus* that are susceptible to clindamycin but resistant to erythromycin. A flattened zone between the disks (positive D-test) indicates inducible clindamycin resistance is present and clindamycin should not be used.

See lab interactions, storage requirements, renal dosage information near the end of this chapter.

Metronidazole and Tinidazole

These antibiotics cause a loss of helical DNA structure and strand breakage resulting in inhibition of protein synthesis.

- Coverage:
  - Metronidazole has activity against anaerobes and protozoal infections. It is effective for bacterial vaginosis, trichomoniasis, giardiasis, amebiasis, *C. difficile*, and is used in combination regimens for intra-abdominal infections.
  - Tinidazole is structurally related to metronidazole, but activity is limited to protozoa (giardiasis, amebiasis), trichomoniasis and bacterial vaginosis organisms.

DRUG	DOSING	SAFETY/SIDE EFFECTS/MONITORING
MetroNIDAZOLE ***(Flagyl,*** *Flagyl ER, Metro)* Tablet, capsule, injection Topical: *MetroCream, MetroGel, MetroLotion, MetroGel Vaginal, Noritate, Nuvessa, Rosadan, Vandazole*	500-750 mg IV/PO Q8-12H or 250-500 mg IV/PO Q6-8H **Mild-to-Moderate CDI:** 500 mg IV/PO TID for 10-14 days No adjustment in renal impairment Take immediate-release tablets with food to ↓ GI upset. Take extended-release tablets on empty stomach	**BOXED WARNING** Possibly carcinogenic based on animal data **CONTRAINDICATIONS** Pregnancy (1st trimester), breastfeeding (tinidazole), use of disulfiram within the past 2 weeks (metronidazole), use of alcohol or propylene glycol-containing products during therapy or within 3 days of therapy discontinuation **WARNINGS** CNS effects – seizures, peripheral/optic neuropathies, aseptic meningitis (metronidazole), encephalopathy (metronidazole) **SIDE EFFECTS** HA, nausea, metallic taste, furry tongue, darkened urine, dizziness, rash/severe skin reactions (SJS/TEN), **NOTES** See Pregnancy chapter for review of safety IV:PO is 1:1 (metronidazole)
Tinidazole *(Tindamax)* Tablet	2 grams PO daily Take with food to minimize GI effects No adjustment in renal impairment	

See lab interactions, storage requirements, renal dosage information near the end of this chapter.

Metronidazole/Tinidazole Drug Interactions

- Metronidazole is an inhibitor of 3A4 (weak) and 2C9 (weak). Tinidazole is a substrate of 3A4 (minor).
- Metronidazole and tinidazole should not be used with alcohol (during and for 3 days after discontinuation of therapy) due to a potential disulfiram-like reaction (abdominal cramping, nausea/vomiting, headaches, and flushing).
- Metronidazole, and potentially tinidazole, can ↑ INR in patients taking warfarin.

Fidaxomicin

Inhibits RNA polymerase resulting in inhibition of protein synthesis and cell death.

- Coverage: used for *Clostridium difficile* infection. It has shown benefit in preventing recurrence of disease, but due to high cost, it is typically reserved for select cases (e.g., recurrent disease, treatment failure with vancomycin or metronidazole).

DRUG	DOSING	SAFETY/SIDE EFFECTS/MONITORING
Fidaxomicin *(Dificid)* Tablet	200 mg PO BID x 10 days No adjustment in renal impairment	**WARNINGS** Not effective for systemic infections – absorption is minimal. **SIDE EFFECTS** N/V, abdominal pain, GI bleeding, anemia

See lab interactions, storage requirements, renal dosage information near the end of this chapter.

Rifaximin

Rifaximin inhibits bacterial RNA synthesis by binding to bacterial DNA-dependent RNA polymerase. It is structurally related to rifampin.

- Coverage: *E. coli*

DRUG	DOSING	SAFETY/SIDE EFFECTS/MONITORING
RifAXIMIN *(Xifaxan)* Tablet	**Travelers' diarrhea:** 200 mg PO TID x 3 days **Reduction of hepatic encephalopathy recurrence:** 550 mg PO BID **Irritable bowel syndrome w/diarrhea (IBS-D):** 550 mg PO TID x 14 days No adjustment in renal impairment	**SIDE EFFECTS** Peripheral edema, dizziness, headache, flatulence, nausea, abdominal pain, rash/pruritus **NOTES** Not effective for systemic infections (< 1% absorption) May be used as salvage treatment in patients with *C. difficile* infection

See lab interactions, storage requirements, renal dosage information near the end of this chapter.

URINARY AGENTS

Fosfomycin

Inhibits bacterial cell wall synthesis by inactivating the enzyme pyruval transferase, which is critical in the synthesis of cell walls. Single-dose regimen used for uncomplicated UTI (cystitis only).

- Coverage: *E. coli* (including ESBLs) and *E. faecalis* (including VRE).

DRUG	DOSING	SAFETY/SIDE EFFECTS/MONITORING
Fosfomycin *(Monurol)* 1 packet granules = 3 grams	**Female, Uncomplicated UTI** 3 grams PO x 1, mixed in 3-4 oz of cold water	**SIDE EFFECTS** Headache, diarrhea, nausea

See lab interactions, storage requirements, renal dosage information near the end of this chapter.

Nitrofurantoin

Bacterial cell wall inhibitor. Used for uncomplicated UTI (cystitis only).

- Coverage: *E. coli, Klebsiella, Enterobacter, S. aureus,* and *Enterococcus* (VRE).

DRUG	DOSING	SAFETY/SIDE EFFECTS/MONITORING
Nitrofurantoin ***(Macrodantin, Macrobid,*** *Furadantin)* Capsule, suspension	*Macrodantin:* 50-100 mg PO QID with food x 3-7 days; 50-100 mg PO QHS with food for prophylaxis *Macrobid:* 100 mg PO BID x 7 days The macrocrystal formulation *(Macrobid)* dissolves more slowly and is given BID CrCl < 60 mL/min: contraindicated Per revised 2015 Beers Criteria: use can be considered when CrCl > 30 mL/min	**CONTRAINDICATIONS** Renal impairment (CrCl < 60 mL/min) due to inadequate urinary concentrations and risk for accumulation of neurotoxins, a previous history of cholestatic jaundice/ hepatic dysfunction, pregnancy (at term) **WARNINGS** Optic neuritis, hepatotoxicity, peripheral neuropathy, pulmonary toxicity, hemolytic anemia (use caution in patients with G6PD deficiency) and positive Coombs test **SIDE EFFECTS** GI upset (take with food), headache, rash, brown urine discoloration (harmless) **NOTES** See Pregnancy chapter for safety discussion

See lab interactions, storage requirements, renal dosage information near the end of this chapter.

TOPICAL DECOLONIZATION

Mupirocin Nasal Ointment

Topical antimicrobial ointment used to eliminate *Staphylococci* (MRSA) colonization of the nares. See Common Skin Conditions chapter for discussion regarding mupirocin topical use for infected skin lesions.

DRUG	DOSING	SAFETY/SIDE EFFECTS/MONITORING
Mupirocin Nasal *(Bactroban Nasal)* 1 g tubes	Decolonization: ½ tube in each nostril BID x 5 days	**SIDE EFFECTS** Headache, burning, localized irritation, rhinitis, pharyngitis

See lab interactions, storage requirements, renal dosage information near the end of this chapter.

DRUGS ACTIVE AGAINST SPECIFIC PATHOGENS

Community-associated methicillin-resistant *Staphylococcus aureus* (CA-MRSA) skin & soft tissue infections (SSTI)
SMX/TMP *(Bactrim DS)*

Doxycycline, minocycline

Clindamycin*

For more severe SSTI requiring IV treatment or hospitalization
Vancomycin

Linezolid, tedizolid

Daptomycin

Ceftaroline

Telavancin

Oritavancin

Dalbavancin

Quinupristin/Dalfopristin

Tigecycline

Nosocomial MRSA
Vancomycin (consider using alternative if MIC ≥ 2)

Linezolid

Telavancin

Daptomycin (not in pneumonia)

Rifampin (for select infections, never used alone)

VRE *(E. faecalis)*
Pen G or ampicillin

Linezolid

Daptomycin

Tigecycline

Cystitis only: nitrofurantoin, fosfomycin, doxycycline

VRE *(E. faecium)*
Daptomycin

Linezolid

Quinupristin/Dalfopristin

Tigecycline

Cystitis only: nitrofurantoin, fosfomycin, doxycycline

Pseudomonas aeruginosa
Piperacillin/Tazobactam

Cefepime

Ceftazidime

Ceftazidime/Avibactam

Ceftolozane/Tazobactam

Carbapenems (not ertapenem)

Ciprofloxacin, levofloxacin

Aztreonam

Aminoglycosides

Colistimethate, polymyxin B

Acinetobacter baumannii
Carbapenems (except ertapenem)

Ampicillin/Sulbactam

Minocycline

Tigecycline

Quinolones

SMX/TMP

Colistimethate, polymyxin B

Extended spectrum beta-lactamase producing Gram-negative rods (ESBL GNR) – *E. coli, Klebsiella pneumoniae, P. mirabilis*
Carbapenems

Ceftolozane/Tazobactam

Ceftazidime/Avibactam

Cefepime (high-dose)

Quinolones

Aminoglycosides

Cystitis only: fosfomycin

Carbapenem-resistant Gram-negative rods (CRE)

Ceftazidime/Avibactam

Colistimethate, polymyxin B

Bacteroides fragilis
Metronidazole

Beta-lactam/Beta-lactamase inhibitor

Cefotetan, cefoxitin

Carbapenems

Tigecycline

Others (reduced activity): clindamycin, moxifloxacin

***C. difficile* Infection**
Metronidazole

Vancomycin (oral)

Fidaxomicin

Atypical Organisms
Azithromycin, clarithromycin

Doxycycline, minocycline

Quinolones

HNPEK
Amoxicillin (if beta-lactamase negative)

Beta-lactam/Beta-lactamase inhibitor

Cephalosporins (except 1st generation)

Carbapenems

SMX/TMP

Aminoglycosides

Quinolones

**A D-test must be performed before using clindamycin. Never use quinolones for MRSA, regardless of susceptibility report.*

STORAGE REQUIREMENTS

REFRIGERATION REQUIRED AFTER RECONSTITUTION (ORAL)		
Penicillin VK	Cefadroxil *(Duricef)*	Cefaclor *(Ceclor)*
Ampicillin	Cefpodoxime *(Vantin)*	Ceftibuten *(Cedax)*
Amoxicillin/Clavulanate *(Augmentin)*	Cefprozil *(Cefzil)*	Vancomycin (oral)
Cephalexin *(Keflex)*	Cefuroxime *(Ceftin)*	Valgancyclovir*

REFRIGERATION RECOMMENDED
Amoxicillin (*Amoxil*) – improves taste

DO NOT REFRIGERATE (ORAL)		
Cefdinir *(Omnicef)*	Ciprofloxacin *(Cipro)*	Acyclovir *(Zovirax)*
Azithromycin *(Zmax)*	Levofloxacin *(Levaquin)*	Fluconazole *(Diflucan)**
Clarithromycin *(Biaxin)* – bitter taste, thickens/gels	Clindamycin *(Cleocin)* – thickens, may crystallize	Posaconazole *(Noxafil)**
Doxycycline *(Vibramycin)*	Linezolid *(Zyvox)*	Voriconazole *(Vfend)**
	Sulfamethoxazole/Trimethoprim *(Septra, Sulfatrim)*	Nystatin*

DO NOT REFRIGERATE (IV)	
Acyclovir (*Zovirax*)* – refrigeration causes crystallization	Moxifloxacin *(Avelox)*
Metronidazole *(Flagyl)*	Sulfamethoxazole/trimethoprim *(Septra, Sulfatrim)*

** These drugs are discussed in Infectious Diseases Chapter III*

RENAL DOSE ADJUSTMENT

Many antibiotics are cleared through the kidneys and require adjustment based on renal function. Most beta-lactams and quinolones require adjustment for renal impairment. See the following table of antibiotics that do not require renal adjustment.

NO RENAL DOSE ADJUSTMENT REQUIRED	
Dicloxacillin, nafcillin, oxacillin	Clindamycin
Ceftriaxone	Metronidazole, tinidazole
Moxifloxacin	Fidaxomicin
Azithromycin, erythromycin	Vancomycin (PO only)
Doxycycline, minocycline, tigecycline	Rifaximin
Linezolid, tedizolid	Rifampin*
Quinupristin/dalfopristin	Chloramphenicol

** This agent is discussed in Infectious Diseases Chapter II*

DRUG-LABORATORY INTERACTIONS

Some anti-infectives can cause abnormalities in laboratory values. An antibiotic can cause a true change in a lab value, which often necessitates a change in therapy (e.g., a positive Coombs test in combination with bleeding indicates that a patient could be experiencing drug-related hemolysis and the antibiotic should be discontinued). In other cases, a drug should not be started in patients with certain conditions (e.g., primaquine in patients with G6PD deficiency). In some situations, medications can interfere with the result of the test, even if there are no clinical effects (e.g., daptomycin can cause a falsely elevated INR, but does not cause bleeding). See Lab Values & Drug Monitoring chapter for other drugs and additional information.

LAB TEST	IMPLICATIONS	ANTIBIOTICS
G6PD deficiency	These drugs have been associated with hemolytic anemia. Consider alternatives in patients with G6PD deficiency when possible. Monitor CBC and discontinue drug if hemolysis or bleeding occurs.	Chloroquine* Primaquine* (avoid in G6PD deficiency) Dapsone** Nitrofurantoin Sulfamethoxazole
Coombs test, positive	Discontinue drug; indicates drug-related hemolysis Increased risk with higher doses/prolonged infusions	Penicillins Cephalosporins Imipenem, meropenem Nitrofurantoin Rifampin Sulfamethoxazole Quinine* Isoniazid**
Drug-Induced Lupus Erythematosus (DILE), evidenced by butterfly rash, achy joints, lab tests (RF+, $\uparrow$ ANA, ESR, CRP)	Discontinue drug; lupus damages joints/organs	Isoniazid** Minocycline Terbinafine**
False-positive urine glucose tests (with copper reduction tests)	Positive urinary glucose may be due to drug (rather than $\uparrow$ BG)	Penicillins Cephalosporins Imipenem Isoniazid**
False elevation of aPTT	Use alternate assay (Factor Xa) or alternative anticoagulant not requiring aPTT or PT/INR monitoring	Oritavancin (IV heparin contraindicated x 5 days after dose) Telavancin (IV UFH contraindicated)
False elevation of INR	Use alternate anticoagulant or see specific drug recommendations for INR	Daptomycin (monitor INR just prior to dose) Oritavancin (monitor INR > 12 hours after dose) Telavancin (monitor INR just prior to dose)
Elevated CPK	Monitor at least weekly, or more if current or prior statin use or renal impairment. DC daptomycin if myopathy symptoms plus CPK > 5x the upper limit of normal (ULN) or 1,000 units/L or when CPK > 10x ULN if asymptomatic.	Daptomycin

** These drugs are discussed in Travelers*
***These drugs are discussed in Infectious Diseases II – IV*

SPECIAL REQUIREMENTS

SPECIAL REQUIREMENTS	DRUG	
Most anti-infectives can be taken with food to ↓ GI upset; except these, which are different	Within one hour of finishing a meal: *Moxatag* (amoxicillin formulation) Empty stomach: ampicillin oral capsules and suspension, azithromycin *(Zmax,* extended-release oral suspension), ceftibuten suspension, levofloxacin oral solution, metronidazole extended-release, penicillin, rifampin*, isoniazid*, itraconazole solution*, voriconazole*	
Oral to IV Dosing Ratios 1:1 (Oral and IV dose is the same)	Levofloxacin, moxifloxacin Doxycycline, minocycline Sulfamethoxazole/trimethoprim Linezolid, tedizolid Metronidazole Fluconazole*, isavuconazonium*, posaconazole* (oral tablets and IV), voriconazole*	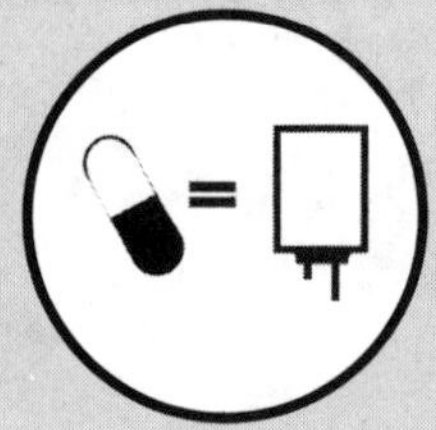
Light Protection Required During Administration	Doxycycline Micafungin* Pentamidine*	
Compatible with Dextrose only	Dalbavancin, oritavancin Pentamidine* Quinupristin/dalfopristin Sulfamethoxazole/trimethoprim Amphotericin B* (conventional, *Abelcet, Amphotec, Ambisome)*	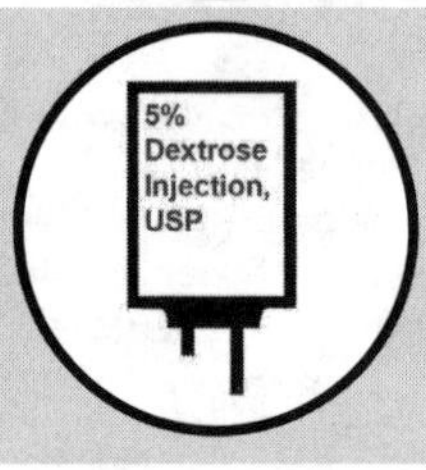
Compatible with Saline only	Ampicillin Ampicillin/sulbactam Ertapenem	
Compatible with NS/LR only	Caspofungin* Daptomycin	

** These drugs are discussed in Infectious Diseases Chapter II-IV*

PATIENT COUNSELING

All Antibiotics

- Antibiotics only treat bacterial infections. They do not treat viral infections such as the common cold and are not recommended in most cases of acute bronchitis and sinusitis.
- Skipping doses or not completing the full course of therapy may ↓ effectiveness of treatment, cause the infection to return, and increase the likelihood that this medicine will not work for you in the future.
- If your symptoms worsen, contact your healthcare provider.
- Many antibiotics can cause rash. If you experience a rash, contact your healthcare provider.
- Many antibiotics can cause GI upset. Taking medication with food will usually help, however some antibiotics need to be taken on an empty stomach.
- Measure liquid doses carefully using a measuring device/syringe which should come with the medicine. Ask your pharmacist if you do not have one. Household spoons should not be used, as they often do not deliver the correct dose.
- Contact your healthcare provider if you have watery diarrhea several times a day, with or without abdominal cramping. This can occur during treatment, or weeks after the antibiotic treatment has finished. You should not self-treat with anti-diarrheal medicine.
- Some oral liquid and chewable dosage forms contain phenylalanine. Let the pharmacist know if you have phenylketonuria (inability to metabolize phenylalanine).

Beta-lactam Antibiotics

Amoxicillin products

- Amoxicillin may be taken with food, usually every 8 or 12 hours. *Moxatag* is taken within 1 hour of finishing a meal. *Augmentin* is taken with food to ↑ what your body absorbs and ↓ stomach upset. Amoxicillin/clavulanate extended release tablets should be taken with food.
- The suspensions should be refrigerated (especially important for *Augmentin*).

Cephalexin *(Keflex)*, Cefuroxime *(Ceftin)*, Cefdinir *(Omnicef)*

- Cephalexin: take this medication by mouth with or without a meal or snack every 6 hours. The suspension should be refrigerated.
- Cefuroxime: take this medication by mouth with a meal or snack every 12 hours. The suspension should be refrigerated.
- Cefdinir: can be taken with or without food. The suspension should not be refrigerated.

Penicillin VK

- Take this medication by mouth one hour before or two hours after a meal, usually every 6 hours.
- The suspension should be refrigerated.

Clindamycin *(Cleocin)*

- Take by mouth with or without food, 3 – 4 times a day.
- Take with a full glass of water to avoid GI irritation.
- The liquid suspension should not be refrigerated.

Macrolides

Azithromycin *(Zithromax)*

- Common dosing is two 250 mg tablets on day 1, followed by one 250 mg tablet daily on days 2 – 5, or 500 mg daily for 3 days.
- The tablets and immediate release oral suspension can be taken with or without food, extended release suspension should be taken on an empty stomach (1 hour before or 2 hours after a meal).
- The suspension should be stored at room temperature and should not be refrigerated.

Clarithromycin *(Biaxin)*

- Common side effects include abnormal (metallic) taste, diarrhea and GI upset.
- The tablets and oral suspension are taken twice daily with or without food or with milk.
- *Biaxin XL* tablets should be taken with food.
- The liquid suspension should not be refrigerated.

Erythromycin

- The liquid suspension combination with sulfisoxazole should be refrigerated.

Metronidazole *(Flagyl)*

- Common side effects include nausea and unusual (metallic) taste.
- Do not use any alcohol products while using this medicine, and for at least 3 days afterward.
- Immediate-release tablets and capsules may be taken with food to minimize stomach upset. Take extended release tablets on an empty stomach (1 hour before or 2 hours after meals); do not split, crush or chew.

Mupirocin Ointment *(Bactroban Nasal)* 1 gram tube

- Place ½ the ointment from the tube into one nostril and the other ½ into the other nostril. Press the nostrils at the same time and let go many times (for about a minute) to spread the ointment into the nose.
- Wash your hands after use.
- The most common side effects are burning and itching.

Nitrofurantoin *(Macrodantin, Macrobid)*

- Take this medication with food to improve absorption and ↓ side effects. Swallow the medication whole.
- Do not use magnesium trisilicate-containing antacids while taking this medication. These antacids can bind with nitrofurantoin, preventing its full absorption into your system.
- Side effects including nausea and headache may occur.
- This medication may cause your urine to turn dark yellow or brown in color. This is usually a harmless, temporary effect and will disappear when the medication is stopped. However, dark brown urine can also be a sign of liver damage. Seek immediate medical attention if you notice dark urine along with any of the following symptoms: persistent nausea or vomiting, pale stools, unusual fatigue or if your skin and whites of your eyes become yellow.
- This medication may rarely cause very serious (possibly fatal) lung problems. Lung problems may occur within the first month of treatment or after long-term use of nitrofurantoin (generally for 6 months or longer). Seek immediate medical attention if you develop symptoms of lung problems including: persistent cough, chest pain, shortness of breath/trouble breathing, joint/muscle pain or bluish/purplish skin.

Quinolones

- Dispense MedGuide and instruct patient to read it.
- Antacids, didanosine *(Videx)*, sucralfate *(Carafate)*, bile acid resins, magnesium, aluminum, calcium, iron, zinc, multivitamins or any product containing these multivalent cations can bind to these drugs and prevent them from working properly.
  - Give ciprofloxacin 2 hours before or 6 hours after these drugs
  - Give levofloxacin 2 hours before or 2 hours after these drugs
  - Give moxifloxacin 4 hours before or 8 hours after these drugs
- Although the actual effect of dairy products on quinolone absorption varies, it is generally recommended to avoid consuming calcium-rich foods (dairy products) with the dose to avoid binding.
- Drink plenty of fluids as this medication can cause crystals to form in the urine.
- This medicine can rarely cause tendon inflammation (tendinitis) or a serious problem called tendon rupture. If you hear or feel a snap or pop or notice pain/swelling in a tendon area: the back of the ankle (Achilles), shoulder, hand or other sites, stop the medicine and contact your healthcare provider immediately. This occurs more frequently in people over age 60, and in patients who have had transplants, or who use steroid medicines, such as prednisone.
- This medications can increase your risk for seizures. This is rare but you should not take this medicine if you have a history of seizures. Other effects include restlessness, anxiousness, nightmares, lightheadedness/dizziness, headaches
- This medicine can make your skin more sensitive to the sun, and you can burn more easily. Use sunscreen, wear protective clothing, and avoid sun exposure.
- Do not take this medicine if you have myasthenia gravis. Breathing problems can occur.
- This medicine can cause weakness or tingling/painful sensations in the arms and legs. If this occurs, contact your healthcare provider immediately.
- If you use blood sugar-lowering medicines, your blood sugar may get unusually low. Be sure to check your blood sugar level frequently and treat low blood sugar if it occurs.

Ciprofloxacin *(Cipro)*

- Do not use this medicine if you take a different medicine called tizanidine *(Zanaflex)*. Please tell your healthcare providers about all medicines you are using.
- The liquid suspension should not be refrigerated. Do not chew the microcapsules.

Levofloxacin *(Levaquin)*

- Take this medication once daily, with or without food. The suspension is taken 1 hour before or 2 hours after eating.
- The liquid formulation should not be refrigerated.

Sulfamethoxazole and Trimethoprim *(Bactrim, Septra)*

- Do not use this medication if you have an allergy to sulfa medicines.
- Take with a full glass of water to prevent crystal formation in the urine. Take with or without food. If stomach upset occurs, take with food or milk.
- Do not use this medication if you are pregnant, if you could become pregnant, or if you are breastfeeding.
- This medicine can make your skin more sensitive to the sun, and you can burn more easily. Use sunscreen, wear protective clothing, and avoid the sun.
- Shake the suspension prior to use. The suspension should not be refrigerated and protected from light.

Tetracyclines

Doxycycline *(Doryx,* others)

- This medication can make your skin more sensitive to the sun, and you can burn more easily. Use sunscreen, wear protective clothing and avoid the sun.
- Take with a full glass of water to avoid GI irritation.
- This medicine should be taken twice daily 1 – 2 hours before, or 4 – 6 hours after taking antacids, vitamins, magnesium, calcium, iron or zinc supplements, dairy products, bismuth subsalicylate.
- *Oracea* should be taken on an empty stomach (1 hour before or 2 hours after meals).
- Do not use this medicine if you are pregnant, if you could become pregnant or if you are breastfeeding.
- The liquid suspension should not be refrigerated.

Minocycline *(Minocin, Solodyn)*

- Take this medication with or without food, 1– 2 times daily.
- Swallow tablet or capsule whole.
- Take with a full glass of water to decrease GI irritation.
- Do not use this medication if you are pregnant, if you could become pregnant, or if you are breast-feeding.

Questions

1. Which of the following statements regarding linezolid is correct?

   a. It is a cyclic lipopeptide.
   b. It is a MAO inhibitor and should be avoided with serotonergic drugs.
   c. It is a combination product consisting of quinupristin and dalfopristin.
   d. It needs to be dose adjusted in patients with renal impairment.
   e. It is not effective for treating infections in the lung.

2. Which of the following statements regarding the intravenous formulation of *Bactrim* is/are correct? (Select **ALL** that apply.)

   a. *Bactrim* IV should be protected from light during administration.
   b. *Bactrim* IV should be refrigerated.
   c. *Bactrim* IV is compatible with Dextrose 5% (D5W).
   d. *Bactrim* IV needs to be dose adjusted . in patients with significant renal impairment.
   e. *Bactrim* IV can be converted to *Bactrim* PO in a 1:1 ratio.

3. Which one of the following antibiotics does not require dose adjustment in renal impairment?

   a. Gentamicin
   b. Clarithromycin
   c. Cefixime
   d. Tigecycline
   e. Daptomycin

4. Which one of the following antibiotics should be refrigerated?

   a. Cipro
   b. Keflex
   c. Levaquin
   d. Septra
   e. Zithromax

5. The pharmacist should counsel a patient to use sunscreen when taking which of the following medication(s)? (Select **ALL** that apply.)

   a. Cleocin
   b. Biaxin
   c. Avelox
   d. Minocin
   e. Ceftin

6. Which one of the following antimicrobials in the IV formulation is stable in and preferred to be reconstituted in normal saline (NS)? (Select **ALL** that apply.)

   a. Quinupristin/dalfopristin
   b. Ertapenem
   c. Ampicillin
   d. SMX/TMP
   e. Azithromycin

7. An infection caused by *E. coli* that produces extended-spectrum beta-lactamases could be treated with which of the following antibiotics: (Select **ALL** that apply.)

   a. Invanz
   b. Rocephin
   c. Unasyn
   d. Zerbaxa
   e. Avycaz

8. All of the following have activity against *Pseudomonas aeruginosa* except: (Select **ALL** that apply.)

   a. Cefepime
   b. Meropenem
   c. Ertapenem
   d. Piperacillin/tazobactam
   e. Aztreonam

9. Which of the following antibiotics can interfere with coagulation assays: (Select **ALL** that apply)

   a. Vibativ
   b. Zithromax
   c. Primaxin
   d. Sivextro
   e. Orbactiv

10. Which of the following antibiotics is **not** matched with a possible side effect/warning/interaction:

   a. Daptomycin – increased CPK/myopathy
   b. Telavancin – fetal risk
   c. Vancomycin – seizures
   d. Metronidazole – disulfiram-like reaction with alcohol consumption
   e. Doripenem – decreased valproic acid concentrations

Answers

1-b, 2-c,d,e, 3-d, 4-b, 5-c,d, 6-b,c, 7-a,d,e, 8-c, 9-a,e, 10-c

29

INFECTIOUS DISEASES II: BACTERIAL INFECTIONS

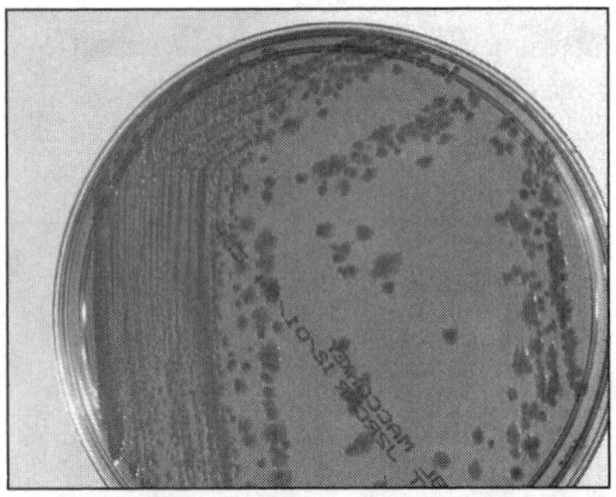

GUIDELINES/REFERENCES

Bratzler DW, Dellinger EP, Olsen KM et al. Clinical practice guidelines for antimicrobial prophylaxis for surgery. *Am J Health-Syst Pharm.* 2013; 70:195-283.

Lieberthal AS, Carroll AE, Chonmaitree T et al. The Diagnosis and Management Acute Otitis Media; *Pediatrics.* 2013; 131:e964-e999.

Workowski KA, Golan GA. Sexually Transmitted Diseases Treatment Guidelines, 2015. MMWR Recomm Rep 2015;64(No. RR-3):1-137

Guidelines available at the Infectious Diseases Society of America website (www.idsociety.org)

Additional references included with the video files (RxPrep Online).

We gratefully acknowledge the assistance of Emi Minejima, PharmD, Assistant Professor and Annie Wong-Beringer, PharmD, FCCP, FIDSA, Associate Dean and Professor, University of Southern California School of Pharmacy, in preparing this chapter.

BACKGROUND

Infectious Diseases I should be reviewed prior to this chapter, to gain a working knowledge of bacterial pathogens, microbiology reports, resistance, and antibiotic agents, including spectrum of activity (coverage), and pharmacokinetics/pharmacodynamics, which play an important role in selecting optimal treatment of infections.

Antibiotic Selection Principles

- Presence of infection is based on signs and symptoms. For example, a positive urine culture does not determine the presence of infection. The diagnosis of an infection must be made initially based on symptoms of dysuria, urgency, leukocytosis, fever, etc. and a urinalysis. Once the diagnosis of infection is made, the culture can help guide an appropriate antibiotic choice.
- A broad spectrum regimen is often used empirically to ensure adequate therapy for likely pathogens. Local resistance patterns and antibiotic use guidelines should always be considered.
- Infection characteristics include infection site, infection severity, and whether it is community- or hospital-acquired.
- Antibiotic characteristics include spectrum of activity and adequate penetration to the site of infection. Lipophilic antimicrobials have enhanced tissue penetration. Antibiotics that are cleared hepatically may not achieve adequate drug concentrations in the urine.

- Patient characteristics also affect treatment choices. These include age, body weight, renal/hepatic function, allergies, recent antibiotic use, colonization with resistant bacteria, recent environmental exposure, vaccination status, pregnancy status, immune function, and comorbid conditions.
- When culture and susceptibilities are available, empiric antibiotics should be streamlined to narrower spectrum treatment in order to limit collateral damage associated with broad spectrum agents.

COMMON BACTERIAL PATHOGENS FOR SELECTED SITES OF INFECTION

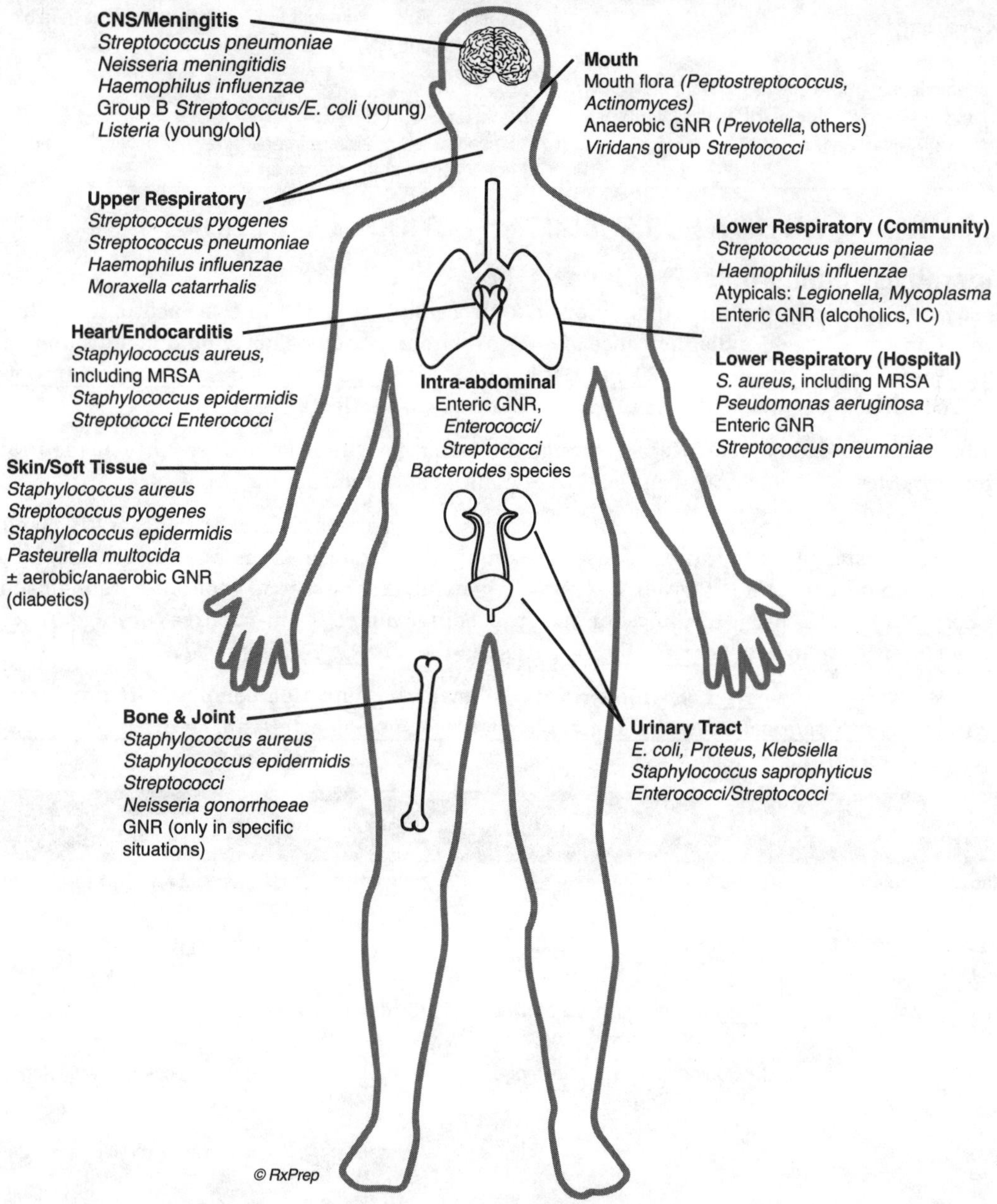

CNS = central nervous system, IC = immunocompromised, GNR = Gram-negative rods, Enteric GNR = *Proteus, E. coli, Klebsiella, Enterobacter*

Assessment of Treatment

MONITORING TREATMENT RESPONSE	REASONS FOR LACK OF RESPONSE
Clinical status of the patient: 1. Fever trend (and other vital signs) 2. WBC trend 3. Reduction in signs and symptoms of infection Radiographic findings (such as CXR) Negative cultures Pain/inflammation – markers of inflammation include procalcitonin levels (more specific to bacterial infection), C-reactive protein (CRP), and the erythrocyte sedimentation rate (ESR)	**Antibiotic factors** Inadequate spectrum and/or dose, poor tissue penetration, drug-drug interaction(s), non-adherence, inadequate duration of therapy **Microbiologic factors** Resistance, superinfection *(C. difficile)*, alternative etiology (viral, fungal, noninfectious cause) **Host factors** Uncontrolled source of infection (e.g., abscess or fluid collection), immunocompromised

ANTIMICROBIAL AGENTS FOR SELECT INFECTIOUS CONDITIONS

Perioperative Antimicrobial Prophylaxis

- A dose of antibiotics given immediately prior to procedures can obtain therapeutic levels in both serum and tissue to reduce the incidence of surgical site infections. This should be initiated within 60 minutes before the incision, or 120 minutes before the incision if using quinolones or vancomycin, which require longer infusion times to avoid serious adverse effects.
- In order to maintain therapeutic levels throughout the surgery, additional doses may be required for longer surgeries (> 3 – 4 hours) or in cases of major blood loss during the procedure.
- Controversy exists regarding the duration of prophylaxis necessary after the surgery is complete. In most circumstances, no additional doses are required. If continued postoperatively, prophylactic agents should be discontinued within 24 hours. In general, first or second generation cephalosporins (e.g., cefazolin) are the drugs of choice for most procedures due to Gram-positive coverage. Vancomycin is an alternative in beta-lactam allergic patients or when MRSA is a concern.
- Surgeries involving the bowel or with a risk of an anaerobic infection commonly require antibiotics with broader Gram-negative and anaerobic coverage such as cefotetan, cefoxitin, ertapenem or (ceftriaxone + metronidazole).

SURGICAL PROCEDURE	RECOMMENDED ANTIBIOTICS*	IF BETA-LACTAM ALLERGY
Cardiac or vascular surgeries	Cefazolin or cefuroxime	Vancomycin or clindamycin
Hip fracture repair/ total joint replacement	Cefazolin	Vancomycin or clindamycin
Colon (colorectal)	Cefotetan, cefoxitin, ampicillin/ sulbactam, ertapenem or Metronidazole + (cefazolin or ceftriaxone)	Clindamycin + (aminoglycoside or quinolone or aztreonam) or Metronidazole + (aminoglycoside or quinolone)
Hysterectomy	Cefotetan, cefoxitin, cefazolin or ampicillin/sulbactam	Clindamycin or vancomycin + (aminoglycoside or quinolone or aztreonam) or Metronidazole + (aminoglycoside or quinolone)

** For procedures and/or patients where MRSA is a likely pathogen consider adding vancomycin to routine prophylaxis.*

Meningitis

Meningitis is inflammation of the meninges (membranes) that cover the brain and spinal cord. The meninges swell, causing three classic symptoms: Severe headache, nuchal rigidity (stiff neck) and altered mental status. Not every patient will demonstrate all three symptoms. Other symptoms could include chills, vomiting and photophobia. Meningitis is mostly caused by viral infections, but can be due to bacteria or fungi. Meningitis symptoms must be quickly recognized and treated to avoid severe complications, including death.

- Diagnosis is made by a lumbar puncture (LP), which is a sampling of the cerebral spinal fluid (CSF) to help guide antibiotic choices before the culture and susceptibility results are available. In some patients a computed tomography (CT) scan is performed prior to the LP to avoid potentially fatal complications. It is preferable to get the LP prior to starting antibiotics; however, antibiotics should be given promptly, even if the LP is delayed.
- Antibiotic dosages are higher to penetrate the CNS.
- The most likely organisms causing bacterial meningitis are *Streptococcus pneumoniae, Neisseria meningitidis, Haemophilus influenzae* and *Listeria monocytogenes.* Likely pathogens and empiric antibiotics largely depend on the patient's age and immune status (see table). If recent surgery or procedure, *S. aureus,* including MRSA, should be considered.

Acute Bacterial Meningitis Treatment (Community-Acquired)

- Dexamethasone is given 15 – 20 min prior to or with the 1st dose of antibiotics to prevent neurological complications of meningitis. The adult dexamethasone dose is 0.15 mg/kg (commonly rounded to 10 mg) IV Q6H x 4 days.
- Antibiotic durations are pathogen-dependent: 7 days for *N. meningitidis* and *H. influenzae*, 10 – 14 days for *S. pneumoniae* and 21 days for *Listeria monocytogenes.*

AGE/RISK GROUP	EMPIRIC THERAPY
Age < 1 month Common pathogens: *S. agalactiae, E. coli, Listeria monocytogenes, Klebsiella* species Avoid ceftriaxone in this age group	Ampicillin* **plus** Cefotaxime or Gentamicin
Age 1-23 months Common pathogens: *S. pneumoniae, N. meningitidis, S. agalactiae, H. influenzae, E. coli*	Cefotaxime or Ceftriaxone **plus** Vancomycin
Age 2-50 years Common pathogens: *S. pneumoniae, N. meningitidis*	Adult doses: Cefotaxime 2 grams IV Q4-6H or Ceftriaxone 2 grams IV Q12H **plus** Vancomycin 30-45 mg/kg/day in divided doses
Age > 50 years or immunocompromised Common pathogens: *S. pneumoniae, N. meningitidis, L. monocytogenes, aerobic gram-negative bacilli*	Vancomycin + ampicillin* + (ceftriaxone or cefotaxime)
If severe PCN allergy	Quinolone (moxifloxacin or levofloxacin) + vancomycin (± SMX/TMP 10-20 mg/kg/day IV divided Q6-12H for *Listeria* coverage)

**Ampicillin is added for Listeria coverage*

UPPER RESPIRATORY TRACT INFECTIONS

Acute Otitis Media

Acute otitis media (AOM) is the most common childhood infection in the United States requiring antibiotic treatment. Signs and symptoms often have a rapid onset and can include bulging tympanic membranes, otorrhea (middle ear effusion/fluid), otalgia (ear pain), fever, crying and tugging or rubbing the ears.

- Systemic agents are preferred for pain (acetaminophen or ibuprofen).
- Many of the infections are viral, therefore antibiotics will be ineffective.
- Observation without antibiotics may be an option for non-severe AOM depending on age, diagnostic certainty, and illness severity. An observation period of 48 – 72 hours is used to assess clinical improvement without antibiotics. The decision for observation should involve both the pediatrician and caregiver.

AOM Treatment

AGE	OTORRHEA WITH AOM	UNILATERAL OR BILATERAL AOM WITH SEVERE SYMPTOMS*	BILATERAL AOM WITHOUT OTORRHEA	UNILATERAL AOM WITHOUT OTORRHEA
6 months-2 years	Antibiotics	Antibiotics	Antibiotics	Antibiotics or additional observation
≥ 2 years	Antibiotics	Antibiotics	Antibiotics or additional observation	Antibiotics or additional observation

**Severe symptoms include otalgia > 48 hrs, temperature ≥ 39°C (102.2°F) in past 48 hrs*

INITIAL ANTIBIOTIC TREATMENT		ANTIBIOTIC TREATMENT AFTER 48-72 HOURS OF FAILURE OF INITIAL THERAPY
Recommended First-line Treatment	**Alternative Treatment (if Penicillin Allergy)**	**Recommended First-line Treatment**
Amoxicillin 80-90 mg/kg/day in 2 divided doses or	Cefdinir 14 mg/kg/day in 1 or 2 doses	Amox/clav* (90 mg/kg/day of amoxicillin with 6.4 mg/kg/day of clavulanate) in 2 divided doses
Amox/clav 90 mg/kg/day of amoxicillin with 6.4 mg/kg/day of clavulanate (amoxicillin to clavulanate ratio is 14:1) in 2 divided doses	Cefuroxime 30 mg/kg/day in 2 divided doses	Ceftriaxone 50 mg/kg IM/IV daily for 3 days
	Cefpodoxime 10 mg/kg/day in 2 divided doses	
	Ceftriaxone 50 mg/kg IM/IV daily for 1 or 3 days	

**May be considered in patients who have received amoxicillin in the past 30 days*

- First line treatment is high-dose amoxicillin (80 – 90 mg/kg/day divided Q12H) or amoxicillin/clavulanate (90 mg/kg/day of amoxicillin divided Q12H). The higher dose will cover most *S. pneumoniae*.
- Recommended agents in the setting of amoxicillin failure include amoxicillin/clavulanate 90 mg/kg/day of amoxicillin component x 5 – 10 days (see recommendations for duration below) or ceftriaxone 50 mg/kg IM/IV daily x 3 days.
- When using high dose amoxicillin/clavulanate, the formulation with less clavulanate should be used, as it is less likely to cause diarrhea. *Augmentin ES-600* (amoxicillin 600 mg and clavulanate 42.9 mg per 5 mL) has a lower ratio of amoxicillin/clavulanate than the other suspension formulations.

- Recommended duration of treatment for amoxicillin, amoxicillin/clavulanate and oral cephalosporins: < 2 years of age = 10 days; 2 – 5 years of age = 7 days; and ≥ 6 years of age = 5 – 7 days.
- Ceftriaxone (50 mg/kg) can be given IM/IV daily for 1 or 3 days (1 or 3 days for initial treatment or 3 days for treatment failure) for those who cannot tolerate oral medication due to GI side effects.
- In patients with a non-severe penicillin allergy, the American Academy of Pediatrics (AAP) recommends use of a cephalosporin, as stated above. Although there is some risk of cross-reactivity, it is thought to be much lower than old estimates and is negligible with second and third generation cephalosporins (cefuroxime, cefdinir, cefpodoxime and ceftriaxone). In addition, non-beta-lactam antibiotics that are suitable for use in children have limited efficacy against typical pathogens, due to resistance.

AOM Prevention

The pneumococcal conjugate vaccine (PCV13, *Prevnar 13*) is recommended for all children, with the series starting at 2 months of age, and pneumococcal polysaccharide vaccine (PPSV23, *Pneumovax 23*) is recommended in select patients. See the Immunizations chapter for detailed information. Annual influenza vaccine should be given to all patients age ≥ 6 months. Prophylactic antibiotics should not be prescribed to reduce frequency of AOM.

Overview of Non-AOM Upper Respiratory Tract Infection Management

The majority of upper respiratory tract infections are viral, therefore, antibiotics will not be beneficial. If severe/chronic symptoms and/or microbiologic/diagnostic evidence of a bacterial infection are present, antibacterials may be used for pharyngitis and sinusitis (see table below).

	COMMON COLD	INFLUENZA	PHARYNGITIS	SINUSITIS
Typical Etiology	Respiratory viruses (Rhinovirus, coronavirus)	Influenza virus	Respiratory viruses *S. pyogenes*	Respiratory viruses, *S. pneumoniae, H. influenzae, Moraxella catarrhalis. Staphylococci* species, anaerobes and Gram-negative rods can also be implicated in chronic sinusitis.
Indications for Anti-infective Treatment	None	< 48 hours since symptom onset Risk factors for severe disease Outbreak scenario	Positive rapid antigen diagnostic test or positive *S. pyogenes* culture	≥ 10 days of symptoms or ≥ 3 days of severe symptoms (fever > 102□, face pain, purulent nasal discharge), or Worsening of symptoms after initial improvement.
Anti-infective options	None	Oseltamivir Zanamivir Peramivir	Penicillin Amoxicillin 1st/2nd generation cephalosporin If beta-lactam allergy: Clarithromycin or azithromycin or clindamycin	**First Line** Amoxicillin/clavulanate **Second Line if Failure to Above** Oral 2nd or 3rd generation cephalosporins + clindamycin, doxycycline Respiratory quinolone (gemifloxacin, moxifloxacin, levofloxacin)
Treatment Duration	Per symptoms	5 days	10 days unless using azithromycin (5 days)	Variable depending on severity and chronicity Acute sinusitis: Adults: 5-7 days Children: 10-14 days Chronic sinusitis: ≥ 21 days ± surgical intervention

LOWER RESPIRATORY TRACT INFECTIONS

Bronchitis

Bronchitis is an inflammation of the mucous membranes of the bronchi. It is classified as acute or chronic. Chronic bronchitis is treated with antibiotics only when exacerbations occur.

Acute Bronchitis

- Symptoms of acute bronchitis are usually self-limited and can include cough lasting more than 5 days (up to 3 weeks) with or without sputum production, fatigue, headache and watery eyes. Systemic symptoms such as fever are rare.
- Acute bronchitis is primarily (90% of cases) caused by respiratory viruses, including respiratory syncytial virus (RSV), adenovirus, rhinovirus, coronavirus, influenza virus, parainfluenza virus.
- In severe cases, a bacterial cause can be considered. Common pathogens include *M. pneumoniae, H. influenzae, B. pertussis, C. pneumoniae.*
- Diagnosis is usually made by ruling out other causes of acute cough (common cold, acute asthma, pneumonia). Cultures are not routinely performed.

Acute Bacterial Exacerbation of Chronic Bronchitis

- Acute bacterial exacerbation of chronic bronchitis (ABECB), or chronic obstructive pulmonary disease (COPD) exacerbations, are diagnosed based on clinical presentation. Exacerbations can be triggered by infections (70 – 80% are due to bacterial or viral causes), environmental pollution, pulmonary embolism, or unknown causes.
- The Global Initiative for Chronic Obstructive Lung Disease (GOLD) defines an acute exacerbation as an acute increase in symptoms beyond normal day-to-day variation and necessitates a change in medications. If there is increased sputum purulence and increased sputum volume, increased dyspnea, or if mechanical ventilation is required, antibiotics should be utilized for 5 – 10 days.

BRONCHITIS NOTES & TREATMENT

Acute Bronchitis (not COPD exacerbation)

Mild-to-moderate disease:

- Supportive treatment – fluids to prevent dehydration, antipyretics for fever, antitussive agents, vaporizers, etc.
- Antibiotics should be considered only if pneumonia is suspected or if patient has confirmed or probable *Bordetella pertussis* (whooping cough)
- Pertussis treatment (choose one):
  - Azithromycin 500 mg x 1, then 250 mg daily on days 2-5
  - Clarithromycin 500 mg BID or 1 g ER daily x 7 days
  - SMX/TMP DS 1 tab BID x 14 days

Acute Bacterial Exacerbation of Chronic Bronchitis (ABECB)

- Supportive treatment – supplemental oxygen, increase dose and/or frequency of short-acting beta-2 adrenergic agonists, anticholinergic agents, IV or PO steroids (prednisone 40 mg PO daily x 5 days)
- Antibiotics indicated if 3 cardinal symptoms present: increase in dyspnea, sputum volume, and sputum purulence*; or if mechanical ventilation is required
  - Amoxicillin/clavulanate or
  - Azithromycin or
  - Doxycycline
  - Duration 5-10 days

**If purulent sputum is present, antibiotics are indicated with only 2 symptoms*

Community-Acquired Pneumonia

Community-acquired pneumonia (CAP) is contracted outside of healthcare facilities and is one of the most common types of pneumonia. Causes can be bacterial, viral or fungal (rare). Most bacterial cases are caused by *Streptococcus pneumoniae, Haemophilus influenzae* and *Mycoplasma pneumoniae.*

Chlamydophila pneumoniae can also cause CAP. Patients often present with fever, productive cough with purulent sputum and pleuritic chest pain. Rales (crackling noises) can be heard over the infected lobe on auscultation. A chest x-ray is the gold standard for the diagnosis of CAP; findings of "infiltrates" or "consolidations" are indicative of pneumonia. The antibiotic recommendations for CAP are designed to provide reliable empiric coverage of *S. pneumoniae*, atypical bacteria and if indicated, risk factors for additional pathogens (*Pseudomonas*, MRSA). There are subtle differences in coverage that are important when treating pneumonia. Coverage must be considered by specific antibiotic, rather than using class trends. A good example is ciprofloxacin; because ciprofloxacin does not reliably cover *S. pneumoniae*, it is not a respiratory quinolone.

Outpatient CAP Treatment

Treatment of outpatient CAP requires an assessment of the patient's risk factors for drug resistant *S. pneumoniae* and the presence of comorbidities. Outpatients who have not recently received antibiotics and who are previously healthy can receive a simple regimen of a macrolide or doxycycline. Patients with a history of recent antibiotic use or the presence of comorbidities or immunosuppression require a regimen with broader coverage due to the possibility of drug-resistant *S. pneumoniae* (DRSP). Monotherapy with a respiratory quinolone is one option, but requires a careful review of the patient profile. Quinolones carry many warnings and risk of side effects is substantial.

PATIENT CHARACTERISTICS	RECOMMENDED EMPIRIC REGIMEN
Step 1: Check for history of antibiotic use in the past 3 months **Step 2:** Look for comorbidities or immunosuppression **Step 3:** Decide whether the patient falls into Category 1 or Category 2 (see below) **Step 4:** Choose one option within the category. Be sure to look for allergies, drug-disease interactions (e.g., quinolone with seizures), drug-drug interactions (QT prolongation), and culture results, if available	
Category 1 – **No antibiotic use in past 3 months and previously healthy**	**Option 1** ■ Macrolide (azithromycin, clarithromycin, erythromycin) **Option 2** ■ Doxycycline
Category 2 – **Risk for drug-resistant *S. pneumoniae* or comorbidities:** ■ Antibiotic use in previous 3 months ■ Chronic diseases: heart, lung, liver, or renal disease; diabetes mellitus; alcoholism; malignancies; asplenia ■ Immunocompromised or use of immunosuppressants	**Option 1** ■ Beta-lactam + macrolide ❑ Amoxicillin (high-dose), amoxicillin/clavulanate, cefpodoxime, cefdinir, cefuroxime, ceftriaxone plus ❑ Macrolide or doxycycline **Option 2** ■ Respiratory quinolone monotherapy ❑ Moxifloxacin, gemifloxacin, or levofloxacin

CLINICAL CASE EXAMPLE

RP is a 46 yo female who presents to the urgent care clinic with shortness of breath, productive cough and temperature of 100.2□. A chest x-ray reveals a left lower lobe infiltrate. Her past medical history (PMH) includes back pain and schizophrenia. Her scheduled medications include *Geodon* 40 mg PO BID and trazodone 50 mg PO QHS. Which empiric antibiotic regimen should she receive for pneumonia?

Stepwise approach: She reports no recent antibiotic use and the PMH does not include any of the chronic comorbidities, risk for drug-resistant *S. pneumoniae* or immunosuppression listed in Category 2. She appears to fall in Category 1. The choice is between a macrolide, such as azithromycin, or doxycycline. Macrolides can prolong QT interval. As *Geodon* and trazodone can also prolong the QT interval, doxycycline would be the best choice in this outpatient with CAP.

Inpatient CAP Treatment

Treatment for patients who are ill enough to require hospitalization for CAP differs from outpatients. Monotherapy with a macrolide or doxycycline is not recommended. Patients who are not in the ICU can be treated with IV or PO antibiotics. IV antibiotics are preferred (for initial therapy) in ICU patients. Monotherapy with a respiratory quinolone provides adequate coverage, but patient safety should be carefully assessed, in light of the risks of quinolones. Regimens include:

- Beta-lactam + macrolide (or + doxycycline)
  - Preferred beta-lactam: ceftriaxone, cefotaxime, ampicillin (IV) plus
  - Macrolide (azithromycin, clarithromycin, erythromycin) or doxycycline
- Respiratory quinolone monotherapy (consider reserving quinolone for beta-lactam allergies)
  - Moxifloxacin, gemifloxacin, or levofloxacin – IV/PO

If a patient with CAP has risk factors for *Pseudomonas,* the beta-lactam or quinolone must be active against both *S. pneumoniae* and *Pseudomonas.* This regimen can include piperacillin/tazobactam, cefepime, imipenem/cilastatin, meropenem, levofloxacin, plus an aminoglycoside and azithromycin. If MRSA is a concern, vancomycin or linezolid should be added.

Duration

The duration of treatment can be as short as 5 days, depending on the patient's condition. Most are treated successfully in 5 – 7 days.

Hospital-Acquired and Ventilator-Associated Pneumonias

Hospitalized patients who develop lower respiratory tract infections (pneumonia) are at risk of becoming infected with nosocomial pathogens (see below). Hospital-acquired pneumonia (HAP) has an onset > 48 hours after hospital admission and occurs in non-ventilated patients. HAP is the leading infectious cause of death in ICUs. Mechanically ventilated patients are at especially high-risk of developing pneumonia. Ventilator-associated pneumonia (VAP) occurs > 48 hours after the start of mechanical ventilation and can negatively impact patient outcomes, including prolonging duration of ventilation up to 11.5 days, and prolonging hospitalization by up to 13.1 days. VAP can be reduced by proper hand-washing, elevating the head of bed by ≥ 30 degrees, weaning off the ventilator, removing nasogastric (NG) tubes when possible, and discontinuing unnecessary stress ulcer prophylaxis.

Common pathogens in HAP and VAP

Nosocomial pathogens occur more commonly in HAP and VAP. MRSA is a common Gram-positive pathogen. Gram-negative pathogens can include *P. aeruginosa, Acinetobacter* species, and other Gram-negative rods (e.g., *Enterobacter* species, *E. coli* and *Klebsiella* species).

Current guidelines recommend a careful assessment of each patient's risk factors for multidrug-resistant pathogens (MDR). These risk factors, along with the risk for patient mortality, are used to select the empiric antibiotic regimen. Coverage of MRSA and double coverage of *P. aeruginosa* are required in specific situations.

RISK FACTORS FOR MDR PATHOGENS

Risk factor for MRSA, MDR *Pseudomonas* or other MDR pathogens in HAP/VAP include

- IV antibiotic use within 90 days
- High prevalence of MRSA in the unit
- Positive MRSA screen

Risk factors for MDR pathogens in VAP

- Hospitalization for ≥ 5 days prior to VAP
- Septic shock at the time of VAP onset
- Acute respiratory distress syndrome (ARDS) preceding VAP
- Acute renal replacement therapy (i.e., hemodialysis) prior to VAP onset

Treatment of HAP and VAP

RISKS	RECOMMENDED EMPIRIC REGIMEN	
Targets *Pseudomonas* and MSSA **Patient has:** HAP without high risk of mortality and with low MRSA risk VAP without risk factors for MDR pathogens or MRSA (see box)	**Choose one:** Piperacillin/Tazobactam Cefepime Levofloxacin Imipenem/Cilastatin or meropenem	
Targets *Pseudomonas* and MRSA **Patient has:** HAP without high risk of mortality with MRSA risk VAP without MDR pathogen risk factors, with MRSA risk factors (see box)	**Single coverage of *Pseudomonas* (choose one):** Piperacillin/Tazobactam Cefepime, ceftazidime Levofloxacin, ciprofloxacin Imipenem/Cilastatin, meropenem Aztreonam	**Plus anti-MRSA agent (choose one):** Vancomycin Linezolid
Targets MDR *Pseudomonas* and MRSA **Patient has:** HAP with high risk of mortality or received antibiotics in the prior 90 days VAP with risk factors for MDR pathogens (see box) or >10% resistance to monotherapy drug	**Double coverage of *Pseudomonas* (choose two, avoid two beta-lactams):** Piperacillin/Tazobactam Cefepime, ceftazidime Levofloxacin, ciprofloxacin Imipenem/Cilastatin, meropenem Aztreonam Tobramycin, gentamicin, amikacin* Colistin, polymyxin B*	

**These agents are always used in combination with another antipseudomonal drug*

Duration of Treatment

Treat for 7 days. Shorter or longer treatment durations may be indicated based on clinical, radiologic and laboratory parameters.

Tuberculosis

Tuberculosis (TB) is caused by *Mycobacterium tuberculosis* (aerobic, non-spore forming bacillus). Active pulmonary TB is transmitted by aerosolized droplets (sneezing, coughing, talking, etc.) and is highly contagious. TB primarily infects the lungs, but can also disseminate to other organs. Tuberculosis can be fatal if not treated properly. Incidence of strains that are resistant to multiple drugs continues to increase. The disease has two phases: latent and active. Latent disease occurs when the immune system is able to contain the disease, and is characterized by a complete lack of symptoms. Active pulmonary disease is highly contagious and most often manifested as cough/hemoptysis (with blood), purulent sputum and fever/night sweats. Hospitalized patients with active pulmonary TB should be isolated in a single negative pressure room and healthcare workers must wear respirator masks (e.g, N95).

Latent Tuberculosis Diagnosis and Treatment

Latent disease is diagnosed using the tuberculin skin test (TST), also called a purified protein derivative (PPD) test. The solution is injected intradermally and the area is inspected for induration (raised area) 48 – 72 hours later. False positive TST can occur in those who have received the bacille Calmette-Guerin (BCG) vaccine (used in areas of the world with high TB rates). A diagnostic blood test for latent tuberculosis is also available. The interferon-gamma release assay (IGRA) does not require a follow-up visit and can be used in patients who have received the BCG vaccine. Treatment of latent TB with one of the following regimens greatly reduces the risk of developing of active disease:

- Isoniazid (INH) 300 mg PO daily (or 15 mg/kg PO twice weekly, max 900 mg/dose) for 9 months. These regimens are preferred for HIV+ patients, pregnant women and children.
- Rifampin 600 mg daily for 4 months if INH-resistant/INH not tolerated.
- INH and rifapentine *(Priftin)* once weekly for 12 weeks (not used in HIV+, children < 2 years old, pregnant women or presumed infection with INR- or rifampin-resistant TB). The older combination of rifampin + pyrazinamide is no longer recommended due to risk of hepatotoxicity.

POSITIVE TB SKIN TEST (TST) CRITERIA FOR LATENT TB

≥ 5 mm induration:
Close contacts of recent TB cases

Significant immunosuppression (e.g., HIV, transplant medications)

≥ 10 mm induration:
Recent immigrants

IV drug users

Residents/employees of "high-risk" congregate settings (e.g., inmates, healthcare workers)

Moderate immunosuppression

≥ 15 mm induration:
Patients with no risk factors

Induration = raised area

Active Tuberculosis Diagnosis and Treatment

Active TB is a public health issue because it is highly contagious and can be difficult to treat. It is diagnosed through a sputum culture (not TST). *M. tuberculosis* (MTB) are acid-fast bacilli (AFB) and can be detected by AFB stain in the laboratory. However, the acid fast test is not specific to MTB; definitive diagnosis must be made using polymerase chain reaction (PCR) testing or culture results. MTB is a slow-growing organism; final culture and susceptibility results can take up to 6 weeks.

Active disease treatment is divided into two treatment phases (intensive and continuation). To avoid treatment failure due to resistance, preferred intensive phase treatment consists of a 4-drug regimen of rifampin, isoniazid, pyrazinamide and ethambutol for 2 months (this regimen is known as "RIPE"). In the continuation phase, the therapy can be scaled back to two drugs depending on the drug susceptibility of the isolate, and continues for 4 months. The continuation phase is extended to 7 months if: 1) there is evidence of cavitary pulmonary TB and the sputum culture remains positive after 2 months of therapy, 2) if intensive phase did not include PZA, or 3) if patient is being treated with once weekly INH and rifapentine and has a positive sputum culture at the end of the intensive phase.

Use of Directly Observed Treatment (DOT) is preferred in select populations (those with positive sputum spears, delayed culture positivity, homeless, drug resistance, among others) to increase medication adherence. Alternate dosing regimens (2 – 3x per week) can be used in this setting. Daily dosing regimens are strongly encouraged if DOT is not possible.

TB can be resistant to INH and/or rifampin; if it demonstrates resistance to both agents it is called multidrug-resistant TB (MDR-TB). Resistant TB requires use of second line agents and longer durations of therapy (up to 24 months). While many agents can be used, preferred drugs include quinolones (moxifloxacin or levofloxacin) or injectables (streptomycin, amikacin, or kanamycin). Streptomycin given IM is an alternative agent to ethambutol, but it has associated toxicities and resistance is increasing. In extremely drug-resistant TB (XDR-TB), bedaquiline *(Sirturo)* may be used, but it has boxed warnings for QT prolongation and increased risk of death compared to placebo.

RIPE THERAPY

Monitoring:

Sputum culture

Chest X-ray

CBC (isoniazid)

LFTs, including total bilirubin (all)

Renal function (pyrazinamide, ethambutol)

Uric acid (pyrazinamide)

Vision tests monthly (ethambutol)

Mental status (ethambutol)

Other:

Pyridoxine 25 mg PO daily is given to reduce risk of INH-associated peripheral neuropathy

Rifabutin is used instead of rifampin if unacceptable drug-drug interactions

TB Disease Treatment Regimens

PREFERRED REGIMEN

Intensive Phase – Take all 4 drugs for 2 months (until cultures and susceptibilities are available)

	RIPE: Rifampin (RIF) + Isoniazid (INH) + Pyrazinamide (PZA) + Ethambutol* Duration: 56 daily doses (8 weeks)

Continuation Phase – Medications are scaled down to 2 drugs that continue for 4 months

Susceptible to INH and RIF	Continue INH and RIF daily or 3x per week (18 weeks) Total treatment duration: 26 weeks (6 months)

**Ethambutol can be discontinued if drug susceptibility studies demonstrate susceptibility to first-line drugs*

RIPE Therapy for Active TB

DRUG	DOSING	SAFETY/SIDE EFFECTS/MONITORING
RifAMPin *(Rifadin)* + isoniazid *(Rifamate)* + isoniazid + pyrazinamide *(Rifater)*	10 mg/kg (max 600 mg) PO daily or 2-3x/ week Doses differ for other indications Take on an empty stomach	**CONTRAINDICATIONS** Concurrent use with protease inhibitors (PIs) **SIDE EFFECTS** ↑ LFTs, orange-red discoloration of body secretions, positive Coombs test, flu-like syndrome, GI upset, rash/pruritus **NOTES** Orange-red discoloration of body secretions (sputum, urine, sweat, tears) – can stain contact lenses and clothing. Rifabutin dosed 5 mg/kg/day (300 mg) can replace rifampin to avoid significant drug-drug interactions (e.g., HIV patient on PIs).
Isoniazid (INH) + rifampin *(Rifamate)* + pyrazinamide/ rifampin *(Rifater)*	5 mg/kg (max 300 mg) PO daily or 15 mg/kg (max 900 mg) 2-3x/ week Take on an empty stomach Use pyridoxine 25 mg PO daily to ↓ risk of INH-associated peripheral neuropathy	**BOXED WARNING** Severe (and fatal) hepatitis **CONTRAINDICATIONS** Active liver disease, previous severe adverse reaction to INH **WARNINGS** Peripheral neuropathy is rare, but occurs more commonly in patients predisposed to neuropathy (diabetes, HIV, renal failure, alcoholism, elderly and malnutrition). Pyridoxine supplementation is recommended for these patients and patients who are pregnant or breastfeeding. **SIDE EFFECTS** Headache, GI upset, ↑ LFTs (usually asymptomatic), drug-induced lupus erythematosus (DILE), positive Coombs test, peripheral neuropathy, hyperglycemia, agranulocytosis, hemolytic and aplastic anemia, thrombocytopenia, pancreatitis, severe skin reactions (SJS/DRESS) **NOTES** Store oral solution at room temperature

RIPE Therapy for Active TB Continued

DRUG	DOSING	SAFETY/SIDE EFFECTS/MONITORING
Pyrazinamide + rifampin + isoniazid *(Rifater)*	20-25 mg/kg/day PO 40-55 kg: 1 g/day 56-75 kg: 1.5 g/day 76-90 kg: 2 g/day (max dose); 3-4 grams given 2-3x/week CrCl < 30 mL/min: extend interval	**CONTRAINDICATIONS** Acute gout, severe hepatic damage **SIDE EFFECTS** Increased LFTs, hyperuricemia, gout, GI upset, malaise, arthralgias, myalgias, rash
Ethambutol *(Myambutol)*	15-20 mg/kg (max 1.6 grams) PO daily or 25-30 mg/kg (max 2.4 grams) 3x/week or 50 mg/kg (max 4 grams) 2x/week Take without regards to meals CrCl < 50 mL/min: extend interval	**CONTRAINDICATIONS** Optic neuritis (risk vs benefit decision); use in young children, unconscious patients, or any patient who cannot discern and report visual changes **SIDE EFFECTS** Optic neuritis (dose-related), ↑ LFTs, ↓ visual acuity, scotoma and/or color blindness (usually reversible); rash, headache, confusion, hallucinations, N/V, abdominal pain

Tuberculosis Agents Drug Interactions

- Rifampin is a potent inducer of CYP450 1A2, 2C8, 2C9, 2C19, 3A4 and P-glycoprotein. Significantly ↓ concentrations and effect of many other drugs (100+ are documented). Some notable interactions involve ↓ serum concentrations of protease inhibitors (substitute rifabutin) and warfarin (a very large ↓ in INR is common) and ↓ efficacy of oral contraceptives. Apixaban, edoxaban, rivaroxaban and dabigatran should be avoided with rifampin. It is important to screen all concurrent medications for drug interactions with rifampin due to its extremely high potential for interactions. See the Drug Interactions chapter.

- INH is an inhibitor of 1A2 (weak), 2C19 (moderate), 2C9 (weak), 2D6 (moderate), and 3A4 (weak). Use of INH can ↑ levels and toxicity of many other drugs. Also notable, enzyme inhibition can decrease activation of other drugs that require conversion to active metabolites. The manufacturer recommends avoiding tyramine and histamine containing foods (low clinical significance). ↑ dietary intake of folic acid, niacin, and magnesium while taking INH.

Infective Endocarditis

Infective endocarditis (IE) is an infection of the inner tissue of the heart, most commonly the heart valves, and is generally fatal if untreated. The majority of patients present with fever with or without heart murmur. IE is diagnosed by the Modified Duke Criteria which includes an echocardiogram, allowing for visualization of the vegetation. The three most common organisms that cause IE are *Staphylococcus*, *Streptococcus*, and *Enterococcus* species.

Empiric treatment often includes vancomycin and ceftriaxone. Definitive treatment and antibiotic duration for IE are dependent on the pathogen, the type of infected valve (native or prosthetic) and the susceptibility results. In general, 4 – 6 weeks of IV antibiotic treatment is required; when prosthetic valves and/or more resistant organisms are involved, durations will be at the upper end of this range.

Gentamicin is added to primary antimicrobial therapy for synergy for specific organisms and clinical situations. It is most important in infections that are more difficult to eradicate, such as prosthetic valve infections, and with more resistant organisms. In some cases the risk of additive nephrotoxicity with vancomycin outweighs the benefit and it is left off of the regimen (e.g., when vancomycin is used for Streptococcal endocarditis in beta-lactam allergy). The duration of gentamicin varies based on the presence of a prosthetic valve (2 weeks), or on the pathogen (4 – 6 weeks for *Enterococcus*). When gentamicin is used for synergy, target peak levels of 3 – 4 mcg/mL and trough levels < 1 mcg/mL. Extended interval dosing is not used for AMG when treating endocarditis.

Some bacteria will form a biofilm (slime layer), especially on prosthetic valves, which can be difficult for some antibiotics to penetrate. Rifampin can be used in cases of *Staphylococcal* prosthetic valve endocarditis, due to its ability to treat organisms in a biofilm.

ORGANISM	PREFERRED ANTIBIOTIC REGIMEN
Viridans group *Streptococci*	Penicillin, ampicillin, or ceftriaxone ± gentamicin for synergy If beta-lactam allergy, use vancomycin monotherapy
Staphylococci (MSSA)	Nafcillin or cefazolin, if beta-lactam allergy, use vancomycin (+ gentamicin if prosthetic valve)
Staphylococci (MRSA)	Vancomycin + (gentamicin if prosthetic valve)
Enterococci	Penicillin or ampicillin (if beta-lactam allergy or resistance, use vancomycin) + gentamicin for synergy

Dental Procedures and IE Prophylaxis

The mouth contains bacteria that are released during dental work and travel into the bloodstream where they can settle on the heart lining, a heart valve or a blood vessel. IE after dental procedures is rare, but risk is increased with certain cardiac conditions. In patients at high risk of IE, antibiotics should be used before all dental procedures that involve manipulation of gingival tissue (gums) or the periapical region (near the root of the tooth) or perforation of the oral mucosa. See the following table for the risk criteria and prophylaxis regimens.

IE Dental Prophylaxis

PATIENTS AT HIGH RISK OF IE	ADULT PROPHYLAXIS REGIMENS*
■ Artificial (prosthetic) heart valve or heart valve repaired with artificial material ■ History of endocarditis ■ Heart transplant with abnormal heart valve function ■ Certain congenital heart defects including: ❑ Cyanotic congenital heart disease (birth defects with oxygen levels lower than normal), that has not been fully repaired, including children who have had surgical shunts and conduits. ❑ Congenital heart defect that has been completely repaired with artificial material or a device for the first six months after the repair procedure. ❑ Repaired congenital heart disease with residual defects, such as persisting leaks or abnormal flow at or adjacent to a prosthetic patch or prosthetic device.	Given as a single dose 30-60 min before dental procedure **Oral:** Amoxicillin 2 grams **If unable to take oral medication:** Ampicillin 2 grams IM/IV or Cefazolin 1 gram IM/IV **If allergic to penicillins and can take oral medication:** Cephalexin or cefadroxil** 2 grams or Clindamycin 600 mg or Azithromycin or clarithromycin 500 mg **If allergic to penicillins and unable to take oral medication:** Cefazolin or ceftriaxone** 1 gram IM/IV Clindamycin 600 mg IM/IV

**In pediatric patients use weight-based doses of the same antibiotics.*

***Cephalosporins should not be used in an individual with a history of anaphylaxis, angioedema, or urticaria with penicillins or ampicillin.*

Intra-Abdominal Infections

Intra-abdominal infections are a common cause of hospital admissions and the second most common cause of infectious mortality in ICUs. Intra-abdominal infections are usually polymicrobial and can occur in any intra-abdominal organ or space. The range of infections includes: primary (spontaneous bacterial), secondary and tertiary peritonitis, and biliary tract infections (cholecystitis and cholangitis).

- Primary peritonitis (AKA spontaneous bacterial peritonitis, SBP) is an infection of the peritoneal space and often occurs in patients with liver disease. The most likely pathogens are *Streptococci* and enteric Gram-negative organisms (PEK) and, rarely, anaerobes. The drug of choice is ceftriaxone for 5 – 7 days. Alternatives include ampicillin, gentamicin or a quinolone, among other options. SMX/TMP, ofloxacin and/or ciprofloxacin can be used for primary or secondary prophylaxis of SBP.
- Secondary peritonitis is caused by a traumatic event (e.g., ulceration, ischemia, obstruction, or surgery). Abscesses are common and should be drained and damaged tissue may require surgery. The most likely pathogens are *Streptococci*, enteric Gram-negatives and anaerobes *(Bacteroides fragilis)*. In more severe cases (critically ill patients in the ICU), coverage of *Pseudomonas* and CAPES organisms may be necessary.
- Cholecystitis is an acute inflammation of the gallbladder due to an obstructive stone and is generally surgically managed through cholecystectomy. Infection may not be the precipitating factor, but complicates half of cases. If infection is present, likely pathogens and antimicrobial selection are similar to primary peritonitis. Cholangitis is an infection of the common bile duct and is generally managed with bile decompression and antimicrobial therapy. Likely pathogens and antimicrobial selection are similar to secondary peritonitis.

Treatment consists of selecting an agent or combination that will cover the likely pathogens, which includes anaerobes. This can be accomplished with a single drug in some cases; however, if the antibiotic selected does not have anaerobic coverage, an additional antibiotic (generally metronidazole) must be added. See Infectious Diseases I chapter for detailed discussion of antibiotic coverage. Duration of treatment is generally 4 – 7 days for mild to moderate cases with adequate source control. Longer courses (7 – 14 days) may be needed in more severe cases. If an intra-abdominal abscess is present, ≥ 14 days may be required.

Management of Secondary Peritonitis and Cholangitis

MILD-TO-MODERATE INFECTIONS	HIGH-SEVERITY INFECTIONS/ICU
Cover PEK + anaerobes + *Streptococci* ± *Enterococci*	Cover PEK + CAPES + anaerobes + *Streptococci* ± *Enterococci*
Possible regimens include: Cefoxitin, ertapenem, moxifloxacin (Cefazolin, cefuroxime or ceftriaxone) + metronidazole (Ciprofloxacin or levofloxacin) + metronidazole	Possible regimens include: Carbapenem (except ertapenem) Piperacillin/tazobactam (Cefepime or ceftazidime) + metronidazole (Ciprofloxacin or levofloxacin) + metronidazole (Aztreonam or AMG) + metronidazole

AMG = aminoglycosides; CAPES (nosocomial GNRs) = Citrobacter, Acinetobacter, Providencia, Enterobacter, Serratia; ICU = intensive care unit; PEK (enteric GNRs) = Proteus, E. coli, Klebsiella

Skin and Soft-Tissue Infections

Skin and soft-tissue infections (SSTIs) may involve any or all layers of the skin (epidermis, dermis, and subcutaneous fat), fascia, and muscle. SSTIs usually result from introduction of bacteria through breaks in the skin barrier, and less frequently from an infection that spreads from the bloodstream to the skin. Minor local trauma (small cuts, insect bites) can be the provoking event, which can progress to deeper infection. SSTIs can be broadly divided into impetigo, nonpurulent (cellulitis, erysipelas, necrotizing infections) and purulent (furuncle, carbuncle, abscess) infections and are further categorized as mild, moderate or severe.

Impetigo is a superficial skin infection that occurs commonly in children and is characterized by honey-colored crusts. It is commonly caused by *S. pyogenes* and *S. aureus* and is treated with topical mupirocin or oral antibiotics (e.g., dicloxacillin or cephalexin, or if MRSA is suspected/confirmed, use doxycycline, clindamycin, or sulfamethoxazole/trimethoprim).

Cellulitis is an acute nonpurulent infection that extends down to the subcutaneous tissues. Lesions are usually painful, erythematous, and feel hot and tender. The infected area has poorly defined margins and may extend. *S. pyogenes* is the most common pathogen; however, in some circumstances (e.g., penetrating trauma) *S. aureus*, including community-associated MRSA (CA-MRSA) may be involved. Non-pharmacologic treatment involves measures to decrease swelling (elevation and immobilization of the area) and cool sterile saline dressings to decrease the pain. Blood culture or wound cultures are not routinely recommended for mild to moderate nonpurulent infections, unless the patient has significant risk factors such as immunosuppression, immersion injuries, or animal bites. Mild nonpurulent infections may be treated with oral antibiotics that primarily target *Streptococci*. If cellulitis is secondary to penetrating trauma, coverage of *S. aureus* and *Streptococci* is recommended.

SSTI CLASSIFICATIONS

Mild infection
Systemic symptoms* absent

Moderate infection
Systemic symptoms* present

Severe infection
Any of the following:

Failed I&D (if purulent) + oral antibiotics

Signs of deeper infection (fluid-filled blisters, skin sloughing, hypotension or evidence of organ dysfunction)

Patient is immunocompromised

**Systemic symptoms: temperature > 100.4° F, heart rate > 90 BPM, WBC > 12,000 or < 400 cells/mm³*

In purulent SSTI, abscesses should have an incision and drainage (I&D) and cultures should be sent for Gram stain and culture in moderate, severe or recurrent infections. If antibiotics are indicated, then target *S. aureus* (including MRSA if patient has previously failed initial antibiotic treatment or is immunosuppressed or septic). For recurrent SSTIs in patients colonized with *S. aureus*, consider decolonization with intranasal mupirocin *(Bactroban Nasal)* BID for 5 days, daily chlorhexidine washes, and daily decontamination of personal items.

SSTI Treatment

INFECTION/ SEVERITY	ADULT TREATMENT OPTIONS	COMMENTS
Empiric antibiotics for nonpurulent infection		
Mild Target *Streptococci*	Penicillin VK 250-500 mg PO Q6H Cephalexin 500 mg PO Q6H or Dicloxacillin 500 mg PO QID or Clindamycin 300-450 mg QID	Duration of therapy: 5 days (extend if infection has not improved within 5 days).
Moderate Target *Streptococci* ± MSSA	Penicillin 2-4 million units IV Q4-6H or Ceftriaxone 1 g IV Q24H or Cefazolin 1 g IV Q8H or Clindamycin 600-900 mg IV Q8H	IV antibiotics are preferred initially. Once the patient is clinically stabile, can transition to PO antibiotics. Duration of therapy: 5 days (extend if infection has not improved within 5 days).

SSTI Treatment Continued

INFECTION/ SEVERITY	ADULT TREATMENT OPTIONS	COMMENTS
Severe or necrotizing Broad coverage	Vancomycin + beta-lactam: Vancomycin 15 mg/kg IV Q12H + Piperacillin/Tazobactam 3.375 g IV Q6H or Imipenem/cilastatin 1 g IV Q6-8H or Meropenem 1 g IV Q8H	Treatment of choice for Group A Strep (*S. pyogenes)* necrotizing fasciitis is penicillin G with clindamycin added for toxin suppression. Management of diabetic foot ulcers/infections is addressed later in this chapter.

Empiric oral therapy for purulent infection. All purulent infections (abscesses) should have I & D.

Moderate purulent SSTI Target CA-MRSA	SMX/TMP 1-2 DS tabs BID or Doxycycline 100 mg BID or Minocycline 200 mg x 1, then 100 mg BID or Clindamycin 300-450 mg QID or Linezolid 600 mg BID	Mild purulent infections – primary treatment is I & D; antibiotics may not be indicated in all cases. If systemic signs and symptoms present (moderate infection), consider oral antibiotics. Defined treatment based on C & S: If MSSA, narrow to cephalexin or dicloxacillin If MRSA, narrow to SMX/TMP
Severe purulent SSTI Target MRSA	Vancomycin 15 mg/kg IV Q12H (goal trough 10-15 mg/L) or Daptomycin 4 mg/kg IV daily or Linezolid 600 mg IV/PO BID or Telavancin 10 mg/kg IV daily or Ceftaroline 600 mg IV Q12H or Tedizolid 200 mg IV/PO daily or Dalbavancin 1,500 mg x1 or 1,000 mg IV x 1, then 500 mg IV 1 week later or Oritavancin 1,200 mg IV x 1	If systemic signs and symptoms present, failed oral antibiotics, or immunocompromised, consider IV antibiotics. Once the patient is clinically stable, can transition to PO antibiotics. Bite infections require broader antibiotic coverage (e.g. ampicillin/sulbactam, amoxicillin/clavulanate) for aerobic Gram-negatives (including *Pasteurella* spp.), Gram-positives and anaerobes. Duration of therapy: 7 to 14 days.

Diabetic Foot Infections

Diabetic patients are at high risk for foot infections because of compromised blood flow to the lower extremities and neuropathic damage. Foot infections are the most common cause of amputation in diabetic patients. Grading systems are used to evaluate ulcers for presence of inflammation, purulence and infection, and to classify severity, which guides management (surgery and/or antibiotics). *Staphylococcus* species and *Streptococcus* species are the predominant pathogens in diabetic foot infections (DFIs), however, they can be polymicrobial infections, thus empiric therapy is usually broad. It is imperative that patients follow proper foot care and evaluation, as discussed in the Diabetes chapter. If deeper infection, such as osteomyelitis, is present, longer courses of antibiotics (often IV) will be required.

ETIOLOGY	GRAM-POSITIVE	GRAM-NEGATIVE
Aerobic	*S. aureus* (including MRSA) Group A *Streptococcus* *Viridans group Streptococci* *S. epidermidis*	*E. coli* *Klebsiella pneumoniae* *Proteus mirabilis* *Enterobacter cloacae* *Pseudomonas aeruginosa*
Anaerobic	*Peptostreptococcus* *Clostridium perfringens*	*Bacteroides fragilis* and others

Treatment of Moderate-Severe (Life or Limb-threatening) Diabetic Foot Infections

TYPE OF REGIMEN	TREATMENT REGIMEN	COMMENTS
Combination therapy	Vancomycin plus one of the following: ceftazidime*, cefepime*, piperacillin/ tazobactam*, aztreonam* or a carbapenem* Vancomycin alternatives: Daptomycin or linezolid Note: consider adding anaerobe coverage (metronidazole) if ceftazidime, cefepime, or aztreonam selected	Duration: 7-14 days More severe, deep tissue infection: treat for 2-4 weeks. Severe, limb-threatening or bone/joint infection: treat for 4-6 weeks. Osteomyelitis requires longer courses of therapy, and may include chronic suppressive therapy.
Monotherapy options	Ampicillin/sulbactam, piperacillin/ tazobactam* or Imipenem/cilastatin*, meropenem*, ertapenem or Tigecycline** or Moxifloxacin	

** Has Pseudomonas coverage*
*** Tigecycline should only be used when all other alternatives have been exhausted*

Urinary Tract Infections

Most urinary tract infections (UTIs) occur in the bladder (cystitis) and urethra, which is called the lower urinary tract. More severe infections can occur in the kidneys (pyelonephritis), or the upper urinary tract. UTIs are more common in females than males, as the female urethra provides a shorter route for organisms to travel up into the bladder. Sexual intercourse can facilitate this movement; women who develop UTIs commonly after intercourse may be prescribed prophylactic antibiotics after sexual intercourse. UTIs are classified as uncomplicated and complicated. Uncomplicated UTIs are those that occur in non-pregnant, premenopausal women who have no urologic abnormalities or comorbidities. An infection in males is considered to be complicated because it is likely due to some type of abnormality or obstruction, such as an enlarged prostate. Complicated infections can also result from a neurogenic bladder (e.g., spinal cord injury, stroke, multiple sclerosis), an obstruction (e.g., a stone) or the presence of an indwelling catheter. All patients are at risk for catheter-associated infections, see the Medication Safety & Quality Improvement chapter for a discussion of ways to reduce this common (and often preventable) infection.

UTI SYMPTOMS

Lower UTI (cystitis)
Dysuria, urgency, frequency, burning, nocturia, suprapubic heaviness, and/or hematuria (fever is uncommon)

Upper UTI (pyelonephritis)
Flank pain/costovertebral angle pain, abdominal pain, fever, nausea, vomiting, and malaise

A urinalysis is considered positive when there is evidence of pyuria (positive leukocyte esterase or > 10 WBC/mm^3) and bacteriuria ($\geq 10^5$ bacteria/mL in asymptomatic patients, $\geq 10^3$ bacteria/mL in symptomatic males, and $\geq 10^2$ bacteria/mL in symptomatic females and catheterized patients).

Aside from antibiotics, other products used for this condition include cranberry, blueberry, bearberry, garlic, echinacea, stinging nettle, asparagus, yogurt and some probiotics (*Bifidobacteria* and *Lactobacillus* strains). See the Dietary Supplements, Natural & Complementary Medicine chapter.

UTI Treatment

DIAGNOSIS	DRUGS OF CHOICE/GUIDELINES	COMMENTS
Acute uncomplicated cystitis in females of child bearing age (~15-45 years of age) Common pathogens: *E. coli* (vast majority), *Proteus, Klebsiella* (PEK) *S. saprophyticus, Enterococcus*	Nitrofurantoin 100 mg BID with food x 5 days (less collateral damage) or SMX/TMP 1 DS tab BID x 3 days (avoid if *E. coli* resistance rate in community/institution is ≥ 20% or if sulfa allergy) or Fosfomycin 3 grams x 1 in 4 oz water (lower efficacy) or Alternatives: Ciprofloxacin 250 mg BID x 3 days or Ciprofloxacin ER 500 mg daily x 3 days or Levofloxacin 250 mg daily x 3 days Beta-lactam (amoxicillin/clavulanate and oral cephalosporins) x 3-7 days are appropriate choices when other recommended agents cannot be used. Treat pregnant women for 3-7 days.	Usually empirically treated as an outpatient If no response with a 3 day course, perform urinary culture and treat accordingly. Do not use moxifloxacin for UTIs (does not reach high levels in the urine) or gemifloxacin (limited activity against normal UTI pathogens). Prophylaxis: If ≥ 3 episodes in 1 year, can use 1 SMX/TMP SS daily, nitrofurantoin 50 mg PO daily, or 1 SMX/TMP DS post coitus. May add phenazopyridine 200 mg PO TID x 2 days to relieve dysuria.
Acute uncomplicated pyelonephritis Common pathogens: *E. coli, Enterococci, P. mirabilis, K. pneumoniae, P. aeruginosa*	Moderately ill outpatient (PO): If local quinolone resistance < 10% - Ciprofloxacin 500 mg PO BID or ciprofloxacin ER 1,000 mg daily x 7 days or levofloxacin 750 mg daily x 5 days If local quinolone resistance > 10% - Ceftriaxone 1 gram IV x 1 or AMG IV x 1, followed by SMX/TMP (if susceptible) or beta-lactam (amox/clav, cefdinir, cefaclor, or cefpodoxime) – treat for 14 days Severe – hospitalized patient (IV): Initial: Ceftriaxone; ampicillin + gentamicin; ciprofloxacin or levofloxacin; or piperacillin/tazobactam. Step down to oral options based on susceptibility results. Treatment duration: 14 days total (including IV & PO)	If risk for or documented *Pseudomonas* infection, consider piperacillin/tazobactam or meropenem ± aminoglycoside.
Complicated UTI Common pathogens: *E.coli, Klebsiella, Enterobacter, Serratia, Pseudomonas, Enterococcus, Staphylococcus*	Similar to options noted above for pyelonephritis If ESBL producers are present, use a carbapenem Treat for 7 days if there is prompt symptom relief Treat for 10-14 days with delayed response	Urinalysis, urine and blood cultures should be done. May be due to obstruction, catheterization – remove or change catheter if possible.

Bacteriuria and Pregnancy

Bacteriuria in pregnant women must be treated (for 3 – 7 days) even if asymptomatic with negative urinalysis. If not treated, bacteriuria can lead to pyelonephritis, premature birth and neonatal meningitis.

- Generally, beta-lactams are used (amoxicillin/clavulanate or oral cephalosporins).

- Nitrofurantoin and SMX/TMP can be used with a beta-lactam allergy. The American College of Gynecology states that nitrofurantoin and SMX/TMP should be last line agents in the 1st trimester, but should be used when needed in a patient that cannot use preferred medications, due to the risks associated with untreated bacteriuria.
- There is concern that SMX/TMP could cause hyperbilirubinemia and kernicterus in the newborn if used close to delivery. Nitrofurantoin labeling lists a contraindication in the late pregnancy (last 2 weeks before delivery), due to the possibility of hemolytic anemia in the infant.
- Fosfomycin can be considered for use in pregnant patients who have drug allergies.
- In pregnant women, avoid quinolones (cartilage toxicity and arthropathies) and tetracyclines (teratogenic). See Drug Use in Pregnancy chapter for more information.

Urinary Analgesic

Phenazopyridine may be given for symptomatic relief of dysuria (pain or burning with urination). Appropriate antibiotic treatment will resolve symptoms promptly. It is occasionally given to reduce pain from vaginal procedures.

DRUG	DOSING	SAFETY/SIDE EFFECTS/MONITORING
Phenazopyridine *(Azo, Uristat, Pyridium,* others) OTC/Rx	200 mg PO TID x 2 days (max) Take with or following food and 8 oz of water to minimize stomach upset.	**CONTRAINDICATIONS** Do not use in patients with renal impairment or liver disease. **SIDE EFFECTS** Headache, dizziness, stomach cramps, body secretion discoloration **NOTES** May cause red-orange coloring of the urine and other body fluids. Contact lenses and clothes can be stained. Can cause hemolytic anemia in patients with G6PD deficiency (discontinue if hemolysis occurs).

Clostridium difficile Infection

The GI tract contains > 1,000 species of organisms. The use of antibiotics eliminates much of the "healthy" bacteria, allowing an overgrowth of *Clostridium difficile* bacteria, a Gram-positive rod, obligate anaerobic, spore-forming bacteria. Some types releases toxins that attack the intestinal lining, causing colitis. Symptoms of *C. difficile* infection (CDI) include abdominal cramps, profuse diarrhea (can be bloody), and fever. *C. difficile* overgrowth can lead to inflammation of the colon and pseudomembranous colitis, which can progress to toxic megacolon and colectomy or death. Rates of CDI have increased in recent years due to overuse of antibiotics. In addition to antibiotics, other risk factors include recent healthcare exposure, use of proton pump inhibitors, advanced age, immunocompromised state, obesity and previous CDI.

CDI Treatment and Isolation Principles

- Discontinue antibiotics, if possible. Review the medication profile for other medications that could cause diarrhea.
- Antimotility agents should not be used for CDI diarrhea due to the risk of toxic megacolon.
- Patient should be isolated to prevent transmission (single-patient rooms, contact precautions: gloves, gowns). Wash hands with soap and water to remove spores from the hands and prevent transmission. Hand sanitizers containing alcohol do not kill or remove *C. difficile* spores.
- Metronidazole should not be used beyond the 1st recurrence or for long-term therapy due to the potential for cumulative neurotoxicity.

- Probiotics *(Lactobacillus, Saccharomyces)* are not beneficial for treatment, but may have some benefit for prophylaxis.
- Although not currently part of the IDSA guidelines, fidaxomicin or fecal stool transplant are alternative therapies for recurrent or relapsing CDI.
- Bezlotoxumab *(Zinplava)* is a monoclonal antibody approved in late 2016 that binds *C. difficile* toxin B. It is used to reduce recurrence of CDI in adults who are receiving antibacterial drug treatment of CDI and are at a high risk for CDI recurrence. It is given as a 1x IV infusion.
- Treatment recommendations vary based on the severity and whether it is the first infection or a recurrence. Review the profile to determine the best treatment.

CDI Treatment*

SEVERITY OF INFECTION	1ST INFECTION	2ND INFECTION (1ST RECURRENCE)	3RD INFECTION (2ND RECURRENCE)
Mild-moderate disease	Metronidazole 500 mg PO TID x 10-14 days	Same as 1st infection if same severity	Vancomycin taper/pulse therapy 125 mg PO QID x 10-14 days, BID x 1 week, daily x 1 week, then 125 mg every 2-3 days/ week for 2-8 weeks
Severe disease Criteria: WBC ≥ 15,000 or SCr ≥ 1.5x baseline	Vancomycin 125 mg PO QID x 10-14 days	Same as 1st infection if same severity	Vancomycin taper/pulse therapy
Severe, complicated disease Criteria: Hypotension, shock, ileus, or toxic megacolon	Vancomycin 500 mg PO QID + metronidazole 500 mg IV Q8H If complete ileus, add vancomycin per rectum (500 mg in 100 mL NS PR Q6H)	Same as 1st infection if same severity	Vancomycin taper/pulse therapy

* *In clinical trials, fidaxomicin was non-inferior to vancomycin oral therapy, but with lower recurrence rates. Consider fidaxomicin instead of vancomycin for patients at high risk of recurrence (patients receiving chemotherapy or immunosuppressed patients) – place in therapy not fully established.*

Traveler's Diarrhea

Traveler's diarrhea (TD) is a common travel-related illness and is primarily related to ingestion of contaminated food or water. Bacteria causes 80% of TD cases, including enterotoxigenic *Escherichia coli*, followed by *Campylobacter jejuni*, *Shigella* species and *Salmonella* species. Viral diarrhea can involve a number of pathogens, most commonly norovirus and rotavirus. Protozoa including *Giardia, Entamoeba histolytica, Cryptosporidium* and *Cyclospora*, less commonly cause TD. Bacterial or viral diarrhea presents with sudden onset of symptoms, including cramps and urgent loose stools to severe abdominal pain, fever, vomiting, and bloody diarrhea. Protozoal diarrhea, such as that caused by *Giardia* or *E. histolytica*, generally has a more gradual onset of low-grade symptoms, with 2 – 5 loose stools per day.

TRAVELER'S DIARRHEA TREATMENT
Ciprofloxacin 750 mg PO x 1 or 500 mg PO BID x 1-3 days or
Levofloxacin 500 mg PO daily x 1-3 days or
Norfloxacin 400 mg PO BID x 1-3 days or
Ofloxacin 200 mg PO BID x 1-3 days or
Rifaximin 200 mg PO TID x 3 days or
Azithromycin 1,000 mg PO x 1 or 500 mg PO daily x 1-3 days (drug of choice in pregnancy and children)

Metronidazole, tinidazole, and nitazoxanide should be reserved for TD caused by Protozoa (e.g., Giardia or Cryptosporidia)

A 1 – 3 day course of quinolones or macrolides are generally effective in treating TD (see box). Adjunctive therapy, including antimotility agents (loperamide) provide symptomatic relief, but generally should be avoided for bloody diarrhea or for patients with a fever. See Travelers chapter for information on prevention and symptomatic treatment.

Sexually Transmitted Infections

Sexually transmitted infections (STIs) encompass a variety of clinical syndromes and infections caused by pathogens acquired through sexual activity and are a major public health concern. Screening and prevention counseling should be done for timely diagnosis of STIs and prevention of complications, including cervical cancer, infertility, or transmission to partners. Sexual partners should be treated concurrently to prevent re-infection, except in bacterial vaginosis. The most common STIs and their treatment recommendations are listed below.

INFECTION	DOC	DOSING/DURATION	ALTERNATIVES/NOTES
Syphilis – caused by *Treponema pallidum*, a spirochete Primary, secondary, or early latent (< 1 year duration)	Penicillin G benzathine (*Bicillin L-A*, do not substitute with *Bicillin C-R)*	2.4 million units IM x 1	Doxycycline 100 mg PO BID or Tetracycline 500 mg PO QID x 14 days Pregnant patients allergic to PCN should be desensitized and treated with PCN Syphilis is diagnosed using the rapid plasma reagin (RPR), also called Venereal Diseases Research Laboratory (VDRL) blood test, and a confirmation test
Syphilis – Late latent (> 1 year duration), tertiary, or latent syphilis of unknown duration	Penicillin G benzathine (*Bicillin L-A*, do not substitute with *Bicillin C-R)*	2.4 million units IM weekly x 3 weeks (7.2 million units total)	Doxycycline 100 mg PO BID or Tetracycline 500 mg PO QID x 28 days Pregnant patients allergic to PCN should be desensitized and treated with PCN
Neurosyphilis (including ocular syphilis)	Penicillin G aqueous crystalline	3-4 million units IV Q4H or continuous infusion (18-24 million units/day) x 10-14 days	Penicillin G procaine 2.4 million units IM daily + probenecid 500 mg PO QID x 10-14 days
Congenital syphilis	Penicillin G aqueous crystalline	Newborns: 50,000 units/kg IV Q12H x 7 days, then Q8H for 10 days total Infants ≥ 1 month old: 50,000 units/kg IV Q4-6H x 10 days	Penicillin G procaine 50,000 units/kg IM daily x 10 days
Gonorrhea – caused by *Neisseria gonorrhoeae*, a Gram-negative diplococcus Urethral, cervical, rectal, pharyngeal	Ceftriaxone plus either Azithromycin (preferred) or Doxycycline	250 mg IM x 1 1 gram PO x 1 100 mg PO BID x 7 days	Monotherapy is not recommended due to resistance Recommended therapy also covers co-infection with *Chlamydia* Ceftriaxone is most effective for pharyngeal infections If ceftriaxone is not available, can use cefixime *(Suprax)* 400 mg PO x 1 + azithromycin (or doxycycline) with a test for cure in 1 week If severe cephalosporin allergy, azithromycin 2 g PO x 1 plus either gemifloxacin 320 mg PO x 1 or gentamicin 240 mg IM x 1 with a test for cure in 1 week

Sexually Transmitted Infections Drugs Continued

INFECTION	DOC	DOSING/DURATION	ALTERNATIVES/NOTES
Chlamydial Infections – caused by *Chlamydia trachomatis*, intracellular obligate Gram-negative organism	Azithromycin or Doxycycline	1 gram PO x 1 100 mg PO BID x 7 days	Erythromycin base 500 mg PO QID x 7 days or Levofloxacin 500 mg PO daily x 7 days or Ofloxacin 300 mg PO BID x 7 days Pregnancy: azithromycin (preferred) or amoxicillin 500 mg PO TID x 7 days
Bacterial Vaginosis – caused by many different organisms	Metronidazole or Metronidazole 0.75% gel or Clindamycin 2% cream	500 mg PO BID x 7 days 5 g intravaginally daily x 5 days 5 g intravaginally at bedtime x 7 days	Clindamycin 300 mg PO BID x 7 days or Clindamycin ovules* 100 mg intravaginally at bedtime x 3 days or Tinidazole 2 g PO daily x 2 days or Tinidazole 1 g PO daily x 5 days
Trichomoniasis – caused by *Trichomonas vaginalis*, a flagellated protozoan	Metronidazole or Tinidazole	2 grams PO x 1 2 grams PO x 1	Metronidazole 500 mg PO BID x 7 days Pregnancy: metronidazole package insert lists contraindication in 1st trimester. Based on additional data indicating safety, CDC recommends metronidazole for trichomoniasis in all trimesters.
Herpes Simplex Virus (HSV 1 and HSV 2)			See Infectious Diseases III chapter

**Clindamycin ovules use a base that can weaken latex or rubber products (i.e., condoms).*
Condom use within 72 hours of clindamycin ovules should not be considered adequate protection.

Rickettsial Diseases and Related Infections

Rickettsial infections are caused by a variety of bacteria that are carried by many ticks, fleas, and lice and cause diseases in humans such as those found below. Rocky Mountain spotted fever is the most common and most fatal rickettsial illness in the U.S. Initial signs and symptoms include fever, headache, muscle pain followed by the development of a rash.

DISEASE	ORGANISM	TREATMENT
Rocky Mountain Spotted Fever	*Rickettsia rickettsii* Gram-negative obligate intracellular bacteria	Doxycycline 100 mg PO/IV BID x 5-7 days
Typhus	*Rickettsia typhi* Gram-negative obligate intracellular bacteria	Doxycycline 100 mg PO/IV BID x 7 days
Lyme Disease	*Borrelia burgdorferi* Spirochete	Doxycycline 100 mg PO BID x 10-21 days or Amoxicillin 500 mg PO TID x 14-21 days or Cefuroxime 500 mg PO BID x 14-21 days
Ehrlichiosis	*Ehrlichia chaffeensis* Obligate intracellular bacteria	Doxycycline 100 mg PO/IV BID x 7-14 days
Tularemia	*Francisella tularensis* Aerobic Gram-negative coccobacilli	Gentamicin or tobramycin 5 mg/kg/d IV divided Q8H x 7-14 days

PRACTICE CASE

MJ is a previously healthy 43 y/o black female who presents to the urgent care clinic with complaints of fever, runny nose, congestion, productive cough and body aches. She reports that she has been feeling this way for the past 36 hours and she needs to get better quickly to return to work. She noticed a lot of people coughing on the bus this week and figures that is where she picked this up. Her past medical history is significant for GERD and depression.

Allergies: Sulfa (extreme rash and hives)

Medications:

Prozac 20 mg PO daily

Zantac 150 mg PO BID

Tums 1-2 tabs PRN heartburn

Vitals:

Height: 5'6" Weight: 192 pounds BMI: 31

BP: 164/81 mmHg HR: 114 BPM RR: 24 BPM Temp: 102.3°F Pain: 2/10

Labs:

Na (mEq/L) = 142 (135 - 145)

K (mEq/L) = 3.5 (3.5 - 5)

Cl (mEq/L) = 97 (95 - 103)

HCO_3 (mEq/L) = 27 (24 - 30)

BUN (mg/dL) = 13 (7 - 20)

SCr (mg/dL) = 1.1 (0.6 - 1.3)

Glucose (mg/dL) = 129 (100 - 125)

Ca (mg/dL) = 10.1 (8.5 - 10.5)

Mg (mEq/L) = 2.0 (1.3 - 2.1)

PO_4 (mg/dL) = 4.2 (2.3 - 4.7)

WBC (cells/mm^3) = 15.3 (4 - 11 x 10^3)

Hgb (g/dL) = 13.3 (13.5 - 18 male, 12 - 16 female)

Hct (%) = 42 (38 - 50 male, 36 - 46 female)

Plt (cells/mm^3) = 315 (150 - 450 x 10^3)

PMNs (%) = 90 (45 - 73)

Bands (%) = 7 (3 - 5)

Eosinophils (%) = 2 (0 - 5)

Basophils (%) = 0 (0 - 1)

Lymphocytes (%) = 37 (20 - 40)

Monocytes (%) = 3 (2 - 8)

Tests:

Chest x-ray: left middle lobe infiltrate

Assessment and Plan:

CAP confirmed by chest x-ray. Start antibiotic and have patient stay home from work for 2 days.

Questions

1. Based on the information provided in the case, what is the most appropriate antibiotic for MJ?

   a. *Zithromax* 500 mg PO x 1, then 250 mg PO daily x days 2-5
   b. *Avelox* 400 mg IV daily x 5-7 days
   c. *Levaquin* 500 mg PO x 1, then 250 mg PO daily x 5-7 days
   d. *Ceftin* 500 mg PO Q12H x 5-7 days
   e. *Bactrim* 1 DS tab PO Q12H x 5-7 days

2. MJ has accidentally lost the prescription and she cannot afford another office visit. She decides to tough it out and goes back to work. Two days later, MJ is admitted to the hospital due to worsening symptoms. What is the best regimen to treat her community-acquired pneumonia in the inpatient setting?

   a. Ciprofloxacin 500 mg PO daily
   b. Ceftriaxone 1 gram IV daily
   c. Ceftriaxone 1 gram IV daily + azithromycin 500 mg IV daily
   d. Vancomycin 1 gram IV Q12H + imipenem/cilastatin 500 mg Q6H
   e. Gemifloxacin 320 mg PO daily + clarithromycin 500 mg PO Q12H

3. While in the hospital, MJ's course is complicated by bacteremia due to an infected central line with *Pseudomonas aeruginosa*. Which of the following antibiotics would be an appropriate treatment for her bacteremia?

   a. Ampicillin
   b. *Cubicin*
   c. *Invanz*
   d. *Merrem*
   e. *Tygacil*

4. MJ improved and was discharged home a few weeks later. After about 3-4 months, she returns to the clinic complaining of intense burning on urination, dysuria, and frequent bathroom visits. The diagnosis is confirmed as a urinary tract infection caused by *E. coli*, which is susceptible to all antibiotics tested. Which of the following is the best choice to treat MJ's UTI?

   a. *Bactrim* SS 1 tab PO BID x 3 days
   b. *Bactrim* DS 1 tab PO BID x 3 days
   c. Nitrofurantoin 100 mg PO BID x 3 days
   d. Nitrofurantoin 100 mg PO BID x 5 days
   e. Phenazopyridine 200 mg TID x 2 days

Questions 5 – 10 do not apply to the case

5. The pharmacist is working in the ER when an intern asks how to treat the patient in room 4 who has gonorrhea. What is the best recommendation to treat this patient?

   a. Levofloxacin 750 mg PO x 1
   b. Doxycycline 100 mg PO BID x 7 days
   c. Benzathine penicillin G 2.4 million units IM x 1
   d. Metronidazole 2 grams PO x 1
   e. Ceftriaxone 250 mg IM x 1 + azithromycin 1 gram PO x 1

6. Tommy is taking isoniazid (INH) for latent tuberculosis treatment. Which of the following is/are correct regarding INH? (Select **ALL** that apply.)

   a. INH should be taken 1 hour before or 2 hours after a meal on an empty stomach.
   b. INH is a potent enzyme inducer.
   c. INH is contraindicated in acute gout.
   d. INH can be used alone to treat latent TB.
   e. INH requires dose adjustments in renal impairment.

7. Which of the following medications can help prevent peripheral neuropathies in patients taking isoniazid?

   a. Pyrazinamide
   b. Pyridoxine
   c. *Pyridium*
   d. Pyridostigmine
   e. Pyrimethamine

8. A patient comes into your clinic. She is 5 months pregnant and has a UTI. She is allergic to cephalexin. Which of the following regimens would be a treatment option for her? (Select **ALL** that apply.)

   a. *Bactrim* 1 DS tab BID x 3 days
   b. *Cipro ER* 500 mg PO daily x 7 days
   c. Nitrofurantoin 100 mg PO BID x 7 days
   d. Cefpodoxime 100 mg PO Q12H x 7 days
   e. Do not treat since she is pregnant

9. A 26 year old male presents to the clinic complaining of pain in his right foot. On exam, there is no focal abscess, just diffuse redness and warmth on the bottom of big toe spreading to the arch of his foot. He recalls stepping on a staple when barefoot the week prior. He denies having a fever and his vital signs are normal. Which one of the following antibiotics would be a good choice for his skin infection? (Select **ALL** that apply.)

   a. *Bactrim* SS 1 tab PO BID x 7 days
   b. Ceftriaxone 1 g IV x 1
   c. Dicloxacillin 500 mg PO Q6H x 5 days
   d. *Sivextro* 200 mg PO Q24H x 7 days
   e. Cephalexin 500 mg PO Q6H x 5 days

10. A 45 year old male with history of Hepatitis C cirrhosis presents to the hospital with a 6 day history of fever and chills. He has significant ascites and he has diffuse tenderness to palpation in his abdomen. The physician orders 2 sets of blood cultures, which grow Gram-negative rods, pending identification and susceptibilities. Which of the following would be the best choice for empiric therapy?

   a. *Bactrim DS* PO BID
   b. Ceftriaxone 1 gram IV daily
   c. Ofloxacin 200 mg IV Q12H
   d. Cefixime 200 mg PO BID
   e. Erythromycin 250 mg IV Q6H

Answers

1-a, 2-c, 3-d, 4-d, 5-e, 6-a,d, 7-b , 8-a,c, 9-c,e, 10-b

30

INFECTIOUS DISEASES III: ANTIFUNGALS & ANTIVIRALS

CDC/Dr. Lucille K. Georg

We gratefully acknowledge the assistance of Emi Minejima, PharmD, Assistant Professor and Annie Wong-Beringer, PharmD, FCCP, FIDSA, Associate Dean and Professor, University of Southern California School of Pharmacy, in preparing this chapter.

GUIDELINES/REFERENCES

Patterson TF, Thompson GR 3rd, Denning DW, et al. Practice Guidelines for the Diagnosis and Management of Aspergillosis: 2016 update by IDSA. *Clin Infect Dis.* 2016;63:e1-e60.

Pappas PG, Kauffman CA, Andes DR, et al. Clinical Practice Guideline for Management of Candidiasis: 2016 Update by IDSA. *Clin Infect Dis.* 2016;62:409-17.

Additional guidelines available at: http://www.idsociety.org

SYSTEMIC FUNGAL INFECTIONS

Fungal infections cause a wide spectrum of disease, from severe infections such as meningitis or pneumonia, to mild infections such as nail bed infections. Invasive fungal infections are associated with high morbidity and mortality. Candidemia, the 4th most common cause of nosocomial bloodstream infections in the U.S., has a mortality rate up to 20%. Diagnosis of fungal infections can be made by culture, serologic studies, or histologic features of a tissue specimen.

Fungi are classified as either yeasts, molds, or dimorphic (see box). Dimorphic fungi exist as mold forms at lower temperatures and yeast forms at higher temperatures ("Mold in the cold, yeast in the heat"). *Zygomycetes* refers to a class of fungi which includes *Mucor* species and *Rhizopus* species; invasive disease with this group is commonly referred to as "mucormycosis".

Certain types of fungi (including yeasts such as *Candida)* may colonize body surfaces and are considered to be normal flora in the intestine. They do not normally cause serious infections unless the immune system is weakened, or compromised, by drugs or diseases (HIV, malignancy). See Infectious Diseases IV for more information on opportunistic infections. Some fungi reproduce by spreading microscopic spores. These spores are often present in the air, where they can be inhaled or come into contact with the skin, causing lung and skin infections and in some cases central

FUNGAL CLASSIFICATIONS

Yeasts
Candida species (includes *C. albicans, C. tropicalis, C. parapsilosis, C. glabrata, C. krusei)*

Cryptococcus neoformans

Molds
Aspergillus species

Zygomycetes (Mucor species, *Rhizopus* species)

Dimorphic fungi
Histoplasma capsulatum

Blastomyces dermatitidis

Coccidioides immitis

nervous system infections. Systemic and long-term therapy is necessary for certain invasive fungal infections in the chronically immunosuppressed patient (e.g., *Cryptococcus, Coccidioides*).

In general, *C. albicans* is the most susceptible of the *Candida* species. *C. glabrata* and *C. krusei* tend to be more difficult to treat due to resistance to certain azole drugs. Of the molds, *Aspergillus* and *Zygomycetes* require the use of specific agents that have adequate activity.

Amphotericin B Deoxycholate and Lipid Formulations

Amphotericin B is a broad spectrum agent, binding to ergosterol, altering cell membrane permeability and causing cell death. Amphotericin B deoxycholate (the conventional form) has many toxicities. Lipid formulations are a complex of the active medication and a lipid component, which are used clinically because they are associated with fewer toxicities. Amphotericin B products are active against yeasts, molds and dimorphic fungi. They are used as initial treatment for many invasive infections, including *Cryptococcal* meningitis, histoplasmosis and mucormycosis.

AMPHOTERICIN B FORMULATIONS	DOSING	SAFETY/SIDE EFFECTS/MONITORING
Conventional Formulation		**BOXED WARNINGS** Medication errors from confusion between lipid-based forms of amphotericin *(Abelcet, Amphotec, AmBisome)* and conventional amphotericin B for injection have resulted in death. Conventional amphotericin B for injection doses should not exceed 1.5 mg/kg/day; verify product name and dosage if dose exceeds 1.5 mg/kg/day. Overdose may result in cardiopulmonary arrest. **SIDE EFFECTS** Infusion-related: fever, chills, HA, malaise, rigors, ↓ K, ↓ Mg, nephrotoxicity, anemia, hypotension/hypertension, thrombophlebitis, N/V *AmBisome* has had rare reports of severe back/chest pain with 1st dose. **MONITORING** Renal function, LFTs, electrolytes (especially K and Mg), CBC **NOTES** Amphotericin B deoxycholate (conventional formulation) requires pre-medication to reduce infusion-related reactions. Give the following 30-60 minutes prior to infusion: ■ Acetaminophen or NSAID ■ Diphenhydramine and/or hydrocortisone ■ Meperidine to ↓ duration of severe rigors ■ NS boluses to ↓ risk of nephrotoxicity Lipid formulations have ↓ infusion reactions and ↓ nephrotoxicity compared to conventional formulation; choice of formulation will depend on infection indication and patient specific risk factors (e.g., renal dysfunction)
Amphotericin B deoxycholate Injection	0.1-1.5 mg/kg/day	
Lipid Formulations		
Amphotericin B Lipid Complex *(Abelcet)* Injection	5 mg/kg/day	
Liposomal Amphotericin B *(AmBisome)* Injection	3-6 mg/kg/day	
Amphotericin B cholesteryl sulfate complex *(Amphotec)* Injection	3-4 mg/kg/day	

Amphotericin B Drug Interactions

- Additive ↑ risk of nephrotoxicity when used with other nephrotoxic agents such as aminoglycosides, cisplatin, colistimethate, cyclosporine, flucytosine, loop diuretics, NSAIDs, radiocontrast dye, tacrolimus, vancomycin and others.
- May ↑ risk of digoxin toxicity due to hypokalemia. Use caution with any agent that ↓ potassium or magnesium since amphotericin decreases both. Scheduled replacement of potassium or magnesium should be considered.

Flucytosine

Flucytosine works by penetrating fungal cells where it is converted to fluorouracil, which competes with uracil, interfering with fungal RNA and protein synthesis. Due to development of resistance when used alone, flucytosine is recommended for use in combination with amphotericin B for treatment of invasive *Cryptococcal* (meningitis) or *Candida* infections.

DRUG	DOSING	SAFETY/SIDE EFFECTS/MONITORING
Flucytosine, 5-FC *(Ancobon)* Spectrum: covers yeasts, including *Candida* and *Cryptococcus*	50-150 mg/kg/day, divided Q6H CrCl < 40 mL/min: adjustment required	**BOXED WARNING** Use with extreme caution in patients with renal dysfunction. Closely monitor hematologic, renal, and hepatic status. **SIDE EFFECTS** Dose-related myelosuppression, (anemia, neutropenia, thrombocytopenia), ↑ SCr, ↑ BUN, hepatitis , ↑ bilirubin, many CNS effects, hypoglycemia, ↓ K, aplastic anemia, and others **NOTES** Avoid use as monotherapy due to rapid resistance.

Azole Antifungals

Azole antifungals decrease ergosterol synthesis and inhibit cell membrane formation. Azoles are inhibitors of the fungal CYP450 system and also interact with the human CYP450 enzymes (mainly 3A4) resulting in significant drug interactions as a class. The coverage and indications of azoles vary widely. Ketoconazole was the first azole, but due to toxicities and many significant drug interactions it is most often used topically. Fluconazole has reliable activity against *Candida albicans* and *Candida tropicalis*. Itraconazole can be used as an alternative to fluconazole in some cases, as it is active against *C. albicans, C. tropicalis* and *Cryptococcus neoformans*, but use is often limited by drug interactions, less data and expense. The primary uses for itraconazole are for the dimorphic fungi *Blastomycosis* and *Histoplasmosis* and for nail bed infections (onychomycosis). See the Common Skin Conditions chapter for treatment of non-invasive fungal infections, including onychomycosis.

STUDY TIP: AZOLE ANTIFUNGALS

All can cause ↑ LFTs

Only fluconazole requires renal dose adjustment

Fluconazole has narrower spectrum

- Covers *C. albicans* well
- Useful for vaginal candidiasis (non-pregnant)
- *C. glabrata* can be resistant and *C. kruseii* is inherently resistant

Voriconazole

- Drug of choice for *Aspergillus*

Posaconazole and isavuconazonium

- Active against molds including *Aspergillus* and *Zygomycetes*

<table>
<tr><th>DRUG</th><th>DOSING</th><th>SAFETY/SIDE EFFECTS/MONITORING</th></tr>
<tr>
<td>Ketoconazole (Nizoral, Nizoral AD, Ketodan, Extina, Xolegel – all brands are topicals)

Tablet, cream, foam, gel, shampoo

Used off-label to treat advanced prostate cancer due to anti-androgenic activity (dosing differs for this indication)</td>
<td>200-400 mg PO daily

No adjustment in renal impairment

See Common Skin Conditions chapter.</td>
<td rowspan="3">BOXED WARNINGS

Ketoconazole
Hepatotoxicity which has led to liver transplantation and/or death

Concomitant use with cisapride, dofetilide, pimozide, and quinidine is contraindicated due risk of life-threatening ventricular arrhythmias such as torsades de pointes

Use oral tablets only when other effective antifungal therapy is unavailable or not tolerated and the benefits outweigh risks (hepatotoxicity, adrenal insufficiency, drug interactions)

Itraconazole
Contraindicated for treatment of onychomycosis in patients with ventricular dysfunction or a history of HF

Coadministration with itraconazole can cause ↑ plasma concentrations of certain drugs and can lead to QT prolongation and ventricular tachyarrhythmias, including torsades de pointes. Coadministration with methadone, disopyramide, dofetilide, dronedarone, quinidine, ergot alkaloids, irinotecan, lurasidone, oral midazolam, pimozide, triazolam, felodipine, nisoldipine, ranolazine, eplerenone, cisapride, lovastatin, simvastatin and, in subjects with renal or hepatic impairment, colchicine, is contraindicated

WARNINGS
Liver dysfunction, hepatotoxicity, exfoliative skin disorders (fluconazole)

SIDE EFFECTS
Headache, N/V, abdominal pain, rash/pruritus ↑ LFTs, ↑ triglycerides, QT prolongation, ↓ K, hypertension, edema, dizziness, hair loss (or possible hair growth) and altered hair texture with ketoconazole shampoo

NOTES
Safety issue – see Pregnancy chapter (fluconazole)

All azoles are cleared hepatically except fluconazole, which requires renal dose adjustment

Fluconazole and voriconazole penetrate the CNS adequately to treat fungal meningitis

Voriconazole is often associated with CNS toxicities (headache, dizziness, hallucinations or ocular toxicity)</td>
</tr>
<tr>
<td>Fluconazole (Diflucan)

Tablet, suspension, injection

Spectrum: yeasts (including Candida albicans Candida tropicalis, Cryptococcus) and Coccidioides

Limited efficacy for C. glabrata due to resistance

C. krusei is considered fluconazole-resistant</td>
<td>50-800 mg PO/IV daily

Vaginal candidiasis: 150 mg PO x 1

CrCl ≥ 50 mL/min: ↓ dose by 50%</td>
</tr>
<tr>
<td>Itraconazole (Sporanox, Sporanox PulsePak, Onmel)

Tablet, capsule, solution

Spectrum: yeasts (C. albicans, C. tropicalis), dimorphic fungi, Aspergillus</td>
<td>200-400 mg PO daily-BID

Capsules and oral solution are not interchangeable.

Solution is taken without food.

Capsule and tablet are taken with food.

Limited data on use in renal impairment (use with caution).

See Common Skin Conditions chapter for use in treatment of onychomycosis.</td>
</tr>
</table>

Azole Antifungals Continued

DRUG	DOSING	SAFETY/SIDE EFFECTS/MONITORING
Voriconazole *(Vfend)* Tablet, suspension, injection Spectrum similar to itraconazole but better coverage of *Aspergillus* species, *C. glabrata,* and *C. krusei,* compared to itraconazole/fluconazole. No activity against *Zygomycetes (Mucor, Rhizopus).* Drug of choice for Aspergillosis	Loading dose: 6 mg/kg IV Q12H x 2 doses Maintenance dose: 4 mg/kg IV Q12H or 200 mg PO Q12H – use actual body weight for dosing Hepatic impairment: adjustment required CrCl < 50 mL/min: oral dosing is preferred after the initial IV loading doses. The IV vehicle, SBECD (sulfobutyl ether beta-cyclodextrin), may accumulate and worsen renal function. **Therapeutic Range** Trough levels: 1-5 mcg/mL	**CONTRAINDICATIONS** Coadministration with barbiturates (long-acting), carbamazepine, efavirenz (≥ 400 mg/day), ergot alkaloids, pimozide, quinidine, rifabutin, rifampin, ritonavir (≥ 800 mg/day), sirolimus and St. John's wort **WARNINGS** Liver damage, visual disturbances (optic neuritis and papilledema), embryofetal toxicity, QT prolongation (correct K, Ca, and Mg prior to initiating treatment), infusion-related reactions, serious skin reactions (SJS/TEN), phototoxicity (malignancy has been reported in patients with prior photosensitivity reactions on long-term voriconazole), skeletal adverse effects (fluorosis, periostitis) **SIDE EFFECTS** Visual changes (~20% – blurred vision, photophobia, altered color perception, altered visual acuity), ↑ LFTs, ↑ SCr, CNS toxicity (hallucinations, headache, dizziness), rash (SJS/TEN), photosensitivity, ↓ K, ↓ Mg, skeletal pain **MONITORING** LFTs, renal function, electrolytes, visual function (for therapy > 28 days), CBC, trough concentrations **NOTES** Safety issue - see Pregnancy chapter Caution driving at night due to vision changes Avoid direct sunlight Hold tube feedings for 1 hour before and 1 hour after doses Suspension – shake for 10 seconds before each use. Do not refrigerate
Posaconazole *(Noxafil)* Tablet, suspension, injection Spectrum similar to voriconazole plus *Zygomycetes (Mucor* and *Rhizopus)*	Suspension: 200 mg TID or 400 mg BID Give with a full meal (during or within 20 minutes following a meal) Tablets: 300 mg PO BID on day 1, then 300 mg PO daily with food. Based on indication, can range from 100-400 mg/day, divided in 1-3 doses IV: 300 mg BID x 1 day, then 300 mg daily CrCl < 50 mL/min: oral dosing is preferred. The IV vehicle, SBECD (sulfobutyl ether beta-cyclodextrin), may accumulate and worsen renal function.	**CONTRAINDICATIONS** Coadministration with sirolimus, ergot alkaloids, pimozide, quinidine, atorvastatin, lovastatin or simvastatin **WARNINGS** QT prolongation – correct K, Ca, and Mg prior to initiating therapy Prescribing and dispensing errors. Suspension and tablet are not interchangeable, as dosing regimens differ (tablet is better absorbed) Neurotoxicity with vincristine due to increased vincristine levels (seizures, peripheral neuropathy, SIADH, paralytic ileus) **SIDE EFFECTS** N/V/D, fever, headache, ↑ LFTs, rash, ↓ K, ↓ Mg, hyperglycemia **MONITORING** LFTs, renal function, electrolytes, CBC

Azole Antifungals Continued

DRUG	DOSING	SAFETY/SIDE EFFECTS/MONITORING
Isavuconazonium sulfate *(Cresemba)* Capsules, injection Prodrug of isavuconazole Similar spectrum to posaconazole	IV/PO: 372 mg Q8H for 6 doses, then 372 mg daily No adjustment for renal dysfunction, use with caution in severe hepatic impairment Can be taken without regard to food Swallow whole, do not crush or open	**CONTRAINDICATIONS** Concurrent use of strong CYP3A4 inhibitors or inducers, familial short QT syndrome **WARNINGS** Hepatic adverse drug reactions, infusion reaction (DC infusion if occurs), hypersensitivity reactions (anaphylaxis, SJS/TEN), embryo-fetal toxicity, drug interactions, particulates (undissolved drug) **SIDE EFFECTS** N/V/D, HA, infusion reactions (hypotension, dyspnea, chills, dizziness, tingling and numbness), peripheral edema, ↓ K, ↑ LFTs **MONITORING** LFTs, electrolytes **NOTES** Requires a filter (0.2-1.2 micron) during administration due to possible particulates

Azole Antifungals Drug Interactions

- All azoles are 3A4 inhibitors (moderate-strong). Itraconazole is an inhibitor of 3A4 (strong) and P-glycoprotein (P-gp). Ketoconazole inhibits 1A2 (weak), 2C9 (moderate), 2C19 (moderate), 2D6 (moderate), 3A4 (strong) and P-gp. Fluconazole is an inhibitor of 2C9 (strong), 2C19 (strong), and 3A4 (moderate). Voriconazole is an inhibitor of 2C9 (moderate), 2C19 (moderate) and 3A4 (strong). Posaconazole is an inhibitor of 3A4 (strong). Isavuconazonium is an inhibitor of 3A4 (moderate), inducer of 2C8/9 (weak/moderate), 3A4 (weak).
- Itraconazole and ketoconazole have pH-dependent absorption; ↑ pH causes ↓ absorption. Antacids should be spaced 2 hours from doses. If PPIs and H2RAs must be used during antifungal therapy, administer itraconazole or ketoconazole with 8 oz. non-diet cola to provide an acidic environment for absorption.
- PPIs and cimetidine can decrease absorption of posaconazole suspension and should be stopped during therapy to avoid treatment failure.
- Voriconazole is metabolized by several CYP 450 enzymes (2C19, 2C9 and 3A4); the voriconazole concentration can ↑ dangerously when given with drugs that inhibit voriconazole's metabolism or with small dose increases – it exhibits first-order, followed by zero-order (non-linear) kinetics.
- Avoid concurrent use of voriconazole with the following drugs: barbiturates (long-acting), carbamazepine, efavirenz (≥ 400 mg/day), ergot alkaloids, pimozide, quinidine, rifabutin, rifampin, ritonavir (≥ 800 mg/day), cobicistat, sirolimus and St. John's wort.
- Avoid use of isavuconazonium with strong 3A4 inhibitors or inducers.
- All azoles can ↑ INR in patients on warfarin – greatest risk with fluconazole, ketoconazole and voriconazole. Monitor INR.
- Strong 3A4 inhibitors may ↑ concentrations of apixaban and rivaroxaban. Monitor for s/s of bleeding.

Echinocandins

Echinocandins inhibit synthesis of beta (1,3)-D-glucan, an essential component of the fungal cell wall. They are effective against most *Candida* species, including non-albicans strains that are resistant to azoles (e.g., *C. glabrata* and *C. krusei*). Activity includes *Aspergillus* spp., but other agents are generally preferred. Should be used as part of a combination regimen if used for *Aspergillus* spp. Echinocandins are generally well-tolerated and are not associated with significant renal or hepatic toxicity. Echinocandins are available only as injections.

DRUG	DOSING	SAFETY/SIDE EFFECTS/MONITORING
Caspofungin ***(Cancidas)*** Injection	70 mg IV on day 1, then 50 mg IV daily Moderate hepatic impairment: 70 mg IV on day 1, then 35 mg IV daily ↑ dose to 70 mg IV daily when used in combination with rifampin or other strong enzyme inducers	**WARNINGS** Histamine-mediated symptoms (rash, pruritus, facial swelling, flushing, hypotension) have occurred; anaphylaxis **SIDE EFFECTS** ↑ LFTs, hypotension, ↓ K, ↓ Mg, fever, N/V/D, hypoglycemia, anemia, ↑ SCr, rash Severe skin reactions, including SJS/TEN (caspofungin) **MONITORING** LFTs **NOTES** All are given once daily and do not require dose adjustment in renal impairment. Very few drug interactions. Caution use of caspofungin with cyclosporine due to ↑ hepatotoxicity.
Micafungin ***(Mycamine)*** Injection	**Candidemia** 100 mg IV daily **Esophageal Candidiasis** 150 mg IV daily	
Anidulafungin *(Eraxis)* Injection	**Candidemia** 200 mg IV on day 1, then 100 mg IV daily **Esophageal Candidiasis** 100 mg IV on day 1, then 50 mg daily	

Other Antifungal Agents

Systemic agents for treatment of superficial fungal infections are typically considered second line to topical products. Griseofulvin is a less favorable agent, as it has a narrow antifungal spectrum, is less effective than other systemic agents (e.g., itraconazole or terbinafine), and requires prolonged courses. Nystatin suspension and clotrimazole troches/lozenges are useful for treating mild, localized *Candida* infections (thrush). Systemic treatment (e.g., fluconazole, micafungin) is required in patients with HIV and in moderate-severe infections, including esophageal candidiasis.

DRUG	DOSING	SAFETY/SIDE EFFECTS/MONITORING
Griseofulvin *(Grifulvin V, Gris-PEG)* Tablet, suspension Griseofulvin binds to the keratin precursor cells which prevents fungal invasion; indicated for dermatomycosis and tinea infections of skin, hair and nails.	*Grifulvin V:* 500-1,000 mg/day in 1-2 divided doses *Gris-PEG:* 375-750 mg/day in 1-2 divided doses Take with a fatty meal to ↑ absorption or with food/milk to avoid GI upset	**CONTRAINDICATIONS** Severe liver disease, porphyria, pregnancy **SIDE EFFECTS** HA, rash, urticaria, dizziness, photosensitivity, ↑ LFTs, leukopenia, severe skin reactions **MONITORING** LFTs, renal function, CBC **NOTES** Safety issue – see Pregnancy chapter Cross reaction possible with PCN allergy Duration of therapy depends on site of infection. Tinea corporis: 2-4 weeks. Tinea pedis: 4-8 weeks

Other Antifungal Agents Continued

DRUG	DOSING	SAFETY/SIDE EFFECTS/MONITORING
Terbinafine *(LamISIL, Terbinex)* Tablet, oral granule, topical Topical forms (Rx, OTC) Inhibits squalene epoxidase, a key enzyme in sterol biosynthesis in fungi, resulting in a deficiency of ergosterol within the cell wall leading to cell death	250 mg/day in 1-2 divided doses without regards to meals Confirm fungal infection prior to use for onychomycosis or dermatomycosis See Common Skin Conditions chapter	**CONTRAINDICATIONS** Chronic or active liver disease **WARNINGS** Hepatotoxicity, taste/smell disturbance (including loss of taste or smell that can be permanent), depression, neutropenia, serious skin reactions (SJS/TEN/DRESS/erythema multiforme) Can cause or exacerbate systemic lupus erythematosus **SIDE EFFECTS** HA, ↑ LFTs, skin rashes, abdominal pain, pruritus, diarrhea, dyspepsia, taste disturbance **MONITORING** CBC, LFTs **NOTES** MedGuide required
Clotrimazole *(Mycelex)* 10 mg troche/lozenge	**Oral Candidiasis** Prophylaxis: 10 mg 3x/day Treatment: 10 mg 5x/day x 14 days Allow troche to dissolve slowly over 15-30 minutes	**SIDE EFFECTS** ↑ LFTs, nausea, dysgeusia **MONITORING** LFTs
Nystatin *(Bio-Statin)* Suspension, tablet	**Oral Candidiasis** Suspension: 400,000-600,000 units 4 times/day; swish in the mouth and retain for as long as possible (several minutes) before swallowing **Intestinal infections** Oral tablets: 500,000-1,000,000 units Q8H	**SIDE EFFECTS** N/V/D, stomach pain

Drug Interactions

- Griseofulvin: induces 1A2, 2C9, 3A4 (all weak/moderate). Griseofulvin may ↓ the metabolism of hormonal (estrogen and progestin) contraceptives which may lead to contraceptive failure. Use an alternative, nonhormonal form of contraception.
- Terbinafine is a strong 2D6 inhibitor and a weak/moderate 3A4 inducer.

Treatment Recommendations for Selected Fungal Pathogens

PATHOGEN	FIRST-LINE TREATMENT
Candida albicans	Oropharyngeal infection (thrush) ■ Mild disease: topical antifungals (clotrimazole, nystatin) ■ If HIV+ or moderate-to-severe disease: fluconazole (PO) Esophageal infection ■ Fluconazole or echinocandin Bloodstream or other invasive infection ■ If patient is not neutropenic: echinocandin (preferred), fluconazole (alternative) ■ If patient is neutropenic: echinocandin (preferred), amphotericin B, fluconazole (alternatives)
Candida glabrata or *Candida krusei*	Echinocandins or amphotericin B
Aspergillus	Voriconazole (preferred), liposomal amphotericin B, isavuconazonium
Cryptococcus neoformans	Induction in serious infections (primarily causes meningitis): amphotericin B + flucytosine (5-FC) Consolidation: fluconazole (prolonged)
Coccidioides immitis	Fluconazole, itraconazole or amphotericin B
Histoplasma capsulatum	Liposomal amphotericin B or itraconazole
Zygomycetes class (*Rhizopus*, *Mucor*, etc.)	Amphotericin B ± posaconazole, isavuconazonium
Dermatophytes	Nail bed infections: itraconazole, terbinafine, or fluconazole (confirm fungal infection prior to treatment); see Common Skin Conditions chapter

Antifungal Patient Counseling

All azoles

- Common side effects include headache, nausea and abdominal pain.
- This drug can (rarely) damage the liver. Get immediate medical help if you develop any of the following: yellowing of the white part of your eyes or yellowing of your skin, dark-colored urine, light colored stool, or severe stomach pain with nausea.
- The liquid suspension should not be refrigerated.

Ketoconazole *(Nizoral)* and itraconazole *(Sporanox)*

- With ketoconazole and itraconazole: do not use with antacids (need two hour separation). These medicines will reduce the amount of the antifungal medicine that gets into your system.
- Itraconazole tablets and capsules should be taken with food.
- Itraconazole solution should be taken on an empty stomach.

Voriconazole *(Vfend)*

- Avoid driving at night because this medicine may cause vision problems like blurry vision. If you have any change in your eyesight, avoid all driving or using dangerous machinery. Vision changes are temporary and reversible.
- Avoid sunlight. Your skin may burn more easily. Your eyes may hurt in bright sunlight.
- Take this medication by mouth on an empty stomach, at least 1 hour before or 1 hour after meals, usually every 12 hours or as directed.
- The liquid suspension should not be refrigerated.
- There are many interactions with this drug and other medicines. Please discuss with your pharmacist to make sure this will not pose a problem.
- This medication can cause harm to a baby if taken during pregnancy. Use effective contraception during treatment.

Posaconazole *(Noxafil)*

- Posaconazole tablets should be taken with food; posaconazole suspension should be administered during or within 20 min following a full meal or oral liquid nutritional supplement to maximize absorption.

Nystatin

- If you are using the suspension form of this medication, shake well before using. Be sure to swish the medication around in your mouth for several minutes before swallowing.

Terbinafine *(Lamisil)*

- The most common side effect is headache. Temporary change or loss of taste and appetite and loss of smell can also occur.
- Terbinafine is used to treat certain types of fungal infections (e.g., fingernail or toenail). It works by stopping the growth of fungus.
- Take this medication by mouth with or without food, usually once a day. Dosage and length of treatment depend on the location of the fungus and the response to treatment.
- It may take several months after you finish treatment to see the full benefit of this drug. It takes time for your new healthy nails to grow out and replace the infected ones.
- Skipping doses or not completing the full course of therapy may ↓ effectiveness of treatment, cause the infection to return, and increase the likelihood that this medicine will not work for you in the future.
- This drug can (rarely) damage the liver. Get immediate medical help if you develop any of the following: yellowing of the white part of your eyes or yellowing of your skin, dark-colored urine, light colored stool, or bad stomach pain with severe nausea.

VIRAL INFECTIONS

Viruses are obligate intracellular parasites, depending on the host cell's metabolic processes for survival. Therapies available to treat viral infections work by either directly inhibiting viruses (antiviral agents) or augmenting or modifying host defenses to the viral infection (immunomodulating agents). Antivirals target critical steps in the viral life cycle, such as entry into the cell or replication. As viruses depend on hosts for metabolism/replication, antivirals may injure or destroy the host cells.

Many viral infections have no effective drug treatment. Medications are available to treat influenza virus, herpes simplex virus [genital herpes, herpes labialis (cold sores), and systemic herpes virus infections], varicella-zoster virus (VZV) and cytomegalovirus (CMV).

INFLUENZA

Influenza is a respiratory virus that affects 5 – 20% of the U.S. population annually, with peak activity between late November and March. Influenza A and B are the strains that commonly infect humans. Both can cause severe illness, leading to hospitalization and death, particularly in at-risk patients (pregnant women, children age < 5 years, adults age > 65 years, immunocompromised patients and those with comorbid conditions such as diabetes, asthma or cardiovascular disease). Influenza spreads via respiratory droplets generated by coughing and sneezing. A person with influenza can be contagious one day prior to developing symptoms and for up to 5 – 7 days after becoming ill. Influenza commonly presents with symptoms that include fever, chills, fatigue, body aches, cough, sore throat and headaches. The seasonal influenza vaccine is the most effective prevention for influenza infection and is recommended for all patients age ≥ 6 months who have no contraindications. See Immunizations chapter.

Antivirals for Influenza

The Centers for Disease Control and Prevention (CDC) updates antiviral treatment recommendations based on the type of circulating virus during influenza season. Neuraminidase inhibitors (oseltamivir, zanamivir and peramivir) reduce the amount of virus in the body by inhibiting the enzyme which enables the release of new viral particles from infected cells. They are active against both influenza A and B and they decrease the duration of symptoms by about 1 day and reduce the risk of complications from influenza. To be most effective, neuraminidase inhibitors should be started within 48 hours of illness onset. In hospitalized, severely ill patients, neuraminidase inhibitors may be beneficial if started within 4 – 5 days after symptom onset. There is less benefit if started later, after the virus has already caused damage to respiratory epithelial cells. Adamantanes (rimantadine and amantadine) are only effective for influenza A, and in recent years have not been recommended as monotherapy due to resistance.

Neuraminidase Inhibitors

DRUG	DOSING	SAFETY/SIDE EFFECTS/MONITORING
Oseltamivir *(Tamiflu)* 30, 45, 75 mg capsules 6 mg/mL (60 mL) suspension 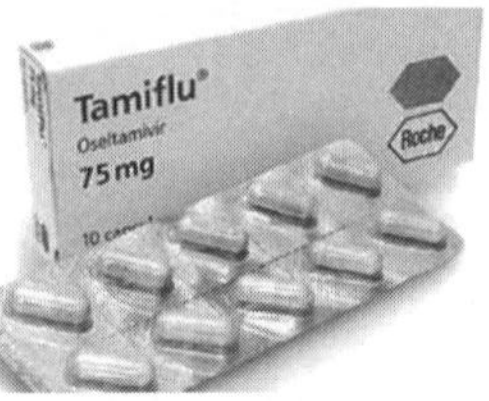	**Treatment, age > 12 years:** 75 mg BID x 5 days **Prophylaxis, age > 12 years:** 75 mg daily x 10 days Pediatric patients (age 2 weeks-12 years): dose is based on body weight. CrCl ≤ 60 mL/min: adjustment required	**WARNINGS** Neuropsychiatric events (sudden confusion, delirium, hallucinations, unusual behavior, or self-injury), serious skin reactions (SJS/TEN), anaphylaxis **SIDE EFFECTS** N/V/D, abdominal pain

Neuraminidase Inhibitors Continued

DRUG	DOSING	SAFETY/SIDE EFFECTS/MONITORING
Zanamivir *(Relenza Diskhaler)* 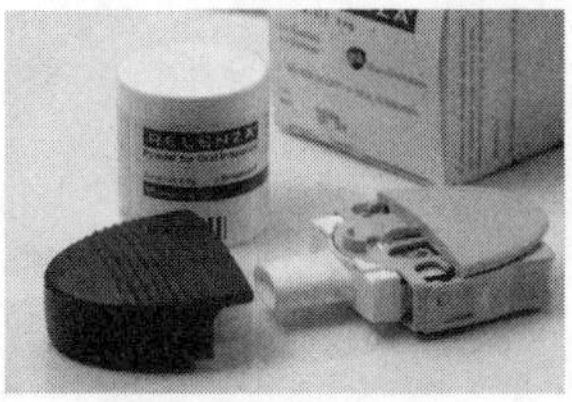	**Treatment, age ≥ 7 years:** 10 mg (two 5 mg inhalations) BID x 5 days **Prophylaxis, age ≥ 5 years:** 10 mg (two 5 mg inhalations) once daily x 10 days (household setting) or 28 days (community outbreak)	**WARNINGS** Neuropsychiatric events, bronchospasm (do not use in asthma/COPD or with any breathing problems). Stop the drug if wheezing or breathing problems develop. **SIDE EFFECTS** Headache, throat pain, cough
Peramivir (*Rapivab*) Injection	**Treatment (adult):** 600 mg IV as a single dose CrCl < 50 mL/min: adjustment required	**WARNINGS** Neuropsychiatric events (sudden confusion, delirium, hallucinations, unusual behavior, or self-injury), serious skin reactions (SJS/TEN), anaphylaxis, hepatic or renal impairment **SIDE EFFECTS** Hypertension, insomnia, increased blood glucose, diarrhea, constipation, neutropenia, ↑ AST/ALT

Adamantanes

Rimantadine *(Flumadine)* Tablet Amantadine - Due to resistance, it is not recommended for influenza prophylaxis and treatment of influenza A.	Treatment/Prophylaxis: 100 mg BID CrCl < 30 mL/min: adjustment required	**WARNINGS** Seizures – use with caution in patients with a history of seizure disorder Psychosis – avoid use **SIDE EFFECTS** N/V, loss of appetite, dry mouth, insomnia, impaired concentration. Amantadine has greater incidence of these side effects. **NOTES** See Parkinson Disease chapter for further information on amantadine

HERPES VIRUSES

There are hundreds of herpes viruses in existence; however, not all are responsible for causing human disease. Clinically significant herpes viruses include: herpes simplex viruses 1 and 2 (HSV-1, HSV-2), varicella-zoster virus (VZV), cytomegalovirus (CMV), Epstein-Barr virus (EBV), Kaposi sarcoma associated herpes virus (HHV-8), HHV-6, and HHV-7.

Both HSV-1 and HSV-2 can cause a variety of infections, including orofacial infection, genital infection, eye infections, encephalitis, esophagitis, and pulmonary infections. HSV-1 is most commonly associated with oropharyngeal disease. HSV-2 is associated more closely with genital disease. However, each virus is capable of causing infections clinically indistinguishable at both anatomic sites.

Infection with varicella zoster virus is commonly called chickenpox. After an occurrence of varicella zoster infection, the virus lies dormant in the nerve root and can later cause herpes zoster infection, often referred to as shingles.

Antivirals for Herpes Simplex Virus and Varicella Zoster Virus

DRUG	SAFETY/SIDE EFFECTS/MONITORING
Acyclovir *(Zovirax, Sitavig)* Capsule, tablet, buccal tablet, suspension, injection, topical *Zovirax* cream, *Sitavig* – for cold sores (herpes simplex labialis) **ValACYclovir *(Valtrex)*** Tablet Prodrug of acyclovir Famciclovir *(Famvir)* Tablet Prodrug of penciclovir	**WARNINGS** Thrombocytopenic purpura/hemolytic uremic syndrome (TTP/HUS) has been reported in immunocompromised patients Caution in patients with renal impairment, the elderly, and/or those receiving nephrotoxic agents. Infuse acyclovir over at least 1 hour and maintain adequate hydration to reduce risk of renal tubular damage **SIDE EFFECTS** Malaise, headache, N/V/D, rash, pruritus, ↑ LFTs, neutropenia, ↑ seizures (especially with IV acyclovir, famciclovir), transient burning or stinging with topical formulation Anaphylaxis (famciclovir) ↑ SCr/BUN with crystal nephropathy (IV acyclovir) **MONITORING** Renal function, LFTs, CBC **NOTES** Acyclovir dose is based on IBW in obese patients Infuse acyclovir over 1 hour to prevent renal damage ↓ dose and/or extend interval in renal impairment In general, 5 mg/kg IV acyclovir = 1,000 mg PO valacyclovir

Genital Herpes

Genital herpes is a chronic, life-long viral infection. One in six people in the U.S. have HSV-2. The first episode of genital herpes usually begins within 2 – 14 days post exposure, but up to 50% of patients are asymptomatic. Symptoms of the first episode can include flu-like symptoms, fever, headache, malaise, myalgia, and development of pustular or ulcerative lesions on external genitalia. Lesions usually begin as papules or vesicles that rapidly spread and clusters of lesions form, crust, and re-epithelialize. Lesions are described as painful. Itching, dysuria, and vaginal or urethral discharge are common symptoms. Recurrent infections are not associated with systemic manifestations. Symptoms are localized to the genital area, milder, and of shorter duration. Patients typically experience a prodrome (which can consist of mild tingling or shooting pain in the legs, hips, thighs or buttocks) occurring hours to days prior to the appearance of lesions.

Treatment must be initiated during prodrome or within 1 day of lesion onset for the patient to experience the full benefit. Suppressive therapy reduces the frequency of genital herpes recurrences by 70-80% among patients who have frequent recurrences (e.g., > 6 recurrences/year) and many report no symptomatic outbreaks. Viral transmission is also reduced. Acyclovir *(Zovirax)* is the least expensive regimen, however, it must be dosed up to 5 times per day. Valacyclovir *(Valtrex)* is a prodrug of acyclovir that results in higher concentrations than with oral acyclovir and less frequent dosing that may enhance adherence. If the virus is found to be resistant to acyclovir, it will be resistant to valacyclovir. Famciclovir *(Famvir)* is a pro-drug of penciclovir. Strains resistant to acyclovir are generally resistant to famciclovir. Infections caused by acyclovir-resistant HSV are treated with foscarnet until the lesions heal.

Genital Herpes Simplex Virus Treatment In Non-HIV Patients

HSV INFECTION	ACYCLOVIR	VALACYCLOVIR	FAMCICLOVIR
Initial episode*	400 mg PO TID x 7-10 days or 200 mg PO 5x daily x 7-10 days	1 gram PO BID x 7-10 days	250 mg PO TID x 7-10 days
Recurrent episodes	400 mg PO TID x 5 days or 800 mg PO BID x 5 days or 800 mg PO TID x 2 days	500 mg PO BID x 3 days or 1 gram PO daily x 5 days	125 mg PO BID x 5 days or 500 mg PO x 1, then 250 mg PO BID x 2 days or 1 gram PO BID x 1 day
Chronic suppression	400 mg PO BID	500 - 1,000 mg PO daily	250 mg PO BID

**Treatment can be extended if healing is incomplete after 10 days of therapy*

HSV Encephalitis Invasive Infections

HSV is the most commonly identified cause of viral encephalitis in U.S. (10 – 20% of all cases). Cases of HSV encephalitis occur more frequently in young patients (ages 5 – 30) and older adults (age > 50 years). Hallmark symptoms include acute onset of fever and focal neurologic symptoms and cause altered mental status. HSV encephalitis is treated with IV acyclovir 10 mg/kg/dose Q8H x 14 – 21 days. Other invasive infections occur infrequently, typically in the immunosuppressed population, such as esophagitis and pneumonitis and are treated with IV acyclovir dosed 5 mg/kg/dose Q8H.

Herpes Simplex Labialis (Cold Sores)

Cold sores are ubiquitous and are highly contagious. Children often pick up the infection from family members. Infection is usually due to HSV-1 in children, but can be caused by HSV-2 when older due to oral/genital sex. Virus can be shed when asymptomatic, but is most commonly spread with active lesions; kissing, sharing drinks should be avoided when lesions are oozing. Sore eruption is preceded by prodromal symptoms (tingling, itching, soreness). In most patients the sore appears in the same location repeatedly. The most common site is the junction between the upper and lower lip. Triggers that cause sore outbreaks include fatigue/stress, stress to the skin (sun exposure, acid peels) and dental work. Patients should identify their own trigger/s and attempt to avoid them. The prodromal period is the optimal time to apply topical or take oral medication to reduce blister duration. If recurrences are frequent (> 4 times/year), chronic suppression can be taken daily. OTC and Rx topicals shorten the duration by up to one day; oral (systemic) antivirals shorten the duration by up to two days.

Topical Treatment of Herpes Labialis

DRUGS	DOSING	NOTES
Docosanol *(Abreva)* OTC	Apply 5x daily at first sign of outbreak, continue until healed.	Systemic antivirals are more effective. 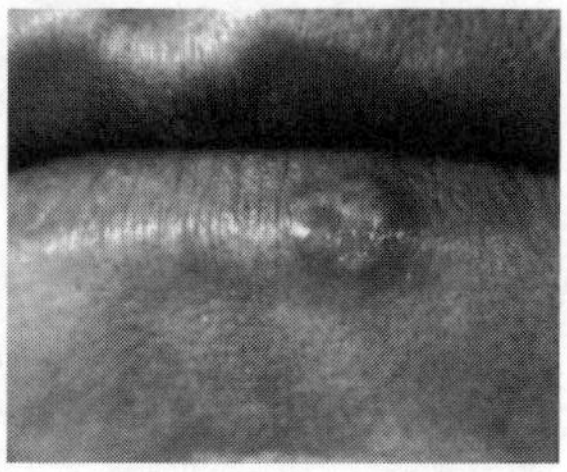
Acyclovir topical cream *(Zovirax)* Rx	Apply 5x daily for 4 days (can be used on genital sores).	
Acyclovir buccal tablet *(Sitavig)* Rx	Apply 50 mg tablet as a single dose to the upper gum region.	
Penciclovir topical cream *(Denavir)* Rx	Apply every 2 hours during waking hours for 4 days.	

Systemic Treatment of Herpes Labialis

HSV INFECTION	ACYCLOVIR	VALACYCLOVIR	FAMCICLOVIR
Initial episode	200-400 mg PO 5x daily or 400 mg TID x 7-10 days	2 grams PO BID x1 day	
Recurrent episode	200-400 mg PO 5x daily x 5 days or 400 mg PO TID x 5 days or 800 mg PO BID x 5 days	2 grams PO BID x 1 day	1.5 grams PO x 1 dose
Chronic suppression	400 mg PO BID		

Varicella Zoster Virus and Herpes Zoster

Most people in the U.S. have had varicella zoster virus (chickenpox) infection during childhood. The virus can lie dormant in the nerve for decades without causing any symptoms. The recurrence of viral symptoms is called herpes zoster or shingles. The risk of herpes zoster increases with age, and older patients are more likely to experience postherpetic neuralgia, non-pain complications, hospitalizations, and interference with activities of daily living. An outbreak may occur as the patient ages, and is often due to acute stress. Although herpes zoster can occur at any age, adults > 60 years old are most often affected. The shingles rash is distinctive – it can be itchy or tingly, is very painful and often manifests unilaterally. Pharmacists should be able to recognize a shingles rash and inform patients to see a physician; refer to the image.

Shingles vaccine *(Zostavax)* can prevent shingles and shingles-related complications. It is FDA approved for use in patients 50+ years of age and is recommended by ACIP for patients age 60+ years of age. It can be used in patients who have experienced a previous shingles outbreak to decrease likelihood of recurrence and postherpetic neuralgia. See Immunizations chapter.

Antiviral therapy should be initiated at the earliest sign or symptom of shingles and is most effective when started within 72 hours of the onset of zoster rash. Pain can be treated with topical agents (*Lidoderm* patch, lidocaine viscous gel) or with neuropathic pain agents (anticonvulsants, antidepressants), and sometimes with NSAIDs or opioids. Most recover without long-term aftereffects; 5 – 10% have chronic pain, which can be debilitating.

Herpes Zoster (Shingles) Treatment

DRUG	DOSING	DESCRIPTION
Acyclovir *(Zovirax)*	800 mg PO 5x daily for 7-10 days	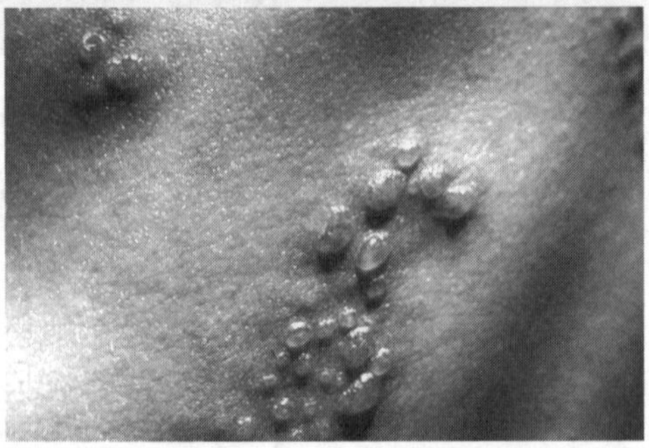
Famciclovir *(Famvir)*	500 mg PO TID for 7 days	
Valacyclovir *(Valtrex)*	1 gram PO TID for 7 days	A cluster of fluid-filled blisters, often in a band around one side of the waist or on one side of the forehead, or around an eye or on the neck (less commonly anywhere else on the body).

Cytomegalovirus

Cytomegalovirus (CMV) is a double-stranded DNA virus within the herpes virus family (HHV-5). It occurs in advanced immunocompromised states (e.g., HIV/AIDS, transplant recipients) and most commonly causes retinitis, colitis or esophagitis. Ganciclovir and valganciclovir are the treatments of choice for CMV disease. Foscarnet and cidofovir should be reserved for refractory cases of CMV infection, treatment limiting toxicities due to ganciclovir, and/or when the CMV strain is found to be resistant to (val)ganciclovir. Secondary prophylaxis (also called maintenance) is necessary in some patients (e.g., HIV patients with CMV retinitis and CD4+ counts < 50 cells/mm^3); valganciclovir is preferred.

DRUG	DOSING	SAFETY/SIDE EFFECTS/MONITORING
Ganciclovir *(Cytovene* injection, *Zirgan* ophthalmic gel)	Treatment: 5 mg/kg IV BID Maintenance/secondary prophylaxis: 5 mg/kg IV daily ↓ dose and extend interval when CrCl < 70 mL/min Prepare in sterile water, not bacteriostatic (ganciclovir) Hazardous agents: special handling required	**BOXED WARNINGS** Myelosuppression; carcinogenic and teratogenic effects and inhibition of spermatogenesis in animals **SIDE EFFECTS** Fever, N/V/D, anorexia, thrombocytopenia, neutropenia, leukopenia, anemia, ↑ SCr, seizures (rare), retinal detachment (valganciclovir) **MONITORING** CBC with differential, PLT, SCr, retinal exam (valganciclovir) **NOTES** Patients of reproductive potential: females should use contraception during treatment and for 30 days after, males for 90 days Safety issue – see Pregnancy chapter (valganciclovir) IV ganciclovir 5 mg/kg = PO valganciclovir 900 mg Ganciclovir and valganciclovir are the drugs of choice for CMV disease
ValGANciclovir *(Valcyte)* Tablet, suspension Prodrug of ganciclovir with better bioavailability than oral ganciclovir.	Treatment: 900 mg PO BID x21 days Maintenance/secondary prophylaxis: 900 mg PO daily ↓ dose and extend interval when CrCl < 60 mL/min Hazardous agents: special handling required Suspension: refrigerate Discard after 49 days.	
Cidofovir *(Vistide)* Injection CMV retinitis in HIV patients only	5 mg/kg/wk IV x 2 weeks, then 5 mg/kg once every 2 weeks Hazardous agent: special handling required Renal impairment: ↓ dose or discontinue based on level of SCr increase (also see Contraindications)	**BOXED WARNINGS** Dose-dependent nephropathy, neutropenia, carcinogenic/teratogenic **CONTRAINDICATIONS** SCr > 1.5 mg/dL, CrCl ≤ 55 mL/min, urine protein ≥ 100 mg/dL (> 2+ proteinuria), sulfa allergy, use with or within 7 days of other nephrotoxic drugs, direct intraocular injection **SIDE EFFECTS** Similar to ganciclovir with risk of nephrotoxicity; lower risk for myelosuppression, metabolic acidosis **NOTES** Patient should receive hydration before each dose Can decrease tenofovir clearance
Foscarnet *(Foscavir)* Injection CMV retinitis, resistant HSV	Induction: 90 mg/kg IV Q12H or 60 mg/kg Q8H x 2-3 weeks Maintenance: 90-120 mg/kg IV daily Resistant HSV infection: 40 mg/kg Q8-12H x 2-3 weeks Renal impairment: ↓ dose and extend interval	**BOXED WARNINGS** Renal impairment occurs to some degree in majority of patients; seizures due to electrolyte imbalances (some leading to status epilepticus or death) **SIDE EFFECTS** Electrolyte abnormalities (↓ K, ↓ Ca, ↓ Mg, ↓ Phos), ↑ SCr, ↑ BUN **NOTES** Vesicant (central line preferred)

Epstein-Barr Virus

This virus, also called EBV, is a member of the herpes virus family. Infectious EBV is called mononucleosis or "mono" and most people get infected with EBV at some point in their lives. It is transmitted through bodily fluids, primarily saliva, and can spread by kissing, sharing drinks or food, or contact with an object that has been in the mouth of an infected person (e.g., children's toys). Common symptoms are fatigue, fever, sore throat and swollen lymph nodes, and usually resolve in 2 – 4 weeks. No drug treatment or vaccine exists for mononucleosis.

Antiviral Patient Counseling

Oseltamivir *(Tamiflu)*

- Treatment should begin within 2 days of onset of influenza symptoms.
- The most common side effects are nausea and vomiting. Take with or without food. There is less chance of stomach upset if you take it with a light snack, milk, or a meal.
- Patients with the flu, particularly children and adolescents, may be at an ↑ risk of self-injury and confusion shortly after taking this medicine and should be closely monitored for signs of unusual behavior. Contact your healthcare provider immediately if you or your loved ones show any signs of unusual behavior.
- Tell your healthcare provider if you have received the nasally administered influenza virus vaccine during the past two weeks (there is a risk that *Tamiflu* may inhibit replication of the live virus vaccine).

Acyclovir *(Zovirax)*

- This medicine works best when taken at the first sign of an outbreak within the first day.
- The most common side effects are malaise (a generally ill feeling), headache, nausea and diarrhea.
- Take this medication by mouth with or without food, usually 2 to 5 times daily, as directed. The intervals should be evenly spaced.
- Drink plenty of fluids while taking this medication.
- The topical cream may cause temporary burning or stinging.

Valacyclovir (*Valtrex)*

- *Valtrex* is used daily to manage herpes simplex, and when used along with the following safer sex practices can lower the chances of passing genital herpes to your partner.
  - Do not have sexual contact when you have any symptom or outbreak of genital herpes.
  - Use a condom made of latex or polyurethane whenever you have sexual contact.
- This medication does not cure herpes infections (cold sores, chickenpox, shingles, or genital herpes).
- This medication can be taken with or without food. If stomach upset occurs, take with meals.
- Start treatment during prodrome or within 24 hours of the onset of symptoms. This medication is less helpful if you start treatment too late.
- The most common side effects are tiredness and headache. These side effects are usually mild and do not cause patients to stop taking the medication.
- Store suspension in a refrigerator. Discard after 21 days.

Questions

1. A patient is on amphotericin B for treatment of cryptococcal meningitis. Which of the following electrolyte abnormalities need to be monitored during therapy?
   a. Hypocalcemia and hypomagnesemia
   b. Hyponatremia and hypokalemia
   c. Hypernatremia and hyperkalemia
   d. Hypokalemia and hypernatremia
   e. Hypokalemia and hypomagnesemia

2. Which of the following statements is/are correct regarding *Vfend*? (Select **ALL** that apply.)
   a. *Vfend* can cause visual changes and patients should be instructed not to operate heavy machinery while taking the medication.
   b. *Vfend* must be taken on an empty stomach.
   c. *Vfend* oral tablets should not be used in patients with poor renal function.
   d. *Vfend* oral suspension should be refrigerated.
   e. *Vfend* is a preferred agent for *Aspergillosis* infections.

3. An intern in the ED asks about treating genital herpes simplex virus (HSV) and *Valtrex*. Which of the following statements is correct regarding *Valtrex*?
   a. *Valtrex* is a prodrug of acyclovir and can be used as suppressive therapy in patients with HSV.
   b. *Valtrex* is a prodrug of penciclovir and should not be used as suppressive therapy in patients with HSV.
   c. *Valtrex* should only be used for herpes zoster virus.
   d. *Valtrex* needs to be taken with a fatty meal for best absorption.
   e. *Valtrex* is contraindicated in patients with a CrCl < 30 mL/min.

4. A patient has been receiving *Noxafil* suspension for antifungal prophylaxis during cancer chemotherapy treatment. She has a new prescription for *Noxafil* tablets because she experienced nausea with the suspension and her mucositis has improved to the point that she can now swallow a tablet. Which of the following statements is incorrect?
   a. An appropriate maintenance dose for posaconazole tablets is 300 mg PO daily.
   b. An appropriate dose for posaconazole suspension is 200 mg PO TID.
   c. The suspension is better absorbed than the tablets.
   d. Atorvastatin is contraindicated with posaconazole.
   e. Posaconazole suspension should not be refrigerated.

5. The medical resident in the clinic asks the pharmacist for a recommendation for shingles treatment in a 71 year old female. She is 5'3" tall, weighs 118 pounds and has a serum creatinine of 1.0 mg/dL. Which of the following would be an appropriate regimen? (Select ALL that apply).
   a. Famciclovir 500 mg PO TID for 7 days
   b. Acyclovir 800 mg PO 5x daily for 7– 10 days
   c. Valganciclovir 1,000 mg PO TID for 7 days
   d. Acyclovir cream applied 5x daily for 7-10 days
   e. Valacyclovir 500 mg PO TID for 10 days

6. A 56 year old patient with a history of HIV presents with severe esophageal candidiasis where it is hard for him to eat or drink. The pharmacist assesses his home medication and sees he is on darunavir, ritonavir, emtricitabine/tenofovir, ibuprofen as needed for pain, and ferrous sulfate. Which of the following will be the best therapy to treat this patient's severe esophageal candidiasis?
   a. Nystatin
   b. Itraconazole
   c. Micafungin
   d. Clotrimazole
   e. Flucytosine

Answers

1-e, 2-a,b,e, 3-a, 4-c, 5-a,b, 6-c

31

INFECTIOUS DISEASES IV: OPPORTUNISTIC INFECTIONS

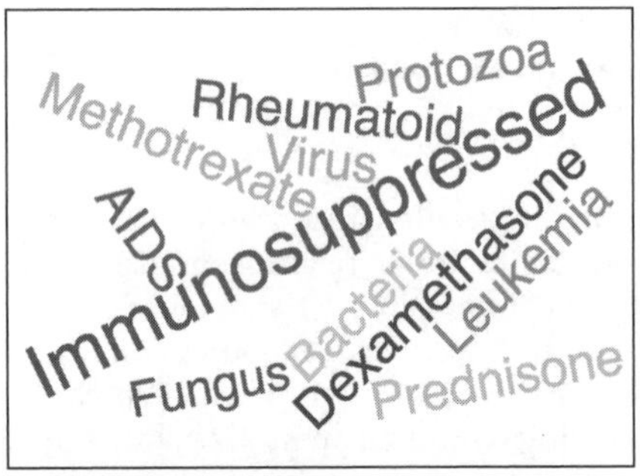

GUIDELINES/REFERENCES

Panel on Opportunistic Infections in HIV-Infected Adults and Adolescents. Guidelines for the Prevention and Treatment of Opportunistic Infections in HIV-Infected Adults and Adolescents: Recommendations from the Centers for Disease Control and Prevention, the National Institutes of Health, and the HIV Medicine Association of the Infectious Diseases Society of America. Available at http://aidsinfo.nih.gov/contentfiles/lvguidelines/adult_oi.pdf. (accessed 2016 August 30).

National Comprehensive Cancer Network (NCCN) Clinical Practice Guidelines in Oncology. Prevention and Treatment of Cancer-Related Infections. Version 2.2016.http://www.nccn.org/professionals/physician_gls/pdf/infections.pdf. (acessed 2016 August 30).

We gratefully acknowledge the assistance of Emi Minejima, PharmD, Assistant Professor, and Annie Wong-Beringer, PharmD, FCCP, FIDSA, Associate Dean and Professor, University of Southern California School of Pharmacy, in preparing this chapter.

BACKGROUND

Immunocompromised patients are predisposed to infections with a variety of pathogens, including bacteria, fungi, viruses and protozoa. These are called opportunistic infections (OIs) because they occur primarily when the immune system is unable to respond in a normal manner. The risk can be related to a disease or to drug treatment that suppresses the immune system. Immunocompromised states include:

- Diseases that destroy key components of the immune response (primarily HIV patients with a CD4+ T lymphocyte count < 200 cells/microliter).
- Use of systemic steroids for 14 days or longer at a prednisone dose (or prednisone equivalent dose) ≥ 20 mg/day or ≥ 2 mg/kg/day.
- Asplenia (lack of a functioning spleen), as with sickle cell disease or following a splenectomy.
- Use of immunosuppressants for autoimmune conditions or transplant (e.g., TNF-alpha inhibitors).
- Use of cancer chemotherapy agents that destroy white blood cells.

PRIMARY PROPHYLAXIS IN PATIENTS WITH MALIGNANCIES

Patients with malignancies undergoing chemotherapy are at high risk for opportunistic infections, which contributes to morbidity and mortality. Severe neutropenia (ANC < 500 cells/microliter) is a major risk factor for the development of infections. Effective strategies to anticipate, prevent, and manage infectious complications can greatly improve outcomes. Without neutrophils, patients are highly susceptible to Gram-negative pathogens, fungal infections, and viral infections.

Antimicrobials are used for the duration of neutropenia to prevent infectious diseases. Antibiotic regimens are chosen based on malignancy type, anticipated duration of neutropenia, and risk for a particular infection. Antibiotic prophylaxis often consists of a quinolone (primarily levofloxacin). Antifungal prophylaxis commonly involves fluconazole or an echinocandin. In higher risk patients where mold/*Mucor* coverage is necessary, amphotericin B, voriconazole or posaconazole may be used. Antivirals targeting HSV and/or VZV are used for patients at intermediate-to-high risk of infection and typical agents include acyclovir, valacyclovir and famciclovir. Patients who develop a fever while neutropenic receive presumptive treatment with specific antimicrobial regimens based on current guidelines.

PRIMARY PROPHYLAXIS IN PATIENTS WITH HIV

HIV-infected patients not taking antiretroviral therapy (ART) are at risk for developing OIs as a result of uncontrolled HIV infection and progressive immunosuppression. Patients are at higher risk for specific OIs as CD4+ counts decline. The table below outlines select OIs, the CD4+ count at which the patient becomes at risk for the infection, and the primary prophylaxis regimen that should be initiated to prevent the first episode of the infection. Oropharyngeal and esophageal *Candida* infections (also called thrush) can occur when the CD4+ count is < 200 cells/mm^3. These infections are generally less severe (low morbidity and mortality) and resolve quickly with fluconazole treatment. No prophylaxis (primary or secondary) is recommended for candidiasis. Note that although the species name of *Pneumocystis* was changed from *carinii* to *jirovecii*, pneumonia caused by this organism is still commonly referred to as PCP (*Pneumocystis* pneumonia), or sometimes PJP.

INFECTION	INDICATION	PRIMARY PROPHYLAXIS REGIMEN	CRITERIA FOR DISCONTINUING PRIMARY PROPHYLAXIS
Pneumocystis pneumonia (PCP)	CD4+ count < 200 cells/mm^3 or oropharyngeal candidiasis or other AIDS-defining illness	Preferred: SMX/TMP DS tab PO daily or SS PO daily Alternative: SMX/TMP DS 3x/week or Dapsone or Dapsone + pyrimethamine + leucovorin or Aerosolized pentamidine or Atovaquone	CD4+ count ≥ 200 cells/mm^3 for > 3 months on ART
Toxoplasma gondii encephalitis	Toxoplasma IgG positive patients with CD4+ count < 100 cells/mm^3	Preferred: SMX/TMP DS tab PO daily Alternative: SMX/TMP DS 3xweek or 1 SS PO daily or (dapsone + pyrimethamine + leucovorin) or (atovaquone alone, or with pyrimethamine + leucovorin)	CD4+ count > 200 cells/mm^3 for > 3 months on ART
Mycobacterium avium complex (MAC) infection	CD4+ count < 50 cells/mm^3 Must rule out active disseminated MAC disease.	Preferred: azithromycin 1,200 mg PO weekly or clarithromycin 500 mg PO BID or azithromycin 600 mg PO twice weekly	CD4+ count > 100 cells/mm^3 for ≥ 3 months on ART

TREATMENT OF OPPORTUNISTIC INFECTIONS

Treatment for each infection remains the same, regardless of the cause of immunosuppression. Newly diagnosed patients with HIV and an OI should be monitored closely for immune reconstitution inflammatory syndrome (IRIS) when antiretroviral therapy (ART) is started (see Human Immunodeficiency Virus chapter). The table below lists select OIs and the recommended agents for treatment. Secondary prophylaxis is given to prevent future episodes/recurrence of the infection, and should be started after completing initial treatment for the infection in patients who continue to be at risk.

Treatment of oropharyngeal candidiasis (thrush) for patients with HIV differs from that in immunocompetent patients. Systemic treatment is preferred first line (rather than localized agents such as miconazole or nystatin) even in mild disease.

INFECTION	PREFERRED REGIMEN	ALTERNATIVE REGIMEN	SECONDARY PROPHYLAXIS
Candidiasis (oropharyngeal/ esophageal)	Fluconazole	Itraconazole, posaconazole	None
Cryptococcal meningitis	Induction: amphotericin B (deoxycholate or liposomal) + flucytosine	Fluconazole ± flucytosine	Fluconazole (low dose)
Cytomegalovirus (CMV)	Valganciclovir Ganciclovir	If toxicities to ganciclovir or resistant strains: Foscarnet, cidofovir	Valganciclovir
Mycobacterium avium complex infection	(Clarithromycin or azithromycin) + ethambutol	Add a 3rd or 4th agent using rifabutin, amikacin or streptomycin, moxifloxacin or levofloxacin	Same as treatment regimens
Pneumocystis pneumonia (PCP)	SMX/TMP ± prednisone or methylprednisolone Duration: 21 days	Atovaquone or (clindamycin + primaquine) or pentamidine IV or (dapsone + trimethoprim)*	SMX/TMP or dapsone or (dapsone + pyrimethamine + leucovorin**) or atovaquone or inhaled pentamidine
Toxoplasmosis gondii encephalitis	Pyrimethamine + leucovorin** ± sulfadiazine	SMX/TMP, (pyrimethamine + leucovorin**) + (either clindamycin or azithromycin) or (atovaquone alone, or with sulfadiazine or with pyrimethamine + leucovorin**)	Same agents at reduced dosed

* *Selection of alternative therapy for PCP depends on severity of illness and patient specific factors (allergies and G6PD deficiency). For example, atovaquone, clindamycin + primaquine or pentamidine are all potential options in the setting of sulfa allergy; however, only atovaquone (mild-to-moderate disease) and pentamidine (moderate-severe disease) are available options in the setting of G6PD deficiency.*

** *Leucovorin added as rescue therapy to reduce risk for myelosuppression associated with pyrimethamine.*

Questions

Questions refer to the following case:

RY is a 24 year old male with AIDS who presents to the HIV clinic for a routine follow-up visit. He states that he was unable to pick up his prescriptions and hasn't taken his antiretroviral therapy for the past 4 months. His CD4+ count is found to be 94 cells/mm^3.

1. Prophylaxis for which opportunistic infection/s should be initiated in RY? (Select **ALL** that apply.)
   a. *Toxoplasmosis* only
   b. *Pneumocystis* pneumonia, *Toxoplasmosis* and *Mycobacterium avium* complex
   c. *Pneumocystis* pneumonia and *Toxoplasmosis*
   d. *Mycobacterium avium* complex only
   e. *Toxoplasmosis* and *Mycobacterium avium* complex

2. Choose the statement/s that are true regarding the prophylaxis regimen that should be started for RY: (Select **ALL** that apply.)
   a. SMX/TMP DS PO daily will cover both *Pneumocystis* pneumonia and *Toxoplasmosis*
   b. SMX/TMP DS PO daily is the preferred regimen
   c. Dapsone could be used in place of SMX/TMP if the patient had G6PD deficiency
   d. Azithromycin should be dosed at 600 mg PO daily
   e. Prophylaxis should continue until the CD4 count is > 200 cells/mm^3

Answers

1-c, 2-a,b,e

32

HUMAN IMMUNODEFICIENCY VIRUS

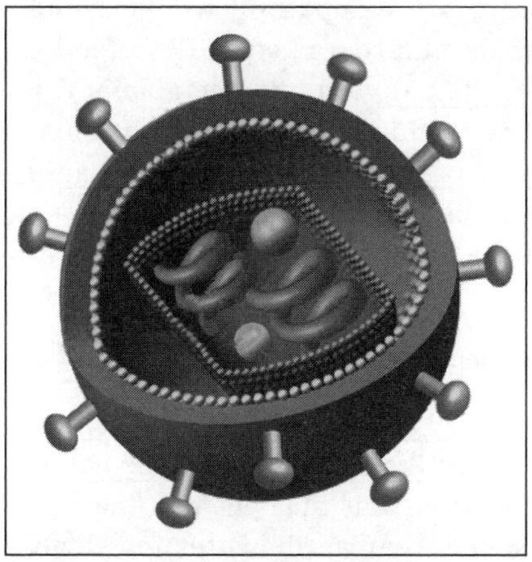

We gratefully acknowledge the assistance of Taylor K. Gill, PharmD, BCPS, AAHIVP, Clinical Education and Development Coordinator, Via Christi Hospitals Wichita, in preparing this chapter.

BACKGROUND

The first cases of Human Immunodeficiency Virus (HIV)/Acquired Immunodeficiency Syndrome (AIDS) were reported in 1981. The Centers for Disease Control and Prevention now estimates that there are more than 1.2 million people in the United States living with HIV infection, and about 1 out of every 8 persons is unaware that they are infected. HIV is a single-stranded RNA retrovirus that attacks the immune system, mainly the CD4+ T-helper cells, causing a progressive decrease in CD4+ T cell count. Once CD4+ counts fall below 200 cells/mm^3, the person becomes more susceptible to opportunistic infections (OIs) and certain malignancies due to the loss of cell-mediated immunity. HIV has two viral subtypes, HIV-1 and HIV-2. Found primarily in South African countries, HIV-2 is a more virulent virus that is more difficult to treat. HIV-1 is the predominant subtype in the United States and will be referred to as simply "HIV" throughout the course book.

GUIDELINES/REFERENCES

Panel on Antiretroviral Guidelines for Adults and Adolescents. Guidelines for the use of antiretroviral agents in HIV-1-infected adults and adolescents. Department of Health and Human Services. Available at: http://aidsinfo.nih.gov/contentfiles/lvguidelines/adultandadolescentgl.pdf. Accessed 2016 Sept 29.

Panel on treatment of HIV-infected pregnant women and prevention of perinatal transmission. Recommendations for use of antiretroviral drugs in pregnant HIV-1-infected women for maternal health and interventions to reduce perinatal HIV transmission in the United States. Available at: http://aidsinfo.nih.gov/contentfiles/lvguidelines/perinatalgl.pdf. Accessed 2016 Sept 29.

Panel on opportunistic infections in HIV-infected adults and adolescents. Guidelines for the prevention and treatment of opportunistic infections in HIV-infected adults and adolescents: recommendations from the Centers for Disease Control and Prevention, the National Institutes of Health, and the HIV Medicine Association of the Infectious Diseases Society of America. Available at: http://aidsinfo.nih.gov/contentfiles/lvguidelines/adult_oi.pdf. Accessed 2016 Sept 29.

Additional guidelines included with the online course.

TRANSMISSION

HIV can be spread through infected blood, semen, and vaginal secretions. Unprotected intercourse and sharing needles with HIV-infected individuals are the two most common means of HIV transmission. Transmission via sexual exposure may be facilitated through the presence of sores or cuts in the vagina, penis, rectum, or mouth. Vertical transmission (from mother to child) may also occur, either during pregnancy, at birth, or through breastfeeding.

SCREENING AND DIAGNOSIS

The CDC recommends routine HIV screening for patients aged 13 – 64 years old in all healthcare settings (unless the patient declines testing). Additionally, pregnant women and patients initiating treatment for tuberculosis or sexually transmitted infections should also be tested for HIV. Persons at high risk for HIV (e.g., injection drug users, persons with high-risk sexual behaviors) should be tested for HIV at least annually.

An acute HIV infection is characterized by an initial burst of viremia (virus in the blood) immediately following infection. Persons with acute HIV infection may experience non-specific flu-like symptoms, such as fever, fatigue/malaise, myalgias/arthralgias, lymphadenopathy (swollen lymph nodes), and rash. Many persons may not recognize that they have developed an acute HIV infection since symptoms, if present, are self-limiting. Anti-HIV antibodies (HIV Ab) are undetectable at this time, however, HIV RNA and HIV p24 antigen will be present. Following this acute phase of the infection, the HIV Ab test will usually become positive about 4 – 8 weeks after contracting the disease; for some individuals, it may take up to 3 – 6 months for HIV Ab to be detected. Recent infection is generally considered the phase up to 6 months after the onset of the infection during which HIV Ab are detectable.

As of June 2014, the CDC recommends the following HIV testing algorithm:

- Perform initial HIV screening using a FDA-approved combination HIV Ab and HIV p24 antigen immunoassay test. This test detects HIV antigens in addition to HIV antibodies. HIV antigens can be detected earlier than HIV antibodies, typically at 2 weeks post infection, thus the benefit of the combination HIV Ab/antigen test is that it can detect HIV infection sooner than antibody testing alone.
- If the initial screening test is reactive (positive), perform confirmatory testing with an HIV-1/HIV-2 antibody differentiation immunoassay test. This test serves two purposes: it serves as a confirmation of the positive screening test and it determines whether a patient has HIV-1 or HIV-2.
- If the initial test is reactive (positive), but the secondary test is non-reactive (negative) or indeterminate, then a third test should be conducted (the HIV nucleic acid test).

If this algorithm cannot be implemented, the recommendations provide alternative testing guidance, which includes using the HIV immunoassay screening test [also referred to as HIV ELISA (enzyme-linked immunosorbent assay)] as an initial screening. This tests only for the presence of HIV Ab in a person's blood sample. Alternative confirmatory tests include the HIV RNA viral load and the Western Blot. Regardless of the test used, a positive HIV screening test may not always represent true infection (due to rare chance of false-positive tests) and therefore all positive screening tests must be followed by a supplemental confirmatory test. Diagnosis of HIV is confirmed when both the HIV immunoassay screening and supplemental confirmatory tests are positive.

Over-the-Counter HIV Testing

There are 2 over-the-counter HIV tests patients can do at home. The *Home Access Express HIV Test System* is a blood test where the patient collects the sample of blood from a fingerstick, ships the sample in a pre-paid overnight envelope, and obtains results the next day (excluding weekends and holidays). The *OraQuick In-Home HIV Test* is an oral swab test where results are obtained in 20 – 40 minutes. Individuals with a positive OTC HIV home test result must follow-up with their healthcare provider for a confirmatory HIV laboratory-based test. These are HIV Ab screening tests, meaning they can detect the presence of HIV Ab which may take up to 6 months after onset of infection to develop.

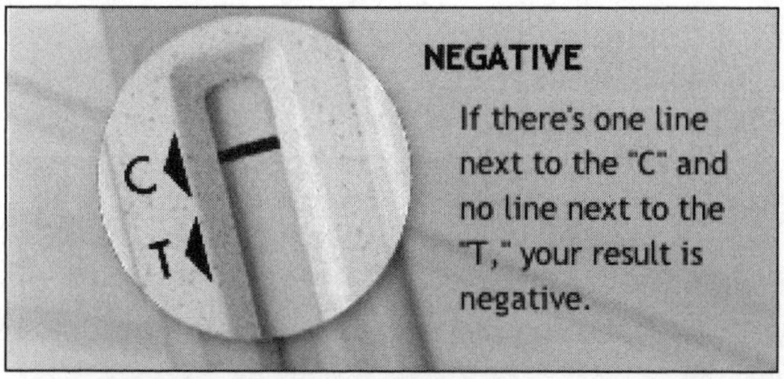
NEGATIVE
If there's one line next to the "C" and no line next to the "T," your result is negative.
C
T

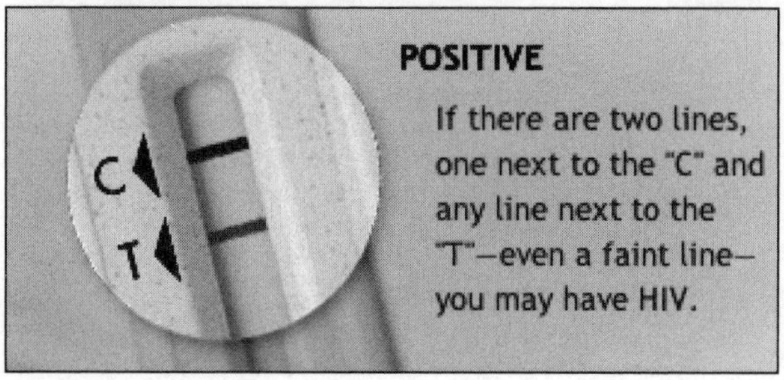
POSITIVE
If there are two lines, one next to the "C" and any line next to the "T"—even a faint line— you may have HIV.
C
T

http://www.oraquick.com/Taking-the-Test/ Understanding-Your-Results

The tests should be used ≥ 3 months from the possible exposure; testing sooner than 3 months can lead to a false negative result.

USE OF THE *ORAQUICK* IN-HOME HIV TEST

- Do not eat, drink, or use oral care products at least 30 minutes before taking the test. Remove dental products such as dentures that cover your gums.
- Tear open the packet labeled "Test Tube". There is liquid in this tube so be careful upon opening not to spill the liquid. Pop off the cap, do not twist.
- Open the packet labeled "Test Stick". Do not touch the pad with your fingers. Gently swipe the pad along your upper gums once and your lower gums once. You may use either side on the flat pad. Make sure you swipe each gum only once or your results could be wrong (do not swab the roof of the mouth, inside of the cheek, or the tongue).
- Insert the test stick into the test tube which contains liquid at the bottom. Write down your start time. Then add 20 minutes and write down this number, which is your read time.
- Read the results after 20 minutes but not later than 40 minutes. Do not remove the test stick from the liquid while the test is running.
- Refer to picture for interpretation. The test is considered invalid if no line appears next to "C" or no lines appear at all.

INITIAL EVALUATION AND MONITORING

After the diagnosis is made, the following laboratory parameters are recommended for all HIV-infected individuals:

- CD4+ count – quantifies the CD4+ cells in the blood. It is the major laboratory indicator of immune function and serves as a key factor in determining the need for opportunistic infection (OI) prophylaxis. CD4+ counts should be measured at baseline, every 3 – 6 months and any time clinical failure is suspected. The treatment goal is a normal CD4+ count (800 – 1200 cells/mm^3).
- HIV viral load – quantifies the copies of HIV RNA in the blood. It is the most important indicator of response to antiretroviral therapy (ART) and is used to assess for possible problems with medication adherence or drug resistance. HIV viral load should be measured at baseline, 2 – 8 weeks post ART initiation or modification, then every 3 – 6 months thereafter. The treatment goal is to have an undetectable HIV viral load.
- Drug resistance testing – genotypic testing that determines the specific genetic mutations of the virus and reports susceptibility information for individual antiretroviral medications. Measured at entry to care, at ART initiation or modification, or if treatment failure is suspected.
- Comprehensive metabolic panel (includes SCr, glucose, LFTs), CBC with differential, lipid panel and urinary analysis prior to ART initiation or medication and every 6 – 12 months thereafter.
- Hepatitis B and C testing – perform at baseline.
- Pregnancy testing – perform at baseline.
- Drug specific testing when required – HLA-B*5701 for abacavir and tropism testing for maraviroc.

HIV Replication Cycle Stages and the Antiretrovirals Site of Action

It is very important to understand the steps (or stages) involved in HIV viral replication and know where each drug class works. See following description and diagram.

STAGE	DESCRIPTION OF STAGE	DRUG CLASS TARGETING THIS STAGE
Stage 1: Binding/Attachment	HIV attaches to a CD4 receptor and the co-receptors (CCR5 and/or CXCR4) on the surface of the CD4+ host cell. The virus must bind/attach to both a CD4 receptor and a co-receptor in order for the next step of viral replication to occur.	CCR5 Antagonist (blocks only the CCR5 co-receptor but not the CXCR4 co-receptor)
Stage 2: Fusion	Fusion of the HIV viral envelope with the CD4+ host cell membrane allows HIV to enter the host cell, where uncoating of the virus releases HIV RNA and viral proteins and enzymes needed for HIV replication into the host cell's cytoplasm.	Fusion Inhibitors
Stage 3: Reverse Transcription	Once inside the cell, single-stranded HIV RNA is converted to double-stranded HIV DNA by reverse transcriptase.	Nucleoside/Nucleotide Reverse Transcriptase Inhibitors (NRTIs) and Non-Nucleoside Reverse Transcriptase Inhibitors (NNRTIs)
Stage 4: Integration	HIV DNA is transported across the host cell nuclear membrane and is integrated into the host cell's DNA.	Integrase Strand Transfer Inhibitors (INSTIs)
Stage 5: Transcription and Translation	HIV DNA is transcribed and translated into new HIV RNA as well as new viral proteins (envelope proteins and non-functional long-chain proteins).	
Stage 6: Assembly	New HIV RNA, viral envelope proteins, and non-functional long-chain viral proteins migrate to the host cell surface to begin forming new, immature HIV virus. Protease enzyme is also incorporated into this newly forming HIV virus.	
Stage 7: Budding and Maturation	Newly formed, immature HIV virus buds off from the host cell. During the maturation process, protease cleaves the long-chain viral proteins into smaller, functional viral proteins and enzymes. The mature HIV virus is now able to move on to infect other CD4+ host cells.	Protease Inhibitors (PIs)

ANTIRETROVIRAL THERAPY

Treatment for HIV requires combination antiretroviral therapy (ART). ART has dramatically reduced HIV-associated morbidity and mortality and, although not curative, has transformed HIV disease into a chronic, manageable condition. Without treatment, the vast majority of HIV-infected individuals will eventually develop progressive immunosuppression (as evident by low CD4+ count), leading to OIs and premature death. The primary goals of ART are to restore and preserve the immune system, suppress HIV viral load to undetectable levels, reduce HIV-associated morbidity, prolong survival and prevent HIV transmission.

ART is recommended in all HIV-infected individuals to reduce risk of disease progression and, in combination with safer sex/behavior risk reduction practices, to prevent transmission of HIV to non-HIV-infected individuals. On a case-by-case basis, ART may be deferred due to clinical and/or psychosocial factors, but therapy should be initiated

HIV Life Cycle

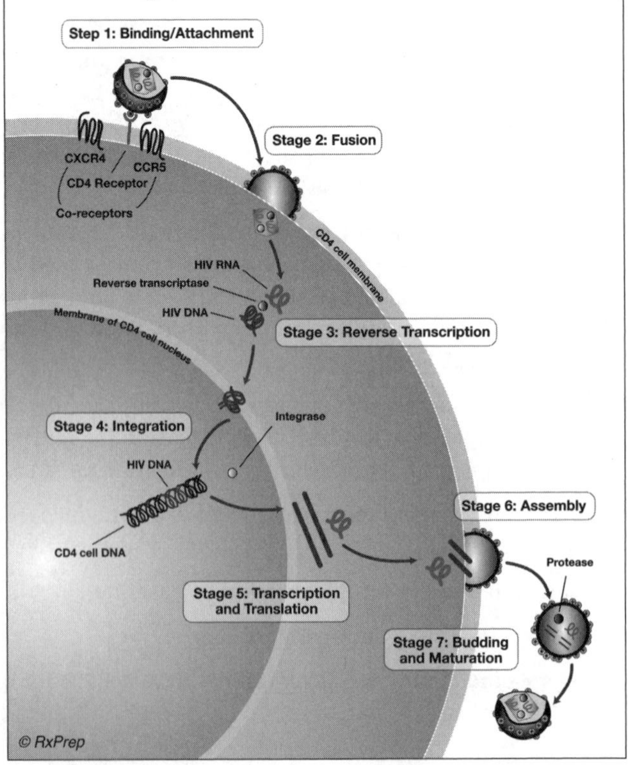

as soon as is feasible. Patients starting ART should be willing and able to commit to treatment and understand the benefits and risks of therapy and the importance of adherence. Patients need to be advised that they need to have an adherence rate of 95% or higher in order for their ART regimen to be effective long-term. An example of 95% or higher adherence is no more than 1 missed dose per month for a patient who is taking a once daily regimen.

Recommended Regimens For Antiretroviral-Naïve HIV Infected Patients

Selection of an ART regimen should be individualized based on efficacy, toxicity, pill burden, dosing frequency, drug interaction potential, resistance test results, and comorbid conditions. Listed below are the currently recommended initial ART regimen options for treatment-naive patients. Recommended regimens have optimal and durable efficacy, favorable tolerability and toxicity profile and ease of use. These regimens are listed in alphabetical order, not by order of preference. [Note: HIV treatment guidelines are updated frequently. Check for guideline updates at: http://aidsinfo.nih.gov]

REGIMENS	COMMENTS
INSTI-BASED REGIMEN Dolutegravir/abacavir/lamivudine	Abacavir should not be used in patients who test positive for HLA-B*5701
Dolutegravir + emtricitabine/tenofovir disoproxil fumarate	Tenofovir disoproxil fumarate should be used with caution in patients with renal insufficiency
Elvitegravir/cobicistat/emtricitabine/tenofovir disoproxil fumarate	Elvitegravir/cobicistat/emtricitabine/tenofovir disoproxil fumarate *(Stribild)* should only be initiated in patients with baseline CrCl ≥ 70 mL/min
Elvitegravir/cobicistat/emtricitabine/tenofovir alafenamide	
Raltegravir + emtricitabine/tenofovir disoproxil fumarate	Elvitegravir/cobicistat/emtricitabine/tenofovir alafenamide *(Genvoya)* should only be initiated in patients with baseline CrCl ≥ 30 mL/min
PI-BASED REGIMEN Darunavir + ritonavir + emtricitabine/tenofovir disoproxil fumarate	Lamivudine and emtricitabine are interchangeable

See table of combination products near the end of the chapter

Recommended Regimens for Antiretroviral-Naïve HIV Infected Pregnant Women

Regimen should include 2 NRTIs plus either a boosted-PI or INSTI. Preferred drugs are listed below. Choose one line from the first column, then add one line from the second or third column.

NRTI COMBINATIONS	PI	INSTI
Abacavir/lamivudine	Atazanavir + ritonavir	Raltegravir
Tenofovir disoproxil fumarate/emtricitabine (or lamivudine)	Darunavir + ritonavir (BID regimen only)	

If an HIV infected woman becomes pregnant while on effective ART, then the effective ART regimen should be continued.

NUCLEOSIDE/NUCLEOTIDE REVERSE TRANSCRIPTASE INHIBITORS

Nucleoside/nucleotide reverse transcriptase inhibitors (NRTIs) are structurally similar to naturally occurring nucleosides/nucleotides needed to synthesize viral DNA. NRTIs work by competitively binding to the enzyme reverse transcriptase, blocking HIV viral RNA-dependent DNA polymerase. This results in DNA

KEY FEATURES OF NRTIs

- Renal dose adjustment required (except abacavir)
- No CYP450 drug interactions
- Take without regards to meals (except didanosine)
- Boxed Warning: lactic acidosis and hepatomegaly with steatosis (zidovudine, stavudine, didanosine > other NRTIs)
- Abacavir – hypersensitivity reactions; test for HLA-B*5701
- Tenofovir toxicities – nephrotoxicity, osteoporosis, Fanconi syndrome. Thought to be ↓ with tenofovir alafenamide

chain termination and stops further viral DNA synthesis (see Stage #3 in the HIV life cycle diagram). All NRTIs have a boxed warning for lactic acidosis and severe hepatomegaly with steatosis, sometimes fatal (especially didanosine, stavudine and zidovudine). If a patient is suspected to have lactic acidosis or hepatotoxicity, a healthcare provider should be contacted for recommendations and the NRTI-containing regimen should be stopped.

DRUG	DOSING	SAFETY/SIDE EFFECTS/MONITORING
Abacavir, ABC ***(Ziagen)*** Tablet, oral solution (20 mg/mL) **+ lamivudine *(Epzicom)*** **+ lamivudine and dolutegravir *(Triumeq)*** + lamivudine and zidovudine *(Trizivir)*	300 mg BID or 600 mg daily No renal dose adjustments required *Epzicom:* 1 tab daily *Triumeq:* 1 tab daily and keep in the original container *Trizivir:* 1 tab BID All formulations: take without regards to food	**BOXED WARNINGS** Screen for the HLA-B*5701 allele before starting abacavir therapy – if positive, use is contraindicated due to ↑ risk for hypersensitivity reactions. Record as abacavir allergy in patient record and do not use. Serious, sometimes fatal, hypersensitivity reactions – fever, rash, fatigue, malaise, GI symptoms (N/V/D, abdominal pain), and/or respiratory symptoms (dyspnea, cough); discontinue drug and do not re-challenge regardless of HLA-B*5701 status. **CONTRAINDICATIONS** Previous hypersensitivity to abacavir, moderate to severe hepatic impairment **WARNINGS** Caution in CVD due to possible ↑ risk of MI **SIDE EFFECTS** N/V, HA, rash, ↑ LFTs, hyperlipidemia **MONITORING** LFTs, s/sx of hypersensitivity **NOTES** Caution with alcohol (↑ abacavir AUC) MedGuide and warning card (summarizing symptoms of hypersensitivity) required Abacavir/lamivudine with either efavirenz or atazanavir + ritonavir should not be used in patients with pre-treatment HIV viral load > 100,000 copies/mL
LamiVUDine, 3TC ***(Epivir)*** Tablet, oral solution (10 mg/mL) + zidovudine *(Combivir)* **+ abacavir *(Epzicom)*** + abacavir and zidovudine *(Trizivir)* **+ abacavir and dolutegravir *(Triumeq)***	150 mg BID or 300 mg daily CrCl < 50 mL/min: ↓ dose 1 tab daily for *Epzicom* and *Triumeq* 1 tab BID for *Combivir* and *Trizivir* Take without regards to food *Triumeq:* keep in original container	**BOXED WARNINGS** Do not use *Epivir-HBV* for treatment of HIV (contains lower dose of lamivudine); can result in HIV resistance Severe acute exacerbation of hepatitis B (HBV) can occur when drug is discontinued in patients with HBV infection **SIDE EFFECTS** HA, N/V/D, fatigue, insomnia, myalgias, ↑ LFTs **MONITORING** LFTs, renal function, HBV status prior to initiation **NOTES** Avoid combining with emtricitabine; antagonistic interaction as both are cytosine analogs: FTC and 3TC) Has activity against HBV. In HIV/HBV co-infection, must dose lamivudine at the higher, HIV treatment dose; use correct dosage strength/product *(Epivir* is not equivalent to *Epivir-HBV)*

Nucleoside Reverse Transcriptase Inhibitors (NRTIs) Continued

DRUG	DOSING	SAFETY/SIDE EFFECTS/MONITORING
Emtricitabine, FTC ***(Emtriva)*** Capsule, oral solution (10 mg/mL) **+ tenofovir disoproxil fumarate *(Truvada)*** **+ tenofovir alafenamide *(Descovy)*** **+ tenofovir disoproxil fumarate and rilpivirine *(Complera)*** **+ tenofovir alafenamide and rilpivirine *(Odefsey)*** **+ tenofovir disoproxil fumarate and elvitegravir and cobicistat *(Stribild)*** **+ tenofovir alafenamide and elvitegravir and cobicistat *(Genvoya)*** **+ efavirenz and tenofovir disoproxil fumarate *(Atripla)***	Cap: 200 mg daily Soln: 240 mg daily (refrigerate; stable for 3 months at room temp) Take without regards to food CrCl < 50 mL/min: ↓ dose or frequency 1 tab daily for *Truvada, Atripla, Complera, Stribild, Descovy, Odefsey* and *Genvoya* Take *Truvada* and *Descovy* without regards to food Take *Atripla* on an empty stomach, preferably at bedtime Take *Complera, Stribilld, Odefsey* and *Genvoya* with food	**BOXED WARNINGS** Severe acute exacerbation of hepatitis B (HBV) can occur when drug is discontinued in patients with HBV infection **SIDE EFFECTS** N/V/D, rash, dizziness, HA, insomnia, hyperpigmentation primarily of palms and/or soles (mainly in children), ↑ CPK, ↑ LFTs **MONITORING** LFTs, renal function, HBV status prior to initiation **NOTES** Avoid combining with lamivudine; antagonistic interaction as both are cytosine analogs: FTC and 3TC Capsule and oral solution are not bioequivalent *Truvada, Atripla, Complera, Stribild, Descovy, Odefsey, Genvoya:* keep in original container (contains desiccant to protect from moisture) MedGuide required *(Truvada)*

Nucleoside Reverse Transcriptase Inhibitors (NRTIs) Continued

DRUG	DOSING	SAFETY/SIDE EFFECTS/MONITORING
Tenofovir disoproxil fumarate, TDF ***(Viread)*** Tablet, oral powder (40 mg/g) **+ emtricitabine *(Truvada)*** **+ emtricitabine and efavirenz *(Atripla)*** **+ emtricitabine and elvitegravir and cobicistat *(Stribild)*** **+ emtricitabine and rilpivirine *(Complera)*** **Tenofovir alafenamide** (TAF) Tablet **+ emtricitabine *(Descovy)*** **+ emtricitabine and elvitegravir and cobicistat *(Genvoya)*** **+ emtricitabine and rilpivirine *(Odefsey)*** *Vemlidy* for hepatitis B	300 mg daily CrCl < 50 mL/min: ↓ frequency 1 tab daily for *Truvada, Atripla, Complera, Stribild* and *Genvoya* Take *Viread* tablets and *Truvada* without regards to food Take *Atripla* on an empty stomach, preferably at bedtime Take *Complera* and *Stribild* with food Dispense in original container 25 mg in *Descovy* and *Odefsey* 10 mg in *Genvoya* Take *Genvoya* and *Odefsey* with a meal Take *Descovy* without regards to food	**BOXED WARNINGS** Tenofovir alafenamide combination products *(Descovy, Genvoya, Odefsey)*: not approved for the treatment of chronic hepatitis B virus (HBV) infection and safety and efficacy have not been established for patients co-infected with HIV and HBV All tenofovir-containing products *(Truvada, Atripla, Complera, Stribild, Descovy, Genvoya, Odefsey, Vemlidy)*: Severe acute exacerbation of hepatitis B (HBV) can occur when drug is discontinued in patients with HBV infection **WARNINGS** Renal toxicity including acute renal failure and/or Fanconi syndrome, osteomalacia and ↓ bone mineral density **SIDE EFFECTS** Tenofovir disoproxil-containing products: N/V/D, HA, depression, renal impairment, ↓ bone mineral density, ↑ LFTs, ↑ CPK Tenofovir alafenamide-containing products: nausea, ↓ bone mineral density HA, fatigue *(Genvoya)* **MONITORING** LFTs, CBC, renal function, CPK, urinalysis, Ca, PO4, bone density (long-term), HBV status prior to initiation **NOTES** Avoid use with didanosine due to resistance and virologic failure as well as ↑ didanosine concentration Consider vitamin D and calcium supplementation **Tenofovir disoproxil fumarate** Approved for treatment of chronic HBV (same treatment dose as HIV infection) Powder should be mixed with 2-4 oz of soft food (applesauce, yogurt) to avoid bitter taste. Do not mix powder with liquid MedGuide required *(Truvada)* **Tenofovir alafenamide** This new form of tenofovir achieves higher intracellular concentrations with lower blood levels, resulting in presumably lower rates of renal and bone toxicity compared to tenofovir disoproxil fumarate Not available as an individual agent, only in combination

Nucleoside Reverse Transcriptase Inhibitors (NRTIs) Continued

DRUG	DOSING	SAFETY/SIDE EFFECTS/MONITORING
Zidovudine, ZDV or AZT *(Retrovir)* Capsule, tablet, oral solution (10 mg/mL), injection + lamivudine *(Combivir)* + abacavir and lamivudine *(Trizivir)*	PO: 300 mg BID IV: 1 mg/kg Q4H CrCl < 15 mL/min: ↓ dose and/or change frequency 1 tab BID for *Combivir* and *Trizivir* Take without regards to food (although generally better tolerated when taken with food)	**BOXED WARNINGS** Hematologic toxicities (neutropenia and anemia) especially in advanced HIV Prolonged use has been associated with symptomatic myopathy and myositis **SIDE EFFECTS** N/V, anorexia, HA, malaise, insomnia, skin/nail hyperpigmentation (blue), myopathy, macrocytic anemia, lipoatrophy, ↑ LFTs, insulin resistance/diabetes, hyperlipidemia **MONITORING** CBC, LFTs, lipids, blood glucose, MCV (if the MCV is not elevated, there is likely an adherence problem) **NOTES** Avoid combining with stavudine; antagonist interaction as both are thymidine analogs: d4T and AZT Erythropoietin is indicated to manage zidovudine-induced anemia Lipoatrophy: stavudine > zidovudine > other NRTIs IV zidovudine should be administered in the setting of labor for HIV-infected pregnant women, with HIV viral load > 1,000 copies/mL (or unknown HIV viral load)
Stavudine, d4T *(Zerit)* Capsule, oral solution (1 mg/mL)	≥ 60 kg: 40 mg Q12H < 60 kg: 30 mg Q12H CrCl ≤ 50 mL/min: ↓ dose and/or frequency Oral soln: stable for 30 days in refrigerator. Shake vigorously before use Take without regards to food	**BOXED WARNINGS** Pancreatitis (sometimes fatal) has occurred during combination therapy with didanosine **WARNINGS** Neurologic symptoms including motor weakness (mimics Guillian-Barrè syndrome) and hepatotoxicity **SIDE EFFECTS** HA, N/V/D, peripheral neuropathy (can be irreversible), ↑ LFTs, hyperbilirubinemia, lipoatrophy, pancreatitis, insulin resistance/diabetes, hyperlipidemia **MONITORING** LFTs, renal function, s/sx of peripheral neuropathy, lipids **NOTES** Avoid stavudine and didanosine combination due to ↑ risk of peripheral neuropathy, pancreatitis, and lactic acidosis Do not combine with zidovudine; antagonist interaction as both are thymidine analogs: d4T and AZT Lipoatrophy: stavudine > zidovudine > other NRTIs MedGuide required

Nucleoside Reverse Transcriptase Inhibitors (NRTIs) Continued

DRUG	DOSING	SAFETY/SIDE EFFECTS/MONITORING
Didanosine, ddI *(Videx, Videx EC)* Capsule, solution (10 mg/mL)	≥ 60 kg: 400 mg daily < 60 kg: 250 mg daily Take on an empty stomach (at least 30 minutes before or 2 hours after a meal) CrCl < 60 mL/min: ↓ dose Oral soln: stable for 30 days if refrigerated	**BOXED WARNING** Pancreatitis (sometimes fatal) **CONTRAINDICATIONS** Concurrent use with allopurinol or ribavirin **WARNINGS** Noncirrhotic portal hypertension, retinal changes and optic neuritis **SIDE EFFECTS** N/V/D, peripheral neuropathy (potentially irreversible), ↑ amylase, ↑ LFTs, rash **MONITORING** LFTs, eye exam, CBC, blood chemistry, renal function, amylase and lipase (with pancreatitis) **NOTES** Avoid didanosine and stavudine combination due to ↑ risk of pancreatitis, peripheral neuropathy, and lactic acidosis Avoid use with tenofovir due to resistance and virologic failure as well as ↑ didanosine concentrations MedGuide required

NRTI Drug Interactions

NRTIs do not undergo hepatic transformations via the CYP metabolic pathway, therefore, they have fewer significant drug interactions compared to PIs and NNRTIs. Some NRTIs have other mechanisms of drug interactions (e.g., P-glycoprotein, overlapping toxicities). Here are a few notable drug interactions:

- Avoid concurrent use of ribavirin with didanosine (↑ risk of liver failure, pancreatitis), and ribavirin with zidovudine (significantly ↑ risk and severity of anemia).
- Avoid didanosine (ddI) and stavudine (d4T) combination due to ↑ risk of peripheral neuropathy, pancreatitis, and lactic acidosis.
- Avoid didanosine and tenofovir combination due to resistance and virologic failure as well as increased didanosine concentration.
- Allopurinol can ↑ didanosine levels; contraindicated.
- Avoid emtricitabine and lamivudine combination (antagonistic interaction as both are cytosine analogs: FTC and 3TC).
- Avoid zidovudine and stavudine (antagonistic interaction as both are thymidine analogs: d4T and AZT).
- Methadone can ↑ zidovudine levels; monitor for zidovudine toxicity.
- Caution when using sofosbuvir/ledipasvir with *Stribild* due to ↑ tenofovir disoproxil fumarate levels; monitor renal function closely.
- Tenofovir alafenamide is a P-gp substrate; avoid rifampin and St. John's wort with *Descovy, Genvoya* and *Odefsey*.

NON-NUCLEOSIDE REVERSE TRANSCRIPTASE INHIBITORS

Non-nucleoside reverse transcriptase inhibitors (NNRTIs) work by non-competitive binding to reverse transcriptase and blocking the RNA-dependent and DNA-dependent DNA polymerase activities including HIV replication (see Stage #3 in the HIV life cycle diagram). None of the currently recommended ART regimens for treatment-naive patients with HIV contain an NNRTI.

KEY FEATURES OF NNRTIs

No renal dose adjustment needed (avoid *Atripla* and *Complera* if CrCl < 50 mL/min)

Primarily CYP450 inducers (exceptions: delavirdine is an inhibitor, efavirenz is an inducer > inhibitor, rilpivirine is a substrate)

Hepatotoxicity and rash, including SJS/TEN (nevirapine > other NNRTIs)

- Monitor for erythema, facial edema, skin necrosis, blisters and tongue swelling

Food requirements:
- With food – etravirine, rilpivirine
- Without food – efavirenz

Efavirenz – CNS effects; ↓ by giving at bedtime on an empty stomach

Rilpivirine – QT prolongation, depression suicidality

DRUG	DOSING	SAFETY/SIDE EFFECTS/MONITORING
Efavirenz, EFV ***(Sustiva)*** Capsule, tablet **+ emtricitabine and tenofovir disoproxil fumarate *(Atripla)***	600 mg daily 1 tab daily for *Atripla* Take on an empty stomach (to ↓ risk of CNS effects), preferably at bedtime Capsule contents may be sprinkled onto 1-2 teaspoons of food *Atripla:* keep in original container (contains desiccant to protect from moisture)	**WARNINGS** Serious psychiatric symptoms (suicidal ideation, depression), CNS symptoms (generally resolve in 2-4 weeks), convulsions, QT prolongation, fetal toxicity **SIDE EFFECTS** CNS effects (impaired concentration, abnormal dreams, confusion, dizziness), rash, HA, N/V, fatigue, insomnia **MONITORING** Lipids, CNS and psychiatric effects, LFTs, ECG **NOTES** Package insert states to avoid in 1st trimester. Based on additional data, guidelines recommend no restrictions on use in pregnancy. May cause false positive for cannabinoid and benzodiazepine on drug screening tests Efavirenz should not be used with abacavir/lamivudine (or emtricitabine) in patients with pre-treatment HIV viral load > 100,000 copies/mL
Delavirdine, DLV *(Rescriptor)* Tablet	400 mg TID Patients with achlorhydria should take with acidic beverage; separate dose from antacids by 1 hour Take without regards to food	**CONTRAINDICATIONS** Concurrent use of alprazolam, ergot alkaloids, midazolam, rifampin, triazolam, others **SIDE EFFECTS** Nausea, HA, depression, fever, rash, ↑ LFTs **NOTES** Rarely used due to TID dosing, drug interactions, and suboptimal response (compared to other antiretrovirals)

Non-Nucleoside Reverse Transcriptase Inhibitors (NNRTIs) Continued

DRUG	DOSING	SAFETY/SIDE EFFECTS/MONITORING
Nevirapine, NVP *(Viramune, Viramune XR)* Tablet, oral suspension (10 mg/mL)	200 mg daily x 14 days, then 200 mg BID *(Viramune)* or 400 mg daily *(Viramune XR)* Requires 14 day lead-in period (may ↓ risk of rash, hepatotoxicity) If treatment is interrupted > 2 weeks, re-initiate titration. Take without regards to food	**BOXED WARNINGS** Hepatotoxicity (liver failure, death) – risk highest during the first 6 weeks of therapy but may be seen out to 18 weeks (or more); more common in women and with higher CD4+ counts as noted below Serious skin reactions (SJS/TEN) – risk highest during the first 18 weeks of therapy and intensive monitoring is required **CONTRAINDICATIONS** Moderate-to-severe hepatic impairment, use in post-exposure prophylaxis regimens **SIDE EFFECTS** Rash (SJS/TEN), nausea, diarrhea, ↑ LFTs **MONITORING** CBC, LFTs, rash **NOTES** Do not initiate therapy in women with CD4+ counts > 250 cells/mm³ or in men with CD4+ counts > 400 cells/mm³ due to ↑ risk of hepatotoxicity MedGuide required
Etravirine, ETR *(Intelence)* Tablet	200 mg BID after meals Protect from moisture Tablets may be dispersed in water to ease administration	**SIDE EFFECTS** Nausea, rash (including SJS/TEN), ↑ cholesterol, ↑ LDL, ↑ TGs, hyperglycemia, ↑ LFTs, peripheral neuropathy **MONITORING** LFTs, lipids, blood glucose **NOTES** Typically used in patients who are treatment-experienced and have resistance to first line ART regimens
Rilpivirine, RPV ***(Edurant)*** Tablet **+ emtricitabine and tenofovir disoproxil fumarate *(Complera)*** **+ emtricitabine and tenofovir alafenamide *(Odefsey)***	25 mg daily with a meal Keep in original container; protect from light 1 tab daily with food *(Complera* and *Odefsey)* Requires acidic environment for absorption: give H2RAs at least 12 hours before or 4 hours after rilpivirine. Give antacids at least 2 hours before or 4 hours after rilpivirine.	**CONTRAINDICATIONS** Concurrent use with PPIs, rifampin, rifapentine, carbamazepine, oxcarbazepine, phenobarbital, phenytoin, St. John's wort, and dexamethasone (more than a single dose) **WARNINGS** QT prolongation, serious skin reactions, multiorgan hypersensitivity reactions (DRESS), depressive disorders, hepatotoxicity **SIDE EFFECTS** Depressive disorders, mood changes, insomnia, HA, rash **MONITORING** LFTs, rash, lipids, CNS effects, QT **NOTES** Higher rates of failure if viral load > 100,000 copies/mL and/or CD4+ counts < 200 cells/mm³ at treatment initiation Protein supplement drinks should not be substituted for normal to high calorie meal (does not increase rilpivirine absorption)

NNRTI Drug Interactions

All NNRTIs are cleared non-renally and metabolized in the liver via the CYP 450 system; they have many drug interactions. They are all 3A4 substrates and may also be an inducer (nevirapine and etravirine), inhibitor (delavirdine) or both inducer and inhibitor (efavirenz). Many of the NNRTIs inhibit other isoenzymes. Always run a drug interaction check for patients receiving NNRTIs. Below are some notable drug interactions:

- Class interactions: avoid with St. John's wort, avanafil, *Viekira Pak* and *Viekira XR*
- Delavirdine: strong inhibitor of 2C9, 2C19 and 2D6, moderate inhibitor of 3A4 and major 3A4 substrate.
- Efavirenz: moderate inhibitor of 2C8/9 and 2C19; moderate inducer of 3A4 and a major substrate of 3A4. Avoid with carbamazepine, flibanserin, itraconazole, ketoconazole, midazolam (PO), posaconazole, simeprevir, *Zepatier*, others. If used with voriconazole, both drugs require dose adjustment.
- Etravirine: moderate inhibitor of 2C9 and 2C19; moderate inducer of 3A4; and major substrate of 3A4, 2C9, and 2C19. Avoid concurrent use with carbamazepine, clopidogrel, flibanserin, phenobarbital, phenytoin, rifampin, simeprevir, *Zepatier*, others.
- Nevirapine: weak 3A4 inducer and major 3A4 substrate. Avoid concurrent use with carbamazepine, itraconazole, ketoconazole, rifampin, simeprevir, others.
- Rilpivirine: major substrate of 3A4. Contraindicated with strong 3A4 inducers (carbamazepine, oxcarbazepine, phenobarbital, phenytoin, rifampin, systemic dexamethasone (> 1 dose) and PPIs. Caution with other acid suppressants: H2RAs should be administered at least 12 hours before or 4 hours after rilpivirine; antacids should be given at least 2 hours before or 4 hours after rilpivirine.
- Methadone levels can be ↓ by efavirenz and nevirapine. Monitor for signs and symptoms of possible methadone withdrawal.
- Hormonal contraceptive levels can be ↓ by efavirenz and nevirapine and result in unintended pregnancy. Patients should be counseled to use alternative or additional contraception.

PROTEASE INHIBITORS/PHARMACOKINETIC BOOSTERS

Protease inhibitors (PIs) work by inhibiting HIV protease and rendering the enzyme incapable of cleaving the Gag-Pol polyprotein, resulting in non-functional viral proteins and preventing the assembly and maturation of HIV virions (see Stage #7 in the HIV life cycle diagram). The PIs are effective even with multiple gene mutations (more resistant viruses).

It is recommended that all PIs be "boosted". Boosting takes advantage of a pharmacokinetic interaction to increase the drug levels and efficacy of PIs. All PIs are substrates of CYP3A4 and when given concurrently with a strong CYP3A4 inhibitor, the PI competes for metabolism and this results in increased PI drug levels. PIs should rarely, if at all, be given unboosted (except nelfinavir) and the boosting agent is not considered part of the three-drug ART regimen. Boosting agents include low dose ritonavir and cobicistat. See Pharmacokinetic Booster comparison chart for differences between the agents.

KEY FEATURES OF PIs

- The generic names end in "-navir"
- Primarily CYP450 inhibitors (always check for drug interactions; also see PI Drug Interactions section)
- No renal dose adjustment needed to PI, but may be used as part of a regimen with renal restrictions
- Hepatotoxicity (highest risk with tipranavir)
- Taken with a pharmacokinetic booster (ritonavir or cobicistat) to increase levels of the PI
- Metabolic abnormalities such as hyperlipidemia, lipohypertrophy (atazanavir, darunavir < other PIs), insulin resistance/hyperglycemia (highest risk with indinavir, lopinavir/ritonavir)
- Increased CVD risk (lowest with atazanavir and darunavir)
- GI upset (N/V/D)
- Generally take with food (also helps decrease GI side effects; exceptions: fosamprenavir and lopinavir/ritonavir)
- Bleeding events (in patients with hemophilia)
- ECG changes (especially saquinavir/ritonavir, lopinavir/ritonavir and atazanavir/ritonavir)
- Rash (including SJS/TEN)

DRUG	DOSING	SAFETY/SIDE EFFECTS/MONITORING
Darunavir, DRV ***(Prezista)*** Tablet, oral suspension (100 mg/mL) + cobicistat *(Prezcobix)*	Treatment naïve: 800 mg + 100 mg ritonavir daily or 150 mg cobicistat Treatment-experienced: 600 mg + 100 mg ritonavir BID 1 tablet daily *(Prezcobix)* Take with food Swallow whole If CrCl < 70 mL/min, do not give *Prezcobix* as part of a regimen that includes tenofovir disoproxil fumarate	**CONTRAINDICATIONS** Use with narrow therapeutic index drugs that are highly dependent on 3A4 for clearance (darunavir + ritonavir) **WARNINGS** Drug-induced hepatitis, serious skin reactions (SJS/TEN), use caution in patients with a sulfa allergy **SIDE EFFECTS** N/V/D, rash, ↑ LFTs, HA, hyperglycemia, ↑ SCr (with *Prezcobix*) **MONITORING** LFTs, rash, blood glucose, lipids, SCr (with *Prezcobix*) **NOTES** Must be given with ritonavir or cobicistat (cobicistat only FDA approved with darunavir daily dose) Less likely to cause lipodystrophy and affect blood glucose/lipids than other PIs

Protease Inhibitors (PIs) Continued

DRUG	DOSING	SAFETY/SIDE EFFECTS/MONITORING
Atazanavir, ATV ***(Reyataz)*** Capsule, oral powder + cobicistat *(Evotaz)*	300 mg + 100 mg ritonavir daily (or 150 mg cobicistat) 400 mg daily if therapy-naïve, not on tenofovir, and unable to tolerate ritonavir 1 tablet daily *(Evotaz)* Take with food (better absorption) If CrCl < 70 mL/min, do not give *Evotaz* as part of a regimen that includes tenofovir disoproxil fumarate	**WARNINGS** PR interval prolongation, severe skin reactions, hyperbilirubinemia, hepatotoxicity, nephrolithiasis and cholelithiasis **SIDE EFFECTS** Indirect hyperbilirubinemia (jaundice or scleral icterus – think "bananavir" – reversible), cholelithiasis, HA, N/V/D, severe skin reactions, depression, myalgia, hyperglycemia, ↑ SCr (with *Evotaz*), kidney stones **MONITORING** ECG in at-risk patients, LFTs (including bilirubin), blood glucose, lipids, SCr (with *Evotaz*) **NOTES** Compared to other PIs, less likely to cause lipodystrophy or affect blood glucose and lipids Caution with acid-suppressive agents as they can reduce the absorption (and blood levels) of atazanavir **With H2RAs** Atazanavir alone (unboosted): Take at least 2 hours before or 10 hours after H2RA Atazanavir with ritonavir: Take together or at least 10 hours after H2RA **With Antacids** Take atazanavir at least 2 hours before or 1 hour after antacids **With PPIs** Atazanavir with ritonavir: Take at least 12 hours after PPIs. The dose should not be > 20 mg of omeprazole (or equivalent) per day (PPIs are not recommended if atazanavir unboosted or in treatment-experienced patients)
Fosamprenavir, FPV *(Lexiva)* Tablet, oral suspension (50 mg/mL)	Treatment naïve: 1,400 mg ± 100-200 mg ritonavir daily or 700 mg + 100 mg ritonavir BID Treatment-experienced: 700 mg + 100 mg ritonavir BID Oral suspension: Take without food (adults) Tablets: take without regards to meals (unboosted); take with food (boosted with ritonavir)	**WARNINGS** Use caution in patients with a sulfa allergy, nephrolithiasis, hemolytic anemia, hypersensitivity reactions (SJS/TEN) **SIDE EFFECTS** N/V/D, HA, rash, hyperlipidemia (especially TG) **MONITORING** LFTs, GI symptoms, blood glucose, lipids **NOTES** Prodrug of amprenavir Caution when dispensing: Potential for medication error among *Lexiva*, *Lexapro*, and *Levitra* Unboosted fosamprenavir not recommended due to inferior potency compared to boosted PIs

Protease Inhibitors (PIs) Continued

DRUG	DOSING	SAFETY/SIDE EFFECTS/MONITORING
Indinavir, IDV *(Crixivan)* Capsule	Without ritonavir: 800 mg every 8 hours. Take on empty stomach (1 hour before or 2 hours after a meal) With ritonavir: 800 mg + 100-200 mg ritonavir BID. Take with food due to ritonavir component and with 48 oz. of water Swallow whole; do not break, crush, or chew	**WARNINGS** Nephrolithiasis/urolithiasis, hyperbilirubinemia, hemolytic anemia **SIDE EFFECTS** N/V/D, HA, nephrolithiasis, ↑ LFTs, rash, metallic taste, abdominal pain **MONITORING** LFTs (including bilirubin), urinalysis, CBC, blood glucose, lipids **NOTES** Compared to other PIs, indinavir (and lopinavir/ritonavir) have highest risk of causing hyperglycemia, including insulin resistance/diabetes Must dispense in the original container with the desiccant to protect from moisture Avoid high fat/high calorie meal as indinavir absorption is decreased
Lopinavir + ritonavir, LPV/r *(Kaletra)* Tablet, oral solution (80 mg lopinavir + 20 mg ritonavir/mL)	Treatment naïve: 800 mg lopinavir/200 mg ritonavir daily or 400/100 mg BID Treatment-experienced: 400/100 mg BID Tablets: take without regards to meals. Swallow whole; do not break, crush, or chew. Store at room temperature. Solution: take with food. Refrigerate; Stable for 2 months at room temp. Contains 42% alcohol.	**WARNINGS** Pancreatitis, hepatotoxicity, QT and/or PR interval prolongation, caution in patients with CVD due to increased risk of MIs **SIDE EFFECTS** N/V/D, abdominal pain, hyperlipidemia (especially TG), hyperglycemia **MONITORING** LFTs, blood glucose, lipids, ECG in at-risk patients **NOTES** Compared to other PIs, lopinavir/ritonavir (and indinavir) have highest risk of causing hyperglycemia, including insulin resistance/diabetes Avoid once daily dosing with carbamazepine, phenytoin, phenobarbital and in pregnant women MedGuide required
Nelfinavir, NFV *(Viracept)* Tablet	750 mg TID or 1,250 mg BID Take with food	**SIDE EFFECTS** Diarrhea (up to 20% in adults), flatulence, nausea, rash, ↑ LFTs **MONITORING** LFTs, GI symptoms (and electrolytes, hydration status if diarrhea), blood glucose, lipids **NOTES** Boosting with ritonavir not recommended (achieves adequate concentrations on its own) If difficulty with swallowing, tablets may be dissolved in small amount of water and consumed immediately Do not use with PPIs

Protease Inhibitors (PIs) Continued

DRUG	DOSING	SAFETY/SIDE EFFECTS/MONITORING
Saquinavir, SQV *(Invirase)* Capsule, tablet	1,000 mg + ritonavir 100 mg BID Take with food (or within 2 hours of a full meal) Must be given with ritonavir	**CONTRAINDICATIONS** Severe hepatic impairment, congenital or acquired QT prolongation, complete AV block or at high-risk for AV block, and refractory hypokalemia or hypomagnesemia **WARNINGS** PR and QT interval prolongation (avoid use if QT > 450 msec), photosensitivity reaction **SIDE EFFECTS** Nausea, vomiting, diarrhea, HA, abdominal pain, fatigue, hyperglycemia **MONITORING** ECG (baseline and ongoing),electrolytes (esp K, Mg), blood glucose, lipids **NOTES** Capsules may be opened and mixed with syrup or jam immediately before taking MedGuide required
Tipranavir, TPV *(Aptivus)* Capsule, oral solution (100 mg/mL)	500 mg + ritonavir 200 mg BID Take with food Swallow whole; do not break, crush, or chew Must be given with ritonavir Capsules: refrigerate; can store at room temp. up to 60 days; need to discard 60 days after opening bottle Solution: store at room temperature; need to discard 60 days after opening bottle	**BOXED WARNINGS** Clinical hepatitis and hepatic decompensation (sometimes fatal) and intracranial hemorrhage **CONTRAINDICATIONS** Moderate or severe hepatic impairment **WARNINGS** Use caution in patients with a sulfa allergy, intracranial hemorrhage (caution in those with bleeding risk) **SIDE EFFECTS** N/V/D, HA, ↑ CPK, hyperlipidemia (especially TG) **MONITORING** LFTs, blood glucose, lipids **NOTES** Capsules contain 7% alcohol Oral solution contains vitamin E; additional vitamin supplements should be avoided

PI Drug Interactions

All PIs are metabolized in the liver via the CYP 450 system; they have many drug interactions. All PIs are 3A4 substrates and most are strong inhibitors of 3A4. The drug interaction list below highlights the most important interactions and contraindications; it is not all-inclusive.

- Avoid with PIs:
  - 3A4 inducers (e.g., rifampin and St. John's wort): they can lower PI concentrations.
  - Antiarrhythmics: dronedarone (contraindicated with all PIs), amiodarone (contraindicated with some), use caution with all antiarrhythmics.
  - Anticoagulants/antiplatelets: apixaban, edoxaban, rivaroxaban, ticagrelor and vorapaxar.
  - Direct-acting antivirals (DAA) for HCV: simeprevir (contraindicated with all PIs), many other DAAs interact; check for interactions when initiating.
  - Other drugs that are contraindicated or should be avoided with all PIs: alfuzosin, cisapride, colchicine (in patients with hepatic or renal impairment), eplerenone, ergot derivatives, flibanserin, ivabradine, lurasidone, midazolam (PO), pimozide, salmeterol, suvorexant, triazolam and voriconazole.
- PIs can alter the INR (mainly ↓) in patients taking warfarin due to 2C9 induction; the INR should be closely monitored.
- Anticonvulsants: carbamazepine, phenytoin, phenobarbital (avoid with darunavir/ritonavir, atazanavir/ritonavir and cobicistat).
- Hormonal contraceptives (especially those containing ethinyl estradiol and norethindrone): ritonavir may ↓ levels via CYP induction. Check for drug-specific recommendations (variable among PIs/contraceptives) and counsel on use of additional/alternative contraceptive methods as appropriate.
- Methadone: ritonavir may ↓ levels (via CYP induction). Monitor for possible methadone withdrawal.
- Phosphodiesterase-5 inhibitors (PDE-5 inhibitors): PIs can ↑ levels of PDE-5 inhibitors and ↑ risk of toxicity. Initiate PDE-5 inhibitors at lowest dose and extend the dosing interval. Sildenafil (used for PAH) is contraindicated.
- Statins: PIs can ↑ statin levels. Lovastatin and simvastatin are contraindicated with PIs. Rosuvastatin and atorvastatin are preferred statins with PIs. Start statin therapy with a low dose and titrate to response. Monitor closely for statin toxicity.
- PIs ↑ the levels of trazodone and many tricyclic antidepressants. Start with low doses and then titrate anti-depressant doses based upon clinical response.
- Atazanavir: caution with the use of acid-suppression. See specific information in the drug table.
- Do not use nelfinavir with PPIs.

Pharmacokinetic Boosters

Ritonavir is a protease inhibitor, but its currently used only for its potent 3A4 inhibition to increase, or boost, the level of other PIs. Cobicistat *(Tybost)* is a strong 3A4 inhibitor and FDA-approved to pharmacokinetically enhance, or boost, levels of atazanavir and darunavir. Cobicistat itself is not a protease inhibitor and is not interchangeable with ritonavir.

	RITONAVIR *(Norvir)*	COBICISTAT *(Tybost)*
Boxed Warning	Interacts with many medications, including antiarrhythmics, ergot alkaloids and sedatives/hypnotics, resulting in potentially serious and/or life-threatening adverse events	None
Dose	100 to 400 mg PO daily (in 1-2 divided doses)	150 mg PO daily with darunavir or atazanavir
Antiretroviral activity	Yes	No
Enzyme activity	Strong inhibitor: 3A4, 2C8 Weak inhibitor: 2C9 (also weak/moderate inducer), 2C19	Strong inhibitor: 3A4 Weak inhibitor: 2D6, BCRP, OATP1B1, OATP1B3
P-glycoprotein inhibition	Strong	Weak
Adverse effects	N/V/D, paresthesias, arthralgias, ↑ CPK, lipid abnormalities	Increase in SCr (average 0.4), without affecting glomerular filtration function
Additional considerations	Take with food Capsules and tablets are not bioequivalent (patients may experience more GI side effects with the tablet form due to higher peak concentrations Tablets: do not break, crush or chew Capsules: refrigerate; stable at room temperature for up to 30 days Solution: 43% alcohol; shake well Keep in original container Difficult to co-formulate with other ARVs	Take with food Can be co-formulated (*Stribild, Genvoya, Prezcobix, Evotaz)*
Contraindicated with both	Alfuzosin, amiodarone, carbamazepine, cisapride, colchicine (with renal or hepatic impairment), dronedarone, ergot derivatives, flecainide, lovastatin, lurasidone, midazolam (PO), phenobarbital, phenytoin, pimozide, propafenone, quinidine, ranolazine, rifampin, simvastatin, sildenafil (used for PAH), St. John's wort, triazolam Cobicistat only: narrow therapeutic index drugs that are highly dependent on 3A4 for clearance	

INTEGRASE STRAND TRANSFER INHIBITORS

Integrase strand transfer inhibitors (INSTIs) block the integrase enzyme needed for viral DNA to integrate with the host cell DNA/ human genome (see Stage #4 in the HIV life cycle diagram).

KEY FEATURES OF INSTIs

The generic names end in "-tegravir"

No renal dose adjustment needed (avoid *Stribild* if CrCl < 70 mL/min, avoid *Genvoya* if CrCl < 30 mL/min)

No major CYP interactions (exception: elvitegravir + cobicistat or ritonavir)

↑ CPK (raltegravir > other INSTIs)

Headache, insomnia

Take without regards to meals (exception: elvitegravir with food)

Interact with polyvalent cations – must separate dose

DRUG	DOSING	SAFETY/SIDE EFFECTS/MONITORING
Elvitegravir, EVG *(Vitekta)* Tablet **+ cobicistat and emtricitabine and tenofovir disoproxil fumarate *(Stribild)*** **+ cobicistat and emtricitabine and tenofovir alafenamide *(Genvoya)***	Rarely used as single agent *Stribild*: 1 tablet daily CrCl < 70 mL/min: do not initiate CrCl < 50 mL/min: discontinue *Genvoya*: 1 tablet daily If CrCl < 30 mL/min: do not initiate Take with food Keep in original container Boosting with cobicistat allows once daily dosing	**BOXED WARNINGS** Lactic acidosis with severe hepatomegaly with steatosis Acute exacerbation of HBV can occur when drug is discontinued in patients with HBV (specific for emtricitabine and tenofovir) **CONTRAINDICATIONS** Concurrent use of alfuzosin, cisapride, ergot derivatives, lovastatin, midazolam (oral), pimozide, rifampin, sildenafil (when used for pulmonary arterial hypertension), simvastatin, St. John's wort and triazolam **WARNINGS** New onset or worsening renal impairment, ↓ bone density **SIDE EFFECTS** Proteinuria, ↑ SCr, nausea and diarrhea, hyperlipidemia, HA, insomnia, **MONITORING** CPK, LFTs, renal function
Dolutegravir, DTG ***(Tivicay)*** Tablet **+ abacavir and lamivudine *(Triumeq)***	For patients ≥ 40 kg only 50 mg PO daily 50 mg PO BID (for treatment-experienced patients or those with INSTI resistance or those taking certain UGT1A or 3A4 inducers) Take without regard to meals	**CONTRAINDICATION** Coadministration with dofetilide **SIDE EFFECTS** Insomnia, HA, diarrhea, rash, ↑ CPK, ↑ LFTs among hepatitis B/C patients, ↑ SCr without affecting GFR **MONITORING** CPK, LFTs (especially in patients with hepatitis B or C)
Raltegravir, RAL ***(Isentress)*** Tablet (including chewable), powder packet for oral suspension	400 mg BID Take without regard to meals Chewable tablets: Keep in original container Oral suspension: Keep in original container, do not open foil packet until ready for reconstitution and use	**SIDE EFFECTS** Nausea, HA, insomnia, fatigue, ↑ CPK, myopathy and rhabdomyolysis **MONITORING** CPK (if symptomatic), LFTs

INSTI Drug Interactions

- INSTIs should be taken 2 hours before or 6 hours after cation-containing antacids or laxatives, sucralfate, iron or calcium supplements or buffered medications. Exception: no dose separation needed for raltegravir and calcium carbonate. H2RAs and PPIs do not pose an interaction with INSTIs.
- Elvitegravir: major 3A4 substrate and an inducer of 2C9 (weak/moderate). It may ↓ the plasma concentrations of 2C9 substrates. Multiple interactions with DAAs used for HCV. Avoid with rifampin.
- Cobicistat: interactions are very similar to ritonavir interactions (see Boosters table following the protease inhibitors). is an inhibitor of 3A4 (strong), 2D6 (weak) and P-gp.
- Raltegravir: metabolized by the UGT1A1-mediated glucuronidation pathway. Rifampin, a strong inducer of UGT1A1, will ↓ levels of raltegravir. When given concurrently with rifampin, use raltegravir 800 mg BID. PPIs can ↑ levels of raltegravir although dosage adjustment is not needed.

CCR5 ANTAGONIST

Maraviroc inhibits binding to the CCR5 co-receptor on the CD4+ cells and prevents HIV from entering the cell (see Stage #1 in the HIV life cycle diagram). Unlike the other antiretroviral drug classes, the CCR5 antagonist does not directly target the HIV cell; it blocks the human host cell receptor.

DRUG	DOSING	SAFETY/SIDE EFFECTS/MONITORING
Maraviroc, MVC *(Selzentry)* Tablet, solution	300 mg BID Adjust dose if concurrent 3A4 inhibitor or inducer; see contraindications for renal impairment. Take without regard to meals Prior to starting therapy, patients must undergo a tropism test, to determine the type of co-receptor present. Patients may have CCR5, CXCR4 or both receptors (dual tropism). Maraviroc will only work in patients with CCR5-tropic disease (patient must be negative for CXCR4- or dual/mixed-tropic disease)	**BOXED WARNING** Hepatotoxicity, may occur with severe rash or other allergic type features **CONTRAINDICATIONS** Patients with severe renal impairment (CrCl < 30 mL/min) taking potent 3A4 inhibitors/inducers **WARNINGS** Hypersensitivity reactions (including SJS), CV events (including MI), orthostatic hypotension in patients with renal impairment **SIDE EFFECTS** URTIs, fever, cough, rash, abdominal pain, dizziness **MONITORING** Tropism testing prior to initiation, LFTs, s/sx of infection, skin reactions **NOTES** Swallow tablets whole; do not chew, break, or crush MedGuide required

CCR5 Antagonist Drug Interactions

Maraviroc is a P-gp and major 3A4 substrate. Maraviroc concentrations can be significantly ↑ in the presence of strong 3A4 inhibitors and ↓ with 3A4 inducers, and maraviroc dosage is determined by the presence of drug interactions. Avoid use with St. John's wort.

FUSION INHIBITOR

Fusion inhibitors block the fusion of the HIV virus with the CD4+ cells by blocking the conformational change in gp41 required for membrane fusion and entry into CD4+ cells (see Stage #2 in the HIV life cycle diagram).

DRUG	DOSING	SAFETY/SIDE EFFECTS/MONITORING
Enfuvirtide, T20 *(Fuzeon)* Powder for injection	90 mg SC BID Reconstituted solution should be refrigerated and used within 24 hours	**WARNINGS** ↑ risk of bacterial pneumonia, hypersensitivity reaction **SIDE EFFECTS** Local injection site reactions in 98% of patients (pain, erythema, nodules and cysts, ecchymosis), diarrhea, nausea, fatigue **NOTES** Patient should be counseled regarding proper reconstitution and injection technique and to rotate injection sites Typically used in patients who are treatment-experienced with resistance to multiple other ART

ADMINISTRATION REQUIREMENTS

With food

- Atazanavir
- *Complera*
- Darunavir
- Etravirine (after meals)
- *Genvoya*
- Indinavir (boosted)
- *Kaletra* oral soln
- Nelfinavir
- *Odefsey*
- Rilpivirine
- Ritonavir
- Saquinavir
- *Stribild*
- Tipranavir
- Tenofovir powder (to avoid bitter taste)

Without food

- *Atripla*
- Didanosine
- Indinavir (unboosted)
- Efavirenz (small amount of non-fatty food is okay)
- Fosamprenavir (oral suspension)

COMBINATION PRODUCTS

Combination products can increase convenience (lower pill burden) and improve adherence. Combination products may not be available, due to differences in dosing schedule (e.g., raltegravir), or formulation requirements (e.g., ritonavir).

GENERIC NAME	BRAND NAME	DOSE
Common NRTI Combination Products		
Abavacir 600 mg + lamivudine 300 mg	*Epzicom*	1 tab daily
Emtricitabine 200 mg + tenofovir alafenamide 25 mg	*Descovy*	1 tab daily
Emtricitabine 200 mg + tenofovir disoproxil fumarate 300 mg	*Truvada*	1 tab daily
Lamivudine 150 mg + zidovudine 300 mg	*Combivir*	1 tab BID
Common PI Combination Products		
Atazanavir 300 mg + cobicistat 150 mg	*Evotaz*	1 tab daily
Darunavir 800 mg + cobicistat 150 mg	*Prezcobix*	1 tab daily
Once-Daily Single Tablet Regimens		
NNRTI-based		
Efavirenz 600 mg + emtricitabine 200 mg tenofovir disoproxil fumarate 300 mg	*Atripla*	1 tab daily at HS
Emtricitabine 200 mg + rilpivirine 25 mg + tenofovir disoproxil fumarate 300 mg	*Complera*	1 tab daily
Emtricitabine 200 mg + rilpivirine 25 mg + tenofovir alafenamide 25 mg	*Odefsey*	1 tab daily
INSTI-based		
Elvitegravir 150 mg + cobicistat 150 mg + emtricitabine 200 mg + tenofovir disoproxil fumarate 300 mg	*Stribild*	1 tab daily
Elvitegravir 150 mg + cobicistat 150 mg + emtricitabine 200 mg + tenofovir alafenamide 10 mg	*Genvoya*	1 tab daily
Abacavir 600 mg + dolutegravir 50 mg + lamivudine 300 mg	*Triumeq*	1 tab daily

SELECT COMPLICATIONS OF ART

Lactic acidosis and severe hepatomegaly with steatosis: stop treatment in any patient who develops clinical or laboratory findings suggestive of lactic acidosis or hepatotoxicity (↑ LFTs may accompany hepatomegaly and steatosis). Most commonly associated with NRTIs.

Immune reconstitution inflammatory syndrome (IRIS): paradoxical worsening of a preexisting OI or malignancy when ART is initiated. Since ART leads to an improvement in immune function, an inflammatory reaction may occur at the site of the preexisting infection. Patients at highest risk for IRIS are those with low CD4+ counts and high viral loads. IRIS generally develops within 1 – 3 months of ART initiation. Common pathogens associated with IRIS include *M. tuberculosis*, *M. avium*, *Pneumocystis jiroveci* pneumonia (PCP), herpes simplex virus (HSV), herpes zoster, cytomegalovirus (CMV), *Cryptococcus*, and HBV. Management of IRIS consists of the following:

- Start or continue therapy for the underlying opportunistic pathogen or malignancy.
- Continue ART if the patient is currently receiving ART. Among patients newly diagnosed with HIV with OI, ART may be intentionally delayed while treating the OI to minimize risk for IRIS. However, ART should be started within 2 weeks of OI treatment initiation the majority of OIs with the exception of cryptococcal meningitis and *M. tuberculosis*.
- In select circumstances, the addition of systemic steroids may be appropriate.

Lipodystrophy: changes in fat distribution in the body and is further subcategorized as lipoatrophy (fat loss or wasting) or lipohypertrophy (fat accumulation).

- Lipoatrophy: loss of subcutaneous fat in the face, arms, legs, and buttocks and is most commonly associated with NRTIs, specifically with stavudine (and zidovudine to a lesser extent).
- Lipohypertrophy: fat accumulation in the upper back and neck ("buffalo hump"), abdominal area, and breast area in both men and women and is most commonly associated with PIs. Breast enlargement with efavirenz has been reported.

Diarrhea: diarrhea is a common side effect of ART. All ARTs have been associated with GI toxicity, however, PIs are generally the most problematic (especially nelfinavir and lopinavir/ritonavir).

ART ADVERSE EFFECTS BY CLASS AND AGENT

This table is a summary of important adverse effects of ART drug classes and individual drugs covered throughout the chapter.

ART	COMMON ADVERSE EFFECT
NRTIs Class Effect: Lactic acidosis	
Abacavir	Hypersensitivity and possible ↑ risk of MI
Didanosine	Pancreatitis and peripheral neuropathy
Emtricitabine	Headache
Lamivudine	Headache
Stavudine	Pancreatitis and peripheral neuropathy
Tenofovir (TDF, TAF)	Renal toxicity (Fanconi syndrome) and ↓ bone mineral density
Zidovudine	Macrocytic anemia and myopathy
NNRTIs Class Effect: Rash	
Efavirenz	CNS effects (impaired concentration, abnormal dreams, confusion)
Nevirapine	Hepatotoxicity and hypersensitivity reaction
Delavirdine	Headache
Etravirine	SJS/TEN
Rilpivirine	Depression and insomnia
PIs Class effects: Metabolic abnormalities (hyperlipidemia, hyperglycemia, lipohypertrophy) and N/V/D	
Darunavir	Headache
Atazanavir	Nephrolithiasis and indirect hyperbilirubinemia
Fosamprenavir	Rash
Indinavir	Nephrolithiasis and urolithiasis
Lopinavir/ritonavir	Hypertriglyceridemia
Nelfinavir	Diarrhea
Ritonavir	N/V/D
Saquinavir	Nausea
Tipranavir	Intracranial hemorrhage
INSTIs	
Raltegravir	↑ CPK, myopathy and rhabdomyolysis
Elvitegravir	Headache and insomnia
Dolutegravir	↑ SCr without affecting GFR

Therapies for HIV Complications

DRUG AND INDICATION	DOSING	SAFETY/SIDE EFFECTS/MONITORING
Poly-L-Lactic Acid *(Sculptra)* Injection Lipoatrophy (facial)	About 20 injections (given intradermal or SC) per cheek Typical treatment course can require 3-6 treatments. Treatments should be separated by ≥ 2 weeks.	**SIDE EFFECTS** Injection site reactions (e.g., bleeding, bruising, erythema, edema, inflammation), photosensitivity, hematoma, discomfort
Calcium hydroxylapatite *(Radiesse, Radiesse Plus)* Injection Lipoatrophy (facial)	Intradermal injection Typical treatment course may require 1-3 treatments. In clinical trials, multiple treatments were separated by at least 1 month.	**SIDE EFFECTS** Injection site reactions (e.g., bruising, erythema, edema), pain, pruritus, nodules
Tesamorelin *(Egrifta)* Injection HIV-associated lipodystrophy (specifically reduction of excess abdominal fat)	2 mg SC daily	**SIDE EFFECTS** Injection site reactions (e.g., pruritus, erythema, bruising, pain), rash, peripheral edema, hyperglycemia, arthralgias, development of IgG antibodies **NOTES** This medication is a growth hormone releasing factor Safety Issue – See Pregnancy chapter
Crofelemer *(Mytesi)* Tablet Non-infectious diarrhea due to ART	125 mg PO BID	**SIDE EFFECTS** URTIs, bronchitis, cough, flatulence, ↑ bilirubin/LFTs **NOTES** Minimal oral absorption Due to cost, first consider trial of loperamide *(Imodium)* or diphenoxylate/atropine *(Lomotil)*
Megestrol *(Megace, Megace ES)* Tablet, suspension *Megace* 40 mg/mL, *Megace ES* 625 mg/5 mL Anorexia or cachexia associated with AIDS	400-800 mg suspension PO daily	**SIDE EFFECTS** Hyperglycemia, adrenal suppression, hypertension, HA, rash, N/V/D **NOTES** Available as oral suspension (used in HIV-associated anorexia/cachexia) and tablets (used in cancer treatment) – dispense correct strength and formulation. *Megace* and *Megace ES* are not equivalent on a mg-per-mg basis. Safety issue – see Pregnancy chapter
Dronabinol *(Marinol, Syndros)* C-III Capsule, oral solution AIDS-related anorexia	Capsules: 2.5 mg PO BID (before lunch and dinner), max 20 mg/day Oral suspension: 2.1 mg PO BID, max 16.8 mg/day Refrigerate capsules and oral solution Swallow capsule whole. Do not chew, break, or crush.	**SIDE EFFECTS** CNS effects (e.g., euphoria, somnolence, abnormal thinking, confusion), dizziness, abdominal pain, paranoia, N/V **NOTES** Causes positive cannabinoid drug test. Caution in patients with underlying cardiac or liver disease or seizure disorders.

HIV PREVENTION STRATEGIES

Various prevention strategies are utilized to reduce the number of new HIV infections. Prevention strategies include pre-exposure prophylaxis, treatment as prevention and post-exposure prophylaxis (occupational and non-occupational). These strategies are often utilized in combination and coupled with continued community education on HIV transmission and risk factors.

Pre-Exposure Prophylaxis (PrEP)

PrEP is an HIV prevention method in which people who do not have HIV take emtricitabine/tenofovir *(Truvada)* 1 tab PO daily, in combination with safer sex/behavior risk reduction practices, to reduce their risk of becoming infected. The effectiveness of PrEP is directly related to medication adherence. PrEP is recommended for both homosexual and heterosexual individuals who are at very high risk for sexual exposure to HIV as well as for active intravenous drug users.

Before Initiating PrEP

- Confirm HIV negative status through HIV antibody test
- Confirm CrCl ≥ 60 mL/min
- Confirm patient very high risk for acquiring HIV
- Screen for hepatitis B and STIs

Once PrEP is initiated, follow-up visits are needed at least every 3 months with the following recommendations during each visit:

- HIV test and document negative result
- Provide no more than 90-day supply at a time (renew Rx only once HIV negative status is confirmed)
- Pregnancy test (for non-HIV-infected women taking PrEP)
- Counseling on PrEP adherence and safe sex/behavior risk reduction practices
- Every 6 months, check SCr and calculate CrCl, and test for bacterial STIs (regardless of symptoms)

Treatment as Prevention

The risk of transmitting HIV to another individual is directly proportional to the HIV viral load. Treatment as Prevention aims to treat the HIV infected individual with effective ART to reduce the HIV viral load thus reducing the risk of transmitting HIV to another person.

NONOCCUPATIONAL POSTEXPOSURE PROPHYLAXIS (nPEP)

Nonoccupational exposure is the use of ART prophylaxis after sexual, injection drug use, or some other nonoccupational exposure to HIV. Regardless of whether or not nPEP is prescribed, the exposed patient should be tested for HIV Ab at baseline, 4 – 6 weeks, 3 months, and 6 months after the exposure event.

Nonoccupational Postexposure Prophylaxis (nPEP) Recommendations

PREFERRED REGIMENS	CRITERIA TO QUALIFY	DURATION
NNRTI-BASED Emtricitabine + tenofovir disoproxil fumarate *(Truvada)* 1 tablet daily + Raltegravir 400 mg PO BID or Dolutegravir 50 mg PO daily **PI-BASED** Emtricitabine + tenofovir disoproxil fumarate *(Truvada)* 1 tablet daily + Darunavir 800 mg + ritonavir 100 mg daily	As soon as possible but within 72 hours since exposure Known HIV (+) status of source (if HIV status unknown, then case-by-case determination) Exposed patient is HIV (–) or being tested for HIV Type of exposure is also factored into decision to initiate nPEP	28 days

OCCUPATIONAL POST-EXPOSURE PROPHYLAXIS RECOMMENDATIONS (PEP)

Occupational exposure typically refers to exposure of health care personnel to blood or body fluids that may potentially be contaminated with HIV. ART prophylaxis for occupational exposure is generally only recommended if the source of contaminated blood or body fluid is known to be HIV infected. If the source patient's HIV status is unknown, the HIV status should be determined, if possible, to guide need for HIV PEP. Therapy should be started right away, ideally within 72 hours, when treatment is indicated. Per the 2013 updated guideline, a three drug regimen including raltegravir *(Isentress)* + tenofovir/emtricitabine *(Truvada)* for a 4-week course is the preferred regimen. The exposed health care personnel should be tested for HIV Ab at baseline, 4 – 6 weeks, 3 months, and 6 months after the exposure event. If PEP is initiated, then CBC, renal and liver function should be tested at baseline and repeated at 2 weeks post-exposure.

PATIENT COUNSELING

All HIV Medications

- This medication is not a cure for HIV and should be used along with other practices to prevent the spread of HIV to others. Avoid sharing needles or personal items that may have blood on them (e.g., razors or toothbrushes) and do not have unprotected sex.
- It is very important to continue taking this medication (and other HIV medications in your regimen) exactly as prescribed by your healthcare provider. Do not skip doses or stop taking any part your HIV medication regimen even for a short time unless directed to do so by your healthcare provider. Skipping or stopping your medication, or taking only some but not all of the HIV medications in your full regimen, may cause the amount of HIV virus to increase and make the infection more difficult to treat (resistant). Refill all HIV medications before you run out.
- If you are taking HIV medications for the first time, you may experience symptoms of an old infection. This can happen as your immune system begins to work better. Contact your healthcare provider immediately if you notice any new occurrence of the following symptoms: fever, cough, trouble breathing, vision problems, headaches or skin problems.
- Rarely, this medication can cause severe liver problems. Tell your healthcare provider immediately if you develop symptoms such as persistent nausea/vomiting, loss of appetite, stomach/abdominal pain, pale stools, dark urine, yellowing eyes/skin, or unusual tiredness.
- This medication can cause changes in body fat, such as increased fat in the upper back and neck, breasts, and belly areas, and loss of fat from legs, arms and face. These symptoms occur after you have been on the medication for a long time.
- Do not breastfeed. HIV can be passed on to your baby through your breastmilk.
- HIV is always treated with more than one medication. Some combination medicines are available to decrease the amount of pills you take each day.

STRATEGIES TO IMPROVE ADHERENCE TO ANTIRETROVIRAL THERAPY
Multidisciplinary team approach (e.g., nurses, social workers, pharmacists, psychologists, physicians)
Accessible, non-judgmental health care team, establish trusting relationship with patient
Evaluate patient's knowledge of HIV disease, prevention and treatment, and provide information as needed; establish patient readiness to start ART and involve in ART regimen selection
Identify potential barriers to adherence (e.g., psychosocial or cognitive issues, substance abuse, low literacy, busy daily schedule, lack of prescription coverage and/or social support)
Assess adherence at every clinic visit, and simplify ART regimen when possible; provide positive reinforcement to foster adherence success
Identify non-adherence and reasons for non-adherence (e.g., adverse effects from medications, complex regimen, difficulty swallowing large pills, forgetfulness, pill fatigue, food requirements, stigma, change or lapse of insurance coverage)
Provide resources (e.g., referrals for mental health and/or substance abuse treatment, prescription drug assistance programs, pillboxes, reminder tools, medication lists or calendars)

NRTIs Patient Counseling

- Take this medication with or without food.
- Rarely, this medication can cause a build-up of acid in your blood; report any symptoms such as stomach pain, nausea, vomiting, troubled breathing, weakness or muscle pain.
- If you have hepatitis B and are taking a regimen containing lamivudine, emtricitabine, and/or tenofovir, your hepatitis symptoms may become suddenly worse if you stop taking any of these medications. This can lead to death. Talk with your healthcare provider before stopping the medication(s). Tell your healthcare provider immediately if you develop symptoms of worsening liver problems.

Abacavir

- Read the MedGuide that has been given to you. Carry the Warning Card (which lists the symptoms of a serious allergic reaction) with you at all times and contact your healthcare provider if you develop the following symptoms: fever, rash, nausea, vomiting, diarrhea, severe stomach pain, extreme tiredness or aches, generalized ill feeling, shortness of breath, cough or sore throat, as you may need to stop taking products that contain abacavir.

Lamivudine

- If you have Hepatitis B and HIV, your healthcare provider will prescribe a higher dose of lamivudine than is present in *Epivir-HBV*, because a higher dose is required to treat HIV.

Emtricitabine

- Headaches are a common side effect of this medication.
- This medication can cause darkening skin color on palms of hands and on soles of feet.
- This medication may cause rash in some people who take it. If you develop a rash, notify your healthcare provider as soon as possible.

Tenofovir disoproxil fumarate and tenofovir alafenamide

- Tell your healthcare provider immediately if any of these rare but serious side effects occur: signs of kidney problems such as a change in the amount of urine, unusual thirst, muscle cramps/weakness
- Bone problems, including bone pain, softening or thinning of the bones, can happen in some people who take this medication. Your healthcare provider may order extra tests to check your bones.
- Tenofovir disoproxil fumarate powder: This medication comes with a dosing scoop; use only the dosing scoop to measure the oral powder. Mix the oral powder with soft foods that can be swallowed without chewing (e.g., applesauce, baby food or yogurt). Do not mix with liquid as the powder may float to the top even after stirring. Give the entire dose right away after mixing to avoid a bad taste.

NNRTIs Patient Counseling

- This medication may cause a rash in some people who take it. It may go away, but if you develop a rash, notify your healthcare provider. If the rash is very severe, accompanied with a fever, or you develop skin blistering, seek care immediately.
- This medication interacts with many other medications. Tell your healthcare provider about all the medications you are taking, including any over-the-counter medications and herbal supplements. Do not start, stop, or change the dosage of any medication before checking with your healthcare provider or pharmacist first.

Efavirenz

- Take this medication on an empty stomach, usually once daily at bedtime. Taking efavirenz with food especially fatty foods, can increase the blood level of this medication, which may increase your risk of certain side effects.

- Headache, nausea, vomiting, and diarrhea may occur.
- Dizziness, drowsiness, abnormal dreams/nightmares, trouble sleeping, tiredness/fatigue, and trouble concentrating may occur. These side effects may begin 1 – 2 days after starting this medication and usually go away in 2 – 4 weeks. They are also reduced by taking efavirenz on an empty stomach at bedtime. If any of these effects persist or worsen, tell your healthcare provider promptly.
- Because efavirenz may cause confusion, make it difficult to concentrate, or slow down your reactions. Use caution when driving or performing tasks that requires you to be awake and alert. Avoid drinking alcohol.
- Serious psychiatric symptoms have been reported during efavirenz treatment, especially in people who have mental health conditions. Tell your healthcare provider immediately if any of these unlikely but serious side effects occur: mental/mood changes such as depression, thoughts of suicide, nervousness, angry behavior, or hallucinations.
- This medication may decrease the effectiveness of hormonal birth control pills, patches, or rings which can result in pregnancy. To reduce the risk of unintended pregnancy, and also the risk of spreading HIV to others, use barrier protection during all sexual activity.
- If you take efavirenz during pregnancy, your baby has a higher and unknown risk for some birth defects. Do not use efavirenz without your healthcare provider's consent if you are pregnant or planning to get pregnant. Use two forms of birth control, including a barrier form (such as a condom and diaphragm with spermicide gel) while you are taking efavirenz, and for at least 12 weeks after your treatment ends. Tell your healthcare provider if you become pregnant during treatment.

Rilpivirine

- This medication may cause depression and trouble sleeping. If you notice changes in your mood, such as feeling sad, hopeless, anxious or have thoughts of suicide, contact your healthcare provider.
- It is very important to take this medication with a full meal as this helps ensure that your body is absorbing enough of the medication to work against the virus. Ideally, your meal should be at least 500 calories. A protein drink should not be used in place of a meal.
- Medications that reduce stomach acid can significantly affect the absorption of this medication and result in failure of HIV treatment. Talk with your healthcare provider or pharmacist before starting any acid suppressant medications.

PI Patient Counseling

- Diarrhea, nausea, vomiting, heartburn, stomach pain, headache, dizziness, fatigue, weakness, or changes in taste may occur. If any of these effects persist or worsen, tell your healthcare provider or pharmacist promptly.
- A mild rash (redness and itching) may occur within the first few weeks after the medicine is started and usually goes away within 2 weeks with no change in treatment. If a severe rash develops with symptoms of fever, body or muscle aches, mouth sores, shortness of breath, or swelling of the face, contact your healthcare provider immediately.
- Before using this medication, tell your healthcare provider your medical history, especially if you have: diabetes, heart problems (coronary artery disease, heart attack), hemophilia, high cholesterol/triglycerides, gout/high uric acid in the blood, liver problems (such as hepatitis B or hepatitis C), kidney problems, and/or pancreatitis.
- Some patients taking this medication have increased blood sugar levels. If you have diabetes, check your blood sugar levels regularly as directed by your healthcare provider. Tell your healthcare provider immediately if you have symptoms of high blood sugar, such as increased thirst, increased urination, confusion, drowsiness, flushing, rapid breathing, or fruity breath odor.
- This medication interacts with many other medications. Tell your healthcare provider about all the medications you are taking, including any over-the-counter medications and herbal supplements. Do

not start, stop or change the dosage of any medicine before checking with your healthcare provider or pharmacist first.

- Seek immediate medical attention if any of these rare but serious side effects occur: symptoms of a heart attack (such as chest/jaw/left arm pain, shortness of breath or profuse sweating), change in heart rhythm, dizziness, lightheadedness, severe nausea or vomiting, severe stomach pain, extreme weakness or trouble breathing.

Atazanavir

- Take this medication once daily with food. If you are also prescribed ritonavir, make sure to take both atazanavir and ritonavir at the same time.
- Acid-lowering medications for indigestion, heartburn, or ulcers (e.g., prescription or over-the-counter medications such as antacids, famotidine or omeprazole) can significantly decrease the amount of atazanavir that gets in your system and result in failure of your HIV treatment. Ask your healthcare provider or pharmacist how to use these medications together with atazanavir safely.
- May cause skin or the whites of eyes to turn yellow. This is usually not a dangerous side effect, however, if this becomes bothersome, talk with your healthcare provider. If you develop yellowing of skin/eyes along with severe abdominal pain and/or nausea/vomiting, contact your healthcare provider immediately as these could be signs of liver problems.
- Although rare, some patients have developed gallstones or kidney stones while on this medication. Take this medication with plenty of water to reduce chances of developing kidney stones. Seek immediate care if you notice signs of a kidney stone (e.g., pain in side/back/abdomen, painful urination or blood in the urine).

Darunavir

- Take darunavir with ritonavir at the same time(s) each day with food.
- Headaches are a common side effect of this medication.
- This medication may cause rash in some people, which is usually mild and will resolve on its own over time. If you develop a severe, bothersome rash, contact your healthcare provider immediately. If you have a sulfa allergy, tell your healthcare provider or pharmacist right away.

INSTI Patient Counseling

- This medication can interact with antacids, multivitamins, iron and other supplements. Talk with your healthcare provider before taking these two medications together. Generally, you should separate this HIV medication at least 2 hours before or 6 hours after the antacids.
- May cause rash in some people. Notify your healthcare provider if it becomes bothersome. If you develop severe rash, accompanied with fever and/or difficulty breathing, seek medical attention immediately.
- May cause muscle pain or tenderness, or weakness. Inform your healthcare provider if you notice these symptoms, especially if you develop these out of proportion to your actual level of activity.
- May cause headache or difficulty sleeping.
- Rarely, may cause kidney or liver problems. Your healthcare provider will be checking your labs from time to time to monitor your kidneys and liver.

Dolutegravir

- Take this medication with or without food.
- Follow the dosing instructions as prescribed by your healthcare provider (once vs. twice a day).
- Do not take this medication if you are also taking dofetilide for a heart rhythm problem. Contact your healthcare provider to discuss alternative HIV therapy options.

Raltegravir

- This medication is to be taken twice a day with or without food.
- Rarely this medication can cause muscle problems. Report any new muscle pain, weakness or extreme tiredness.

Elvitegravir

- This medication should be taken with food.
- Headaches and trouble sleeping can happen with this medication.

***Stribild* and *Genvoya* (also see emtricitabine and tenofovir disoproxil fumarate counseling points)**

- This medication contains 4 medications in one pill: elvitegravir, cobicistat, emtricitabine, and tenofovir.
- Take this medication once a day with food. Keep the medication in the original container.
- If you have hepatitis B, it's very important that you do not suddenly stop this medication unless instructed to do so by your healthcare provider. Abruptly stopping this medication may result in worsening of your hepatitis symptoms.
- This medication interacts with many medications. Tell your healthcare provider and pharmacist about all the medications you are taking, including any over-the-counter medications and herbal supplements. Do not start, stop, or change the dosage of any medication before checking with your healthcare provider or pharmacist first.

33

PULMONARY ARTERIAL HYPERTENSION

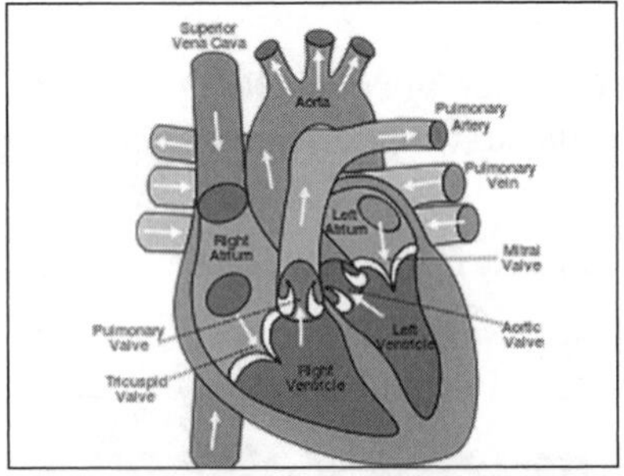

We gratefully acknowledge the assistance of Heather R. Bream-Rouwenhorst, PharmD, BCPS, Clinical Assistant Professor, University of Iowa College of Pharmacy, in preparing this chapter.

BACKGROUND

Pulmonary hypertension (PH) is characterized by continuous high blood pressure in the pulmonary arteries. A normal pulmonary artery pressure (PAP) ranges from 8 – 20 mmHg when a person is resting. PH is defined as a mean PAP (mPAP) ≥ 25 mmHg in the setting of normal fluid status. Other hemodynamic parameters are affected as well.

Classification

PH may occur secondary to various disease states. The World Health Organization (WHO) classifies PH into five groups (see box on following page). The primary focus of this chapter is Group 1, pulmonary artery hypertension (PAH). When there is no identifiable cause, it is called primary, or idiopathic, PAH. Secondary causes include genetic inheritance, connective tissue diseases, advanced liver disease, and HIV, among others. Less commonly, medications can be the causative factor. The PH treatments discussed in this chapter are only approved for the treatment of PAH, with the exception of riociguat *(Adempas)*.

Treatment of the other PH groups is aimed at the underlying causes. Group 2 is pulmonary venous hypertension, which arises from left-sided heart disease (e.g., left ventricular systolic or diastolic dysfunction, valvular disease, congenital heart disease). Group 3 is PH due to hypoxia or chronic lung diseases, such as COPD or pulmonary fibrosis and emphysema. Group 4 is chronic thromboembolic PH (CTEPH), which occurs in a minority of pulmonary embolism (PE) survivors. Warfarin, with an INR goal of 2 – 3, is recommended for CTEPH; for patients who are not thrombectomy candidates, riociguat *(Adempas)* is an approved treatment. Group 5 is PH caused by conditions that do not fit in the above categories (e.g., sarcoidosis).

GUIDELINES/REFERENCES

Pharmacologic therapy for pulmonary arterial hypertension in adults. *Chest.* 2014;146:449-475.

2015 ESC/ERS guidelines for the diagnosis and treatment of pulmonary hypertension. *Eur Heart J.* 2016;37:67-119.

SELECT DRUGS THAT CAN CAUSE PAH

Cocaine

Dasatinib *(Sprycel)*

Diazoxide *(Proglycem)*

Methamphetamines

SSRI use during pregnancy (↑ risk in newborns)

Weight loss agents (diethylpropion, lorcaserin, phendimetrazine, phentermine)

The WHO also has a functional classification system for PAH, similar to the NYHA classification used in heart failure.

WORLD HEALTH ORGANIZATION (WHO) CLINICAL CLASSIFICATION OF PULMONARY HYPERTENSION

Group 1: pulmonary arterial hypertension (PAH) – includes idiopathic, heritable, drug- and toxin-induced, disease-associated (e.g., connective tissue diseases, HIV infection, portal hypertension), and persistent pulmonary hypertension of a newborn

Group 2: pulmonary hypertension due to left heart disease

Group 3: pulmonary hypertension due to lung diseases and/or hypoxia

Group 4: chronic thromboembolic pulmonary hypertension (CTEPH)

Group 5: pulmonary hypertension with unclear or multifactorial mechanisms

PATHOPHYSIOLOGY

PAH stems from an imbalance in vasoconstrictor and vasodilator substances. Vasoconstrictor substances [e.g., endothelin-1 and thromboxane A2 (TXA2)] are increased and vasodilating substances (e.g., prostacyclins, others) are decreased. Vasoconstriction results in reduced blood flow and high pressure within the pulmonary vasculature. In addition, there is an imbalance between cell proliferation and apoptosis (cell death) in the walls of the pulmonary arteries. The increasing amount of pulmonary artery smooth muscle cells causes pulmonary artery walls to thicken and form scar tissue (vasoproliferation). As the walls thicken and scar, the arteries become increasingly narrower. These changes make it difficult for the right ventricle to pump blood through the pulmonary arteries and into the lungs due to the increased pressure. As a result of working harder, the right ventricle becomes enlarged and right heart failure develops. Heart failure is the most common cause of death in people who have PAH.

Symptoms of PAH include fatigue, dyspnea, chest pain, syncope, edema, tachycardia and/or Raynaud's phenomenon. In Raynaud's, reduced blood supply causes discoloration and coldness in the fingers, toes, and occasionally other areas.

There is no cure for PAH, but in the last decade, knowledge of the disease has increased significantly and many more treatment options have become available. Without treatment, life expectancy is three years. In some cases, a lung or heart-lung transplant may be an option, at least for younger patients.

NON-DRUG TREATMENT

Patients with PAH should follow a sodium restricted diet (< 2.4 grams/day) to help manage volume status, especially if they have right ventricular failure. Routine immunizations against influenza and pneumococcal pneumonia are advised. Exposure to high altitudes may contribute to hypoxic pulmonary vasoconstriction and may not be tolerated by patients. Oxygen is used when needed to maintain oxygen saturation above 90%.

DRUG TREATMENT

The biochemical changes mentioned above (↑ TXA2, ↓ prostacyclin), along with other altered pathways, lead to a pro-thrombotic state. Anticoagulation with warfarin, titrated to an INR of 1.5 – 2.5, can be considered to prevent blood clots from forming; this lower than usual INR goal is based on observational evidence and expert opinion assessing the risks and benefits of anticoagulation therapy in PAH. Other supportive therapies includes loop diuretics, if needed for volume overload, and possibly digoxin (to improve cardiac output or control heart rate in atrial fibrillation). Patients should be referred to a PAH specialty center for further management, including right heart catheterization to confirm the PAH diagnosis and determine responsiveness to acute vasoreactivity testing. During right heart catheterization, short-acting vasodilators (e.g., inhaled nitric oxide, IV epoprostenol, or IV adenosine) are administered. If the mPAP falls by at least 10 mmHg to an absolute value less than 40 mmHg, patients are considered responders and should be initiated on calcium channel blockers (CCBs). Approximately 10% of patients are candidates for CCB therapy, though only half of these will have a sustained response. The CCBs used most frequently are long-acting nifedipine, diltiazem, and amlodipine. The use of verapamil is not recommended due to its more pronounced negative inotropic effects, relative to diltiazem.

Non-responders to vasoreactivity testing, and positive responders who fail CCB therapy, need to be treated with one or more vasodilating drugs approved for PAH. These include prostacyclin analogues and receptor agonists, endothelin receptor antagonists (ERAs), phosphodiesterase-5 inhibitors (PDE-5), the same drugs used for erectile dysfunction but with different brand names and doses, and a soluble guanylate cyclase (sGC) stimulator. In most cases, drug therapy will reduce symptoms and improve exercise tolerance. Parenteral prostacyclin analogues, specifically IV epoprostenol, have been shown to decrease mortality. Some patients may benefit from combination therapy.

PAH Treatment Algorithm

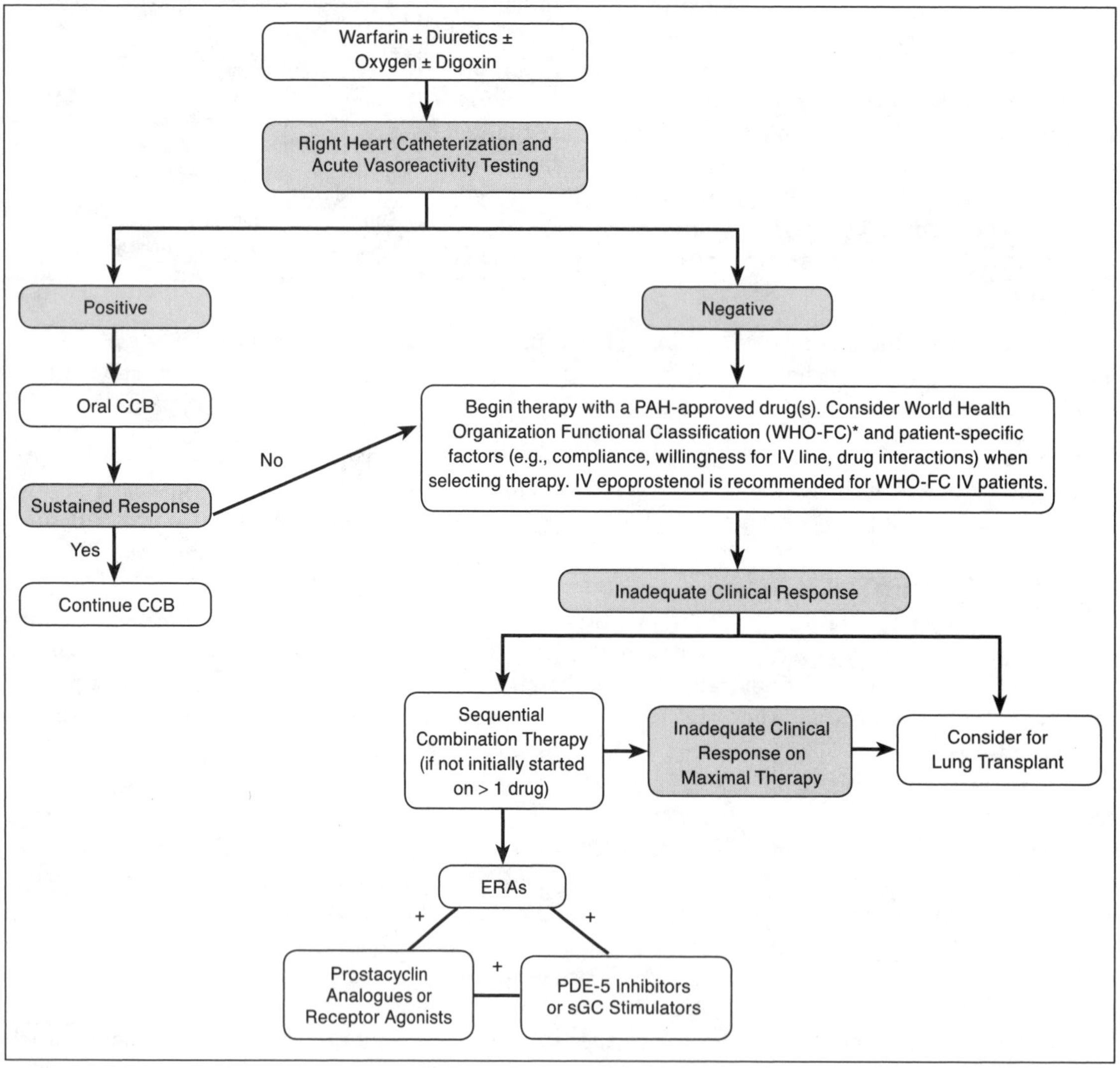

**WHO-FC: Class I = patients with PH but without limitation of physical activity; Class II = patients with PH resulting in slight limitation of physical activity (symptoms with ordinary physicial activity); Class III = patients with PH with marked limitation of physical activity (symptoms with less than ordinary physical activity); Class IV = patients with PH unable to be physically active and with signs of right heart failure (may be present at rest)*

Prostacyclin Analogues (or Prostanoids) and Receptor Agonists

Prostacyclin synthase is reduced in patients with PAH, causing decreased production of prostacyclin I_2, a vasodilator with anti-proliferative effects, in pulmonary artery smooth muscle cells. Prostacyclin analogues are potent vasodilators (of both pulmonary and systemic vascular beds) and inhibitors of platelet aggregation. The prostacyclin receptor agonist selexipag *(Uptravi)* is structurally different but works similarly. Drugs which decrease prostaglandins (e.g., NSAIDs) should be avoided in patients with PAH.

DRUG	DOSING	SAFETY/SIDE EFFECTS/MONITORING
Epoprostenol *(Flolan, Veletri)* AKA prostacyclin Continuous IV infusion via central venous catheter	Start at 2 ng/kg/min and ↑ by 1-2 ng/kg/min in 15 minute intervals based on clinical response; usual dose is 25-40 ng/kg/min but it can be titrated higher	**CONTRAINDICATIONS** Epoprostenol: heart failure with ↓ left ventricular ejection fraction Treprostinil (oral): severe hepatic impairment (Child-Pugh Class C) **WARNINGS** Rebound PH (do not ↓ dose or discontinue abruptly - see Notes), increased risk of bleeding Chronic IV infusions: sepsis and blood stream infections
Treprostinil *Remodulin:* continuous SC or IV (central venous catheter) infusion *Tyvaso:* inhalation *Orenitram*: oral, ER tablet	*Remodulin:* start at 1.25 ng/kg/min and ↑ by 1.25 ng/kg/min at weekly intervals for the first month then by 2.5 ng/kg/min at weekly intervals thereafter, up to 40 ng/kg/min (and possibly more) *Tyvaso:* start with 18 mcg (3 inhalations) 4 times/day and ↑ by 18 mcg (3 inhalations) per dose every 1-2 weeks to target of 54 mcg (9 inhalations) 4 times/ day; doses should be taken Q4hrs during waking hours *Orenitram:* start at 0.25 mg BID or 0.125 mg TID, ↑ by 0.25-0.5 mg BID or 0.125 mg TID every 3-4 days up to the maximum tolerated dose; take with food	Treprostinil (oral): tablet shell does not dissolve and can lodge in diverticuli **SIDE EFFECTS** Vasodilation reactions (hypotension, headache, dizziness, flushing, N/V/D), edema, jaw pain, musculoskeletal pain (e.g., myalgias), tachycardia, flu-like syndrome, anxiety, tremor, thrombocytopenia IV/SC infusions: infusion-site pain (especially SC *Remodulin* - see Notes) Treprostinil (inhaled) and iloprost: cough and mouth/throat irritation **NOTES** Parenteral agents are considered the most potent of all PAH medications. Avoid interruptions in therapy. Immediate access to a back up pump, infusion sets and medication is essential for parenteral products (particularly for epoprostenol). Epoprostenol half-life is ~6 minutes and treprostinil half-life is ~4 hours. Avoid large, sudden reductions in dose. Decrease dose gradually if side effects occur. Epoprostenol: must protect from light before reconstitution and during infusion. *Flolan:* reconstituted solutions require use of ice packs for stability. *Veletri* is thermostable (no need for ice packs). *Remodulin:* infusion site pain can occur in up to 85% of patients with SC administration (may need an analgesic to tolerate). Thermostable (no ice packs needed). To ↓ infections, patients must be instructed on how to care for infusion sites and use of sterile technique when preparing the drug for parenteral use. Lower starting doses required with mild or moderate hepatic impairment for selexipag and treprostinil; avoid selexipag with severe hepatic impairment.
Iloprost *(Ventavis)* Inhalation	2.5-5 mcg/inhalation given 6-9 times/day, no more than once every 2 hrs	
Selexipag *(Uptravi)* Tablet	Start with 200 mcg BID and ↑ by 200 mcg BID at weekly intervals to maximum dose of 1600 mcg BID	

Prostacyclin Analogue and Receptor Agonist Drug Interactions

- The effects of antihypertensive, antiplatelet and anticoagulant agents can be increased.
- Treprostinil levels are increased by CYP450 2C8 inhibitors (e.g., gemfibrozil) and decreased by 2C8 inducers (e.g., rifampin). Strong 2C8 inhibitors should be avoided with selexipag.

Endothelin Receptor Antagonists

Endothelin is a vasoconstrictor with cellular proliferative effects. Endothelin receptor antagonists (ERAs) block endothelin receptors on pulmonary artery smooth muscle cells.

DRUG	DOSING	SAFETY/SIDE EFFECTS/MONITORING
Bosentan *(Tracleer)*	< 40 kg: 62.5 mg BID ≥ 40 kg: 62.5 mg BID (for 4 wks), then 125 mg BID	**BOXED WARNINGS** Embryo-fetal toxicity (women of childbearing potential must have a negative pregnancy test prior to initiation of therapy and monthly thereafter) Bosentan: hepatotoxicity (↑ ALT/AST and liver failure) Available only through individual REMS programs *(Tracleer* REMS Program, *Letairis* REMS Program and *Opsumit* REMS Program); prescribers, pharmacies and patients must enroll (only female patients required to be enrolled in the *Letairis* and *Opsumit* REMS programs)
Ambrisentan *(Letairis)*	5 mg daily, may ↑ to 10 mg daily after 4 weeks if tolerated	**CONTRAINDICATIONS** Pregnancy Bosentan: use with cyclosporine or glyburide Ambrisentan: idiopathic pulmonary fibrosis **WARNINGS** Hepatotoxicity, ↓ Hgb/Hct, fluid retention (e.g., pulmonary edema, peripheral edema), decreased sperm counts
Macitentan *(Opsumit)*	10 mg daily	**SIDE EFFECTS** Headache, upper respiratory tract infections (e.g., nasal congestion, cough, bronchitis), flushing, hypotension **MONITORING** LFTs, bilirubin, Hgb/Hct, pregnancy tests **NOTES** Safety issue - see Pregnancy chapter. MedGuide required.

Endothelin Receptor Antagonist Drug Interactions

- Bosentan is a substrate and inducer of 3A4 and 2C9; monitor for drug interactions. Levels of bosentan can increase with 2C9 (e.g., amiodarone, fluconazole) and 3A4 (e.g., ritonavir) inhibitors. Avoid concurrent use of cyclosporine or glyburide. Bosentan can decrease the effectiveness of hormonal contraceptives (at least one barrier method of contraception, if not two, is recommended).
- Ambrisentan is a substrate of 3A4 (major), 2C19 (minor) and P-gp. Cyclosporine can increase the serum concentration of ambrisentan; limit the dose of ambrisentan to 5 mg daily when given with cyclosporine.
- Macitentan is a substrate of 3A4 (major) and 2C19 (minor). Strong 3A4 inhibitors and inducers should be avoided with macitentan.

Phosphodiesterase-5 Inhibitors

PDE-5 is responsible for the degradation of cyclic guanosine monophosphate (cGMP); increased cGMP concentrations lead to pulmonary vasculature relaxation and vasodilation.

<table>
<tr><th>DRUG</th><th>DOSING</th><th>SAFETY/SIDE EFFECTS/MONITORING</th></tr>
<tr><td>Sildenafil (Revatio)
Viagra - ED
Tablet, oral suspension, intravenous</td><td>IV: 2.5-10 mg TID
Oral: 5-20 mg TID, taken 4-6 hours apart</td><td rowspan="2">CONTRAINDICATIONS
Use with nitrates or riociguat
Revatio: avoid taking with protease inhibitors (e.g., atazanavir, ritonavir, others)

WARNINGS
Hearing loss (with or without tinnitus and dizziness); vision loss, rare but may be due to nonarteritic anterior ischemic optic neuropathy (NAION); priapism – seek emergency medical care if erection lasts > 4 hours; hypotension, pulmonary edema
Revatio: not recommended for pediatric use due to increased mortality

SIDE EFFECTS
Headache, flushing, dyspepsia, extremity or back pain, N/D, epistaxis

NOTES
Adcirca: avoid use in severe hepatic impairment.</td></tr>
<tr><td>Tadalafil (Adcirca)
Cialis - ED, BPH
Tablet</td><td>40 mg daily
20 mg daily if mild to moderate renal or hepatic impairment
CrCl < 30 mL/min: avoid use</td></tr>
</table>

PDE-5 Inhibitor Drug Interactions

- Do not give with other PDE-5 inhibitors used for erectile dysfunction.
- Do not use with nitrate medications (any formulation – see Ischemic Heart Disease chapter) or the sGC stimulator riociguat as the potential for excessively low blood pressure is increased. Taking nitrates is an absolute contraindication to the use of PDE-5 inhibitors; this includes the illicit drugs such as amyl nitrate and butyl nitrate ("poppers").
- Use caution with alpha blocker therapy (or other antihypertensives) as PDE-5 inhibitors can increase the hypotensive effects of these agents. When tadalafil is used for PAH, alpha 1-blockers are not recommended for the treatment of BPH.
- PDE-5 inhibitors are major substrates of 3A4; avoid use of strong 3A4 inhibitors and inducers.

Soluble Guanylate Cyclase Stimulator

Soluble guanylate cyclase (sGC) is a receptor for endogenous nitric oxide. Riociguat *(Adempas)* sensitizes sGC to endogenous nitric oxide and directly stimulates the receptor at a different binding site. This increases cGMP, leading to relaxation and antiproliferative effects in the pulmonary artery smooth muscle cells. Riociguat is approved for use in both PAH and CTEPH.

DRUG	DOSING	SAFETY/SIDE EFFECTS/MONITORING
Riociguat *(Adempas)*	Start with 0.5-1 mg TID, increasing by 0.5 mg TID every 2 weeks if SBP > 95 mmHg; max dose is 2.5 mg TID	**BOXED WARNING** Embryo-fetal toxicity (women of childbearing potential must have a negative pregnancy test prior to initiation of therapy and monthly thereafter) Available only through the *Adempas* REMS Program; prescribers, pharmacies and female patients must enroll **CONTRAINDICATIONS** Pregnancy, use of PDE-5 inhibitors or nitrates **WARNINGS** Hypotension, bleeding, pulmonary edema **SIDE EFFECTS** Headache, dyspepsia, dizziness, N/V/D **NOTES** Safety issue - see Pregnancy chapter. MedGuide required.

Riociguat Drug Interactions

- Do not use with nitrate medications (any formulation – see Ischemic Heart Disease chapter) or PDE-5 inhibitors as the potential for excessively low blood pressure is increased.
- Smoking increases riociguat clearance; the dose may need to be decreased with smoking cessation.
- Separate from antacids by > 1 hour.
- Riociguat is a major substrate of 3A4, 2C8 and P-gp; monitor for drug interactions and dose adjustments.

PULMONARY FIBROSIS

Pulmonary fibrosis (PF) is scarred and damaged lung tissue. The common presentation is exertional dyspnea with a nonproductive cough. As the condition worsens, breathing becomes more labored. There are a variety of causes of PF, including toxin exposure (e.g., asbestos, silica, others), medical conditions, and drugs (see box) among others. Often the contributing factor is not identified and the PF is called idiopathic pulmonary fibrosis (IPF).

SELECT DRUGS THAT CAN CAUSE PF	
Amiodarone	Nitrofurantoin
Methotrexate	Sulfasalazine

If the condition is drug-induced, the offending drug should be discontinued. Aside from treatment with chronic oxygen supplementation, two drugs are now available for IPF. Both pirfenidone *(Esbriet)* and nintedanib *(Ofev)* slow the rate of decline in lung function. In addition to these two drugs, several of the drugs approved for PAH (particularly sildenafil) may be used off-label for PF. The prognosis of IPF is poor; 5 year survival is approximately 20 – 30% once diagnosed.

ALLERGIC RHINITIS, COUGH & COLD

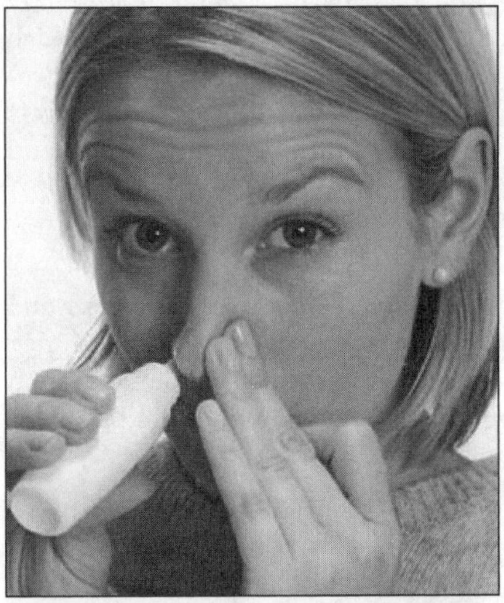

ALLERGIC RHINITIS

Background

Allergic rhinitis is inflammation of the nasal airways and is very common, affecting up to 20% – 40% of the population. It is classified as intermittent (infrequent or seasonal) or persistent (chronic or perennial), and symptoms can be mild, moderate or severe. It represents an opportunity for pharmacists to help patients select self care over the counter products, and to use prescription medication correctly. Allergic rhinitis is a major reason for decreased work productivity, or lost work or school days each year. Symptoms include sneezing, itchy nose, eyes or throat, watery eyes, rhinorrhea (runny nose), nasal congestion, and postnasal drip. It can also result in fatigue, irritability, sleep disturbance and reduced cognitive ability. Untreated allergic rhinitis can lead to sinusitis, otitis media (in children) and asthma exacerbation in susceptible people. Unlike the common cold or the flu, onset of symptoms occurs quickly (within minutes) after allergen exposure.

GUIDELINES/REFERENCES

Seidman MD, Gurgel RK, Lin SY et al. Clinical Practice Guideline: Allergic Rhinitis. *Otolaryngology-Head and Neck Surgery.* 2015;152(IS):S1-S43.

Krinsky DL, Berardi RR, Ferreri SP, eds. Handbook of Nonprescription Drugs. 18th ed. Washington DC: APhA; 2015:172-208.

NON-DRUG TREATMENT

Environmental control is required to minimize allergic symptoms and involves avoiding exposure to known or suspected allergens, if possible. An IgE-mediated skin or blood allergy test by an allergy or pulmonary specialist can help determine patient-specific allergens. Common allergens include house-dust mites, outdoor mold spores, pollen from trees and ragweed, cat-derived allergens, cockroaches, and urban pollutants such as a diesel exhaust particles. Ventilation systems with high-efficiency particulate air (HEPA) filters can help with some allergens (pollen, mold), however, these systems are expensive and ineffective for some patients. Vacuuming carpets, drapes, and upholstery with a HEPA vacuum cleaner weekly or more often will reduce household allergens. Removing carpets, upholstered furniture, encasing pillows, mattresses and box springs in allergen-impermeable covers, and washing bedding and soft toys in hot water weekly reduces dust mite allergens. Patients with air pollutants as triggers should be aware of the air quality index (AQI) and plan outdoor activities accordingly. Patients with pollen as a trigger should monitor pollen counts and plan accordingly. Staying indoors, closing windows in the house or car and using air-conditioning can help reduce exposure. However, keeping an environment that is "too clean" reduces exposure to microbes and helminths and may not be ideal: children need exposure to various "germs" to build a healthy immune system.

Nasal Irrigation and Wetting Agents

Nasal wetting agents (saline, propylene and polyethylene glycol sprays) or nasal irrigation with warm saline (isotonic or hypertonic) may reduce symptoms. Nasal irrigation rinses out allergens and mucus, increases ciliary function and reduces swelling. Saline solutions are either isotonic (0.9%) or hypertonic (2 – 3.5%). A popular product, the "neti pot", looks like a small genie lamp or teapot. It is used to hold salt water (saline solution) that is poured into one nostril and drained out of the other nostril. Nasal irrigation is safe for children and pregnant women. Tap water contains some organisms that are safe to ingest orally (they are killed by stomach acid), but when it is used for nasal irrigation, these can rarely cause fatal infections. Instruct the patient to use only boiled or distilled water (not directly from the faucet). The most common side effects are nasal burning, stinging, pain or irritation, which are increased with higher concentrations of saline. The pots or bottles should be rinsed with safe water after every use ad left to air dry. Pots and bottles should never be shared with others. Nasal gels with petrolatum *(Allergen Block)* can be applied around the nostrils to physically block pollens and allergens from entering the nose.

DRUG TREATMENT

Selecting appropriate pharmacologic management depends on the person's severity of illness and symptoms. Intranasal corticosteroids are first-line for chronic, moderate-to-severe rhinitis. Milder, intermittent symptoms can be treated with oral antihistamines. Decongestants are used for congestion (if present) and come in nasal and oral formulations. Agents for itchy eyes can be found in the Glaucoma, Ophthalmics & Otics chapter. A variety of other agents can be modestly useful.

Intranasal Corticosteroids

Intranasal corticosteroids work by decreasing inflammation. They are the most effective medication class in controlling symptoms of chronic allergic rhinitis and are considered first-line treatment for moderate-severe rhinitis. They are especially effective in reducing the nasal symptoms of allergic rhinitis (sneezing, itching, rhinorrhea, congestion). Triamcinolone (*Nasacort* Allergy 24HR), fluticasone (*Flonase Allergy Relief*) and budesonide *(Rhinocort Allergy Spray)* are approved for nonprescription use to treat nasal allergy symptoms. Take note that steroids used to treat chronic allergic rhinitis have different brand names and delivery vehicles than those used to treat asthma. For example, fluticasone for nasal allergy relief is *Flonase* ("-nase" for nose) and for asthma is *Flovent*.

DRUG	DOSING	SAFETY/SIDE EFFECTS/MONITORING
Beclomethasone *(Beconase AQ, Qnasl)*	Adult: 1-2 sprays per nostril BID *(Beconase AQ)*; 2 sprays per nostril daily *(Qnasl)* Age 6-11 yrs.: 1-2 sprays per nostril BID *(Beconase AQ)*	**WARNINGS** Adrenal suppression: Can occur when used in high doses for prolonged periods Delayed wound healing: Avoid use if recent nasal septal ulcers, nasal surgery, or nasal trauma until healing has occurred. Pediatrics: can ↓ growth velocity in pediatric patients (~1 centimeter/yr and is dose and duration related). To minimize, use lowest effective dose. Monitor growth. Infections: Prolonged use can ↑ the risk of secondary infection or limit response to vaccines. Avoid exposure to chickenpox. Caution in patients with untreated fungal, viral, or bacterial infections. Ocular disease: Caution in patients with cataracts and/or glaucoma; ↑ intraocular pressure, open-angle glaucoma, and cataracts have occurred with prolonged use. Consider routine eye exams in chronic users. **SIDE EFFECTS** Headache, dry nose, epistaxis (nose bleeds), unpleasant taste, localized infection **NOTES** Can take up to one week to get full relief. Budesonide is the preferred nasal steroid in pregnancy. If using regularly for several months, recommend periodic nasal exams to evaluate for nasal septal perforation or ulcers. Advise patients to discontinue if they come into contact with a person who has chickenpox, measles or TB, if they develop symptoms of an infection, have a change in vision, or experience frequent nose bleeds. Instruct patients to shake bottle well before each use and discard product after total number of estimated doses, even if bottle does not feel completely empty.
Budesonide ***(Rhinocort Aqua, Rhinocort Allergy Spray OTC)***	Adult: 1 spray per nostril daily (max 4 sprays per nostril daily) Age ≥ 6 yrs.: 1 spray per nostril daily (max 2 sprays per nostril daily)	
Ciclesonide *(Omnaris, Zetonna)*	Adult: 2 sprays per nostril daily *(Omnaris)*; 1 spray per nostril daily *(Zetonna)* Age ≥ 6 yrs.: use adult dose	
Flunisolide	Adult: 2 sprays per nostril BID or TID Age 6-14 yrs.: 1 spray per nostril TID or 2 sprays per nostril BID	
Fluticasone ***(Flonase)*** *OTC products: Flonase Allergy Relief, Flonase Sensimist, Children's Flonase* + azelastine *(Dymista)*	Adult: 1-2 sprays per nostril daily *(Flonase, Flonase Allergy Relief, Flonase Sensimist)* Age 4-11 yrs.: 1 spray per nostril daily *(Children's Flonase)* Age ≥ 2 yrs.: 1-2 sprays per nostril daily *(Sensimist)* *Dymista:* Adult and age ≥ 6 yrs: 1 spray per nostril BID	
Mometasone *(Nasonex)*	Adult: 2 sprays per nostril daily Age 2-11 yrs.: 1 spray per nostril daily	
Triamcinolone *(Nasacort AQ,* ***Nasacort Allergy 24HR OTC)***	Adult: 1-2 sprays per nostril daily Age ≥ 6 yrs.: use adult dose Age 2-5 yrs.: 1 spray per nostril daily	

Oral Antihistamines

Oral antihistamines are considered first-line agents for patients with mild-moderate disease. They are effective in reducing symptoms of itching, sneezing, rhinorrhea, and other types of immediate hypersensitivity reactions, but have little effect on nasal congestion. Antihistamines work by blocking histamine at the histamine-1 (H1) receptor site. The second-generation agents are generally preferred since they cause less sedation and cognitive impairment. Antihistamines can help if symptoms of allergic conjunctivitis (itchy, red eyes) are present. See Glaucoma, Ophthalmics & Otics chapter.

SELECT FIRST GENERATION ORAL ANTIHISTAMINES

DRUG	DOSING	SAFETY/SIDE EFFECTS/MONITORING
Clemastine *(Tavist Allergy, Dayhist Allergy 12 HR Relief)* Tablet, syrup	Adult: 1.34-2.68 mg PO Q8-12H (max 8.04 mg/day) Age 6-11 yrs.: 0.67-1.34 mg PO BID (max 4.02 mg/day)	**CONTRAINDICATIONS** Newborns or premature infants, lactating women, narrow-angle glaucoma, acute asthma exacerbation, stenosing peptic ulcer, symptomatic BPH, and bladder-neck and pyloroduodenal obstruction. Avoid concurrent use of MAO inhibitors. **WARNINGS** Due to strong anticholinergic effects, avoid use in elderly (Beers criteria), caution with cardiovascular disease, prostate enlargement, glaucoma, asthma, pyloroduodenal obstruction, thyroid disease. Caution for excessive sedation. In 2008 the FDA advised that OTC cough and cold preparations, including first generation antihistamines (chlorpheniramine, diphenhydramine, brompheniramine and clemastine) should not be used in children < 2 years due to the risk of potentially serious and life threatening side effects. **SIDE EFFECTS** Somnolence, cognitive impairment, strong anticholinergic effects (dry mouth, blurred vision, urinary retention, constipation), and seizures/arrhythmias in higher doses **NOTES** First generation antihistamines should not be taken by lactating women; second generation agents, such as loratadine or fexofenadine, are preferred. All antihistamines should be discontinued at least 4 days prior to allergy skin testing. 1st generation antihistamines are photosensitizing; advise patients to use sunscreens and wear protective clothing while taking them.
DiphenhydrAMINE HCl *(Benadryl*, many others) Capsule, tablet, chewable, elixir, strip, syrup, suspension, injection, cream, gel, solution, stick	Adult: 25-50 mg PO Q4-6H (max 300 mg/day) Age 6-11 yrs.: 12.5-25 mg PO Q4-6H (max 150 mg/day) Age < 6 yrs.: do not use for self care	
Carbinoxamine *(Arbinoxa, Karbinal ER)* Capsule, tablet, solution	**IR** Adult: 4-8 mg PO Q6-8H 6-11 yrs.: 2-4 mg PO Q6-8H 2-5 yrs.: 1-2 mg PO Q6-8H **ER** Adult: 6-16 mg PO Q12H 6-11 yrs.: 6-12 mg PO Q12H 4-5 yrs.: 3-8 mg PO Q12H 2-3 yrs.: 3-4 mg PO Q12H	
Chlorpheniramine *(Chlor-Trimeton, Chlorphen, Ed ChlorPed,* others) Tablet, liquid, suspension, syrup	**IR** Adult: 4 mg PO Q4-6H (max 24 mg/day) 6-11 yrs.: 2 mg PO Q4-6H (max 12 mg/day) 2-5 yrs.: 1 mg PO Q4-6H (max 6 mg/day) **ER** Adult: 12 mg PO Q12H (max 24 mg/day) no pediatric dosing	

Oral Antihistamines Continued

DRUG	DOSING	SAFETY/SIDE EFFECTS/MONITORING

SECOND GENERATION ORAL ANTIHISTAMINES

DRUG	DOSING	SAFETY/SIDE EFFECTS/MONITORING
Cetirizine *(ZyrTEC, ZyrTEC-D*, others) Capsule, tablet, solution, syrup, chewable, ODT	Adult: 5-10 mg PO daily (max 5 mg daily in elderly) ≥ 6 yrs.: use adult dose 2-5 yrs.: 2.5-5 mg PO daily	**CONTRAINDICATIONS** Levocetirizine: end-stage renal disease (CrCl < 10 mL/min), hemodialysis, infants and children 6 months to 11 years of age with renal impairment **WARNINGS** CNS depression: can cause sedation when used with other sedating drugs **SIDE EFFECTS** Somnolence can still be seen occasionally with the 2nd generation agents (more with cetirizine and levocetirizine) **NOTES** Fexofenadine: take with water (not juice due to ↓ absorption). Avoid concurrent administration with aluminum or magnesium-containing products. All antihistamines should be discontinued at least 4 days prior to allergy skin testing. If a 2nd generation antihistamine is preferred in pregnancy, loratadine and cetirizine are considered low risk.
Levocetirizine (*Xyzal*) Tablet, solution	Adult: 5 mg PO QHS 6-11 yrs.: 2.5 mg PO QHS 6 mos-5 yrs.: 1.25 mg PO QHS	
Fexofenadine *(Allegra, Allegra D 12H, Allegra D 24H, Children's Allegra ODT, Mucinex Allergy)* Tablet, suspension, ODT	Adult: 60 mg PO BID or 180 mg daily 2-11 yrs.: 30 mg PO BID	
Loratadine (*Claritin, Claritin-D 24 hour, Claritin RediTabs, Alavert)* Tablet, capsule, chewable, solution, syrup, ODT	Adult: 10 mg PO daily or 5 mg PO BID *(RediTabs)* Age ≥ 6 yrs.: use adult dose 2-5 yrs.: 5 mg PO daily	
Desloratadine *(Clarinex, Clarinex D, Clarinex RediTabs)* Tablet, syrup, ODT	Adult: 5 mg PO daily 6-11 yrs.: 2.5 mg PO daily 12 mos-5 yrs.: 1.25 mg PO daily 6-11 mos.: 1 mg PO daily	

INTRANASAL ANTIHISTAMINES

DRUG	DOSING	SAFETY/SIDE EFFECTS/MONITORING
Azelastine *(Astelin, Astepro)* + fluticasone *(Dymista)*	Adult: 1-2 sprays per nostril BID 6-11 yrs.: 1 spray per nostril BID	**SIDE EFFECTS** Bitter taste, headache, somnolence, nasal irritation, minor nosebleed, sinus pain **NOTES** Helps with nasal congestion as well.
Olopatadine *(Patanase)*	Adult: 2 sprays per nostril BID 6-11 yrs.: 1 spray per nostril BID	

Decongestants

These agents are effective in reducing sinus and nasal congestion. Decongestants are alpha-adrenergic agonists (sympathomimetics) that work by causing vasoconstriction that decreases sinusoid vessel engorgement and mucosal edema. If a product contains a D after the name (such as *Mucinex D* or *Robitussin D*), it usually contains a decongestant (phenylephrine or pseudoephedrine).

DRUG	DOSING	SAFETY/SIDE EFFECTS/MONITORING

SYSTEMIC (ORAL)

DRUG	DOSING	SAFETY/SIDE EFFECTS/MONITORING
Phenylephrine HCl ***(Sudafed PE***, others) Tablet, liquid, solution, injection	Adult: 10 mg PO Q4H PRN (max 60 mg/day) 6-11 yrs.: 5 mg PO Q4H PRN (max 30 mg/day) 4-5 yrs.: 2.5 mg PO Q4H PRN (max 15 mg/day)	**CONTRAINDICATIONS** Do not use within 14 days of MAO inhibitors. **WARNINGS** Avoid in children < 2 years Use with caution in patients with CV disease and uncontrolled hypertension (can ↑ BP), hyperthyroidism (can worsen), diabetes (can ↑ blood glucose), bowel obstruction, glaucoma (can ↑ IOP), BPH (can cause urinary retention), and in the elderly
Pseudoephedrine *(Sudafed, Nexafed, Zephrex-D*, others) Tablet, liquid, syrup	Adult: 60 mg PO Q4-6H PRN, or 120 mg PO ER Q12H, or 240 mg PO ER daily (max 240 mg/day) 6-12 yrs.: 30 mg PO Q4-6H PRN (max 120 mg/day) 4-5 yrs.: 15 mg PO Q4-6H PRN (max 60 mg/day)	**SIDE EFFECTS** Cardiovascular stimulation (tachycardia, palpitations, ↑ BP), CNS stimulation (anxiety, tremors, insomnia, nervousness, restlessness, fear, hallucinations), dizziness, headache, anorexia **NOTES** Phenylephrine has low bioavailability (~38%); pseudoephedrine is more effective Onset of 15-60 minutes

TOPICALS (INTRANASAL)

DRUG	DOSING	SAFETY/SIDE EFFECTS/MONITORING
Naphazoline 0.05% *(Privine)*	Adult: 1-2 sprays per nostril Q6H PRN	**CONTRAINDICATIONS** Phenylephrine: hypertension, ventricular tachycardia
Oxymetazoline 0.05% ***(Afrin**, Neo-Synephrine Nighttime 12-Hour, Vicks Sinex, Zicam Extreme Congestion Relief)*	Adult: 2-3 sprays per nostril Q12H PRN ≥ 6 yrs.: use adult dose	**WARNINGS** Do not use with MAO inhibitors, or if have closed angle glaucoma
Phenylephrine 0.125%, 0.25%, 0.5%, 1% *(Neo-Synephrine 4-Hour, Little Noses Decongestant Drops)*	Adult: 2-3 sprays of 0.25% to 1% per nostril Q4H PRN 6-12 yrs.: 2-3 sprays of 0.25% per nostril Q4H PRN 2-5 yrs.: 2-3 sprays of 0.125% per nostril Q4H PRN	**SIDE EFFECTS** Stinging, burning, sneezing, dryness (vehicle-related), trauma from the tip of the device, rhinitis medicamentosa (rebound congestion if used longer than 3 days) **NOTES** Effective with a fast onset of 5-10 minutes
Tetrahydrozoline 0.05%, 0.1% *(Tyzine)* – Rx	Adult: 3-4 sprays of 0.1% per nostril Q3-4H PRN or 2-4 drops per nostril Q3-4H PRN > 6 yrs.: use adult dose 2-6 yrs.: 2-3 drops of 0.05% per nostril Q4-6H PRN	Limit use to ≤ 3 days to prevent rebound congestion

Additional Allergy Agents

Intranasal cromolyn *(Nasalcrom)*

Cromolyn is a mast cell stabilizer used for treatment and prophylaxis. It must be started at the onset of allergy season and used regularly (not PRN), 1 spray per nostril every 6 – 8 hours, to be effective. Symptoms start to improve in 3 – 7 days but can take as long as 2 – 4 weeks of continued use to see maximal effect. Although generally not as effective as other agents, it is used in children 2 years and older and pregnancy due to its safety profile.

Intranasal ipratropium bromide *(Atrovent Nasal Spray)*

This agent is effective for decreasing rhinorrhea by causing nasal dryness (not effective for other nasal symptoms).

Oral antileukotrienes (Montelukast – *Singulair*)

Montelukast has similar efficacy to antihistamines or pseudoephedrine and can be recommended for adjunctive relief. The dose of montelukast is 10 mg PO daily (15 years and up), 5 mg chewable tablet PO daily (ages 6 – 14 years), 4 mg chewable tablet PO daily (ages 2 – 5 years), or one packet of 4 mg oral granules PO daily (ages 6 months-5 years). See Asthma chapter for more information.

Sublingual Immunotherapy

In 2014 the FDA approved 3 new sublingual (SL) treatments for allergic rhinitis due to specific types of grass pollen. They are alternatives to allergy shots, which must be given in a physician office. The first dose must be given in the doctor's office with all 3 of these agents, but subsequent doses can be taken at home. The patient must be monitored for at least 30 minutes for signs of allergic reactions (boxed warning) and the patient should be prescribed epinephrine auto-injector.

- *Oralair* contains 5 different grass pollen extracts. Place 1 SL tablet under the tongue daily; initiate treatment 4 months before and during grass pollen season.
- *Grastek* contains Timothy grass pollen extract. Place 1 SL tablet under the tongue daily; initiate treatment 3 months before and during grass pollen season.
- *Ragwitek* contains ragweed pollen extract. Place 1 SL tablet under the tongue daily; initiate treatment 3 months before and during pollen season.

COMBAT METHAMPHETAMINE EPIDEMIC ACT 2005

The sale of non-prescription pseudoephedrine (PSE) is restricted as part of the "Combat Meth Act" (CMEA) to crack down on the methamphetamine epidemic. Meth causes unpredictable and often violent behavior. The waste created in the production is very toxic and is usually dumped illegally. The act applies to any non-prescription product containing pseudoephedrine, phenylpropanolamine and ephedrine, all of which can be converted rather easily into methamphetamine.

These products must be kept behind the counter or in a locked cabinet. They often are, but do not need to be, located in the pharmacy. Stores must keep a logbook of sales (the exception is the single dose package that contains a maximum of 60 mg). For any sale above this amount, the customer must show a government-issued photo ID (e.g., driver's license, ID card, US passport).

Customers record their name, date and time of sale, and sign the logbook. The store staff must verify that the name matches the photo ID and that the date and time are correct. The store staff must also record the address; some stores can swipe the driver's license electronically to do this. The store staff must record what the person received as well as the quantity purchased. Under federal law the maximum amount allowed for purchase is 3.6 grams per day, and 9 grams in a 30-day period. The logbook must be kept for a minimum of 2 years and must be kept secured and readily available upon request by board inspectors or law enforcement. The logbook cannot be shared with the public.

Many states now have their own restrictions in addition to the federal restriction, such as age restrictions, prescription required or stricter limits.

COUGH AND COLD

Background

The common cold, a viral infection of the upper respiratory tract, is caused by over 200 viruses including rhinoviruses and coronaviruses. It is transmitted primarily by mucus secretions via patient's hands or by the air from coughing or sneezing. Coughing or sneezing into the elbow or into a tissue is preferable over coughing into a hand, which can then touch surfaces and spread illness. Frequent hand cleansing with soap or soap substitutes (e.g., hand sanitizer) should be encouraged. Refer to the Medication Safety and Quality Improvement chapter for correct hand washing technique. Refer to the Infectious Diseases II chapter for a table of common upper and lower respiratory infections. Although colds are usually self-limiting, they are the leading cause of absenteeism in work and school due to bothersome symptoms.

Natural Products used for Colds

Zinc, in various formulations including lozenges, is used for cold prevention and treatment. There is little efficacy data for cold prevention, but zinc lozenges or syrup may decrease cold duration if used correctly (taken every 2 hours while awake, starting within 24 hours of symptom onset). For this purpose zinc supplements are rated as "possibly effective" by the *Natural Medicines Database*. Zinc lozenges can cause mouth irritation, a metallic taste and nausea. Do not use for more than 5 – 7 days as long term use can cause copper deficiency. Due to loss of smell, zinc nasal formulations were removed from the market. Vitamin C (ascorbic acid) supplements are commonly used, with no efficacy for cold prevention. Some data has shown a decrease in the duration of the cold by 1 – 1.5 days at doses of 1 – 3 grams/day. There may also be a dose-dependent response; doses of at least 2 grams/day appears to work better than 1 gram/day. Vitamin C is rated as "possibly effective" for cold treatment by the *Natural Medicines Database*. However, high doses of vitamin C (4 g/day or greater) may cause diarrhea as well as kidney stones in male patients. Echinacea is also rated as "possibly effective" for cold treatment. With any of these products it is important to use the correct dose from a reputable manufacturer. *Airborne* and *Emergen-C Immune+* are popular products that contains a variety of ingredients, including vitamins C, vitamin E, zinc and echinacea. They are costly and have no proven benefit in the combinations provided.

Expectorants

Cough associated with colds is usually nonproductive. However, expectorants can be used for a productive cough to ↓ phlegm viscosity in the lower respiratory tract and ↑ secretions in the upper respiratory tract to help move phlegm upwards and out.

DRUG	DOSING	SAFETY/SIDE EFFECTS/MONITORING
GuaiFENesin *(Mucinex, Robitussin Mucus + Chest Congestion)* Tablet, caplet, liquid, syrup, granule	200-400 mg Q4H PRN, or 600-1,200 mg ER Q12H (max 2.4 g/day) Age 6-11 yrs:1,200 mg/day (max) Age 4-5 yrs: 600 mg/day (max)	**WARNINGS** Some formulations may contain phenylalanine. **SIDE EFFECTS** Nausea (dose-related), vomiting, dizziness, headache, rash, diarrhea, stomach pain **NOTES** Not for OTC use in children < 2 years of age

Cough Suppressants

Cough suppressants are used for dry, unproductive cough, or to suppress productive cough at night to allow for restful sleep. Dextromethorphan (DM) and codeine have high affinity to several regions of the brain, including the medullary cough center, suppressing the cough reflex. DM also acts as a serotonin reuptake inhibitor. DM is a nonopioid agent without analgesic, sedative, respiratory depressant, or addictive properties when used at usual antitussive doses. However, DM is a drug of abuse as it acts as an NMDA-receptor blocker in high doses leading to euphoric and hallucinogenic properties similar to PCP, termed "robo-tripping". Its safety and efficacy in children has not been established and due to it's abuse potential, California became the first state to ban the sale of DM to minors < 18 years of age. A few other states have followed, some with more stringent requirements. Codeine products scheduled as C-V drugs must contain one or more noncodeine active ingredients and no more than 200 mg of codeine/100 mL. Codeine is commonly abused, particularly in combination with promethazine, known by street names "purple drank" and "lean". Benzonatate suppresses cough by topical anesthetic action on the respiratory stretch receptors.

DRUG	DOSING	SAFETY/SIDE EFFECTS/MONITORING
Dextromethorphan *(Delsym, DayQuil Cough)* Capsule, liquids, lozenge, strips	10-20 mg Q4H PRN, or 30 mg Q6-8H PRN, or 60 mg ER Q12H PRN (max 120 mg/day) Age 6-12 yrs: 60 mg/day max Age 4-6 yrs: 30 mg/day max	**CONTRAINDICATIONS** All dextromethophan-containing products should not be used within 14 days of MAO inhibitor use. **SIDE EFFECTS** N/V, drowsiness, serotonin syndrome if co-administered with other serotonergic drugs **NOTES** If the product name has DM at the end, such as *Robitussin DM*, it contains dextromethorphan. Additive CNS depression may occur with alcohol, antihistamines, and psychotropic medications.
Codeine C-II	Adults: 10-20 mg Q4-6H PRN (max 120 mg/day)	**BOXED WARNING** Respiratory depression and death have occurred in children who received codeine following tonsillectomy and/or adenoidectomy and had evidence of being ultra-rapid metabolizers of codeine due to a CYP2D6 polymorphism, avoid. **CONTRAINDICATIONS** Paralytic ileus, children who have undergone tonsillectomy and/or adenoidectomy, known codeine hypersensitivity, during labor when a premature birth is anticipated **SIDE EFFECTS** N/V, sedation, constipation, hypotension **NOTES:** Use with CNS depressants causes additive CNS depression
Benzonatate *(Tessalon Perles, Zonatuss)*	100-200 mg TID PRN (max 600 mg/day)	**WARNINGS** Accidental ingestion and fatal overdose has been reported in children < 10 years of age, avoid. **SIDE EFFECTS** Somnolence, confusion, hallucinations
Diphenhydramine *(Benadryl)*	25 mg Q4H PRN (max 150 mg/day)	See First Generation Oral Antihistamine table

Decongestants

Systemic and nasal decongestants are used to relieve congestion and rhinorrhea. These agents are discussed in the previous section.

Analgesics/Antipyretics

Analgesics and antipyretics such as acetaminophen and ibuprofen are used to relieve sore throat, body malaise, and/or fever. See Pain chapter for more information.

Select Cough and Cold Combination Products

DRUG	ADULT DOSING
Dextromethorphan/promethazine	15 mg/6.25 mg per 5 mL; 5 mL Q4-6H PRN (max 30 mL/day)
Brompheniramine/pseudoephedrine/ dextromethorphan *(Bromfed DM)*	2 mg/30 mg/10 mg per 5 mL; 10 mL Q4H PRN (max 60 mL/day)
Promethazine/phenylephrine/codeine (Promethazine VC/Codeine) C-V	6.25 mg/5 mg/10 mg per 5 mL; 5 mL Q4-6H PRN (max 30 mL/day)
GuaiFENesin/codeine *(Robafen AC, Virtussin AC)* C-V	100 mg/10 mg per 5 mL; 10 mL PO Q4H PRN (max 60 mL/day)
GuaiFENesin/codeine/pseudoephedrine *(Cheratussin DAC, Mytussin DAC)* C-V	100 mg/10 mg/30 mg per 5 mL; 10 mL Q4H PRN (max 40 mL/day)
Chlorpheniramine/hydrocodone *(TussiCaps, Tussionex, Vituz)* C-II	8 mg/10 mg ER per 5 mL; 5 mL Q12H PRN (max 10 mL/day)
Chlorpheniramine polistirex/codeine polistirex *(Tuzistra XR)*, C-III	10 mL PO Q12H PRN (max 20 mL/day)

Cough and Cold Products in Children

In 2008, the FDA warned that OTC cough and cold products should not be used in children under 2 years old due to safety concerns. Later that same year, many manufacturers voluntarily re-labeled these cough and cold products to state: "do not use in children under 4 years of age." The American Academy of Pediatrics has recommended against their use in children under 6 years old, due to inadequate data on efficacy and the potential for errors and adverse effects.. These cough and cold products include any product containing decongestants and the antihistamines diphenhydramine, brompheniramine or chlorpheniramine. Do not use promethazine in any form in children less than 2 years old. The FDA advises against the use of promethazine with codeine cough syrups in children ≤ 6 years of age, due to the risk of respiratory depression, cardiac arrest and neurological problems.

If a young child has a cold, it is safe and useful to recommend proper hydration, nasal bulbs for gentle suctioning, saline drops/sprays (*Ocean* and generics), vaporizers/humidifiers, and ibuprofen and acetaminophen, if needed for fever or pain. Do not use aspirin in children due to the risk of Reye's syndrome. OTC cough and cold medications have not been shown to work in young children and can be dangerous. Over the past year there have been rare cases of severe skin reactions in patients using acetaminophen and NSAIDs. Symptoms of the common cold usually resolve in a few days (up to 2 weeks). If the child is a small infant, seems seriously ill, or if symptoms worsen or do not go away, the child should be seen by a pediatrician.

Non-pharmacological treatments should be initiated first. A cool mist humidifier helps nasal passages shrink, allowing for easier breathing. Avoid using warm mist humidifiers as they can cause nasal passages to swell (making breathing more difficult) and can cause burns if spilled. Wash humidifiers daily when in use. Saline nose drops or sprays keep nasal passages moist and reduce congestion. Nasal suctioning with a bulb syringe, either with or without saline nose drops, works especially well for infants less than a year old. Older children often resist its use.

Acetaminophen or ibuprofen can be used to reduce fever, aches and pains. If a parent purchases OTC infant drops for fever (let pediatrician recommend if under age 2), remind them to use the calibrated dropper or oral syringe that came with the bottle and do not mix and match dosing devices or overdose can occur. Advise against using kitchen teaspoons to measure out medication since these come in different sizes.

- Acetaminophen infants' or children's liquid suspensions (both 160 mg/5 mL): 10 - 15 mg/kg/dose Q4-6H PRN, max 5 doses/24H.
- Ibuprofen infants' drops (50 mg/1.25 mL) or children's liquid suspensions (100 mg/5 mL): 5 – 10 mg/kg/dose Q6-8H PRN. Max daily dose 40 mg/kg/day for both formulations.

Some doctors recommend alternating ibuprofen with acetaminophen at each dosing interval to avoid acetaminophen toxicity or ibuprofen-induced GI discomfort.

Menthol and camphor used topically, such as in *Vick's VapoRub*, do not work well and should not be used in children less than 2 years. Menthol can result in aspiration and cardiac and CNS toxicity if ingested. Camphor is generally considered safe but lacks sufficient data. *Vick's BabyRub* contains petrolatum, eucalyptus oil, lavender oil, rosemary oil and aloe extract and is also considered relatively safe but lacks sufficient efficacy data.

Patient Counseling for *Flonase* (Fluticasone Nasal Inhaler) and *Nasacort 24 HR* (Triamcinolone Nasal Spray)

Before using

- Shake the bottle gently and then remove the dust cover/cap.
- It is necessary to prime the pump into the air the first time it is used, or when you have not used it for awhile (7 days for *Flonase*, 14 days for *Nasacort*). To prime the pump, hold the bottle with the nasal applicator pointing away from you, with your forefinger and middle finger on either side of the nasal applicator and your thumb underneath the bottle. When you prime the pump for the first time, press down and release the pump a few times. The pump is now ready for use. If the pump is not used for awhile (7 days for *Flonase*, 14 days for *Nasacort*) prime until a fine spray appears.

Using the spray

- Blow your nose to clear your nostrils.
- Close one nostril. Tilt your head forward slightly and, keeping the bottle upright, carefully insert the nasal applicator into the other nostril.
- Start to breathe in through your nose, and while breathing in, press firmly and quickly down once on the applicator to release the spray. To get a full actuation, use your forefinger and middle finger to spray while supporting the base of the bottle with your thumb. Avoid spraying in eyes. Breathe gently inwards through the nostril.
- Breathe out through your mouth. If a second spray is needed in that nostril, repeat the above 3 steps. Repeat the above 3 steps in the other nostril.

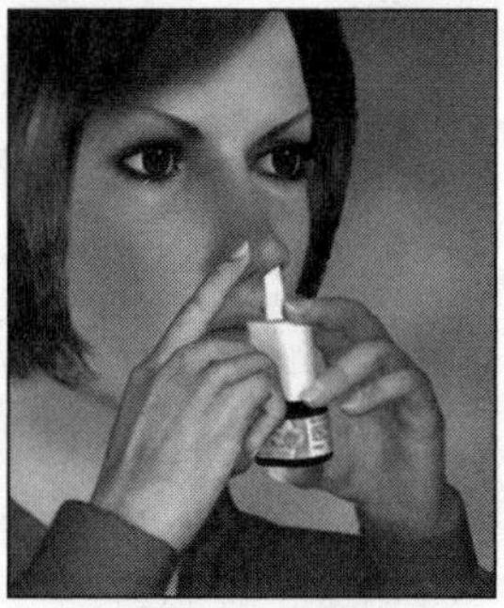

- Wipe the nasal applicator with a clean tissue and replace with dust cover.
- Do not use the bottle for more than the labeled number of sprays even though the bottle is not completely empty.
- Do not blow your nose right after using the nasal spray. Clean the nasal applicator tip regularly (at least once a week for *Flonase*, after every use for *Nasacort)* by gently pulling it off and rinsing it under warm water. Let it air dry before replacing back onto the bottle.

35

ASTHMA

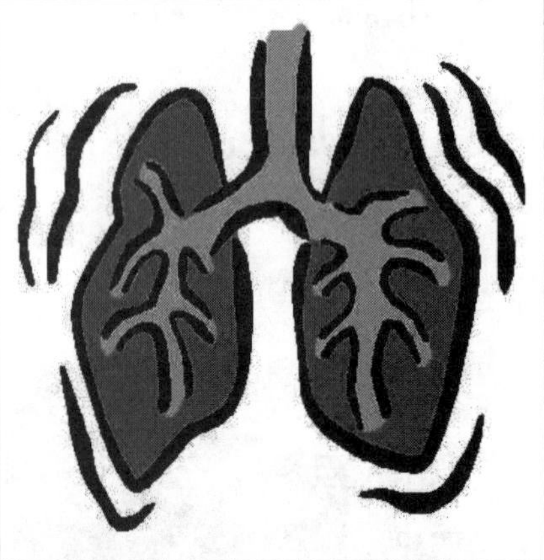

GUIDELINES/REFERENCES

Expert Panel Report 3. Guidelines for the Diagnosis and Management of Asthma. National Heart, Lung and Blood Institute, August 2007. http://www.nhlbi.nih.gov/guidelines/asthma (accessed 2016 Nov 6).

The Global Strategy for Asthma Management and Prevention, Global Initiative for Asthma (GINA) 2016. http://www.ginasthma.org (accessed 2016 Nov 6).

We gratefully acknowledge the assistance of Catrina Derderian, BS, PharmD, BCACP, Clinical Pharmacist, Cambridge Health Alliance, in preparing this chapter.

BACKGROUND

Asthma is a disease that affects the airways (bronchi) of the lungs. It is one of the most common, chronic diseases among children and the prevalence is increasing each year. Asthma is characterized by a predisposition to chronic airway inflammation leading to bronchoconstriction (narrowed airways), airway wall thickening, and increased mucous. This inflammation causes recurrent episodes of the classic signs and symptoms of asthma such as wheezing, breathlessness, chest tightness, and coughing, particularly at night or early in the morning. These symptoms vary over time and in intensity, and can be triggered by a variety of factors, including exercise, allergens, tobacco smoke, and stress (see table on the following page). The expiratory airflow limitation (difficulty with exhalation) that results is reversible with medication and most can live successful and active lives with asthma.

PATHOPHYSIOLOGY

The development of asthma can be attributed to two main factors - host factors (genetic factors such as cytokine response profiles) and environmental exposure (allergens, pollution, infections, stress). Atopy, the genetic predisposition for the development of an immunoglobulin E (IgE)-mediated response to common allergens, is the strongest identifiable factor associated with developing asthma. Proinflammatory mediators and cytokines are produced or released by many cells within the airways (e.g., mast cells, eosinophils, neutrophils, T lymphocytes, macrophages, epithelial cells) leading to airway inflammation. This airway inflammation contributes to bronchial hyperresponsiveness, bronchial constriction, airflow limitation, and respiratory symptoms. Chronic inflammation can be associated with permanent changes in the airway structure, referred to as airway remodeling. These structural changes (subepithelial fibrosis, mucous gland hypersecretion, etc.) increase airflow obstruction and are often less responsive to currently available treatments.

Environmental factors and comorbid conditions (Triggers)

CATEGORIES	EXAMPLES
Airborne Allergens	Airborne pollens (grass, trees, weeds), house-dust mites, animal dander, cockroaches, fungal spores, tobacco smoke
Medication Sensitivities	Aspirin, NSAIDs, non-selective beta blockers
Sulfite Sensitivity	Processed potatoes, shrimp, dried fruit, beer, wine
Environment	Cold air, fog, ozone, sulfur dioxide, nitrogen dioxide, tobacco smoke, wood smoke
Exercise	Particularly cold, dry air
Occupational	Bakers (flour dust), farmers (hay mold), spice and enzyme workers; painters (arabic gum), chemical workers (azo dyes, toluene diisocyanates, polyvinyl chloride); plastics, rubber, and wood workers (formaldehyde, dimethyethanolamine)
Respiratory Infections	Respiratory syncytial virus (RSV), rhinovirus, influenza, others
Comorbid Conditions	Allergic bronchopulmonary Aspergillosis, gastroesophageal reflux, obesity, obstructive sleep apnea, rhinitis/sinusitis, chronic stress/depression

DIAGNOSIS AND ASSESSMENT

Spirometry measures the forced expiratory volume (FEV) or how fast and how much a person can breathe out. Spirometry testing is used to measure airflow obstruction and assess reversibility. Bronchodilator reversibility is documented when forced expiratory volume in one second (FEV1) increases by more than 12% from baseline after using a short acting bronchodilator or when average daily peak expiratory flow (PEF) rate variability is greater than 10%. A detailed medical history, physical exam, assessment of the patient's signs and symptoms and other tests may be done to exclude other conditions. Classification of the severity of asthma is important in the selecting the appropriate pharmacologic treatment. See the table below.

Classifying Asthma Severity and Initiating Treatment in Patients ≥ 12 Years of Age

The table is used to assess severity and determine <u>initial treatment in patients not currently taking long-term control medications</u>. Severity components are assessed by both risk and impairment during the previous 2 – 4 weeks. Drug therapy is recommended based on Step classification at the bottom of the table.

Components of Severity		Classification of Asthma Severity (patients ≥ 12 years of age)			
		Intermittent	Persistent		
			Mild	Moderate	Severe
Impairment	Symptoms	≤ 2 days/week	> 2 days/week but not daily	Daily	Throughout the day
	Nighttime awakenings	≤ 2x/month	3–4x/month	> 1x/week but not nightly	Often 7x/week
	Short-acting beta-2 agonist use for symptom control (not prevention of EIB)	≤ 2 days/week	> 2 days/week, not daily and not more than 1x on any day	Daily	Several times per day
	Interference with normal activity	None	Minor limitation	Some limitation	Extremely limited
	Lung function Normal FEV1/FVC 8–19 yr 85% 20–39 yr 80% 40–59 yr 75% 60–80 yr 70%	▪ Normal FEV1 between exacerbations ▪ FEV1 > 80% predicted ▪ FEV1/FVC normal	▪ FEV1 > 80% predicted ▪ FEV1/FVC normal	▪ FEV1 > 60% but < 80% predicted ▪ FEV1/FVC reduced 5%	▪ FEV1 < 60% predicted ▪ FEV1/FVC reduced 5%
Risk	Exacerbations requiring oral systemic corticosteroids	0–1/year	≥ 2/year →		
		← Consider severity and interval since last exacerbation. → Frequency and severity may fluctuate over time for patients in any severity category.			
Recommended Step for Initiating Treatment		Step 1	Step 2	Step 3 and consider short course of oral systemic corticosteroids	Step 4 or 5 and consider short course of oral systemic corticosteroids
Adapted from NHLBI 2007 EPR.		In 2–6 weeks, evaluate level of asthma control that is achieved and adjust therapy accordingly.			

FEV1: forced expiratory volume in 1 second, FVC: forced vital capacity, ICU: intensive care unit

After initiating therapy, it is important to continuously assess asthma control. The Global Initiative for Asthma (GINA), a scientific committee that partners with the National Heart, Lung, and Blood Institute (NHLBI), provides a global strategy for the management and prevention of asthma. GINA recommends assessing both symptom control and risk factors at every follow-up visit. Proper medication technique and adherence should also be assessed at every visit. Lung function is most useful as an indicator of future risk after the diagnosis of asthma has been made.

DRUG TREATMENT

Long term asthma management should focus on reducing impairment (symptoms, frequent rescue inhaler use) and reducing risk (exacerbations, emergency care, loss of lung function). Drugs used to treat asthma are classified as controllers (maintenance) or relievers (rescue). All patients with asthma need a "rescue" inhaler for acute asthma symptoms. Relievers, or rescue inhalers, are used as-needed to quickly reverse bronchoconstriction, or preventively for exercise-induced bronchospasm (EIB). An example of a rescue inhaler is albuterol *(ProAir)*. Within minutes of inhalation, these agents quickly open airways to make breathing easier. Increased use of a short-acting beta-2 agonist indicates worsening asthma control and a need to reassess treatment.

Controllers are taken on a chronic, daily basis to keep asthma under control, primarily by reducing inflammation. Inhaled corticosteroids and long acting bronchodilators are commonly used as controller inhalers. These agents open the airways and reduce swelling for at least 12 hours. In most cases, a low dose inhaled corticosteriod (ICS) will be initiated, such as fluticasone *(Flovent)*. ICS agents are the most effective and the recommended first-line maintenance medication for long-term control therapy.

Asthma drugs come in oral, inhaled and injectable formulations. Inhaled forms deliver drugs directly into the lungs, have reduced toxicity, and are the preferred delivery vehicle. Steroids can be given by injection in acute cases, and oral steroids are used for severely uncontrolled asthma, but the use of steroids in formulations other than inhaled are limited by the risk of adverse effects. Theophylline can be helpful in some cases, but has significant adverse effects and drug interactions.

Adults aged 19 – 64 years with asthma should receive pneumococcal polysaccharide vaccine (PPSV23, *Pneumovax 23)*. Children 2 – 18 years of age with asthma, treated with high-dose oral corticosteroid therapy, should receive the pneumococcal conjugate vaccine (PCV13, *Prevnar 13)*, if they have not received it before, and PPSV23. An annual influenza vaccine should be given to those with asthma.

"RESCUERS" – COMMONLY USED IN ASTHMA EXACERBATIONS	"CONTROLLERS" – LONG-TERM, MAINTENANCE THERAPY
Short-acting beta-2 agonists (SABA)	Inhaled steroids
Systemic steroids (injection or oral)	Long-acting beta-2 agonists (taken with inhaled steroids)
Inhaled anticholinergics	Leukotriene modifying agents
	Theophylline
	Inhaled anticholinergics
	Omalizumab *(Xolair)*, mepolizumab *(Nucala)*

After classifying the patients asthma severity, the table on the next page provides a stepwise approach to asthma therapy. Ongoing treatment is based on continuous patient assessment, adjustment of treatments and patient response. Controller medications are adjusted up or down in a step wise approach.

ASSESS CONTROL

STEP UP IF NEEDED (1ST CHECK INHALER TECHNIQUE, ADHERENCE, ENVIRONMENTAL CONTROL, AND COMORBIDITIES)

STEP DOWN IF POSSIBLE (IF ASTHMA IS WELL CONTROLLED FOR AT LEAST 2-3 MONTHS)

		Step 1	Step 2	Step 3	Step 4	Step 5	Step 6
		Each step: patient education, environmental control, and management of comorbidities.					
0-4 YEARS		Intermittent Asthma	Persistent Asthma: Daily Medication Consult with Asthma specialist if step ≥ 3 is needed. Consider consult at step 2.				
0-4 YEARS	Preferred	SABA prn	Low-dose ICS	Medium-dose ICS	Medium-dose ICS + either LABA or Montelukast	High-dose ICS + either LABA or Montelukast	High-dose ICS + either LABA or Montelukast
0-4 YEARS	Alternative		Cromolyn or Montelukast				
0-4 YEARS	Rescue Medication	With viral respiratory symptoms: SABA every 4-6 hours up to 24 hours (longer with provider consult). Consider short course of corticosteroids if exacerbation is severe or history of severe exacerbations.					
5-11 YEARS		Intermittent Asthma	Persistent Asthma: Daily Medication Consult with Asthma specialist if step ≥ 4 is needed. Consider consult at step 3.				
5-11 YEARS	Preferred	SABA prn	Low-dose ICS	Low-dose ICS + either LABA, LTRA, or Theophylline OR Medium-dose ICS	Medium-dose ICS + LABA	High-dose ICS + LABA	High-dose ICS + LABA + oral corticosteroids
5-11 YEARS	Alternative		Cromolyn, LTRA, Nedrocromil, or Theophylline		Medium-dose ICS + either LTRA or Theophylline	High-dose ICS + either LTRA or Theophylline	High-dose ICS + LTRA or Theophylline + oral corticosteroids
≥ 12 YEARS OF AGE		Intermittent Asthma	Persistent Asthma: Daily Medication Consult with Asthma specialist if step ≥ 4 is needed. Consider consult at step 3.				
≥ 12 YEARS OF AGE	Preferred	SABA prn	Low-dose ICS	Low-dose ICS + LABA, or Medium-dose ICS	Medium-dose ICS + LABA	High-dose ICS + LABA AND consider Omalizumab for allergic asthma	High-dose ICS + LABA + oral corticosteroids AND consider Omalizumab for allergic asthma
≥ 12 YEARS OF AGE	Alternative		Cromolyn, LTRA, Nedrocromil, or Theophylline	Low-dose ICS + either LTRA, Theophylline or Zileuton	Medium-dose ICS + either LTRA, Theophylline or Zileuton		
ALL PATIENTS	Rescue Medication	SABA prn for symptoms (patients > 5 years – adult: up to 3 treatments at 20 minute intervals initially); treatment intensity depends on symptom severity. Consider short course of oral corticosteroids if needed. Increasing SABA use or use > 2 days/week for symptom relief (not prevention of EIB) generally indicates inadequate control and the need to step up treatment.					
ALL PATIENTS	Notes	In the treatment of all patients, if an alternative treatment is used and response is inadequate, discontinue and use the preferred treatment before stepping up. Consider subcutaneous allergen immunotherapy in patients ≥ 5 years of age with persistent, allergic asthma in step 2 or higher.					

EIB: exercise-induced bronchospasm, ICS: inhaled corticosteroids, LABA: long-acting beta-2 agonist, LTRA: leukotriene receptor antagonist.

Adapted from NHLBI 2007 EPR-3 Quick Reference.

STEP UP AND STEP DOWN THERAPY

If symptoms and/or exacerbations persist for 2 – 3 months despite controller treatment, a step up in therapy should be considered following the NHLBI/GINA step up recommendations. A step down in therapy may be considered when asthma is well-controlled for 3 months. A reduction in ICS dose by 25 – 50% at 2 – 3 month intervals in conjunction with a written action plan and close follow-up is warranted.

Asthma exacerbations

An episodic flare-up, called an asthma exacerbation, can occur, particularly when the disease state worsens due to exposure of allergen(s) or non-adherence to the medication regimen. Viral respiratory infections are one of the most important causes of asthma exacerbations and may also contribute to the development of asthma.

Short courses of oral systemic steroids are used in asthma exacerbations. As steroid use can increase bone fracture risk, consider smoking cessation, regular exercise and the use of the lowest, effective steroid dose to decrease risk. Calcium and vitamin D supplementation should be considered, if needed, along with regular bone density screenings.

Beta-2 Agonists

These agents bind to beta-2 receptors, causing relaxation of bronchial smooth muscle, therefore leading to bronchodilation. Inhalation is the preferred route of administration. Inhaled devices come as a metered-dose inhalers (MDIs) or dry powder inhalers (DPIs), including a breath-actuated DPI. Short acting Beta-2 Agonist (SABA) agents are only used as needed for monotherapy in Step 1, when symptoms are rare, there are no night wakings, no exacerbations in the last year, and FEV1 is normal. SABAs can also be used for other reversible airway diseases such as colds, allergies and bronchitis.

Long-acting beta-2 agonists are used as maintenance therapy only in combination with an ICS. LABAs should not be used as monotherapy. When a medium dose of a ICS alone fails to achieve good asthma control, the addition of a LABA to the ICS improves symptoms and lung function while reducing risk of exacerbation more rapidly than increasing to a high dose ICS monotherapy.

DRUG	DOSING	SAFETY/SIDE EFFECTS/MONITORING
Short-Acting Beta-2 Agonists (SABAs)		
Albuterol ***(ProAir HFA,*** *ProAir RespiClick, Proventil HFA,* ***Ventolin HFA,*** *VoSpire ER)* 90 mcg/inh, 0.5% and 0.083% nebulizer solution, syrup, tablet	MDI/DPI: 1-2 inhalations Q4-6H PRN Nebulizer: 1.25-5 mg Q4-8H PRN IR: 2-4 mg Q4-6H PO PRN ER: 8 mg Q12H PRN	**WARNINGS** Caution in CVD, glaucoma, hyperthyroidism **SIDE EFFECTS** Nervousness, tremor, tachycardia, palpitations, cough, hyperglycemia, ↓ K **MONITORING** Number of days of SABA use, symptom frequency, peak flow, pulmonary function tests, BP, HR, blood glucose, K **NOTES** MDIs: Shake well before use. Levalbuterol contains R-isomer of albuterol. Most albuterol inhalers contain 200 inhalations/canister.
Levalbuterol ***(Xopenex, Xopenex Concentrate, Xopenex HFA)*** 45 mcg/inh, nebulizer solution	MDI: 1-2 inhalations Q4-6H PRN Nebulizer: 0.63-1.25 mg Q6-8H PRN	
Racepinephrine *(Asthmanefrin EZ Breathe Atomizer)* OTC	Should not be used since it is non-selective	

Beta-2 Agonists continued

DRUG	DOSING	SAFETY/SIDE EFFECTS/MONITORING

Long-Acting Beta-2 Agonists (LABAs)

DRUG	DOSING	SAFETY/SIDE EFFECTS/MONITORING
Salmeterol *(Serevent Diskus)* 50 mcg/inh **+ fluticasone *(Advair Diskus, Advair HFA)***	DPI: 1 inhalation BID	**BOXED WARNING** ↑ risk of asthma-related deaths, should only be used in asthma patients as adjunctive therapy in patients who are currently receiving but are not adequately controlled on a long-term asthma control medication (an inhaled corticosteroid). **CONTRAINDICATIONS** Monotherapy in the treatment of asthma, treatment of status asthmaticus or other acute episodes of asthma or COPD **SIDE EFFECTS** and **MONITORING** - same as SABAs **NOTES** Formoterol nebulizer solution is the only LABA in nebulizer formulation. Vilanterol (LABA) available in combination with fluticasone *(Breo Ellipta),* is discussed on the next page. MedGuide required.
Advair Diskus – 100, 250, 500 mcg fluticasone + 50 mcg salmeterol/inh	DPI: 1 inhalation BID	
Advair HFA – 45, 115, 230 mcg fluticasone + 21 mcg salmeterol/inh	MDI: 2 inhalations BID	
Formoterol (Perforomist) nebulizer solution **+ budesonide *(Symbicort)***	Nebulized	
Symbicort – 80, 160 mcg budesonide + 4.5 mcg formoterol/inh	MDI: 2 inhalations BID	
+ mometasone *(Dulera)* 100, 200 mcg mometasone + 5 mcg formoterol/inh	MDI: 2 inhalations BID	
+ glycopyrrolate *(Bevespi Aerosphere)* (glycopyrrolate 9 mcg/formoterol 4.8 mcg per inhalation); only for COPD	MDI: 2 inhalations BID	

STUDY TIP: MDIs AND DPIs

MDIs

- How to identify: products that end in aerosolized or HFA
- Deliver dose of aerosolized liquid medication
- Some use a propellant (HFA)
- Shake well (except *QVAR* and *Alvesco)*
- Administration requires a slow deep inhalation at the same time the dose is delivered
- A spacer can be used for patients who cannot coordinate breath with dose delivery

DPIs

- How to identify: products that end in *Diskus, Handihaler, Neohaler, Aerolizer*
- Deliver a dose of fine powdered medication
- No propellant
- Do not shake
- Administration requires a quick and forceful inhalation
- Spacers cannot be used, the drug is delivered by the breath and no coordination is needed

**Additional devices are discussed at the end of the chapter.*

Corticosteroids

Corticosteroids inhibit the inflammatory response, depressing migration of polymorphonuclear (PMN) leukocytes and fibroblasts, and reversing capillary permeability and lysosomal stabilization at the cellular level. They block late-phase reaction to the allergen, reduce airway hyperresponsiveness and are the potent and effective anti-inflammatory medications. ICSs have the ability to reduce symptoms, increase lung function, improve quality of life, and reduce the risk of exacerbations.

Inhaled Corticosteroids

DRUG	DOSING	SAFETY/SIDE EFFECTS/ MONITORING
Beclomethasone HFA *(QVAR)* 40, 80 mcg/inh	MDI: 1-2 inhalations BID	**CONTRAINDICATIONS** Primary treatment of status asthmaticus or acute episodes of asthma (not for relief of acute bronchospasm) **WARNINGS** Adrenal suppression with high doses for prolonged period of time **SIDE EFFECTS (INHALED)** Dysphonia (difficulty speaking), oral candidiasis (thrush), cough, HA, hoarseness, URTIs, hyperglycemia, ↑ risk of fractures and pneumonia (with high dose, long-term use), growth retardation (in children with high doses) **MONITORING** Use of SABA, symptom frequency, peak flow, growth (children/adolescents) and signs/symptoms of HPA axis suppression/adrenal insufficiency, signs/ symptoms of oral candidiasis, bone mineral density **NOTES** To prevent oral candidiasis, rinse mouth and throat with warm water and spit out or use a spacer device if using a MDI *QVAR* and *Alvesco* are MDIs that do not need to be shaken before use Only use *Pulmicort Respules* with a jet nebulizer machine that is connected to an air compressor. Do not use an ultrasonic nebulizer
Budesonide *(Pulmicort Flexhaler,* *Pulmicort Respules)* ***Pulmicort Flexhaler*** 90, 180 mcg/in *Pulmicort Respules* nebulizer suspension **+ formoterol *(Symbicort)*** 80, 160 mcg budesonide + 4.5 mcg formoterol/inh	DPI: 1-2 inhalations BID *Pulmicort Respules* (ages 1-8 years): 0.25-0.5 mg via jet nebulizer daily or BID *Symbicort* MDI: 2 inhalations BID	
Ciclesonide *(Alvesco)* 80, 160 mcg/inh	MDI: 1-2 inhalations BID	
Flunisolide HFA *(Aerospan HFA)* – has built-in spacer 80 mcg/inh	MDI: 2 inhalations BID	
Fluticasone *(Flovent HFA,* *Flovent Diskus, Arnuity Ellipta)* *Flovent HFA* 44, 110, 220 mcg/inh *Flovent Diskus* 50, 100, 250 mcg/inh *Arnuity Ellipta* 100, 200 mcg/inh + vilanterol *(Breo Ellipta)* 100, 200 mcg fluticasone + 25 mcg vilanterol/inh **+ salmeterol *(Advair Diskus, Advair HFA)***	MDI: 2 inhalations BID *Flovent Diskus* DPI: 1-2 inhalations BID *Arnuity Ellipta* DPI: 1-2 inhalations daily *Breo Ellipta* DPI: 1 inhalation daily *Advair Diskus*: 1 inhalation BID *Advair HFA*: 2 inhalations BID	
Mometasone *(Asmanex HFA, Asmanex Twisthaler)* *HFA* 100, 200 mcg/inh *Twisthaler* 110, 220 mcg/inh + formoterol *(Dulera)* 100, 200 mcg mometasone + 5 mcg formoterol/inh	MDI: 1-2 inhalations BID DPI: 1-2 inhalations daily or BID MDI: 2 inhalations BID	

DPI: dry powder inhaler, HFA: hydrofluoroalkane, MDI: metered dose inhaler

Daily Dosages for Inhaled Corticosteroids in Patients ≥ 12 Years of Age

DRUG	LOW DAILY DOSE	MEDIUM DAILY DOSE	HIGH DAILY DOSE
Beclomethasone HFA 40 or 80 mcg/inh	80–240 mcg	> 240–480 mcg	> 480 mcg
Budesonide DPI 90, 180, or 200 mcg/inh	180–600 mcg	> 600–1,200 mcg	> 1,200 mcg
Ciclesonide 80, 160 mcg/inh	80–160 mcg	> 160–320 mcg	> 320 mcg
Flunisolide HFA 80 mcg/inh	320 mcg	> 320–640 mcg	> 640 mcg
Fluticasone			
HFA/MDI: 44, 110, or 220 mcg/inh	88–264 mcg	> 264–440 mcg	> 440 mcg
DPI: 50, 100, or 250 mcg/inh	100–300 mcg	> 300–500 mcg	> 500 mcg
Mometasone DPI 200 mcg/inh	200 mcg	400 mcg	> 400 mcg

Leukotriene Modifying Agents

Leukotriene receptor antagonists (LTRAs) target one part of the inflammatory pathway in asthma. Zafirlukast is a LTRA that inhibits both leukotriene D4 (LTD4) and E4 (LTE4). Montelukast only inhibits LTD4. Zileuton is a 5-lipoxygenase inhibitor which inhibits leukotriene formation. All agents help ↓ airway edema, constriction and inflammation.

LTRA monotherapy is less effective than low dose ICS monotherapy. ICS/LTRA combination therapy is less effective than ICS/LABA combination therapy. LTRAs are used most commonly in children.

DRUG	DOSING	SAFETY/SIDE EFFECTS/MONITORING
Zafirlukast *(Accolate)*	20 mg BID Age 5-11 years: 10 mg BID Taken 1 hr before or 2 hrs after meals (empty stomach)	**CONTRAINDICATIONS** Hepatic impairment – zafirlukast Active liver disease or LFTs ≥ 3 x ULN – zileuton **WARNINGS** Neuropsychiatric events; monitor for signs of aggressive behavior, hostility, agitation, depression, suicidal thinking Systemic eosinophilia, sometimes presenting with clinical features of vasculitis consistent with Churg-Strauss syndrome (rare) **SIDE EFFECTS** Headache, dizziness, abdominal pain, ↑ LFTs, URTIs, pharyngitis, sinusitis **MONITORING** Zileuton – LFTs at baseline, every month for first 3 months, every 2-3 months for the rest of the first year, then periodically; use of SABAs **NOTES** Zafirlukast: keep in the original container
Montelukast ***(Singulair)***	10 mg daily in the evening Age 6-14 years: 5 mg daily in the evening Age 1-5 years: 4 mg daily in the evening	
Zileuton *(Zyflo, Zyflo CR)*	*Zyflo*: 600 mg QID *Zyflo CR*: 1,200 mg BID within 1 hour of morning and evening meals Age < 12 years: not recommended	

Leukotriene Modifying Agents Drug Interactions

- Zafirlukast: substrate of 2C9 (major); inhibitor of 1A2 (weak), 2C9 (moderate), 2C19 (weak), 2D6 (weak), 2C8 (weak) and 3A4 (weak) – may ↑ levels of carvedilol, pimozide, theophylline, warfarin and 2C9 substrates. Levels of zafirlukast may be ↑ by erythromycin, theophylline, and food (↓ bioavailability by 40%) – take 1 hour before or 2 hours after meals.
- Montelukast: substrate of 3A4 (minor) and 2C8/9 (minor); inhibitor of 2C8/9 (weak). Gemfibrozil may ↑ levels of montelukast and lumacaftor may ↓ levels of montelukast.
- Zileuton: substrate of 1A2 (minor), 2C9 (minor), 3A4 (minor); inhibitor of 1A2 (weak) – may ↑ levels of pimozide, propranolol, theophylline, and warfarin.

Theophylline

Blocks phosphodiesterase causing ↑ cyclic adenosine monophosphate (cAMP) which promotes release of epinephrine from adrenal medulla cells. This results in bronchodilation, mild anti-inflammatory effects, diuresis, CNS and cardiac stimulation and gastric acid secretion. Theophylline may help as add-on therapy, but use is limited by ↓ effectiveness, drug interactions and adverse effects.

DRUG	DOSING	SAFETY/SIDE EFFECTS/MONITORING
Theophylline *(Elixophyllin, Theo-24, Theochron)* Capsule, tablet, elixir, solution, injection Active metabolites are caffeine and 3-methylxanthine	300-600 mg daily Therapeutic range: 5-15 mcg/mL (measure peak level after 3 days of oral dosing, at steady state)	**WARNINGS** Caution in patients with cardiovascular disease, hyperthyroidism, PUD and seizure disorder since use may exacerbate these conditions **SIDE EFFECTS** Nausea, loose stools, headache, tachycardia, insomnia, tremor, and nervousness Signs of toxicity – persistent and repetitive vomiting, ventricular tachycardias, seizures **MONITORING** Theophylline levels, use of SABA, HR, respiratory rate, CNS effects **NOTES** Narrow therapeutic index medication. Dosing is based on IBW, unless TBW < IBW, then dose on TBW (to minimize overdose risk). If no theophylline given within past 24 hrs, LD = 5 mg/kg. Aminophylline contains 80% theophylline; converting aminophylline to theophylline, multiply by 0.8; converting theophylline to aminophylline, divide by 0.8.

Theophylline Drug Interactions

Theophylline is a substrate of 1A2 (major), 3A4 (major), 2E1 (major), 2C9 (minor) and 2D6 (minor) and an inhibitor of 1A2 (weak). It has first order kinetics, followed by zero order kinetics. A small increase in dose can result in a large increase in the theophylline concentration (see Pharmacokinetics chapter).

- Drugs that can ↑ theophylline levels due to 1A2 inhibition: ciprofloxacin, fluvoxamine, propranolol, zafirlukast, zileuton and possibly others.
- Drugs that can ↑ theophylline levels due to 3A4 inhibition: clarithromycin, conivaptan, erythromycin and possibly others.
- Drugs that can ↑ theophylline levels due to other mechanisms: alcohol, allopurinol, antithyroid agents, disulfiram, estrogen-containing oral contraceptives, methotrexate, pentoxifylline, propafenone, verapamil and possibly others. Also conditions such as acute pulmonary edema, CHF, cirrhosis or liver disease, cor-pulmonale, fever, hypothyroidism or shock can ↓ clearance.

- Drugs that may ↓ theophylline levels: carbamazepine, fosphenytoin, phenobarbital, phenytoin, primidone, rifampin, ritonavir, tobacco/marijuana smoking, St. John's wort, thyroid hormones (levothyroxine), high-protein diet and charbroiled meats. Conditions such as hyperthyroidism and cystic fibrosis can ↑ clearance.
- Theophylline will ↓ lithium (theophylline ↑ renal excretion of lithium) and will ↓ zafirlukast.

Anticholinergics

Anticholinergics inhibit muscarinic cholinergic receptors and reduce intrinsic vagal tone of the airway, leading to bronchodilation. These agents are mainly used with other medications in the emergency department in acute exacerbations. In September 2015, tiotropium *(Spiriva Respimat)* was approved for asthma in patients 12 years of age and older with a history of exacerbations despite ICS/LABA therapy. Refer to the COPD chapter for more information on anticholinergics.

Omalizumab *(Xolair)*

IgG monoclonal antibody that inhibits IgE binding to the IgE receptor on mast cells and basophils. Omalizumab is indicated for moderate to severe persistent, allergic asthma in patients 12 years of age and older with a positive skin test to perennial aeroallergen and inadequately controlled symptoms on inhaled steroids (Step 5 or 6 per guidelines).

DRUG	DOSING	SAFETY/SIDE EFFECTS/MONITORING
Omalizumab ***(Xolair)***	Dose and frequency based on pretreatment total IgE serum levels and body weight – given SC every 2 or 4 weeks Drug should always be given in a healthcare setting Dosing should be adjusted during therapy for significant changes in body weight	**BOXED WARNING** Anaphylaxis, including delayed-onset, can occur. Anaphylaxis has occurred after the first dose but also has occurred beyond 1 year after beginning treatment. Closely observe patients for an appropriate period of time after administration and be prepared to manage anaphylaxis that can be life-threatening. **WARNING** Slight ↑ risk of serious cardiovascular and cerebrovascular adverse events Malignancies have been observed in clinical studies **SIDE EFFECTS** Injection site reactions, arthralgias, pain, dizziness, fatigue, leg pain, arm pain, pruritus, dermatitis, bone fracture, earache **MONITORING** Baseline IgE, FEV1, peak flow, s/sx of anaphylaxis and infection **NOTES** Doses > 150 mg should be divided over more than one injection site

Interleukin-5 (IL-5) Receptor Antagonist Agents

IL-5 is the major cytokine responsible for the growth and differentiation, recruitment, activation, and survival of eosinophils (a cell type associated with inflammation and an important component in the pathogenesis of asthma). Mepolizumab and reslizumab are two agents used for asthma management in this therapeutic class. Both agents are used as add-on maintenance treatment of severe asthma in adults with an eosinophilic phenotype.

Mepolizumab *(Nucala)*

An interleukin-5 (IL-5) receptor antagonist monoclonal antibody (IgG1 kappa) that inhibits IgE binding to the IgE receptor on mast cells and basophils. Mepolizumab is indicated in ages > 12 years and dosed 100 mg SC once every 4 weeks. Headache and injection site reactions are common, but minor.

Reslizumab *(Cinqair)*

Inhibits IL-5 signaling, reduces the production and survival of eosinophils; however, the mechanism of action of reslizumab in asthma has not been definitively established. The dose is 3 mg/kg by IV route once every 4 weeks.

SPECIAL SITUATIONS

Exercise-Induced Bronchospasm

- In most cases, SABAs are preferred. SABAs can be taken 5 – 15 minutes before exercise and have a duration of 2 – 3 hours.
- If a longer duration of symptom control is needed, LABAs can be used. These agents need to be taken 15 minutes (formoterol) or 30 minutes (salmeterol) prior to exercise. If already using a LABA for asthma maintenance, then do not use additional doses for EIB. Remember, LABAs should not be used as monotherapy in patients with persistent asthma.
- Montelukast must be taken 2 hours prior to exercise and lasts up to 24 hours. However, it is effective in only 50% of patients. Daily administration to prevent EIB has not been evaluated. Patients receiving montelukast for asthma or another indication should not take an additional dose to prevent EIB.
- If indicated, appropriate long-term control therapy with anti-inflammatory medication is associated with a reduction in the frequency and severity of exercise-induced bronchospasm (EIB).

Pregnancy

Asthma should be monitored in pregnant women as the condition may become worse. To ensure oxygen supply to the fetus, it is safer to be treated with asthma medications than to have poorly controlled asthma. Albuterol is the preferred short-acting beta-2 agonist and budesonide is the preferred inhaled corticosteroid due to more data in pregnancy.

Asthma-COPD Overlap Syndrome (ACOS)

Asthma diagnosis may be difficult in the elderly, due to lack of fitness, reduced activity, and shortness of breath due to heart failure. If there is a history of smoking, COPD or asthma-COPD overlap syndrome (ACOS) should be considered. ACOS has worse outcomes than asthma or COPD alone.

PEAK FLOW METERS

Peak flow meters are devices that measure a patient's peak expiratory flow rate (PEFR) – the greatest velocity attained during a forced expiration starting from fully inflated lungs. The patient's best PEFR is known as a Personal Best (PB) and is determined by spirometry, taking into account the patient's height, gender, and age. Patients may also find their PB by taking peak flow readings twice a day (morning and evening) for 2 – 3 weeks. The most frequent highest reading is the PB. Typically, a PB can be found after a short burst of steroids to maximize lung function. Peak flow meters are beneficial in patients with frequent asthma exacerbations, worsening asthma, persistent asthma (Step 3 – 6), poor perception of airflow obstruction and unexplained response to environmental factors. These devices can identify exacerbations early (even before the patient is symptomatic), allowing the patient to initiate treatment sooner. A treatment action plan, is developed by the health care provider so the patient can manage symptoms and avoid hospitalizations due to an exacerbation (see next page).

Technique

- Use the peak flow meter every morning upon awakening and before the use of any asthma medications. Proper technique and best effort are essential. Less than best effort can lead to false 'exacerbation' and unnecessary medication treatment.
- Move the indicator to bottom of numbered scale. Stand up straight. Exhale comfortably.
- Inhale as deeply as possible. Place lips firmly around mouthpiece, creating a tight seal.
- Blow out as hard and as fast as possible. Write down the PEFR.
- Repeat the steps two more times, allowing enough rest in between. Record the highest value.

Peak Flow Meter Care

- Patients should always use the same brand of peak flow meter.
- Peak flow meters should be cleaned at least once a week; if the patient has an infection, they should clean it more frequently. Wash peak flow meters in warm water with mild soap. Rinse gently but thoroughly. Do not use brushes to clean inside the peak flow meters. Do not place peak flow meters in boiling water. Allow to air dry before taking next reading.

ZONES

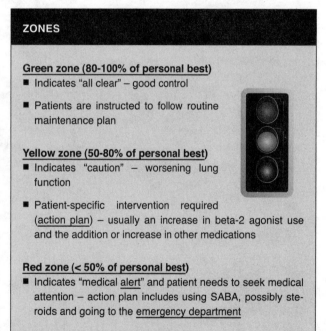

Green zone (80-100% of personal best)
- Indicates "all clear" – good control
- Patients are instructed to follow routine maintenance plan

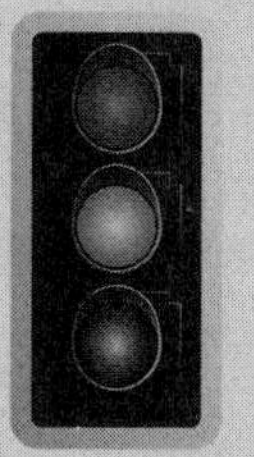

Yellow zone (50-80% of personal best)
- Indicates "caution" – worsening lung function
- Patient-specific intervention required (action plan) – usually an increase in beta-2 agonist use and the addition or increase in other medications

Red zone (< 50% of personal best)
- Indicates "medical alert" and patient needs to seek medical attention – action plan includes using SABA, possibly steroids and going to the emergency department

SPACERS

Spacer is a generic term that refers to simple open tubes that are placed on the mouthpiece of a MDI to extend it away from the mouth of the patient. A valve holding chamber (VHC), one type of spacer, has a one-way valve that does not allow the patient to exhale into the device. This benefits patients who have difficulty coordinating actuation (pressing down on the canister) and inhalation as they can press and have a short time delay before the need for inhalation. Therefore, VHC spacers make it easier to administer inhaled medication from an MDI into the lungs. Patients should use the same combination of an MDI and VHC. Flunisolide *(Aerospan)* has a built-in spacer.

- Spacer devices help prevent thrush from ICSs and can reduce cough associated with some inhalers.
- Clean at least once a week in warm, soapy water.
- Spacer devices should not be shared.

Sample Asthma Action Plan (Adult)

My Asthma Action Plan

Patient Name: ____________________

Medical Record #: ____________________

Physician's Name: ____________________ DOB: ____________________

Physician's Phone #: ____________________ Completed by: ____________________ Date: __________

Long-Term-Control Medicines	How Much To Take	How Often	Other Instructions
		_____ times per day **EVERY DAY!**	
		_____ times per day **EVERY DAY!**	
		_____ times per day **EVERY DAY!**	
		_____ times per day **EVERY DAY!**	

Quick-Relief Medicines	How Much To Take	How Often	Other Instructions
		Take ONLY as needed	NOTE: If this medicine is needed frequently, call physician to consider increasing long-term-control medications.

Special instructions when I feel ● *good,* ○ *not good,* and ● *awful.*

GREEN ZONE

I feel ***good.***

(My peak flow is in the GREEN zone.)

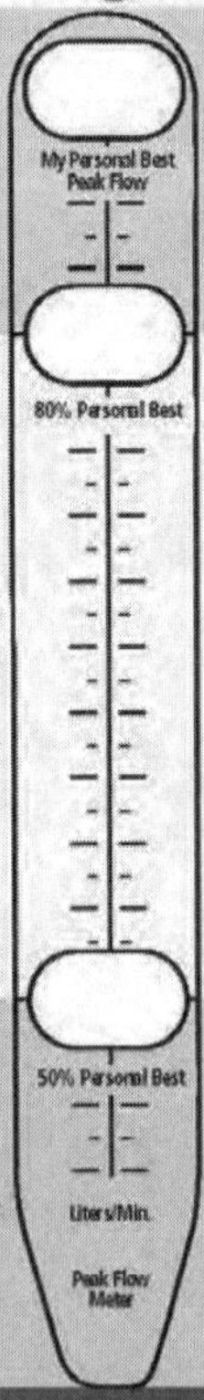

PREVENT asthma symptoms everyday:

- ☐ Take my long-term-control medicines (above) every day.
- ☐ Before exercise, take _____ puffs of __________
- ☐ Avoid things that make my asthma worse like:

____

YELLOW ZONE

I do ***not*** feel ***good.***

(My peak flow is in the YELLOW zone.)

My symptoms may include one or more of the following:

- Wheeze
- Tight chest
- Cough
- Shortness of breath
- Waking up at night with asthma symptoms
- Decreased ability to do usual activities
- __________

____

CAUTION. I should continue taking my long-term-control asthma medicines every day AND:

- ☐ Take __________

____

If I still do not feel good, or my peak flow is not back in the ***Green Zone*** within 1 hour, then I should:

- ☐ Increase __________

____

- ☐ Add __________

____

- ☐ Call __________

RED ZONE

I feel ***awful.***

(My peak flow is in the RED zone.)

Warning signs may include one or more of the following:

- It's getting harder and harder to breathe
- Unable to sleep or do usual activities because of trouble breathing

MEDICAL ALERT! Get help!

- ☐ Take __________ until I get help immediately.
- ☐ Take __________

____

- ☐ Call __________

Danger! Get help immediately! Call 9-1-1 if you have trouble walking or talking due to shortness of breath or lips or fingernails are gray or blue.

Adapted from NHLBI 2007 EPR.

DEVICES

Nebulizers

A nebulizer is a device that turns liquid medication into a fine mist. This fine mist can be inhaled through a face mask or mouthpiece and into the lungs. Nebulizers use natural breathing, making medication delivery easy for infants, children and the elderly. There are two types of nebulizers, jet nebulizers and ultrasound nebulizers. Check the medication information to see which nebulizer device is indicated.

Albuterol comes as a nebulized solution in 2 common concentrations (0.083% solution containing 2.5 mg/3mL and a 0.5% solution containing 2.5 mg/0.5 mL as a unit-dose and in a 20 mL vial). The 0.083% solution is a ready-to-use preparation that can be placed directly into the nebulizer without further dilution. The 0.5% concentrated solution must be diluted with 2.5 mL of normal saline prior to use. Nebulizers are covered by CMS' Durable Medical Equipment (DME) under the medical insurance component (Part B).

INHALER USE

Little or no medicine reaches the lungs if the inhaler is used incorrectly, therefore patient counseling is essential. Most patients (up to 80%) cannot use their inhaler correctly. This contributes to poor symptom control and increased exacerbations. Assessing inhaler technique is essential to asthma control.

Additionally, up to 50% of adults and children do not take their controller medications as prescribed. Many times, this is unintentional and due to lack of education, cost, or forgetfulness. Again, assessing adherence is important for successful asthma control. Patient should also be aware of how to monitor the doses remaining in an inhaler. Some inhalers have an internal dose counter that is displayed for the patient. Most inhalers are designed to last one month when the patient is adherent to therapy; rescue inhalers can vary depending on use. It is useful for patients to know when the inhaler should run out. Refer to the table below for examples of the number of days that an inhaler will last for commonly used inhalers.

Patients should be educated to wait the correct time between puffs when using inhalers. If prescribed more than 1 puff of medication at a time, the patient should wait 60 seconds between puffs.

If using more than one inhaler, the sequence of inhalers is important. Bronchodilators work faster than inhaled steroids. Using bronchodilators first will allow airways to open quickly. By using the inhaled steroids last, the medication will be able to travel deeper into the lungs.

General rules:

- First: SABA (albuterol).
- Second: use any other bronchodilators prescribed for regular use (e.g., *Atrovent* or *Serevent*).
- Last: steroid inhaler.

DRUG	DOSES	DOSAGE	DAYS SUPPLY
Maintenance inhalers			
Advair Diskus	60 doses	1 puff BID	1 puff x 2x/day x 30 days = 60 puffs
QVAR	120 puffs	1-2 puffs BID	2 puffs x 2x/day x 30 days = 120 puffs
Stiolto Respimat	60 puffs	2 puffs daily	2 puffs x 1x/day x 30 days = 60 puffs
Rescue inhalers			
Albuterol MDI, Levalbuterol MDI	200 puffs	1-2 puffs per dose, used every 4-6 hrs as needed	2 puffs x 3x/day x 30 days = 180 puffs

Metered-Dose Inhalers

Ventolin, ProAir HFA, Proventil, Symbicort, QVAR, Flovent HFA, Alvesco, others

STEP 1

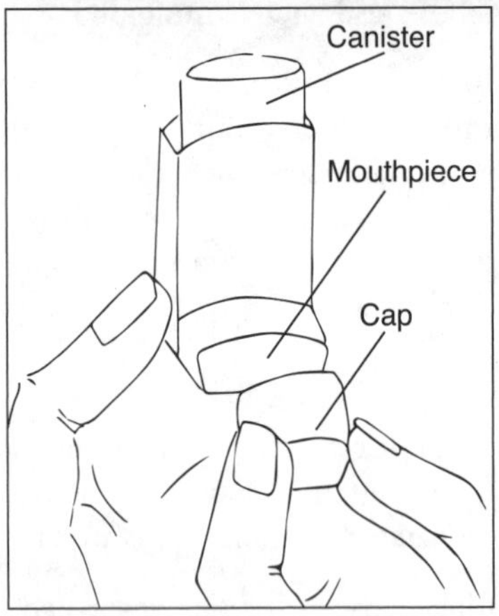

Make sure the canister is fully inserted into the actuator (if it comes separately). Always use the actuator that came with the canister. Shake the inhaler well for 5 seconds immediately before each spray (except for *QVAR* or *Alvesco* which do not need to be shaken). Remove cap from the mouthpiece and check mouthpiece for foreign objects prior to use.

STEP 2

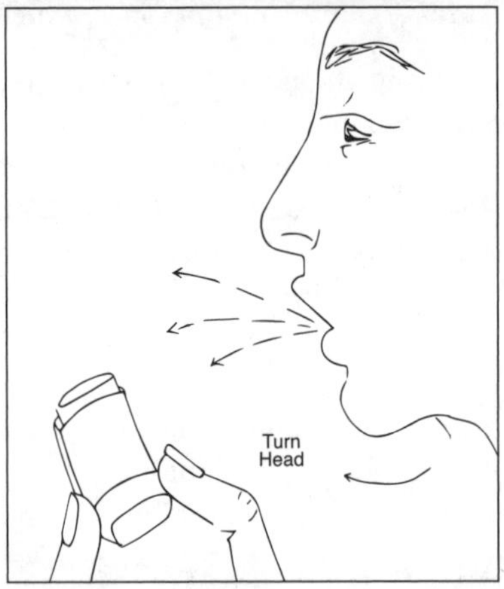

Breathe out fully through your mouth expelling as much air from your lungs as possible. Holding the inhaler upright (as shown in the picture), place the mouthpiece into your mouth and close your lips around it.

STEP 3

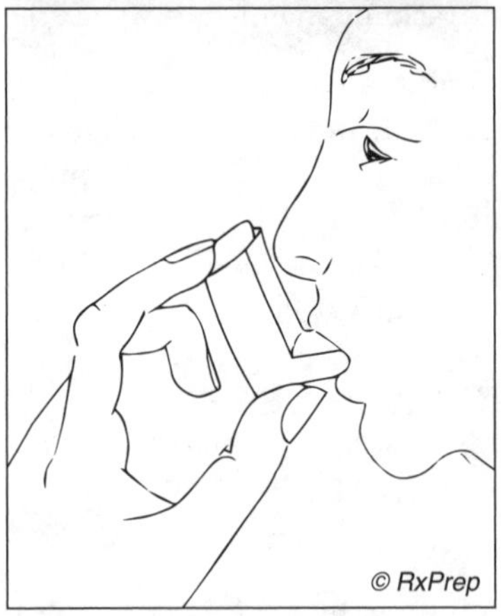

While breathing in slowly and deeply through your mouth, press the top of the canister all the way down with your index finger. Right after the spray comes out, take your finger off the canister. After you have inhaled all the way, take the inhaler out of your mouth and close your mouth. Hold your breath as long as possible, up to 10 seconds, then breathe normally. If another inhalation is needed, wait 1 minute and repeat Steps 1-3. Place cap back on the mouthpiece after use.

TO PRIME

Ventolin
Spray 4 times (shaking between sprays) away from the face. Prime again if >14 days from last use or if you drop it.

Flovent HFA
Spray 4 times (shaking between sprays) away from the face. Prime again if > 7 days from last use with just 1 spray.

Symbicort
Spray 2 times (shaking between sprays) away from the face. Prime again if > 7 days from last use.

TO CLEAN

Ventolin
Rinse mouthpiece under warm running water (but not the metal canister) for 30 seconds to prevent medication buildup and blockage. Shake to remove excess water and let air dry. Clean weekly.

Flovent HFA
Use a clean cotton swab dampened with water to clean the small circular opening where the medicine sprays out. Gently twist the swab in a circular motion to remove the medicine buildup. Do not take the canister out of the plastic actuator. Wipe the inside of the mouthpiece with a damp tissue. Let air dry overnight.

Symbicort
Wipe the inside and outside of the mouthpiece opening with a clean, dry cloth. Do not put into water.

Dry Powder Inhalers

Advair Diskus

STEP 1

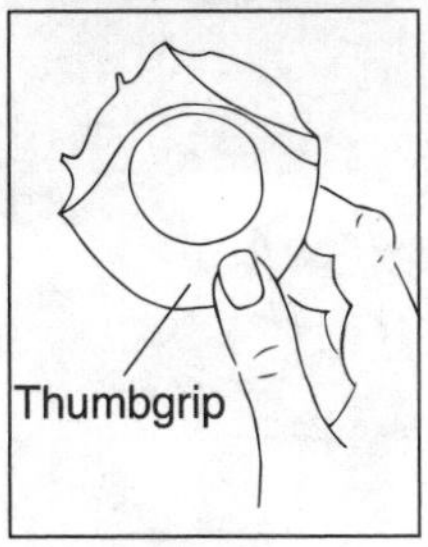

Hold the *Diskus* in your left hand and put the thumb of your right hand in the thumb grip. Push the thumb grip away from you as far as it will go until the mouthpiece appears and the *Diskus* snaps into position.

STEP 2

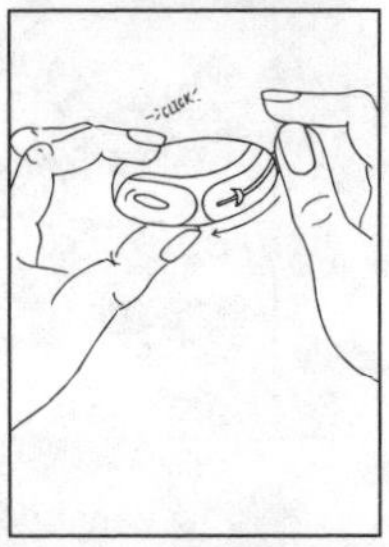

Hold the *Diskus* in a level, flat position with the mouthpiece towards you. Slide the lever away from the mouthpiece until it clicks.

STEP 3

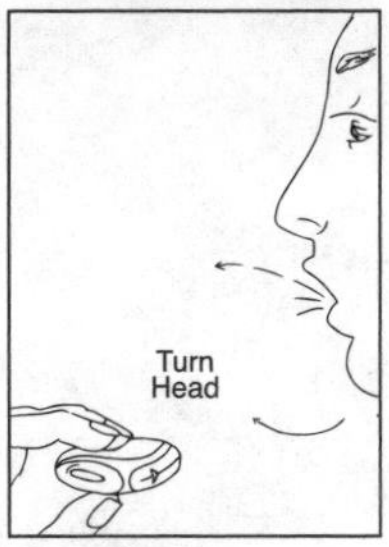

Before using, breathe out fully while holding the *Diskus* away from your mouth. Do not tilt the *Diskus*.

STEP 4

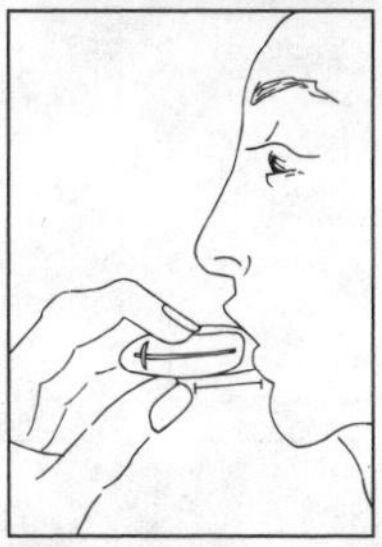

Put the mouthpiece to your lips. Breathe in quickly and deeply through the inhaler. Do not breathe in through your nose. Remove the *Diskus* from your mouth and hold your breath for 10 seconds, or as long as comfortable. Then, breathe out slowly.

STEP 5

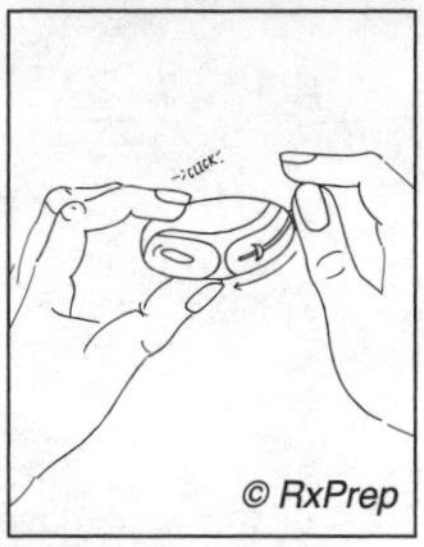

Close the *Diskus* inhaler by putting your thumb in the thumb grip and slide as far back towards you as it will go, until the *Diskus* clicks shut. Rinse your mouth with water and spit out the water to prevent thrush.

TO CLEAN

Do not wash the *Diskus* and store in a dry place.

Pulmicort Flexhaler

STEP 1

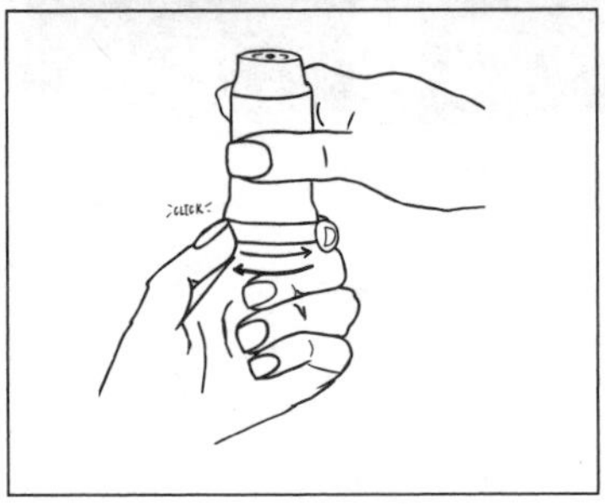

Twist off the white cover. Holding the middle of the inhaler with one hand, twist the brown base fully in one direction as far as it will go with the other hand. Twist it fully back again in the other direction as far as it will go. You will hear a "click" during one of the twisting movements. The dose is now loaded. Do not shake the inhaler after it is loaded. (Of note, only one dose is loaded at a time, no matter how often you twist the brown base, but the dose counter will continue to advance).

STEP 2

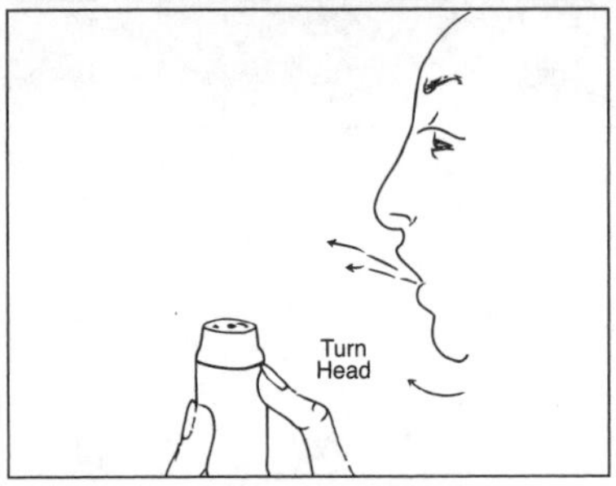

Turn your head away from the inhaler and breathe out fully.

STEP 3

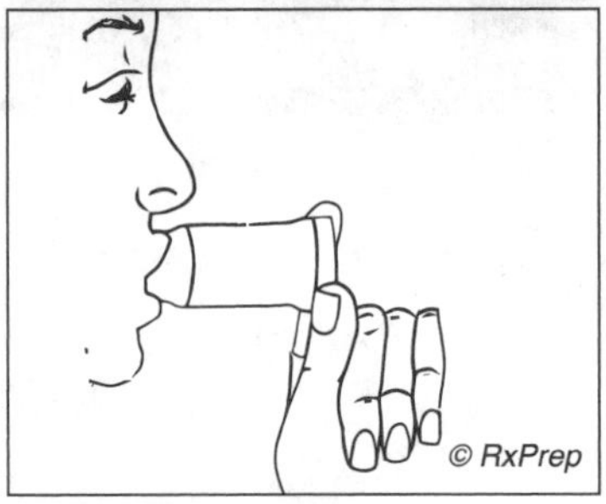

Place the mouthpiece in your mouth and close your lips around the mouthpiece. Breathe in deeply and forcefully through the inhaler. Remove the inhaler from your mouth and breathe out. Replace the white cover on the inhaler and twist shut. Rinse your mouth with water and spit out the water to prevent thrush.

TO PRIME

Twist off the white cover. Holding the inhaler upright, twist the brown base fully in one direction as far as it will go and then fully back. You will hear a click during one of the twisting motions. Repeat twisting motion again (back and forth). The inhaler is now primed and ready to load your first dose. This inhaler does not need to be primed again (even after long periods of no use).

TO CLEAN

Wipe the mouthpiece with a dry tissue weekly. Do not use water or immerse it in water.

ProAir RespiClick

STEP 1

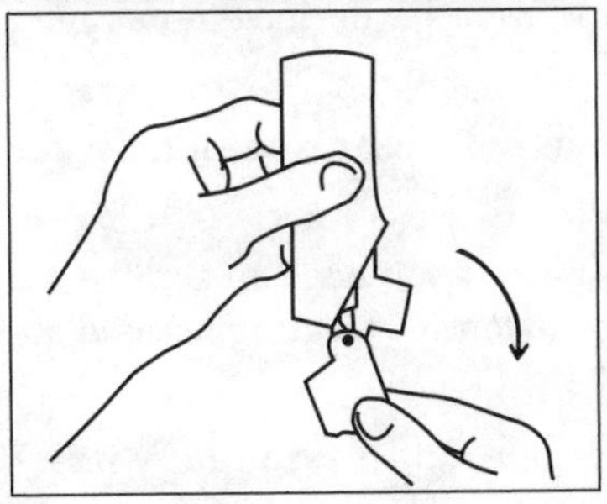

Make sure the cap is closed before each dose. Hold the inhaler upright as you open the cap fully. Open the cap all the way back until you hear a "click". Your inhaler is now ready to use. Do not open the cap unless you are taking a dose. Note: Opening and closing the cap without inhaling a dose will waste the medicine and may damage your inhaler.

STEP 2

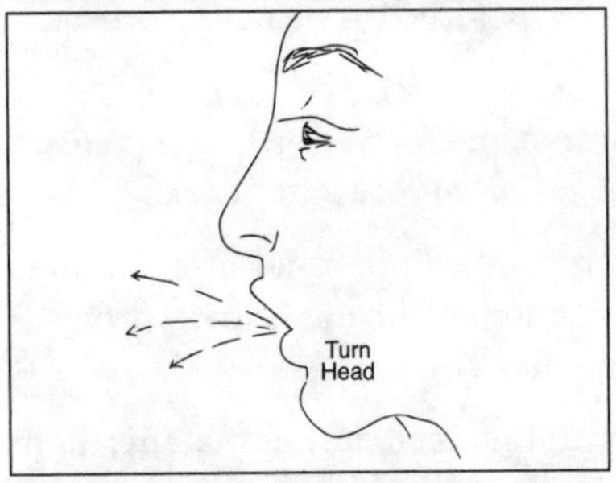

Breathe out through your mouth and push as much air from your lungs as you can. Be careful not to breathe out into the inhaler mouthpiece.

STEP 3

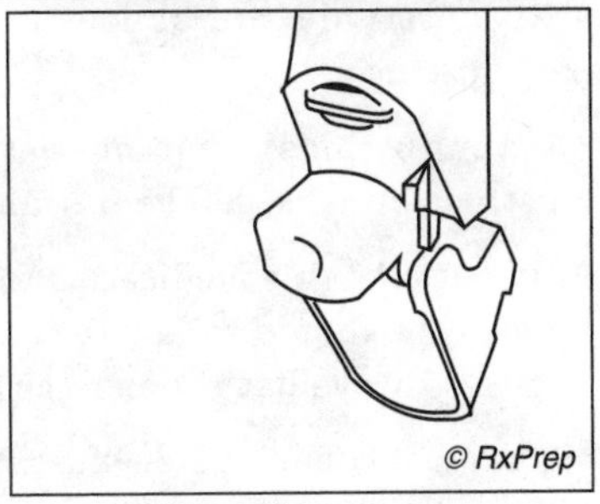

Put the mouthpiece in your mouth and close your lips around it. Breathe in deeply through your mouth, until your lungs feel completely full of air. Do not let your lips or fingers block the vent above the mouthpiece. Hold your breath for about 10 seconds or as long as you comfortably can. Remove the inhaler from your mouth. Check the dose counter on the back of the inhaler to make sure you received the dose. Close the cap over the mouthpiece after each use of the inhaler. Make sure the cap closes firmly into place.

TO PRIME

None needed.

TO CLEAN

Keep your inhaler dry and clean at all times. Do not wash or put any part of your inhaler in water. If the mouthpiece needs cleaning, gently wipe it with a dry cloth or tissue after using. Opening and closing the cap without inhaling a dose will waste the medicine and may damage your inhaler.

Patient Counseling for *Singulair*

For adults and children 12 months of age and older with asthma:

- Take this medication once a day in the evening. You may take this medication with or without food.
- Take every day for as long as your healthcare provider prescribes it, even if you have no asthma symptoms.
- If your asthma symptoms get worse, or if you need to increase the use of your rescue inhaler for asthma attacks, call your healthcare provider right away.
- Do not take this medication for the immediate relief of an asthma attack. If you have an asthma attack, you should follow the instructions your healthcare provider gave you for treating asthma attacks. Always have your rescue inhaler with you.
- The most common side effects with this medication include: stomach pain, upper respiratory infections, headache and sinus infection.
- Rarely, this medication has been associated with behavior and mood changes such as aggressive behavior, hostility, anxiousness, depression and/or suicidal thoughts and actions. Please report any of these symptoms to your healthcare provider immediately.

For patients 6 years of age and older for the prevention of exercise-induced asthma:

- Take this medication at least 2 hours before exercise.
- Always have your rescue inhaler with you for asthma attacks.
- If you are taking *Singulair* daily for chronic asthma or allergies, do not take another dose to prevent exercise-induced asthma. Talk to your healthcare provider about your treatment of exercise-induced asthma.
- Do not take an additional dose of *Singulair* within 24 hours of a previous dose.
- *Singulair* 4 mg oral granules can be given:
  - directly in the mouth
  - dissolved in 1 teaspoonful (5 mL) of cold or room temperature baby formula or breast milk
  - mixed with 1 spoonful of one of the following soft foods at cold or room temperature
  - applesauce, mashed carrots, rice, or ice cream. Give the child all of the mixture right away (within 15 minutes)
- Important for *Singulair* oral granules: never store any oral granules mixed with food, baby formula, or breast milk for use at a later time. Throw away any unused portion. Do not mix *Singulair* oral granules with any liquid drink other than baby formula or breast milk.

Patient Counseling for *Pulmicort Respules*

- Take one ampule out of the sealed aluminum envelope, recording the date you opened the envelope.
- Place any unused ampules back into the envelope and store upright, protected from light, at room temperature. Keep in mind, any remaining ampules should be used within two weeks.
- Gently swirl the ampule using a circular motion, making sure to not squeeze the ampule and keeping it in an upright position.
- Twist off the top of the ampule and squeeze all the liquid into the nebulizer and use right away. If using a face mask, make sure it fits snugly.
- Turn the compressor on and continue treatment until the mist stops, generally within 5 to 10 minutes.
- Rinse mouth with water after each dose, and wash face after treatment if a face mask was used.

PRACTICE CASE

Patient Profile

Patient Name Terri Price
Address 108 Morning Road
Age 22
Sex Female
Race White
Height 5'3"
Weight 130 lbs
Allergies NKDA

DIAGNOSES

Asthma - Step 3	GERD
Anemia	

MEDICATIONS

Date	No.	Prescriber	Drug and Strength	Quantity	Sig	Refills
7/15	35421	May	*ProAir HFA*	#1	1-2 puffs Q4-6H PRN	6
7/15	35422	May	*Flovent Diskus* 100 mcg/inh	#1	2 inh BID	6
7/15	35423	May	*Singulair* 10 mg	#30	1 PO daily	6
7/15	35424	May	*Aciphex* 20 mg	#30	1 PO daily	6
7/15	35425	May	*Advil* 200 mg		TID PRN headaches	
7/15	35426	May	Ferrous sulfate 325 mg		1 PO daily	
1/18	87242	Horowitz	Albuterol 0.5% solution	#60	2 nebulizations daily	0

LAB/DIAGNOSTIC TESTS

Test	Reference Value	Results 4/1/13	Results 7/4/15
Glu	65-99 mg/dL		
Na	135-146 mEq/L	135	137
K	3.5-5.3 mEq/L	4.2	4.7
Cl	98-110 mEq/L	102	105
CO_2	21-33 mmHg	26	26
BUN	7-25 mg/dL	10	12
Creatinine	0.6-1.2 mg/dL	0.6	0.7
Calcium	8.6-10.2 mg/dL		9.8
WBC	4-11 cells/mm3		10.2
RBC	3.8-5.1 mL/mm3		4.6

10/29/15 Here for refills on all her asthma medications. Using *ProAir* 4 x/week. Last refilled *ProAir* 18 days ago. Last refilled *Flovent, Singulair* and *Aciphex* 27 days ago. Requests recommendation for sleep agent. Also buying OTC ferrous sulfate, aspirin, *Dexatrim,* Sucrets lozenges and *Maalox.* Per discussion, she is a college student who lives at home with her parents.

Questions

1. TP seems to be exhibiting signs of uncontrolled asthma. Which of the following would be the best recommendation for better control?
   a. Take *ProAir* on a scheduled basis.
   b. Add *Serevent Diskus* 1 inhalation BID.
   c. Take *Singulair* 10 mg BID.
   d. Go to the emergency room as she is having an acute asthma attack.
   e. Elevate the head of the bed by 30 degrees when she sleeps.

2. TP states that she doesn't understand why her asthma is worsening. Which of the following could be contributing to her symptoms?
   a. Living in the same place for many years
   b. NSAID use
   c. Ferrous sulfate use
   d. *Aciphex* use
   e. She could be sleeping on her stomach more

3. TP asks you if the *Sucrets* lozenges will help the sore throat. She was told by her doctor that she has signs of thrush. Which of the following recommendations would you give that would help prevent this from happening in the future?
   a. Take the *Sucrets* lozenges because they will help with her sore throat and cure thrush.
   b. Recommend that she switch to *Symbicort* instead of *Flovent*.
   c. Recommend that she rinse her mouth after her *Flovent Diskus*, if not already doing so.
   d. Recommend that she rinse her mouth after using her *ProAir HFA*, if not already doing so.
   e. Tell her to purchase a spacer device for the *Flovent Diskus*.

4. Which of the following side effects is most likely to occur when using *Serevent Diskus* therapy?
   a. Neuropsychiatric behavior
   b. Palpitations
   c. Stomach upset
   d. Enuresis
   e. Depression

5. TP is placed on theophylline therapy for treatment of her asthma. Which of the following can decrease theophylline levels? (Select **ALL** that apply.)
   a. Ciprofloxacin
   b. Carbamazepine
   c. Erythromycin
   d. Cirrhosis
   e. High protein diet

Questions 6-7 do not relate to the above case.

6. Emi is a patient weighing 55 lbs. with a prescription for 0.1 mg/kg albuterol in 2.5 mL of normal saline. How many mL of the 0.5% albuterol solution is needed to fill this prescription?
   a. 0.1 mL
   b. 0.4 mL
   c. 0.5 mL
   d. 0.7 mL
   e. 1 mL

7. Omalizumab has a boxed warning for:
   a. Increased risk of MI
   b. Stevens-Johnson syndrome
   c. Thrombocytopenia
   d. GI ulcers
   e. Anaphylaxis

Answers

1-b, 2-b, 3-c 4-b, 5-b,e, 6-c, 7-e

36

CHRONIC OBSTRUCTIVE PULMONARY DISEASE

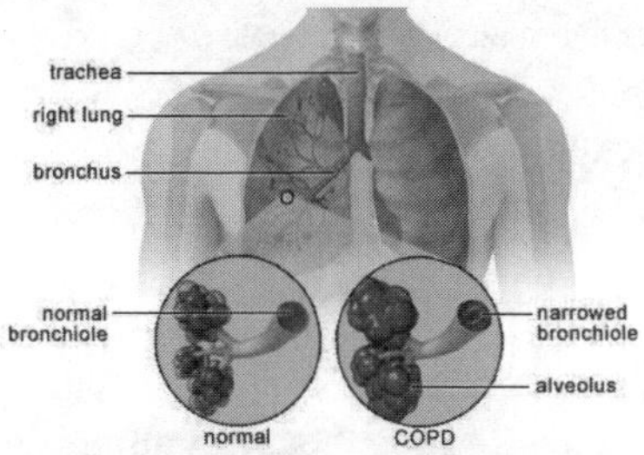

GUIDELINES/REFERENCES

Global Strategy for the Diagnosis, Management and Prevention of COPD, Global Initiative for Chronic Obstructive Lung Disease (GOLD) 2017. http://www.goldcopd.org (accessed 2016 Dec 1).

We gratefully acknowledge the assistance of Catrina Derderian, BS, PharmD, BCACP, Clinical Pharmacist, Cambridge Health Alliance, in preparing this chapter.

BACKGROUND

Chronic obstructive pulmonary disease (COPD) is the 3rd leading cause of death in the United States. It is a primarily preventable and somewhat treatable disease, which is characterized by persistent airflow limitation that is usually progressive. In contrast to asthma, the limitation of airflow is not fully reversible and generally worsens over time, leading to gradual loss of lung function.

COPD is most commonly caused by inhalation of tobacco smoke, however other air pollutants (noxious particles, smoke from biomass fuels, cigars, pipes, marijuana, etc.) can also trigger an abnormal inflammatory response in the lungs. This chronic inflammatory response can lead to lung tissue destruction and alter normal repair and defense mechanisms. The lung tissue destruction can result in emphysema, while the altered repair and defense mechanisms can result in small airway narrowing and fibrosis. Both changes lead to air trapping and worsened airflow limitation, and to the breathlessness and other classic symptoms of COPD.

Individuals with alpha-1 antitrypsin (AAT) deficiency, a rare inherited disorder in which the body does not produce enough AAT, are also at higher risk of developing COPD. AAT helps to protect the lungs from damage caused by inflammation.

DIAGNOSIS

When COPD is suspected, it is important to rule out other common reasons for shortness of breath and cough. Shortness of breath can be the presenting symptom for many different conditions including asthma. Asthma onset is usually earlier in life (childhood) versus the usual mid-life onset of COPD. Asthma symptoms are usually worse at certain times of the days or when certain triggers are present while COPD symptoms are slowly progressive. Other potential diagnoses are usually easier to distinguish from COPD and may include congestive heart failure or tuberculosis.

A clinical diagnosis of COPD should be considered in any individual over the age of 40 who has dyspnea (shortness of breath, which is chronic and progressive), chronic cough or sputum production, and a history of exposure to risk factors for the disease (smoking). Spirometry (a test to measure lung function) is required to make a diagnosis of COPD. Spirometry measures the amount of air a person can breathe out and the amount of time taken to do so. It is the most reproducible and objective measurement of airflow limitation available. The presence of a post-bronchodilator FEV1/FVC < 0.70 confirms the presence of persistent airflow limitation and thus of COPD. Spirometry is used as a diagnostic tool, evidence does not support periodic spirometry after initiation of therapy to monitor ongoing disease status or modify therapy.

STUDY TIP: COPD VS. ASTHMA

COPD

- Age of onset: usually > 40 years
- Usually a smoking history > 10 years
- Sputum production is common
- Allergies are uncommon
- Persistent and progressive symptoms that worsen over time (with exacerbations)
- Bronchodilators are mainstay of therapy

ASTHMA

- Age of onset: usually < 40 years
- Smoking history uncommon, worsens control
- Infrequent sputum production
- Allergies are common
- Symptoms are intermittent and variable and course of disease is stable (with exacerbations)
- Inhaled corticosteroids are mainstay of therapy

ASSESSMENT OF COPD

The goals of COPD assessment are to determine the severity of disease, the impact on the patient's health status and the risk of future events. Future events include exacerbations, hospital admissions and death. The following aspects of the disease should be assessed separately:

- Symptoms
- Degree of airflow limitation (using spirometry)
- Risk of exacerbations
- Presence of comorbidities

Symptoms

The classic symptoms of chronic cough and sputum production, that varies from day to day, may appear years before airflow limitation occurs. Comprehensive symptom assessment is recommended using validated questionnaires, such as the COPD Assessment Test (CAT) or the COPD Control Questionnaire (CCQ). The Modified British Medical Research Council (mMRC) is used to assess breathlessness.

Degree of Airflow Limitation

The spirometry results may be useful to identify patients who may benefit from initiation of medication therapy. The most commonly used classification system for COPD was developed by the Global Initiative for Chronic Obstructive Lung Disease or GOLD.

Classification of Severity of Airflow Limitation in COPD (Based on Post-Bronchodilator FEV1)

CLASSIFICATION	SEVERITY	AIRFLOW
IN PATIENTS WITH FEV1/FVC < 0.70		
GOLD 1	Mild	FEV1 ≥ 80% predicted
GOLD 2	Moderate	50% ≤ FEV1 < 80% predicted
GOLD 3	Severe	30% ≤ FEV1 < 50% predicted
GOLD 4	Very Severe	FEV1 < 30% predicted

Risk of Exacerbations

An exacerbation of COPD is defined as an acute event characterized by a worsening of the patient's respiratory symptoms that is beyond normal day-to-day variations. Those who experience 2 or more exacerbations per year are considered frequent exacerbators. The risk of exacerbations will increase as airflow limitation worsens. Hospitalization for an exacerbation is associated with an increased risk of death, therefore taking measures to prevent and quickly treat COPD exacerbations is of high importance.

Comorbidities

Comorbid conditions such as cardiovascular diseases, osteoporosis, diabetes, depression, anxiety, skeletal muscle dysfunction, metabolic syndrome, GERD and lung cancer may influence mortality and hospitalizations, and should be monitored routinely and treated appropriately.

Combined Assessment of COPD

The combined assessment of COPD takes into account the symptoms, airflow limitation and exacerbation risk of the patient (see table below). When assessing risk, choose the highest risk according to GOLD grade or exacerbation history.

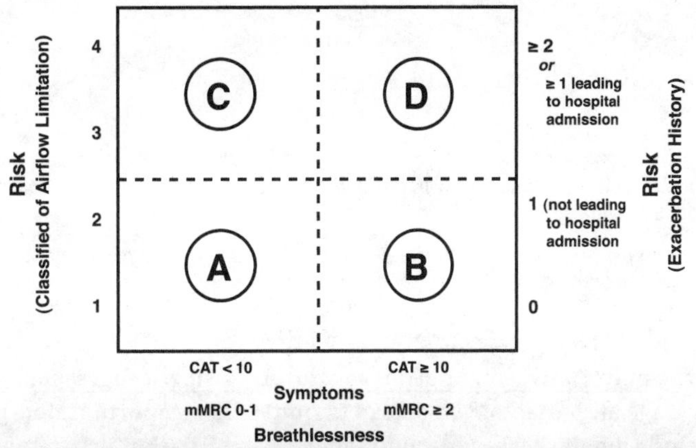

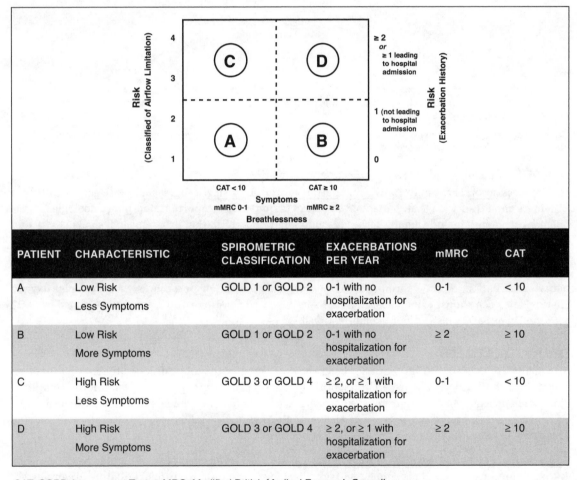

PATIENT	CHARACTERISTIC	SPIROMETRIC CLASSIFICATION	EXACERBATIONS PER YEAR	mMRC	CAT
A	Low Risk Less Symptoms	GOLD 1 or GOLD 2	0-1 with no hospitalization for exacerbation	0-1	< 10
B	Low Risk More Symptoms	GOLD 1 or GOLD 2	0-1 with no hospitalization for exacerbation	≥ 2	≥ 10
C	High Risk Less Symptoms	GOLD 3 or GOLD 4	≥ 2, or ≥ 1 with hospitalization for exacerbation	0-1	< 10
D	High Risk More Symptoms	GOLD 3 or GOLD 4	≥ 2, or ≥ 1 with hospitalization for exacerbation	≥ 2	≥ 10

CAT: COPD Assessment Test, mMRC: Modified British Medical Research Council

Pharmacologic Therapy for Stable COPD

PATIENT GROUP	RECOMMENDED FIRST CHOICE	STEP UP IN THERAPY	FURTHER EXACERBATIONS
A	SABA or LABA	LA anticholinergic or LABA or SABA and SA anticholinergic	
B*	Long-acting bronchodilator (LA anticholinergic or LABA)	LA anticholinergic and LABA	
C	LA anticholinergic	LA anticholinergic and LABA (preferred) or LA anticholinergic and ICS	
D	LABA + LA anticholinergic (preferred) or LABA + ICS	ICS + LABA and LA anticholinergic (preffered)	Consider roflumilast if FEV1 < 50% predicted and patient has chronic bronchitis Consider adding a macrolide (in former smokers)

**Dual LABA therapy can be considered in patients with persistent breathlessness on monotherapy. Patient with severe breathlessness may begin initial therapy with two bronchodilators.*

SA: short-acting, LA: long-acting, SABA: short-acting beta-2 agonist, LABA: long-acting beta-2 agonist, ICS: inhaled corticosteroid, PDE-4: phosphodiesterase-4, PRN: when necessary.

NON-DRUG TREATMENT

Smoking cessation is the only management strategy proven to slow progression of disease. Healthcare providers should encourage all patients who smoke to quit. Other important non-pharmacological management strategies include inhaler technique, pulmonary rehabilitation programs, physical activity and assessment of comorbidities. Pulmonary rehabilitation helps improve quality of life and symptoms and should be recommended to all patients who become short of breath when walking their own pace on level ground. Some patients go on to require long-term oxygen therapy, either given in the hospital for acute exacerbation, or used chronically outpatient with the use of portable oxygen systems. Oxygen therapy has been shown to increase survival in patients with severe resting hypoxemia (defined by $PaO2 \leq 55$ mmHg or $SaO2 \leq 88\%$ without complications).

DRUG TREATMENT

The medications used in COPD have not been shown to modify the long-term decline in lung function nor reduce mortality. Therefore, pharmacotherapy is used to decrease symptoms and/or complications such as exacerbations and hospitalizations. Each treatment regimen should be patient-specific, as severity of symptoms and severity of airflow limitation is also influenced by other factors such as frequency of exacerbations and the presence of comorbidities.

Bronchodilators (beta-2 agonists, anticholinergics) are used as-needed or on a regular basis, depending on symptom severity. If used on a regular basis, long-acting inhaled bronchodilators are preferred, more effective and more convenient than frequent treatment with short-acting inhaled bronchodilators. Combining bronchodilators of different pharmacologic classes may improve efficacy and decrease the risk of side effects compared to increasing the dose of a single agent.

Long term monotherapy with oral or inhaled corticosteroids is not recommended. However, inhaled corticosteroids can be added in severe and very severe COPD and have been shown to improve symptoms, lung function, quality of life, and reduce exacerbation frequency.

An inhaled corticosteroid combined with a long acting beta-2 agonist is most effective in improving lung function and reduces exacerbations in patients with moderate to very severe COPD.

PDE-4 inhibitor use is limited. Treatment with theophylline is not recommended unless other long-term treatment bronchodilators are unavailable or unaffordable.

If patients have severe hereditary alpha-1 antitrypsin deficiency, they may be placed on an alpha-1 proteinase inhibitor *(Prolastin, Aralast* or *Zemaira)* for chronic augmentation therapy. These agents are very expensive, given as weekly IV infusions, and are associated with many side effects, including anaphylaxis.

Vaccines are used to prevent infections and reduce the risk of acute exacerbations. Influenza vaccine (annually) and pneumococcal vaccine (PPSV23, *Pneumovax 23*) x 1 should be given to all smokers from age 19 – 64 years and those with COPD. Refer to Immunizations chapter for additional information regarding vaccines.

COPD exacerbations may be caused by respiratory tract infections (viral, bacterial) or other factors such as increased air pollution. If there is increased sputum purulence and increased sputum volume or increased dyspnea, or if mechanical ventilation is required, antibiotics should be utilized for 5 – 10 days. Outside of antibiotics, an inhaled short-acting beta-2 agonist with or without a short-acting anticholinergic plus oral steroids (e.g., prednisone 40 mg/day) are effective treatments. For treatment of acute COPD exacerbations, see the Infectious Diseases II chapter.

INHALER DEVICES

There are 2 categories of inhaler devices, metered-dose inhalers (MDIs) and dry powder inhalers (DPIs). Up to 94% of patients with asthma and COPD use their inhalers incorrectly. Poor adherence or incorrect use of inhalers due to poor education may lead to decreased quality of life, worsened health outcomes, and increased frequency of exacerbations and hospitalizations. See the MDI and DPI Study Tip in the Asthma chapter for a review of these devices and the online video course for demonstration of the devices.

ANTICHOLINERGIC AGENTS

Anticholinergics block the action of acetylcholine and ↓ cyclic guanosine monophosphate (cGMP) at parasympathetic sites in bronchial smooth muscle causing bronchodilation. Anticholinergic agents block muscarinic receptors, so they may be referred to as antimuscarinics.

DRUG	DOSING	SAFETY/SIDE EFFECTS/MONITORING
Short-acting anticholinergics		**WARNINGS** Use with caution in patients with myasthenia gravis, narrow-angle glaucoma, urinary retention, benign prostatic hyperplasia and bladder neck obstruction **SIDE EFFECTS** Dry mouth (much more common with tiotropium), upper respiratory tract infections (nasopharyngitis, sinusitis), cough, bitter taste **MONITORING** S/sx at each visit, smoking status, COPD questionnaires, annual spirometry **NOTES** Avoid spraying in the eyes Do not swallow capsules of glycopyrrolate, glycopyrrolate/indacaterol or tiotropium *Tudorza* – Discard product 45 days after opening pouch, when device locks out or when dose indicator displays "0", whichever comes first.
Ipratropium bromide *(Atrovent HFA)* 17 mcg/inh, 0.02% nebulizer solution **+ albuterol *(Combivent Respimat,*** *DuoNeb)* 20 mcg ipratropium + 100 mcg albuterol/inh 0.5 mg ipratropium + 2.5 mg albuterol per 3 mL nebulizer solution	***Atrovent*** MDI: 2 inhalations QID Nebulizer: 0.5 mg TID-QID ***Combivent Respimat*** MDI: 1 inhalation QID Nebulizer *(DuoNeb)*: 3 mL QID	
Long-acting anticholinergics		
Aclidinium *(Tudorza Pressair)* 400 mcg/inh	DPI: 1 inhalation BID	
Glycopyrrolate *(Seebri Neohaler)* 15.6 mcg/inh + indacaterol *(Utibron Neohaler)* 15.6 mcg glycopyrrolate + 27.5 mcg indacaterol/inh	DPI: 1 capsule via *Neohaler* device BID DPI: 1 capsule via *Neohaler* device BID	
Tiotropium *(Spiriva HandiHaler,* *Spiriva Respimat)* 18 mcg capsule, 2.5 mcg/inh, (1.25 mcg/inh for asthma) + olodaterol *(Stiolto Respimat)* 2.5 mcg tiotropium + 2.5 mcg olodaterol/inh	DPI: 1 capsule inhaled daily via the *HandiHaler* device (requires 2 puffs) **Both *Respimat* devices** MDI: 2 inhalations daily	
Umeclidinium *(Incruse Ellipta)* 62.5 mcg/inh + vilanterol *(Anoro Ellipta)* 62.5 mcg umeclidinium + 25 mcg vilanterol/inh	**Both *Ellipta* devices** DPI: 1 inhalation daily	

BETA-2 AGONISTS

These agents bind to beta-2 receptors causing relaxation of bronchial smooth muscle, resulting in bronchodilation; the inhaled route is the preferred route of administration. Short-acting beta-2 agonists are often used for other reversible airway diseases such as colds, allergies and bronchitis. For short-acting beta-2 agonists, see the Asthma chapter.

DRUG	DOSING	SAFETY/SIDE EFFECTS/MONITORING
Long-acting beta-2 agonists		**BOXED WARNING** Long-acting beta-2 agonists (LABAs) increase the risk of asthma-related deaths and should only be used in asthma patients who are currently on a long-term asthma control medication (inhaled corticosteroid) but are not adequately controlled **CONTRAINDICATIONS** Status asthmaticus, acute episodes of asthma or COPD, monotherapy in treatment of asthma **SIDE EFFECTS** Tachycardia, tremor, shakiness, lightheadedness, cough, palpitations, hypokalemia and hyperglycemia **MONITORING** S/sx at each visit, smoking status, COPD questionnaires, annual spirometry **NOTES** Bronchodilators are used on a PRN or scheduled basis to reduce symptoms. Do not swallow capsules of indacaterol, indacaterol/gylcopyrrolate or formoterol. All steroid-containing inhalers – rinse mouth with water after use and spit. Long-acting inhaled bronchodilators are more effective and convenient. Combination therapy with inhaled steroids can ↑ the risk of pneumonia, however, the combination showed a ↓ in exacerbations and improvement in lung function when compared to the individual components. Indacaterol is more effective than formoterol and salmeterol. Arformoterol contains R-isomer of formoterol. ***Advair*** Discard Diskus device 1 month after removal from pouch or when dose counter reads "0" (whichever comes first). ***Symbicort*** Discard inhaler after the labeled number of inhalations have been used or within 3 months after removal from foil pouch. ***Serevent Diskus* and all *Ellipta* devices** Discard device 6 weeks after removal from the foil tray or when the dose counter reads "0" (whichever comes first). **All *Respimat* devices** Discard device 3 months after cartridge is inserted into the inhaler or when the inhaler locks (which indicates no doses are left).
Salmeterol *(Serevent Diskus)* 50 mcg/inh	DPI: 1 inhalation BID	
+ fluticasone *(Advair Diskus, Advair HFA)*		
Advair Diskus: 100, 250, 500 mcg fluticasone + 50 mcg salmeterol/inh (250/50 is approved for COPD)	DPI: 1 inhalation BID	
Advair HFA: 45, 115, 230 mcg fluticasone + 21 mcg salmeterol/inh	MDI: 2 inhalation BID	
Formoterol *(Perforomist – nebulizer)* 12 mcg capsule, 20 mcg/2 mL nebulizer solution	Nebulizer: 20 mcg BID	
+ budesonide *(Symbicort)* 80, 160 mcg budesonide + 4.5 mcg formeterol/inh (160/4.5 is the only strength approved for COPD)	MDI: 2 inhalations BID	
+ glycopyrrolate *(Bevespi Aerosphere)* (glycopyrrolate 9 mcg/formoterol 4.8 mcg per inhalation)	MDI: 2 inhalations BID	
Arformoterol *(Brovana)* 15 mcg/2 mL nebulizer solution	Nebulizer: 15 mcg BID	
Indacaterol *(Arcapta Neohaler)* 75 mcg capsule	DPI: 1 capsule via *Neohaler* device daily	
+ glycopyrrolate *(Utibron Neohaler)* 27.5 mcg indacaterol + 15.6 mcg glycopyrrolate/inh	DPI: 1 capsule via *Neohaler* device BID	
Fluticasone/vilanterol *(Breo Ellipta)* 100, 200 mcg fluticasone + 25 mcg vilanterol/inh (100/25 is the only one approved for COPD)	DPI: 1 inhalation daily	
Olodaterol *(Striverdi Respimat)* 2.5 mcg/inh	**Both *Respimat* devices** MDI: 2 inhalations daily	
+ tiotropium *(Stiolto Respimat)* 2.5 olodaterol + 2.5 mcg tiotropium/inh		

PHOSPHODIESTERASE-4 INHIBITOR

Roflumilast is a PDE-4 inhibitor that ↑ cAMP levels, leading to a reduction in lung inflammation. This medication should always be used in combination with at least one long-acting bronchodilator. Consider roflumilast in patients with severe to very severe COPD, chronic bronchitis, and a history of exacerbations and chronic bronchitis.

DRUG	DOSING	SAFETY/SIDE EFFECTS/MONITORING
Roflumilast *(Daliresp)* Tablet	500 mcg PO daily	**CONTRAINDICATIONS** Moderate to severe liver impairment **WARNINGS** Psychiatric events (depression, mood changes) including suicidality **SIDE EFFECTS** Diarrhea, weight loss, nausea, ↓ appetite, insomnia, HA **MONITORING** S/sx at each visit, LFTs, smoking status, COPD questionnaires, annual spirometry **NOTES** Use only in severe COPD due to modest benefit

See Asthma chapter for details on theophylline and inhaled corticosteroids.

Roflumilast Drug Interactions

Roflumilast is a substrate of 3A4 (major) and 1A2 (minor). Use with strong enzyme inducers (e.g., carbamazepine, phenobarbital, phenytoin, rifampin) is not recommended. Use with 3A4 inhibitors or dual 3A4 and 1A2 inhibitors (erythromycin, ketoconazole, fluvoxamine, cimetidine) will ↑ roflumilast levels.

PATIENT COUNSELING - METERED DOSE INHALERS

Atrovent HFA

STEP 1

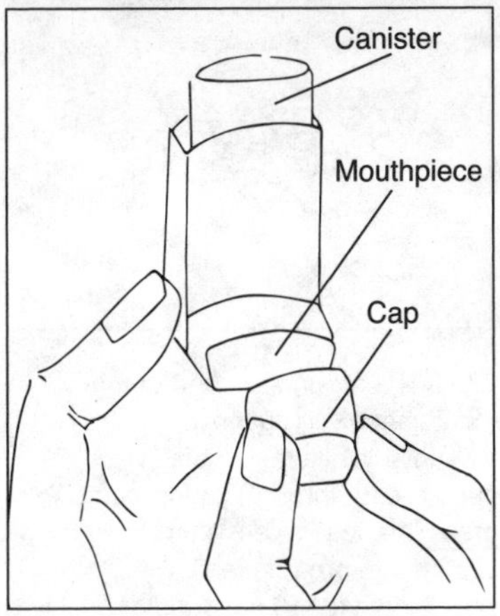

Insert the metal canister into the actuator. The *Atrovent HFA* plastic actuator should only be used with the *Atrovent HFA* canister. Remove the protective dust cap from the mouthpiece and check mouthpiece for foreign objects prior to use.

STEP 2

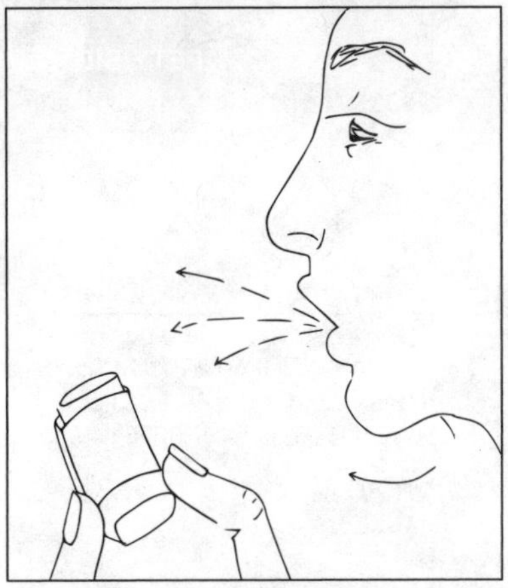

Breathe out deeply through your mouth. Holding the inhaler upright (as shown in the picture), place the mouthpiece into your mouth and close your lips around it. Keep your eyes closed so that no medicine will be sprayed into your eyes.

STEP 3

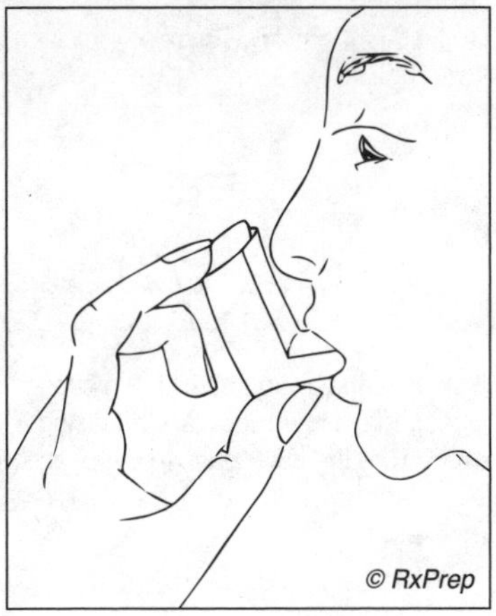

While breathing in slowly and deeply through your mouth, press the top of the canister all the way down with your index finger. Hold your breath as long as possible, up to 10 seconds, then breathe normally. If another inhalation is needed, wait at least 15 seconds and repeat Steps 1-3. Place cap back on the mouthpiece after use.

TIPS

PRIMING

Spray 2 times away from the face. Prime again if > 3 days from last use.

CLEANING

Rinse mouthpiece under warm running water (but not the metal canister) for 30 seconds to prevent medication buildup and blockage. Shake to remove excess water and let air dry. Clean at least weekly.

Combivent Respimat, Stiolto Respimat, Striverdi Respimat

STEP 1

Hold the inhaler upright with the cap closed to avoid accidentally releasing a dose. Turn the clear base in the direction of the arrows on the label until it clicks (half a turn).

STEP 2

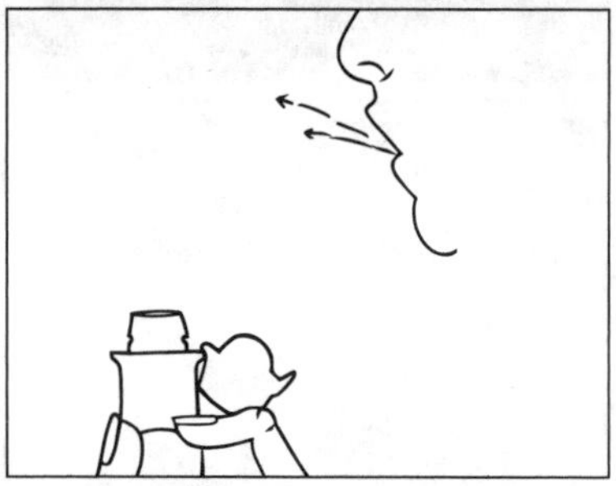

Flip the cap until it snaps fully open. Turn head away from the inhaler and breathe out slowly and fully.

STEP 3

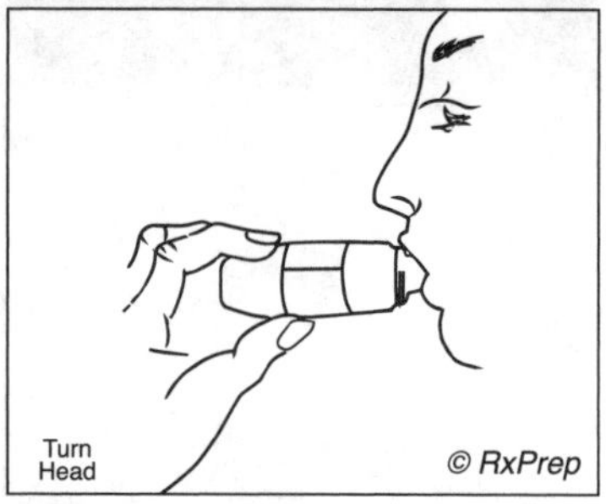

Close lips around the end of the mouthpiece without covering the air vents. While taking a slow, deep breath through your mouth, press the dose release button and continue to breathe in slowly. Hold your breath for 10 seconds or as long as comfortable. Close the cap when finished.

TIPS

ASSEMBLE DEVICE FOR FIRST TIME USE

With the cap closed, press the safety catch while pulling off the clear base. Do not touch the piercing element located inside the bottom of the clear base. Write the discard by date on the label of the inhaler (which is 3 months from the date the cartridge is inserted). Push the narrow end of the cartridge into the inhaler. The base of the cartridge will not sit flush with the inhaler; about 1/8 of an inch will stick out when the cartridge is correctly inserted.

PRIMING

Hold the inhaler upright with the cap closed to avoid accidentally releasing a dose. Turn the clear base in the direction of the arrows on the label until it clicks (half a turn). Flip the cap until it snaps fully open. Point the inhaler toward the ground away from your face. Press the dose release button. Close cap. Repeat these steps over again until a spray is visible. Once the spray is visible, repeat the steps 3 more times to make sure inhaler is prepared for use. If inhaler is not used for > 3 days, spray 1 puff toward the ground to prepare the inhaler. If inhaler has not been used for > 21 days, follow priming for initial use instructions.

CLEANING

Clean the mouthpiece, including the metal part inside the mouthpiece, with a damp cloth or tissue weekly.

PATIENT COUNSELING - DRY POWDER INHALERS

Spiriva HandiHaler

STEP 1

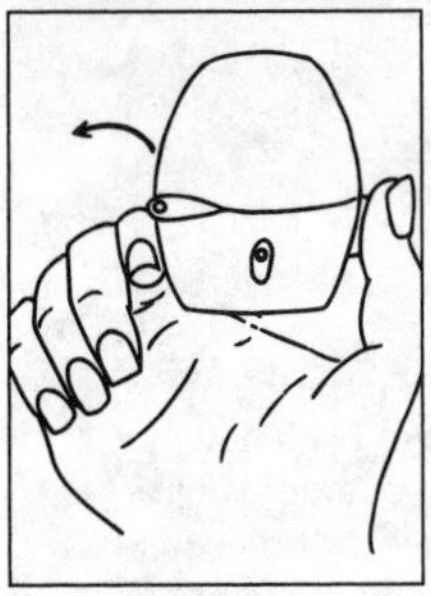

Open the Handi-Haler device by pressing on the green button and lifting the cap upwards. Open the mouthpiece by pulling up and away from the base.

STEP 2

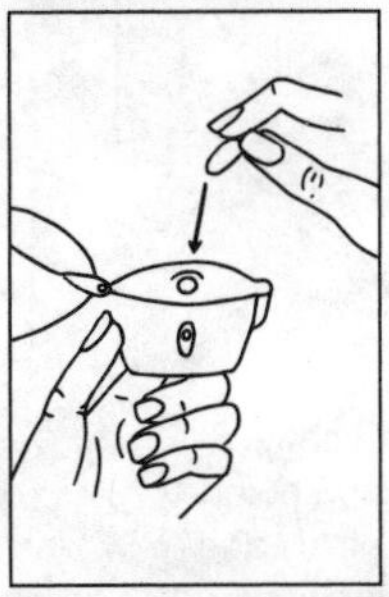

Insert the *SPIRIVA* capsule in the chamber and close the mouthpiece firmly against the gray base until you hear a click.

STEP 3

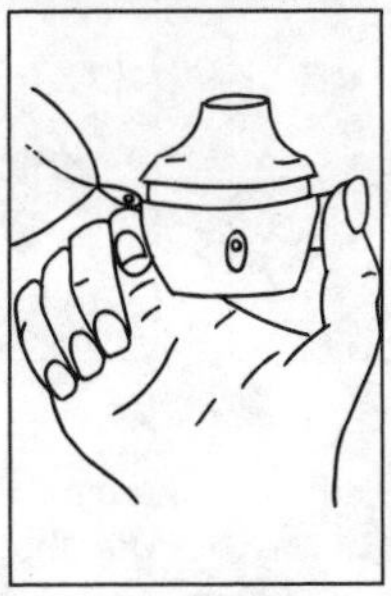

Press the green piercing button once until it is flat (flush) against the base, then release. Do not shake the device.

STEP 4

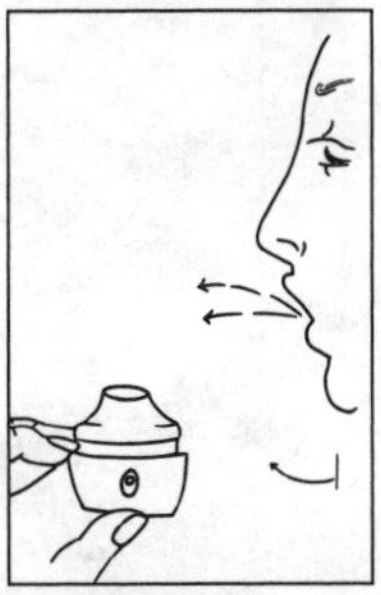

Turn head away from the inhaler and breathe out fully.

STEP 5

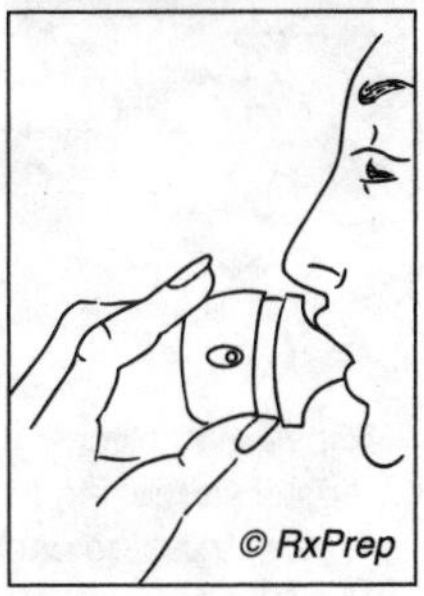

Raise your *Handihaler* to your mouth in a horizontal position and close your lips around the mouthpiece. Breathe in deeply and fully. You should hear or feel the *SPIRIVA* capsule vibrate (rattle). Remove inhaler from your mouth and hold your breath for a few seconds. Breathe normally. Breathe out again and breathe in deeply and fully through the inhaler (you must inhale twice from each capsule). Discard capsule after 2 inhalations. Close the lid of the device.

TIPS

CLEANING

Clean inhaler as needed. Rinse inhaler with warm water, pressing the green button a few times so the chamber and piercing needle are under the running water. Make sure any powder build up is removed. Air dry. It takes 24 hours to air dry the *Handihaler* device after it is cleaned.

Tudorza

STEP 1

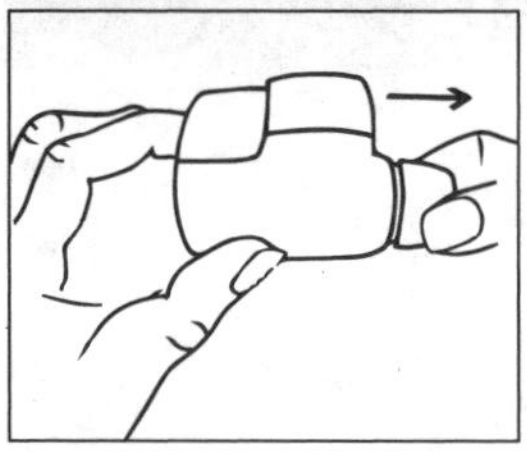

Remove the protective cap by lightly squeezing the arrows marked on each side of the cap and pulling outwards. Check the mouthpiece for foreign objects.

STEP 2

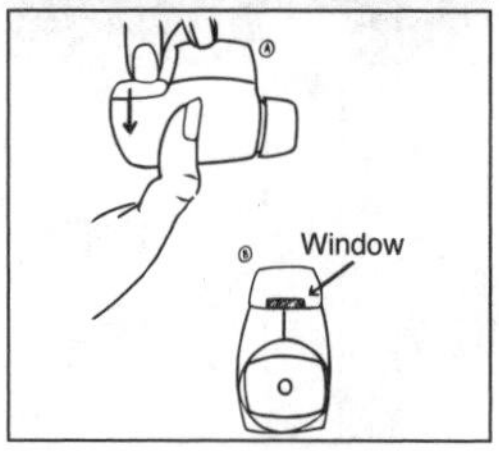

A. Before putting into mouth, press the back (green) button all the way down and release.

B. Check the control window to make sure the dose is ready for inhalation; the window will change from red to green. Breathe out completely, away from the inhaler.

STEP 3

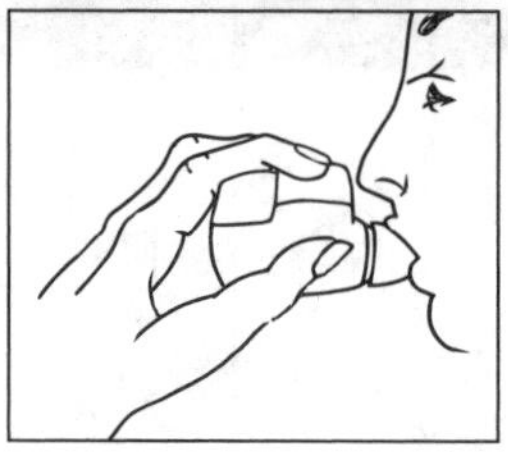

Put your lips tightly around the mouthpiece. Breathe in quickly and deeply through your mouth. Breathe in until you hear a "click" sound and keep breathing in to get the full dose.

Note. Do not hold down the back (green) button while breathing in.

STEP 4

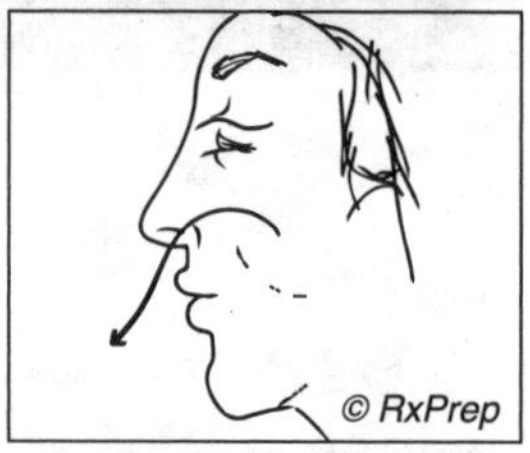

Remove the inhaler from your mouth and hold your breath for as long as comfortable. Then breathe out slowly through your nose. Place the protective cap on the inhaler.

Note. Check that the control window has turned to red which indicates the full dose has been inhaled correctly.

TIPS

CLEANING
You do not need to clean your inhaler. If you wish to clean it, wipe the outside of the mouthpiece with a dry tissue or paper towel. Do not use water.

Anoro Ellipta, Breo Ellipta, Incruse Ellipta

STEP 1

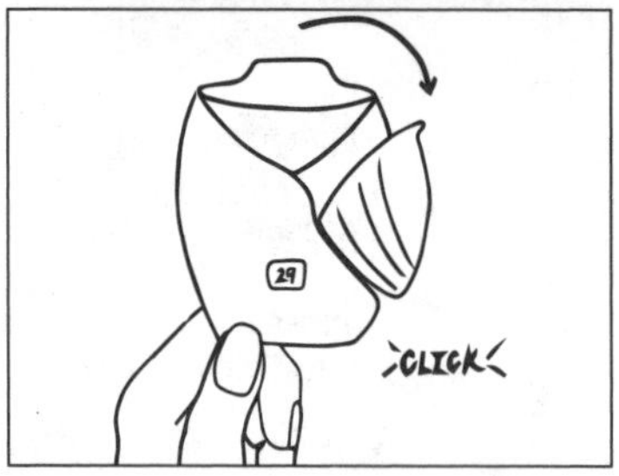

Open the cover of the inhaler by sliding the cover down to expose the mouthpiece. You should hear a "click." The counter will count down by 1 number, indicating that the inhaler is ready to use. Note: if you open and close the cover without inhaling the medicine, the dose will be lost. It is not possible to accidentally take a double dose or an extra dose in 1 inhalation.

STEP 2

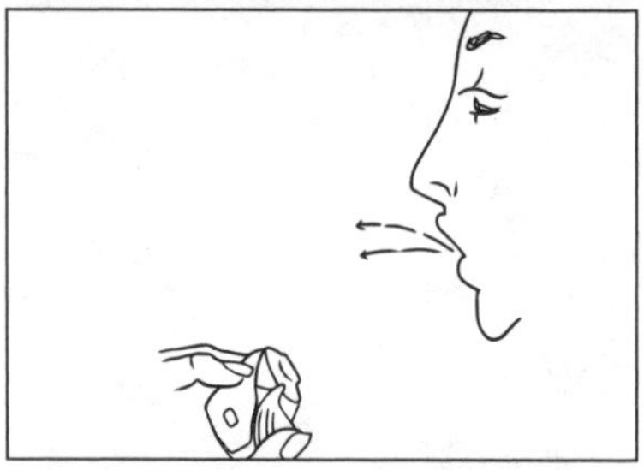

While holding the inhaler away from your mouth, breathe out fully. Do not breathe out into the mouthpiece.

STEP 3

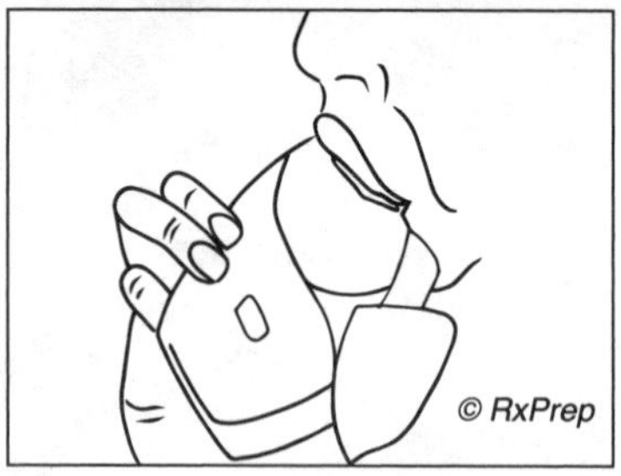

Put the mouthpiece between your lips and close your lips firmly around it. Take one long, steady, deep breath in through your mouth. Do not block the air vent with your fingers. Remove inhaler from mouth and hold your breath for 3-4 seconds or as long as comfortable. Breathe out slowly and gently. Close the inhaler. Rinse your mouth.

TIPS

CLEANING
You can clean the mouthpiece if needed, using a dry tissue, before you close the cover. Routine cleaning is not required.

Arcapta Neohaler, Seebri Neohaler, Utibron Neohaler

STEP 1

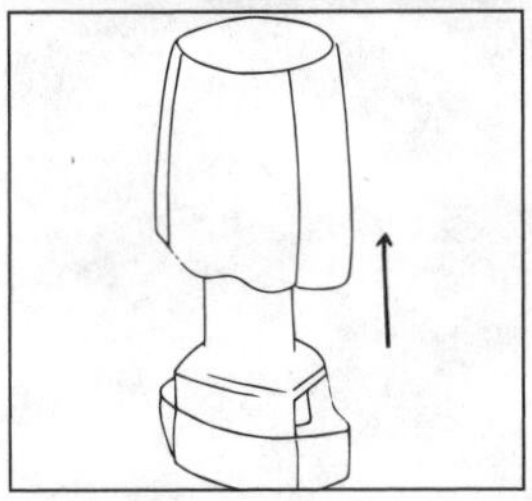

Pull off cap.

STEP 2

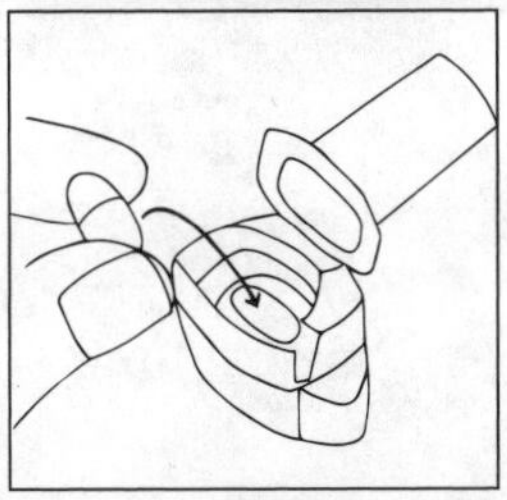

Hold the base of the inhaler firmly and tilt the mouthpiece to open the inhaler. Place the capsule into the capsule chamber. Close the inhaler fully, until you hear a "click" sound.

STEP 3

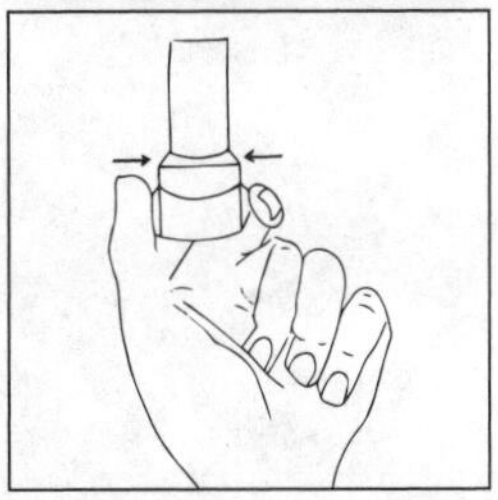

Hold the inhaler upright. Press both buttons fully one time. You should hear a "click" as the capsule is being pierced. Release the buttons fully. The inhaler is now ready to be used. Before using, breathe out fully, away from the inhaler.

STEP 4

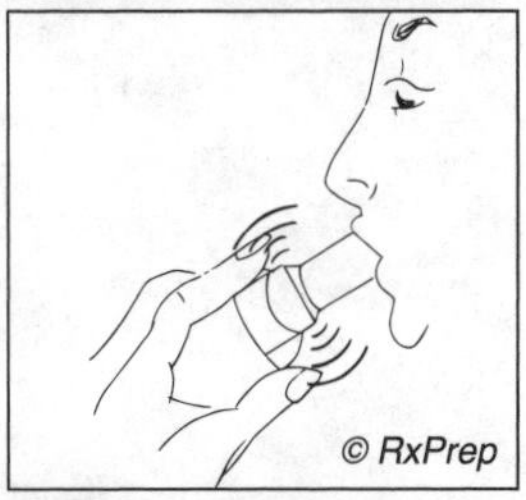

Place the mouthpiece in your mouth and close your lips around the mouthpiece. Hold the inhaler with the buttons to the side (not up and down). Breathe in rapidly and deeply (you should hear a whirring sound when breathing in). Hold your breath as long as comfortable while removing the inhaler from your mouth. Then, breathe out. The capsule should be empty of all powder. If it is not, inhale again. Remove capsule and replace the cap.

TIPS

CLEANING

Cleaning the device is not necessary, however, if desired, a clean, dry, lint-free cloth or a clean, dry soft brush may be used to wipe the inhaler between uses.

37

TOBACCO CESSATION

GUIDELINES/REFERENCES

Treating Tobacco Use and Dependence. 2008 Update. Content last reviewed June 2015. Agency for Healthcare Research and Quality, Rockville, MD. http://www.ahrq.gov/professionals/clinicians-providers/guidelines-recommendations/tobacco/index.html (accessed 2016 Sept 22).

Fiore MC, Baker TB. Treating smokers in the health care setting. *N Engl J Med* 2011;365:1222-31.

We gratefully acknowledge the assistance of Beth A. Martin, PhD, MS, RPh, Associate Professor, University of Wisconsin-Madison School of Pharmacy, and Megan Heim, PharmD, BCACP, TTS, Clinical Pharmacist, William S. Middleton Memorial Veterans Hospital, in preparing this chapter.

BACKGROUND

Smoking is the leading cause of preventable death in the U.S. and a known cause of multiple cancers, heart disease, stroke, pregnancy complications, COPD, and many other diseases. Tobacco dependence is a chronic disease that often requires repeated interventions and multiple attempts to quit. Effective treatments exist that can significantly increase rates of long-term abstinence. It is essential for healthcare providers to ask patients about tobacco use, document the response and provide treatment. A national network of tobacco quitlines is available for patients at 1-800-QUIT-NOW (1-800-784-8669).

The combination of counseling and medication is more effective than either counseling or medication alone. Two counseling components that are especially effective are behavioral counseling (problem-solving/skills training) and social support. There is a strong correlation between counseling intensity (length and number of counseling sessions) and quitting success.

There are several effective, first-line medications for tobacco dependence, including five nicotine replacement therapies (NRTs) and two non-nicotine therapies. Combination therapy, such as using a long-acting nicotine patch with a short-acting formulation (e.g., gum, lozenge) or nicotine patch with bupropion sustained release (SR), can be used first-line. Medications reduce withdrawal symptoms, including anxiety, irritability, depression, insomnia, poor concentration, restlessness, increased appetite, and an urge to smoke. Medications should be encouraged for all patients attempting to quit, except when medically contraindicated.

Electronic Cigarettes

The risks and benefits of electronic cigarettes, also known as e-cigarettes and "electronic nicotine delivery systems" (ENDS), continues to be investigated. Prior to August 2016, e-cigarettes were not regulated by the FDA and high nicotine variability was found between and within brands. There is some risk for nicotine addiction when non-smokers use them. Carcinogens and other chemicals can be present in the nicotine vapors. The attractiveness of the cartridge flavors has increased adolescent use and contributed to accidental poisonings in children. At this time, e-cigarettes should not be recommended as an alternative to approved smoking cessation treatments.

Smoking and Drug Interactions

Non-nicotine compounds in tobacco smoke induce CYP450 enzymes, primarily CYP450 1A2. Smokers who quit can experience side effects from supratherapeutic levels of caffeine, theophylline, fluvoxamine, olanzapine, clozapine and the R-isomer of warfarin. The R-isomer is the less potent isomer, but due to warfarin's narrow therapeutic range, bleeding could occur. Smoking increases the risk of bleeding with clopidogrel. Women ≥ 35 years of age who smoke should not be taking oral contraceptives due to an increased risk of cardiovascular events.

Exceptions to Drug Treatment

The guidelines promote the use of behavioral counseling over drugs for the following populations: pregnant women, adolescents, smokeless tobacco users (e.g., chewing tobacco), and "light" smokers using < 10 cigarettes a day. This is consistent with the American College of Obstetricians and Gynecologists (ACOG) recommendations.

THE "5 A'S" MODEL FOR TREATING TOBACCO USE AND DEPENDENCE

Ask about tobacco use
Identify and document tobacco use status for every patient at every visit.

Advise to quit
In a clear, strong, and personalized manner, urge every tobacco user to quit.

Assess willingness to make a quit attempt
Is the tobacco user willing to make a quit attempt at this time (e.g., in the next month)?

Assist in quit attempt
For the patient willing to make a quit attempt, offer medication (if appropriate) and provide or refer for behavioral counseling.

For patients unwilling to quit at this time, provide motivational interventions designed to increase future quit attempts.

For the recent quitter, or any patient with remaining challenges, provide relapse prevention.

Arrange follow up
For the patient willing to make a quit attempt, arrange for follow up visits beginning within the first week after the quit date.

For patients unwilling to make a quit attempt at this time, address tobacco dependence and willingness to quit at next clinic visit.

Vaccinations in Smokers

Smokers 19 – 64 years of age should receive the pneumococcal polysaccharide vaccine *(Pneumovax 23)* and an annual influenza vaccine. Additional immunizations depend on the patient's age and risk factors, per the ACIP recommendations. See the Immunizations chapter for further discussion.

DRUG TREATMENT

Nicotine Replacement Therapy (NRT)

DRUG	DOSING	SAFETY/SIDE EFFECTS/MONITORING
Nicotine patch ***(NicoDerm CQ,*** others) OTC	Apply upon waking on quit date If > 10 cigarettes/day: Weeks 1-6: use 21 mg patch Weeks 7-8: use 14 mg patch Weeks 9-10: use 7 mg patch If ≤ 10 cigarettes/day: Weeks 1-6: use 14 mg patch Weeks 7-8: use 7 mg patch	**WARNINGS** Immediate post-MI period, life-threatening arrhythmia, severe or worsening angina, pregnancy Inhaler/Nasal Spray: bronchospastic or reactive airway disease **SIDE EFFECTS** Headache, dizziness, nervousness, insomnia, dyspepsia Patch: skin irritation Inhaler: mouth and throat irritation, cough, rhinitis Nasal Spray: nasal irritation, watery eyes, sneezing, transient changes in taste and smell **NOTES** The FDA prohibits sale of nicotine products to individuals < 18 years of age. Identification required to purchase. The nicotine patch has the highest adherence rate. Combination therapy with short-acting NRT is the most effective. The patch should not be cut and should be removed before an MRI. Patch is typically worn for 24 hours, but can be removed at bedtime to avoid insomnia and bothersome, vivid dreams. The gum and lozenge are sugar-free. The gum and lozenge (4 mg strengths) have been shown to reduce or delay weight gain. The inhaler mimics the hand to mouth smoking action, providing a coping mechanism. The nasal spray has the fastest delivery and is useful for rapid relief of withdrawal symptoms. It has the highest dependence potential among NRTs. Safety issue (Rx products) – see Pregnancy chapter.
Nicotine polacrilex **gum *(Nicorette,*** others) and **lozenge *(Nicorette, Nicorette Mini,*** others) OTC	1st cigarette > 30 min after waking up: use 2 mg gum or lozenge 1st cigarette ≤ 30 min after waking up: use 4 mg gum or lozenge Additional guidelines for dosing gum: < 25 cigarettes daily use 2 mg gum, ≥ 25 cigarettes daily use 4 mg gum Weeks 1-6: 1 piece Q1-2H Weeks 7-9: 1 piece Q2-4H Weeks 10-12: 1 piece Q4-8H Min: 9 pieces/day for 1st 6 wks Max (gum): 24 pieces/day Max (lozenge): 20 pieces/day Generally used up to 12 wks	
Nicotine inhaler *(Nicotrol Inhaler)* Rx	6-16 cartridges daily up to 12 wks, then taper frequency of use over 6-12 wks Use up to 6 months	
Nicotine nasal spray *(Nicotrol NS)* Rx	1 dose = 2 sprays (1 spray in each nostril), use 1-2 doses per hour, ↑ PRN for symptom relief Min: 8 doses/day Max: 5 doses/hr or 40 doses/day Use up to 3 months	

Bupropion and Varenicline

Bupropion blocks neuronal reuptake of dopamine and/or norepinephrine resulting in reduced cravings and other withdrawal symptoms. Varenicline is a partial neuronal alpha-4 beta-2 nicotinic receptor agonist. It causes low-level stimulation of the receptor, while blocking the ability of nicotine to bind. This relieves symptoms of nicotine withdrawal and inhibits the surges of dopamine responsible for the reinforcement and reward associated with smoking. These agents do not need to be tapered when they are discontinued.

DRUG	DOSING	SAFETY/SIDE EFFECTS/MONITORING
BuPROPion SR ***(Zyban)*** Tablet *Aplenzin*, Bupropion IR, *Wellbutrin SR*, *Wellbutrin XL*, *Forfivo XL* - for depression *Aplenzin*, *Wellbutrin XL* - for seasonal affective disorder (SAD)	Start at least 1 week before quit date 150 mg QAM for 3 days, then 150 mg BID Max dose: 300 mg/day Use up to 6 months To ↓ insomnia and risk of seizures, take 1st dose upon awakening and 2nd dose 8 hours after 1st dose If no significant progress by week 7, consider discontinuation	**BOXED WARNINGS** Serious neuropsychiatric events (e.g., depression, mania, suicidal or homicidal thoughts, psychosis), risk of suicidal thinking and behavior is increased in children, adolescents, and young adults taking antidepressants **CONTRAINDICATIONS** Seizure disorder, history of anorexia/bulimia, use within 14 days of discontinuing MAO inhibitors, use in patients receiving linezolid or IV methylene blue, abrupt discontinuation of alcohol, benzodiazepines, barbiturates or antiepileptic drugs **WARNINGS** Hypertension, angle-closure glaucoma, activation of mania/hypomania, suicidal thinking and behavior, hypersensitivity reactions [e.g., anaphylactic shock, rash (including SJS), angioedema, dyspnea] **SIDE EFFECTS** Dry mouth, insomnia, nausea, constipation, sweating, agitation, anxiety, tachycardia, tremors, dizziness, headache, blurred vision **NOTES** Do not use with other forms of bupropion. Delays weight gain. MedGuide required. See Depression chapter for more information.
Varenicline ***(Chantix)*** Tablet	Start 1 week before quit date or start, then quit between days 8 and 35 Days 1-3: 0.5 mg daily Days 4-7: 0.5 mg BID Days 8 (quit date) and beyond: 1 mg BID CrCl < 30 mL/min: 0.5 mg daily titrated to 0.5 mg BID Use for 12 weeks, can use another 12 weeks to maintain success	**BOXED WARNINGS** Serious neuropsychiatric events, including suicidal thinking and behavior (stop if patient becomes agitated, hostile, depressed, or has other abnormal behavior) **WARNINGS** Seizures, ↑ effects of alcohol and risk of blackout, accidental injury (e.g., traffic accidents) – use caution operating machinery or driving, CVD risk, angioedema, rash (including SJS), somnambulism (sleepwalking) **SIDE EFFECTS** Nausea (~30% and dose dependent), insomnia, abnormal dreams, constipation, flatulence, vomiting, headache **NOTES** To ↓ nausea, use lower dosage and take with food and a full glass of water. To ↓ insomnia, take 2nd dose earlier than bedtime. MedGuide required. For patients unable to quit abruptly on day 8, the goal should be to decrease smoking by 50% in the first 4 weeks, an additional 50% in weeks 5-8, with complete cessation by week 12.

PATIENT COUNSELING

Nicotine Patch

- At the start of each day, place the patch on a clean, dry and relatively hairless area of the skin between the neck and the waist, such as the upper arm, shoulder or back; press onto skin for ~10 seconds.
- If you have vivid dreams or trouble sleeping, remove the 24-hour patch prior to bedtime and apply a new one in the morning, or use the 16-hour patch.
- Skin reactions can occur. They are usually mild and go away after a few days, but occasionally they may worsen over the course of therapy. Rotate patch sites and apply hydrocortisone cream if needed. Do not apply patch to the same area of skin where cream was applied as it will not stick well.
- Wash hands after applying and removing the patch. Discard patches by folding the sticky ends together, replace in pouch and put in the trash with a lid to keep away from children and pets.

Weeks 1-6	Weeks 7-8	Weeks 9-10
≥ 10 cigarettes/day: 21 mg patch	14 mg patch	7 mg patch
< 10 cigarettes/day: 14 mg patch	7 mg patch	No recommendation

Nicotine Gum, Inhaler and Lozenge

- Acidic beverages (e.g., coffee, juices, soft drinks) interfere with the buccal absorption of nicotine; you should wait 15 minutes after eating or drinking before use.

Nicotine Gum

- Gum should be chewed slowly, until there is a "tingle" or "flavored" taste in the mouth, then "parked" between the cheek and gum to help more of the drug get into your body. When the "tingle" or "flavored" taste goes away, begin chewing slowly again until it returns, then "park" the gum again.
- The gum should be chewed slowly several times, with breaks while "parked", for about 30 minutes total time or until the taste or tingle goes away completely.
- For best results, use at least 1 piece every 1 – 2 hours (minimum of 9 pieces per day) for the first 6 weeks.

Weeks 1-6	Weeks 7-9	Weeks 10-12
1 piece every 1 to 2 hours	1 piece every 2 to 4 hours	1 piece every 4 to 8 hours

Nicotine Lozenge

- Place the lozenge in your mouth and let it dissolve slowly rather than chewing or swallowing it. You may feel a warm or tingling sensation. Move the lozenge from one side of the mouth to the other until it has completely dissolved (this could take 20 – 30 minutes).
- Do not use more than one lozenge at a time, or one lozenge after another continuously, as you may experience side effects, including hiccups, heartburn and nausea.
- For best results, use at least 1 lozenge every 1 – 2 hours (minimum of 9 lozenges per day) for the first 6 weeks.

Weeks 1-6	Weeks 7-9	Weeks 10-12
1 lozenge every 1 to 2 hours	1 lozenge every 2 to 4 hours	1 lozenge every 4 to 8 hours

Nicotine Inhaler

- Puff on the inhaler in short, frequent, breaths (similar to a pipe or cigar) and inhale deeply into the back of the throat.
- Each cartridge provides about 20 minutes of continuous puffing and is only good for one day after opening.
- You may develop a cough and mild irritation in the mouth and throat when you first use the inhaler. These side effects usually improve after a short time.
- Clean mouthpiece with soap and water regularly.
- Keep the inhaler at room temperature. The amount of nicotine inhaled decreases in cold temperatures. In cold weather, keep the inhaler and cartridge in an inside pocket or other warm area.

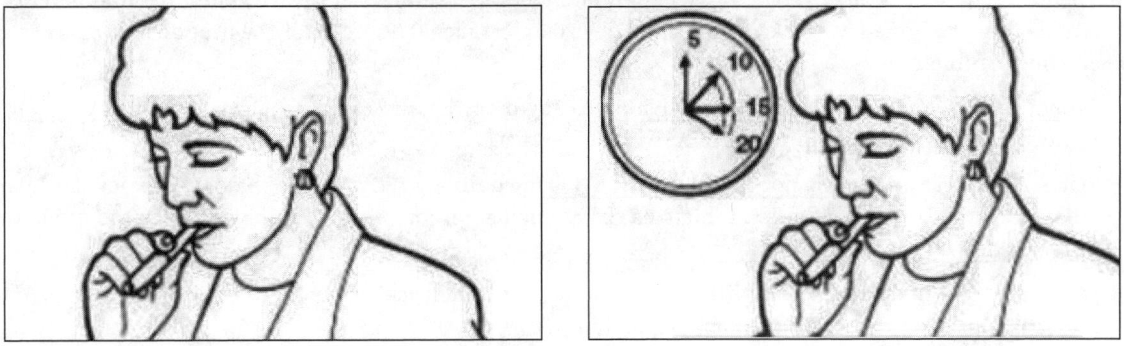

Nicotrol Inhaler (nicotine inhalation system) package insert. New York, NY: Pharmacia & Upjohn CO; 2008 Dec.

Nicotine Nasal Spray

- Blow your nose before use, if needed. Tilt head back slightly and insert the tip of the bottle into the nostril. Spray once in each nostril while breathing through the mouth. Do not sniff, swallow, or inhale through the nose.
- You may experience sneezing, coughing, watery eyes, runny nose and a hot peppery feeling in the back of the throat when you first use the nasal spray. Wait 5 minutes after use before driving or operating heavy machinery. These side effects should lessen in a few days.

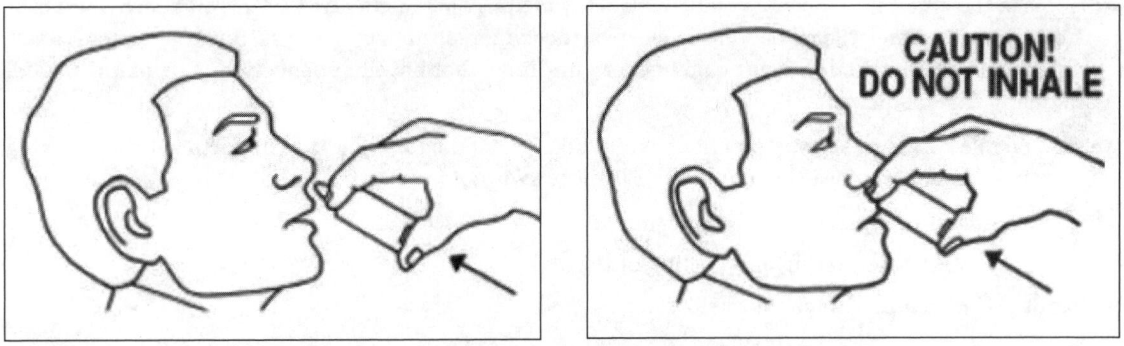

Nicotrol NS (nicotine nasal spray) package insert. New York, NY: Pharmacia & Upjohn CO; 2010 Jan.

Bupropion and Varenicline

- Start the medication 1 week before your quit date. This allows the medication to build up in the body to work. You can continue to use tobacco during this time. Try to stop using tobacco on your quit date.
- With varenicline, you may set a quit date between day 8 and 35, or gradually reduce the amount you smoke over 12 weeks until you have completely stopped.
- If behavior changes are noticed, such as agitation, hostility, depression or other abnormal thoughts or behaviors, stop the medication and call your healthcare provider right away.

Bupropion

- The most common side effects are dry mouth and trouble sleeping. These are generally mild and often disappear after a few weeks. The second dose can be taken 8 hours after the first dose to decrease sleeping problems.
- Do not take if you have a seizure disorder, an eating disorder, are taking other forms of bupropion, or have taken an MAO inhibitor within the last 14 days.
- To decrease seizure risk, do not take more than 300 mg daily, or 150 mg at each dose. Swallow tablets whole; do not chew, cut, or crush tablets as the medicine will be released into your body too quickly. Take the doses at least 8 hours apart.
- If you are able to quit smoking with this medicine, your healthcare provider may keep you on it for several months so you do not go back to smoking.

Varenicline

- The most common side effects are nausea and trouble sleeping. These are generally mild and often disappear after a few weeks. The second dose can be taken 8 hours after the first dose to decrease insomnia.
- Take the medication after eating and with a full glass (8 ounces) of water.
- Most people will take this medicine for up to 12 weeks. If you do not quit using tobacco by 12 weeks, reaffirm your motivation to quit smoking and consider another 12 weeks of therapy.
- Decrease the amount of alcohol you drink when you start this medication until you know whether it affects your tolerance. Some people have experienced increased drunkenness, unusual or sometimes aggressive behavior, and/or having no memory of things that have happened while drinking alcohol and using this medication.
- Some people can have serious reactions while taking this medication. It is important to stop taking Chantix and contact a healthcare provider if these symptoms occur:
    - Swelling of the face, mouth, tongue and neck.
    - Rash, redness, blistering and peeling of the skin.
- Do not use with other drugs that help you quit smoking.

38

CYSTIC FIBROSIS

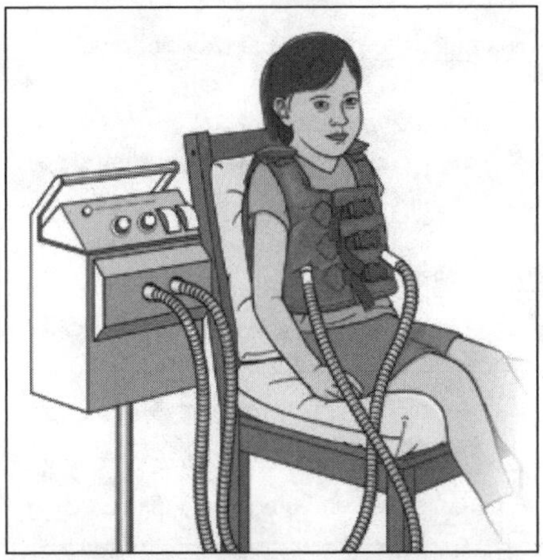

We gratefully acknowledge the assistance of Paul Beringer, PharmD, BCPS, FASHP, Associate Professor of Clinical Pharmacy and Clinical Medicine, University of Southern California, in preparing this chapter.

GUIDELINES/REFERENCES

Cystic Fibrosis Pulmonary Guidelines: Chronic Medications for Maintenance of Lung Health. *Am J Respir Crit Care Med.* 2013; 187:680–689.

Cystic Fibrosis Pulmonary Guidelines: Treatment of Pulmonary Exacerbations. *Am J Respir Crit Care Med.* 2009; 180:802–808.

BACKGROUND

Cystic fibrosis (CF) is a genetic disorder that leads to abnormal transport of chloride, bicarbonate, and sodium ions across the epithelium, leading to thick, viscous secretions. The thick mucus affects the lungs, pancreas, liver and intestine, primarily causing difficulty breathing and lung infections as well as digestive complications. The name cystic fibrosis refers to the characteristic scarring (fibrosis) and cyst formation that occurs within the pancreas. More than 75% of people with CF are diagnosed by 2 years of age.

CF is caused by a mutation in the gene for the protein cystic fibrosis transmembrane conductance regulator (CFTR). This protein is required to regulate the components of sweat, digestive juices, and mucus. CFTR regulates the movement of chloride, bicarbonate, and sodium ions across epithelial membranes, and mutations can lead to a chronic cycle of lung infection, inflammation, and obstruction which results in a progressive loss of pulmonary function and eventual respiratory failure. CFTR dysfunction also leads to pancreatic dysfunction that can lead to insulin deficiency and diabetes. Infertility, biliary cirrhosis and other defects can occur as well.

CLINICAL PRESENTATION

The classic symptoms of CF are salty tasting skin, poor growth and poor weight gain despite adequate food intake, thick and sticky mucus production, frequent lung infections, coughing and shortness of breath. Digital clubbing is often present. Digestive symptoms include steatorrhea (fatty stools) and malnutrition due to poor absorption of nutrients, including fat-soluble vitamins, and a failure to thrive if not treated.

DRUG TREATMENT

Early diagnosis of CF and a comprehensive treatment plan can improve survival and quality of life. Specialty clinics for cystic fibrosis are helpful and are found in many communities. The prevention and treatment of lung infections are essential; antibiotics (inhaled if possible) are a mainstay of therapy. Patients experience obstruction of pancreatic ducts and cannot digest essential nutrients. Advances in research have led to the development of two new targeted gene therapy medications, ivacaftor and ivacaftor/lumacaftor.

Treatment for Lung Complications

Multiple medications are used to help manage the thick mucus and reduce the risk of infection in the lungs (see table at right). When patients are taking several medications, the order is critical to maximize absorption and effect. The recommended order is as follows: bronchodilator, hypertonic saline, dornase alfa, chest physiotherapy, then inhaled antibiotics.

INTERVENTION	PURPOSE
Inhaled bronchodilators	Open the airways
Hypertonic saline (e.g., *HyperSal*)	Mobilize mucus to improve airway clearance
Dornase alfa *(Pulmozyme)*	Thins mucus to promote airway clearance
Chest physiotherapy	Mobilize mucus to improve airway clearance
Inhaled antibiotics	Control airway infection
Oral azithromycin	Reduce airway inflammation and disrupt *Pseudomonas aeruginosa* biofilm formation
Transplantation	For patients with end-stage lung disease

Infection Management

Intermittent Infection

Impaired mucus clearance predisposes patients with CF to bacterial colonization and lung infections. The most common organisms early in the disease are *Staphylococcus aureus* and *Haemophilus influenzae* followed by *Pseudomonas aeruginosa* in adolescents and adults. Acute pulmonary exacerbations characterized by an increase in cough, sputum production with a change in sputum color (greenish), shortness of breath, a rapid decline in FEV1, loss of appetite and weight are a frequent complication of CF. Treatment often includes an extended course of antibiotics (2 – 4 weeks), modalities to increase airway clearance and nutritional therapies.

If the patient has a *Pseudomonas aeruginosa* infection, two IV drugs are recommended to provide potential synergy and prevent resistance. These include aminoglycosides, beta-lactams, quinolones, and others that cover *Pseudomonas aeruginosa*. See Infectious Diseases I chapter for a complete discussion on treatment options of *Pseudomonas aeruginosa*. Doses tend to be larger than normal due to the need to obtain a therapeutic concentration in lung tissue and the reduced susceptibility of the bacteria chronically colonizing the airways of these patients.

Chronic Infection

Lung infections occur intermittently at first, but eventually become chronic. In particular, chronic lung infections with *Pseudomonas aeruginosa* are associated with more rapid decline in pulmonary function. Inhaled antibiotics are recommended for patients with chronic *Pseudomonas aeruginosa* lung infections to reduce the bacterial burden. Treatment is cycled with 28 days on therapy, followed by 28 days off, and is associated with an improvement in lung function and a reduction in the frequency of acute pulmonary exacerbations. The frequency of exacerbations is strongly associated with lung function decline and shortened survival in CF. If a patient is using a bronchodilator and/or mucolytic, these should be given prior to the antibiotic inhalation. See agents in the following chart.

Treatment for Lung Complications

DRUG	DOSING	SAFETY/SIDE EFFECTS/MONITORING
Agents to Promote Mucus Clearance		
Bronchodilator (e.g, **albuterol**)	2-4 times daily	Refer to Asthma chapter
Hypertonic saline *(HyperSal, PulmoSal)* 4 mL unit dose vials	4 mL via a nebulizer 2-4 times daily	Hypertonic saline is a high-alert drug, especially with IV administration. For CF therapy, hypertonic saline is supplied as small ampules that are delivered via a nebulizer. *PulmoSal* is buffered to match physiologic pH of the airway surface liquid.
Dornase alfa *(Pulmozyme)* 2.5 mg single use ampule	2.5 mg daily with recommended nebulizer and compressor system Do not mix with any other drug in the nebulizer	**CONTRAINDICATIONS** Hypersensitivity to Chinese Hamster Ovary (CHO) products **SIDE EFFECTS** Chest pain, fever, rash, rhinitis, laryngitis, voice alteration, throat irritation **NOTES** Store the ampules in the refrigerator (do not expose to room temperature ≥ 24 hours). Protect from light.
Antibiotics, Inhaled		
Tobramycin Inhalation Solution *(TOBI, Bethkis, Kitabis Pak)* *TOBI, Kitabis:* 300 mg/5 mL single use ampule *Bethkis:* 300 mg/4 mL single use ampule	300 mg via nebulizer Q12H x 28 days, followed by 28 days off cycle Indicated in patients ≥ 6 years who are colonized with *Pseudomonas aeruginosa* to reduce infection/hospitalization Do not mix with any other drug in the nebulizer	**SIDE EFFECTS** Ototoxicity, tinnitus, voice alteration, dizziness, bronchospasm, mouth and throat pain **NOTES** Little systemic absorption *TOBI:* Use with *PARI LC Plus* reusable nebulizer and *DeVilbiss Pulmo-Aide* air compressor *Bethkis:* Use with *PARI LC Plus* nebulizer and *Vios* air compressor Doses should be taken at least 6 hours apart Refrigeration recommended; can be kept at room temperature up to 28 days In foil pouch to protect from light Not studied in patients colonized with *Burkholderia cepacia,* if FEV1 < 40% or > 80% predicted *(Bethkis, TOBI)* or < 25% or > 80% predicted *(Kitabis Pak)*
Tobramycin Inhalation Powder *(TOBI Podhaler)* 28 mg capsules in blister card	112 mg (4 x 28 mg caps) Q12H x 28 days, followed by 28 days off cycle Indicated in patients ≥ 6 years who are colonized with *Pseudomonas aeruginosa* to reduce infection/hospitalization	**SIDE EFFECTS** Similar to above **NOTES** Little systemic absorption Use with *Podhaler* (device that comes with the capsules) Do not swallow capsules Doses should be taken at least 6 hours apart Store capsules at room temperature in a dry place Not for use if FEV1 < 25% or > 80% predicted, or if colonized with *Burkholderia cepacia*

Treatment for Lung Complications Continued

DRUG	DOSING	SAFETY/SIDE EFFECTS/MONITORING
Aztreonam *(Cayston* - inhalation solution, ***Azactam*** - IV)	75 mg via nebulizer TID x 28 days, followed by 28 days off cycle Indicated in patients ≥ 7 years who are colonized with *Pseudomonas aeruginosa* to reduce infection/hospitalization Do not mix with any other drug in the nebulizer	**SIDE EFFECTS** Allergic reactions (may be severe), bronchospasm, fever, wheezing, cough, chest discomfort **NOTES** Doses should be taken at least 4 hours apart Use with *Altera* nebulizer system Reconstitute with 1 mL of sterile diluent (provided); give immediately Refrigeration recommended (can be kept at room temperature up to 28 days) Protect from light

Antibiotic, Oral

Azithromycin ***(Zithromax)*** Off-label	< 40 kg: 250 mg 3 times/ week > 40 kg: 500 mg 3 times/ week Used to decrease inflammation and reduce exacerbations	**SIDE EFFECTS** In CF patients: tinnitus, nausea, risk of QT prolongation **NOTES** Do not use as monotherapy in individuals with nontuberculous mycobacteria lung infections

Treatment of Malabsorption

Malabsorption, increased energy needs, and reduced appetite are common in CF patients. Correction of maldigestion and malabsorption are essential to meet the increased energy requirements for normal growth, optimal pulmonary function and to prolong life.

- A high-fat and calorically-dense diet: to help with nutrition and normal weight and growth, increased energy needs and to prolong survival
- Pancreatic enzyme replacement: to improve digestion, optimize growth and nutritional status
- Proton pump inhibitors: required with *Viokace* and used with other pancreatic enzymes to reduce symptoms and for the treatment of GERD
- Vitamin supplements: especially the fat-soluble vitamins A, D, E, and K for normal cellular function
- Insulin: for treatment of CF-related diabetes mellitus

Pancreatic Enzyme Products

The thick mucus obstructs pancreatic enzyme flow, resulting in a lack of these enzymes reaching the gastrointestinal tract. Frequent, greasy, oily, foul-smelling stools are manifestations of pancreatic insufficiency. Most CF patients need to supplement their diet with appropriate amounts of pancreatic enzyme products (PEPs).

Pancrelipase is a natural product harvested from porcine pancreatic glands which contains a combination of lipase, amylase, and protease. PEPs are formulated to dissolve in the more basic pH of the duodenum so they can act locally to break down fat, starches and protein. The dose is individualized for each patient and is based on the lipase component. Once PEP therapy is started, the dose is adjusted every 3 – 4 days until stools are normalized. Do not use doses > 6,000 units/kg/meal of lipase due to risk of colonic stricture.

Enzymes are given prior to meals and snacks: full doses are given before meals and 50% of the mealtime dose is given with snacks. Meals with high fat content require higher doses. Retention in the mouth before swallowing may cause mucosal irritation and stomatitis. If infants spit them out, immediately follow with liquid until swallowed.

DRUG	DOSING	SAFETY/SIDE EFFECTS/MONITORING
Pancrelipase *(Creon, Lip-Prot-Amyl, Pancreaze, Pertzye, Ultresa, Viokace, Zenpep)*	**Initial** Age < 1 year: varies by product Age 1- 3 years: Lipase 1,000 units/kg/meal Age ≥ 4 years: Lipase 500 units/kg/meal **Max (all ages)** Lipase ≤ 2,500 units/kg/meal or ≤ 10,000 units/kg/day. Doses > 6,000 units/kg/meal are associated with colonic stricture. Take before or with food, avoid foods with high pH such as dairy. Use ½ meal-time dose with snacks. Keep in original container; protect from moisture.	**WARNINGS** Fibrosing colonopathy advancing to colonic strictures (rare: higher risk with doses > 10,000 lipase units/kg/day), mucosal irritation, hyperuricemia **SIDE EFFECTS** Abdominal pain, flatulence, nausea, HA, neck pain **MONITORING** Abdominal symptoms, nutritional intake, weight, height (children), stool, fecal fat **NOTES** *Viokace* is the only formulation not enteric coated and needs to be given with a PPI. All formulations are porcine derived and are not interchangeable. Do not crush or chew contents of capsules. Delayed-release capsules with enteric coated microspheres or microtablets may be opened and sprinkled on soft, acidic foods (pH ≤ 4.5). Pancreatic enzymes do not require refrigeration. MedGuide required.

Cystic Fibrosis Transmembrane Conductance Regulator Potentiator

Two therapies are available that work at the cellular level where the chloride transport defect occurs. Ivacaftor *(Kalydeco)* works by increasing the time CFTR channels remain open, augmenting chloride transport activity. It is currently indicated in patients ≥ 2 years of age who have one of the following mutations in the CFTR gene: G551D, G1244E, G1349D, G178R, G551S, S1251N, S1255P, S549N, S549R or R117H (which represents 5% of the CF population worldwide). Lumacaftor/ivacaftor (*Orkambi*) is a combination of a CFTR corrector and potentiator therapies. Lumacaftor works by correcting the CFTR folding defect, resulting in an increase in the presence of the protein at the cell surface. Ivacaftor/lumacaftor is approved in patients 6 years and older who are homozygous (two copies of the same allele) for the CFTR F508del mutation (the most common mutation) in the CFTR gene.

DRUG	DOSING/INDICATIONS	SAFETY/SIDE EFFECTS/MONITORING
Ivacaftor *(Kalydeco)* Tablet, oral packet	150 mg PO Q12H with high fat containing food With CYP 3A4 moderate inhibitors or moderate-severe hepatic impairment: 150 mg daily With CYP 3A4 strong inhibitors: 150 mg twice weekly	**WARNINGS** ↑ LFTs, cataracts in children *Orkambi* only: respiratory events (dyspnea, chest discomfort, abnormal respiration upon initiation), hypertension **SIDE EFFECTS** Headache, dizziness, URTIs, nasopharyngitis, oropharyngeal pain, abdominal pain, nausea, diarrhea, rash, ↑ CPK, flatulence (*Orkambi* only) **MONITORING** LFTs (baseline, every 3 months for 1 year, then annually), eye exam (peds), pulmonary tests
Lumacaftor/ivacaftor *(Orkambi)* Tablet	≥ 12 yrs: 2 tablets (each containing 200/125 mg) PO Q12H with high fat containing food 6-11 yrs: 2 tablets (each containing 100/125 mg) PO Q12H with high fat containing food Moderate hepatic impairment: 2 tablets QAM, 1 tablet QPM Severe hepatic impairment: 1 tablet Q12H With CYP 3A4 strong inhibitors: 1 tablet daily x 1 week, titrate to 2 tablets Q12H	

Cystic Fibrosis Transmembrane Conductance Regulator Drug Interactions

Ivacaftor is a substrate of 3A4 (major) and lumacaftor is an inducer of 3A4 (strong); see dosing recommendations above. Inducers of 3A4 will decrease the level of both these medications and should be avoided.

Patient Counseling

TOBI Podhaler

- Do not swallow the capsules.
- Use the *Podhaler device* to inhale the powder in the capsules. This medication is not used with a nebulizer.
- Use a new *Podhaler* device every 7 days.
- One dose consists of 4 capsules, 1 at a time. Take doses as close to 12 hours but no less than 6 hours apart. Remove 1 capsule at a time from the packaging immediately before administration. Inhale one capsule through the *Podhaler* device before removing the next capsule from the packaging.
- Make sure to finish the whole dose of *TOBI*. Do not leave any medication in the capsules.

- The medication comes in 4 weekly packs containing 7 blister cards of 8 capsules each (4 for each morning and evening). Store capsules at room temperature in a dry place.

TOBI Inhalation for Nebulization

- Open the ampule by twisting off the top. Squeeze all the contents of the ampule into the nebulizer cup.
- Sit or stand in an upright position and breathe through your mouth (may need to use nose clips if easier) and continue until all the medicine is gone and there is no longer any mist being produced.
- Clean the nebulizer as instructed after each use. Wash all parts (except tubing) with warm water and soap, rinse thoroughly and allow to air dry or dry with a lint-free cloth. The nebulizer parts (except tubing) can be washed on the top rack in a dishwasher (in a dishwasher basket).
- Every other treatment day, disinfect the nebulizer parts (except tubing) by boiling them in water for a full 10 minutes.
- Do not share nebulizers.

Pancreatic Enzyme Counseling (Children)

- The most common side effects include stomach pain, bloating, gas, nausea, headache, and neck pain.
- Read the MedGuide that was given to you, this discusses a rare bowel disorder that can happen with some people.
- This medication is taken at the beginning of a meal or snack. At snacks give half of the meal-time dose.
- Have your child swallow whole. Do not let your child chew or crush or hold the medicine in the mouth or the medicine will cause the mouth to become sore.
- If it is difficult to swallow the capsules, the contents can be sprinkled on a spoonful of soft food such as applesauce, pureed bananas, or pears. Once the contents are sprinkled on the food, it needs to be used right away. Do not let your child chew it, just swallow.
- Do not mix with dairy products such as milk or yogurt.
- Have your child drink lots of non-caffeinated liquids every day.
- It is important to follow the diet plan you received for your child to get adequate nutrition and to keep as healthy as possible.
- If you forget to give the medicine with the meal, wait until the next scheduled dose. Do not make up for missed doses.

PRACTICE CASE

PATIENT PROFILE

Patient Name	**Gina Alossi**
Address	**390 Frost Ave**
Age	**13** **Sex** **F** **Race** **Height** **4'8"** **Weight** **76 lbs**
Allergies	

DIAGNOSES

Cystic Fibrosis

MEDICATIONS

Date	No.	Prescriber	Drug & Strength	Quantity	Sig	Refills
3/21		Sanchez	ZenPep	20,000 units	TID	5
3/21		Sanchez	Albuterol 0.5% nebulization solution	2.5 mg/0.5 mL	BID	5
3/21		Sanchez	Multivitamin		QD	

LAB/DIAGNOSTIC TESTS

Test	Normal Value	Results Date 2/9	Date 3/21	Date 4/8
Alk Phos	33-115 u/L	48		
AST	10-35 IU/L	22		
ALT	10-40 IU/L	27		
GLU	65-99 mg/dL	89		
NA	135-146 mEq/L	141		
K	3.5-5.3 mEq/L	4.7		
CL	98-110 mEq/L	104		
HCO3-	22-28 mEq/L	24		
BUN	7-25 mg/dL	19		
Creatinine	0.6-1.2 mg/dL	0.6		
Calcium	8.6-10.2 mg/dL			
WBC	4-11 cells/mm^3	5.5		
CFTR gene testing			F508del/F508del	
Sputum culture (x 2)				*Pseudomonas aeruginosa*

Questions

1. Based on the laboratory testing on 3/21, which of the following medications would be appropriate to add to Gina's regimen?
   a. *TOBI Podhaler*
   b. *HyperSal*
   c. *Pulmozyme*
   d. *Kalydeco*
   e. *Orkambi*

2. Based on the above culture, which of the following represents the best pharmacologic intervention at the present time?
   a. Cephalexin
   b. *Biaxin*
   c. *Kalydeco*
   d. *Cayston*
   e. *Amoxil*

3. Which of the following is a correct patient counseling recommendation for pancreatic enzyme replacement therapy?
   a. If the patient has difficulty swallowing the capsules, the microspheres can be crushed and sprinkled over food.
   b. The enzymes should be taken with meals.
   c. The enzyme products are equivalent and can be interchanged, depending on formulary requirements.
   d. *Viokace* should be administered with an acidic liquid such as orange juice.
   e. Pancreatic enzymes should not be taken if the meal contains little or no fat content.

Questions 4-7 do not apply to the above case.

4. Which of the following are potential adverse effects associated with *TOBI* therapy? (Select **ALL** that apply.)
   a. Voice alteration
   b. Bronchospasm
   c. Ototoxicity
   d. Tinnitus
   e. Pulmonary infiltrates

5. Which of the following is an appropriate counseling recommendation for *TOBI Podhaler* therapy?
   a. Store capsules in the freezer at all times.
   b. Capsules should be taken orally on an empty stomach.
   c. Take twice daily; doses may be taken 4 hours apart.
   d. Remove only 1 capsule at a time immediately before administration.
   e. Instruct the patient to thoroughly chew (or crush) the tablets.

6. Which of the following therapies are used in promoting mucus clearance in patients with cystic fibrosis?
   a. Pseudoephedrine
   b. Hypertonic saline
   c. Tiotropium
   d. Inhaled aztreonam
   e. Inhaled tobramycin

7. Which of the following are correct statements regarding ivacaftor? (Select **ALL** that apply).
   a. Ivacaftor is used to treat pulmonary infections caused by *Pseudomonas aeruginosa*.
   b. Ivacaftor should be administered with a high fat containing meal.
   c. Dosage adjustment is necessary when co-administered with CYP3A4 inhibitors.
   d. Ivacaftor is nephrotoxic and is contraindicated in severe renal insufficiency.
   e. The normal dose is 150 mg by mouth every 12 hours.

Answers

1-e, 2-d, 3-b, 4-a,b,c,d, 5-d, 6-b, 7-b,c,e

39

DIABETES

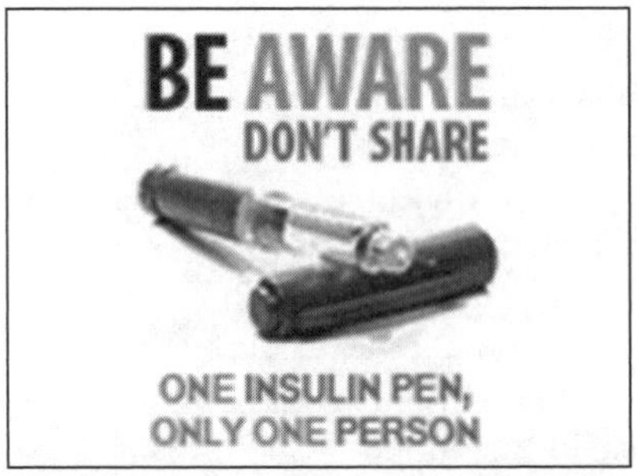
BE AWARE
DON'T SHARE
ONE INSULIN PEN,
ONLY ONE PERSON

We gratefully acknowledge the assistance of Bethany L. Murphy, PharmD, BCACP, BC-ADM, Assistant Professor of Pharmacy Practice, Union University School of Pharmacy, in preparing this chapter.

GUIDELINES/REFERENCES

American Diabetes Association (ADA) Position Statement. Standards of Medical Care in Diabetes – 2016. *Diabetes Care.* 2016;39 (suppl 1):S1-S112.

American Association of Clinical Endocrinologists (AACE)/American College of Endocrinology. Clinical practice guidelines for developing a diabetes mellitus comprehensive care plan. *Endocr Pract.* 2015;21 (suppl 1):1-87.

Additional guidelines included with the online course.

BACKGROUND

Diabetes is a common condition in the United States, affecting ~29 million Americans, or 9.3% of the population. Of these, 21 million are diagnosed, and 8 million remain undiagnosed.

Diabetes is characterized by hyperglycemia due to decreased insulin secretion (from the pancreas), decreased insulin sensitivity (primarily in muscle cells), or both. Chronic hyperglycemia leads to many complications, including organ and nerve damage.

Most patients have type 2 diabetes; of the 29 million cases, 1.25 million are children and adults with type 1 diabetes. In some patients, it is difficult to distinguish between type 1 and type 2, especially early in the disease.

CLASSIFICATION/TYPES OF DIABETES

Type 1 Diabetes

Type 1 diabetes is caused by autoimmune destruction of the beta cells in the pancreas. These are the cells that produce insulin; once the beta cells are destroyed, there is no more insulin production. The C-peptide test is used to determine if the patient is still producing insulin. Without insulin, glucose cannot enter muscle cells and fat is used as an alternative energy source. Fat breakdown produces ketones, and the ketones can cause diabetic ketoacidosis (DKA), which is life-threatening. Type 1 diabetes usually presents in younger, thinner patients, but it can also appear in older patients; family history is the biggest risk factor. Patients with type 1 diabetes must be treated with insulin.

Type 2 Diabetes

Type 2 diabetes accounts for ~95% of cases and is due to both insulin resistance (decreased insulin sensitivity) and insulin deficiency. The pancreatic beta cells produce less insulin over time as they become damaged. This is why the onset of type 2 diabetes is often not noticed; the patient is producing some insulin, which helps some glucose enter into the cells. Type 2 diabetes is strongly associated with obesity, physical inactivity, family history and the presence of other comorbid conditions (see Risk Factors box). Type 2 diabetes can be managed with lifestyle modifications alone (in a small minority of patients), or lifestyle modifications in combination with medication(s).

Prediabetes

Prediabetes indicates that there is an increased risk of developing diabetes. Meeting dietary and exercise recommendations reduces the risk of progression from prediabetes to diabetes. Metformin can be used to help improve blood glucose levels, especially in those with a BMI > 35 kg/m^2, age < 60 years and women with a history of gestational diabetes mellitus (GDM). Annual monitoring for development of diabetes and treatment of modifiable CVD risk factors is recommended.

Diabetes in Pregnancy

Diabetes in pregnancy consists of two different types: women who develop diabetes during pregnancy (gestational diabetes mellitus or GDM), or women who had diabetes prior to becoming pregnant (pregestational diabetes). In both groups, the blood glucose targets are more stringent than the targets for the non-pregnant population with diabetes (see Goals box); they are closer to normal levels to help keep the mother and the baby healthy. If the blood glucose is high, the baby can be large (macrosomia), will be at risk for hypoglycemia at birth, and will become a child with high risk for obesity and type 2 diabetes. The first step in diabetes management during pregnancy should be lifestyle modifications (diet and exercise). Frequent self-monitoring of blood glucose (SMBG) is used to assess if the lifestyle modifications are adequate; if not, insulin or metformin are preferred for add-on treatment. Glyburide may be used but it is associated with higher rates of neonatal hypoglycemia and macrosomia. Long-term safety data for both metformin and glyburide is not available.

RISK FACTORS FOR TYPE 2 DIABETES

- First-degree relative with diabetes
- High-risk race/ethnicity (African American, Latino, Native American, Asian American, Pacific Islander)
- Overweight (BMI ≥ 25 kg/m^2 or ≥ 23 kg/m^2 in Asian Americans)
- Physical inactivity
- Hypertension (≥ 140/90 mmHg or taking medications for hypertension)
- HDL < 35 mg/dL and/or TG > 250 mg/dL
- History of CVD
- A1C ≥ 5.7%, impaired glucose tolerance or impaired fasting glucose on previous testing
- Women who delivered a baby weighing > 9 lbs or who had gestational diabetes mellitus
- Women with polycystic ovary syndrome
- Other clinical conditions associated with insulin resistance (e.g., severe obesity, acanthosis nigricans)

GOALS FOR DIABETES IN PREGNANCY

Gestational Diabetes

Fasting: ≤ 95 mg/dL

1 hour post-meal: ≤ 140 mg/dL

2 hours post-meal: ≤ 120 mg/dL

Pregestational Diabetes

A1C: < 6-6.5%

Fasting: ≤ 95 mg/dL

1 hour post-meal: ≤ 130-140 mg/dL

2 hours post-meal: ≤ 120 mg/dL

DIAGNOSIS/SCREENING

Clinical Signs and Symptoms

Classic symptoms of diabetes that occur due to hyperglycemia include polyuria (excessive urination), polyphagia (excessive hunger or increased appetite), polydipsia (excessive thirst), blurred vision and fatigue. In type 1 diabetes, especially in children, DKA is commonly the initial presentation and is caused by a total deficiency in insulin. DKA seldom occurs in type 2 diabetes unless it is associated with the stress of another illness, such as an infection.

Type 2 diabetes frequently goes undiagnosed for years because hyperglycemia develops gradually and the early symptoms may not be severe enough for the patient to notice; however, the hyperglycemia puts the person at increased risk for developing complications. Screening can help identify these patients.

Screening

Testing for type 2 diabetes and prediabetes should be done in all adults who are overweight or obese (BMI $\geq 25\ kg/m^2$ or $\geq 23\ kg/m^2$ in Asian Americans, as this group has a higher risk of diabetes at a lower BMI) and who have one or more additional risk factors for diabetes (see Risk Factors box on previous page). In patients without risk factors, testing should start at 45 years of age. The criteria for diagnosis varies based on the type of test used (see Diagnostic Criteria box); no single test is preferred over another.

> **DIAGNOSTIC CRITERIA**
>
> **Diagnosis of Prediabetes**
> - Fasting plasma glucose (FPG) 100-125 mg/dL
>   or
> - 2-hr plasma glucose after a 75-g oral glucose tolerance test (OGTT) 140-199 mg/dL
>   or
> - A1C 5.7-6.4%
>
> **Diagnosis of Diabetes**
> - Classic symptoms of hyperglycemia (e.g., polyuria, polydipsia, unexplained weight loss) or hyperglycemic crisis AND a random plasma glucose ≥ 200 mg/dL
>   or
> - FPG ≥ 126 mg/dL – fasting is defined as no caloric intake for at least 8 hours*
>   or
> - 2-hr plasma glucose after a 75-g OGTT ≥ 200 mg/dL*
>   or
> - A1C ≥ 6.5%*
>
> * *In the absence of unequivocal hyperglycemia, results should be confirmed by repeat testing*

NON-DRUG (LIFESTYLE) TREATMENT

Lifestyle modifications should be used alone or in combination with medications when necessary to meet treatment goals. All patients who smoke should quit (see Tobacco Cessation chapter). Psychosocial assessment and emotional well-being are important components of diabetes care and self-management.

Nutrition

Patients with diabetes should receive individualized medical nutrition therapy (MNT). There is no one-size-fits-all recommendation. Various diets have been shown to provide benefit, including Mediterranean-style diets, the Dietary Approaches to Stop Hypertension (DASH) plan, plant-based diets (vegan or vegetarian), and lower-fat or lower-carbohydrate diets. Carbohydrates from vegetables, fruits, whole grains, legumes and dairy products should be selected over other carbohydrate sources, especially those that contain added fat, sugar or sodium. Increased intake of long-chain omega-3 fatty acids (EPA and DHA) from foods such as fatty fish (2 or more servings per week), and omega-3 linolenic acid (ALA) from foods such as flaxseed and soy, is recommended. The recommendations for saturated fat, cholesterol and *trans* fat intake are the same as that for the general population. Sugar-sweetened beverages should be avoided.

Overweight or obese patients should be encouraged to lose weight by reducing energy intake (decreasing calories), while choosing healthy foods; weight loss improves blood glucose, blood pressure and cholesterol levels. Reducing weekly calorie intake by 3,500 kcal will result in a 1 pound weight loss. The waist circumference should be < 35 inches for females and < 40 inches for males. The recommendation for maximum sodium intake is the same as the general population (< 2,300 mg per day). Reducing sodium intake is important for blood pressure control.

Patients with type 1 diabetes should use the carbohydrate-counting meal planning approach. If the insulin dose is fixed (not adjusted based on the grams of carbohydrates in the meal), then the carbohydrate intake will need to be constant. A carbohydrate serving is measured as 15 grams which is approximately one small piece of fruit, 1 slice of bread, ⅓ cup of cooked rice/pasta, or ½ cup of oatmeal. Many patients with type 1 diabetes match the prandial (mealtime) insulin dose to the carbohydrate intake.

Physical Activity

Adults should perform at least 150 minutes of moderate-intensity aerobic activity per week, spread over at least 3 days, with no more than 2 consecutive days off. Changing sedentary habits reduces hyperglycemia and is important for those who watch long hours of television, or who have jobs where they sit all day. Patients should be instructed to "get up and move" every 90 minutes, at a minimum. Resistance training, such as weight lifting, is recommended at least twice weekly.

COMPREHENSIVE CARE

In addition to glycemic control, many of the treatments in patients with diabetes are aimed at preventing long-term macrovascular and microvascular complications. The development of macrovascular complications is dependent on atherosclerotic cardiovascular disease (ASCVD) risks; these include diabetes, dyslipidemia, hypertension, smoking, a family history of premature ASCVD, and overweight/obesity. ASCVD is defined as a history of acute coronary syndrome (MI, unstable angina), stable angina, coronary or other arterial revascularization, stroke/transient ischemic attack (TIA) or peripheral arterial disease (PAD). ASCVD is the leading cause of morbidity and mortality in patients with diabetes.

LONG-TERM COMPLICATIONS OF DIABETES
Microvascular Disease
Retinopathy (most common)
Diabetic kidney disease (may progress to ESRD)
Peripheral neuropathy (↑ risk for foot infections and amputations)
Autonomic neuropathy (erectile dysfunction, gastroparesis, loss of bladder control/ UTIs)
Macrovascular Disease
Coronary artery disease (e.g., MI, stable angina)
Cerebrovascular disease (e.g., TIA/stroke)
Peripheral artery disease

Antiplatelet Therapy

Aspirin (75 – 162 mg/day) should be considered for primary prevention in patients with type 1 and type 2 diabetes who have increased ASCVD risk (10-year risk > 10%) and are not at increased risk of bleeding. This includes most men and women ≥ 50 years of age who have diabetes and at least one additional ASCVD risk factor. Aspirin (75 – 162 mg/day) should be used for secondary prevention unless the patient has an allergy or contraindication to use. If the patient has an aspirin allergy, clopidogrel 75 mg/day is recommended.

Cholesterol Control

Obtain a lipid profile at diagnosis, at initial medical evaluation, and/or at age 40, then periodically thereafter (every five years, or more frequently if indicated). Lifestyle modification should focus on increasing physical activity and reducing saturated fat, *trans* fat and cholesterol intake while increasing consumption of omega-3 fatty acids, viscous fiber, and plant stanols/sterols. Patients with a fasting TG level ≥ 500 mg/dL should be evaluated for secondary causes and medical therapy should be considered to reduce the risk of pancreatitis and MI. Statin therapy is indicated and intensity of dosing is based on age and ASCVD risk (see below); these recommendations from the ADA closely align with the 2013 ACC/AHA Guideline on the Treatment of Blood Cholesterol. In addition, the most recent ADA guidelines give consideration to the addition of ezetimibe to moderate-intensity statin therapy in patients with a recent acute coronary syndrome and LDL level > 50 mg/dL, or in patients who cannot tolerate high-intensity statin therapy.

AGE	RISK FACTORS*	RECOMMENDED STATIN INTENSITY DOSE**	MONITORING LIPID PANEL
< 40 years	None	None	Annually or as needed to monitor adherence
	ASCVD risk factors	Moderate or high	
	ASCVD	High	
40-75 years	None	Moderate	As needed to monitor adherence
	ASCVD risk factors	High	
	ASCVD	High	
> 75 years	None	Moderate	As needed to monitor adherence
	ASCVD risk factors	Moderate or high	
	ASCVD	High	

** ASCVD risk factors include, in addition to diabetes, LDL-C ≥ 100 mg/dL, high blood pressure, smoking, overweight/ obesity and family history of premature ASCVD; ASCVD indicates a history of acute coronary syndromes, stable angina (e.g., IHD), coronary or other arterial revascularization, stroke/TIA or PAD*

***In addition to lifestyle modification*

Blood Pressure Control

Blood pressure (BP) should be measured at every routine visit. Goal BP for patients with diabetes is < 140/90 mmHg. A lower target, < 130/80 mmHg, may be appropriate for certain individuals if it can be reached without undue treatment burden; this includes younger patients, patients with albuminuria, and those with hypertension plus one additional ASCVD risk factor. An ACE inhibitor or ARB is first-line due to the reduction of CVD outcomes and delayed progression of diabetic kidney disease in patients with albuminuria (see below). Most patients with diabetes will require two or more medications to achieve BP targets. Choice of additional agents (e.g., thiazide diuretics and dihydropyridine CCBs) will depend on the patient's comorbidities (see Hypertension chapter for JNC 8 recommendations). The JNC 8 and ADA guidelines recommend that one or more antihypertensive medications be taken at bedtime.

CLINICAL SCENARIOS (JNC 8)

Patient with diabetes and hypertension, but no albuminuria

- Thiazide, CCB, ACE inhibitor or ARB*

Patient with diabetes and albuminuria, but no hypertension

- ACE inhibitor or ARB

Patient with diabetes, hypertension and albuminuria

- ACE inhibitor or ARB (add thiazide or CCB as needed for BP control)

** ADA guidelines specify preference for ACE inhibitor or ARB*

Diabetic Kidney Disease

Diabetic kidney disease is the leading cause of end-stage renal disease (ESRD). An annual urine test is used to measure urine albumin excretion as an indicator of disease progression. Regardless of the presence of hypertension, either an ACE inhibitor or ARB (but not both in combination) should be started in nonpregnant patients with a urinary albumin excretion ≥ 30 mg/24 hours [or urine albumin-to-creatinine ratio (UACR) ≥ 30 mg/g]. A level < 30 mg/24 hours is considered normal. Optimizing blood glucose and BP helps to slow the progression of diabetic kidney disease and delay or prevent renal failure.

Retinopathy Screening and Treatment

Diabetic retinopathy is the leading cause of blindness in adults. An annual dilated, comprehensive eye exam, performed by an ophthalmologist or optometrist, is recommended. If the patient has one or more normal eye exams and their blood glucose is well controlled, screening can be done every 2 years. More frequent exams may be required if retinopathy is progressing. Cessation of smoking and optimizing blood glucose, BP and cholesterol helps to reduce the risk or slow the progression of retinopathy.

Neuropathy Screening and Treatment

All patients should be assessed at least annually for diabetic peripheral neuropathy using the 10-g monofilament and at least one additional test (pinprick, temperature, or vibration sensation). Signs and symptoms of autonomic neuropathy (e.g., gastroparesis, neurogenic bladder, erectile dysfunction) should be assessed in those who have peripheral neuropathic complications. Optimizing blood glucose helps avoid and delay the progression of neuropathy. FDA approved options for the treatment of peripheral neuropathic pain include pregabalin, duloxetine and tapentadol. The ADA guidelines also suggest that tricyclic antidepressants (TCAs), gabapentin, venlafaxine, carbamazepine, tramadol and topical capsaicin may be considered.

Foot Care

Patients with diabetes are at increased risk for foot ulcers and amputations due to the loss of protective sensation (LOPS) that occurs, most commonly, with peripheral neuropathy and PAD. All adults with diabetes should have a comprehensive foot exam, at least once per year with visual examination of the skin for dryness/cracking, signs of infection, ulcers, bunions, calluses and other deformities, such as claw toes. Screening for peripheral neuropathy (as previously described) and PAD [e.g., assessment of claudication, pedal pulses and an ankle-brachial index (ABI)] is recommended.

Patients with insensate (without feeling) feet, foot deformities and ulcers should have their feet inspected at every healthcare visit. Patients who smoke, have LOPS, structural abnormalities, PAD or a prior lower-extremity complication should be referred to a foot care specialist. All patients with diabetes should inspect their feet daily (or have a family member do so if they are unable).

Foot Care Counseling

- Check your feet every day for any changes (red spots, cuts, swelling, blisters and cracks). Be sure to look between the toes. Use a mirror, if needed, to inspect the bottom of the feet. Call or see a healthcare provider if there are cuts or breaks in the skin, ingrown nail(s) or signs of an infection (redness, swelling).
- Wash your feet every day and dry them completely, especially between the toes. Rub a thin coat of skin moisturizer over the tops and bottoms of dry feet, but not between your toes due to an increased risk of a fungal infection called tinea pedis.
- Trim your toenails straight across and file the nail edges with an emery board in the same shape or outline as the toe.
- Avoid walking barefoot. Wear socks and shoes at all times.
- Wear properly fitting, comfortable, supportive shoes (with inserts or insoles if needed). Use extra-wide shoes to accommodate any deformities such as bunions or hammertoes. Use caution when breaking in new shoes and inspect your shoes for foreign objects before inserting feet.
- Keep blood flowing to the feet. Put your feet up when sitting. Wiggle your toes and move your ankles up and down for 5 minutes, 2 – 3 times/day. Do not cross your legs for long periods of time.
- Protect your feet from hot and cold. Wear shoes at the beach or on hot pavement. Keep your feet away from items that may cause burning such as fireplaces, electric blankets, or heating pads. Use another part of the body to test water (bath or shower) temperature.

Vaccinations

Patients with chronic illnesses, including diabetes, have increased rates of hospitalizations and mortality from influenza and pneumococcal diseases. In addition, patients with diabetes have higher rates of hepatitis B. Routine vaccines, for both children and adults, should be given according to ACIP age-specific recommendations (see Immunizations chapter). In addition, patients with diabetes should receive an annual influenza vaccine (if ≥ 6 months of age), pneumococcal vaccines [PPSV23 *(Pneumovax 23* x 1 between age 2 – 64 years and, at age ≥ 65 years, PCV13 *(Prevnar)* and *Pneumovax 23*, spaced at least 12 months apart and with *Pneumovax 23* spaced at least ≥ 5 years after any previous administrations], and hepatitis B vaccine (if unvaccinated and aged 19 – 59 years; may also consider in unvaccinated adults ≥ 60 years).

Durable Medical Equipment

Durable Medical Equipment (DME) covered by CMS under the Part B medical benefit includes glucose monitors, test strips, lancet devices and lancets, and diabetic shoes or inserts. Medicare has an anti-switching rule that prohibits suppliers from encouraging patients to switch glucose meters or test strips. If the supplier does not have the test strip that the meter requires the patient can ask about alternative brands, but the supplier cannot initiate the discussion. CMS does not cover continuous glucose monitoring (CGM) devices. Part B covers some other diabetes services, including self-management training, annual eye exam, foot exam every 6 months, glaucoma tests and nutrition therapy.

GLYCEMIC (BLOOD GLUCOSE) CONTROL

Glycemic Targets For Non-Pregnant Adults with Diabetes

Two primary techniques for assessing glycemic control are SMBG, using a glucose meter to test capillary plasma glucose, and measurement of glycosylated hemoglobin, or A1C. CGM may be used in combination with SMBG in select patients (e.g., frequent hypoglycemia). Patients on a multiple-dose insulin regimen, or those using insulin pumps, should perform SMBG prior to meals and snacks, occasionally postprandially, at bedtime, prior to exercise or other critical tasks such as driving, when low blood glucose is suspected, and after treating low blood glucose, until normoglycemic. In patients on basal insulin or oral medications, there is not enough evidence regarding when to perform SMBG and how often testing is needed.

The A1C should be measured quarterly in patients who are not at goal, or when therapy has recently changed, and at least twice per year if patients are at goal and have stable glycemic control. Use of point-of-care (POC) testing for A1C allows for more timely treatment changes.

ADULT TREATMENT GOALS	PER ADA GUIDELINES	PER AACE GUIDELINES
A1C	< 7%*	< 6.5%
Preprandial capillary plasma glucose	80-130 mg/dL	< 110 mg/dL
Peak postprandial capillary plasma glucose (1-2 hours after the start of a meal)	< 180 mg/dL	< 140 mg/dL

** Individualize target goals: per the ADA, a more stringent A1C goal (e.g., < 6.5%) may be appropriate for patients not experiencing hypoglycemia or other adverse effects of treatment, those with a short duration of diabetes, and those with long life expectancy or with no significant CVD. A less stringent A1C goal (e.g., < 8%) may be appropriate for patients with a history of severe hypoglycemia, limited life expectancy, extensive comorbid conditions, advanced complications, or longstanding diabetes where the goal A1C is difficult to attain despite optimal efforts.*

While SMBG measures the blood glucose at a given moment, the A1C measures the average blood glucose over the past 2 – 3 months. This estimated average glucose (eAG) may be easier for patients to understand over A1C. The eAG goal is < 154 mg/dL per the ADA guidelines.

A1C and Average Glucose (estimated)

A1C (%)	ESTIMATED PLASMA GLUCOSE (MG/DL)
6	126
7	154
8	183
9	212
10	240
11	269
12	298

Drug-Induced Hyperglycemia

When assessing glycemic control in patients with diabetes, it is important to review the full medication profile for drugs that can cause hyperglycemia. Key drugs that can increase blood glucose are shown in the box. In most cases, the mechanism is reduced insulin secretion or sensitivity. Use of some of these agents may be necessary in patients with diabetes (e.g., to control BP or cholesterol) and the benefits may outweigh the risks. Use of other agents (e.g., corticosteroids, antipsychotics, protease inhibitors) will require close monitoring; dose reductions, or selection of an alternate agent, may be necessary. Patients should be counseled about the risks of hyperglycemia when using these agents, as well as symptoms of hyperglycemia (previously described). Some medications can cause hypoglycemia or hyperglycemia (see Hypoglycemia section for further discussion).

DRUGS THAT CAN RAISE BLOOD GLUCOSE

KEY DRUGS

- Beta-blockers*
- Diuretics (thiazides/loops)
- Immunosuppressants (e.g., cyclosporine, tacrolimus)
- Niacin
- Protease inhibitors
- Quinolones*
- Second-generation (atypical) antipsychotics (e.g., clozapine, olanzapine, quetiapine)
- Statins
- Systemic steroids

Others:

- Azole antifungals (esp. posaconazole)
- Beta-agonists
- Cough syrups (OTC and Rx)
- Diazoxide
- Inteferon alfas
- Octreotide*

** May also cause hypoglycemia (see Hypoglycemia section)*

ADA TREATMENT GUIDELINES FOR TYPE 2 DIABETES

MONOTHERAPY

Lifestyle modifications + metformin* (unless contraindicated)

** If A1C ≥ 9%, consider starting with dual therapy*
If BG ≥ 300 mg/dL and/or A1C ≥ 10%, consider starting combination injectable therapy

↓ *If not at target A1C after 3 months, consider adding a 2nd agent*

DUAL THERAPY

Choose one (see Study Tips Box below for factors to consider):

SU	DPP-4 inhibitor	GLP-1 agonist
TZD	SGLT2 inhibitor	Basal insulin

↓ *If not at target A1C after 3 months, consider adding a 3rd agent*

TRIPLE THERAPY

Most 3-drug combinations are acceptable.

Combinations that are not recommended include:**
Metformin + DPP-4 inhibitor + GLP-1 agonist
Metformin + SGLT2 inhibitor + GLP-1 agonist
Metformin + basal insulin + SU

↓ *If not at target A1C after 3 months of triple therapy*

1) If on oral combination regimen, switch to injectables
2) If on GLP-1 agonist, add basal insulin
3) If on optimally titrated basal insulin, add GLP-1 agonist or mealtime insulin
4) In refractory patients, add TZD or SGLT2 inhibitor

COMBINATION INJECTABLE THERAPY

Basal insulin + mealtime insulin or GLP-1 agonist

SU = sulfonylurea, TZD = thiazolidinediones, DPP-4 = dipeptidyl peptidase 4, SGLT2 = sodium glucose co-transporter 2, GLP-1 = glucagon-like peptide 1
***These combinations contain drugs with similar mechanisms of action and/or they have not been adequately studied*

STUDY TIPS: FACTORS TO CONSIDER WHEN SELECTING AN ADDITIONAL AGENT

EFFICACY	COST	HYPOGLYCEMIA RISK	WEIGHT	FORMULATION
Moderate: DPP-4 inhibitors, SGLT2 inhibitors **High:** metformin, SUs, TZDs, GLP-1 agonists, meglitinides **Highest:** insulin	**Low:** metformin, SUs, TZDs **Moderate:** meglitinides **High:** SGLT2 inhibitors, DPP-4 inhibitors, GLP-1 agonists **Variable:** insulin (depends on formulation)	**Low:** metformin, TZDs, DPP-4 inhibitors, GLP-1 agonists, SGLT2 inhibitors **Moderate:** SUs, meglitinides **High:** insulin	**Weight loss:** GLP-1 agonists, SGLT2 inhibitors **Weight neutral:** metformin, DPP-4 inhibitors **Weight gain:** insulin, SUs, meglitinides, TZDs	**Injectable:** insulin, GLP-1 agonists **Oral:** all others

Primary Mechanism of Action of the Drug Classes

↑/REPLACES INSULIN SECRETION	↓ HEPATIC GLUCOSE OUTPUT	↓ GLUCAGON WHICH ↓ GLUCOSE PRODUCTION (LIVER)	↓ GLUCOSE ABSORPTION	↑ GLUCOSE EXCRETION	↑ INSULIN SENSITIVITY
Insulin SUs Meglitinides	Metformin	GLP-1 agonists DPP-4 inhibitors Pramlintide	Alpha-glucosidase inhibitors	SGLT2 inhibitors	TZDs Metformin

BIGUANIDE

Metformin primarily works by ↓ hepatic glucose production, ↓ intestinal absorption of glucose and ↑ insulin sensitivity. Metformin is first-line therapy in type 2 diabetes and can be used in prediabetes; use is dependent on estimated glomerular filtration rate (eGFR); see Renal Disease chapter.

DRUG	DOSING	SAFETY/SIDE EFFECTS/MONITORING
MetFORMIN *(Glucophage, Glucophage XR,* *Fortamet, Glumetza, Riomet)* IR: 500, 850, 1,000 mg ER: 500, 750, 1,000 mg *Riomet* liquid (500 mg/5 mL) + glipizide + glyburide *(Glucovance)* + pioglitazone *(Actoplus Met, Actoplus Met XR)* + rosiglitazone *(Avandamet)* + repaglinide *(PrandiMet)* **+ sitagliptin *(Janumet, Janumet XR)*** + saxagliptin *(Kombiglyze XR)* + linagliptin *(Jentadueto, Jentadueto XR)* + alogliptin *(Kazano)* + canagliflozin *(Invokamet, Invokamet XR)* + dapagliflozin *(Xigduo XR)* + empagliflozin *(Synjardy, Synjardy XR)*	IR: 500 mg BID or 850 mg daily initially ER: 500-1,000 mg with dinner initially Titrate by 500 mg weekly or 850 mg every 2 weeks Max dose: 2,000-2,550 mg/day (varies by product) Give with a meal to ↓ GI upset ER: swallow whole; do not crush, break or chew	**BOXED WARNING** Lactic acidosis – risk ↑ with acute HF, dehydration, hypoxemia, sepsis, excessive alcohol intake, hepatic or renal impairment, advanced age (≥ 80 years – check renal function before starting) **CONTRAINDICATIONS** eGFR < 30 mL/min/1.73 m^2, renal dysfunction due to acute MI, sepsis, cardiovascular collapse (shock), acute or chronic metabolic acidosis (includes DKA) **WARNINGS** Not recommended to initiate with eGFR 30-45 mL/min/1.73 m^2; assess benefits of continuing if already taking metformin and eGFR falls below 45 mL/min/1.73 m^2 Use of intravascular iodinated contrast media (see Drug Interactions) Decreased vitamin B12 absorption (rarely leads to anemia and reversible with B12 supplementation) **SIDE EFFECTS** N/V/D, flatulence, abdominal cramping **MONITORING** BG, A1C, renal function, B12 **NOTES** ↓ A1C 1-2% ER formulations can leave a ghost tablet (empty shell) in the stool – see Patient Counseling section

Metformin Drug Interactions

- Alcohol can ↑ the risk for lactic acidosis; excessive intake, acute or chronic, should be avoided.
- Intravenous iodinated contrast media used for imaging studies can ↑ the risk of lactic acidosis. Discontinue metformin, at the time of or before the imaging procedure, in patients with an eGFR between 30 – 60 mL/min/1.73 m^2 or a history of hepatic disease, alcoholism, or heart failure. Metformin may be restarted 48 hours after the procedure if the eGFR has been confirmed to be stable.
- The combination of metformin and topiramate can ↑ the risk of metabolic acidosis.

Metformin Counseling

- Diarrhea, nausea, vomiting, abdominal discomfort and flatulence can occur, but these side effects often go away with time. Taking this medication with food can help.
- Some people have developed a very rare, life-threatening condition called lactic acidosis while taking metformin. Seek emergency medical help if you have any of these symptoms: feeling weak or tired, slow or irregular heartbeat, unusual muscle pain, trouble breathing, unusual stomach pain, dizziness, lightheadedness or feeling cold. Drinking alcohol while taking this medication increases your risk of lactic acidosis.
- If you need to have any type of X-ray or procedure using a contrast dye, you may need to temporarily stop taking metformin.
- Do not crush, chew, or break an extended-release tablet. Swallow the pill whole as it is made to release the medication slowly into the body. Breaking the pill would cause too much of the drug to be released at one time.
- If using *Glumetza, Fortamet* or *Glucophage XR*, you may see a shell of the medication in the stool. This is normal, the drug is in your body and the tablet is empty.

INSULIN SECRETAGOGUES

Sulfonylureas (SUs) and meglitinides are known as insulin secretatogues; they work by stimulating insulin secretion from the pancreatic beta cells to decrease postprandial blood glucose. Meglitinides have a faster onset (15 – 60 minutes) and shorter duration of action compared to the SUs. They require multiple daily dosing so use is typically restricted to patients with irregular meal schedules or those who develop late postprandial hypoglycemia with SUs. Older, first generation SUs (chlorpropamide, tolazamide and tobutamide) should not be used as they can cause prolonged hypoglycemia.

Meglitinides

DRUG	DOSING	SAFETY/SIDE EFFECTS/MONITORING
Repaglinide *(Prandin)* + metformin *(PrandiMet)*	A1C < 8% or not previously treated: 0.5 mg before each meal (TIDAC) A1C ≥ 8% and previously treated: 1-2 mg before each meal (TIDAC) Titrate at weekly intervals to max dose of 16 mg daily Take 15-30 minutes before meals	**CONTRAINDICATIONS** Type 1 diabetes, DKA Repaglinide: co-administration of gemfibrozil **WARNINGS** Hypoglycemia, caution with severe liver/renal impairment **SIDE EFFECTS** Weight gain, upper respiratory tract infections (URTIs) **MONITORING** BG, A1C **NOTES** ↓ A1C 0.5-1.5% Nateglinide is slightly less effective than repaglinide
Nateglinide *(Starlix)*	60-120 mg before each meal (TIDAC) Take 1-30 minutes before meals	

Sulfonylureas

DRUG	DOSING	SAFETY/SIDE EFFECTS/MONITORING
GlipiZIDE ***(Glucotrol, Glucotrol XL, GlipiZIDE XL)*** + metformin	IR: 5 mg daily, ↑ by 2.5-5 mg every few days; max dose = 40 mg/day; daily doses > 15 mg should be divided BID XL: 5 mg daily, titrate to a max dose of 20 mg/day	**CONTRAINDICATIONS** Type 1 diabetes, DKA, sulfa allergy (not likely to cross-react – see Drug Allergies & Adverse Drug Reactions chapter) Glyburide: use with bosentan **WARNINGS** Hypoglycemia, G6PD deficiency Glimepiride: hypersensitivity reactions (e.g., anaphylaxis, angioedema, SJS) **SIDE EFFECTS** Weight gain, nausea **MONITORING** BG, A1C **NOTES** ↓ A1C 1-2% ↓ efficacy after long-term use (as pancreatic beta cell function declines) Glipizide IR is taken 30 minutes before a meal; all other products take with breakfast or the first meal of the day; may need to hold doses if NPO *Glucotrol XL* is in an OROS formulation (see Drug Formulations chapter) and can leave a ghost tablet (empty shell) in the stool Glyburide has a weakly active metabolite that is renally cleared, and is not a preferred agent in patients with renal insufficiency Glyburide tablets cannot be used interchangeably with micronized tablet formulations, which have better absorption
Glimepiride ***(Amaryl)*** + pioglitazone *(Duetact)* + rosiglitazone	1-2 mg daily, ↑ by 1-2 mg every 1-2 weeks; max dose = 8 mg/day	
GlyBURIDE ***(DiaBeta)*** Micronized glyburide *(Glynase)* + metformin *(Glucovance)*	*DiaBeta:* 2.5-5 mg daily, ↑ by 2.5 mg weekly; max dose = 20 mg/day *Glynase:* 1.5-3 mg daily, ↑ by 1.5 mg weekly; max dose = 12 mg/day	

Sulfonylurea and Meglitinide Drug Interactions

- Insulin, SUs and meglitinides should never be used in combination due to an ↑ risk of hypoglycemia.
- A reduction in SU or meglitinide dose may be required when a TZD, GLP-1 agonist, DPP-4 inhibitor or SGLT2 inhibitor is initiated. Use caution with other drugs that can decrease blood glucose (see Hypoglycemia section).
- Sulfonylureas are CYP 2C9 substrates; use caution with drugs that are 2C9 inducers or inhibitors.
- Gemfibrozil can ↑ repaglinide concentrations and can ↓ blood glucose.
- Alcohol may ↑ the risk for delayed hypoglycemia, especially if taking insulin or insulin secretagogues.

Sulfonylurea and Meglitinide Counseling

- Sulfonylureas should be taken with breakfast (except for glipizide IR which is taken 30 minutes before meals). Do not crush, chew, or break an extended-release tablet. Swallow the pill whole as it is made to release the medication slowly into the body. Breaking the pill would cause too much of the drug to be released at one time.
- Take repaglinide 15 – 30 minutes before meals and nateglinide 1 – 30 minutes before meals. If you forget to take a dose until after eating, skip that dose and take only your next regularly scheduled dose, before a meal. If you plan to skip a meal, skip the dose for that meal.
- Keep this medication away from children, even one tablet can be dangerous.

- This medication can cause low blood sugar, which is more likely if you skip a meal, exercise too long, drink alcohol or are under stress. Symptoms of low blood sugar including shakiness, irritability, hunger, headache, confusion, feeling weak or sleepy, dizziness, sweating and fast heartbeat. Very low blood sugar can cause seizures (convulsions), fainting or coma. Always keep a source of sugar available in case you have symptoms of low blood sugar.

THIAZOLIDINEDIONES

Thiazolidinediones (TZDs) are peroxisome proliferator-activated receptor gamma (PPARγ) agonists that cause ↑ peripheral insulin sensitivity (↑ uptake and utilization of glucose by the peripheral tissues, also known as insulin sensitizers).

DRUG	DOSING	SAFETY/SIDE EFFECTS/MONITORING
Pioglitazone *(Actos)* + metformin *(Actoplus Met, Actoplus Met XR)* + glimepiride *(Duetact)* + alogliptin *(Oseni)*	Initial: 15-30 mg daily NYHA Class I/II heart failure: start with 15 mg daily Max dose: 45 mg daily Take without regard to meals	**BOXED WARNINGS** May cause or exacerbate heart failure Rosiglitazone: increased risk of MI **CONTRAINDICATIONS** NYHA Class III/IV heart failure **WARNINGS** Hepatic failure, edema (including macular edema), risk of fractures Ovulation, in premenopausal anovulatory women, can occur which can lead to unintended pregnancy; contraception is recommended in all premenopausal women Pioglitazone: do not use in patients with active bladder cancer; bladder cancer risk is increased with duration of use **SIDE EFFECTS** Peripheral edema, weight gain, URTIs, myalgia Pioglitazone: ↑ HDL, ↓ TGs and ↓ total cholesterol **MONITORING** LFTs, BG, A1C, s/sx of heart failure **NOTES** ↓ A1C 0.5-1.4% MedGuide required
Rosiglitazone *(Avandia)* + metformin *(Avandamet)* + glimepiride	4-8 mg daily Max dose: 8 mg daily Take without regard to meals	

Thiazolidinedione Drug Interactions

- These agents can reduce the amount of insulin or insulin secretagogue required. Monitor blood glucose closely after initiation of therapy.
- These agents are major substrates of CYP 2C8; use caution with drugs that are 2C8 inducers (e.g., rifampin) or inhibitors (e.g., gemfibrozil).

Thiazolidinedione Counseling

- Take once daily, with or without food. It may take several weeks for this medication to lower blood sugar.
- This drug can cause your body to keep extra fluid (water retention), which can cause swelling, weight gain, and heart problems such as heart failure. Inform your healthcare provider right away if you have trouble breathing (especially when you lie down), swelling in the ankles or legs, unusual or fast weight gain, or if you feel unusually tired.
- Women may be more likely than men to have bone fractures in the upper arm, hand or foot while taking this medication. Talk with your healthcare provider if you are concerned about this possibility.

- Contact your healthcare provider right away if you are passing dark-colored urine, have decreased appetite, stomach pain, nausea or vomiting, feel more tired than usual, or if your skin and/or whites of your eyes become yellow. These may be signs of liver damage.
- Tell your healthcare provider if you have heart failure, heart disease or liver problems. For pioglitazone, tell your healthcare provider if you have or have had bladder cancer.

SODIUM GLUCOSE CO-TRANSPORTER 2 INHIBITORS

The sodium glucose co-transporter 2 (SGLT2) protein, expressed in the proximal renal tubules, is responsible for the majority of the reabsorption of filtered glucose from the tubular lumen. By inhibiting SGLT2, these agents reduce reabsorption of filtered glucose and lower the renal threshold for glucose; this ↑ urinary glucose excretion and ↓ plasma glucose concentrations. SGLT2 inhibitors are dosed based on eGFR; see Renal Disease chapter.

DRUG	DOSING	SAFETY/SIDE EFFECTS/MONITORING
Canagliflozin *(Invokana)* + metformin *(Invokamet, Invokamet XR)*	100 mg daily prior to the first meal of the day; can ↑ to 300 mg daily eGFR 45-59 mL/min: 100 mg max dose eGFR 30-44 mL/min: not recommended eGFR < 30 mL/min: contraindicated	**CONTRAINDICATIONS** Severe renal impairment (eGFR < 30 mL/min), ESRD, or on dialysis **WARNINGS** Ketoacidosis (including fatal cases), genital mycotic infections, hypotension (due to intravascular volume depletion), ↑ LDL, urosepsis and pyelonephritis Canagliflozin and dapagliflozin: acute kidney injury and renal impairment (due to intravascular volume depletion) Canagliflozin: hyperkalemia, risk of fractures Dapagliflozin: risk of bladder cancer **SIDE EFFECTS** Hypoglycemia, weight loss, ↑ urination, ↑ thirst, ↑ Mg/PO4 **MONITORING** Renal function, BG, A1C, LDL, BP, volume status **NOTES** ↓ A1C 0.7-1% Do not monitor BG with urine glucose tests as SGLT2 inhibitors increase urinary glucose excretion MedGuide required
Dapagliflozin *(Farxiga)* + metformin *(Xigduo XR)*	5 mg daily in the morning; can ↑ to 10 mg daily eGFR 30-59 mL/min: not recommended eGFR < 30 mL/min: contraindicated	
Empagliflozin *(Jardiance)* + linagliptin *(Glyxambi)* + metformin *(Synjardy, Synjardy XR)*	10 mg daily in the morning; can ↑ to 25 mg daily eGFR 30-44 mL/min: not recommended eGFR < 30 mL/min: contraindicated	

SGLT2 Inhibitor Drug Interactions

- To reduce the risk of hypoglycemia, consider a lower dose of insulin or insulin secretagogue when initiating SGLT2 inhibitors. Monitor blood glucose closely after initiation of therapy.
- The risk of intravascular volume depletion (causing hypotension and acute kidney injury) can be increased if used in combination with diuretics, RAAS inhibitors or NSAIDs.
- UGT inducers (e.g., rifampin) can ↓ levels of canagliflozin; consider using 300 mg dose if used in combination and CrCl ≥ 60 mL/min.
- Canagliflozin can ↑ the AUC of digoxin; monitor digoxin levels if used in combination.
- Monitor potassium levels closely in patients taking canagliflozin with other medications that can ↑ potassium (e.g., ACE inhibitors, ARBs, aldosterone antagonists).

SGLT2 Inhibitor Patient Counseling

- Take this medication in the morning (canagliflozin should be taken before the first meal).

- This medication can cause increased urination and dehydration (loss of too much body water) resulting in dizziness, lightheadedness, weakness, fainting, and thirst. This can lead to sudden injury of the kidneys; tell your healthcare provider right away if you are sick, and cannot eat or drink, or if you lose liquids due to vomiting, diarrhea or being in the sun too long.
- This medication can cause yeast infections of the penis or vagina; tell your healthcare provider if you develop an odor, discharge, itchiness or pain in the genital area.
- This medication can cause a serious condition called ketoacidosis, which can lead to death. Tell your healthcare provider right away if you develop nausea, vomiting, tiredness, trouble breathing, or stomach pain.
- This medication can cause serious infections of the urinary tract. Tell your healthcare provider if you have burning or pain when urinating, a need to urinate frequently and urgently, have pain in the lower part of your stomach or blood in the urine, especially if you also have a fever.

DIPEPTIDYL PEPTIDASE 4 INHIBITORS

Dipeptidyl peptidase 4 (DPP-4) inhibitors prevent the enzyme DPP-4 from breaking down incretin hormones, glucagon-like peptide 1 (GLP-1) and glucose-dependent insulinotropic polypeptide (GIP). These hormones help to regulate blood glucose levels by ↑ insulin release from the pancreatic beta cells and ↓ glucagon secretion from pancreatic alpha cells. A reduction in glucagon results in ↓ hepatic glucose production. These medications enhance the effects of the body's own incretins.

DRUG	DOSING	SAFETY/SIDE EFFECTS/MONITORING
SITagliptin *(Januvia)* **+ metformin *(Janumet, Janumet XR)***	100 mg daily CrCl 30-49 mL/min: 50 mg daily CrCl < 30 mL/min: 25 mg daily	**WARNINGS** Acute pancreatitis, severe and disabling arthralgia (joint pain), hypersensitivity reactions [anaphylaxis, angioedema, severe skin reactions (SJS)]
SAXagliptin *(Onglyza)* + metformin *(Kombiglyze XR)*	2.5-5 mg daily CrCl < 50 mL/min: 2.5 mg daily *Kombiglyze XR* is given daily with the evening meal	Saxagliptin and alogliptin: risk of heart failure (especially in patients with a history of heart failure or renal impairment) Alogliptin: hepatotoxicity
Linagliptin *(Tradjenta)* + metformin *(Jentadueto, Jentadueto XR)* + empagliflozin *(Glyxambi)*	5 mg daily No renal dose adjustment	**SIDE EFFECTS** Nasopharyngitis, URTIs, UTIs, peripheral edema, rash **MONITORING** BG, A1C, renal function
Alogliptin *(Nesina)* + metformin *(Kazano)* + pioglitazone *(Oseni)*	25 mg daily CrCl 30-59 mL/min: 12.5 mg daily CrCl < 30 mL/min: 6.25 mg daily	**NOTES** ↓ A1C 0.5-0.8%; ↓ postprandial BG; weight neutral Alogliptin available in generic (may be lower cost) MedGuide required

DPP-4 Inhibitor Drug Interactions

- To reduce the risk of hypoglycemia, consider a lower dose of insulin or insulin secretagogue when initiating DPP-4 inhibitors. Monitor blood glucose closely after initiation of therapy.
- Saxagliptin is a major substrate of CYP 3A4 and P-gp. Limit the dose to 2.5 mg with strong 3A4 inhibitors, including atazanavir, clarithromycin, indinavir, itraconazole, ketoconazole, nefazodone, nelfinavir, ritonavir, and saquinavir.
- Linagliptin is a major substrate of 3A4 and P-gp. Linagliptin levels are ↓ by strong 3A4 inducers (e.g., carbamazepine, efavirenz, phenytoin, rifampin, St. John's wort).

DPP-4 Inhibitor Counseling

- Take this medication once daily in the morning, with or without food.
- Seek immediate medical help if you develop symptoms of a severe allergic reaction: severe rash with itching, redness or swelling, swelling in your face, lips, tongue or throat, wheezing or trouble breathing or severe dizziness.
- This medication can cause pain and inflammation in your pancreas. Stop taking it and tell your healthcare provider right away if you have severe stomach pain, with or without vomiting. The pain can radiate from the abdomen through to the back.
- Saxaliptin and alogliptin: this medication can cause heart failure. Inform your healthcare provider right away if you have trouble breathing (especially when you lie down), swelling in the ankles or legs, unusual or fast weight gain, or if you feel unusually tired.

GLUCAGON-LIKE PEPTIDE 1 AGONISTS

Glucagon-like peptide 1 (GLP-1) agonists are analogs of the incretin hormone GLP-1 which ↑ glucose-dependent insulin secretion, ↓ glucagon secretion, slows gastric emptying, improves satiety and may result in weight loss. These are incretin mimetics.

<table>
<tr><th>DRUG</th><th>DOSING</th><th>SAFETY/SIDE EFFECTS/MONITORING</th></tr>
<tr><td>Exenatide (Byetta)

5 mcg/dose, 10 mcg/dose multidose pen</td><td>Start: 5 mcg SC BID for 1 month, then 10 mcg SC BID

Give within 60 minutes before the morning and evening meal</td><td rowspan="7">BOXED WARNING
All (except Byetta and Adlyxin): risk of thyroid C-cell carcinomas – seen in rats, unknown if risk applies to humans

CONTRAINDICATIONS
All (except Byetta and Adlyxin): personal or family history of medullary thyroid carcinoma (MTC) or patients with Multiple Endocrine Neoplasia syndrome type 2 (MEN 2)

WARNINGS
Pancreatitis (can be fatal, usually in patients with risk factors: history of pancreatitis, gallstones, alcoholism or ↑ TGs)

Not recommended in patients with severe GI disease

Renal impairment – use with caution in patients with renal impairment, not recommended if CrCl < 30 mL/min (Byetta, Bydureon)

Bydureon: serious injection-site reactions (e.g., abscess, cellulitis, necrosis) with or without SC nodules

SIDE EFFECTS
Nausea (primary side effect), vomiting, diarrhea, constipation, antibodies, hypoglycemia, weight loss, injection site reactions

Trulicity: cardiovascular effects (tachycardia, 1st degree AV block, PR interval prolongation)

MONITORING
BG, A1C, renal function

NOTES
↓ A1C 0.5-1.1%; ↓ postprandial BG

Safety issue (Saxenda) – see Pregnancy chapter

Byetta, Victoza, and Adlyxin multidose pens: needles are not included and a separate prescription may be needed

Pen injection devices should never be shared (even when the needle is changed) due to the risk for transmission of blood-borne pathogens

MedGuide required</td></tr>
<tr><td>Exenatide extended release (Bydureon)

2 mg single-dose vial/tray or single-dose pen</td><td>2 mg SC once weekly

Give without regard to meals</td></tr>
<tr><td>Liraglutide (Victoza)

18 mg/3 mL multidose pen

Saxenda – for weight loss</td><td>Start: 0.6 mg SC daily x 1 week, then 1.2 mg SC daily x 1 week; can ↑ to 1.8 mg SC daily, if needed

Give without regard to meals</td></tr>
<tr><td>Dulaglutide (Trulicity)

0.75 mg/0.5 mL, 1.5 mg/0.5 mL single-dose pen</td><td>Start: 0.75 mg SC once weekly, can ↑ to 1.5 mg SC once weekly

Give without regard to meals</td></tr>
<tr><td>Albiglutide (Tanzeum)

30 mg/0.5 mL, 50 mg/0.5 mL single-dose pen for reconstitution</td><td>Start: 30 mg SC once weekly, can ↑ to 50 mg SC once weekly

Give without regard to meals

Use within 8 hours of reconstitution</td></tr>
<tr><td>Lixisenatide (Adlyxin)

10 mcg/dose, 20 mcg/dose multidose pen</td><td>Start: 10 mcg SC daily x 14 days, then ↑ to 20 mcg daily

Give within 60 minutes of the first meal of the day</td></tr>
</table>

GLP-1 Agonist Drug Interactions

- To reduce the risk of hypoglycemia, consider a lower dose of insulin or insulin secretagogue when initiating GLP-1 inhibitors. Monitor blood glucose closely after initiation of therapy.
- These drugs slow gastric emptying and can reduce the extent and rate of absorption of orally administered drugs. Caution is warranted, especially with narrow therapeutic index drugs or medications that require threshold concentrations for efficacy (e.g., antibiotics, oral contraceptives). Patients should be advised to take oral contraceptives at least 1 hour before exenatide or *Adlyxin* and at least 11 hours after *Adlyxin*.
- Can ↑ the INR in patients on warfarin, monitor INR.

GLP-1 Agonist Counseling

- This medication can cause pain and inflammation in your pancreas. Stop taking it and tell your healthcare provider right away if you have severe stomach pain, with or without vomiting. The pain can radiate from the abdomen through to the back.
- The most common side effects include nausea, vomiting, diarrhea and headache. These symptoms will decrease over time. Talk to your healthcare provider about any side effect that bothers you or does not go away.
- Store in the refrigerator (never freeze) and protect from light.
- Administer (using a new needle) by SC injection in the stomach area, upper leg (thigh) or the back of the upper arm. Rotate sites with each injection.
- Do not store your pen with the needle attached. Remove the needle from the pen immediately after injection; this helps prevent leaking of the medication from the pen and air bubbles from forming in the cartridge. Keep pens and needles out of the reach of children and pets.
- Used needles should be placed in a sharps disposal container or in a puncture-resistant household container with a tight-fitting lid (e.g., detergent bottle or empty metal coffee container). See the Medication Safety & Quality Improvement chapter.

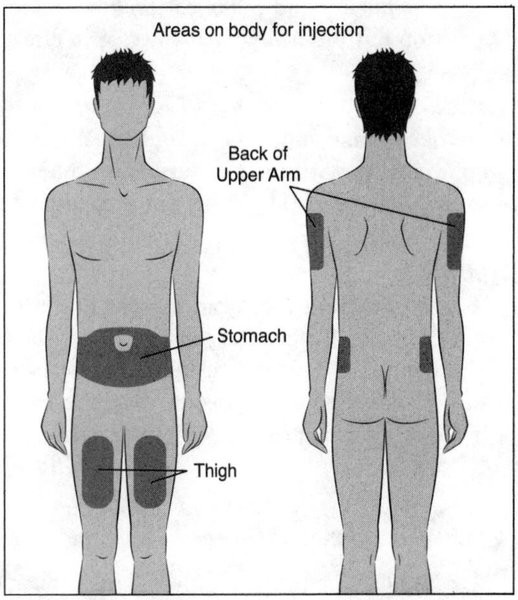

For all except *Byetta* and *Adlyxin*:

- Do not take this medication if you or any family members have had thyroid cancer, especially medullary thyroid cancer. While taking this medication, tell your healthcare provider if you get a lump or swelling in your neck, hoarseness, have trouble swallowing, or develop shortness of breath. These may be symptoms of thyroid cancer.

Byetta

- Inject two times each day, within 60 minutes before the morning and evening meals (or before the two main meals of the day, at least 6 hours apart). Never inject after a meal due to the risk of low blood sugar.
- Insert the needle into the skin, push the inject button firmly, count to 5, then remove the needle from the skin.
- Each pen contains enough drug for injection twice daily for 30 days. Mark the date when you first use your pen and the date 30 days later. After 30 days, throw away the *Byetta* pen, even if it is not completely empty.

Bydureon

- *Bydureon* single-dose vial/tray requires you to mix the powder medication with a liquid in a syringe. Once mixed, it must be injected immediately otherwise clumps will form. Insert the needle into the skin, push down on the syringe plunger with your thumb until it stops, then withdraw the needle.
- *Bydureon* pen: remove one pen from the refrigerator and let it stand at room temperature for at least 15 minutes. Check the liquid inside the inspection window to make sure it is clear and free of particles. Do not use if the liquid is colored, has particles, or is not clear. Air bubbles are normal.
  - Screw the needle onto the pen. With the pen upright, slowly turn the knob at the end of the pen until you hear the click and the green label disappears.
  - Hold the pen by the end with the orange label and tap the pen firmly against the palm of your hand. Tap about 80 times, rotating the pen every 10 taps. When mixed, *Bydureon* (both formulations) will be a uniformly cloudy solution with no clumps.
  - Hold the pen with the needle pointing straight up and turn the white knob until the orange label disappears and the injection button is released. Insert the needle into the skin, press the injection button firmly until you hear a click, count to 10 before withdrawing the needle.

Victoza

- *Victoza* is taken once daily. Turn the dose selector on your pen until your needed dose (0.6, 1.2 or 1.8 mg) lines up with the pointer, insert the needle into the skin, press down firmly on the dose button until 0 mg lines up with the pointer, count to 6 before withdrawing the needle.

Trulicity

- Remove the Base Cap from the pen and place the Clear Base flat and firmly against the skin at the injection site. Unlock the pen by turning the Lock Ring. Press and hold the green injection button; you will hear a loud click. Continue to hold the Clear Base against the skin until a second click is heard; this happens when the needle starts retracting in about 5 – 10 seconds. You will know the injection is complete when the gray plunger is visible. You can then remove the pen from your skin.

Tanzeum

- This pen has medication powder in one compartment and water in another for mixing.
  - Remove the pen from the refrigerator and let it stand at room temperature for 15 minutes.
  - Check that the pen has a "1" in the number window. Hold the pen upright and twist the clear cartridge in the direction of the arrow until you hear a click and see a "2" in the number window. This will mix the medication powder and liquid in the clear cartridge.
  - Slowly and gently rock the pen side to side (like a windshield wiper) 5 times to mix. Do not shake hard to avoid foaming.
  - Place the pen into an empty cup with the clear cartridge pointing up for 15 minutes (30 mg pen) or 30 minutes (50 mg pen). After this time has passed, slowly and gently rock the pen again from side to side 5 times to mix the medication. Do not shake hard to avoid foaming.
  - Look through the viewing window to make sure the solution is clear and slightly yellow in color. There will be large air bubbles but it should be free of particles.
- Attach the needle, then slowly twist the clear cartridge in the direction of the arrow until it clicks and you see a "3" in the number window. Insert the needle into the skin, press the injection button down slowly and steadily until you hear a click, then count to 5 before withdrawing the needle.

Bydureon, Trulicity, Tanzeum

- These medications are taken once weekly. If a dose is missed, take it as soon as you remember, as long as the next regularly scheduled dose is at least 3 days (72 hours) later. If the next dose is < 3 days later, skip the missed dose entirely and continue with the next regularly scheduled dosing day.

- Each prefilled pen comes with 1 dose of medication and should be disposed of after a single use.

Adlyxin

- This medication is taken once daily within one hour of the first meal of the day. Each pen contains 14 doses. After 14 days, the pen should be discarded, even if there is some medication left.
- The starter pack contains two different colored pens; the green pen contains 10 mcg/dose and the burgundy pen contains 20 mcg/dose. You must start with the green pen and use all 14 doses before using the burgundy pen.
- Before each dose, check to make sure the activation window is white and the liquid is clear and colorless with no particles. Air bubbles are normal.
- Attach a needle then pull the injection button out firmly until it stops (the arrow in the window will now be pointing towards the needle). Insert the needle into the skin then press the injection button until you feel or hear a click, count to 2 then withdraw the needle.

OTHER NON-INSULIN DRUGS FOR DIABETES

The following classes of drugs may be used in specific situations but given their modest efficacy, side effects and/or frequency of administration, they are not used routinely.

Alpha-Glucosidase Inhibitors

These agents reversibly inhibit membrane-bound intestinal alpha-glucosidases, which hydrolyze oligosaccharides and disaccharides to glucose and other monosaccharides in the brush border of the small intestine. This delays glucose absorption and decreases postprandial hyperglycemia. Since these agents inhibit the metabolism of sucrose to glucose and fructose, glucose should be used to treat hypoglycemia (not sucrose).

DRUG	DOSING	SAFETY/SIDE EFFECTS/MONITORING
Acarbose *(Precose)* Miglitol *(Glyset)*	25 mg TID; ↑ dose every 1-2 months Max dose: 100 mg TID, 50 mg TID if ≤ 60 kg (acarbose) SCr > 2 mg/dL: not recommended Start low and titrate slow to ↓ GI effects Take each dose with the first bite of each main meal	**CONTRAINDICATIONS** Inflammatory bowel disease (IBD), colonic ulceration, partial or complete intestinal obstruction, DKA Acarbose: cirrhosis **SIDE EFFECTS** GI effects (flatulence, diarrhea, abdominal pain) Acarbose: ↑ LFTs **MONITORING** BG, A1C, LFTs (acarbose) **NOTES** ↓ A1C 0.5-0.8%; ↓ postprandial BG, weight neutral Most effective with diets rich in complex carbohydrates

Alpha-Glucosidase Inhibitor Counseling

- Take this medication three times daily with the first bite of food for each meal (the medication needs to be in the stomach with your food). If you plan to skip a meal, skip the dose for that meal.
- This medication can cause flatulence (gas), diarrhea and abdominal pain, but this usually goes away with time. The dose may be increased as you get over these side effects.
- These agents, by themselves, do not cause low blood sugar. If you get low blood sugar after taking acarbose or miglitol, you cannot treat it with sucrose (present in fruit juice), table sugar or candy. If you are using this agent with a drug that causes low blood sugar (such as insulin, SUs or meglitinides), you will need to purchase glucose tablets or gel to treat episodes of low blood sugar.

Pramlintide

Pramlintide is a synthetic analog of the human neuroendocrine hormone, amylin. Amylin is produced by pancreatic beta cells; it helps control postprandial glucose by slowing gastric emptying, suppressing glucagon secretion following a meal and increasing satiety. This is an amylinomimetic agent.

DRUG	DOSING	SAFETY/SIDE EFFECTS/MONITORING
Pramlintide *(SymlinPen)* 60 mcg/dose, 120 mcg/dose multidose pen Can use in type 1 and 2 diabetes	Type 1: start at 15 mcg/dose, ↑ in 15 mcg increments every 3 days (if no significant nausea) Max = 60 mcg/dose Type 2: start at 60 mcg/dose, ↑ to 120 mcg/dose after 3 days (if no significant nausea) Administer SC in abdomen or thigh prior to each major meal (≥ 250 kcal or ≥ 30 grams of carbohydrates – if consuming less than the above quantities, skip dose)	**BOXED WARNING** Severe hypoglycemia when used with insulin (usually within 3 hours following administration) **CONTRAINDICATIONS** Gastroparesis, hypoglycemia unawareness **WARNINGS** Hypoglycemia – reduce mealtime insulin by 50% when starting **SIDE EFFECTS** N/V, anorexia, headache, weight loss **MONITORING** BG, A1C **NOTES** ↓ A1C 0.5-1% MedGuide required

Pramlintide Drug Interactions

- Slows gastric emptying; administer oral medications at least 1 hour before and 2 hours after if rapid onset or threshold concentration is critical (e.g., analgesics, antibiotics, oral contraceptives).

Bile Acid Binding Resins

The mechanism by which colesevelam improves glycemic control is unknown. The other indication is for the treatment of hyperlipidemia. It binds to bile acids and reduces bile acid absorption.

DRUG	DOSING	SAFETY/SIDE EFFECTS/MONITORING
Colesevelam *(Welchol)* Tablets: 625 mg Packets for oral suspension: 3.75 gram Also approved for hyperlipidemia	3.75 grams/day: 6 tablets daily or 3 tablets BID or 3.75 gram packet daily Tablets need to be taken with a meal and liquid Powder packets need to be dissolved in 4-8 oz of water, fruit juice, or diet soft drink and taken with a meal	**CONTRAINDICATIONS** History of bowel obstruction, TG > 500 mg/dL, history of hypertriglyceridemia-induced pancreatitis **WARNINGS** ↑ TGs, ↓ absorption of fat-soluble vitamins or other drugs, GI disorders (not recommended in patients with gastroparesis, motility disorders, GI tract surgery or risk for bowel obstruction) Oral suspension contains phenylalanine – avoid in patients with phenylketonuria **SIDE EFFECTS** Constipation, dyspepsia, nausea, bloating **MONITORING** BG, A1C, LDL, TG **NOTES** ↓ A1C 0.5%, weight neutral

Colesevelam Drug Interactions

- The following medications should be taken 4 hours prior to colesevelam: cyclosporine, glimepiride, glipizide, glyburide, levothyroxine, olmesartan, phenytoin, and oral contraceptives containing ethinyl estradiol and norethindrone.
- Colesevelam ↑ levels of metformin extended release; monitor when co-administered.
- Colesevelam can ↓ INR, monitor INR frequently during initiation and after dose changes.

Colesevelam Counseling

- This drug may cause you to feel constipated. Talk to your healthcare provider to see if you need a laxative (e.g., senna) or stool softener (e.g., docusate). Be sure to drink enough water while taking this medication.
- Take this medication at a different time than your multivitamin because it ↓ the absorption of vitamins A, D, E and K.

BROMOCRIPTINE

Bromocriptine is a dopamine agonist. The mechanism by which it improves glycemic control is unknown; it is thought to reset hypothalamic circadian activities which have been altered in obesity, resulting in decreased insulin resistance and decreased glucose production.

DRUG	DOSING	SAFETY/SIDE EFFECTS/MONITORING
Bromocriptine *(Cycloset)* *Parlodel* – for acromegaly, hyperprolactinemia, Parkinson's Disease	Start with 0.8 mg daily, ↑ in 0.8 mg increments weekly to usual dose of 1.6-4.8 mg daily Take dose within 2 hours of waking in the morning; take with food to ↓ nausea	**CONTRAINDICATIONS** *Cycloset:* syncopal migraines, breast feeding **WARNINGS** Hypotension (including orthostatic hypotension), particularly upon initiation and dose titration Psychosis – not recommended in patients with severe psychotic disorders Somnolence **SIDE EFFECTS** Nausea, constipation, dizziness, fatigue, headache, ↓ prolactin levels **MONITORING** BG, A1C **NOTES** ↓ A1C by 0.5%, weight neutral

Bromocriptine Drug Interactions

- Bromocriptine is a major substrate of CYP 3A4; avoid use with strong 3A4 inhibitors and do not exceed 1.6 mg daily with moderate 3A4 inhibitors.
- May ↑ ergot-related side effects (e.g., nausea, vomiting, fatigue) or reduce ergot effectiveness for migraines; use within 6 hours of other ergot-related drugs is not recommended.
- Use with metoclopramide or other dopamine antagonists is not recommended.
- Bromocriptine is highly protein bound and may ↑ the unbound fraction of other highly protein-bound drugs.
- May decrease the vasodilatory effects of nitroglycerin.

INSULIN

Insulin is a hormone required by muscle and adipose tissue for glucose uptake. Insulin also has a role in regulating fat storage and inhibits the breakdown of fat for energy. Commercially available insulins differ in their onset and duration of action. Insulins are high-risk medications.

INSULIN TYPE	UNIQUE CONCERNS	SAFETY/SIDE EFFECTS/MONITORING
Rapid-acting insulins		
Aspart *(NovoLOG, NovoLOG FlexPen)* Glulisine *(Apidra, Apidra SoloStar)* **Lispro *(HumaLOG, HumaLOG KwikPen)*** All: 100 units/mL Vials (10 mL) Multidose pens (3 mL) **Other concentrations:** *HumaLog KwikPen* also comes in 200 units/mL	Give up to 15 minutes before meals or immediately after meals Onset: 10-30 minutes Duration: 3-5 hours Faster onset and shorter duration of action than regular (short-acting) insulin	**WARNINGS** Hypoglycemia, hypokalemia (shifts K from extracellular space to intracellular space), renal/hepatic impairment (may need to ↓ dose) Pen devices should never be shared (even when the needle is changed) due to the risk for transmission of blood-borne pathogens **SIDE EFFECTS** Weight gain, lipodystrophy (thickening or thinning of adipose tissue), injection site reactions, peripheral edema, antibodies **MONITORING** BG, A1C, weight
Afrezza Oral inhalation powder Available as 4, 8, and 12 unit cartridges (single inhalation)	Inhale at the beginning of meals Onset: ~15 minutes Duration: 2-3 hours Has a shorter duration of action compared to 3-5 hours for the injectable rapid-acting insulins Replace the inhaler every 15 days to maintain accurate drug delivery	Same as above plus: **BOXED WARNING** Acute bronchospasm in patients with chronic lung disease such as asthma or COPD – detailed medical history, physical examination, and spirometry (FEV1) required before initiation **CONTRAINDICATIONS** Asthma, COPD, other chronic lung disease **WARNINGS** Decline in pulmonary function (FEV1), lung cancer, DKA **SIDE EFFECTS** Cough, throat pain **MONITORING** Pulmonary function tests (FEV1) **NOTES** Not recommended in patients who smoke or who have recently stopped smoking MedGuide required
Short-acting insulins (regular insulin)		
Regular insulin *(HumuLIN R, NovoLIN R, NovoLIN R ReliOn)* Available without a prescription 100 units/mL Vials (3 mL, 10 mL)	Give 30 minutes before meals Onset: 15-30 minutes Duration: 4-12 hours	Same as rapid-acting injectables above plus: **NOTES** Can be used in IV solutions Available alone or combined with intermediate-acting insulins (N, NPH)

Insulin Products Continued

INSULIN TYPE	UNIQUE CONCERNS	SAFETY/SIDE EFFECTS/MONITORING
Concentrated regular insulin *(HumuLIN R U-500, HumuLIN R U-500 KwikPen)* 500 units/mL Vial (20 mL) Multidose pens (3 mL)	5 times as concentrated; recommended when patient requires > 200 units/day of insulin Give 30 minutes before meals Onset: 15-30 minutes Duration: 13-24 hours All patients using the U-500 insulin vial must also be prescribed a U-500 insulin syringe to avoid dosing errors	Same as rapid-acting injectables above plus: **WARNINGS** The prescribed dose of *Humulin R U-500* should always be expressed in units of insulin; if using the vial, use the U-500 insulin syringe (each marking represents 5 units and no dose conversions are needed) – do not use any other type of syringe **NOTES** Do not transfer insulin from the *KwikPen* into a syringe, the dose window shows the number of units Do not mix with other insulins Do not administer IV, IM or in an insulin pump

Intermediate-acting (NPH) insulins

Intermediate insulin *(HumuLIN N, HumuLIN N KwikPen, NovoLIN N, NovoLIN N ReliOn)* Available without a prescription 100 units/mL Vials (3 mL, 10 mL) Multidose pens (3 mL)	Typically given once or twice daily NPH insulins are cloudy (including pre-mixed preparations) Onset: 1-2 hours Duration: 14-24 hours	Same as rapid-acting injectables above plus: **NOTES** Can mix with rapid and short-acting insulins – draw up rapid and short acting insulin first (clear before cloudy)

Long-acting (basal) insulins

Detemir *(Levemir, Levemir FlexTouch)* **Glargine *(Lantus, Lantus SoloStar, Basaglar KwikPen, Toujeo SoloStar)*** **+ lixisenatide 33 mcg/mL *(Soliqua 100/33)*** Degludec *(Tresiba FlexTouch)* **+ liraglutide 3.6 mg/mL *(Xultophy 100/3.6)*** All (except *Toujeo SoloStar*): 100 units/mL Vials (10 mL) Multidose pens (3 mL) **Other concentrations:** *Tresiba FlexTouch* also comes in 200 units/mL *Toujeo SoloStar* only comes in 300 units/mL (1.5 mL pen)	Give once (at bedtime) or twice daily Onset: 3-4 hours (6 hours for *Toujeo)* Duration – product dependent: Detemir: 6-23 hours (higher doses have longer duration) Glargine and degludec: 24 hours or longer	Same as rapid-acting injectables above plus: **NOTES** Do not mix with other insulins Glargine has an acidic pH and may sting upon injecting *Soliqua 100/33* should be given once daily within 60 minutes prior to the first meal of the day

Insulin Products Continued

INSULIN TYPE	UNIQUE CONCERNS	SAFETY/SIDE EFFECTS/MONITORING
Pre-mixed insulins		
70% insulin aspart protamine suspension, 30% insulin aspart solution *(NovoLOG Mix 70/30)* 75% insulin lispro protamine suspension, 25% insulin lispro solution *(HumaLOG Mix 75/25)* 50% insulin lispro protamine suspension, 50% insulin lispro solution *(HumaLOG Mix 50/50)* 70% NPH, 30% regular *(HumuLIN 70/30, NovoLIN 70/30)* 70% insulin degludec, 30% insulin aspart *(Ryzodeg)*	Typically given twice daily *(Ryzodeg* can be given once daily) Timing of administration before meals is according to rapid or short-acting insulin component NPH and protamine insulins are cloudy	Same as rapid-acting injectables above plus: **NOTES** *HumuLIN 70/30, HumuLIN 70/30 KwikPen* and *NovoLIN 70/30* are available without a prescription Protamine components are intermediate acting All products available in vials (10 mL) and/or pens (3 mL)

Summary of Insulin Properties by Product Type

INSULIN	ONSET	PEAK	DURATION
Rapid-acting insulins			
Insulin aspart *(NovoLOG)* Insulin glulisine *(Apidra)* **Insulin lispro *(HumaLOG)***	10-30 minutes	0.5-3 hours	3-5 hours
Inhaled insulin *(Afrezza)*	~15 minutes	~1 hour	2-3 hours
Short-acting insulins			
Regular *(HumuLIN R, NovoLIN R)*	15-30 minutes	2.5-5 hours	4-12 hours
Concentrated regular *(HumuLIN R U-500)*	15-30 minutes	4-8 hours	13-24 hours
Intermediate-acting insulins			
NPH *(HumuLIN N, NovoLIN N)*	1-2 hours	4-12 hours	14-24 hours
Insulin NPH/insulin regular *(HumuLIN 70/30, NovoLIN 70/30)*	30 minutes	2-12 hours	18-24 hours
Long-acting insulins			
Insulin detemir *(Levemir)*	3-4 hours	–	6-23 hours (dose-dependent)
Insulin glargine *(Lantus, Basaglar, Toujeo SoloStar)*	3-4 hours (*Toujeo* – 6 hours)	–	≥ 24 hours
Insulin degludec *(Tresiba FlexTouch)*	1 hour	–	> 24 hours

Insulin Drug Interactions

Many drugs can increase the risk of hypoglycemia when used in combination with insulin. Meglitinides and SUs should never be used with insulin. When used in combination with TZDs, SGLT2 inhibitors, DDP-4 inhibitors, GLP-1 agonists, and pramlintide, insulin doses may need to be decreased. Use caution with use of other drugs known to cause hypoglycemia (see Hypoglycemia section).

Insulin Vials, Pens and Pumps

Most insulin products contain 100 units/mL of insulin with few exceptions (see Box). Most insulin vials contain 10 mL, except *Humulin R U-500* insulin which comes in a 20 mL vial. Most insulin pen cartridges contain 3 mL, except *Toujeo SoloStar* pens which contain 1.5 mL. In general, pens are easier to use and cause fewer dosing errors if used correctly. They are easier to use for patients with hand tremor, arthritis or vision difficulty. Insulin pumps are devices that deliver SC insulin; they consist of a pump, insulin reservoir, tubing and cannula. Only rapid acting injectable insulin or regular insulin should be used in an insulin pump. The devices can be programmed to mimic the insulin secretion of the pancreas, by providing a continuous infusion (basal rate) throughout the day and boluses of rapid-acting or regular insulin as needed (e.g., mealtimes). Pumps are most often used by patients with type 1 diabetes but are increasingly used by patients with type 2. Candidates for insulin pumps must be receiving multiple daily doses of insulin, be experienced in carbohydrate counting, be highly motivated, understand how to operate the pump, and be willing to test their blood sugar frequently throughout the day. Insulin pumps are not appropriate for newly diagnosed patients.

CONCENTRATED INSULIN PRODUCTS

Rapid-Acting Insulin
Humalog KwikPen: 200 units/mL

Regular (Short-Acting) Insulin
Humulin R U-500: 500 units/mL

Long-Acting Insulins
Tresiba FlexPen (insulin degludec): 200 units/mL

Toujeo SoloStar (insulin glargine): 300 units/mL

INSULIN DOSING

Initiating Insulin for Patients with Type 1 Diabetes

Most people with type 1 diabetes should be treated with an insulin pump or multiple daily injections of insulin [3-4 injections/day between long-acting (basal) and rapid- or short-acting (bolus/prandial) insulin]. Patients should be educated on matching the prandial insulin dose to carbohydrate intake, premeal blood glucose and anticipated activity. Insulin analogs are preferred, to reduce hypoglycemia risk and to mimic the physiologic pattern of the insulin made by the body. Insulin analogs include rapid-acting injectable insulins and basal insulins. Patients with type 1 diabetes should be screened for other autoimmune disorders (e.g., thyroid disorders, vitamin B12 deficiency, celiac disease).

Insulin should be started at a total daily dose (TDD) of 0.6 units/kg/day based on actual body weight (ABW). A basal-bolus strategy, using long-acting (basal) insulin and rapid-acting (bolus) insulin, can be determined as shown in the Study Tip box. If using NPH and regular insulins (NPH/R strategy), use $^2/_3$ of the TDD as the intermediate-acting (NPH) dose and $^1/_3$ as the regular insulin dose. These are generally dosed together twice daily, 30 minutes prior to breakfast and dinner (evening meal).

INITIATING BASAL-BOLUS INSULIN

Start a basal-bolus regimen with *Lantus* and *Humalog* in a 70 kg patient

Step 1: calculate TDD (0.6 units/kg/day using ABW)

Example: 0.6 units/kg/day x 70 kg = 42 units

Step 2: divide the TDD into 50% basal (long-acting) insulin and 50% bolus (rapid-acting) insulin

Example: 21 units Lantus and 21 units Humalog

Step 3: divide the bolus insulin among 3 meals*

Example: 7 units of Humalog TIDAC

Final regimen = 21 units *Lantus* QHS plus 7 units *Humalog* TIDAC

* *May divide evenly or give more insulin for larger meals and less insulin for smaller meals*

Insulin-to-Carbohydrate Ratio

Every person responds differently to insulin (some are more sensitive to the effects than others); because of this, mealtime insulin may be adjusted based on the number of carbohydrates an individual is eating with a meal. An insulin-to-carbohydrate ratio (ICR) is patient specific and helps determine the units of insulin required to cover the grams of carbohydrate included in a meal. It can be calculated using the Rule of 500 (for rapid-acting insulins) or Rule of 450 (for regular insulin):

$$\frac{500}{\text{total daily dose of insulin (TDD)}} = \text{grams of carbohydrate covered by 1 unit of rapid-acting insulin}$$

$$\frac{450}{\text{total daily dose of insulin (TDD)}} = \text{grams of carbohydrates covered by 1 unit of regular insulin}$$

Correction Factor and Correction Dose

Patients with diabetes should know how to calculate their correction dose, which is the amount of insulin needed to return their blood glucose to normal range. For example, if a patient's glucose is higher than desired before a meal, a correction dose of insulin can be given. The correction dose of insulin would be added to the dose they would normally take for that meal, in order to ensure that the patient will reach his or her glycemic target after the meal. The correction dose of insulin is determined based on an individual's correction factor, which provides the number of points that each unit of insulin will decrease the glucose.

Correction Factor – 1,800 Rule (Rapid-Acting Insulin)

$$\frac{1{,}800}{\text{total daily dose of insulin (TDD)}} = \text{correction factor for 1 unit of rapid-acting insulin}$$

Correction Factor – 1,500 Rule (Regular Insulin)

$$\frac{1{,}500}{\text{total daily dose of insulin (TDD)}} = \text{correction factor for 1 unit of regular insulin}$$

Correction Dose

$$\frac{\text{(blood glucose now) - (target blood glucose)}}{\text{correction factor}} = \text{correction dose}$$

Initiation and Adjustment of Insulin for Patients with Type 2 Diabetes

In patients with type 2 diabetes, basal insulin is often initiated when a patient fails to reach glycemic targets with multiple oral agents. Basal insulin is started at 0.1 – 0.2 units/kg/day (using ABW) or 10 units/day. This dose is titrated by 10 – 15% or 2 – 4 units once or twice weekly to reach the fasting blood glucose goal. If the A1C remains above goal, despite control of fasting glucose levels, the addition of one to three injections of rapid-acting mealtime insulin (basal-bolus strategy) and titration to achieve post-prandial targets is recommended. Alternative strategies are to try a GLP-1 agonist with basal insulin, or use a pre-mixed insulin product twice daily. If converting between insulin agents, use the conversions shown; these assume blood glucose is under good control.

Insulin Conversions

INSULIN TYPE	CONVERSION
Rapid-acting to regular (or vice versa)	1:1
NPH to long-acting (or vice versa)	1:1
NPH BID to glargine	↓ daily dose by 20%
Long-acting to long-acting*	1:1

**Lantus to Toujeo: may need to increase Toujeo dose*

Insulin Stability

For all insulins: discard insulin if it is frozen, discolored, or contains particulates. If a needle is attached for use, discard used needle immediately after use. Do not store under direct sunlight or heat. All insulins should be refrigerated until first use. If refrigerated and unopened, the insulin is stable until the expiration date on the label. Stability of the different injectable products at room temperature, including insulins, is shown in the table.

Insulin Administration Counseling

- Wash your hands and lay out all supplies.
- Check the insulin for any discoloration, crystals or particles.
- If the insulin is a suspension, roll the bottle gently between the hands (do not shake). If it is a pen, invert it 4 – 5 times.
- Clean the injection site (area of the skin) and wipe the top of the insulin vial (if using) with an alcohol swab.
- If using a vial, inject an equal volume of air into the vial before withdrawing the insulin out. Make sure to limit bubbles in the syringe.
  - If mixing two types of insulin in the same syringe, the clear insulin should be drawn into the syringe before the cloudy insulin.
- The abdomen is the preferred injection site. For alternate sites, see the diagram on the following page. Inject at least two fingers away from the belly button.
- Rotate injection sites around the abdomen regularly to prevent inflammation and/or thinning of fat tissue.
- To inject subcutaneously, gently pinch a 2 inch portion of the skin and fat between your thumb and first finger and insert the needle all the way at a 90 degree angle (or 45 degrees if you are thin).
  - If using a syringe, inject the insulin by pushing all the way down on the plunger then remove the needle slowly.
  - If using an insulin pen, turn the dosing knob to select the correct number of units, inject the insulin and count 5 – 10 seconds before removing the needle.
- Properly dispose of needles or entire syringes in a sharps container. These containers can be taken to any proper disposal site (e.g., public health clinic or local needle exchange). Ask the local health department for guidelines or visit www.safeneedledisposal.org. See the Medication Safety & Quality Improvement chapter for more information.

Syringe and Needle Sizes

Choosing the correct syringe is important. The smallest syringe that will hold the dose should be used. The smaller the syringe barrel, the easier it is to read the scale markings in order to draw up an accurate dose. This is also helpful for patients with vision problems. If the patient's largest dose is close to the maximum syringe capacity, choose the next syringe size up.

STABILITY OF INJECTABLES AT ROOM TEMPERATURE

3 Days

Afrezza (inhaled insulin) – if opened

10 Days

Afrezza (inhaled insulin) – if unopened
Humalog 50/50, 75/25 and *Humulin 70/30* (pens)

14 days

Humulin N (pens)
Novolog 70/30 (pen)
Soliqua 100/33 (pen)
Trulicity and *Adlyxin* (pens)

21 days

Xultophy 100/3.6 (pen)

~4 Weeks (28-31 days)

Apidra, Humalog, Novolog (vials and pens)
Humulin R (U-100 vial)
Humulin R U-500 (pen)
Humulin N (vial)
Humalog 50/50, 75/25, Novolog 70/30, Humulin 70/30 (vials)
Lantus (vial and pen), *Basaglar* (pen)
Bydureon (vial and pen), *Tanzeum, Symlin, Victoza, Byetta* (pens)

~6 Weeks (40-42 days)

Humulin R U-500 (vial)
Novolin R (U-100 vial)
Novolin N (vial)
Novolin 70/30 (vial)
Toujeo (pen)
Levemir (vial and pen)

8 Weeks (56 days)

Tresiba (pens)

Syringe Size/Volume

- If injecting < 30 units of insulin, use a 0.3 mL syringe (markings in 1 unit increments).
- If injecting 30 – 49 units of insulin, use a 0.5 mL syringe (markings in 1 unit increments).
- If injecting ≥ 50 units of insulin, use a 1 mL syringe (markings in 2 unit increments; holds up to 100 units).

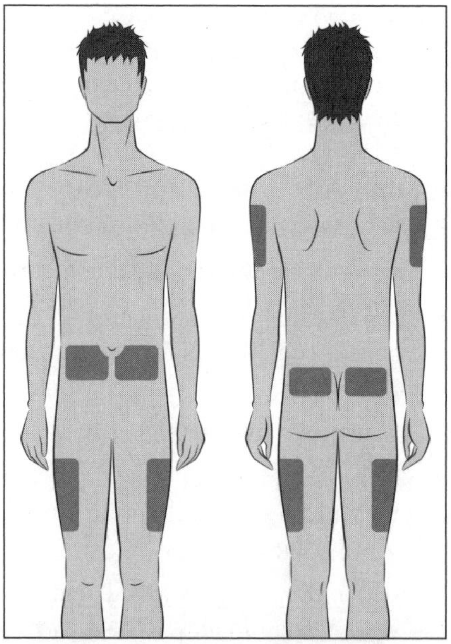

Needle Length

- ½″ (12.7 mm), 5/16″ (8 mm), 3/16″ (5 mm), 5/32″ (4 mm).
- Many users feel that shorter needles are more comfortable. Use ½″ needles for obese patients or if back leakage of insulin is a problem.

Insulin Injection Sites

Insulin absorption is fastest and most predictable when injected into the abdomen followed by the posterior upper arm, superior buttocks area and lateral thigh area; because of these variations, injections should be rotated within a specific region to limit fluctuations in blood glucose.

SLIDING SCALE EXAMPLE

BLOOD GLUCOSE READING (MG/DL)	INSTRUCTION
< 60	Hold insulin; contact MD
150-200	Give 2 units of insulin
201-250	Give 4 units of insulin
251-300	Give 6 units of insulin
301-350	Give 8 units of insulin
351-400	Give 10 units of insulin
401-450	Call MD

Hospitalized Patients

Hospitalized patients on insulin should have BG maintained between 140 – 180 mg/dL. More stringent goals may be appropriate for select patients. The use of sliding scale insulin (SSI) alone in the hospital setting is strongly discouraged. A more physiological insulin regimen including basal, bolus and correction dose insulin is preferred over sliding scales, however many hospitals currently use sliding scales despite this being against ADA and AACE recommendations.

HYPOGLYCEMIA

Normal fasting blood glucose in a person without diabetes is 70 – 99 mg/dL. Hypoglycemia is defined as a blood glucose < 70 mg/dL. The lower the level, the more symptomatic the patient. Seizures, coma and death can occur if the blood glucose drops below 20 mg/dL.

Hypoglycemic Symptoms

Hypoglycemic symptoms include dizziness, headache, anxiety, irritability, shakiness, diaphoresis (sweating), hunger, nausea, confusion, lack of coordination, tremors, palpitations or fast heart rate, and blurred vision.

Drugs That Cause Hypoglycemia

Insulin is the primary cause of drug-induced hypoglycemia. Drugs that make the body secrete more insulin, such as SUs and meglitinides (insulin secretagogues), are also high-risk for causing hypoglycemia. Pramlintide is high risk since it is used with insulin at mealtimes. Patients are at risk if food intake is decreased and mealtime insulin is not reduced appropriately, or if a patient continues taking mealtime insulin, SUs or meglitinides when not eating.

The GLP-1 agonists, DPP-4 inhibitors, TZDs and SGLT2 inhibitors can increase the risk of hypoglycemia, primarily in patients using a hypoglycemic agent (e.g., insulin or an insulin secretagogue); use in combination may necessitate a dose reduction. Some other drugs, not used to treat diabetes, that have package insert warnings for hypoglycemia are shown in the box. All beta-blockers can mask the symptoms of shakiness, palpitations and anxiety (sweating and hunger are not masked). That is why beta-blockers are sometimes used for stage fright. This can prevent prompt recognition of low blood glucose and can result in more severe hypoglycemia. The non-selective agents, such as carteolol, carvedilol, propranolol and others can also exacerbate insulin-induced hypoglycemia and delay recovery of blood glucose to normal levels.

SELECT DRUGS THAT CAN LOWER BLOOD GLUCOSE
Linezolid
Lorcaserin *(Belviq)*
Octreotide*
Pentamidine
Propranolol and other non-selective beta-blockers*
Quinine
Quinolones*

** Can also cause hyperglycemia (see Drug-Induced Hyperglycemia section)*

Hypoglycemia Treatment

Glucose is the preferred treatment of hypoglycemia, but any form of carbohydrate that contains glucose will raise blood sugar (see box). Added fat will slow absorption and prolong the hypoglycemia.

1. Consume 15 – 20 grams of glucose or simple carbohydrates.
2. Recheck blood glucose after 15 minutes.
3. If hypoglycemia continues, repeat treatment (step #1).
4. Once blood glucose returns to normal, the patient should eat a small meal or snack to prevent recurrence.

15 GRAMS OF SIMPLE CARBOHYDRATES USED TO TREAT HYPOGLYCEMIA
3-4 glucose tablets (follow package instructions)
1 serving of gel tube (follow package instructions)
2 tablespoons of raisins
4 ounces (1/2 cup) of juice or regular soda (not diet)
1 tablespoon sugar, honey, or corn syrup
8 ounces (1 cup) of milk

Glucagon

Glucagon should be prescribed for all patients at significant risk of severe hypoglycemia. Glucagon administration is not limited to healthcare professionals; caregivers and family members should be instructed on its administration. Glucagon *(GlucaGen)* is only used if the patient is unconscious or not conscious enough to self-treat the hypoglycemia. If using glucagon, place the patient in a lateral recumbent position (on side) to protect the airway and prevent choking when consciousness returns. Glucagon 1 mg is given by SC, IM or IV injection. Of note, glucagon must be reconstituted prior to administration. Once conscious, administer a carbohydrate source; this can be in the form of glucose given intravenously (Dextrose 25%, Dextrose 50%).

Recheck the blood glucose 15 minutes after treatment. If it is < 70 mg/dL, or if the patient is still symptomatic, give another dose of glucagon and check the blood glucose again in 15 minutes. All episodes of hypoglycemia are dangerous and should be reported to the physician. Hypoglycemia unawareness, or one or more episodes of severe hypoglycemia, should trigger re-evaluation of the treatment regimen.

SELF-MONITORING BLOOD GLUCOSE

Self-monitoring blood glucose (SMBG) is important to prevent hypo- and hyperglycemia and associated complications. Patients on multiple-dose insulin or insulin pump therapy should perform SMBG prior to meals and snacks, occasionally post-prandially, at bedtime, prior to exercise or other critical tasks such as driving, when low blood glucose is suspected, and after treating low blood glucose, until normoglycemic. For patients using less frequent insulin injections, non-insulin therapies or medical nutrition therapy, SMBG may be useful as an indicator of treatment success.

Preparing to Test

- Some blood glucose meter devices require calibration before first use. Recalibration may be needed if a new package of strips is opened, the meter is left in extreme conditions, the meter is dropped, or if the level does not match how the patient is feeling.
- Read the test strip packaging to make sure the strips are compatible with the glucose meter.
- Do not use test strips from a damaged or expired bottle.
- Enter the correct calibration code, if required.
- Thoroughly wash hands vigorously with warm water and mild soap to clean the site and increase circulation at the fingertips.
- Dry hands thoroughly since water can affect the blood sample and create an error or false reading.
- Allow arm to hang down at the side of the body for 30 seconds so blood can pool into the fingertips.

Testing Blood Glucose

- Use a new test strip for each test.
- Insert the test strip completely into the glucose meter prior to applying the blood sample.
- In order to minimize pain, lance the finger on the side (where there are fewer nerves), instead of on the finger pads. Keep the hand below the level of the heart.
- Make sure there is a large enough drop of blood as directed by the meter. Allow the blood to flow freely and do not squeeze the finger.
- Apply the blood to the test strip.
- Properly dispose of lancets in a sharps container.

Maintaining Blood Glucose Meter

- Clean the meter regularly.
- Test the meter regularly with the control solution.
- Store the meter and supplies properly, away from heat and humidity.
- Keep extra batteries charged and ready.
- Close the lid of the strips container after every use, as air and moisture can destroy the strips and affect results.

Alternative Site Testing

- Select meters are approved for testing on other areas, most commonly the forearm, palm or thigh. Always verify which sites are appropriate according to the individual meter instructions. A different end cap on the lancing device may be required for alternative site testing.
- Alternative sites, such as the forearm or thigh, can give a test result that is 20 to 30 minutes old. Alternative testing sites are not recommended in cases where the blood glucose is changing rapidly (e.g., after a meal or after exercise) or when hypoglycemia is suspected.

HYPERGLYCEMIC CRISES

Diabetic Ketoacidosis

Diabetic ketoacidosis (DKA) is a hyperglycemic crisis that most commonly presents in patients with type 1 diabetes and rarely in type 2 diabetes. DKA occurs due to insulin non-compliance (e.g., ran out, lost medication, homeless, refused to take), subtherapeutic insulin dosing, a condition that can cause hyperglycemia (e.g., a stressor, such as infection, MI or trauma), or as the initial presentation in a patient with type 1 diabetes. Ketones are present because triglycerides and amino acids are used for energy, which produces free fatty acids (FFAs). Glucagon converts the FFAs into ketones. Normally, insulin prevents this conversion; but in DKA, insulin is absent.

- DKA symptoms: BG > 250 mg/dL, ketones (urine and serum, or picked up as "fruity" breath), with an anion gap metabolic acidosis (arterial pH < 7.35, anion gap > 12).
- DKA treatment:
  - Fluids first: normal saline (NS) infused at a rate of 15 – 20 mL/kg/hr (1 – 2 liters) during the first hour. Continue fluids (the type of fluid will be based on hydration, Na and BG status). When blood glucose reaches 250 mg/dL, D5W with 1/2 NS is used (along with insulin).
  - Give regular insulin 0.15 units/kg bolus, followed by an IV infusion at a rate of 0.1 units/kg/hr.
  - Potassium replacement when needed (to prevent hypokalemia due to intracellular shifts caused by insulin). Monitor K frequently.
  - Sodium bicarbonate may be used if pH < 7.

Hyperglycemia Hyperosmolar State

Hyperglycemia hyperosmolar state (HHS) is a hyperglycemic crisis that most often occurs in type 2 diabetes due to some type of severe stress. Serum ketones would be negligible or not present because the patient with type 2 diabetes has enough insulin to suppress ketogenesis. The blood glucose is usually much higher at presentation because acidosis is not present and the patient can endure the symptoms longer.

- HHS symptoms: BG > 600 mg/dL, high serum osmolality > 320 mOsm/L, extreme dehydration, altered consciousness (confusion, dizziness, seizures), pH > 7.3, bicarbonate > 15 mEq/L.
- HHS Treatment: NS and insulin; potassium (as needed).

PRACTICE CASE

PATIENT PROFILE

Patient Name	EH							
Address	577 Ridge Rd							
Age	21	Sex	F	Race	White	Height	5'9"	Weight 65 kg
Allergies	NKDA							

DIAGNOSES

Type 1 Diabetes
General Anxiety Disorder

Date	Prescriber	Drug & Strength	Sig
4/26	Callihan	Apidra SoloStar	3 units AC meals
4/26	Callihan	Lantus SoloStar	15 units QHS
4/26	Callihan	Ativan	1 mg BID
5/8	Wong	Regular Insulin 100 units/100 mL NS	6.5 units/hr x 6 hrs
5/8	Wong	0.9% NaCl	15 mL/kg/hr x 1 hr, followed by
5/8	Wong	0.45% NaCl	500 mL/hr x 2 hrs, followed by
		D5W1/2NS	200 mL/hr x 3 hrs

LAB/DIAGNOSTIC TESTS

Test	Normal Value	Results		
		Date	Date	Date
		5/8 @ 1300	5/8 @ 1400	5/8 @ 1500
NA	135-146 mEq/L	139	140	141
K	3.5-5.3 mEq/L	4.5	3.9	3.3
CL	98-110 mEq/L	107	106	107
HCO3-	22-28 mEq/L	17	17	18
BUN	7-25 mg/dL	45	39	32
Creatinine	0.6-1.2 mg/dL	0.8	0.7	0.9
Glucose	65-99 mg/dL	593	361	301
Calcium	8.6-10.2 mg/dL			
WBC	4-11 cells/mm^3			
Urine ketones		Positive		

Questions

1. Which of the following is the most likely diagnosis for EH on 5/8?

   a. Sepsis
   b. Diabetic ketoacidosis
   c. Hyperglycemia hyperosmolar state
   d. Serotonin syndrome
   e. Insulin overdose

2. What is EH's anion gap on 5/8 at 1300?

   a. 16
   b. 15
   c. 13
   d. 9
   e. 8

3. On 5/8, how much total fluid volume from all sources did EH receive?

   a. 2,614 mL
   b. 2,575 mL
   c. 1,615 mL
   d. 1,600 mL
   e. 1,000 mL

4. According to EH's labs on 5/8 at 1500, which of the following should be administered?

   a. Magnesium sulfate
   b. Calcium gluconate
   c. 3% hypertonic saline
   d. 5% albumin
   e. Potassium chloride

5. Per the ADA guidelines, what is EH's goal blood glucose while she remains in the hospital?

   a. < 180 mg/dL
   b. 140 – 180 mg/dL
   c. 110 – 140 mg/dL
   d. 100 – 120 mg/dL
   e. 80 – 130 mg/dL

6. EH is being transitioned to her outpatient regimen but the hospital does not have *Apidra* or *Lantus* on formulary. Which therapeutic interchange would be most appropriate?

   a. Tresiba, Toujeo
   b. Humulin R U-500, Toujeo
   c. Humulin N, Levemir
   d. Humalog, Levemir
   e. Humalog 70/30, Novolog

Questions 7-11 do not apply to the case.

7. A patient currently uses 30 units of *Lantus* daily and 10 units of *Humalog* with breakfast, lunch, and dinner. She is going to be started on pramlinitide and needs to be counseled on how to adjust her dose of insulin. Select the correct adjustments.

   a. Reduce *Lantus* to 15 units and *Humalog* to 5 units with meals.
   b. Reduce *Lantus* to 10 units and *Humalog* to 5 units with meals.
   c. Reduce *Lantus* to 15 units and keep *Humalog* at 10 units with meals.
   d. Do not adjust *Lantus* and reduce *Humalog* to 5 units with meals.
   e. Do not adjust *Lantus* or *Humalog.*

8. A patient is taking *Novolog Mix* 70/30, 10 units twice a day. How many units of insulin aspart does the patient inject in the morning?

   a. 20 units
   b. 10 units
   c. 7 units
   d. 6 units
   e. 3 units

9. Which of the following insulins has the shortest duration?

   a. Glulisine
   b. Detemir
   c. Regular
   d. Glargine
   e. NPH

10. A patient is prescribed *Glucovance*. What are the individual components?

   a. Metformin/glyburide
   b. Metformin/pioglitazone
   c. Metformin/sitagliptin
   d. Metformin/repaglinide
   e. Metformin/glipizide

11. A patient with newly diagnosed Type 1 diabetes is to be initiated on a basal-bolus insulin regimen with *Levemir* and *Novolog FlexPen*. If the patient weighs 50 kg, how much *Levemir* should be injected daily?

   a. 5 units
   b. 10 units
   c. 15 units
   d. 20 units
   e. 30 units

Answers

1-b, 2-b, 3-a, 4-e, 5-b, 6-d, 7-d, 8-e, 9-a, 10-a, 11-c

40

THYROID DISORDERS

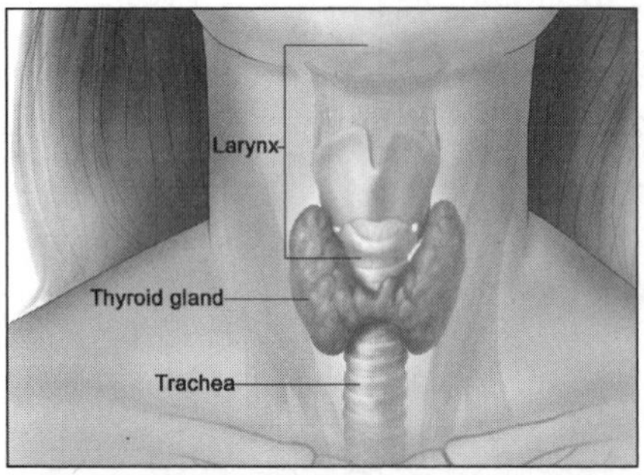

GUIDELINES/REFERENCES

2016 American Thyroid Association Guidelines for Diagnosis and Management of Hyperthyroidism and Other Causes of Thyrotoxicosis. *Thyroid.* 2016; 26(10):1343-1422.

Guidelines for the Treatment of Hypothyroidism: Prepared by the American Thyroid Association Task Force on Thyroid Hormone Replacement. http://online.liebertpub.com/doi/full/10.1089/thy.2014.0028 (accessed 2016 Nov 25).

Garber JR, Cobin RH, Gharib H, et al. Clinical Practice Guidelines for Hypothyroidism in Adults: Cosponsored by the American Association of Clinical Endocrinologists and the American Thyroid Association. *Endocr Pract.* 2012; 18(6):988-1028.

BACKGROUND

The thyroid gland is a butterfly-shaped organ composed of two symmetrical lobes, one on each side of the windpipe, connected by the isthmus. The thyroid gland synthesizes and releases thyroid hormones, and is the only organ containing cells that have the ability to absorb iodine. Thyroid hormones affect metabolism, brain development, respiration, cardiac and nervous system functions, body temperature, muscle strength, skin dryness, menstrual cycles, body weight, and cholesterol levels. Hyperthyroidism (overactive thyroid) and hypothyroidism (underactive thyroid) are the most common problems of the thyroid gland. Hypothyroidism occurs more commonly in women, and its incidence increases with age.

PATHOPHYSIOLOGY

The thyroid gland produces two thyroid hormones, triiodothyronine (T3) and thyroxine (T4). Iodine and tyrosine are used to form both T3 and T4. Less than 20% of T3 is produced by the thyroid gland; T3 is primarily formed from the breakdown of T4 by peripheral tissues. T3 is more potent than T4 but has a shorter half-life. Thyroid hormone production is regulated by thyroid-stimulating hormone (TSH or thyrotropin), which is secreted by the pituitary gland in the brain. Elevations in T4 levels will inhibit the secretion of TSH, and create a negative feedback loop. Since T3 and T4 are transported in the blood and bound by proteins, it is important to measure the free T4 (FT4) levels as this is the active form. In hypothyroidism, there is a deficiency in T4, and consequently,

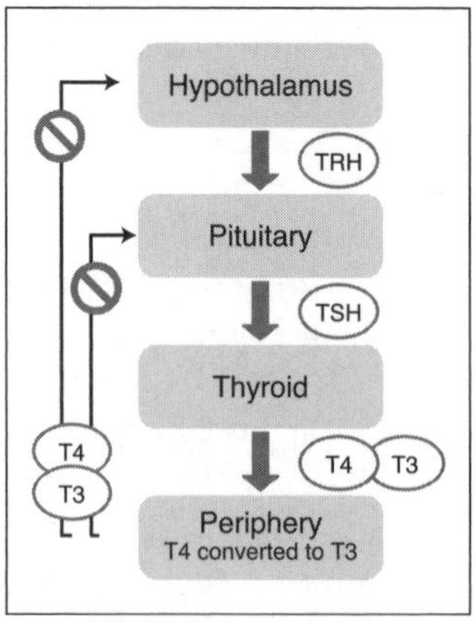

TRH = thyrotropin-releasing hormone

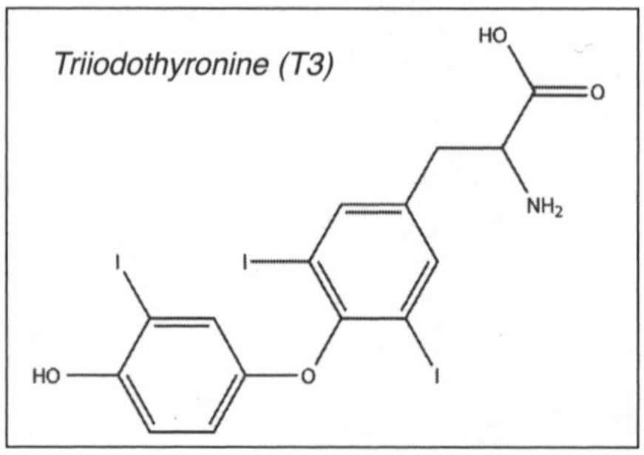

an elevation in TSH. In hyperthyroidism, there is over-secretion of T4, and consequently, a decrease in TSH.

HYPOTHYROIDISM

In hypothyroidism, the decrease in thyroid hormone causes the body to slow down and the classic symptoms of low metabolism appear (fatigue and weight gain). Other signs and symptoms are included in the box to the right. The most common cause of hypothyroidism is Hashimoto's disease, an autoimmune condition in which a patient's antibodies attack their own thyroid gland. Drugs and other conditions that can cause hypothyroidism are included in the box. Complications of hypothyroidism include depression, infertility and cardiovascular disease. When hypothyroidism decompensates or goes untreated for a long period, myxedema coma can result. Myxedema coma is a life-threatening emergency characterized by poor circulation, hypothermia, and hypometabolism. Due to unpredictable absorption of oral thyroid hormone from the gastrointestinal tract, intravenous thyroid hormone products should be administered.

S/SX OF HYPOTHYROIDISM

Cold intolerance/sensitivity	Myalgias
Dry skin	Weakness
Fatigue	Depression
Muscle cramps	Bradycardia
Voice changes	Coarseness or loss of hair
Constipation	Menorrhagia (heavier than normal menstrual periods)
Weight gain	Memory and mental impairment
Goiter (possible, can be due to low iodine intake)	

SELECT DRUGS AND CONDITIONS THAT CAN CAUSE HYPOTHYROIDISM

Hashimoto's disease – most common cause

Pituitary failure

Surgical removal of part or all of the thyroid gland

Congenital hypothyroidism

Thyroid gland ablation with radioactive iodine

External irradiation

Iodine deficiency

Drugs (e.g., amiodarone, carbamazepine, eslicarbazepine, interferons, lithium, oxcarbazepine, phenytoin, tyrosine kinase inhibitors – most notably sunitinib)

Diagnosis

Low free thyroxine (↓ FT4): normal range 0.9 – 2.3 ng/dL

High thyroid stimulating hormone (↑ TSH): normal range 0.3 – 3 mIU/L

Screening for hypothyroidism should be considered in patients > 60 years old.

Monitoring Parameters

TSH is the primary screening test for thyroid function and it is the most reliable therapeutic endpoint for treatment. Check TSH levels (rarely serum FT4) and clinical symptoms every 4 – 6 weeks until levels are normal, then 4 – 6 months later, then yearly. It is important to monitor as the person ages; they may need a dose reduction. Too high of a dose of thyroid hormone replacement in elderly patients leads to atrial fibrillation and fractures. Serum FT4 is monitored, in addition to TSH, in central hypothyroidism (rare) because the defect is pituitary production of TSH. FT4 is also monitored when treating hypothyroidism in pregnancy.

Pregnancy and Hypothyroidism

Levothyroxine is FDA Pregnancy Category A. Pregnant women with thyroid hormone deficiency or TSH elevation during pregnancy may have children at risk of impairment in their intellectual function and motor skills, unless properly treated. Pregnant women being treated with thyroid hormone replacement will require a 30 – 50% increase in the dose throughout the course of their pregnancy. The mother will need an elevated dose for several months after giving birth. In 2011, the guidelines called for more aggressive control of hypothyroidism in pregnancy. Preferably, treatment should start prior to pregnancy.

Drug Treatment

The goals of therapy are to resolve signs and symptoms of hypothyroidism, normalize serum TSH, and avoid overtreatment (causing hyperthyroidism). Patients should be counseled on clinical symptoms of both hypo- and hyperthyroidism as the dose will be titrated to the individual's needs. Levothyroxine (T4) is the drug of choice and current recommendations encourage the use of a consistent preparation for an individual patient to minimize variability from refill to refill. There are patients who state they just do not "feel right" on T4 alone, and may supplement with other formulations, such as liothyronine (T3, *Cytomel* and *Triostat*) or desiccated thyroid (T3 and T4, *Armour Thyroid*). Desiccated thyroid is not favored since the preparations can contain variable amounts, although newer formulations have become standardized. This is called "natural thyroid" and it is dosed in grains. Some patients choose to use these alternatives alone.

Levothyroxine should be taken with water consistently at least 60 minutes before breakfast or at bedtime (at least 3 hours after the last meal) for optimal absorption. It should be stored properly and patients should be counseled regarding drug interactions.

Iodine supplementation, including kelp or other iodine-containing functional foods, is not required in the U.S. because most of the salt has iodine added (iodized salt). This has eliminated almost all cases of iodine deficiency goiter. Individuals who are restricting salt intake can consume foods high in iodine (dairy, seafood, meat, some breads), and can take a multivitamin containing iodine.

Hypothyroidism Treatment

DRUG	DOSING	SAFETY/SIDE EFFECTS/MONITORING
Levothyroxine (T4) ***(Synthroid**, Levothroid, Levoxyl, Tirosint, Unithroid)* Capsule, tablet, injection Available strengths: 13, 25, 50, 75, 88, 100, 112, 125, 137, 150, 175, 200, 300 mcg Check the therapeutic equivalence of a generic to a brand in the *Orange Book*. Not all generic levothyroxine formulations are A-rated to various brands.	Full replacement dose = 1.6 mcg/kg/day (IBW) Start with full replacement dose in otherwise healthy, young (< 50 years of age) and middle age patients with markedly ↑ TSH. Start with partial replacement dose in milder hypothyroidism and those with comorbidities. If known CAD, start with 12.5-25 mcg daily. Elderly often need 20-25% less per kg; may require < 1 mcg/kg/day	**BOXED WARNING** Thyroid supplements are ineffective and potentially toxic when used for the treatment of obesity or for weight reduction, especially in euthyroid patients. High doses can cause serious or even life-threatening toxic effects particularly when used with some anorectic drugs (e.g., sympathomimetic amines). **CONTRAINDICATIONS** Acute MI, thyrotoxicosis, uncorrected adrenal insufficiency **WARNINGS** ↓ dose in cardiovascular disease (chronic hypothyroidism predisposes to coronary artery disease), ↓ bone mineral density which can lead to osteoporosis **SIDE EFFECTS** If patient is euthyroid, no side effects should exist. If dose is too high, patient will experience hyperthyroid symptoms such as ↑ HR, palpitations, sweating, weight loss, arrhythmias, irritability, others. **MONITORING** Check TSH levels (rarely FT4) and clinical symptoms every 4-6 weeks until levels are normal, then 4-6 months later, then yearly. Monitor as the patient ages; dose reduction may be necessary. Assessment of serum FT4, in addition to TSH, can be used selectively in some patients. **SEE NOTES ON NEXT PAGE**

Hypothyroidism Treatment continued

DRUG	DOSING	SAFETY/SIDE EFFECTS/MONITORING
Thyroid, Desiccated USP (T3 and T4) ***(Armour Thyroid,** Nature-Throid, Westhroid, NP Thyroid, WP Thyroid)* Tablet	Start 15-30 mg daily (15 mg in cardiac disease); titrate in 15 mg increments. Usual dose is 60-120 mg daily	**SEE WARNINGS, SIDE EFFECTS AND MONITORING IN PREVIOUS TABLE** **NOTES** Pregnancy Category A Highly protein bound (> 99%) Levothyroxine is the drug of choice due to chemical stability, once-daily dosing, low cost, lack of antigenicity and more uniform potency
Liothyronine (T3) *(Cytomel, Triostat)* Tablet, injection	Start 25 mcg daily; titrate in 12.5-25 mcg increments. Usual dose is 25-75 mcg daily	**Levothyroxine IV** Use immediately upon reconstitution. IV to PO ratio is 0.75:1
Liotrix (T3 and T4 in 1:4 ratio) *(Thyrolar)* Tablet	Start 25 mcg levothyroxine/6.25 mcg liothyronine daily. Usual dose is 50-100 mcg levothyroxine/12.5-25 mcg liothyronine	**Thyroid USP** Natural porcine-derived thyroid that contains both T3 and T4; less predictable potency and stability. Not preferred, but some feel better using it **Liothyronine** Shorter t½ causes fluctuations in T3 levels

Levothyroxine Drug Interactions

STUDY TIP: LEVOTHYROXINE TABLET COLORS

Orangutans Will Vomit On You Right Before They Become Large, Proud Giants.

25 mcg – orange
50 mcg – white (no dye)
75 mcg – violet
88 mcg – olive
100 mcg – yellow
112 mcg – rose
125 mcg – brown
137 mcg – turquoise
150 mcg – blue
175 mcg – lilac
200 mcg – pink
300 mcg – green

Drugs that ↓ Thyroid Hormone Levels

- These drugs can ↓ absorption:
  - Aluminum (antacids), calcium, cholestyramine, iron, magnesium, multivitamins (containing ADEK, folate, iron), orlistat *(Xenical, Alli)*, sevelamer, sodium polystyrene *(Kayexalate)*, sucralfate: separate doses by 4 hours from thyroid replacement therapy
  - Lanthanum: separate doses by 2 hours from thyroid replacement therapy
  - Patiromer *(Veltassa)*: separate doses by 6 hours from thyroid replacement therapy
- Estrogen, SSRIs and hepatic inducers ↓ thyroid hormone levels
- Beta-blockers, amiodarone, systemic steroids, and propylthiouracil (PTU) can ↓ the effectiveness of levothyroxine by ↓ the conversion of T4 to T3
- Thyroid hormone is highly-protein bound (> 99%). Drugs that can cause protein-binding site displacement include salicylates (> 2 g/day), heparin, phenytoin, NSAIDs, others

Thyroid hormone can change concentrations/effects of these drugs:

- ↑ effect of anticoagulants (e.g., ↑ PT/INR with warfarin)
- ↓ digoxin levels
- ↓ theophylline levels
- ↓ effect of antidiabetic agents

Levothyroxine Counseling

- Levothyroxine is a replacement for a hormone that is normally produced by your body to regulate your energy and metabolism. Levothyroxine is given when the thyroid does not produce enough of this hormone on its own.
- There are many medicines that can alter levothyroxine effects; tell the pharmacist about all medications you are taking. This includes over-the-counter vitamins, supplements and heartburn medications.
- Different brands of levothyroxine may not work the same. If you get a prescription refill and your new pills look different, ask the pharmacist.
- This medicine is safe to use while you are pregnant. It is also safe to use while you are breast-feeding a baby. It does pass into breast milk, but it is not harmful to a nursing infant.
- Tell your healthcare provider if you become pregnant during treatment; it is likely that your dose will need to be increased during pregnancy or if you plan to breast-feed.
- Take this medication with water 60 minutes before breakfast or at bedtime at least 3 hours after your last meal.
- If you are taking other medicines on an empty stomach first thing in the morning, discuss the best dosing with your pharmacist. Medications for your bones (osteoporosis) like *Actonel* or *Fosamax* should be taken 30 minutes before your thyroid medicine.
- Some patients will notice a slight reduction in symptoms within 1 to 2 weeks, but the full effect from therapy is often delayed for a month or two before people start to feel normal.
- Even if you feel well, you still need to take this medicine every day for the rest of your life to replace the thyroid hormone your body cannot produce.
- To be sure the dose being used is optimal for you, your blood will need to be tested on a regular basis (at least annually).

HYPERTHYROIDISM

Hyperthyroidism (overactive thyroid or thyrotoxicosis) occurs when there is over-production of thyroid hormones. Instead of low FT4 and high TSH, FT4 is high and TSH is low and symptoms are nearly opposite of those seen in hypothyroidism. Hyperthyroidism can significantly accelerate metabolism, causing sudden weight loss, a rapid or irregular heartbeat, sweating, nervousness, irritability, diarrhea and insomnia. Goiter and exophthalmos (protrusion of the eyeballs) can occur. Without treatment, hyperthyroidism can lead to tachycardia, arrhythmias, heart failure and osteoporosis. No one should use thyroid hormone to lose weight; it can lead to irritability and severe cardiac complications.

Causes

The most common cause of hyperthyroidism is Graves' disease, which tends to occur in females in their 30's and 40's. Graves' disease is an autoimmune disorder (like Hashimoto's) but instead of destroying the gland, the antibodies stimulate the thyroid to produce too much T4. Less commonly, a single nodule is responsible for the excess hormone secretion. Thyroiditis (inflammation of the thyroid) can also cause

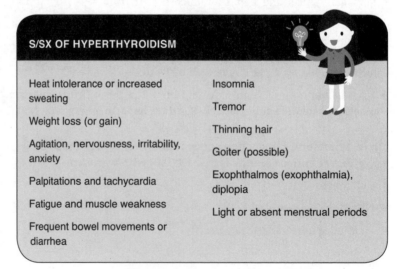

S/SX OF HYPERTHYROIDISM

Heat intolerance or increased sweating	Insomnia
Weight loss (or gain)	Tremor
Agitation, nervousness, irritability, anxiety	Thinning hair
Palpitations and tachycardia	Goiter (possible)
Fatigue and muscle weakness	Exophthalmos (exophthalmia), diplopia
Frequent bowel movements or diarrhea	Light or absent menstrual periods

hyperthyroidism. Drugs that can cause hyperthyroidism include iodine, amiodarone and interferons. Iodine-induced hyperthyroidism can occur after intake of excess iodine in the diet, exposure to radiographic contrast media, or medications. Excess iodine increases the synthesis and release of thyroid hormone in iodine-deficient patients and in older patients with preexisting multinodular goiters. Hyperthyroidism can also occur in patients who take excessive doses of any of the available forms of thyroid hormone.

Drug Treatment

Treatment involves anti-thyroid medications, destroying part of the gland via radioactive iodine (RAI-131) or surgery. RAI-131 has historically been considered the preferred treatment in Graves' disease, but all three treatment options are effective and relatively safe. With any option, the patient can be treated with beta blockers first for symptom control (to reduce palpitations, tremors and tachycardia). Propylthiouracil (PTU) or methimazole can be used as a temporary measure until surgery is complete. Initially, when treating with drugs, it takes 1 – 3 months at higher doses to control symptoms, at which point the dose is reduced to prevent hypothyroidism from occurring.

Hyperthyroidism Treatment

DRUG	DOSING	SAFETY/SIDE EFFECTS/MONITORING
Thionamides – inhibit synthesis of thyroid hormones by blocking the oxidation of iodine in the thyroid gland; PTU also inhibits peripheral conversion of T4 to T3		
Propylthiouracil (PTU) Tablet	50-150mg Q8H initially until euthyroid (higher doses for more severe hyperthyroidism), followed by dose reduction	**BOXED WARNING** Severe liver injury and acute liver failure (with PTU) Safety issue – see Pregnancy chapter. PTU preferred in 1st trimester – change to methimazole for 2nd and 3rd trimesters (due to increased risk of liver toxicity from PTU and fetal abnormalities from methimazole) **SIDE EFFECTS** GI upset, headache, rash (exfoliative dermatitis, pruritus), fever, constipation, loss of taste/taste perversion, drug-induced lupus erythematosus (DILE), lymphadenopathy, bleeding Hepatitis, agranulocytosis (rare): see MD at once for yellow skin, abdominal pain, high fever, or severe sore throat **MONITORING** CBC, LFTs, PT and thyroid function tests (TSH, FT4, total T3) every 4-6 weeks until euthyroid **NOTES** PTU is preferred in thyroid storm Take with food to reduce GI upset Patient must monitor for liver toxicity (abdominal pain, yellow skin/eyes, dark urine, nausea, weakness) PTU is not a first line treatment for hyperthyroidism except in patients who cannot tolerate other options or conditions where other antithyroid therapies are contraindicated.
MethIMAzole *(Tapazole)* Tablet	Mild hyperthyroidism: 5 mg Q8H initially until euthyroid initially until euthyroid (↑ doses for more severe hyperthyroidism), then 5-15 mg daily	

Hyperthyroidism Treatment continued

DRUG	DOSING	SAFETY/SIDE EFFECTS/MONITORING
Iodides – temporarily inhibit secretion of thyroid hormones; T4 and T3 levels will be reduced for several weeks but effect will not be maintained		
Potassium iodide and iodine solution *(Lugol's Solution)* Oral solution	Preparation for thyroidectomy: 5-7 drops Q8H for 10 days prior to surgery (off-label)	**CONTRAINDICATIONS** Hypersensitivity to iodide or iodine; dermatitis herpetiformis; hypocomplementemic vasculitis, nodular thyroid condition with heart disease **SIDE EFFECTS** Rash, metallic taste, sore throat/gums, GI upset, urticaria, hypo/hyperthyroidism with prolonged use
Saturated solution of potassium iodide *(SSKI, ThyroShield)* Oral solution	Preparation for thyroidectomy: 1-2 drops Q8H for 10 days prior to surgery (off-label)	**MONITORING** Thyroid function tests, s/sx of hyperthyroidism **NOTES** Safety issue - see Pregnancy chapter Dilute in a glassful of water, juice, or milk. Take with food or milk to reduce GI upset *SSKI* is also used as an expectorant

Thionamide Drug Interactions

- Can ↓ the anticoagulant effect of warfarin; monitor.

POTASSIUM IODIDE USE AFTER EXPOSURE TO RADIATION

Potassium iodide (KI) blocks the accumulation of radioactive iodine in the thyroid gland; thus preventing thyroid cancer. Potassium iodide should be taken as soon as possible after radiation exposure on the advice of public health or emergency management personnel only. The correct dose must be used and higher doses do not offer greater protection. The doses below provide protection for 24 hours. If the radiation exposure is longer, refer to the CDC website for repeat-dose instructions. Iodized salt and foods do not contain enough iodine to block radioactive iodine and are not recommended.

- Birth – 1 month: 16.25 mg KI
- Infants and children between 1 month – 3 years: 32.5 mg KI
- Children 3 – 12 years: 65 mg KI
- Children > 12 – 18 years weighing < 68 kg: 65 mg KI
- Children > 12 – 18 years weighing ≥ 68 kg : 130 mg KI
- Adults: 130 mg KI

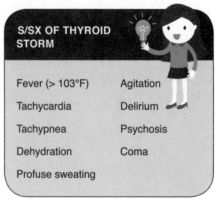

S/SX OF THYROID STORM

Fever (> 103°F)	Agitation
Tachycardia	Delirium
Tachypnea	Psychosis
Dehydration	Coma
Profuse sweating	

THYROID STORM

Thyroid storm is a life-threatening medical emergency characterized by decompensated hyperthyroidism that can be precipitated by infection, trauma, surgery, radio-active iodine treatment or non-adherence to antithyroid medication. The following treatment measures must be implemented promptly.

Drug Treatment

- Antithyroid drug therapy (PTU is preferred; 500 – 1,000 mg loading dose, then 250 mg PO Q4H) PLUS
    - Can crush tablets and administer through NG-tube if needed
    - Given ≥ 1 hour before iodide to block synthesis of thyroid hormone

- Inorganic iodide therapy such as *SSKI* 5 drops (in water or juice) PO Q6H or *Lugol's Solution* 4 – 8 drops PO Q6 – 8H PLUS
- Beta blocker (e.g., propranolol 40 – 80 mg PO Q6H) PLUS
- Systemic steroid (e.g., dexamethasone 2 – 4 mg PO Q6H) PLUS
- Aggressive cooling with acetaminophen and cooling blankets and other supportive treatments (e.g., antiarrhythmics, insulin, fluids, electrolytes, etc.)

PRACTICE CASE

MT is a 45 y/o white female who comes to the clinic complaining of more fatigue than normal and constipation. On exam, the patient has some dry skin patches and looks a bit depressed. Her past medical history is significant for GERD.

Allergies: NKDA

Medications:
Dexilant 30 mg capsule PO daily
Maalox 2 tablespoonfuls PRN heartburn

Vitals:
Height: 5'4" Weight: 122 lbs
BP: 139/82 mmHg HR: 62 BPM RR: 15 BPM Temp: 38°C Pain: 0/10

Labs: Na (mEq/L) = 138 (135 - 145)
K (mEq/L) = 4.5 (3.5 - 5)
Cl (mEq/L) = 98 (95 - 103)
HCO3 (mEq/L) = 29 (24 - 30)
BUN (mg/dL) = 11 (7 - 20)
SCr (mg/dL) = 0.9 (0.6 - 1.3)
Glucose (mg/dL) = 87 (100 - 125)
Ca (mg/dL) = 10.1 (8.5 - 10.5)
Mg (mEq/L) = 1.8 (1.3 - 2.1)
PO4 (mg/dL) = 3.0 (2.3 - 4.7)
TSH (mIU/L) = 44 (0.3 - 3)
Free T4 (ng/dL) = 0.5 (0.9 - 2.3)

Initiate therapy for new diagnosis of hypothyroidism and educate patient.

Questions

1. The physician is considering starting thyroid medication for MT. Which of the following options is considered most appropriate for initial therapy?

   a. *Levoxyl*
   b. *Armour Thyroid*
   c. *Thyrolar*
   d. RAI 131
   e. Propranolol

2. What is the full replacement starting dose of *Synthroid* for MT?

   a. 12.5 mcg daily
   b. 25 mg daily
   c. 75 mg daily
   d. 88 mcg daily
   e. 125 mg daily

Questions 3 – 10 do not relate to the case.

3. Which of the following medications can decrease the levels of levothyroxine? (Select **ALL** that apply.)
   a. Magnesium – Aluminum hydroxide *(Maalox)*
   b. Iron
   c. Warfarin
   d. *Kayexalate*
   e. *Dilantin*

4. Propylthiouracil is associated with which of the following serious adverse effects?
   a. Angioedema
   b. Liver failure
   c. Renal failure
   d. Rhabdomyolysis
   e. Priapism

5. What is the most common cause of hypothyroidism?
   a. Graves' disease
   b. Hashimoto's disease
   c. Surgery
   d. Amiodarone
   e. Lithium

6. A patient is beginning levothyroxine therapy. Patient counseling points should include the following:
   a. You should feel much better by this afternoon or tomorrow morning.
   b. Your healthcare provider will need to recheck your thyroid hormone levels in 4-6 weeks.
   c. If you get pregnant, stop using this medicine.
   d. A and C only
   e. All of the above

7. Which of the following are symptoms of hypothyroidism? (Select **ALL** that apply.)
   a. Fatigue
   b. Weight gain or increased difficulty losing weight
   c. Diarrhea
   d. Tachycardia
   e. Exophthalmos

8. Which of the following is the best way to instruct a patient to take levothyroxine?
   a. First thing in the morning, with food
   b. First thing in the morning, about 60 minutes before food or other medicines
   c. With the largest meal to reduce nausea
   d. With dinner since levothyroxine is sedating
   e. At bedtime

9. A female patient taking levothyroxine therapy plans to become pregnant. What change in her levothyroxine dose will be required during pregnancy?
   a. An increase in dose by 10-20%
   b. An increase in dose by 30-50%
   c. A decrease in dose by 10-20%
   d. A decrease in dose by 30-50%
   e. No change is required during pregnancy

10. What is the most common cause of hyperthyroidism?
   a. Hashimoto's disease
   b. Pituitary failure
   c. Lithium
   d. Amiodarone
   e. Graves' disease

Answers

1-a, 2-d, 3-a,b,d,e, 4-b, 5-b, 6-b, 7-a,b, 8-b, 9-b, 10-e

SYSTEMIC STEROIDS & AUTOIMMUNE CONDITIONS

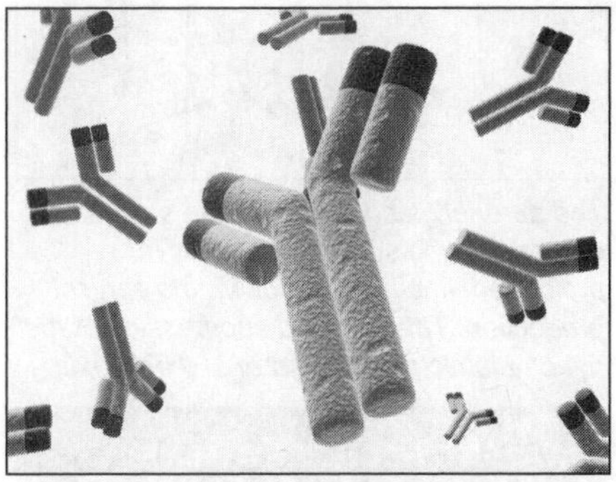

We gratefully acknowledge the assistance of Ann Snyder Franklin, PharmD, MEd, BCPS, in preparing this chapter.

GUIDELINES/REFERENCES

Singh, JA, Saag, KG, Bridges Jr, SL, et al. 2015 American College of Rheumatology Guideline for the Treatment of Rheumatoid Arthritis. Arthritis Care & Research DOI 10.1002/acr.22783. Available at http://www.rheumatology.org/Portals/0/Files/ACR%202015%20RA%20Guideline.pdf (accessed 2016 Oct 17).

King, A. Gluten Content of the Top 200 Medications: Follow-Up to the Influence of Gluten on a Patient's Medication Choices. *Hospital Pharmacy*. 2013;48(9): 736-743.

Hahn BH, McMahon MA, Wilkinson A, et al. American College of Rheumatology Guidelines for Screening, Treatment and Management of Lupus Nephritis. *Arthritis Care Res.* 2012;64(6):797-808.

Additional guidelines included with the video files (RxPrep Online).

SYSTEMIC STEROIDS

There are several big guns used to treat inflammation, including drugs that target the chemical pathway of the inflammation (various biologics), cancer drugs that have strong anti-inflammatory properties, steroids and NSAIDs. Steroids are strong anti-inflammatory drugs. NSAIDs are anti-inflammatory, but are weaker than steroids. Despite all the health risks with using chronic NSAIDs, they are safer than steroids used long-term. The side effect profile of steroids given both acutely and chronically is important to review.

Steroids are used:

1. To treat inflammation from a chronic inflammatory condition, such as rheumatoid arthritis, or topical conditions (with topical steroids), such as psoriasis.

2. To treat acute inflammation, such as a severe asthma attack or allergic reaction.

3. To treat various conditions that involve inflammation, including chemo-induced nausea.

4. To replace endogenous (our own) steroids that the adrenal gland is not producing in adequate amounts. There are two primary endogenous steroids that may need replacement:

- Cortisol, which can be replaced by any of the common steroids.
- Aldosterone, which is replaced by giving fludrocortisone, which mimics aldosterone. Addison's disease is the only common use of fludrocortisone.

Fludrocortisone has more mineralocorticoid activity, which is used to maintain a balance of water and electrolytes. This helps to keep blood pressure in balance. The others that are used commonly (prednisone and others) have more glucocorticoid activity, which has more anti-inflammatory effects. The rest of this section discusses only the commonly used glucocorticoids, which will be referred to as steroids.

Cushing's Syndrome

Cushing's syndrome develops when the adrenal gland produces too much cortisol, or when exogenous steroids are taken in doses higher than the amount of cortisol that would have been produced naturally. Steroids taken exogenously, for 2 weeks or longer, will cause the adrenal gland to stop producing cortisol, due to feedback inhibition. When the steroid is discontinued, it will need to be tapered off to give the adrenal gland time to resume cortisol production. Addison's can be thought of as the opposite of Cushing's; in Addison's, the adrenal gland is not making enough cortisol. If exogenous steroids are stopped suddenly, it causes "Addisonian Crisis," which can be fatal.

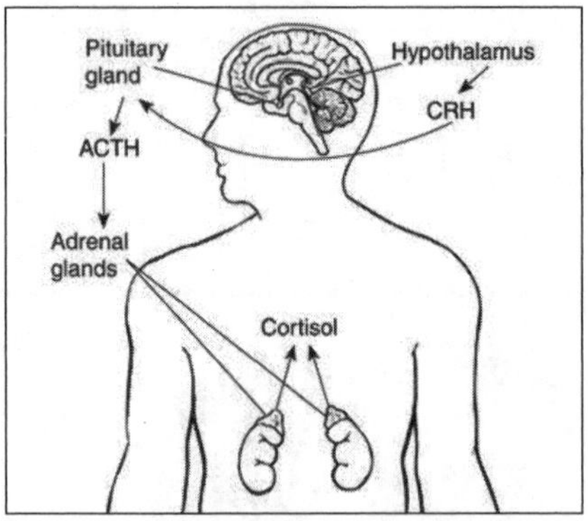

The adrenal gland produces the steroid cortisol. Taking systemic steroids for a prolonged time can shut down the cortisol production. This is called suppression of the hypothalamic-pituitary-adrenal (HPA) axis.

CUSHING'S SYNDROME:
High steroid intake or production

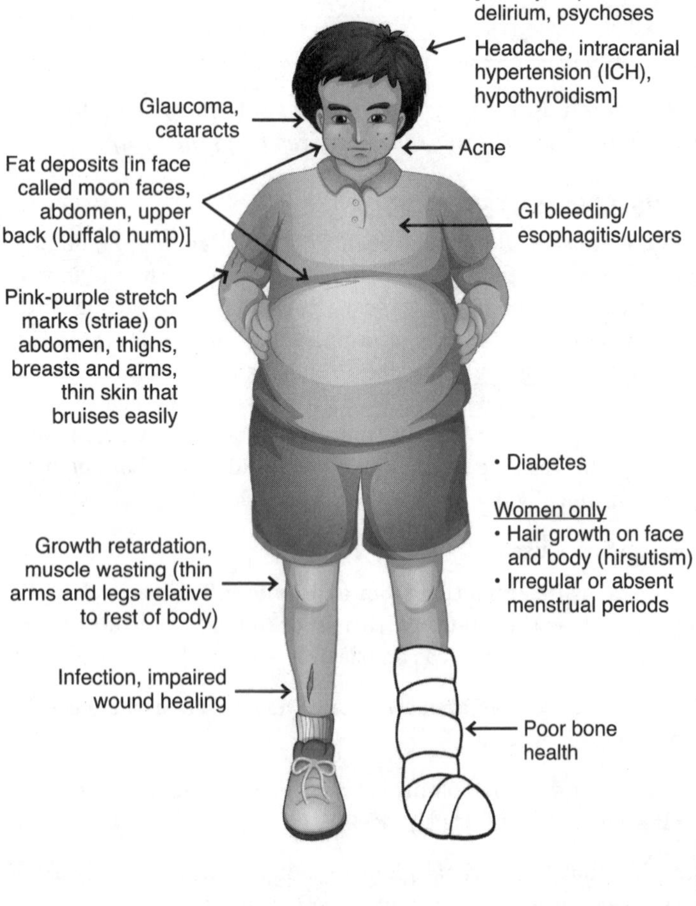

WAYS TO REDUCE SYSTEMIC STEROID RISKS

- Use alternate day dosing (skip every other day); this decreases Cushing-like side effects.
- Give a high dose initially (to wham-bam the inflammation down), and then taper the dose down to treat the remaining inflammation, while preventing a rebound attack. This is commonly done with prednisone or the dexamethasone "dose-paks".
- If treating joint inflammation, inject into the joint; this can damage the joint, but the drug stays local.
- For a condition in the gut, use a steroid with low systemic absorption, such as budesonide (*Entocort EC*).
- For treating asthma, use inhaled steroids that mostly stay in the lungs.

A medical condition may require long-term steroids (e.g., transplant, or severe autoimmune condition).

- If continual treatment is needed, use the lowest possible dose for the shortest possible time.

SYSTEMIC STEROIDS (PO, IV) DOSE EQUIVALENCE		
Cortisone	25 mg	Short-acting
Hydrocortisone	20 mg	
Prednisone	5 mg	Intermediate-acting
Prednisolone	5 mg	
Methylprednisolone	4 mg	
Triamcinolone	4 mg	
Dexamethasone	0.75 mg	Long-acting & Highest potency
Betamethasone	0.6 mg	

STUDY TIP

Cortisol/Hydrocortisone (HC) (25/20)

HC divided by Prednisone or Prednisolone (5) gives the potency of Methylprednisolone/Triamcinolone (4), and then the little bitty (but potent) babies Dexa (0.75) and Beta (0.6)

Cute Hot Pharmacists & Physicians Marry Together & Deliver Babies

Determining if a Patient is Immune-Suppressed

A patient is immune-suppressed when using ≥ 2 mg/kg/day or ≥ 20 mg/day of prednisone for ≥ 2 weeks. Immune-suppressed patients cannot receive live vaccines and have a high risk of infection. If not using prednisone, calculate the prednisone-equivalent dose using the above table. The systemic steroid will need to be tapered off, even if switching to an inhaled steroid.

Glucocorticoids (Systemic Steroids)

DRUG	DOSING	SAFETY/SIDE EFFECTS/MONITORING
Cortisone Betamethasone *(Celestone Soluspan, Celestone, Beta1 Kit)* **Dexamethasone** *(Dexamethasone Intensol,* ***DexPak 6, 10 or 13 day,*** *DoubleDex)* Hydrocortisone *(Solu-CORTEF, Cortef)* **MethylPREDNISolone (Medrol, *Medrol Dosepak, Solu-MEDROL, A-Methapred, Depo-Medrol)*** **PredniSONE** ***(PredniSONE Intensol, Deltasone,*** *Rayos)* **PrednisoLONE** ***(Millipred, Orapred ODT, Pediapred,*** *Veripred)* **Triamcinolone** ***(Kenalog,*** *Aristospan, Arze-Ject-A, Pro-C-Dure 5, Pro-C-Dure 6)*	Dosing varies by condition Many formulations: liquids, ODT (children), injections (fast-acting, joints, etc.), regular tablets If once daily, take between 7-8 AM to mimic the natural diurnal cortisol release Short-term side effects can lead to medical conditions: ↑ Blood glucose → can lead to diabetes ↑ High blood pressure → can lead to hypertension ↑ Intraocular pressure → can lead to glaucoma Emotional instability, euphoria, mood swings → can lead to psychiatric conditions	**CONTRAINDICATIONS** Live vaccines, serious systemic infections **WARNINGS** Adrenal suppression - HPA axis suppression may lead to adrenal crisis and death. If taking longer than 10-14 days, must taper slowly Immunosuppression, psychiatric disturbances, caution in HF, DM, HTN, osteoporosis, others **SIDE EFFECTS** Short-term side effects (used < 1 month) ↑ appetite/weight gain, fluid retention, emotional instability (euphoria, mood swings, irritability), insomnia, indigestion, bitter taste. Higher doses ↑ in BP and ↑ blood glucose Long-term side effects; see Cushing's Syndrome figure **MONITORING** BP, weight, appetite, mood, growth (children/adolescents), bone mineral density, blood glucose, electrolytes, infection, IOP if > 6 weeks **NOTES** Cortisone is prodrug of cortisol. Prednisone is prodrug of prednisolone. Prednisolone is used most commonly in children (many formulations).

AUTOIMMUNE CONDITIONS

Autoimmune diseases are conditions that occur when the body's immune system attacks and destroys healthy body tissue. The immune system is a complex organization of cells and antibodies designed to "seek and destroy" invaders of the body, particularly infections. Symptoms vary based on the type of autoimmune disease and the location of the immune response. Common symptoms of all autoimmune diseases include fatigue, weakness and pain.

Rheumatoid arthritis (RA), systemic lupus erythematosus (SLE), multiple sclerosis (MS), celiac disease, Sjögren's syndrome, Raynaud's and psoriasis are discussed in this chapter. Other autoimmune diseases covered elsewhere in the book include type 1 diabetes (discussed in the Diabetes chapter), Hashimoto's thyroiditis and Graves disease (discussed in the Thyroid Disorders chapter).

TREATMENT

Treatment of autoimmune diseases is typically with drugs that suppress the immune system, which decrease the immune response. The use of strong immunosuppressants can increase the risk of certain conditions including:

- Tuberculosis and hepatitis B, C (if present) re-activation; testing (and treatment if needed) must be done prior to the start of immunosuppressive agents.
- Viruses; if the virus can be prevented by a live vaccine, the vaccine must be given prior to the start of immunosuppressive treatment.
- Lymphomas and certain skin cancers: these cancer types are normally suppressed by a competent immune system.
- Infections of various types (e.g., bacterial, fungal); this requires CBC monitoring, symptom monitoring (by the patient) and may require infection control mechanisms.

RHEUMATOID ARTHRITIS

Rheumatoid arthritis (RA) is a chronic, progressive autoimmune disorder that primarily affects joints. It typically results in warm, tender, swollen, and painful joints. Other organs in the body, including the kidneys, eyes, heart, and lungs can be affected. Like many of the autoimmune conditions discussed in this chapter, the disease course is highly variable and some patients have much more aggressive disease than others.

ARTICULAR (JOINT) SYMPTOMS OF RA	
Joint swelling	Difficulty with movement, weakness
Pain	Edema
Stiffness	Redness
Bone deformity	

Clinical Presentation

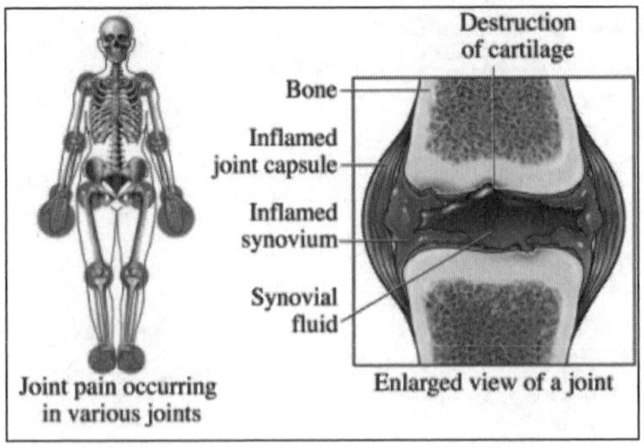

RA typically presents first with the smaller joints in the fingers, wrist, ankles, and feet. Bilateral, symmetrical disease can help with an RA diagnosis, in contrast to osteoarthritis (OA) in which one side of the body, such as the right hand, is involved or one side is more damaged than the other. The classic symptoms include joint swelling, stiffness, pain, and eventually, bone deformity (see box). RA is a systemic disease and systemic symptoms, such as fever, weakness, and loss of appetite can be present. Stiffness and pain are worse after rest, which is why "morning stiffness" is a common complaint. In contrast, OA does not cause prolonged stiffness. Diagnosis will depend on a combination of signs, symptoms, lab tests, and x-rays.

When a patient presents with joint pain and swelling, it can be challenging to identify the type of arthritis that is causing the symptoms. Joint erosion and rheumatoid nodules can be absent if RA is caught early. Anti-citrullinated peptide antibody (ACPA) has high specificity for RA, but can be absent in early disease. Rheumatoid factor (RF) has lower specificity for RA and can be positive due to another autoimmune disorder. Eventually, as the condition progresses, most patients will be positive for both ACPA and RF.

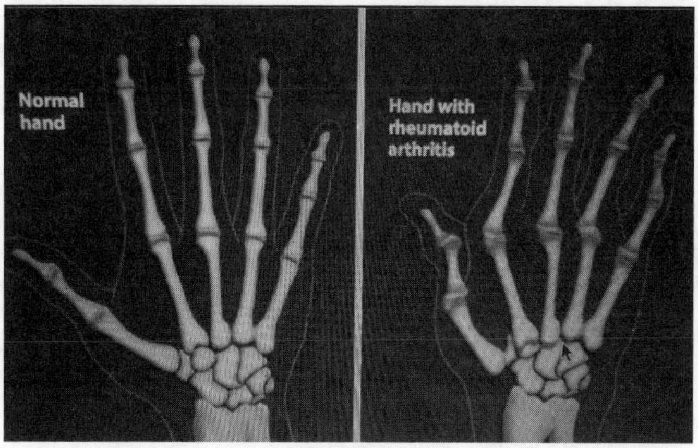

Non-Drug Treatment

Non-drug treatments include rest, physical therapy, occupational therapy, exercise, diet and weight control, and surgical intervention (e.g., a joint replacement).

Drug Treatment

RA is classified as mild, moderate or severe. Patients with symptomatic RA should be started on a disease-modifying antirheumatic drug (DMARD), regardless of the severity of disease. DMARDs work via various mechanisms to slow the disease process and help prevent further joint damage. The ideal treatment target goal is remission of the disease (or low disease activity). Methotrexate (MTX) is the preferred initial therapy for most patients. For patients with moderate or high disease activity despite MTX (with or without a systemic steroid), a combination of DMARDs or a tumor necrosis factor (TNF) inhibitor biologic or a non-TNF biologic, with or without MTX, is recommended. Never use two biologics in combination due to the risk of serious (fatal) infection. Low dose steroids (defined as ≤ 10 mg/day of prednisone or equivalent) can be added in patients with moderate or high disease activity when starting a DMARD (as a "bridging" option to provide relief while waiting for the effect of the DMARD to be felt) and in patients with DMARD failure. Steroids are commonly used in RA flares and should be used at the lowest dose for the shortest duration possible.

NSAIDs are a weaker option for bridging than steroids, but are less toxic, and often used for this purpose; anti-inflammatory (higher) doses are required. NSAID toxicity (GI bleeds, CVD risk, danger in heart failure, etc.) must be considered.

Traditional (Non-Biologic) Disease-Modifying Anti-Rheumatic Drugs (DMARDs)

DRUG	DOSING	SAFETY/SIDE EFFECTS/MONITORING
Methotrexate *(Otrexup, Rasuvo, Rheumatrex, Trexall)* *Otrexup* and *Rasuvo* are SC auto-injectors used weekly *Rheumatrex* and *Trexall* are oral tablets; *Rheumatrex* comes as in Dose Packs of 2.5 mg tablets, in various weekly dosages Injection (IV/IT) - for oncology use Irreversibly binds and inhibits dihydrofolate reductase, inhibiting folate, thymidylate synthetase and purine; has immune modulator and anti-inflammatory activity	7.5-20 mg once weekly Low weekly doses are used for RA (divided oral dosages of 2.5 mg Q12H x 3 doses as a course once weekly) never dose daily for RA; numerous incidences of adverse events (mouth sores, intestinal bleeding, liver damage, etc.) have occurred due to patients taking daily. PO, SC or IM	**BOXED WARNINGS** Hepatotoxicity, acute renal failure, pneumonitis, myelosuppression, mucositis/stomatitis, dermatologic reactions, malignant lymphomas, potentially fatal opportunistic infections, others – renal and lung toxicity more likely when using oncology doses **CONTRAINDICATION** Pregnancy, breastfeeding, alcoholism, chronic liver disease, blood dyscrasias, immunodeficiency syndrome **SIDE EFFECTS** (vary by route and dosage) N/V/D, ↑ LFTs, stomatitis, alopecia, photosensitivity, arthralgia, myalgia **MONITORING** CBC, SCr, LFTs at baseline and Q2-4 weeks for first 3 months or following dose increases, then Q8-12 weeks for 3-6 months, then less frequently. Also at baseline: chest X-ray, hepatitis B and C serologies (if at high risk); pulmonary function tests (if lung-related symptoms), TB test **NOTES** Safety issue – see Pregnancy Chapter. Folate can be given to ↓ hematological, gastrointestinal and hepatic side effects associated with MTX. Give 5 mg PO weekly on the day following MTX administration (some take 1 mg daily on non-MTX days).
Hydroxychloroquine *(Plaquenil)* +/- MTX Tablet Immune modulator	400 mg/day initially, then 300 mg/day for maintenance dose Take with food or milk	**CONTRAINDICATIONS** Retinopathy, hypersensitivity to 4-aminoquinoline compounds, long-term use in children **WARNINGS** Loss of visual acuity/macular pigment changes, neuromuscular weakness, cardiomyopathy and hematologic reactions with prolonged use; caution in patients with G6PD deficiency **SIDE EFFECTS** N/V/D, abdominal pain, rash, pruritus, HA, vision changes (dose-related), pigmentation changes of the skin and hair (rare), anemia, leukopenia, thrombocytopenia **MONITORING** CBC and LFTs at baseline and periodically. Eye exam and muscle strength at baseline and every 3 months during prolonged therapy If no or inadequate response after 6 months consider alterative **NOTES** Should be avoided in pregnancy Monotherapy: if low disease activity and symptoms < 24 months

Traditional (Non-Biologic) Disease-Modifying Anti-Rheumatic Drugs (DMARDs) Continued

DRUG	DOSING	SAFETY/SIDE EFFECTS/MONITORING
SulfaSALAzine *(Azulfidine, Azulfidine EN-tabs)* Tablet +/- MTX Immune modulator	500-1,000 mg/day initially, then 1,000 mg BID for maintenance dose (max 3 grams/day) Take with food and 8 oz. of water to prevent crystalluria	**CONTRAINDICATION** Patients with a sulfa or salicylate allergy, GI or GU obstruction, porphyria **WARNINGS** Blood dyscrasias, severe skin reactions (SJS/TEN), hepatic failure, and pulmonary fibrosis; use caution **in** patients with G6PD deficiency **SIDE EFFECTS** HA, rash, anorexia, dyspepsia, N/V/D, oligospermia (reversible); folate deficiency, arthralgia, crystalluria **MONITORING** CBC and LFTs (baseline, then every other week for first 3 months, then monthly for 3 months, then once every 3 months), renal function **NOTES** Safety issue – see Pregnancy Chapter Can cause yellow-orange coloration of skin/urine Impairs folate absorption, may give 1 mg/day folate supplement
Leflunomide *(Arava)* Tablet +/- MTX Inhibits pyrimidine synthesis resulting in anti-proliferative and anti-inflammatory effects Prodrug	100 mg PO x 3 days, then 20 mg PO daily, can use 10 mg PO daily if unable to tolerate 20 mg (may omit loading dose if at higher risk of liver or myelosuppression) Must have negative pregnancy test prior and use 2 forms of birth control. If pregnancy is desired, must wait 2 years after discontinuation or use accelerated drug elimination procedure	**BOXED WARNINGS** Embryo-Fetal Toxicity: Exclude pregnancy prior to starting therapy Hepatotoxicity: Avoid in pre-existing liver disease or ALT > 2x upper limit of normal (ULN) **CONTRAINDICATION** Pregnancy, severe hepatic impairment, current teriflunomide therapy **WARNINGS** Severe infections, serious skin reactions (SJS/TEN), peripheral neuropathy, interstitial lung disease, hypertension Upon discontinuation of treatment, use accelerated drug elimination procedure to reduce levels of active metabolite, teriflunomide **SIDE EFFECTS** ↑ LFTs, nausea, diarrhea, respiratory infections, rash, HA **MONITORING** LFTs and CBC at baseline and monthly for first 6 months, BP at baseline and regularly. Screen for TB and pregnancy prior to starting therapy **NOTES** Pregnancy: Contraindicated. Females/Males of Reproductive Potential: May cause fetal harm; consider discontinuing use. Accelerated drug elimination options: 1. Cholestyramine 8 gms PO TID x 11 days (Use 4 gms if 8 gms dose is not tolerated), 2. Activated charcoal suspension 50 gms PO Q12H x 11 days Transient acute renal failure typically occurs 12 weeks to 2 years

Traditional (Non-Biologic) Disease-Modifying Anti-Rheumatic Drugs (DMARDs) Continued

DRUG	DOSING	SAFETY/SIDE EFFECTS/MONITORING
Tofacitinib *(Xeljanz, Xeljanz XR)* Tablet +/- non-biologic DMARDs (MTX), do not use with biologic DMARDs or potent immunosuppressants Inhibits Janus Kinase (JAK) enzymes, which stimulate immune cell function	5 mg PO BID XR: 11 mg PO daily With strong 3A4 inducers: avoid use With strong 3A4 inhibitors or with concomitant moderate 3A4 inhibitors and strong 2C19 inhibitors: 5 mg daily (immediate release only) ↓ dose to 5 mg daily (immediate release only) in moderate hepatic impairment and mod-severe renal impairment Do not start therapy if: absolute lymphocyte count < 500 cells/mm^3, Hgb < 9 gm/dL, or ANC < 1,000 cells/mm^3	**BOXED WARNINGS** Serious infections including tuberculosis, fungal, viral, bacterial, or other opportunistic infections; screen for active and latent TB and treat before starting therapy Malignancy: ↑ risk for lymphomas and other malignancies **WARNINGS** GI perforation, ↑ LFTs, not studied in patients with a baseline CrCl < 40 ml/min, avoid live vaccines **SIDE EFFECTS** Upper respiratory tract infections (URTIs), urinary tract infections (UTIs), diarrhea, HA, hypertension, ↑ lipids **MONITORING** CBC (for lymphopenia, neutropenia and anemia) and lipids at baseline, then 4-8 weeks later, then Q3 months; LFTs (at baseline and periodically thereafter), new onset abdominal pain, signs of infection **NOTES** Safety issue – see Pregnancy Chapter MedGuide required Caution in patients of Asian descent (↑ frequency of side effects) When transitioning from immediate release to extended release, begin extended release the day following the last dose of 5 mg immediate release Available through specialty/network pharmacies

Methotrexate Drug Interactions

- Methotrexate should not be taken with alcohol; this combination ↑ the risk of liver toxicity.
- Active transport renal elimination is ↓ by aspirin/NSAIDs, beta-lactams, and probenecid, resulting in toxicity. Caution if using concurrently.
- Sulfonamides and topical tacrolimus ↑ adverse effects of methotrexate. Avoid concurrent use.
- Methotrexate can ↓ effectiveness of loop diuretics; loop diuretics can ↑ the methotrexate concentration. Use caution if using these agents concomitantly.
- Methotrexate and cyclosporine concentrations will both ↑ when used concomitantly, leading to toxicity; avoid.
- Levetiracetam and methotrexate coadministration may lead to higher amounts of serum methotrexate, which may cause serious adverse events, including acute kidney failure.

Methotrexate Patient Counseling

- Common side effects of this medication include nausea, vomiting, abdominal pain, diarrhea, mouth sores, and rash.
- If you are receiving this medicine for rheumatoid arthritis or psoriasis, the dosage is usually given once weekly. Some patients are told to divide the once weekly dose in half and take it over two consecutive days per week for better tolerability. Do not use this medicine daily or double-up on doses. Serious side effects could occur if it is used more frequently than directed. Choose a day of the week to take your medicine that you can remember.
- Methotrexate has caused birth defects and death in unborn babies (Pregnancy Category X). If you are pregnant or plan on becoming pregnant, you should not use this medicine. Use an effective form of birth control, whether you are a man or a woman. Tell your healthcare provider if you or your sexual partner become pregnant during treatment.
- Do not use methotrexate if you are breast-feeding.
- If you have kidney problems or excess body water (ascites, pleural effusion), you must be closely monitored and your dose may be adjusted or stopped by your healthcare provider. Talk to your provider about appropriate hydration and urine alkalinization.
- Your healthcare provider will perform periodic blood tests to measure your liver function to ensure it stays healthy. Tell your healthcare provider right away if you develop any new or worsening symptoms, including black, tarry stools or symptoms of liver damage (unusual tiredness or weakness, yellow skin or eyes or darkened urine, stomach upset or pain).
- Methotrexate (usually at high dosages) has rarely caused severe (sometimes fatal) bone marrow suppression (decreasing your body's ability to fight infections) and stomach/intestinal disease (e.g., bleeding) when used at the same time as NSAIDs. Therefore, NSAIDs should not be used with high-doses of methotrexate. Caution is advised if you also take aspirin. If you are using low-dose aspirin (81-325 milligrams per day) for heart attack or stroke prevention, continue to take it unless directed otherwise.
- Methotrexate use has rarely resulted in serious (sometimes fatal) lung problems, such as scarring and lung infections (*Pneumocystis* pneumonia).
- For *Rasuvo* and *Otrexup* auto-injectors: Inspect syringe. Liquid should be yellow (*Otrexup*) to yellow-brown (*Rasuvo*). Discard if cloudy or containing particles. Select an injection site on the abdomen (2 inches from navel) or upper thigh only. Do not inject in the arms or any other areas of the body. Swab with alcohol pad and allow to dry – do not fan or blow on the area. For *Otrexup*, twist cap to break seal and remove the safety clip. For *Rasuvo* pull the yellow cap directly off without twisting. Pinch the skin and inject at a 90° angle. Press firmly until you hear a click. Hold 3 seconds for *Otrexup* and 5 seconds for *Rasuvo*. Check the viewing window to be sure the medicine was given. Dispose of the used injector in a sharps container. Store at room temperature.

Biologic Agents

Tumor Necrosis Factor (TNFα) Inhibitors (Anti-TNF biologics)

TNF inhibitor dosing is provided for RA. Recommended dosing for psoriatic arthritis, plaque psoriasis, Crohn's disease, ulcerative colitis, and other indications may vary. Each agents has their own pregnancy registry.

DRUG	DOSING	SAFETY/SIDE EFFECTS/MONITORING
Etanercept (***Enbrel***, *Enbrel SureClick, Erelzi*-biosimilar) Pre-filled syringe, auto-injector and starter kit +/- MTX	50 mg SC weekly	**BOXED WARNINGS** Serious infections, some fatal, including TB, fungal, viral, bacterial or opportunistic; screen for latent TB and treat prior to therapy Lymphomas and other malignancies **CONTRAINDICATION** Active systemic infection, dose > 5 mg/kg in mod-severe heart failure (infliximab), sepsis (etanercept) **WARNINGS** TNF inhibitors can cause demyelinating disease, seizures, hepatitis B reactivation, heart failure, hepatotoxicity, lupus-like syndrome, myelosuppression and severe infections. Do not use with other biological DMARDs or live vaccines. **SIDE EFFECTS** Infections and injection site reactions (redness, rash, swelling, itching, or bruising), positive anti-nuclear antibodies, headache, nausea, ↑ CPK (adalimumab) **MONITORING** TB test (prior to initiation and annually if risk factors for TB are present), signs of infection, CBC, LFTs, HBV (HBsAg and Anti-HBc prior to initiation and during treatment), HF, malignancies, vitals (during infliximab infusion) **NOTES** Safety issue – see Pregnancy Chapter. Do not shake or freeze, requires refrigeration (biologics will denature if hot). Etanercept and adalimumab can be stored at room temperature for a maximum of 14 days, do not refrigerator once warmed, allow to reach room temperature before injecting (15-30 minutes). MTX is used 1st-line and these agents are add-on therapy. However, if the initial presentation is severe, these can be started as initial therapy. Do not use two biologics concurrently. Do not use live vaccines if using these drugs. Antibody induction can occur and will ↓ usefulness of drug. *Erelzi*, *Amjevita*, and *Inflectra* are biosimilar agents. Rotate injection sites. MedGuide required.
Adalimumab (***Humira***, *Humira Pen, Amjevita*-biosimilar) Pre-filled syringe and pen +/- MTX	40 mg SC every other week (if not taking MTX, can ↑ dose to 40 mg SC weekly)	
InFLIXimab (***Remicade***, *Inflectra*-biosimilar) Injection (IV) + MTX	3 mg/kg IV at weeks 0, 2, and 6, then every 8 weeks (can ↑ dose to 10 mg/kg or treat as often as every 4 weeks based on need but ↑ infection risk) IV infliximab requires a filter and is stable in NS only Infusion reactions: hypotension, fever, chills, pruritus (may pre-medicate with acetaminophen, antihistamine, steroids) Delayed hypersensitivity reaction 3-12 days after administration (fever, rash, myalgia, HA, sore throat)	
Certolizumab pegol (***Cimzia***, *Cimzia Pen, Cimzia Starter Kit*) Pre-filled syringe and syringe kit +/- MTX	400 mg SC at weeks 0, 2, and 4, then 200 mg SC every other week (may consider 400 mg every 4 weeks)	
Golimumab (***Simponi***, *Simponi Aria*) Auto-injector and injection (IV) + MTX	SC: 50 mg monthly *(Simponi)* IV: 2 mg/kg infused over 30 minutes at weeks 0 and 4, then every 8 weeks *(Simponi Aria)* IV golimumab requires a filter	

Other Biologics (Non-TNF Biologics)

Rituximab

Depletes CD20 B cells. B cells are believed to have a role in RA development and progression.

DRUG	DOSING	SAFETY/SIDE EFFECTS/MONITORING
RiTUXimab ***(Rituxan)*** Injection (IV) + MTX	1,000 mg IV on day 1 and 15 in combination with MTX for 2 doses Can repeat treatment if needed at 24 weeks (or no sooner than every 16 weeks) Pre-medicate with a steroid, acetaminophen, and an antihistamine Start infusion at 50 mg/hr; can ↑ by 50 mg/hr every 30 minutes if no reaction (max 400 mg/hr) Gently invert the bag to mix the solution, do not shake	**BOXED WARNINGS** Serious, and fatal, infusion-related reactions usually with first infusion Progressive multifocal leukoencephalopathy (PML) due to JC virus infection, may be fatal Hepatitis B virus (HBV) reactivation; some cases resulting in fulminant hepatitis, hepatic failure and death; Screen for HBV and HCV (high risk groups) prior to initiating therapy; monitor patients for clinical and laboratory signs (HBsAg and Anti-HBc) several months after treatment Serious skin reactions (SJS/TEN) **WARNINGS** Infections; do not use with other biological DMARDs or live vaccines **SIDE EFFECTS** In patients treated for RA: infusion-related reactions, URTIs, UTIs, N/V/D, peripheral edema, weight gain, hypertension, HA, angioedema, fever, insomnia, pain **MONITORING** ECG, vitals, infusion reactions, CBC, SCr, electrolytes **NOTES** Safety issue – see Pregnancy Chapter; MedGuide required

Anakinra

IL-1 receptor antagonist. During inflammation, endogenous IL-1 is induced which mediates immunologic reactions in RA (degrades cartilage, increases bone resorption). Not recommended as a first line option in the guidelines.

DRUG	DOSING	SAFETY/SIDE EFFECTS/MONITORING
Anakinra *(Kineret)* Pre-filled syringe	100 mg SC daily (same time each day) Give only after failure of one or more DMARDs CrCl < 30 mL/min: 100 mg SC every other day	**WARNINGS** Malignancies and serious infections, discontinue if a serious infection develop, screen for TB prior to initiating therapy, do not give with other biological DMARDs or live vaccines **SIDE EFFECTS** URTIs, HA, N/D, abdominal pain, injection site reactions, antibody development, arthralgias **MONITORING** CBC, SCr, signs of infection **NOTES** Safety issue – see Pregnancy Chapter. Do not shake or freeze, refrigerate and protect from light.

Abatacept

Selective T cell costimulator; inhibits T cell activation by binding to CD80 and CD86 on cells that present these antigens (activated cells are detected in the synovium of RA joints).

DRUG	DOSING	SAFETY/SIDE EFFECTS/MONITORING
Abatacept *(Orencia, Orencia Clickject)* Pre-filled syringe, pen, injection (IV)	IV: 500-1,000 mg (based on body weight) at 0, 2, and 4 weeks, then every 4 weeks, infuse over 30 minutes SC: 125 mg weekly SC with IV loading dose: give first IV dose as above, followed by 125 mg SC within 24 hours, then 125 mg SC weekly	**WARNINGS** Malignancies and serious infections, discontinue if a serious infection develops, screen for latent TB and HBV prior to initiating therapy, do not give with other biologics or live vaccines, caution in patients with COPD - may worsen symptoms. **SIDE EFFECTS** Headache, nausea, injection site reactions, infections, nasopharyngitis, antibody development **MONITORING** Signs of infection, hypersensitivity **NOTES** Safety issue – see Pregnancy Chapter. Stable in NS only, requires a filter and light protection during administration; do not shake.

Tocilizumab

IL-6 receptor antagonist. IL-6 mediates immunologic reactions in RA.

DRUG	DOSING	SAFETY/SIDE EFFECTS/MONITORING
Tocilizumab *(Actemra)* Pre-filled syringe, injection (IV) +/- MTX	IV: 4 mg/kg every 4 weeks given over 60 minutes (may ↑ to 8 mg/kg based on clinical response). Max: 800 mg SC: If < 100 kg, 162 mg every other week (may ↑ to weekly based on response) If ≥ 100 kg, 162 mg SC weekly Do not start if: ALT or AST are > 1.5 times ULN, ANC < 2,000 cells/mm^3, or platelets < 100,000 cell/mm^3	**BOXED WARNING** Serious infections, discontinue if a serious infection develops, screen for latent TB prior to initiating therapy **WARNINGS** GI perforation, can cause demyelinating diseases, hypersensitivity reactions, lipid abnormalities, ↑ LFTs, neutropenia, thrombocytopenia, do not give with other biological DMARDs or live vaccines **SIDE EFFECTS** URTIs, HA, hypertension, injection-site reactions, ↑ LDL and total cholesterol, ↑ LFTs **MONITORING** LFTs, CBC (baseline, 4-8 weeks after start of therapy, and every 3 months thereafter), lipid panel, signs of infection **NOTES** Safety issue – see Pregnancy Chapter. Do NOT use SC inj. for IV infusion; SC products contain polysorbate 80. Dose adjustments available for LFTs, neutropenia, and thrombocytopenia.

Patient Counseling

SC injectable Anti - TNF biologics (Adalimumab, Etanercept and Golimumab)

- Read the medication guide that comes with this medicine.
- Common side effects include injection site reactions, such as redness, swelling, itching, or pain. These symptoms usually go away within 3 to 5 days. If you have pain, redness, or swelling around the injection site that does not go away or gets worse, call your healthcare provider. Other side effects can include upper respiratory infections (sinus infections), headache, dizziness, or coughing.
- People taking this medicine should not get live vaccines. Make sure your vaccines are up-to-date before starting this medicine. You can continue receiving the annual influenza shot but not the influenza nasal vaccine, since this is a live vaccine.
- Because this medicine works by blocking the immune system it lowers your ability to fight infections. This may make you more likely to get a serious (rarely fatal) infection or can make any infection you have worse. You should be tested for tuberculosis (TB skin test or chest X-ray) before treatment with this medicine. Tell your healthcare provider immediately if you have any signs of infection, such as a fever of 100.5°F (38°C) or higher, chills, very bad sore throat, ear or sinus pain, a cough, or more sputum or a change in the color of sputum.
- This medicine has a possibility of causing liver damage. Call your healthcare provider right away if you have any of these symptoms: feeling very tired, yellowing of your skin or eyes, poor appetite, vomiting, or pain on the right side of your stomach (abdomen).
- This medicine may worsen heart failure (HF). Notify your healthcare provider if you experience sudden weight gain or shortness of breath.
- This medicine is injected subcutaneously (SC) under the skin of the thigh or abdomen (or upper arm for etanercept and golimumab), exactly as prescribed by your healthcare provider (once weekly for etanercept, every 1 – 2 weeks for adalimumab, monthly for golimumab).
- Store the medication (single-use syringes or multiple-use vials) in the refrigerator (etanercept and adalimumab can be stored at room temperature for a maximum of 14 days with protection from light and sources of heat). Allow the medicine to warm to room temperature. Do not warm to room temperature any other way than letting the product sit at room temperature outside the carton before injecting (takes 15 – 30 minutes). Once warmed do not return to the refrigerator. Do not shake the medicine. Before using, check for particles or discoloration. If either is present, do not use the medicine. Injectors require protection from light prior to administration.
- Before injecting each dose, clean the injection site with rubbing alcohol. Do not wave the hand over the wet area to dry. It is important to change the location of the injection site each time you use this drug to prevent problems under the skin. New injections should be given at least 1 inch (2.5 centimeters) from the last injection site. Do not inject into areas of the skin that are sore, bruised, red, broken or hard. Do not bend or place the white cap back onto the auto injector.
- For adalimumab *(Humira)*: Inject into the abdomen or thigh. A loud click is heard when the plum-colored activator button is pressed. Continue to hold injector against the skin until the yellow marker fully appears in the window view and stops moving (may take 10 seconds).
- For etanercept *(Enbrel)* syringe or auto-injector: Inject into abdomen, thigh, or upper arm. A loud click is heard when injection begins, continue to hold auto-injector against skin for 15 seconds. You may hear a second click as the purple button pops back up, indicating all of the medicine has been injected.
- For etanercept *(Enbrel)* vials for reconstitution: When reconstituting *Enbrel* powder from the multi-dose vial, some foaming is normal. The final solution should be clear and colorless with no particulate matter. After use, the window will turn yellow. If it does not, contact your healthcare provider for instructions.
- For golimumab *(Simponi)*: Inject into abdomen, thigh, or upper arm. A loud click is heard when the injection begins, continue to hold auto-injector against skin until second click is heard (3-15 seconds).

SYSTEMIC LUPUS ERYTHEMATOSUS

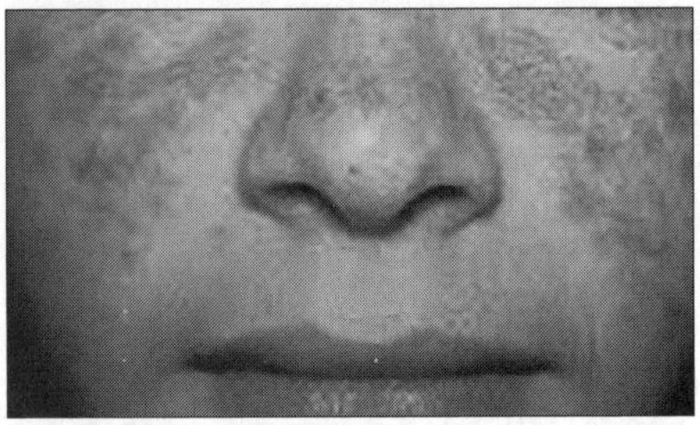

Background

Systemic lupus erythematosus (SLE), or lupus, is a multi-system autoimmune disease that affects primarily young women, with a female-to-male ratio of 10:1. The disease predominantly occurs in persons 15-45 years of age, and it is more common in women of African-American and Asian descent. Patients experience flare-ups to varying degrees as well as periods of disease remission. Although factors such as sunlight, certain drugs and viral infections are known to trigger SLE, the underlying cause is not fully understood. As the disease progresses, symptoms may be present in almost every organ system, with the heart, lungs, kidneys, and brain being most affected. Drug-induced lupus erythematosus (DILE) can have similar clinical and laboratory features as SLE, but usually resolves within weeks after drug discontinuation. A few common drugs are listed in thbox below.

Clinical Presentation

The most common symptoms include fatigue, depression, anorexia, weight loss, muscle pain, arthritis, discoid rash, malar rash (butterfly rash), photosensitivity, and joint pain and stiffness. Over half of the people with SLE develop a characteristic red, flat facial rash over the bridge of their nose and cheeks. Because of its shape, it is frequently referred to as the SLE "butterfly rash." Usually, the rash is not painful or itchy. The facial rash, along with inflammation in other organs, can be precipitated or worsened by exposure to sunlight. Arthritis and cutaneous manifestations are most common, but renal, hematologic, and neurologic manifestations contribute largely to morbidity and mortality. Lupus nephritis (kidney disease) develops in over 50% of patients with SLE. Common laboratory findings may include positive antinuclear antibodies (ANA - with titers ≥ 1:160), positive anti-single stranded DNA (anti-ssDNA), positive anti-double stranded DNA (anti-dsDNA), positive anti-Sm, positive antiphospholipid antibodies, low complement (C3, C4, CH50), and elevated acute phase reactants (such as ESR, CRP).

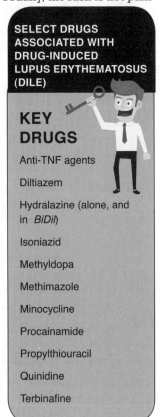

SELECT DRUGS ASSOCIATED WITH DRUG-INDUCED LUPUS ERYTHEMATOSUS (DILE)

KEY DRUGS

Anti-TNF agents

Diltiazem

Hydralazine (alone, and in *BiDil*)

Isoniazid

Methyldopa

Methimazole

Minocycline

Procainamide

Propylthiouracil

Quinidine

Terbinafine

NON-DRUG AND DRUG TREATMENT

Non-drug treatment consists of rest and proper exercise to manage the fatigue. Smoking cessation is encouraged since tobacco smoke can be a trigger for disease flare. Photosensitivity is common with the condition and the treatment; sunscreens and sun protection/avoidance is required. Drug treatment for SLE consists of immunosuppressants, cytotoxic agents, and/or anti-inflammatory agents. Treatment approaches emphasize using a combination of drugs to minimize chronic exposure to steroids.

Patients with mild disease may do well on an NSAID (dosed at anti-inflammatory doses to ↓ swelling and pain) but use caution since the doses are high and these patients are more sensitive to the GI and renal side effects. Concurrent use with a PPI is generally recommended to reduce GI side effects. Other agents are discussed below.

Agents Used in SLE

DRUG	DOSING	SAFETY/SIDE EFFECTS/MONITORING
Antimalarial agents – impair complement-dependent antigen-antibody reactions; have anti-inflammatory, immunomodulatory and antithrombotic properties		
Hydroxychloroquine *(Plaquenil)*	Oral: 200 to 400 mg Take with food or milk	Hydroxychloroquine has less adverse effects (preferred); takes 6 months to see maximal effect Effective for cutaneous symptoms, joint pain, fatigue, and fever Use as chronic therapy See RA section for additional labeling
Chloroquine	250 mg PO daily CrCl < 10 mL/min: 125 mg PO daily	
Steroids		
PredniSONE (or **methylPREDNISolone**)	0.5-1 mg/kg/day PO; then taper	Used acutely to control flares at higher doses; taper to lower doses for chronic, suppressive therapy
Select cytotoxic agents – used in severe disease (flares)		
Cyclophosphamide	500-1,000 mg/m^2 IV monthly for 6 months, then every 3 months for 2.5 years; or 1-1.5 mg/kg daily if using PO	**SIDE EFFECTS** Myelosuppression, infections, hemorrhagic cystitis, malignancy, sterility, teratogenesis, nausea, vomiting **MONITORING** CBC and urinalysis **NOTES** Safety issue – see Pregnancy Chapter
AzaTHIOprine *(Azasan, Imuran)*	2 mg/kg PO daily CrCl 10-50 mL/min: 75% of dose CrCl < 10 mL/min: 50% of dose	**BOXED WARNING** Malignancy (especially lymphomas) **WARNINGS** Severe N/V/D, hematologic (leukopenia, thrombocytopenia, anemia) toxicities, hepatotoxicity, infections; patients with genetic deficiency of thiopurine methyltransferase (TPMT) are at ↑ risk for myelosuppression and may require lower dose **SIDE EFFECTS** N/V/D, rash, ↑ LFTs, myelosuppression **MONITORING** LFTs, CBC, renal function, screen for TPMT deficiency **NOTES** Safety issue – see Pregnancy Chapter
Mycophenolate mofetil *(CellCept)* Off-label	Initial: 2-3 grams PO daily (can be divided BID) in combination with a glucocorticoid for 6 months Maintenance: 0.5-3 grams daily (can be divided BID)	See Transplant chapter

Agents Used in SLE Continued

DRUG	DOSING	SAFETY/SIDE EFFECTS/MONITORING
CycloSPORINE ***(Gengraf, Neoral)*** Capsule, Solution	Inital oral cyclosporine (modified): 4 mg/kg daily for 1 month; (reduce dose if trough concentrations >200 ng/mL); reduce dose by 0.5 mg/kg every 2 weeks until maintenance dose Maintenance: 2.5-3 mg/kg daily	See Transplant chapter

IgG1-lambda monoclonal antibody that prevents the survival of B lymphocytes by blocking the binding of soluble human B lymphocyte stimulator protein (BLyS) to receptors on B lymphocytes. This reduces the activity of B-cell mediated immunity and the autoimmune response.

Belimumab *(Benlysta)*	10 mg/kg IV Q2 weeks x 3 doses, then Q4 weeks thereafter; infuse over 1 hour Consider giving pre-medication for infusion reactions and hypersensitivity reactions Stable in NS only	**WARNINGS** Serious (sometimes fatal) infections, PML, acute hypersensitivity reactions, malignancy, psychiatric events, do not give with other biologics, do not give live vaccines 30 days prior or concurrently with therapy **SIDE EFFECTS** Infections, nausea, diarrhea, fever, depression, insomnia **NOTES** Safety issue – see Pregnancy Chapter Black/African-American patients: May have a lower response rate; use with caution. MedGuide required

MULTIPLE SCLEROSIS

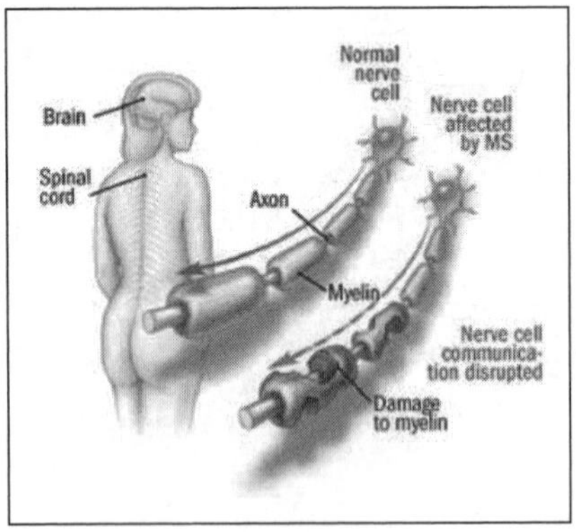

Background

Multiple sclerosis (MS) is a chronic, progressive autoimmune disease in which the patient's immune system attacks the myelin sheath, the fatty substance that surrounds and insulates nerve fibers, of the axons in the brain and spinal cord (CNS). As demyelination progresses, the symptoms worsen because the nerves can no longer properly conduct electrical transmission. Similar to other autoimmune conditions, most patients experience periods of disease activity followed by intervals of remission. The presentation is highly variable with some patients having a much more aggressive course while others have occasional discrete attacks.

Clinical Presentation

Early symptoms include fatigue, weakness, tingling, numbness, and blurred vision. As the condition worsens, a variety of physical and psychological issues can make life very challenging, including deterioration of cognitive function, muscle spasms, pain, incontinence, depression, heat sensitivity, sexual dysfunction, difficulty walking with gait instability, and visual disturbances. If left untreated, about 30% of patients will develop significant physical disability. Up to 10% of patients have a milder phenotype in which no significant physical disability develops, although these patients may develop mild cognitive dysfunction. Male patients with primary progressive MS generally have the worst prognosis. Symptoms are characterized as primary (muscle weakness), secondary (which result from primary symptoms, such as incontinence due to muscle impairment) and tertiary, which involve psychological and social concerns, such as depression.

MS occurs in both men and women, but as other autoimmune conditions is more common in women (ratio 2:1). The typical age of onset is between 20 to 40 years old. Various tests are performed to make a diagnosis including magnetic resonance imaging (MRI), spinal fluid analysis, and evoked potentials (tests that measure electrical conduction of the brain). A primary goal of therapy is prevention of disease progression; what is lost in neuronal function cannot be regained. The agents that can modify disease progression are costly. The beta interferons cost on average about $68,000 - 77,000/year. The newer oral immune modulator fingolimod costs about $65,000/year. The newest agent, dimethyl fumarate, costs about $76,000/year.

Treatment

Promoting functional rehabilitation and emotional health are important for all stages of MS. Programs exist to support cognitive and vocational rehabilitation. Physical and occupational therapy programs are available for motor, speech, and swallowing. Medications are used to modify disease, treat relapses, and manage symptoms. Mitoxantrone (*Novantrone*) is a chemotherapeutic agent that may be used for MS and is approved for this condition; a review of mitoxantrone can be found in the Oncology II chapter. Steroids are used to help with relapses. Corticotropin (*HP Acthar*) can be administered SC or IM daily for 2 – 3 weeks. Other drugs used for various related symptoms are summarized at the end of this chapter, and detailed information on these agents can be found in other chapters.

Disease-Modifying Therapies

Interferon beta formulations (*Betaseron, Avonex, Rebif, Extavia, Plegridy*) and glatiramer acetate (*Copaxone, Glatopa*) have been the mainstay of treatment for patients with relapsing forms of MS. Fingolimod (*Gilenya*) and teriflunomide (*Aubagio*) were the first oral disease-modifying agents to be approved for MS. In 2013, a third oral agent, dimethyl fumarate (*Tecfidera*) was approved. Pegylated interferon beta (*Plegridy*) was approved in 2014. It allows for more convenient SC dosing every 14 days. For SC injections rotate administration site to prevent lipoatrophy and rare necrosis. If these are not effective the monoclonal antibodies or chemotherapy drugs can be tried; these have significant toxicities and are used in refractive cases.

If the drug is a powder that is reconstituted, the drug powder may require refrigeration or be kept at room temperature. If a drug is reconstituted, immediate use is necessary (at most within a few hours; a few reconstituted injections permit short storage in the refrigerator). Some of the powders that are reconstituted contain albumin and some patients will not wish to or cannot use albumin-containing products.

Glatiramer acetate is an immune modulator thought to induce and activate T-lymphocyte suppressor cells in relapsing form of MS. Exact mechanism not well-defined.

DRUG	DOSING	SAFETY/SIDE EFFECTS/MONITORING
Glatiramer acetate *(Copaxone, Glatopa)* Pre-filled syringes (20 and 40 mg/mL), these are not interchangeable Same auto-injector can be used for both concentrations	20 mg SC daily or 40 mg SC 3 times per week (at least 48 hours apart) If increasing dose to 40 mg start 48 hrs after the 20 mg dose	**WARNINGS** Immediate post-injection reaction, chest pain, lipoatrophy **SIDE EFFECTS** Injection site reactions (inflammation, erythema, pain, pruritus, residual mass), infection, pain, flushing, diaphoresis, dyspnea, weakness, anxiety, rash, nausea, nasopharyngitis, vasodilation, antibody development **NOTES** Preferred agent if treatment is necessary during pregnancy Check solution for discoloration; if present, discard Can be kept at room temp for up to one month, or in the refrigerator (preferred); If cold, let stand to room temp for 20 minutes prior to injecting
Interferon beta-1a *(Avonex, Avonex Pen, Rebif, Rebif Rebidose)* Powder (for reconstitution), pre-filled syringe and pen	*Avonex* IM: 30 mcg weekly *Rebif* SC: 22 mcg or 44 mcg three times per week (at least 48 hours apart)	**WARNINGS** Psychiatric disorders (depression/suicide), injection site necrosis, myelosuppression, ↑ LFTs, thyroid dysfunction (hyper and hypo), infections, anaphylaxis, worsening cardiovascular disease, seizure risk **SIDE EFFECTS** Flu-like symptoms following administration (lasting min to hrs and ↓ with continued treatment - can use acetaminophen or NSAIDs prior to injection or start with lower doses titrating weekly to target dose) Injection site reactions: mild erythema to severe skin necrosis Visual disturbances, fatigue, depression, pain, urinary tract infections, HA **MONITORING** LFTs, CBC (at 1, 3 and 6 months, then periodically); thyroid function every 6 months (in patients with thyroid dysfunction or as clinical necessary) **NOTES** Refrigerate all except *Betaseron* and *Extavia* (which can be stored at room temp). If refrigerated, let stand to room temp prior to injection. Do not expel small air bubble in pre-filled syringes due to loss of dose. Do not shake *Avonex, Betaseron or Extavia.* Some formulations contain albumin – risk of Creutzfeldt-Jakob disease transmission (rare); avoid in albumin-sensitive patients. MedGuide required.
Interferon beta-1b *(Betaseron, Extavia, Betaconnect)* Powder (for reconstitution), and auto-injector	SC: 0.25 mg every other day (use within 3 hrs of reconstitution)	
Peginterferon beta-1a *(Plegridy, Plegridy Starter Pack)* Pre-filled syringe and pen	SC: 63 mcg on Day 1, 94 mcg on Day 15, then 125 mcg every 14 days starting on Day 29	

Multiple Sclerosis Drugs Continued

DRUG	DOSING	SAFETY/SIDE EFFECTS/MONITORING
ORAL IMMUNE MODULATORS		
Teriflunomide *(Aubagio)* Tablet Active metabolite of leflunomide	7 mg or 14 mg PO daily	**BOXED WARNINGS** Severe hepatotoxicity and teratogenicity **CONTRAINDICATIONS** Severe hepatic impairment, pregnancy, current leflunomide treatment **WARNINGS** Severe infections, peripheral neuropathy, neutropenia, hypertension, serious risk reactions (SJS/TEN), interstitial lung disease Can use accelerated elimination to remove drug - see leflunomide **SIDE EFFECTS** ↑ LFTs, alopecia, N/D, hypophosphatemia, HA, renal impairment **MONITORING** Hepatic and renal function, CBC **NOTES** Safety issue – see Pregnancy Chapter. MedGuide required
Fingolimod *(Gilenya)* Capsules	0.5 mg PO daily Blister packs; protect from moisture Patient must be monitored for at least 6 hours after the first dose	**CONTRAINDICATIONS** Recent (within the last 6 months) MI, unstable angina, stroke, TIA, HF requiring hospitalization, or NYHA Class III/IV HF; history of 2nd or 3rd degree heart block or sick sinus syndrome (without a functional pacemaker), QT interval ≥ 500 msec, concurrent use of Class Ia or III anti-arrhythmics **WARNINGS** Bradycardia (must monitor), BP, macular edema, PML, severe infections, posterior reversible encephalopathy syndrome (PRES - rare but can cause stroke/hemorrhage), decrease in pulmonary function tests, hepatotoxicity **SIDE EFFECTS** Headache, diarrhea, flu-like syndrome, back pain, ↑ LFTs **MONITORING** CBC, ECG, eye exam **NOTES** Safety issue – see Pregnancy Chapter Caution when used with drugs that slow HR, monitor continuous ECG overnight after first dose if concomitant use is necessary MedGuide required

Multiple Sclerosis Drugs Continued

DRUG	DOSING	SAFETY/SIDE EFFECTS/MONITORING
Dimethyl fumarate (*Tecfidera*) Capsules NrF2 activator	120 mg PO BID for 7 days, then 240 mg BID Do not crush, chew, or sprinkle capsule contents on food	**WARNINGS** PML, anaphylaxis and angioedema, and lymphopenia/infection risk Flushing: can give aspirin 30 minutes prior and administer with food to prevent flushing, temporary dose reduction may decrease symptoms **SIDE EFFECTS** Flushing, N/V/D, abdominal pain, neutropenia (reversible) **MONITORING** CBC, ↑ LFTs and proteinuria for 6 months then every 6-12 months **NOTES** Safety issue – see Pregnancy Chapter

Dalfampridine: Potassium channel blocker that may increase nerve signal conduction; indicated to improve walking. Takes up to 6 weeks to show efficacy; most patients do not respond.

Dalfampridine (*Ampyra*) Tablet	10 mg BID Take tablets whole; do not crush, chew, divide, or dissolve	**CONTRAINDICATION** History of seizures, CrCl ≤ 50 mL/min **WARNINGS** Seizures can occur especially with higher doses, anaphylaxis **SIDE EFFECTS** UTI, insomnia, dizziness, HA, nausea, weakness, back pain **MONITORING** ECG, walking ability, SCr (baseline and annually) **NOTES** Safety issue – see Pregnancy Chapter; MedGuide required

Monoclonal Antibodies

Natalizumab (*Tysabri*) Injection (IV) Monoclonal antibody that binds to the alpha-4 subunit of integrins expressed on the surface of leukocytes	300 mg IV given over 1 hour, every 4 weeks Stable in NS only REMS: Only available through the TOUCH prescribing program	**BOXED WARNING** PML - risk factors include anti-JC virus antibodies, duration of therapy and prior use of immunosuppressants **CONTRAINDICATION** History of PML **WARNINGS** Herpes encephalitis and meningitis, hepatotoxicity, immunosuppression/infections, immune reconstitution inflammatory syndrome (IRIS) **SIDE EFFECTS** Infusion-related reactions, HA, fatigue, arthralgia, respiratory infections, UTIs, vaginitis, nausea, depression, gastroenteritis, abdominal pain **MONITORING** MRI for PML, CBC, LFTs, hypersensitivity rxns **NOTES** Safety issue – see Pregnancy Chapter; MedGuide required

Multiple Sclerosis Drugs Continued

DRUG	DOSING	SAFETY/SIDE EFFECTS/MONITORING
Recombinant humanized monoclonal antibody		
Alemtuzumab *(Lemtrada)* Injection (IV) CD52-directed cytolytic monoclonal antibody For inadequate response to ≥ 2 MS drugs	First course: 12 mg IV (over 4 hours) daily x 5 days Second course: 12 mg IV daily x 3 days 12 months after first course Pre-medicate with 1 gram methylprednisolone	**BOXED WARNINGS** Serious, sometimes fatal, autoimmune conditions; infections; cytopenias; serious, sometimes fatal, infusion reactions; malignancies REMS program: only available through *Lemtrada* REMS **CONTRAINDICATION** HIV (causes prolonged ↓ CD4 count) **SIDE EFFECTS** Rash, HA, fever, fatigue, infection, insomnia, urticaria, pruritus, N/V/D, abdominal pain, muscle pain, paresthesia, dizziness, flushing, BP, PML **MONITORING** CBC with differential and SCr, TSH, ECG, HPV screen, baseline and annual skin exams (for melanoma), signs of infection or PML **NOTES** Safety issue – see Pregnancy Chapter Complete all vaccinations 6 weeks before therapy Start antiviral prophylaxis on first day of each course and continue for 2 months or until CD4 count ≥ 200 (whichever is later) Do not shake; MedGuide required
Daclizumab *(Zinbryta)* Pre-filled syringe IL-2 recepor antagonist	150 mcg SC monthly Pre-medicate with acetaminophen or antihistamine if missed dose >2 weeks hold until next dose	**BOXED WARNINGS** Serious, sometimes fatal, autoimmune conditions; hepatic injury including autoimmune hepatitis REMS program: only available through *Zinbryta* REMS **CONTRAINDICATION** Pre-existing hepatic disease (e.g., ALT>2x UNL, autoimmune liver) **SIDE EFFECTS** Hepatotoxicity; if severe autoimmune disease or infusion related rash consider stopping; N/V/D, abdominal pain, dark urine, infections, severe depression, suicide **MONITORING** LFTs (prior to initiation, monthly, up to 6 months after last dose), HBV screening; Screen for TB treat prior to therapy, CBC with differential and SCr, sign of infection **NOTES** Safety issue – see Pregnancy Chapter Indicated for those with inadequate response to ≥ 2 MS drugs Complete all vaccinations 6 weeks before therapy Protect from light

Glatiramer Counseling

- This medication is given by injection under the skin as directed by your healthcare provider. This medication is available in 2 different doses. Depending on your dose, this medication is injected daily or 3 times a week at least 48 hours apart. Administer consistently on the same three days each week (e.g., M, W, F schedule).
- Common side effects include redness, warmth and itchy skin where you inject. Other common side effects include sweating, chest pain, weakness and anxiety. These should be mild; if they are not, contact your healthcare provider.
- The syringes can be kept at room temperature for up to one month. If it has been in the refrigerator keep the syringe at room temperature for 20 minutes. Do not inject the medication cold because this will be painful. The liquid in the syringe should be clear and colorless to slightly yellow. If particles or discoloration are present, do not use it.

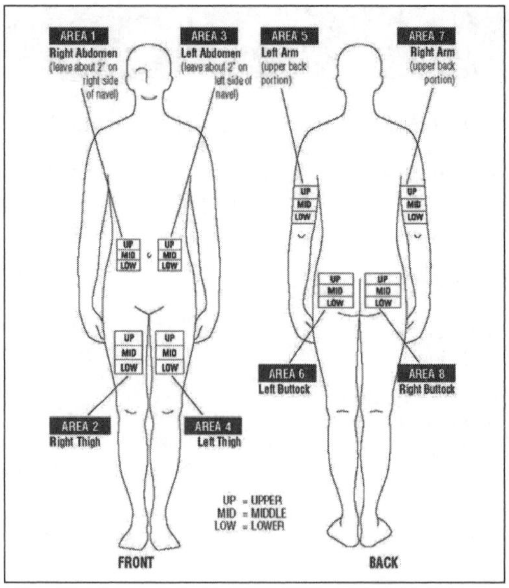

- Change the injection site daily to prevent skin problems (rotate injection sites between your arms, abdomen, hips and thighs). Keep track of your injections and do not inject into the same site for at least 1 week.
- After pulling out the needle, apply gentle pressure on the injection site. Do not rub the area. Discard any unused portion after a single use and put the used syringe into a sharps container.

Drugs Used for Symptom Control

Patients with MS may use a variety of medications for symptom control. The individual agents used can be found in different chapters in this book. Commonly used symptom-control agents for MS include anticholinergics for incontinence, laxatives for constipation (or loperamide if diarrhea), skeletal muscle relaxants for muscle spasms/spasticity, or various pain agents for muscle spasms and pain. For localized pain and spasms botulinum toxin (*Botox*) injections can provide relief for up to three months. Propranolol can help with tremor. For depression many antidepressants are used; if an SNRI is chosen it may help both neuropathic pain and depression. Fatigue is often treated with modafinil or similar agents, or stimulants used for ADHD, such as methylphenidate. Meclizine and scopolamine are used for dizziness and vertigo. Acetylcholinesterase inhibitors, including donepezil, are used to help cognitive function. Erectile dysfunction can be treated with the phosphodiesterase inhibitors.

Notice that the drugs used for symptom control can worsen other symptoms. For example, anticholinergics can mildly worsen cognitive function (not all of them do, and this is patient-specific), but it happens. The vertigo agents can worsen cognitive function. Propranolol can worsen cognitive function, depression and cause problems with sexual performance. The SSRI and SNRI antidepressants can worsen sexual concerns. Clozapine can worsen cardiac and neutropenia concerns. Opioids, if used for pain, will worsen constipation, can decrease cognition and have dependence concerns. Managing the various medications used for MS requires competent pharmacists.

RAYNAUD'S PHENOMENON

Raynaud's is a common condition which does not have drug tables discussed separately because the drugs used for treatment are common and are used for several other conditions. It is useful to know the presentation and which drugs are used for symptom relief. Raynaud's is triggered by exposure to cold and/or stress, which causes vasospasm in the extremities (most commonly in the fingers and/or toes). Laboratory findings that can signify other autoimmune conditions are generally absent. The vasospasm causes the skin to turn white and then blue, which is followed by painful swelling when the affected areas warm. The calcium channel blocker (CCB) nifedipine is commonly used for prevention – other CCBs can be used. Additional agents used for vasodilation include iloprost, topical nitroglycerin, and the phosphodiesterase-5 inhibitors. Various other classes are used less commonly.

CELIAC DISEASE

Background

Celiac disease (celiac sprue) is an immune response to eating gluten, a protein found in wheat, barley and rye. The primary and effective treatment is to avoid gluten entirely. Gluten is present in many foods, food additives and in many drug excipients. Pharmacists assist patients in avoiding gluten-containing drugs completely, even a small exposure will trigger a reaction. To emphasize this point, the FDA permits food products to be labeled "gluten-free' only if the food contains less gluten than 20 parts per million.

Clinical Presentation

The common symptoms of celiac disease are diarrhea, abdominal pain, bloating, and weight loss. Constipation (rather than diarrhea) can be present, and is more common in children. Because antibodies attack and damage the lining of the small intestine vitamin and nutritional deficiencies are common due to decreased absorption in the small intestine. Other complications include small bowel ulcers, amenorrhea and infertility, and increased risk of cancer (primarily lymphomas). Ninety-five percent of cases will respond well to dietary changes, although avoiding gluten entirely is not a simple task.

Dermatitis herpetiformis is an extremely itchy, blistery skin rash with chronic eruptions that is present in 20-25% of celiac patients, and occurs more often in males. The rash can be present with or without overt intestinal symptoms. The rash is often mistaken for eczema or psoriasis, which leads to a delay in diagnosis and treatment.

Treatment

The FDA has strict regulations regarding the active ingredients in drug formulations, but there is little oversight for the excipients in a formulation, making the identification of gluten difficult. The active drug is gluten-free, however the excipients may contain gluten. And, it is not safe to assume that the generic formulations will contain the same excipients as the brand; there is no legal requirement to match the excipients.

Package inserts may contain information on the excipient components. Look for the key word "starch" which will be either corn, potato, tapioca, or wheat. If the package insert lists "starch" alone then the manufacturer must be consulted to find out if the starch is wheat. The manufacturer may report that they do not use gluten in the manufacturing process, but they cannot state whether the excipients purchased from outside vendors are gluten-free. The risk of cross-contamination is low, but not absent, and this information should be provided to the patient who ultimately must decide, hopefully in consult with the prescriber, whether to take the drug or not.

SJÖGREN'S SYNDROME

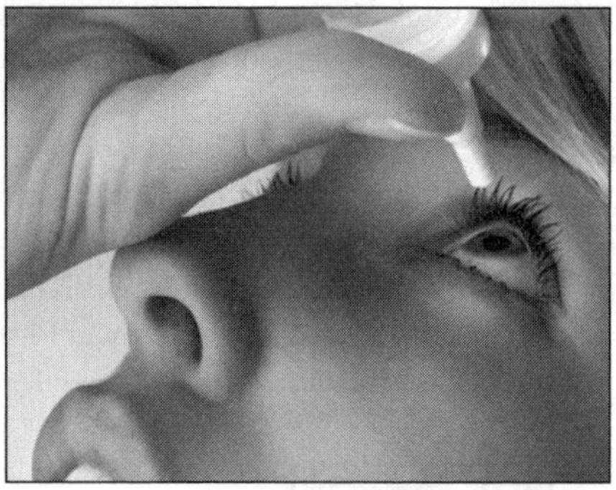

Sjögren's syndrome is an autoimmune disease, most often characterized by severe dry eyes and dry mouth. Many other symptoms can be associated with Sjögren's, including thyroiditis, Raynaud's phenomenon, neuropathy, and lymphadenopathy. Sjögren's syndrome can be primary or secondary and associated with another autoimmune disease, such as RA or SLE. Dry mouth and dry eyes are a source of significant morbidity for these patients and can lead to complications, such as dental caries, corneal ulceration, and chronic oral infections. There is no known cure for Sjögren's; therefore, treatment focuses on reducing the symptoms of dry eyes and dry mouth.

Dry Eyes Treatment

The use of artificial teardrops is the primary treatment for dry eyes. Popular OTC artificial teardrops available are *Systane, Refresh, Clear Eyes,* and *Liquifilm*. It may be necessary to try a couple of different OTC eye drops before finding one that provides the most comfort. If the preservative is irritating (likely benzalkonium chloride) preservative-free artificial tear drops packaged in individual use containers are available. If the eyes dry out while sleeping an ointment is preferable. Cyclosporine eye drops *(Restasis)* can be used in patients who do not have satisfactory relief from other measures, including ductal occlusion (lacrimal duct plugs). *Restasis* provides benefit for a small percentage of users and is expensive. Patients should be instructed to monitor a reduction in symptoms and a reduction in the use of OTC eye drops and to use properly to avoid infection, which is more likely due to the dry eye state. Counsel patients that it may take up to 3 – 6 months to notice an increase in tear production. Lifitegrast *(Xiidra)* was approved in 2016 for the treatment of signs and symptoms of dry eye disease. It is a new drug class.

Eye Drops for Dry Eyes

DRUG	DOSING	SAFETY/SIDE EFFECTS/MONITORING
CycloSPORINE Emulsion Eye Drops *(Restasis)*	1 drop in each eye Q12H	**SIDE EFFECTS** Burning, stinging, redness, pain, blurred vision, foreign body sensation, discharge, itching eye **NOTES** Prior to use, invert the vial several times to make uniform emulsion. One single-use vial is to be used immediately after opening in one or both eyes, and the remaining contents should be discarded immediately after administration. Do not allow the tip of the vial to touch the eye or any surface, as this can contaminate the emulsion. Remove contact lenses prior to administration, re-insert 15 minutes afterwards. Separate from artificial tears by 15 minutes

Eye Drops for Dry Eyes continued

DRUG	DOSING	SAFETY/SIDE EFFECTS/MONITORING
Lifitegrast *(Xiidra)*	1 drop in each eye Q12H	**SIDE EFFECTS** Eye irritation, discomfort, blurred vision, unusual taste **NOTES** Safety issue – see Pregnancy Chapter One single-use foil container to protect from light is to be used immediately after opening in each eye, and the remaining contents should be discarded immediately after administration. Do not allow the tip of the vial to touch the eye or any surface Remove contact lenses prior to administration, re-insert 15 minutes afterwards. Separate from artificial tears by 15 minutes

Dry Mouth Treatment

Non-drug treatment for dry mouth includes salivary stimulation, using sugar-free chewing gum (with xylitol) and lozenges, and daily rinses with antimicrobial mouthwash. Salivary substitutes are available in lozenges, rinses, sprays, and swabs (*Plax, Oralube, Salivart*). These contain carboxymethylcellulose or glycerin. If OTC treatments do not provide sufficient relief, prescription muscarinic agonists, such as pilocarpine or cevimeline (*Evoxac*), can be used. Glycopyrrolate is an anticholinergic agent used to decrease excessive salivation; this may be used in a few conditions, such as myasthenia gravis. Check that the dry mouth is not due to inappropriate use of glycopyrrolate.

Muscarinic Agonists for Dry Mouth

DRUG	DOSING	SAFETY/SIDE EFFECTS/MONITORING
Pilocarpine *(Salagen)* Tablet **Pilocarpine ophthalmic** *(Isopto Carpine, Pilopine HS)* is used for glaucoma	5 mg PO four times daily Fat decreases absorption, avoid taking with a high-fat meal Moderate hepatic impairment: 5 mg BID adjust dose based on response and tolerability	**CONTRAINDICATIONS** Uncontrolled asthma, narrow-angle glaucoma, severe hepatic impairment **WARNINGS** Cardiovascular disease, cholelithiasis, nephrolithiasis, hepatic impairment, respiratory disorders **SIDE EFFECTS** Diaphoresis, flushing, nausea, urinary frequency, chills, weakness, rhinitis, dizziness **MONITORING** Intraocular pressure, fundoscopic exam, visual acuity testing **NOTES** Safety issue – see Pregnancy Chapter
Cevimeline *(Evoxac)* Capsule	30 mg PO TID	**CONTRAINDICATIONS** Uncontrolled asthma, narrow-angle glaucoma, acute iritis **WARNINGS** Cardiovascular disease, cholelithiasis, nephrolithiasis, hepatic impairment, respiratory disorders, CYP2D6 deficiency **SIDE EFFECTS** Diaphoresis, nausea, URTIs (sinusitis, rhinitis) **NOTES** Safety issue – see Pregnancy Chapter

PSORIASIS

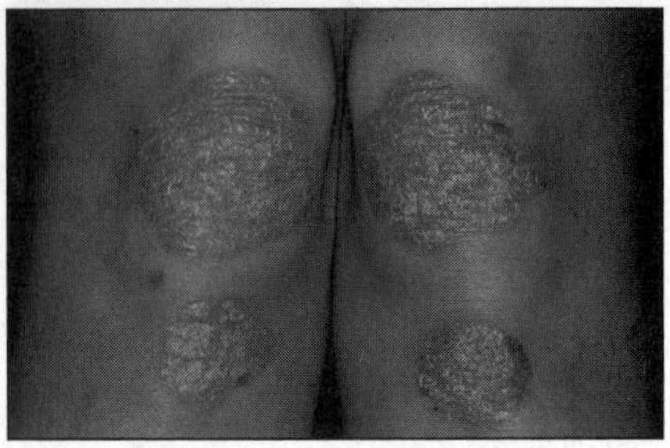

Background

Psoriasis is a chronic, autoimmune disease that appears on the skin. There are several types of psoriasis. The most common is plaque psoriasis, which appears as raised, red patches covered with a silvery white buildup of dead skin cells, on any part of the body. Treatments can be divided into three main types: topical, light therapy, and systemic medications. Most psoriasis is treated with topicals and UV light therapy. Soaking helps loosen and remove the plaques.

Non-Drug Treatment

Ultraviolet (UV) light exposure causes activated T cells in the skin to die. This slows skin turnover and ↓ scaling and inflammation. Brief, daily exposures to small amounts of sunlight can improve psoriasis, but intense sun exposure can worsen symptoms and cause skin damage. UVB phototherapy, in controlled doses from an artificial source, can improve mild to moderate psoriasis symptoms. Other non-drug treatments include photochemotherapy (ultraviolet A light with psoralen, a light sensitizer), and laser light therapy.

Drug Treatment

There are many topical options for treating psoriasis including steroids, vitamin D analogues (calcipotriene), anthralin, retinoids (some of the same drugs used for acne), salicylic acid (primarily in medicated shampoo), coal tar, and moisturizers. Topical vitamin D analogues, tazorotene, and salicylic acid are used in combination with topical steroids. If these fail, calcineurin inhibitor topicals (Protopic, Elidel) can be tried and are preferred agents for apply to the face. Treatment for more severe symptoms may require immune suppressing agents including methotrexate, cyclosporine, hydroxyurea, and the immunomodulators, such as etanercept and infliximab. Newer systemic agents approved for plaque psoriasis include *Stelara, Otezla, Cosentyx, and Taltz.*

DRUG	DOSING	SAFETY/SIDE EFFECTS/MONITORING
Topical Steroids	Monotherapy: 1-2 times daily (product dependent)	Use high-potency steroids only short-term due to risk of side effects. Can be used with other therapies See Common Skin Conditions chapter
Topical retinoids Tazorotene *(Tazorac)*		See Common Skin Conditions chapter
Coal tar, in many products, including *Neutrogena T, Denorex, Psoriasin, Pentrax Gold* Topical (cream, foam, emulsion, ointment, oil, shampoo), bath products (topicals, bar soap) + salicylic acid (*Sebutone, Tarsum, X-Seb T*, others)	Body: Apply 1-4 times per day, usually at bedtime Scalp psoriasis: Apply sparingly to lesions 3-12 hrs before each shampoo	Coal tar products are messy, time consuming and can stain clothing and bedding. Some patients get relief at a reasonable cost. Also used for dandruff and dermatitis Do not use salicylic acid products with other salicylates, systemic absorption can occur **SIDE EFFECTS** Skin irritation, photosensitivity
Anthralin (*Zithranol, Dritho-Crème HP*, others)	Body: once daily or as directed	**NOTES** Keratolytic containing salicylic acid with irritant potential, ↑ contact time as tolerated up to 30 min

Psoriasis Drug Treatment continued

DRUG	DOSING	SAFETY/SIDE EFFECTS/MONITORING
Calcipotriene (*Dovonex, Calcitrene, Sorilux)* Cream, foam, ointment, solution + betamethasone *(Taclonex* ointment, *Taclonex* scalp suspension, *Enstilar* foam*)*	Plaque psoriasis: Cream, foam, solution: Apply BID Ointment: Apply daily-BID *Taclonex*: Apply once daily for up to 4 weeks for ointment or up to 8 weeks suspension. Do not use > 100 gm ointment weekly or use on > 30% of BSA	**CONTRAINDICATIONS** Avoid in hypercalcemia or vitamin D toxicity, do not use on face **NOTES** Vitamin D analog If suspension shake well Do not apply to face, axillae or groin
Acitretin *(Soriatane)* Tablet Retinoid	25-50 mg daily with main meal of the day (lower doses ↓ side effects)	**BOXED WARNING** Hepatotoxicity, pregnancy, female (must sign informed consent before dispensing) **NOTES** Used only in severe cases when patient is unresponsive to other therapies due to numerous contraindication and side effects Safety issue – see Pregnancy Chapter. MedGuide required
Apremilast *(Otezla)* Tablet Phosphodiesterase-4 inhibitor	10 mg daily in the morning, titrate daily to 30 mg BID ↓ dose in severe renal impairment	**WARNINGS** Depression and suicidal ideation, weight loss **SIDE EFFECTS** Diarrhea, N/V, headache **NOTES** Safety issue – see Pregnancy Chapter

Apremilast Drug Interactions

- Apremilast is a major CYP450 3A4 substrate. Strong 3A4 inducers should be avoided concomitantly.

Interleukin (IL) receptor antagonist

Chimeric (murine/human) monoclonal antibodies that inhibit IL-17A *(Cosentyx, Taltz)* and IL-12/IL-23 *(Stelara)* receptors on the surface of activated T-lymphocytes are used for moderate-severe plaque psoriasis and psoriatic arthritis to prevent inflammation. Because the protein is humanized, infusion-related reactions are unlikely, and pre-medication is generally not necessary. These agents require refrigeration, do not shake or freeze, protect from light, warm prior to administration and avoid injecting into areas where psoriasis is present.

DRUG	DOSING	SAFETY/SIDE EFFECTS/MONITORING
Ixekizumab *(Taltz)* Pre-filled syringe, auto-injector	160 mg (two 80 mg injections) SC at week 0, then every 2 weeks until week 12 then monthly	**WARNINGS** Serious infections (including active TB); screen for latent TB and treat before starting; exacerbation of Crohn's disease, latex hypersensitivity, avoid live vaccines **SIDE EFFECTS** Diarrhea, URTIs **NOTES** Safety issue – see Pregnancy Chapter MedGuide required
Secukinumab *(Cosentyx)* Pre-filled syringe,Sensoready pen Injection single use vial	300 mg SC at weeks 0, 1, 2, 3, and 4, then every 4 weeks thereafter Each dose is given as two SC injections of 150 mg For some patients 150 mg dose is acceptable	**WARNINGS** Serious infections (including active TB); screen for latent TB and treat before starting; exacerbation of Crohn's disease, latex hypersensitivity, avoid live vaccines **SIDE EFFECTS** Diarrhea, URTIs **NOTES** Safety issue – see Pregnancy Chapter MedGuide required
Ustekinumab *(Stelara)* Pre-filled syringe, both doses Monoclonal antibody	≤ 100 kg: 45 mg SC at 0 and 4 weeks, then every 12 weeks thereafter > 100 kg: 90 mg SC at 0 and 4 weeks, then every 12 weeks thereafter	**WARNINGS** Serious infections (including active TB, fungal, viral, bacterial or opportunistic infections; screen for latent TB and treat before starting therapy, no live vaccines, reversible posterior leukoencephalopathy syndrome (RPLS), lymphomas and other malignancies, IL-12/IL-23 deficiency **SIDE EFFECTS** Infection, headache, fatigue, diarrhea **NOTES** Safety issue – see Pregnancy Chapter MedGuide required

PRACTICE CASE

PATIENT PROFILE

Patient Name	Jennifer Cranford
Address	4780 Valley Drive
Age	46 Sex F Race Height 5'3" Weight 140 lbs
Allergies	

DIAGNOSES

Rheumatoid Arthritis
Hypertension
Depression

MEDICATIONS

Date	No.	Prescriber	Drug & Strength	Quantity	Sig	Refills
5/1/15	48201	Pepper	Lisinopril 20 mg	30	1 PO daily	9
5/1/15	48202	Pepper	Methotrexate 7.5 mg	8	2 tabs weekly	3
5/1/15	48290	Pepper	Prednisone 10 mg	30	1 PO daily	3
5/1/15	51025	Lai	Alendronate 70 mg	4	1 PO weekly	5
			Calcium 500+ D 400 IU	OTC	1 tab daily	

LAB/DIAGNOSTIC TESTS

Test	Normal Value	Results		
		Date 5/22/15	Date	Date
Rheum Fact	<40 IU/mL	88		
ESR	≤30 mm/hr	81		
Alk Phos	33-115 u/L			
AST	10-35 IU/L	48		
ALT	6-40 mEq/L	82		
GLU	65-99 mg/dL			
NA	135-146 mEq/L			
K	3.5-5.3 mEq/L			
CL	98-110 mEq/L			
HCO3-	22-28 mEq/L			
BUN	7-25 mg/dL			
Creatinine	0.6-1.2 mg/dL			
Calcium	8.6-10.2 mg/dL			
WBC	4-11 cells/mm^3	6.5		
TB test, PPD		Negative		

ADDITIONAL INFORMATION

Date	Notes
6/14/15	BP on this visit is 129/85 mmHg. Patient reports morning stiffness for past 2 months which improves as the day progresses. Reports wrists, arms and feet joints are sore and tender and is tired all the time. No chest pain or breathing problems reported.

Questions

1. The prescriber is deciding whether to change the dose of methotrexate to daily therapy or begin etanercept. Choose the correct response:

   a. The methotrexate can be increased safely to 50 mg daily for rheumatoid arthritis.
   b. The methotrexate can be increased safely to 100 mg daily for rheumatoid arthritis.
   c. The methotrexate can be increased safely to 150 mg daily for rheumatoid arthritis.
   d. The methotrexate can be increased safely to 200 mg daily for rheumatoid arthritis.
   e. Methotrexate is not given daily for this.

2. The pharmacist will counsel the patient on her methotrexate therapy. She should include the following counseling points: (Select **ALL** that apply.)

   a. Common side effects include GI upset, nausea and diarrhea.
   b. She should not get pregnant while using this medication.
   c. Her liver will need to be checked periodically with a blood test.
   d. Choose a day of the week that you will remember to take the medicine.
   e. She should be taking leucovorin as well.

3. The patient is using prednisone 10 mg daily and weekly bisphosphonate therapy. Choose the correct statement:

   a. She does not need supplemental calcium and vitamin D with the alendronate.
   b. The prednisone may improve her blood pressure control
   c. If she is able, her healthcare provider should try and help her decrease the prednisone dose.
   d. Prednisone is not bad for bones; in fact, it builds strong bones.
   e. A, B and C.

4. The physician decides to begin etanercept therapy. Choose the correct administration route for this medication:

   a. Oral tablets
   b. Suppository
   c. Subcutaneous injection
   d. Intramuscular injection
   e. Intravenous infusion

Questions 5-7 are NOT based on the above case.

5. The pharmacist will counsel the patient on the etanercept therapy. She should include the following counseling points: (Select **ALL** that apply.)

   a. Store the medication in the freezer.
   b. Inject subcutaneously in the deltoid muscle.
   c. This medication can activate latent tuberculosis; you will need to have a TB test prior to starting therapy.
   d. This medication does not cause increased risk of infections, except for tuberculosis.
   e. You can receive live vaccines, but not the annual influenza vaccine.

6. A physician has written a prescription for *Humira*. Choose the appropriate therapeutic interchange:

   a. Adalimumab
   b. Etanercept
   c. Rituximab
   d. Anakinra
   e. Infliximab

7. A physician has written a prescription for *Remicade*. Choose the appropriate therapeutic interchange:

   a. Adalimumab
   b. Etanercept
   c. Rituximab
   d. Anakinra
   e. Infliximab

Answers

1-e, 2-a,b,c,d, 3-c, 4-c, 5-c, 6-a, 7-e

42

TRANSPLANT

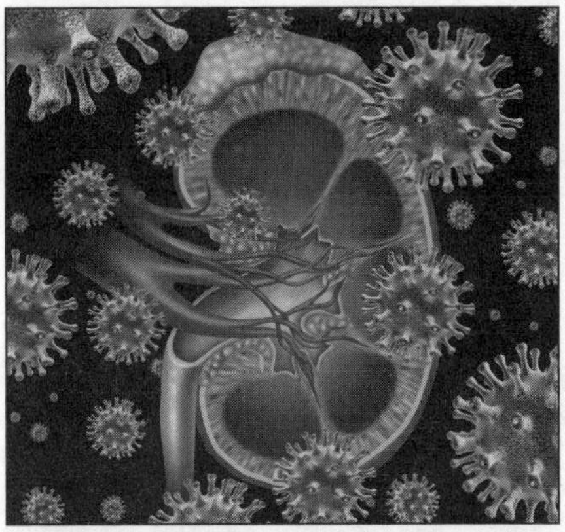

GUIDELINES/REFERENCES

Kidney Disease: Improving Global Outcomes (KDIGO) Transplant Work Group. KDIGO clinical practice guideline for the care of kidney transplant recipients. *Am J Transplant.* 2009; 9 (Suppl 3):S1-155.

Lucey MR, Terrault N, Ojo L et al. Long-Term Management of the Successful Adult Liver Transplant: 2012 Practice Guideline by AASLD and the American Society of Transplantation. http://www.aasld.org/sites/default/files/guideline_documents/managementadultltenhanced.pdf (accessed 2016 Dec 13).

Costanzo MR, Dipchand A, Starling R et al. The International Society of Heart and Lung Transplantation Guidelines for the care of heart transplant recipients. *J Heart Lung Transplant.* 2010; 29:914-56.

We gratefully acknowledge the assistance of Heather R. Bream-Rouwenhorst, PharmD, BCPS, Clinical Assistant Professor, University of Iowa College of Pharmacy, in preparing this chapter.

BACKGROUND

Transplantation is one of the most challenging and complex areas of modern medicine. Some of the key areas for medical management are the problems surrounding transplant rejection. If rejection occurs, the body is having an immune response to the transplanted organ, which can lead to transplant failure and can require immediate removal of the transplanted organ. The majority of transplant cases are kidneys (1st) and livers (2nd), in addition to others such as pancreases, hearts, lungs, etc. Prior to any transplant, tissue typing or crossmatching is performed to assess donor-recipient compatibility for human leukocyte antigen (HLA) and ABO blood group. A mismatch in either instance would lead to a fast, acute rejection. This is followed by a Panel Reactive Antibody (PRA) test that is taken to gauge the degree to which the recipient is "sensitized" to foreign (or "non-self") proteins. A high score correlates with the likelihood of graft rejection and could necessitate some type of desensitization protocol prior to the transplant. Patients with a higher PRA result are likely to wait longer for a suitable donor.

An allograft is the transplant of an organ or tissue from one individual to another of the same species with a different genotype. This can also be called an allogenic transplant or homograft. A transplanted organ from a genetically identical donor (such as an identical twin) is called an isograft. An autograft is when a tissue is a transplant from one site to another on the same patient, also termed autologous transplant (or autologous stem cell transplant).

AVOIDING AN "ABO MISMATCH" OR INCOMPATIBILITY REACTION

Type A blood will react against type B or type AB blood.

Type B blood will react against type A or type AB blood.

Type O blood will react against type A, type B, or type AB blood (Type O can only receive Type O).

Type AB blood will not react against type A, type B, or type AB blood.

Type O blood does not cause an immune response when it is received by people with type A, type B, or type AB blood. This is why type O blood cells can be given to patients of any blood type. People with type O blood are called "universal donors."

Hyperacute rejection occurs in the operating room within hours of the transplant and is due to some type of mismatch; no treatment exists, and the transplanted organ must be removed to avoid death.

Induction immunosuppressant therapy is given before or at the time of transplant to prevent an acute rejection during the early post-transplant period by providing a high degree of immune suppression. It consists of a short course of very effective intravenous (IV) agents using either a biological drug or monoclonal antibody (these end in -mab) sometimes combined with high-dose IV steroids. The most commonly used induction drug is basiliximab, an interleukin-2 (IL-2) receptor antagonist. The IL-2 receptor is expressed on activated T-lymphocytes and is a critical pathway for activating cell-mediated rejection. As an alternative to basiliximab, patients at higher risk of rejection will receive the lymphocyte-depleting agent antithymocyte globulin. In some cases, induction can be achieved with higher doses of the same drugs used for maintenance. Induction agents may not be required if the transplant is from an identical twin.

Maintenance immunosuppressant therapy is generally provided by the combination of:

- A calcineurin inhibitor (CNI; tacrolimus is the 1st line CNI), plus:
  - An antiproliferative agent (mycophenolate is 1st line in most protocols), or everolimus, sirolimus, belatacept or azathioprine.
  - ± steroids (typically prednisone).

If the patient is low immunological risk, the steroids will be discontinued; otherwise, they are not, and the long-term adverse effects will need to be considered. Suppressing the immune system via multiple mechanisms through different drug classes is designed to both lower toxicity risk of the individual immunosuppressants and to reduce the risk of graft rejection.

Cardiovascular Disease: The Common Cause of Death in Transplant Patients

A concerted effort must be made to reduce risk factors for cardiovascular disease (CVD). This is challenging considering that the patient is using transplant-rejection drugs that cause metabolic syndrome. Nonetheless, these patients are among the highest risk for CVD, and blood pressure, blood glucose, cholesterol and weight must be tightly controlled. For instance, in a renal transplant patient, the blood pressure must be well-controlled with goals provided by the transplant center. Specific goals based on transplant protocols are managed by specialists, including pharmacists, that specialize in transplant medicine. Blood glucose is managed to the ADA guidelines and cholesterol to the NCEP guidelines. Weight is measured at each visit, with reduction programs used as-needed. Refer to the individual chapters for treatment of these conditions.

Cancer: Higher Risk in Transplant Patients

Cancer risk is higher in transplant recipients compared to the general population. Some cancer types are viral-mediated and related to the immune suppression, which causes increased cancer incidence. The cancer risk is similar to that seen with the use of the stronger agents used for autoimmune conditions. For example, the Epstein-Barr virus infects most people without serious consequences. In transplant recipients, there is a marked increase in the risk of malignancies associated with the infection. Age-appropriate cancer screening should be performed prior to getting on the list as a transplant candidate, and post-transplant, according to nationally recognized guidelines. Screening for common cancers should be routine, along with lifestyle measures known to reduce risk. Skin cancer is common with transplant, and sunscreen must be used routinely, along with sun avoidance or sun protection with clothing. In addition, CNIs cause photosensitivity. The skin should be assessed professionally at least annually.

TRANSPLANT DRUGS: WHAT'S USED, WHEN

Immunosuppression protocols will vary by center and type of transplant.

Induction Drugs (to avoid acute early rejection):
Basiliximab, an interleukin-2 (IL-2) receptor antagonist (the primary induction agent), or antithymocyte globulin in patients at higher risk of rejection, or the maintenance drugs at higher doses.

Primary Immunosuppressive Drugs
The calcineurin inhibitors (CNIs), which are tacrolimus (primarily) or cyclosporine.

Adjuvant Agents (given with the primary drugs), also called Antiproliferative or Antimetabolite Agents
Given with the CNI (to enable lower doses of the CNI to reduce nephrotoxicity risk). These include steroids, azathioprine or mycophenolate mofetil (*CellCept*). The majority of transplant patients use a CNI + *CellCept* ± steroids. Or, patients may be using one of the drugs that bind to the mTOR protein (such as everolimus) to reduce the CNI nephrotoxicity risk. This class may act synergistically with the CNIs.

With the use of adjuvants, adequate immunosuppression can be achieved while decreasing the dose and toxicity of the individual agents.

Infection Risk Reduction
Protocols for which prophylactic drugs to use will vary by the transplant center and the type of transplant. See separate box for the discussion of vaccines. Treatment of opportunistic infections is the same as in HIV; see Infectious Diseases IV chapter.

All transplant recipients must self-monitor for symptoms of infection: fever of 100.5°F (38°C) or higher (lower if elderly), chills, sore throat, ear or sinus pain, cough, more sputum or change in color of sputum, pain with passing urine, mouth sores, or a wound that will not heal.

Monitoring by Patient & Health Care Team

In addition to drug toxicity symptoms, patients will need to monitor for symptoms of organ rejection. Common symptoms of an acute rejection include flu-like symptoms, such as chills, body aches, nausea, cough, shortness of breath and organ-specific symptoms that depend on the transplant type. For example, heart failure symptoms or a new arrhythmia could be due to a heart transplant rejection. A decrease in urine output, fluid retention, blood pressure elevation or graft tenderness could be due to a kidney transplant rejection.

Monitoring Questions
Is it a symptom of drug **toxicity**?

Is it a symptom of **organ rejection**?

Is it a symptom of an **infection**?

All immunosuppressive medications require careful monitoring (including drug trough levels) to minimize toxicities and decrease the incidence of rejection. Keep in mind which maintenance agents have the highest incidence of certain adverse effects:

- Nephrotoxicity (tacrolimus and cyclosporine)
- Worsening or new onset diabetes (tacrolimus, steroids and cyclosporine)
- Worsening lipid parameters (mTOR inhibitors, steroids and cyclosporine)
- Hypertension (steroids, cyclosporine and tacrolimus)

Reducing Infection Risk

The use of potent drugs has made solid organ transplant widely available and successful. However, the use of strong agents correlates with infection risk. The majority of infections are opportunistic, and these are a major cause of death in transplant recipients. Opportunistic infections are caused by organisms that are ubiquitous (everywhere) in the environment, but rarely cause disease in the immunocompetent host (persons with a functional immune system). Infection prophylaxis is essential; review the basics in the sidebars. Infection control must include reducing risk from transmission, such as proper hand-washing techniques (see Medication Safety chapter), air filtration systems, keeping the mouth clean, and keeping away from dusty, crowded areas and sick people. Often the drugs used for opportunistic infection prophylaxis are used for treatment, but in larger doses and possibly given IV. Treatment may require drugs used in combination. Vaccine-preventable illness is an important consideration pre-transplant since live vaccines cannot be given post-transplant.

VACCINE-PREVENTABLE ILLNESS

Required vaccines should be given pre-transplant if the recipient is not current. The inactivated vaccines can be given post-transplant in 3-6 months (once the immune system has recovered from the induction immunosuppression), if needed; live vaccines cannot be given post-transplant.

Influenza (inactivated, not live) annually (recurring, each October-November) should be given when the vaccine is available.

Pneumococcal vaccine in adults ≥ 19 years who are immunocompromised: receive PCV13 first, followed by PPSV23 at least 8 weeks later. Subsequent doses of PPSV23 should follow current PPSV23 recommendations for adults at high risk (5 years after the first PPSV23 dose). Some transplant centers recommend PPSV23 every 5 years.

Transplant patients are at high risk for serious varicella infections, with a very high risk of disseminated disease if infection occurs. The best protection is to vaccinate the close contacts (in addition to the recipient pre-transplant). Although there is a small risk that transmission could occur (from the vaccine recipient to the transplant recipient), ACIP states that "the benefits of vaccinating susceptible household contacts of immunocompromised persons outweigh the potential risk for transmission of vaccine virus to immunocompromised contacts."

If a vaccinated household contact develops a rash they are considered contagious. They should avoid contact with the transplant recipient and should contact their physician. If the transplant patient develops a rash, they will need to be seen right away.

INDUCTION AGENTS

DRUG	SAFETY/SIDE EFFECTS/MONITORING

Antithymocyte globulins – Reverse rejection by binding to antigens on T-lymphocytes (killer cells) and interfering with their function. These drugs are made by injecting human T-lymphocytes into animals, allowing the animals to make antibodies against the T-lymphocytes, and then administering the animals' purified antibodies back to the human transplant recipients. Because they deplete both mature and immature T-lymphocytes, they may be used for both induction and treatment of rejection.

Antithymocyte Globulin *(ATGAM-Equine)* *(Thymoglobulin-Rabbit)*	**BOXED WARNING** Should be administered under the supervision of a physician experienced in immunosuppressive therapy. Adequate laboratory and supportive medical resources must be readily available (e.g., epinephrine). Anaphylaxis (intradermal skin testing recommended prior to 1st dose). **SIDE EFFECTS** Infusion-related reactions (fever, chills, pruritus, rash, hypotension; particularly common with the first dose), leukopenia, thrombocytopenia, chest pain, hypertension, edema and others **MONITORING** Lymphocyte profile (T-cell count), CBC with differential, vital signs during administration **NOTES** Pre-medicate (diphenhydramine, acetaminophen and steroids) to lessen infusion-related reactions. Epinephrine and resuscitative equipment should be nearby. There is a difference in dosing. Normal equine doses are approximately 10-fold greater than the rabbit product (10-15 mg/kg/day vs. 1-1.5 mg/kg/day IV, respectively, for 5-14 days).

Interleukin 2 (IL-2) receptor antagonist – Chimeric (murine/human) monoclonal antibody that inhibits the IL-2 receptor on the surface of activated T-lymphocytes preventing cell-mediated allograft rejection. Basiliximab does not deplete immature T-lymphocytes and therefore cannot be used for treatment of rejection. Because the protein is humanized, infusion-related reactions are unlikely, and pre-medication is generally not necessary.

Basiliximab *(Simulect)* Dosing: 20 mg IV post-op day 1 then repeat dose 4 days after transplant	**BOXED WARNING** Should only be used by physicians experienced in immunosuppressive therapy. **SIDE EFFECTS** Well tolerated; side effects listed are rated as severe and >10%: hypertension, fever, weakness, stomach upset/nausea/vomiting/cramping, peripheral edema, dyspnea/upper respiratory irritation/infection, cough, tremor, painful urination **MONITORING** Signs and symptoms of hypersensitivity and infection.

MAINTENANCE MEDICATIONS

DRUG	DOSING	SAFETY/SIDE EFFECTS/MONITORING

Systemic steroids – Naturally occurring hormones that prevent or suppress inflammation and humoral immune responses

PredniSONE, others	2.5-5 mg PO daily, or on alternate days (dose individualized to patient's history of rejection and other factors)	**SHORT-TERM SIDE EFFECTS** Fluid retention, stomach upset, emotional instability (euphoria, mood swings, irritability), insomnia, ↑ appetite, weight gain, acute rise in blood glucose and blood pressure with high dose **LONG-TERM SIDE EFFECTS** Adrenal suppression/Cushing's syndrome, impaired wound healing, hypertension, diabetes, acne, osteoporosis, impaired growth in children. See Autoimmune chapter for further information on chronic steroid use.

Antiproliferative Agents – Inhibit T-lymphocyte proliferation by altering purine synthesis

Mycophenolate Mofetil (*CellCept*) **Mycophenolic Acid (*Myfortic*)**	1-1.5 g PO/IV BID *(Cellcept)* or 360-720 mg PO BID *(Myfortic)*, depending on transplant type	**BOXED WARNINGS** ↑ risk of infection; ↑ development of lymphoma and skin malignancies; ↑ risk of congenital malformations and spontaneous abortions when used during pregnancy; should only be prescribed by healthcare providers experienced in immunosuppressive therapy. **SIDE EFFECTS** Diarrhea, GI upset, vomiting, leukopenia, hyper- and hypotension, edema, tachycardia, pain, hyperglycemia, hypo/hyperkalemia, hypomagnesemia, hypocalcemia, hypercholesterolemia, tremor, acne, infections **MONITORING** CBC, intolerable diarrhea, renal function, LFTs, signs of infection **NOTES** MedGuide required REMS drug Safety Issue – see Pregnancy chapter *CellCept* and *Myfortic* should not be used interchangeably due to differences in absorption. Myfortic is enteric coated to decrease diarrhea (1% absolute difference in rates of reported diarrhea with *Cellcept* vs. *Myfortic*). Protect tablets from moisture and light. *CellCept IV* is stable in D5W only. Do not use IV if allergy to polysorbate 80. Should be taken on an empty stomach to avoid variability in absorption. Decreases efficacy of oral contraceptives.

Maintenance Medications Continued

DRUG	DOSING	SAFETY/SIDE EFFECTS/MONITORING
AzaTHIOprine (*Azasan, Imuran*)	1-3 mg/kg PO daily, for maintenance CrCl < 50 mL/min: adjustment required	**BOXED WARNINGS** Chronic immunosuppression can ↑ risk of neoplasia (esp. lymphomas); hematologic toxicities (leukopenia, thrombocytopenia) and mutagenic potential. **WARNINGS** GI (severe N/V/D), hematologic (leukopenia, thrombocytopenia, anemia) and hepatotoxicity; patients with genetic deficiency of thiopurine methyltransferase (TPMT) are at ↑ risk for myelosuppression and may require lower dose. **SIDE EFFECTS** GI upset (N/V), rash, ↑ LFTs, myelosuppression **MONITORING** LFTs, CBC, renal function **NOTES** Safety Issue – see Pregnancy chapter

Calcineurin inhibitors – Suppress cellular immunity by inhibiting T-lymphocyte activation

Tacrolimus (*Prograf,* *Astagraf XL, Envarsus XR*) *Protopic* – topical for eczema	Initial: 0.1-0.2 mg/kg/day PO (depending on transplant type) in 2 divided doses for *Prograf*, given every 12 hours Goal trough level varies, dependent on: Transplant type Time since transplant Concurrent medications 4. Center's protocol Goal trough 3-15 ng/mL	**BOXED WARNINGS** ↑ susceptibility to infection; possible development of lymphoma; should be administered under the supervision of a physician experienced in organ transplantation in a facility appropriate for monitoring and managing therapy; extended-release tacrolimus associated with increased mortality in female liver transplant recipients (*Astagraf XL*) **SIDE EFFECTS** Hypertension, nephrotoxicity, hyperglycemia, neurotoxicity, (tremor, headache, dizziness, paresthesias), hyperkalemia, hypomagnesemia, edema, chest pain, insomnia, generalized pain, rash/pruritus, diarrhea, abdominal pain, nausea, dyspepsia, anorexia, constipation, urinary tract infection, anemia, leukopenia, leukocytosis, thrombocytopenia, elevated liver enzymes, arthralgia, hypophosphatemia, hyperlipidemia, QT prolongation **MONITORING** MedGuide required Trough levels, serum electrolytes (K and Mg), renal function, LFTs, BP, blood glucose, lipid profile **NOTES** Consistently take with or without food; food decreases absorption. Higher fat food decreases absorption the most. Do not interchange XL to immediate release. PO IR doses are 3-4 times that of IV. Start oral dosing 8-12 hours after last IV dose. Numerous drug interactions: this is a CYP 3A4 and P-gp substrate. Avoid alcohol.

Maintenance Medications Continued

DRUG	DOSING	SAFETY/SIDE EFFECTS/MONITORING
CycloSPORINE (modified: *Neoral, Gengraf;* non-modified: *SandIMMUNE)* *Restasis* – drops for dry eyes	Dose depends on transplant type and formulation Cyclosporine (modified): initial dosing of ~8 ± 4 mg/kg/day, divided BID and then individualized to achieve target trough level Cyclosporine (non-modified): 3-10 mg/kg/day, divided BID, for maintenance, individualized to achieve target trough level IV cyclosporine (*Sandimmune*) is available; the IV dose is 1/3 of the PO dose Conversion to cyclosporine (modified) from cyclosporine (non-modified): Start with daily dose previously used and adjust to obtain pre-conversion cyclosporine trough concentration; monitor every 4-7 days and dose adjust as necessary Goal trough 100-400 ng/mL (nephrotoxicity can occur at any level)	**BOXED WARNINGS** Renal impairment (with high doses); ↑ risk of lymphoma and other malignancies; ↑ risk of skin cancer; ↑ risk of infection; may cause hypertension; dose adjustments should only be made under the direct supervision of an experienced physician, cyclosporine (modified – *Gengraf/Neoral)* has 20-50% greater bioavailability compared to cyclosporine (non-modified – *Sandimmune)* and cannot be used interchangeably. **SIDE EFFECTS** Hypertension, nephropathy, hyperkalemia, hypomagnesemia, hirsutism, gingival hyperplasia, edema, hyperglycemia, neurotoxicity (tremor, headache, paresthesia), abdominal discomfort/nausea/diarrhea, increased triglycerides, viral infections, QT prolongation **MONITORING** Trough levels, serum electrolytes (K and Mg), renal function, LFTs, BP, blood glucose, lipid profile **NOTES** Numerous drug interactions: this is a CYP 3A4 and P-gp substrate.

Mammalian target of rapamycin (mTOR) kinase inhibitor) – Inhibits T-lymphocyte activation and proliferation; may be synergistic with CNIs

Everolimus *(Zortress, Afinitor)* *Afinitor Disperz* is available for treatment of breast, pancreatic, and renal cancers	Initial: 0.75-1 mg PO BID; adjust maintenance dose if needed to reach serum trough of 3-8 ng/mL	**BOXED WARNINGS** Only experienced prescribers should prescribe everolimus; ↑ risk of infection and cancers; reduced doses of cyclosporine are recommended when used concomitantly; ↑ risk of renal thrombosis may result in graft loss; not recommended in heart transplant. **SIDE EFFECTS** Peripheral edema, hypertension, constipation, N/V/D, HA, hyperglycemia, hyperlipidemia/hypertriglyceridemia, impaired wound healing, pneumonitis (discontinue drug if this develops), proteinuria, fatigue, fever, rash/pruritus, xeroderma, acne, onychoclasis (nail disease), abdominal discomfort, stomatitis, dysgeusia, weight loss, dry mouth, anemia, lymphocytopenia, thrombocytopenia, risk of renal and hepatic artery thrombosis (do not use within 30 days of transplant), angioedema **MONITORING** Trough levels, renal function, LFTs, lipids, blood glucose, BP, CBC, signs of infection **NOTES** MedGuide required Everolimusis a 3A4 substrate; concomitant use of inducers or inhibitors will necessitate everolimus dose adjustments.

Maintenance Medications Continued

DRUG	DOSING	SAFETY/SIDE EFFECTS/MONITORING
Sirolimus (*Rapamune*)	Usually 1-5 mg/day Serum trough concentrations should be determined 3-4 days after loading doses and 7-14 days after dosage adjustments; approximate range 4-12 ng/mL, level dependent on concurrent drug use, including potent inhibitors or inducers of CYP 3A4 or P-gp.	**BOXED WARNINGS** ↑ risk of infection; ↑ risk of lymphoma; not recommended for use in liver transplantation (hepatic artery thrombosis); not recommended for use in lung transplantation (anastomotic dehiscence) **SIDE EFFECTS** Impaired wound healing, irreversible pneumonitis/bronchitis/cough (discontinue therapy if this develops), hyperglycemia, hyperlipidemia/hypertriglyceridemia, peripheral edema, hypertension, headache, pain, insomnia, acne, constipation, abdominal pain, diarrhea, nausea, anemia, thrombocytopenia, arthralgia **MONITORING** Trough levels, LFTs, renal function, blood glucose, lipids, BP, CBC, signs of infection **NOTES** Tablets and oral solution are not bioequivalent due to differences in absorption. Sirolimus is a CYP 3A4 substrate; concomitant use of inducers or inhibitors will necessitate sirolimus dose adjustments.

Belatacept binds to CD80 and CD86 to ultimately block T-cell costimulation and production of inflammatory mediators

Belatacept (*Nulojix*) Administer with silicone-free disposable syringe (comes with drug)	Initial: 10 mg/kg on days 1, 5 and then at the end of weeks 2, 4, 8, and 12 after transplantation Maintenance: 5 mg/kg at the end of week 16 after transplantation and then monthly thereafter Dose using TBW and round dose to the nearest 12.5 mg	**BOXED WARNINGS** Increased risk of post-transplant lymphoproliferative disorder (PTLD) with highest risk in recipients without immunity to Epstein-Barr Virus (EBV). Use in EBV seropositive patients only. Increased susceptibility to infection and malignancies; avoid use in liver transplant patients due to risk of graft loss and death; should be administered under the supervision of a prescriber experienced in immunosuppressive therapy. **WARNINGS** Increased risk of opportunistic infections, sepsis, and/or fatal infections. Increased risk of tuberculosis (TB); test patients for latent TB prior to initiation, and treat latent TB infection prior to use **SIDE EFFECTS** Headache, anemia, leukopenia, constipation, diarrhea, nausea, peripheral edema, hypertension, cough, photosensitivity, insomnia, urinary tract infection, pyrexia, hypo/hyperkalemia **MONITORING** New-onset or worsening neurological, cognitive, or behavioral signs/symptoms (consider progressive multifocal leukoencephalopathy (PML), post-transplant lymphoproliferative disorder (PTLD), or CNS infection); signs/symptoms of infection, TB screening prior to therapy initiation, EBV seropositive verification prior to therapy initiation **NOTES** MedGuide required

Drug Interactions

Transplant drugs affect the levels of each other and the following interactions must be considered: Cyclosporine will ↓ mycophenolate and ↑ sirolimus and everolimus (and will increase some of the statins, which transplant patients are usually taking). Both cyclosporine and tacrolimus are CYP 3A4 and P-glycoprotein (P-gp) substrates. Inducers of either enzyme (examples: carbamazepine, nafcillin, rifampin, etc.) will decrease the CNI concentration, and inhibitors (examples: azole antifungals, diltiazem, erythromycin, etc.) will increase the CNI concentration. Both will interact with the majority of drugs. Consistency is essential; the drug dose will be adjusted to the trough level. Tacrolimus absorption is decreased by food; take with or without, but be consistent.

- Azathioprine is metabolized by xanthine oxidase. The dose will need to be reduced by 75% if concomitant allopurinol, a xanthine oxidase inhibitor, is used.
- ACE inhibitors should not be used with azathioprine due to a risk of severe anemia.
- Use of azathioprine with other drugs that can cause myelosuppression should be done cautiously.
- Mycophenolate – can ↓ levels of hormonal contraception; mycophenolate levels can be ↓ by antacids and multivitamins, cyclosporine, metronidazole, PPIs, quinolones, sevelamer, bile acid resins, and rifampin and derivatives. Monitor for additive myelosuppression when using mycophenolate with other marrow suppressing drugs.
- Avoid grapefruit juice and St. John's wort with either CNI.
- Caution with additive drugs that are nephrotoxic with tacrolimus and cyclosporine.
- Caution with additive drugs that raise blood glucose with tacrolimus, steroids, cyclosporine and the mTOR inhibitors (everolimus/sirolimus).
- Caution with additive drugs that worsen lipids with the mTOR inhibitors, steroids and cyclosporine.
- Caution with additive drugs that raise blood pressure with steroids, cyclosporine and tacrolimus.

Patient Counseling for All Immunosuppressants

- Take the medication exactly as prescribed by your healthcare provider. It is important that you take your medication at the same time every day. Also, stay consistent on how you take your medication.
- Never change or skip a dose of medication. Remember, if you stop taking your immunosuppressive medications, your body will reject your transplanted organ.
- Monitor your health at home and keep daily records of your temperature, weight, blood pressure, and glucose (if diabetes is present).
- Do not take any NSAIDs (e.g., *Advil, Naprosyn, Aleve*) as these drugs could cause harm to your kidney.
- Do not take any over-the-counter, herbal, or alternative medications without consulting with your healthcare provider.
- Do not get immunizations/vaccinations without the consent of your healthcare provider. The use of live vaccines should definitely be avoided. Avoid contact with people who have recently received oral polio vaccine, nasal flu vaccine, or zoster vaccine.
- Patients are vulnerable to developing infections (severe infections) due to their suppressed immune system. Avoid contact with people who have the flu or other contagious illness. Practice infection control techniques such as good hand washing and staying away from sick people.
- Chronic immunosuppression has been associated with an increased risk of cancer, particularly lymphoma and skin cancer. Protect and cover your skin from the sun. Be sure to use sunscreen with an SPF of 30 or higher. Avoid using tanning beds or sunlamps. People who take immunosuppressive medications have a higher risk of getting skin cancer.
- If getting a blood test to measure the drug level, take your medication after you had your blood drawn (not before). It is important to measure the lowest (trough) level of drug in your blood.

Patient Counseling for Mycophenolate

- Take exactly as prescribed, every 12 hours (8 AM and 8 PM). It is important that you take your medication at the same time every day.
- If you miss a dose and it is less than 4 hours after the scheduled dose, take the missed dose and continue on your regular schedule. If you miss a dose and it is more than 4 hours after your scheduled dose, skip the missed dose, and return to your regular dosing schedule. Never take 2 doses at the same time. Record any missed doses.
- Take capsules, tablets and oral suspension on an empty stomach, either 1 hour before or 2 hours after a meal.
- Do not open or crush tablets or capsules. If you are not able to swallow tablets or capsules, your healthcare provider may prescribe an oral suspension. Your pharmacist will mix the medicine before giving it to you.
- Do not mix the oral suspension with any other medicine.
- This medication can cause diarrhea. Call your healthcare provider right away if you have diarrhea. Do not stop the medication without first talking with your healthcare provider. Other side effects include nausea, vomiting, abdominal pain/cramping, headache, and decreased white blood cells and platelets.
- Do not get pregnant while taking this medication. Women who take this medication during pregnancy have a higher risk of losing a pregnancy (miscarriage) during the first 3 months (first trimester), and a higher risk that their baby will be born with birth defects. Birth control pills do not work as well with this drug.
- Do not take with antacids or multivitamins concurrently. Separate the doses by 2 hours. Avoid use with bile acid resins.
- Limit the amount of time you spend in sunlight. Avoid using tanning beds or sunlamps. Use sunscreen with a SPF of 30 or higher. People who take this medicine have a higher risk of getting skin cancer.
- Mycophenolic acid *(Myfortic)* and mycophenolate mofetil *(CellCept)* are not interchangeable. Do not switch between products unless directed by your healthcare provider. These medicines are absorbed differently. This can affect the amount of medicine in your blood.

Patient Counseling for Tacrolimus

- Take this medication as directed by your healthcare provider, usually every 12 hours. It is best to take on an empty stomach for best absorption. However it is taken, you must be consistent (with food or without food), and take this medication the same way every day so that your body always absorbs the same amount of drug.
- It is important to take all doses on time to keep the amount of medicine in your body at a constant level. Remember to take it at the same times each day. You will need repeated appropriate laboratory tests while receiving tacrolimus; at a minimum, expect a monthly trough level with renal function and electrolyte monitoring. Follow your prescriber's dosage instructions exactly, and do not change your dose without first discussing it with your prescriber. Tacrolimus increases your risk of cancer; do not become pregnant without discussing pregnancy with your prescriber first.
- If you miss a dose and it is less than 4 hours after the scheduled dose, take the missed dose and continue on your regular schedule. If you miss a dose and it is more than 4 hours after your scheduled dose, skip the missed dose, and return to your regular dosing schedule. Never take 2 doses at the same time. Record any missed doses.
- As with other immunosuppressive drugs, owing to the potential risk of malignant skin changes, exposure to sunlight and ultraviolet (UV) light should be limited by wearing protective clothing and using a sunscreen with a SPF of 30 or higher.

- Avoid eating grapefruit or drinking grapefruit juice while being treated with tacrolimus. Grapefruit can increase the amount of tacrolimus in your bloodstream. Tacrolimus has many drug interactions; never start or stop any medication without first discussing the change with the transplant team FIRST.
- Tacrolimus may cause your blood pressure to increase. You may be required to check your blood pressure periodically and/or take another medication to control your blood pressure.
- Side effects of tacrolimus also include tremors/shaking, headache, diarrhea, nausea/vomiting, upset stomach, loss of appetite, tingling of the hands/feet, increased blood pressure, increased cholesterol, increased blood sugar, decreased kidney function, and an increase in potassium levels.
- Tacrolimus can cause diabetes. Tell your healthcare provider if you experience any of the following symptoms of high blood sugar: increased thirst/hunger or frequent urination.
- Tacrolimus may cause a condition that affects the heart rhythm (QT prolongation). QT prolongation can infrequently result in serious fast/irregular heartbeat and other symptoms (such as severe dizziness, fainting) that require immediate medical attention.
- High (or low) levels of potassium or magnesium in the blood may also increase your risk of certain heart abnormalities called QT prolongation. This risk may increase if you use certain drugs (such as diuretics/"water pills") or if you have conditions such as severe sweating, diarrhea, or vomiting. This drug may increase your potassium and lower your magnesium levels.

Patient Counseling for Cyclosporine (using *Neoral* as an example)

- Because different brands deliver different amounts of medication, do not switch brands of cyclosporine without your prescriber's permission and directions.
- Take *Neoral* on a consistent schedule with regard to time of day and relation to meals. Avoid eating grapefruit or drinking grapefruit juice while being treated with this medication. Grapefruit can increase the amount of the cyclosporine in your bloodstream. Cyclosporine has many drug interactions; never start or stop any medication without first discussing the change with the transplant team.
- If you miss a dose and it is less than 4 hours after the scheduled dose, take the missed dose and continue on your regular schedule. If you miss a dose and it is more than 4 hours after your scheduled dose, skip the missed dose, and return to your regular dosing schedule. Never take 2 doses at the same time. Record any missed doses.
- Repeated laboratory tests (trough blood levels, renal function, and electrolytes) will be needed while you take cyclosporine. If getting a blood test to measure the drug level, take your medication after you had your blood drawn.
- *Neoral* oral solution (cyclosporine oral solution [USP Modified]) should be diluted, preferably with orange or apple juice that is at room temperature. Do not administer oral liquid from plastic or styrofoam cup. The combination of *Neoral* Oral Solution (cyclosporine oral solution, USP) Modified with milk can be unpalatable. (*Sandimmune* can be diluted with milk, chocolate milk, or orange juice). Avoid changing diluents frequently. Mix thoroughly and drink at once. Use the syringe provided to measure the dose, mix in a glass container, and rinse the container with more diluent to ensure the total dose was taken.
- Cyclosporine can also cause high blood pressure and kidney problems. The risk of both problems increases with higher doses and longer treatment with this drug.
- Side effects of cyclosporine also include increased cholesterol, headache, nausea, vomiting, diarrhea, stomach upset, increased hair growth on the face/body, tremor, and acne. If any of these effects persist or worsen, notify your healthcare provider promptly.

- This drug can increase your risk for developing skin cancer. Avoid prolonged sun exposure, tanning booths and sunlamps. Use a sunscreen, SPF 30 or higher, and wear protective clothing when outdoors.
- This medication may cause swelling and growth of the gums (gingival hyperplasia). Brush your teeth and floss daily to minimize this problem. See your dentist regularly.

REJECTION

Rejection of the transplanted organ arises from either T-cell (cellular) or B-cell (humoral or antibody) mediated mechanisms. Both types can occur simultaneously. Distinguishing the type of rejection via biopsy is essential in order to determine treatment.

In general, the initial approach is administration of high-dose corticosteroids. For cellular rejection, the steroids and increased levels of maintenance immunosuppression may be adequate to treat the rejection. For steroid-resistant rejection, administration of antithymocyte globulin is often the next step.

Humoral rejection is more challenging to treat as the preformed antibodies against the graft must be removed and then suppressed from recurring. This process if often done via a course of plasmapheresis and administration of immunomodulatory intravenous immunoglobulin (IVIG), followed by a dose of rituximab. Rituximab, a monoclonal antibody against the CD20 antigen on B-cells, will prevent further antibody development.

43

CONTRACEPTION & INFERTILITY

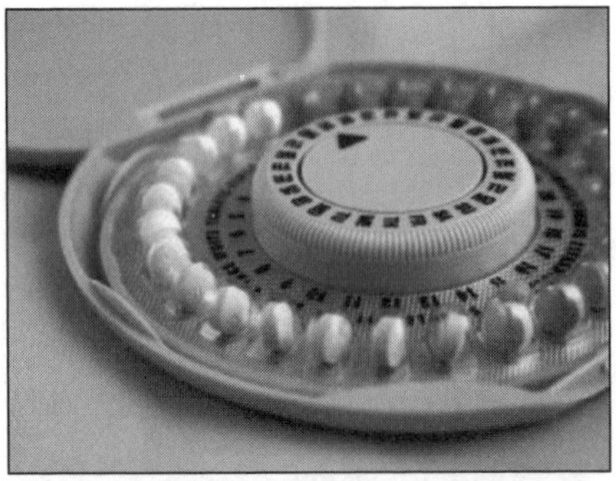

We gratefully acknowledge the assistance of Sally Rafie, PharmD, BCPS, Assistant Clinical Professor, University of California San Diego Skaggs School of Pharmacy and Pharmaceutical Sciences, in preparing this chapter.

GUIDELINES/REFERENCES

Emergency Contraception Information http://ec.princeton.edu/index.html (accessed 2016 Nov 19).

Association of Reproductive Health Professionals (ARHP) http://www.arhp.org/topics/contraception (accessed 2016 Nov 19).

Additional guidelines included with the online course.

BACKGROUND

There are 61 million U.S. women in their childbearing years (ages 15 – 44 years). Seven in 10 women of reproductive age (43 million) are sexually active and do not want to become pregnant, but could become pregnant if they or their partner fails to use a contraceptive method. The typical U.S. woman wants two children. To achieve this goal, she must use contraceptives for roughly three decades of her life.

Among the 43 million women who do not want to become pregnant and are at risk of unintended pregnancy, 68% use some form of contraception correctly and consistently (accounting for 5% of unintended pregnancies), 18% use their contraceptive method incorrectly or inconsistently (accounting for 41% of unintended pregnancies), and 14% do not use any form of contraception or have long gaps in use (accounting for 54% of unintended pregnancies). Of the women using contraception, 67% use reversible methods, including hormonal methods (such as the pill, patch, implant, injectable, vaginal ring, and hormonal IUDs) and nonhormonal methods (such as the copper IUD and barrier methods). The remaining women use permanent female or male sterilization. Hormonal methods provide health benefits, including a decrease in menstrual pain, menstrual irregularity, endometriosis, acne, ectopic pregnancy, noncancerous breast cysts/lumps, and risk of endometrial and ovarian cancer.

Contraceptive choices vary markedly with age. For women in their teens and 20's, the pill is the leading method. Among women 35 years and older, more rely on sterilization, which is often performed immediately post-partum (following a birth). Male contraception options are limited. Presently, male condoms and vasectomy are the only options. Several contraceptive methods for men are in development.

MENSTRUAL CYCLE PHASES AND TEST KITS

A normal menstrual cycle ranges from 23 – 35 days (average 28 days). Menstruation starts on day 1 and typically lasts several days. Refer to the diagram on female sex hormones and cycle in the Drug Mechanisms chapter.

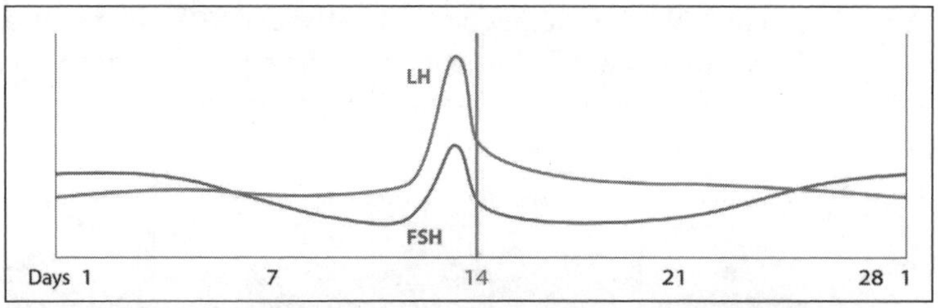

An ovulation predictor kit is positive when the LH surge is detected. This indicates that the egg will be released in ~24 hours. The egg survives for 24 hours. Sperm can survive for ~3 days. A couple wishing to conceive should have intercourse when the LH surge is detected, and for the following 2 days.

Ovulation

The mid-cycle luteinizing hormone (LH) surge results in release of the oocyte (egg) from the ovary into the fallopian tube. The oocyte lives for one day once released. Ovulation kits test for LH in the urine and are positive if LH is present. There are also kits to help women track basal body temperature where a spike in temperature predicts ovulation the following day, and others to identify a fern-shaped pattern in the saliva that occurs 3 – 5 days prior to ovulation. They predict the best time for intercourse based on ovulation in order to try to conceive (get pregnant).

Pregnancy

Human chorionic gonadotropin (hCG) is produced by the placenta during pregnancy and can be detected in blood and urine. A home urine test can pick up pregnancy sooner if the woman uses the first urine in the morning for the test, when the hCG level is highest.

Preconception Health

The U.S. currently has high infant and maternal morbidity and mortality rates. Although not all adverse perinatal outcomes can be prevented, women can increase their chances of having a healthy pregnancy by taking precautionary steps prior to conception. Any woman planning to conceive (and all women of child-bearing age) should be taking a folic acid (folate) supplement (400 mcg/day) to help prevent birth defects of the brain and spinal cord (neural tube defects). Folate is in many healthy foods, including fortified cereals, dried beans, leafy green vegetables and orange juice. Similarly, men can play a role in increasing the chances of having a healthy baby by maintaining their health. Preconception care refers to a set of preventative interventions that identify and address biomedical, behavioral, and social risks to a woman's health that may negatively affect a future pregnancy. These interventions include counseling on health behaviors, vaccinations, safe medication use, and screening and managing medical conditions. See the Pregnancy chapter for a review of these topics.

CONTRACEPTION

Contraception should be used until ready to conceive. A prompt return to fertility occurs when most contraceptives are discontinued. The only reversible contraceptive method that has a delay in return to fertility is the shot.

Effectiveness of Contraceptive Methods

The figure on the next page provides a comparison of the efficacy of contraceptive methods that are available as OTC or Rx products in pharmacies. Under the sponge, parous refers to women who have given birth and nulliparous refers to women who have not given birth. Contraceptive methods, except for condoms, do not provide protection from sexually transmitted diseases (STDs). Condoms provide some protection – female internal condoms provide more protection than male external condoms.

Hormonal Contraceptives

These contain progestin only (pill, injectable, implant, and IUD) or estrogen/progestin combinations (pills, patch, and ring). Non-oral contraceptives that contain both estrogen and progestin are referred to as combined hormonal contraceptives (CHC). The patch and the ring have unique considerations (such as how to apply) but contain the same hormones that are present in pill formulations. A contraindication to use of the pill will remain a contraindication for the patch or the ring.

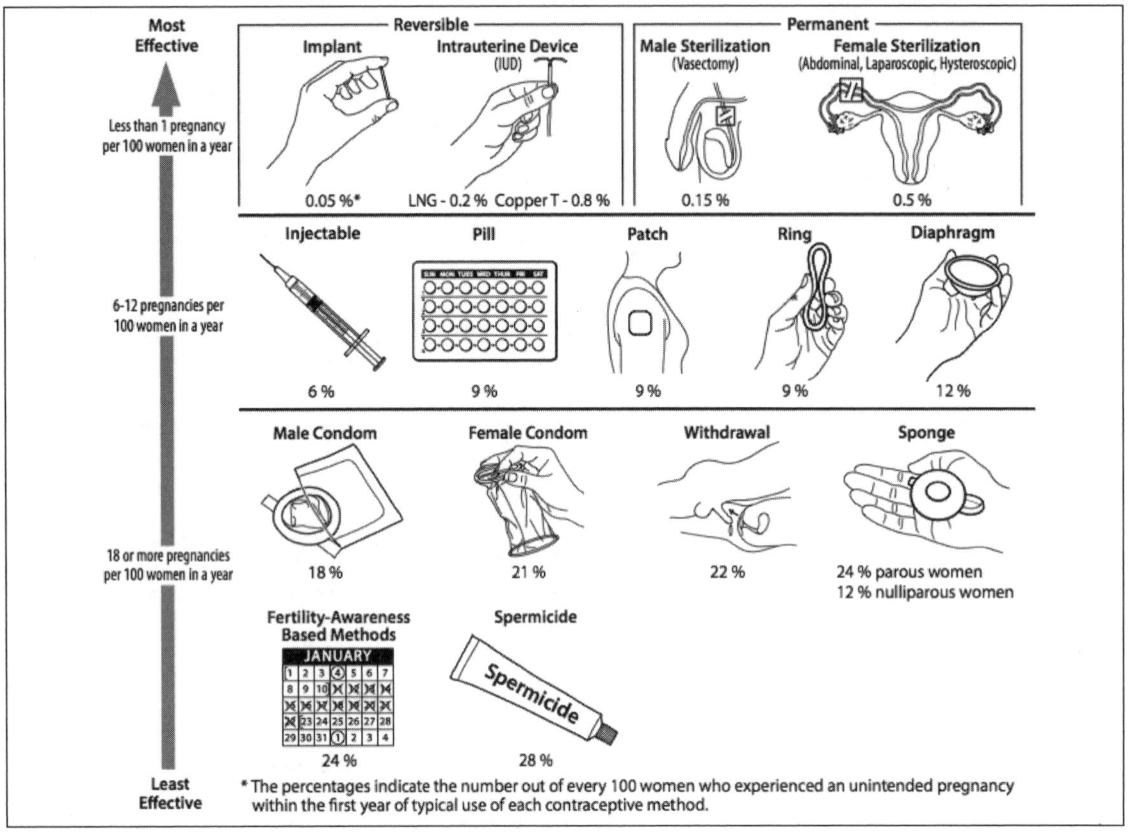

Estrogen and progestin combination oral contraceptives

The primary method of the combination oral contraceptives (COCs) involves inhibition of follicle stimulating hormone (FSH) and LH production, which in turn prevents ovulation. COCs may also prevent pregnancy by altering the endometrial lining, altering cervical mucus, interfering with fertilization or transport of an egg, or preventing implantation. There are many different formulations of COCs. Monophasic COCs have the same dose of estrogen and progestin throughout the pill pack. Biphasic, triphasic and quadriphasic pill packs were developed to mimic the estrogen and progesterone levels during a menstrual cycle and the name is based on the number of dose changes in the pill pack. Most COCs contain the estrogen ethinyl estradiol (EE) and a progestin [e.g., norethindrone, levonorgestrel (LNG), norgestimate, drospirenone].

COCs are used for various indications, including dysmenorrhea, PMS, peri-menopausal pregnancy prevention and symptoms (hot flashes, night sweats), anemia due to excessive blood loss, acne (in females), and premenstrual migraine prophylaxis. The use of COCs to regulate menses is first-line treatment for polycystic ovary syndrome (PCOS), a common condition (~5 – 10% of women) with a typical presentation of infrequent or prolonged menstrual periods, hirsutism, acne and excessive weight, often with insulin resistance. COCs are used as first-line treatment for endometriosis, a common condition (~10 - 20% of women) with a typical presentation of heavy and extremely painful menses due to the presence of endometrial tissue (uterine lining) out the uterus.

Progestin only pills

This continuous progestin exposure suppresses ovulation in about half of users, thickens the cervical mucus to inhibit sperm penetration, lowers the mid-cycle LH and FSH peaks, slows movement of the ovum through the fallopian tubes, and alters the endometrium. The use of progestin only pills (POPs) as a contraceptive method is primarily recommended for lactating (breastfeeding) women, because estrogen reduces the milk production and the risk of thrombosis is highest during the 6 weeks postpartum. They are sometimes used for women who cannot tolerate or have a contraindication to estrogen. POPs must be taken on a tight schedule and are less "forgiving" if a pill is late or forgotten; it is easier to get pregnant on a POP if the woman is not breastfeeding. They are sometimes used for reduction in premenstrual migraine (a common migraine in women). The POPs are useful for migraine prophylaxis, and are safe for women who have migraines with aura (in this type of migraine, avoid estrogen due to risk of stroke).

Contraceptive Types and Names*

Estrogen + progestin

PRODUCT TYPE	DESCRIPTION
PILLS**	
Monophasic	All active pills with same dose of hormones during the 21-24 active days
MonoNessa, Microgestin Fe 1/20, Ortho-Cyclen, Yasmin, Sprintec 28	21/7 pill packs contains 21 active hormonal pills, 7 inactive pills
Gildess Fe, Junel Fe 1/20, Loestrin 24 Fe, Yaz, Minastrin 24 Fe	24/4 pill packs contains 24 active hormonal pills, 4 inactive pills
Biphasic, Triphasic	Hormone dose changes over the 21-24 days to mimic menstrual cycle
Necon 10/11, Ortho Tri-Cyclen, Necon 7/7/7, Cyclessa, Trinessa	Tri or 7/7/7 or Cycl- are Triphasic pills
Quadriphasic	Hormone dose changes over the 21-24 days to mimic menstrual cycle (four phases of estradiol valerate and progestin dienogest)
Natazia	
Extended cycle	91 day pack
Jolessa	84 days of EE + LNG followed by 7 days of placebo
Amethyst	84 days of EE + LNG followed by 7 days of low dose EE in "placebo" week
Amethia Lo, Seasonique, Quartette	84 days of a lower dose EE + LNG followed by 7 days of low dose EE in "placebo" week
PATCH	
Transdermal patch	Weeks 1-3: apply once weekly; week 4: off
Xulane	Higher AUC than pills
RING	
Vaginal Ring	Insert monthly: in x 3 weeks; remove x 1 week
NuvaRing	Lower AUC than pills

Progestin Only

PRODUCT TYPE	DESCRIPTION
PILLS	
Camila, Errin, Micronor, Nora-BE, Heather, Jolivette	All contain norethindrone; take active tablet daily (no placebo days and no change in dose) "Nor" in the name indicates it contains norethindrone
INJECTION	
Depo-Provera	Contains depot medroxyprogesterone; injected every 3 months (150 mg IM or 104 mg SC) "Pro" in the name indicates it contains a progestin

**This is not a comprehensive list. For exam purposes, focus on unique formulations and consider patient specific factors when selecting an agent.*

***Agents with Lo in the name contain a lower dose of estrogen (< 30 mcg); agents with Fe in the name contain iron.*

Adverse Effects Due to Estrogen

Estrogen can cause nausea, breast tenderness/fullness, bloating, weight gain and elevated blood pressure. The incidence of side effects correlates with the dose; low-dose estrogen formulations are chosen for this purpose, which are generally well-tolerated, but can result in spotting in some women. There can also be insufficient estrogen if the woman is a fast metabolizer, or is using an enzyme inducer. If the spotting (breakthrough bleeding) occurs early or mid-cycle, it may require a higher estrogen dose. The general practice is to wait three monthly cycles prior to changing the dose to see if spotting dissipates.

Serious adverse effects are rare but can include thrombosis, including heart attack, stroke and DVT/PE. The risk for clots increases as the woman ages, if she smokes, if she has diabetes or hypertension, if she requires prolonged bed rest, and if she is overweight. The higher the estrogen dose or exposure (e.g., with *Xulane* transdermal patch), the higher the clotting risk. Refer to the box on risks of hormonal contraceptives. When evaluating risks from use of the pill, consider risks with an unintended pregnancy: the risk of blood clots during pregnancy and postpartum is much higher than clotting risk with any birth control pill formulation.

Adverse Effects Due to Progestin

Progestin can cause breast tenderness, headache, fatigue or changes in mood. If late cycle breakthrough bleeding occurs, a higher progestin dose may be required.

Drospirenone has a slightly higher risk of clotting, and should be avoided in women with clotting risk. The injectable depot medroxyprogesterone acetate can cause a transient loss in bone mineral density. This can be especially important for teens and young women who are still accumulating bone mass. Advise users to supplement their diets as needed to obtain their daily recommended doses of calcium and vitamin D (see recommendations in the Osteoporosis chapter).

STUDY TIP

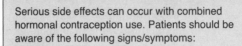

Serious side effects can occur with combined hormonal contraception use. Patients should be aware of the following signs/symptoms:

Abdominal (stomach) pain that is severe.
- Can be a sign of possible ruptured liver tumor, cyst, or ectopic pregnancy.

Chest pain.
- Sharp, crushing, or heavy pain may be a sign of a possible heart attack. Shortness of breath could be a sign of possible blood clot in the lungs.

Headaches.
- Sudden and severe with vomiting or weakness/numbness on one side of the body can be a sign of possible stroke.

Eye problems.
- Blurring vision, flashing lights or partial/complete vision loss may be a sign of possible blood clot in the eye.

Swelling or sudden pain in legs.
- May be a sign of possible blood clots in legs.

Mnemonic: ACHES

If a patient experiences any of these warning signs, they should call or see a healthcare provider as soon as possible.

RISKS OF HORMONAL CONTRACEPTIVES*

BOXED WARNINGS
All estrogen-containing products (pills, ring, patch)

- Avoid use in women > 35 years old who smoke due to risk of serious cardiovascular events

Estrogen + progestin transdermal patch *(Xulane)*

- Increased risk of of venous thromboembolism (DVT, PE) compared to COCs

Depo-Provera

- Loss of bone mineral density with long-term use

DO NOT USE ESTROGEN WITH THESE CONDITIONS*
History of DVT/PE, stroke, CAD, thrombosis of heart valves or acquired hypercoagulopathies

History of breast, ovarian, or liver cancer; liver disease; uncontrolled hypertension (e.g., > 160/100 mmHg); severe headaches or migraines with aura (especially if > 35 years of age); diabetes with vascular disease; unexplained uterine bleeding; others

** Risks vary by method. Consult product-specific package labeling. Refer to CDC Medical Eligibility Criteria for contraceptive use.*

Formulation Considerations

TYPE OF PATIENT	PRODUCT SELECTION CONSIDERATIONS
Breastfeeding	Choose POP or nonhormonal method for the first 42 days postpartum (first 21 days if no VTE risk factors).
Migraine	If with aura, choose progestin only or nonhormonal method; avoid estrogen. If no aura, choose any method.
Estrogen contraindication (including clotting risk)	Choose progestin only or nonhormonal method.
Overweight	Choose any method. Counsel patient about the possibility of reduced effectiveness with CHC and POP. Avoid depot medroxyprogesterone acetate (DMPA) if trying to avoid further weight gain.
Hypertension	If BP is uncontrolled, some estrogen formulations may be contraindicated. Choose progestin only pill or nonhormonal method.
Mood changes or disorder	Use monophasic CHC – extended cycle or continuous with drospirenone is preferred.
Premenstrual dysphoric disorder	Choose Yaz or antidepressant – see Depression chapter.
Acne	Use COC with lower androgenic activity (e.g., *Ortho-Cyclen)* or no androgenic activity (i.e., *Yaz, Yasmin).*
Spotting/"breakthrough bleeding"	More common with extended or continuous cycles. When starting conventional formulations, wait 3 cycles before switching. If early or mid-cycle spotting occurs, the estrogen dose may need to be increased. If later in the cycle, the progestin dose may need to be increased.
Avoiding monthly cycle/ menses	Use extended (91-day) or continuous formulations. Alternative: monophasic 28-day formulation and skip placebo pills.
Heavy menstrual bleeding	The COC *Natazia* and the levonorgestrel-releasing IUD *Mirena* are indicated for this condition (menorrhagia). COCs with only 4 placebo pills (rather than 7) or continuous/ extended regimens will minimize bleeding time.
Fluid retention/bloating	Choose a product containing drospirenone. Progestin component helps reduce water retention (progestin component is a mild diuretic). It retains potassium, and is contraindicated with renal or liver disease. Check potassium, renal function and use of other potassium-retaining agents.
Nausea	Take at night, with food, can consider decreasing estrogen dose or switching to a progestin-only product, *NuvaRing*, or nonhormonal method (ideally after a 3 month trial).

Drug Interactions with Hormonal Contraceptives

The birth control injection does not have drug interactions since it bypasses first-pass metabolism. Other forms of contraception may have decreased efficacy when used with other drugs; this may require use of a back-up contraception method such as condoms/spermicide, an IUD or the birth control injection. With all new drugs being dispensed to a patient using contraception, the package insert should be checked to avoid missing an interaction that could decrease the contraceptive efficacy.

Drug Interactions that Decrease Hormonal Contraception Efficacy

- Some antibiotics have package labelings that recommend use of a back-up method with contraception pills. Antibiotics with evidence of decreased efficacy include rifampin, rifapentine and rifabutin; these are all strong inducers. With rifampin, the induction can be prolonged so a back-up method of contraception is needed for 6 weeks after rifampin has been discontinued. Other strong inducers, if used long-term, will require an alternate form of birth control. If in doubt, it is safest to use back-up.
- Anticonvulsants (barbiturates, carbamazepine, oxcarbazepine, phenytoin, primidone, topiramate and lamotrigine).

- St. John's wort.
- Ritonavir-boosted protease inhibitors (PIs), bosentan *(Tracleer)*, mycophenolate *(CellCept, Myfortic)*.
- Use of sugammadex *(Bridion)* for neuromuscular blockade reversal requires back up for the following 7 days.
- Separate from colesevelam by at least 4 hours.
- Take at least 1 hour prior to *Byetta* injection.
- Smoking tobacco.

Risks with Hepatitis C Agents

The hepatitis C antivirals, *Technivie* and *Viekira Pak*, cannot be used with any formulation containing ethinyl estradiol due to the risk of liver toxicity. With all new hepatitis C drugs being dispensed to a patient using contraception, the package insert should be checked to avoid missing an interaction that could cause toxicity or a decrease in contraceptive efficacy.

Drospirenone Drug Interactions and Use

- Risk of increased K; caution must be used with K-sparing agents, including aldosterone antagonists, potassium supplements, salt substitutes (KCl), ACE inhibitors, angiotensin receptor blockers, heparin, canaglifozin and calcineurin inhibitors (see hyperkalemia discussion in Renal chapter).
- Avoid use with kidney, liver, or adrenal gland disease as these can increase potassium. On a case, check the potassium level. It should be in the safe range of 3.5 – 5 mEq/L.

Starting Oral Contraceptive Therapy

Combination Oral Contraception (COCs)

- Start today. Best practice recommendation. Requires back-up method for 7 days. Maximizes time protected from unintended pregnancy. Known as "quick start."
- Sunday start. Starts the Sunday after onset of menstruation. This is most common because patients often prefer that menstruation occur during the week and is complete before the following weekend. It is not ideal and can lead to missed doses if the patient inadvertently runs out of refills over the weekend. Requires a back-up method for 7 days.
- Start on 1st day of menses – if COCs are started within 5 days after the start of the period, no back-up method of birth control is needed; protection is immediate. If not within 5 days, use back-up for first week of use.

POP Start Day Options

- Start at any time. Use another method of birth control for the first 48 hours of progestin-pill use – protection begins after two days. All come in 28-day packs and all pills are active.
- POPs need to be taken at or around the same time of day, everyday; if 3 hours have elapsed from the regular scheduled time, back-up is needed for 48 hours after taking the late pill. If a dose is missed, there is a risk of pregnancy and emergency contraception (EC) may be an option.

COC Specific Drug Information and Patient Counseling

This section contains information specific to individual products along with patient counseling.

Combination Oral Contraceptives

The FDA requires that the Patient Package Insert (PPI) be dispensed with oral contraceptives – it will be in the product packaging. The PPI has important safety information and instructions how to use them properly and what to do if pills are missed. Dispense the PPI and instruct the patient to read it.

- Most women can take birth control pills safely. However, some women are at high risk of developing certain serious conditions that can be life-threatening. The risks increase significantly if you:
  - Have or have had clotting disorders, heart attack, stroke, angina, cancer of the breast or sex organs, jaundice, or malignant or benign liver tumors.
  - Smoke; cigarette smoking increases the risk of serious effects on the heart and blood vessels. This risk increases with age and with heavy smoking and is quite marked in women over 35 years of age. Women who use oral contraceptives should not smoke.
- You should not take the pill if you have unexplained vaginal bleeding.
- Most side effects of the pill are mild and not serious. The most common are nausea, bleeding between menstrual periods (spotting), weight gain and breast tenderness. These side effects, especially nausea, often improve after 3 months of use. Taking the pill with food or at night helps to reduce the nausea.
- For any estrogen-containing product: Watch for severe pain in your leg/calf, severe abdominal (stomach) pain, chest pain/shortness of breath/cough, blurred or loss of vision – which can be due to a blood clot. If this occurs you will need to get medical care right away. Discuss with your pharmacist if you start any new medicines, including over-the-counter products or antibiotics for an infection.
- Take the pill at the same time every day and pick a time of day that you will remember.

Missed COC Pills – Instructions for Typical Formulations

Missed pills (particularly if the seven-day hormone-free interval is extended on either end) are a common cause of contraceptive failure. Unintended pregnancies are often due to picking up the refill late. There may be different instructions in the package insert of the formulation dispensed. These are the standard instructions from the CDC.

PILLS MISSED	NOTES
If **one** pill is **late** (< 24 hrs since it should have been taken) or **missed** (24 to < 48 hrs since a pill should have been taken)	Take the late or missed dose as soon as possible. Continue taking remaining pills at the usual time. No back-up contraception needed. EC not needed but can be considered if hormonal pills were missed earlier in the cycle or in the last week of the previous cycle and unprotected intercourse occurred in the previous 5 days.
If **two or more** consecutive pills have been **missed** (≥ 48 hours since a pill should have been taken)	Continue taking remaining pills at the usual time (even if it means two pills in one day). Use back-up contraception or avoid intercourse for 7 days. If hormonal pills were missed in the last week of the cycle: Omit the hormone-free interval by finishing the hormonal pills in current pack and start new pack next day. If unable to start a new pack, use back-up contraception or avoid intercourse until first 7 days of new pack taken. Consider EC if missed pills were during the first week and unprotected intercourse occurred in the previous 5 days. Consider EC at other times as appropriate.

Continuous Pills With No Monthly Cycle *(Amethyst)*

- *Amethyst* comes in 28 day packets of all active (yellow) pills, with no placebo pills; the packets are taken continuously. When finished, start the next pack.
- With this formulation, it can be difficult to tell if a woman is pregnant.
- There is a higher discontinuation rate with the continuous formulations than with other COCs, due to spotting. Spotting should decrease over time.

Drospirenone Formulations: *Yasmin, Yaz, Gianvi, Loryna, Ocella, Zarah, Angeliq, Nikki, Safyral, Syeda, Vestura, Beyaz (Safyral* & *Beyaz* contain folate)

These are popular COCs, since they decrease bloating, PMS symptoms, acne and weight gain. This is due to the progestin drospirenone, which is a potassium-sparing diuretic.

Specific Drug Information and Patient Counseling for Other Formulations

Xulane Contraceptive Patch

Has the same side effects, contraindications and drug interactions as the pills except that the patch causes a higher systemic estrogen exposure; avoid use in anyone with clotting risk factors. Less effective in women > 198 pounds. Do not use if smoker and over 35 years old.

- This is a thin, beige, plastic patch that is placed on clean, dry skin of buttocks, stomach, upper arm, or upper torso once a week for 21 out of 28 days. Do not apply to breasts.
- Start on either Day 1 (no back-up needed) or Sunday (back-up 7 days if not day 1).
- If patch becomes loose or falls off > 24 hours during the 3 weeks of use or if > 7 days have passed during the 4th week where no patch is required, there is a risk of pregnancy; thus a back-up method should be used for 1 week while a new patch is put in place.

NuvaRing Vaginal Contraceptive Ring

Has the same side effects, contraindications and drug interactions as the pills.

- Small flexible ring inserted into the vagina once a month.
- The ring is inserted in place for 3 weeks and taken out for 1 week before replacement with a new ring. The ring can be kept in place for up to 4 weeks for women who want an extended or continuous cycle.
- For starting therapy and no hormonal contraceptive use in preceding cycle: insert the ring the first day of menstrual bleeding. If inserted on days 2 – 5 of cycle, a back-up method should be used for the first seven days in the first cycle.
- Exact position of ring in vagina does not matter.
- If ring is out < 48 hours during week 1, rinse with cool to lukewarm water and reinsert; use back-up method for 1 week while the ring is in place, consider EC if intercourse within last 5 days.
- If ring is out < 48 hours during week 2 or 3, rinse and re-insert ring.
- If ring is out ≥ 48 hours during week 2 or 3, rinse and re-insert ring and use back-up for 7 days.
- Store for up to 4 months at room temperature (refrigerated at pharmacy).

Injectable Contraception

The injection *(Depo-Provera, Depo-subQ Provera)* is depot medroxyprogesterone acetate (DMPA), a progestin. Suppresses ovulation, thickens cervical mucus, and causes thinning of the endometrium. Given by IM (150 mg) or SC (104 mg) injection every 3 months. About half of users will be amenorrheic (no menses) after 1 year of use; this is an advantage for some and a disadvantage for others.

- This medication can decrease the amount of mineral stored in your bones. This can increase your risk of developing bone fractures. You should consume the recommended daily intake of calcium and vitamin D.
- You may experience a change in your normal menstrual cycle. With continued use of this medication, some women experience a decrease in bleeding and many women stop having periods after 1 year of use.

ADDITIONAL METHODS OF BIRTH CONTROL AND "SAFE" OR "SAFER SEX"

Abstinence is the only 100% way to prevent pregnancy and STDs. Safer sex recommendations:

- Alcohol and other drugs can make people forget safer sex; use should be avoided when in high-risk situations.
- Condoms form a barrier between the penis and anus, vagina or mouth. The barrier keeps one partner's fluids from getting into or on the other. Latex or synthetic plastic (not natural sheepskin) condoms must be used for maximum protection. Male or female condoms can be used. Skin-to-skin contact not covered by the condom is not protected from transmission of infection.
- Oral sex is safer than vaginal or anal sex to reduce HIV risk, but will still put the person at risk for herpes, syphilis, hepatitis B, gonorrhea, and HPV. The *Sheer Glyde* dental dam is FDA-approved for safer sex; it blocks passage of infectious organisms during oral contact.
- Lubricant is important for safer sex because it makes condoms and dams slippery and less likely to break by reducing dry friction. Never recommend oil-based lubricant (called "lube") with a latex or non-latex synthetic condom; only recommend water or silicone-based lubricants. These products are discussed in the Osteoporosis chapter.

Condoms

- Male condoms are a thin latex or plastic sheath worn on the penis. Female condoms are inserted into the vagina. Both are OTC and most effective when used with spermicide for contraception. Condoms help protect against many STDs (only if latex or synthetic condoms, not "natural" sheepskin).
- To increase the efficacy for contraception, use with nonoxynol-9 spermicide.
- Do not use spermicide with anal sex. It is irritating and can increase the risk of STDs. Some of the condoms are lubricated with nonoxynol-9.

Other OTC Contraceptive Methods

- Available as foams, film, creams, suppositories, and jellies. These contain the spermicide nonoxynol-9.
- Place deep into the vagina right before intercourse where they melt (except for foam, which bubbles).

Diaphragm, Caps and Shields

These three options are soft latex or silicone barriers that cover the cervix and prevent sperm passage. The new *Caya* diaphragm is a single size and does not require fitting.

Diaphragm Directions for Use

- Wash hands thoroughly.
- Place 1 tablespoon of spermicide in the diaphragm and disperse inside and around the rim.
- Pinch the ends of the cup and insert the pinched end into the vagina.
- Leave in for six hours after intercourse.
- Reapply spermicide if intercourse is repeated or diaphragm is in place for more than two hours before sex, by inserting jelly with applicator.
- Diaphragms should not be in place greater than 24 hours.

- Wash with mild soap and warm water after removal, air dry.
- Can be used for up to 2 years.

Long-Acting Reversible Contraceptives

- These devices are generally not dispensed from community pharmacies. They must be placed and removed by trained healthcare professionals. They are the most effective forms of contraception that are reversible, and as effective as sterilization.
- Intrauterine devices *(Mirena, Skyla, Kyleena, Liletta)* are both hormonal IUDs. These cause lighter menstrual bleeding and minor or no cramping. *Mirena* is FDA-approved for heavy menstrual bleeding. *Mirena* and *Kyleena* can be used up to 5 years and *Skyla and Liletta* up to 3 years. About 20% of women using *Mirena* will become amenorrheic.
- The copper-T IUD *(Paragard)* can be used for EC and/or regular birth control, and can be used up to 10 years, but causes heavier menstrual bleeding and cramping, which can be painful. Some women prefer this nonhormonal method.
- Implant *(Nexplanon)* is a plastic rod that is placed subdermally *and* releases the progestin etonogestrel for 3 years.

EMERGENCY CONTRACEPTION (EC)

Emergency contraception (EC) is a form of hormonal or nonhormonal contraception that prevents pregnancy after unprotected intercourse. The copper IUD *(Paragard)* is the most effective form of EC if inserted within 5 days. There are two oral EC (also known as the "morning after pill") options, levonorgestrel *(Plan B One-Step)* and ulipristal acetate *(Ella)*, that can be used within 5 days, with effectiveness diminishing over time. This means that the sooner EC is used, the higher the efficacy. The use of higher doses of combination oral contraceptives is no longer a common practice as it is less effective than these options, leads to more nausea/vomiting, and has more contraindications. EC has been available for 30 years and there have been no reports of serious complications or birth defects.

EC can be an important resource after unprotected sex, such as from missed pills, a condom breaking during intercourse, a diaphragm or cap that moved out of place during intercourse, or if a woman may have been sexually assaulted. If sexual assault has occurred the woman may require STD treatment, including HIV prevention, HBV and HPV vaccines, and empiric antimicrobial treatment for chlamydia, gonorrhea, and trichomonas. Pharmacists should have referrals for other providers available to provide to patients.

Occasionally, women may be using EC after sex as their regular method of birth control; this may be done when a woman has occasional (not regular) sexual activity and is willing to accept the effectiveness of the method. Depending on insurance coverage, it may also be more expensive. If it is prescribed, it will be covered by insurance plans as required by the Affordable Care Act (ACA), except grandfathered plans, which are exempt.

Levonorgestrel

Plan B One-Step and generics, which come as one 1.5 mg tab of levonorgestrel. This formulation of EC reduces the risk of pregnancy by up to 89 percent when started within 72 hours after unprotected intercourse. The sooner it is started, the higher the efficacy.

Plan B One-Step and generics *(Take Action, Next Choice One-Dose, Aftera, My Way)* are OTC with no age or other restrictions. The pharmacy does not need to be present or open to sell these products. Per the FDA, these should be placed in the OTC aisles with the other family-planning products, such as condoms and spermicides. The generics cost $35 - $45, about $10 less than the brand *Plan B One-Step*. There is no reason to use a prescription with the formulations available OTC (unless someone wanted the 2 pill formulation), except to use insurance coverage.

If the EC is purchased OTC, there is no requirement for purchasers to sign a registry. They can receive multiple doses and the American College of Obstetrics and Gynecologists (ACOG) recommends an additional dose for future use, if needed, since EC is more effective the sooner it is used.

- Mechanism of action: primarily works by preventing or delaying ovulation, but also thickens the cervical mucus.
- This type of EC is indicated for up to 5 days (the sooner, the better) after unprotected intercourse. The package indicates use within 3 days, but is used up to 5 days off-label according to evidence-based guidelines.
- Preferred regimen is 1.5 mg as a single dose *(Plan B One-Step)*.
- Primary side effect is nausea, which occurs in 23% of women, and 6% have vomiting. If the women is easily nauseated, an OTC anti-emetic (1 hour prior to use, and caution if driving home due to sedation) should be recommended to avoid losing the dose. If a patient vomits within 2 hours of taking the pill(s), she should consider repeating the dose.

Ulipristal acetate *(Ella)*

Some patients may not wish to use this EC option because it is a chemical cousin to mifepristone *(Mifeprex)*, also known as the "abortion pill" or RU-486. They are not the same drug and are used differently. The mifepristone product available in the US is used primarily for pregnancy terminations and other noncontraceptive uses. The dose of ulipristal is much lower potency and is used to delay ovulation. It may also prevent implantation and this is a cause of concern for some.

- Single 30 mg dose. Requires a prescription.
- Works primarily by delaying ovulation. May also prevent implantation in the uterus – this mechanism is more controversial than levonorgestrel.
- Indicated for up to 5 days after unprotected intercourse. More effective than levonorgestrel if 72 – 120 hours since unprotected intercourse or if woman is overweight.
- Primary side effects are headache, nausea and abdominal pain. Some women have changes in their menstrual cycle, but all should get their period within a week. Can only use once per cycle. Use a barrier method of contraception the rest of the cycle as ovulation may occur later than normal.

Patient Counseling for EC

- If you vomit after taking EC you may need to take another dose. Before you do, contact a pharmacist or other healthcare provider immediately. If you get easily nauseated, the pharmacist can recommend an OTC medication that helps to lessen nausea that you can use before you take the EC pill.
- If you do not get your period in 3 weeks (or it is more than a week late), a pregnancy test should be taken. If you develop severe abdominal pain or irregular bleeding, you may have an ectopic pregnancy (outside of the uterus) and will need immediate medical attention.
- It is important to visit your healthcare provider for a regular birth control method and information about preventing sexually transmitted infections. If you may have contracted an infection, you should get care right away.
- You may wish to get a package of EC for future use, if needed.
- Regular hormonal contraceptives (OCs, shot, ring, patch), should be started on the same or the following day as taking the EC.
- You should only use one type of oral EC pill. Do not use the two different types together since they can cancel eachother out.

INFERTILITY

About 10 – 15% of women (6.1 million) have difficulty getting pregnant or staying pregnant annually. One in sixteen babies are now conceived by women using fertility medications. From a business perspective, the sale of infertility medications is profitable. Detailed knowledge of this topic is a "specialty" area; this section provides "basic competency" knowledge.

The chance of pregnancy in couples attempting pregnancy is about 25% per month, and 85% will become pregnant within a year. If pregnancy has not occurred at one year's time, the couple should be referred for medical consultation. Infertility can be due to either the male or female. Males can be contributory due to various problems with sperm production. Females could have one or more contributory factors, including congenital defects, infectious pathogens (including damage from chlamydia or trichomoniasis), abdominal conditions, ectopic pregnancy, scarring from previous surgeries, hypothyroidism or polycystic ovary syndrome (PCOS).

In the beginning part of this chapter there is a brief description of ovulation kits; these are a reasonable place to start, prior to outside referral. Ovulation kits test for luteinizing hormone (LH), which is present in the urine and surges 24 – 48 hours prior to ovulation. The LH surge triggers the release of an egg from an ovary (ovulation). Ovulation is the most fertile time of the cycle. The three days immediately following the positive result is the highest chance for pregnancy. The kits are simple to use and require either running the test stick under the urine stream, or collecting the urine in a small container and dipping the test strip.

There are other more complex ways to assess ovulation, including testing body temperature, cervical mucus, and using fertility monitors. Any women trying to conceive should have possible teratogens discontinued, if possible. The pharmacist should check the woman's OTC and Rx medication use and consult with the prescriber. It may also be necessary to eliminate medications from the male partner's regimen. Possible teratogens are discussed in more detail in the Drug Use in Pregnancy chapter.

Patient-Specific Infertility Treatment Goals

- Address any underlying medical condition.
- Increase quantity of quality sperm
- Increase number of eggs
- In-vitro fertilization (IVF) and other assisted reproductive technologies (ART) (e.g., cervical or intrauterine insemination)

The common fertility medications are in the table. They are either oral, or must be given by injection.

DRUG	DOSING	SAFETY/SIDE EFFECTS/MONITORING

Oral

Clomiphene *(Clomid, Serophene)* GnRH ↑ FSH & ↑ LH, to ↑ ovulation Selective Estrogen Receptor Modulator (SERM)	50 mg x 5 days, taken on days 3, 4 or 5 after period starts. Can increase to 100 mg, 5 days/ cycle.	**CONTRAINDICATIONS** Liver disease, pregnancy, ovarian cyst, uncontrolled adrenal or thyroid disorders. History of breast cancer as a contraindication is controversial. **SIDE EFFECTS** Hot flashes, ovarian enlargement, abdominal bloating/ discomfort, blurred vision, headache, fluid retention. Increases chance of multiple births (but less than injectables), increases thrombosis risk.

Injectable

Human Chorionic Gonadotropin (hCG) *(Ovidrel)*, SC *(Pregnyl, Novarel)*, IM **Gonadotropins** Follitropin Beta *(Follistim AQ)*, IM, SC **Urofollitropin** *(Bravelle, Fertinorm HP)*, IM, SC **Follitropin Alpha** *(Gonal-F), Gonal-F RFF,* SC **Menotropins** *(Menopur, Repronex)*, IM, SC **Gonadotropin Releasing Hormone Agonist (GnRH agonist)** Sometimes used: Leuprolide *(Lupron)*, Goserelin *(Zoladex)*, Nafarelin (*Synarel)*, IM, SC **Gonadotropin Releasing Hormone Antagonist (GnRH antagonist)** Cetrorelix *(Cetrotide)*, SC	These come in either prefilled syringes, or as pens that may be preloaded, or pens with prefilled cartridges, or in ampules that are reconstituted, with supplied diluent. If reconstituting: insert syringe needle into vial, invert, slowly draw entire contents into syringe. Make sure tip of needle is not sticking through the solution or it will not be pulled into the syringe. Remove needle and syringe, replace syringe with injection needle. If air bubbles they can be tapped out. Some multiple dose pens require priming – these pens have dose counters on them and the instructions will designate the priming dose. The pen is primed when liquid appears at the tip. All SC injections: keep needle in skin for at least 5 seconds; some are longer, to avoid the drug "popping" out onto the skin. If multiple use, recap. Otherwise, discard entire device without recapping into appropriate container (sharps container, milk container, unbreakable plastic container).	**SIDE EFFECTS** Injection site pain, CNS (depression, fatigue, headache), ovarian hyper-stimulation syndrome (ovaries become enlarged and tender, small risk multiple pregnancies). **NOTES** SC: abdomen is generally preferred due to a more even absorption, or other SC sites. Instructions will indicate either 45 or 90 degrees. See immunization chapter for more details: these are short needles (½" or less). For IM: Upper outer quadrant is often used, as marked in this picture. These are 1" or longer needles; more information on injections in the Immunization chapter. 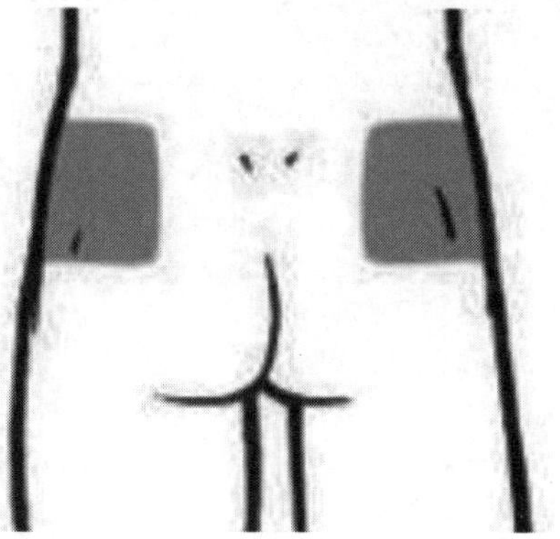

44

OSTEOPOROSIS, MENOPAUSE & TESTOSTERONE USE

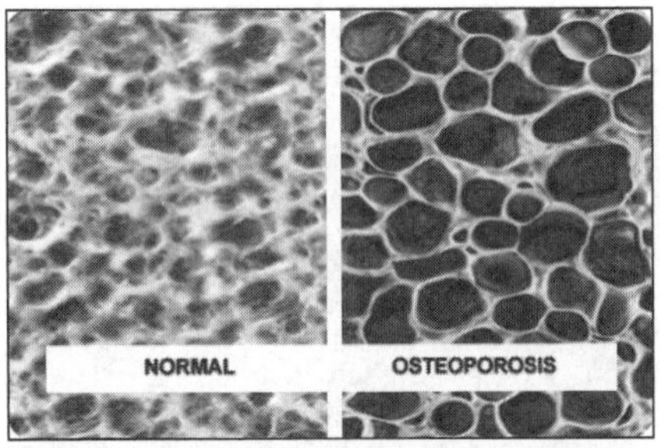

GUIDELINES/REFERENCES

Clinician's Guide to Prevention and Treatment of Osteoporosis. National Osteoporosis Foundation; 2014. https://www.cme.nof.org/resources.aspx (accessed 2016 Nov 21).

American College of Obstetricians and Gynecologist's Practice Bulletin No. 141: Management of Menopausal Symptoms. 2014;123(1):202-216.

Critical Update of the 2010 Endocrine Society Clinical Practice Guidelines for Male Hypogonadism. *Mayo Clin Proc.* 2015;90(8):1104-1115.

Additional guidelines included with the online course.

We gratefully acknowledge the assistance of Sally Rafie, PharmD, BCPS, Assistant Clinical Professor, University of California San Diego Skaggs School of Pharmacy and Pharmaceutical Sciences, in preparing this chapter.

OSTEOPOROSIS

Background

Osteoporosis, which means "porous bones," is a condition that causes bones to become weak and fragile. It is estimated that more than one-quarter of all adults in the U.S., and over half of those > 50 years of age, have osteoporosis, low bone density, or low bone mass. Although osteoporosis can occur in both men and women of all races, it is most common in postmenopausal women and is frequently underdiagnosed in men. About one in two women and one in five men will have an osteoporosis-related fracture during their lifetime. Falls are the most common cause of fractures, but with extremely porous bones, coughing or rolling over in bed can result in fractures. The most common locations for fractures are the vertebrae (spine), proximal femur (hip), and distal forearm (wrist).

Vertebral fractures can often occur without a fall and can initially be painless. The only clue to collapsing vertebrae may be a gradual loss of height. Hip fractures are the most devastating type of fractures, with higher costs, disability, and mortality than all other fractures combined. They are also more common after age 75. A hip fracture in a woman has a 25% risk of mortality at one year; the mortality risk is higher in men, since they may be in poorer health at baseline. Wrist fractures, or other fractures, appear in younger people and serve as an early indicator of poor bone health.

Risk Factors

Osteoporosis can occur as a result of normal age-related bone loss. Bone accumulates until approximately age 30. After that, men lose bone at a rate of 0.2 – 0.5% per year and women lose bone at a similar rate, except in the 10 years after menopause when bone loss is accelerated (1-5% per year). In addition to age-related bone loss, patient-specific characteristics, lifestyle habits, diseases, and medications can contribute to osteoporosis risk (see table on the following page).

SELECT FACTORS AND CONDITIONS WITH OSTEOPOROSIS RISK

Patient Characteristics

Advanced age

Ethnicity (white and Asian American women at ↑ risk)

Family history

Gender (females > males)

Low body weight

Lifestyle Factors

Smoking

Excessive alcohol intake (≥ 3 drinks per day)

Low calcium intake

Low vitamin D intake

Physical inactivity

Medical Diseases/Conditions

Anorexia nervosa

Diabetes

Gastrointestinal diseases (e.g., IBD, celiac disease, gastric bypass, other malabsorption syndromes)

Hyperthyroidism

Hypogonadism in men

Menopause

Rheumatoid arthritis and other autoimmune diseases

Others (e.g., epilepsy, HIV/AIDS, Parkinson's Disease)

Medications

Anticonvulsants (e.g., carbamazepine, phenytoin, phenobarbital)

Aromatase inhibitors

Depo-medroxyprogesterone

GnRH (gonadotropin-releasing hormone) agonists

Lithium

PPIs (↓ Ca absorption with ↑ gastric pH)

Steroids* (≥ 5 mg daily of prednisone or equivalent for ≥ 3 months)

Thyroid hormones (in excess)

Others (e.g., heparin, loop diuretics, SSRIs, TZDs)

**Long-term use of steroids is the major drug-contributing factor to poor bone health*

Diagnosis

Bone Mineral Density

Bone is not "dead tissue"; it is living and undergoes constant remodeling, although some types of bone remodel very slowly and others remodel at a faster rate. Osteoblasts are the cells involved in bone formation. Osteoclasts are the cells involved in bone resorption; that is they break-down tissue in the bone. Bone health is evaluated by measuring bone mineral density (BMD). The gold standard test to measure BMD and diagnose osteoporosis is a dual energy x-ray absorptiometry (DEXA, or DXA). This measures BMD of the spine and hip and calculates a T-score or a Z-score. The T-score compares a person's measured BMD to the average peak BMD of a healthy, young, white adult of the same sex. Z-scores are calculated the same way, but they compare the patient's measured BMD to the mean BMD of an age, sex and ethnicity-matched population.

The threshold T-scores for diagnosing osteoporosis and osteopenia are shown in the box. Notice that T-scores are negative; a score at or above -1 (closer to zero) correlates with stronger (denser) bones, which are less likely to fracture. Scores less than -1 reflect the standard deviation of the patient's BMD from the average BMD for healthy, young, white adults (e.g., a patient T-score of < -2.5 indicates that the BMD is at least 2.5 standard deviations below an average BMD for healthy, young, white adults).

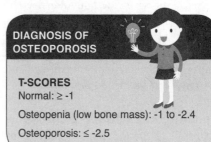

DIAGNOSIS OF OSTEOPOROSIS

T-SCORES

Normal: ≥ -1

Osteopenia (low bone mass): -1 to -2.4

Osteoporosis: ≤ -2.5

All women ≥ 65 years and men ≥ 70 years should have BMD measured, preferably with a DXA scan. Women < 65 years and men aged 50 – 69 years should have BMD checked if there is a history of a fragility fracture (e.g., a fall from standing height or less that results in a fracture) after age 50, risk for disease- or drug-induced bone loss, parental history of hip fracture, or other clinical risk factors for fracture (e.g., smoking, alcoholism, low body weight).

If a DXA scan is unavailable, an ultrasound may be performed; ultrasounds are less expensive, portable and do not emit radiation, but they are less than optimal. Ultrasound readings provide bone density in one location, such as the heel; if low, the patient should be encouraged to get a DXA scan. Since vertebral fractures are so common in older adults, and usually lack symptoms, vertebral imaging may be done if height loss is observed or if BMD testing indicates osteopenia. In addition to monitoring the BMD over time, biochemical markers of bone turnover are also useful.

Fracture Risk Assessment Tool (FRAX)

The FRAX tool is a computer-based algorithm developed by the World Health Organization (WHO) that estimates the risk of osteoporotic fracture in the next 10 years (available at www.nof.org or www.shef.ac.uk/FRAX). It has been well-validated and the U.S. tool has adapted versions available for Caucasian, Black, Hispanic, and Asian patients. Clinical risk factors included in the tool are: age, sex, weight, height, previous fracture, parental hip fracture, femoral neck BMD, smoking status, steroid use, alcohol intake, disorders strongly associated with osteoporosis (e.g., type I diabetes, chronic liver disease, premature menopause), and diagnosis of rheumatoid arthritis. The tool is intended for postmenopausal women and men > 50 years of age.

TREATMENT AND PREVENTION OF OSTEOPOROSIS

Fall Prevention Measures

If the bone density is low, care must be taken to avoid falls. Factors that put a patient at increased fall risk include: a history of recent falls, medications that cause sedation or orthostasis (e.g., antihypertensives, sedatives and hypnotics, narcotic analgesics, psychotropics), neurologic disorders or any condition that causes physical instability or poor coordination (e.g., Parkinson's Disease, dementia, prior stroke, peripheral neuropathy), impaired vision or hearing, poor health/frailty, and urinary or fecal urgency. A home safety assessment should ensure that lighting is appropriate, floors are safe (throw rugs/clutter/cords have been removed), storage is at reasonable heights, bathrooms have safety bars and nonskid floors, handrails are present on all stairs, and the stairs are well-lit with non-skid treads or carpet.

Preventing falls requires measures to improve muscle strength, balance and vision. Adequate corrective lenses, safe shoes and appropriate clothing (that will not cause falls) are required. If a disability is present, canes or walkers should be strongly recommended.

Recommended Daily Intake for Calcium

AGE	MALE	FEMALE
0-6 months	200 mg	200 mg
7-12 months	260 mg	260 mg
1-3 years	700 mg	700 mg
4-8 years	1,000 mg	1,000 mg
9-18 years	1,300 mg	1,300 mg
19-50 years	1,000 mg	1,000 mg
51-70 years	1,000 mg	1,200 mg
> 70 years	1,200 mg	1,200 mg

Lifestyle Measures

All patients with low bone density should be encouraged to perform regular weight-bearing exercise (e.g., walking, jogging, Tai-Chi) and muscle-strengthening exercises (e.g., weight training, yoga), stop smoking and avoid secondhand smoke, reduce alcohol intake and adopt fall prevention strategies as described previously.

Calcium and Vitamin D Intake

Over half of the U.S. population has low calcium and vitamin D intake. Adequate calcium intake (see table) is required throughout life. It is critically important in children (who can build bone stores), in pregnancy (when the fetus can deplete the mother's stores) and during the years around menopause, when bone loss is rapid. Dietary intake of calcium is preferred, with supplements used if needed. Intake in excess of recommended allowances may contribute to kidney stones, cardiovascular disease, and stroke, though the evidence remains controversial.

Vitamin D is required for calcium absorption, and low levels contribute to various health conditions, including autoimmune conditions and cancer. Vitamin D deficiency in children causes rickets, and in adults causes osteomalacia (softening of the bones, with low levels of collagen and calcium). The National Osteoporosis Foundation (NOF) recommends 800 – 1,000 international units (IU) of vitamin D daily for adults ≥ 50 years. Other organizations recommend 600 international units daily for people up to age 70 years and 800 international units daily for people ≥ 71 years. However, these levels are currently controversial and many endocrinologists suggest a higher intake of 800 – 2,000 international units daily. The Institute of Medicine has a recommended safe upper limit of 4,000 international units daily for adolescents and adults.

Calcium Supplementation

- Dietary calcium is generally not sufficient; most women need an additional 600 – 900 mg daily (2 to 3 dairy portions) to reach recommended levels.
- Calcium absorption is saturable; doses above 500 – 600 mg should be divided.
- Although calcium citrate has a lower amount of elemental calcium, it has better absorption and may be preferable when gastric pH is increased (e.g., elderly patients, use of PPIs).
- Calcium products are available in many forms (e.g., capsules, tablets, chewables, liquids, granules/powder).
- There is no known benefit of using more expensive formulations. Untested products may contain lead, especially those containing calcium from dolomite, oyster shell, or bone meal. Recommend products made by reputable manufacturers. Constipation is a common side effect.

STUDY TIPS:
CALCIUM AND VITAMIN D

CALCIUM

- Do not exceed 500-600 mg per dose
- Calcium carbonate (e.g., *Tums*, others)
  - 40% elemental calcium
  - Absorption: acid-dependent
  - Must take with meals
- Calcium citrate (e.g., *Calcitrate*, others)
  - 21% elemental calcium
  - Absorption: not acid dependent
  - Can take with or without food

VITAMIN D

- Required for calcium absorption
- Deficiency: serum vitamin D [25(OH)D] < 30 ng/mL
- Treat deficiency with cholecalciferol (vitamin D3) or ergocalciferol (vitamin D2), dosed daily or weekly

Vitamin D Deficiency

- A few years ago vitamin D levels were not routinely tested; now it has become commonplace. A serum vitamin D level [25(OH)D] should be measured and supplements given to maintain levels of approximately 30 ng/mL (75 nmol/L).
- Vitamin D2 (ergocalciferol) or vitamin D3 (cholecalciferol) 50,000 international units weekly, or 5,000 – 7,000 international units daily, for 8 to 12 weeks is recommended in adults with deficiency to replenish stores. This should be followed by maintenance therapy (1,000 – 2,000 international units daily, or dosed to maintain target levels). See the Renal Disease chapter for information on vitamin D analogs (e.g., calcitriol).
- Sunlight exposure is another source of vitamin D3. Patients should be advised to obtain any required intake from food and supplements, rather than sunlight, due to the risk of skin cancer.

Drug Treatment

There are a number of FDA-approved options for the treatment and prevention of osteoporosis. Agents approved for treatment and prevention include the bisphosphonates (except IV ibandronate) and raloxifene. Teriparatide, denosumab and calcitonin are for treatment only and estrogen-based therapies, including *Duavee*, are only indicated for prevention. These medications have primarily been studied in postmenopausal women with osteoporosis, and there is limited data in men or in those with glucocorticoid-induced osteoporosis. Men are typically treated for 3 – 5 years with bisphosphonates; other agents can be considered depending on the patient's risk and condition. All prescription medications for low bone density require adequate calcium and vitamin D intake and levels should be evaluated before initiating therapy. Other important facts about each drug/drug class are shown in the Study Tips box below.

Criteria for Initiating Treatment

Osteoporosis	■ Postmenopausal women or men > 50 years of age with a BMD T-score of ≤ -2.5 at the femoral neck, total hip or lumbar spine ■ Presence of a fragility fracture, regardless of BMD
Osteopenia, if high risk	■ Low bone density (T-score between -1 and -2.5) at the femoral neck, total hip or lumbar spine AND ■ FRAX score indicates a 10-year probability of a major osteoporosis-related fracture ≥ 20% or a 10-year hip fracture probability ≥ 3%

STUDY TIPS: SUMMARY OF OSTEOPOROSIS TREATMENT AND PREVENTION OPTIONS

BISPHOSPHONATES

- 1st line for treatment or prevention of osteoporosis in most patients
- Oral administration requires staying upright for 30 minutes and, for most products, drinking 6-8 oz of plain water
- Common side effects: esophagitis, musculoskeletal symptoms, hypocalcemia
- Rare side effects: osteonecrosis of the jaw (ONJ) and atypical femur fractures
- Weekly/monthly oral options if adherence to administration instructions is difficult; quarterly/yearly parenteral options if there are GI side effects or adherence issues with oral options
- Treatment duration 3 – 5 years in patients at low risk of fracture (due to rare risk of femur fracture and ONJ)

ESTROGEN AGONIST/ANTAGONISTS

- Raloxifene *(Evista)*
  - Can be used for treatment or prevention
  - Decreases risk of breast cancer but causes vasomotor symptoms
- Conjugated equine estrogen/bazedoxifene *(Duavee)*
  - For prevention only in postmenopausal women with a uterus
  - Helps vasomotor symptoms but increases risk of breast cancer
- Both products increase the risk of venous thromboembolism (VTE) and stroke (boxed warnings)

TERIPARATIDE *(FORTEO)* AND DENOSUMAB *(PROLIA)*

- Treatment of high risk patients only
- Teriparatide causes hypercalcemia; denosumab causes hypocalcemia

LAST LINE OR NOT RECOMMENDED THERAPIES

- Estrogen (with or without progestin): for prevention only in postmenopausal women with vasomotor symptoms; use lowest possible dose for the shortest duration of time
- Calcitonin: for treatment only if other options are not suitable (less effective and has cancer risk with long term use)

Bisphosphonates

Bisphosphonates increase bone density by inhibiting osteoclast activity and bone resorption. They reduce both vertebral and hip fracture risk, except ibandronate which has only been shown to reduce vertebral fractures. Bisphosphonates are first-line for most patients for prevention or treatment of osteoporosis. They are also used to treat Paget's disease, glucocorticoid-induced osteoporosis (in men and women taking ≥ 7.5 mg of prednisone or equivalent), and hypercalcemia of malignancy.

Oral Bisphosphonates

DRUG	DOSING	SAFETY/SIDE EFFECTS/MONITORING
Alendronate *(Fosamax, Binosto)* Tablet, oral solution, effervescent tablet **+ cholecalciferol *(Fosamax Plus D)*** Tablet	**Prevention (postmenopausal women)** 5 mg PO daily, or 35 mg PO weekly **Treatment (postmenopausal women and men)** 10 mg PO daily, or 70 mg PO weekly *Fosamax Plus D:* 70 mg/2,800 IU or 70 mg/5,600 IU PO weekly **Glucocorticoid-Induced Osteoporosis** 5 mg PO daily Postmenopausal women not on estrogen: 10 mg PO daily	**CONTRAINDICATIONS** Inability to stand or sit upright for at least 30 minutes (60 minutes with once-monthly *Boniva);* abnormalities of the esophagus (e.g., esophageal stricture, achalasia); difficulty swallowing or at high risk for aspiration; hypocalcemia **WARNINGS** Osteonecrosis of the jaw (ONJ) – risk ↑ with invasive dental procedures, poor dental hygiene, cancer diagnosis, use of chemotherapy or corticosteroids, and duration of exposure Atypical femur fractures; bone, joint or muscle pain (may be severe) Esophagitis, esophageal ulcers, erosions, stricture or perforation (rare) – follow administration instructions (see Patient Counseling section) Hypocalcemia must be corrected prior to use Renal impairment – do not use or use not recommended: CrCl < 35 mL/min: alendronate CrCl < 30 mL/min: ibandronate, risedronate **SIDE EFFECTS** Hypocalcemia, hypophosphatemia (mild, transient), abdominal pain, dyspepsia, N/V, dysphagia, heartburn, musculoskeletal pain Risedronate: headache, hypertension, skin rash, UTI, infection **NOTES** Check calcium and vitamin D levels prior to initiating therapy Due to risk of jaw decay/necrosis, dental work should be done prior to starting therapy Aspirin or NSAIDs can worsen GI irritation – use with caution Separate calcium, antacids, iron and magnesium supplements from all oral bisphosphonates by at least 2 hours *Binosto* (effervescent alendronate tablet) contains 650 mg Na (use with caution in Na restricted patients, such as those with heart failure, hypertension or cirrhosis) *Atelvia* is a delayed release form that requires an acidic gut for absorption; H2RAs and PPIs should be avoided completely MedGuide required
Risedronate *(Actonel, Atelvia)* Tablet, delayed-release tablet *(Atelvia)*	**Prevention and Treatment (postmenopausal women)** 5 mg PO daily, or 35 mg PO weekly, or 75 mg PO on two consecutive days/month, or 150 mg PO monthly **Treatment (males)** 35 mg PO weekly **Glucocorticoid-Induced Osteoporosis** 5 mg PO daily	
Ibandronate *(Boniva)* Tablet, injection	**Prevention and Treatment (postmenopausal women)** PO: 150 mg monthly (on the same date every month)	

Bisphosphonates Continued

DRUG	DOSING	SAFETY/SIDE EFFECTS/MONITORING

Injectable Bisphosphonates

Ibandronate ***(Boniva)*** Tablet, injection	**Treatment (postmenopausal women)** 3 mg IV every 3 months Administer over 15 – 30 seconds	**CONTRAINDICATIONS** Hypocalcemia Zoledronic acid: CrCl < 35 mL/minute or evidence of acute renal impairment **WARNINGS** Same as oral bisphosphonates (except no GI problems) plus: Renal impairment (including injury and death due to renal failure); monitor serum creatinine before each dose; use with caution in dehydrated patients, in patients with comorbid conditions or those taking medications that can cause renal impairment Ibandronate: do not use if CrCl < 30 mL/min Zoledronic acid: use caution in patients with aspirin-sensitive asthma (can cause bronchoconstriction) **SIDE EFFECTS** Same as oral bisphosphonates (except no esophageal problems) plus: Acute phase reaction (flu-like symptoms such as fever, achiness, runny nose, headache) Zoledronic acid: edema, hypotension, fatigue, dehydration, ↓ PO4, K, and Mg **NOTES** Injectable bisphosphonates preferred if esophagitis is present, due to the risk for esophageal cancer Zoledronic acid: safety issue – see Pregnancy chapter MedGuide required
Zoledronic Acid ***(Reclast)*** *Zometa* – for hypercalcemia of malignancy	**Prevention (postmenopausal women)** 5 mg IV every 2 years **Treatment (postmenopausal women and men)** 5 mg IV once yearly **Glucocorticoid-Induced Osteoporosis** 5 mg IV once yearly Administer over ≥ 15 minutes	

Estrogen Agonist/Antagonist Containing Products

Raloxifene is an estrogen agonist/antagonist [a selective estrogen receptor modulator (SERM)], that ↓ bone resorption. Conjugated estrogens/bazedoxifene (*Duavee*) is an equine (horse) estrogen/SERM combination indicated for osteoporosis prevention in postmenopausal women with a uterus.

DRUG	DOSING	SAFETY/SIDE EFFECTS/MONITORING
Raloxifene ***(Evista)***	**Prevention and Treatment (postmenopausal women)** 60 mg PO daily	**BOXED WARNINGS** ↑ risk of VTE (DVT, PE); ↑ risk of death due to stroke in women at risk for coronary events or with CAD **CONTRAINDICATIONS** VTE, pregnancy **SIDE EFFECTS** Hot flashes, peripheral edema, arthralgia, leg cramps/muscle spasms, flu symptoms, infection **NOTES** Separate raloxifene and levothyroxine by several hours Discontinue 72 hours prior to and during prolonged immobilization Safety issue – see Pregnancy chapter MedGuide required
Conjugated Estrogens/ Bazedoxifene ***(Duavee)***	**Prevention (postmenopausal women with a uterus)** 1 tablet (0.45/20 mg) PO daily Also indicated for treatment of moderate-severe vasomotor symptoms associated with menopause (same dose)	**BOXED WARNINGS** Endometrial cancer (due to unopposed estrogen use in a women with a uterus); dementia (women ≥ 65 years); ↑ risk of VTE and stroke in postmenopausal women 50-79 years of age (do not use to prevent cardiovascular disease), do not use with additional estrogens **CONTRAINDICATIONS** Breast cancer (any history); undiagnosed uterine bleeding; active VTE, arterial thromboembolic disease, or known protein C, S or antithrombin deficiency; hepatic impairment; pregnancy **WARNINGS** ↑ risk of breast cancer (from use of estrogen alone) and ovarian cancer, ↑ risk of retinal vascular thrombosis, lipid effects (↑ HDL, ↑ TG, ↓ LDL) **SIDE EFFECTS** Nausea, diarrhea, dyspepsia, abdominal pain, muscle spasms **NOTES** Not recommended for women > 75 years of age As with other estrogens, use for the shortest duration possible Safety issue – see Pregnancy chapter

Calcitonin

Calcitonin directly inhibits osteoclastic bone resorption. It is considered less effective than other agents for the treatment of osteoporosis and, with long term use, the risk of cancer is increased. For these reasons, it is rarely used.

DRUG	DOSING	SAFETY/SIDE EFFECTS/MONITORING
Calcitonin ***(Miacalcin)*** Nasal spray, injection	**Treatment (women > 5 years postmenopause)** Nasal spray: 1 spray (200 units) in one nostril daily (alternate nostril daily) SC or IM: 100 units daily	**CONTRAINDICATION** Allergy to calcitonin-salmon **WARNINGS** Hypocalcemia (associated with tetany and seizures); ↑ risk of malignancy with long-term use; hypersensitivity reactions to salmon-derived product (e.g., bronchospasm, anaphylaxis, swelling of the tongue or throat); antibody formation Nasal spray: nasal reactions (e.g., ulceration, epistaxis, rhinitis) – nasal exams recommended **SIDE EFFECTS** Back pain, myalgia, nausea, dizziness Injection: flushing, injection site reactions **NOTES** Keep injection and unopened nasal spray bottles refrigerated

Parathyroid Hormone 1-34

Teriparatide is a recombinant form of endogenous parathyroid hormone which stimulates osteoblast activity and increases bone formation. It is used for the treatment of osteoporosis when there is a high risk of fracture.

DRUG	DOSING	SAFETY/SIDE EFFECTS/MONITORING
Teriparatide ***(Forteo)*** Injection	**Treatment (postmenopausal women and men)** 20 mcg SC daily **Glucocorticoid-Induced Osteoporosis** 20 mcg SC daily Use > 2 years is not recommended	**BOXED WARNING** Osteosarcoma (bone cancer) in rat studies – risk dependent on dose and duration of treatment **WARNINGS** Hypercalcemia, orthostatic hypotension, do not use in patients with bone malignancy or metabolic bone diseases, use cautiously in patients with urolithiasis (urinary stones) **SIDE EFFECTS** Arthralgias, leg cramps, pain, nausea, orthostasis/dizziness **NOTES** Keep refrigerated and protect from light MedGuide required

Receptor Activator of Nuclear Factor kappa-B Ligand (RANKL) Inhibitor

Denosumab is a monoclonal antibody that binds to RANKL and blocks its interaction with RANK (a receptor on osteoclasts) to prevent osteoclast formation; this leads to ↓ bone resorption and ↑ bone mass. It is used for treatment of osteoporosis when there is a high risk of fracture.

DRUG	DOSING	SAFETY/SIDE EFFECTS/MONITORING
Denosumab ***(Prolia)*** Injection *Xgeva* – hypercalcemia of malignancy, bone cell tumor, prevention of bone metastasis	**Treatment (postmenopausal women and men)** 60 mg SC every 6 months Other indications: treatment of bone loss in men receiving androgen deprivation therapy for prostate cancer and women receiving aromatase inhibitor therapy for breast cancer Must be administered by a healthcare professional	**CONTRAINDICATIONS** Hypocalcemia (must be corrected prior to using), pregnancy **WARNINGS** Osteonecrosis of the jaw (ONJ) – risk ↑ with invasive dental procedures, poor dental hygiene, cancer diagnosis, use of chemotherapy or corticosteroids, and duration of exposure Atypical femur fractures; bone, joint or muscle pain (may be severe) Hypocalcemia - use caution in patient's predisposed (e.g., hypoparathyroidism, thyroid surgery, malabsorption syndromes, CrCl < 30 mL/min) Serious infections (e.g., skin, abdomen, urinary tract), dermatologic reactions (e.g., dermatitis, eczema, rash) **SIDE EFFECTS** Hypertension, fatigue, edema, dyspnea, headache, N/V/D, ↓ PO4 **NOTES** Safety issue – see Pregnancy chapter If/when discontinued, bone loss can be rapid; consider alternative agents to maintain BMD MedGuide required

Patient Counseling

All Osteoporosis Medications

- This medication does not work well if you are not taking enough calcium and vitamin D. Some products used to treat or prevent osteoporosis contain calcium or vitamin D. Discuss with your healthcare provider to see if you need to use calcium or vitamin D supplements.
- If you are using a proton pump inhibitor (e.g., *Prilosec, Prevacid)* for heartburn, discuss with your healthcare provider. These drugs may decrease the amount of calcium that is able to get into your body and increase fracture risk. You may need to use calcium citrate as your calcium supplement.
- Your bone and muscle strength will improve faster if you exercise. Your healthcare provider should discuss safe and healthy ways to exercise with you.

Bisphosphonates

- Take this medication first thing in the morning, before you eat or drink anything, with 6 – 8 oz (1 cup) of plain water. If using weekly or monthly, you must take it on the same day each week or month; choose a day that is easy to remember (e.g., Sunday if going to church, bridge day, book club).
- You must take this medication while you are sitting up or standing, and stay upright for at least 30 minutes after (60 minutes with monthly *Boniva)*. During this time, you cannot eat or drink anything else except more plain water. You cannot take any other medications or vitamins. You must not lie down again until after the first food of the day.

- This medication must be swallowed whole, and washed down with water. Do not crush or chew the tablet.
- For *Binosto*, dissolve one tablet in 4 oz (1/2 cup) of room temperature plain water. Wait 5 minutes to allow the tablet to dissolve, then stir for 10 seconds before drinking.
- If using an oral solution, drink at least 2 oz (1/4 cup) of plain water after taking the medication.
- *Atelvia*: this is a long-acting form of risedronate. Take the medication after breakfast with 4 oz (1/2 cup) of plain water. Sit or stand upright for at least 30 minutes after taking. Do not use acid suppressing "heartburn" therapy with this medication.
- Common side effects of this medication include GI upset (e.g., heartburn, upset stomach, pain in the stomach area), and pain in the bones, joints or muscles.
- Stop taking this medication if you develop difficult or painful swallowing, have chest pain, have very bad heartburn that does not go away, or have severe pain in the bones, joints or muscles.
- Rarely, some patients have developed serious jaw-bone problems from taking this medication, which may include infection and slower healing after teeth are pulled. Tell your healthcare providers, including your dentist, right away if you have these symptoms. If you are scheduled to have dental work, you should have it done before starting the medication.
- Rarely, this medication can cause fractures in the thigh bone. Tell your healthcare provider right away if you develop thigh, hip or groin pain while on this medication.
- Do not take calcium, iron, magnesium, antacids or multivitamin supplements until later in the day.
- Missed doses:
  - Daily dosing schedule: if you miss a dose, skip that dose. Take the next dose at the regularly scheduled time.
  - Weekly dosing schedule: if you miss a dose, take the it the morning after you remember (but do not take two doses on the same day).
  - Monthly dosing schedule: if you miss a dose, take it the morning after you remember, except if it is less than one week to the next dose, then skip it (do not take two doses in the same week).

Raloxifene

- Take with or without food.
- This medication can cause dangerous blood clots. If any of the following symptoms occur, it could be due to a blood clot and you should get medical treatment quickly: sudden leg pain, chest pain, shortness of breath, vision changes, an inability to speak or slurred speech, or loss of movement on any side of your body.
- This medication can cause hot flashes, leg cramps, flu-like symptoms, joint pain, sweating, and swelling in the feet, ankles or legs. If these occur and are bothersome, discuss with your healthcare provider.
- Discontinue this medication at least 72 hours prior to and during prolonged immobilization, such as after a surgery or with prolonged bed rest.

Teriparatide

- This medication helps to form new bone and increase bone strength. When tested in animals, it caused a rare form of bone cancer. It is not known if people who take the medication have the same risk. Inform your healthcare provider right away if you develop bone or joint pain.
- You may feel dizzy or lightheaded after the first few doses. This usually happens within 4 hours of taking the medication and goes away within a few hours. For the first few doses, inject this medication in a place where you can sit or lie down right away if these symptoms occur.

- The medication comes in a prefilled injection pen that lasts 28 days. Each injection provides the set dose of 20 mcg dose. Do not transfer the medication from the delivery device to a syringe.
- Using a new needle, inject the medication once daily in your thigh or abdomen (lower stomach area). The injection sites must be rotated.
- After injecting, discard the needle in a puncture-resistant container with a tight-fitting lid (see the Medication Safety & Quality Improvement chapter). The pen should be re-capped after each use and kept in the refrigerator.
- You can inject at any time of the day, but should pick the same time each day. If you forget, or cannot take the medication at your usual time, take it as soon as you can on that day. Do not take more than one injection in the same day.
- After 28 days, the pen should be discarded even if some medication remains. Mark the date in the user manual when the pen is started and the date (28 days later) when the pen should be thrown away.
- Do not use for more than 2 years.

Calcitonin Nasal Spray

- Keep unused bottles in the refrigerator; once in use, the bottle may be kept at room temperature for 30 days.
- When using a new bottle, allow it to reach room temperature prior to use. Before you take the first dose, hold the bottle upright and press the two white side arms toward the bottle to release at least 5 sprays and until a full spray is produced (this called "priming the pump"). Once the pump is primed, it does not have to be primed again if the bottle is stored in an upright position.
- To use the nasal spray, remove the protective cap, keep the head upright, and insert the tip of the nozzle into a nostril. Press down firmly on the pump to deliver the medication. Use the other nostril the next day.
- After 30 doses, the pump may not deliver the correct amount of medication with each spray and should be discarded.
- Call 911 if you have an allergic reaction (e.g., swelling of your face or throat, or trouble breathing).
- Some nose irritation may occur. Discuss with your healthcare provider if you get nasal crusting, dryness, redness, swelling, nose sores (ulcers) or nose bleeds.

MENOPAUSE

Menopause means that the last menstrual period was over 12 months ago. Menopause usually occurs between the ages of 40 and 58 (average age is 52 years). A decrease in estrogen and progesterone causes an increase in follicle stimulating hormone (FSH), resulting in vasomotor symptoms (recurrent transient episodes of flushing and sensation of heat in the upper body and face, sometimes followed by chills). More than half of women experience vasomotor symptoms during the menopause transition period (known as perimenopause) as estrogen production by the ovaries declines. These are often described as hot flashes and night sweats (hot flashes that occur during sleep). Sleep can be disturbed, and mood changes may be present. Due to a decline in estrogen in the vaginal mucosa, vaginal dryness, burning and painful intercourse can occur.

Some women remain largely asymptomatic during menopause, while others suffer from severe symptoms that significantly impact their quality of life. Vasomotor symptoms can last up to 7 years. Women who have both of their ovaries removed, or receive chemotherapy or radiation for cancer, will experience induced menopause; the symptoms are similar but often more acute initially due to a sudden, rather than a gradual, decline in estrogen.

Treatment of Vasomotor Symptoms: Estrogen-Progestin Products

Health Risks and Considerations For Use

The most effective therapy for vasomotor symptoms is systemic hormone therapy with estrogen, which causes a decrease in luteinizing hormone (LH) and more stable temperature control. Estrogen improves bone density as well. In women with a uterus, estrogen should never be used alone and should always be accompanied by a form of progesterone (e.g., a progestin); unopposed estrogen will place the woman at increased risk for endometrial cancer. Progestins can cause mood disturbances in some women, and may be hard to tolerate. If given intermittently, for two weeks each month, rather than continuously (such as with *Premphase)*, spotting can be a nuisance. Progestins (e.g., norethindrone, levonorgestrel, norgestimate, drospirenone) are given in combination with the estrogen, or as a separate tablet (generally medroxyprogesterone, MPA).

In 2002, data from large trials on hormone therapy became available; these were the Women's Health Initiative (WHI) postmenopausal hormone therapy trials. Initially, the data led to several boxed warnings on the use of hormone therapy (HT), including warnings for increased risk of stroke, heart attacks and probable risk of dementia. As the data was reanalyzed, it became apparent that the elevated risk was generally isolated to older women. Currently, the following considerations for use should be followed according to the North American Menopause Society:

- To maximize safety, consider HT for healthy symptomatic women who are within 10 years of menopause, or aged younger than 60 years, and who do not have contraindications to use of HT.
- Extending HT beyond age 60 is acceptable under some circumstances (e.g., osteoporosis), provided that the lowest effective dose is used and the woman has been advised of the risks of HT.
- Consideration should be given to the woman's quality-of-life priorities and personal risk factors (e.g., age, time since menopause, risk of blood clots, heart disease, stroke, and breast cancer).

Formulation Considerations

Both transdermal and low-dose oral estrogen therapy have been associated with lower risks of venous thromboembolism (VTE) and stroke than standard doses of oral estrogen. Estrogen is generally well tolerated, but can cause nausea, dizziness, headaches, mood changes, vaginal bleeding, bloating and breast tenderness/fullness. Topical formulations (e.g., patch, gel, emulsion) bypass first pass metabolism, and lower doses can be used. Topical formulations may decrease the systemic estrogen exposure, cause less nausea, and have little or no effect on cholesterol levels.

Local estrogen products are preferred for patients who have vaginal symptoms only (vaginal dryness and/or painful intercourse). Any of the vaginal products included in this chapter (creams, vaginal tablets, vaginal rings) or OTC lubricants can be helpful. Common OTC lubricants and moisturizers include *Replens* and *Luvena*. A lubricant marketed specifically for dyspareunia (dry, painful intercourse) is *Astroglide*. Oil-based lubricants should not be used with condoms as they can cause the condom to tear. *Astroglide* or silicon-based lubricants are safe to recommend with condoms.

Common Hormone Therapy Products

Estradiol-containing products and conjugated estrogens are used primarily for vasomotor symptoms, vaginal atrophy and osteoporosis prevention. Oral contraceptives, used for contraception, contain ethinyl estradiol.

COMPONENTS	FORMULATION
Topical Hormone Therapies	
17-Beta-Estradiol	Vaginal cream ***(Estrace)*** Vaginal ring ***(Estring)*** Vaginal tablet ***(Vagifem)***
Systemic Hormone Therapies	
Estradiol	Topical gel *(Elestrin)* Transdermal patch ***(Alora, Climara, Minivelle, Vivelle-Dot, Menostar)*** Vaginal ring ***(Femring)***
17-Beta-Estradiol	Oral tablet, micronized ***(Estrace)*** Topical gel *(Divigel, EstroGel)* Topical spray *(Evamist)*
Estradiol and Levonorgestrel	Transdermal patch *(Climara Pro)* *"Pro" in the name indicates a progestin
Estradiol and Norethindrone	Transdermal patch *(CombiPatch)* Oral tablet *(Activella, Amabelz, Mimvey, Mimvey Lo)*
Estradiol and Norgestimate	Oral tablet *(Prefest):* cyclic treatment – estradiol x 3 days, estradiol + norgestimate x 3 days, then repeat
Estradiol and Drospirenone	Oral tablet *(Angeliq)*
Conjugated Equine Estrogens	Oral tablet ***(Premarin)*:** 0.3, 0.45, 0.625, 0.9, 1.25 mg Vaginal cream ***(Premarin)*:** 0.625 mg/gram Injection ***(Premarin)***
Conjugated Equine Estrogens and MedroxyPROGESTERone (MPA)	Oral tablet ***(Prempro)*:** 0.3/1.5, 0.45/1.5, 0.625/2.5, 0.625/0.5 mg Oral tablet ***(Premphase)*:** phasic dosing – 0.625 mg on days 1-14, then 0.625/5 mg on days 15-28
MedroxyPROGESTERone *Depo-Provera* – SC or IM for contraception	Oral tablets ***(Provera)*:** 2.5, 5, 10 mg
Conjugated Estrogens/Bazedoxifene	Oral tablet ***(Duavee)***

SAFETY/SIDE EFFECTS/MONITORING

BOXED WARNINGS

Endometrial cancer (if estrogen used without progestin in a women with a uterus); dementia (women ≥ 65 years); ↑ risk of VTE and stroke in postmenopausal women 50-79 years of age (do not use to prevent cardiovascular disease), breast cancer; use lowest effective dose for shortest duration consistent with treatment goals and risks

Evamist: secondary exposure can cause breast budding and breast masses in prepubertal females, and gynecomastia and breast masses in prepubertal males; keep children away from spray

CONTRAINDICATIONS

Estrogen-containing products: breast cancer (any history); undiagnosed uterine bleeding; active VTE, arterial thromboembolic disease, or known protein C, S or antithrombin deficiency; hepatic impairment; pregnancy

WARNINGS

↑ risk of breast cancer (from use of estrogen alone) and ovarian cancer, ↑ risk of retinal vascular thrombosis, lipid effects (↑ HDL, ↑ TG, ↓ LDL)

SIDE EFFECTS

Edema, hypertension, headache, weight gain, depression, nausea, abdominal pain

Patch: redness/irritation of the skin

NOTES

Topical (vaginal) hormone therapies may have lower systemic absorption than systemic hormone therapies; safety issues above should still be considered, although risk may be lower

Patch formulations may need to be removed prior to an MRI (see Drug Formulations chapter)

Vivelle-Dot, Alora, Minivelle patches are applied twice weekly; *Climara* and *Menostar* patches are once weekly

Gels and *Evamist* spray are flammable

Safety issue - see Pregnancy chapter

"Bioidentical" Nomenclature

The warnings for hormone therapy are based on the analysis of the WHI data. Until more information is available to refine these warnings, it is safest to assume that the known risks for one estrogen formulation may apply to other formulations. Some women will prefer to use bioidentical hormones, that include commercially available products approved by the FDA, and others will prefer compounded preparations.

The term "bioidentical" has different meanings; some use it to refer to hormones that have an identical structure to those found in the female body, while others use it to refer to plant-derived hormones that are compounded. Many woman, physicians and compounding pharmacists believe that bioidentical HT is safer, but there are no well-designed studies to confirm risk or benefit and compounded preparations are not regulated by the FDA. Compounded products allow for patient specific formulations when the patient's needs are not met by the FDA approved commercially available products.

Estrogen Patient Counseling

- Estrogen products help control menopausal symptoms but they have risks and should not be continued indefinitely. The goal is to use the lowest dose possible for the shortest period of time. When you are ready to stop treatment, discuss the best way to do so with your healthcare provider.
- This product does not contain a progestin; women with a uterus should not take estrogen alone as it increases the risk of cancer of the uterus.
- Report any unusual vaginal bleeding right away while you are taking estrogen. Vaginal bleeding after menopause may be a warning sign of cancer of the uterus and your healthcare provider will need to evaluate any unusual vaginal bleeding promptly.
- Using estrogens may increase your risk for heart attacks, strokes, breast cancer, dementia and blood clots. You should talk with your healthcare provider regularly about whether you still need treatment. Do not use hormone therapy to prevent heart disease, heart attacks, or strokes.
- Estrogen can help keep your bones healthy. If you are using estrogen for this reason, ask your healthcare provider for help deciding if you need to take calcium and vitamin D, which are also important for healthy bones.
- Topical gels: these are applied once daily. *Divigel* should be applied to the right or left upper thigh, (alternate sides daily); *Elestrin* should be applied to the upper arm and shoulder; *EstroGel* should be applied to the entire arm from wrist to shoulder. It is important that you wash your hands after applying estrogen gels.
- *Evamist* spray: each morning, spray on the inside of the forearm between the elbow and the wrist.
- If you are in the transition period of menopause (called perimenopause), you may be at risk of accidental pregnancy as your menstrual cycle has become irregular; speak with you healthcare provider about effective birth control options.

Patch Application

- Mark the schedule you plan to follow on the inner flap of your medication package, or on your calendar. If you forget to change your patch on the correct date, apply a new one as soon as you remember.
- Apply the patch to the lower abdomen, below the waistline (avoid the waistline, since clothing may cause the patch to rub off). Make sure the skin is clean, dry, and free of powder, oil or lotion. Do not apply the patch to cut or irritated skin.
- Do not apply the patch to the breasts.
- If any adhesive residue remains on your skin after removing the patch, allow the area to dry for 15 minutes. Then, gently rub the area with oil or lotion to remove the adhesive from your skin.

Other Products Used to Treat Vasomotor Symptoms

Natural Products

Natural products used for vasomotor symptoms include black cohosh, red clover, soy, flaxseed, dong quai, St. John's wort, and evening primrose oil. The mild "plant estrogens," found in soy and red clover, are called phytoestrogens; phyto means plant. These natural products may help with mild symptoms, but do not usually provide the same benefit seen with estrogens.

SSRIs and Other Drugs

Paroxetine *(Brisdelle)* is the first non-hormonal FDA approved treatment of moderate-severe vasomotor symptoms associated with menopause. The dose of paroxetine used is lower than the recommended dose for depression. Women who use *Brisdelle* should not use tamoxifen or warfarin. Paroxetine is a CYP 2D6 inhibitor, and it will block the effectiveness of tamoxifen. SSRIs can increase the risk of bleeding in patients using warfarin, but the mechanism is unknown. SNRIs (e.g., desvenlafaxine), clonidine and gabapentin have also shown effectiveness for treating vasomotor symptoms related to menopause, but they are not FDA approved for this indication.

Ospemifene

Ospemifene *(Osphena)*, is an oral estrogen agonist/antagonist indicated for dyspareunia (painful intercourse), which is a symptom of vulvar and vaginal atrophy due to menopause. Due to the risks associated with use, it is not indicated for mild symptoms (topical vaginal products are safer for this purpose) and should only be used for a short treatment period for moderate-to-severe symptoms. *Intrarosa* (prasterone), a vaginally inserted steroid, was also approved for the treatment of moderate-severe dyspareunia in late 2016.

DRUG	DOSING	SAFETY/SIDE EFFECTS/MONITORING
PARoxetine *(Brisdelle)* *Paxil, Paxil CR, Pexeva* – for depression, panic disorder	7.5 mg PO QHS	**BOXED WARNING** Suicide risk (same as with other SSRIs – see Depression chapter) **CONTRAINDICATIONS/WARNINGS** Same as with other SSRIs (see Depression chapter) **SIDE EFFECTS** Same sexual side effects as other SSRIs (see Depression chapter); *Brisdelle* trials showed > 10% incidence of sedation, insomnia, restlessness, tremor, dizziness/weakness, nausea, dry mouth, constipation, diaphoresis **NOTES** Lag time to effect (~4 weeks) Do not use with warfarin (↑ bleeding risk) or tamoxifen (↓ tamoxifen efficacy)
Ospemifene *(Osphena)*	60 mg PO daily Take with food	**BOXED WARNINGS/CONTRAINDICATIONS** Same as for other estrogen-containing products (see Hormone Therapy table above) **WARNING** Should not be used in women with severe hepatic impairment **SIDE EFFECTS** Hot flashes, vaginal discharge, hyperhidrosis, muscle spasms

HYPOGONADISM IN MALES

Hypogonadism in older males can be due to a normal age related decline in testosterone, or it can be secondary to a medical condition, surgical procedure, or medication that lowers testosterone. Medications that can lower testosterone include opioids (especially methadone when used for opioid dependence), chemotherapy drugs used for prostate cancer (see Oncology II chapter), cimetidine and spironolactone.

Testosterone Use

The increased use of testosterone over the past few years is largely due to older males requesting testosterone therapy for "Low T" symptoms in order to increase sexual interest (↑ libido) and improve sexual performance, increase muscle mass, increase bone density, sharpen memory and concentration, and increase energy. The use of testosterone replacement for conditions other than the accepted medical uses is controversial, and a clear benefit of improved sexual function has not been established. In 2015, the FDA released a warning about cardiovascular risks associated with testosterone use and included a recommendation to only use it in men with low testosterone levels caused by certain medical conditions and confirmed by laboratory tests.

In addition, there have been reports of increased clotting risk in men using testosterone therapy; most men who experienced clotting may have had a higher risk at baseline and, at present, the link to testosterone use is unclear. Testosterone increases hematocrit, which can cause polycythemia and an increase in clotting risk. Testosterone can cause noncancerous prostate growth in men with benign prostatic hypertrophy (BPH); for this reason, testosterone replacement is restricted in men with severe BPH. However, even with mild or moderate BPH, if dispensing a 5-alpha-reductase inhibitor for BPH (e.g., finasteride) that blocks the conversion of testosterone to the active form, it would not make sense to dispense another drug that provides testosterone directly. Common side effects of testosterone include increased male pattern baldness, acne and gynecomastia.

In October 2016, the FDA approved class wide labeling changes for all prescription testosterone and anabolic androgenic steroids (AAS) to alert prescribers of the potential for abuse and serious adverse events. Abuse of testosterone, at doses higher than those typically prescribed and usually in conjunction with other AAS, is associated with serious safety risks affecting the heart, brain, liver, mental health, and endocrine system. Reported serious adverse outcomes include heart attack, heart failure, stroke, depression, hostility, aggression, liver toxicity, and male infertility. Individuals abusing high doses of testosterone have also reported withdrawal symptoms, such as depression, fatigue, irritability, loss of appetite, decreased libido, and insomnia.

Testosterone Formulations

Testosterone comes in many formulations including parenteral (IM or SC) injections, topic gels and solutions, buccal tablets and transdermal patches. The injectable forms are painful and require medical visits; patients may complain that they feel symptomatic when it is getting close to the time for the next dose. The injections may increase the hematocrit more than topical formulations. The SC pellets in *Testopel* are a little smaller than a *Tic-Tac* mint and have the unfortunate tendency of popping out.

The gel formulations *(AndroGel* and other topical gels) are the most popular formulations and are relatively well-tolerated. *AndroGel* is the top-selling "Low-T" product and it is applied to the upper body. Men who use the gel need to let it dry prior to dressing and be careful not to let others touch the application area, as this increases the risk of drug transfer. If drug transfers to a female or male child, it can cause "early virilization" and, depending on the dose received, the child could have enlarged genital organs, aggressive behavior and premature pubic hair growth. The risk of early virilization is a boxed warning and requires counseling (see Testosterone Patient Counseling section). There are new topical formulations that reduce accidental exposure risk: *Axiron* is applied to the underarms using an applicator that looks like deodorant, *Fortesta* is applied to the thighs with one finger (the amount is small) and *Natesto* is applied to the nostrils.

Testosterone Products: C-III

TESTOSTERONE	COUNSELING
Topical Gels and Solutions	
Testosterone gel ***AndroGel*** (1%, 1.62%), ***AndroGel Pump*** (1.62%)	*AndroGel* 1% is applied daily to the upper arms, shoulders, and/or abdomen; 1.62% should only be applied to the upper arms or shoulders (not the abdomen)
Testosterone gel 1% *(Vogelxo, Vogelxo Pump)*	Applied to upper arms and shoulders daily
Testosterone gel 1% *(Testim)*	Applied to arms and shoulders daily
Testosterone gel 2% *(Fortesta)*	Applied to front and inner thighs daily
Testosterone solution *(Axiron)*	Applied to armpits daily
Testosterone nasal gel *(Natesto)*	1 spray per nostril TID
Alternative Formulations	
Transdermal patch *(Androderm)*	2 mg, 4 mg Apply to back, abdomen, thighs or upper arms each night
Buccal tabs *(Striant)*	30 mg to the gum region BID
Implantable pellets *(Testopel)*	SC every 3-6 months
Injections	
Testosterone undecanoate *(Aveed)*	IM every 4 weeks (2 doses), then every 10 weeks
Testosterone cypionate *(Depo-Testosterone)*	IM every 2-4 weeks
Testosterone enanthate	IM every 2-4 weeks
Testosterone ointment/ cream *(First-Testosterone)*	Apply as directed

SAFETY/SIDE EFFECTS/MONITORING

BOXED WARNINGS

Secondary exposure to testosterone in children can occur resulting in virilization; children should avoid contact with any unwashed or unclothed application sites in men using testosterone gel

Aveed: pulmonary oil microembolism (POME) reactions (cough, dyspnea, throat tightening, anaphylaxis) – can be life-threatening; requires observation in a healthcare setting for 30 minutes after each injection

CONTRAINDICATIONS

Breast cancer, prostate cancer, pregnancy, breast-feeding women

Aveed: allergy to castor oil or benzyl benzoate

Depo-Testosterone: serious cardiac, hepatic or renal disease

WARNINGS

↑ risk of breast cancer, prostate cancer, cardiovascular events, VTE, dyslipidemia, gynecomastia, hepatic impairment, polycythemia, priapism; may worsen BPH (↑ PSA)

SIDE EFFECTS

↑ appetite, ↑ SCr, sensitive nipples, acne, edema, hepatotoxicity, reduced sperm count, sleep apnea

Additional Issues By Formulation Type

Androderm: skin irritation

Striant: buccal irritation

Natesto: nasal irritation

Injections: injection site pain

MONITORING

Testosterone levels, PSA, liver function, cholesterol, some products recommend checking hematocrit

NOTES

Gels: apply at the same time each morning; they are flammable until dry.

Androderm: do not use two 2 mg patches for a 4 mg dose. After removal, can treat irritation with OTC hydrocortisone. Remove patch before MRI.

Testosterone Patient Counseling

Testosterone Gels

- This medication should not be used by women or children. To avoid transferring the testosterone drug to women or children, it is important that you wash your hands after applying this medication and to be careful that no one touches the areas of application, especially when wet.
  - Topical testosterone is absorbed through the skin and can cause side effects or symptoms of male features in a child or woman who comes into contact with the medication. Symptoms include enlarged genitals, premature pubic hair, increased libido, aggressive behavior, male-pattern baldness, excessive body hair growth, increased acne, irregular menstrual periods, or any signs of male characteristics.
- Testosterone can cause birth defects in unborn babies. A pregnant woman should avoid coming into contact with testosterone topical gel, or with areas of a man's skin where a testosterone topical patch has been worn or the gel has been applied. If contact does occur, wash with soap and water right away.

How to apply topical gels

- Apply the medication as directed (see application sites in table) to clean, dry skin once daily in the morning. Apply only to areas that would be covered with clothing (e.g., a short sleeve t-shirt for *Androgel*). Avoid applying this medication to broken, irritated skin. Do not apply to the genitals (penis or scrotum) or breasts. Do not let others apply this medication to your body.
- Before dressing, wait a few minutes for the application site to dry completely. Keep the application site covered with clothing until you wash the areas well with soap and water.
- If you expect to have skin-to-skin contact with another person, first wash the application area well with soap and water.
- For best effects, wait at least 2 to 6 hours after applying the medication before showering or swimming.
- This medication is flammable until dry. Let the gel dry before smoking or going near an open flame.
- *AndroGel Pump*: before using the pump for the first time, you will need to prime the pump. To do this, push down fully on the pump 3 times. Do not use any *AndroGel* that came out while priming. Wash it down the sink or throw it in the trash to avoid accidental exposure to others. Your healthcare provider will tell you the number of times to press the pump for each dose.
- *AndroGel* packets: tear open the packet completely at the dotted line. Squeeze all of the *AndroGel* out of the packet into the palm of your hand. Squeeze from the bottom of the packet to the top.
- *Axiron* (applied to underarms): apply deodorant first.
- *Fortesta:* apply to the front and inner thighs with one finger.
- *Natesto:* prime the pump ten times first, insert the actuator into the nostril, depress slowly until the pump stops, remove from the nose while wiping the tip to transfer gel to the lateral side of the nostril, then press on the nose and lightly massage. Try not to blow your nose or sniff for one hour.

Androderm Patch

- Apply the patch each night to a clean, dry area of the skin (see table for application sites). Avoid showering, washing the application site, or swimming for at least 3 hours after application. Do not use the same site for at least seven days.
- Dispose of used patches by folding adhesive ends together, place in a pouch or sealed container, and place in the trash away from children and pets.
- The testosterone transdermal patch may burn your skin if you wear the patch during an MRI (magnetic resonance imaging). Remove the patch before undergoing such a test.

PAIN

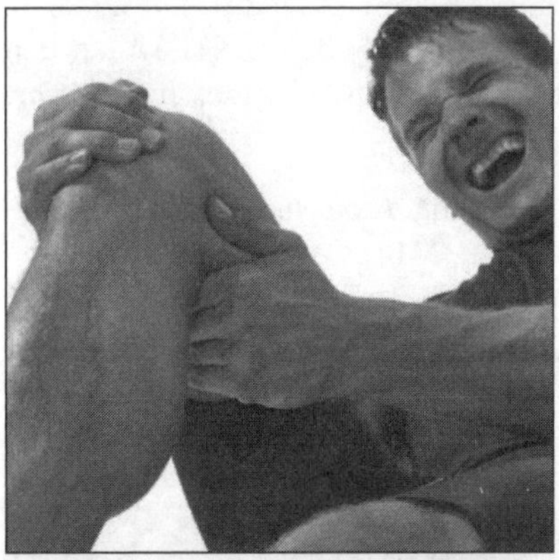

We gratefully acknowledge the assistance of Jeffrey Fudin, BS, PharmD, DAAPM, FCCP, FASHP, and Erica L. Wegrzyn, BA, BS, PharmD, in preparing this chapter.

BACKGROUND

The word pain is derived from the Latin term "poena" which means "punishment". Despite the literal translation, pain should never be viewed as a form of punishment. Acute pain is a protective mechanism to prevent further injury. For example, when skin is exposed to something very hot, the pain causes the person to pull away very quickly. Pain can be defined as the physical suffering caused by an illness or injury.

GUIDELINES/REFERENCES

CDC Guideline for Prescribing Opioids for Chronic Pain. http://www.cdc.gov/drugoverdose/prescribing/common-elements.html (accessed 2016 Dec 6).

American Pain Society's Principles of Analgesic Use in the Treatment of Acute Pain and Cancer Pain, 6th Edition, 2008.

Pain Treatment Resources, at www.paindr.com (accessed 2016 Dec 6).

Nociceptive and Neuropathic Pain

Nociceptive pain occurs when sensory nerves (nociceptors) identify damage in tissues from changes such as temperature, swelling and vibration. The nociceptors send impulses to the brain that result in feeling pain. Nociceptive pain is classified by whether it comes from injury to internal organs (visceral pain) or from an injury to the skin, muscles, bones, joints or ligaments (somatic pain, which is commonly referred to as musculoskeletal pain).

Neuropathic pain means that the damage (the pathology) is due to the nerve itself (the neuron). The common cause of neuropathic pain is years of chronically elevated blood glucose. Neuropathies can be due to drugs, such as the vinka alkaloids, or disease states.

Acute and Chronic Pain

The difference between acute and chronic pain is important because they are treated differently. Acute pain begins suddenly and usually feels sharp. It is due to some type of injury, such as a fracture, burn or cut, or the pain associated with surgery or childbirth. The pain can last just a few moments, or longer, and usually resolves (goes away) when the cause of the pain has resolved. The acute pain can cause anxiety and physical symptoms, including sweating and tachycardia.

Chronic Pain

The term chronic refers to a condition that lasts a long time. Chronic pain can persist with a visible injury (such as crushed lumbar vertebrae, causing lower back pain) or when no visible injury is present, such as with diabetic neuropathy. Other common types of chronic pain include recurring headaches, including migraine headaches, and pain in the joints due to damage from osteoarthritis. Chronic pain that does not remit is miserable, and causes depression and physical symptoms, including muscle tension and fatigue.

Pharmacists and prescribers must address inadequate pain treatment, and balance the drug use with potential abuse issues with opioids. Additionally, analgesics (pain drugs) have many drug interactions, and require side effect management.

The Joint Commission (TJC) standards require that pain be treated in the same manner as vital signs, making it compulsory to inquire about, measure, and treat pain, as would be done for blood pressure, pulse or respiratory rate. Pain is considered to be the "fifth vital sign".

CDC Guideline for Prescribing Opioids for Chronic Pain

The guideline for using opioids for chronic non-cancer pain treatment were released in March 2016, and should be followed when prescribing and dispensing opioids. See Study Tip below. [The American Society for Clinical Oncology (ASCO) issues the guidelines for treating cancer pain, which have differences, and include consideration for terminal illness.]

An opioid prescription requires a risk/benefit assessment, and monitoring. An assessment is also required when increasing the daily morphine milligram equivalent dose (MME) to ≥ 50 MME/day. Doses ≥ 90 MME/day should be avoided, or well-justified. A prescription for in-home naloxone should be offered to patients with elevated risk factors for opioid-induced respiratory depression (OIRD). Risk factors include a history of previous overdose, substance abuse, using ≥ 50 MME/day or concurrent benzodiazepines. Comorbid illness such as respiratory and psychiatric disease increases risk.

TREATMENT PRINCIPLES

Pain is subjective, and the primary measurement is the patient's own report, along with observations. Patients should be taught to monitor and document their pain. This helps evaluate and adjust medications and doses. Pain scales (see figures) are useful to assess pain severity. The patient records the pain level, the type or quality (using words such as burning, shooting, stabbing, aching) and the time of day that the pain is better or worse. Anything that worsens or lessens the pain should be noted.

It is preferable to prevent severe pain since delaying treatment until the pain worsens may require a higher total analgesic dose and could lead to a chronic pain disorder. When initially using any class of analgesic including opioids, start low, and stop at the lowest dose that adequately reduces the pain. Using medicines with multiple mechanisms of action (multimodal pain control) often produces improved pain control via additive or synergistic effects. Opioids in

OPIOIDS & CHRONIC NON-CANCER PAIN

Opioids are not first-line for chronic pain treatment and should not be used routinely. In some cases, they have benefit. When used, follow safe use recommendations:

- Establish and measure goals for pain and function. *Reaching low pain rather than no pain may be reasonable.*
- If using opioids, start with immediate-release. *Start low and go slow.*
- Follow-up, taper the dose, consider discontinuation.
- Evaluate risk factors for opioid-related harm.
- Pharmacists should check their states Prescription Drug Monitoring Program (PDMP) data. *Look for high dosages and prescriptions from other providers.*
- Use urine drug testing, and watch for false positives and negatives.
- Use adjunctive medications to enable a lower opioid dose.
- Avoid benzodiazepine and opioids given together, except in rare cases. *Quadruples the risk of overdose death.*

particular can be difficult to manage, even for the patient who needs them, and an appropriate goal may be to try and reduce or avoid the use of opioids altogether. The addition of non-opioids (e.g., acetaminophen) to a regimen often reduces the total opioid dose required, while providing superior analgesia. Acetaminophen works synergistically with opioids, which means that the benefit is greater than the sum benefit from each additional agent. IV acetaminophen and ibuprofen are used in hospital settings for similar reasons.

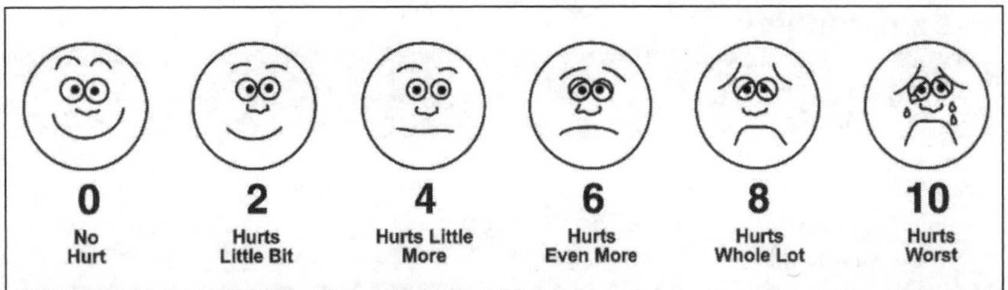

© 1983, Wong-Baker FACES™ Foundation. Used with permission.

Non-drug measures that help with pain control include physical exercise, smoking cessation and weight loss. Patients with excess weight have a higher incidence of back, joint and muscle pain. Smokers have a higher incidence of all types of pain, and smoking can lower some analgesic serum concentrations. Physical exercise improves mood, which lessens pain, plus it can build bone and strengthen muscles, which support joints and helps decrease musculoskeletal pain.

Selecting an Analgesic

Choosing the correct analgesic is important; opioids are, in general, strong analgesics, but they are not the strongest or the best option for treating certain types of pain. NSAIDs are usually preferable for bone and connective tissue pain. Amitriptyline (a tricyclic antidepressant, TCA) and duloxetine (an SNRI) block norepinephrine reuptake, which is beneficial for neuropathic pain. These drugs are commonly use for this purpose, with occasional use of other TCAs and SNRIs. SSRIs do not have this benefit. Antiepileptic drugs (AEDs) (notably pregabalin and gabapentin) are useful for neuropathic pain. In severe cases, other classes of agents, including opioids, can provide benefit.

Pain can be treated using a stepwise approach, where the choice of drug depends on the patient's self-reported pain severity. Adjuvants (e.g., antidepressants, AEDs, muscle relaxants) should be considered with all steps.

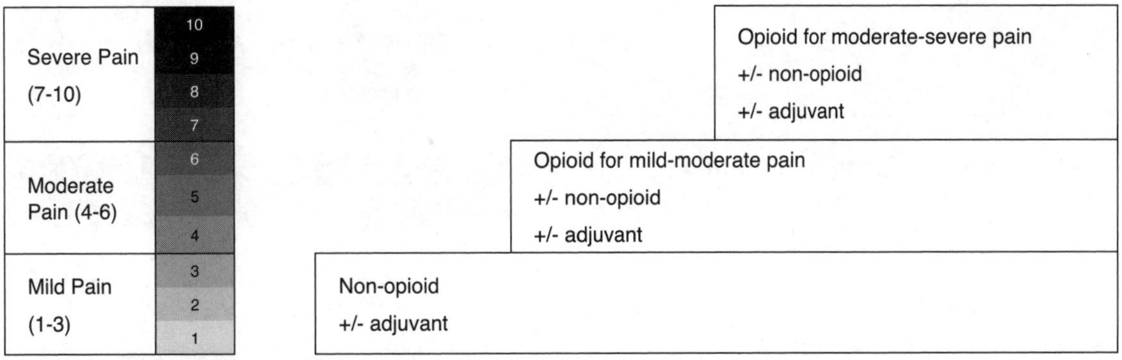

ACETAMINOPHEN

Acetaminophen reduces pain (provides analgesia) and reduces fever (is an antipyretic) but does not provide an anti-inflammatory effect. Acetaminophen does not inhibit thromboxane and therefore has very little effect on platelets. The mechanism of action is not well defined but is thought to involve inhibition of prostaglandin synthesis in the CNS and reduced pain impulse generation. Other mechanisms may include the endogenous cannabinoid system and inhibition of N-methyl-D-aspartate (NMDA) receptors.

Acetaminophen

DRUG	DOSING	SAFETY/SIDE EFFECTS/MONITORING
Acetaminophen ***(Tylenol,*** most "Non-Aspirin" pain relievers, ***Ofirmev, FeverAll)*** Tablet/caplet, chewable tablet, ODT, injection, suspension, infant drops, suppository *FeverAll:* Rectal suppository ***Ofirmev:*** Injection used inpatient to enable ↓ opioid doses, and when other routes are not feasible **+ Hydrocodone *(Norco,*** *Vicodin, Lortab)* **+ OxyCODONE *(Percocet, Endocet)*** **+ Codeine**: ***(Tylenol #2, 3, 4)*** **+ TraMADol *(Ultracet)*** + Diphenhydramine *(Tylenol PM)* And in multiple cough & cold products and OTC combos	**Adults** Max < 4,000 mg/day and max of 325 mg per prescription dosing unit in combo products, per the FDA. OTC dosing ranges depend on the formulation or are weight-based. 325 mg, max 2 tabs Q4-6H, NTE 10 tabs per 24 hr (3,250 mg) 500 mg, max 2 tabs Q6H, NTE 6 tabs per 24 hr (3,000 mg) 650 ER, max 2 tabs Q8H, NTE 6 tabs per 24 hr (3,900 mg) Rectal supp: 650 mg supp Q4-6H, NTE 6 supp per 24 hr (3,900 mg) IV (≥ 50 kg): 650 mg Q4H or 1,000 mg Q6H, max dose 4 grams/day *Recommended doses and max doses may differ for combination products.* **Pediatrics (< 12 yrs)** 10-15 mg/kg Q4-6H, max 5 doses/day or use weight and age based dosing table on container Infant drops are now the same concentration as the children's suspension (160 mg/5 mL) to ↓ dosing confusion and thus ↓ toxicity risk Rectal supp: 80, 120, 325, 650 mg	**BOXED WARNING** May cause severe hepatotoxicity (potentially requiring liver transplant or resulting in death), usually associated with excessive acetaminophen intake (> 4 grams/day) or use of more than one acetaminophen-containing product; risk of 10-fold dosing errors with injection. **SIDE EFFECTS** Hepatotoxicity (can be fatal) Cases of severe skin rash (rare) including SJS, TEN, AGEP. Stop drug, seek immediate medical help. Nephrotoxicity (rare, usually with chronic overdose); generally safer than NSAIDs in renal disease **NOTES** Pregnancy Category C (IV formulation); often used for mild pain in pregnancy. Avoid the "APAP" abbreviation on labels so patients understand that they are getting acetaminophen. **SAFETY CONSIDERATIONS** Use dosing syringe or cup provided with the medicine. Caution with dosing IV acetaminophen: Concentration is 10 mg/mL (in 100 mL vials). Order in mg, not mLs (for example, a 75 mg dose is not 75 mL, it is 7.5 mL). Do not permit nurses to prepare doses in the units. All IV acetaminophen doses should be prepared in the pharmacy.

Acetaminophen Drug Interactions

- May be used with warfarin; however, if used chronically (doses > 2 grams/day), can ↑ INR. Monitor accordingly.
- Avoid or limit alcohol use due to the risk of hepatotoxicity. See counseling section.

Acetaminophen Counseling

- Contact your healthcare provider right away for any condition that is being self-treated if the condition worsens, if it lasts for more than two days, if there is a high fever (> 102.5°F), or with rash, nausea, vomiting or blood in the stool. These are true also for children. Infants should be seen by a pediatrician.

ACETAMINOPHEN OVERDOSE
Antidote: N-Acetylcysteine (NAC, *Mucomyst, Cetylev)* PO and *Acetadote* IV (more costly)
MOA: Restores intracellular glutathione (acts as a glutathione substitute)
Administer immediately, even before the results of APAP level are obtained; within 8 hours of ingestion
Give 140 mg/kg PO loading dose, followed by 70 mg/kg PO Q4H x 17 doses (unless the initial APAP level is non-toxic)
Has an odor of rotten eggs and often causes N/V

- Many products contain acetaminophen, including prescription pain medicines and over-the-counter pain and cough-and-cold products. The name may be written as acetaminophen, *Tylenol*, APAP, non-aspirin pain reliever, etc. The total daily dose of all products should not exceed safe amounts.
- Too much acetaminophen can cause kidney damage, and can permanently harm the liver. This can be worsened by the use of too much alcohol. Women should not exceed more than 1 drink per day, and men should not exceed more than 2 drinks per day.

NON-STEROIDAL ANTI-INFLAMMATORY DRUGS

Non-steroidal anti-inflammatory drugs (NSAIDs) include the traditional (non-selective) NSAIDs such as ibuprofen, the salicylates, which includes aspirin, and the specific cyclooxygenase 2 (COX-2) inhibitors. The cyclooxygenase (COX) 1 and 2 enzymes catalyze the conversion of prostaglandins (PGs) and thromboxane A2 (TxA2) from arachidonic acid. The non-selective NSAIDs block the synthesis of both COX enzymes. The COX-2 selective agents block the synthesis of COX-2 only, which ↓ GI risk because COX-1 protects the gastric mucosa. Both groups ↓ the formation of the PGs that are involved in ↓ inflammation, ↓ pain and ↓ fever. Blocking COX-1 ↓ the synthesis of PG-H2, which ↓ the formation of TxA2, which is required for both platelet activation and aggregation. Blocking TxA2 ↓ clotting and provides the cardiovascular benefit. Aspirin is a more effective antiplatelet agent than other non-selective NSAIDs because aspirin inhibits COX-1 irreversibly (with a covalent, irreversible bond). The other non-selective NSAIDs bind to COX-1 reversibly.

NSAID Boxed Warnings

A MedGuide is required for all NSAIDs (even OTC written on a prescription) due to these risks below. These boxed warnings are not repeated in the tables that follow.

All NSAIDs, Including Aspirin

- GI Risk: NSAIDs cause an ↑ risk of serious GI adverse events including bleeding, ulceration and perforation of the stomach and intestines, which can be fatal. These events can occur at any time during use and without warning. Elderly patients, those with history of GI bleed, patients taking systemic steroids, SSRIs or SNRIs are at greatest risk for serious GI events.

All Non-Aspirin NSAIDs

- Cardiovascular Risk: NSAIDs can ↑ risk of serious cardiovascular thrombotic events, MI and stroke, which can be fatal. Risk may be ↑ with duration of use and in patients with CV disease or risk factors for CV disease.
    - In 2015, the FDA mandated updates to labeling of all non-aspirin NSAIDs (prescription and OTC) to reflect the following: ↑ risk of MI or stroke (as early as the first weeks of NSAID use). Increased risk with higher doses/longer duration of use and is present in patients without history or risk factors. NSAIDs can also ↑ risk of heart failure.
- CABG: Use is contraindicated for the treatment of perioperative pain in the setting of CABG surgery.

NSAIDs, Salicylates

DRUG	DOSING	SAFETY/SIDE EFFECTS/MONITORING
Aspirin/ Acetylsalicylic Acid *(Ascriptin, Bufferin, Ecotrin, Durlaza)* Tablet/caplet, chewable tablet, suppository ***Ascriptin, Bufferin, Ecotrin:*** EC/buffered ***Durlaza*** (Rx): ER capsule *Bayer "Advanced" Aspirin:* dissolves slightly faster + acetaminophen and caffeine *(Excedrin, Excedrin Migraine)* + antacid *(Alka-Seltzer)* + calcium *(Bayer Women's Low Dose)* + omeprazole ***(Yosprala)*** And in multiple other OTC combos	Primarily used for cardioprotection: 81-162 mg *Durlaza* (Rx): 162.5 mg once daily Analgesic dosing: 325-650 mg Q4-6H All NSAIDs: known risk factors for GI bleeding: Elderly, previous bleed, chronic or high dose use, hypoxic gut. Check for dark, tarry stool, stomach upset, weakness, coffee-ground emesis (indicates a more serious, fast GI bleed).	**WARNINGS** Avoid with NSAID hypersensitivity (past reaction with trouble breathing), nasal polyps, asthma. Avoid aspirin (not other NSAIDs) in children and teenagers with any viral infection due to potential risk of Reye's syndrome (symptoms include somnolence, N/V, lethargy, confusion). Severe skin rash (rare) including SJS/TEN. Stop drug, seek immediate medical help. Upper GI events (ulcers), avoid if possible 1-2 weeks before surgery due to antiplatelet effects. **SIDE EFFECTS** Dyspepsia, heartburn, bleeding, renal impairment, ↑ blood pressure, CNS effects (fatigue, confusion, dizziness; caution in the elderly), photosensitivity, fluid retention/edema, hyperkalemia (in renal impairment or with potassium-retaining agents), blurred vision **NOTES** Pregnancy Category: most are C/D (avoid, esp in 3rd trimester). To ↓ nausea, use EC/buffered product or take with food. PPIs may be used to protect the gut with chronic NSAID; consider the risks from chronic PPI use (↓ bone density, ↑ infection risk). Do not use *Durlaza* or *Yosprala* (ER aspirin) when immediate effect is needed (e.g., MI). **Salicylate-Specific** Salicylate overdose can cause tinnitus. Take with food or water or milk to minimize GI upset. All NSAIDs should be taken with food, but salicylates usually cause more nausea. Methyl salicylate is a popular OTC topical found in *Bengay, Icy Hot, Flexal, Thera-Gesic, Salonpas*. See end of chapter.
Non-Acetylated Salicylates		
Salsalate	Up to 3 grams/day, divided BID-TID	
Magnesium Salicylate *(Doans, Doans ES, Momentum, Keygesic)*	ES: 580 mg/tablet 2 tablets Q6H, max 8 tablets/day	
Choline Magnesium Trisalicylate	1 gram BID-TID or 3 grams at bedtime	
Diflunisal	500 mg BID-TID (max 1.5 grams daily)	
Salicylate salts *(Arthropan, Asproject, Magan, Mobidin, Rexolate, Tusal)*	No longer commonly used	

NSAIDs, Others

DRUG	DOSING	SAFETY/SIDE EFFECTS/MONITORING
Ibuprofen ***(Motrin, Advil, Caldolor,*** *Neoprofen)* Tablet/capsule, chewable tablet, suspension, injection ***Caldolor:*** IV injection For mild-mod pain, can ↓ opioid dose, and can be used when oral routes are not available; must be diluted	**Adult** OTC: 200-400 mg Q4-6H, max 1.2 grams/day, limit self-treatment to ≤ 10 days Rx: 400-800 mg Q6-8H, max 3.2 grams/day ↑ doses required for inflammation **Pediatric** 5-10 mg/kg/dose Q6-8H (as an antipyretic), max daily dose 40 mg/kg/day	**NOTES** Similar to aspirin except for the risk of Reye's in children is not present (ibuprofen is used in pediatrics). Take with food to ↓ nausea. *Neoprofen* injection is indicated for closure of patent ductus arteriosis (PDA) in premature infants.
Naproxen (OTC: ***Aleve,*** Rx: ***Naprelan, Naprosyn, Anaprox***) Tablet/capsule, suspension + sumatriptan *(Treximet)* + esomeprazole *(Vimovo)* And in OTC combos with diphenhydramine and pseudoephedrine	**OTC** Pain, fever: 200 mg (or 220 mg, if naproxen Na) 1 tab Q8-12H (may take 2 tabs for 1st dose); do not exceed 3 tabs in 24 hours **Rx** Inflammation, mild-mod pain: 500 mg Q12H (or occasionally 250 mg Q6-8H); max daily dose is 1,250 mg (Day #1) followed by 1,000 mg thereafter	**NOTES** Prescribers and patients sometimes prefer naproxen since it can be dosed BID. Naproxen base 200 mg = Naproxen Na 220 mg. The PPI in *Vimovo* is used to protect the gut from damage caused by the NSAID.
Diclofenac *(Cambia,* ***Dyloject****, Flector, Pennsaid, Zorvolex, Zipsor)* Tablet/capsule, packet, gel, patch, topical solution, injection ***Voltaren****, Solaraze* gel *Pennsaid* topical solution + misoprostol *(Arthrotec)*	Oral tablets: 50-75 mg BID-TID *Zipsor* capsules: 25 mg four times per day *Zorvolex* capsules: 18 mg or 35 mg TID *Dyloject* IV: 37.5 mg Q6H *Flector* patch: 1 patch (180 mg) to most painful area BID *Cambia* packet: 1 packet (50 mg) mixed in water for acute migraine	**BOXED WARNING** *Arthrotec:* not to be used in women of childbearing potential unless woman is capable of complying with effective contraceptive measures. **NOTES** Possible risk of GI/renal issues; *Zorvolex* is lower dose. Oral diclofenac formulations are not bioequivalent even if mg strength is the same. Misoprostol is used to replace the gut-protective prostaglandin to ↓ the risk of GI damage from the NSAID. This used to be more popular before the advent of PPIs. In addition to ↑ uterine contractions (which can terminate pregnancy), misoprostol component causes cramping and diarrhea.
Indomethacin ***(Indocin,*** *Tivorbex)* Capsule, oral suspension, suppository, injection	IR: 25-50 mg BID-TID CR: 75 mg daily-BID *Tivorbex:* 20 mg TID or 40 mg BID-TID	High risk for CNS SEs (avoid in psych conditions) and GI toxicity. The IR formulation is an older NSAID approved for gout; any NSAID can be used. *Tivorbex* is micronized for faster dissolution. Injection indicated for closure of patent ductus arteriosis (PDA) in premature infants.
Piroxicam *(Feldene)*	10-20 mg daily	High risk for GI toxicity and severe skin reactions, including SJS/TEN Used when other NSAIDs have failed; may need agent to protect gut (PPI, misoprostol)

NSAIDs, Others Continued

DRUG	DOSING	SAFETY/SIDE EFFECTS/MONITORING
Ketorolac *(Sprix, Toradol)* Tablet, injection, nasal spray, ophthalmic *Acular:* ophthalmic	Oral: 10-20 mg x 1, then 10 mg Q4-6H PRN (max 40 mg/day) IV (≥ 50 kg): 30 mg x 1 or 30 mg Q6H (↓ dose if ≥ 65 y/o) IM (≥ 50 kg): 60 mg x 1 or 30 mg Q6H (↓ dose if ≥ 65 y/o) *Sprix:* < 65 y/o and ≥ 50 kg: 1 spray in each nostril Q6-8H ≥ 65 y/o or < 50 kg: 1 spray in one nostril Q6-8H Always start IV, IM or nasal spray and continue with oral, if necessary. Not to be used in any situation with increased bleeding risk. 5 days total max treatment.	**BOXED WARNINGS** For short-term moderate to severe acute pain only as continuation of IV or IM ketorolac (max combined duration IV/IM and PO/nasal is 5 days in adults), not for intrathecal or epidural use, contraindicated in advanced renal impairment or risk due to volume depletion; ↓ dose if ≥ 65 years old, < 50 kg and ↑ SCr. **NOTES** Can cause severe adverse effects including GI bleeding and perforation, post-op bleeding, acute renal failure, liver failure and anaphylactic shock. Usually used in post-op setting (never pre-op). Prime *Sprix* nasal spray 5 times before 1st dose each day.
Sulindac *(Clinoril)*	150-200 mg BID	Sometimes used with reduced renal function, and in patients on lithium who require an NSAID.
Other less-commonly used NSAIDs include: meclofenamate, mefenamic acid *(Ponstel)*, ketoprofen, fenoprofen *(Nalfon)*, flurbiprofen *(Ansaid)*, oxaprozin *(Daypro* – caution similar to piroxicam – higher risk of side effects).		

COX-2 Selective: Lower risk for GI complications (but still present), ↑ risk MI/stroke (avoid with CVD risk, avoid ↑ doses and longer duration in patients at risk for CVD), same risk for renal complications

Celecoxib *(Celebrex)* Capsule	OA: 100 mg BID or 200 mg daily RA: 100-200 mg BID Indications: OA, RA, juvenile RA, acute pain, primary dysmenorrhea, ankylosing spondylitis	Highest COX-2 selectivity Contraindicated with sulfonamide allergy Same Boxed Warnings as other NSAIDs Pregnancy Category C prior to 30 weeks gestation; Category D starting at ≥ 30 weeks gestation
Meloxicam *(Mobic,* *Vivlodex)* Tablet/capsule, oral suspension	*Mobic:* 7.5-15 mg once daily *Vivlodex:* 5-10 mg once daily	These agents have some COX-2 selectivity. *Vivlodex* capsules and other meloxicam formulations are not interchangeable.
Etodolac *(Lodine)* Tablet/capsule	300-500 mg Q6-8H	
Nabumetone *(Relafen)* Tablet	1,000-2,000 mg daily (can be divided BID)	

NSAID Drug Interactions

- Caution for additive bleeding risk with other agents that can ↑ bleeding risk. See Drug Interactions chapter. Do not use NSAIDs with steroids due to increased risk of GI bleeding.
- Caution with use of aspirin and other ototoxic agents (e.g., aminoglycosides, IV loop diuretics).
- There is no reason to use two different NSAIDs concurrently (exception: low dose aspirin for cardioprotection but the cardioprotective effects may be blocked by ibuprofen and other NSAIDs – see above). If using aspirin for cardioprotection and ibuprofen for pain, take aspirin one hour before or eight hours after ibuprofen.

- NSAIDs can ↑ the levels of lithium (avoid concurrent use) and methotrexate. If an NSAID must be used with lithium, there is less of an affect from aspirin and sulindac however this is not included in their package inserts and therefore would be an off-label preference.

NSAID Patient Counseling

- Dispense MedGuide and instruct patient to read it. This medicine can increase the chance of a heart attack or stroke that can lead to death. The risk increases in people who have heart disease. If you have heart disease, please discuss using this medicine with your healthcare provider.
- This medicine can cause ulcers and bleeding in the stomach and intestines at any time during treatment. The risk is highest if you use higher doses, and when used long-term. To help reduce the risk, limit alcohol use while taking this medicine, and use the lowest possible dose for the shortest possible time. This medicine should not be used with steroids (such as prednisone) or anticoagulants (such as warfarin, *Pradaxa* or *Xarelto)*. There are some exceptions in very high risk (clotting) patients who use both aspirin and warfarin but in general, using them together is not recommended.
- Do not use after coronary heart surgery, unless you have been instructed to do so by your healthcare provider. Do not use this medicine before any elective surgery.
- Take with food if this medicine upsets your stomach.
- The risk of bleeding with these medicines is higher with many antidepressants, including SSRIs and SNRIs.
- Do not use this medicine if you have experienced breathing problems or allergic-type reactions after taking aspirin or other NSAIDs.
- This medicine can raise your blood pressure. If you have high blood pressure, you will need to check your blood pressure regularly; you may have to stop using this medicine if your blood pressure increases too much.
- This medicine can cause fluid and water to accumulate, particularly in your ankles. If you have heart disease, discuss the use of this medicine with your healthcare provider and monitor your weight.
- Photosensitivity: Limit sun exposure, including tanning booths, wear protective clothing, use sunscreen that blocks both UVA and UVB (this applies to some of the NSAIDs, but there is a class risk).
- Do not use this medicine if you are pregnant.
- Diclofenac gel: use the dosing card that is inside the package to correctly measure each dose. The dosing card is reusable so do not throw it away. Do not use more than 32 grams total of diclofenac gel each day. You should add up the amount applied to each area to make sure it is less than 32 grams:
  - The dose for your hands, wrists, or elbows is 2 grams with each application; apply four times daily and do not exceed 8 grams each day to these areas.
  - The dose for your feet, ankles, or knees is 4 grams with each application; apply four times daily but do not exceed more than 16 grams each day to these areas.

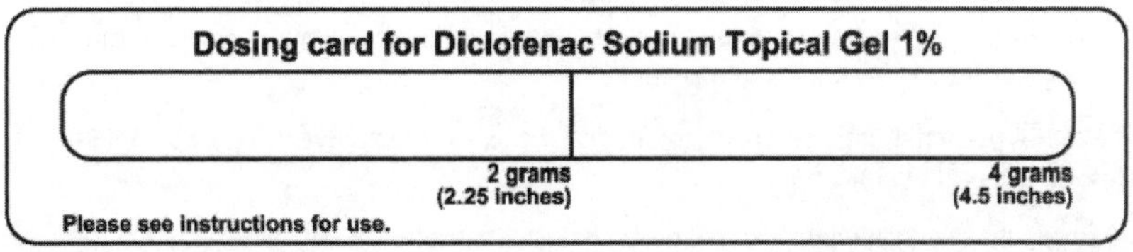

Diclofenac sodium topical gel package insert. Piscataway, NJ: Amneal Pharmaceuticals; 2016 May.

- Place the dosing card on a flat surface so that you can read the print. Squeeze the diclofenac gel onto the dosing card evenly; cover the 2 gram or 4 gram dosing area up to the dosing line.
- Using the dosing card, apply the gel to clean, dry skin that does not have any cuts or open wounds; then gently rub the gel into the skin with your hands, making sure to cover the affected area fully.
- Do not shower, bathe or wash your treated hands for at least 1 hour after application.

OPIOIDS

Opioid drugs interact in a variety of ways with the three primary types of opioid receptors: μ (mu), κ (kappa) and δ (delta). Opioids are mu receptor agonists in the CNS; this is the primary mechanism for pain relief, but also causes euphoria and respiratory depression.

Opioids are available in many formulations (e.g., IR, ER, solution, patch, SL spray and film, transmucosal lozenge "lollipop", injection, suppository, nasal spray, iontophoretic transdermal system and abuse-deterrent formulations) and in many combination products. Brand names for some discontinued products (e.g., *Avinza*) are included here so they can be recognized. The names may continue to be used in clinical practice.

Opiod Terminology

TERM	DEFINITION
Physiological Adaptation (Physical Dependence)	Almost all patients using chronic opioids, including abusers, become physiologically adapted to the opioid, and experience physical withdrawal symptoms when the opioid is stopped or a dose is late or missed. The symptoms include anxiety, tachycardia, shakiness and shortness of breath. The withdrawal causes much suffering. Physiological adaptation is not addiction.
Addiction	A strong desire or compulsion to take the drug despite harm. Involves drug-seeking behavior, including exaggerating the pain or physical problems, getting prescriptions from multiple prescribers and/or prescription forgery.
Pseudo-Addiction	On occasion, a patient is seen at the pharmacy who appears anxious and states they ran out of medication or are afraid of running out too early. The person seems similar to an addict, but is actually a legitimate pain patient with poorly controlled pain. The remedy is adequate analgesics, such as ER opioids, for pain control.
Tolerance	A higher opioid dose is needed to produce the same level of analgesia that a lower dose previously provided. Tolerance develops over time with chronic opioid use. It is important to distinguish whether the higher pain severity is due to a condition (e.g., cancer that has spread), or a decrease in the drug's effectiveness due to tolerance, or both. If tolerance develops, it may be preferable to switch to another opioid, rather than increase the dose.
Opioid Hyperalgesia	Is present when the opioid dose is increased to treat the pain, but the pain becomes worse rather than better. This occurs occasionally. If suspected, a different class of analgesic or a switch to another opioid should be tried.
Break-Through Pain [(BTP), end of dose pain]	Sharp spikes of severe pain that occur despite the use of an extended release (ER) opioid. Must be treated with a fast acting pain agent, such as an injection, transmucosal immediate-release fentanyl (TIRF) drugs (for cancer BTP only) or (less expensive, but not preferable) immediate-release (IR) opioids. When multiple doses are required for BTP, a higher baseline dose may be required, or possibly a switch to a different opioid. Baseline opioids are dispensed with a BTP medication until the dose of the scheduled opioid is adequate.
Opioid-Induced Respiratory Depression (OIRD)	Usual cause of fatality in opioid overdose. Hospitalized patients receiving IV opioids must be carefully monitored for sedation and oxygen saturation, which precedes the usual cause of fatality in opioid overdose.
Opioid-Induced Constipation (OIC)	One of the most bothersome side effects of chronic opioid use, OIC does not lessen and requires prophylactic treatment.
Peripherally-Acting Mu Opioid Receptor Antagonists (PAMORA)	Drugs that selectively block the mu-opioid receptors in the GI tract but not in the CNS. They reverse OIC without reducing analgesia.
Centrally-Acting Opioid Antagonists	There are two drugs in this group; both block opioids from binding to the mu receptor. Naloxone is used to reverse respiratory depression. Naltrexone is most commonly used in combination with an opioid or buprenorphine to block the use of other opioids that may be taken (inappropriately) at the same time.

Opioid Boxed Warnings and Warnings

On July 9, 2012, the FDA approved a risk evaluation and mitigation strategy (REMS) for all ER and LA opioid medications. Included in that warning is methadone, however technically methadone does not fit either category, as it generally needs to be dosed 3 – 4 times daily for pain, and it stays in the blood by virtue of it's long and variable half-life and large volume of distribution - not because of any pharmaceutical formulation. Primary components of the REMS: Education for prescribers, and requirement that the prescribers counsel the patients. Common boxed warnings include:

- Addiction, abuse and misuse with ER products, which can lead to overdose and death especially when attempting to manipulate the dosage form for dose dumping orally and nasal insufflation. Assess risk before prescribing and monitor regularly for these behaviors or conditions.
- Respiratory depression (highest risk at initiation and with dosage increases). Swallow whole. Crushing, dissolving, or chewing of the long acting products can cause the delivery of a potentially fatal dose. Accidental ingestion/exposure of even one dose in children can be fatal. Never give this medication to anyone else (includes patch formulations).
- Life-threatening neonatal opioid withdrawal with prolonged use during pregnancy.
- *Avinza, Kadian, Embeda, Zohydro, Opana ER and Nucynta ER:* Do not consume alcohol or alcohol containing products while taking this medication. Doing so can cause increased plasma levels and a potentially fatal overdose. *MS Contin, MorphaBond, Hysingla and Exalgo* have a similarly worded warning regarding alcohol, but it is not a boxed warning.

Warnings For All Opioids

- Additive sedation: Concomitant use with CNS depressants (including alcohol) may cause profound sedation, respiratory depression and death.
- Monitor closely in elderly, debilitated, cachectic patients and patients with chronic pulmonary disease (conditions associated with hypoxia) or head injury/increased intracranial pressure. All are at increased risk of respiratory depression.
- Risk of hypotension.

OPIOID AUXILIARY LABELS

Controlled substance: Do not share with others.

May cause dizziness or drowsiness.

Do not operate machinery.

Keep away from children and animals.

If ER: Do not crush, chew or dissolve. Swallow whole.

Do not drink alcoholic beverages.

Take with food or milk.

Common Side Effect Management

Opioid side effects (see Drug Table) usually lessen over time, except for constipation. If a patient has a problem that persists or is bothersome, such as pruritus, switching to another opioid may be reasonable. Postoperative nausea and vomiting (PONV) occurs in surgical patients due primarily to the use of anesthesia and opioids. PONV is treated in the hospital with a 5HT3-receptor antagonist such as ondansetron, or a phenothiazine such as prochlorperazine. All oral opioids should be taken with food to lessen nausea.

Hydroxyzine is used primarily for pruritus, and also helps with nausea. Diphenhydramine is also used for pruritus.

MORPHINE-TYPE ALLERGY

The common drugs in the same chemical class that cross-react with each other have **cod** or **morph** in the name. Buprenorphine has **norph** instead of **morph**.

Codeine	**Morph**ine	Bupre**norph**ine
Hydro**cod**one	Hydro**morph**one	Heroin (diacetyl-morphine)
Oxy**cod**one	Oxy**morph**one	

What to do if a morphine-type allergy is reported: In practice, make sure it is an actual allergy, and not nausea or itching. If it seems to be accurate, choose a drug in a different chemical class, such as methadone or fentanyl. Meperidine is also in a different class, but is likely not the correct choice to use in a patient with a morphine-type allergy. It's too toxic.

Sedation and cognitive effects occur when the opioid is started or the dose is increased, and generally lessen over time. Pharmacists advise patients not to drive or do anything potentially hazardous until they are accustomed to the medication. The use of other CNS depressants should be minimized. Alcohol should not be used concurrently with opioids.

Constipation does not dissipate with time, and is the most bothersome complication of opioid treatment. When opioids are dosed around-the-clock (ATC, such as with an ER opioid), prophylaxis is required. Stimulant laxatives, including senna, are the typical first-line laxative, with or without a stool softener (which are helpful if the stool is hard). The stimulant laxative bisacodyl comes as a tablet (for prophylaxis) or suppository (to expel stool right away, i.e., treatment).

Opioid Allergy

True opioid allergies are rare. Most complaints of itching or rash are not a true allergic response. Symptoms of an opioid allergy (rare, but dangerous if present) include difficulty breathing, severe drop in blood pressure, serious rash, swelling of face, lips, tongue and larynx. In a true opioid allergy, use an agent in a different chemical class (see box on previous page).

Tramadol package labeling warns of increased risk of reactions to tramadol in those with previous anaphylatoid reactions to opioids. Tapentadol does not have this warning in the U.S., though tramadol and tapentadol are structurally similar. If allergic to tramadol, an allergy to tapentadol is likely, and vice versa.

DRUG	DOSING	SAFETY/SIDE EFFECTS/MONITORING
Morphine (ER: ***MS Contin, Kadian,*** *MorphaBond AVINza;* IR solution: ***Roxanol;*** injection: *Astramorph, Duramorph, Infumorph)* C-II Tablet (IR/ER), capsule (ER), injection, solution, suppository + naltrexone *(Embeda)* ER formulations, including *Embeda*, are REMS drugs.	Common dosing IR (including solution): 10-30 mg Q4H PRN ER: 15, 30, 60, 100, 200 mg Q8-12H *MorphaBond* BID, *Kadian* daily or BID IV (opioid naïve): 2.5-5 mg Q3-4H PRN Do not crush or chew any ER/CR opioids. Can open and sprinkle contents on applesauce, soft food. If renally impaired, start at a lower dose, or avoid morphine, oxycodone, tramadol or tapentadol due to accumulation of parent drug and/or active metabolite(s).	**BOXED WARNINGS** Medication errors with oral solution (note strength), appropriate staff and equipment needed for intrathecal/epidural administration **SIDE EFFECTS** **GI effects** Constipation, N/V (may need anti-emetics) **CNS effects** Somnolence, dizziness, changes in mood, confusion, delirium **Skin reactions** Flushing, pruritus, diaphoresis; may need antihistamine **Respiratory depression** Caused by opioid overdose or combination with other sedatives and CNS depressants, and can be fatal (see opioid antagonist section that follows). **NOTES** Do not use MSO4 or MS abbreviations for morphine or magnesium, due to risk of errors. **Constipation** Tolerance usually develops to opioid side effects except constipation. When opioids are used around the clock (ATC), docusate alone will rarely be enough to treat constipation. It will likely require stimulant laxatives (senna, bisacodyl), osmotic laxatives (e.g., MOM) or commonly docusate + stimulant combinations. Methylnaltrexone (*Relistor*) is a laxative (given SC) for constipation due to opioids (it blocks gut opioid-receptors). The patient must have failed DSS + laxative (senna, bisacodyl). Alternatives to *Relistor* include oral naloxone solution, lubiprostone and naloxegol (see Opioid-Induced Constipation in this chapter).

Opioids Continued

DRUG	DOSING	SAFETY/SIDE EFFECTS/MONITORING
FentaNYL ***(Duragesic, Sublimaze***, others below) C-II Injection, buccal/ SL tablet, lozenge, SL film, SL spray, nasal spray, patch, iontophoretic transdermal system *Actiq* oral transmucosal lozenge (on a stick "lollipop"): Always start with 200 mcg, can titrate to 4 BTP episodes/day. Only for cancer BTP. *Lazanda:* nasal spray *Fentora*: buccal tabs *Ionsys:* iontophoretic transdermal system *Abstral:* tabs, SL *Subsys:* spray, SL Fentanyl transmucosal forms and *Ionsys* system (not patch or injection) are REMS drugs.	Patch: Apply 1 patch Q72H (occas. Q48H) 12 (delivers 12.5 mcg/hr), 25, 50, 75, 100 mcg/h patch strengths Do not ↑ dose if pain is controlled but doesn't last long enough. In this case shorten the interval (change to Q48H) as you would do with any ER opioid. Otherwise, you risk overdose or higher degree of side effects.	**BOXED WARNINGS** Potential for medication errors when converting between different dosage forms, use with strong or moderate CYP 3A4 inhibitors may result in increased effects and potentially fatal respiratory depression **SIDE EFFECTS** Constipation, bradycardia, confusion, dizziness, somnolence, diaphoresis, dehydration, dry mouth, N/V, muscle rigidity, weakness, miosis, dyspnea **NOTES** Fentanyl, in any form, is for chronic pain management only. Can convert a patient who has been using morphine 60 mg/day or equivalent for at least 7 days. Fentanyl is not used in opioid-naïve patients (especially the potent SL forms, which are for cancer-related BTP). Cut off stick and flush unused/unneeded *Actiq.* Short t½ when given IV. IV boluses are given Q1-2H, but commonly given as continuous infusion or PCA. *Ionsys:* iontophoretic transdermal system for hospital use only (for short-term post-op pain); patient presses button to deliver on-demand doses. Healthcare providers must wear gloves when handling the device. Remove before discharge. Similar drugs (IV only): alfentanil *(Alfenta)*, remifentanil *(Ultiva)*, sufentanil *(Sufenta)*

Fentanyl Patch Information

- Analgesic effect can be seen 8 – 16 hrs after application. Do not stop other analgesic immediately (↓ dose 50% for the first 12 hrs).
- Do not apply > 1 patch each time.
- Do not heat patch or skin area before or after applying. Do not cover with heating pad or any bandage. Caution with fever (tell patient to call healthcare provider if they have a fever).
- Do not switch generic fentanyl patches. Try to use the same one.
- Some patches need to be removed prior to MRI.
- Apply to hairless skin (cut short if necessary) on flat surface (chest, back, flank, upper arm) and change every 72 hrs. Press in place for 30 seconds.
- Do not use soap, alcohol, or other solvents to remove transdermal gel if it accidentally touches skin. Use large amount of water.
- Dispose of patch in toilet.
- Keep away from children and animals, including used patches.
- Keep in child-resistant box.

Opioids Continued

DRUG	DOSING	SAFETY/SIDE EFFECTS/MONITORING
Hydrocodone IR (combination products only) C-II (including combo products) **+ acetaminophen (*Norco,* *Lorcet, Lortab, Vicodin, Zydone, Anexsia, Co-Gesic)*** Select combination products: + chlorpheniramine *(TussiCaps)* + chlorpheniramine and pseudoephedrine *(Zutripro)* + pseudoephedrine *(Rezira)* + homatropine *(Tussigon)* + ibuprofen *(Vicoprofen, Reprexain)*	*Norco:* 2.5, 5, 7.5, 10 mg hydrocodone + 325 mg acetaminophen Usual starting dose: 5/325 or 10/325 PO Q6H (or 4 times per day)	**BOXED WARNING** Acetaminophen may cause severe hepatotoxicity (potentially requiring liver transplant or resulting in death), usually associated with excessive acetaminophen intake (> 4 grams/day) or use of more than one acetaminophen-containing product. **WARNINGS** Those that apply to acetaminophen and opioids: respiratory and/or CNS depression, constipation, hypotension, skin reactions (rare), caution in liver disease (avoid or limit alcohol intake) and in 2D6 poor metabolizers **SIDE EFFECTS** N/V, dizziness, lightheadedness, sedation, constipation, risk of respiratory depression and rare side effects related to acetaminophen **NOTES** Products with > 325 mg acetaminophen per dosage unit are no longer considered safe by the FDA.
Hydrocodone ER *(Zohydro, Hysingla ER)* C-II REMS drugs	*Zohydro* (capsule): start at 10 mg Q12H (opioid-naïve) Range 10-50 mg *Hysingla ER* (tablet): start at 20 mg Q24H (opioid-naïve) Range 20-120 mg	**BOXED WARNINGS** Initiation of 3A4 inhibitors (or stopping 3A4 inducers) can cause fatal overdose. **NOTES** Both are substrates of 3A4 (major) & 2D6 (minor). Preferably avoid use if breast feeding. Monitor for respiratory depression and sedation. Abuse-deterrent formulations. ***Hysingla*** QT prolongation has occurred at doses > 160 mg/day.
HYDROmorphone *(Dilaudid, Dilaudid-HP)* C-II Tablet, injection, solution *Exalgo:* ER tablet *Exalgo* is a REMS drug.	Initial (opioid-naïve) Oral: 2-4 mg Q4-6H PRN IV: 0.2-1 mg Q2-3H PRN May cause less nausea, pruritus	**BOXED WARNINGS** Risk of medication error with high potency (HP) injection (use in opioid-tolerant patients only) **NOTES** Potent; start low, convert carefully. High risk for overdose. Caution with 3A4 inhibitors, use lower doses initially. Commonly used in PCAs and epidurals. *Dilaudid HP* (10 mg/mL) is a higher potency injection than *Dilaudid* (1 mg/mL). *Exalgo* is an abuse-deterrent formulation (crush and extraction resistant). *Exalgo* is contraindicated in opioid-naïve patients. Two week washout required between *Exalgo* and MAO inhibitors.

Opioids Continued

DRUG	DOSING	SAFETY/SIDE EFFECTS/MONITORING
OxyCODONE C-II (full opioids and combos) Tablet/capsule (IR), tablet (ER), solution IR: *Oxaydo*, ***Roxicodone*** CR: ***OxyCONTIN*** ER**:** *Xtampza* **+ acetaminophen *(Endocet, Percocet, Roxicet,*** *Xartemis XR)* + naloxone *(Targiniq ER)* + naltrexone (*Troxyca ER*)	IR: 5-20 mg Q4-6H CR: 10-80 mg Q12H (60, 80 mg only for opioid-tolerant patients) Do not use or ↓ dose with renal impairment. If ER ↓ by ½ - ⅓	**BOXED WARNINGS** Initiation of 3A4 inhibitors (or stopping 3A4 inducers) can cause fatal overdose, caution with oxycodone oral solution and oral concentrate (confusion between mg and mL and different concentrations) **NOTES** *Oxaydo, OxyContin, Targiniq ER, Troxyca ER and Xtampza ER*: abuse-deterrent formulations. *Xtampza ER* capsules can be opened and contents administered with soft food or through a GI tube. Avoid high fat meals with higher doses (except re-formulated *OxyContin).*
OxyMORphone *(Opana, Opana ER)* C-II Tablet (IR/ER), injection *Opana ER* is a REMS drug.	IR (opioid-naïve): 5-10 mg Q4-6H PRN ER (opioid-naïve): 5 mg Q12H Take on empty stomach (most other analgesics are with food to help avoid stomach upset)	**NOTES** Do not use with moderate-to-severe liver impairment. Use low doses in elderly, renal or mild liver impairment; there will be higher drug concentrations in these patients. *Opana ER:* abuse-deterrent formulation. *Opana ER* is not suitable for use as an "as needed" analgesic. Tablets should not be broken, chewed, dissolved, or crushed; tablets should be swallowed whole. *Opana ER* is intended for use in long-term, continuous management of moderate-to-severe chronic pain.
Methadone *(Dolophine, Methadone Intensol, Methadose*) C-II Tablet, soluble tablet, solution Methadone is a REMS drug.	Initial: 2.5-10 mg Q8-12H Methadone 40 mg is indicated for detox and maintenance treatment of opioid-addicted patients. Useful for detox because it relieves opioid craving and blocks euphoric effects of abusable opioids.	**BOXED WARNINGS** Life-threatening QT prolongation and serious arrhythmias (e.g., TdP) have occurred during treatment (most involve large, multiple daily doses). Should be prescribed by professionals who know requirements for safe use. **NOTES** Due to variable half-life from 15-60 hrs and in some cases up to 150 hrs due to polymorphism, methadone is hard to dose safely and has a risk of QT prolongation (proarrhythmic) which will be aggravated if dosed incorrectly. Can ↓ testosterone and contribute to sexual dysfunction (others opioids can also, but methadone is notable). In combo with other drugs, it is serotonergic and can raise risk of serotonin syndrome. Methadone also blocks reuptake of norepinephrine. Methadone is a major 3A4 substrate; avoid inhibitors concurrently or lower methadone dose.

Opioids Continued

DRUG	DOSING	SAFETY/SIDE EFFECTS/MONITORING
Meperidine ***(Demerol)*** C-II Tablet, solution, injection	Oral/IM: 50-150 mg Q3-4H PRN Short duration of action (pain controlled for max 3 hrs)	**WARNING** Renal impairment/elderly at risk for CNS toxicity, avoid with or within 2 weeks of MAO inhibitor **SIDE EFFECTS** Lightheadedness, dizziness, somnolence, N/V, sweating **NOTES** Normeperidine (metabolite) is renally cleared and can accumulate and cause CNS toxicity, including seizures. In combo with other drugs, it is serotonergic and can raise risk of serotonin syndrome. No longer recommended as an analgesic (especially in elderly and renally impaired). Avoid for chronic pain management and even short-term in elderly. Acceptable for short-term acute or single use (e.g., sutures in ER) and used off-label for post-operative rigors (shivering).
Codeine **+ acetaminophen** ***(Tylenol #2, 3, 4)*** C-II: codeine C-III: combos (w/ acetaminophen) C-V: antitussives (anti-cough), codeine cough syrups	*Tylenol #3:* 1 tab (acetaminophen 300 mg + codeine 30 mg) Q4-6H PRN, range 15-120 mg codeine	**BOXED WARNING** Respiratory depression and death have occurred in children who received codeine following tonsillectomy and/or adenoidectomy and were found to have evidence of being ultra-rapid metabolizers of codeine due to a 2D6 polymorphism. Deaths have also occurred in nursing infants after being exposed to high concentrations of morphine because the mothers were ultra-rapid metabolizers. Use is contraindicated in the postoperative pain management of children who have undergone tonsillectomy and/or adenoidectomy. **SIDE EFFECTS** Codeine has a high degree of GI side effects: constipation, N/V/D

Centrally Acting Analgesics

Both tramadol and tapentadol are mu-opioid receptor agonists and inhibitors of norepinephrine reuptake. Tramadol also inhibits reuptake of serotonin. Tapentadol has the same boxed warnings as other opioids (see previous discussion), while tramadol has no boxed warnings.

DRUG	DOSING	SAFETY/SIDE EFFECTS/MONITORING
TraMADol ***(Ultram, Conzip)*** C-IV Tablet (IR/ER), capsule (ER) **+ acetaminophen** ***(Ultracet)***	IR: 50-100 mg Q4-6H, max 400 mg/day ER: 100 mg once daily, max 300 mg/day CrCl < 30 mL/min: IR: ↓ dose ER: do not use	**WARNINGS** Seizure risk (avoid in patients with seizure history, head trauma), risk of serotonin syndrome when used alone or with other serotonergic drugs or inhibitors of 2D6 or 3A4, CNS depression (avoid alcohol and do not crush/chew/dissolve ER capsules), respiratory depression (rare), avoid in patients who are suicidal; misuse, abuse and diversion (similar to opioids) **SIDE EFFECTS** Dizziness, nausea, constipation, loss of appetite, flushing, dry mouth, dyspepsia, pruritus, insomnia (some patients find tramadol sedating but for most it is not; this can be an advantage over hydrocodone), possible headache, ataxia. Lower severity of GI side effects versus strong opioids. **NOTES** Tramadol requires conversion to active metabolite by 2D6. Use with 2D6 inhibitors can have variable effects due to mixed MOA of tramadol. Off-label use of tramadol in children < 17 years of age can cause slowed or difficult breathing; ↑ risk following tonsillectomy/adenoidectomy and/or ultra rapid metabolizers.

Centrally Acting Analgesics Continued

DRUG	DOSING	SAFETY/SIDE EFFECTS/MONITORING
Tapentadol *(Nucynta, Nucynta ER)* C-II Tablet (IR/ER) *Nucynta ER* is a REMS drug.	IR: 50-100 mg Q4-6H PRN ER: 50-250 mg BID CrCl < 30 mL/min: Use not recommended (not studied). Use with severe renal insufficiency is a CI in Canada.	**CONTRAINDICATIONS** Use of MAO inhibitors concurrently or within 14 days **WARNINGS** May increase seizure risk (avoid in patients with seizure history or seizure risk), risk of serotonin syndrome when used alone or with other serotonergic drugs **SIDE EFFECTS** Dizziness, somnolence, nausea but lower severity of GI side effects than stronger opioids

Opioid Drug Interactions

- Caution with use of concurrent CNS depressants: Additive somnolence, dizziness, confusion, increased risk of respiratory depression. These include alcohol, hypnotics, benzodiazepines, muscle relaxants, etc. Avoid alcohol with all opioids, especially ER formulations. Boxed warning to avoid alcohol with *Avinza, Kadian, Embeda, Zohydro, Opana ER and Nucynta ER.*
- Increased risk of hypoxemia with underlying respiratory disease (e.g., COPD) and sleep apnea.
- Methadone: Caution with agents that worsen cardiac function or increase arrhythmia risk. Caution with other serotonergic agents.
- Meperidine: Caution with agents that worsen renal function, elderly and those with seizure history. Caution with other serotonergic agents.
- Tramadol and tapentadol: Caution with other agents that lower seizure threshold. Caution with other serotonergic agents. Avoid tramadol with 2D6 inhibitors (requires conversion). Possibility of increased INR with warfarin; monitor. Tapentadol may enhance the adverse/toxic effect of MAO inhibitors; avoid concurrent use.

Opioid Counseling

- Do not crush, chew, break, or open controlled-release forms. Breaking them would cause too much drug to be released into your blood at one time.
- *Avinza* and *Kadian* must be swallowed whole or may be opened and the entire bead contents sprinkled on a small amount of applesauce immediately prior to ingestion. The beads must not be chewed, crushed, or dissolved due to the risk of exposure to a potentially toxic dose of morphine. *Avinza* can be put down a G-tube.
- *Opana* and *Opana ER*: take on empty stomach (1 hr before, 2 hr after eating).
- Avoid alcohol with all opioids, especially ER formulations. Boxed warning to avoid alcohol with *Avinza, Kadian, Embeda, Zohydro, Opana ER* and *Nucynta ER*.
- To ensure that you get a correct dose, measure liquid forms with a special dose-measuring spoon or cup, not with a regular tablespoon. If you do not have a dose-measuring device, ask your pharmacist.
- This medicine will cause drowsiness and fatigue. Avoid alcohol, sleeping pills, antihistamines, sedatives, and tranquilizers that may also make you drowsy, except under the supervision of your healthcare provider.
- Take with a full glass of water. Take with food or milk if it upsets your stomach.
- Do not stop taking suddenly if you have been taking it continuously for more than 5 to 7 days. If you want to stop, your healthcare provider will help you gradually reduce the dose.

- This medicine is constipating. Increase the amount of fiber and water (at least six to eight full glasses daily) in your diet to prevent constipation (if not fluid restricted due to heart failure). Your pharmacist or healthcare provider will recommend a stronger agent for constipation if this is not adequate.
- Do not share this medication with anyone else.
- Never take more pain medicine than prescribed. If your pain is not being adequately treated, talk to your healthcare provider.

Abuse Deterrent Opioid Formulations

There have been a number of FDA approved opioids designed to help mitigate drug abuse and misuse. It is important to note that these formulations do not eliminate the ability to abuse or misused opioids. Some formulations such as *Suboxone*, *Troxyca ER*, or *Embeda* are compounded with a secondary medication such as naloxone or naltrexone while others such as *OxyContin*, *Hysingla ER*, or *Opana ER* are manufactured using specific technology designed to deter crushing, dissolving or other modifications.

Opioid Dose Conversions

The correct dose is the lowest dose that provides effective pain relief. If the dose has been increased and the pain relief is not adequate or if the side effects are intolerable (patients react differently to different opioids) or if the drug is unaffordable or not included on formulary, then switch. Switch safely and monitor for hyperalgesia, which should be suspected when opioids increase pain (rather than decreasing pain) due to a paradoxical situation. This happens occasionally, and if so, increasing the dose will not work. If switching to morphine and the patient has renal insufficiency, a 50% reduction in the total daily dose or similar would be wise; morphine has an active metabolite that is renally cleared, thus a lower dose is required. Always use breakthrough medication, as-needed, when converting.

For opioid conversions (not methadone) you can use ratio conversion (see table below). Make sure the units and route in the numerator match, and the units and route in the denominator match. Converting to a fentanyl patch is most commonly done using a dosing table (see table on the following page and example). If converting to fentanyl using the chart below, remember that you are finding the total daily dose in mg, and will then need to convert it to mcg (multiply by 1,000) and then divide by 24 to get the patch dose; fentanyl is dosed in mcg per hour (note: no oral dose conversion as fentanyl is not absorbed orally). Some clinicians use this estimation: morphine 60 mg total daily dose = 25 mcg/hr fentanyl patch.

When converting one opioid to another, round down (do not round up) and use breakthrough doses for compensation. A patient may respond better to one agent than another (likely due to less tolerance) and estimating lower will reduce the risk of overdose.

DRUG	IV/IM (MG)	ORAL (MG)
Morphine	10	30
Hydromorphone	1.5	7.5
Oxycodone	–	20
Hydrocodone	–	30
Codeine	130	200
Fentanyl	0.1	–
Meperidine	75	300
Oxymorphone	1	10

If the medicine is effective, but runs out too fast, do not increase the dose. This will cause a risk of respiratory depression. Rather, shorten the dosing interval.

Steps to convert

- Calculate total 24 hr dose requirement of the current drug.
- Use ratio-conversion to calculate the dose of the new drug: make sure the numerators and denominators match in both drug and route of administration.
- Calculate 24 hr dose of new drug and reduce dose at least 25%. (If the problem on the exam does not specify to reduce it, but just to find the equivalent dose, then do not reduce it.)
- Divide to attain appropriate interval and dose for new drug.
- Always have breakthrough pain (BTP) medication available while making changes. Guideline recommendation for BTP dosing ranges from 5 – 17% of the total daily baseline opioid dose.

Example of Opioid Conversion

A hospice patient has been receiving 12 mg/day of IV hydromorphone. The pharmacist will convert the hydromorphone to morphine ER, to be given Q12H. The hospice policy for opioid conversion is to reduce the new dose by 50%, and to use 5 – 17% of the total daily dose for breakthrough pain.

The conversion factors (the left fraction) are taken from the above table. The right fraction has the patient's current total daily IV dose of hydromorphone in the denominator, and the total daily dose of morphine in the numerator:

$$\frac{\text{30 mg oral morphine}}{\text{1.5 mg IV hydromorphone}} = \frac{\text{X mg oral morphine}}{\text{12 mg IV hydromorphone}} \qquad \text{X = 240 mg of oral morphine}$$

Multiply the top left numerator (30) by the bottom right denominator (12), and then divide by the left denominator (1.5). This will give a total daily dose of morphine (PO) of 240 mg.

Reduce by 50%, as instructed in the problem:

50% of 240 mg = 120 mg, the correct dose of morphine ER would be 60 mg BID

Whenever possible, use an immediate release version of the long-acting opioid for BTP. Typically 10 – 15% of the total daily dose is administered Q1 – 2H for BTP (~5% administered Q4H in the elderly). For example, a rescue dose of 15 mg IR morphine Q1 – 2H could be used with morphine ER 60 mg BID in the example above and this would adhere to the hospice policy stated in the question. Other agents commonly used for BTP include combo agents, such as hydrocodone/acetaminophen. In an inpatient setting, injections can be given. Injections will have a faster onset and since BTP is typically severe, they may be preferable. However, if the patient does not have a port, the injection itself will cause discomfort. In real life, morphine IR may not be available. Hydrocodone/acetaminophen is often used for breakthrough pain. The hydrocodone dose is roughly the same as the morphine dose. If the patient is using acetaminophen alone for more mild pain, or the combination for moderate pain, the total daily acetaminophen intake will need to be monitored. Keep in mind that any drug that requires oral absorption will take time; if the patient has cancer pain (in which case the breakthrough pain is likely to be quite severe) a sublingual form of fentanyl may be used, which has faster onset.

Example of Conversion to Fentanyl Patch using a Fentanyl Patch Conversion Table

MJ is a 52 year old male patient who has been using *OxyContin* 40 mg BID and *Endocet* 5-325 mg as-needed for breakthrough pain. He uses the breakthrough pain medication 2 – 3 times weekly. Using the *OxyContin* dose only select the fentanyl patch strength that should be chosen for this patient, using the following table:

Conversion chart for oral opioid to fentanyl patch

Table 1: DOSE CONVERSION TO DURAGESIC

Current Analgesic	Daily Dosage (mg/day)			
Oral morphine	60–134	135–224	225–314	315–404
Intramuscular or Intravenous morphine	10–22	23–37	38–52	53–67
Oral oxycodone	30–67	67.5–112	112.5–157	157.5–202
Oral codeine	150–447			
Oral hydromorphone	8–17	17.1–28	28.1–39	39.1–51
Intravenous hydromorphone	1.5–3.4	3.5–5.6	5.7–7.9	8–10
Intramuscular meperidine	75–165	166–278	279–390	391–503
Oral methadone	20–44	45–74	75–104	105–134
	↓	↓	↓	↓
Recommended DURAGESIC Dose	25 mcg/hour	50 mcg/hour	75mcg/hour	100 mcg/hour

Table 1 should not be used to convert from DURAGESIC to other therapies because this conversion to DURAGESIC is conservative. Use of Table 1 for conversion to other analgesic therapies can overestimate the dose of the new agent. Overdosage of the new analgesic agent is possible

Answer: Oxycodone 80 mg daily is in the range of 67.5 – 112 mg daily which correlates to the 50 mcg/hr patch.

Methadone Conversion: Not straight-forward; should be done by pain specialists

Methadone conversion from morphine ranges from 1 – 20:1; this is highly variable due to patient tolerance and duration of therapy. The half-life of methadone varies widely. There are separate conversion charts for pain specialists to estimate methadone dosing. This should be done only by specialists with experience in using methadone. In addition to the variable half-life, methadone is proarrhythmic and has other safety issues. Methadone is used both for the treatment of opioid addiction and for chronic pain. When used for chronic pain syndromes, it is administered 2 – 3 times per day after the proper dose is determined by titration. It should be started at very low doses of no more than 2.5 mg PO BID or TID, and escalated slowly.

PERIPHERALLY-ACTING MU-OPIOID RECEPTOR ANTAGONISTS (PAMORAS)

Methylnaltrexone and naloxegol are indicated for opioid-induced constipation (OIC). These drugs block opioid receptors in the gut to reduce constipation without affecting analgesia. Another option for OIC is lubiprostone *(Amitiza)*; refer to Constipation and Diarrhea chapter for further information.

DRUG	DOSING	SAFETY/SIDE EFFECTS/MONITORING
Methylnaltrexone *(Relistor)* Injection, tablet	OIC with chronic non-cancer pain: 12 mg SC daily or 450 mg PO once daily OIC with advanced illness: weight-based dose SC every other day Administer SC in the upper arm, abdomen or thigh CrCl < 30 mL/min: ↓ dose Discontinue all laxatives prior to use	**CONTRAINDICATION** GI obstruction **WARNINGS** Risk of GI perforation (rare reports; monitor for severe abdominal symptoms), risk of opioid withdrawal (evaluate risk vs benefit and monitor), use > 4 months has not been studied, discontinue if opioid is discontinued or if severe/persistent diarrhea **SIDE EFFECTS** Abdominal pain, flatulence, N/D **NOTES** Stay close to toilet after injecting. Only for patients on opioids who have failed DSS + laxative (senna, bisacodyl). Do not use routinely; can often increase laxative to obtain effect. MedGuide required.
Naloxegol *(Movantik)* Tablet	OIC with chronic non-cancer pain: 25 mg once daily in the morning on empty stomach CrCl < 60 mL/min: 12.5 mg once daily Discontinue all laxatives prior to use; can reintroduce laxatives as needed if suboptimal response to naloxegol after 3 days	**CONTRAINDICATIONS** GI obstruction, use with strong 3A4 inhibitors **WARNINGS** Risk of GI perforation (rare reports; monitor for severe abdominal symptoms), risk of opioid withdrawal (evaluate risk vs benefit and monitor) **SIDE EFFECTS** Abdominal pain, diarrhea, headache, flatulence **NOTES** Discontinue if opioid is discontinued. Do not use with strong 3A4 inhibitors. Avoid use or reduce dose to 12.5 mg daily with moderate 3A4 inhibitors. Do not use with grapefruit juice. MedGuide required.
Lubiprostone *(Amitiza)* Tablet	OIC: 24 mcg BID	**CONTRAINDICATION** GI obstruction **NOTES** See Constipation & Diarrhea chapter

BUPRENORPHINE AND NALOXONE FORMULATIONS

Buprenorphine is a partial mu-opioid agonist. It is an agonist at low doses and an antagonist at higher doses. It is used in lower doses to treat pain and higher doses to treat addiction. Naloxone is an opioid antagonist; it replaces the opioid on the mu receptor. Given by itself, naloxone (injection or nasal spray) is used for opioid overdose. Buprenorphine/naloxone combination products are used as alternatives to methadone for opioid dependence (buprenorphine suppresses withdrawal symptoms and naloxone helps prevents misuse). Naltrexone is an opioid blocker normally used to help treat alcoholism *(ReVia)*; the IV form *(Vivitrol)* is used for alcohol and opioid dependence.

S/SX OF ACUTE OPIOID OVERDOSE
Somnolence
Respiratory depression with shallow breathing
Constricted (pinpoint) pupils (miosis)
Cold and clammy skin
Overdose can lead to coma and death

The new auto-injector *Evzio* has visual and voice instructions that make administration quite simple, although the protocol covers the use of all FDA-approved naloxone formulations, including the injection (generic naloxone) and the nasal spray (*Narcan*).

Naloxone can be given if opioid overdose is suspected due to respiratory symptoms and/or symptoms of CNS depression. Similar to epinephrine, if there is a question about whether the drug should be used, use it, since fatality could result from lack of use. It is important to call 911 if naloxone is used. The opioid will last longer than the antidote, and respiratory depression can recur. Emergency help should be en-route.

DRUG	DOSING	SAFETY/SIDE EFFECTS/MONITORING
Naloxone *(Narcan, Evzio)* Injection, nasal spray *Narcan* nasal spray *Evzio* auto-injector	IV/IM/SC: 0.4-2 mg Q2-3 min or IV infusion at 100 mL/hr (0.4 mg/hr) Nasal spray: 1 spray (4 mg), may repeat Repeat dosing may be required (opioid may last longer than blocking agent) The *Evzio* auto-injector has voice directions. Can be given by patients or friends for overdose emergency; give in thigh through clothing, hold for 5 seconds, if any doubt, inject, then call 911.	**NOTES** Naloxone will cause an acute withdrawal syndrome (pain, anxiety, tachypnea) in patients physically dependent on opioids. Due to low bioavailability, can be given orally to prevent opioid-induced constipation (off-label). Highest risk of respiratory depression from opioids: opioid-naïve patients (new users), if dose is ↑ too rapidly, and in illicit substance abuse (e.g., heroin).
Buprenorphine C-III Injection, patch, buccal film ***Butrans:*** patch (only for mod-severe pain in patients who need ATC opioid) *Buprenex:* injection *Probuphine* implant kit ***Belbuca:*** buccal film **+ naloxone** *(Bunavail:* buccal tablets, ***Suboxone:*** buccal film, ***Zubsolv***: sublingual tablets) REMS drugs (all)	*Butrans* (opioid-naïve): 5 mcg/hr patch once weekly *Belbuca* (opioid-naïve): 75 mcg daily or Q12H *Bunavail, Suboxone, Zubsolv:* Used daily for addiction, and have been used legally off-label as long as prescriber is not a certified buprenorphine prescriber for substance abuse disorder. To prescribe for opioid dependence: Prescribers need Drug Addiction Treatment Act (DATA 2000) waiver. If they have it, the DEA number will start with X. **Patch Application** Apply to upper outer arm, upper chest, side of chest, upper back. Change weekly. Do not use same site for at least 3 weeks. Disposal: Fold sticky sides together, flush or put in disposal unit that comes with drug. **FILM APPLICATION** *Belbuca* is a small film that has one white side and one yellow side. The white side should be placed on fingertip and the film is inserted between gum and cheek on the cheek. The cheek must be wet from saliva or water and patient should be instructed not to eat or drink for 30 minutes after placement of film.	**BOXED WARNINGS (*BUTRANS* PATCH)** Risk of addiction, abuse and misuse; risk of serious or fatal respiratory depression; life-threatening neonatal opioid withdrawal with prolonged use during pregnancy, accidental ingestion (especially in children) can be fatal **WARNINGS** CNS depression, QT prolongation (do not exceed one 20 mcg/hr patch) **SIDE EFFECTS** Sedation, dizziness, headache, confusion, mental and physical impairment, diaphoresis, QT prolongation, respiratory depression (dose-dependent) Patch: nausea, headache, application site pruritus/rash, dizziness, constipation, somnolence, vomiting, application site erythema, dry mouth **NOTES** Do not expose patch to heat.

Buprenorphine Drug Interactions

- Caution with use of concurrent CNS depressants: Additive sedation (somnolence), dizziness, confusion. These include alcohol, hypnotics, benzodiazepines, skeletal muscle relaxants, etc.
- Prolongs the QT interval. Use with caution in patients also taking QT-prolonging agents or in patients at risk of arrhythmia.

MUSCLE RELAXANTS

Muscle relaxants have various, poorly-understood mechanisms of action. Some work predominantly by CNS depression leading to relaxation of skeletal muscles (carisoprodol, chlorzoxazone, metaxalone, methocarbamol), while others work by decreasing transmission of reflexes at the spinal level.

DRUG	DOSING	SAFETY/SIDE EFFECTS/MONITORING
Antispasmodics with analgesic effects		
Baclofen *(Lioresal)* Tablet, injection **AUX LABELS** May cause drowsiness. Do not operate machinery....	5-20 mg TID-QID PRN Injection given via intrathecal pump for severe spasticity	**BOXED WARNING** Abrupt withdrawal of intrathecal baclofen has resulted in severe effects (hyperpyrexia, obtundation, rebound/exaggerated spasticity, muscle rigidity, and rhabdomyolysis), leading to organ failure and some fatalities. **SIDE EFFECTS** For all muscle relaxants: excessive sedation, dizziness, confusion **NOTES** Do not overdose in elderly (e.g., start low, titrate carefully), watch for additive side effects.
Cyclobenzaprine *(Fexmid,* *Amrix* ER, *Flexeril)* Tablet/capsule	IR: 5-10 mg TID PRN ER: 15-30 mg once daily	Dry mouth. May have efficacy with fibromyalgia. Serotonergic: should not be combined with other serotonergic agents. May precipitate or exacerbate cardiac arrhythmias; caution in elderly or those with heart disease (similar to TCAs -Is chemically a tricylclic almost identical to amitriptyline.).
TiZANidine *(Zanaflex)* Tablet/capsule	2-4 mg Q6-8H PRN (max 36 mg/day)	Central alpha-2 agonist: hypotension, dizziness, xerostomia, weakness, QT prolongation
Drugs that exert their effects by sedation		
Carisoprodol *(Soma)* C-IV (due to dependence, withdrawal symptoms, and diversion and abuse)	250-350 mg QID PRN	Somnolence Poor 2C19 metabolizers will have higher carisoprodol concentrations (up to 4-fold). Rapid 2C19 metabolizer will convert to the active metabolite meprobamate, which is far more toxic and has greater sedative properties.
Metaxalone *(Skelaxin)*	800 mg TID-QID PRN	Decreased cognitive/sedative effects; hepatotoxic; monitor
Methocarbamol *(Robaxin, Robaxin-750)*	1,500-2,000 mg QID PRN	Hypotension; monitor BP

Rarely used muscle relaxants include dantrolene *(Dantrium,* sometimes used for malignant hyperthermia), chlorzoxazone *(Parafon Forte DSC)* and orphenadrine *(Norflex).*

Muscle Relaxant Drug Interactions

- Caution with use of concurrent agents that are CNS depressants: Additive somnolence, dizziness, confusion. These include alcohol, hypnotics, benzodiazepines, opioids, etc.
- Carisoprodol: Poor 2C19 metabolizers will have higher carisoprodol concentrations (up to 4-fold).
- Tizanidine: Contraindicated with moderate-strong 1A2 inhibitors (e.g., ciprofloxacin and fluvoxamine) due to elevated tizanidine levels.

Muscle Relaxant Counseling

- This medicine will cause somnolence and fatigue and can impair your ability to perform mental and physical activities. Do not drive when using this medicine.
- Avoid alcohol, sleeping pills, antihistamines, sedatives, pain pills and tranquilizers that may also make you drowsy, except under the supervision of your healthcare provider.

COMMON ADJUVANTS FOR PAIN MANAGEMENT

Adjuvants [e.g., antiepileptic drugs (AEDs), antidepressants, topical anesthetics] are useful in pain management though they are not classified as analgesics. They can be added to opioid or non-opioid analgesics (multimodal treatment). Adjuvants are commonly used in pain associated with neuropathy (from diabetes or spinal cord injury), fibromyalgia, postherpetic neuralgia (PHN), and other disorders. See Epilepsy/Seizure and Depression chapters for more detail on these drugs.

DRUG	DOSING	SAFETY/SIDE EFFECTS/MONITORING
Pregabalin ***(Lyrica)*** C-V Capsule, solution	Initial: 75 mg BID or 50 mg TID, max 450 mg/day CrCl < 60 mL/min: ↓ dose and/or extend interval	**WARNINGS** Angioedema, hypersensitivity reactions, risks of suicidal thoughts or behavior (all AEDs), ↑ seizure frequency if rapidly discontinued in those with seizures; can cause peripheral edema, dizziness and somnolence **SIDE EFFECTS** Dizziness, somnolence, peripheral edema, weight gain, ataxia, diplopia, blurred vision, dry mouth, mild euphoria **NOTES** Approved for use in fibromyalgia, PHN and neuropathic pain associated with diabetes and spinal cord injury. MedGuide required.
Gabapentin ***(Neurontin,*** *Fanatrex* compounding kit) Capsule, tablet, solution, suspension *Gralise* (tablet): for PHN *Horizant* (ER tablet): for PHN and restless legs syndrome	Initial: 300 mg TID, max 3,600 mg/day CrCl < 60 mL/min: ↓ dose and/or extend interval IR, ER and gabapentin enacarbil are not interchangeable	**WARNINGS** Angioedema/anaphylaxis, mulitorgan hypersensitivity (DRESS) reactions, suicidal thoughts or behavior (all AEDs), ↑ seizure frequency if rapidly discontinued in those with seizures, CNS effects **SIDE EFFECTS** Dizziness, somnolence, ataxia, peripheral edema, weight gain, diplopia, blurred vision, dry mouth **NOTES** Used more often off-label for fibromyalgia, pain (neuropathic), headache, drug abuse, alcohol withdrawal. Take ER formulation with food. MedGuide required.

Common Adjuvants for Pain Management Continued

DRUG	DOSING	SAFETY/SIDE EFFECTS/MONITORING
DULoxetine ***(Cymbalta)*** Capsule	30-60 mg/day	**BOXED WARNING** Antidepressants ↑ risk of suicidal thoughts and behaviors in children, adolescents and young adults. **CONTRAINDICATIONS** Concomitant use or within 2 weeks of MAO inhibitors, avoid with linezolid or IV methylene blue **SIDE EFFECTS** **Common to all SNRIs** ↑ BP, HR; sexual side effects (20-50%) include ↓ libido, ejaculation difficulties, anorgasmia; increased sweating (hyperhidrosis), restless leg (see if began when therapy was started) **Duloxetine-Specific Side Effects** Nausea, dry mouth, somnolence, fatigue, ↓ appetite **NOTES** MedGuide required
Milnacipran *(Savella, Savella* Titration Pack) Tablet	Day 1: 12.5 mg daily Days 2-3: 12.5 mg BID Days 4-7: 25 mg BID Then 50 mg BID (CrCl < 30 mL/min, max dose is 25 mg BID)	**BOXED WARNINGS** Milnacipran is a SNRI similar to SNRIs used to treat depression and other psychiatric disorders. Antidepressants ↑ the risk of suicidal thinking and behavior in children, adolescents, and young adults (18-24 years of age) with major depressive disorder (MDD) and other psychiatric disorders (not approved for depression or in pediatric patients). **CONTRAINDICATIONS** Concomitant use or within 2 weeks of MAO inhibitors, avoid with linezolid or IV methylene blue **SIDE EFFECTS** Nausea, headache, constipation, dizziness, insomnia, hot flashes **DRUG INTERACTIONS** Digoxin: Milnacipran may enhance the adverse/toxic effect of digoxin. The risk of postural hypotension and tachycardia may be increased, particularly with IV digoxin. Do not use IV digoxin in patients receiving milnacipran. Increased bleeding risk with anticoagulants or antiplatelets. **NOTES** Indicated for fibromyalgia only.

Common Adjuvants for Pain Management Continued

DRUG	DOSING	SAFETY/SIDE EFFECTS/MONITORING
CarBAMazepine *(Tegretol, Carbatrol, Carnexiv)* Tablet IR or ER, capsule ER, suspension, injection	Initial: 100 mg BID Max: 1,200 mg/day	**BOXED WARNINGS** Patients of Asian descent should be screen for HLA-B*1502 allele due to increased risk of Stevens-Johnson Syndrome (SJS) or toxic epidermal necrolysis (TEN) Must monitor frequently (weekly during titration and every 3 months for stable dosing) for aplastic anemia and agranulocytosis **CONTRAINDICATIONS** Patients with a history of bone marrow suppression **SIDE EFFECTS** CNS – dizziness, drowsiness, decreased coordination Dermatologic – SJS or TEN Aplastic anemia, pancytopenia, thrombocytopenia, leukopenia **DRUG INTERACTIONS** Potent CYP450 auto-inducer **NOTES** Only FDA approved medication for the treatment of Trigeminal Neuralgia
Amitriptyline *(Elavil)* Tablet	10-50 mg QHS, sometimes higher	**SIDE EFFECTS** Uncommon with low doses used for pain, but could include: QT prolongation (with overdose), orthostatic hypotension, tachycardia, anticholinergic (dry mouth, blurred vision, urinary retention, constipation, delirium in elderly) **NOTES** TCAs can be used for suicide. Counsel carefully.
Desipramine *(Norpramin)* Tablet	Initial: 25 mg daily Titrate every 3-7 days Max: 150 mg/day	**SIDE EFFECTS** TCA like amitriptyline, with similar side effect profile, but much less sedating **NOTES** Higher norepinephrine to serotonin ratio

Topical Pain Agents, For Localized Pain

DRUG	DOSING/NOTES	SAFETY/SIDE EFFECTS/MONITORING
Lidocaine 5% patches *(Lidoderm)* Lidocaine viscous gel (Rx) *LidoPatch*, OTC, 3.99%	Apply to affected area 1-3 patches/day for up to 12 hrs/day (5% patch) Approved for postherpetic neuralgia (shingles)	**SIDE EFFECTS** Minor topical burning, pruritus, rash **NOTES** Can cut into smaller pieces (before removing backing). Do not apply more than 3 patches at one time. Caution with used patches; can harm children and pets; fold patch in half and discard safely. Do not cover with heating pads/electric blankets.

Topical Pain Agents, For Localized Pain Continued

DRUG	DOSING/NOTES	SAFETY/SIDE EFFECTS/MONITORING
Capsaicin 0.025% and 0.075% *(Zostrix, Zostrix HP)* *Qutenza 8%:* Rx capsaicin patch	Apply to affected area TID-QID ↓ TRPV1-expressing nociceptive nerve endings (↓ substance P)	**SIDE EFFECTS** Topical burning, which dissipates with continued use **NOTES** *Qutenza* is given in the healthcare provider's office only – it causes topical burning and requires pre-treatment with lidocaine – applied for 1 hour and lasts for months – works in ~ 40% of patients to reduce pain, indicated for post-herpetic neuralgia (PHN) pain.
Diclofenac topical *(Voltaren* gel, *Flector* patch)	Gel: Apply to affected area TID-QID Patch: Apply Q12H	**NOTES** *Voltaren* gel: approved for OA and sprains, strains, and contusions Flector patch: apply to most painful area, twice daily. Remove if bathing/showering. Remove for MRI. FDA approved for sprains, strains, and contusions
Methyl salicylate topical OTCs *(BenGay, Icy Hot, Precise, SalonPas, Thera-Gesic,* store brands) Methyl salicylate plus other ingredients	Patches, creams	**NOTES** OTC counseling: contact healthcare provider if rash, pruritus, or excessive skin irritation occurs, or symptoms persist for > 7 days. Do not apply over wounds or damaged skin and do not cover with tight bandage or apply heat source. Occasionally the topicals have caused first to third-degree burns, mostly in patients with neuropathic damage: Discontinue use and seek medical attention if signs of skin injury (pain, swelling, or blistering) occur following application.

Lidoderm Patient Counseling

- Patches may be cut into smaller sizes with scissors before removal of the release (plastic) liner.
- Safely discard unused portions of cut patches where children and pets cannot get to them.
- Apply up to three (3) patches at one time to cover the most painful area. Apply patches only once for up to 12 hr in a 24-hr period (12 hr on and 12 hr off).
- Remove patch if skin irritation occurs.
- Fold used patches so that the adhesive side sticks to itself and safely discard used patches or pieces of cut patches where children and pets cannot get to them. Even a used patch contains enough medicine to harm a child or pet.
- Do not use on broken, abraded, severely burned or skin with open lesions (can significantly increase amount absorbed).

Capsaicin Patient Counseling

- Apply a thin film of cream to the affected area and gently rub in until fully absorbed.
- Apply 3 to 4 times daily.
- Best results typically occur after 2 to 4 weeks of continuous use. Do not use as-needed, since frequent, long-term use is required for benefit.
- Unless treating hand pain, wash hands thoroughly with soap and water immediately after use.
- If treating hands, leave on for 30 minutes, then wash hands as above.
- Do not touch genitals, nasal area, mouth or eyes with the medicine; it will burn the sensitive skin.
- The burning pain should dissipate with continual use; starting at the lower strength will help.
- Never cover with bandages or a heating pad; serious burning could result.

PRACTICE CASE

PATIENT PROFILE

Patient Name	Gene Schneider								
Address	11188 Country Club Drive								
Age:	50	**Sex:**	Male	**Race:**	Caucasian	**Height:**	5'6"	**Weight:**	239 lbs
Allergies	Sulfa								

DIAGNOSES

Hypertension
Osteoarthritis

MEDICATIONS

Date	No.	Prescriber	Drug & Strength	Quantity	Sig	Refills
12/13	57643	Suhlbach	Atenolol 100 mg	30	1 PO daily	11
12/13	57647	Suhlbach	Amlodipine 5 mg	30	1 PO daily	11
12/13	57648	Suhlbach	HCTZ 25 mg	30	1 PO daily	11
OTC			Acetaminophen 500 mg		1-2 PO prn 4-5x daily	
OTC			Capsaicin cream 0.025%		Apply QID	

LAB/DIAGNOSTIC TESTS

Test	Normal Value	Results		
		Date: 12/11	**Date:**	**Date:**
Na	135-146 mEq/L	130		
K	3.5-5.3 mEq/L	3.7		
Cl	98-110 mE1/L	104		
C02	21-33 mmHg	28		
BUN	7-20 mg/dL	24		
Creatinine	0.6-1.3 mg/dL	1.5		
Glucose	65-99 mg/dL	118		

ADDITIONAL INFORMATION

Date	Notes
12/15	BP today 152/92. Patient reports pain at 5-7 out of 10 throughout day, describes knee as "grating." Capsaicin and APAP used regularly; asking for stronger pain medicine.

Questions

1. Gene's wife asks if OTC ibuprofen would be useful when the pain is not relieved with acetaminophen. The pharmacist counsels Gene and his wife that this may be unsafe due to the following reasons. (Select **ALL** that apply).
   a. It could cause acute kidney problems.
   b. It could cause his blood pressure to increase.
   c. It could cause an interaction with the acetaminophen.
   d. Ibuprofen is contraindicated with a sulfa allergy.
   e. Ibuprofen is not safe to use with concurrent capsaicin.

2. Gene's physician prescribes *Ultracet*. This drug contains the following ingredients:
   a. Tramadol + acetaminophen
   b. Tramadol + ibuprofen
   c. Hydrocodone + acetaminophen
   d. Hydrocodone + ibuprofen
   e. Codeine + acetaminophen

3. Gene's wife uses *Percocet*, and she suggests that this might help Gene. Which of the following statements is correct?
   a. This drug contains an NSAID.
   b. It is no more effective for pain than aspirin and can be dangerous.
   c. There are no significant side effects.
   d. It is more effective for pain than acetaminophen alone, but you should discuss with the prescribing physician before starting a previously prescribed drug.
   e. It may raise blood pressure.

4. Gene fills a prescription for *Ultracet*, and finds that the pain relief is satisfactory for about one year. After this time, the physician tries *MS Contin*, and eventually switches Gene over to the *Duragesic* patch. Choose the correct statement:
   a. *Duragesic* is the brand name for hydromorphone.
   b. This is a poor choice due to his degree of renal insufficiency.
   c. This medication can only be used in patients who have dysphagia.
   d. The starting application frequency is one patch Q48 hours.
   e. The starting application frequency is one patch Q72 hours.

Questions 5-11 are not based on the above case.

5. Tramadol is not a good choice in patients with the following condition:
   a. Muscle spasticity
   b. Aspirin allergy
   c. Seizures
   d. Peptic ulcer disease
   e. Gout

6. A physician has called the pharmacist. He has a patient on morphine sulfate extended-release who is having difficulty with regular bowel movements. The patient is using docusate sodium 100 mg BID. The patient reports that his stools are difficult to expel, although they are not particularly hard or condensed. Which of the following recommendation is appropriate to prevent the constipation?
   a. Senna
   b. Bismuth subsalicylate
   c. *Relistor*
   d. Mineral oil
   e. Phosphate soda

7. A patient with cancer is using the fentanyl patch along with the *Actiq* transmucosal formulation for breakthrough pain. Which statement is correct?

   a. *Actiq* contains hydromorphone for sublingual absorption.
   b. No more than 4 BTP episodes per day should be treated with *Actiq*; if more are required, the patient should consult with his/her physician.
   c. A patient who is not taking an extended-release version of an opioid may still use *Actiq* for occasional, breakthrough cancer pain.
   d. *Actiq* contains oxymorphone for sublingual absorption.
   e. This drug is contraindicated in patients older than 65 years of age.

8. Which of the following brand-generic combinations is correct?

   a. Celecoxib *(Mobic)*
   b. Naproxen *(Motrin)*
   c. Morphine *(Opana)*
   d. Hydromorphone *(Dilaudid)*
   e. Methadone *(Demerol)*

9. Choose the correct statement regarding the medication *Celebrex*:

   a. This may be a safer option for patients with GI bleeding risk.
   b. This may be a safer option for patients with reduced renal function.
   c. This is a non-selective NSAID, and has a better safety profile.
   d. This drug is safe to use in patients with any type of sulfonamide allergy.
   e. The maximum dose for inflammatory conditions, such as RA, is 200 mg daily.

10. A patient with poor pain control has been taking hydrocodone-acetaminophen 10 mg-325 mg 8 tablets daily. The physician will convert the patient to *Kadian* to provide adequate pain relief. Using the hydrocodone component only, calculate the total daily dose of *Kadian* that is equivalent to the hydrocodone dose, and then reduce the dose by 25% (to lessen the possibility of excessive side effects from the initial conversion). The final daily dose of *Kadian* is:

    a. 10 mg *Kadian*
    b. 40 mg *Kadian*
    c. 60 mg *Kadian*
    d. 80 mg *Kadian*
    e. 110 mg *Kadian*

11. Which is the correct antidote for acetaminophen toxicity?

    a. Flumazenil
    b. N- Acetylcysteine
    c. Pyridoxine
    d. Physostigmine
    e. Atropine

Answers

1-a,b, 2-a, 3-d, 4-e, 5-c, 6-a, 7-b, 8-d, 9-a, 10-c, 11-b

MIGRAINE

GUIDELINES/REFERENCES

Evidence-Based Guideline Update: Pharmacologic Treatment for Episodic Migraine Prevention in Adults. http://www.neurology.org/content/78/17/1337.full.pdf+html (accessed 2016 Oct 4).

ICSI Health Care Guideline: Diagnosis and Treatment of Headache. Updated January 2013. https://www.icsi.org/_asset/qwrznq/Headache.pdf (accessed 2016 Oct 4).

BACKGROUND

Headache treatment is a common concern in the community pharmacy, one of the most common complaints in neurologists' offices and the most common pain complaint seen in family practice. Most headaches are migraine and tension-type headaches.

Migraines are chronic headaches that can cause significant pain for hours or days. In addition to severe pain, most migraines cause nausea, vomiting, and sensitivity to light and sound. Some migraines are preceded or accompanied by sensory warning symptoms or signs (auras), such as flashes of light, blind spots or tingling in the arms or legs. Most migraines do not have an aura.

A headache accompanied by fever, stiff neck, rash, confusion, seizures, double vision, weakness, numbness, chest pain, shortness of breath or aphasia (trouble speaking) could indicate a serious cardiovascular, cerebrovascular or infectious event. Patients with these symptoms should seek immediate medical attention.

MIGRAINE CAUSES

The cause of migraines is not well-understood. They may be caused by changes in the trigeminal nerve and imbalances in neurotransmitters, including serotonin, which decrease during a migraine, causing a chemical release of neuropeptides that trigger vasodilation in cranial blood vessels.

Identifying "triggers" can be useful so the patient can avoid them and reduce migraine incidence. A common type of migraine is a menstrual-associated migraine (MAM) in women. These may be treated with oral contraceptives or the estradiol patch or creams to decrease migraine frequency. Women who have migraine with aura are at higher risk for stroke and should not use estrogen-containing contraceptives.

DIAGNOSIS

Migraine can be diagnosed when an adult has at least 5 attacks (not attributed to another disorder) fulfilling the following criteria:

1. Headaches last 4 – 72 hrs and recur sporadically.
2. Headaches have ≥ 2 of the following characteristics: unilateral location, pulsating, moderate-severe pain and aggravated by (or causing avoidance of) routine physical activity.
3. One of the following occurs during the headache: nausea and/or vomiting, photophobia and phonophobia.

NON-DRUG TREATMENT

A headache diary can assist patients in identifying triggers. Non-pharmacologic interventions involve avoiding triggers, stress management, massage, spinal manipulation or applying cold compresses/ice to the head. Acupuncture can be helpful for reducing migraines in some patients.

NATURAL PRODUCTS

Caffeine is effective in combination with acetaminophen or aspirin for migraine headaches and is available in combination products for this purpose. Butterbur, coenzyme Q10, feverfew, magnesium, peppermint (applied topically) and riboflavin (alone or in combination) have been used.

COMMON MIGRAINE TRIGGERS

Hormonal Changes in Women
Fluctuations in estrogen trigger headaches in many women. Some women use monophasic oral contraceptive formulations to keep estrogen levels more constant and help reduce menstrual-associated migraines, the most common type of female migraine. Progestin-only pills are recommended for women with migraine with aura, due to stroke risk with estrogen-containing contraceptives.

Foods
Common offending agents include alcohol, especially beer and red wine, aged cheeses, chocolate, aspartame, overuse of caffeine, monosodium glutamate (MSG), salty foods and processed foods.

Stress
Stress is a major cause of migraines.

Sensory Stimuli
Bright lights, sun glare, loud sounds and scents (which may be pleasant or unpleasant odors).

Changes in Wake-Sleep Pattern
Either missing sleep or getting too much sleep (including jet lag).

Changes in the Environment
A change of weather or barometric pressure.

DRUG TREATMENT

Acute Treatment

Acute or abortive treatment is used for a headache that is already present. There are many drug options for acute treatment, including OTC options: acetaminophen, *Advil Migraine* (which contains only ibuprofen), *Excedrin Migraine* (aspirin, acetaminophen and caffeine), *Aleve* (naproxen) or other agents, including store brands of these options. OTC agents can be tried for migraines that are mild to moderate. Prescription options for acute treatment include: serotonin receptor agonists (triptans), ergotamine- and butalbital-containing medications, opioids and opioid-combination products (*Vicodin*, etc.) and diclofenac *(Cambia)* in a packet formulation that is specifically indicated for migraine treatment. Refer to the Pain chapter for a more detailed discussion of many of these medications. Opioids, butalbital-containing products, tramadol, and tapentadol are not recommended due to abuse/dependence issues. If other agents have failed, these are used in select cases.

Some patients get more relief from OTC products, some from triptans and others need to use combinations of both. Always ask the patient what they have tried in the past, and if it was useful. Patients with nausea/vomiting may benefit from combined treatment with an antiemetic.

Triptans

Triptans are selective agonists for the 5-HT1 receptor and cause vasoconstriction of cranial blood vessels, inhibit neuropeptide release and decrease pain transmission. They are first-line for acute treatment. The safety of treating > 3 – 5 headaches per month (product-specific) has not been established.

DRUG	DOSING	SAFETY/SIDE EFFECTS/MONITORING
Almotriptan *(Axert)* Tablet	Initial: 6.25-12.5 mg, can repeat x 1 after 2 hrs (max 25 mg/day)	**CONTRAINDICATIONS** Cerebrovascular disease (stroke/TIA), uncontrolled hypertension, ischemic heart disease, peripheral vascular disease, history of hemiplegic or basilar migraine, use within 24 hrs of another triptan or ergotamine-type medication. See Drug Interactions for products contraindicated with MAO inhibitors and 3A4 inhibitors. **WARNINGS** Risk of ↑ blood pressure, cardiac and cerebrovascular events, arrhythmias, serotonin syndrome, medication overuse headache (MOH), seizures (sumatriptan only); caution in hepatic or renal impairment (product specific) **SIDE EFFECTS** Paresthesia (tingling/numbness), dizziness, hot/cold sensations, chest pain/tightness, dry mouth, somnolence, nausea Triptan sensations (pressure in the chest or heaviness or pressure in the neck region) usually dissipate after administration. **NOTES** ODTs, nasal sprays and injections are useful if nausea is present. No water is required for ODTs. Nasal sprays and injections work faster. *Imitrex* and *Zomig* nasal sprays contain only 1 dose (do not prime). *Treximet:* keep in original container (contains desiccant). See Pain chapter for boxed warning and additional information related to naproxen. **Children and Adolescents** Almotriptan tablets, zolmitriptan nasal spray and *Treximet* are approved for children and adolescents ≥ 12 years of age; rizatriptan is approved for children and adolescents 6-17 years of age. **Duration of Action** Frovatriptan has the longest half-life (26 hrs). Both frovatriptan and naratriptan are considered long-acting, but onset is slower. These can be chosen if headache recurs after dosing, lasts a long time or can be anticipated (e.g., MAM). Triptans with a shorter half-life have a faster onset: almotriptan, eletriptan, rizatriptan, sumatriptan and zolmitriptan. **Sumatriptan Injections** All are injected SQ. Preferred site is lateral thigh or upper arm for all except *Sumavel DosePro* (use abdomen or lateral thigh). Protect from light. Prefilled syringe *(Imitrex)*, prefilled autoinjector *(Zembrace)*, needle-free system *(Sumavel)*.
Eletriptan *(Relpax)* Tablet	Initial: 20-40 mg, can repeat x 1 after 2 hrs (max 80 mg/day)	
Frovatriptan *(Frova)* Tablet	Initial: 2.5 mg, can repeat x 1 after 2 hrs (max 7.5 mg/day)	
Naratriptan *(Amerge)* Tablet	Initial: 1-2.5 mg, can repeat x 1 after 4 hrs (max 5 mg/day)	
Rizatriptan *(Maxalt, Maxalt-MLT)* Tablet, ODT	Initial: 5-10 mg, can repeat x 1 after 2 hrs (max 30 mg/day)	
SUMAtriptan *(Imitrex, Imitrex STATdose, Onzetra Xsail,* *Sumavel DosePro,* ***Zembrace SymTouch)*** Tablet, SC (autoinjector and needle-free injector), nasal spray, nasal powder + naproxen 85-500 mg and 10-60 mg ***(Treximet)***	PO: 25, 50 or 100 mg, can repeat x 1 after 2 hrs Max 200 mg/day **Subcutaneous:** *Imitrex, Sumavel*: 4 or 6 mg, can repeat x 1 after 1 hr Max 12 mg/day *Zembrace*: 3 mg, can repeat up to 4 times per day (1 hr between doses) Max 12 mg/day **Intranasal:** Spray *(Imitrex)*: 5, 10, or 20 mg in one nostril can repeat x 1 after 2 hrs Max 40 mg/day Powder *(Onzetra Xsail)*: 11 mg in each nostril using nosepiece, can repeat x 1 after 2 hrs Max 44 mg/day ***Treximet*** Adults: *Treximet* (85-500 mg) 1 tab, can repeat x 1 after 2 hrs Max 2 tabs/24 hrs Pediatric (12-17 yrs): *Treximet* (10-60 mg) 1 tab x 1 dose	
ZOLMitriptan (*Zomig, Zomig-ZMT*) Tablet, ODT, nasal spray	PO: 1.25-5 mg, can repeat x 1 after 2 hrs Intranasal: 2.5-5 mg, can repeat x 1 after 2 hrs Max 10 mg/day (all formulations)	

Triptan Drug Interactions

- FDA warning about combining triptans with serotonergic drugs such as SSRIs and SNRIs. Many patients take both safely, since the triptan is only taken PRN. It may present a problem when a third serotonergic agent is added. See Patient Counseling.
- Sumatriptan, rizatriptan and zolmitriptan are contraindicated with MAO inhibitors (or within 2 weeks of stopping), the others are not. All of the product labels discuss the risk of serotonin syndrome.
- Eletriptan is contraindicated with strong CYP 3A4 inhibitors; reduce the dose of almotriptan.

Ergotamine Drugs

Ergotamine is a nonselective agonist of serotonin receptors, which causes cerebral vasoconstriction. In patients with contraindications to triptans or who do not find benefit with a triptan, ergotamine is generally used next.

DRUG	DOSING	SAFETY/SIDE EFFECTS/MONITORING
Dihydroergotamine ***(D.H.E. 45, Migranal)*** Injection, nasal spray	IM/SC/IV *(D.H.E. 45)*: 1 mg at first sign of headache, repeat hourly to a max dose of 2 mg/day (IV) and 3 mg/day (IM/SC) and max 6 mg/week Intranasal *(Migranal)*: 1 spray (0.5 mg) into each nostril, can repeat after 15 minutes, up to a total of 4 sprays (2 mg)	**BOXED WARNING** Contraindicated with potent CYP 3A4 inhibitors (e.g., protease inhibitors, azoles and some macrolide antibiotics) due to serious and life-threatening peripheral ischemia. **CONTRAINDICATIONS** Uncontrolled hypertension, pregnancy, ischemic heart disease, angina, MI, peripheral vascular disease, hemiplegic or basilar migraine, renal/hepatic impairment, sepsis, use with pressors/vasoconstrictive drugs. Dihydroergotamine: avoid use within 24 hours of serotonin agonists or other ergotamine-type drugs. Avoid during or within 2 weeks of discontinuing MAO inhibitors.
Ergotamine + caffeine *(Cafergot, Migergot)* Tablet, suppository	*Cafergot* (1 mg ergotamine + 100 mg caffeine): take 2 tablets at onset of migraine, then 1 tablet every 30 min PRN to a max of 6 tablets per attack *Migergot:* 1 suppository at first sign of migraine, may repeat x 1 after 1 hr. Max: 2 suppositories per attack	**WARNINGS** Cardiovascular effects (avoid in any patient with baseline risk, cerebrovascular events, ergotism (intense vasoconstriction resulting in peripheral vascular ischemia and possible gangrene), cardiac valvular fibrosis, potentially serious drug interactions. **SIDE EFFECTS** Nasal spray: rhinitis, dysgeusia, nausea, dizziness **NOTES** Nasal spray: prime by pumping 4 times. Do not inhale deeply (to let drug absorb into skin in nose). Use at first sign of attack, but can be used at any time during migraine. Safety issue – see Pregnancy chapter

Butalbital-Containing Combination Products

Butalbital is a barbiturate. Acetaminophen/butalbital/caffeine *(Fioricet)* and aspirin/butalbital/caffeine *(Fiorinal)* are both available in combinations with codeine: *Fioricet with Codeine* and *Fiorinal with Codeine*. All of these products are federally classified as C-III, except *Fioricet* (which is exempt). *Fioricet* remains a popular drug, but butalbital-containing products are not recommended for treating acute migraines due to abuse/dependence issues and lower efficacy. If used regularly, and long-term, they must be tapered off or the patient will get worsening of headache, tremors, and be at risk for delirium and seizures. Pharmacists should make sure patients do not exceed safe doses of acetaminophen and counsel on the potential for nausea and constipation with the codeine-containing formulations and additive sedation with alcohol.

Prophylactic Treatment

Some patients will require a prophylactic medication to decrease the frequency of migraines. Consider using a prophylactic medication if the patient requests it, if they use acute treatments ≥ 2 days/week or ≥ 3 times per month, if the migraines decrease their quality of life or if acute treatments are ineffective or contraindicated. Typically, the reduction in migraines is ~50% with prophylaxis, but a patient may have to try more than one agent to find one that works well for them. A full trial, at a reasonable dose, should be 2 – 6 months.

Choose the prophylactic agent based on patient characteristics and the side effect profile of the medications because the efficacy data is similar. Prophylactic therapies include:

- Antihypertensives: Most experience is with beta blockers (best evidence with propranolol, timolol, metoprolol). Lisinopril, verapamil and other beta blockers have been used.
- Antiepileptic drugs: Topiramate *(Topamax)* and valproic acid.
- Antidepressants: Tricyclic antidepressants (most evidence with amitriptyline) are effective. TCAs are used at lower doses for migraine prophylaxis. Venlafaxine may also be effective.
- MAM: Extended-cycle oral contraceptives, or start NSAIDs or triptan (specifically those with longer half life: frovatriptan or naratriptan) prior to menses, continue for 5 – 7 days.
- Other: Natural products (see beginning of chapter) and botulinum toxin type A *(Botox)* injections. *Botox* is for chronic migraines only (≥ 15 headache days per month).

DRUG	TYPICAL DOSING RANGE	COMMENTS/SIDE EFFECTS
Beta Blockers (see Hypertension chapter for complete discussion)		
Propranolol *(Inderal LA)*	80-240 mg, divided Q6-8H	Fatigue, ↓ HR, possible depression with propranolol (most lipophilic and non-selective)
Timolol	10 mg twice daily	Both propranolol and timolol are non-selective beta blockers; do not use in COPD, emphysema
Metoprolol *(Lopressor, Toprol XL)*	100-200 mg daily	Metoprolol is beta-1 selective. Caution with all beta blockers if low HR (they will ↓ HR), monitor for hypotension, dizziness
Antiepileptic Drugs (see Epilepsy/Seizures chapter for complete discussion)		
Divalproex *(Depakote,* others), Valproic acid *(Depakene,* others)	250-500 mg twice daily	Liver toxicity, pancreatitis, sedation, weight gain, tremor, teratogenicity, thrombocytopenia, alopecia, nausea (less with divalproex), polycystic ovarian syndrome Safety issue – see Pregnancy chapter
Topiramate *(Topamax)*	Start 25 mg QHS, titrate to 50 mg BID	Weight loss (6-13%), paresthesia, cognitive impairment, metabolic acidosis, nephrolithiasis, open angle glaucoma, hypohidrosis (children), depression, reduced efficacy of oral contraceptives, Safety issue – see Pregnancy chapter

MEDICATION-OVERUSE ("REBOUND") HEADACHES

Medication overuse headaches (MOH) result from overuse of most headache medications (e.g., NSAIDs, opioids, the butalbital-containing drugs, analgesic combination products, triptans and ergotamines, except DHE) and are characterized by headaches that occur > 10 – 15 days per month. Pharmacists are in a position to see many patients who chronically use headache medicines, and have daily headaches. It may be best to consult with another healthcare provider if the patient seems at risk or is unlikely to successfully reduce analgesic use independently. To prevent MOH, educate patients to limit acute treatment medications to 2 or 3 times per week, at most. The most important thing is to stop the "over-used" medication. If the drug is an opioid or contains butalbital *(Fioricet, Fiorinal)*, a slow taper will be needed.

Patient Counseling

All Triptans

- Side effects that you may experience include sleepiness, nausea, numbness, throat or neck pressure, dizziness, hot or cold sensations and a heaviness or pressure in the chest or neck region. These usually occur after the drug is taken and go away quickly.
- If nausea prevents you from swallowing or holding down your medication, your healthcare provider can prescribe a tablet that dissolves in your mouth, an injection or a nasal spray.
- If you have migraines that come on very quickly, a nasal spray or injection will provide faster relief.
- Serious, but rare, side effects such as heart attacks and strokes have occurred in people who have used this type of medication because of this, triptans cannot be used in patients who have had a stroke, have heart disease or have blood pressure that is not well-controlled. If any of this applies to you, inform your healthcare provider.
- This medication increases the levels of a chemical in your blood called serotonin. If it is taken with other OTC or prescription medications that also increase serotonin, toxicity can occur. Seek urgent medical care if you have symptoms of toxicity: severe nausea, dizziness and headache, diarrhea, feeling very agitated, a racing heartbeat or hallucinations.
- Take the medication with or without food, at the first sign of a migraine. It will not work as well if you wait to use it.
- If you use the orally disintegrating tablets *(Maxalt-MLT* and *Zomig-ZMT)*, peel open the blister pack and place the orally disintegrating tablet on your tongue, where it will dissolve and be swallowed with saliva. You do not need to use water. These formulations should not be used in patients with phenylketonuria, due to the sweetener.
- If your symptoms are only partly relieved, or if your headache comes back, you may take a second dose in the time period explained to you by the pharmacist.
- If you use migraine treatments more than twice a week or if they are severe, you should be using a daily medication to help prevent migraines. Discuss this with your healthcare provider.

Imitrex STATdose System

- Inject the medication just below the skin as soon as the symptoms of your migraine appear.
- The *STATdose* system includes a carrying case, a *STATdose* pen and two syringe cartridges.
- Clean the area of skin (upper outside arm or lateral thigh) with rubbing alcohol prior to administering the injection.
- Open the carrying case and pull off the tamper-proof seal from one of the syringe cartridges. Open the lid of the cartridge.
- Take the pen out of the carrying case. Load the *STATdose* pen by inserting it into the syringe cartridge and turning it clockwise. The cartridge is loaded when you are no longer able to turn the pen clockwise.
- Gently pull the loaded pen out of the carrying case. The blue button on the side triggers the injection. There is a safety feature that does not allow the injection to be triggered unless it is against your skin.
- Hold the loaded pen to the area that you have cleaned to receive the shot. Push the blue button on the top of the pen. To make sure you receive all of the medicine, you must continue to hold the pen against the skin for 5 seconds.
- Follow safety procedures and return the used injection needle to the cartridge. Insert the pen into the empty cartridge container. This time, turn it counterclockwise to loosen the needle. Remove the empty *STATdose* pen from the cartridge and store it in the carrying case.
- Replace the cartridge pack after both doses have been used. Discard the pack and insert a new refill.

Zembrace SymTouch

- Remove the autoinjector from the carton and check the expiration date. Inspect the medicine through the medicine window. It should be a clear, colorless to pale yellow solution.
- Clean the injection site (lateral thigh or upper arm) with an alcohol pad.
- Pull the red cap off to expose the yellow needle guard. Do not put thumb, fingers or hand over yellow needle guard.
- Press the yellow needle guard gently against the skin at a 90 degree angle.
- Press and hold the autoinjector against skin. The first "click" is the start of the injection. Continue to hold down until you hear the second "click". After the second click, hold the autoinjector against the skin for 5 seconds to get the full dose.
- Lift the autoinjector away from the skin. The yellow needle guard will cover the needle. Do not rub the injection site.
- Verify that you can see the red plunger in the medicine window. That means the full dose was given. Never reuse the autoinjector.
- Dispose of the autoinjector in a sharps container or heavy-duty plastic container (secure lid, leak-resistant and properly labeled as hazardous waste).

Sumavel DosePro

- Select a delivery site on the stomach area or thigh. Do not deliver *Sumavel DosePro* in the arm or within 2 inches of the navel (belly button). Change delivery sites with each use.
- Snap: When ready to take the dose, hold the device firmly in one hand. Grip the top and bottom of the snap-off tip where the finger grips are located. Break off the tip by snapping it in a downward motion. You do not need to pull or twist it.
- Flip: Firmly press the lever down until it clicks and locks into the handle. Once the lever has been flipped, do not touch the end of the chamber and keep it pointed away from your face and eyes.
- Pinch and Press: Pinch about 2 inches of the skin at the selected delivery site (abdomen or thigh only) and place the end of the device with the clear medication chamber against your skin. Steadily press straight down against skin until you hear a burst of air.
- There is no button to push. Once you hear the burst of air, you can remove the device from the skin.

Onzetra Xsail Nasal Powder

- Open the pouch and remove the first nosepiece. Insert the nosepiece into the device until you hear it click.
- Press and release the white button to pierce the medication capsule.
- Insert the nosepiece deeply into the nose (first nostril). Rotate the device to place the mouthpiece into your mouth.
- Blow into the device with your mouth for 2 – 3 seconds to deliver medication into your nose.
- Press the clear tab to remove the first nosepiece. Check the capsule to be sure the medication is gone. Discard the first nosepiece.
- Insert the second nosepiece into the device and repeat the steps above using the second nostril.

Zomig Nasal Spray

- Blow your nose gently before use.
- Remove the protective cap.
- Hold the nasal sprayer device gently with your fingers and thumb.
- There is only one dose in the nasal sprayer. Do not prime (test) the nasal sprayer or you will lose the dose.
- Do not press the plunger until you have put the tip in your nostril or you will lose the dose. Insert into nose about a half an inch, close your mouth, press the plunger, keep head level for 10 – 20 seconds, and gently breathe in through your mouth.

GOUT

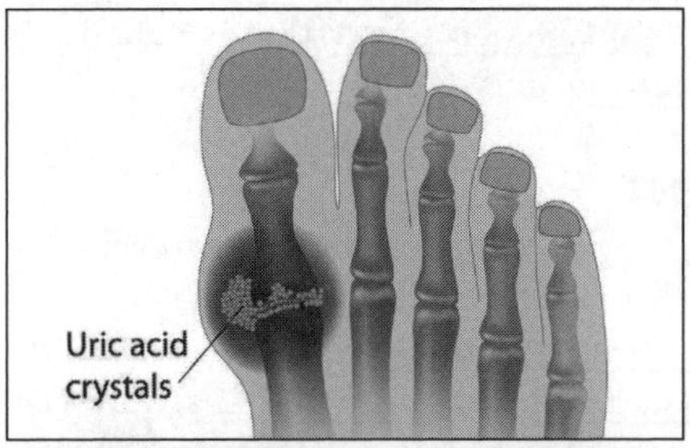

BACKGROUND

Gout is a type of arthritis caused by a buildup of uric acid crystals, primarily in the joints. Uric acid is a breakdown product of purines, which are one of the base pairs of DNA and are present in many foods. Gout attacks are sudden with severe pain, burning, and swelling. Gout typically occurs in one joint, which is most often the metatarsophalangeal joint (MTP, the big toe). If left untreated, the attacks can occur over and over, and will eventually damage the joints, tendons and other tissues.

Another type of "gout" is an acute condition called tumor lysis syndrome (TLS). This is a potentially life-threatening complication of aggressive chemotherapy. When cells are "lysed" open, many purines are released into the blood and are quickly converted to uric acid, which can cause acute gout as well as electrolyte abnormalities (hyperkalemia, hyperphosphatemia, and hypocalcemia).

GUIDELINES/REFERENCES

Khanna D, Fitzgerald JD, Khanna PP, et al. 2012 American College of Rheumatology Guidelines for Management of Gout. *Arthritis Care and Research.* 2012;64(10):1431-1461.

CAUSES

Uric acid is produced as an end-product of purine metabolism (see following figure). Under normal conditions, uric acid is excreted ⅔ renally and ⅓ by the GI tract. When uric acid builds up in the blood, the patient may remain asymptomatic (many people with high uric acid, or hyperuricemia, never get gout) or the uric acid can crystallize in the joints, resulting in a severe, painful gout attack. Gout typically strikes after many years of persistent hyperuricemia.

Risk Factors

Risk factors for gout include male sex, obesity, excessive alcohol consumption (particularly beer), hypertension, chronic kidney disease (CKD), lead intoxication, advanced age and using medications that increase uric acid. To reduce the risk of recurrent gout attacks patients should avoid organ meats, high-fructose corn syrup and alcohol. Servings of fruit juices, table sugar, sweetened drinks and desserts, salt, beef, lamb, pork and seafood with high purine content (sardines, shellfish) should be limited. A healthy diet (including low fat dairy products and vegetables), hydration, weight control, smoking cessation and exercise reduce the risk of gout attacks.

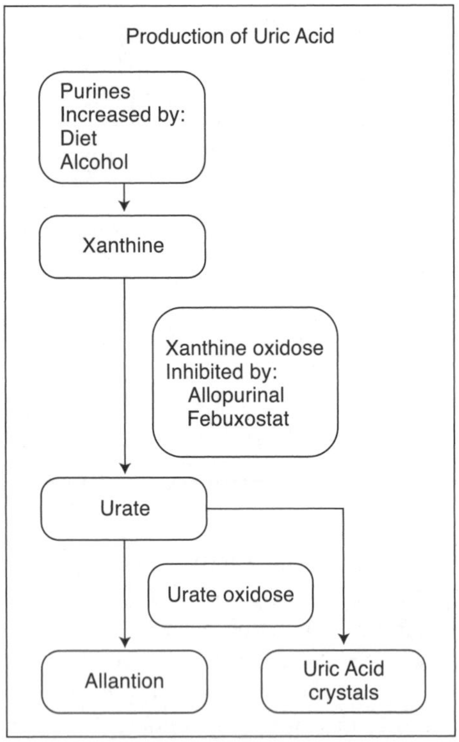

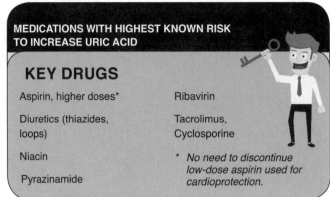

MEDICATIONS WITH HIGHEST KNOWN RISK TO INCREASE URIC ACID

KEY DRUGS

Aspirin, higher doses*	Ribavirin
Diuretics (thiazides, loops)	Tacrolimus, Cyclosporine
Niacin	* *No need to discontinue low-dose aspirin used for cardioprotection.*
Pyrazinamide	

Laboratory Parameters

A normal serum uric acid (urate) level is ~2.0 – 7.2 mg/dL. The treatment goal is a uric acid level < 6 mg/dL. Do not start treatment until gout has occurred; this is called asymptomatic hyperuricemia, and it is not treated.

DRUG TREATMENT

The goal of treatment is to treat acute attacks, prevent future flare-ups, and reduce uric acid levels. Note that the drugs used to treat an acute attack (colchicine, NSAIDs, steroids) are different than the drugs used to prevent further attacks. Colchicine or NSAIDs, however, are recommended when prophylactic treatment is started to reduce the risk of acute attacks which can occur when uric acid is lowered rapidly. Colchicine is on the Beer's list of potentially harmful drugs in the elderly if the CrCl is < 30 mL/min.

Acute Gout Attack Treatment

Gout attacks are painful and treatment should be started within 24 hours. Single agent treatment with an NSAID, systemic steroid or oral colchicine is recommended for most cases. In more severe disease, combination therapy is used, with colchicine and either an NSAID or an oral steroid. Another option (with 1 or 2 joints affected), is an intra-articular steroid injection (injected into the joint/s), which is given with one of the oral drugs.

If an acute attack occurs in a patient using chronic urate-lowering therapy (ULT) (allopurinol, or febuxostat), they should continue the ULT without interruption.

Topical ice applied to the affected joints is helpful.

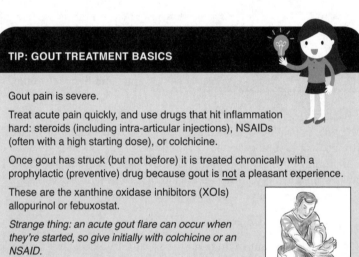

TIP: GOUT TREATMENT BASICS

Gout pain is severe.

Treat acute pain quickly, and use drugs that hit inflammation hard: steroids (including intra-articular injections), NSAIDs (often with a high starting dose), or colchicine.

Once gout has struck (but not before) it is treated chronically with a prophylactic (preventive) drug because gout is not a pleasant experience.

These are the xanthine oxidase inhibitors (XOIs) allopurinol or febuxostat.

Strange thing: an acute gout flare can occur when they're started, so give initially with colchicine or an NSAID.

The XOI didn't work well enough? (UA remain > 6 mg/dL)

2 options:

✓ Add on lesinurad (*Zurampic*)—take with the daily XOI

✓ Replace the XOI with pegloticase (*Krystexxa*)—that's IV & has risk of anaphylaxis

*Rasburicase is similar to pegloticase, but that's for gout prevention with tumor lysis syndrome only (i.e., as part of cancer treatment).

Acute Gout Attack Treatment

DRUG	DOSING	SAFETY/SIDE EFFECTS/MONITORING

Colchicine

DRUG	DOSING	SAFETY/SIDE EFFECTS/MONITORING
Colchicine *(Colcrys, Mitigare)* + probenecid Patients receiving prophylaxis with colchicine who receive colchicine for acute gout should wait 12 hours before resuming prophylaxis dose	**Treatment** 1.2 mg orally (this is two 0.6 mg tablets) followed by 0.6 mg in 1 hr (do not exceed a total of 1.8 mg in 1 hr, or 2.4 mg/day Dose to be repeated no earlier than 3 days CrCl < 30 mL/min: the treatment dose is the same, but do not give again for 2 weeks **Prophylaxis** 0.6 mg once or twice daily CrCl < 30 mL/min, ↓ to 0.3 mg/day	**CONTRAINDICATIONS** Do not use with a P-gp or strong CYP 3A4 inhibitor with renal and/or hepatic impairment. **WARNINGS** Myelosuppression, gastrointestinal symptoms (↓ dose if anorexia, diarrhea, N/V), neuromuscular toxicity (including rhabdomyolysis), use with cyclosporine, diltiazem, verapamil, gemfibrozil, statins; these drugs ↑ myopathy risk **SIDE EFFECTS** Diarrhea, nausea, vomiting, ↓ vitamin B12 Myelosuppression, myopathy, neuropathy (dose-related) **NOTES** Recommended only when treatment is started within 36 hrs of onset of symptoms (preferably sooner). Beer's criteria in elderly with CrCl < 30 mL/min: risk of myelosuppression, GI and neuromuscular adverse effects. ↓ dose and monitor, or use steroid as an alternative.

NSAIDs

DRUG	DOSING	SAFETY/SIDE EFFECTS/MONITORING
Indomethacin *(Indocin)*	50 mg TID until attack resolved	See Pain chapter for more complete information. **NOTES** Avoid use in severe renal disease (uric acid is renally cleared and patients with gout may have renal insufficiency); consider risk of bleeding (however risk of GI bleeding is less due to short duration of therapy), CVD risk (most with celecoxib). Indomethacin was the 1st NSAID approved and is the traditional DOC; however, it is more toxic than ibuprofen (↑ risk for GI toxicity) and has psychiatric side effects. Indomethacin, naproxen and sulindac are approved for gout; the ACR guideline does not limit treatment to these NSAIDs.
Naproxen *(Naprosyn, others)*	750 mg x 1, then reduce to 250 mg Q8H until attack resolved	
Sulindac *(Clinoril)*	200 mg BID, until attack resolved	
Celecoxib *(CeleBREX)*	800 mg x 1, then 400 mg x 1 (later in day), then 400 mg BID x 1 week	

Steroids: Can be given PO, IM, IV, intra-articular or via ACTH (adrenocorticotropic hormone) which triggers endogenous glucocorticoid secretion.

DRUG	DOSING	SAFETY/SIDE EFFECTS/MONITORING
PredniSONE/ PredniSOLONE	0.5 mg/kg/day PO for 5-10 days (no taper) or 0.5 mg/kg/day for 2-5 days, then taper (reduce dose by 5 mg each day) over 7-10 days	See Systemic Steroids & Autoimmune Disease chapter for more complete information. **NOTES** Acute side effects of steroids (e.g., hyperglycemia, hypertension, insomnia, increased appetite). Systemic side effects with intra-articular steroid injections are infrequent. There may be mild pain at the injection site. Repeated injections increase the risk of joint damage.
MethylPREDNISolone *(Medrol, Solu-Medrol)*	Intra-articular: If 1-2 large joints involved Oral: Methylprednisolone dose pack	
Triamcinolone	IM: Triamcinolone 60 mg, then start PO prednisone	

Colchicine Drug Interactions

- Colchicine is a substrate (major) of CYP 3A4 and the efflux transporter P-glycoprotein (P-gp). Fatal toxicity can occur if colchicine is combined with strong 3A4 inhibitors, such as clarithromycin or a strong inhibitor of P-gp, such as cyclosporine. Check for inhibitors prior to dispensing drug. If using a moderate 3A4 inhibitor, the maximum dose for acute treatment is 1.2 mg (2 tablets).
- Patients are at higher risk of myopathy and rhabdomyolysis if given together with cyclosporine, diltiazem, verapamil, gemfibrozil and statins; have patients monitor muscle pain/soreness.

Colchicine Counseling

- At the first sign of an attack, take 2 tablets. You can take 1 more tablet in one hour. Do not use more than this amount in an hour, and do not use more than 4 tablets in 24 hours. Taking too much colchicine can lead to serious side effects.
- You should not take the 2nd dose if you have upset stomach, nausea or diarrhea.
- Report any serious nausea, vomiting, diarrhea, fatigue, unusual bleeding, tingling in your fingers or toes or muscle soreness to your healthcare provider right away.
- Do not start treatment course again for at least 3 days.

Chronic Urate Lowering Therapy

Chronic urate lowering therapy (ULT) should be started in all patients with gout who experience intermittent symptoms or tophi (uric acid crystals that can form under the skin in long-term gout). First-line agents for ULT are the xanthine oxidase (XO) inhibitors allopurinol or febuxostat. Blocking XO stops the production of uric acid and produces a non-toxic end product. These agents are titrated up (slowly for allopurinol) to lower the uric acid to a target level of $<$ 6 mg/dL. Allopurinol is started at a lower dose with moderate or severe CKD. Patients who are at high risk of a severe allopurinol hypersensitivity reaction (including certain Asian groups) should be screened prior to use for the HLA-B*5801 allele. Probenecid is a 2nd line agent and can be used if XO inhibitors are contraindicated or not tolerated, or can be added when the uric acid level is not at goal despite maximal doses of XO inhibitors. Probenecid inhibits reabsorption of uric acid in the proximal tubule of the nephron, thus promoting uric acid excretion. It requires adequate renal function to be effective, which many gout patients do not have. Another option when the XO inhibitor treatment is inadequate (uric acid > 6 mg/dL) is to use daily zurampic. It is taken with the XO inhibitor. Pegloticase is a recombinant uricase enzyme, which converts uric acid to an inactive metabolite that can be easily excreted. Pegloticase is reserved for severe, refractory disease.

Prophylaxis for tumor lysis syndrome is given in high-risk patients receiving certain types of chemotherapy. If TLS occurs, treatment to lower uric acid is initiated, and the electrolyte levels are corrected. The usual prophylaxis and treatment medication is high-dose allopurinol. Another option is rasburicase (urate oxidase), which has a mechanism of action similar to pegloticase (converts uric acid to water-soluble allantoin).

Xanthine Oxidase Inhibitors, zurampic *(Lesinurad)*

DRUG	DOSING	SAFETY/SIDE EFFECTS/MONITORING
Allopurinol *(Zyloprim,* *Aloprim)* Due to the high rate of gout attacks when beginning ULT, colchicine at a dose of 0.6 mg once or twice daily or NSAIDs are used concurrently for the first 3 – 6 months.	Start at 100 mg daily, then slowly titrate up until uric acid is < 6 mg/dL (doses > 300 mg may be necessary and should be divided BID) Take after a meal (with food in stomach) to ↓ nausea	**WARNINGS** Hypersensitivity reactions can occur, including severe rash (SJS/TEN). Can test for HLA-B*5801 prior to use, esp in Koreans, Han Chinese or Thai. Hepatotoxicity, caution in liver impairment, bone marrow suppression. Do not use to treat asymptomatic hyperuricemia (high uric acid, no history gout). **SIDE EFFECTS** Rash, acute gout attacks, nausea, diarrhea, ↑ LFTs **MONITORING** UA level, with goal < 6 mg/dL, CBC, LFTs, renal function **NOTES** Higher doses used for tumor lysis syndrome (in chemotherapy).
Febuxostat *(Uloric)*	Start at 40 mg daily, ↑ to 80 mg if UA not < 6 mg/dL at 6 weeks	**CONTRAINDICATIONS** Do not use with didanosine, mercaptopurine, pegloticase (↑ toxicity) **WARNINGS** Hepatotoxicity, possible ↑ thromboembolic events Give with NSAID or colchicine (up to 6 months) to prevent gout flare **SIDE EFFECTS** Rash, nausea, ↑ LFTs, arthralgia **MONITORING** LFTs **NOTES** Tablet contains lactose. Expensive compared to allopurinol, but no dose reduction necessary in renal impairment and ↓ risk hypersensitivity.
Zurampic *(Lesinurad)* Use only with XOI if UA goals not reached with XOI alone	200 mg daily, in the morning, with (allopurinol or febuxostat); if XOI stopped, stop zurampic Do not start if CrCl < 30 mL/min, discontinue if CrCl < 45 mL/min	**CONTRAINDICATIONS** CrCl < 30 mL/min, ESRD, dialysis, kidney transplant **BOXED WARNING** Acute renal failure; more common if used alone; only use with XOI **SIDE EFFECTS** HA, ↑ SCr (mostly transient), renal failure (≤4%), nephrolithiasis (3%) **MONITORING** SCr, CrCl **NOTES** Take in the morning with XOI, food and water; must stay hydrated.

Chronic UA – Lowering Therapy Continued

Probenecid is a uricosuric and inhibits reabsorption of UA in kidneys.

DRUG	DOSING	SAFETY/SIDE EFFECTS/MONITORING

Probenecid (a uricosuric) inhibits reabsorption of uric acid in the kidneys, which ↑ uric acid excretion.

DRUG	DOSING	SAFETY/SIDE EFFECTS/MONITORING
Probenecid 2nd line agent	Start 250 mg BID, can increase to 2 g/day	**CONTRAINDICATIONS** Concomitant aspirin therapy, blood dyscrasias, uric acid kidney stones (nephrolithiasis), children < 2 years, initiation in acute gout attack **WARNINGS** ↓ effectiveness with < 30 mL/min (ACR guidelines: do not use < 50 mL/min) ↑ risk of hemolytic anemia in patients with G6PD deficiency **SIDE EFFECTS** Hypersensitivity reactions, hemolytic anemia **NOTES** Requires adequate renal function; not recommended as monotherapy in patients with CrCl < 50 mL/min; avoid use in patients with CrCl < 30 mL/min. Used to ↑ beta lactam levels; ↓ beta lactam renal excretion.
Colchicine-Probenecid	0.5/500 mg daily for 1 week, then BID (for starting probenecid, to reduce risk acute attack)	

Pegloticase is a pegylated form of uricase, an enzyme which converts uric acid to allantoin (an inactive and water soluble metabolite of uric acid); it does not block uric acid formation.

DRUG	DOSING	SAFETY/SIDE EFFECTS/MONITORING
Pegloticase (*Krystexxa*) – injection, costly, refractory gout cases only	8 mg IV every 2 weeks	**BOXED WARNING** Anaphylactic reactions; monitor, and premedicate with antihistamines and steroids. Risk is highest if uric acid is > 6 mg/dL. **CONTRAINDICATIONS** G6PD deficiency **WARNINGS** Acute gout flares can occur upon initiation; an NSAID or colchicine should be given 1 week prior to infusion; continue for at least 6 months. **SIDE EFFECTS** Antibody formation, gout flare, infusion reactions, nausea, bruising, urticaria, erythema, pruritus **NOTES** Do not use in combination with allopurinol (increased risk of anaphylaxis).

Chronic UA – Lowering Therapy Continued

DRUG	DOSING	SAFETY/SIDE EFFECTS/MONITORING
Rasburicase ***(Elitek)*** For tumor lysis syndrome; top hospital drug due to use in cancer treatment.	IV: 0.2 mg/kg daily, max 5 days	**BOXED WARNINGS** Anaphylaxis, hemolysis, methemoglobinemia, interference with uric acid measurements **CONTRAINDICATIONS** History of anaphylaxis or severe hypersensitivity to rasburicase, history of hemolytic reaction or methemoglobinemia associated with rasburicase, G6PD deficiency **WARNINGS** Patients at risk for tumor lysis syndrome should receive appropriate IV hydration as part of uric acid management **SIDE EFFECTS** Peripheral edema, headache, anxiety, rash, N/V abdominal pain, diarrhea or constipation (both 20%), mucositis, hypophosphatemia, hypovolemia, hyperbilirubinemia, ↑ ALT, ↑ antibodies, sepsis, pharyngolaryngeal pain **MONITORING** Uric acid, CBC

Allopurinol Drug Interactions

- Allopurinol ↑ the concentration of mercaptopurine, the active metabolite of azathioprine. Do not use either drug with allopurinol, or ↓ dose, and monitor for toxicity.
- Antacids ↓ allopurinol absorption.
- Avoid use with didanosine; allopurinol can ↑ didanosine levels.

Probenecid Drug Interactions

- Probenecid decreases the renal clearance of other medications taken concurrently, including aspirin (do not use salicylates concurrently), methotrexate, penicillins, cephalosporins and carbapenems.
- Probenecid is sometimes used with beta lactams to ↑ the concentration; this will ↑ adverse reactions. This is occasionally done with penicillin when treating neurosyphilis or other penicillin-treated infections.
- Probenecid decreases the efficacy of loop diuretics, but increases the loop's toxicity.

Allopurinol Counseling

- Take after a meal to reduce stomach upset (higher doses can be divided). Drink plenty of fluids.
- If you feel ill or get a rash, you should seek medical help quickly. The rash could become serious.

PRACTICE CASE

BK is a 62 y/o white male with hypertension. He presents to the clinic today with pain described as 10/10. He is trying to avoid putting weight on his right foot. Physical exam reveals a swollen, tender, enlarged big toe. His blood pressure has a daily range of 155-178/88-99 mmHg. The patient reports that he consumes low fat yogurt with berries or nuts for breakfast each day. He walks each night around the track at the neighborhood high school. He reports "weekend" alcohol use (3-4 beers on Saturday/ Sunday). No past or present history of tobacco use.

Allergies: NKDA

Medications:
Norvasc 10 mg PO daily
Zestril 10 mg PO daily
Chlorthalidone 25 mg PO daily
Aspirin EC 81 mg daily
Fish oil capsule with dinner
Coenzyme Q10 with dinner

Vitals:
Height: 5'11" Weight: 255 pounds
BP: 177/95 mmHg HR: 89 BPM RR: 16 BPM Temp: 98.8ΥF Pain: 10/10

Labs: Na (mEq/L) = 142 (135 - 145)
K (mEq/L) = 4.8 (3.5 - 5)
Cl (mEq/L) = 100 (95 - 103)
HCO_3 (mEq/L) = 28 (24 - 30)
BUN (mg/dL) = 22 (7 - 20)
SCr (mg/dL) = 1.4 (0.6 - 1.3)
Glucose (mg/dL) = 119 (100 - 125)
Ca (mg/dL) = 10.2 (8.5 - 10.5)
Mg (mEq/L) = 1.8 (1.3 - 2.1)
PO_4 (mg/dL) = 4.2 (2.3 - 4.7)

AST (IU/L) = 12 (8 - 48)
ALT (IU/L) = 14 (7 - 55)
Albumin (g/dL) = 4.8 (3.5 - 5)
Uric Acid (mg/dL) = 18.3 (3.5 - 7.2 male, 2 - 6.5 female)

April 1st: 62 y/o male with first episode of acute gout in right great toe. Provide therapy for gout and optimize therapy for uncontrolled HTN. Prescription written for *Dilacor XR* 120 mg daily.

Questions

1. Which of the following are risk factors for gout? (Select **ALL** that apply.)
   - *a.* Male sex
   - *b.* Hypertension
   - *c.* Weekend alcohol use
   - *d.* Hypertension
   - *e.* Dairy consumption (lowfat yogurt)

2. The physician is considering allopurinol to treat the acute attack. Choose the correct statement:
   - *a.* This is not appropriate therapy for an acute attack.
   - *b.* He should receive a starting dose of 50 mg daily.
   - *c.* He should receive a starting dose of 75 mg daily.
   - *d.* He should receive a starting dose of 100 mg daily.
   - *e.* He should receive a starting dose of 150 mg daily.

3. BK will receive a short-course of prednisone therapy, with taper, that will last less than 2 weeks. Which of the following side effects are possible and should be explained to BK?
   - *a.* Growth suppression
   - *b.* Insomnia/spaciness
   - *c.* Osteoporosis
   - *d.* Cataracts
   - *e.* Seizures

4. Choose the correct dosing regimen for colchicine for an acute gout attack:
   - *a.* 1.2 mg followed by 0.6 mg every 2 hours, not to exceed 6 tablets/24 hours
   - *b.* 1.2 mg followed by 0.6 mg every 2 hours, not to exceed 8 tablets/24 hours
   - *c.* 1.2 mg followed by 0.6 mg in 2-4 hours (total 1.8 mg)
   - *d.* 1.2 mg followed by 0.6 mg in 1 hours, then as-needed for 3 additional doses (total 3.6 mg)
   - *e.* 1.2 mg followed by 0.6 mg in 1 hours (total 1.8 mg)

Questions 5 – 8 do not apply to the above case.

5. A pharmacist receives a prescription for *Zyloprim*. Which medication is an acceptable alternative?
   - *a.* Probenecid
   - *b.* Colchicine
   - *c.* Allopurinol
   - *d.* Naproxen
   - *e.* Febuxostat

6. Which of the following are true regarding pegloticase? (Select **ALL** that apply.)
   - *a.* The brand name is *Krystexxa*
   - *b.* The recommended dose is 8 mg PO daily
   - *c.* It should not be given in combination with allopurinol
   - *d.* It is a first-line treatment for acute gout
   - *e.* Patients must be monitored for anaphylactic reactions when receiving this agent

7. Which of the following side effects are likely to occur with colchicine therapy?
   - *a.* Nausea, cramping, loose stools
   - *b.* Xerostomia, xerophthalmia
   - *c.* Mental confusion
   - *d.* Skeletal bone loss
   - *e.* Risk of severe rash/hypersensitivity reactions

8. A pharmacist has just attended an education program on the use of febuxostat. He wants to present the main points about this drug to his pharmacy colleagues. He should include the following points: (Select **ALL** that apply.)
   - *a.* Febuxostat works by increasing the renal excretion of uric acid.
   - *b.* Febuxostat appears to have lower risk of hypersensitivity reactions than allopurinol, including less of a risk of serious rash.
   - *c.* Febuxostat should only be taken with allopurinol.
   - *d.* The brand name of febuxostat is *Zyloprim*.
   - *e.* Febuxostat is a xanthine oxidase inhibitor.

Answers

1-a,b,c,d, 2-a, 3-b, 4-e, 5-c, 6-a,c,e, 7-a, 8-b,e

48

DYSLIPIDEMIA

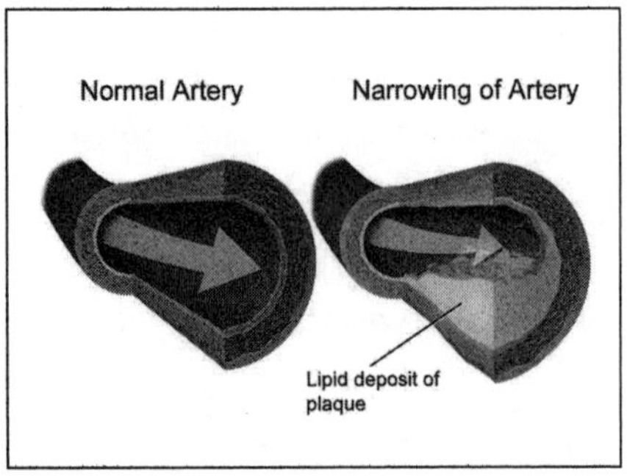

We gratefully acknowledge the assistance of Joel C. Marrs, PharmD, FCCP, FASHP, FNLA, BCPS-AQ Cardiology, BCACP, CLS, Associate Professor at the University of Colorado Skaggs School of Pharmacy and Pharmaceutical Sciences, in preparing this chapter.

BACKGROUND

Cholesterol is required for good health. It is a structural component of cells, is a precursor in hormone synthesis, and is used in the production of bile acids. The liver produces cholesterol, and uses it to make bile acids. The bile acids travel from the liver through the bile ducts (along with free cholesterol and waste products) and into the small intestine. Bile acids present in the small intestine are required for fat absorption. The acid in the intestine converts the bile acids into bile salts, which are continually recycled from the intestine and returned to the liver. This process involves the gut (enteric system) and the liver (hepatic), and is referred to as enterohepatic recycling.

The recycling system decreases the liver's requirement for new cholesterol. Cholesterol has two primary methods of exiting the body: either as free cholesterol or as bile acid. If the absorption of free cholesterol is blocked in the intestine (such as with ezetimibe) or the enterohepatic recirculation of bile salts is blocked (by bile acid sequestrants, such as colesevelam), the end result is a decrease in cholesterol.

GUIDELINES/REFERENCES

Stone NJ, Robinson JG, Lichtenstein AH, et al. 2013 ACC/AHA Guideline on the Treatment of Blood Cholesterol to Reduce Atherosclerotic Cardiovascular Risk in Adults: A Report of the American College of Cardiology/American Heart Association Task Force on Practice Guidelines. *Circulation.* 2014; 129:S1-S45.

Eckel RH, Jakicic JM, Ard JD, et al. 2013 AHA/ACC guideline on lifestyle management to reduce cardiovascular risk: a report of the American College of Cardiology/American Heart Association Task Force on Practice Guidelines. *Circulation.* 2014; 129 (25 Suppl 2):S76-99.

Jacobson TA, Ito MK, Maki KC, et al. National Lipid Association Recommendations for Patient-Centered Management of Dyslipidemia: Part 1 - Executive Summary. *J Clin Lipidol.* 2014; 8(5):473-488.

Goff DC Jr, Lloyd-Jones DM, Bennett G, et al. 2013 ACC/AHA Guideline on the Assessment of Cardiovascular Risk: A Report of the American College of Cardiology/American Heart Association Task Force on Practice Guidelines. JACC 2014;63:2935-59.

Additional guidelines included with the online course.

Cholesterol cannot dissolve in the blood; it is transported in lipoproteins (lipid + a protein carrier). Cholesterol is an umbrella term for different types of lipoproteins. The three major types of lipoproteins are low-density lipoproteins (LDL), high-density lipoproteins (HDL) and very-low density lipoproteins (VLDL), which serve as a carrier for triglycerides (TG). Total cholesterol (TC) encompasses all of the different lipoproteins.

Non-HDL is the difference between the TC and the HDL concentration: non-HDL = TC – HDL. Non-HDL includes atherogenic cholesterol such as LDL, intermediate density lipoproteins (IDL), VLDL, chylomicron remnants and lipoprotein(a). Additionally, apolipoprotein B (apoB) is both a high-risk marker and an indicator of the progression of atherosclerosis, which begins when an apoB particle becomes trapped within the vascular wall.

Elevations in non-HDL, LDL and TG place a patient at increased risk for atherogenic disease, including coronary, cerebrovascular and peripheral artery disease. With each of these conditions, fatty deposits accumulate in the arteries (atherosclerosis). Of note, non-HDL cholesterol has emerged as a stronger predictor of atherosclerotic cardiovascular disease (ASCVD) than LDL. It is helpful to identify areas of risk, but it is also important to realize that the process itself is generally systemic and occurs throughout the body. Elevated TGs can cause acute pancreatitis.

CLASSIFICATION OF DYSLIPIDEMIA

Abnormalities in specific lipoprotein levels are called dyslipidemias and can include ↑ TC, ↑ LDL, ↑ TGs and/or ↓ HDL. Dyslipidemias can be inherited, which are called primary or familial, but are most often secondary to poor diet, lifestyle, medications or other causes.

Primary (or Familial)

- Familial dyslipidemias are classified according to the Fredrickson classification. Familial hypercholesterolemias (FH) are genetic defects resulting in severe cholesterol elevations and increased risk of premature ASCVD. FHs include heterozygous familial hypercholesterolemia (HeFH) and homozygous familial hypercholesterolemia (HoFH), which is much more difficult to treat.

Secondary (or Acquired)

- Some common causes of secondary dyslipidemia are listed in the table below. Severe elevations (including LDL ≥ 190 mg/dL and TG ≥ 500 mg/dL) must be evaluated and treated appropriately. When dyslipidemia is due to diet and lifestyle, improving eating habits, obtaining regular exercise and, when required, using medications, can correct the dyslipidemia.

Secondary Causes of Dyslipidemia

SECONDARY CAUSE	↑ LDL	↑ TRIGLYCERIDES
Diet	Weight gain, saturated or *trans* fats, anorexia	Weight gain, very low-fat diets, high intake of refined carbohydrate, excessive alcohol intake
Drugs	Cyclosporine, tacrolimus, protease inhibitors, 2nd generation (atypical) antipsychotics, glucocorticoids, anabolic steroids, some progestins, diuretics, amiodarone, danazol, isotretinoin, thiazolidinediones, SGLT2 inhibitors, fibric acids (with ↑ TGs)	Cyclosporine, tacrolimus, protease inhibitors, atypical antipsychotics, glucocorticoids, oral estrogen, bile acid sequestrants, retinoids, anabolic steroids, sirolimus, raloxifene, tamoxifen, beta blockers, thiazides, alpha interferons, propofol
Diseases	Nephrotic syndrome, biliary obstruction	Nephrotic syndrome, chronic renal failure, lipodystrophies
Disorders and altered states of metabolism	Obesity, hypothyroidism, pregnancy, polycystic ovary syndrome	Obesity, hypothyroidism, pregnancy, diabetes (poorly controlled)

Cholesterol (Lipoprotein) Types and Normal Values

See table for normal ranges. Many clinicians recommend checking lipoprotein levels after a 9 – 12 hour fast. If it is not reported, LDL may need to be calculated using the Friedewald equation: LDL = TC – HDL – (TG/5). This formula is not used when the TGs are > 400 mg/dL.

If the patient is not fasting, the TG level can be falsely elevated resulting in a falsely low calculation of LDL using the above equation. Non-HDL and apoB do not require fasting for accurate assessment.

CLASSIFICATION OF CHOLESTEROL AND TG LEVELS (MG/DL)

NON-HDL*

< 130	Desirable
130-159	Above desirable
160-189	Borderline high
190-219	High
≥ 220	Very high

LDL

< 100	Desirable
100-129	Above desirable
130-159	Borderline high
160-189	High
≥ 190	Very high

HDL

< 40 (men)	Low
< 50 (women)	Low

Triglycerides

< 150	Normal
150-199	Borderline high
200-499	High
≥ 500	Very high†

HDL = high-density lipoprotein cholesterol, LDL = low-density lipoprotein cholesterol, non-HDL = non-high-density lipoprotein cholesterol

* *Non-HDL = total cholesterol minus HDL*

† *Severe hypertriglyceridemia is another term used for very high triglycerides in pharmaceutical product labeling.*

Natural Products

Red yeast rice is the product of yeast grown on rice that contains naturally occurring HMG-CoA reductase inhibitors, and is similar in efficacy to low-dose statins. The *Natural Medicines Database* recommends against the use of red yeast rice products. Some contain too little drug, some contain too much, and some contain contaminants that have caused renal damage. Plant stanols, sterols, fibrous foods (found in psyllium, barley, oat bran) and a specific type of artichoke extract are each effective in lowering LDL to various extents. OTC fish oils can be used to lower TGs. They can increase LDL in some patients. Garlic used to be recommended for this purpose but the effect is not significant. Fish oils and niacin are discussed later in this chapter. With any of these products, a benefit may have been observed with a specific formulation and dose, but may not be replicated with every product, due to a lack of required quality control for natural products. See the *Natural Medicines Database* for guidance.

NON-DRUG TREATMENT

Lifestyle modifications are an important part of management. These recommendations apply to adults with and without ASCVD and should be emphasized, monitored and reinforced. Consuming a diet rich in vegetables and fruits, choosing whole-grain, high-fiber foods, consuming fish, especially oily fish, and limiting intake of saturated fat, *trans* (partially hydrogenated) fat and cholesterol by choosing lean meats, non-meat alternatives and low-fat dairy products. The consumption of added sugars and salt should be minimized. The diet should be modified for the individual's calorie requirements, personal preferences and in consideration of other medical conditions. Specific targets include:

- Aim for 5 – 6% of calories from saturated fat; ↓ % of calories from *trans* fat.
- Engage in aerobic physical activity 3 – 4 times per week, lasting 40 minutes/session and involving moderate-to-vigorous intensity (↓ LDL 3 – 6 mg/dL).
- Maintain a healthy weight (BMI 18.5 – 24.9 kg/m^2).
- Avoid tobacco products, limit alcohol consumption.

TREATING DYSLIPIDEMIAS

There are two national organizations that have developed guidelines to address cholesterol management: the American College of Cardiology and the American Heart Association guidelines (ACC/AHA) and the National Lipid Association (NLA) guidelines. A primary difference involves a focus on statin use by risk (ACC/AHA) rather than treating to LDL target levels (NLA).

ACC/AHA GUIDELINES

The ACC/AHA national cholesterol treatment guidelines include significant changes from the previous cholesterol guidelines (NCEP ATP III), which had focused on treating LDL and non-HDL to target values. The current guideline identifies four key patient groups in which statin initiation with appropriate intensity (high, moderate or low) should be considered to obtain relative reductions in LDL. For example, a target could be a 50% reduction, rather than a specific LDL value. Non-statins are not recommended unless statins are not tolerated. The IMPROVE-IT study, published after the 2014 guideline, showed a further reduction in CV events in stable patients with a recent ACS when ezetimibe was added to a statin, compared to using a statin alone. This represented a change in thought processes, as previously, ezetimibe was not widely used due to a lack of demonstrated benefit. In 2016, the ACC published consensus recommendations, which were endorsed by the NLA, focused on the role of non-statin therapy, with specific recommendations for ezetimibe and PCSK9 inhibitors.

KEY POINT: ACC/AHA

The ACC/AHA guidelines state that there is no evidence to support continued use of specific LDL treatment targets. Statins (primarily), dosed at the appropriate intensity, are used in patients with ASCVD and patients at risk for ASCVD.

Identification of 4 Statin Benefit Groups

Patients who fall in any of the following four groups should be initiated on statin therapy:

1. Presence of clinical atherosclerotic cardiovascular disease (ASCVD), including coronary heart disease (ACS, S/P MI, stable or unstable angina, coronary or other arterial revascularization), stroke, TIA or peripheral arterial disease thought to be of atherosclerotic origin
2. Primary elevations of LDL ≥ 190 mg/dL
3. Diabetes and age 40 – 75 years with LDL between 70 – 189 mg/dL
4. Patients 40 – 75 years of age with LDL between 70 – 189 mg/dL and estimated 10-year ASCVD risk of ≥ 7.5% (using the global risk assessment tool)

Global Risk Assessment Tool

The global risk assessment tool is used to provide an estimate of an individual's risk of having a cardiovascular event (e.g., MI, stroke or death) during the next 10 years. This is called the 10-year ASCVD risk. When healthcare providers understand the risk level of a patient they are better prepared to determine whether they should prescribe risk-reducing treatments, including statins and antihypertensives. An elevated risk level can also motivate the patient to address modifiable risk factors. To calculate a patient's risk, the clinician inputs the patient's gender, age (20 – 79 years), race, TC, HDL, systolic blood pressure, whether antihypertensive treatment is used, the presence of

ADDITIONAL FACTORS* PER ACC/AHA GUIDELINES

If after quantitative risk assessment, a risk-based treatment decision is uncertain, additional factors may be considered to assist with decision making. These factors include:

- LDL ≥ 160 mg/dL or other evidence of genetic hyperlipidemia
- Family history of premature ASCVD with onset < 55 years in a first degree male relative or < 65 years in a first degree female relative
- High-sensitivity C-reactive protein ≥ 2 mg/L
- Coronary Artery Calcium score ≥ 300 Agatston units or ≥ 75 percentile for age, sex and ethnicity
- Ankle Brachial Index < 0.9

* *These factors support revising risk assessment upward*

diabetes and smoking status. A 10-year ASCVD risk of ≥ 7.5% is an indication to start statin therapy for primary prevention in individuals age 40 – 75 years. This risk assessment should be repeated every 4 – 6 years in those who are found to be at a low 10-year risk (< 7.5%). Other factors may be included to measure risk and those are found in the additional factors box. Note that the risk score is not used for patients who have clinical ASCVD, as all patients in this group should be started on a statin.

Determining Appropriate Statin Treatment Intensity Based on Patient Risk

PREVENTION LEVEL	STATIN TREATMENT
Secondary Prevention	
Clinical ASCVD ≤ 75 years	High-intensity*
Clinical ASCVD > 75 years	Moderate-intensity
Primary Prevention	
Primary elevation of LDL ≥ 190 mg/dL	High-intensity*
Diabetes and age 40-75 years with LDL between 70-189 mg/dL and estimated 10-year ASCVD risk ≥ 7.5%	High-intensity*
Ages 40-75 years with LDL between 70-189 mg/dL and estimated 10-year ASCVD risk ≥ 7.5%	Moderate-to-high intensity
Diabetes and 40-75 years with LDL between 70-189 mg/dL and estimated 10-year ASCVD risk < 7.5%	Moderate-intensity
Ages 40-75 years with LDL between 70-189 mg/dL with estimated 10-year ASCVD risk < 7.5%	Consider risk benefit

**Use moderate-intensity statin if not a candidate for high-intensity*

Statin Treatment Intensity Definitions and Selection Options

HIGH-INTENSITY	MODERATE-INTENSITY	LOW-INTENSITY
Daily dose ↓ LDL ≥ 50%	**Daily dose ↓ LDL 30% – 49%**	**Daily dose ↓ LDL < 30%**
Atorvastatin 40-80 mg daily	Atorvastatin 10-20 mg daily	Simvastatin 10 mg daily
Rosuvastatin 20-40 mg daily	Rosuvastatin 5-10 mg daily	Pravastatin 10-20 mg daily
	Simvastatin 20-40 mg daily	Lovastatin 20 mg daily
	Pravastatin 40-80 mg daily	Fluvastatin 20-40 mg daily
	Lovastatin 40 mg daily	Pitavastatin 1 mg daily
	Fluvastatin XL 80 mg daily	
	Fluvastatin 40 mg BID	
	Pitavastatin 2-4 mg daily	

NLA Expert Panel Recommendations

In the year following the ACC/AHA guideline, the NLA released part 1 of their cholesterol recommendations, which emphasize treating cholesterol to specific goal values. The focus was shifted from targeting LDL (such as had been done with ATP III), to primarily targeting non-HDL and LDL, but, like ATP III, it includes target values rather than percentage reductions. The NLA released part 2 of the recommendations in June 2015, which included an emphasis on active participation of the patient in both lifestyle management and in drug treatment. Part 2 includes specific advice for certain groups, such as advice based on race or gender. First, the patient's ASCVD risk is calculated, then lifestyle counseling is initiated, and statins, when indicated, are started. Non-statins are recommended only as add-on therapy in select patients, and only after the statin has been titrated to the maximally tolerated dose.

ACC Consensus Decision Pathway on Non-Statin Therapy

As previously mentioned, in 2016, the ACC released an expert consensus decision pathway, endorsed by the NLA, on the role of non-statin therapies for LDL cholesterol lowering in the management of ASCVD. This consensus decision pathway reviewed the four statin benefit groups and the major recommendations from the 2013 ACC/AHA guidelines. It reinforced recommendations related to intensity of statin therapy (i.e., high, moderate, low) and reviewed strategies for non-statin therapies to consider in the management of LDL related ASCVD risk. Lastly, they discussed factors to consider in the clinician-patient discussion around lipid lowering therapy. The document provides key recommendations for the use of ezetimibe and PCSK9 inhibitors as add-ons to statin therapy in high risk individuals with established ASCVD. The goal was to provide practical guidance for clinicians and patients regarding the use of non-statin therapies to further reduce ASCVD risk in situations not covered by the 2013 ACC/AHA guideline until such time as the scientific evidence expands and cardiovascular outcomes trials are completed with newer agents for ASCVD risk reduction.

DRUG TREATMENT

Statins are the drugs of choice in treating ↑ non-HDL and LDL. Although statins ↑ the risk of diabetes and myalgias (see box), they are still recommended given their reduction in cardiovascular disease and mortality.

If a patient is completely statin intolerant, it is reasonable to use other cholesterol-lowering drugs. Many of the cholesterol-lowering drugs can cause liver damage (niacin, fibrates, ezetimibe and potentially statins). Liver enzymes should be monitored and the drug stopped if the AST (10 – 40 units/L) or ALT (10 – 40 units/L) is > 3 times the upper limit of normal. Increases in liver enzymes in patients using statins are similar to that of the population not using statins; however, LFTs should be monitored at baseline and periodically thereafter.

In 2015, alirocumab *(Praluent)* and evolocumab *(Repatha)* were FDA approved for treating familial hypercholesterolemia or for patients with ASCVD who require additional ↓ in LDL. Both drugs are PCSK9 inhibitors which block the protein that binds the LDL receptors in the liver. This increases the amount of the receptors, which ↑ LDL degradation, and ↓ LDL by ~60%. These are monoclonal antibodies which must be given by SC injections, are costly, and at present lack long-term safety data. Trials evaluating the impact of PCSK9 inhibitors on the occurrence of cardiovascular events are ongoing; results are expected to be available in 2017.

STATINS & MUSCLE DAMAGE

TERMINOLOGY

Myopathy: muscle weakness +/- ↑ CPK

Myalgia: muscle soreness, tenderness

Myositis: muscle inflammation

Rhabdomyolysis: muscle symptoms + very high CPK > 10,000 + muscle protein in the urine (myoglobinuria), which leads to acute renal failure

SYMPTOMS

Most often occur within 6 weeks of starting tx but can occur after years of tx, and include myalgias, weakness, stiffness/cramps.

Often symmetrical (on both sides of the body) and in large adjacent muscle groups in the legs, back or arms.

REDUCE THE RISK

Check for drug interactions.

Do not use simvastatin 80 mg/day.

Do not use gemfibrozil + statin.

MANAGE MYALGIAS

First, hold statin if intolerable, check CPK, investigate other possible causes.

2-4 weeks: Re-challenge with same statin at same or ↓ dose.

Most patients who did not tolerate a statin will tolerate it when re-challenged, or will tolerate a different statin.

If myalgias return when the original statin is reinitiated, discontinue original statin. Once muscle symptoms resolve, use a low dose of a different statin.

If low dose of a different statin is tolerated, gradually ↑ dose.

Metreleptin *(Myalept)* is not discussed in the drug tables. This is a recombinant human leptin analog, used as an adjunct to diet, to treat leptin deficiency with lipodystrophy. The drug may be a breakthrough for some patients with leptin deficiency, but has safety issues, including the development of leptin antibodies and lymphoma risk. It is a REMS drug, with restricted use.

Statins

Statins inhibit the enzyme 3-hydroxy-3-methylglutaryl coenzyme A (HMG-CoA) reductase, which prevents the conversion of HMG-CoA to mevalonate. This is the rate-limiting step in cholesterol synthesis. Evidence supports the use of statin treatment to ↓ ASCVD risk, in those most likely to benefit (i.e., 4 statin benefit groups). It is important to recognize the statin doses (intensity) are necessary to provide patients the most benefit from these drugs.

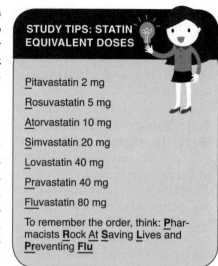

STUDY TIPS: STATIN EQUIVALENT DOSES

Pitavastatin 2 mg

Rosuvastatin 5 mg

Atorvastatin 10 mg

Simvastatin 20 mg

Lovastatin 40 mg

Pravastatin 40 mg

Fluvastatin 80 mg

To remember the order, think: **Ph**armacists **R**ock **A**t **S**aving **L**ives and **Pr**eventing **Flu**

DRUG	DOSING	SAFETY/SIDE EFFECTS/MONITORING
AtorvaSTATin *(Lipitor)* + amlodipine *(Caduet)* + ezetimibe *(Liptruzet)*	10-80 mg daily	**CONTRAINDICATIONS** Active liver disease (including any unexplained ↑ LFTs), pregnancy, breastfeeding; concurrent use of strong 3A4 inhibitors (simvastatin and lovastatin); concurrent use with cyclosporine (pitavastatin) **WARNINGS** Skeletal muscle effects (e.g., myopathy, rhabdomyolysis) – risk ↑ with higher concentrations, advanced age (≥ 65 years), CYP 3A4 inhibitors, niacin, uncontrolled hypothyroidism and renal impairment Diabetes, ↑ A1C and fasting blood glucose; benefits of statin therapy far outweigh the risk of hyperglycemia Hepatotoxicity, ↑ LFTs (rare) Immune-mediated necrotizing myopathy (IMNM) can occur in rare cases Proteinuria, hematuria – usually transient (rosuvastatin) **SIDE EFFECTS** Myalgias, arthralgias, myopathy, diarrhea, cognitive impairment **MONITORING** LFTs at baseline and as clinically indicated thereafter; obtain a lipid panel 4-12 weeks after initiation or up titration of therapy to assess for medication adherence; then every 3-12 months thereafter **NOTES** Safety risk – see Pregnancy chapter. Can take *Crestor, Lipitor, Livalo, Lescol XL* and *Pravachol* at any time of day. When CrCl < 30 mL/min, use lower starting doses (lovastatin, simvastatin, rosuvastatin). When CrCl < 60 mL/min, use lower starting dose of pitavastatin. Rosuvastatin exposures are 2x higher in Asian patients – consider 5 mg starting dose. **Lipid Effects** ↓ LDL ~20-55%, ↑ HDL ~5-15%, ↓ TG ~10-30%
Fluvastatin *(Lescol, Lescol XL)*	20-80 mg *Lescol* is taken in the evening *Lescol XL* is taken daily	
Lovastatin *(Mevacor, Altoprev)*	20-80 mg *Mevacor* (immediate release) is taken with evening meal *Altoprev* (extended release) is taken at bedtime	
Pitavastatin *(Livalo)*	1-4 mg daily	
Pravastatin *(Pravachol)*	10-80 mg daily	
Rosuvastatin *(Crestor)*	5-40 mg daily	
Simvastatin *(Zocor)* Tablet, suspension **+ ezetimibe *(Vytorin)***	10-40 mg daily in the evening	

Statin Drug Interactions

All Statins

- ↑ risk of myopathies when used with fibrates (avoid statins with gemfibrozil) and niacin products containing ≥ 1 gram.
- Myopathy, including rhabdomyolysis, has been reported when coadministered with colchicine.

DRUG	SIGNIFICANT DRUG INTERACTIONS
Simvastatin 3A4 substrate (major), inhibits 2C8 (weak), 2C9 (weak)	Contraindicated with strong 3A4 inhibitors (see box below) plus conivaptan, tacrolimus, gemfibrozil Max 10 mg/day – verapamil, diltiazem, dronedarone Max 20 mg/day – amiodarone, amlodipine, lomitapide, ranolazine Max 40 mg/day – ticagrelor Warfarin – monitor PT/INR after initiation/dose change
Lovastatin 3A4 substrate (major), P-gp substrate, inhibits 2C9 (weak)	Contraindicated with strong 3A4 inhibitors (see box below) plus conivaptan, tacrolimus, gemfibrozil Max 20 mg/day – danazol, diltiazem, dronedarone, verapamil, amlodipine Max 40 mg/day – amiodarone, ticagrelor
Atorvastatin 3A4 substrate (major), P-gp substrate	Avoid – cyclosporine, gemfibrozil, tipranavir + ritonavir Max 20 mg/day – clarithromycin, itraconazole, darunavir + ritonavir, fosamprenavir ± ritonavir, saquinavir + ritonavir Max 40 mg/day – nelfinavir Caution (use lowest dose) with lopinavir + ritonavir Levels of norethindrone and ethinyl estradiol can increase
Rosuvastatin 3A4 and 2C9 substrate (minor), BCRP substrate	Max 5 mg/day – cyclosporine Max 10 mg/day – gemfibrozil, atazanavir + ritonavir, lopinavir + ritonavir, simeprevir Warfarin – can ↑ INR
Pravastatin 3A4 substrate (minor), P-gp substrate, inhibits 2C9 (weak)	Max 20 mg/day – cyclosporine Max 40 mg/day – clarithromycin
Fluvastatin 2C9, 2D6, 3A4 substrate (all minor); inhibits 1A2 (weak), 2C8 (weak), 2C9 (moderate)	Max 40 mg/day – cyclosporine, fluconazole ↑ levels of glyburide, phenytoin Warfarin – can ↑ INR
Pitavastatin Substrate UGT1A3, UGT2B7	Cyclosporine contraindicated Max 1 mg/day – erythromycin Max 2 mg/day – rifampin Warfarin – monitor PT/INR after dose change/initiation

STRONG 3A4 INHIBITORS – AVOID WITH SIMVASTATIN AND LOVASTATIN			
Itraconazole Ketoconazole Posaconazole Voriconazole	Erythromycin Clarithromycin HIV protease inhibitors	Cobicistat-containing regimens Nefazodone Cyclosporine	Danazol (with simvastatin) Grapefruit juice

Ezetimibe

Inhibits absorption of cholesterol at the brush border of the small intestine. Recently (early 2015), the IMPROVE-IT study showed that the addition of ezetimibe to moderate-intensity statin therapy in stable patients with recent ACS, and who had LDL cholesterol levels within guideline recommendations, further lowered the risk of cardiovascular events.

DRUG	DOSING	SAFETY/SIDE EFFECTS/MONITORING
Ezetimibe *(Zetia)* **+ simvastatin *(Vytorin)*** + atorvastatin *(Liptruzet)*	10 mg daily If CrCl < 60 mL/min, do not exceed simvastatin 20 mg/day when using combination product *(Vytorin)*	**CONTRAINDICATIONS** Statin contraindications apply when used with a statin: active liver disease (including any unexplained ↑ in LFTs), pregnancy/breastfeeding **WARNINGS** Avoid use in moderate-or-severe hepatic impairment Skeletal muscle effects (e.g., myopathy, including risk of rhabdomyolysis), risk ↑ when combined with a statin **SIDE EFFECTS** Diarrhea, URTIs, arthralgias, myalgias, pain in extremities, sinusitis **MONITORING** When used with a statin and/or fibrate, obtain LFTs at baseline and as clinically indicated thereafter **NOTES** **Lipid effects with ezetimibe monotherapy** ↓ LDL 18-23%, ↑ HDL 1-3%, ↓ TG 5-10%

Ezetimibe Drug Interactions

- When ezetimibe and cyclosporine are given together, the concentration of both can ↑; monitor levels of cyclosporine.
- Concomitant bile acid sequestrants ↓ ezetimibe; give ezetimibe 2 hours before or 4 hours after bile acid sequestrants.
- Can ↑ risk of cholelithiasis when used with fenofibrate; avoid use with gemfibrozil.
- If using warfarin, monitor INR/bleeding after ezetimibe initiation.

Bile Acid Sequestrants/Bile Acid Binding Resins

Binds bile acids in the intestine, forming a complex that is excreted in the feces. This non-systemic action results in a partial removal of the bile acids from the enterohepatic circulation, preventing their reabsorption.

DRUG	DOSING	SAFETY/SIDE EFFECTS/MONITORING
Cholestyramine *(Questran, Questran Light, Prevalite)* Also approved for pruritus due to increased levels of bile acids, and regression of arteriosclerosis 4 gram powder packet	Initial: 4 grams 1-2x/day Maintenance: 8-16 grams/day divided BID with meals (max 24 grams/day)	**CONTRAINDICATIONS** Cholestyramine – complete biliary obstruction Colesevelam – bowel obstruction, TG > 500 mg/dL, history of hypertriglyceridemia-induced pancreatitis **WARNINGS** Cholestyramine "light" formulations and colesevelam granules contain phenylalanine and should not be used in patients with PKU ↑ bleeding tendency due to vitamin K deficiency **SIDE EFFECTS** Constipation (may need dose reduction or laxative), dyspepsia, nausea, abdominal pain, cramping, gas, bloating, ↑ TGs, esophageal obstruction, ↑ LFTs **NOTES** ACC/AHA guidelines do not recommend using these agents when TGs are ≥ 300 mg/dL. Cholestyramine packet – Mix powder with 2-6 oz. water or non-carbonated liquid. Sipping or holding the resin suspension in the mouth for prolonged periods may lead to changes in the surface of the teeth resulting in discoloration, erosion of enamel or decay; good oral hygiene should be maintained. Colesevelam packet – Empty 1 packet into a glass; add 4-8 oz. of water, fruit juice, or a diet soft drink and mix well. Colestipol packet - Empty 1 packet into at least 3 oz. of liquid and stir until completely mixed. Colesevelam may be considered as an option in a pregnant patient. **Lipid Effects** ↓ LDL ~10-30%, ↑ HDL ~3-5%, no change or ↑ TG (~5%)
Colesevelam *(Welchol)* 625 mg tablet, 3.75 gram granule packet Also approved to improve glycemic control in Type 2 DM (↓ A1C ~ 0.5%)	Tablets/granules: 3.75 grams daily or in divided doses with a meal and liquid	
Colestipol *(Colestid)* 1 gram tablet, 5 gram packet and granules	Tablets: 2 grams daily or BID (max 16 grams/day) Packet and Granules: 5 grams daily or BID (max 30 grams/day)	

Bile Acid Sequestrants Drug Interactions

- Colesevelam has less drug interactions than the other 2 bile acid sequestrants and is more commonly used. For cholestyramine or colestipol, take all other drugs at least 1 – 4 hours before or 4 – 6 hours after the bile acid sequestrants.
- The following medications should be taken 4 hours prior to colesevelam: cyclosporine, glimepiride, glipizide, glyburide, levothyroxine, olmesartan, phenytoin, and oral contraceptives containing ethinyl estradiol and norethindrone. Consider separation with other drugs as well. Colesevelam ↑ levels of metformin ER.
- With warfarin, monitor INR frequently during initiation and after dose change.
- Bile acid sequestrants may ↓ absorption of fat-soluble vitamins (A, D, E, K), folate and iron. Separate administration times with concurrent multivitamin use as noted above.

Fibrates

Fibrates are peroxisome proliferator receptor alpha (PPARα) activators, which upregulate the expression of apolipoprotein C2 (apoC-II) and apolipoprotein A1 (apoA-I). ApoC-II ↑ lipoprotein lipase activity leading to ↑ catabolism of VLDL particles. This will ↓ TG significantly, but in the setting of high TG (increased VLDL particles) fibrate therapy may lead to an ↑ LDL particles and subsequently an ↑ LDL cholesterol. The ↓ TG may lead to an ↑ in HDL cholesterol. Also ↑ apoA-1 will lead to ↑ HDL since apoA-I is the building block of HDL particles. The ACCORD Lipid Study showed no significant difference in experiencing a major cardiac event between patients treated with fenofibrate plus simvastatin compared with simvastatin alone.

DRUG	DOSING	SAFETY/SIDE EFFECTS/MONITORING
Fenofibrate, Fenofibric Acid *(Antara, Fenoglide, Fibricor, Lipofen, Lofibra, TriCor, Triglide, Trilipix,* generics)	*Antara* (micronized capsule): 30-90 mg daily Fenofibrate (micronized): 43-130 mg daily *Antara*, micronized (brand) and fenofibrate, micronized (generic) have slightly different dosing regimens for treatment of hypertriglyceridemia *Fenoglide:* 40-120 mg daily with meals *Fibricor:* 35-105 mg daily *Lofibra* (micronized capsule): 67-200 mg daily with meals *Lofibra* (tablet): 54-160 mg daily *Lipofen:* 50-150 mg daily with meals *TriCor:* 48-145 mg daily *Triglide:* 160 mg daily *Trilipix:* 45-135 mg daily	**CONTRAINDICATIONS** Severe liver disease including primary biliary cirrhosis Severe renal disease (CrCl < 30 mL/min) Gallbladder disease Nursing mothers (fenofibrate derivatives only) Concurrent use with repaglinide (gemfibrozil only) **WARNINGS** Myopathy, ↑ risk when co-administered with a statin particularly in the elderly, diabetes, renal failure, or hypothyroidism Cholelithiasis Reversible ↑ SCr (> 2 mg/dL); clinical significance unknown **SIDE EFFECTS** ↑ LFTs (dose-related), abdominal pain, ↑ CPK, dyspepsia, URTIs **MONITORING** LFTs, renal function **NOTES** Reduce dose if CrCl 30-80 mL/min (fenofibrates) **Lipid Effects** ↓ TGs ~20-50%, ↑ HDL ~15%, ↓ LDL ~5-20% (but can ↑ LDL when TG are high)
Gemfibrozil *(Lopid)*	600 mg BID, 30 minutes before breakfast and dinner	

Fibrate Drug Interactions

- Fibrates (especially gemfibrozil) can ↑ the risk of myopathies and rhabdomyolysis. Gemfibrozil should not be given concurrently with ezetimibe, statins or tizanidine.
- Fibrates may ↑ cholesterol excretion into the bile, leading to cholelithiasis.
- Colchicine can ↑ the risk of myopathy when coadministered with fenofibrate.
- Gemfibrozil is contraindicated with repaglinide as it may ↑ hypoglycemic effects.
- Fibrates may increase the effects of sulfonylureas and warfarin.

Niacin

Decreases the rate of hepatic synthesis of VLDL (↓ TGs) and LDL; may also ↑ rate of chylomicron TG removal from plasma. Alters the binding of HDL particles to scavenger receptor B-1 in the liver, which removes the cholesterol inside, but does not take up the HDL particle which leaves it free to return to the circulation for reverse cholesterol transport. Niacin is also known as nicotinic acid or vitamin B3, although doses for cholesterol reduction are much higher than doses found in multivitamin products.

DRUG	DOSING	SAFETY/SIDE EFFECTS/MONITORING
Immediate-release (crystalline) niacin *(Niacor)* – OTC	100 mg TID Can ↑ every 4-7 days to max dose of 3 grams daily in 2-3 divided doses	**CONTRAINDICATIONS** Active liver disease, active PUD, arterial bleeding **WARNINGS** Use with caution in patients with unstable angina or in the acute phase of an MI Rhabdomyolysis with niacin doses ≥ 1 gram/day combined with statins Hepatotoxicity **SIDE EFFECTS** Flushing, pruritus (itching), N/V/D, hyperglycemia, hyperuricemia (or gout), cough, orthostatic hypotension, hypophosphatemia, ↓ platelets **MONITORING** Check LFTs at the start (baseline), every 6 to 12 weeks for the first year, and then ~ every 6-months; blood glucose (if have diabetes); uric acid (if have gout); INR (if on warfarin), lipid profile **NOTES** Immediate-release niacin has poor tolerability due to flushing/itching. Controlled- and sustained-release forms (CR and SR) have less (but still significant) flushing but more hepatotoxicity. The best clinical choice is extended-release *Niaspan*, with less flushing and less hepatotoxicity – but it is the most expensive. To reduce flushing: take aspirin 325 mg (or ibuprofen 200 mg) 30-60 minutes before the dose. Take with food, but avoid spicy food and hot beverages (which can worsen flushing). Formulations of niacin (IR vs ER) are not interchangeable. Flush-free niacins (inositol hexaniacinate or hexanicotinate), niacinamide or nicotinamide are not effective. **Lipid Effects** ↓ LDL 5-25%, ↑ HDL 15-35%, ↓ TG 20-50%
Extended-Release Niacin *(Niaspan)* 500, 750, 1,000 mg	500 mg QHS x 4 weeks Can ↑ weekly to a max dose of 2 grams daily	
Controlled- or Sustained-Release Niacin *(Slo-Niacin,* OTC) 250, 500, 750 mg	250-750 mg daily	

Niacin Drug Interactions

- Monitor for other concurrent drugs that are potentially hepatotoxic.
- Take niacin 4 – 6 hours after bile acid sequestrants.

Fish Oils

The mechanism is not completely understood; may reduce hepatic synthesis of TGs. These are indicated as an adjunct to diet in patients with TGs ≥ 500 mg/dL. Also known as omega-3 fatty acids.

DRUG	DOSING	SAFETY/SIDE EFFECTS/MONITORING
Omega-3 Acid Ethyl Esters *(Lovaza)* 1 gram capsule contains 465 mg eicosapentaenoic (EPA) acid and 375 mg docosahexaenoic acid (DHA)	4 capsules daily or 2 capsules BID	**WARNINGS** Use with caution in patients with known hypersensitivity to fish and/or shellfish. *Lovaza* and *Epanova* can ↑ levels of LDL; monitor. Monitor LFTs (in patients with hepatic impairment) and LDL periodically during therapy There is a possible association between *Lovaza* and more frequent recurrences of symptomatic atrial fibrillation or flutter in patients with paroxysmal or persistent atrial fibrillation, particularly within the first months of initiating therapy. **SIDE EFFECTS** Eructation (burping), dyspepsia, taste perversions *(Lovaza, Epanova)*, arthralgias *(Vascepa)* **NOTES** There are many OTC omega-3 fatty acid products marketed as dietary supplements. Only prescription medications *Epanova, Lovaza, Omtryg* and *Vascepa* are FDA approved for TG lowering, in addition to diet, when TG ≥ 500 mg/dL. Stop prior to elective surgeries due to increased risk of bleeding. **Lipid Effects** ↓ TGs up to 45%, ↑ HDL ~9% Can ↑ LDL (up to 44% with *Lovaza*; 25% with *Omtryg*, and 15% with *Epanova*). No ↑ seen with *Vascepa*.
Icosapent ethyl *(Vascepa)* contains 0.5 or 1 gram of icosapent ethyl, an ethyl ester of omega-3 fatty acid EPA	0.5 gram capsules- 4 BID with food or 1 gram capsules- 2 BID with food	
Omega-3-carboxylic acids *(Epanova)* 1 gram capsule contains omega-3-carboxylic acids with 850 mg of polyunsaturated fatty acids (mostly EPA + DHA)	2-4 capsules daily	
Omega-3-acid ethyl esters A *(Omtryg)* 1.2 gram capsule contains 465 mg EPA and 375 mg DHA	4 capsules daily or 2 capsules BID with meals	

Fish Oil Drug Interactions

- Omega-3-fatty acids may prolong bleeding time. Monitor INR if patients are taking warfarin at dose initiation or dose change. Caution with other medications that can ↑ bleeding risk.

Proprotein Convertase Subtilisin Kexin Type 9 Inhibitors

Alirocumab and evolocumab are human monoclonal antibodies that bind to proprotein convertase subtilisin kexin type 9 (PCSK9). PCSK9 binds to the LDL receptors on hepatocyte surfaces to promote LDLR degradation. LDLR is the primary receptor that clears circulating LDL; therefore, the decrease in LDLR levels by PCSK9 results in higher blood levels of LDL. By inhibiting the binding of PCSK9 to LDLR, these agents increase the number of LDLRs available to clear LDL, thereby lowering LDL levels. Both medications are indicated for heterozygous familial hypercholesterolemia (HeFH) or ASCVD as an adjunct to diet and maximally tolerated statin therapy (or other therapies in HeFH), when additional LDL lowering is required. Evolocumab is also indicated as an adjunct in homozygous familial hypercholesterolemia (HoFH).

<table>
<tr><th>DRUG</th><th>DOSING</th><th>SAFETY/SIDE EFFECTS/MONITORING</th></tr>
<tr><td>Alirocumab
(Praluent)
75 mg/mL, 150 mg/mL prefilled syringes or pen-injector</td><td>HeFH or ASCVD
75-150 mg SC once every 2 weeks</td><td rowspan="2">WARNING
Allergic reactions

SIDE EFFECTS
Nasopharyngitis, injection site reactions, influenza; URTIs, UTI, back pain (evolocumab), ↑ LFTs (alirocumab)

MONITORING
LDL-C at baseline and at 4-8 weeks to assess response

NOTES
Special storage and handling required (see Patient Counseling)
Long-term cardiovascular outcome data is lacking (anticipated in 2017)
Expensive (~$14,000/yr)

Lipid Effects
↓ LDL ~60%, ↓ non-HDL ~35%, ↓ apoB ~50%, ↓ TC ~36%</td></tr>
<tr><td>Evolocumab
(Repatha, Repatha SureClick, Pushtronex)
140 mg/mL prefilled syringe or autoinjector
420mg/3.5ml prefilled cartridge</td><td>HeFH or ASCVD
140 mg SC once every 2 weeks or 420 mg monthly

HoFH
420 mg SC once monthly
The 420 mg dose is given as three140 mg injections consecutively within 30 minutes or as a 420 mg single injection.</td></tr>
</table>

Lomitapide

Lomitapide binds to and inhibits microsomal triglyceride transfer protein (MTP) in the endoplasmic reticulum. MTP inhibition prevents the assembly of apoB containing lipoproteins in enterocytes and hepatocytes, resulting in reduced production of chylomicrons and VLDL, and subsequently reduced plasma LDL concentrations.

DRUG	DOSING	SAFETY/SIDE EFFECTS/MONITORING
Lomitapide *(Juxtapid)* Capsule Due to the risk of hepatotoxicity, this agent is only available through a *Juxtapid* Risk Evaluation and Mitigation Strategy (REMS) program.	5-60 mg daily Initiate at 5 mg daily; if tolerated, increase after 2 weeks to 10 mg daily. Double the dose at 4 week intervals to a max of 60 mg daily. Mild hepatic impairment or ESRD: dosage adjustment required Take whole, with water, but without food, at least two hours after the evening meal	**BOXED WARNING** Hepatotoxicity (↑ LFTs, steatosis). **CONTRAINDICATIONS** Pregnancy; concomitant use with moderate or strong CYP 3A4 inhibitors; moderate or severe hepatic impairment; active liver disease, including unexplained persistent ↑ LFTs **WARNINGS** Diarrhea and vomiting occur commonly and can affect absorption of other oral medications Embryo-fetal toxicity **SIDE EFFECTS** N/V/D, dyspepsia, abdominal pain, constipation, flatulence, ↑ LFTs, chest pain, back pain, fatigue, weight loss, influenza, nasopharyngitis **MONITORING** LFTs (including total bilirubin) and pregnancy test in females of reproductive potential at baseline; measure LFTs prior to any increase in dose or monthly (whichever occurs first) during the first year, and then every 3 months and prior to dosage increases **NOTES** Safety issue – see Pregnancy chapter MedGuide required Expensive: ~ $440,000/yr

Lomitapide Drug Interactions

- Strong and moderate CYP 3A4 inhibitors are contraindicated with lomitapide. Refer to the Drug Interactions chapter for a complete list of moderate and strong 3A4 inhibitors.
- If using weak 3A4 inhibitors, do not exceed 30 mg/day of lomitapide. See Drug Interactions chapter.
- Warfarin: ↑ INR; monitor after dose initiation or dose change.
- Simvastatin, lovastatin: concomitant use may increase risk of myopathy. Do not exceed simvastatin 20 mg/day (may use 40 mg/day if patients have previously tolerated simvastatin 80 mg/day for 12 months or more without evidence of muscle toxicity). Lovastatin dose should also be reduced when starting lomitapide.
- Lomitapide is an inhibitor of P-glycoprotein (P-gp), which may increase concentration of drugs that are P-gp substrates (see Drug Interactions chapter). Dose reduction of P-gp substrates should be considered when used.
- Monitor for other drugs that are potentially hepatotoxic. This includes isotretinoin, amiodarone, high dose acetaminophen, methotrexate, tetracyclines and tamoxifen.
- Lomitapide reduces absorption of fat soluble vitamins and fatty acids. Supplementation is required.

Mipomersen

Mipomersen is an oligonucleotide inhibitor of apoB-100 synthesis. ApoB is the main component of LDL and VLDL, which is the precursor to LDL.

DRUG	DOSING	SAFETY/SIDE EFFECTS/MONITORING
Mipomersen *(Kynamro)* Prefilled syringe Due to the risk of hepatoxicity, this agent is only available through a *Kynamro* REMS program.	200 mg SC once weekly Maximal LDL reduction seen after ~ 6 months	**BOXED WARNING** Hepatotoxicity (↑ LFTs, steatosis). **CONTRAINDICATIONS** Active liver disease (including unexplained ↑ LFTs), moderate or severe hepatic impairment **WARNINGS** Injection site reactions and flu-like symptoms **SIDE EFFECTS** Nausea, headache, ↑ ALT, antibody formation, fatigue **MONITORING** LFTs (including total bilirubin), alkaline phosphatase at baseline; then monthly for the first year of treatment, then every 3 months thereafter; lipids every 3 months for the first year **NOTES** Expensive: ~ 433,000/yr MedGuide required

Mipomersen Drug Interactions

- Monitor for other drugs that are potentially hepatotoxic. This includes isotretinoin, amiodarone, high dose acetaminophen, methotrexate, tetracyclines, and tamoxifen.

PATIENT COUNSELING

All Cholesterol Medications

- For all cholesterol medicines: your healthcare provider should recommend lifestyle changes including a heart healthy eating habits and exercise.

Statins

- Contact your healthcare provider right away if you have muscle weakness, tenderness, aching, cramps, stiffness or pain that happens without a good reason, especially if you also have a fever or feel more tired than usual. These may be symptoms of muscle damage.
- Contact your healthcare provider right away if you are passing brown or dark-colored urine, have pale stools, feel more tired than usual or if your skin and/or whites of your eyes become yellow. These may be symptoms of liver damage.
- Take *Zocor* and *Lescol* in the evening, *Mevacor* with the evening meal, and *Altoprev* at bedtime. All other statins may be taken at any time of day.
- Grapefruit and grapefruit juice may interact with this medication. This could lead to higher amounts of the drug in your body. Do not consume grapefruit products without discussing with your health-care provider (for lovastatin, simvastatin, atorvastatin).
- Do not use if pregnant or nursing or if you think you may be pregnant. This drug may harm your unborn baby. If you become pregnant, stop statin therapy and call your healthcare provider right away.

Ezetimibe

- Contact your healthcare provider right away if you are passing brown or dark-colored urine, have pale stools, feel more tired than usual or if your skin and/or whites of your eyes become yellow. These may be symptoms of liver damage.
- Contact your healthcare provider right away if you have muscle weakness, tenderness, aching, cramps, stiffness or pain that happens without a good reason, especially if you also have a fever or feel more tired than usual. These may be symptoms of muscle damage.
- Take this medication once daily, with or without food.

Fish Oil

- *Lovaza* and *Omtryg* can be taken once daily, or split BID. *Epanova* is taken once daily.
- Take *Omtryg* and *Vascepa* with food. Take *Epanova* and *Lovaza* with or without food.
- Take whole; do not break, crush, dissolve or chew.
- This medication does not usually cause side effects, but can cause indigestion (stomach upset), burping or abnormal sense of taste *(Lovaza)* or joint pain *(Vascepa)*.

Niacin

- *Niaspan*: take at bedtime after a low-fat snack. Other niacins: take with food.
- Do not crush or chew long-acting formulations.
- Contact your healthcare provider right away if you are passing brown or dark-colored urine, feel more tired than usual or if your skin and/or whites of your eyes become yellow. These may be symptoms of liver damage.
- Flushing (warmth, redness, itching and/or tingling of the skin) is a common side effect that may subside after several weeks of consistent use. Taking 325 mg of aspirin (or 200 mg of ibuprofen) 30 – 60 minutes before the dose (for a few weeks) may help to ↓ flushing. With *Niaspan*, flushing will occur mostly at night; use caution if awakened, due to possible dizziness.
- Avoid drinking alcohol or hot beverages or eating spicy foods around the time of taking this medicine to help reduce flushing.
- If you have diabetes, check your blood sugar when starting this medication because there may be a mild increase.

Bile Acid Sequestrant

- See notes section in drug table for instructions regarding food/fluid intake for specific agents.
- Take this medication at mealtimes with plenty of water or other liquid. Never take dry.
- This medication can cause constipation, your pharmacist can recommend a laxative (senna) or stool softener (docusate). Drink plenty of water and eat food with fiber such as fruits, vegetables and grains.
- Separate the dose of this medication from multivitamins, due to ↓ absorption of vitamins A, D, E and K (mostly K), folate and iron. You may need to take a multivitamin (especially women and children) while taking this medication.

Fibrate

- *Antara, Fibricor, TriCor, Triglide* and *Trilipix*: take once daily, with or without food.
- *Fenoglide, Lofibra* (micronized capsules) and *Lipofen*: Take once daily, with food.
- *Lopid*: Take twice daily, 30 minutes before breakfast and dinner.
- Do not crush or chew.
- Contact your healthcare provider if you experience muscle aches.
- Contact your healthcare provider right away if you experience abdominal pain, nausea or vomiting. These may be signs of inflammation of the gallbladder or pancreas.
- Contact your healthcare provider right away if you are passing brown or dark-colored urine, feel more tired than usual or if your skin and/or whites of your eyes become yellow. These may be signs of liver damage.

PCSK9 Inhibitors

- The most common side effects include runny nose, sore throat, symptoms of the common cold or flu, back pain, and redness, pain, or bruising at the injection site.
- This medication may cause an allergic reaction. Seek emergency medical care right away if you develop symptoms of rash, redness, severe itching, a swollen face or trouble breathing.
- Prior to administration, allow prefilled pen/syringe to warm to room temperature (30 to 45 minutes) and inspect visually for particulate matter and discoloration.
- Do not freeze, expose to extreme heat or shake.
- Rotate the injection sites. Do not inject into areas that are injured, tender, bruised, red, firm or hot. Avoid scars, visible veins or stretch marks.
- If you miss a dose, inject the missed dose as soon as you remember, within 7 days of your missed dose. Then, take the next dose 2 weeks from the missed dose. If the missed dose is not given within 7 days, skip the dose and wait until the next scheduled dose.

Alirocumab

- Administer by subcutaneous injection into the thigh, abdomen or upper arm using a single-dose prefilled pen/syringe. It may take up to 20 seconds to inject all contents of the pen.
- Store in the refrigerator in the outer carton in order to protect from light. This drug should be used as soon as possible after it has warmed up (it should not be out of the refrigerator for > 24 hours).

Evolocumab

- Given as an injection under the skin (subcutaneously), every 2 weeks or 1 time each month.
- Available as a single-use (1 time) prefilled autoinjector or as a single-use prefilled syringe.
- Store in the refrigerator. Can be kept at room temperature (up to 77°F) in the original carton; it must be used within 30 days if removed from refrigerator.
- If your healthcare provider prescribes the monthly dose, you will give yourself 3 separate injections in a row, using a different syringe or autoinjector for each injection. Give all of these injections within 30 minutes.
- Or you can give the once monthly injection as one injection using the *Pushtronex* system, which is available as an on-body infusor with a cartridge. Do not inject together with other medications at the same injection site.

PRACTICE CASE

PATIENT PROFILE

Patient Name DA

Address 1882 Peekaborn

Age 57 **Sex** Male **Race** White **Height** 5'11" **Weight** 246 lbs

Allergies NKDA

DIAGNOSES

Coronary Heart Disease, stent placement 7/16

Dyslipidemia

Hypertension

Type 2 Diabetes

MEDICATIONS

Date	No.	Prescriber	Drug & Strength	Quantity	Sig	Refills
5/15	77328	Gallagher	*Actos* 45 mg	#30	1 PO daily	2
5/15	73768	Gallagher	Metformin 1000 mg	#60	1 PO BID	2
5/15	73554	Gallagher	Lisinopril-HCT 20-25 mg	#30	1 PO daily	2
			Fish oils 1000 mg cap		1 PO BID	
			Aspirin 81 mg EC		1 PO daily	
			Multivitamin		1 PO daily	

LAB/DIAGNOSTIC TESTS

Test	Normal Value	Results		
		Date 5/12	Date	Date
Protein, T	6.2-8.3 g/dL			
Albumin	3.6-5.1 g/dL			
Alk Phos	33-115 units/L			
AST	10-35 units/L	32		
ALT	6-40 units/L	20		
TC	125-200 g/dL	224		
TG	<150 g/dL	248		
HDL	> 40 mg/dL	36		
LDL	< 100 mg/dL			
GLU	65-99 mg/dL	114		
Na	135-146 mEq/L	131		
K	3.5-5.3 mEq/L	3.8		
Cl	98-110 mEq/L	105		
HCO3-	22-28 mEq/L	25		
BUN	7-25 mg/dL	18		
Creatinine	0.6-1.2 mg/dL			
Calcium	8.6-10.2 mg/dL			
WBC	4-11 x 10^3 cells/mm^3	4.6		
RBC	3.8-5.1 x 10^6 mL/mm^3			
Hemoglobin	Male: 13.8- 17.2 g/dL Female: 12.1-15.1 g/dL	14.2		
Hematocrit	Male: 40.7-50.3% Female: 36.1- 44.3%	38		
MCHC	32-36 g/dL			
MCV	80-100 μm			
Platelet count	140-400 x 10^3/mm^3	210		
TSH	0.4-4.0 mIU/L	3.2		
FT4	4.5- 11.2 mcg/dL			
Hgb A1c	4-6%	7.2%		

ADDITIONAL INFORMATION

Date	Notes
11/11	Patient reports walking more since heart procedure. He has lost 13 lbs in last 5 months by decreasing "donuts and sugar." No EtOH, no tobacco use (past Hx smoking). Patient states he prefers not to take more pills, and is scared about his heart. BP today is 145/88 mmHg.

Questions

1. What is DA's calculated LDL?
   - *a.* 188
   - *b.* 176
   - *c.* 138
   - *d.* 105
   - *e.* 99

2. DA needs to be placed on statin therapy. According to the ACC/AHA Treatment of Blood Cholesterol Guideline, which would be the most appropriate statin regimen for DA?
   - *a.* Pravastatin 40 mg daily
   - *b.* Rosuvastatin 10 mg daily
   - *c.* Lovastatin 40 mg daily
   - *d.* Atorvastatin 40 mg daily
   - *e.* Pitavastatin 4 mg daily

3. DA returns to the clinic for follow up and complains of pain in his legs with occasional weakness. The statin therapy is stopped and the pain resolves. What is the best course of action to take for treatment of DA's dyslipidemia according to the ACC/AHA Treatment of Blood Cholesterol Guideline?
   - *a.* Restart the same statin at a lower dose
   - *b.* Switch to a different statin
   - *c.* Consider the patient unable to tolerate statin therapy and start a non-statin cholesterol medication
   - *d.* Recommend angiography to evaluate the leg for claudication
   - *e.* Recommend a venous ultrasound to evaluate the leg for a DVT

Questions 4-8 do not relate to the case.

4. Which of the following cholesterol medications are available as injectable agents? (Select **ALL** that apply.)
   - *a. Praluent*
   - *b. Juxtapid*
   - *c. Kynamro*
   - *d. Livalo*
   - *e. Vascepa*

5. A patient is going to be started on *Niaspan* therapy. Which of the following statements is correct?
   - *a. Niaspan* is immediate-release niacin.
   - *b. Niaspan* has a higher degree of hepatotoxicity than all the other niacin formulations.
   - *c. Niaspan* must be taken on an empty stomach.
   - *d. Niaspan* is taken with breakfast.
   - *e. Niaspan* causes less flushing than immediate-release niacin.

6. A physician has called the pharmacist. He has a patient on phenytoin who cannot tolerate statins. He wishes to begin *Welchol.* Which of the following statements is correct?
   - *a.* The phenytoin should be given 4 hours before *Welchol.*
   - *b.* He cannot use this class of drugs with phenytoin.
   - *c. Questran* would be a better option due to a lower risk of drug interactions.
   - *d.* The dose of *Welchol* is 5 g twice daily, with food and water.
   - *e.* There is no drug interaction between phenytoin and *Welchol.*

7. Which of the following medications has been shown to further lower the risk of cardiovascular events when added to statin treated patients with recent ACS?
   - *a. TriCor*
   - *b. Lovaza*
   - *c. Praluent*
   - *d. Zetia*
   - *e. Niacor*

8. Which of the following generic/brand combinations is correct?
   - *a.* Alirocumab (*Repatha*)
   - *b.* Fenofibric Acid (*Trilipix*)
   - *c.* Amlodipine/Rosuvastatin (*Caduet*)
   - *d.* Fluvastatin (*Crestor*)
   - *e.* Pitavastatin (*Lescol*)

Answers

1-c, 2-d, 3-a, 4-a,c, 5-e, 6-a, 7-d, 8-b

49

HYPERTENSION

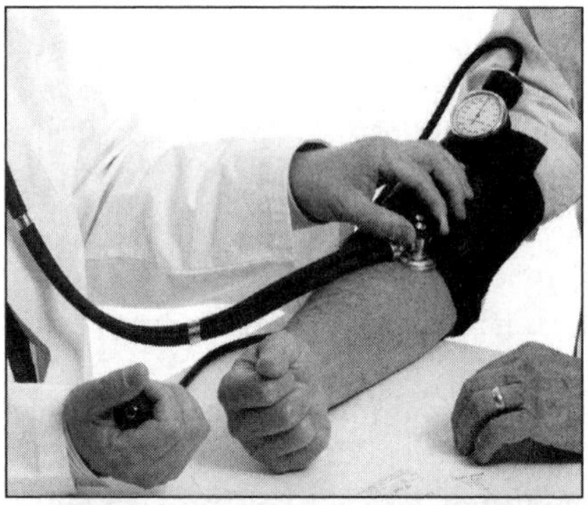

GUIDELINES/REFERENCES

2014 Evidence-Based Guideline for the Management of High Blood Pressure in Adults: Report From the Panel Members Appointed to the Eighth Joint National Committee (JNC 8). *JAMA.* 2014;311:507-520.

2013 AHA/ACC Guideline on Lifestyle Management to Reduce Cardiovascular Risk: A Report of the American College of Cardiology/American Heart Association Task Force on Practice Guidelines. *Circulation.* 2014;129:S76-S99.

Additional guidelines included with the online course.

We gratefully acknowledge the assistance of Kim M. Jones, PharmD, BCPS, Assistant Dean of Student Services and Associate Professor of Pharmacy Practice, Union University, in preparing this chapter.

BACKGROUND

Hypertension, a condition of high blood pressure (BP), affects one in three American adults and is the most common disease state managed in primary care. Hypertension is largely asymptomatic, which can delay detection and treatment and place the patient at greater risk for heart disease, stroke and kidney disease. Only when the BP is very high (e.g., hypertensive crisis) are symptoms such as throbbing headache, fatigue and shortness of breath likely to appear. The absence of symptoms can contribute to medication non-adherence in some patients as there is a lack of understanding about the necessity for treatment. Medication side effects, cost and pill burden can also lead to discontinuation of treatment or non-compliance. Pharmacists can play a vital role, by screening patients for hypertension and providing counseling about the importance of lifestyle measures (e.g., healthy diet, sodium restriction, physical activity, smoking cessation) and medication adherence. Involving the patient, with use of a home blood pressure monitoring device, can improve motivation and success of therapy.

ETIOLOGY AND PATHOPHYSIOLOGY

Most patients (~95%) have primary hypertension, also known as essential hypertension. The cause is unknown, but environmental factors (e.g., obesity, sedentary lifestyle, excessive salt intake) and genetics can contribute. Secondary hypertension can be caused by renal disease (e.g., chronic kidney disease), adrenal disease (e.g., excess aldosterone secretion), sleep apnea or drugs (see Key Drugs box). There is usually increased activity of the sympathetic nervous system (SNS) and the renin-angiotensin-aldosterone system (RAAS); this produces elevated levels of various neurohormones (e.g., norepinephrine, angiotensin II, aldosterone) which can increase blood pressure [due to increased heart rate (HR), contractility, systemic vascular resistance (SVR), and/or blood volume (sodium and water retention)].

Compensatory Mechanisms in Hypertension

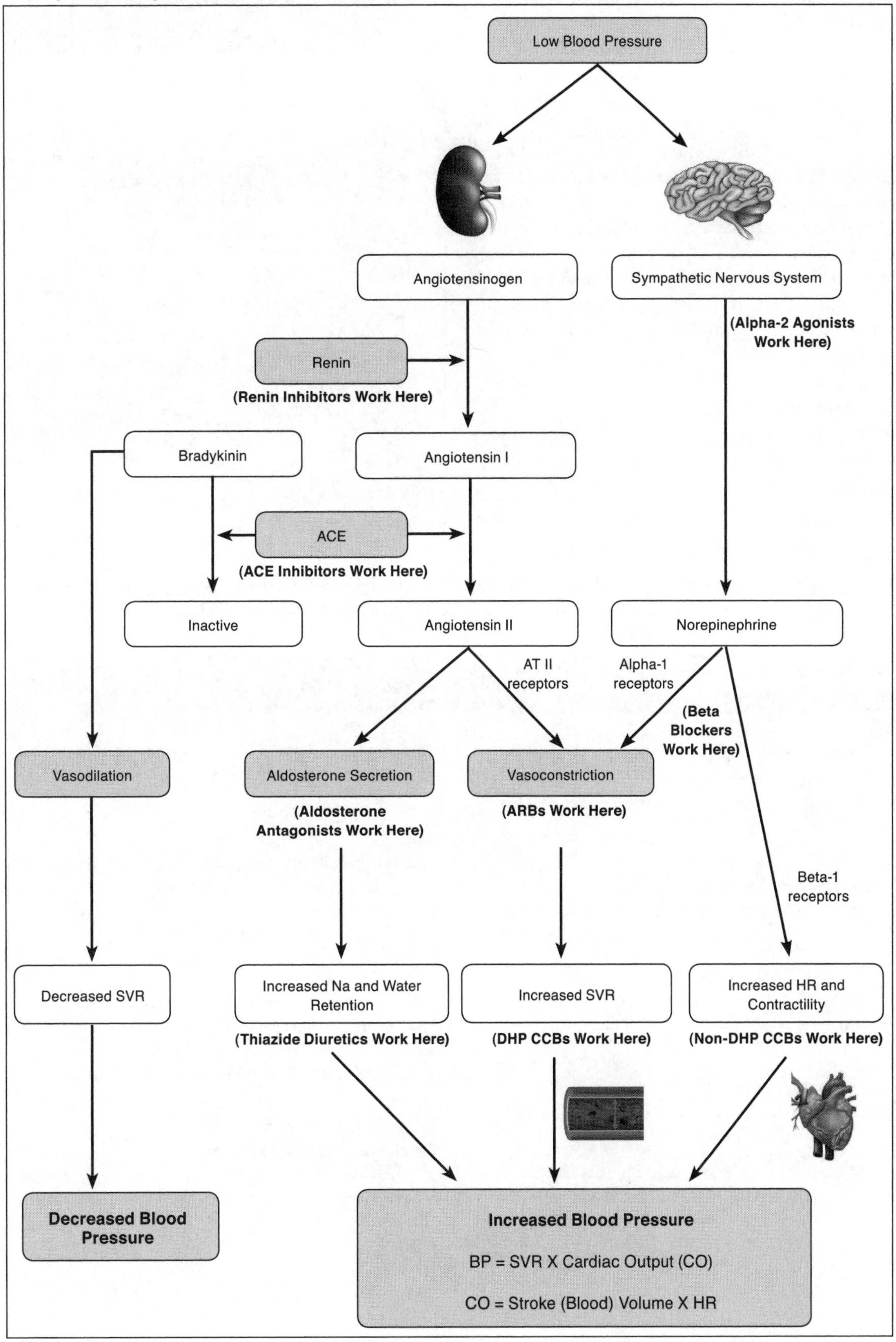

THE EIGHTH JOINT NATIONAL COMMITTEE GUIDELINE

The Eighth Joint National Committee (JNC 8) has simplified the treatment of hypertension in adults. Recommendations for treatment, and BP goals, are based on age, race (black or non-black), the presence of diabetes (DM) and/or the presence of chronic kidney disease (CKD). Black patients are given special consideration because they have a higher risk of stroke than non-blacks, and a better response (lower BP and prevention of stroke) to thiazide diuretics and calcium channel blockers (CCBs) than to angiotensin converting enzyme (ACE) inhibitors or angiotensin receptor blockers (ARBs).

DRUGS THAT CAN INCREASE BLOOD PRESSURE

KEY DRUGS

Amphetamines and other ADHD drugs

Cocaine

Decongestants (e.g., pseudoephedrine, phenylephrine)

Erythropoiesis-stimulating agents

Immunosuppressants (e.g., cyclosporine, tacrolimus)

NSAIDs

Systemic steroids

Others:

Alcohol (excessive)

Appetite suppressants (e.g., phentermine)

Caffeine

Herbals (e.g., ginseng, licorice, yohimbine)

Mirabegron

Oral contraceptives

Select oncology agents (e.g., bevacizumab, tyrosine kinase inhibitors)

SNRIs

Treatment Principles (JNC 8)

- Medication adherence and lifestyle modifications should be emphasized throughout treatment.
- Whenever possible, once daily regimens are preferred for increased patient compliance.
- Drug therapy should be initiated when either the systolic BP (SBP) or the diastolic BP (DBP) is above the target goal based on age and comorbid conditions (see Study Tips box on the following page).

LIFESTYLE MANAGEMENT

Weight
Maintain a normal BMI (18.5-24.9 kg/m^2) and waist circumference (< 35 inches for females and < 40 inches for males).

Limit Alcohol Consumption
1 drink/day for women and ≤ 2 drinks/day for men.

Increase Physical Activity
Engage in moderate-vigorous intensity exercise, lasting 30-40 minutes per session, on most days of the week.

Reduce Sodium Intake
Limit intake to < 1,500 mg/day.

Smoking Cessation
See Tobacco Cessation chapter.

Diet
Emphasize intake of vegetables, fruits, whole grains, low-fat dairy products, poultry, fish, legumes, nontropical vegetable oils and nuts. Aim for 5-6% of calories from saturated fat, and reduce intake of *trans* fats, sweets, sugar-sweetened beverages and red meats. Adapt diet to appropriate calorie requirements, personal and cultural food preferences and nutrition therapy for other medical conditions (e.g., diabetes). This can be achieved by following plans such as the DASH dietary pattern, the USDA Food Pattern or the AHA Diet.

Control Blood Glucose and Lipids to Reduce Cardiovascular Disease Risk!

AHA - American Heart Association, DASH - Dietary Approaches to Stop Hypertension, USDA - United States Department of Agriculture

- Four preferred drug classes are recommended by JNC 8 for initial therapy (ACE inhibitors, ARBs, CCBs or thiazide diuretics). See the Study Tips box below for initial drug selection based on patient-specific criteria.
- Note that selection of an ACE inhibitor or ARB first is only recommended when the patient has CKD with or without albuminuria. This is a deviation from the ADA guidelines which give preference to ACE inhibitors or ARBs to manage blood pressure in patients with diabetes.

STUDY TIPS: JNC 8 TREATMENT RECOMMENDATIONS

BP GOALS

- BP < 140/90 mmHg: age 18-59 years (no DM or CKD)
- BP < 140/90 mmHg: CKD and/or DM* (all ages)
- BP < 150/90 mmHg: age ≥ 60 years (no DM or CKD)
  - If treatment results in a lower SBP (e.g., < 140 mmHg) and is well tolerated, it does not need to be adjusted

INITIAL DRUG SELECTION

- Non-black ± diabetes: thiazide or CCB or ACE inhibitor or ARB
- Black ± diabetes: thiazide or CCB
- CKD ± albuminuria ± diabetes (all races): ACE inhibitor or ARB (to slow the progression of CKD to ESRD)
- BP > 160/100 mmHg or > 20/10 mmHg above goal (all patients): consider starting with 2 drugs**

DRUG TITRATION AND COMBINATION THERAPY**

- Maximize the dose of the 1st medication before adding a 2nd OR add a 2nd medication before reaching the maximum dose of the 1st medication

* *According to the ADA, a BP goal of < 130/80 mmHg can be considered in select patients (see Diabetes chapter); KDIGO recommends a BP goal of < 130/80 mmHg in CKD patients with albuminuria (see Renal Disease chapter); exam questions should specify if you should follow ADA versus JNC 8 recommendations*

** *Do not use ACE inhibitors and ARBs together*

Drug Titration and Combination Therapy

- BP should be checked every 2 – 4 weeks after starting therapy and until goal BP is reached. Most patients will require more than one drug to reach goal BP.
- If goal BP is not reached within a month, drug titration will be needed. When choosing a titration strategy (see Study Tips box above), consider that using two drugs at lower doses may cause less side effects than a higher dose of one agent.
- When starting with two drugs as initial therapy (e.g., when BP is > 20/10 mmHg above goal at baseline), titrate both agents to the maximum tolerated dose before adding a third agent.
- When starting additional antihypertensive agents, select a drug from one of the four preferred drug classes (thiazides, CCBs, ACE inhibitors or ARBs) if they are not already part of the regimen, but do not use ACE inhibitors and ARBs together.
- After addition, or consideration for addition, of the four preferred drug classes, other antihypertensives may be used (e.g., beta-blockers, aldosterone antagonists).
- Many of the common (and a few less common) drugs are available in combinations products. These are shown in the table on the following page, with the more commonly used combination products bolded. Notice that for many diuretic combinations, the brand name often has HCT, -ide or -etic at the end. Agents without a brand name listed are only available as generics.

COMBINATION BLOOD PRESSURE DRUGS

ACE INHIBITOR OR ARB + DIURETIC

Losartan/Hydrochlorothiazide *(Hyzaar)*

Lisinopril/Hydrochlorothiazide *(Zestoretic)*

Olmesartan/Hydrochlorothiazide *(Benicar HCT)*

Valsartan/Hydrochlorothiazide *(Diovan HCT)*

Azilsartan/Chlorthalidone *(Edarbyclor)*

Benazepril/Hydrochlorothiazide *(Lotensin HCT)*

Candesartan/Hydrochlorothiazide *(Atacand HCT)*

Captopril/Hydrochlorothiazide

Enalapril/Hydrochlorothiazide *(Vaseretic)*

Eprosartan/Hydrochlorothiazide *(Teveten HCT)*

Fosinopril/Hydrochlorothiazide *(Monopril HCT)*

Irbesartan/Hydrochlorothiazide *(Avalide)*

Moexipril/Hydrochlorothiazide

Quinapril/Hydrochlorothiazide *(Accuretic, Quinaretic)*

Telmisartan/Hydrochlorothiazide *(Micardis HCT)*

ACE INHIBITOR OR ARB + CCB

Benazepril/Amlodipine *(Lotrel)*

Olmesartan/Amlodipine *(Azor)*

Perindopril/Amlodipine *(Prestalia)*

Valsartan/Amlodipine *(Exforge)*

Telmisartan/Amlodipine *(Twynsta)*

Trandolapril/Verapamil *(Tarka)*

DIRECT RENIN INHIBITOR + DIURETIC

Aliskiren/Hydrochlorothiazide *(Tekturna HCT)*

ALPHA AGONIST + DIURETIC

Clonidine/Chlorthalidone *(Clorpres)*

Methyldopa/Hydrochlorothiazide

BETA BLOCKER + DIURETIC

Atenolol/Chlorthalidone *(Tenoretic)*

Bisoprolol/Hydrochlorothiazide *(Ziac)*

Metoprolol tartrate/Hydrochlorothiazide *(Lopressor HCT)*

Metoprolol succinate/Hydrochlorothiazide *(Dutoprol)*

Nadolol/Bendroflumethiazide *(Corzide)*

Propranolol/Hydrochlorothiazide

BETA BLOCKER + ARB

Nebivolol/Valsartan *(Byvalson)*

K-SPARING DIURETIC + THIAZIDE DIURETIC

Triamterene/Hydrochlorothiazide *(Maxzide, Maxzide-25, Dyazide)*

Amiloride/Hydrochlorothiazide

Spironolactone/Hydrochlorothiazide *(Aldactazide)*

TRIPLE COMBINATIONS

Olmesartan/Amlodipine/Hydrochlorothiazide *(Tribenzor)*

Valsartan/Amlodipine/Hydrochlorothiazide *(Exforge HCT)*

PREGNANCY AND HYPERTENSION

Planning for pregnancy includes the discontinuation of teratogenic drugs that could cause fetal harm. If pregnancy is detected, ACE inhibitors, ARBs, and the direct renin inhibitor aliskiren, should be discontinued immediately as they are contraindicated in pregnancy. When making antihypertensive treatment recommendations in pregnancy, it must first be determined if the patient is experiencing preeclampsia or chronic hypertension, as these are treated differently. Preeclampsia occurs after week 20 of the pregnancy and is evident by elevated blood pressures and proteinuria in the majority of cases. It is more common in women who are overweight, and/or have pre-existing hypertension, renal disease or diabetes. Drug therapy is recommended in pregnant patients with chronic hypertension if SBP is ≥ 160 mmHg or DBP is ≥ 105 mmHg. Recommended first line agents, according to the American College of Obstetricians and Gynecologists (ACOG), include labetalol, nifedipine extended-release and methyldopa. BP should be maintained between 120 – 160 mmHg systolic and 80 – 105 mmHg diastolic.

THIAZIDE-TYPE DIURETICS

Thiazide-type diuretics are inexpensive, effective and have mild side effects in most patients. They are no longer the only class of agents recommended first line for uncomplicated hypertension, but are one of four drug classes that can be considered initially. Loop diuretics are used primarily in heart failure (see Chronic Heart Failure chapter).

Thiazides and thiazide-type diuretics inhibit Na reabsorption in the distal convoluted tubules (see nephron diagram), causing increased excretion of Na, Cl, and water, as well as K and H ions.

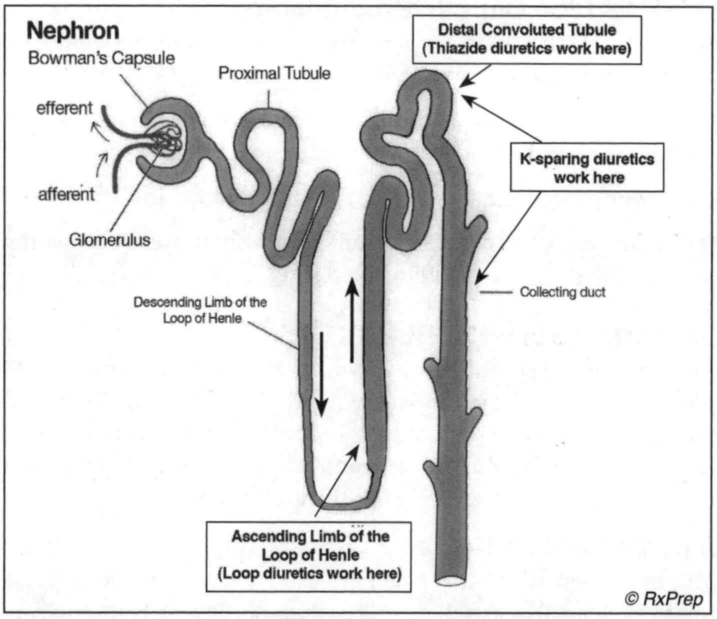

DRUG	DOSING	SAFETY/SIDE EFFECTS/MONITORING
Chlorothiazide *(Diuril)* Tablet, oral suspension, injection	500-2,000 mg daily in 1-2 divided doses	**CONTRAINDICATIONS** Hypersensitivity to sulfonamide-derived drugs (not likely to cross-react – see Drug Allergies & Adverse Drug Reactions chapter); anuria
Chlorthalidone Tablet	12.5-25 mg daily (max dose is 100 mg daily but doses > 25 mg/day have limited clinical benefit)	**WARNINGS** Sulfa allergy (see above), progressive liver disease (fluid and electrolyte changes may precipitate hepatic coma), may precipitate or exacerbate other conditions (e.g., gout, DM, SLE, CKD) Hydrochlorothiazide: acute myopia and angle-closure glaucoma
HydroCHLOROthiazide *(Microzide)* Tablet, capsule	12.5-50 mg daily (max dose is 100 mg daily but doses > 50 mg/day have limited clinical benefit and ↑ risk of adverse effects)	**SIDE EFFECTS** Hypokalemia (↓ K), hypomagnesemia (↓ Mg), hyponatremia (↓ Na), hypercalcemia (↑ Ca), hyperuricemia (↑ UA), elevated lipids (↑ LDL, ↑ TG), hyperglycemia (↑ BG), dizziness, photosensitivity, rash, hypochloremic alkalosis (rare)
Indapamide Tablet	1.25-5 mg daily	**MONITORING** BP, electrolytes, renal function, fluid status (input and output, weight), BG (in patients with diabetes)
Methyclothiazide Tablet	2.5-5 mg daily	**NOTES** Chlorthalidone and indapamide have better evidence than hydrochlorothiazide and may be preferred by some clinicians (but if a patient is on hydrochlorothiazide and is doing well, do not switch) Thiazides may not be effective when CrCl < 30 mL/min (except metolazone, which may work in patients with reduced renal function or diuretic resistance)
MetOLazone *(Zaroxolyn)* Tablet	2.5-5 mg daily	Should be taken early in the day to avoid nocturia Chlorothiazide is the only medication in this class available IV Hypokalemia can usually be avoided with regular intake of potassium rich foods or potassium supplements

Thiazide-Type Diuretic Drug Interactions

- All antihypertensives can potentiate the blood pressure lowering effects of other drugs; BP should be carefully monitored when adding on therapy.
- Patients with hypertension should avoid agents that can cause Na and water retention (e.g., NSAIDs) as these agents can lower the effectiveness of antihypertensive medications.
- Thiazide diuretics may ↓ lithium renal clearance and ↑ the risk of lithium toxicity. Avoid if possible.
- Thiazide diuretics can ↑ dofetilide serum concentrations leading to an ↑ risk of QT prolongation; use in combination is contraindicated.

CALCIUM CHANNEL BLOCKERS

There are two types of CCBs, dihydropyridines (DHP) and non-dihydropyridines (non-DHP). There are many long-acting formulations of nifedipine (a DHP CCB) and diltiazem (a non-DHP CCB). Not all generic products are therapeutically equivalent to the brand name products. If the pharmacist is substituting a generic product for a brand name product, they should check the Orange Book and choose a generic product that is A-rated to the brand product.

Dihydropyridine CCBs

DHP CCBs, which end in "-pine", are used for hypertension, stable angina and Prinzmetal's angina (see Ischemic Heart Disease chapter). They inhibit Ca ions from entering vascular smooth muscle and myocardial cells; this causes peripheral arterial vasodilation, which ↓ SVR and BP, and coronary artery vasodilation. The peripheral vasodilation leads to reflex tachycardia, headache, flushing, and peripheral edema. The intravenous products, nicardipine and clevidipine, are most commonly used in hypertensive crises or other urgent/emergent situations, when oral therapy is not feasible (e.g., blood pressure lowering in acute stroke).

DRUG	DOSING	SAFETY/SIDE EFFECTS/MONITORING
AmLODIPine *(Norvasc)*	2.5-10 mg daily	**WARNINGS** Hypotension (especially in patients with severe aortic stenosis); worsening angina and/or MI has occurred with initiation or dosage titration (due to reflex tachycardia); severe hepatic impairment (start low and titrate slowly); use caution in heart failure (see Notes) Nifedipine IR: not indicated for chronic hypertension and should not be used for acute BP reduction in non-pregnant adults (profound hypotension, MI and/or death has occurred) **SIDE EFFECTS** Peripheral edema, dizziness, flushing, headache, palpitations/ tachycardia, fatigue, gingival hyperplasia **MONITORING** BP, HR, peripheral edema
Felodipine ER	2.5-10 mg daily	
Isradipine	2.5-10 mg BID	
NIFEdipine ER *(Adalat CC, Procardia XL,* others) NIFEdipine IR *(Procardia)*	30-90 mg daily	
Nisoldipine ER *(Sular)*	8.5-34 mg daily	
Nisoldipine ER (original formulation)	10-60 mg daily	
NiCARdipine ER NiCARdipine IR **NiCARdipine IV *(Cardene IV)*** Capsule, injection	ER: 30-60 mg BID IR: 20-40 mg TID IV: 5 mg/hr, ↑ by 2.5 mg/hr every 5-15 minutes to max dose of 15 mg/hr	**NOTES** Amlodipine and felodipine are considered the safest if a CCB must be used in patients with heart failure with reduced ejection fraction Most products must be protected from light and moisture (except amlodipine); this includes *Cardene IV* which requires light protection during administration *Adalat CC* and *Procardia XL:* OROS/gel matrix formulation (see Drug Formulations chapter) can leave a ghost tablet (empty shell) in the stool

Dihydropyridine CCBs Continued

DRUG	DOSING	SAFETY/SIDE EFFECTS/MONITORING
Clevidipine *(Cleviprex)* Injection	1-21 mg/hr	**CONTRAINDICATIONS** Allergy to soybeans, soy products or eggs; defective lipid metabolism (e.g., lipoid nephrosis, hyperlipidemia with acute pancreatitis); severe aortic stenosis **WARNINGS** Hypotension and reflex tachycardia, lipid intake (see Notes), hypertriglyceridemia, infections (see Notes) **SIDE EFFECTS** Headache, atrial fibrillation, nausea, fever **MONITORING** BP, HR **NOTES** In a lipid emulsion (provides 2 kcal/mL); it is milky-white in color Use strict aseptic technique due to infection risk; maximum time of use after vial puncture is 12 hours

Non-Dihydropyridine CCBs

The non-DHP CCBs, verapamil and diltiazem, are primarily used to control HR in certain arrhythmias (e.g., atrial fibrillation), and are sometimes used for hypertension and angina. They inhibit Ca ions from entering vascular smooth muscle and myocardial cells, but they are more selective for the myocardium than the DHP CCBs. The decrease in BP produced by non-DHP CCBs is due to negative inotropic (↓ force of ventricular contraction) and negative chronotropic (↓ HR) effects.

DRUG	DOSING	SAFETY/SIDE EFFECTS/MONITORING
DilTIAZem *(Cardizem, Cardizem CD, Cardizem LA, Cartia XT, Diltzac, Dilt-XR, Taztia XT, Tiazac,* others) Tablet, ER tablet (24-HR), ER capsule (12-HR), ER capsule (24-HR), injection	120-360 mg daily; max dose varies with product IR tablet: daily dose given in 4 divided doses ER capsule (12-HR): daily dose given in 2 divided doses	**CONTRAINDICATIONS** Hypotension (SBP < 90 mmHg) or cardiogenic shock; 2nd or 3rd degree AV block or sick sinus syndrome (unless the patient has a functioning artificial ventricular pacemaker); acute MI and pulmonary congestion **WARNINGS** Sinus bradycardia, AV block (1st, 2nd or 3rd), hypotension, heart failure (may worsen symptoms), ↑ LFTs **SIDE EFFECTS** Edema, headache, dizziness, constipation (more with verapamil), gingival hyperplasia **MONITORING** BP, HR, ECG, LFTs **NOTES** Diltiazem IR: indicated for angina *Covera HS:* OROS/gel matrix formulation (see Drug Formulations chapter) can leave a ghost tablet (empty shell) in the stool
Verapamil *(Calan, Calan SR, Covera HS, Verelan, Verelan PM)* Tablet, ER tablet, ER capsule (24-HR), injection	240-480 mg daily IR tablet: daily dose given in 3 divided doses *Calan SR:* daily dose can be given in 2 divided doses (QAM and QPM) *Covera HS* and *Verelan PM:* daily dose given QHS	

Calcium Channel Blocker Drug Interactions

- All CCBs, both DHP and non-DHP, are major substrates of CYP450 3A4. Strong inducers and inhibitors of 3A4 should be used with caution in combination with CCBs, and in some cases avoided completely. It is important to check for drug interactions when initiating CCB therapy or when other medications are added in a patient who is taking a CCB. Grapefruit juice should be avoided.
- Diltiazem and verapamil are also substrates of P-gp and moderate inhibitors of 3A4. They can increase the concentration of many other drugs.

RENIN-ANGIOTENSIN ALDOSTERONE SYSTEM INHIBITORS

Angiotensin II (Ang II) causes vasoconstriction and increased release of aldosterone, resulting in Na and water retention. RAAS inhibitors decrease BP by inhibiting the effects of Ang II. Some agents have also shown benefit in kidney disease and heart failure. Facts to know about all RAAS inhibitors include:

- Do not use RAAS inhibitors in combination (ACE inhibitor ± ARB ± aliskiren) to lower BP, due to an increased risk for adverse effects (see RAAS Inhibitor Drug Interactions).
- Angioedema can develop with any agent; it occurs more frequently with ACE inhibitors, than with ARBs or aliskiren, and in black patients. If a patient develops angioedema with any RAAS inhibitor, other agents in the class are contraindicated, since angioedema can be fatal.

Angiotensin-Converting Enzyme Inhibitors

ACE inhibitors block the conversion of angiotensin I to Ang II, resulting in ↓ vasoconstriction and ↓ aldosterone secretion. They also block degradation of bradykinin, which is thought to contribute to the vasodilatory effects (and side effects of cough and angioedema). ACE inhibitors have been shown to slow the progression of kidney disease in patients with albuminuria (due to diabetes, hypertension, or other causes of CKD). This is because Ang II constricts the efferent arterioles of the nephron to a greater extent than the afferent arterioles (see nephron diagram), causing increased perfusion pressure (workload) in the glomeruli and resulting in kidney damage over time. Blocking Ang II formation causes efferent arteriole vasodilation and decreases glomerular filtration pressure. ACE inhibitors protect the myocardium from the remodeling effects of Ang II, which helps in heart failure.

DRUG	DOSING	SAFETY/SIDE EFFECTS/MONITORING
Benazepril *(Lotensin)*	5-40 mg daily	**BOXED WARNING** Can cause injury and death to the developing fetus when used in the 2nd and 3rd trimesters; discontinue as soon as pregnancy is detected **CONTRAINDICATIONS** History of angioedema, use with aliskiren in patients with diabetes **WARNINGS** Angioedema, cough, hyperkalemia, hypotension (↑ risk if salt- or volume-depleted), renal impairment, bilateral renal artery stenosis (avoid use) **SIDE EFFECTS** Dizziness, headache, rash **MONITORING** BP, K, renal function, s/sx of angioedema **NOTES** Safety issue – see Pregnancy chapter Once daily agents can be used BID if needed
Captopril	12.5-100 mg BID	
Enalapril, Enalaprilat *(Vasotec, Epaned)* Tablet, oral solution, injection	PO: 5-20 mg daily or BID IV (enalaprilat): 0.625-5 mg Q6H	
Fosinopril	10-40 mg daily	
Lisinopril *(Prinivil, Zestril, Qbrelis)* Tablet, oral solution	5-40 mg daily	
Moexipril	3.75-30 mg daily	
Perindopril *(Aceon)*	4-16 mg daily	
Quinapril *(Accupril)*	5-40 mg daily	
Ramipril *(Altace)*	2.5-20 mg daily	
Trandolapril *(Mavik)*	1-8 mg daily	

Angiotensin Receptor Blockers

ARBs block angiotensin II from binding to the angiotensin II type-1 (AT1) receptor on vascular smooth muscle, preventing vasoconstriction. ARBs have been shown to slow the progression of renal disease and heart failure for similar reasons as ACE inhibitors.

DRUG	DOSING	SAFETY/SIDE EFFECTS/MONITORING
Azilsartan *(Edarbi)*	40-80 mg daily	**BOXED WARNING** Can cause injury and death to the developing fetus when used in the 2nd and 3rd trimesters; discontinue as soon as pregnancy is detected **CONTRAINDICATIONS** History of angioedema **WARNINGS** Angioedema, hyperkalemia, hypotension (↑ risk if salt- or volume-depleted), renal impairment, bilateral renal artery stenosis (avoid use) Olmesartan: sprue-like enteropathy – severe, chronic diarrhea with substantial weight loss can occur months to years after drug initiation **SIDE EFFECTS** Dizziness, headache, diarrhea **MONITORING** BP, K, renal function **NOTES** Safety issue – see Pregnancy chapter Azilsartan: keep in original container to protect from light and moisture
Candesartan *(Atacand)*	8-32 mg daily in 1-2 divided doses	
Eprosartan *(Teveten)*	400-800 mg daily in 1-2 divided doses	
Irbesartan *(Avapro)*	75-300 mg daily	
Losartan *(Cozaar)*	25-100 mg daily in 1-2 divided doses	
Olmesartan *(Benicar)*	10-40 mg daily	
Telmisartan *(Micardis)*	40-80 mg daily	
Valsartan *(Diovan)*	80-320 mg daily	

RAAS Inhibitor Drug Interactions

- All RAAS inhibitors ↑ the risk of hyperkalemia. Other medications that increase potassium (e.g., potassium-sparing diuretics) should be used cautiously. Patients should avoid salt substitutes that contain potassium chloride (instead of sodium chloride).
- Avoid using more than one RAAS inhibitor together (ACE inhibitor ± ARB ± aliskiren) due to an ↑ risk of renal impairment, hypotension, and hyperkalemia. The use of aliskiren in combination with an ACE inhibitor or ARB is specifically contraindicated in patients with diabetes and should be avoided when eGFR is < 60 mL/min.
- ACE inhibitors and ARBs can ↓ lithium renal clearance and ↑ the risk of lithium toxicity.

ADDITIONAL AGENTS FOR TREATING HYPERTENSION

Potassium-Sparing Diuretics

Potassium-sparing diuretics have traditionally been viewed as having minimal BP lowering effects and are most commonly used in combination with hydrochlorothiazide (e.g., *Maxzide, Dyazide)* to counteract the mild potassium losses seen with thiazide diuretics. More recent evidence suggests that spironolactone may be a preferred agent in patients with resistant hypertension (uncontrolled BP despite maximum tolerated doses of a CCB + thiazide diuretic + ACE inhibitor or ARB). The aldosterone receptor antagonists, spironolactone and eplerenone, are also used in heart failure.

Spironolactone is a non-selective aldosterone receptor blocker (also blocks androgen), while eplerenone is a selective aldosterone receptor blocker that does not exhibit endocrine side effects. These agents compete with aldosterone at receptor sites in the distal convoluted tubule and collecting ducts of the nephron (see nephron diagram), increasing Na and water excretion and conserving K and H ions.

<table>
<tr><th>DRUG</th><th>DOSING</th><th>SAFETY/SIDE EFFECTS/MONITORING</th></tr>
<tr><td>AMILoride</td><td>5-10 mg daily, max dose is 20 mg daily</td><td rowspan="4">BOXED WARNINGS
Amiloride and triamterene: hyperkalemia (K > 5.5 mEq/L) – more likely in patients with diabetes, renal impairment, or elderly patients
Spironolactone: tumorigenic in chronic toxicity studies with rats; avoid unnecessary use

CONTRAINDICATIONS
Hyperkalemia (K > 5.5 mEq/L), anuria, renal impairment, co-administration of potassium supplements or potassium sparing diuretics, Addison's disease or other conditions that ↑ K
Eplerenone: type 2 diabetes with microalbuminuria, SCr > 2 mg/dL in males or > 1.8 mg/dL in females, CrCl < 50 mL/min, co-administration of strong 3A4 inhibitors (see Drug Interactions)

SIDE EFFECTS
Dehydration, hyponatremia, dizziness, hyperchloremic metabolic acidosis (rare)
Eplerenone: hypertriglyceridemia
Spironolactone: gynecomastia, breast tenderness, impotence, irregular menses, amenorrhea

MONITORING
BP, electrolytes (check K before starting and frequently thereafter), renal function, fluid status (input and output, weight)</td></tr>
<tr><td>Eplerenone (Inspra)</td><td>50 daily or BID

Heart failure
25-50 mg daily</td></tr>
<tr><td>Spironolactone (Aldactone)</td><td>25-100 mg daily in 1-2 divided doses

Heart failure
12.5-25 mg daily, max dose is 50 mg daily</td></tr>
<tr><td>Triamterene (Dyrenium)
+ HCTZ (Maxzide, Maxzide-25, Dyazide)</td><td>100-300 mg daily in 1-2 divided doses
+ HCTZ: 37.5 mg/25 mg daily or BID
+ HCTZ: 75/50 mg daily</td></tr>
</table>

Potassium-Sparing Diuretic Drug Interactions

- Potassium-sparing diuretics ↑ the risk of hyperkalemia. Additive potassium accumulation can occur when these agents are used with other potassium-sparing drugs (see Drug Interactions chapter).
- Diuretics can ↓ lithium renal clearance and ↑ the risk of lithium toxicity.
- Eplerenone is a major substrate of 3A4; use with strong 3A4 inhibitors (e.g., ketoconazole, itraconazole, clarithromycin, ritonavir) is contraindicated.

Beta Blockers

Beta blockers are no longer recommended as first-line agents for uncomplicated hypertension unless the patient has a comorbid condition for which beta blockers are recommended first-line (e.g., post-MI, stable ischemic heart disease, heart failure, others). These agents decrease BP by competitively blocking beta-1 and beta-2 adrenergic receptors resulting in decreases in HR and myocardial contractility. Some agents also have alpha-1 blocking properties, which decreases peripheral vasoconstriction, as another mechanism of lowering BP. Beta blockers with intrinsic sympathomimetic activity (ISA) partially stimulate beta receptors while blocking against the effects of catecholamines such as norepinephrine; because they do not decrease HR to the same degree as beta blockers without ISA, they are not recommended in post-MI patients. Carteolol, acebutolol, penbutolol, and pindolol (CAPP) are the beta blockers with ISA. The intravenous products, esmolol, labetalol and metoprolol tartrate, are most commonly used in hypertensive crises or other urgent/emergent situations when oral therapy is not feasible.

Beta-1 Selective Blockers

DRUG	DOSING	SAFETY/SIDE EFFECTS/MONITORING
Acebutolol *(Sectral)*	200-800 mg daily in 1-2 divided doses	**BOXED WARNING** Do not discontinue abruptly (particularly in patients with CAD/IHD); gradually taper dose over 1-2 weeks to avoid acute tachycardia, hypertension, and/or ischemia **CONTRAINDICATIONS** Severe bradycardia; 2nd or 3rd degree AV block or sick sinus syndrome (unless a permanent pacemaker is in place); overt cardiac failure or cardiogenic shock Esmolol: pulmonary hypertension; use of IV non-DHP CCBs in close proximity **WARNINGS** Caution in patients with diabetes (may potentiate hypoglycemia and/or mask hypoglycemic symptoms – see Diabetes chapter); may mask signs of hyperthyroidism (e.g., tachycardia); use caution with bronchospastic diseases (e.g., asthma, COPD), peripheral vascular disease, pheochromocytoma, and heart failure; may exacerbate CNS depression **SIDE EFFECTS** $\downarrow$ HR, hypotension, fatigue, dizziness, depression, $\downarrow$ libido, impotence **MONITORING** HR ($\downarrow$ dose if HR < 55 BPM), BP **NOTES** Oral agents: titrate doses every 1-2 weeks (as tolerated), take without regard to meals (except *Lopressor* and *Toprol XL* should be taken with or immediately following food) Atenolol: safety issue - see Pregnancy chapter Metoprolol tartrate IV is not equivalent to PO (IV:PO ratio 1:2.5) When switching from metoprolol tartrate to metoprolol succinate, the same total daily dose of metoprolol should be used Beta-1 selective agents (AMEBBA) – Atenolol, Metoprolol, Esmolol, Bisoprolol, Betaxolol, Acebutolol
Atenolol *(Tenormin)*	25-100 mg daily	
Betaxolol *Betoptic-S* – ophthalmic solution	5-20 mg daily	
Bisoprolol *(Zebeta)*	2.5-20 mg daily	
Esmolol *(Brevibloc)* Injection	0.5-1 mg/kg IV bolus followed by 50-150 mcg/kg/min via continuous IV infusion, titrate as needed to a maximum of 300 mcg/kg/min	
Metoprolol tartrate *(Lopressor)* Tablet, injection **Metoprolol succinate extended release *(Toprol XL)*** Tablet	IR: 100-450 mg daily in 2-3 divided doses XL: 25-100 mg daily; max dose is 400 mg daily **Heart failure *(Toprol XL)*** start with12.5-25 mg daily (target 200 mg daily)	

Beta-1 Selective Blocker and Nitric Oxide-Dependent Vasodilation

Nebivolol *(Bystolic)*	5-10 mg daily; max dose is 40 mg daily CrCl < 30 mL/min or moderate liver impairment, start at 2.5 mg daily	Same as above plus: **CONTRAINDICATIONS** Severe liver impairment (Child-Pugh > B) **SIDE EFFECTS** Nausea, diarrhea, $\uparrow$ TGs, $\downarrow$ HDL **NOTES** Nitric oxide causes peripheral vasodilation

DRUG	DOSING	SAFETY/SIDE EFFECTS/MONITORING

Beta-1 and Beta-2 Blockers (Non-Selective)

Nadolol *(Corgard)*	40-320 mg daily	Same as above for beta-1 selective blockers plus **WARNINGS** May cause hyperglycemia in patients with type 2 diabetes by decreasing insulin release **NOTES** Propranolol has high lipid solubility (lipophilic) and crosses the blood brain barrier; it may be associated with more CNS side effects but this makes it useful for other conditions (e.g., migraine prophylaxis, essential tremor)
Pindolol	5-30 mg BID	
Propranolol *(Inderal LA, Inderal XL, InnoPran XL,* *Hemangeol)* Tablet, ER capsule, oral solution, injection	IR: 40-160 mg BID, max dose is 640 mg daily LA: 80-160 mg daily, same max dose as IR XL: 80 mg daily; max dose is 120 mg daily	
Timolol *Timoptic* – opthalmic solution	10-30 mg BID	

Non-Selective Beta Blocker and Alpha-1 Blockers

Carvedilol *(Coreg, Coreg CR)* Tablet, ER capsule	IR: 6.25-25 mg BID CR: 20-80 mg daily **Heart failure** IR: 3.125-25 mg BID (max dose is 25 mg BID if ≤ 85 kg and 50 mg BID if > 85 kg) CR: 10-80 mg daily	Same as above for beta-1 selective and non-selective blockers plus **CONTRAINDICATIONS** Severe hepatic impairment **WARNINGS** Intraoperative floppy iris syndrome has occurred in cataract surgery patients who were on or were previously treated with an alpha-1 blocker **SIDE EFFECTS** Edema, weight gain, ↑ TGs, ↓ HDL **NOTES** Take all forms of carvedilol with food to ↓ the rate of absorption and the risk of orthostatic hypotension Carvedilol CR has less bioavailability than carvedilol IR, therefore dosing conversions are not 1:1 Dosing conversion from *Coreg* to *Coreg CR:* *Coreg* 3.125 mg BID = *Coreg CR* 10 mg daily *Coreg* 6.25 mg BID = *Coreg CR* 20 mg daily *Coreg* 12.5 mg BID = *Coreg CR* 40 mg daily *Coreg* 25 mg BID = *Coreg CR* 80 mg daily
Labetalol Tablet, injection	PO: 100-1,200 mg BID	Same as above for carvedilol Injection is commonly used in the hospital setting and can be administered by repeated IV injection or slow continuous infusion

Beta Blocker Drug Interactions

- Beta blockers can enhance the hypoglycemic effects of insulin and sulfonylureas and can mask some of the symptoms of hypoglycemia (e.g., shakiness, palpitations, anxiety); sweating and hunger are symptoms that are not masked. In addition, non-selective beta blockers can ↓ insulin secretion in type 2 diabetes causing hyperglycemia. Monitor blood glucose in patients with diabetes.
- Use caution when administering other drugs that ↓ HR (e.g., diltiazem, verapamil, digoxin).
- Carvedilol, propranolol and metoprolol are major substrates of 2D6 and nebivolol is a minor substrate of 2D6. Monitor for drug interactions.
- Carvedilol and propranolol are inhibitors of P-gp and may increase the serum concentration of P-gp substrates (e.g., cyclosporine, dabigatran, digoxin, ranolazine).

Direct Renin Inhibitor

Aliskiren directly inhibits renin, which is responsible for the conversion of angiotensinogen to angiotensin I (Ang I). A decrease in the formation of Ang I results in a decrease in the formation of Ang II.

DRUG	DOSING	SAFETY/SIDE EFFECTS/MONITORING
Aliskiren *(Tekturna)*	150-300 mg daily Take with or without food but be consistent in administration with regard to meals Avoid high fat foods (reduces absorption) Protect from moisture	**BOXED WARNING** Can cause injury and death to the developing fetus when used in the 2nd and 3rd trimesters; discontinue as soon as pregnancy is detected **CONTRAINDICATIONS** Do not use with ACE inhibitors or ARBs in patients with diabetes **WARNINGS** Angioedema (discontinue immediately and do not readminister), hyperkalemia, hypotension (↑ risk if salt- or volume-depleted), renal impairment, bilateral renal artery stenosis (avoid use) **SIDE EFFECTS** Diarrhea **MONITORING** BP, K, renal function **NOTES** Safety issue – see Pregnancy chapter

Direct Renin Inhibitor Drug Interactions

- All RAAS inhibitors ↑ the risk of hyperkalemia. Other medications that increase potassium (e.g., potassium-sparing diuretics) should be used cautiously. Patients should avoid salt substitutes that contain potassium chloride (instead of sodium chloride).
- Avoid using more than one RAAS inhibitor together (ACE inhibitor ± ARB ± aliskiren) due to an ↑ risk of renal impairment, hypotension, and hyperkalemia. The use of aliskiren in combination with an ACE inhibitor or ARB is specifically contraindicated in patients with diabetes and should be avoided when eGFR is < 60 mL/min.
- Aliskiren is a minor substrate of 3A4 and a substrate of P-gp; P-gp inhibitors (e.g., cyclosporine or itraconazole) can increase aliskiren levels and 3A4 inhibitors can increase aliskiren levels. Avoid grapefruit juice.
- Aliskiren ↓ the levels of furosemide; monitor effectiveness.

Centrally-Acting Alpha-2 Adrenergic Agonists

These agents decrease BP by stimulating alpha-2 adrenergic receptors in the brain and reducing sympathetic outflow of norepinephrine, which decreases SVR and HR. Clonidine is commonly used for resistant hypertension and in patients who can not swallow (e.g., due to dysphagia, dementia) since it is available as a patch formulation. Since the patch is changed weekly, it can help with adherence.

DRUG	DOSING	SAFETY/SIDE EFFECTS/MONITORING
CloNIDine *(Catapres, Catapres-TTS patch,* *Duraclon* inj) *Kapvay* – for ADHD Tablet, patch, injection	0.1-0.2 mg PO BID, max dose is 2.4 mg daily **Weekly patch** *Catapres-TTS-1* = 0.1 mg/24 hr *Catapres-TTS-2* = 0.2 mg/24 hr *Catapres-TTS-3* = 0.3 mg/24 hr	**CONTRAINDICATIONS** Methyldopa: active liver disease and concurrent use with MAO inhibitors **WARNINGS** Do not discontinue abruptly (can cause rebound hypertension, sweating, anxiety, tremors); must taper gradually over 2-4 days Methyldopa: positive Coombs test (risk for hemolytic anemia), hepatic necrosis **SIDE EFFECTS** Dry mouth, somnolence, headache, fatigue, dizziness, constipation, ↓ HR, hypotension, depression, behavioral changes, sexual dysfunction Clonidine patch: skin rash, pruritus, erythema, contact dermatitis Methyldopa: edema or weight gain (control with diuretics), hypersensitivity reactions [myocarditis, drug-induced fever, drug-induced lupus erythematosus (DILE)], ↑ prolactin levels **MONITORING** BP, HR, mental status **NOTES** Clonidine patch: apply weekly; remove before MRI
GuanFACINE IR *(Tenex)* GuanFACINE ER *(Intuniv)* – for ADHD	1-2 mg QHS	
Methyldopa Tablet, injection	250 mg BID-TID; max dose is 3 grams daily	

Direct Vasodilators

These agents cause direct vasodilation of arterioles, with little effect on veins, causing a decrease in SVR and a reduction in BP.

DRUG	DOSING	SAFETY/SIDE EFFECTS/MONITORING
HydrALAZINE Tablet, injection	PO: 10-50 mg QID, max dose is 300 mg daily IV: 10-20 mg Q4-6H PRN	**CONTRAINDICATIONS** Mitral valvular rheumatic heart disease, CAD **WARNING** Drug-induced lupus erythematosus (DILE – dose and duration related) **SIDE EFFECTS** Headache, hypotension, reflex tachycardia, palpitations, peripheral neuritis **MONITORING** HR, BP, ANA titer
Minoxidil *Men's Rogaine, Women's Rogaine* – OTC topical for hair growth	5-40 mg daily in 1-2 divided doses, max dose is 100 mg daily	**BOXED WARNING** Potent antihypertensive – can cause pericardial effusion and angina exacerbations; administer with a beta blocker and loop diuretic **CONTRAINDICATION** Pheochromocytoma **SIDE EFFECTS** Fluid retention, tachycardia, hair growth

Alpha Blockers

Alpha blockers bind to alpha-1 adrenergic receptors which results in peripheral vasodilation of arterioles and veins. They are not recommended by JNC 8 and should only be considered for resistant hypertension or in men who also have benign prostatic hypertrophy.

DRUG	DOSING	SAFETY/SIDE EFFECTS/MONITORING
Doxazosin *(Cardura, Cardura XL)*	IR: 1-4 mg daily; max dose is 16 mg daily XL: 4-8 mg daily	**WARNINGS** Orthostatic hypotension and syncope (especially with the 1st dose, dose increases, or when used with other anti-hypertensive agents or PDE-5 inhibitors) Intraoperative floppy iris syndrome has occurred in cataract surgery patients who were on or were previously treated with an alpha-1 blocker Priapism Doxazosin: not recommended in severe hepatic impairment; use caution with strong 3A4 inhibitors **SIDE EFFECTS** Dizziness, fatigue, headache, edema **NOTES** *Cardura XL:* OROS formulation (see Drug Formulations chapter) can leave a ghost tablet (empty shell) in the stool
Prazosin *(Minipress)*	1-5 mg BID; max dose is 20 mg daily in divided doses	
Terazosin	1-2 mg QHS; max dose is 20 mg daily	

Hypertensive Urgencies and Emergencies

A hypertensive urgency or emergency is defined as a rapidly accelerating BP with (emergency) or without (urgency) target organ damage (see table below). There are many treatment options for hypertensive urgency and emergency; drug selection often depends on the patient's other medical conditions and the type of target organ damage identified. IV medications from the various drug classes, and vasodilators (discussed in the Critical Care & Fluid/Electrolytes chapter), are used in hypertensive emergencies, while oral therapy is preferred in hypertensive urgencies. Below is a summary of both conditions and treatment goals.

	URGENCY: NOT LIFE-THREATENING	EMERGENCY: POTENTIALLY LIFE-THREATENING
Definition	↑ BP (generally ≥ 180/120 mmHg) without acute target organ damage	↑ BP (generally ≥ 180/120 mmHg) with acute target organ damage (e.g., encephalopathy, acute coronary syndrome, pulmonary edema, stroke, aortic dissection, acute kidney injury)
Treatment	Any oral medication with an onset of action within 15-30 minutes; ↓ BP gradually over 24-48 hrs	↓ BP by no more than 10-25% (within the first hour), then if stable, ↓ to 160/100 mmHg within the next 2-6 hrs; use IV medications (e.g., esmolol, labetalol, hydralazine, nicardipine, nitroglycerin, nitroprusside)

PATIENT COUNSELING

All Hypertension Medications

- You may not feel that you have high blood pressure, as often there are no obvious symptoms. It is important that you continue using this medication, even if you feel well. You may need to use blood pressure medication for the rest of your life to prevent serious complications, such as kidney damage, stroke and heart attack.
- If you miss a dose, take the missed dose as soon as you remember. If it is almost time for your next dose, skip the missed dose and take the medication at the next regularly scheduled time. Do not take extra medication to make up the missed dose.
- To be sure this medication is helping your condition, your blood pressure will need to be checked on a regular basis. It is important that you do not miss any scheduled visits to your healthcare provider.
- This medication is only one part of a complete treatment program for your high blood pressure; it is important that you follow the recommended diet, exercise, and weight control plans closely.
- You may have been instructed to check your blood pressure at home. Record the measurements in a notebook and bring them to your appointments for your provider to see.

Diuretics

- This medication will cause you to urinate more throughout the day. If you need to take the medication twice daily, be sure to take your second dose no later than 4 P.M. to avoid getting up at night to go to the bathroom.
- This medication may make you feel dizzy and lightheaded when getting up from a sitting or lying position. Get up slowly. Let your feet hang over the bed for a few minutes before getting up. Hang on to the bed or nearby dresser when standing from a sitting position.
- This medication can decrease the amount of potassium in your body. Potassium supplements may be needed while you are on this medication to ensure you have enough potassium for your heart.
- If you have diabetes, your blood sugar may need to be monitored more frequently when you start this medication as it can affect your blood sugar.

Calcium Channel Blockers

- This medication can cause a few side effects, including swelling of the ankles, feeling tired, dizziness, headache, a hot or warm feeling in your face, and an irregular or fast heart beat.
- Other medications can alter how this drug works. Do not start any new medications, including over-the-counter drugs or supplements, unless you check with your healthcare provider first. Avoid eating grapefruit or drinking grapefruit juice while using this medication.
- *Adalat CC:* should be taken on an empty stomach.
- *Adalat CC, Procardia XL* and *Covera HS:* this medication can leave an empty shell in your stool. If you see the tablet in your stool, it is nothing to worry about.

ACE Inhibitors, ARBs, and Aliskiren

- This medication can cause birth defects if taken during pregnancy. Use an effective form of birth control while taking this medication. If you become pregnant during treatment, stop using this medication and tell your healthcare provider right away.
- This medication can increase the amount of potassium in your body. Do not use salt substitutes or potassium supplements while taking this medication, unless your healthcare provider has told you to do so.

- Get emergency medical help if you have any of these signs of an allergic reaction: hives, difficulty breathing, or swelling of your face, lips, tongue, and/or throat.
- ACE inhibitors: tell your healthcare provider if you develop a dry, hacking cough that is bothersome while taking this medication.

Beta Blockers

- Take this medication at the same time every day. Do not discontinue your medication without consulting your healthcare provider as stopping suddenly may make your condition worse.
- This medication can cause a few side effects, including dizziness, fatigue, and rarely, sexual problems. If these side effects bother you, let your healthcare provider know.
- If you have diabetes, this medication may cause you to miss some of the symptoms of low blood sugar (e.g., shakiness, palpitations, anxiety). You will still experience sweating and hunger if your blood sugar is low.
- Non-selective beta blockers: contact your healthcare provider if you experience any difficulty breathing while taking this medication.
- *Coreg/Coreg CR*: take this medication with food.
- *Lopressor/Toprol XL:* take with or immediately after meals.

Clonidine

- Do not stop clonidine suddenly; this can cause your blood pressure to become dangerously high. Make sure you do not run out of medication.
- Clonidine can cause a variety of side effects, including drowsiness, dizziness, fatigue, dry mouth, depression and sexual dysfunction. If the side effects bother you, let your healthcare provider know but do not stop taking this medication suddenly.
- The clonidine patch *(Catapres-TTS)* is changed weekly. Apply the patch to a hairless area of the skin on the upper outer arm or chest every 7 days. The white adhesive cover can be applied over the patch to keep it in place. Do not place the patch on broken or irritated skin. After 7 days, remove the used patch and apply a new patch to a different area than the previous site to avoid skin irritation. When removing the patch, be sure to discard it safely, away from the reach of any children or pets. The patch will need to be removed before an MRI to prevent a potential burn.

PRACTICE CASE

FP is a 58 y/o black male at the clinic today for a routine follow-up visit. His past medical history includes hypertension and chronic lower back pain. He states that he feels fine, except for his back pain, and does not understand why he has to take any other medications. His diet consists of mostly processed and pre-packaged foods. He is a non-smoker and does not drink alcohol.

Allergies: NKDA

Medications:
Norco 1-2 tabs PRN pain NTE 8 tabs/day
Zestoretic 20/25 mg 1 tab daily

Vitals:
BP: 162/95 mmHg HR: 88 BPM RR: 18 BPM Temp: 38°C Pain: 3/10

Labs:
Na (mEq/L) = 141 (135 - 145)
K (mEq/L) = 3.8 (3.5 - 5)
Cl (mEq/L) = 100 (95 - 103)
HCO_3 (mEq/L) = 27 (24 - 30)
BUN (mg/dL) = 35 (7 - 20)
SCr (mg/dL) = 1.2 (0.6 - 1.3)
Glucose (mg/dL) = 160 (100 - 125)
Ca (mg/dL) = 9.1 (8.5 - 10.5)
Mg (mEq/L) = 1.7 (1.3 - 2.1)
PO_4 (mg/dL) = 4.1 (2.3 - 4.7)

Reinforce disease state education and adjust medication.

Questions

1. Which of the following medication combinations is *Zestoretic*?
   a. Benazepril and hydrochlorothiazide
   b. Enalapril and hydrochlorothiazide
   c. Irbesartan and hydrochlorothiazide
   d. Lisinopril and hydrochlorothiazide
   e. Triamterene and hydrochlorothiazide

2. Which of the following increases FP's risk for developing angioedema?
   a. Age
   b. Gender
   c. Ethnicity
   d. Medications
   e. Electrolyte profile

3. Which of the following is the best medication to add for BP control in FP?
   a. *Lasix*
   b. Metolazone
   c. Terazosin
   d. *Avalide*
   e. *Norvasc*

4. Which of the following is true regarding BP management for FP? (Select **ALL** that apply.)
   a. His goal BP is < 150/90 mmHg.
   b. He should decrease his sodium intake.
   c. He should use salt substitutes with potassium.
   d. If he misses a dose of medication, he should double the next dose.
   e. If his BP is controlled, he is less likely to have a stroke.

Questions 5-10 do not apply to the above case.

5. What is the mechanism of action for *Bystolic*? (Select **ALL** that apply.)
   a. Beta-2 selective blocker
   b. Beta-1 selective blocker
   c. Increases nitric oxide production
   d. Alpha-1 selective blocker
   e. Alpha-2 agonist

6. Choose the correct statement(s) concerning *Coreg CR*. (Select **ALL** that apply.)
   a. The generic name is nebivolol.
   b. The starting dose for hypertension is 12.5 mg BID.
   c. The drug is a non-selective beta blocker and alpha-1 blocker.
   d. The drug decreases heart rate.
   e. The drug should be taken without food.

7. Shantal is a 62 year old black female who comes to the clinic for a regular check up. She has chronic kidney disease with proteinuria and is taking *Accupril* 20 mg daily. Her 3 BP readings on this visit are 143/93, 149/91 and 146/95. What would be the best recommendation to make at this time?
   a. Discontinue *Accupril* and start *Norvasc*.
   b. Add *Diovan*.
   c. Add hydrochlorothiazide.
   d. Discontinue *Accupril* and start labetalol.
   e. No additional medication is needed at this time.

8. A patient comes to the pharmacy with a new prescription for *Exforge*. Which of the following medications are the correct match for this prescription?
   a. Aliskiren and hydrochlorothiazide
   b. Aliskiren and valsartan
   c. Amlodipine and benazepril
   d. Valsartan, amlodipine, and hydrochlorothiazide
   e. Amlodipine and valsartan

9. A patient develops angioedema while taking *Altace*. Which of the following medications would be a safe, alternative agent to use for BP control?
   a. *Maxzide*
   b. *Atacand*
   c. *Lotrel*
   d. *Lotensin*
   e. *Tekturna*

10. Which one of the following beta blockers has intrinsic sympathomimetic activity (ISA)?
   a. Atenolol
   b. Acebutolol
   c. Carvedilol
   d. Timolol
   e. Nadolol

Answers

1-d, 2-c,d, 3-e, 4-b,e, 5-b,c, 6-c,d, 7-c, 8-e, 9-a, 10-b

50

ISCHEMIC HEART DISEASE

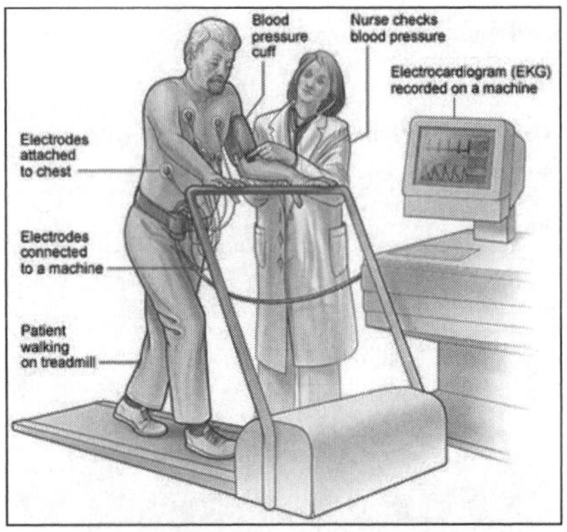

GUIDELINES/REFERENCES

2014 ACC/AHA/AATS/PCNA/SCAI/STS focused update of the guideline for the diagnosis and management of patients with stable ischemic heart disease. *Circulation*. 2014;130:1749-1767.

2012 ACCF/AHA/ACP/AATS/PCNA/SCAI/STS guideline for the diagnosis and management of patients with stable ischemic heart disease. *Circulation*. 2012;126(25):e354-e471.

Additional guidelines included with the online course.

We gratefully acknowledge the assistance of Kim M. Jones, PharmD, BCPS, Assistant Dean of Student Services and Associate Professor of Pharmacy Practice, Union University, in preparing this chapter.

BACKGROUND

Angina is chest pain, pressure, tightness or discomfort, usually caused by ischemia of the heart muscle or spasm of the coronary arteries. The chest pain is described as "squeezing," "grip-like," "heavy," or "suffocating," and typically does not vary with position or respiration. Stable angina, also known as stable ischemic heart disease (SIHD), is associated with predictable chest pain often brought on by exertion or emotional stress and relieved within minutes by rest or with nitroglycerin. Unstable angina (UA) is a type of acute coronary syndrome (ACS); this is a medical emergency where the chest pain is increasing (in frequency, intensity or duration) and is not relieved with nitroglycerin or rest (see the Acute Coronary Syndromes chapter).

Some patients (women, elderly and those with diabetes) may not experience the classic symptoms of SIHD; because of this, they may not recognize the need for medical attention or they may be misdiagnosed with another condition (e.g., GERD).

When chest pain is caused by vasospasm of the coronary arteries, it is called Prinzmetal's (variant or vasospastic) angina. This type of angina can occur at rest and is often caused by illicit drug use, particularly cocaine.

PATHOPHYSIOLOGY

Chest pain occurs when there is an imbalance between myocardial oxygen demand (workload) and supply (blood flow). In SIHD, myocardial oxygen supply is often decreased due to plaque build up (atherosclerosis) within the inner walls of the coronary arteries. This is known as coronary artery disease (CAD) and causes narrowing of the arteries and reduced blood flow to the heart. Myocardial oxygen demand increases when the heart is working harder as a result of increased heart rate, contractility and left ventricular wall tension [due to increased preload (volume of blood returning to the heart) and/or afterload (systemic vascular resistance, or SVR)].

DIAGNOSIS

A cardiac stress test is performed to assess the likelihood of CAD and diagnose SIHD. The cardiac stress test increases myocardial oxygen demand, either by exercise on a treadmill, pedaling a stationary exercise bicycle, or with intravenous pharmacological stimulation (when disabilities or medical conditions limit exercise), using dipyridamole, adenosine *(Adenoscan)*, regadenoson *(Lexiscan)* or dobutamine. As myocardial oxygen demand increases, the patient is monitored for the development of symptoms (e.g., chest pain, dyspnea, lightheadedness), changes in heart rate and blood pressure, and transient rhythm disturbances or ST segment abnormalities on an ECG. In patients for whom the diagnosis of SIHD is certain, stress testing can be used to determine if coronary angiography should be performed to assess the extent of atherosclerosis and need for revascularization.

EVALUATION OF SIHD
History and physical
CBC, CK-MB, troponins (I or T), aPTT, PT/INR, lipid panel, glucose
ECG (at rest and during chest pain)
Cardiac stress test/stress imaging
Cardiac catheterization/angiography

NON-DRUG TREATMENT

Multiple risk factors for heart disease, vascular disease and stroke are typically present in patients with SIHD, including hypertension, smoking, dyslipidemia, diabetes, obesity and physical inactivity. Patients should be encouraged to follow a heart healthy diet (e.g., saturated fats < 7% and *trans* fats < 1% of total calories, adequate intake of fresh fruits and vegetables, low-fat dairy products), maintain a BMI of 18.5 – 24.9 kg/m^2, and maintain a waist circumference < 35 inches in females and < 40 inches in males. To improve cardiopulmonary fitness, 30 – 60 minutes of moderate-intensity aerobic activity 5 – 7 days per week, supplemented by an increase in daily lifestyle activities (e.g., walking breaks at work, gardening), is recommended. Medically supervised programs such as cardiac rehabilitation, and physician-directed, home-based programs are encouraged for at-risk patients at first diagnosis. Please note these recommendations are different from the obesity guideline recommendations (see Weight Loss chapter for more information).

Patients who smoke should quit, and secondhand smoke should be avoided. Alcohol intake should be limited to 1 drink/day (4 oz wine, 12 oz beer, or 1 oz of spirits) for women and 1 – 2 drinks/day for men.

ANGINAL PRESENTATIONS
Stable Ischemic Heart Disease Chest pain that is predictable; it occurs with activity or stress and is relieved promptly by rest or nitroglycerin; underlying cause is atherosclerosis (CAD)
Prinzmetal's Angina Chest pain due to vasospasm of coronary arteries; it is unpredictable and can occur at rest but is not usually associated with underlying CAD
Acute Coronary Syndromes Acute chest pain that is severe and not relieved by rest or nitroglycerin; acute medical care is needed (includes UA, NSTEMI and STEMI – refer to Acute Coronary Syndromes chapter)
Silent Ischemia Transient myocardial ischemia without symptoms of chest pain

DRUG TREATMENT

The treatment goals for SIHD are to improve functional capacity (by eliminating anginal pain), prevent future cardiovascular events (e.g., MI, heart failure) and reduce the risk of cardiovascular death. An antiplatelet agent and an antianginal regimen are used together for this purpose. Aspirin is the recommended antiplatelet agent; clopidogrel *(Plavix)* is used in patients with an allergy or other contraindication to aspirin or in combination in select patients (see Dual Antiplatelet Therapy section).

Antianginal therapy is aimed at decreasing myocardial oxygen demand or increasing myocardial oxygen supply (see Antianginal Treatment table). Beta blockers are first-line; CCBs (both DHPs and non-DHPs) or long-acting nitrates should be used when beta blockers are contraindicated or when additional symptomatic relief is needed. Ranolazine can also be used as a substitute for, or in addition to, beta blocker therapy. Short-acting nitroglycerin, as a sublingual (SL) tablet, powder or translingual (TL) spray, is recommended for immediate relief of angina in all patients.

SIHD is one of the atherosclerotic cardiovascular diseases (ASCVD), as defined by the 2013 ACC/AHA Guideline on the Treatment of Blood Cholesterol. Patients ≤ 75 years of age with ASCVD should be placed on high-intensity statin therapy. For patients > 75 years of age with ASCVD, a moderate-intensity statin is recommended. Patients with hypertension, heart failure and diabetes should be aggressively managed with the guideline-driven therapies for each of these conditions. An annual influenza vaccine is recommended; pneumococcal vaccines *(Prevnar 13* and *Pneumovax 23)* should be administered per ACIP recommendations (see Immunizations chapter).

TREATMENT APPROACH FOR SIHD

- **A** – Antiplatelet and antianginal drugs
- **B** – Blood pressure and beta blockers
- **C** – Cholesterol (statins) and cigarettes (cessation)
- **D** – Diet and diabetes
- **E** – Exercise and education

Antiplatelet Agents

Aspirin binds irreversibly to cyclooxygenase-1 and 2 (COX-1 and 2) enzymes which results in decreased prostaglandin (PG) and thromboxane A2 (TXA2) production; TXA2 is a potent vasoconstrictor and inducer of platelet aggregation. Aspirin has antiplatelet, antipyretic, analgesic and anti-inflammatory properties. Clopidogrel is a prodrug that irreversibly inhibits P2Y12 ADP-mediated platelet activation and aggregation.

DRUG	DOSING	SAFETY/SIDE EFFECTS/MONITORING
Aspirin *(Ascriptin, Bayer, Bufferin, Ecotrin,* *Durlaza,* others) **+ omeprazole *(Yosprala)*** OTC: tablet, chewable tablet, enteric-coated tablet, suppository Rx: ER capsule *(Durlaza),* delayed-release tablet *(Yosprala)* See Pain chapter for more information on aspirin products	75-162 mg daily *Yosprala:* 81 mg/40 mg daily	**CONTRAINDICATIONS** NSAID or salicylate allergy; patients with asthma (due to risk of urticaria, angioedema, or bronchospasm), rhinitis, and nasal polyps; children and teenagers with viral infection (due to risk of Reye's syndrome) **WARNINGS** Bleeding (including GI bleed/ulceration) – risk increased with heavy alcohol use or other drugs that ↑ bleeding risk (e.g., NSAIDs, anticoagulants, other antiplatelet agents) **SIDE EFFECTS** Dyspepsia, heartburn, nausea, tinnitus (in toxicity) **MONITORING** Bleeding, bruising **NOTES** Shown to ↓ incidence of MI, CV events, and death; used in all SIHD patients indefinitely (unless contraindicated) *Yosprala* is indicated for patients who require aspirin but are at risk of developing aspirin-associated gastric ulcers; MedGuide required Enteric coated aspirin (325 mg) must be chewed if patient is having an ACS *Durlaza* and *Yosprala* should not be used when rapid onset is needed (e.g., ACS, pre-PCI)

Antiplatelet Agents Continued

DRUG	DOSING	SAFETY/SIDE EFFECTS/MONITORING
Clopidogrel *(Plavix)* Tablet	75 mg daily	**BOXED WARNING** Clopidogrel is a prodrug. Effectiveness depends on the conversion to an active metabolite, mainly by CYP450 2C19. Poor metabolizers of 2C19 exhibit higher cardiovascular events than patients with normal 2C19 function. Tests to check 2C19 genotype can be used as an aid in determining a therapeutic strategy. Consider alternative treatments in patients identified as 2C19 poor metabolizers. Refer to Pharmacogenomics chapter. **CONTRAINDICATIONS** Serious bleeding (e.g., GI bleed, intracranial hemorrhage) **WARNINGS** 2C19 inhibitors: avoid concomitant use of omeprazole or esomeprazole ↑ bleeding risk, stop 5 days prior to elective surgery (e.g., CABG) Premature discontinuation (↑ risk of thrombosis) Thrombotic thrombocytopenic purpura (TTP) has been reported **SIDE EFFECTS** Gastrointestinal hemorrhage, hematoma, pruritus **MONITORING** Symptoms of bleeding, Hgb/Hct as necessary **NOTES** Used in SIHD patients with a contraindication to aspirin; may be used in combination with aspirin (see Dual Antiplatelet Therapy section) MedGuide required

Dual Antiplatelet Therapy

Monotherapy with aspirin or clopidogrel is used in the vast majority of patients with SIHD. In 2016, the ACC/AHA released a guideline update on dual antiplatelet therapy (DAPT). The primary benefit in SIHD is after placement of a bare metal stent (DAPT for at least one month), a drug-eluting stent (DAPT for at least 6 months), or post-CABG (DAPT for 12 months). When using DAPT in SIHD, clopidogrel is the only P2Y12 inhibitor recommended and the dose of aspirin should be 81 mg daily; aspirin, at doses of 75 – 162 mg, should be continued indefinitely after the course of DAPT has been completed.

Antiplatelet Drug Interactions

- Most drug interactions are due to additive effects with other agents that can ↑ bleeding risk. See Drug Interactions chapter for drugs that can increase bleeding risk.

Aspirin

- Salicylates may ↑ the serum concentration of methotrexate, by inhibiting its renal clearance.
- Use caution in combination with other ototoxic agents (see Drug Interactions chapter).

Clopidogrel

- Avoid concomitant use with omeprazole and esomeprazole and use caution with other 2C19 inhibitors.

Antianginal Treatment

DRUG	MECHANISM OF CLINICAL BENEFIT	CLINICAL NOTES
Beta Blockers Used 1st line in SIHD See Hypertension chapter for a complete review of these agents	Reduce myocardial oxygen demand: ↓ HR, ↓ contractility and ↓ left ventricular wall tension	Start low, go slow; titrate to resting HR of 55-60 BPM; avoid abrupt withdrawal All agents are equally effective; can be used as monotherapy or in combination with DHP CCBs, long-acting nitrates, and/or ranolazine Provide mortality reduction and symptom improvement More effective than nitrates and CCBs in silent ischemia; avoid in Prinzmetal's angina
Calcium Channel Blockers Preferred agents for Prinzmetal's (variant) angina See Hypertension chapter for a complete review of these agents	Reduce myocardial oxygen demand: non-DHPs ↓ HR and contractility; DHPs ↓ SVR (afterload) Increase myocardial oxygen supply: CCBs ↑ blood flow through coronary arteries	Can be used in SIHD when beta blockers are contraindicated or as add-on therapy to beta-blockers for continued anginal symptoms Slow-release or long-acting DHPs and non-DHPs are effective; avoid short-acting DHPs (e.g., nifedipine IR) DHPs are preferred when CCBs are used in combination with beta blockers (due to risk of excessive bradycardia when non-DHPs are used with beta blockers)
Nitrates	Reduce myocardial oxygen demand: ↓ preload (free radical nitric oxide produces vasodilation of veins more than arteries) Increases myocardial oxygen supply: ↑ blood flow through collateral (non-atherosclerotic) arteries	**SL tablets, SL powder or TL spray** Recommended for all patients for fast relief of angina; call 911 if chest pain does not go away after the first dose of SL tablet, SL powder or TL spray; nitrate tolerance does not develop with SL/TL products **Long-acting nitrates** Long-acting nitrates are used when beta blockers are contraindicated or as add-on therapy for treatment of symptoms; a nitrate-free interval is required to prevent tolerance (see Nitroglycerin Formulations table on next page)
Ranolazine *(Ranexa)*	Selectively inhibits the late phase Na current and ↓ intracellular Ca; may decrease myocardial oxygen demand by decreasing ventricular tension and oxygen consumption	**CONTRAINDICATIONS** Liver cirrhosis, concurrent use of strong 3A4 inhibitors and inducers **WARNINGS** Can cause QT prolongation Acute renal failure has been observed in some patients with CrCl < 30 mL/min **SIDE EFFECTS** Dizziness, headache, constipation, nausea **MONITORING** ECG, K, renal function **NOTES** Can use in place of beta blockers or as add-on therapy for treatment of symptoms Has little to no clinical effects on HR or BP Do not crush, break, or chew

Nitroglycerin Formulations Used in SIHD

FORMULATIONS*	SAFETY/SIDE EFFECTS/MONITORING
Short-acting nitrates	**CONTRAINDICATIONS** Hypersensitivity to organic nitrates, concurrent use with PDE-5 inhibitors or riociguat (see Drug Interactions) SL tablets, powder and spray: ↑ intracranial pressure, severe anemia, circulatory failure and shock (SL powder only) **WARNINGS** Hypotension, headache, tachyphylaxis (↓ effectiveness/tolerance), may aggravate angina caused by hypertrophic cardiomyopathy **SIDE EFFECTS** Dizziness, lightheadedness, flushing, syncope **MONITORING** BP, HR, chest pain **NOTES** **Short-acting nitrates** Used PRN for immediate relief of chest pain; all patients with SIHD should have a short-acting product available and be familiar with use in urgent or emergent situations (see Patient Counseling section) Keep nitroglycerin SL tablets in the original amber glass bottle **Long-acting nitrates** Long-acting or scheduled products require a 10-12 hour nitrate-free period to ↓ tolerance (some products require a longer nitrate-free interval) Ointment: dosed BID (6 hours apart with a 10-12 hour nitrate-free interval) Patch: wear on for 12-14 hours, off for 10-12 hours; rotate sites; dispose of safely, away from children and pets Isosorbide mononitrate: use IR product BID at least 7 hours apart (e.g., 8 AM and 3 PM) and ER product QAM Isosorbide dinitrate: IR product is dosed BID-TID; when used TID, take at 8 AM, 12 PM and 4 PM for a 14 hour nitrate-free interval (or similar); take SR/ER product daily in the morning or divided BID with an 18 hour nitrate-free interval Isosorbide dinitrate is the preferred formulation for systolic HF (in combination with hydralazine)
Nitroglycerin SL tablet *(Nitrostat)* **0.3, 0.4, 0.6 mg**	
Nitroglycerin translingual spray *(NitroMist, Nitrolingual Pump Spray)* **0.4 mg/spray**	
Nitroglycerin SL powder *(GoNitro)* **0.4 mg/packet**	
Long-acting nitrates	
Nitroglycerin ointment 2% *(Nitro-BID)*	
Nitroglycerin transdermal patch *(Nitro-Dur, Minitran)* 0.1, 0.2, 0.3, 0.4, 0.6, 0.8 mg/hr	
Isosorbide mononitrate IR/ER tablet *(Monoket)* IR: 10 mg, 20 mg ER: 30 mg, 60 mg, 120 mg	
Isosorbide dinitrate IR/ER *(Isordil Titradose, Dilatrate-SR)* IR: 5 mg, 10 mg, 20 mg, 30 mg, 40 mg ER: 40 mg	

**IV nitroglycerin discussed in the Critical Care & Fluids/Electrolyte Chapter*

Nitrate Drug Interactions

- Avoid concurrent use of long-acting nitrates with PDE-5 inhibitors and riociguat; use caution with other antihypertensive medications and alcohol as these combinations can cause a significant decrease in BP.
  - If a patient does not use long-acting nitrates but has short-acting nitroglycerin available for immediate relief of angina, it should not be used if the patient has recently taken a PDE-5 inhibitor (avanafil in the past 12 hours, sildenafil or vardenafil in the past 24 hours, or tadalafil in the past 48 hours). Occasionally, and with careful monitoring, nitrates may be used in an acute emergency in a patient who has recently taken a PDE-5 inhibitor.

Ranolazine Drug Interactions

- Ranolazine is a substrate of 3A4 (major), 2D6 (minor) and P-gp and an inhibitor of 3A4 (weak), 2D6 (weak) and P-gp. Do not use with strong 3A4 inhibitors or inducers. Limit the dose to 500 mg BID in patients taking moderate 3A4 inhibitors (e.g., diltiazem, verapamil, fluconazole). Limit simvastatin to 20 mg/day if used together.

PATIENT COUNSELING

Antiplatelet Agents

- Take this medication once daily with or without food.
- This medication helps prevent platelets from sticking together and forming a clot that can block an artery. Do not stop taking it without talking to your healthcare provider. Stopping this medication can put you at risk of developing a clot which can be life-threatening.
- If you miss a dose, take it as soon as you remember. If it is almost time for your next dose, skip the missed dose and take the next dose at your regular scheduled time. Do not take two doses at the same time unless instructed by your healthcare provider.
- You may bleed and bruise more easily while taking this medication, even from a minor scrape. It may take longer to stop bleeding. Call your healthcare provider at once if you have black or bloody stools, or if you cough up blood or vomit that looks like coffee grounds. These could be signs of serious bleeding in the stomach or intestines.
- Your risk of bleeding in the stomach or intestines may be increased if you drink alcohol, have a history of stomach ulcers, or take other medications that increase the risk of bleeding (e.g., blood thinners or ibuprofen). Do not take other over-the-counter pain relievers without consulting your healthcare provider.

Aspirin

- Stop taking this medication and tell your healthcare provider right away if you develop signs of an allergic reaction (e.g., hives, swelling in the face, wheezing), ringing in the ears or loss of hearing.

Clopidgrel

- One rare but serious side effect is thrombotic thrombocytopenic purpura (TTP). Seek prompt medical attention if you experience any of these symptoms that cannot otherwise be explained: fever, weakness, extreme skin paleness, purplish spots or skin patches (called purpura), yellowing of the skin or eyes (jaundice), or mental status changes.
- If you need to have any type of surgery or dental work, tell the surgeon or dentist ahead of time that you are using clopidogrel. You may need to stop using the medication for at least 5 days before having major surgery, to prevent excessive bleeding.
- Some acid-reducing medications can decrease the beneficial effects of clopidogrel. Do not take heartburn medications without consulting your healthcare provider.

All Nitroglycerin Products

- This drug should not be used with the following medications: sildenafil *(Viagra, Revatio)*, tadalafil *(Cialis, Adcirca)*, vardenafil *(Levitra, Staxyn)*, avanafil *(Stendra)* and riociguat *(Adempas)*. A dangerous drop in blood pressure could occur.
- Side effects can include headache, dizziness, lightheadedness, redness, mild warmth, or nausea. Headache is often a sign that this medication is working. The redness and mild warmth is called flushing; flushing and headache should become less bothersome as your body gets used to the medication. Your healthcare provider may recommend treating headaches with the over-the-counter pain reliever acetaminophen. If headaches continue or become severe, tell your healthcare provider.

- To reduce the risk of dizziness and lightheadedness with this medication: get up slowly when rising from a sitting or lying position. Hold onto the side of the bed or chair to avoid falling. Limit alcoholic beverages.

Nitroglycerin Sublingual Tablets, Powder and Translingual Spray

- At the first sign of chest pain: take one dose immediately (one SL tablet, one SL powder packet or one TL spray). Call 911 immediately if chest pain persists after this first dose. Continue to take two additional doses at 5 minute intervals while waiting for the ambulance to arrive. Do not take more than three doses within 15 minutes.
- This medication may be taken 5 – 10 minutes before activities that bring on chest pain.
- Take these medications while sitting or lying down to avoid dizziness and lightheadedness.

Nitroglycerin SL Tablets

- Nitroglycerin SL tablets should not be chewed, crushed or swallowed. Place the tablet under the tongue, or in the area between the inside of the cheek and the gums/teeth, and let it dissolve.
- You may feel a slight burning or tingling sensation with SL tablets. This is not a sign of how well the medication is working. Do not use more medication because you do not feel these sensations.
- Keep nitroglycerin SL tablets tightly capped in the original amber glass bottle, and store at room temperature. Shake out 1 tablet only; do not let the other tablets get wet.

Nitroglycerin SL Powder

- Empty the contents of a packet under the tongue, close your mouth and breath normally through your nose. Let the powder dissolve without swallowing. Do not rinse the mouth or spit for 5 minutes after the dose.

Nitroglycerin TL Spray

- The pump must be primed before first use (5 sprays for *Nitrolingual Pump Spray* and 10 sprays for *NitroMist)*. If not used within 6 weeks, prime the pump with 1 spray *(Nitrolingual Pump Spray)* or 2 sprays *(NitroMist)* before use.
- Do not shake. Press the button firmly with the forefinger to release the spray onto or under the tongue. Close your mouth after the spray. Do not inhale the spray and try not to swallow too quickly afterwards. Do not spit or rinse the mouth for 5 – 10 minutes after the dose.

Nitroglycerin Ointment

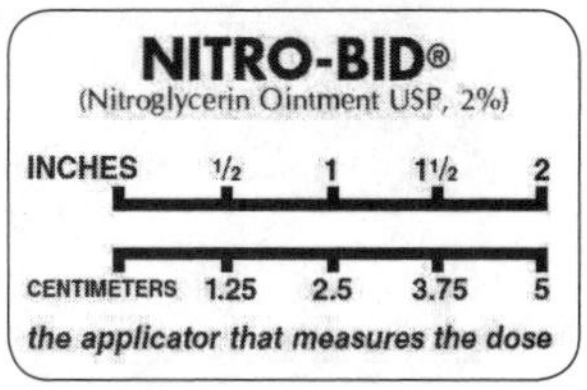

- Measure dosage of ointment with the dose measuring applicator supplied with the tube. Place the applicator on a flat surface, printed side down. Squeeze the needed amount of ointment onto the applicator, and place the applicator (ointment side down) on the desired area of the skin.
- Spread the ointment, using the dose measuring applicator, lightly onto the chest (or other area of skin if preferred). Do not rub into the skin. Tape the applicator into place.
- This medication can stain clothing. Care should be taken to completely cover the dose measuring applicator.

Nitroglycerin Patches

- Remove the patch from its pouch and remove the protective clear liner. Apply the patch to a clean, dry, and hairless area of the skin and press it firmly in place with the palm of your hand. Any area may be selected except the extremities below the knees or elbows; the chest is the preferred site. Hair in the area may be clipped, but not shaved. Avoid areas with cuts or irritation. Do not apply the patch immediately after bathing or showering; wait until your skin is completely dry. You may bathe, shower, and swim while wearing the patch.
- Apply one new patch each morning and wear for 12 – 14 hours. For the medication to work well, there must be a 10 – 12 hour "patch free" interval where the patch is left off.
- To reduce skin irritation, apply each new patch to a different area of skin.
- After removing the old patch, fold it in half with the sticky sides together, and discard out of the reach of children and pets.

Ranolazine

- Ranolazine is used to decrease the number of times you may get chest pain. It works differently than other drugs for chest pain, so it can be used with your other medications (beta blockers, nitrates and calcium channel blockers).
- Take this medication by mouth twice daily with or without food. Swallow the tablet whole. Do not crush or chew the tablets.
- Use this medication regularly to get the most benefit from it. Take it at the same times each day. It should not be used to treat chest pain when it occurs. Use other medications (e.g., SL nitroglycerin) to relieve chest pain, as directed by your healthcare provider.
- Dizziness, headache, lightheadedness, nausea, and constipation may occur. If any of these effects persist or worsen, notify your healthcare provider promptly.
- Ranolazine may cause a condition that affects the heart rhythm (QT prolongation). This heart rhythm can infrequently result in serious fast/irregular heartbeat and other symptoms (such as severe dizziness, fainting) that require immediate medical attention. The risk may be increased if you are taking other drugs that may affect the heart rhythm. Check with your healthcare provider before using any herbal or OTC medications.
- Other drugs may interfere with this medication. Avoid grapefruit and grapefruit juice and inform your healthcare provider and pharmacist that you are taking this medication before starting new drugs.

ACUTE CORONARY SYNDROMES

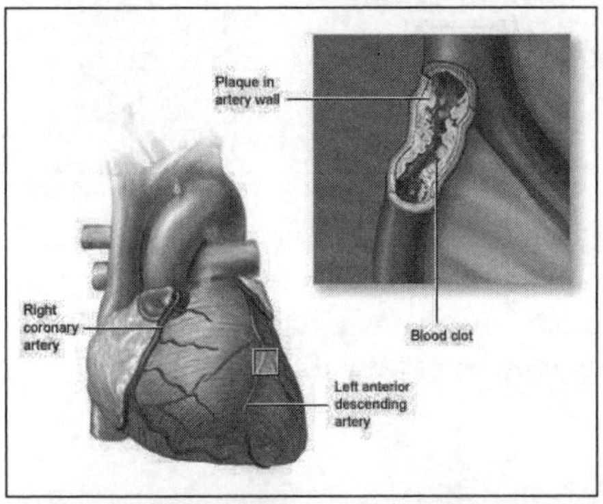

GUIDELINES/REFERENCES

2016 ACC/AHA Guideline Focused Update on Duration of Dual Antiplatelet Therapy in Patients With Coronary Artery Disease. *J Am Coll Cardiol.* 2016; doi:10.1016/j.jacc.2016.03.513.

2014 AHA/ACC Guideline for the Management of Patients with Non-ST-Elevation Acute Coronary Syndromes: A Report of the American College of Cardiology/ American Heart Association Task Force on Practice Guidelines. *Circulation.* 2014.130:e344-e426.

2013 ACCF/AHA Guideline for Management of ST-Elevation Myocardial Infarction: A Report of the American College of Cardiology Foundation/American Heart Association Task Force on Practice Guidelines. *Circulation.* 2013; 127:e362-e425.

We gratefully acknowledge the assistance of Kim M. Jones, PharmD, BCPS, Assistant Dean of Student Services and Associate Professor of Pharmacy Practice, Union University, in preparing this chapter.

BACKGROUND

Acute coronary syndrome (ACS) refers to a set of clinical conditions brought on by sudden, reduced blood flow causing an imbalance between myocardial oxygen supply and demand. This results from plaque buildup in the coronary arteries (coronary atherosclerosis). These plaques are made up of fatty deposits that cause the arteries to narrow, making blood flow more difficult. The surface of the plaque can rupture, leading to clot formation and an acute reduction in blood flow (ischemia). Ischemia may ultimately lead to cardiac muscle cell death (myocyte necrosis).

ACS encompasses the clinical conditions of non-ST segment elevation acute coronary syndromes (NSTE-ACS) and ST segment elevation myocardial infarction (STEMI). NSTE-ACS describes both unstable angina (UA) and non-ST-segment elevation myocardial infarction (NSTEMI), since patients are indistinguishable upon presentation and the term emphasizes the continuum between UA and NSTEMI.

Signs and Symptoms of ACS

The classic symptoms of ACS include chest pain ("pain" also encompasses symptoms of discomfort, pressure and squeezing) lasting ≥ 10 minutes, severe dyspnea, diaphoresis, syncope/presyncope and/or palpitations. The pain may radiate to the arms, back, neck, jaw or epigastric area. Female, elderly and diabetic patients may be less likely to experience the classic symptoms. Symptoms can occur at rest, with minimal exertion, or may be precipitated by exercise, cold weather, extreme emotions, stress or sexual intercourse. ACS is a medical emergency. Patients with a prescription for sublingual nitroglycerin (NTG) should use one dose every 5 minutes for up to 3 doses for relief of chest pain. If the chest pain or discomfort is not improved or is worse 5 minutes after the first dose, 911 should be called immediately.

Diagnosis

A 12-lead ECG should be performed and evaluated within 10 minutes at the site of first medical contact. Patients having an acute MI (STEMI or NSTEMI) should be urgently transported to a hospital with percutaneous coronary intervention (PCI) capability, if possible. If the ECG is not diagnostic, but the patient remains symptomatic, serial ECGs should be performed every 15 – 30 minutes during the first hour to detect ischemic changes.

Biochemical markers are released into the bloodstream when myocardial cells die. The measurement of these cardiac enzymes helps establish the diagnosis. The cardiac troponins I and T (TnI and TnT) are the most sensitive and specific biomarkers for ACS. They are detectable in the blood within 2 – 12 hours (depending on the assay) after myocardial necrosis and can remain detectable for up to 5 – 14 days. Creatine kinase myocardial isoenzyme (CK-MB) and myoglobin are less sensitive markers than troponins, but may still be monitored in clinical practice. Cardiac troponin I or T levels should be obtained at presentation and 3 – 6 hours after symptom onset in all patients with ACS symptoms. B-type natriuretic peptide (BNP) or N-terminal pro-B-type natriuretic peptide (NT-proBNP) levels may be obtained to assess risk.

RISK FACTORS

Age (men > 45 years of age, women > 55 years of age or with early hysterectomy)

Family history (1st degree relative) of coronary event before 55 years of age (men) or 65 years of age (women)

Smoking

Hypertension

Dyslipidemia

Diabetes

Chronic angina

Known coronary artery disease

Lack of exercise

Excessive alcohol

Comparison Between UA, NSTEMI and STEMI

	UA	NSTEMI	STEMI
Symptoms	Chest pain (described in text)		
Cardiac Enzymes	Negative	Positive	Positive
ECG Changes	None or transient ischemic changes*		ST segment elevation**
Blockage	Partial blockage		Complete blockage

**ST segment depression or prominent T-wave inversion*

***Meeting defined criteria and in ≥ 2 contiguous leads (e.g., leads looking at the same area of the heart)*

DRUG TREATMENT

The medical team selects a treatment strategy for the patient depending on the diagnosis and symptom severity. In NSTE-ACS, patients may be treated with medications alone (referred to as medical management) or with PCI (referred to as an early invasive strategy). PCI is a coronary revascularization procedure that involves inflating a small balloon inside a coronary artery to widen it and improve blood flow. Usually metal mesh, called a stent, is placed into the artery afterward to keep the artery open. Because a STEMI results from complete blockage of one or more coronary arteries, the blocked arteries need to be opened as quickly as pos-

STUDY TIP: DRUG TREATMENT OF ACS

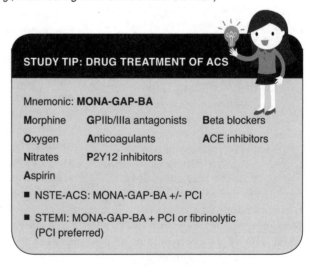

Mnemonic: **MONA-GAP-BA**

Morphine	**G**PIIb/IIIa antagonists	**B**eta blockers
Oxygen	**A**nticoagulants	**A**CE inhibitors
Nitrates	**P**2Y12 inhibitors	
Aspirin		

- NSTE-ACS: MONA-GAP-BA +/- PCI
- STEMI: MONA-GAP-BA + PCI or fibrinolytic (PCI preferred)

sible. For patients with a STEMI, a fibrinolytic should be administered if the patient is not able to receive PCI within 2 hours (120 minutes) of first medical contact (see fibrinolytic section of this chapter). Patients may also go directly for urgent coronary artery bypass graft (CABG) surgery if there is significant multi-vessel disease within the coronary arteries.

Acute treatment is aimed at providing immediate relief of ischemia and preventing MI expansion and death. Drug treatment includes the use of antianginal, antiplatelet and anticoagulant therapy (see Study Tip on previous page and summary table below). High-intensity statin therapy should be initiated or continued in all patients, if there are no contraindications to use, per the NSTE-ACS and STEMI guidelines. An MI is considered atherosclerotic cardiovascular disease (ASCVD) according to the 2013 ACC/AHA Guideline on the Treatment of Blood Cholesterol (refer to Dyslipidemia chapter).

Summary of Drugs Used Acutely for ACS (MONA-GAP-BA)

DRUG	MOA OF CLINICAL BENEFIT	CLINICAL COMMENTS
Morphine	Produces arterial and venous dilation; leading to a ↓ in myocardial O2 demand; provides pain relief	Morphine sulfate (2-5 mg IV repeated at 5- to 30-minute intervals PRN) may be used in patients with ongoing chest discomfort despite NTG therapy. Side effects: hypotension, bradycardia, N/V, sedation and respiratory depression. See Pain chapter for additional information.
Oxygen		Administer to patients with arterial oxygen saturation < 90% (SaO2 < 90%) or those in respiratory distress.
Nitrates	Dilate coronary arteries and improve collateral blood flow; ↓ cardiac O2 demand by ↓ preload, ventricular wall tension and afterload (modestly)	Sublingual NTG (0.3-0.4 mg) as previously described, if not already administered. Start IV NTG (start at 10 mcg/min, titrate as needed) for persistent ischemic pain, hypertension or heart failure. Do not use NTG if SBP < 90 mmHg, HR < 50 BPM or if patient is experiencing a right ventricular infarction. NTG should not be administered concurrently with PDE-5 inhibitors for erectile dysfunction. See Ischemic Heart Disease and Sexual Dysfunction chapters for additional details.
Aspirin	Inhibits platelet aggregation/ clot formation by inhibiting production of thromboxane A2 (TXA2) via irreversible COX-1 and COX-2 inhibition	Non-enteric-coated, chewable aspirin (162-325 mg) should be given to all patients immediately, if no contraindications are present (do not use extended-release aspirin products). A maintenance dose of aspirin 81-162 mg daily should be continued indefinitely. If intolerant to aspirin, may use clopidogrel or ticagrelor (discussed later in this chapter).
Glycoprotein (GP) IIb/IIIa receptor antagonists	Block fibrinogen from binding to the GPIIb/IIIa receptors on platelets, preventing platelet aggregation	Agents include abciximab, eptifibatide or tirofiban. Option for medical management (eptifibatide or tirofiban) or for patients going for PCI +/- stent (all agents). If used in PCI, they are given concurrently with heparin.
Anticoagulants	Inhibit clotting factors and can reduce infarct size	Agents include LMWHs (preferred for NSTEMI) and UFH or bivalirudin (preferred for STEMI). See Anticoagulation chapter.
P2Y12 Inhibitors	Inhibit P2Y12 receptor on platelets, preventing platelet aggregation	Agents include clopidogrel, prasugrel and ticagrelor. Ticagrelor or clopidogrel can be given in medical management as well as with PCI (ticagrelor given preference per guidelines). Prasugrel should only be given if the patient is going for PCI. Administer the loading dose followed by a maintenance dose. Do not give a P2Y12 inhibitor if patient is going for urgent CABG surgery.

Summary of Drugs Used Acutely for ACS Continued

DRUG	MOA OF CLINICAL BENEFIT	CLINICAL COMMENTS
Beta Blockers	↓ O2 demand by ↓ BP, HR, and contractility; ↓ ischemia, reinfarction, and arrhythmias; prevent cardiac remodeling; ↑ long-term survival	An oral, low dose beta blocker (beta-1 selective blocker without intrinsic sympathomimetic activity preferred) should be started within the first 24 hours in patients who do not have any of the following: 1) signs of HF, 2) evidence of a low-output state, 3) ↑ risk for cardiogenic shock, 4) other contraindications to beta blockade [e.g. severe bradycardia (usually defined as HR < 45 BPM in ACS)]. If the patient has concomitant HFrEF that is stable, choose 1 of the 3 beta blockers used in HFrEF (bisoprolol, metoprolol succinate or carvedilol; Chronic Heart Failure chapter). IV beta blocker therapy may be reasonable in STEMI patients, especially if ongoing ischemia or hypertension is present. If beta blockers and nitrates are ineffective, oral long-acting nondihydropyridine calcium channel blockers (verapamil or diltiazem) are reasonable to use for recurrent ischemia, if there are no contraindications. See Hypertension chapter.
ACE Inhibitors	Inhibit angiotensin converting enzyme and block the production of angiotensin II; prevent cardiac remodeling; ↓ preload and afterload	An oral ACE inhibitor should be started within the first 24 hours and continued indefinitely in all patients with left ventricular ejection fraction (LVEF) < 40%, those with HTN, DM or stable CKD unless contraindicated (use ARB if patient is ACE inhibitor intolerant). Use in other patients may be reasonable. Do not use an IV ACE inhibitor within the first 24 hours due to the risk of hypotension. See Hypertension chapter.

Medications to Avoid in the Acute Setting

- NSAIDs (except for aspirin), whether nonselective or COX-2-selective, should not be administered during hospitalization due to ↑ risk of mortality, reinfarction, hypertension, cardiac rupture, renal insufficiency and heart failure associated with their use.
- Immediate-release nifedipine should not be used due to ↑ risk of mortality.

P2Y12 Inhibitors

P2Y12 inhibitors bind the adenosine diphosphate (ADP) P2Y12 receptor on the platelet surface which prevents ADP-mediated activation of the GPIIb/IIIa receptor complex, thereby reducing platelet aggregation. Clopidogrel and prasugrel are structurally similar and classified as thienopyridines; they are prodrugs that irreversibly bind to the receptor. Ticagrelor is not a prodrug and has reversible binding to the receptor. P2Y12s are associated with bleeding and there is no antidote. They are commonly used with aspirin after an ACS, which is called dual antiplatelet therapy (DAPT).

DRUG	DOSING	SAFETY/SIDE EFFECTS/MONITORING
Clopidogrel *(Plavix)* Tablet Indicated for ACS, recent MI, stroke and PAD	LD: 300-600 mg PO (600 mg for PCI) MD: 75 mg PO daily If patient received fibrinolytic therapy for STEMI and is > 75 years of age, omit the loading dose and start 75 mg daily	**BOXED WARNING** Clopidogrel is a prodrug. Effectiveness depends on the conversion to an active metabolite, mainly by CYP450 2C19. Poor metabolizers of 2C19 exhibit higher cardiovascular events than patients with normal 2C19 function. Tests to check 2C19 genotype can be used as an aid in determining a therapeutic strategy. Consider alternative treatments in patients identified as 2C19 poor metabolizers. Refer to Pharmacogenomics chapter. **CONTRAINDICATIONS** Serious bleeding (e.g., GI bleed, intracranial hemorrhage) **WARNINGS** CYP2C19 inhibitors: avoid concomitant use of omeprazole or esomeprazole ↑ bleeding risk, stop 5 days prior to elective surgery (e.g., CABG) Premature discontinuation (↑ risk of thrombosis) Thrombotic thrombocytopenic purpura (TTP) has been reported **SIDE EFFECTS** Bleeding, hematoma, pruritus **NOTES** MedGuide required
Prasugrel *(Effient)* Tablet Indicated for patients with ACS who are to be managed with PCI	LD: 60 mg PO (no later than 1 hour after PCI) MD: 10 mg PO daily (5 mg daily if patient weighs < 60 kg) Once PCI is planned, give the dose promptly and no later than 1 hour after the PCI Keep in original container	**BOXED WARNING** Significant, sometimes fatal, bleeding **CONTRAINDICATIONS** Serious bleeding; history of TIA or stroke **WARNINGS** ↑ bleeding risk, stop 7 days prior to elective surgery (e.g., CABG) Premature discontinuation TTP has been reported **SIDE EFFECTS** Bleeding (more than clopidogrel) **NOTES** Not recommended in patients ≥ 75 years due to high bleeding risk, unless patient is considered high risk (DM or prior MI) MedGuide required

P2Y12 Inhibitors Continued

DRUG	DOSING	SAFETY/SIDE EFFECTS/MONITORING
Ticagrelor *(Brilinta)* Tablet Indicated for patients with ACS	LD: 180 mg MD: 90 mg PO BID for 1 year. After 1 year, give 60 mg BID Tablets can be crushed and mixed with water to be swallowed or given via NG tube	**BOXED WARNINGS** Significant, sometimes fatal, bleeding Maintenance doses of aspirin above 100 mg reduce the effectiveness of ticagrelor and should be avoided; after any initial aspirin dose, maintenance aspirin dose should not exceed 100 mg daily **CONTRAINDICATIONS** Serious bleeding, history of intracranial hemorrhage **WARNINGS** ↑ bleeding risk, stop 5 days prior to elective surgery (e.g., CABG) Severe hepatic impairment Bradyarrhythmias **SIDE EFFECTS** Bleeding, dyspnea (> 10%), ↑ SCr, ↑ uric acid **NOTES** MedGuide required
Cangrelor *(Kengreal)* Injection Indicated as adjunct to PCI to ↓ risk of periprocedural MI, repeat revascularization and stent thrombosis in patients who are P2Y12 inhibitor naïve and are not receiving a GP IIb/IIIa inhibitor	30 mcg/kg IV bolus prior to PCI, then 4 mcg/kg/min IV infusion for 2 hours or duration of procedure (whichever is longer)	**CONTRAINDICATIONS** Significant active bleeding **SIDE EFFECTS** Bleeding **NOTES** Effects are gone 1 hour after drug discontinuation Transition to oral P2Y12 inhibitor as follows: ticagrelor 180 mg given during or immediately after stopping cangrelor infusion; prasugrel 60 mg or clopidogrel 600 mg immediately after stopping cangrelor (do not give prior to stopping cangrelor)

LD = loading dose, MD = maintenance dose

P2Y12 Inhibitor Drug Interactions

- All P2Y12 inhibitors: most drug interactions are due to additive effects with other agents that can ↑ bleeding risk. See Drug Interactions chapter for drugs that can ↑ bleeding risk. If an ACS patient experiences bleeding while on a P2Y12 inhibitor, it should be managed without discontinuing the P2Y12 inhibitor, if possible. Stopping the P2Y12 inhibitor (particularly within the first few months after ACS) ↑ the risk of subsequent cardiovascular events.
- Avoid using clopidogrel in combination with omeprazole and esomeprazole and use caution with other 2C19 inhibitors.
- Ticagrelor is a 3A4 (major) substrate; avoid use with strong 3A4 inhibitors and inducers. See Drug Interactions chapter for more information. Avoid simvastatin and lovastatin doses greater than 40 mg/day. Monitor digoxin levels with initiation of or any change in ticagrelor dose.

Glycoprotein IIb/IIIa Receptor Antagonists

Glycoprotein IIb/IIIa receptor antagonists block the platelet glycoprotein IIb/IIIa receptor, which is the binding site for fibrinogen, von Willebrand factor and other ligands. Inhibition of binding at this final common receptor blocks platelet aggregation and prevents further thrombosis. Eptifibatide and tirofiban have reversible blockade and abciximab has irreversible blockade.

DRUG	DOSING	SAFETY/SIDE EFFECTS/MONITORING
Abciximab ***(ReoPro)*** Injection	LD: 0.25 mg/kg IV bolus MD: 0.125 mcg/kg/min (max 10 mcg/min) IV infusion for 12 hrs (PCI, STEMI with PCI) or 18-24 hrs (NSTE-ACS unresponsive to conventional medical therapy with planned PCI within 24 hrs) Not recommended for medical management (NSTE-ACS without PCI)	**CONTRAINDICATIONS** Thrombocytopenia (platelets < 100,000/mm^3) History of bleeding diathesis (predisposition) Active internal bleeding Severe uncontrolled HTN Recent major surgery or trauma (within past 4 weeks for tirofiban, past 6 weeks for abciximab//eptifibatide) History of stroke within 2 years (abciximab); history of stroke within 30 days or any history of hemorrhagic stroke (eptifibatide)
Eptifibatide ***(Integrilin)*** Injection	LD: 180 mcg/kg IV bolus (max 22.6 mg), repeat bolus in 10 mins if undergoing PCI MD: 2 mcg/kg/min (max 15 mg/hour) IV infusion started after the first bolus. Continue for 18-24 hours after PCI or for 12-72 hours if PCI was not performed CrCl < 50 mL/min: same LD, reduce MD to 1 mcg/kg/min (max 7.5 mg/hour)	**For abciximab** Recent (within 6 weeks) GI or GU bleeding of clinical significance ↑ prothrombin time Hypersensitivity to murine proteins Intracranial neoplasm, arteriovenous malformation or aneurysm **For eptifibatide** Dependency on renal dialysis **SIDE EFFECTS** Bleeding, thrombocytopenia (especially abciximab), hypotension
Tirofiban *(Aggrastat)* Injection	LD: 25 mcg/kg IV bolus over 5 min or less MD: 0.15 mcg/kg/min IV infusion for up to 18 hours CrCl ≤ 60 mL/min: same LD, reduce MD to 0.075 mcg/kg/min	**MONITORING** Hgb, Hct, platelets, s/sx of bleeding, renal function **NOTES** Do not shake vials upon reconstitution Must filter abciximab Platelet function returns in ~24-48 hours after discontinuing abciximab and ~4-8 hours after stopping eptifibatide/tirofiban

LD = loading dose, MD = maintenance dose

Fibrinolytics

These agents cause fibrinolysis (clot breakdown) by binding to fibrin in a thrombus (clot) and converting entrapped plasminogen to plasmin. Fibrinolytics are used only for STEMI. Once a STEMI is confirmed on a 12-lead ECG performed by emergency medical services (EMS), timing is critical. The blocked artery or arteries must be opened as quickly as possible with either PCI or fibrinolytic therapy. PCI is preferred if it can be performed within 90 minutes (optimal door-to-balloon time) or within 120 minutes of first medical contact. If PCI is not possible within 120 minutes of first medical contact, fibrinolytic therapy is recommended and should be given within 30 minutes of hospital arrival (door-to-needle time). In the absence of contraindications and when PCI is not available, fibrinolytic therapy is reasonable in STEMI patients who are still symptomatic within 12 – 24 hours of symptom onset.

DRUG	DOSING	SAFETY/SIDE EFFECTS/MONITORING
Alteplase *(Activase)* Recombinant tissue plasminogen activator (tPA, rtPA) *Cathflo Activase* (single-use 2 mg vial) used to restore function of potentially clotted central lines and devices	**Accelerated Infusion** > 67 kg: 100 mg IV over 1.5 hrs; given as 15 mg bolus, 50 mg over 30 min, 35 mg over 1 hr ≤ 67 kg: 15 mg bolus, 0.75 mg/kg (max 50 mg) over 30 min, 0.5 mg/kg (max 35 mg) over 1 hr (max 100 mg total)	**CONTRAINDICATIONS** Active internal bleeding or bleeding diathesis History of recent stroke Any prior intracranial hemorrhage (ICH) Recent intracranial or intraspinal surgery or trauma (last 2-3 months) Intracranial neoplasm, arteriovenous malformation, or aneurysm Severe uncontrolled hypertension (unresponsive to emergency therapy) **SIDE EFFECTS** Bleeding (including ICH), hypotension **MONITORING** Hgb, Hct, s/sx of bleeding **NOTES** Door-to-needle time should be < 30 minutes Contraindications for the use of alteplase in ischemic stroke differ (refer to Stroke chapter)
Tenecteplase *(TNKase)*	Single IV bolus dose: < 60 kg: 30 mg 60-69 kg: 35 mg 70-79 kg: 40 mg 80-89 kg: 45 mg ≥ 90 kg: 50 mg	
Reteplase *(Retavase)*	2 dose regimen: 10 units IV, followed by 10 units IV given 30 minutes later	

PROTEASE-ACTIVATED RECEPTOR-1 ANTAGONIST

Vorapaxar is a reversible antagonist of the protease-activated receptor-1 (PAR-1) expressed on platelets, but its long half-life makes it effectively irreversible. Vorapaxar is indicated in patients with a history of MI or with peripheral arterial disease (PAD) to reduce thrombotic cardiovascular events (CV death, MI, stroke and urgent coronary revascularization). This agent was used in addition to aspirin and/or clopidogrel in clinical trials. It has not yet been incorporated into clinical guidelines.

DRUG	DOSING	SAFETY/SIDE EFFECTS/MONITORING
Vorapaxar *(Zontivity)* Tablet	2.08 mg (one tablet) PO daily	**BOXED WARNING** Bleeding risk (including ICH and fatal bleeding); contraindicated in patients with history of stroke, TIA, ICH or active serious bleeding **WARNING** Do not use in severe liver impairment **SIDE EFFECTS** Bleeding, anemia **NOTES** No antidote MedGuide required

Vorapaxar Drug Interactions

- Vorapaxar is a substrate of 3A4 and inhibitor of P-gp. Avoid concomitant use with strong 3A4 inhibitors and strong 3A4 inducers.

STUDY TIP: LONG-TERM MANAGEMENT AFTER ACS (SECONDARY PREVENTION)

Aspirin
- Indefinitely (81 mg per day), unless contraindicated

P2Y12 Inhibitor
- Medical Therapy Patients: ticagrelor or clopidogrel with aspirin 81 mg for at least 12 months
- PCI-Treated Patients (including any type of stent): clopidogrel, prasugrel or ticagrelor with aspirin 81 mg for at least 12 months
    - Continuation of DAPT beyond 12 months may be considered in patients who are tolerating DAPT and are not at high risk of bleeding following coronary stent placement

Nitroglycerin
- Indefinitely (SL tabs or spray PRN)

Beta Blocker
- 3 years; continue indefinitely if HF or if needed for management of HTN

ACE Inhibitor
- Indefinitely if EF < 40%, HTN, CKD or diabetes; consider for all MI patients with no contraindications

Aldosterone Antagonist (see Chronic Heart Failure chapter)
- Indefinitely if EF ≤ 40% and either symptomatic HF or DM receiving target doses of an ACE inhibitor and beta blocker
- Contraindications: significant renal impairment (SCr > 2.5 mg/dL in men, SCr > 2 mg/dL in women) or hyperkalemia (K > 5 mEq/L)

Statin (see Dyslipidemia chapter)
- Patients ≤ 75 years of age, use high-intensity statin therapy
- Patients > 75 years of age, use moderate-intensity statin therapy

Other Considerations for ACS Patients

- Pain relief – patients with chronic musculoskeletal pain should use acetaminophen, nonacetylated salicylates, tramadol or small doses of narcotics before considering the use of NSAIDs. If these options are insufficient, it is reasonable to use nonselective NSAIDs such as naproxen (lowest CV risk). COX-2 selective agents have high CV risk and should be avoided.
- Warfarin use – if patients require warfarin (e.g., patients with AFib) along with aspirin and a P2Y12 inhibitor, it may be reasonable to lower the INR goal to 2 – 2.5. Use this triple combination for the shortest time possible to limit the risk of bleeding. Clopidogrel is the preferred P2Y12 for triple therapy. Proton pump inhibitors should be prescribed in any patient with a history of GI bleeding while taking triple antithrombotic therapy.
- Lifestyle counseling – should include smoking cessation, managing chronic conditions (such as HTN, DM), avoiding excessive alcohol intake, encouraging physical exercise and a healthy diet. All patients should be referred to a comprehensive cardiovascular rehabilitation program.

Patient Counseling

Refer to the Ischemic Heart Disease chapter for patient counseling on aspirin, nitrates and clopidogrel.

52

CHRONIC HEART FAILURE

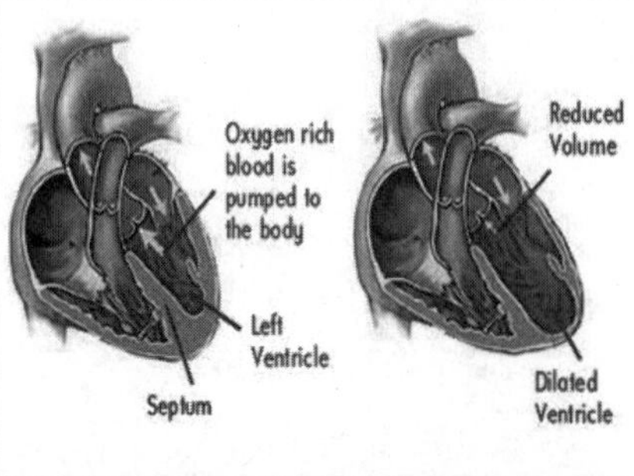

GUIDELINES/REFERENCES

Yancy CW, Jessup M, Bozkurt B, et al. 2016 ACC/AHA/HFSA Focused Update on New Pharmacological Therapy for Heart Failure: An Update of the 2013 ACCF/AHA Guideline for the Management of Heart Failure. *J Card Fail.* 2016; 22:659-69.

Yancy CW, Jessup M, Bozkurt B, et al. 2013 ACCF/AHA Guideline for the Management of Heart Failure: A Report of the American College of Cardiology Foundation/American Heart Association Task Force on Practice Guidelines. *Circulation.* 2013; 128:e240-e327.

We gratefully acknowledge the assistance of Tien M. H. Ng, PharmD, FHFSA, FCCP, BCPS (AQ-Cardiology), Associate Professor, University of Southern California School of Pharmacy, in preparing this chapter.

BACKGROUND

Heart failure (HF) is a common condition in the U.S., especially in older adults. It is the primary diagnosis in over 1 million hospitalizations each year. Heart "failure" occurs when the heart is not able to supply sufficient oxygen-rich blood to the body, because of impaired ability of the ventricle to either fill or eject blood. HF is commonly classified as either ischemic (due to a decrease in blood supply, such as from an MI) or non-ischemic, such as from long-standing uncontrolled hypertension. Other less common causes include valvular disease, excessive alcohol intake or illicit drug use, congenital heart defects, viral infections, diabetes, and cardiotoxic drugs/chest radiation. In the U.S., most cases are due to damage from an MI or from long-standing hypertension.

DIAGNOSIS

Symptoms of HF (see table on next page) can occur due to problems with systolic (contraction) or diastolic (relaxation) functions of the heart. Patients with HF cycle through periods of stability and exacerbation (increased symptoms). Exacerbations frequently result in hospitalization and negatively impact the patient's quality of life.

An ultrasound of the heart (echocardiography or ECHO) provides useful information when HF is suspected, including an estimate of left ventricular ejection fraction (LVEF). LVEF is a measurement of how much blood is pumped out of the left ventricle (the main pumping chamber of the heart) with each contraction. The term LVEF is used interchangeably with the general term, ejection fraction (EF). An EF less than 40% indicates systolic dysfunction, or heart failure with a reduced ejection fraction (HFrEF); this type of heart failure is the focus of this chapter, since it is most widely studied and has well-defined treatment guidelines. Other types of HF and associated EF ranges are shown in the table. Many patients have components of both systolic and diastolic dysfunction.

Ejection Fraction Ranges and Associated Terminology

EF	TERM	PRIMARY PROBLEM
55-70%	Normal	Normal
≥ 50%	Heart Failure with Preserved EF (HFpEF) Diastolic Dysfunction	Impaired ventricular relaxation and filling during diastole
40-49%	Heart Failure with Mid-Range EF (HFmrEF)	Likely mixed systolic and diastolic dysfunction
< 40%	Heart Failure with Reduced EF (HFrEF) Systolic Dysfunction	Impaired ability to eject blood during systole

SIGNS AND SYMPTOMS OF SYSTOLIC HEART FAILURE

Labs

↑ BNP (B-type natriuretic peptide): normal < 100 pg/mL

↑ NT-proBNP (N-terminal pro B-type natriuretic peptide): normal < 300 pg/mL

BNP and proBNP are used to distinguish between cardiac and non-cardiac causes of dyspnea

General Signs and Symptoms

Dyspnea [shortness of breath (SOB); at rest or upon exertion]

Cough

Fatigue, weakness

Reduction in exercise capacity

Left-Sided Signs and Symptoms

Orthopnea: SOB when lying flat

Paroxysmal nocturnal dyspnea (PND): nocturnal cough and SOB

Bibasilar rales: crackling lung sounds heard on lung exam with a stethoscope

S3 gallop: abnormal heart sound

Hypoperfusion (renal impairment, cool extremities)

Right-Sided Signs and Symptoms

Peripheral edema

Ascites: abdominal fluid accumulation

Jugular venous distention (JVD): neck vein distention

Hepatojugular reflux (HJR): neck vein distention that occurs when pressure is placed on the abdomen

Hepatomegaly: enlarged liver due to fluid congestion

Classification Systems

Two classification systems are currently recommended for HFrEF. The American College of Cardiology and the American Heart Association (ACC/AHA) recommend categorizing patients by the HF stage (see table). The staging system is used to guide treatment in order to slow progression in asymptomatic patients (stages A and B) or in symptomatic patients (stages C and D). HF patients can also be classified by the level of limitation in physical functioning using the New York Heart Association (NYHA) classification system. Many drug therapies were studied based on the NYHA functional classification of the patients, so this remains extremely relevant to drug therapy decisions.

ACC/AHA STAGING SYSTEM		NYHA FUNCTIONAL CLASS	
A	At high risk for development of HF, but without structural heart disease or symptoms of HF (e.g., patients with HTN, CAD, DM, obesity, metabolic syndrome)		No corresponding category
B	Structural heart disease present, but without signs or symptoms of HF (e.g., LVH, low EF, valvular disease, previous MI)	I	No limitations of physical activity. Ordinary physical activity does not cause symptoms of HF (e.g., fatigue, palpitations, dyspnea)

Clinical Diagnosis of HF

C	Structural heart disease with prior or current symptoms of HF (e.g., patients with known structural heart disease, SOB and fatigue, reduced exercise tolerance)	I	No limitations of physical activity. Ordinary physical activity does not cause symptoms of HF
		II	Slight limitation of physical activity. Comfortable at rest, but ordinary physical activity results in symptoms of HF
		III	Marked limitation of physical activity. Comfortable at rest but minimal exertion (bathing, dressing) causes symptoms of HF
D	Advanced structural heart disease with symptoms of HF at rest despite maximal medical treatment (refractory HF requiring specialized interventions)	IV	Unable to carry on any physical activity without symptoms of HF, or symptoms of HF at rest

PATHOPHYSIOLOGY

Terminology

Cardiac output (CO) is the volume of blood that is pumped by the heart in one minute. CO is a function of the heart rate (HR) and the stroke volume (SV), or the volume of blood ejected from the left ventricle during one complete heartbeat (cardiac cycle). SV depends on preload, afterload and contractility. The cardiac index (CI) relates the CO to the size of the patient, and is calculated by dividing the CO by the body surface area (BSA).

CO = HR x SV	CI = CO / BSA

Compensatory Mechanisms

During low cardiac output states (the main problem in HFrEF), neurohormones are released that increase the blood volume or increase the force or speed of contractions. These compensatory mechanisms temporarily increase CO, but over time will further compromise the heart. Chronic neurohormonal activation increases the workload of the heart which causes damage to the myocytes and produces changes in the size, composition and shape of the heart (e.g., hypertrophy, dilatation). This is called cardiac remodeling.

The three main neurohormonal pathways activated in heart failure are: the renin angiotensin aldosterone system (RAAS), sympathetic nervous system (SNS) and vasopressin. Refer to the Hypertension chapter for a diagram of the RAAS. Briefly, renin splits angiotensinogen to produce angiotensin I. Angiotensin I is further converted into angiotensin II (Ang II) by the angiotensin-converting enzyme (ACE). There are also non-ACE pathways for the formation of Ang II. Ang II causes blood vessel constriction (vasoconstriction), and stimulates the release of aldosterone (from the adrenal gland) and vasopressin (from the pituitary gland). Aldosterone causes sodium and water retention, and increases potassium excretion. Vasopressin causes vasoconstriction and water retention. Activation of the SNS results in the release of norepinephrine (NE) and epinephrine (EPI). These catecholamines cause an increase in heart rate, contractility (positive inotropy) and vasoconstriction. All three neurohormonal systems also promote cardiac remodeling. Each neurohormonal system potentiates the others, contributing to the vicious cycle of chronic neurohormonal activation. Importantly, neurohormones that normally balance these systems (e.g., natriuretic peptides) are insufficiently expressed.

NON-DRUG (LIFESTYLE) TREATMENT

Patients with heart failure should be instructed to:

- Monitor and document body weight daily, in the morning after voiding and before eating.
- Notify the provider when weight ↑ by 2 – 4 pounds in 1 day or 3 – 5 pounds in 1 week, or when the symptoms have worsened: ↑ SOB with activity, ↑ in cough or wheezing, ↑ swelling in the feet/ankles/legs, ↑ number of pillows needed to sleep, needing to sleep in a chair (upright), or feeling more fatigued than usual. A HF action plan should be provided and explained to the patient.
- Maintain sodium restriction of less than 1,500 mg/day in stage A and B HF (maintain some degree of sodium restriction in other patients).
- Maintain fluid restriction (1.5 – 2 L/day) in stage D, especially in patients with hyponatremia.
- Stop smoking. Limit alcohol intake. Avoid illicit drug use.
- Obtain recommended vaccines: Influenza (annually), pneumococcal vaccines if 65 years of age or older, and any patient-specific requirements.
- Consider weight reduction to BMI < 30 kg/m^2. Weight reduction is important to reduce the heart's workload and preserve function.

SELECT DRUGS THAT CAUSE OR WORSEN HEART FAILURE

KEY DRUGS

Antiarrhythmics
Avoid Class I agents (e.g., procainamide, quinidine, flecainide) in HF

Amiodarone and dofetilide have less risk of worsening HF

Oncology agents
Anthracyclines (doxorubicin, daunorubicin)

Nondihydropyridine CCBs
Diltiazem and verapamil (specifically in systolic HF)

Thiazolidinediones
↑ risk of edema

NSAIDs
All (including celecoxib)

Immunosuppressants
TNF inhibitors (etanercept and rituximab) and interferons

Itraconazole

Others

Systemic steroids

Amphetamines, other sympathomimetics (stimulants), illicit drugs (e.g., cocaine)

Triptans
Contraindicated with history of cardiovascular disease or uncontrolled hypertension

Oncology agents:
Some tyrosine kinase inhibitors (lapatinib, sunitinib) and agents that cause fluid retention (e.g., trastuzumab, imatinib, docetaxol)

Excessive alcohol use

- Exercise training (or regular physical activity) is recommended as safe and effective in patients who are able to participate. Cardiac rehabilitation can be useful in stable HF patients.

OTC and Alternative Medications

- Omega-3 polyunsaturated fatty acid (PUFA) supplementation is reasonable to use as adjunctive therapy in patients with NYHA Class II – IV symptoms to ↓ mortality and cardiovascular hospitalizations. The dose of 1 gram daily is commonly used, although the optimal dose has not been established.
- Hawthorn and coenzyme Q10 may improve HF symptoms based on small studies; patients should consult with their healthcare provider prior to use.
- Avoid the use of products containing ephedra (ma huang) or ephedrine. Patients should consult with their healthcare provider prior to the use of sympathomimetics (stimulants), such as decongestants.

DRUG TREATMENT

The cornerstones of HF treatment are ACE inhibitors or ARBs, beta blockers and loop diuretics. The following diagram reviews the pathophysiology and the Study Tip summarizes current recommendations.

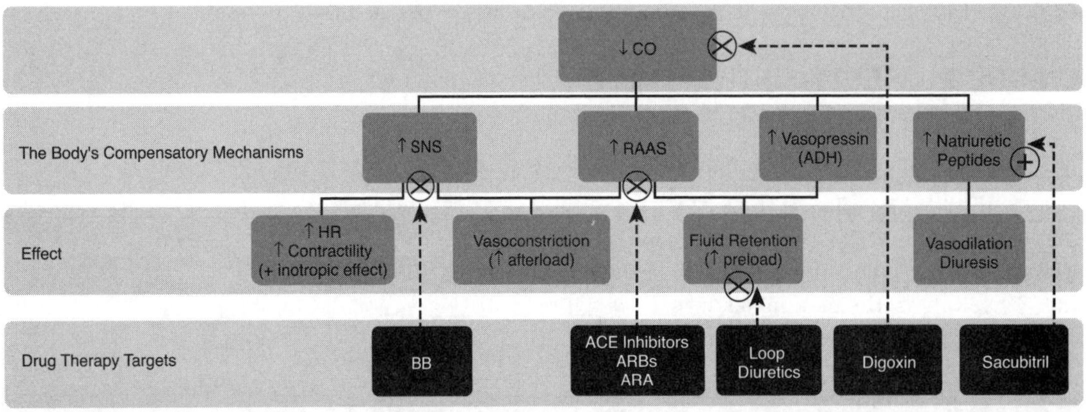

STUDY TIP: TREATMENT OF CHRONIC SYSTOLIC HEART FAILURE

Treatments that ↓ mortality (recommended for all patients without contraindications)

- **ACE inhibitors or angiotensin receptor blockers (ARBs)**
  - Block neurohormonal activation of the RAAS, resulting in vasodilation and improved EF
- **Beta blockers**
  - Block the activation of the SNS by blocking EPI and NE; also provide benefit in controlling heart rate and reducing arrhythmia risk
- **Aldosterone receptor antagonists (ARAs)**
  - Provide added diuresis; improve symptoms and EF
  - ↓ morbidity and mortality in NYHA Class II-IV
- **Angiotensin receptor and neprilysin inhibitor (ARNI)**
  - Sacubitril/valsartan *(Entresto)* ↓ the risk of cardiovascular death and hospitalization for HF in NYHA Class II-IV patients who have a decreased EF
  - In patients with chronic symptomatic HF (NYHA Class II-III) who tolerate an ACE inhibitor or ARB, an ARNI is preferred to an ACE inhibitor/ARB to further reduce morbidity and mortality

Treatments that ↓ mortality for select patients

- **Hydralazine and nitrates *(BiDil)***
  - ↓ morbidity and mortality in black patients with NYHA Class III-IV (when added to an ACE inhibitor or ARB) and in other patients who cannot tolerate an ACE inhibitor or ARB

Treatments that improve other aspects of HF (these are not proven to ↓ mortality)

- **Loop diuretics**
  - Reduce blood volume, which ↓ edema and congestion; most HF patients need a loop diuretic for symptom relief
- **Digoxin**
  - Provides a small increase in cardiac output, improves symptoms and decreases cardiac hospitalizations
- **Ivabradine *(Corlanor)***
  - ↓ risk of hospitalization in patients with stable NYHA Class II-III HF in normal sinus rhythm with a resting heart rate ≥ 70 BPM (refer to drug table for specific criteria for use)

Loop Diuretics

Loop diuretics are used to ↓ fluid volume to make it easier for the heart to pump. Loop diuretics block sodium and chloride reabsorption in the thick ascending limb of the loop of Henle, interfering with the chloride-binding co-transport system. They ↑ excretion of sodium, chloride, magnesium, calcium, and water. They are used to reduce congestive symptoms (reduce preload) and restore euvolemia (or "dry" weight). Loop diuretics have not been shown to alter the survival of stable heart failure patients, but most patients require them for symptom control. Care must be taken not to over-diurese patients, which can lead to hypotension or renal impairment; the lowest effective dose should be used. If the response to the loop is poor, a combination with a thiazide-type diuretic, such as metolazone, can be useful. Loops can be used for BP reduction in patients with renal impairment when other options are not adequate.

DRUG	DOSING	SAFETY/SIDE EFFECTS/MONITORING
Furosemide *(Lasix)* Tablet, injection	Oral: 20-40 mg daily or BID Max 600 mg/day	**BOXED WARNING** Can lead to profound diuresis resulting in fluid and electrolyte depletion **CONTRAINDICATIONS** Anuria **WARNINGS** Sulfa allergy (not likely to cross-react – see cautionary statement in Drug Allergies & Adverse Drug Reactions chapter); this warning does not apply to ethacrynic acid **SIDE EFFECTS** Hypokalemia, orthostatic hypotension, ↓ Na, ↓ Mg, ↓ Cl, ↓ Ca (different than thiazides which ↑ Ca), ↑ HCO3/metabolic alkalosis, hyperuricemia (↑ UA), hyperglycemia (↑ BG), ↑ TGs, ↑ total cholesterol, photosensitivity, ototoxicity (more with ethacrynic acid) including hearing loss, tinnitus and vertigo **MONITORING** Renal function, fluid status (input and output, weight), BP, electrolytes, audiology testing with high doses or rapid IV administration, s/sx of HF **NOTES** Take early in the day to avoid nocturia. Store furosmide injection at room temp (refrigeration causes crystals to form, which may dissolve upon warming). Do not use furosemide solutions if they are yellow in color; must be clear. Furosemide and bumetanide are light-sensitive (in amber bottles); IV admixtures do not require light protection. **Dose Conversions** Oral equivalent dosing: furosemide 40 mg = bumetanide 1 mg = torsemide 20 mg = ethacrynic acid 50 mg Furosemide IV:PO ratio 1:2 (furosemide 20 mg IV = furosemide 40 mg PO). Bumetanide, torsemide and ethacrynic acid IV:PO ratio 1:1.
Bumetanide *(Bumex)* Tablet, injection	Oral: 0.5-1 mg daily or BID Max 10 mg/day	
Torsemide *(Demadex)* Tablet Injection on prolonged shortage; rarely available	Oral: 10-20 mg daily Max 200 mg/day	
Ethacrynic Acid *(Edecrin)* Tablet, injection	Oral: 50-200 mg daily or divided Max 400 mg/day	

Loop Diuretic Drug Interactions

- Can acutely ↓ blood pressure; risk for additive hypotension with other drugs that lower blood pressure. Monitor blood pressure carefully.
- Can ↑ the ototoxic potential of other ototoxic drugs (see Drug Interactions chapter), especially in patients with impaired renal function. This combination should be avoided if possible.
- Diuretics can ↓ renal clearance of lithium and ↑ risk of lithium toxicity.
- Avoid NSAIDs (including COX-2 inhibitors) in patients with HF. NSAIDs ↑ sodium and water retention, which ↓ the effect of the loop diuretics and can lead to renal impairment.
- The combination of a loop and a thiazide-type diuretic may ↑ diuretic response. Electrolyte abnormalities are more likely and must be monitored closely.

ACE Inhibitors and Angiotensin Receptor Blockers

ACE inhibitors block the conversion of angiotensin I to angiotensin II (Ang II) resulting in ↓ vasoconstriction and ↓ aldosterone secretion (refer to the Hypertension chapter for a diagram of the RAAS). They block the degradation of bradykinin, which is thought to contribute to the vasodilatory effects (and the side effects of cough and angioedema). ARBs block Ang II from binding to the angiotensin II type-1 (AT1) receptor. Overall, these agents ↓ RAAS activation (a major compensatory mechanism in HF), resulting in decreased preload and afterload. They ↓ cardiac remodeling, improve left ventricular function, and ↓ morbidity and mortality. The clinical benefits appear to be a drug class effect. An ACE inhibitor (or ARB if intolerant to ACE inhibitors) is indicated for all HF patients regardless of symptoms (NYHA Class I – IV). Other important points include:

- The target doses for these medications for HF are the doses used in clinical trials demonstrating their benefit or the maximum tolerated dose for a given patient. Titrate the drug to the target dose (if possible). Titrate to reduce symptoms, not BP.
- The combination of an ACE inhibitor and ARB has been shown to ↓ hospitalizations for HF, however, this is not frequently done as it is more common to combine either with an aldosterone receptor antagonist (ARA). Triple combination of ACE inhibitor + ARB + ARA is not recommended due to a higher risk of hyperkalemia and renal insufficiency.
- Angioedema can develop with any RAAS inhibitor; it occurs more frequently with ACE inhibitors (than with ARBs or aliskiren) and in black patients. If a patient develops angioedema with any RAAS inhibitor, other agents in the class are contraindicated, since angioedema can be fatal.

DRUG	DOSING	SAFETY/SIDE EFFECTS/MONITORING
ACE Inhibitors – only those mentioned in the guidelines (see complete list in Hypertension chapter)		
Captopril *(Capoten)*	Start 6.25 mg TID, 1 hr before meals Target dose: 50 mg TID	**BOXED WARNING** Can cause injury and death to the developing fetus when used in the 2nd and 3rd trimesters; discontinue as soon as pregnancy is detected **CONTRAINDICATIONS** History of angioedema **WARNINGS** Angioedema, renal impairment, hyperkalemia, hypotension (↑ risk if salt- or volume-depleted), bilateral renal artery stenosis (avoid use) **SIDE EFFECTS** Cough, hyperkalemia, hypotension, dizziness, HA, rash **MONITORING** BP, K, renal function, s/sx of HF **NOTES** Safety issue – see Pregnancy chapter
Enalapril *(Vasotec, Epaned* powder for oral solution) Enalaprilat (*Vasotec IV*)	Start 2.5 mg PO BID Target dose: 10-20 mg PO BID	
Fosinopril	Start 5-10 mg daily Target dose: 40 mg daily	
Lisinopril *(Prinivil, Zestril, Qbrelis* oral solution)	Start 2.5-5 mg daily Target dose: 20-40 mg daily	
Perindopril *(Aceon)*	Start 2 mg daily Target dose: 8-16 mg daily	
Quinapril *(Accupril)*	Start 5 mg BID Target dose: 20 mg BID	
Ramipril *(Altace)*	Start 1.25-2.5 mg daily Target dose: 10 mg daily	
Trandolapril *(Mavik)*	Start 1 mg daily Target dose: 4 mg daily	
ARBs – only those mentioned in the guidelines (see complete list in Hypertension chapter)		
Candesartan *(Atacand)*	Start 4-8 mg daily Target dose: 32 mg daily	Same as above except lack of cough and less angioedema with ARBs
Losartan *(Cozaar)* – benefit in clinical trials but no FDA indication	Start 25-50 mg daily Target dose: 50-150 mg daily	
Valsartan *(Diovan)*	Start 20-40 mg BID Target dose: 160 mg BID	

Angiotensin Receptor and Neprilysin Inhibitor

Entresto is a combination of a neprilysin inhibitor (sacubitril) and an ARB (valsartan). Neprilysin is the enzyme responsible for degradation of several beneficial vasodilatory peptides, including natriuretic peptides, adrenomedullin, substance P, and bradykinin. These peptides counteract the effects of RAAS activation, and produce vasodilation. An ARNI is indicated in NYHA Class II-IV patients to reduce HF hospitalizations and cardiovascular death, and is recommended as a potential first-line option (in place of an ACE inhibitor or ARB as monotherapy) in select symptomatic HF patients (NYHA Class II-III) who tolerate an ACE inhibitor or ARB to further improve morbidity and survival.

DRUG	DOSING	SAFETY/SIDE EFFECTS/MONITORING
Sacubitril/valsartan ***(Entresto)*** Tablet	Start: 50-100 mg BID Target dose: 200 mg BID CrCl < 30 mL/min = 50 mg BID The dose is the sum of the two components: 50 mg = 24/26 mg sacubitril/valsartan 100 mg = 49/51 mg sacubitril/valsartan 200 mg = 97/103 mg sacubitril/valsartan	**BOXED WARNING** Can cause injury and death to the developing fetus when used in the 2nd and 3rd trimesters; discontinue as soon as pregnancy is detected **CONTRAINDICATIONS** Concurrent use with ACE inhibitors or ARBs, history of angioedema **WARNINGS** Angioedema, renal impairment, hyperkalemia, hypotension (↑ risk if salt- or volume-depleted), bilateral renal artery stenosis (avoid use) **SIDE EFFECTS** Hypotension, hyperkalemia, cough, dizziness, renal failure **MONITORING** BP, K, renal function, s/sx of HF **NOTES** Do not use concomitantly with an ACE inhibitor or another ARB. Must have 36 hour wash-out period between stopping an ACE inhibitor and starting sacubitril/valsartan. Safety issue – see Pregnancy chapter

ACE Inhibitor, ARB and ARNI Drug Interactions

- All RAAS inhibitors ↑ the risk of hyperkalemia (most significant side effect). Monitor for additive hyperkalemia with drugs that ↑ potassium (e.g., potassium-sparing diuretics, ARAs, others). Avoid using salt substitutes (which contain KCl rather than NaCl) or OTC potassium supplements. Monitor K and renal function frequently.
- Avoid using more than one RAAS inhibitor together (ACE inhibitor ± ARB ± aliskiren) due to an ↑ risk of renal impairment, hypotension and hyperkalemia. The use of aliskiren in combination with an ACE inhibitor, ARB or ARNI is specifically contraindicated in patients with diabetes or when eGFR is < 60 mL/min. Combining an ACE inhibitor or ARB with an ARA is common in HF.
- The triple combination of ACE inhibitor, ARB and ARA is not recommended due to a higher risk of hyperkalemia and renal insufficiency.
- Additive antihypertensive effects with other drugs that ↓ BP; monitor BP.
- Use with NSAIDs (especially in patients who are elderly, volume depleted or with compromised renal function) can worsen renal function.
- ACE inhibitors and ARBs can ↓ lithium's renal clearance and ↑ risk of lithium toxicity.

Beta Blockers

Beta-adrenergic receptor antagonists, or simply beta blockers, antagonize the effects of catecholamines (especially NE) at the beta-1 and beta-2 adrenergic receptors. Beta blockers ↓ vasoconstriction, improve cardiac function and ↓ morbidity and mortality; they are recommended for all HF patients. Unlike ACE inhibitors (or ARBs), the clinical benefits of beta blockers are not considered a class effect. Only bisoprolol, carvedilol (IR and ER), and metoprolol succinate ER are recommended in the guidelines. The target doses for these agents are the doses used in clinical trials demonstrating their benefit, or the maximum tolerated dose for a given patient. Beta blockers with intrinsic sympathomimetic activity (ISA) should be avoided. Beta blockers should only be stopped in ADHF if hypotension or hypoperfusion is present.

DRUG	DOSING	SAFETY/SIDE EFFECTS/MONITORING
Beta blockers – only those mentioned in the guidelines (see complete list in Hypertension chapter)		
Bisoprolol *(Zebeta)* Benefit in clinical trials, but not FDA approved for HF	Start 1.25 mg daily Target dose: 10 mg daily Titrate every 2 weeks as tolerated	**BOXED WARNING** Beta blockers should not be withdrawn abruptly (particularly in patients with CVD), gradually taper over 1-2 weeks to avoid acute tachycardia, HTN, and/or ischemia **CONTRAINDICATIONS** Severe bradycardia, 2nd or 3rd degree heart block, or sick sinus syndrome (unless patient has a functioning artificial pacemaker) or cardiogenic shock **WARNING** Caution in patients with diabetes (may potentiate hypoglycemia and/or mask hypoglycemia symptoms); may mask signs of hyperthyroidism; use caution with bronchospastic diseases (e.g., asthma, COPD), peripheral vascular disease and Raynaud's disease; may aggravate psychiatric conditions **SIDE EFFECTS** ↓ HR, hypotension, fatigue, dizziness, depression, ↓ libido, impotence, ↑ TGs, ↓ HDL; weight gain and edema especially with carvedilol **MONITORING** HR (↓ dose if HR < 55 BPM), BP, s/sx of HF **NOTES** Metoprolol IV is not equivalent to PO (IV:PO ratio 1:2.5) *Toprol XL* can be cut at the score line; preferably taken with or immediately after meals
Metoprolol succinate extended-release *(Toprol XL)* Metoprolol tartrate *(Lopressor)* is not recommended in HF guidelines	Start 12.5-25 mg/day Target dose: 200 mg daily Titrate every 2 weeks as tolerated	

Beta Blockers Continued

DRUG	DOSING	SAFETY/SIDE EFFECTS/MONITORING
Non-Selective Beta Blocker and Alpha-1 Blocking Agent		
Carvedilol *(Coreg, Coreg CR)*	**Immediate release** Start 3.125 mg BID Target dose: ≤ 85 kg: 25 mg BID > 85 kg: 50 mg BID **Controlled release** Start 10 mg daily Target dose: 80 mg daily Titrate every 2 weeks as tolerated	Same as above **CONTRAINDICATION** Severe hepatic impairment **WARNING** Intraoperative floppy iris syndrome has occurred in cataract surgery patients who were on or were previously treated with an alpha-1 blocker **NOTES** Take with food (all forms) to ↓ the rate of absorption and the risk of orthostatic hypotension Dosing conversion from *Coreg* to *Coreg CR:* *Coreg* 3.125 mg BID = *Coreg CR* 10 mg daily *Coreg* 6.25 mg BID = *Coreg CR* 20 mg daily *Coreg* 12.5 mg BID = *Coreg CR* 40 mg daily *Coreg* 25 mg BID = *Coreg CR* 80 mg daily The IR and CR dose doubles with each increment from the starting dose

Beta Blocker Drug Interactions

- Beta blockers can enhance the hypoglycemic effects of insulin and sulfonylureas and can mask the symptoms of hypoglycemia (e.g., shakiness, palpitations, anxiety); sweating and hunger are symptoms that are not masked. In addition, non-selective beta blockers can ↓ insulin secretion in type 2 diabetes causing hyperglycemia. Monitor blood glucose in patients with diabetes.
- Use caution with other drugs that ↓ HR (e.g., digoxin, verapamil, diltiazem).
- 2D6 inhibitors can ↑ carvedilol levels and rifampin can ↓ carvedilol levels.
- Carvedilol is an inhibitor of P-gp and can ↑ concentrations of P-gp substrates (e.g., digoxin, cyclosporine, dabigatran, ranolazine).

Aldosterone Receptor Antagonists

Aldosterone is a mineralocorticoid, with receptors in the kidneys, as well as on the heart, brain, vasculature, adipose tissue and immune cells; it causes retention of Na and water. Aldosterone receptor antagonists (ARAs), also referred to as mineralocorticoid receptor antagonists (MRAs), compete with aldosterone at receptor sites in the distal convoluted tubule and collecting ducts. Spironolactone is a non-selective ARA (also blocks androgen), while eplerenone is a selective ARA that does not exhibit endocrine side effects. ARAs reduce sodium and water retention, cardiac remodeling (especially myocardial fibrosis) and the risk of sudden cardiac death. ARAs reduce morbidity and mortality and should be added to standard treatment in patients with NYHA Class II – IV.

DRUG	DOSING	SAFETY/SIDE EFFECTS/MONITORING
Spironolactone (*Aldactone*)	Start 12.5-25 mg daily Target dose: 25 mg daily or BID	**BOXED WARNING** Spironolactone: tumorigenic in chronic toxicity studies with rats; avoid unnecessary use **CONTRAINDICATIONS** Hyperkalemia, anuria, significant renal impairment (CrCl ≤ 30 mL/min), (Addison's disease or other conditions that ↑ K) **WARNINGS** Do not initiate treatment in heart failure patients with K > 5 mEq/L; SCr > 2.0 mg/dL (females) or SCr > 2.5 mg/dL (males) **SIDE EFFECTS** Hyperkalemia, ↑ SCr, dizziness, hyperchloremic metabolic acidosis (rare) Spironolactone: gynecomastia, breast tenderness, impotence, irregular menses Eplerenone: ↑ TGs **MONITORING** BP, electrolytes (check K before starting and frequently thereafter), renal function; fluid status (input and output, weight), s/sx of HF
Eplerenone *(Inspra)*	Start 25 mg daily Target dose: 50 mg daily, titrate based on K level	

ARA Drug Interactions

- ARAs ↑ the risk of hyperkalemia (most significant side effect). Monitor for additive hyperkalemia with drugs that ↑ potassium. Monitor K and renal function frequently.
- The triple combination of ACE inhibitor, ARB and ARA is not recommended due to a higher risk of hyperkalemia and renal insufficiency.
- Additive antihypertensive effects with other drugs that ↓ BP; monitor BP.
- Use with NSAIDs in patients with impaired renal function can cause severe hyperkalemia and ↓ antihypertensive effect.
- Diuretics can ↓ lithium's renal clearance and ↑ risk of lithium toxicity.
- Eplerenone is a major substrate of CYP 3A4; use with strong 3A4 inhibitors is contraindicated.

Hydralazine/Nitrate

Hydralazine is a direct arterial vasodilator which ↓ afterload. Nitrates ↑ the availability of nitric oxide which causes venous vasodilation and ↓ preload. Hydralazine also decreases the development of nitrate tachyphylaxis (tolerance). The combination improves the survival of heart failure patients, although not as much as ACE inhibitors. Therefore, this combination is used as alternative treatment for patients who cannot tolerate ACE inhibitors or ARBs due to poor renal function, angioedema, or hyperkalemia. The combination product, *BiDil*, is indicated in self-identified black patients with NYHA Class III or IV who are symptomatic despite optimal treatment with ACE inhibitors and beta blockers. Hydralazine or oral nitrates may be used as monotherapy for other indications, however, they have not individually been shown to affect HF outcomes. Isosorbide dinitrate was the oral nitrate used in clinical trials; there are no data with isosorbide mononitrate, although it is used in practice. As with ACE inhibitors or ARBs, the target doses are those shown to be beneficial in clinical trials.

DRUG	DOSING	SAFETY/SIDE EFFECTS/MONITORING
HydrALAZINE **+ isosorbide dinitrate *(BiDil)***	Start 25-50 mg TID-QID Target dose: 300 mg/day in divided doses	**CONTRAINDICATION** Mitral valve rheumatic heart disease, CAD **WARNING** Drug-induced lupus erythematosus (DILE – dose and duration related) **SIDE EFFECTS** Headache, reflex tachycardia, palpitations, fluid retention, peripheral neuritis **MONITORING** HR, BP, s/sx of HF, ANA titer
Isosorbide dinitrate *(Isordil Titradose, Dilatrate SR)* Preferred formulation for systolic HF **Isosorbide mononitrate *(Monoket, Imdur)*** Not listed in HF guidelines	Dinitrate: Start 20-30 mg TID-QID Target dose: 120 mg daily in divided doses	**CONTRAINDICATIONS** Concurrent use with PDE-5 Inhibitors and riociguat **SIDE EFFECTS** Headache, dizziness, lightheadedness, flushing, hypotension, tachyphylaxis (need 10-12 hour nitrate-free interval), syncope **MONITORING** HR, BP, s/sx of HF
Isosorbide dinitrate + hydralazine *(BiDil)*	Start 20/37.5 mg TID (1 tab TID) Target dose: 40/75 mg TID (2 tabs TID) No nitrate tolerance	As above

Hydralazine/Nitrate Drug Interactions

- Must avoid nitrate administration within 12 hours of avanafil, within 24 hours of sildenafil or vardenafil and within 48 hours of tadalafil. Do not dispense nitrates to patients using PDE-5 inhibitors. Avoid use with riociguat.

Digoxin

Digoxin inhibits the Na/K ATPase pump which results in a positive inotropic effect (↑ in CO). It also exerts a parasympathetic effect which provides a negative chronotropic effect (↓ HR). Digoxin is added in patients who remain symptomatic despite receiving standard treatment of an ACE inhibitor (or ARB) with a beta blocker. Digoxin improves symptoms, exercise tolerance, and quality of life. Overall, digoxin does not improve survival of heart failure patients, but it does reduce hospitalizations for heart failure. Dosing should take into account the patient's renal function, body size, age and gender (lower dose for renal insufficiency, smaller, older, female), with the majority of patients being on no more than 0.125 mg daily. Serum digoxin concentrations for HF should be kept < 1 ng/mL (range 0.5 – 0.9 ng/mL). Patients on digoxin should maintain a serum potassium between 4 – 5 mEq/L and magnesium > 2 mEq/L.

DRUG	DOSING	SAFETY/SIDE EFFECTS/MONITORING
Digoxin *(Digitek, Digox, Lanoxin)* Tablet, solution, injection	Available as 0.0625, 0.125, 0.1875, 0.25 mg Typical dose: 0.125-0.25 mg daily Loading doses not used in HF Therapeutic range for HF = 0.5-0.9 ng/mL (higher range for AFib) CrCl < 50 mL/min; ↓ dose or frequency ↓ dose by 20-25% when going from PO to IV Antidote: *DigiFab*	**CONTRAINDICATIONS** Ventricular fibrillation **WARNINGS** 2nd/3rd degree heart block without a pacemaker, Wolff-Parkinson-White syndrome (WPW) with AFib, vesicant (avoid extravasation) **SIDE EFFECTS** Dizziness, mental disturbances, headache, N/V/D **MONITORING** ECG, HR, BP, electrolytes, renal function and digoxin level (drawn optimally 12-24 hrs after dose) **TOXICITY** Initial s/sx of toxicity are N/V, loss of appetite and bradycardia. Severe s/sx of toxicity include blurred/double vision, altered color perception, greenish-yellow halos around lights or objects, abdominal pain, confusion, delirium, prolonged PR interval, arrhythmias

Digoxin Drug Interactions

- Use caution when administering other drugs that ↓ HR.
- Digoxin is mostly renally cleared and partially cleared hepatically. Decreased renal function requires a ↓ digoxin dose. In acute renal failure, digoxin is held.
- Digoxin is a P-gp and 3A4 substrate (minor). Digoxin levels ↑ with amiodarone, dronedarone, quinidine, verapamil, erythromycin, clarithromycin, itraconazole, cyclosporine, propafenone, and many other drugs. Reduce digoxin dose by 50% if patient is on amiodarone or dronedarone.
- Hypokalemia, hypomagnesemia, and hypercalcemia ↑ risk of digoxin toxicity.
- Hypothyroidism can ↑ digoxin levels.

Ivabradine

High resting heart rate is associated with increased morbidity and mortality in heart failure. Ivabradine is an inhibitor of the "funny" current (I_f) in the sinus node and belongs to a class of drugs known as hyperpolarization-activated cyclic nucleotide-gated channel blockers (HCN blockers). Inhibition of this current results in a reduction in sinus rate and hence heart rate. Ivabradine reduces the risk of hospitalizations for worsening heart failure, but does not affect mortality. It is recommended as a potential adjunctive therapy to reduce HF hospitalizations in symptomatic stable chronic HF patients (NYHA Class II-III), with EF ≤ 35% who are treated with all appropriate first-line medications, are in sinus rhythm and have a resting HR ≥ 70 BPM.

DRUG	DOSING	SAFETY/SIDE EFFECTS/MONITORING
Ivabradine *(Corlanor)* Indicated in patients with: - stable, symptomatic chronic HF - LVEF ≤ 35% - sinus rhythm with resting heart rate ≥ 70 BPM - either are on maximally tolerated doses of beta blockers or have a contraindication to beta blocker use	Starting dose: 5 mg PO twice daily; after two weeks, adjust dose based on heart rate Maintenance dose: 2.5-7.5 mg PO twice daily Target: resting heart rate between 50-60 BPM	**CONTRAINDICATIONS** Acute decompensated HF; BP < 90/50 mmHg; sick sinus syndrome, sinoatrial block or 3rd degree AV block unless patient has a functioning pacemaker; resting heart rate < 60 BPM prior to treatment; severe hepatic impairment; pacemaker dependence (heart rate maintained exclusively by the pacemaker); use in combination with strong 3A4 inhibitors **WARNINGS** Fetal toxicity (females should use effective contraception as drug can cause fetal harm); monitor for atrial fibrillation, ↓ HR, and bradycardia; not recommended in patients with 2nd degree AV block unless patient has a functioning pacemaker **SIDE EFFECTS** Bradycardia, hypertension, atrial fibrillation, luminous phenomena (phosphenes - seeing flashes of light) **MONITORING** HR, ECG, BP **NOTES** MedGuide required

Ivabradine Drug Interactions

- Ivabradine is a substrate of CYP3A4 and is contraindicated with strong 3A4 inhibitors. Ivabradine should be avoided in patients taking strong 3A4 inducers and moderate 3A4 inhibitors.

Potassium Oral Supplementation

Potassium supplementation is an important aspect of managing HF since loop diuretics cause ↓ K while other HF drugs (RAAS inhibitors, ARAs) ↑ K. Maintenance of potassium levels is essential to reduce the proarrhythmic risk of digoxin, especially as HF ↑ arrhythmia risk. There are different formulations (tablets, capsules and liquids) which also vary by salt form (acetate, bicarbonate, citrate, chloride, gluconate and phosphate). The salt used depends on patient factors including acid-base status and deficiency of other electrolytes such as phosphate. Potassium chloride is used most commonly.

Frequency of monitoring serum potassium depends on renal function (and stability), medication regimen, and clinical status. Check potassium levels if the renal function changes, and after any change in diuretic, ACE inhibitor, ARB or ARA dose. Magnesium deficiency aggravates hypokalemia. The magnesium level should be checked and corrected (as needed) prior to correcting the potassium level.

The usual range of K is 3.5 – 5 mEq/L. Supplementation may not be needed in patients who are able to supplement their intake of potassium through dietary sources (e.g., bananas, potatoes, orange juice, beans, dark leafy greens, apricots, peaches, avocados, white mushrooms, tomatoes, and some varieties of fish).

DRUG	DOSING	SAFETY/SIDE EFFECTS/MONITORING
Potassium chloride *(Klor-Con,* *Klor-Con 10, Klor-Con M10, Klor-Con M15,* ***Klor-Con M20, Micro-K,*** *K-Tab, Kaon-Cl,* others)	**Prevention of hypokalemia:** 20-40 mEq/day in 1-2 divided doses **Treatment of mild hypokalemia:** 40-100 mEq/day in 2-5 divided doses; adjust dose according to laboratory values No more than 20-25 mEq should be given as a single dose to avoid GI discomfort	**CONTRAINDICATIONS** Severe renal impairment, hyperkalemia Oral solid dosage forms are contraindicated in patients with delayed or obstructed passage through the GI tract **WARNINGS** Caution in patients with mild-moderate renal impairment, patients with disorders that alter K (untreated Addison's disease, heat cramps, severe tissue trauma/burns) and in patients taking other medications that ↑ K **SIDE EFFECTS** N/V/D, abdominal pain, flatulence, hyperkalemia **MONITORING** K, Mg, Cl, pH, urine output **NOTES** Take with meals and a full glass of water or other liquid to minimize the risk of GI irritation *Micro-K*: capsules can be opened and contents sprinkled on a spoonful of applesauce or pudding and immediately swallowed without chewing *K-Tab, Klor-Con*: swallow whole; do not crush, cut, chew, or suck on tablet *Klor-Con M:* swallow whole; do not crush, chew, or suck on tablet; tablet can also be cut in half and swallowed separately, or can dissolve the whole tablet in 4 oz. of water – stir for 2 mins. and drink immediately

HEART FAILURE EXACERBATIONS AND QUALITY IMPROVEMENT

HF is the most common condition causing hospitalization in patients greater than 65 years old. HF admissions are caused by either new-onset HF (known as acute HF) or worsening HF (known as acute decompensated HF, or ADHF). ADHF presents with either worsening congestion and/or hypoperfusion. Treatment consists of IV loop diuretics, vasodilators and/or inotropes, which are discussed in the Critical Care & Fluids/Electrolytes chapter. The majority of HF hospitalizations are due to nonadherence with medications and/or lifestyle recommendations.

Avoidable HF admissions are a major cause of increased healthcare costs. Medicare now penalizes hospitals for excessive readmissions due to HF exacerbations. Pharmacists are actively involved in quality improvement initiatives directed at decreasing hospital readmissions, such as medication optimization (making sure the right medications are being used and harmful medications are not being used) and medication adherence strategies. Despite all of this, up to 25% of HF patients do not fill one or more discharge medications, and ~34% stop taking one or more medications within a month of discharge. Lifestyle adherence is essential (discussed at the beginning of the chapter), including healthy eating and sodium restriction. Patients need to know what steps to take if symptoms worsen. The steps are outlined in the sample HF action plan on the next page.

Patient Counseling

All Heart Failure Patients

- Monitor body weight daily, in the morning before eating and after using the restroom. Weight should be recorded in a notebook.

Congestive Heart Failure Management/Action Plan

1. Green means Go. Follow medication, weight and diet advice.

2. Yellow means Caution. You may need to change your medicines.

3. Red means Danger. Get help from a doctor today. Call 911.

1. Green – Go

- No shortness of breath
- Usual amount of swelling in legs
- No weight gain
- No chest pain
- No change in usual activity

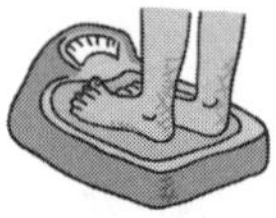

Weigh yourself every day

Take all your medicines

Eat a low salt diet

Go to your doctor appointments

Bring all your medicines to every appointment

2. Yellow – Caution

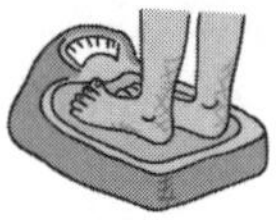

Weight gain of:
- 2-4 pounds in 1 day
- 3-5 pounds in a week

Increased number of pillows to sleep

Increased swelling or coughing

Shortness of breath with activity

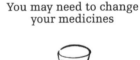

You may need to change your medicines

Call your doctor for instructions

3. Red – Danger

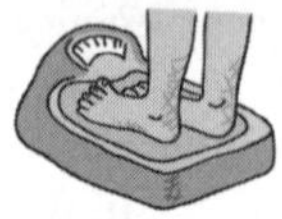

Weight gain of more than 5 pounds in 1 week

Dizziness or falling

Waking at night due to shortness of breath

Shortness of breath at rest, chest tightness or wheezing

Call your doctor today to report symptoms and request an appointment.

Call 911 if having severe chest pain

www.ccwjc.com

- Follow the steps in your HF action plan or contact your healthcare provider if your symptoms worsen or if you gain weight (2 – 4 pounds in one day or 3 – 5 pounds in one week).
- Follow a sodium restricted diet. Foods high in sodium include:
  - Prepared sauces and condiments (such as soy sauce, BBQ sauce, Worcestershire sauce or salsa)
  - Canned vegetables and soups
  - Frozen dinners
  - Deli meats (sandwich meats, bacon, ham, hot dogs, sausage or salami)
  - Salty foods (pickles, olives, cheese, nuts, chips or crackers)
- Take nutrition classes and learn to read nutrition labels. Choose "no sodium added" or "low sodium" options. Healthy ways of cooking include broiling, baking, poaching, and steaming without added salt.
- Stop smoking. Do not use any illegal drugs; they can badly damage the heart. Alcohol, including beer and wine, should be avoided or limited to 1 drink per day for females and 2 drinks per day for males.
- Avoid pain medicines like ibuprofen (NSAIDs) without checking with a healthcare provider. Also, do not use nutritional supplements, vitamins or herbals for HF without discussing with the pharmacist if they are safe to use.
- Take your medications as directed. Discuss with your healthcare provider if the medications are too expensive. Not taking the medications and not following the food and salt recommendations will usually cause worsening of the HF symptoms and possible hospitalization.

Beta Blockers in HF

- Do not stop taking the medication unless your healthcare provider tells you to do so.
- If you miss a dose, take your dose as soon as you remember, unless it is time to take your next dose. Do not double the dose.
- This medication can cause you to feel dizzy, tired or faint. Do not drive a car, use machinery or do anything that requires you to be alert until you adjust to the medication and the symptoms subside. These effects will go away in a few days. However, call your healthcare provider if the symptoms feel severe or you have weight gain or increased shortness of breath.
- This medication can cover up some of the signs and symptoms of low blood sugar (hypoglycemia); make sure to test your blood sugar often and take a fast-acting sugar source if needed.
- Medications used to treat severe allergic reactions may not work as well while taking this medication.

Toprol XL

- If you have been told to cut the *Toprol XL* or its generic equivalent tablet in half, you must use a pill cutter and cut only at the score line. Otherwise, the medicine will enter your body too quickly. Swallow the ½ tablet whole. The tablets cannot be crushed or chewed and should be taken preferably with or following a meal.

Coreg CR

- Take with food, to help reduce dizziness.
- Swallow *Coreg CR* capsules whole. Do not chew or crush the capsules.

- If you have trouble swallowing *Coreg CR* whole, the capsule can be carefully opened and the beads sprinkled over a spoonful of applesauce which should be taken right away. The applesauce should not be warm. Only use applesauce.

Digoxin

- This medicine helps make the heart beat stronger. Keep taking as directed, even if you feel well.
- Do not stop taking this medicine without talking to your healthcare provider. Stopping this medication suddenly may make your condition worse.
- Avoid becoming overheated or dehydrated as an overdose can easily occur if you are dehydrated.
- Symptoms of overdose include poor or no appetite, nausea, vomiting, diarrhea, vision changes (such as blurred or yellow/green vision), uneven heartbeats and feeling like you might pass out. If any of these occur, see a healthcare provider right away.
- There are many medications that can interact with digoxin. Check with your physician or pharmacist before starting any new medicines, including over the counter, vitamin and/or herbal products.
- To be sure that this medication is not causing harmful effects, your blood may need to be tested on a regular basis. Your kidney function will also need to be monitored.

Sacubitril/valsartan

- This medication is used with other heart failure therapies, in place of an ACE inhibitor or other ARB therapy.
- Do not take this medication if you have had an allergic reaction including swelling of your face, lips, tongue, throat or trouble breathing while taking a type of medicine called an angiotensin-converting enzyme (ACE) inhibitor or angiotensin II receptor blocker (ARB).
- This medication cannot be used for at least 36 hours after stopping an ACE inhibitor.
- Do not take this medication if you have diabetes and take a medicine that contains aliskiren.
- Tell you healthcare provider if you are pregnant, plan to become pregnant or are breastfeeding or plan to breastfeed.
- Tell you healthcare provider about all the medications that you take, especially if you take potassium supplements or salt substitutes, non-steroidal anti-inflammatory drugs (NSAIDs), lithium or other medications for high blood pressure or heart problems.

Ivabradine

- This medication can cause an abnormal heart rhythm. Tell your healthcare provider if you have symptoms of an irregular heartbeat, such as feeling that your heart is pounding or racing (palpitations), chest pressure or pain, or worsened shortness of breath.
- This medication can cause a low heart rate. Contact your healthcare provider if you have symptoms such as dizziness, fatigue, lack of energy, or have low blood pressure.
- Tell your healthcare provider if you are pregnant, plan to become pregnant or are breastfeeding or plan to breastfeed.
- Avoid drinking grapefruit juice and taking St. John's wort during treatment with ivabradine. Tell your pharmacist all the medications, herbals and OTC medications you are taking.

PRACTICE CASE

PATIENT
JF
DOB 08/29/1940
AGE 75 yrs
SEX Female
PRN JF120303

FACILITY
San Diego Medical Group Tower
T (444) 444-4444
F (444) 444-5555
35 La Jolla Drive
San Diego, CA 92130

ENCOUNTER
NOTE TYPE SOAP Note
SEEN BY Alison James
DATE 10/06
Not signed

Chief complaint

"Shortness of breath and puffy legs"

Vitals Height: 61 in Weight: 148 lb BMI: 27.96 BP: 117/75 mmHg
Temperature: 98.7 °F Pulse: 104 BPM Respiratory rate: 23 BPM

Subjective

JF is a pleasant 74 y/o female accompanied by her husband.

HPI: Per her husband, JF was doing well with her heart failure regimen over the past several months. Over the weekend, they visited family and ate ham, canned vegetables, and casseroles. JF's shortness of breath started to get worse at that time and continued to worsen over the next 2 days. JF reports a 5 pound weight gain over the last 2 days. She gets short of breath with activity. Her legs and feet are puffy by noon. Her urine output is good, but the fluid is not going away. If she sits in a chair and does nothing, she does not have shortness of breath. She states that she is compliant with her medications. Review of the prescription bottles and refill history support this statement.

JF consulted her heart failure action plan, which instructed her to visit the clinic if her weight increased by > 5 pounds in one week.

Allergies: NKDA

Objective

Past Medical History:
HF (LVEF 35% documented by ECHO in 2014) / HTN / Type 2 DM (diet controlled) / Depression

Medications:
Lasix 40 mg PO daily / Prinivil 40 mg PO daily / Digox 0.25 mg PO daily / Toprol XL 100 mg PO daily / Celexa 20 mg PO daily

Social History: No alcohol, drugs, or tobacco
Family History: Mother with HTN, dyslipidemia, and MI. Father with HTN. Both deceased. Sister with Type 2 DM.

Labs (reference range)
Na 142 (135 - 145 mEq/L)
K 4.7 (3.5 - 5.0 mEq/L)
Cl 101 (95 - 103 mEq/L)
HCO3 25 (24 - 30 mEq/L)
BUN 30 (7 - 20 mg/dL)
SCr 1.5 (0.6 - 1.3 mg/dL)
Glu 218 (70 - 110 mg/dL)
Digoxin 1.8 ng/mL (indication specific)
BNP 372 pg/mL (< 100 pg/mL)

Tests
ECG: sinus tachycardia, no ST or T wave changes
Chest xray: cardiomegaly and bilateral pleural effusions

Assessment

1) Symptomatic heart failure likely secondary to recent dietary indiscretion
2) Hypertension
3) Type 2 Diabetes
4) Depression

Plan

JF has taken all of her home medications for today. An additional 40 mg of *Lasix* was given in clinic today.

Questions

1. Looking at JF's chart note, how much total *Lasix* will JF receive on October 6?

   a. 10 mg
   b. 20 mg
   c. 40 mg
   d. 80 mg
   e. 100 mg

2. JF is taking *Digox* for her heart failure. Which of the following statements is the best interpretation for the use of *Digox* for JF?

   a. She is receiving the correct amount of *Digox* for her condition.
   b. She is receiving too much *Digox* for her condition.
   c. She is not receiving enough *Digox* given her current HR.
   d. She has a contraindication to *Digox* at this time.
   e. She is receiving too much *Digox* given her current HR.

3. The equivalent dose of *Lasix* JF is receiving on a daily basis when converted to the IV route:

   a. 5 mg
   b. 10 mg
   c. 20 mg
   d. 40 mg
   e. None of the above.

4. Which of the following objective findings support the diagnosis of HF in JF? (Select **ALL** that apply.)

   a. Echo results
   b. BNP level
   c. ECG results
   d. Chest X-ray
   e. Pulse

5. Which of the following medications should JF generally avoid as they may worsen her heart failure? (Select **ALL** that apply.)

   a. Celecoxib
   b. Verapamil
   c. Amiodarone
   d. Pioglitazone
   e. Naproxen

6. The healthcare provider decides to increase the *Toprol XL* dose to 200 mg daily. Which of the following patient counseling points should be discussed with JF regarding this change? (Select **ALL** that apply.)

   a. The increase in medication may make you feel more tired and dizzy at first and should disappear over time.
   b. This increase in medication can cause a loss of appetite, blurred vision, lightheadedness, and/or visual changes.
   c. This medication may be cut in half (if directed to do so) with a pill cutter, but do not crush or chew the tablets.
   d. This medication can cause metabolic acidosis.
   e. The increase in medication will cause an increase in your heart rate. Call your healthcare provider if you feel your heart racing.

Questions 7-8 do not pertain to the above case.

7. A 70 kg patient is beginning carvedilol therapy for heart failure. The starting dose is 3.125 mg BID. What should the target dose for carvedilol be in this patient?

   a. 6.25 mg BID
   b. 12.5 mg BID
   c. 25 mg BID
   d. 50 mg BID
   e. 100 mg BID

8. What is the trade name for eplerenone?

   a. *Invega*
   b. *Invanz*
   c. *Invirase*
   d. *Isuprel*
   e. *Inspra*

Answers

1-d, 2-b, 3-c, 4-a,b,d, 5-a,b,d,e, 6-a,c, 7-c, 8-e

53

ARRHYTHMIAS

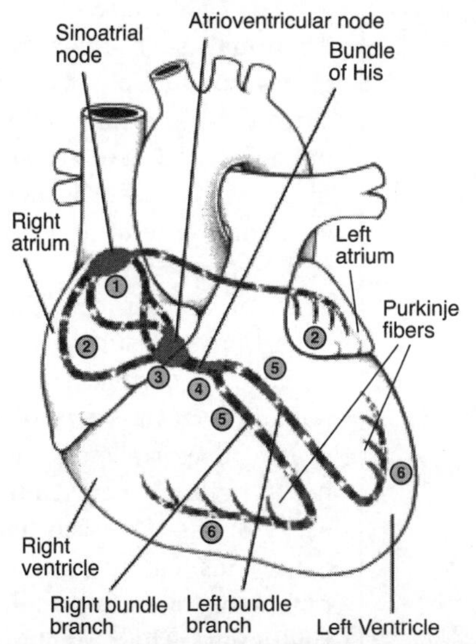

GUIDELINES/REFERENCES

2014 AHA/ACC/HRS Guideline for the Management of Patients With Atrial Fibrillation: A Report of the American College of Cardiology/American Heart Association Task Force on Practice Guidelines and the Heart Rhythm Society. *J Am Coll Cardiol.* 2014; 64(21):2246-80.

We gratefully acknowledge the assistance of Tien M. H. Ng, PharmD, FHFSA, FCCP, BCPS (AQ-Cardiology), Associate Professor at the University of Southern California School of Pharmacy, in preparing this chapter.

BACKGROUND

A normal heart beats in a regular, coordinated way because electrical impulses traveling down the cardiac conduction system trigger a sequence of organized contractions. Arrhythmias are caused by abnormalities in the formation and/or conduction of these electrical impulses. Because the electrical impulses are not visible, an electrocardiogram (ECG) is used to diagnose arrhythmias.

Heart rate (HR) describes the frequency of depolarization of the ventricles. The normal resting HR in adults is 60 to 100 beats per minute (BPM). Arrhythmias can occur with a slow HR (bradyarrhythmias) or a fast HR (tachyarrhythmias). An arrhythmia can be silent (asymptomatic) and may only be detected during a routine physical exam, but most patients experience symptoms. Common complaints of patients experiencing arrhythmias include palpitations (feeling like the heart is fluttering or racing), dizziness, lightheadedness, shortness of breath, chest pain and fatigue. In severe cases, arrhythmias can lead to syncope, heart failure and death.

NORMAL SINUS RHYTHM

Activation of the heart in the normal sequence, through the cardiac conduction system, and at the usual rate of 60 to 100 BPM, is called normal sinus rhythm (NSR). The diagram above traces the normal sequence of formation and conduction of an electrical impulse in the heart. The sinoatrial (SA) node (1) initiates an electrical impulse (this is called automaticity). The impulse spreads throughout the right and left atria (2), resulting in atrial contraction. The electrical impulse reaches the atrioventricular (AV) node (3), where its conduction is slowed. Once through the AV node, the impulse travels down the bundle of His (4), which divides into the right bundle branch for the right ventricle (5) and the left bundle branch for the left ventricle (5). The impulse then spreads through the ventricles via Purkinje fibers (6), resulting in a coordinated and rapid contraction of both ventricles. Any disruption in the normal sequence of impulse formation or conduction can result in an arrhythmia.

Cardiac Action Potential

The cardiac action potential of ventricle muscle cells (myocytes) is generated by the movement of ions through channels in the cardiac cells. The ventricular action potential is depicted below and consists of 5 phases (numbered 0 – 4); the parts of the ECG that correspond with each phase of the action potential is also shown.

- Phase 0: Rapid ventricular depolarization, which initiates the heartbeat in response to an influx of Na; this causes ventricular contraction (represented by the QRS complex on the ECG)
- Phase 1: Early rapid repolarization; Na channels close
- Phase 2: Plateau in response to an influx of Ca and efflux of K
- Phase 3: Rapid ventricular repolarization in response to an efflux of K (represented by the T wave on the ECG)
- Phase 4: Resting membrane potential; atrial depolarization occurs (represented by the P wave on the ECG)

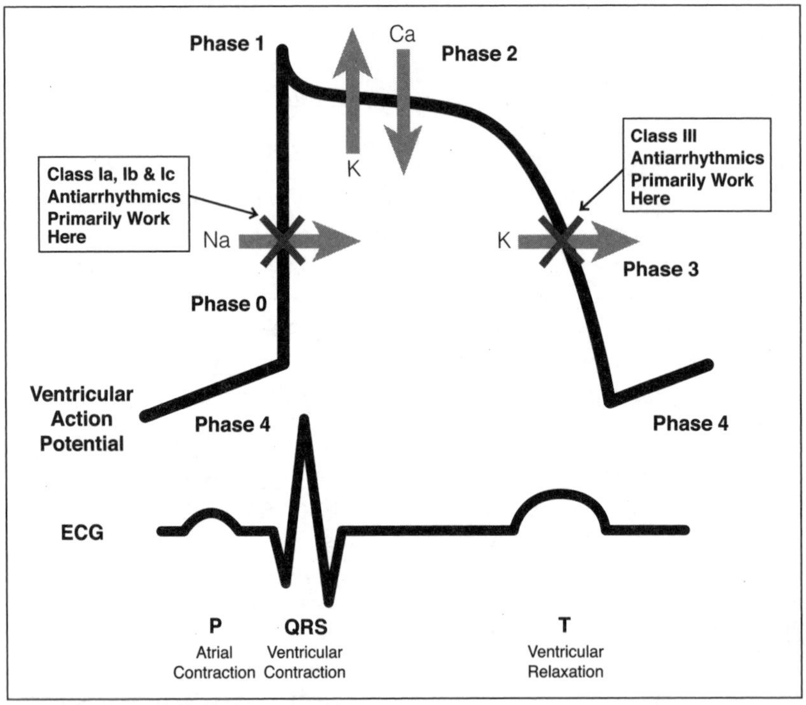

Depolarization/repolarization of cardiac cells must be properly sequenced and coordinated to produce the net ECG effects shown

ARRHYTHMIAS

Abnormalities of the heart, or its conduction system, can alter the cardiac action potential and lead to cardiac arrhythmias. The most common cause of arrhythmias is myocardial ischemia or infarction. Other conditions resulting in damage to cardiac tissue, including heart valve disorders, hypertension and heart failure, can cause arrhythmias. Non-cardiac conditions can trigger or predispose a patient to arrhythmias. These include electrolyte imbalances (especially those important to cardiac electrophysiology, like potassium, magnesium, sodium and calcium), elevated sympathetic states (e.g., hyperthyroidism, infection) and drugs (both illicit drugs and drugs used to treat arrhythmias).

Arrhythmias are generally classified based on their location of origin into two broad categories: supraventricular (originating above the atrioventricular node) or ventricular (originating below the atrioventricular node). Arrhythmias originating in or just below the atrioventricular node are called junctional rhythms, but these are less common.

Supraventricular Arrhythmias

Supraventricular tachyarrhythmias include sinus tachycardia, atrial fibrillation, atrial flutter, focal atrial tachycardias and supraventricular re-entrant tachycardias (formerly known as paroxysmal supraventricular tachycardias or PSVTs). Many patients have ongoing supraventricular arrhythmias (especially atrial fibrillation) without realizing it.

Atrial fibrillation (AFib) is the most common type of arrhythmia. AFib results from multiple waves of electrical impulses in the atria, resulting in an irregular and usually rapid ventricular response. The rapid ventricular rate can result in hypotension and worsen underlying ischemia and heart failure. Due to the disorganized depolarization of the atria, coordinated atrial contraction is impaired. This results in suboptimal blood in the atria, increasing the risk of clot formation, which can embolize to the brain causing a stroke. Refer to the Anticoagulation chapter.

Atrial flutter is usually more organized and regular than atrial fibrillation. This arrhythmia occurs most often with heart disease, and in the first week after heart surgery. Atrial flutter often leads to AFib.

Ventricular Arrhythmias

Common ventricular arrhythmias include premature ventricular contractions (PVCs), ventricular tachycardia and ventricular fibrillation. Premature ventricular contractions (PVCs) are relatively common and occur in people with and without heart disease. This is a "skipped heartbeat" that anyone can experience. These electrical impulses are generated from within the ventricular tissue. In some people, it can be related to stress or too much caffeine, nicotine or exercise.

A series of PVCs in a row, resulting in a heart rate of greater than 100 BPM, is known as ventricular tachycardia (VT). VT is further classified based on the presence or absence of a detectable peripheral pulse. VT with a pulse is treated with certain antiarrhythmics, whereas, pulseless VT is a medical emergency and advanced cardiac life support (ACLS) should be initiated. Untreated VT can degenerate into ventricular fibrillation (completely disorganized electrical activation of the ventricles) which is always a medical emergency.

QT Prolongation & Torsade de Pointes

The QT interval is measured from the beginning of the QRS complex to the end of the T wave on an ECG. It reflects ventricular depolarization and repolarization. The QT interval varies with the heart rate, so a QT interval corrected for heart rate (QTc) is reported. A QTc interval is considered prolonged when it is > 440 milliseconds (msec), but is more worrisome when markedly prolonged (> 500 msec). Prolongation of the QT interval is a risk factor for Torsade de Pointes (TdP), a particularly lethal ventricular tachyarrhythmia which is commonly associated with medications and can result in sudden cardiac death.

SELECT DRUGS THAT CAN INCREASE OR PROLONG THE QT INTERVAL

KEY DRUGS

Antiarrhythmics
Class I (especially Class Ia and Class III)

Antibiotics
Quinolones and macrolides

Azole antifungals (most)

Antidepressants
Tricyclics (amitriptyline, clomipramine, desipramine, doxepin, imipramine), SSRIs (citalopram, escitalopram, others), SNRIs, mirtazapine and trazodone. Sertraline is preferred in cardiac patients.

Antiemetic agents
5-HT3 receptor antagonists, droperidol and phenothiazines

Antipsychotics
Aripiprazole, asenapine, chlorpromazine, clozapine, haloperidol, iloperidone, olanzapine, paliperidone, pimozide, quetiapine, risperidone, thioridazine and ziprasidone

Other agents
Donepezil, methadone

Others

Antibiotics:
Foscarnet, telavancin and others

Oncology agents:
Arsenic, bortezomib, bosutinib, ceritinib, crizotinib, dasatinib, lapatinib, nilotinib, sorafenib, sunitinib

HIV agents:
Protease inhibitors (atazanavir, saquinavir) and rilpivirine

Other agents:
Alfuzosin, apomorphine, atomoxetine, buprenorphine, chloroquine, diphenhydramine, ezogabine, fingolimod, galantamine, mirabegron, pentamidine, propofol, quinine, ranolazine, sevoflurane, solifenacin, tacrolimus, tizanidine

Drug-induced QT prolongation is dose-dependent (concentration-dependent) and additive (combining different drugs that can cause QT prolongation increases the risk). Reduced drug clearance and drug interactions can contribute to QT prolongation. Hypokalemia and/or hypomagnesemia also increase the risk of QT prolongation. Drugs that prolong the QT interval must be used with caution in patients with any arrhythmia risk (including those with any pre-existing cardiac condition or history of arrhythmia, electrolyte abnormalities or those taking other proarrhythmic drugs.

If a patient is using a low dose of amitriptyline for neuropathic pain, this may not be considered particularly risky; but if the same patient is admitted to the hospital with hypokalemia and started on fluconazole and ondansetron, the level of concern would be heightened.

ANTIARRHYTHMIC DRUGS

Antiarrhythmic drugs work by affecting the electrical currents in the cells of the heart. By blocking the movement of ions in different phases of the cardiac action potential (discussed previously), select drugs can reduce conduction velocity and/or automaticity, or prolong the refractory period, which can slow or terminate the abnormal electrical activity causing the arrhythmia. They can also occasionally worsen the existing arrhythmia or cause other arrhythmias.

STUDY TIP: VAUGHAN WILLIAMS CLASSIFICATION

Class I
Ia: disopyramide, quinidine, procainamide
Ib: lidocaine, mexiletine
Ic: flecainide, propafenone

Class II
Beta blockers

Class III
Dronedarone, dofetilide, sotalol, ibutilide, amiodarone

Class IV
Verapamil, diltiazem

Try this memory tool:

Double Quarter Pounder, Lettuce, Mayo, Fries Please! Because Dieting During Stress Is Always Very Difficult

Vaughan Williams Classification

The Vaughan Williams classification system is the most commonly used classification system for antiarrhythmic drugs. Here the drugs are split into categories based on their dominant electrophysiological effect. It has the virtue of simplicity, although many drugs overlap into more than one category.

DRUG TREATMENT

Though ventricular arrhythmias are typically managed in hospital settings, virtually all pharmacists will have an opportunity to care for patients with AFib (even in the community setting). This overview of "Drug Treatment" specifically reviews the guideline-recommended treatment of AFib, which involves two main strategies: rate control and rhythm control (refer to Study Tip on the next page).

Rate Control

The goal resting HR is < 80 BPM in patients with symptomatic AFib; however, a more lenient rate-control strategy of < 110 BPM may be reasonable in patients who are asymptomatic and have preserved left ventricular function. Beta blockers (preferred) or nondihydropyridine (non-DHP) calcium channel blockers are recommended for controlling ventricular rate in patients with AFib. Of note, patients with heart failure and reduced ejection fraction (HFrEF) should not receive a nondihydropyridine calcium channel blocker. Digoxin is not first-line for ventricular rate control, but may be added for refractory patients or in those who cannot tolerate beta blockers or calcium channel blockers.

TYPE OF AFIB	DEFINITION
Paroxysmal	AFib that terminates spontaneously or with intervention within 7 days of onset; episodes may recur with variable frequency
Persistent	Continuous AFib that is sustained > 7 days
Long-standing Persistent	Continuous AFib of > 12 months duration
Permanent	Term used when a joint decision has been made by the clinician and patient to cease further attempts to restore and/or maintain NSR; this is a treatment choice rather than a characteristic of the arrhythmia itself

Rhythm Control

Rhythm-control consists of 1) methods for conversion to NSR and 2) maintenance of NSR. Conversion to NSR is most effective with direct current cardioversion. Medications can be used as well and include amiodarone (oral and IV), dofetilide, flecainide, ibutilide and propafenone. For maintenance of NSR, dofetilide, dronedarone, flecainide, propafenone or sotalol is recommended. Due to toxicities, amiodarone is recommended only when other agents have failed or are contraindicated (e.g., heart failure); despite this, amiodarone remains a top-seller in the U.S. Prior to starting any medication for a non-life-threatening arrhythmia, electrolytes and a toxicology screen should be checked to identify easily reversible causes of the arrhythmia.

CLASS I ANTIARRHYTHMICS

Class I antiarrhythmics are sodium channel blockers. They are further sub-classified based on the duration of time they bind to the sodium channel. Class Ia are intermediate on-off sodium channel blockers and they also block the potassium channels. Class Ib are fast on-off sodium channel blockers. Class Ic are slow on-off sodium channel blockers. All Class I agents are proarrhythmic and have the potential for negative inotropic effects (weakened contractility of the heart).

The Cardiac Arrhythmia Suppression Trial (CAST) was a negative study in which patients with PVCs after an MI were randomized to flecainide, encainide (discontinued) or placebo. Those taking flecainide or encainide had increased mortality compared to patients taking placebo. This led to a boxed warning (summarized below) for all the Class I antiarrhythmics, particularly the Class Ic agents:

AFIB RATE VS RHYTHM CONTROL

Rate Control

- Patient remains in AFib and takes medications to control ventricular rate (HR).
  - Beta blockers or non-DHP CCBs (sometimes digoxin)

Rhythm Control

- Restore and maintain NSR.
  - Ia, Ic or III antiarrhythmic or electrical cardioversion
- If AFib is permanent, avoid rhythm control antiarrhythmic drugs (risk > benefit).

Stroke Prophylaxis (see Anticoagulation chapter)

- Clots can form when a patient is in AFib and embolize (causing stroke) when the patient returns to NSR. Studies show that, for many patients, it is safer to remain in AFib with proper stroke prophylaxis and rate control than to try to restore NSR.
- A rate control strategy requires anticoagulation or aspirin (indefinitely) for stroke prevention in most patients.
- When a rhythm control strategy is chosen, restoration and maintenance of NSR is not guaranteed. Long-term anticoagulation decisions depend on the patient's clot risk.

"In the Cardiac Arrhythmia Suppression Trial (CAST), recent (> 6 days but < 2 years ago) myocardial infarction patients with asymptomatic, non-life-threatening ventricular arrhythmias did not benefit and may have been harmed by attempts to suppress the arrhythmia with flecainide or encainide." This boxed warning is not repeated in the following charts.

Class Ia Antiarrhythmics

Class Ia antiarrhythmics block both sodium channels and potassium channels. Quinidine and disopyramide have strong anticholinergic effects. Procainamide is metabolized by acetylation to N-acetylprocainamide (active metabolite). Class Ia antiarrhythmic drugs ↓ conduction velocity, ↑ refractory period and ↓ automaticity.

DRUG	DOSING	SAFETY/SIDE EFFECTS/MONITORING
Disopyramide (*Norpace, Norpace CR*) Capsule	IR: 100-200 mg PO Q6H CR: 200-400 mg PO Q12H CrCl ≤ 40 mL/min: decrease frequency of IR and do not use CR formulation Take on an empty stomach	**CONTRAINDICATIONS** 2nd/3rd degree heart block (unless patient has a functional artificial pacemaker), cardiogenic shock, congenital QT syndrome, sick sinus syndrome **WARNINGS** Proarrhythmic, HF, BPH/urinary retention/narrow-angle glaucoma, myasthenia gravis (due to anticholinergic effects) **SIDE EFFECTS** Anticholinergic effects (> 10%) (dry mouth, constipation, urinary retention), hypotension **MONITORING** ECG, electrolytes, BP, s/sx of HF

Class Ia Antiarrhythmic Agents Continued

DRUG	DOSING	SAFETY/SIDE EFFECTS/MONITORING
QuiNIDine Tablet, injection	IR: 400 mg PO Q6H ER: 300-648 mg PO Q8-12H Take with food or milk to ↓ GI upset Different salt forms are not interchangeable (267 mg of gluconate = 200 mg of sulfate form)	**BOXED WARNING** May ↑ mortality in treatment of AFib or flutter; control AV conduction before initiating **CONTRAINDICATIONS** Concurrent use of quinolones that prolong the QT interval or ritonavir; 2nd/3rd degree heart block or idioventricular conduction delays (unless patient has a functional artificial pacemaker), thrombocytopenia, thrombotic thrombocytopenic purpura (TTP), myasthenia gravis **WARNINGS** Proarrhythmic, hepatotoxicity, drug-induced lupus erythematosus (DILE), hemolysis risk (avoid in G6PD deficiency), can cause positive Coombs test **SIDE EFFECTS** Diarrhea (35%), stomach cramping (22%), lightheadedness, N/V, cinchonism (tinnitus, hearing loss, blurred vision, headache, delirium), rash **MONITORING** ECG, electrolytes, BP, CBC, LFTs, renal function **NOTES** Avoid changes in Na intake; ↓ Na intake can ↑ quinidine levels Alkaline foods/alkaline urine ↑ quinidine levels and can lead to toxicity
Procainamide Injection	Active metabolite, N-acetyl procainamide (NAPA), is renally cleared; ↓ dose when CrCl < 50 mL/min **Therapeutic levels:** Procainamide: 4-10 mcg/mL NAPA: 15-25 mcg/mL Combined: 10-30 mcg/mL Draw levels 6-12 hours after IV infusion has started	**BOXED WARNINGS** Potentially fatal blood dyscrasias (e.g., agranulocytosis); monitor patient closely in the first 3 months of therapy and periodically thereafter. Long-term use leads to positive antinuclear antibody (ANA) in 50% of patients which may result in drug-induced lupus erythematosus (DILE) in 20-30% of patients **CONTRAINDICATIONS** 2nd/3rd degree heart block (unless patient has a functional artificial pacemaker), SLE, TdP, hypersensitivity to procaine or other ester-type local anesthetics **WARNINGS** Proarrhythmic **SIDE EFFECTS** Hypotension, rash **MONITORING** ECG, electrolytes, BP, renal function, procainamide and NAPA levels, CBC, ANA titers

Class Ia Antiarrhythmic Drug Interactions

- Quinidine is a substrate of CYP450 3A4 (major), 2C9 (minor) and P-gp; it inhibits 2D6 (strong), 2C9 (weak), 3A4 (weak) and P-gp. Some major drug interactions with quinidine include digoxin (↓ digoxin dose by 50%), warfarin (↑ INR), and potent 3A4 inhibitors which will ↑ quinidine levels (e.g., avoid grapefruit juice). Drugs that alkalinize the urine (carbonic anhydrase inhibitors, sodium bicarbonate, thiazide diuretics) ↓ renal elimination of quinidine.
- Procainamide is a substrate of 2D6 (major). Moderate and strong 2D6 inhibitors ↑ levels of procainamide.
- Disopyramide is a substrate of 3A4 (major). Inhibitors of 3A4 and drugs with anticholinergic side effects can ↑ the risk of side effects; 3A4 inducers can ↓ the effects of disopyramide.
- All Class Ia antiarrhythmic agents can cause additive QT prolongation when used with other agents that also prolong the QT interval.

Class Ib Antiarrhythmics

Class Ib antiarrhythmics are pure sodium channel blockers. They are only useful for ventricular arrhythmias (no efficacy for supraventricular arrhythmias such as AFib). They cross the blood-brain-barrier and can cause CNS adverse effects. Class Ib antiarrhythmics ↓ conduction and automaticity at high heart rates, but have little effect on refractory period.

DRUG	DOSING	SAFETY/SIDE EFFECTS/MONITORING
Lidocaine *(Xylocaine)* Injection Available in many formulations for local anesthetic effects	1-1.5 mg/kg IV bolus; can repeat bolus with 0.5-0.75 mg/kg every 5-10 mins up to 3 mg/kg (cumulative dose); follow with 1-4 mg/min IV infusion Can be given via endotracheal tube (requires higher dose: 2-2.5x the IV dose)	**BOXED WARNINGS** Mexiletine: hepatotoxicity **CONTRAINDICATIONS** 2nd/3rd degree heart block (unless patient has a functional artificial pacemaker) Lidocaine: Wolff-Parkinson-White syndrome, Adam-Stokes syndrome, allergy to corn or corn-related products or amide type anesthetic Mexiletine: cardiogenic shock, blood dyscrasias, severe skin reactions (DRESS) **WARNINGS** Caution in the elderly, hepatic impairment and in patients with HF **SIDE EFFECTS** Lightheadedness, dizziness, incoordination, N/V, tremor, CNS (hallucinations, disorientation, confusion, ataxia) **MONITORING** ECG, BP, LFTs, mental status, electrolytes
Mexiletine Capsule	200 mg PO Q8H; max 1.2 g/day Take with food	

Class Ib Antiarrhythmic Drug Interactions

- Lidocaine is a substrate of 3A4 (major), 1A2 (major) and 2C9 (minor); it inhibits 1A2 (weak). Amiodarone, beta blockers and 3A4 inhibitors (e.g., diltiazem, verapamil, grapefruit juice, erythromycin, clarithromycin, itraconazole, ketoconazole, protease inhibitors) ↑ lidocaine levels.
- Mexiletine is a substrate of 1A2 (major) and 2D6 (major); it inhibits 1A2 (strong).

Class Ic Antiarrhythmics

Class Ic antiarrhythmic agents are sodium channel blockers. Propafenone also has significant beta-adrenergic receptor blocking effects. These drugs are absolutely contraindicated in patients with heart failure, significant left ventricular hypertrophy or with a recent myocardial infarction (due to negative inotropic and proarrhythmic properties). Class Ic antiarrhythmic drugs significantly ↓ conduction velocity and automaticity, but have little, if any, effect on the refractory period.

DRUG	DOSING	SAFETY/SIDE EFFECTS/MONITORING
Flecainide Tablet	50-100 mg PO Q12H; max 400 mg/day Store in tight, light-resistant container	**BOXED WARNINGS** When treating atrial flutter, 1:1 atrioventricular conduction may occur; pre-emptive negative chronotropic therapy (e.g., digoxin, beta blockers) may ↓ the risk Proarrhythmic **CONTRAINDICATIONS** $2^{nd}/3^{rd}$ degree heart block (unless patient has a functional artificial pacemaker), cardiogenic shock, structural heart disease (e.g., heart failure, myocardial infarction), concurrent use of ritonavir **SIDE EFFECTS** Dizziness, visual disturbances, dyspnea **MONITORING** ECG, BP, HR, electrolytes
Propafenone *(Rythmol, Rythmol SR)* Capsule, tablet	IR: 150-300 mg PO Q8H SR: 225-425 mg PO Q12H	**CONTRAINDICATIONS** Sinoatrial and atrioventricular disorders (unless patient has a functional artificial pacemaker), sinus bradycardia, cardiogenic shock, hypotension, bronchospastic disorders **SIDE EFFECTS** Taste disturbance (metallic), dizziness, visual disturbances, N/V **MONITORING** ECG, BP, HR, electrolytes

Class Ic Antiarrhythmic Drug Interactions

- Flecainide is a substrate of 2D6 (major) and 1A2 (minor); it inhibits 2D6 (weak).
- Propafenone is a substrate of 2D6 (minor), 3A4 (minor) and 1A2 (minor); it inhibits 1A2 and 2D6 (weak).

Class II Antiarrhythmics

Class II antiarrhythmic drugs are beta blockers, which block beta-adrenergic receptors and indirectly block calcium channels in the SA and AV nodes, resulting in ↓ automaticity and conduction velocity. These drugs are used to slow the ventricular rate in supraventricular tachyarrhythmias. Beta blockers with intrinsic sympathomimetic activity should be avoided, since they do not slow ventricular rate. Refer to the Hypertension chapter for a complete review of the beta blockers.

Class III Antiarrhythmics

Class III antiarrhythmic drugs all significantly prolong the refractory period. Most drugs in this class act through blockade of potassium channels. Ibutilide is the exception; it works by activating the late inward sodium current, which also results in a significant ↑ in refractory period. Amiodarone and dronedarone also block alpha- and beta-adrenergic receptors, and calcium and sodium channels. Sotalol has significant beta-adrenergic receptor blocking activity.

DRUG	DOSING	SAFETY/SIDE EFFECTS/MONITORING
Amiodarone ***(Cordarone, Pacerone, Nexterone)*** Tablet, injection	**Pulseless VT/VF** 300 mg IV push x 1, may repeat 150 mg x 1 if needed **VT with pulse** 150 mg IV bolus, 1 mg/min x 6 hours, then 0.5 mg/min x 18 hours or longer **Ventricular arrhythmias** 800-1,600 mg/day x 1-3 weeks, then 600-800 mg/day x 4 weeks, then 400 mg/day **AFib: Cardioversion (off label)** 600-800 mg/day for a 10 gram loading dose, followed by 200 mg daily **AFib: Maintenance of NSR (off label)** 400-600 mg/day for 2-4 weeks; then 100-200 mg daily t½ = 40-60 days	**BOXED WARNINGS** Proarrhythmic, pulmonary and hepatotoxicity, use only for life-threatening arrhythmias due to toxicities (patients should be hospitalized when loading dose is given) **CONTRAINDICATIONS** Severe sinus-node dysfunction causing marked bradycardia, 2nd/3rd degree heart block (unless patient has a functional artificial pacemaker), bradycardia causing syncope, cardiogenic shock, hypersensitivity to iodine **WARNINGS** Hyper- and hypo-thyroidism (hypo is more common) - amiodarone partially inhibits peripheral conversion of T4 to T3, neurotoxicity (peripheral neuropathy), optic neuropathy (visual impairment), severe skin reactions (SJS/TEN), photosensitivity (slate blue skin discoloration) **SIDE EFFECTS** Hypotension, bradycardia, corneal microdeposits, dizziness, ataxia, N/V constipation, tremor **MONITORING** ECG, BP, HR, electrolytes, pulmonary function (including chest X-ray) at baseline and annually, LFTs at baseline and every 6 months, thyroid function at baseline and every 3-6 months, ophthalmic exams **NOTES** Infusions longer than 2 hours must be administered in a non-polyvinyl chloride (PVC) container such as polyolefin or glass. Premixed *Nexterone* comes in GALAXY containers (non-PVC and non-DEHP) that can be stored up to 24 months at room temperature. PVC tubing is fine to use. Use a 0.22 micron filter. Incompatible with heparin (flush with saline). Premixed IV bag advantages: longer stability, PVC bag not an issue, available in most commonly used concentrations. Slow infusion rate or discontinue if hypotension or bradycardia occurs. Recommended as antiarrhythmic drug of choice in patients with heart failure. Oral and IV amiodarone can provide rate control (due to beta blocking properties) when other measures are unsuccessful or contraindicated. Safety issue – see Pregnancy chapter MedGuide required

Class III Antiarrhythmic Agents Continued

DRUG	DOSING	SAFETY/SIDE EFFECTS/MONITORING
Dronedarone *(Multaq)* Tablet	400 mg PO BID with meals t½ = 13-19 hrs (less lipophilic than amiodarone)	**BOXED WARNINGS** Increased risk of death, stroke and HF in patients with decompensated HF (NYHA Class IV or any Class with a recent hospitalization due to HF) or permanent AFib **CONTRAINDICATIONS** 2nd/3rd degree heart block (unless patient has a functional artificial pacemaker), symptomatic HF, HR < 50, concomitant use of strong 3A4 inhibitors, concomitant use of drugs that prolong the QT interval, QT ≥ 500 msec, PR interval > 280 msec, lung or liver toxicity related to previous amiodarone use, severe hepatic impairment, pregnancy, nursing mothers **WARNINGS** Hepatic failure (especially in the first 6 months), lung disease (including pulmonary fibrosis and pneumonitis), marked ↑ SCr, prerenal azotemia and acute renal failure (usually in the setting of heart failure or hypovolemia), hypokalemia or hypomagnesemia with concomitant administration of potassium-depleting diuretics **SIDE EFFECTS** QT prolongation, ↑ SCr, N/V/D, abdominal pain, diarrhea, bradycardia, asthenia **MONITORING** ECG, BP, HR, electrolytes, renal function, LFTs (especially in the first 6 months) **NOTES** Safety issue – see Pregnancy chapter Noniodinated derivative of amiodarone MedGuide required
Sotalol *(Betapace, Betapace AF, Sotylize, Sorine)* Tablet, solution, injection Non-selective beta blocker	80 mg PO BID; can ↑ to 160 mg PO BID (monitor QT interval and renal function closely) CrCl 40-60 mL/min: ↓ frequency CrCl < 40 mL/min: varies by formulation	**BOXED WARNINGS** To minimize risk of life-threatening ventricular arrhythmias (TdP), initiation (or reinitiation) and dosage increase should be done in a hospital with continuous ECG monitoring and experienced staff Adjust dosing interval based on creatinine clearance to ↓ risk of proarrhythmia; QT prolongation is directly related to sotalol concentration *Betapace* should not be substituted with *Betapace AF* since *Betapace AF* is distributed with educational information specifically for patients with AFib/Atrial flutter **CONTRAINDICATIONS** 2nd/3rd degree heart block (unless patient has a functional artificial pacemaker), congenital or acquired long QT syndrome, sinus bradycardia, uncontrolled HF, cardiogenic shock, asthma For *Betapace AF, Sotylize*, sotalol injection: QTc > 450 msec, bronchospastic conditions, CrCl < 40 mL/min, K < 4 mEq/L, sick sinus syndrome **SIDE EFFECTS** Bradycardia, palpitations, chest pain, dizziness, fatigue, dyspnea, N/V, hypotension, TdP, HF, bronchoconstriction **MONITORING** ECG, BP, HR, electrolytes, renal function

Class III Antiarrhythmic Agents Continued

DRUG	DOSING	SAFETY/SIDE EFFECTS/MONITORING
Ibutilide *(Corvert)* Injection	≥ 60 kg: 1 mg IV over 10 min < 60 kg: 0.01 mg/kg over 10 min, may repeat x 1 after 10 minutes	**BOXED WARNING** Potentially fatal arrhythmias can occur; confirm that benefits of maintaining NSR outweigh the risks of ibutlide **SIDE EFFECTS** Ventricular tachycardias (e.g., TdP), headache, hypotension, QT prolongation
Dofetilide *(Tikosyn)* Capsule	500 mcg PO BID CrCl 40-60 mL/min: 250 mcg BID CrCl 20-39 mL/min: 125 mcg BID CrCl < 20 mL/min: avoid	**BOXED WARNING** Must be initiated (or reinitiated) in a setting with continuous ECG monitoring, experienced staff and ability to assess CrCl for a minimum of 3 days **CONTRAINDICATIONS** Patients with congenital or acquired long QT syndromes; concurrent use of cimetidine, dolutegravir, hydrochlorothiazide, itraconazole, ketoconazole, megestrol, prochlorperazine, trimethoprim, verapamil; HR < 50, CrCl < 20 mL/min, QTc > 440 msec **SIDE EFFECTS** Headache, dizziness, ventricular tachycardias (e.g., TdP), ↑ QT interval **MONITORING** ECG, BP, HR, electrolytes, renal function; QT interval and CrCl every 3 months (discontinue if QTc > 500 msec) **NOTES** A recommended option in patients with heart failure MedGuide required REMS program discontinued in 2016

Class III Antiarrhythmic Drug Interactions

- All Class III antiarrhythmic agents can have additive QT prolongation with other agents that also prolong the QT interval.
- Use extreme caution with other negative chronotropes (e.g., beta blockers, verapamil, diltiazem, ivabradine) which can ↑ risk of bradycardia with sotalol, amiodarone and dronedarone.
- Electrolyte abnormalities (K, Na, Ca, Mg, etc.) should be corrected before any antiarrhythmic treatment is initiated or the risk of arrhythmia is ↑ (true for all antiarrhythmics).
- Do not use grapefruit juice/products. Avoid ephedra and St. John's wort (P-gp inducer).

Amiodarone Drug Interactions

- Amiodarone is an inhibitor of 2C9 (moderate), 2D6 (moderate), 3A4 (weak) and P-gp; it is a major substrate of 3A4 and 2C8 and P-gp. Strong/moderate inhibitors of 3A4, 2C8 and P-gp will ↑ levels of amiodarone and strong/moderate inducers of 3A4, 2C8 and P-gp will ↓ levels of amiodarone.
- When starting amiodarone, ↓ dose of digoxin by 50% and ↓ dose of warfarin by 30 – 50%. Do not exceed 20 mg/day of simvastatin or 40 mg/day of lovastatin in patients taking amiodarone.
- Sofosbuvir may enhance the bradycardic effect of amiodarone.

Dronedarone Drug Interactions

- Dronedarone is a moderate inhibitor of 2D6, 3A4 and P-gp; it is a major substrate of 3A4. Avoid use with strong inhibitors and inducers of 3A4 and other drugs that prolong the QT interval. If using digoxin, reduce dose of digoxin by 50%. Caution with the use of statins at higher doses (see above under amiodarone).
- Monitor INR after initiating dronedarone in patients taking warfarin.

Dofetilide Drug Interactions

- Dofetilide is a minor 3A4 substrate and is cleared renally. Avoid concurrent use with cimetidine, dolutegravir, hydrochlorothiazide, itraconazole, ketoconazole, megesterol, prochlorperazine, trimethoprim and verapamil.

Class IV Antiarrhythmics

Class IV antiarrhythmic drugs block L-type calcium channels, slowing SA and AV nodal conduction velocity. These drugs are used to slow the ventricular rate in supraventricular tachyarrhythmias. Non-dihydropyridine calcium channel blockers should not be used in patients with LV systolic dysfunction (HFrEF) and decompensated HF due to their negative inotropic effects, but they may be used in patients with HF with preserved LV systolic function (HFpEF).

DRUG	DOSING	SAFETY/SIDE EFFECTS/MONITORING
DilTIAZem *(Cardizem, Cardizem CD, Cardizem LA*, *Cartia XT, Dilt-XR, Diltzac Tiazac, Taztia XT)* Tablet, capsule, injection	120-360 mg PO daily	**CONTRAINDICATIONS** Severe hypotension (systolic < 90 mmHg), 2nd/3rd degree heart block or sick sinus syndrome (unless the patient has a functioning artificial pacemaker), cardiogenic shock, systolic HF, Wolff-Parkinson-White syndrome (WPW) with AFib **WARNINGS** 1st degree AV block with sinus bradycardia, ↑ LFTs
Verapamil *(Calan, Calan SR, Covera HS, Verelan, Verelan PM)* Tablet, capsule, injection	180-480 mg PO daily	**SIDE EFFECTS** Edema, headache, dizziness, hypotension, arrhythmias, HF, constipation (more with verapamil), gingival hyperplasia **MONITORING** ECG, BP, HR, electrolytes, LFTs, renal function **NOTES** Only non-dihydropyridine CCBs are used as antiarrhythmics

For drug interactions/counseling of calcium channel blockers, see Hypertension chapter.

Drugs Not Included In Vaughan Williams Classification

- Adenosine slows conduction through the AV node via activation of adenosine-1 receptors. Adenosine is used to restore NSR in supraventricular re-entrant tachycardias (paroxysmal supraventricular tachyarrhythmias or PSVTs).
- Digoxin causes direct AV node suppression, ↑ refractory period and ↓ conduction velocity. Digoxin enhances vagal tone, resulting in ↓ ventricular rate in supraventricular tachyarrhythmias. Digoxin reduces the resting heart rate, but it is ineffective at controlling the ventricular response during exercise; therefore, it is not used first line for rate control.

DRUG	DOSING	SAFETY/SIDE EFFECTS/MONITORING
Adenosine *(Adenocard)* Injection	6 mg IV push (may increase to 12 mg if not responding) t½: less than 10 sec Used in paroxysmal supraventricular tachycardia (PSVTs) and not for converting AFib/Atrial flutter or ventricular tachycardia	**CONTRAINDICATIONS** 2nd/3rd degree heart block, sick sinus syndrome or symptomatic bradycardia (except in patients with a functional pacemaker), bronchospastic lung disease **SIDE EFFECTS** Transient new arrhythmia, facial flushing, chest pain/pressure, neck discomfort, dizziness, headache, GI distress, transient ↓ in blood pressure, dyspnea
Digoxin *(Digitek, Digox, Lanoxin)* Tablet, solution, injection	Typical dose: 0.125-0.25 mg PO daily Tablet strengths: 0.0625, 0.125, 0.1875, 0.25 mg Loading dose [called total digitalizing dose (TDD)] is: 8-12 mcg/kg. Give ½ of the TDD as the initial dose, followed by ¼ of the TDD in 2 subsequent doses at 4-8 hour intervals. Alternatively, give 0.25 mg IV and repeat dosing to a max of 1.5 mg over 24 hours Therapeutic range for AFib = 0.8-2 ng/mL (lower range for heart failure) When CrCl < 50 mL/min, ↓ dose or ↓ frequency ↓ dose by 20-25% when going from oral to IV Antidote: *DigiFab*	**CONTRAINDICATIONS** Ventricular fibrillation **WARNINGS** 2nd/3rd degree heart block without a pacemaker, Wolff-Parkinson-White syndrome (WPW) with AFib, vesicant - avoid extravasation **SIDE EFFECTS** Dizziness, mental disturbances, headache, N/V/D **MONITORING** ECG, HR, BP, electrolytes, renal function and digoxin level (drawn optimally 12-24 hrs after dose) **Toxicity** Initial s/sx of toxicity are N/V, loss of appetite and bradycardia; severe s/sx of toxicity include blurred/double vision, altered color perception, greenish-yellow halos around lights or objects, abdominal pain, confusion, delirium, prolonged PR interval, arrhythmias **NOTES** Not usually given alone for rate control (used in combination with a beta blocker or CCB)

Digoxin Drug Interactions

- Use caution when administering other drugs that ↓ HR.
- Digoxin is 50 – 70% cleared by the kidney (unchanged) and partially cleared hepatically. Decreased renal function requires a ↓ digoxin dose. In acute renal failure, digoxin is held.
- Digoxin is a substrate of 3A4 (major) and P-gp. Digoxin levels ↑ with amiodarone, dronedarone, quinidine, verapamil, erythromycin, clarithromycin, itraconazole, propafenone and many other drugs. Reduce digoxin dose by 50% if patient is on amiodarone or dronedarone.
- Hypokalemia, hypomagnesemia and hypercalcemia ↑ the risk of digoxin toxicity.
- Hypothyroidism can ↑ digoxin levels.

PATIENT COUNSELING

Amiodarone Patient Counseling

- Read the MedGuide that has been given to you. This medication can cause severe lung or liver problems in some rare instances. Get immediate medical help if you experience any of these serious side effects: cough, fever, chills, chest pain, difficult or painful breathing, coughing up blood, severe stomach pain, nausea, vomiting, fatigue, yellowing eyes or skin, or dark-colored urine and new shortness of breath. Your blood will need to be checked, and possibly a chest X-ray, during treatment.
- This medication is used to treat certain types of serious (possibly fatal) irregular heartbeat problems called arrhythmias. It is used to restore and maintain the normal heart rhythm and keep a regular, steady heartbeat. Amiodarone works by blocking certain electrical signals in the heart that can cause an irregular heartbeat. This medication has not been shown to help people with these arrhythmias live longer.
- Take this medication by mouth, usually once or twice daily or as directed by your healthcare provider. If stomach upset occurs, take the medication with food.
- Like other medications used to treat irregular heartbeats, amiodarone can infrequently cause them to become worse. Seek immediate medical attention if your heart continues to pound or skips a beat.
- This drug may infrequently cause serious vision changes. Tell your healthcare provider immediately if you develop any vision changes (such as seeing halos or blurred vision). You will need to have your eyes checked before and during the time you are taking amiodarone.
- You may develop "pins and needles" or numbness in your legs, hands and feet, or muscle weakness or trouble walking. Discuss with your healthcare provider if this happens.
- This drug can change how your thyroid gland works and may cause your metabolism to speed up or slow down. Tell your healthcare provider if you develop any symptoms of low or overactive thyroid including cold or heat intolerance, unexplained weight loss/gain, thinning hair, unusual sweating, nervousness, irritability or restlessness. Discuss this with your healthcare provider; tests can be ordered to check your thyroid function.
- This drug may cause your skin to be more sensitive to the sun. Stay out of the sun during the mid-day and use protective clothing and broad spectrum sunscreen. Infrequently, this medication has caused the skin to become a blue-gray color. This effect is not harmful and usually goes away months after the drug is stopped.
- Avoid eating grapefruit or drinking grapefruit juice while using this medication. Grapefruit will cause too much of the medication to get into your body.
- This drug can interact with other medications. Before starting a new medication, including any over-the-counter medications, discuss with your healthcare provider if it is safe to use with amiodarone.
- If you miss a dose, do not take a double dose to make up for the dose you missed. Continue with your next regularly scheduled dose.

Digoxin Patient Counseling

- This medicine helps the heart beat with a more regular rate. Keep taking as directed, even if you feel well.
- Do not stop taking this medicine without talking to your healthcare provider. Stopping suddenly may make your condition worse.
- Avoid becoming overheated or dehydrated as an overdose can occur more easily if you are dehydrated.

- Symptoms of overdose may include nausea, vomiting, diarrhea, loss of appetite, vision changes (such as blurred or yellow/green vision), confusion and hallucinations and feeling like you might pass out. If any of these occur, see your healthcare provider right away.
- There are many medications that can interact with digoxin. Check with your healthcare provider before starting any new medications, including over the counter, vitamin and/or herbal products.
- To be sure that this medication is not causing harmful effects, your blood may need to be tested on a regular basis. Your kidney function will also need to be monitored.

PRACTICE CASE

AH is a 57 y/o Hispanic male who had an appointment in the clinic this morning. He has asked to speak to the pharmacist at the clinic pharmacy. He tells you that he went to the clinic because he felt like his heart was racing and he felt dizzy. The doctor told him that he has atrial fibrillation. He is concerned that this will affect his life span. You are able to access his clinic records and learn that his past medical history includes heart failure (NYHA Class 3) and hypertension. He is a smoker.

Allergies: Sulfa

Medications:
Digox 0.25 mg PO daily
Lasix 40 mg PO daily
Spironolactone 12.5 mg PO daily
Coreg CR 20 mg PO daily
Lisinopril 40 mg PO daily

Vitals:
BP: 152/83 mmHg HR: 84 BPM RR: 15 BPM Temp: 98.5°F

Labs:
Na (mEq/L) = 137 (135 - 145)
K (mEq/L) = 5.2 (3.5 - 5)
Cl (mEq/L) = 99 (95 - 103)
HCO_3 (mEq/L) = 28 (24 - 30)
BUN (mg/dL) = 43 (7 - 20)
SCr (mg/dL) = 1.4 (0.6 - 1.3)
Glucose (mg/dL) = 112 (100 - 125)
Ca (mg/dL) = 9.5 (8.5 - 10.5)
Mg (mEq/L) = 1.8 (1.3 - 2.1)
PO_4 (mg/dL) = 3.8 (2.3 - 4.7)

The cardiologist has written a new prescription for amiodarone 200 mg PO daily that AH would like to have filled.

Questions

1. Before the prescription for amiodarone is filled, the pharmacist should call the prescriber to decrease the dose of which of AH's medications?
   a. *Digox*
   b. *Lasix*
   c. Spironolactone
   d. *Coreg CR*
   e. Lisinopril

2. When counseling AH on the use of amiodarone, he should be told to expect periodic monitoring of these organ systems:
   a. Liver, kidney, and eyes
   b. Liver, colon, and kidney
   c. Kidney, gall bladder, and CNS
   d. Thyroid, kidney, and liver
   e. Thyroid, liver, and lungs

3. Which of the following are side effects of amiodarone? (Select **ALL** that apply.)
   a. Skin discoloration
   b. Corneal deposits
   c. Pulmonary fibrosis
   d. Taste perversions
   e. Hypothyroidism

4. AH develops thyroid dysfunction. His doctor switches him to *Multaq* to try and alleviate the problem. Choose the correct therapeutic equivalent for *Multaq*:
   a. Mexiletine
   b. Flecainide
   c. Lidocaine
   d. Dronedarone
   e. Dofetilide

Questions 5-8 do not apply to the above case.

5. What class of antiarrhythmic is disopyramide in the Vaughan Williams classification system?
   a. Ia
   b. Ib
   c. Ic
   d. III
   e. IV

6. A patient has a long QT interval. She is at risk for fatal arrhythmias. Which of the following medications will increase her risk of further QT prolongation? (Select **ALL** that apply.)
   a. *Biaxin*
   b. Ketorolac
   c. Docusate
   d. Escitalopram
   e. Ondansetron

7. A patient is taking *Betapace AF*. Which of the following statements is true of *Betapace AF*?
   a. It is a beta-1 selective beta blocker.
   b. It is a recommended option in decompensated heart failure.
   c. Reduce frequency of administration to once daily if CrCl is 40 – 60 mL/min.
   d. It is contraindicated if CrCl > 60 mL/min.
   e. Thyroid function should be monitored during treatment.

8. A patient is beginning digoxin 0.125 mg daily in addition to her *Lopressor* therapy. After a few weeks, the patient develops an infection with nausea and vomiting. She is weak and dehydrated and is admitted to the hospital. Her work up is significant for new onset acute renal failure, mental confusion, pneumonia and atrial fibrillation. She is started on levofloxacin for her pneumonia. Which of the following statements regarding this patient and her digoxin therapy is true? (Select **ALL** that apply.)
   a. The digoxin may have become toxic due to her decreased renal function.
   b. An elevated digoxin level can worsen nausea and vomiting.
   c. The digoxin level will increase due to the initiation of levofloxacin.
   d. Mental confusion may be due to an elevated digoxin level.
   e. The patient will need to stay on digoxin therapy regardless of the level.

Answers

1-a, 2-e, 3-a,b,c,e, 4-d, 5-a, 6-a,d,e, 7-c, 8-a,b,d

ANTICOAGULATION

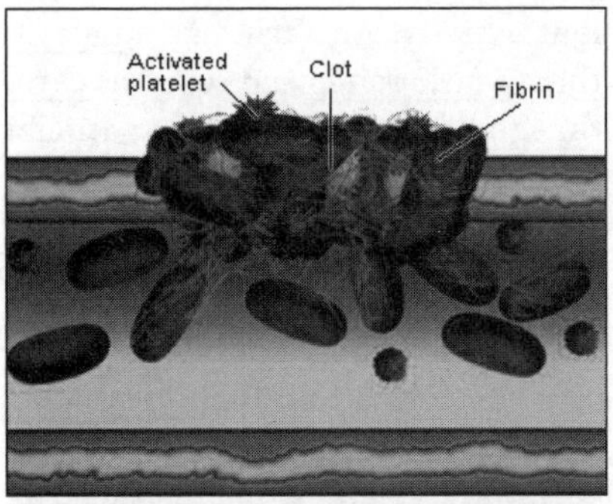

GUIDELINES/REFERENCES

Antithrombotic Therapy for VTE Disease: CHEST Guideline Expert Panel Report. *Chest.* 2016; 149(2):315-52.

2014 AHA/ACC/HRS Guideline for the Management of Patients With Atrial Fibrillation: A Report of the American College of Cardiology/American Heart Association Task Force on Practice Guidelines and the Heart Rhythm Society. *J Am Coll Cardiol.* 2014; 64(21):e1-e76.

Executive Summary of Antithrombotic Therapy and Prevention of Thrombosis, 9th ed: American College of Chest Physicians Evidence-Based Clinical Practice Guidelines. *Chest.* 2012; 141(2):7S-47S.

BACKGROUND

Anticoagulants are used to prevent blood clots from forming and to keep existing clots from becoming larger. They do not break down existing clots (like thrombolytics such as tPA). Anticoagulants are most commonly used for acute coronary syndrome (ACS), prevention of cardioembolic stroke and prevention/treatment of venous thromboembolism (VTE), which refers to deep vein thrombosis (DVT) and/or pulmonary embolism (PE). A DVT is a blood clot (thrombus) in a vein. DVTs can occur anywhere in the body but are most frequently found in the deep veins of the legs, thighs, and pelvis. When a clot forms in a deep vein, the clot or a piece of the clot can break off, travel to the heart and be pumped into the arteries of the lung. This can cause a PE. Patients with atrial fibrillation (AFib) or patent foramen ovale (PFO) can form clots in the heart which can travel to the brain causing a transient ischemic attack (TIA) or ischemic stroke. Anticoagulants are high risk medications which must be carefully monitored due to the risks involved with either clotting or bleeding.

CLOT FORMATION

Coagulation is the process by which blood clots form. A number of factors can lead to activation of the coagulation process such as blood vessel injury, blood stasis, and pro-thrombotic conditions. The coagulation process involves activation of platelets and the clotting cascade. All of the clotting factors have an inactive and an active form. Once activated, the clotting factor will serve to activate the next clotting factor in the sequence until fibrin is formed. The coagulation cascade has two pathways which lead to fibrin formation: the contact activation pathway (or the intrinsic pathway) and the tissue factor pathway (or the extrinsic pathway). Anticoagulants are used to inhibit the clotting cascade, thereby preventing or reducing clot formation.

DRUG TREATMENT

Anticoagulants work by various mechanisms. Unfractionated heparin (UFH), low molecular weight heparins (LMWHs), and fondaparinux work by binding to antithrombin (AT) causing a conformational

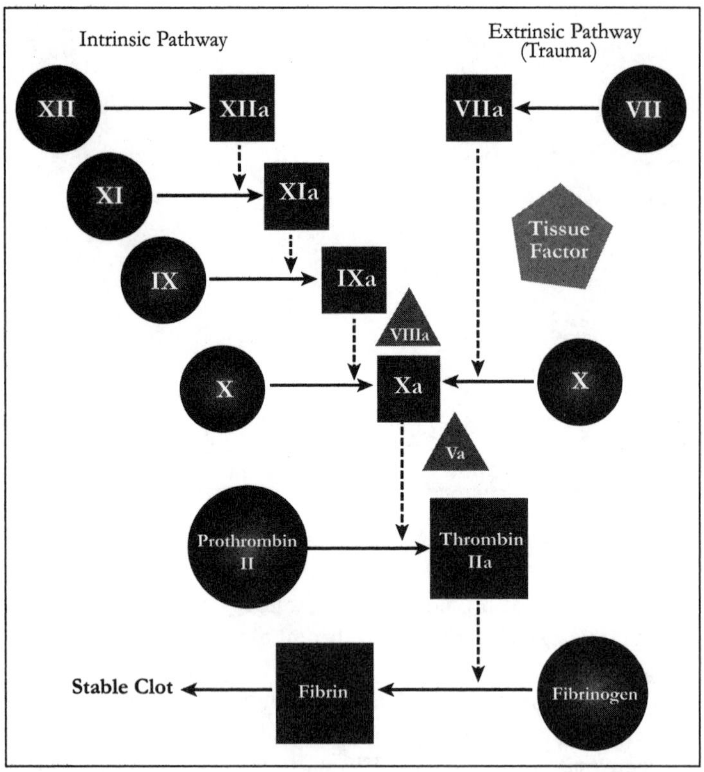

change which increases AT activity 1,000-fold. AT inactivates thrombin and other proteases involved in blood clotting, including factor Xa. LMWHs inhibit factor Xa more specifically than unfractionated heparin. Fondaparinux *(Arixtra)* is a synthetic pentasaccharide that requires AT binding to selectively inhibit Factor Xa.

Warfarin is a vitamin K antagonist. Vitamin K is required for the carboxylation of clotting factors II, VII, IX, and X. Without adequate vitamin K, the liver produces the clotting factors, but they have reduced coagulant activity. Warfarin has a narrow therapeutic range and requires careful monitoring of the international normalized ratio (INR), which is affected greatly by many drugs and changes in dietary vitamin K intake.

Direct thrombin inhibitors (DTIs) block thrombin directly, decreasing the amount of fibrin available for clot formation. The intravenous DTIs are important clinically since they do not cross-react with heparin-induced thrombocytopenia (HIT) antibodies. Once HIT develops in the hospital setting, the injectable DTI argatroban is the drug of choice. Dabigatran *(Pradaxa)* is an oral DTI.

Rivaroxaban *(Xarelto)*, apixaban *(Eliquis)* and edoxaban *(Savaysa)* work by inhibiting Factor Xa. These newer oral agents are taken once or twice daily and require no laboratory monitoring for efficacy.

Injectable anticoagulants are used for ACS and VTE (treatment and prevention), while oral anticoagulants are used mainly for VTE (treatment and prevention) and stroke prevention in patients with AFib. An overview of these indications is included at the end of the chapter.

EXAM SCENARIO

When studying the Anticoagulation, Acute Coronary Syndrome, Ischemic Heart Disease and Stroke chapters, it can be difficult to determine when a fibrinolytic, antiplatelet or anticoagulant would be appropriate.

- Fibrinolytics break down existing clots, but are associated with very high risk of bleeding. They are used for STEMI and acute ischemic stroke, when the patient could die without rapid restoration of blood flow.
- Antiplatelet agents (aspirin, clopidogrel, etc.) are used mainly for ACS and to prevent stroke/TIA. Dual antiplatelet therapy (DAPT) refers to using both aspirin and a P2Y12 inhibitor together, which is very common in patients who have had an ACS. Antiplatelet agents are not sufficient for treating acute DVT/PE.
- Oral anticoagulants are used mainly in AFib (for stroke prevention) and for DVT/PE (treatment and prevention). The popular oral medications *(Xarelto, Eliquis, Savaysa* and *Pradaxa)* are not indicated for ACS where platelet aggregation is the main target of drug therapy.

High Alert Medications

All anticoagulants can cause significant bleeding and are classified as "High Alert" medications by the Institute for Safe Medication Practices (ISMP). Bleeding events associated with anticoagulants put patients at risk for increased mortality. The Joint Commission's National Patient Safety Goals require the implementation of policies and protocols to properly initiate and manage anticoagulant therapy. Patients receiving anticoagulants should receive individualized care through a defined process that includes standardized ordering, dispensing, administration, monitoring and patient/caregiver education (for treatment doses). Refer to the Medication Safety & Quality Improvement chapter for additional information. When pharmacists are involved in managing anticoagulants, patient care and outcomes are improved and costs are decreased. Pharmacists are also involved with ensuring that patients who need anticoagulants for VTE prophylaxis (e.g., orthopedic and cardiac surgical patients) receive them (this is discussed later in this chapter).

UNFRACTIONATED HEPARIN

Unfractionated heparin (UFH) binds to antithrombin (AT), which then inactivates thrombin (Factor IIa) and Factor Xa (as well as factors IXa, XIa, XIIa, and plasmin) and prevents the conversion of fibrinogen to fibrin.

DRUG	DOSING	SAFETY/SIDE EFFECTS/MONITORING
Unfractionated Heparin Anticoagulation Treatment/ Prophylaxis Many strengths and volumes (ranging from 1 unit/mL to 20,000 units/mL), including total units of 5,000, 10,000, 12,500, 20,000, 25,000 & others. Usual infusion for treatment is 25,000 units in 250 mL (concentration: 100 units/mL) in D5W, ½ NS or NS. Line Flush 10 units/mL, 100 units/mL syringes (in 1, 2, 2.5, 3, 5, 10, 30 mL), others **SAFETY NOTE** Heparin lock-flushes *(HepFlush)* are used to keep IV lines open (patent), not used for anticoagulation. There have been fatal errors, especially in neonates, made by choosing the incorrect heparin strength. Heparin injection 10,000 units/mL and heparin flushes 10 or 100 units/mL look and sound alike. Using a higher dose to flush a line could cause fatal hemorrhage. Refer to the Medication Safety & Quality Improvement chapter for safe use of antithrombotics.	**Prophylaxis of VTE** 5,000 units SC Q8-12H **Treatment of VTE** 80 units/kg IV bolus followed by 18 units/kg/hr infusion or a fixed dose of 5,000 units IV bolus followed by 1,000 units/hr infusion. If treating as an outpatient, give 333 units/kg x 1 dose SC, then 250 units/kg SC Q12H **Treatment of ACS/STEMI** 60 units/kg IV bolus (max 4,000 units); 12 units/kg/hr (max 1,000 units/hr) infusion Use actual body weight for dosing Onset IV: immediate; SC: 20-30 min t½ = 1.5 hrs. HIT antibodies have cross-sensitivity with LMWHs Antidote: protamine – 1 mg protamine will reverse ~100 units of heparin; max dose 50 mg	**CONTRAINDICATIONS** Uncontrolled active bleed (ICH), severe thrombocytopenia, history of HIT, hypersensitivity to pork products. Some products contain benzyl alcohol as a preservative (do not use in neonates, infants, pregnancy and breastfeeding) **WARNING** Fatal medication errors: verify that the correct concentration is chosen **SIDE EFFECTS** Bleeding (epistaxis, ecchymosis, gingival, GI), thrombocytopenia, HIT, hyperkalemia and osteoporosis (with long-term use) **MONITORING** aPTT (or anti-Xa level: 0.3-0.7 units/mL) aPTT is taken 6 hours after initiation, every 6 hours until therapeutic range of 1.5-2.5 x control (patient's baseline) is reached, then every 24 hours. Also check aPTT after every dosage change. Platelets, Hgb, Hct at baseline and daily (↓ in platelets > 50% from baseline suggests possible HIT) **NOTES** Unpredictable anticoagulant response (has variable and extensive binding to plasma proteins and cells) Do not give IM due to hematoma risk

LOW MOLECULAR WEIGHT HEPARINS

Low molecular weight heparins (LMWHs) bind to AT and have a greater affinity of inhibiting Factor Xa than Factor IIa.

DRUG	DOSING	SAFETY/SIDE EFFECTS/MONITORING
Enoxaparin ***(Lovenox)*** Multidose vial (300 mg/3 mL) and prefilled syringes: 30 mg/0.3 mL, 40 mg/0.4 mL, 60 mg/0.6 mL, 80 mg/0.8 mL, 100 mg/mL, 120 mg/0.8 mL, 150 mg/mL 1 mg = 100 units anti-Xa activity	**Prophylaxis of VTE** 30 mg SC Q12H or 40 mg SC daily CrCl < 30 mL/min: 30 mg SC daily **Treatment of VTE and UA/NSTEMI** 1 mg/kg SC Q12H (or 1.5 mg/kg SC daily only for inpatient VTE treatment) CrCl < 30 mL/min: 1 mg/kg SC daily Use actual body weight for dosing **Treatment for STEMI** Patients < 75 years: 30 mg IV bolus plus a 1 mg/kg SC dose followed by 1 mg/kg SC Q12H (max 100 mg for the first two SC doses only) CrCl < 30 mL/min: 30 mg IV bolus plus a 1 mg/kg SC dose, followed by 1 mg/kg SC daily Patients ≥ 75 years: 0.75 mg/kg SC Q12H (no bolus – max 75 mg for the first two SC doses only) CrCl < 30 mL/min: 1 mg/kg SC daily (no bolus) Patients managed with percutaneous coronary intervention (PCI): if the last SC dose was given 8-12 hours before balloon inflation, give 0.3 mg/kg IV bolus	**BOXED WARNING** Patients receiving neuraxial anesthesia (epidural, spinal) or undergoing spinal puncture are at risk of hematomas and subsequent paralysis. **CONTRAINDICATIONS** History of HIT, active major bleed, hypersensitivity to pork **SIDE EFFECTS** Bleeding, anemia, ↑ LFTs, thrombocytopenia, hyperkalemia, injection site reactions (bruising) **MONITORING** Platelets, Hgb, Hct, SCr Anti-Xa level monitoring is recommended in pregnancy. Monitoring may be done in obesity, low body weight, pediatrics, elderly or renal insufficiency. aPTT is not used. Obtain peak anti-Xa levels 4 hours post dose. VTE treatment (enoxaparin daily): 1-2 anti-Xa units/mL VTE treatment (enoxaparin Q12H): 0.6-1 anti-Xa units/mL Recurrent VTE prophylaxis in pregnancy: 0.2-0.6 anti-Xa units/mL **NOTES** More predictable anticoagulant response than UFH; does not require anti-Xa level monitoring in most cases. This makes LMWH more cost effective even though the actual drug costs more than UFH. Do not expel air bubble from syringe prior to injection (can cause loss of drug). Do not administer IM. Store at room temperature. Largely neutralized by protamine.
Dalteparin *(Fragmin)*	**Prophylaxis of VTE** 2,500-5,000 units SC daily **Treatment of UA/NSTEMI** 120 units/kg (max 10,000 units) SC Q12H	

UFH/LMWH Drug Interactions

- Most drug interactions are due to additive effects with other drugs that can ↑ bleeding risk (other anticoagulants, antiplatelet drugs, some herbals, NSAIDs, SSRIs, SNRIs, thrombolytics, others). See the Drug Interactions chapter.

HEPARIN-INDUCED THROMBOCYTOPENIA OVERVIEW

Heparin-induced thrombocytopenia (HIT) is an immune-mediated IgG drug reaction that is associated with a high risk of venous and arterial thrombosis. The immune system forms antibodies against heparin when it binds to platelet factor 4 (PF 4). These IgG antibodies form a complex with heparin and PF 4. In HIT, this complex binds to the Fc receptors on platelets, which leads to further platelet activation, and causes a release of PF 4 and other pro-coagulant microparticles from platelet granules. If left untreated, HIT can lead to a prothrombotic state causing many complications including heparin-induced thrombocytopenia and thrombosis (HITT). HITT causes amputations, post-thrombotic syndrome, and/or death. The estimated incidence of HIT is ~3% of those patients exposed to heparin for more than four days. It is lower with a shorter duration of treatment. The typical onset of HIT occurs 5 – 14 days after the start of heparin or within hours if a patient has been exposed to heparin within the past 3 months. A diagnosis is made by a compatible clinical picture, a profound, unexplained drop in platelet count (defined as > 50% drop from baseline) and laboratory confirmation of antibodies or platelet activation by heparin. Although thrombocytopenia is the most common presenting feature of HIT, in up to 25% of patients with HIT, the development of thrombosis precedes the development of thrombocytopenia.

Management of HIT Complicated by Thrombosis (HITT)

- If HIT is suspected or confirmed, stop all forms of heparin and LMWH including heparin flushes (can use regional citrate) and heparin-coated catheters. If the patient is on warfarin and diagnosed with HIT, the warfarin should be discontinued and vitamin K should be administered. Although the patient is at a high risk of thrombosis, warfarin use with a low platelet count has a high correlation with warfarin-induced limb gangrene and necrosis.
- In patients with HIT, nonheparin anticoagulants are recommended, in particular, argatroban, over the further use of heparin or LMWH or initiation/continuation of vitamin K antagonists.
- Do not start warfarin therapy until the platelets have recovered to at least 150,000/mm^3. Warfarin should be initiated at lower doses (5 mg maximum). Overlap warfarin with a nonheparin anticoagulant for a minimum of 5 days and until the INR is within target range for 24 hours.
- If urgent cardiac surgery or PCI is required, bivalirudin is the preferred anticoagulant.

FACTOR Xa INHIBITORS

Rivaroxaban *(Xarelto)*, apixaban *(Eliquis)* and edoxaban *(Savaysa)* are direct Factor Xa inhibitors and are available orally. Fondaparinux *(Arixtra)* is an injectable synthetic pentasaccharide that selectively inhibits Factor Xa via antithrombin (AT), making it an indirect inhibitor of Factor Xa. Fondaparinux is often used off label in clinical practice for HIT.

DRUG	DOSING	SAFETY/SIDE EFFECTS/MONITORING

Oral Direct Factor Xa Inhibitors

DRUG	DOSING	SAFETY/SIDE EFFECTS/MONITORING
Rivaroxaban *(Xarelto)* Tablet *Xarelto Starter Pack:* 30-day blister pack containing 15 mg and 20 mg tablets (for ease of prescribing for DVT/PE treatment) **Missed Dose** Administer the dose as soon as possible on the same day as follows: If taking 15 mg twice daily: take immediately to ensure intake of 30 mg/day. In this particular instance, two 15 mg tablets may be taken at once. Then resume regular schedule on the following day. If taking 10, 15 or 20 mg once daily: take immediately on the same day; otherwise skip.	Doses ≥ 15 mg must be taken with food; 10 mg dose can be taken without regard to meals **Nonvalvular AFib** CrCl > 50 mL/min: 20 mg PO daily with evening meal CrCl 15-50 mL/min: 15 mg PO daily with evening meal CrCl < 15 mL/min: avoid use **Treatment of DVT/PE** 15 mg PO BID x 21 days, then 20 mg PO daily. CrCl < 30 mL/min: avoid use **Prophylaxis for DVT (after knee/hip replacement)** 10 mg PO daily (for 12 days after knee or 35 days after hip replacement surgery). Give first dose 6-10 hours after surgery CrCl < 30 mL/min: avoid use **Reduction in the Risk of Recurrence of DVT and PE** 20 mg PO daily CrCl < 30 mL/min: avoid use	**BOXED WARNINGS** Patients receiving neuraxial anesthesia (epidural, spinal) or undergoing spinal puncture are at risk of hematomas and subsequent paralysis Premature discontinuation ↑ risk of thrombotic events **CONTRAINDICATIONS** Active pathological bleeding **WARNINGS** Not recommended with prosthetic heart valves, avoid in patients with moderate to severe hepatic impairment **SIDE EFFECTS** Bleeding, anemia **MONITORING** Hgb, Hct, SCr, LFTs; no monitoring of efficacy required **NOTES** No antidote Discontinue 24 hours prior to elective surgery (rivaroxaban) Discontinue 48 hours prior to elective surgery with moderate-high bleeding risk or 24 hours prior with a low bleeding risk (apixaban) Can be crushed and put on applesauce (rivaroxaban, apixaban); crushed and mixed in water, D5W or apple juice (apixaban) or suspended in water or D5W to administer by NG tube (rivaroxaban, apixaban) MedGuide required
Apixaban *(Eliquis)* Tablet **Missed Dose** Take immediately on the same day and twice daily administration should be resumed. The dose should not be doubled to make up for a missed dose.	**Nonvalvular AFib** 5 mg BID Unless patient has at least 2 of the following: age ≥ 80 years, body weight ≤ 60 kg, or SCr ≥ 1.5 mg/dL, give 2.5 mg BID **Treatment of DVT/PE** 10 mg PO BID x 7 days, then 5 mg PO BID **Prophylaxis for DVT (after knee/hip replacement)** 2.5 mg PO BID (for 12 days after knee or 35 days after hip replacement surgery). Give first dose 12-24 hours after surgery **Reduction in the Risk of Recurrence of DVT and PE** 2.5 mg PO BID after at least 6 months of treatment for DVT or PE	

Factor Xa Inhibitors continued

DRUG	DOSING	SAFETY/SIDE EFFECTS/MONITORING
Edoxaban *(Savaysa)* Tablet **Missed Dose** Take immediately on the same day. The dose should not be doubled to make up for a missed dose.	**Nonvalvular AFib** CrCl > 95 mL/min: do not use CrCl 51-95 mL/min: 60 mg daily CrCl 15-50 mL/min: 30 mg daily CrCl < 15 mL/min: not recommended **Treatment of DVT/PE** 60 mg daily, start after 5-10 days of parenteral anticoagulation CrCl 15-50 mL/min or body weight ≤ 60 kg or on certain P-gp inhibitors: 30 mg daily CrCl < 15 mL/min: not recommended	**BOXED WARNINGS** Reduced efficacy in nonvalvular AFib patients with CrCl > 95 mL/min Patients receiving neuraxial anesthesia (epidural, spinal) or undergoing spinal puncture are at risk of hematomas and subsequent paralysis Premature discontinuation ↑ risk of ischemic events **CONTRAINDICATIONS** Active pathological bleeding **WARNINGS** Not recommended with prosthetic heart valves, moderate to severe hepatic impairment **SIDE EFFECTS** Bleeding, anemia, rash, ↑ LFTs **MONITORING** Hgb, Hct, SCr, LFTs; no monitoring of efficacy required **NOTES** No antidote Discontinue 24 hours prior to elective surgery MedGuide required

Injectable (SC) Indirect Factor Xa Inhibitor

Fondaparinux *(Arixtra)* Prefilled syringes: 2.5 mg/0.5 mL, 5 mg/0.4 mL, 7.5 mg/0.6 mL, 10 mg/0.8 mL Store at room temperature	**Prophylaxis of VTE** ≥ 50 kg: 2.5 mg SC daily < 50 kg: contraindicated **Treatment of VTE** < 50 kg: 5 mg SC daily 50-100 kg: 7.5 mg SC daily > 100 kg: 10 mg SC daily **Both indications** CrCl 30-50 mL/min: use caution CrCl < 30 mL/min: contraindicated	**BOXED WARNING** Patients receiving neuraxial anesthesia (epidural, spinal) or undergoing spinal puncture are at risk of hematomas and subsequent paralysis. **CONTRAINDICATIONS** Severe renal impairment (CrCl < 30 mL/min), active major bleed, bacterial endocarditis, thrombocytopenia with positive test for anti-platelet antibodies in presence of fondaparinux **SIDE EFFECTS** Bleeding (epistaxis, ecchymosis, gingival, GI, etc.), anemia, local injection site reactions (rash, pruritus, bruising), thrombocytopenia, hypokalemia, hypotension **MONITORING** Anti-Xa levels (3 hrs post-dose), platelets, Hgb, Hct, SCr **NOTES** Do not expel air bubble from syringe prior to injection No antidote Do not administer IM

Factor Xa Inhibitor Drug Interactions

- Avoid using with other anticoagulants (unless benefit outweighs risk). Monitor for additive effects with other drugs that can ↑ bleeding risk (antiplatelet drugs, some herbals, NSAIDs, SSRIs, SNRIs, thrombolytics, others). See the Drug Interactions chapter.
- Rivaroxaban is a substrate of 3A4 (major) and P-gp. Avoid concomitant use with drugs that are combined P-gp and strong 3A4 inducers (e.g., carbamazepine, phenytoin, rifampin, St. John's wort) or combined P-gp and strong 3A4 inhibitors (e.g., ketoconazole, itraconazole, lopinavir/ritonavir, ritonavir, indinavir, and conivaptan). The benefit must outweigh the potential risks in these situations: CrCl 15-80 mL/min who are receiving combined P-gp and moderate 3A4 inhibitors (e.g., diltiazem, verapamil, dronedarone, erythromycin).
- Apixaban is a substrate of 3A4 (major) and P-gp. Avoid concomitant use with strong dual inducers of 3A4 and P-gp (e.g., carbamazepine, phenytoin, rifampin, St. John's wort). For patients receiving doses > 2.5 mg BID, the dose of apixaban should be decreased by 50% when coadministered with drugs that are strong dual inhibitors of 3A4 and P-gp (e.g., clarithromycin, itraconazole, ketoconazole, or ritonavir). For patients taking 2.5 mg BID, avoid these strong dual inhibitors.
- Edoxaban is a substrate of P-gp; avoid concomitant use with rifampin. When treating DVT/PE, reduce dose to 30 mg daily with verapamil, macrolides (azithromycin, clarithromycin, erythromycin) and oral itraconazole or ketoconazole.

Conversion Between Anticoagulants

ORAL FACTOR XA INHIBITORS	
Oral Factor Xa inhibitors to warfarin	Stop Factor Xa inhibitor and start parenteral anticoagulant and warfarin at next scheduled dose of the Factor Xa inhibitor
Warfarin to apixaban	Stop warfarin and start apixaban when INR < 2
Warfarin to edoxaban	Stop warfarin and start edoxaban when INR ≤ 2.5
Warfarin to rivaroxaban	Stop warfarin and start rivaroxaban when INR < 3
ORAL DIRECT THROMBIN INHIBITOR	
Dabigatran to warfarin	CrCl > 50 mL/min: Start warfarin 3 days before stopping dabigatran CrCl 30-50 mL/min: Start warfarin 2 days before stopping dabigatran CrCl 15-30 mL/min: Start warfarin 1 day before stopping dabigatran CrCl < 15 mL/min: No recommendations can be made
Warfarin to dabigatran	Stop warfarin and start dabigatran when INR < 2

DIRECT THROMBIN INHIBITORS

These agents directly inhibit thrombin (Factor IIa); they bind to the active thrombin site of free and clot-associated thrombin.

DRUG	DOSING	SAFETY/SIDE EFFECTS/MONITORING
Oral Direct Thrombin Inhibitor		
Dabigatran *(Pradaxa)* Capsules **Missed Dose** Take immediately unless it is within 6 hours of next scheduled dose; the dose should not be doubled to make up for a missed dose.	**Nonvalvular AFib** 150 mg BID CrCl 15-30 mL/min: 75 mg BID CrCl < 15 mL/min: no recommendations **Treatment of DVT/PE and Reduction in the Risk of Recurrence of DVT and PE** 150 mg BID, start after 5-10 days of parenteral anticoagulation CrCl ≤ 30 mL/min: no recommendations **Prophylaxis of DVT/PE following hip replacement surgery** 110 mg on day 1, then 220 mg daily CrCl ≤ 30 mL/min: no recommendations Take with a full glass of water (with or without food). Swallow capsules whole. Do not break, chew, crush or open.	**BOXED WARNINGS** Patients receiving neuraxial anesthesia (epidural, spinal) or undergoing spinal puncture are at risk of hematomas and subsequent paralysis. Premature discontinuation ↑ risk of thrombotic events. **CONTRAINDICATIONS** Active pathological bleeding, treatment of patients with mechanical prosthetic heart valve(s) **SIDE EFFECTS** Dyspepsia, gastritis-like symptoms, bleeding (including more GI bleeding) **MONITORING** Hgb, Hct, SCr; no monitoring of efficacy required **NOTES** Antidote: idarucizumab *(Praxbind)* Keep in original container and discard 4 months after opening. Keep the bottle tightly closed to protect from moisture. Blister packs are good until the date on the pack. Do not administer by NG tube Can ↑ aPTT, PT/INR Discontinue if undergoing invasive surgery (1-2 days before if CrCl ≥ 50 mL/min, 3-5 days before if CrCl < 50 mL/min) Dabigatran prevents 5 more strokes per 1,000 patients/year than warfarin (therefore preferred by CHEST guidelines for stroke prevention in nonvalvular AFib). These guidelines came out before rivaroxaban and apixaban were approved MedGuide required

Direct Thrombin Inhibitors Continued

DRUG	DOSING	SAFETY/SIDE EFFECTS/MONITORING
Injectable (IV or SC) Direct Thrombin Inhibitors		
Argatroban Indicated for HIT and in patients undergoing PCI who are at risk for HIT **Bivalirudin *(Angiomax)*** Indicated for patients with ACS undergoing PCI and are at risk for HIT	**HIT** Argatroban: initial: 2 mcg/kg/min – titrate to target aPTT. Max: 10 mcg/kg/min **PCI** IV drugs given as a bolus followed by an infusion; all are weight-based Used in patients with a history of HIT Argatroban – ↓ dose in hepatic impairment Bivalirudin – ↓ dose when CrCl < 30 mL/min	**CONTRAINDICATIONS** Active major bleeding **SIDE EFFECTS** Bleeding, anemia, hematoma **MONITORING** aPTT and/or ACT (for bivalirudin), platelets, Hgb, Hct, renal function **NOTES** No cross-reaction with HIT antibodies. No antidote. Argatroban can ↑ INR; if starting on warfarin concurrently do not use a loading dose of warfarin; dose cautiously.
Desirudin *(Iprivask)* Indicated for VTE prevention after hip arthroplasty	15 mg SC Q12H CrCl < 60 mL/min: ↓ dose	**BOXED WARNING** Patients receiving neuraxial anesthesia (epidural, spinal) or undergoing spinal puncture are at risk of hematomas and subsequent paralysis. **MONITORING** aPTT, renal function, CBC **NOTES** No antidote

Dabigatran Drug Interactions

- Avoid using with other anticoagulants (unless benefit outweighs risk). Monitor for additive effects with other drugs that can ↑ bleeding risk (antiplatelet drugs, some herbals, NSAIDs, SSRIs, SNRIs, thrombolytics, others). See the Drug Interactions chapter.
- Dabigatran is a substrate of P-gp; avoid concomitant use with rifampin.
- Nonvalvular AFib: if CrCl 30-50 mL/min and patient is taking P-gp inhibitors (dronedarone or systemic ketoconazole), reduce dose to 75 mg BID. In severe renal impairment (CrCl 15-30 mL/min), avoid concomitant use of any P-gp inhibitors.
- Other indications: avoid any concomitant P-gp inhibitors in patients with CrCl < 50 mL/min.

WARFARIN

Warfarin competitively inhibits the C1 subunit of the multi-unit vitamin K epoxide reductase (VKORC1) enzyme complex, thereby reducing the regeneration of vitamin K epoxide and causing depletion of active clotting factors II, VII, IX and X and proteins C and S.

DRUG	DOSING	SAFETY/SIDE EFFECTS/MONITORING
Warfarin *(Coumadin, Jantoven)* Tablet Racemic mixture of R- and S-enantiomers with the S- enantiomer being 2.7-3.8 times more potent **Missed Dose** Take immediately on the same day. Do not double the dose the next day to make up for a missed dose.	Healthy outpatients: 10 mg daily for first 2 days, then adjust dose per INR values Lower doses (≤ 5 mg) for elderly, malnourished, taking drugs which can ↑ warfarin levels, liver disease, heart failure, or have a high risk of bleeding Take at the same time each day Highly protein bound (99%) See Study Tip for tablet colors	**BOXED WARNING** Major or fatal bleeding **CONTRAINDICATIONS** Pregnancy (except with mechanical heart valves at high risk for thromboembolism), hemorrhagic tendencies, blood dyscrasias, uncontrolled hypertension, noncompliance, recent or potential surgery of the eye or CNS, major regional lumbar block anesthesia or traumatic surgery resulting in large open surfaces, pericarditis or pericardial effusion, bacterial endocarditis, (pre-) eclampsia, threatened abortion **WARNINGS** Tissue necrosis/gangrene, systemic atheroemboli and cholesterol microemboli, HIT (contraindicated as monotherapy in the initial treatment of active HIT), presence of 2C9*2 or *3 alleles and/or polymorphism of VKORC1 gene may increase bleeding risk (routine genetic testing is not currently recommended; see Pharmacogenomics chapter) **SIDE EFFECTS** Bleeding, skin necrosis, purple toe syndrome **MONITORING** Goal INR is 2-3 (target 2.5) for most indications (DVT, AFib, bioprosthetic mitral valve, mechanical aortic valve, antiphospholipid syndrome) and should be 2.5-3.5 for some high-risk indications such as a mechanical mitral valve or 2 mechanical heart valves. Begin INR monitoring after the initial 2 or 3 doses, or if on a chronic, stable dose of warfarin, monitor at intervals up to 12 weeks. Hct, Hgb, signs of bleeding **NOTES** Antidote: vitamin K Dental cleanings and single tooth extraction do not generally require a change in warfarin dosing, if INR is in therapeutic range MedGuide required

Warfarin – Pharmacokinetic Drug Interactions

- Warfarin is a substrate of CYP 2C9 (major), 1A2 (minor), 2C19 (minor) and 3A4 (minor) and an inhibitor of 2C9 (weak) and 2C19 (weak). Avoid use with tamoxifen.
- 2C9 inducers can ↓ INR; these include aprepitant, bosentan, carbamazepine, phenobarbital, phenytoin, primidone, rifampin (large ↓ INR), licorice and St. John's Wort.
- 2C9 inhibitors can ↑ INR; these include amiodarone, azole antifungals (e.g., fluconazole, ketoconazole, voriconazole), capecitabine, etravirine, fluvastatin, fluvoxamine, macrolide antibiotics, metronidazole, tigecycline, TMP/SMX and zafirlukast. See Drug Interactions chapter.
  - When starting amiodarone, ↓ the dose of warfarin by 30-50%.

- Other antibiotics: penicillins, including amoxicillin, some cephalosporins, fluoroquinolones and tetracyclines can enhance the anticoagulant effect of warfarin – monitor INR.
- Check for 1A2, 2C19 and 3A4 interactions; these occur, but usually have less of an effect on INR.

Warfarin – Pharmacodynamic Drug Interactions

- The most common pharmacodynamic interactions are with NSAIDs, antiplatelet agents, other anticoagulants, SSRIs and SNRIs. These interactions ↑ bleeding risk, but the INR may not be increased.
- Drugs that ↑ clotting risk (e.g., estrogen and SERMs) should be discontinued if possible.

Herbal/Natural Product Drug Interactions

- Many natural products can ↑ bleeding risk, but not all of them ↑ INR. Examples include bromelain, danshen (can ↑ INR), dong quai (can ↑ INR), vitamin E, evening primrose oil, high doses of fish oils, garlic, ginger, ginkgo biloba, ginseng, glucosamine (can ↑ INR), goldenseal, grapefruit (can ↑ INR), policosanol, willow bark and wintergreen oil (can ↑ INR).
- Some products may ↓ the effectiveness of warfarin including alfalfa, American ginseng, green tea and coenzyme Q10. Per the package insert, American ginseng may decrease the effects of warfarin. There is evidence that both American and Panax ginseng inhibit platelet aggregation, which potentially has the opposite effect. Monitor INR closely if patients are taking ginseng.
- Any additions of vitamin K will ↓ the INR. Check any nutritional products for vitamin K content. Stay consistent with the amount of vitamin K consumed through the diet (see foods high in vitamin K box).

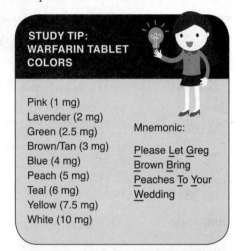

STUDY TIP: WARFARIN TABLET COLORS

Pink (1 mg)
Lavender (2 mg)
Green (2.5 mg)
Brown/Tan (3 mg)
Blue (4 mg)
Peach (5 mg)
Teal (6 mg)
Yellow (7.5 mg)
White (10 mg)

Mnemonic:

Please Let Greg Brown Bring Peaches To Your Wedding

FOODS HIGH IN VITAMIN K

Broccoli	Lettuce (red leaf or butterhead)
Brussel sprouts	Mustard greens
Cabbage	Parsley
Canola oil	Soybean oil
Cauliflower	Spinach
Chickpeas	Swiss chard
Cole slaw	Tea (green or black)
Collard greens	Turnip greens
Coriander	Watercress
Endive	
Green kale	

Warfarin Use – Key Points from CHEST 2012 Guidelines

- In healthy outpatients, the initial starting dose of warfarin should be 10 mg daily for the first 2 days, then adjust per INR values.
- Start warfarin on the same day as the parenteral anticoagulant (e.g., enoxaparin or UFH) and continue both anticoagulants for a minimum of 5 days and until the INR is ≥ 2 for at least 24 hours. Once the INR is therapeutic for 24 hours, the parenteral anticoagulant can be discontinued.
- Routine pharmacogenomic testing is not recommended at this time.
- Routine use of vitamin K supplementation is not recommended in patients taking warfarin.
- For patients with stable therapeutic INRs presenting with a single subtherapeutic INR value, routinely bridging with UFH or LMWH is not recommended.
- For patients with consistently stable INRs on warfarin therapy, INR testing can be done up to every 12 weeks rather than every 4 weeks.

- For patients with previously stable therapeutic INRs who present with a single out-of-range INR of ≤ 0.5 below or above the therapeutic range, continue current dose and obtain another INR within 1 – 2 weeks.
- Warfarin is highly protein bound, therefore caution is advised with other highly protein bound drugs that may displace warfarin such as phenytoin, valproic acid and others.

ANTICOAGULANT ANTIDOTES AND REVERSAL

Bleeding is the major adverse effect of anticoagulants. Bleeding can be serious and fatal. Anticoagulation commonly needs to be reversed if a patient experiences life-threatening bleeding or requires surgery.

Protamine combines with strongly acidic heparin to form a stable salt complex neutralizing the anticoagulant activity of both drugs. Phytonadione (vitamin K) provides an essential vitamin for liver synthesis of clotting factors (II, VII, IX, X). *Kcentra* is a newer product indicated for the urgent reversal of warfarin and *Praxbind* is a recently approved antidote for dabigatran. The oral factor Xa inhibitors have no approved antidote at this time. Prothrombin complex concentrates (PCCs) are sometimes used (off label) in an attempt to reverse factor Xa inhibitors. If PCCs are used in this manner, monitoring clotting tests (PT, PTT, INR, anti-Xa) to assess reversal is not useful and is not recommended.

ANTIDOTE	DOSING	SAFETY/SIDE EFFECTS/MONITORING
For UFH/LMWH reversal		
Protamine Injection 10 mg/mL (5 mL, 25 mL)	1 mg protamine will reverse ~100 units of heparin – reverse the amount of heparin given in the last 2-2.5 hours; max dose: 50 mg Enoxaparin given within last 8 hours: 1 mg protamine per 1 mg of enoxaparin Enoxaparin given > 8 hours ago: 0.5 mg protamine per 1 mg of enoxaparin Dalteparin: 1 mg protamine for each 100 anti-Xa units of dalteparin	**BOXED WARNING** Hypotension, cardiovascular collapse, non-cardiogenic pulmonary edema, pulmonary vasoconstriction, and pulmonary hypertension may occur. **SIDE EFFECTS** Hypotension, bradycardia, flushing, anaphylaxis **MONITORING** aPTT, anti-Xa levels, cardiac monitoring required (ECG, BP, HR) **NOTES** Rapid IV infusion causes hypotension. Administer slow IV push (50 mg over 10 minutes). Inject without further dilution over 1-3 minutes.
For dabigatran reversal - binds only to dabigatran molecules without interfering with the coagulation cascade		
IdaruCIZUmab *(Praxbind)* Injection 2.5 g/50 mL single-use vial	5 grams IV (given as 2 separate 2.5 gram doses no more than 15 minutes apart) Do not confuse with IDArubicin	**WARNINGS** Thromboembolic risk, risk of serious adverse events with hereditary fructose intolerance due to sorbitol excipient **SIDE EFFECTS** HA, ↓ K, delirium, constipation, fever

Anticoagulant Antidotes and Reversal Continued

ANTIDOTE	DOSING	SAFETY/SIDE EFFECTS/MONITORING
For warfarin reversal		
Vitamin K or phytonadione *(Mephyton)* 5 mg tablets 1 mg/0.5 mL, 10 mg/mL injection	1-10 mg PO/IV If given IV, infuse slowly; rate of infusion should not exceed 1 mg/min To ↓ risk of anaphylaxis, dilute dose in a minimum of 50 mL of compatible solution and administer using an infusion pump over at least 20 minutes	**BOXED WARNINGS** Severe reactions resembling hypersensitivity reactions (e.g., anaphylaxis) have occurred rarely during or immediately after IV administration (even with proper dilution and rate of administration); some patients had no previous exposure to phytonadione **SIDE EFFECTS** Anaphylaxis, flushing, rash, dizziness **NOTES** Requires light protection during administration SC route not recommended due to variable absorption; IM route not recommended due to risk of hematoma Orlistat and mineral oil ↓ absorption of oral vitamin K See specific recommendations in Warfarin Reversal section
Four Factor Prothrombin Complex Concentrate (Human) *(Kcentra)* Injection Factors II, VII, IX, X, Protein C, Protein S	IV dose is based on patient's INR and body weight Do not let drug back-up into line; will clot. Refrigerate; allow to reach room temp prior to administration. Do not repeat dose	**BOXED WARNING** Arterial and venous thromboembolic complications have been reported **CONTRAINDICATIONS** Disseminated intravascular coagulation (DIC) and known HIT (contains heparin) **WARNINGS** Made from human blood and may carry risk of transmitting infectious agents **SIDE EFFECTS** HA, N/V/D, arthralgia, hypotension, ↓ K, thrombotic events **NOTES** Administer vitamin K concurrently
Three Factor Prothrombin Complex Concentrates (Human) *(Bebulin, Profilnine)* Off label	Weight-based dosing given IV slowly Given with fresh frozen plasma (FFP) or factor VIIa	**BOXED WARNINGS** HIT *(Bebulin)* **WARNINGS** *Bebulin* and *Profilnine* contain Factors II, IX and X but low or nontherapeutic levels of factor VII and should not be confused with Prothrombin Complex Concentrate (Human) [(Factors II, VII, IX, X), Protein C, Protein S] *(Kcentra)* which contains therapeutic levels of factor VII. Made from human blood and may carry risk of transmitting infectious agents (e.g., viruses) **SIDE EFFECTS** Chills, fever, flushing, nausea, headache, risk of thrombosis **NOTES** Slow infusion and give antihistamine to minimize side effects Administer vitamin K concurrently

Anticoagulant Antidotes and Reversal Continued

ANTIDOTE	DOSING	SAFETY/SIDE EFFECTS/MONITORING
Factor VIIa Recombinant *(NovoSeven RT)* Off label	10-20 mcg/kg IV bolus over 5 minutes	**BOXED WARNING** Serious thrombotic events are associated with the use of factor VIIa outside labeled indications.

Warfarin Reversal

Variable INRs are common in clinical practice. Elevated INRs are concerning due to increased risk of bleeding. Vitamin K is used to reverse warfarin (to ↓ INR quickly); it can be used by itself or with other agents for life-threatening bleeding. Bleeding, at any INR, will warrant more serious intervention.

Oral formulations of vitamin K (generally at doses of 2.5 – 5 mg) are preferred for reversal in patients without significant or major bleeding. Vitamin K given subcutaneous (SC) has a slow onset and a variable response; therefore, SC injections should be avoided. The intramuscular (IM) route should also be avoided due to the risk of hematoma formation. Intravenous vitamin K should be used only when the patient is experiencing serious bleeding. IV injection is reported to cause anaphylaxis in 3 of out 100,000 patients: infuse slowly.

Use of Vitamin K for Overanticoagulation

SYMPTOMS/INR VALUE	WHAT TO DO
INR above therapeutic range but < 4.5 without bleeding	Reduce or skip warfarin dose. Monitor INR. Resume warfarin when INR therapeutic. Dose reduction may not be needed if only slightly above therapeutic range.
For patients with a supratherapeutic INR of 4.5-10 without bleeding	Routine use of vitamin K is not recommended if no evidence of bleeding. Hold 1-2 doses of warfarin. Monitor INR. Resume warfarin at lower dose when INR therapeutic. Vitamin K can be used if urgent surgery needed (≤ 5 mg, with additional 1-2 mg in 24 hours if needed) or bleeding risk is high (1-2.5 mg).
For patients with INR > 10 without bleeding	Hold warfarin. Give oral vitamin K 2.5-5 mg even if not bleeding. Monitor INR. Resume warfarin at a lower dose when INR is therapeutic.
For patients with major bleeding from warfarin	Hold warfarin therapy. Give vitamin K 5-10 mg by slow IV injection and four-factor prothrombin complex concentrate (PCC). PCC suggested over fresh frozen plasma (FFP) due to risks of allergic reactions, infection transmission, longer preparation time, slower onset and higher volume.

PERIOPERATIVE MANAGEMENT OF PATIENTS ON WARFARIN

- Stop warfarin therapy approximately 5 days before major surgery. In patients with a mechanical heart valve, AFib, or VTE at high risk for thromboembolism, bridging therapy with LMWH or UFH is recommended (bridging means stopping the warfarin and using anticoagulant doses of the LMWH or UFH for a short period to prevent clotting). Discontinue therapeutic-dose SC LMWH 24 hours before surgery (stop the UFH IV therapy 4 – 6 hours before surgery). Patients at low risk for thromboembolism do not require bridging; stop the warfarin and restart after surgery when hemostasis is achieved (see below).
- If INR is still elevated 1 – 2 days before surgery, give low-dose vitamin K (1 – 2 mg).
- If reversal of warfarin is needed in a patient requiring an urgent surgical procedure, give low-dose (2.5 – 5 mg) IV or oral vitamin K.
- Resume warfarin therapy 12 – 24 hours after the surgery, when there is adequate hemostasis.

VTE TREATMENT AND PROPHYLAXIS

VTE Prophylaxis

Risk factors for the development of VTE are shown in the box. The CHEST guidelines provide specific recommendations for the prevention of VTE depending on the patient's level of risk. UFH, LMWHs, fondaparinux, rivaroxaban, apixaban and dabigatran are all approved for VTE prophylaxis (refer to recommended doses in the drug tables). If patients have a contraindication to anticoagulants (such as an active bleed) or have a high risk for bleeding, they will need non-drug alternatives to prevent VTE. These options include intermittent pneumatic compression (IPC) devices or graduated compression stockings (GCS).

RISK FACTORS FOR THE DEVELOPMENT OF VENOUS THROMBOEMBOLISM	
Surgery	Inherited or acquired thrombophilia (e.g., antithrombin deficiency, Factor V Leiden, antiphospholipid syndrome)
Major trauma or lower extremity injury	Increasing age
Immobility	Venous compression (tumor, hematoma, arterial abnormality)
Cancer or chemotherapy	Inflammatory bowel disease
Previous venous thromboembolism	Nephrotic syndrome
Pregnancy and postpartum period	Myeloproliferative disorders
Estrogen-containing medications or selective estrogen receptor modulators	Paroxysmal nocturnal hemoglobinuria
Erythropoiesis-stimulating agents	Central venous catheterization
Acute medical illness	
Obesity	

For long distance travelers at risk for VTE (previous VTE, recent surgery or trauma, active malignancy, pregnancy, estrogen use, advanced age, limited mobility, severe obesity, or known thrombophilic disorder), the following recommendations will ↓ VTE risk: frequent ambulation, calf muscle exercise, sitting in an aisle seat and using graduated compression stockings with 15 – 30 mmHg of pressure at the ankle during travel. Aspirin or anticoagulants should not be used.

VTE Treatment

Any VTE that is caused by surgery or a reversible risk factor should be treated for 3 months. If the VTE is unprovoked (unknown cause), extending therapy longer than 3 months is recommended, as long as the patient's bleeding risk is low-to-moderate. If the risk of bleeding is high, limit the treatment to 3 months. When patients have 2 episodes of unprovoked VTE, long-term treatment may be warranted. Estrogen-containing medications and selective estrogen receptor modulators (SERMs) are contraindicated in patients with history of, or current, VTE and should be discontinued.

VTE guidelines were updated in 2016. Important changes include the following:

- For patients without cancer, dabigatran and the oral factor Xa inhibitors (rivaroxaban, apixaban and edoxaban) are preferred over warfarin for the first 3 months of treatment for a DVT in the leg or a PE.
- For patients with cancer, LMWH is preferred over all oral anticoagulants (including warfarin).
- In patients with an unprovoked DVT or PE who are stopping anticoagulation, aspirin is recommended to prevent recurrence (if there are no contraindications).

ATRIAL FIBRILLATION

Anticoagulation for Patients with Nonvalvular Atrial Fibrillation/Atrial Flutter

Patients with atrial fibrillation or atrial flutter (AFib/AFlutter) can experience pooling of blood in the heart. When the blood doesn't move effectively, clots can form. If a clot is ejected during the heart's contraction, the clot can travel to the brain causing a stroke (cardioembolic stroke) or TIA. Stroke prevention is an important goal in patients with AFib/AFlutter (see Arrhythmias chapter). AFib and AFlutter are common in patients with heart valve problems, which may or may not require valve replacement surgery (replacing the damaged valve with a mechanical or animal valve). Patients with mechanical heart valves have the highest risk for clotting/strokes and are treated with warfarin only. Importantly, none of the factor Xa inhibitors or DTIs are approved for this patient population.

The majority of patients with AFib/AFlutter do not have heart valve involvement (called nonvalvular AFib) and may require anticoagulation depending on their risk of having a cardioembolic stroke. The 2012 CHEST guideline uses the $CHADS_2$ scoring system to estimate risk of stroke in AFib/AFlutter and to guide anticoagulation therapy. They do not address the newer oral factor Xa inhibitors. After the 2012 CHEST guideline was released, a newer guideline by the ACC/AHA/HRS was released that does include the newer drugs and uses a different scoring system. This means there are currently two current guidelines for the same condition. First, focus on the simpler CHEST guideline recommendations (1st set of boxes), and then focus on the differences in the newer guideline (the 2nd set of boxes).

ANTICOAGULATION FOR PATIENTS WITH AFIB WHO WILL UNDERGO CARDIOVERSION

- AFib > 48 hours or unknown duration: anticoagulation (if warfarin, target INR 2–3) for at least 3 weeks prior to and 4 weeks after cardioversion (regardless of method – electrical or pharmacologic) when normal sinus rhythm is restored.
- AFib ≤ 48 hours duration undergoing elective cardioversion: start full therapeutic anticoagulation at presentation, do cardioversion, and continue full anticoagulation for at least 4 weeks while patient is in normal sinus rhythm.
- For patients staying in AFib, chronic anticoagulation therapy may be needed for stroke prevention. Treatment depends on the number of risk factors present. See text.

$CHADS_2$ Scoring System (CHEST Guidelines)

First, count the number of risk factors the patient has (see box on the left). Second, use the box on the right to select the recommended therapy. The higher the value, the higher the risk and the more intensive anticoagulation that is required to reduce the chance that the patient will have a stroke.

$CHADS_2$ SCORING SYSTEM

Add up the total number of risk factors for a given patient.

C – CHF	1
H – HTN	1
A – Age ≥ 75 years	1
D – Diabetes	1
S_2 – Prior Stroke/TIA*	2

**Does not include thromboembolism (TE) per CHEST guideline*

RISK CATEGORY	RECOMMENDED THERAPY
$CHADS_2$ score = 0	No therapy. For patients wanting anticoagulant therapy, ASA 75-325 mg daily should be used over oral anticoagulation or combination therapy with ASA and clopidogrel.
$CHADS_2$ score = 1	Oral anticoagulation* rather than ASA 75 mg-325 mg daily or combination therapy with ASA and clopidogrel. For patients unable to take oral anticoagulants, ASA and clopidogrel should be used.
$CHADS_2$ score ≥ 2	Oral anticoagulation*. For patients unable to take oral anticoagulants, ASA and clopidogrel should be used.

** Oral anticoagulation favors dabigatran 150 mg BID rather than adjusted dose warfarin therapy (target INR 2-3).*

CHA_2DS_2-VASc Scoring System (ACC/AHA/HRS Guideline)
Notice that more risk factors are included in this scoring system (vascular disease, age and sex category). The newer agents rivaroxaban and apixaban are included as treatment options if the score is ≥ 2. Anticoagulation for patients with AFib who are undergoing cardioversion is the same in both guidelines.

CHA_2DS_2-VASc SCORING SYSTEM	
Add up the total number of risk factors for a given patient.	
C – CHF	1
H – HTN	1
A – Age ≥ 75 years	2
D – Diabetes	1
S_2 – Prior Stroke/TIA	2
V – Vascular Disease (prior MI, PAD, aortic plaque)	1
A – Age 65-74 years	1
S – Sex category, female	1

RISK CATEGORY	RECOMMENDED THERAPY
CHA_2DS_2-VASc Score = 0	No anticoagulation recommended.
CHA_2DS_2-VASc Score = 1	No anticoagulation or oral anticoagulation or ASA may be considered.
CHA_2DS_2-VASc Score ≥ 2	Oral anticoagulation is recommended. Options include warfarin, dabigatran, rivaroxaban and apixaban.

For patients who are unable to maintain a therapeutic INR on warfarin, a direct thrombin inhibitor or factor Xa inhibitor is recommended.

Patient Counseling: For All Anticoagulants

- This medication can interact with many other drugs. Check with your healthcare provider before taking any other medication, including over the counter medications, vitamins, or herbal products.
- This medication can cause you to bruise and/or bleed more easily. Report any unusual bleeding, bruising, or rashes to your healthcare provider.
- Tell physicians and dentists that you are using this medication before any surgery is performed.
- Call your healthcare provider right away if you fall or injure yourself, especially if you hit your head
- Alcoholic drinks should be avoided.
- Do not start, stop, or change any medicine without talking with your healthcare provider.
- This medication is very important for your health, but it can cause serious and life-threatening bleeding problems.
- Call your healthcare provider right away if you develop any of these symptoms:
    - Unexpected pain, swelling, or discomfort
    - Headaches, dizziness, or weakness
    - Unusual bruising that develops without known cause
    - Frequent nose bleeds
    - Unusual bleeding gums
    - Bleeding from cuts that take longer than normal to stop
    - Menstrual bleeding or vaginal bleeding that is much heavier than normal
    - Pink or brown urine
    - Red or black stools that look like tar
    - Coughing up blood or blood clots
    - Vomiting blood or material that looks like coffee grounds

Enoxaparin

- Wash and dry hands.
- Sit or lie in a comfortable position so you can see your abdomen. Choose an area on the right or left side of your abdomen, at least 2 inches from the belly button.
- Clean the injection site with an alcohol swab and allow the site to dry.
- Remove the needle cap by pulling it straight off the syringe and discard it in a sharps collector. Do not twist the cap off as this can bend the needle.
- Hold the syringe like a pencil in your writing hand.
- Do not expel the air bubble in the syringe prior to injection unless your healthcare provider has advised you to do so.
- With your other hand, pinch an inch of the cleansed area to make a fold in the skin. Insert the full length of the needle straight down – at a 90 degree angle – into fold of skin.
- Press the plunger with your thumb until the syringe is empty.
- Pull the needle straight out at the same angle that it was inserted, and release the skin fold.
- Point the needle down and away from yourself and others, and push down on the plunger to activate the safety shield.
- Do not rub the site of injection as this can lead to bruising. Place the used syringe in the sharps collector.

Dabigatran

- Do not stop taking dabigatran without talking to your prescriber. Stopping dabigatran increases your risk of having a stroke.
- Take with a full glass of water and swallow the capsules whole. Do not break, chew, or empty the pellets from the capsule. It is fine to take with or without food.
- Common side effects of dabigatran include indigestion, upset stomach or stomach burning and/or pain.
- Only open 1 bottle of dabigatran at a time. Finish your opened bottle of dabigatran before opening a new bottle. After opening a bottle of dabigatran, use within 4 months.
- Keep dabigatran in the original bottle or blister package to keep it dry and protect the capsules from moisture. Do not put dabigatran in pill boxes or pill organizers.
- Tightly close your bottle of dabigatran right after you take your dose.
- If you miss a dose of dabigatran, take it as soon as you remember. If your next dose is less than 6 hours away, skip the missed dose. Do not take two doses of dabigatran at the same time.
- Dabigatran is not for patients with artificial heart valves.

Rivaroxaban

- Rivaroxaban is not for patients with artificial heart valves.
- If you take rivaroxaban for atrial fibrillation: Take rivaroxaban once daily with your evening meal.
  - If you miss a dose of rivaroxaban, take it as soon as you remember on the same day. Take your next dose at your regularly scheduled time.

- If you take rivaroxaban for blood clots in the veins of your legs or lungs: take rivaroxaban once or twice daily as prescribed with food at the same time each day.
  - If you miss a dose of rivaroxaban and take rivaroxaban twice daily: take rivaroxaban as soon as you remember on the same day. You may take 2 doses at the same time to make up for the missed dose. Take your next dose at your regularly scheduled time.
  - If you miss a dose of rivaroxaban and take rivaroxaban once daily: take rivaroxaban as soon as you remember on the same day. Take your next dose at your regularly scheduled time.
- If you take rivaroxaban for hip or knee replacement surgery: take rivaroxaban once daily with or without food.
  - If you miss a dose of rivaroxaban, take it as soon as you remember on the same day. Take your next dose at your regularly scheduled time.

Warfarin

- Take warfarin at the same time every day as prescribed by your doctor. You can take warfarin either with food or on an empty stomach.
- Warfarin lowers the chance of blood clots forming in your body.
- If you miss a dose, take the dose as soon as possible on the same day. Do not take a double dose the next day to make up for a missed dose.
- You will need to have your blood tested frequently to monitor your response to this medication. This test is called an INR. Your dose may be adjusted to keep you INR in a target range.
- Do not make changes in your diet, such as eating large amounts of green, leafy vegetables. Be consistent with the amount of leafy green vegetables and other foods rich in vitamin K.
- Avoid drinking alcohol.
- Other side effects besides bleeding include purple toe syndrome that can cause your toes to become painful and purple in color. Also, death of skin tissue can occur. Report any unusual changes or pain immediately to your healthcare provider.

PRACTICE CASE

AM is a 57 y/o female who has been admitted to the hospital with shortness of breath, difficulty breathing, chest pain, coughing and sweating. She states she saw blood in a tissue that she coughed into while coming to the hospital. Her past medical history includes hypertension, neuropathic pain in her feet and atrial fibrillation. She is recovering from a bad fall two days ago but reports "no broken bones, just bruises." She states that she is having difficulty taking care of her grandson who she watches during the day because she is "too tired."

Medications:
Aspirin 325 mg one EC tablet daily
Cordarone 200 mg one daily
Lyrica 75 mg one capsule BID
Chlorthalidone 25 mg one daily
Effexor XR 150 mg one daily

Labs: Ca (mg/dL) = 8.3 (8.5 - 10.5)
Cl (mEq/L) = 98 (95 - 103)
Mg (mEq/L) = 1.3 (1.3 - 2.1)
K (mEq/L) = 4.2 (3.5-5)
PO_4 (mg/dL) = 3.9 (2.3 - 4.7)
Na (mEq/L) = 142 (135 - 145)
HCO_3 (mEq/L) = 22 (24 - 30)
BUN (mg/dL) = 41 (7 - 20)
SCr (mg/dL) = 1.5 (0.6 - 1.3)

AST (U/L) = 27 (0-33)
ALT (U/L) = 23 (0-45)

INR = 1.1 (0.00-1.2)
PTT (seconds) = 27.4 (24.8-35.6)

BP: 152/96 Temp: 98.4°F, Wt 176 lbs. Ht 5'4". Computerized tomography and ultrasound are ordered. Acute PE and DVT are confirmed. The patient will be started on a heparin drip.

Adult Heparin Drip Protocol

PTT	Rebolus or Hold	Rate Adjustment	Recheck PTT
≤ 60	Bolus: 80units/kg	↑ 4 units/kg/hr	6hrs
61-78	Bolus: 40units/kg	↑ 2 units/kg/hr	6hrs
GOAL 79-118	**NONE**	**NONE**	**In AM**
119-135	NONE	↓ 2 units/kg/hr	6hrs
≥136	HOLD 60 minutes	↓ 3 units/kg/hr	6hrs

Questions

1. The medical team asks the clinical pharmacist to dose the heparin for AM. Using the protocol provided, what should the correct bolus and infusion rate of heparin be for AM?

   a. 10,000 units bolus, followed by 2,300 units/hr infusion
   b. 14,000 units bolus, followed by 3,500 units/hr infusion
   c. 7,000 units bolus, followed by 1,400 units/hr infusion
   d. 6,400 units bolus, followed by 1,440 units/hr infusion
   e. None of the above

2. The bolus and infusion are given. After 6 hours, the aPTT comes back at 66 sec. Per the protocol, what is the correct dose adjustment for heparin?

   a. Give a 6,400 unit bolus now and increase the infusion rate to 1,900 units/hr
   b. Give a 3,200 unit bolus now and increase the infusion rate to 1,600 units/hr
   c. Make no change to the dose
   d. Do not give a bolus and reduce the infusion rate to 1,500 units/hr
   e. None of the above

3. The pulmonary embolism was confirmed. It is AM's third day in the hospital, and the medical team would like to discharge her. She starts bridge therapy and receives 5 mg of warfarin at bedside. Which of the statements is true regarding warfarin? (Select **ALL** that apply.)

   a. Warfarin is a direct thrombin inhibitor that helps to prevent clot formation.
   b. Warfarin has a high risk of bleeding. Careful monitoring is advised.
   c. Warfarin should be taken with a low fat meal and never double up on the dose.
   d. Warfarin is a racemic mixture and the R-isomer is more potent than the S-isomer.
   e. Warfarin should overlap the heparin therapy until she is at a therapeutic INR for 24 at least hours.

4. In addition to warfarin, what other medication will AM need for bridge therapy until her INR is therapeutic? Select the appropriate agent, route of administration, and dose for AM's treatment of PE.

   a. *Lovenox* 30 mg SC daily
   b. *Lovenox* 30 mg SC Q12H
   c. *Lovenox* 80 mg SC Q12H
   d. *Lovenox* 80 mg SC daily
   e. *Lovenox* 180 mg SC daily

5. AM will need to be counseled on subcutaneous administration of enoxaparin. List the steps in order that the patient should take to administer the drug.

   a. Place injection in the abdomen at least 2″ from the navel.
   b. Insert full length of the needle at a 90 degree angle.
   c. Place the used syringe in a sharps container.
   d. Wash hands thoroughly.
   e. The patient should clean the injection site with alcohol.

6. AM should be careful not to take other products that can increase the bleeding risk while on warfarin. Which of the following would *not* increase her risk of bleeding? (Select **ALL** that apply.)

   a. Calcium with Vitamin D
   b. Large amounts of garlic
   c. Dong quai
   d. Fidaxomicin
   e. Ginkgo biloba

Questions 7-10 do not relate to the case.

7. Which of the following medications can significantly interact with warfarin? (Select **ALL** that apply.)

   a. Amiodarone
   b. Morphine
   c. Rifampin
   d. Levetiracetam
   e. Fluconazole

8. A patient comes to the hospital with a DVT. He has developed HIT with thrombosis in the past. Which of the following agents is considered first-line treatment in this patient?

    a. *Arixtra*
    b. Argatroban
    c. *Xarelto*
    d. *Fragmin*
    e. Desirudin

9. Which of the following is a possible side effect of heparin? (Select **ALL** that apply.)

    a. Xerostomia
    b. Thrombocytopenia
    c. Osteoporosis
    d. Hyperkalemia
    e. Bleeding

10. Which of the following parameters need to be monitored during heparin therapy?

    a. Hematocrit, hemoglobin, platelets, AST, and ALT
    b. Hematocrit, hemoglobin, platelets, and aPTT
    c. Hematocrit, hemogloblin, platelets, and PT
    d. CBC and Chem 7 panel
    e. Chem 7 panel and aPTT

Answers

1-d, 2-b, 3-b,e, 4-c, 5-d,e,a,b,c, 6-a,d, 7-a,c,e, 8-b, 9-b,c,d,e, 10-b

55

ONCOLOGY I: OVERVIEW & SIDE EFFECT MANAGEMENT

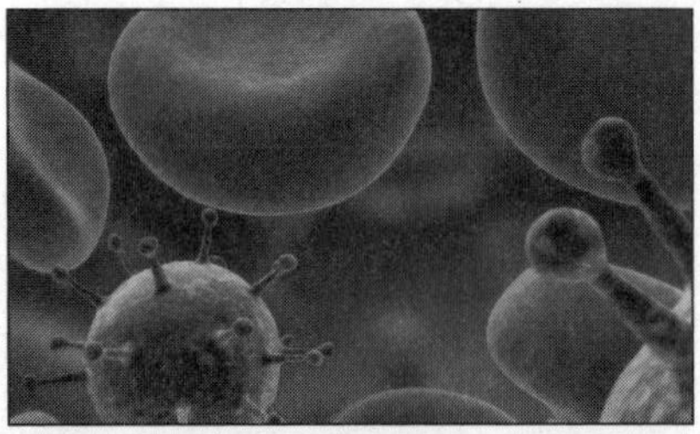

We gratefully acknowledge the assistance of Doreen Pon, PharmD, BCOP, BCPS, Assistant Professor at Western University of Health Sciences and Muoi Gi, PharmD, BCPS, BCOP, Oncology Pharmacy Residency Director, VA San Diego Healthcare System and D. Raymond Weber, PharmD, BSPharm, BCOP, BCPS, RPh, Associate Professor, Notre Dame of Maryland University School of Pharmacy, in preparing this chapter.

GUIDELINES/REFERENCES

American Cancer Society. Cancer Screening Guidelines http://www.cancer.org/healthy/findcancerearly/cancerscreeningguidelines/american-cancer-society-guidelines-for-the-early-detection-of-cancer (accessed 2016 November 14)

National Comprehensive Cancer Network (NCCN). www.nccn.org (accessed 2016 October 5)

American Society of Clinical Oncology (ASCO). www.asco.org (accessed 2016 October 15)

BACKGROUND

Cancer is a group of diseases characterized by uncontrolled growth and spread of abnormal cells and is also referred to as malignancy. The process by which abnormal cells spread to other parts of the body is called metastasis, and this process can result in death. Cancer is caused by both external factors (such as chemicals, radiation, bacteria and viruses) and internal factors (heredity, hormones, immune disorders, and genetic mutations). Sunlight exposure, tobacco use, excessive alcohol intake, obesity, older age, poor diet and low physical activity level increases the risk for certain cancers.

CLASSIFICATION

There are more than 100 types of cancer. Types of cancer are usually named for the organs or tissues where the cancer forms. Malignancies are classified based on the tissue type as epithelial, connective, lymphoid or nerve. Most malignant cells retain enough traits to identify their basic tissue type, and therefore a sample of tissue (biopsy) should be taken for diagnosis along with X-rays, CT scans, MRIs and other diagnostic tools to evaluate the stage of cancer. Lab work is required for blood chemistries, urine analysis and tumor markers.

WARNING SIGNS

The American Cancer Society lists seven warning signs of cancer in an adult. Any of these warning signs should warrant referral to a physician. Remember **CAUTION:**

Change in bowel or bladder habits

A sore that does not heal

Unusual bleeding or discharge

Thickening or lump in breast or elsewhere

Indigestion or difficulty swallowing

Obvious change in wart or mole

Nagging cough or hoarseness

CANCER SCREENING RECOMMENDATIONS

Cancer Screening Guidelines for Average Risk Patients (American Cancer Society)

CANCER	SEX	AGE	SCREENING
Breast	F	40-44 years	Talk with healthcare provider; women may choose to start annual screening with mammograms
		45-54 years	Begin yearly mammograms
		≥ 55 years	Mammograms every 2 years or continue yearly
Cervical	F	21-29 years	Pap smear every 3 years
		30-65 years	Pap smear + HPV test every 5 years
			or
			Pap smear every 3 years
Colon	M/F	≥ 50 years	Preferred tests (find polyps and cancer) - choose one of the following:
			Colonoscopy every 10 years
			Flexible sigmoidoscopy every 5 years
			Double-contrast barium enema every 5 years
			CT colonography every 5 years
			Alternative tests (find only cancer) - choose one of the following:
			Stool DNA test every 3 years
			Fecal occult blood test every year
			Fecal immunochemical test every year
Lung	M/F	55-74 years	Low dose CT scan of the chest every year can be considered if (all of the following):
			In good health
			Have at least a 30 pack-year smoking history
			Still smoking or quit smoking within the past 15 years

HPV: Human papillomavirus

Skin Cancer

Skin cancer is the most common cancer in the United States. Risk factors for skin cancer include history of ultraviolet (UV) light exposure [natural (sun) and/or artificial (tanning beds)], light skin tone or skin that burns easily, light hair color, such as blonde or red, immune suppressing drugs or diseases, and a history of skin cancer.

There are three types of skin cancer: basal cell, squamous cell, and melanoma. Basal cell and squamous cell skin cancers (non-melanoma skin cancer) are common and very survivable if detected and treated early. Melanoma, although much less common than non-melanoma skin cancer, commonly metastasizes and accounts for approximately 75% of all deaths related to skin cancer. Recommendations for reducing the risk of developing skin cancer include:

- Seek shade – especially between the hours of 10 AM and 4 PM when the UV radiation is strongest.
- Slip on a shirt – tightly woven fabrics will protect better than loosely woven fabrics.
- Slop on sunscreen – use a broad spectrum sunscreen with an SPF of at least 15 – 30 and reapply every 2 hours.
- Slap on a hat – wear a hat with at least a 2″ – 3″ brim all around.
- Wrap on sunglasses – to protect the skin around the eyes and help prevent cataracts.

The "ABCDE" mnemonic can be used to educate patients about suspicious skin spots that could be melanoma. Patients should be examined by a physician if they note a suspicious skin spot, a spot that is changing over time, or a spot that looks different from all the other spots on their skin.

ABCDE – Warning Signs of Melanoma Skin Cancer

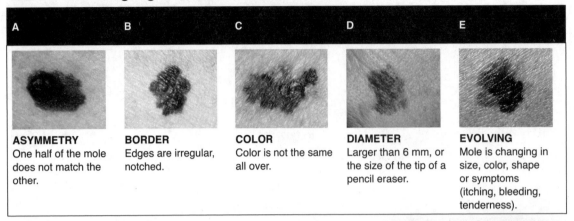

A	B	C	D	E
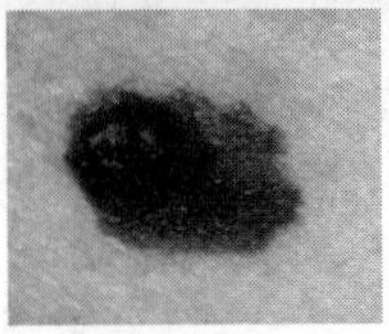	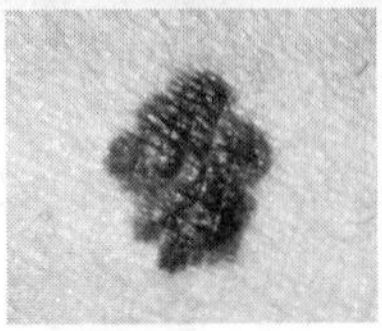	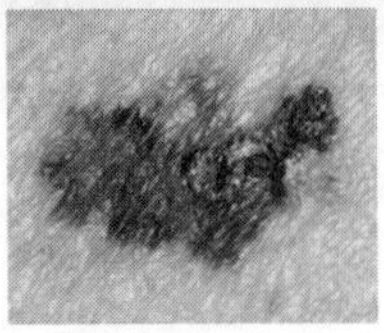	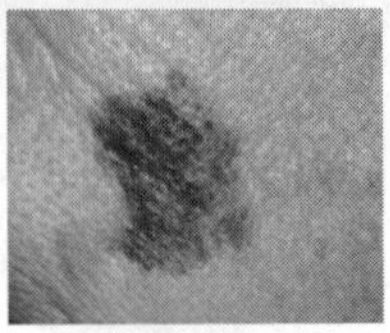	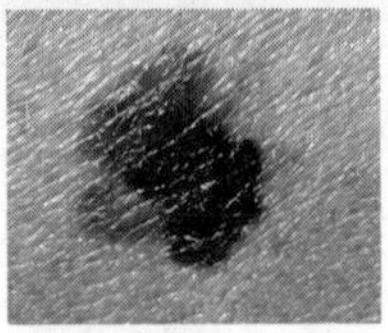
ASYMMETRY One half of the mole does not match the other.	**BORDER** Edges are irregular, notched.	**COLOR** Color is not the same all over.	**DIAMETER** Larger than 6 mm, or the size of the tip of a pencil eraser.	**EVOLVING** Mole is changing in size, color, shape or symptoms (itching, bleeding, tenderness).

TREATMENT OVERVIEW

Cancer can be treated with surgery, radiation, chemotherapy, hormone therapy, biological therapy, targeted therapy, immunotherapy and/or vaccines. Treatment decisions are based on the cancer type and stage and patient characteristics such as tumor markers. For most cancers (including breast, lung, prostate and colon cancer), the stage is classified by the size of the tumor and whether it has spread. As a cancer grows, it can invade nearby tissues and enter the lymphatic system. Cancer cells can travel through the blood or lymphatic system to distant organs, such as the lungs, liver and brain. This process of metastasis usually represents the most advanced stage of cancer, or stage IV. Stage IV cancers are rarely curable. Goals of treatment depend on prognosis. The plan may attempt to achieve remission (with curative intent) or be palliative (to reduce tumor size and symptoms). If a patient remains cancer-free for 5 years, it is unlikely that their cancer will recur. Although these patients may be "cured," they are typically considered cancer-free survivors. Response to treatment is classified as complete (no evidence of disease for at least 1 month) or partial (≥ 30% ↓ in tumor size). Stable disease means < 30% decrease or < 20% increase in tumor size, and progression is ≥ 20% increase in tumor size or tumor growth in a new site.

Often, the primary treatment modality is surgery if the cancer is resectable. Neoadjuvant therapy (e.g., radiation or chemotherapy) may be used prior to surgery to shrink the tumor initially. Adjuvant therapy (may include radiation and/or chemotherapy) is given after surgery in an attempt to eradicate residual disease and ↓ recurrence.

Sometimes, surgery is not an option for initial treatment and the treatment regimen begins with chemotherapy.

TO REDUCE RISK OF DEVELOPING CANCER

Everyone should be encouraged to maintain a healthy lifestyle:

- Avoid tobacco (enroll in smoking cessation program if needed).
- Maintain a healthy weight.
- Exercise regularly.
- Eat healthy with plenty of fruits and vegetables.
- Limit alcohol intake.
- Protect skin from harmful UV rays.
- Assess cancer risk, family history, and individual history.
- Have regular check-ups and cancer screening tests.
- Low-dose aspirin is recommended for prevention of colorectal cancer and CVD in patients who are age 50-59, have ASCVD risk ≥ 10%, have ≥ 10 year life expectancy and are at low risk of bleeding.

Terminology Used in Cancer Therapy

TYPE OF THERAPY	DEFINITION
Curative	Therapy given with the intention of curing the cancer.
Palliative	Therapy given with the intention of reducing symptoms and/or slowing the growth of the cancer.
Adjuvant	Therapy given after the primary therapy (usually surgery) to eradicate residual disease and ↓ recurrence.
Neoadjuvant	Therapy given before the primary therapy (usually surgery) to shrink the size of the tumor.

Chemotherapeutic regimens are usually designed for synergism. Drugs with different mechanisms of action that complement each other are chosen. Synergy will not work unless each drug is active on the tumor independently. Most drugs are more effective at killing rapidly dividing cancer cells since they work by interfering with the DNA replication cycle.

Through various mechanisms of actions, chemotherapeutic regimens can be highly toxic. The majority of adverse effects are due to damaging effects on non-cancerous, rapidly dividing cells in the GI tract, hair follicles and bone marrow (where the production of blood cells takes place). Thus, diarrhea, alopecia, and myelosuppression are common side effects of most chemotherapeutic regimens. Pharmacists can play an important role in helping patients manage the side effects of chemotherapeutic regimens.

Due to these severe side effects, the patient's physical functioning must be assessed with rating systems such as the Karnofsky and the ECOG (Eastern Cooperative Oncology Group) performance status scales. Many patient factors can affect treatment choice such as: age, comorbidities and/or previous treatments. A patient's quality of life may lead the clinician and family to choose palliative measures (to reduce the symptoms) over a more aggressive treatment plan with side effects that could be intolerable to the patient.

Pregnancy & Breastfeeding

Chemotherapy should be avoided during pregnancy and breastfeeding. Chemotherapy may be teratogenic. Counsel both male and female patients to avoid conceiving during treatment and to consider using barrier methods to avoid contact with body fluids. Pregnant women should avoid handling chemotherapeutic drugs. Some of the medications can cause long-term sterility.

SUMMARY OF TOXICITIES

For studying purposes, it is helpful to know the common toxicities of chemotherapy drugs and the specific agents most commonly associated with those toxicities. It is important to know the chemoprotectant drugs (or antidotes) and the situations in which they should be used, along with maximum doses of select chemotherapy drugs. These common toxicities are discussed here and the drugs are discussed in more detail in the next chapter.

Dosing Considerations for Cancer Therapeutic Agents

DRUG	MAXIMUM DOSES	REASON
Bleomycin	Lifetime cumulative dose: 400 units	Pulmonary toxicity
Doxorubicin	Lifetime cumulative dose: 450-550 mg/m^2	Cardiotoxicity
Cisplatin	Dose per cycle not to exceed 100 mg/m^2	Nephrotoxicity
Vincristine	Single dose "capped" at 2 mg	Neuropathy

Common Toxicities of Select Chemotherapeutic Agents

TOXICITY	COMMON DRUGS	MONITORING	MANAGEMENT
Myelosuppression	Almost all, except: Asparaginase, bleomycin, vincristine, most monoclonal antibodies and many tyrosine kinase inhibitors (TKIs)	Complete blood count (CBC) with differential, temperature, bleeding, fatigue, shortness of breath	Neutropenia: colony-stimulating factors (CSFs) Anemia: RBC transfusions and erythropoiesis-stimulating agents (ESAs) Thrombocytopenia: platelet transfusions
Nausea & Vomiting	Cisplatin, doxorubicin, epirubicin, cyclophosphamide and ifosfamide are highly emetogenic	Patient symptoms of nausea and vomiting and hydration status	Neurokinin-1 receptor antagonist (NK1-RA), serotonin-3 receptor antagonist (5HT3-RA), dexamethasone IV/PO fluid hydration
Mucositis	Fluorouracil, capecitabine, irinotecan, methotrexate and many TKIs including afatinib, ponatinib, sorafenib, sunitinib	S/sx of superinfection of oral ulcers with herpes simplex virus or thrush *(Candida* species)	Symptomatic treatment: mucosal coating agents, topical local anesthetics
Diarrhea	Fluorouracil, capecitabine, irinotecan and many TKIs	Frequency of bowel movements, hydration status, potassium and other electrolytes	IV/PO fluid hydration, antimotility agents (e.g., loperamide) Irinotecan: atropine for early onset diarrhea
Constipation	Vincristine, pomalidomide, thalidomide	Frequency of bowel movements	Stimulant laxatives, polyethylene glycol
Xerostomia	Caused by radiation therapy to the head or neck regions.	Dry mouth	Artificial saliva substitutes, pilocarpine
Cardiotoxicity	**Cardiomyopathy** Anthracyclines, HER2 inhibitors (ado-trastuzumab, trastuzumab, pertuzumab), fluorouracil, lapatinib **QT prolongation** Arsenic trioxide, many tyrosine kinase inhibitors (dasatinib, nilotinib, vemurafenib, dabrafenib, trametinib, crizotinib, ceritinib, erlotinib, gefitinib, lapatinib, sorafenib, sunitinib) and leuprolide	**Cardiomyopathy** Left ventricular ejection fraction (LVEF), lifetime cumulative dose of anthracycline **QT prolongation** ECG, K, Mg, Ca	**Cardiomyopathy** Do not exceed recommended lifetime cumulative dose of 450-550 mg/m^2 for doxorubicin, dexrazoxane can be administered prophylactically in select patients receiving doxorubicin. **QT prolongation** Ensure K, Mg, Ca within normal limits, consider holding therapy if QTc > 500 msec.

Common Toxicities of Select Chemotherapeutic Agents Continued

TOXICITY	COMMON DRUGS	MONITORING	MANAGEMENT
Hepatotoxicity	Antiandrogens (bicalutamide, flutamide, nilutamide), folate antimetabolites (methotrexate, pemetrexed, pralatrexate), pyrimidine analog antimetabolites (cytarabine, gemcitabine), many tyrosine kinase inhibitors, ipilimumab, pembrolizumab, nivolumab, atezolizumab	LFTs, jaundice, ascites	Symptomatic management. Consider stopping therapy. Corticosteroids if an autoimmune mechanism for PD-1 immunotherapy agents.
Nephrotoxicity	Cisplatin, methotrexate (especially high doses), pemetrexed, pralatrexate, carfilzomib, bevacizumab, nivolumab, pembrolizumab, ipilimumab, atezolizumab	BUN, SCr, urinalysis, urine output, creatinine clearance	Amifostine *(Ethyol)* may be given prophylactically with cisplatin to reduce the risk of nephrotoxicity. Ensure adequate hydration. Do not exceed maximum dose of 100 mg/m^2/cycle for cisplatin.
Hemorrhagic Cystitis	Ifosfamide (all doses), cyclophosphamide (higher doses, e.g., > 1 gram/m^2)	Urinalysis for blood, symptoms of dysuria	Mesna (*Mesnex*) is always given prophylactically with ifosfamide (and sometimes with cyclophosphamide) to reduce the risk of hemorrhagic cystitis. For both, always ensure adequate hydration.
Neuropathy	**Peripheral Sensory Neuropathy** Vinca alkaloids (vincristine, vinblastine, vinorelbine), platinums (cisplatin, oxaliplatin), taxanes (paclitaxel, docetaxel, cabazitaxel), proteasome inhibitors (bortezomib, carfilzomib), thalidomide, ado-trastuzumab, cytarabine (high doses), brentuximab **Autonomic Neuropathy** Vinca alkaloids		Symptomatic treatment with drugs for neuropathic pain. **Vincristine** Many recommend limiting the dose of vincristine to 2 mg per week (regardless of BSA calculated dose). **Oxaliplatin** Causes an acute cold-mediated sensory neuropathy. Instruct patients to avoid cold temperatures and avoid drinking cold beverages. **Bortezomib** SC administration is associated with less peripheral neuropathy than IV administration.
Clotting Risk	Aromatase inhibitors (e.g., anastrozole, letrozole), SERMs (e.g., tamoxifen), immunomodulators (thalidomide, lenalidomide, pomalidomide)	S/sx of DVT/PE, stroke, MI	Consider thromboprophylaxis based on patient's risk factors.

Prevalent Toxicities of Common Chemotherapy Agents

This is a visual way to remember the toxicities associated with common chemotherapy agents. Students are encouraged to draw a chemo person to help make connections and learn the material.

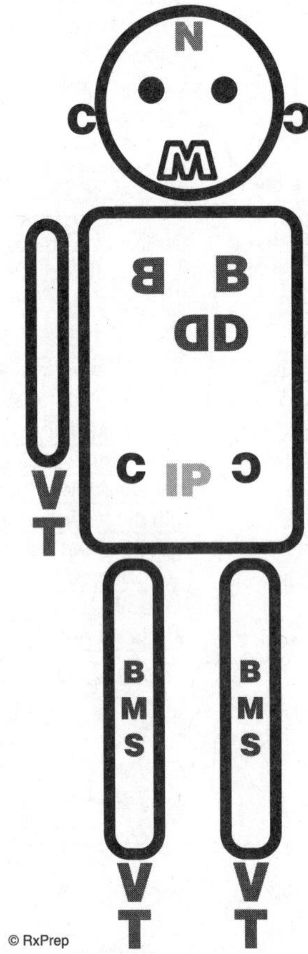

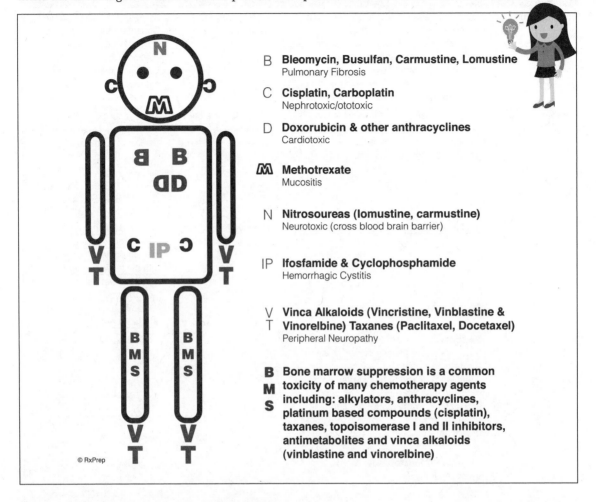

B **Bleomycin, Busulfan, Carmustine, Lomustine**
Pulmonary Fibrosis

C **Cisplatin, Carboplatin**
Nephrotoxic/ototoxic

D **Doxorubicin & other anthracyclines**
Cardiotoxic

M **Methotrexate**
Mucositis

N **Nitrosoureas (lomustine, carmustine)**
Neurotoxic (cross blood brain barrier)

IP **Ifosfamide & Cyclophosphamide**
Hemorrhagic Cystitis

V T **Vinca Alkaloids (Vincristine, Vinblastine & Vinorelbine) Taxanes (Paclitaxel, Docetaxel)**
Peripheral Neuropathy

B M S Bone marrow suppression is a common toxicity of many chemotherapy agents including: alkylators, anthracyclines, platinum based compounds (cisplatin), taxanes, topoisomerase I and II inhibitors, antimetabolites and vinca alkaloids (vinblastine and vinorelbine)

Chemotherapy Adjunctive Medications

CHEMOTHERAPEUTIC AGENT	ADJUNCTIVE MEDICATION	INDICATION FOR ADJUNCTIVE MEDICATION
Cisplatin	Amifostine *(Ethyol)*	Prophylaxis to prevent nephrotoxicity
Doxorubicin	Dexrazoxane *(Zinecard)*	Prophylaxis to prevent cardiomyopathy
	Dexrazoxane *(Totect)*	Treatment for extravasation
Fluorouracil	Leucovorin or levoleucovorin *(Fusilev)*	Given with fluorouracil to enhance efficacy
Fluorouracil or capecitabine	Uridine triacetate *(Vistogard)*	Use within 96 hours for any overdose or to treat severe, life-threatening or early onset toxicity
Ifosfamide	Mesna *(Mesnex)*	Prophylaxis to prevent hemorrhagic cystitis
Irinotecan	Atropine	Prophylaxis to prevent acute diarrhea
Methotrexate	Leucovorin or levoleucovorin *(Fusilev)*	Given after methotrexate (MTX) to reduce myelosuppression and mucositis
	Glucarpidase *(Voraxaze)*	Given in acute renal failure/high concentration of MTX

MANAGEMENT OF SIDE EFFECTS

Myelosuppression Overview

Myelosuppression (↓ in bone marrow activity resulting in fewer RBCs, WBCs and platelets) is a complication of most chemotherapeutic agents. Neutrophils and platelets are often affected since these cells have shorter life spans and thus, the turnover is rapid. If WBCs decrease, the immune system will become depressed and the patient will have trouble fighting an infection. If RBCs decrease, the patient becomes anemic, experiencing weakness and fatigue. If platelets decrease, there is an increased risk of severe bleeding.

The lowest point that WBCs and platelets reach (the nadir) occurs about 7 – 14 days after chemotherapy, although some agents have a delayed effect. RBC nadir is much later, generally after several months of therapy, due to the long life span of RBCs (~120 days). WBCs and platelets generally recover 3 – 4 weeks post treatment. The next dose of chemotherapy is given after the WBCs and platelets have returned to a safe level. If the WBCs and/or platelets have not recovered to a safe level, the next cycle of chemotherapy may need to be delayed to allow for recovery. Medications may be necessary to help restore blood cell counts. Severe cases may require a transfusion (providing the deficient cell line directly, such as giving packed RBCs for severe anemia). All agents used for myelosuppression discussed here are usually given by subcutaneous injection, either by the patient, caregiver or healthcare provider.

Neutropenia

A low neutrophil count ↑ infection risk and makes it difficult for the human body to fight an infection. The more neutropenic the patient is, the higher the risk of infection.

Neutropenia Definition (American Society of Clinical Oncology)

CATEGORY	ABSOLUTE NEUTROPHIL COUNT (ANC)
Neutropenia	< 1,000 cells/mm^3
Severe Neutropenia	< 500 cells/mm^3
Profound Neutropenia	< 100 cells/mm^3

Know how to calculate the ANC; this is reviewed in the Calculations II chapter.

Colony stimulating factors (CSFs), also called "myeloid growth factors," are a class of biologic agents that regulate the proliferation, differentiation, survival, and activation of cells in the myeloid lineage. Myeloid refers to the granulocyte precursor cell, which differentiates into neutrophils, eosinophils, and basophils. These agents are expensive and have not been shown to improve overall survival outcomes. They do shorten the time that a patient is at risk for infection due to neutropenia and reduce mortality from infections when given prophylactically in patients at high risk for febrile neutropenia. The National Comprehensive Cancer Network (NCCN) recommends that all patients with > 20% chance of developing chemotherapy-induced febrile neutropenia receive myeloid growth factors. There are three primary types: GM-CSF (sargramostim), G-CSF (filgrastim) and pegylated G-CSF (pegfilgrastim). GM-CSF is limited to use in stem cell transplantation. Both forms of G-CSF are indicated for prevention of febrile neutropenia.

Effect of CSF Prophylaxis on the Duration of Chemotherapy-Induced Neutropenia

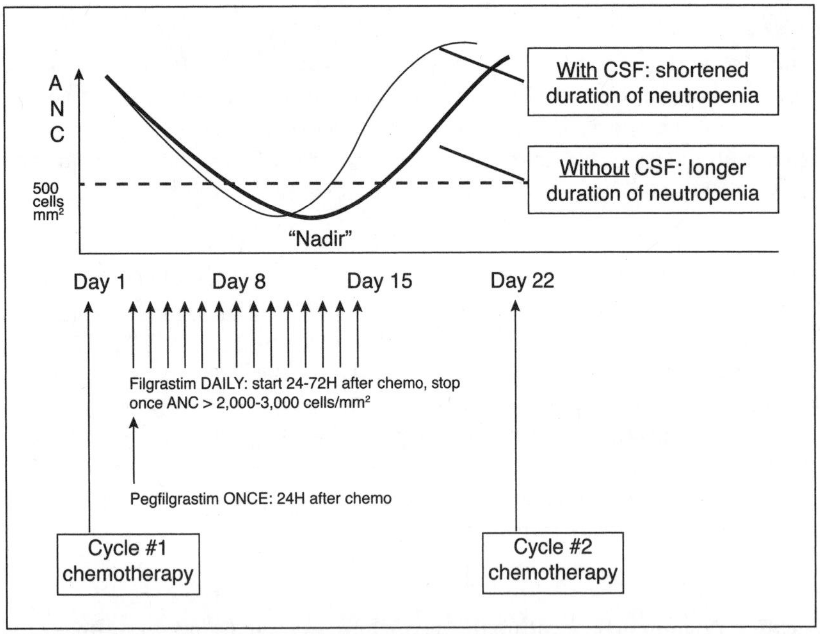

DRUG	DOSING	SAFETY/SIDE EFFECTS/MONITORING
G-CSF **Filgrastim** ***(Neupogen, Zarxio)*** **Tbo-filgrastim** ***(Granix)***	5 mcg/kg/day given IV/SC daily (round to the nearest 300 mcg or 480 mcg vial size); treat through post-nadir recovery (until ANC > 2,000-3,000 cells/mm³) 10 mcg/kg/day used for bone marrow transplant	**SIDE EFFECTS** Filgrastim/pegfilgrastim/tbo-filgrastim: bone pain, fever, glomerulonephritis, generalized rash, injection site reaction Sargramostim: fever, bone pain, arthralgias, myalgias, rash, dyspnea, peripheral edema, pericardial effusion, cardiovascular edema, HTN, chest pain **MONITORING** CBC with differential, pulmonary function, weight, vital signs **NOTES** Store in refrigerator. Protect vials from light. Administer first dose 24-72 hours after chemo. Patients should report any signs of enlarged spleen (pain in left upper abdomen or respiratory distress syndrome). Must document when pegfilgrastim was given. Pegfilgrastim should not be given until 24 hours after the end of chemo infusion or within 14 days prior to the next cycle of chemo. Filgrastim and sargramostim should not be given within 24 hours before or after chemo.
Pegylated G-CSF **Pegfilgrastim** ***(Neulasta)*** Long acting: relatively equivalent to 14 daily doses of filgrastim	1 prefilled syringe (6 mg) SC once per chemo cycle	
GM-CSF **Sargramostim** ***(Leukine)*** Limited to use in stem cell transplantation	250 mcg/m²/day given IV/SC daily; treat through post-nadir recovery	

Febrile Neutropenia

Patients receiving cytotoxic chemotherapy are at risk for infections with enteric bacteria and fungi due to alterations in gastrointestinal mucosa caused by chemotherapy. These patients also commonly have central venous access devices, which places them at risk for infections due to skin flora. When these patients become neutropenic following cytotoxic chemotherapy, they may be unable to fight off these infections, placing them at risk for death due to sepsis syndrome. Because a fever may be the only sign of infection in a neutropenic patient, appropriate empiric antibiotics must be started immediately when a fever occurs.

The Infectious Diseases Society of America defines febrile neutropenia as:

FEVER	NEUTROPENIA
Single oral temperature > 38.3° C (101° F) or	Absolute neutrophil count (ANC) < 500 cells/mm³ or
Oral temperature > 38.0° C (100.4° F) sustained for greater than 1 hour	ANC that is expected to decrease to < 500 cells/mm³ during the next 48 hours

Although both Gram-positive and Gram-negative bacteria may be isolated from patients with febrile neutropenia, infection with Gram-negative bacteria pose the greatest risk for causing sepsis syndrome in these patients. Therefore, initial empiric antibiotics in febrile neutropenia should provide adequate coverage against Gram-negative bacteria, including *Pseudomonas aeruginosa*. The individual patient's risk of developing serious complications should also be considered when determining the initial empiric antibiotic regimen. Modification of the initial empiric antibiotic regimen may be necessary based on culture results, if a patient continues to have fever or clinical deterioration.

PATIENT RISK	RISK DEFINITION	INITIAL EMPIRIC ANTIBIOTICS
Low-risk	Expected ANC < 500 cells/mm³ for ≤ 7 days No comorbidities	**Oral anti-pseudomonal antibiotics** Ciprofloxacin + amoxicillin-clavulanate or Ciprofloxacin +/– clindamycin or Levofloxacin
High-risk	Expected ANC ≤ 100 cells/mm³ for > 7 days Presence of comorbidities Evidence of renal or hepatic impairment (CrCl < 30 mL/min or LFTs > 5x ULN)	**Intravenous anti-pseudomonal beta-lactams** Cefepime or Ceftazidime or Meropenem or Imipenem-cilastatin or Piperacillin-tazobactam

Anemia

Hemoglobin (Hgb) levels are used to assess anemia. Normal Hgb levels are 12 – 16 g/dL for females and 13.5 – 18 g/dL for males (hematocrit is 36 – 46% females; 38 – 50% males). Anemia may recover on its own, be treated with a RBC transfusion, or rarely, with an erythropoiesis-stimulating agent (ESA). ESAs can shorten survival and ↑ tumor progression or recurrence as shown in clinical studies of patients with breast, non-small cell lung, head and neck, lymphoid, and cervical cancers. Therefore, ESAs are not recommended to be used in patients receiving chemotherapy with curative intent. To make sure that patients are aware of the risks, MedGuides are dispensed at the initiation of therapy. For cancer, the use of ESAs must fulfill the requirements of the ESA APPRISE Oncology Program. This is a Risk Evaluation and Mitigation Strategies (REMS) program to make sure healthcare providers are trained and patients receive proper counseling on the risks and benefits of therapy. To minimize the risks of ESAs in patients with chemotherapy-induced anemia, the following requirements from the ESA APPRISE Oncology Program must be met:

- Use ESA therapy only in patients with non-myeloid malignancies where anemia is due to the effect of concomitant myelosuppressive chemotherapy
- Upon initiation of ESA therapy, there is a minimum of 2 additional months of planned chemotherapy
- Initiate ESA therapy when the Hgb is < 10 g/dL
- Use the lowest dose needed to avoid RBC transfusions

Serum ferritin, transferrin saturation (TSAT) and total iron-binding capacity (TIBC) may be ordered to assess iron storage and transport since the ESAs will not work well to correct the anemia if iron levels are inadequate. Levels of folate and vitamin B12 may need to be evaluated, especially if there is a poor response to the ESA. For further information regarding ESAs and ESA dosing in cancer, refer to the Anemia chapter.

Thrombocytopenia

Low platelets (thrombocytes) can result in spontaneous, uncontrolled bleeding. The normal range for platelets is 150,000 – 450,000/mm^3. The risk for spontaneous bleeding is increased when the platelet count is <10,000 cells/mm^3. Platelet transfusions are generally indicated when the count falls below 10,000 cells/mm^3 (or 20,000 cells/mm^3 if active bleed is present). Chemotherapy doses may be reduced or placed on hold until the platelet count recovers. Intramuscular injections and medications that affect platelet functioning, such as NSAIDs, should be avoided in patients who are thrombocytopenic.

Chemotherapy-Induced Nausea and Vomiting (CINV)

Nausea and vomiting are common with chemotherapy. Patient factors which ↑ risk of nausea and vomiting include: female gender, < 50 years of age, dehydration, history of motion sickness, and history of nausea and vomiting with prior regimens. For chemotherapy-induced nausea and vomiting (CINV), administer antiemetics at least 30 minutes prior to chemotherapy and provide take-home antiemetic medication (such as ondansetron, prochlorperazine, or metoclopramide) for breakthrough nausea and vomiting. There are 3 subtypes of CINV: acute, delayed and anticipatory.

SUBTYPE	RISK FACTORS	ONSET	MAJOR NEURO-TRANSMITTERS	DRUG THERAPY
Acute	See text above for patient risk factors and the table below for high risk drugs	Within 24 hours after chemo	Serotonin	5HT3 receptor antagonists (5HT3-RA)
Delayed	Anthracyclines, platinum analogs, cyclophosphamide, ifosfamide, any chemo regimens with a high risk for causing acute CINV	1 to 7 days after chemo	Substance P	NK1 receptor antagonists (NK1-RA), corticosteroids, palonosetron (the only 5HT3-RA with a labeled indication for delayed emesis)
Anticipatory	History of CINV with previous chemo regimen	Before chemo		Benzodiazepines

Emetic Risk Potential

Chemotherapy regimens are divided into risk groups for emetogenicity. Regimens with high emetic risk cause emesis at a frequency > 90%. Cisplatin is a high emetic risk drug. Other risk categories include moderate (30 – 90%), low (10 – 30%) and minimal risk (< 10%). The majority of the monoclonal antibodies and TKIs have minimal emetic risk.

Antiemetic Regimens for Acute/Delayed Nausea & Vomiting

The goal is to prevent nausea and vomiting and antiemetic regimens are started before chemotherapy. Risk of nausea and vomiting persists for 3 days after receiving the last dose of high emetic risk chemotherapy and for at least 2 days following the last dose of moderate emetic risk regimens.

5HT3RA	NK1-RA	COMBINATION	OTHER	STEROID
Ondansetron Granisetron Dolasetron Palonosetron	Aprepitant PO Fosaprepitant IV Rolapitant	Netupitant/ palonosetron *(Akynzeo)*	Olanzapine	Dexamethasone

CHEMOTHERAPY REGIMEN	ANTIEMETIC REGIMEN
High emetic risk*	**3 drugs** ■ NK1-RA + 5HT3-RA + Dexamethasone ■ Netupitant/palonosetron *(Akynzeo)* + Dexamethasone ■ Olanzapine + Palonosetron + Dexamethasone
Moderate emetic risk*	**2 or 3 drugs** ■ NK1-RA + 5HT3-RA + Dexamethasone ■ 5HT3-RA + Dexamethasone ■ Netupitant/palonosetron *(Akynzeo)* + Dexamethasone ■ Olanzapine + Palonosetron + Dexamethasone
Low emetic risk	**1 drug (any except NK1-RA)** ■ 5HT3-RA ■ Dexamethasone ■ Prochlorperazine ■ Metoclopramide

**May add lorazepam PRN, H2RA or PPI*

Antiemetics for Breakthrough CINV

Despite receiving antiemetic prophylaxis for acute and/or delayed CINV, some patients may experience breakthrough nausea and vomiting. Various antiemetics may be used, including 5HT3-RAs, dopamine receptor antagonists, and cannabinoids. 5HT3-RAs are usually well-tolerated by most patients, with migraine-like headaches and constipation being common side effects. They also cause minimal sedation, compared to dopamine receptor antagonists and cannabinoids. Dopamine receptor antagonists, such as prochlorperazine, promethazine, and metoclopramide, are commonly prescribed, although some patients may experience unpleasant side effects. These agents commonly cause sedation and some anticholinergic side effects. Extrapyramidal symptoms (EPS), such as acute dystonic reactions, can occur, especially in younger patients. Acute dystonic reactions should be treated with anticholinergics (benztropine, diphenhydramine). Note that droperidol is not used for CINV, but is included here only to complete the discussion of antiemetics.

Cannabinoids, such as Dronabinol *(Marinol, Syndros)* and nabilone *(Cesamet)* can be used as second line agents. These are synthetic analogs of delta-9-tetrahydrocannabinol, a naturally occurring component of *Cannabis sativa* (marijuana). Although these agents may be legally prescribed, they may cause side effects similar to *Cannabis*, such as sedation, dysphoria, or euphoria. The DEA classifies *Cannabis*, (marijuana, used in the plant form) as a schedule I drug, however it can be purchased for medical and nonmedical use in some states, and in some jurisdictions can be purchased for medical use only.

Antiemetic Agents

<u>Substance P/Neurokinin-1 Receptor Antagonists:</u> inhibit the substance P/neurokinin 1 receptor, therefore augmenting the antiemetic activity of 5HT3 receptor antagonists and corticosteroids to inhibit acute and delayed phases of chemotherapy-induced emesis.

DRUG	DOSING	SAFETY/SIDE EFFECTS/MONITORING
Aprepitant *(Emend)* Capsule, suspension	PO: 125 mg 1 hour before chemo on day 1, then 80 mg daily x 2 days	**CONTRAINDICATIONS** Aprepitant/fosaprepitant: do not use with pimozide or cisapride (CYP3A4 substrates) Rolapitant: do not use with thioridazine (CYP2D6 substrate) **SIDE EFFECTS** Dizziness, fatigue, constipation, weakness, hiccups **NOTES** Aprepitant/fosaprepitant/netupitant are CYP3A4 inhibitors. Dose of dexamethasone should be decreased when used concurrently as an antiemetic. Rolapitant is a CYP2D6 inhibitor. Dose of dexamethasone should not be decreased when used concurrently as an antiemetic.
Fosaprepitant *(Emend)* Injection	IV: 150 mg 30 minutes before chemo	
Netupitant + palonosetron *(Akynzeo)* Capsule	PO: 300/0.5 mg 1 hour before chemo	
Rolapitant *(Varubi)* Tablet	PO: 180 mg 1-2 hours before chemo	

<u>5HT-3 Receptor Antagonists</u>: work by blocking serotonin, both peripherally on vagal nerve terminals and centrally in the chemoreceptor trigger zone. All may be given once prior to chemotherapy on day 1, with the exception of the granisetron transdermal patch.

DRUG	DOSING	SAFETY/SIDE EFFECTS/MONITORING
Ondansetron *(Zofran, Zuplenz* film)	PO: 16-24 mg IV: 8-16 mg	**CONTRAINDICATIONS** Concomitant use of apomorphine *(Apokyn)* with ondansetron (enhances hypotensive effects of apomorphine) **WARNINGS** Dose-dependent ↑ in QT interval (torsade de pointes) - more common with IV Serotonin syndrome when used in combination with other serotonergic agents Constipation, progressive ileus and gastric distension *(Sustol)* **SIDE EFFECTS** Headache, fatigue, dizziness, constipation, injection site reactions *(Sustol)* **NOTES** MedGuide required *(Sustol)* Palonosetron only available PO in combination with netupitant *(Akynzeo)*
Granisetron *(Kytril, Sancuso, Sustol)*	PO: 2 mg IV: 10 mcg/kg or 1 mg SC *(Sustol)*: 10 mg over 20-30 seconds Patch *(Sancuso)*: 3.1 mg/24hr patch, apply 24-48 hours before chemo; may leave in place up to 7 days	
Dolasetron *(Anzemet)*	PO: 100 mg IV: <u>Not indicated</u> for CINV due to ↑ risk for <u>QT prolongation</u>	
Palonosetron *(Aloxi)* **+ netupitant *(Akynzeo)***	IV *(Aloxi)*: 0.25 mg	

Antiemetic Agents Continued

Corticosteroids: unknown

DRUG	DOSING	SAFETY/SIDE EFFECTS/MONITORING
Dexamethasone ***(Decadron)***	All off label dosing High risk: 12 mg PO/IV on day 1 of chemo, then 8 mg PO daily days 2-4 (with aprepitant or netupitant) or 8 mg PO day 2, then 8 mg PO BID days 3 and 4 (with fosaprepitant) or 20 mg PO/IV on day 1, then 8 mg PO BID on days 2-4 (with rolapitant) Moderate risk: 12 mg PO/IV on day 1 of chemo, then 8 mg PO/IV days 2-3 Low risk: 12 mg PO/IV on day(s) of chemo	**CONTRAINDICATIONS** Systemic fungal infections, cerebral malaria **SIDE EFFECTS** Short-term side effects include ↑ appetite/weight gain, fluid retention, emotional instability (euphoria, mood swings, irritability, acute psychosis), insomnia, GI upset. Higher doses can cause ↑ in BP and blood glucose (especially in patients with diabetes).

Dopamine Receptor Antagonists: work by blocking dopamine receptors in the CNS, including the chemoreceptor trigger zone (among other mechanisms).

<table>
<tr><th>DRUG</th><th>DOSING</th><th>SAFETY/SIDE EFFECTS/MONITORING</th></tr>
<tr><td>Prochlorperazine
(Compazine, Compro)</td><td>10 mg IV/PO Q6H PRN
May give 25 mg suppository PR Q12H PRN</td><td rowspan="4">BOXED WARNING
Prochlorperazine: ↑ mortality in elderly patients with dementia-related psychosis.
Promethazine: do not use in children age < 2 years due to risk of respiratory depression. Do not give via intra-arterial or SC administration. IV route can cause serious tissue injury if extravasation occurs. Deep IM injection is preferred (see Notes).
Metoclopramide: tardive dyskinesia (TD) that can be irreversible. Discontinue metoclopramide if signs or symptoms of TD. ↑ risk of developing TD with ↑ duration of treatment and total cumulative dose. Avoid treatment with metoclopramide for > 12 weeks.
Droperidol: QT prolongation and serious arrhythmias. All patients should have a 12-lead ECG prior to receiving droperidol and continue for 2-3 hours after completing treatment. Contraindicated if baseline QT is prolonged.

WARNINGS
Symptoms of Parkinson disease may be exacerbated. Avoid use in patients with Parkinson disease.

SIDE EFFECTS
Sedation, lethargy, hypotension, neuroleptic malignant syndrome (NMS), QT prolongation, acute EPS (common in children – antidote is diphenhydramine or benztropine), can lower seizure threshold, strong anticholinergic side effects (not metoclopramide or droperidol)

NOTES
MedGuide required (metoclopramide)
Droperidol has not been used for CINV. It is included here only for completeness of antiemetic discussion
IM injections not feasible with ↓ PLT</td></tr>
<tr><td>Promethazine
(Phenergan, Phenadoz, Promethegan)</td><td>12.5-25 mg PO/IM/IV/PR Q4-6H PRN</td></tr>
<tr><td>Metoclopramide
(Reglan, Metozolv ODT)</td><td>10-40 mg PO/IV Q6H PRN
For highly emetic regimens: 0.5-2 mg/kg/dose PO/IV Q6H PRN
CrCl < 40 mL/min: Give 50% of the dose</td></tr>
<tr><td>Droperidol
Injection</td><td>0.625-1.25 mg x1
Indicated only for post-operative N/V</td></tr>
</table>

Antiemetic Agents Continued

DRUG	DOSING	SAFETY/SIDE EFFECTS/MONITORING

Cannabinoids: may work by activating cannabinoid receptors within the central nervous system and/or by inhibiting the vomiting control mechanism in the medulla oblongata.

Dronabinol *(Marinol, Syndros)* Capsules, solution Refrigerate C-III	Labeled dosing: 5 mg/m² PO prior to chemo and Q2-4H after chemo for up to 6 doses/day. Most patients respond to 5 mg 3-4 times/day.	**SIDE EFFECTS** Somnolence, euphoria, ↑ appetite, orthostatic hypotension, dysphoria, lowering of the seizure threshold, use with caution in patients with histories of substance abuse or psychiatric disorders **NOTES** Solution contains 50% alcohol
Nabilone *(Cesamet)* No refrigeration needed C-II	1-2 mg PO BID, continue for up to 48H after last chemo dose	

Patient Counseling for Ondansetron

- Common side effects of this medication include headache, constipation, fatigue and dizziness.
- Take this medicine by mouth with a glass of water. It may be taken as needed or at scheduled times. Follow the directions on your prescription label. Do not take your medicine more often than directed.
- Do not take this medicine if you are taking apomorphine.
- If you are prescribed the oral disintegrating tablets: do not attempt to push the tablets through foil backing. With dry hands, peel back the foil of 1 blister and remove the tablet. Place tablet on the tongue; it will dissolve in seconds. Once dissolved, you may swallow with saliva. Administration with liquid is not necessary. Wash hands after administration.
- If you are prescribed the oral soluble film *(Zuplenz)*: with dry hands, fold the pouch along the dotted line to expose the tear notch. While still folded, tear the pouch carefully along the edge and remove the oral soluble film just prior to dosing. Place the film on the tongue, it will dissolve in a few seconds. Allow each film to dissolve completely before taking the next film if more than one is needed to reach the desired dose (i.e., 16 mg given as two 8 mg films).

Other Gastrointestinal Complications

Cells of the GI tract are rapidly dividing and are therefore susceptible to being killed by chemotherapy agents that interfere with DNA replication or cell division. Damage to the epithelium of the GI tract results in diarrhea. Damage to oral mucosal epithelial cells leads to painful oral ulcerations, also called oral mucositis. Damage to the salivary glands usually caused by radiation therapy to the head or neck regions may cause dry mouth, also called xerostomia.

Chemotherapy-Induced Diarrhea

Chemotherapy-induced diarrhea (CID) can lead to life-threatening dehydration and electrolyte imbalances. Antimotility agents, such as loperamide and diphenoxylate + atropine may be prescribed to treat CID. Although the usual maximum dose of loperamide is 16 mg/day, this dose may be increased to 24 mg/day when treating CID under medical supervision. Fluorouracil, capecitabine, and irinotecan commonly cause CID that occurs several days after chemotherapy. The risk of diarrhea is increased when fluorouracil (or the prodrug capecitabine) is used in combination with leucovorin or when used in patients with dihydropyrimidine dehydrogenase (DPD) deficiencies (not common). Irinotecan also causes an early onset diarrhea that occurs during the infusion of the drug and is often accompanied by symptoms of cholinergic excess such as abdominal cramping, rhinitis, lacrimation and salivation. The treatment is the anticholinergic drug atropine. Many TKIs, especially those targeting VEGFR or EGFR, such as sorafenib and sunitinib, commonly cause diarrhea.

Oral Mucositis

Oral mucositis usually occurs several days after chemotherapy, with the severity of symptoms usually peaking around 7 days after chemotherapy and slowly resolving approximately 4 – 8 days later. Many chemotherapy agents that cause diarrhea also cause oral mucositis. No therapy is approved for the prevention of oral mucositis caused by standard doses of chemotherapy. Patients should be instructed to practice good oral hygiene to help reduce the risk of oral complications. Agents that coat or anesthetize the oral mucosa may be prescribed for control of oral pain and discomfort. Patients who develop oral mucositis may also develop oral infections with herpes simplex virus or *Candida spp*. Antiviral or antifungal medications may be prescribed.

Medications for Oral Complications of Chemotherapy

DRUG	DOSING	SAFETY/SIDE EFFECTS/MONITORING
Oral Mucositis		
Mucosal Barrier Gel Spray, solution, wafer *(Episil, Gelclair, Mucotrol, MuGard, Orafate, ProThelial)*	Varies depending on product. Most are applied to the oral mucosa several times per day.	**SIDE EFFECTS** Burning, stinging sensation in the mouth
Lidocaine 2% topical solution for mouth/throat	15 mL swish and spit/swallowed Q3H PRN	**BOXED WARNING** Avoid use in patients < 3 years of age due to reports of seizures, cardiopulmonary arrest and death. **WARNINGS** Exceeding the recommended dose can result in high plasma levels and serious adverse effects (seizures, cardiopulmonary arrest) **SIDE EFFECTS** Dizziness, drowsiness, confusion, hypotension **NOTES** Avoid ingestion of food for 60 minutes following dose due to risk of impaired swallowing and aspiration.
Xerostomia		
Artificial Saliva Substitutes Spray, solution, lozenge *(Aquoral, Biotene, Caphosol, Entertainer's Secret, Moi-Stir, Mouth Kote, NeutraSal, Numoisyn, Oasis, SalivaSure)*	Varies depending on product. Most can be applied to oral mucosa PRN.	
Pilocarpine *(Salagen)*	5-10 mg PO TID <u>Hepatic impairment</u> Moderate: 5 mg PO BID Severe: avoid use	**WARNINGS** Use with caution in patients with cholelithiasis, nephrolithiasis, cardiovascular disease, asthma, bronchitis, COPD **SIDE EFFECTS** Cholinergic side effects: flushing, sweating, nausea, urinary frequency **NOTES** Avoid administering with high-fat meal

Hand-Foot Syndrome

Hand-foot syndrome (also known as palmar-plantar erythrodysesthesia) frequently occurs following treatment with fluorouracil, capecitabine, cytarabine, and liposomal doxorubicin. It can also occur following treatment with multitargeted TKIs, such as sorafenib and sunitinib. The mechanism for this toxicity is unclear. Patients may present with redness, swelling, tenderness, pain, blisters and possibly peeling of the palms and soles. Dose reductions or delays in treatment are recommended if symptoms do not improve.

Cooling procedures with cold compresses provide temporary relief of pain and tenderness. Emollients provide excellent moisturizing for hands and feet. Corticosteroids and pain medications may be used to help alleviate inflammation and pain.

HAND-FOOT SYNDROME PREVENTION
Limit daily activities to reduce friction and heat exposure to hands and feet for 1 week after IV medication (e.g., 5-Fluorouracil) or during the duration of oral exposure (e.g., capecitabine).
Avoid long exposure to hot water (washing dishes, showers). Take short showers in luke warm water.
Avoid use of dishwashing gloves as the rubber will hold in the heat.
Avoid increased pressure on soles of feet (no jogging, aerobics, power walking, jumping).
Avoid increased pressure on palms of hands (do not use garden tools, screwdrivers, knives for chopping or performing other tasks that require squeezing hand(s) on a hard surface).

Hypercalcemia of Malignancy

Hypercalcemia occurs commonly in patients with breast cancer, lung cancer and multiple myeloma and causes significant symptoms for the patient, including nausea, vomiting, fatigue, dehydration, renal failure and mental status changes. Because of the risk of intravascular volume depletion due to hypercalcemia, all patients should be treated with hydration. Patients with mild hypercalcemia (corrected calcium < 12 mg/dL and no symptoms) may receive oral or IV hydration, all others should receive IV hydration. Loop diuretics, such as furosemide, should only be given after dehydration is corrected. Patients with moderate to severe hypercalcemia (corrected calcium > 12 mg/dL or symptomatic) should be treated with an IV bisphosphonate. Denosumab is an alternative in patients who cannot receive or have not responded to bisphosphonates. Calcium lowering effects of bisphosphonates and denosumab are expected to be observed in 1 – 3 days. Calcitonin lowers serum calcium in 2-6 hours and can be used concurrently with bisphosphonates or denosumab in patients with symptomatic hypercalcemia. Tachyphylaxis to calcitonin develops with repeated dosing, so therapy should be limited to 48 hours. Long term bone resorption of calcium due to cancer can cause significant bone pain and a high risk of skeletal damage (fractures, spinal cord compression, etc.). Bisphosphonates or denosumab are used early in metastatic disease to prevent skeletal related events.

Hypercalcemia of Malignancy Treatment

TREATMENT	MOA	ONSET	DURATION	DEGREE OF HYPERCALCEMIA*
Hydration with normal saline and loop diuretics	↑ renal calcium excretion	Minutes to hours	Only during length of infusion	Mild (oral or IV hydration) Moderate Severe
Calcitonin *(Miacalcin)* 4-8 units/kg IM/SC Q12H	Inhibits bone resorption, ↑ renal calcium excretion	2-6 hours	48 hours max (risk of tachyphylaxis)	Moderate Severe

Hypercalcemia of Malignancy Treatment Continued

TREATMENT	MOA	ONSET	DURATION	DEGREE OF HYPERCALCEMIA*
IV Bisphosphonates **Zoledronic acid *(Zometa)*** 4 mg IV once, may repeat in 7 days if needed. Do not infuse over < 15 minutes due to increased risk of renal toxicity. Dose does not need to be adjusted for mild-moderate renal insufficiency when used for hypercalcemia. (Do not confuse with *Reclast*, which is dosed at 5 mg IV yearly for osteoporosis - see Osteoporosis chapter) Pamidronate *(Aredia)* 60-90 mg IV over 2-24 hrs once, may repeat in 7 days if needed.	Inhibits bone resorption by stopping osteoclast function	24-72 hours	2-4 weeks	Mild Moderate Severe
Denosumab *(Xgeva)* 120 mg SC on days 1, 8 and 15 of the first month, then monthly (Do not confuse with *Prolia*, which is dosed at 60 mg SC every 6 months for osteoporosis - see Osteoporosis chapter)	Monoclonal antibody that blocks the interaction between RANKL and RANK (a receptor on osteoclasts), preventing osteoclast formation	24-72 hours	~1 month	Moderate Severe

* *Degree of hypercalcemia – Mild: corrected calcium < 12 mg/dL, Moderate: corrected calcium 12-14 mg/dL, Severe: corrected calcium >14 mg/dL. Corrected Calcium = Calcium (reported) + [(4 – Albumin) x 0.8 mg/dL]*

SAFE HANDLING OF HAZARDOUS AGENTS

Chemotherapy agents are hazardous drugs that are considered carcinogenic, mutagenic, and teratogenic. To limit exposure to these agents, pharmacies should have written procedures for handling these drugs safely. The United States Pharmacopeia (USP) chapters 797 and 800 are standards for the preparation and handling of hazardous drugs and should be used by facilities that prepare chemotherapy agents. Refer to the Sterile Compounding chapter for further information.

Routes of exposure include inhalation, ingestion, dermal contact, and accidental injections. The most common type of accidental exposure is inhalation of the aerosolized drug. A vertical flow class II biological safety cabinet (chemo hood) or compounding aseptic containment isolator (glove box/isolator) should be used at all times in addition to chemo-gowns and chemo-block gloves (preferably double gloving). The gowns should be made of lint-free, low-permeability fabric with a solid front, long sleeves, and tight-fitting elastic cuffs. Drug preparation should take place in a negative-pressure environment. Chemotherapy spill kits should be readily available and located in areas of the institution in which chemotherapy agents are handled. Cytotoxic waste should be disposed of properly, IV bags should be labeled "Chemotherapeutic: Dispose of Properly" or similar, and patients should be informed of proper methods of disposing of potentially contaminated body waste (such as flushing the toilet twice). Patients should be advised not to split or crush oral chemotherapy agents, as this may present a hazard to others in the household. Caregivers should wear gloves when handling oral chemotherapy agents. Unused oral chemotherapy agents should not be flushed down the toilet.

Many chemotherapy agents are vesicants, which means they may cause tissue necrosis if the IV drug accidentally leaks from the vein into the surrounding tissue (also called extravasation). Major vesicant drug classes include anthracyclines and vinca alkaloids. Care should be taken to avoid extravasation of these drugs by administering them through freshly started peripheral IVs or central venous catheters. If extravasation occurs, apply cold compresses (except with the vinca alkaloids and etoposide, use warm compresses) and the antidotes below depending on the drug extravasated:

- Anthracyclines: dexrazoxane (*Totect*) or dimethyl sulfoxide (off label use)
- Vinca alkaloids: hyaluronidase (off label use)

Based on clinical experience, a limited number of chemotherapy agents may be administered intrathecally. This is usually accomplished by performing a lumbar puncture and injecting the drug into the cerebrospinal fluid. Drugs that may be administered intrathecally include cytarabine, methotrexate, hydrocortisone, and thiotepa and they must be preservative-free.

Unfortunately, accidental intrathecal administration of vincristine has been reported. Intrathecal administration of vincristine is fatal. Care must be taken to properly label vincristine to avoid accidental intrathecal administration. Do not dispense vincristine in a syringe. Vincristine is prepared in small volume IVPB solutions (50 – 100 mL) to avoid the risk of accidental intrathecal administration.

TIMING OF VACCINATIONS

Vaccination during chemotherapy should be avoided because the antibody response is suboptimal. When chemotherapy is being planned, vaccination should precede the initiation of chemotherapy by ≥ 2 weeks. Patients on chemotherapy may receive the inactivated seasonal influenza vaccine in between cycles of chemotherapy. The administration of live vaccines to immunocompromised patients must be avoided. Live vaccines can generally be administered at least 3 months after discontinuation of chemotherapy.

56

ONCOLOGY II: COMMON CANCER TYPES & TREATMENT

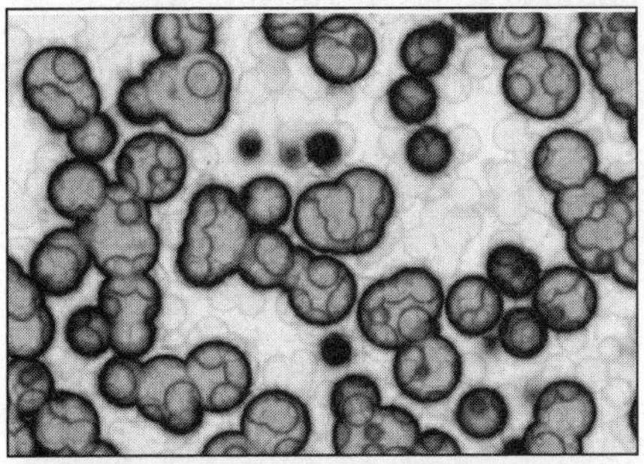

GUIDELINES/REFERENCES

National Comprehensive Cancer Network (NCCN). www.nccn.org (accessed 2016 November 28)

American Society of Clinical Oncology (ASCO). www.asco.org (accessed 2016 November 28)

We gratefully acknowledge the assistance of Doreen Pon, PharmD, BCOP, BCPS, Assistant Professor at Western University of Health Sciences and Muoi Gi, PharmD, BCPS, BCOP, Oncology Pharmacy Residency Director at the VA San Diego Healthcare System and D. Raymond Weber, PharmD, BSPharm, BCOP, BCPS, RPh, Associate Professor, Notre Dame University of Maryland School of Pharmacy, in preparing this chapter.

BREAST AND PROSTATE CANCER

Treatment for most specific malignancies is outside the scope of basic competency. However, treatment of prostate cancer and breast cancer often includes oral medications that are routinely dispensed from community pharmacies. It is important that the pharmacist is familiar with proper use of these medications, side effects and the primary counseling points.

Breast Cancer

Breast cancer is the most commonly diagnosed cancer and the second most common cause of cancer deaths among females in the US.

Treatment of Early Stage Breast Cancer (Stage I-II)

Most patients with early stage breast cancer are treated with multi-modality therapy, including surgery, radiation therapy, chemotherapy, and hormonal therapy. Adjuvant treatment with chemotherapy and hormonal therapy (given after the primary treatment) will help to decrease the risk of disease recurrence and improve long-term survival. Patients whose breast cancer cells overexpress HER2 should receive a HER2-targeted monoclonal antibody, such as trastuzumab, in addition to cytotoxic chemotherapy. Breast cancers are classified by the presence or absence of hormone receptors, estrogen receptors (ER) and progesterone receptors (PR); most breast cancers are hormone receptor positive. Patients who are estrogen and/or progesterone receptor positive (ER+/PR+) are candidates for adjuvant hormonal therapy. The choice of therapy depends on the menopausal status of the patient.

- Patients who are premenopausal should be treated with tamoxifen for 5 years. Their menopausal status should then be reassessed. If they are still premenopausal, they should receive tamoxifen for an additional 5 years. If they are now postmenopausal, they may receive either tamoxifen or an aromatase inhibitor (AI) for an additional 5 years.

- Patients who are postmenopausal should be treated with an aromatase inhibitor or tamoxifen for 5 years. However, treatment with an aromatase inhibitor is preferred.
- Patients who are hormone receptor negative (ER-/PR-) do not benefit from adjuvant hormonal therapy.

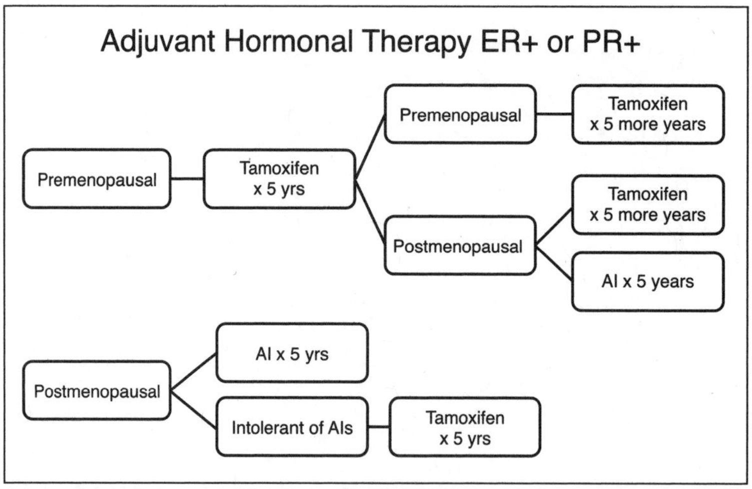

Treatment of Metastatic Breast Cancer (Stage IV)

Treatment of patients with metastatic breast cancer is influenced by the site of metastases and HER2 status. Patients with metastatic breast cancer may have visceral metastases (involvement of vital organs, such as the lungs, liver, brain) and/or nonvisceral metastases (involvement of the skin or bone).

- Patients with visceral metastases that are immediately life-threatening are usually treated with cytotoxic chemotherapy, which acts rapidly. HER2-targeted monoclonal antibodies should be given in addition to cytotoxic chemotherapy for patients who are HER2-positive.
- Patients with nonvisceral metastases or non-life-threatening visceral metastases can be treated with hormonal therapy, which acts more slowly but is better tolerated than cytotoxic chemotherapy.
- Fulvestrant with palbociclib is currently the preferred treatment in postmenopausal Stage IV hormone positive breast cancer.

Hormonal Therapies for Breast Cancer

Hormonal therapies for breast cancer work by interfering with estrogen-stimulated growth of breast cancer cells. In premenopausal women, the ovaries are the primary producers of endogenous estrogen. In postmenopausal women and women who have had their ovaries removed, the adrenal glands are the primary producers of endogenous estrogen.

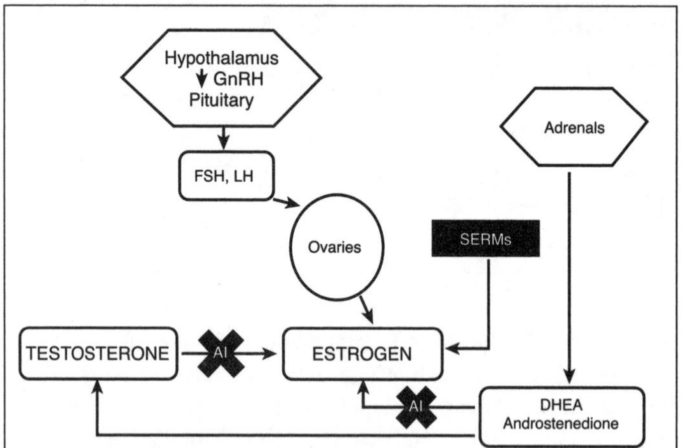

SERMs: selective estrogen receptor modifiers
AI: aromatase inhibitors

- Selective estrogen receptor modifiers (SERMs) have estrogen antagonist activity in breast tissue, but act as estrogen agonists in some other tissues, including bone. These are used for breast cancer in hormone receptor positive tumors. Most SERMs are used in postmenopausal women, however, tamoxifen is used in both pre- and postmenopausal women and in men with breast cancer.
- Aromatase inhibitors (AIs) block the enzyme required for the peripheral conversion of adrenally produced estrogen precursors to estrogen. Since the majority of estrogen in premenopausal women is produced in the ovaries, not the adrenal glands, AIs are ineffective in adequately suppressing estrogen-stimulated cancer cell growth in premenopausal women. Therefore, AIs are approved for

postmenopausal women only (and not in men with breast CA). AIs may occasionally be used in premenopausal women, but must be used in combination with a gondaotropin-releasing hormone (GnRH) agonist to suppress ovarian production of estrogen.

DRUG	UNIQUE CONCERNS	SAFETY/SIDE EFFECTS/MONITORING

Selective Estrogen Receptor Modulators

DRUG	UNIQUE CONCERNS	SAFETY/SIDE EFFECTS/MONITORING
Tamoxifen ***(Nolvadex, Soltamox)*** 20 mg PO daily **Fulvestrant** ***(Faslodex)*** 500 mg IM days 1, 15, 29, then monthly Raloxifene *(Evista)* 60 mg PO daily Toremifene *(Farestron)* 60 mg PO daily	Tamoxifen ↑ risk of uterine or endometrial cancers, others decrease risk Tamoxifen is a major substrate of CYP 3A4, 2C9 and 2D6. Watch for drug interactions, particularly with 2D6 inhibitors; recommend venlafaxine for hot flashes over fluoxetine and paroxetine (strong 2D6 inhibitors) for patients on tamoxifen	**BOXED WARNINGS** ↑ risk of uterine or endometrial cancers (tamoxifen), ↑ risk of thromboembolic events such as VTE, PE, stroke (tamoxifen, raloxifene), QT prolongation (toremifene) **CONTRAINDICATIONS** Concomitant warfarin therapy (tamoxifen), history of DVT/PE (tamoxifen, raloxifene), pregnancy and breastfeeding (raloxifene), QT prolongation, hypokalemia, hypomagnesemia (toremifene) **SIDE EFFECTS** DVT/PE, menopausal symptoms, hot flashes, flushing, edema, weight gain, hypertension, mood changes, amenorrhea, vaginal bleeding/discharge, arthralgia/myalgia, skin changes, cataracts (tamoxifen) **NOTES** Safety issue – see Pregnancy Category MedGuide required (tamoxifen, raloxifene)

Aromatase Inhibitors

DRUG	UNIQUE CONCERNS	SAFETY/SIDE EFFECTS/MONITORING
Anastrozole ***(Arimidex)*** 1 mg PO daily **Letrozole** ***(Femara)*** 2.5 mg PO daily **Exemestane** ***(Aromasin)*** 25 mg PO daily	Higher risk of osteoporosis due to decreased bone mineral density; consider Ca and vitamin D supplementation, weight bearing exercise, DEXA screening Higher risk of CVD compared to SERMs	**CONTRAINDICATIONS** Pregnancy **SIDE EFFECTS** Arthralgia/myalgia, bone pain, lethargy/fatigue, menopausal symptoms, hot flashes, N/V, rash, hepatotoxicity, hypertension, dyslipidemia

Cyclin-Dependent Kinase Inhibitor – inhibits downstream signaling and tumor growth

DRUG	UNIQUE CONCERNS	SAFETY/SIDE EFFECTS/MONITORING
Palbociclib *(Ibrance)* 125 mg PO daily for 21 of 28 day cycle	Take with food Avoid with CYP3A4 inhibitors or inducers Use with letrozole or fulvestrant significantly improves outcomes	**SIDE EFFECTS** Myelosuppression (mild), N/V/D, thromboembolic events (PE), fatigue, alopecia, infection, blurred vision

Patient Counseling

Tamoxifen

- This medication can be used to reduce your chance of getting breast cancer, reduce the spread of breast cancer or be used to cure breast cancer.
- Swallow the tablet whole daily, with water or another non-alcoholic liquid. You can take it with or without food.

- If you forget a dose, take it when you remember, then take the next dose as usual. If it is almost time for your next dose or you remember at your next dose, do not take extra tablets to make up the missed dose.
- Do not become pregnant while taking this medication or for 2 months after you stop. This medication can stop hormonal birth control methods from working correctly (birth control pills, patches, injections, rings and implants). Therefore, while taking this medication, another method of contraception should be used, such as condoms, diaphragms with spermicide, or IUDs.
- If you become pregnant, stop taking this medication right away and call your healthcare provider.
- Be sure to have regular gynecology check-ups, breast exams and mammograms to check for signs of breast cancer and cancer of the endometrium (lining of the uterus). Your healthcare provider will tell you how often.
- Read the MedGuide that has been given to you. This medication can cause some serious, but rare, side effects such as endometrial cancer, stroke, or a blood clot. This medication can also increase the risk of getting cataracts.
- The most common side effects include hot flashes, hypertension, peripheral edema, mood changes, depression, skin changes, and vaginal discharge.
- You should call your healthcare provider right away if you develop:
  - Vaginal bleeding or bloody discharge that is a rusty or brown color, change in your monthly bleeding, such as in the amount or timing of bleeding or increased clotting, or pain or pressure in your pelvis (below your belly button).
  - Sudden chest pain, shortness of breath, coughing up blood, pain, tenderness, or swelling in one or both of your legs.
  - Sudden weakness, tingling or numbness (in your face, arm or leg, especially on one side of your body), sudden confusion, trouble speaking or sudden trouble seeing in one or both eyes, sudden trouble walking, dizziness, loss of balance or coordination, or sudden severe headache with no known cause.
  - Signs of liver problems like lack of appetite and yellowing of your skin or whites of your eyes.
- For raloxifene *(Evista)* – discontinue at least 72 hours prior to and during prolonged immobilization (e.g., post-surgical recovery, prolonged bed rest), and avoid prolonged restrictions of movement during travel because of the increased risk of blood clots.

Aromatase Inhibitors

- This medication is used to treat breast cancer in women who have finished menopause. This medication does not work in women who have not finished menopause. It can be taken with or without food.
- If you miss a dose, take it as soon as you remember. If it is almost time for your next dose, skip the missed dose. Take your next regularly scheduled dose. Do not take two doses at the same time.
- Common side effects include hot flashes, weakness, joint pain, bone pain, osteoporosis, mood changes, high blood pressure, depression, and rash.
- This medication can cause rare, but serious, adverse effects such as heart disease, increased cholesterol, skin reactions, allergic reactions, and liver problems.
- Call your healthcare provider right away if you develop:
  - Chest pain, shortness of breath.
  - Any skin lesions, ulcers, or blisters.
  - Swelling of the face, lips, tongue, or throat, trouble swallowing, or trouble breathing.
  - A general feeling of not being well with yellowing of the skin or whites of the eyes or pain on the right side of your abdomen.

- Tell your healthcare provider about all the medications you take, including prescription and non-prescription medicines, vitamins, and herbal supplements. This medication should not be taken with tamoxifen or any medicines containing estrogen (e.g., pills, patches, creams, rings, or suppositories).

Prostate Cancer

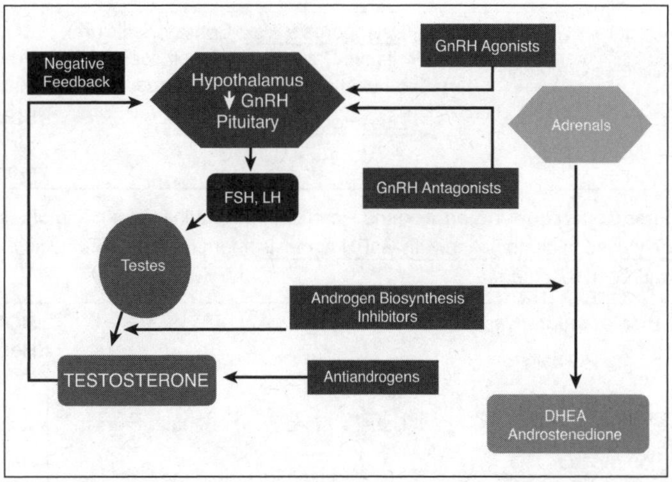

Prostate cancer is the most commonly diagnosed cancer and the second most common cause of cancer deaths among males in the US. Most patients are diagnosed at earlier stages of the disease, before the prostate cancer has metastasized to other organs. At 5 years after diagnosis, almost all patients with nonmetastatic prostate cancer will still be alive, whereas only approximately one-third of patients with metastatic prostate cancer will still be alive. Nonmetastatic prostate cancer can be treated with surgery, radiation, with or without pharmacologic androgen deprivation therapy (ADT), or watchful waiting. First-line treatment for metastatic prostate cancer is usually pharmacologic ADT ("chemical castration") with a gonadotropin releasing hormone (GnRH) agonist or antagonist. Metastatic prostate cancer that has failed to respond to ADT is called "castration-resistant" and may be treated with additional hormonal agents listed below or cytotoxic chemotherapy.

Hormonal Therapies for Prostate Cancer

Hormonal therapy for prostate cancer is referred to as ADT. The goal is to reduce the concentration of testosterone in the body. As a result, ADT causes symptoms of hypogonadism, such as hot flashes, loss of libido/impotence, gynecomastia, hair thinning and peripheral edema. Long term therapy can be associated with osteoporosis and metabolic complications, such as weight gain, hyperlipidemia, and diabetes. They are also associated with QT prolongation.

DRUG	UNIQUE CONCERNS	SAFETY/SIDE EFFECTS/MONITORING
Gonadotropin-Releasing Hormone (GnRH) Agonists – also referred to as luteinizing hormone releasing hormone (LHRH) agonists. These drugs reduce testosterone synthesis through a negative feedback mechanism. They cause an initial surge in testosterone concentrations, followed by a gradual reduction in testosterone concentrations. This initial surge in testosterone may cause symptoms of "tumor flare" in patients with metastatic prostate cancer. Symptoms of tumor flare may include bone pain or problems with urination. To prevent symptoms of tumor flare, antiandrogens are given for several weeks in conjunction with the initiation of GnRH agonists.		
Leuprolide *(Lupron, Lupron Depot,* *Eligard)* **Goserelin *(Zoladex)*** Histrelin *(Supprelin LA, Vantas)* Triptorelin *(Trelstar)* Given SC or IM monthly or less frequently (up to once yearly) depending on formulation	Osteoporosis Risk: Consider calcium, vitamin D supplementation, weight bearing exercise, DEXA screening Tumor Flare: Consider antiandrogen therapy when initiating GnRH agonists in patients with metastatic prostate cancer Leuprolide and goserelin can be used to treat breast cancer in women	**CONTRAINDICATIONS** Pregnancy (all) Breastfeeding, vaginal bleeding (leuprolide) **SIDE EFFECTS** Hot flashes, impotence, gynecomastia, peripheral edema, bone pain, injection site pain, QT prolongation, dyslipidemia, hyperglycemia

Prostate Cancer Treatment Continued

DRUG	UNIQUE CONCERNS	SAFETY/SIDE EFFECTS/MONITORING
Gonadotropin Releasing Hormone Antagonist – does not cause an initial surge in testosterone concentrations.		
Degarelix *(Firmagon)* Given SC monthly	Osteoporosis Risk: Consider calcium, vitamin D supplementation, weight bearing exercise, DEXA screening Does not cause tumor flare	**CONTRAINDICATIONS** Pregnancy **SIDE EFFECTS** Similar to GnRH agonists plus hypersensitivity reactions
First Generation Antiandrogens – competitively inhibit the binding of testosterone to prostate cancer cells. They are only used in combination with GnRH agonists. Monotherapy is ineffective due to an up-regulation in the expression of androgen receptors.		
Bicalutamide *(Casodex)* 50 mg PO daily		**BOXED WARNINGS** Hepatotoxicity (flutamide), interstitial pneumonitis (nilutamide) **CONTRAINDICATIONS** Use in women, especially in pregnancy (bicalutamide); severe hepatic impairment (flutamide, nilutamide) **SIDE EFFECTS** Hot flashes, gynecomastia, edema, asthenia, hepatotoxicity, ↑ risk of CVD, N/V/D
Flutamide *(Eulexin)* 250 mg PO Q8H	Causes more diarrhea than others in class	
Nilutamide *(Nilandron)*	Can cause night blindness and disulfiram reactions (avoid alcohol)	
Second Generation Antiandrogen – unlike first generation antiandrogens, it does not cause an upregulation in the expression of androgen receptors and can be used as monotherapy.		
Enzalutamide *(Xtandi)* 160 mg (4 x 40 mg capsules) daily		**CONTRAINDICATIONS** Pregnancy (partner to use effective contraception) **WARNINGS** Seizures **SIDE EFFECTS** Hypertension, peripheral edema, hot flashes, fatigue
Androgen Biosynthesis Inhibitor - interferes with specific enzymes involved in the biosynthesis of steroid hormones in the testes and adrenal gland to decrease testosterone production. Must give with prednisone to cause a negative feedback on the production of aldosterone and prevent symptoms of hyperaldosteronism (hypertension, fluid retention and hypokalemia).		
Abiraterone *(Zytiga)* 1,000 mg (4 x 250 mg tablets) daily on an empty stomach (1 hr before or 2 hrs after food) Given with prednisone 5 mg BID	Avoid concurrent use with strong CYP3A4 inducers; if used with a strong 3A4 inducer, dose adjustment required	**CONTRAINDICATIONS** Pregnancy **SIDE EFFECTS** Mineralocorticoid excess: fluid retention, HTN, hypokalemia, hepatotoxcity Hyperglycemia, ↑ TGs, hypophosphatemia, hot flashes

Patient Counseling

Leuprolide for Prostate Cancer

- This medication is used to treat your prostrate cancer and will lower sex hormones (testosterone and estrogen) produced by the body.

- If you are taking this medication for metastatic prostate cancer, then some patients experience worsening of their prostate cancer symptoms upon starting this medication due to "tumor flare". To minimize this side effect, an antiandrogen (such as bicalutamide) may be started at least 1 week prior to your injection.
- Common side effects include hot flashes and impotence.
- During the first few weeks of treatment you may experience increased bone pain and increased difficulty in urinating.
- If you have a change in strength on one side of your body that is greater than the other side, trouble speaking or thinking, change in balance, or blurred eyesight you will need to see a healthcare provider right away.

CHEMOTHERAPY REGIMENS AND DOSING

Cancer treatment depends on multiple factors, including cancer type, extent of disease and patient factors. When chemotherapy is used, the regimens are usually in combinations chosen for efficacy, synergy and ability to target cells with different resistance mechanisms and different stages of replication. Regimens are usually administered in cycles involving one or more drugs, given once, or multiple times, such as over several consecutive days, followed by days or weeks without treatment. The break in treatment will allow the patient time to recover from side effects.

CANCER THERAPEUTIC AGENTS

Traditional cytotoxic cancer therapeutic agents kill cancer cells by interfering with cellular replication. Cell cycle specific agents, such as antimetabolites and microtubule inhibitors, kill cancer cells during specific phases of the cell cycle, while cell cycle non-specific agents, such as alkylating agents and anthracyclines, can kill cancer cells in any phase of the cell cycle. Regardless of cell cycle specificity, traditional cytotoxic cancer therapeutic agents are more effective at killing cells undergoing cell division. Therefore, cancers that are characterized by more rapid cell growth, such as acute leukemias, are very susceptible to the cytotoxic effects of traditional cytotoxic cancer therapeutic agents. However, because other cells in the body are also rapidly dividing, such as those in the gastrointestinal tract and bone marrow, they are also susceptible to being killed by cytotoxic chemotherapy. This is

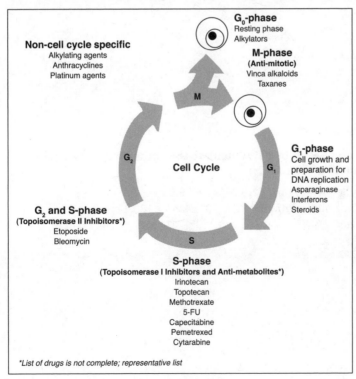

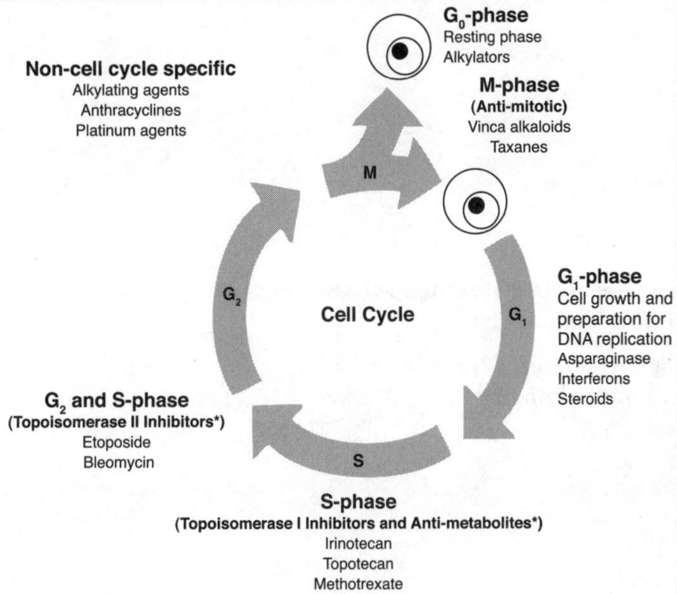

List of drugs is not complete; representative list

PHASES OF THE CELL CYCLE

M
Mitosis – cell divides into 2 daughter cells

G_0
Resting phase post mitosis – no cell division occurs

G_1
Post-mitotic phase – where enzymes and proteins are synthesized

S
DNA synthesis and duplication occurs

G_2
Pre-mitotic phase – RNA and proteins are produced to prepare for cell division

why many cytotoxic cancer therapeutic agents cause common toxicities such as diarrhea, mucositis, and myelosuppression.

Some of the other cancer therapeutic agents are considered to be more targeted. Rather than non-specifically affecting any cell undergoing replication, these agents are designed to recognize specific biomarkers that are present on cancer cells or other cells that are essential for cancer cell growth. Drugs that are considered "targeted" include monoclonal antibodies and kinase inhibitors (TKIs). In general, these targeted agents have side effect profiles that are very different from traditional cytotoxic agents.

Body Surface Area (BSA) Calculations

Chemotherapy may be dosed using flat or fixed dosing, patient's weight (mg/kg), or patient's body surface area (BSA). There are several BSA formulas, but the most commonly used are: DuBois and DuBois, and **Mosteller**. Actual body weight that is commonly used for calculating the dose in oncology. Use the patient's actual body weight for BSA and dosage calculations in oncology unless instructed otherwise.

Dubois and Dubois Equation

$$\text{BSA (m}^2\text{)} = 0.007184 \times [\text{Height (cm)}]^{0.725} \times [\text{Weight (kg)}]^{0.425}$$

Example

A patient has a weight of 175 pounds and height of 6'1". Calculate the patient's BSA using the DuBois and DuBois formula. Round to the nearest hundredth.

Convert weight in pounds to kilograms by dividing by 2.2: 175/2.2 = 79.5 kg
Convert height in inches to centimeters by multiplying by 2.54: 73 inches x 2.54 = 185.4 cm

$$\text{BSA (m}^2\text{)} = 0.007184 \times [\text{Height(cm)}]^{0.725} \times [\text{Weight(kg)}]^{0.425}$$

$$\text{BSA (m}^2\text{)} = 0.007184 \times (185.4)^{0.725} \times (79.5)^{0.425}$$

$$\text{BSA (m}^2\text{)} = 2.03\ \text{m}^2$$

Mosteller Equation

$$\text{BSA (m}^2\text{)} = \sqrt{\frac{\text{Ht (cm)} \times \text{Wt (kg)}}{3{,}600}}$$

Example

A patient has a weight of 175 pounds and height of 6'1". Calculate the patient's BSA using the Mosteller formula. Round to the nearest hundredth.

Convert weight in pounds to kilograms by dividing by 2.2: 175/2.2 = 79.5 kg
Convert height in inches to centimeters by multiplying by 2.54: 73" x 2.54 = 185.4 cm

$$\text{BSA (m}^2\text{)} = \sqrt{\frac{185.4\ \text{cm} \times 79.5\ \text{kg}}{3{,}600}} = 2.02\ \text{m}^2$$

A patient with a BSA of 2.02 m^2 is going to receive paclitaxel for lung cancer at a dose of 175 mg/m^2. Calculate the dose of paclitaxel that this patient will receive. Round to the nearest whole number.

$$175\ mg/m^2 \times 2.02\ m^2 = 354\ mg$$

A patient with a BSA of 2.02 m^2 is going to receive paclitaxel for lung cancer at a dose of 175 mg/m^2. Paclitaxel is available as a 6 mg/mL solution. If the patient's dose is 354 mg, how many milliliters will be needed for the dose?

$$354\ mg \times \frac{1\ mL}{6\ mg} = 59\ mL$$

TRADITIONAL CYTOTOXIC CANCER THERAPEUTIC AGENTS

The discussion that follows highlights the more commonly encountered "prototype drugs" in each class, but is not intended to be comprehensive in scope. Throughout this section, the traditional cytotoxic cancer chemotherapy agents will be categorized into either cell cycle non-specific agents or cell cycle specific agents.

CELL CYCLE NON-SPECIFIC AGENTS

Alkylating Agents

Alkylating agents work by cross-linking DNA strands and inhibiting protein synthesis and DNA synthesis.

- Many of the agents are available in oral and/or intravenous formulations.
- Can cause DNA mutations that lead to "secondary malignancies" (usually acute leukemia).
- Cyclophosphamide and ifosfamide produce a metabolite, acrolein, that concentrates in the bladder and can cause hemorrhagic cystitis. Mesna is a chemoprotectant that inactivates this toxic metabolite in the bladder without interfering with the cytotoxic efficacy.

<table>
<tr><th>DRUG</th><th>UNIQUE CONCERNS</th><th>SAFETY/SIDE EFFECTS/ MONITORING</th></tr>
<tr><td>Cyclophosphamide (Cytoxan)
Ifosfamide (Ifex)</td><td>Hemorrhagic cystitis: Ensure adequate hydration and give mesna
Mesna (Mesnex) is a chemoprotectant that must be given prophylactically with ifosfamide and with high doses of cyclophosphamide</td><td rowspan="5">BOXED WARNINGS
Myelosuppression
Hemorrhagic cystitis (ifosfamide, cyclophosphamide)
Pulmonary toxicity (carmustine)
Neurotoxicity (ifosfamide)
Hepatic necrosis (dacarbazine)

WARNINGS
Severe skin reactions, including SJS/TEN; reactivation of infections, including HBV, CMV, TB, HSV; hepatotoxicity (bendamustine)

SIDE EFFECTS
Pulmonary toxicity (busulfan, carmustine, lomustine)
SIADH (cyclophosphamide)
Mucositis, moderate-high emetic potential, alopecia, secondary malignancies, neurotoxicity</td></tr>
<tr><td>Carmustine (BiCNU, Gliadel Wafer)</td><td>Use non-PVC bag and tubing due to absorption to PVC</td></tr>
<tr><td>Dacarbazine (DTIC-Dome)</td><td>Protect from light (decomposed drug turns pink)</td></tr>
<tr><td>Procarbazine (Matulane)</td><td>MAO inhibitor, avoid interacting drugs/foods</td></tr>
<tr><td>Altretamine (Hexalen)
Bendamustine (Bendeka, Treanda)
Busulfan (Myleran, Busulfex)
Lomustine (CeeNU, Gleostine)
Mechlorethamine (Mustargen, Valchlor topical gel)
Melphalan (Alkeran, Evomela)
Temozolomide (Temodar)</td><td>Lomustine: fatal toxicity occurs with overdosage. Do not dispense more than one dose at a time. Both healthcare provider and pharmacist should emphasize to the patient that only one dose of lomustine is taken every 6 weeks.</td></tr>
</table>

Platinum-Based Compounds

Similar to alkylating agents in that they cross-link DNA and interfere with DNA synthesis and cell replication.

- Due to the platinum content, they can cause a few toxicities that are similar to symptoms of heavy metal poisoning, such as peripheral sensory neuropathy, ototoxicity, and nephrotoxicity.
- Cisplatin is associated with the highest incidence of nephrotoxicity and chemotherapy-induced nausea and vomiting (CINV).
- All platinum-based compounds are renally eliminated and require dose adjustments for renal impairment.

DRUG	UNIQUE CONCERNS	SAFETY/SIDE EFFECTS/MONITORING
CISplatin *(Platinol)*	Nephrotoxicity, ototoxicity (both cumulative) Doses are usually limited to ≤ 100 mg/m²/cycle Nephrotoxicity: Monitor renal function, intake/output, Mg and K (levels may decrease) and ensure adequate IV hydration (1-2 L) before each dose Amifostine *(Ethyol)* is a chemoprotectant that may be given prophylactically to prevent nephrotoxicity Ototoxicity: perform audiograms at baseline and before each dose Highly emetogenic: 3 drug antiemetic regimen required for prevention	**BOXED WARNINGS** Anaphylactic-like reactions – risk increases with repeated exposure; caution when > 6 cycles of carboplatin are used Myelosuppression (carboplatin and cisplatin) Renal toxicity, ototoxicity, doses > 100 mg/m²/cycle must be confirmed with prescriber (cisplatin) **CONTRAINDICATIONS** Pre-existing renal impairment, hearing impairment (cisplatin) Myelosuppression (cisplatin and carboplatin) **SIDE EFFECTS** Peripheral neuropathy (cumulative dose-related), myelosuppression, ↑ LFTs N/V (cisplatin, carboplatin)
CARBOplatin *(Paraplatin)*	Myelosuppression is dose-related. Doses for adults are commonly calculated by target AUC using the Calvert Formula: Total carboplatin dose (mg) = (Target AUC) x (GFR + 25) where: - AUC can range from 2-8 mg/mL x min - GFR is commonly "capped" at 125 mL/min	
Oxaliplatin *(Eloxatin)*	Acute sensory neuropathy: Occurs 1-7 days after administration and can be exacerbated by exposure to cold, including drinking cold beverages	

Anthracyclines

Work by several mechanisms, including intercalation into DNA, inhibiting topoisomerase II, and creating oxygen-free radicals that damage cells.

- Cardiotoxicity is associated with all anthracyclines and is manifested as cardiomyopathy and heart failure. The risk for cardiotoxicity is related to the total cumulative anthracycline dose the patient has received over their lifetime. The recommended lifetime maximum cumulative anthracycline dose differs for each anthracycline, but is best defined for

TO REDUCE DOXORUBICIN CARDIOTOXICITY:

1. Keep track of the lifetime cumulative doxorubicin dose for each patient

[Doxorubicin Dose in mg/m²/cycle] x [total number of cycles received] = Cumulative Doxorubicin Dose in mg/m²

Example: [Doxorubicin 50 mg/m²/cycle] x [6 cycles] = 300 mg/m²

2. Lifetime maximum cumulative doxorubicin dose = 450-550 mg/m²
3. Monitor left ventricular ejection fraction (LVEF) before and after treatment (using echocardiogram or MUGA scan)
4. Dexrazoxane *(Zinecard)*, a chemoprotectant, may be considered when the doxorubicin cumulative dose > 300 mg/m²

doxorubicin. Dexrazoxane (*Zinecard)* is a chemoprotectant indicated for prevention of doxorubicin-induced cardiotoxicity (see box).

- Anthracyclines are potent vesicants, however, liposomal anthracyclines are not. Dexrazoxane *(Totect)* is an antidote that can be used for accidental doxorubicin extravasation. Note that dexrazoxane has two brand names, each used for a different indication.

DRUG	UNIQUE CONCERNS	SAFETY/SIDE EFFECTS/MONITORING
DOXOrubicin *(Adriamycin)* DAUNOrubicin *(Cerubidine)* EpiRUBicin *(Ellence)* IDArubicin *(Idamycin PFS)* Valrubicin *(Valstar)*- only used as bladder instillation, but can have systemic toxicity	Potent vesicants (tissue necrosis if extravasated) Red urine discoloration Doxorubicin: do not exceed 450-550 mg/m^2 (total lifetime cumulative dose) Dexrazoxane *(Totect)* for extravasation; *(Zinecard)* for cardioprotection at higher doses N/V - give antiemetics	**BOXED WARNINGS** Myocardial toxicity, vesicant, myelosuppression, secondary malignancy Hepatotoxicity (daunorubicin) Renal impairment (daunorubicin, idarubicin) Hepatic impairment - dose reduction (except valrubicin) **CONTRAINDICATIONS** Pre-existing myocardial insufficiency Severe hepatic impairment
DOXOrubicin liposomal *(Doxil, Lipodox50)*	Not a vesicant Red urine discoloration Not interchangeable with non-liposomal formulation	**BOXED WARNINGS** Myocardial toxicity, infusion-related reactions, myelosuppression **SIDE EFFECTS** Hand-foot syndrome
MitoXANTRONE *(Novantrone)* an anthracenedione, related to the anthracyclines	Irritant with vesicant-like properties Blue urine discoloration	**BOXED WARNINGS** Myocardial toxicity, myelosuppression, secondary malignancy

CELL CYCLE SPECIFIC AGENTS

Vinca Alkaloids

Vinca alkaloids inhibit the function of microtubules during M phase.

FOR INTRAVENOUS USE ONLY.
FATAL IF GIVEN BY OTHER ROUTES.

- Peripheral sensory and autonomic neuropathies (constipation) are common. Neuropathies are common side effects because microtubules play an important role in axonal transport in neurons.
  - VinCristine is associated with more CNS toxicity (neuropathy) than the other vinca alkaloids. Accidental intrathecal administration will cause a progressive paralysis and death. Label products to prevent accidental intrathecal administration.
- VinBlastine and vinorelBine are associated with more Bone marrow suppression (myelosuppression) than vincristine.
- Vinca alkaloids are potent vesicants. Use warm compresses and hyaluronidase (off-label use) if extravasation occurs.

DRUG	UNIQUE CONCERNS	SAFETY/SIDE EFFECTS/MONITORING
VinCRIStine *(Vincasar PFS)*	Not myelosuppressive Often "capped" at 2 mg/dose, regardless of the calculated mg/m^2 dose; higher doses may be associated with ↑ risk of neuropathy	**BOXED WARNINGS** Vesicants For IV administration only (intrathecal administration is fatal) **SIDE EFFECTS** Peripheral sensory neuropathy (paresthesias), autonomic neuropathy (gastroparesis, constipation), SIADH
VinBLASTine *(Velban)* VinORELbine *(Navelbine)*	Myelosuppressive	
VinCRIStine liposomal *(Marqibo)*	Not interchangeable with vincristine	

Taxanes

Taxanes inhibit the function of microtubules during M phase.

- Peripheral sensory neuropathies are common side effects since the microtubules play an important role in axonal transport in neurons.
- Severe infusion-related hypersensitivity reactions (HSR) and fatal anaphylaxis can occur with all taxanes. Premedication regimens vary depending on the specific taxane.
- All taxanes are metabolized by the liver and require adjustment for hepatic impairment.
- Drug interaction: elimination of taxanes is reduced when given after cisplatin/carboplatin. Give taxanes before platinum-based compounds.

DRUG	UNIQUE CONCERNS	SAFETY/SIDE EFFECTS/MONITORING
PACLitaxel *(Taxol)*	HSR: Premedicate with diphenhydramine, corticosteroid, H2RA	**BOXED WARNINGS** Severe hypersensitivity reactions (except *Abraxane)*, myelosuppression Fluid retention (docetaxel) **SIDE EFFECTS** Peripheral sensory neuropathy, myalgias, arthralgias, hepatotoxicity, alopecia (less with cabazitaxel) **NOTES** Hypersensitivity reactions are due to the solvent systems, not the taxane. To maintain solubility, paclitaxel contains polyoxyl35/polyoxethylated castor oil (Cremophor EL); docetaxel contains Polysorbate 80. *Abraxane* is paclitaxel bound to albumin without a solvent system. Only isolated case reports of allergic reaction; no need to premedicate. Use non-PVC bag and tubing due to leaching of DEHP (except *Abraxane).*
DOCEtaxel *(Taxotere, Docefez)*	HSR: Premedicate with corticosteroids for 3 days, starting 1 day prior to docetaxel Causes severe fluid retention (characterized by pleural effusion, cardiac tamponade and/or edema); premedicate with dexamethasone Some formulations contain alcohol and may cause symptoms of alcohol intoxication	
Cabazitaxel *(Jevtana)*	HSR: Premedicate with diphenhydramine, corticosteroid, H2RA	
Paclitaxel albumin-bound *(Abraxane)*	No premedication required (see Notes)	

Topoisomerase I Inhibitors

These agents block the coiling and uncoiling of the double-stranded DNA helix during S phase; causes single and double strand breaks in the DNA and prevents religation (sealing the DNA strands back together again) of single strand breaks.

DRUG	UNIQUE CONCERNS	SAFETY/SIDE EFFECTS/MONITORING
Irinotecan ***(Camptosar)***	Acute cholinergic symptoms: Flushing, sweating, abdominal cramps, diarrhea (treat with atropine) Delayed diarrhea: Treat with loperamide (up to 24 mg/day) Pharmacogenomics: Patients homozygous for the UGT1A1*28 allele are at ↑ risk for neutropenia and delayed diarrhea	**BOXED WARNINGS** Myelosuppression Use only when ANC > 1,500 cells/mm^3 and platelets > 100,000 cells/mm^3 (topotecan) Diarrhea (early and late) (irinotecan) **SIDE EFFECTS** N/V/D, alopecia, diarrhea, abdominal pain
Topotecan *(Hycamtin)*		

Topoisomerase II Inhibitors

Block the coiling and uncoiling of double-stranded DNA during the G2 phase; this causes single and double strand breaks in the DNA and prevents religation (sealing the DNA strands back together again) of single strand breaks.

DRUG	UNIQUE CONCERNS	SAFETY/SIDE EFFECTS/MONITORING
Etoposide IV *(Toposar)*	Infusion rate-related hypotension: Infuse over at least 30-60 minutes IV preparation: Prepare solution to a concentration ≤ 0.4 mg/mL to avoid precipitation (due to poor water solubility) Use non-PVC IV bag and tubing due to leaching of DEHP	**BOXED WARNING** Myelosuppression **SIDE EFFECTS** Hypersensitivity reactions, anaphylaxis, secondary malignancies
Etoposide phosphate *(Etopophos)*	Does not have solution concentration limits like etoposide (primarily used if the concentration needs to be ≥ 0.4 mg/mL) Helpful in patients with fluid restriction	
Etoposide capsules ***(VePesid)***	Refrigerate capsules Etoposide IV:PO ratio is 1:2 (50% bioavailability) Doses > 200 mg need to be given in divided doses due to reduced bioavailability	

Pyrimidine Analog Antimetabolites

These agents inhibit pyrimidine synthesis during S phase; an active metabolite (F-UMP) is incorporated into RNA to replace uracil and inhibits cell growth, while another active metabolite (5-dUMP) inhibits thymidylate synthetase.

DRUG	UNIQUE CONCERNS	SAFETY/SIDE EFFECTS/MONITORING
Fluorouracil, "5-FU" *(Adrucil)* *Efudex, Carac, Tolak* and *Fluoroplex* are topical formulations used for actinic keratosis *Efudex* is also used for basal cell carcinoma	Leucovorin: Given with fluorouracil to $\uparrow$ the efficacy of fluorouracil; helps fluorouracil bind more tightly to its target enzyme, thymidylate synthetase Pharmacogenomics: Dihydropyrimidine dehydrogenase (DPD) deficiency $\uparrow$ risk of severe toxicity	**BOXED WARNINGS** Significant $\uparrow$ in INR during and up to 1 month after treatment, monitor INR frequently (capecitabine) **CONTRAINDICATIONS** Severe renal impairment (CrCl < 30 mL/min) (capecitabine) **SIDE EFFECTS** Hand-foot syndrome, cardiotoxicity, diarrhea, photosensitivity, dermatitis, mucositis **NOTES** Uridine triacetate *(Vistogard)* can be given as an antidote for overdose or severe or early toxicity due to DPD deficiency
Capecitabine *(Xeloda)* 2 divided doses 12 hrs apart, given with water within 30 min after a meal	Oral prodrug of fluorouracil Pharmacogenomics: Dihydropyrimidine dehydrogenase (DPD) deficiency $\uparrow$ risk of severe toxicity	
Cytarabine conventional (called "ara-C") Cytarabine liposomal *(DepoCyt)* for intrathecal administration	Cytarabine Syndrome: Fever, flu-like symptoms, myalgia, bone pain, rash	**BOXED WARNINGS** Myelosuppression, hepatotoxicity and GI toxicities (conventional) Chemical arachnoiditis (N/V, HA, fever) is common and can be fatal if untreated - give dexamethasone (liposomal formulation) **SIDE EFFECTS** Pulmonary toxicity, encephalopathy, hand-foot syndrome, neuropathy, conjunctivitis (higher doses require use of steroid eye drops)
Gemcitabine *(Gemzar)*	Infusion rate affects efficacy and toxicity; infuse per institutional protocol	**SIDE EFFECTS** Myelosuppression, flu-like symptoms, hepatotoxicity, pulmonary toxicity

Folate Antimetabolites

Interfere with the enzymes involved in the folic acid cycle, blocking purine and pyrimidine biosynthesis during S phase.

- Folic acid or folic acid analogs +/- vitamin B12 may be required to reduce toxicity caused by interference with the folic acid cycle (myelosuppression, mucositis, diarrhea). With high doses of methotrexate, leucovorin (or levoleucovorin) "rescue" must be given. Leucovorin is the active form of folic acid that is able to bypass the enzyme block of dihydrofolate reductase caused by methotrexate. Note that folic acid is ineffective for high dose methotrexate "rescue".
- Nephrotoxicity is associated with all the folate antimetabolites, but most frequently with high doses of methotrexate (≥ 1 gram/m^2).

DRUG	UNIQUE CONCERNS	SAFETY/SIDE EFFECTS/ MONITORING
Methotrexate *(Trexall, Otrexup, Rasuvo, Rheumatrex)* Doses used for cancer are much higher than doses used for RA or psoriasis. RA/psoriasis doses are given weekly, not daily. If given intrathecally, use only the preservative-free formulation of methotrexate Avoid use of MTX – this is an error prone abbreviation	"High-dose" methotrexate (≥ 500 mg/m^2) requires leucovorin (folinic acid) "rescue". "Moderate-dose" methotrexate (100-499 mg/m2) may require leucovorin rescue. LEVOleucovorin *(Fusilev)* is also available as the levo (L) isomer (the active biological moiety) of leucovorin and is dosed at 1/2 the dose of leucovorin. Monitor methotrexate levels and renal function daily and continue leucovorin until level is ≤ 0.05-0.1 micromolar. Hydration and IV sodium bicarbonate must be given to alkalinize the urine and ↓ risk of nephrotoxicity caused by high doses. Ensure patient does not have 3rd spacing (ascites, pleural effusions, severe edema) prior as this can cause delayed clearance of drug. Glucarpidase *(Voraxaze)* can rapidly lower methotrexate levels that remain high despite adequate hydration and urinary alkalinization; turns extracellular methotrexate into inactive metabolites (DAMPA and glutamate); it is very expensive Drug interactions: NSAIDs, salicylates, beta-lactams, proton pump inhibitors, sulfonamide antibiotics, probenecid – all can ↓ clearance of methotrexate	**BOXED WARNINGS** Myelosuppression and aplastic anemia, renal damage, hepatotoxicity (fibrosis and cirrhosis with long-term use), interstitial pneumonitis, dermatologic reactions (SJS/TEN), diarrhea, stomatitis, immunosuppression, tumor lysis syndrome, fetal death or teratogenicity Renal impairment or ascites/pleural effusions: requires dose adjustments or discontinuation **SIDE EFFECTS** Nephrotoxicity (dose related), hepatotoxicity (more common with chronic use), hand-foot syndrome
PEMEtrexed *(Alimta)*	To ↓ risk of side effects, give folic acid, vitamin B12 and dexamethasone	**SIDE EFFECTS** Nephrotoxicity, hepatotoxicity, dermatologic toxicity (premedicate with dexamethasone)
PRALAtrexate *(Folotyn)*	To ↓ risk of side effects, give folic acid and vitamin B12	**SIDE EFFECTS** Nephrotoxicity, hepatotoxicity

Miscellaneous Agents

DRUG	UNIQUE CONCERNS	SAFETY/SIDE EFFECTS/MONITORING
Tretinoin, AKA **All-trans Retinoic Acid,** *ATRA* ↓ proliferation and ↑ differentiation of acute promyelocytic leukemia (APL) cells First line therapy for APL	Retinoids (vitamin A analogues) Safety issue – see Pregnancy chapter Retinoic Acid-Acute Promyelocytic Leukemia (RA-APL) differentiation syndrome: fever, dyspnea, weight gain, edema, pulmonary infiltrates, pericardial or pleural effusions – treat with dexamethasone	**BOXED WARNINGS** RA-APL differentiation syndrome, leukocytosis, pregnancy **SIDE EFFECTS** Leukocytosis, RA-APL differentiation syndrome, QT prolongation, N/V/D, skin/mucous membrane dryness, hyperlipidemia, GI bleeding
Arsenic trioxide ***(Trisenox)*** ↑ apoptosis of APL cells and damages fusion protein PML-RAR alpha Second line therapy for acute promyelocytic leukemia (APL)	QT prolongation: monitor ECG, avoid concurrent QT prolonging agents, keep Mg, Ca, and K within normal range If acute vasomotor reactions (lightheadedness, dizziness, or hypotension) occur, prolong infusion	**BOXED WARNINGS** RA-APL differentiation syndrome, ECG abnormalities (AV block, QT prolongation), ECG and electrolyte monitoring **SIDE EFFECTS** Leukocytosis, APL differentiation syndrome, QT prolongation, N/V/D, GI bleeding, stomatitis, electrolyte imbalance, acute vasomotor reactions (lightheadedness, dizziness, or hypotension), fatigue, edema, HA, insomnia, anxiety, infection
Asparaginase ***(Erwinaze)*** – derived from *Erwinia chrysanthemi* **Pegaspargase** ***(Oncaspar)*** – modified form of L-asparaginase (derived from *E. coli)* and conjugated with polyethylene glycol	Deprives leukemia cells of asparagine, which is an essential amino acid in leukemia. The pegylated form (pegaspargase) allows for every 2 week dosing and ↓ incidence of allergic reactions Monitor fibrinogen, PT, aPTT, LFTs	**CONTRAINDICATIONS** Bleeding, thrombosis or pancreatitis with prior asparaginase treatment **SIDE EFFECTS** Hypersensitivity reactions, pancreatitis, hyperglycemia, hepatotoxicity, CNS toxicity (lethargy, somnolence), encephalopathy, N/V, prolonged prothrombin time (PT/INR)
Bleomycin Intercalating agent blocking topoisomerase II	Due to risk of anaphylactoid reactions, a test dose may be given May premedicate with acetaminophen to ↓ incidence of fever or chills ↑ risk of pulmonary fibrosis when given with G-CSF (filgrastim); recommend to not use G-CSF on days of bleomycin administration Not myelosuppressive Maximum lifetime dose of 400 units due to pulmonary toxicity risk	**BOXED WARNINGS** Pulmonary fibrosis, anaphylaxis **SIDE EFFECTS** Hypersensitivity reaction, pulmonary reactions (such as pneumonitis which may progress to pulmonary fibrosis), mucositis, hyperpigmentation, fever, chills, N/V (mild)
Mitomycin ***(Mutamycin)*** Free radical formation and alkylator	Vesicant, do not extravasate. Antidote is dimethyl sulfoxide (DMSO) and cool compresses Mitomycin IV solutions are a hazy blue in color and can make the urine blue-green	**BOXED WARNINGS** Bone marrow suppression, hemolytic-uremic syndrome **CONTRAINDICATIONS** Thrombocytopenia, coagulopathy, bleeding **SIDE EFFECTS** Leukopenia, thrombocytopenia, N/V, fatigue, alopecia, mucous membrane toxicity, cystitis or dysuria (from intravesical administration into bladder)

Miscellaneous Agents Continued

DRUG	UNIQUE CONCERNS	SAFETY/SIDE EFFECTS/MONITORING

Mammalian Target of Rapamycin (mTOR) Inhibitors – Inhibit downstream regulation of vascular endothelial growth factor (VEGF) reducing cell growth, metabolism, proliferation and angiogenesis.

Everolimus *(Afinitor)* Tablet *Zortress* is indicated for transplantation and used in various doses	CYP 3A4 major substrate	**BOXED WARNINGS** See Transplant chapter for *Zortress* **CONTRAINDICATIONS** Hypersensitivity to rapamycin derivatives **SIDE EFFECTS** Dyslipidemia, hyperglycemia, myelosuppression, rash, pruritus, hand-foot syndrome, stomatitis, fatigue, N/V/D, peripheral edema, interstitial lung disease, renal impairment, ↑ LFTs MedGuide required
Temsirolimus *(Torisel)* Injection	CYP 3A4 major substrate Premedicate with diphenhydramine Use non-PVC bag & tubing due to leaching of DEHP	**CONTRAINDICATION** Moderate to severe hepatic impairment **SIDE EFFECTS** Dyslipidemia, hyperglycemia, myelosuppression, interstitial lung disease, acute hypersensitivity reactions (polysorbate 80 solvent system), N/V/D, peripheral edema, renal impairment

Immunomodulators – oral agents that block angiogenesis and kill abnormal cells in the bone marrow while stimulating the bone marrow to produce normal healthy cells. Usually indicated for multiple myeloma. These agents cause severe birth defects and patients must not become pregnant while using these drugs. All three have strict REMS programs.

Lenalidomide *(Revlimid)* **Pomalidomide *(Pomalyst)*** **Thalidomide *(Thalomid)***	Severe birth defects. Only available under restricted distribution program: patient, prescriber and pharmacist must be registered with *Revlimid* REMS program, *Pomalyst* REMS program and/or *Thalomid* REMS program if using drug. MedGuide required Consider prophylactic anticoagulation due to ↑ VTE risk, seek medical care if signs and symptoms of DVT/PE develop: shortness of breath, chest pain, or arm or leg swelling. Pharmacogenomics: myelodysplastic syndrome with a deletion 5q (del 5q) cytogenetic abnormality (lenalidomide)	**BOXED WARNINGS** Fetal risk/pregnancy, thrombosis (DVT/PE), hematologic toxicity (lenalidomide) **CONTRAINDICATIONS** Pregnancy **SIDE EFFECTS** Neutropenia, thrombocytopenia, constipation, N/V/D, fatigue, fever, cough, pruritus, rash, arthralgias, back pain, peripheral edema, DVT/PE Neuropathy, confusion, somnolence (thalidomide) Hypercalcemia (pomalidomide)

Miscellaneous Agents Continued

DRUG	UNIQUE CONCERNS	SAFETY/SIDE EFFECTS/MONITORING
Proteasome Inhibitors – Inhibit proteasomes, which help to regulate intracellular protein homeostasis by inhibiting cell cycle progression and inducing apoptosis.		
Bortezomib *(Velcade)* SC administration has less neuropathy than IV administration	Give antiviral (acyclovir, valacyclovir) to prevent herpes (zoster and simplex) reactivation	**CONTRAINDICATIONS** Hypersensitivity to boron or mannitol, intrathecal administration (fatal) **SIDE EFFECTS** Peripheral neuropathy, psychiatric disturbances, insomnia, weakness, paresthesias, arthralgias/myalgias, cardiotoxicity, pulmonary toxicity, hypotension, thrombocytopenia, neutropenia, N/V/D, tumor lysis syndrome
Carfilzomib *(Kyprolis)*	Premedicate with dexamethasone and fluids ↑ alkaline phosphatase correlates with ↑ efficacy	**SIDE EFFECTS** Peripheral neuropathy (but less than bortezomib), fatigue, pulmonary toxicity, acute renal failure, tumor lysis syndrome, hepatotoxicity, anemia, thrombocytopenia, N/V/D, pyrexia, cardiotoxicity

TARGETED THERAPIES

Monoclonal Antibodies

Monoclonal antibodies work in various ways to inhibit cancer cell growth. Some bind to specific antigens or receptors on the surface of cancer cells and cause cell death. Others agents are conjugated to cytotoxic drugs or radioactive compounds. Some help to activate the immune system to recognize and destroy tumor cells. Representative monoclonal antibody targets and the associated drugs are included in the following tables (not a complete list).

- All are given as intravenous infusions.
- Most are associated with infusion-related reactions, including hypersensitivity reactions, anaphylaxis, hypotension, and bronchospasm. Some infusion-related reactions may be fatal. Premedication is usually required.
- Agents that are conjugated to cytotoxic drugs are associated with additional side effects due to the cytotoxic conjugate.
- Agents that activate the immune system can be associated with potentially life-threatening autoimmune-mediated side effects.

Hints for Understanding Monoclonal Antibodies Used in Oncology

SUBSTEM	EXAMPLES	TARGET	MECHANISM OF ACTION	COMMON TOXICITIES
"ci" Circulatory System	Bevacizumab Ramucirumab	Vascular endothelial growth factor (VEGF) or VEGF receptor	Inhibits growth of blood vessels. Used to treat certain solid tumors, such as colon cancer and non-small cell lung cancer.	■ Inhibition of blood vessel growth → HTN → proteinuria ■ Hemorrhage or thrombosis may occur ■ Impaired wound healing (due to decreased blood flow)
"tu" Tumor	Cetuximab Panitumumab	Epidermal growth factor receptor (EGFR)	Inhibits growth factor from binding to surface of tumor cell and promoting cell growth. Used to treat certain solid tumors, such as colon cancer.	■ EGFR → epidermis → skin toxicity (acneiform rash) ■ Development of rash is correlated with response to therapy
"tu" Tumor	Trastuzumab Pertuzumab	Human epidermal growth factor receptor 2 (HER2)	Inhibits growth factor from binding to surface of tumor cell and promoting cell growth. Used to treat certain solid tumors, such as breast cancer.	■ Cardiotoxicity ■ Embryo-fetal toxicity
"tu" Tumor	Rituximab Brentuximab Daratumumab	Cluster of differentiation (e.g., CD20, CD38) antigens expressed on cell surface of hematopoietic cells	Binds to antigens expressed on specific hematopoietic cells and causes cell death. Used to treat certain hematologic malignancies, such as non-Hodgkin's lymphoma, Hodgkin's lymphoma, multiple myeloma.	■ CD antigens are expressed on normal, as well as malignant, hematopoietic cells → suppression of specific hematopoietic cells → bone marrow suppression, increased risk for reactivation of viral infections
"li" Immune System	Ipilimumab Atezolizumab Nivolumab Pembrolizumab	Immune system (PD-1, PDL-1, CTLA-4)	Interferes with the body's ability to "down-regulate" the immune system. Results in increased immune recognition of tumor antigens. Used to treat certain solid tumors, such as non-small cell lung cancer and melanoma.	■ Patient's immune system becomes overactive → potentially life-threatening immune-mediated reactions, such as colitis, hepatic toxicity, thyroid dysfunction and myocarditis

DRUG	UNIQUE CONCERNS	SAFETY/SIDE EFFECTS/MONITORING

Vascular Endothelial Growth Factor (VEGF) Inhibitors

DRUG	UNIQUE CONCERNS	SAFETY/SIDE EFFECTS/MONITORING
Bevacizumab *(Avastin)*	Use 0.22 micron filter for ramucirumab Impairs wound healing: Do not administer for 28 days before or after surgery	**BOXED WARNINGS** Severe/fatal bleeding, GI perforation, surgical wound dehiscence (splitting)
Ramucirumab *(Cyramza)*	Monitor blood pressure and proteinuria prior to each dose	**SIDE EFFECTS** Hypertension, proteinuria, nephrotic syndrome, heart failure, thrombosis

Monoclonal Antibodies Continued

DRUG	UNIQUE CONCERNS	SAFETY/SIDE EFFECTS/MONITORING

Human Epidermal Growth Factor Receptor 2 (HER2) Inhibitors

DRUG	UNIQUE CONCERNS	SAFETY/SIDE EFFECTS/MONITORING
Trastuzumab *(Herceptin)* **Pertuzumab *(Perjeta)*** **Ado-Trastuzumab Emtansine *(Kadcyla)*** Trastuzumab conjugated to a microtubule inhibitor	Use 0.22 micron filter for ado-trastuzumab emtansine Pharmacogenomics: Test for HER2 gene expression; must have HER2 overexpression to use Monitor LVEF (using echocardiogram or MUGA scan) at baseline and during treatment.	**BOXED WARNINGS** Heart failure, embryo-fetal death and birth defects (avoid pregnancy x 7 months after receiving) Severe infusion-related reactions and pulmonary toxicity (trastuzumab) Hepatotoxicity (ado-trastuzumab emtansine) Ado-trastuzumab emtansine and conventional trastuzumab are not interchangeable **SIDE EFFECTS** Infusion-related reactions, N/V/D, alopecia Ado-trastuzumab emtansine: myelosuppression, hepatotoxcitiy, neuropathy, pulmonary toxicity

Epidermal Growth Factor Receptor (EGFR) Inhibitors

DRUG	UNIQUE CONCERNS	SAFETY/SIDE EFFECTS/MONITORING
Cetuximab *(Erbitux)* **Panitumumab *(Vectibix)***	Premedicate 1st dose with diphenhydramine Use 0.22 micron filter Pharmacogenomics: Test for EGFR gene expression and KRAS mutation. EGFR positive expression correlates with better response rates in NSCLC; must be KRAS wild type to use. KRAS mutation predicts poor response to treatment in colorectal cancer. *NSCLC = non-small cell lung cancer*	**BOXED WARNINGS** Severe/fatal infusion-related reactions, cardiac arrest (cetuximab) Dermatologic toxicities (panitumumab) **SIDE EFFECTS** Acneiform rash, serious skin toxicities (SJS/TEN), ocular toxicities, infusion-related reactions, N/V/D, Mg and Ca wasting **NOTES** Acneiform rash usually occurs within the 1st 2 weeks of treatment and may correlate with response. Advise patients to avoid direct sunlight, use sunscreen and topical emollients. Contact MD if skin blistering, bullae, or exfoliation occur.

Leukocyte Cluster of Differentiation (CD) Antigens (CD20, CD30, CD19, CD3, CD38) Inhibitors

DRUG	UNIQUE CONCERNS	SAFETY/SIDE EFFECTS/MONITORING
Rituximab *(Rituxan)* Ofatumumab *(Arzera)* Obinutuzumab *(Gazyva)*	Premedicate with diphenhydramine, acetaminophen, corticosteroid; slowly titrate rate of first infusion to lower risk of infusion reactions Pharmacogenomics: Test for B-cell antigen CD20; must be CD20 positive to use MedGuide required	**BOXED WARNINGS** Hepatitis B reactivation, progressive multifocal leukoencephalopathy (all) Serious skin reactions (SJS/TEN), severe/fatal infusion-related reactions (rituximab) **SIDE EFFECTS** Rash, peripheral edema, hypertension, renal impairment, tumor lysis syndrome **NOTES** Check hepatitis B panel prior to administration Can cause severe infusion-related reactions (urticaria, hypotension, angioedema, bronchospasm, hypoxia, anaphylaxis)

Monoclonal Antibodies Continued

DRUG	UNIQUE CONCERNS	SAFETY/SIDE EFFECTS/MONITORING
Brentuximab Vedotin *(Adcetris)* Conjugated to MMAE, a microtubule inhibitor	Pharmacogenomics: CD30 angiten must be positive for use	**BOXED WARNINGS** Progressive multifocal leukoencephalopathy **CONTRAINDICATIONS** Concurrent use with bleomycin **SIDE EFFECTS** Myelosuppression, neuropathy, pulmonary toxicity, hepatotoxicity, infusion-related reactions, SJS/TEN
Blinatumomab *(Blincyto)* Bispecific antibody targeting CD19 on B-cells and engaging CD3 on T-cells, causing lysis of B-cells	Pharmacogenomics: CD19 and CD3 antigens must be positive for use MedGuide required	**BOXED WARNINGS** Cytokine release syndrome, neurotoxicity **SIDE EFFECTS** Myelosuppression, hepatotoxicity, leukoencephalopathy, tumor lysis syndrome
Daratumumab *(Darzalex)* Anti-CD38 monoclonal antibody	Pharmacogenomics: CD38 antigen must be positive for use Premedicate with systemic steroid, acetaminophen and diphenhydramine	**SIDE EFFECTS** Myelosuppression, infusion-related reactions

Programmed Death Receptor-1 (PD-1) Inhibitors – when the programmed cell death (PD-1) receptor binds the PD-L1 ligand, the end result is decreased T-cell activation. PD-1 inhibitors are monoclonal antibodies that selectively inhibit PD-1 activity. This allows increased T-cell activation. Activated T-cells are capable (to some extent) of recognizing cancer cells as "non-self" or foreign, and activating the immune system against them (antitumor responses).

Pembrolizumab *(Keytruda)*	MedGuide required	**SIDE EFFECTS** Immune-mediated toxicities including: colitis, hepatotoxicity, pulmonary toxicity, nephrotoxicity (pembrolizumab), thyroid disorders, myocarditis, encephalitis, endocrinopathies, rash, weakness **NOTES** Immune-mediated toxicities may require interruption or permanent discontinuation of treatment and treatment with corticosteroids
Nivolumab *(Opdivo)*	MedGuide required	
Atezolizumab *(Tecentriq)*	MedGuide required	

Cytotoxic T-Lymphocyte Antigen-4 (CTLA-4) Inhibitor – monoclonal antibody that binds to the cytotoxic T-lymphocyte associated antigen 4 (CTLA-4) receptors, which effectively removes the "brake" from T-cell activation. Induces antitumor responses through increased T-cell recognition of cancer cells.

Ipilimumab *(Yervoy)*	MedGuide required REMS program	**BOXED WARNINGS** Fatal immune-mediated reactions (enterocolitis, hepatitis, dermatitis, endocrinopathy, neuropathy) **SIDE EFFECTS** Pneumonitis, nephrotoxicity, ocular toxicity **NOTES** Immune-mediated toxicities may require interruption or permanent discontinuation of treatment and administration of corticosteroids.

Tyrosine Kinase Inhibitors

There are a large number of different tyrosine kinase proteins that play roles in intracellular signaling pathways that control the growth and differentiation of cells. Tyrosine kinase inhibitors (TKIs) are orally administered small molecules that are active against different types of cancers. Some TKIs are "targeted" to inhibit specific abnormal tyrosine kinases that are associated with certain types of cancers. Pharmacogenomic testing must be done to identify patients likely to respond to these targeted TKIs. Other TKIs are considered to be "multitargeted". They inhibit multiple different tyrosine kinases involved in the cell signaling pathway and/or cell growth. Many TKIs have limited distribution through specialty pharmacies. The list below is not a complete list, but contains representative TKI targets and the associated drugs. For many of the TKIs, oral bioavailability may be altered if taken with food. It is very important for patients to follow the dosing instructions with regards to taking the specific TKI with or without food.

DRUG	MECHANISM/GENETICS	SAFETY/SIDE EFFECTS/MONITORING
USED IN CHRONIC MYELOGENOUS LEUKEMIA (CML)		
BCR-ABL Inhibitors		
Imatinib *(Gleevec)* Dasatinib *(Sprycel)* Nilotinib *(Tasigna)* PONATinib *(Iclusig)* Bosutinib *(Bosulif)*	BCR-ABL gene translocation (Philadelphia Chromosome) → abnormal tyrosine kinase (occurs in ~95% of CML patients) Pharmacogenomics: Must be Philadelphia chromosome (BCR-ABL) positive to use	**BOXED WARNINGS** QT prolongation (nilotinib) Vascular occlusions (strokes, MIs), heart failure, hepatotoxicity (ponatinib) **SIDE EFFECTS** Myelosuppression, N/V/D, fluid retention, edema, skin rash, ↑ LFTs, HF, QT prolongation (dasatinib, nilotinib, bosutinib); HBV reactivation (dasatinib, nilotinib) **NOTES** MedGuide required (nilotinib, ponatinib)
USED IN MELANOMA		
BRAF Inhibitors		
Vemurafenib *(Zelboraf)* Dabrafenib *(Tafinlar)*	BRAF mutation → abnormal tyrosine kinase that is always "on", → melanoma (occurs in ~50% of melanoma patients) Pharmacogenomics: Must be BRAF V600E or V600K mutation positive to use	**WARNINGS** New malignancies such as squamous cell carcinoma and basal cell carcinoma, QT prolongation, serious skin reactions, hepatotoxicity **SIDE EFFECTS** Skin rash, photosensitivity, N/V/D, peripheral edema, fatigue, arthralgia
Mitogen-Activated Extracellular Kinase (MEK) 1 and 2 Inhibitors		
Trametinib *(Mekinist)* Cobimetinib *(Cotellic)*	Inhibits MEK, a cell signaling protein downstream from RAF Used in combination with BRAF inhibitors in patients with BRAF V600E or V600K mutations	**SIDE EFFECTS** Hypertension, HF, hepatotoxicity, skin rash, N/V/D, myelosuppression Hand-foot syndrome, QT prolongation (trametinib) Visual impairment (cobimetinib)

Tyrosine Kinase Inhibitors Continued

DRUG	MECHANISM/GENETICS	SAFETY/SIDE EFFECTS/MONITORING
USED IN NON-SMALL CELL LUNG CANCER (NSCLC)		
Epidermal Growth Factor Receptor (EGFR) Inhibitors		
Afatinib *(Gilotrif)* Erlotinib *(Tarceva)* Gefitinib *(Iressa)*	EGFR mutation → abnormal tyrosine kinase that is always "on" → NSCLC (occurs in ~15% of NSCLC patients) Pharmacogenomics: Must be EGFR mutation positive (exon 19 or 21) to use	**WARNINGS** Interstitial lung disease, hepatotoxicity, GI perforation, skin reactions (SJS/TEN), ocular toxicity (keratitis), fetal harm; diarrhea (afatinib/gefitinib) Renal impairment requires dose adjustment (afatinib) **SIDE EFFECTS** Acneiform rash, dry skin, pruritus, N/V/D, mucositis **NOTES** Acneiform rash usually occurs within the 1st 2 weeks of treatment and may correlate with response. Advise patients to avoid direct sunlight, use sunscreen and topical emollients. Report if skin blistering, bullae or exfoliation occur.
Anaplastic Lymphoma Kinase (ALK) Inhibitors		
Crizotinib *(Xalkori)* Ceritinib *(Zykadia)* Alectinib *(Alecensa)*	ALK gene translocation → abnormal tyrosine kinase that is always "on" → NSCLC (occurs in ~5% of NSCLC patients) Pharmacogenomics: Must be ALK mutation positive to use	**WARNINGS** Hepatotoxicity, bradycardia, interstitial lung disease, QT prolongation; ocular toxicities (crizotinib), pancreatitis (ceritinib), myalgia and photosensitivity (alectinib) **SIDE EFFECTS** Skin rash, N/V/D, edema, hyperglycemia (ceritinib)
OTHER TKIs (not a complete list)		
Lapatinib *(Tykerb)*	Human Epidermal Growth Factor Receptor 2 (HER-2) inhibitor (also inhibits EGFR) Pharmacogenomics: Must have HER2 overexpression to use in breast cancer	**BOXED WARNINGS** Hepatotoxicity **WARNINGS** Decreased LVEF, serious skin reactions (SJS/TEN), interstitial lung disease, QT prolongation **SIDE EFFECTS** Diarrhea, N/V, skin rash, hand-foot syndrome
SORAfenib *(NexAVAR)* SUNItinib *(Sutent)*	Multiple targets Useful in cancers where traditional therapy has little benefit, such as hepatocellular, renal and thyroid cancers	**BOXED WARNINGS** Hepatotoxicity (sunitinib) **WARNINGS** Hepatotoxicity, cardiac toxicity, hypertension, proteinuria, hemorrhagic events, SJS/TEN, impaired wound healing **SIDE EFFECTS** Skin changes, hand-foot syndrome, N/V/D, QT prolongation, thyroid dysfunction, mucositis

Common Toxicities of Tyrosine Kinase Inhibitors

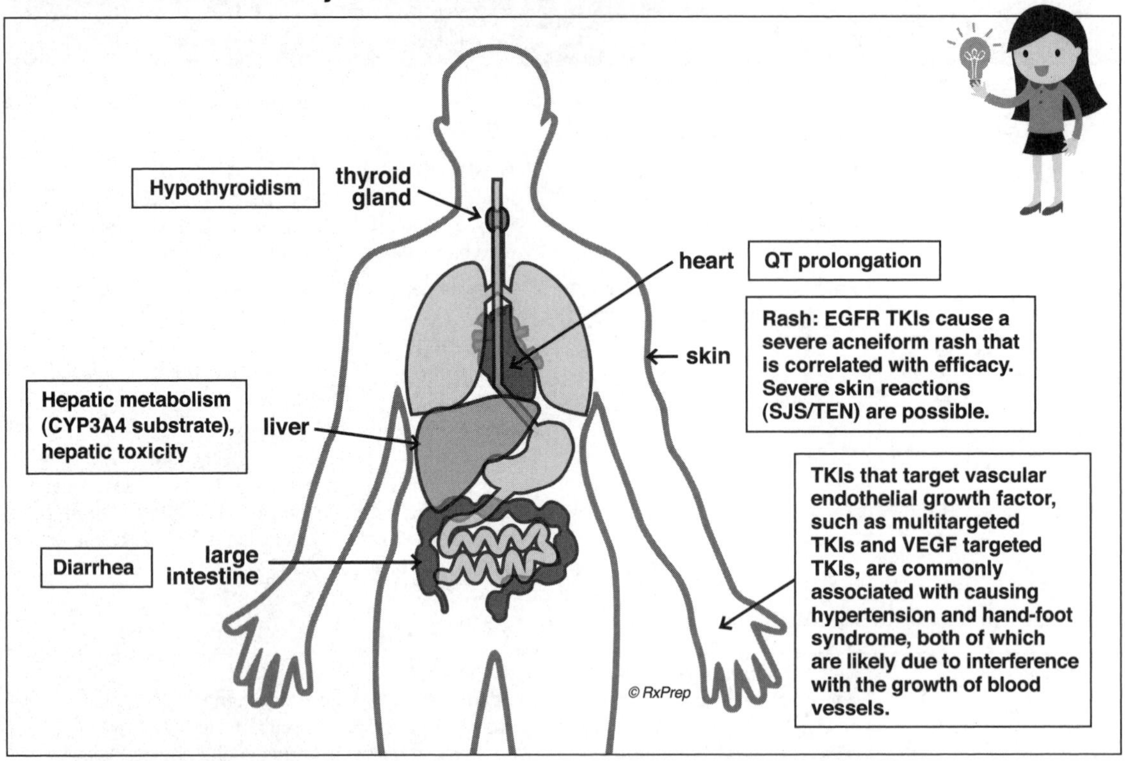
Hypothyroidism
thyroid gland
heart
QT prolongation
skin
Rash: EGFR TKIs cause a severe acneiform rash that is correlated with efficacy. Severe skin reactions (SJS/TEN) are possible.
Hepatic metabolism (CYP3A4 substrate), hepatic toxicity
liver
Diarrhea
large intestine
TKIs that target vascular endothelial growth factor, such as multitargeted TKIs and VEGF targeted TKIs, are commonly associated with causing hypertension and hand-foot syndrome, both of which are likely due to interference with the growth of blood vessels.
© RxPrep

Administration and Safe Handling of Oral Chemotherapeutic Agents

GENERIC (BRAND)	ADMINISTRATION	SPECIAL HANDLING
Imatinib *(Gleevec)*	Take with food or within 1 hour after a meal	Thalidomide, pomalidomide, and lenalidomide: female patients of reproductive potential must have 2 negative pregnancy tests prior to starting treatment and use 2 forms of birth control. REMS drugs only available through a specialty pharmacy. Safety risk – see Pregnancy chapter
Thalidomide *(Thalomid)*		
Capecitabine *(Xeloda)*		
Nilotinib *(Tasigna)*	Take on an empty stomach (1 hour before or 2 hours after food, pomalidomide is taken 2 hours before or 2 hours after food)	
Erlotinib *(Tarceva)*		
Sorafenib *(Nexavar)*		
Temozolomide *(Temodar)*		
Abiraterone *(Zytiga)*		
Pomalidomide *(Pomalyst)*		
Dasatinib *(Sprycel)*	Take without regards to food	
Sunitinib *(Sutent)*		
Tamoxifen *(Nolvadex, Soltamox)*		
Anastrozole *(Arimidex)*		
Bicalutamide *(Casodex)*		
Lenalidomide *(Revlimid)*		

PRACTICE CASE

TO is a 53 y/o Indian male diagnosed with non-Hodgkin's lymphoma. His past medical history is significant for mild heart failure (NYHA Class I). He is to receive 6 cycles of "CHOP" chemotherapy.

Allergies: NKDA

Chemotherapy Regimen:
Cyclophosphamide 750 mg/m^2 IV on Day 1
Doxorubicin 50 mg/m^2 IV on Day 1
Vincristine 1.4 mg/m^2 IV on Day 1
Prednisone 100 mg PO on Days 1-5 given first

Vitals:
Height: 5'10" Weight: 200 pounds
BP: 145/97 mmHg HR: 79 BPM RR: 15 BPM Temp: 98.5°F Pain: 0/10

Labs: Na (mEq/L) = 136 (135 - 145)
K (mEq/L) = 3.7 (3.5 - 5)
Cl (mEq/L) = 98 (95 - 103)
HCO_3 (mEq/L) = 26 (24 - 30)
BUN (mg/dL) = 15 (7 - 20)
SCr (mg/dL) = 1.1 (0.6 - 1.3)
Glucose (mg/dL) = 106 (100 - 125)
Ca (mg/dL) = 9.1 (8.5 - 10.5)
Mg (mEq/L) = 1.5 (1.3 - 2.1)
PO_4 (mg/dL) = 2.9 (2.3 - 4.7)
AST (IU/L) = 20 (8 - 48)
ALT (IU/L) = 12 (7 - 55)
Albumin (g/dL) = 3.4 (3.5 - 5)
T Bili (mg/dL) = 0.8 (0.1 - 1.2)

Start chemotherapy today. Monitor for acute toxicities from chemotherapy regimen and begin any supportive care as needed.

Questions

Questions 1-4 refer to the above case.

1. The pharmacist must first calculate the patient's BSA and will use the Dubois and Dubois equation: BSA (m^2) = 0.007184 x [weight (kg)$^{0.425}$] x [height (cm)$^{0.725}$]. The patient's BSA is:

   a. 1.15 m^2
   b. 1.03 m^2
   c. 2.09 m^2
   d. 2.18 m^2
   e. 3.15 m^2

2. What is the correct milligram dose of doxorubicin that the patient should receive on Day 1?

   a. 104.5 mg
   b. 510 mg
   c. 949.5 mg
   d. 948.5 mg
   e. 300 mg

3. The physician wants to know if there are any medications that can reduce the likelihood of cardiotoxicity with doxorubicin therapy. Which of the following would you suggest?

   a. *Totect*
   b. *Zinecard*
   c. *Lasix*
   d. *Epogen*
   e. *Mesna*

4. What is the dose limiting toxicity of vincristine?

   a. Neuropathy
   b. Nephrotoxicity
   c. Hypersensitivity reaction
   d. Ototoxicity
   e. Pulmonary toxicity

Questions 5-13 do not relate to the above case.

5. A patient is using apomorphine *(Apokyn)* injections for advanced Parkinson's disease. The patient has been suffering from nausea. Which of the following antiemetics should be avoided with apomorphine?

   a. Lorazepam
   b. Metoclopramide
   c. Prochlorperazine
   d. Granisetron
   e. Dexamethasone

6. A patient will begin raloxifene therapy. Choose the correct counseling points: (Select **ALL** that apply.)

   a. This drug can increase your risk of breast cancer.
   b. Avoid long periods of immobility, such as during long airplane flights – get up and move when you can.
   c. This medication can cause weakened bones and fractures.
   d. This medication should only be used by men.
   e. This drug should be taken once daily.

7. Which of the following medications should be taken with food? (Select **ALL** that apply.)

   a. *Gleevec*
   b. *Xeloda*
   c. *Nexavar*
   d. *Votrient*
   e. *Zytiga*

8. An antidote for toxicity from high-dose methotrexate is:

   a. Folic acid
   b. Leucovorin
   c. Vitamin B12
   d. Cholestyramine
   e. Vitamin D

9. A pharmacist received a prescription for *Gleevec*. An appropriate generic interchange is:

   a. Aprepitant
   b. Imatinib
   c. Temozolomide
   d. Anastrozole
   e. Capecitabine

10. A pharmacist receives a prescription for *Arimidex*. An appropriate generic interchange is:

    a. Aprepitant
    b. Anastrozole
    c. Exemestane
    d. Letrozole
    e. Tamoxifen

11. A patient is receiving dronabinol for nausea. Appropriate counseling points should include:

    a. The capsules should be kept in the refrigerator.
    b. Your appetite may increase.
    c. This medication cannot be shared with others.
    d. A and B only.
    e. A, B and C.

12. A patient has chemotherapy-induced anemia. She states she is weak. The pharmacist has access to her labs and finds that the current hemoglobin level is 11 g/dL. Ferritin, serum iron, TIBC, folate and vitamin B12 are all at acceptable levels. Her oncologist has prescribed *Procrit*. The patient has brought the *Procrit* prescription to the pharmacy. Choose the correct statement:
    a. The prescription can be filled after the pharmacist confirms that the patient is registered with the ESA APPRISE program.
    b. The generic name of *Procrit* is darbepoetin.
    c. The patient should be aware that they may experience euphoria and increased appetite.
    d. The prescription should not be filled; the pharmacist should contact the prescriber.
    e. A and B only.

13. A patient with end stage breast cancer has been experiencing fatigue and dehydration. She has a corrected calcium of 11.5 mg/dL. What is most appropriate for treating her hypercalcemia?
    a. Instruct patient to drink 8 glasses of water
    b. IV hydration, loop diuretic, and zoledronic acid
    c. Calcitonin
    d. Vitamin D
    e. No treatment is necessary since her calcium is within the normal range

Answers

1-c, 2-a, 3-b, 4-a, 5-d, 6-b,e, 7-a,b, 8-b, 9-b, 10-b, 11-e, 12-d, 13-b

57

ANEMIA

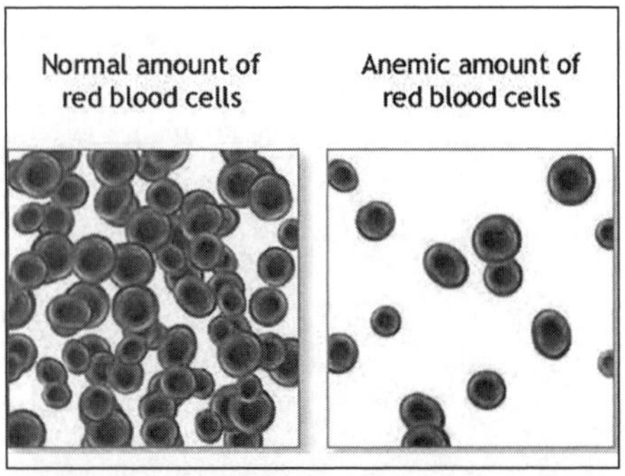

GUIDELINES/REFERENCES

Kidney Disease: Improving Global Outcomes (KDIGO) Anemia Work Group. KDIGO Clinical Practice Guideline for Anemia in Chronic Kidney Disease. Kidney Int Suppl. 2012;2:279-335.

National Kidney Foundation. KDOQI Clinical Practice Guideline and Clinical Practice Recommendations for Anemia in Chronic Kidney Disease. http://www2.kidney.org/professionals/KDOQI/guidelines_anemia/ (accessed 2016 November 8)

Additional guidelines included with the online course.

BACKGROUND

Anemia is the most common blood disorder worldwide and it affects approximately 3.5 million Americans. It is characterized by a decrease in hemoglobin (Hgb) and hematocrit (Hct) concentration below the normal range for age and gender. Hgb is an iron-rich protein found in red blood cells (RBCs); its main purpose is to carry oxygen from the lungs to the tissues. RBCs are formed in the bone marrow, where they take up Hgb and iron, and then they are released into the circulation as immature RBCs, known as reticulocytes. After 1 – 2 days, the reticulocytes mature into erythrocytes. These mature RBCs have a lifespan of about 120 days, after which they are removed from circulation by macrophages, mainly in the spleen.

Anemia can occur due to impaired RBC production, increased RBC destruction (hemolysis), or blood loss. Either way, a decrease in Hgb or RBC volume results in decreased oxygen carrying capacity of the blood. Anemia can result from nutritional deficiencies (e.g., iron, folate, vitamin B12) or it can occur as a complication of another medical disorder, such as chronic kidney disease (CKD) or malignancy. Therefore, diagnosis of the underlying cause is essential.

SYMPTOMS OF ANEMIA

Most patients with mild or early stage anemia are asymptomatic. If anemia becomes severe and/or prolonged, the lack of oxygen in the blood can lead to classic symptoms of fatigue, weakness, shortness of breath, exercise intolerance, headache, dizziness, anorexia, and/or pallor. If sudden blood loss occurs, the patient may experience acute symptoms, such as chest pain, angina, fainting, palpitations, and tachycardia. Glossitis (an inflamed, sore tongue), koilonychias (thin, concave, spoon-shaped nails), or pica (craving and eating non-foods such as chalk or clay) may develop in iron deficiency anemia. Patients with vitamin B12 (cobalamin) deficiency can present with neurologic symptoms, including peripheral neuropathies, visual disturbances, and/or psychiatric symptoms.

A decreased oxygen supply can cause ischemic damage to many organs. In chronic anemia, the heart tries to compensate for low oxygen levels by pumping faster (tachycardia), thereby increasing the mass of the ventricular wall, which can eventually lead to heart failure.

TYPES OF ANEMIA

The type of anemia, and underlying cause, cannot be determined based on signs and symptoms alone. Once the decreased Hgb is recognized, the most common way to classify anemia is by the mean corpuscular volume (MCV). The MCV reflects the size, or average volume, of RBCs. The most common clinical scenarios describing the different types of anemia are shown in the box. In addition, certain genetic conditions can cause anemia due to dysfunctional RBCs (see Sickle Cell Disease chapter for more information).

ANEMIA CLINICAL SCENARIOS

The patient has low Hgb and signs and symptoms of anemia. The next step is to evaluate the MCV.

Clinical scenario 1: low Hgb, low MCV (< 80 mm^3)

- Likely diagnosis: microcytic anemia caused by iron deficiency

Clinical scenario 2: low Hgb, high MCV (> 100 mm^3)

- Likely diagnosis: macrocytic anemia caused by vitamin B12 and/or folate deficiency

Clinical scenario 3: low Hgb, normal MCV (80-100 mm^3)

- Likely diagnosis: normocytic anemia, evaluate for underlying causes [e.g., CKD, malignancy, acute blood loss (surgery or trauma), bone marrow failure (aplastic anemia), hemolysis]

Common laboratory tests used to determine the type and cause of anemia are shown in the table below. Iron studies are used to further evaluate microcytic anemia due to iron deficiency; they include serum iron (bound to transferrin), serum ferritin (iron stores), transferrin saturation (amount of transferrin binding sites occupied by iron) and total iron binding capacity (amount of transferrin binding sites available to bind iron, or unbound sites). Vitamin B12 and folate levels can further evaluate macrocytic anemia; since vitamin B12 is required for enzyme reactions involving methylmalonic acid and homocysteine, they may also be useful in confirming a diagnosis. Reticulocyte counts are a measure of RBC production, which is usually impaired in anemia.

COMMON LABORATORY TESTS IN ANEMIA*

Relevant Components of the CBC	**Iron Studies**
Hemoglobin (Hgb)	Serum Iron
Hematocrit (Hct)	Serum Ferritin
Red Blood Cell (RBC) Count	Total Iron Binding Capacity (TIBC)
Reticulocyte Count	Transferrin Saturation (TSAT)
RBC Indices	**Additional Tests**
Mean Corpuscular Volume (MCV)	Serum Folate
Mean Corpuscular Hemoglobin (MCH)	Serum Vitamin B12
Mean Corpuscular Hemoglobin Concentration (MCHC)	Methylmalonic Acid
Red Blood Cell Distribution Width (RDW)	Homocysteine

**Refer to the Lab Values & Monitoring chapter for normal laboratory ranges in adults*

IRON DEFICIENCY ANEMIA

Iron deficiency is the most common nutritional deficiency in the United States. Common causes of iron deficiency are shown in the box. Dietary iron is available in two forms: heme iron (found in meat and seafood) and non-heme iron (found in nuts, beans, vegetables and fortified grains, such as cereals). Heme iron is more readily absorbed than non-heme iron, the absorption of which can vary greatly depending on other foods being consumed as well as gastric pH. Meat, seafood, poultry and ascorbic acid increase the absorption of non-heme iron, while foods that contain phytate and polyphenols (e.g., grains, beans, cereals and legumes), can decrease non-heme iron absorption. This is particularly important for patients who follow a vegetarian diet, since they are more likely to consume foods with a less absorbable form of iron along with foods that decrease the absorption of iron; for this reason, vegetarians may require iron supplementation, even if dietary intake of iron seems adequate.

Preventative measures can be used for some of the at-risk patient populations. For example, women who use hormonal contraception may experience less bleeding during menstrual periods and their risk of developing iron deficiency may be lower. In addition, the CDC recommends low-dose iron supplementation (30 mg/day) for all pregnant women, beginning at the first prenatal visit. Usually this low iron dose is provided in the prenatal vitamin. Larger doses of iron are required if iron deficiency anemia (IDA) is diagnosed in pregnancy.

CAUSES OF IRON DEFICIENCY

Inadequate Dietary Intake
- Iron-poor diets (e.g., vegetarian, vegan)
- Malnutrition
- Disease-related (e.g., dementia, psychosis)

Blood Loss
- Acute (e.g., GI hemorrhage)
- Chronic (e.g., heavy menses, blood donations, PUD, IBD, intestinal cancer, hemorrhoids)
- Drug-induced bleeding (e.g., NSAIDs, steroids, antiplatelets, anticoagulants)

Decreased Iron Absorption
- High gastric pH (e.g., PPIs)
- Gastrointestinal diseases (e.g., celiac disease, IBD, gastrectomy, gastric bypass)

Increased Iron Requirements
- Pregnancy, lactation, infants*, rapid growth (e.g., adolescence)

**See the Dietary Supplements, Natural & Complimentary Medicine chapter for infant iron requirements*

Diagnosis of Iron Deficiency Anemia

In addition to low Hgb and low MCV, iron studies will show a ↓ in serum iron, iron stores (ferritin), and TSAT (less iron available to bind to transferrin), and an ↑ in TIBC (more transferrin binding sites available). Reticulocyte counts are also reduced as there is not enough iron available to produce new RBCs.

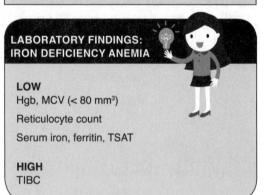

LABORATORY FINDINGS: IRON DEFICIENCY ANEMIA

LOW
Hgb, MCV (< 80 mm^3)
Reticulocyte count
Serum iron, ferritin, TSAT

HIGH
TIBC

Treatment of Iron Deficiency Anemia

Oral Iron Therapy

- Oral iron supplementation can adequately treat most patients with IDA; parenteral iron therapy is typically reserved for select patient populations due to a higher risk of side effects, cost and burden of administration (see Parenteral Iron Therapy section).
- The recommended dose is 100 – 200 mg of elemental iron per day, typically taken in divided doses.
- There is no evidence that one oral formulation is better than another, if dosed appropriately based on elemental iron needs.

- Since there are several salt forms and iron preparations available, it is important to know the % elemental iron in each product (see Study Tips box).

% ELEMENTAL IRON IN ORAL PRODUCTS	
IRON FORMULATION	**ELEMENTAL IRON**
Ferrous gluconate	12%
Ferrous sulfate	20%
Ferrous sulfate, dried	30%
Ferrous fumurate	33%
Carbonyl iron	100%
Polysaccharide iron complex	100%

- Iron absorption can be impacted by numerous factors:
  - Food ↓ the absorption of iron (by as much as 50%). It is best to take iron on an empty stomach, at least 1 hour before or 2 hours after meals. However, many patients take iron with food to decrease GI side effects.
  - Iron absorption is ↑ in an acidic environment. Giving iron with ascorbic acid (vitamin C 200 mg) may enhance the absorption to a minimal extent.
  - Ferrous iron (Fe^{2+}) is absorbed more readily than the ferric (Fe^{3+}) form. However, polysaccharide iron complex, the only oral product in the ferric form, may have less GI irritation.
  - Sustained-release or enteric-coated formulations have a lower risk of GI irritation but have ↓ absorption, as they do not release iron until they reach the small intestine and insoluble complexes can form in the alkaline environment. For this reason, they are not recommended as initial therapy.
- Iron therapy should increase the Hgb level by 1 g/dL every 2 – 3 weeks. Treatment should continue for 3 – 6 months after the anemia has resolved to allow for iron stores to return to normal and to prevent relapse.

DRUG	DOSING	SAFETY/SIDE EFFECTS/MONITORING
Ferrous sulfate *(Ferro-Bob, FeroSul, Fer-In-Sol,* many OTC multivitamins with iron) Tablet, elixir, oral solution, syrup	325 mg (65 mg elemental iron) PO daily to TID Most commonly prescribed and is the least expensive (other doses available)	**BOXED WARNING** Accidental overdose of iron-containing products is a leading cause of fatal poisoning in children under 6; keep iron out of reach of children; in the case of an accidental overdose, go to the ED or call a poison control center immediately **CONTRAINDICATIONS** Hemochromatosis, hemolytic anemia, hemosiderosis **SIDE EFFECTS** Nausea, stomach upset, constipation (dose-related), dark and tarry stools **MONITORING** Hgb, iron studies, RBC indices, reticulocyte count **NOTES** Although fiber is the first line treatment for constipation, a stool softener such as docusate is often recommended to prevent iron-induced constipation
Ferrous sulfate, dried *(Slow Fe, Slow Iron)* ER tablet	160 mg (50 mg elemental iron) PO daily to TID (other doses available)	
Ferrous fumarate *(Ferretts, Ferrimin 150, Hemocyte)*	324 mg (106 mg elemental iron) PO daily to TID (other doses available)	
Ferrous gluconate *(Ferate)*	324 mg (38 mg elemental iron) PO daily to TID (other doses available)	
Carbonyl iron *(FerraPlus 90, Ferralet 90, Iron Chews)*	90 mg (90 mg elemental iron) PO daily or as directed (other doses available)	
Polysaccharide iron complex *(iFerex 150, Ferrex 150,* others) Capsules, liquid	150 mg PO daily (other doses available)	

Oral Iron Drug Interactions

- Antacids, H2RAs, and PPIs ↓ iron absorption by ↑ gastric pH. Patients should take iron 2 hours before or 4 hours after taking antacids. H2RAs and PPIs raise gastric pH for up to 24 hours, therefore separating the administration of these agents from iron supplements does not improve absorption.
- Iron is a polyvalent cation that can ↓ the absorption of other drugs by binding with them in the GI tract to form nonabsorbable complexes. It is important to separate administration of iron supplements from the following agents (general guidance is provided but prescribing information should be consulted for exact details):
  - Quinolone and tetracycline antibiotics (less concern with doxycycline and minocycline) – take iron products 2 hours before or 4 – 8 hours after these agents.
  - Bisphosphonates – take iron products 60 minutes after oral ibandronate or 30 minutes after alendronate/risedronate.
  - Cefdinir, dolutegravir, levothyroxine, levodopa, and methyldopa – separate from iron products by 2 – 4 hours.
- Vitamin C ↑ the absorption of iron and food ↓ the absorption, especially cereals, fiber, tea, coffee, eggs or milk (avoid these if taking iron with food to prevent GI upset).

Oral Iron Patient Counseling

- This medication is used to treat a condition called anemia which is caused by low levels of iron in your body. It needs to be taken for at least a few months for your symptoms to improve; do not stop until directed by your healthcare provider.
- This medication should be taken on an empty stomach. If stomach upset occurs, it can be taken with food, but avoid cereals, tea, coffee, eggs, milk and high fiber products, as these can decrease iron absorption.
- Iron can cause your stool to become dark. This is expected.
- If you develop constipation, ask your healthcare provider to recommend a stool softener (such as docusate sodium) and/or a fiber product (such as psyllium).

Iron Toxicity

Accidental iron poisoning is the leading cause of poisoning deaths in children < 6 years of age. Even small doses can lead to poisoning in a small child. The child can initially appear asymptomatic or may quickly develop severe nausea, vomiting, gastrointestinal bleeding (most often vomiting blood) and diarrhea. If a parent suspects their child ingested iron pills or liquid, they should be directed to the nearest emergency room immediately, whether symptomatic or not. Left untreated, iron overdose can lead to liver damage, heart failure, coma or death. The antidote for iron overdose is deferoxamine *(Desferal)*.

Parenteral Iron Therapy

Parenteral iron therapy, by providing elemental iron and avoiding the issues with iron absorption, is more effective and increases Hgb levels more quickly than oral iron. Another advantage is that the total dose needed to replenish iron stores (e.g., 1,000 mg) can be provided in a single infusion, if desired. Due to the risk of more severe adverse reactions, as well as cost of therapy, IV administration of iron is typically restricted to the following situations:

- Patients with CKD on hemodialysis (most common use of IV iron).
- Use of erythropoiesis-stimulating agents (ESAs) in CKD.
- Unable to tolerate oral iron or failure of oral therapy (e.g., as seen with IBD, celiac disease, certain gastric bypass procedures, achlorhydria and bacterial overgrowth syndromes such as *H. pylori*).
- Losing iron too fast for oral replacement.
- As an alternative when blood transfusions are not accepted by the patient (e.g., for religious reasons).

Intravenous (Parenteral) Iron Therapy

DRUG	SAFETY/SIDE EFFECTS/MONITORING
Iron dextran *(INFeD)*	**BOXED WARNING (IRON DEXTRAN AND FERUMOXYTOL)** Serious and sometimes fatal anaphylactic reactions have occurred with the use of iron dextran or ferumoxytol; all patients receiving iron dextran should be given a test dose prior to the first full therapeutic dose; fatal reactions have occurred even in patients who tolerated the test dose; a history of drug allergy or multiple drug allergies may ↑ the risk **SIDE EFFECTS** Muscle aches, flushing, hypotension, hypertension, tachycardia, chest pain and peripheral edema All parenteral iron products carry a risk for hypersensitivity reactions (including anaphylaxis) **MONITORING** Hgb, iron studies, reticulocyte count, vital signs, signs and symptoms of anaphylaxis **NOTES** Give by slow IV injection or infusion to ↓ the risk of hypotension All agents are stable in NS; *Feraheme* is stable in NS or D5W *Triferic* is only indicated for iron replacement in patients with hemodialysis-dependent CKD; it should be added to the bicarbonate concentrate of the hemodialysate for patients receiving hemodialysis
Sodium ferric gluconate *(Ferrlecit)*	
Iron sucrose *(Venofer)*	
Ferumoxytol *(Feraheme)*	
Ferric carboxymaltose *(Injectafer)*	
Ferric pyrophosphate citrate *(Triferic)*	

MACROCYTIC ANEMIA

Macrocytic anemia is caused by vitamin B12 or folate deficiency, or both. Pernicious anemia, the most common cause of vitamin B12 deficiency, occurs due to a lack of intrinsic factor, which is required for adequate vitamin B12 absorption in the small intestine. Pernicious anemia can be diagnosed using the Schilling test and requires lifelong parenteral vitamin B12 replacement. Other causes of macrocytic anemia include alcoholism, poor nutrition, gastrointestinal disorders (e.g., Crohn's disease, celiac disease) and pregnancy.

Vitamin B12 deficiency can result in serious neurologic dysfunction, including cognitive impairment and peripheral neuropathies. If vitamin B12 deficiency goes undiagnosed for more than 3 months, then neurologic symptoms may become irreversible. Folic acid deficiency does not result in neurologic symptoms; rather, it causes ulcerations of the tongue and oral mucosa, and changes to skin, hair and fingernail pigmentation.

Diagnosis of Macrocytic Anemia

In addition to low Hgb and high MCV, serum levels of vitamin B12 and/or folate will be low. Since vitamin B12 is required for enzyme reactions involving methylmalonic acid and homocysteine, they accumulate when vitamin B12 is deficient. Homocysteine levels can also be elevated in folate deficiency.

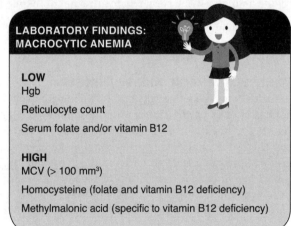

LABORATORY FINDINGS: MACROCYTIC ANEMIA

LOW

Hgb

Reticulocyte count

Serum folate and/or vitamin B12

HIGH

MCV (> 100 mm^3)

Homocysteine (folate and vitamin B12 deficiency)

Methylmalonic acid (specific to vitamin B12 deficiency)

Treatment of Macrocytic Anemia

In most cases, the initial treatment of vitamin B12 deficiency involves vitamin B12 injections, to bypass absorption barriers, followed by oral supplements, if appropriate. Vitamin B12 injections are recommended first line for anyone with a severe deficiency or neurological symptoms.

DRUG	DOSING	SAFETY/SIDE EFFECTS/MONITORING
Cyanocobalamin, vitamin B12 ***(Physicians EZ Use B-12, B-12 Compliance, Nascobal,*** oral generics) Injection, lozenge, tablets (including ER and SL forms), liquid, nasal solution	IM or deep SC: 100-1,000 mcg daily/weekly/monthly (varies depending on severity of deficiency) Oral/sublingual: 1,000-2,000 mcg daily *Nascobal*: 500 mcg in one nostril once weekly	**CONTRAINDICATIONS** Cobalt allergy **WARNINGS** Parenteral products may contain aluminum which can accumulate and become toxic if renal function is impaired **SIDE EFFECTS** Pain with injection, rash **MONITORING** Hgb, Hct, vitamin B12, reticulocyte count
Folic acid, folate *(FA-8)* Tablet, capsule, injection	0.4-1 mg daily	**WARNINGS** Parenteral products may contain aluminum which can accumulate and become toxic if renal function is impaired **SIDE EFFECTS** Bronchospasm, flushing, rash, pruritus, malaise (rare) **MONITORING** Hgb, Hct, folate, reticulocyte count

Drug Interactions

Vitamin B12

- Chloramphenicol, colchicine, heavy alcohol use, and long-term use of metformin, H2RAs or PPIs (≥ 2 years) may ↓ vitamin B12 absorption.

Folic Acid

- Folic acid can ↓ the efficacy of raltitrexed (a chemotherapeutic agent); avoid combination.
- Folic acid may ↓ the serum concentration of fosphenytoin, phenytoin, primidone and phenobarbital.
- Green tea and sulfasalazine may ↓ the serum concentration of folic acid.

NORMOCYTIC ANEMIA

Anemia Of Chronic Kidney Disease

Anemia of chronic kidney disease (CKD) is primarily due to a deficiency in erythropoietin (EPO), a hormone produced by the kidneys that stimulates the bone marrow to produce RBCs. To a lesser degree, this type of anemia is also attributed to a shortened RBC survival and reduced responsiveness to EPO. Iron therapy and erythropoiesis-stimulating agents (ESAs) are the mainstay of treatment in patients with anemia of CKD. Most patients receiving hemodialysis (HD) will require iron therapy, due to repeated blood loss (e.g., retention of blood in the dialyzer, venipuncture losses); IV iron is first line in these patients. Non-HD CKD patients with anemia can be treated with oral iron supplements. ESAs help maintain Hgb levels and reduce the need for blood transfusions.

The KDIGO (Kidney Disease Improving Global Outcomes) guidelines recommend iron therapy in both non-HD and HD patients if TSAT is ≤ 30% and ferritin levels are ≤ 500 ng/mL. On the other hand, the KDOQI (Kidney Disease Outcomes Quality Initiative) guidelines recommend iron therapy if TSAT is ≤

20% (non-HD and HD patients) and ferritin levels are ≤ 100 ng/mL in non-HD patients and ≤ 200 ng/mL in HD patients. These criteria are especially important when using ESAs because ESAs are ineffective if iron stores are low. The KDOQI guideline recommendations are consistent with the package labeling for ESAs.

Erythropoiesis-Stimulating Agents (ESAs)

DRUG	DOSING	SAFETY/SIDE EFFECTS/MONITORING
Epoetin alfa *(Epogen, Procrit)* IV, SC	**Chronic Kidney Disease** 50-100 units/kg IV or SC 3x/week Initiate when Hgb < 10 g/dL ↓ or interrupt dose when Hgb approaches or exceeds 11 g/dL (CKD on HD), or > 10 g/dL (CKD not on HD) If Hgb increases > 1 g/dL in any 2-week period, interrupt or ↓ dose by ≥ 25% If Hgb ↑ is less than 1 g/dL after 4 weeks, ↑ dose by 25% **Patients on Cancer Chemotherapy** 150 units/kg SC 3x/week or 40,000 units SC weekly Initiate when Hgb < 10 g/dL and when at least 2 additional months of chemotherapy are planned If Hgb increases > 1 g/dL in any 2-week period, interrupt or ↓ dose by 25% If Hgb ↑ is less than 1 g/dL after 4 weeks, ↑ dose to 300 units/kg SC 3x/week or 60,000 units SC weekly	**BOXED WARNINGS** ↑ risk of death, MI, stroke, VTE, thrombosis of vascular access, and tumor progression or recurrence **Chronic Kidney Disease** ↑ risk of death, serious cardiovascular events, and stroke when target Hgb level > 11 g/dL; use the lowest effective dose to reduce the need for blood transfusions **Cancer** Shortened overall survival and/or ↑ risk of tumor progression or recurrence in clinical studies of patients with breast, head and neck, non-small cell lung, lymphoid, and cervical cancers Prescribers and hospitals must enroll in and comply with the ESA APPRISE Oncology Program to prescribe and/or dispense these agents to cancer patients Not indicated when the anticipated outcome is cure; use the lowest effective dose to avoid blood transfusions and discontinue following completion of chemotherapy **Perisurgery** DVT prophylaxis is recommended due to ↑ risk of DVT **CONTRAINDICATIONS** Uncontrolled hypertension, pure red cell aplasia (PRCA) that begins after treatment Epoetin alfa: multidose vials contain benzyl alcohol (contraindicated in neonates, infants, pregnancy and lactation) **WARNINGS** Hypertension, seizures, serious allergic reactions Epoetin alfa: contains albumin from human blood (remote risk for transmission of viral diseases) **SIDE EFFECTS** Arthralgia/bone pain, fever, headache, pruritus/rash, N/V, cough, dyspnea, edema, injection site pain, dizziness **MONITORING** Hgb, Hct, TSAT, serum ferritin, BP **NOTES** IV route is recommended for patients on hemodialysis Do not ↑ the dose more frequently than once every 4 weeks Store in the refrigerator; protect vials from light The t½ of darbepoetin is 3-fold longer than epoetin alfa (hence it can be given less frequently) MedGuide required
Darbepoetin *(Aranesp)* IV, SC	**Chronic Kidney Disease on HD** 0.45 mcg/kg IV or SC weekly or 0.75 mcg/kg IV or SC every 2 weeks **Chronic Kidney Disease Not on HD** 0.45 mcg/kg IV or SC every 4 weeks Initiate when Hgb < 10 g/dL ↓ or interrupt dose when Hgb approaches or exceeds 11 g/dL (CKD on HD), or > 10 g/dL (CKD not on HD) If Hgb increases > 1 g/dL in any 2-week period, interrupt or ↓ dose by ≥ 25% If Hgb ↑ is less than 1 g/dL after 4 weeks, ↑ dose by 25% **Cancer** 2.25 mcg/kg SC weekly or 500 mcg SC every 3 weeks Initiate when Hgb < 10 g/dL and when at least 2 additional months of chemotherapy are planned If Hgb increases > 1 g/dL in any 2-week period, ↓ dose by 40% If Hgb ↑ is less than 1 g/dL after 6 weeks, ↑ dose to 4.5 mcg/kg/week	

ESA Patient Counseling

- This medication is used to treat a condition called anemia, which is when your body is not producing enough red blood cells. It can help reduce your need for a blood transfusion, but to be sure it is working properly, your blood will need to be tested on a regular basis. It is important that you do not miss any scheduled appointments.
- This medication can increase your risk of life-threatening conditions, including heart attack, heart failure, stroke or blood clots. Seek emergency medical help if you have symptoms such as: chest pain, shortness of breath, leg pain (with or without swelling), a cool or pale arm or leg, sudden confusion, trouble speaking, numbness or weakness on one side of your body (e.g., face, arm, or leg), trouble seeing, or loss of consciousness.
- For people with cancer: this medication may make your tumor grow faster. Talk with your healthcare provider about your individual risk.
- This medication may cause other serious side effects such as high blood pressure, seizures or serious allergic reactions (causing rash, shortness of breath, wheezing, fainting, sweating, and/or facial swelling). Stop the medication and contact your healthcare provider right away if you have any of these symptoms.
- Less serious side effects include body aches, headache, fever, and pain or tenderness at areas of the skin where you injected the medication.
- This medication comes in a single-dose vial and must be drawn up into a syringe *(Aranesp* also comes in a pre-filled syringe). Instructions for use include (read the complete instructions for use provided before administration):
  - ❑ Do not shake the vial or syringe as this will ruin the medication and it will not work.
  - ❑ Do not use the medication if it has changed color or has any particles in it.
  - ❑ Do not draw up the dose into a syringe until you are ready to give yourself an injection.
  - ❑ Recommended sites for injection into the skin include the outer areas of the upper arms, the abdomen (except for 2 inches around the navel), the front of the middle thighs, and the upper outer area of the buttocks.

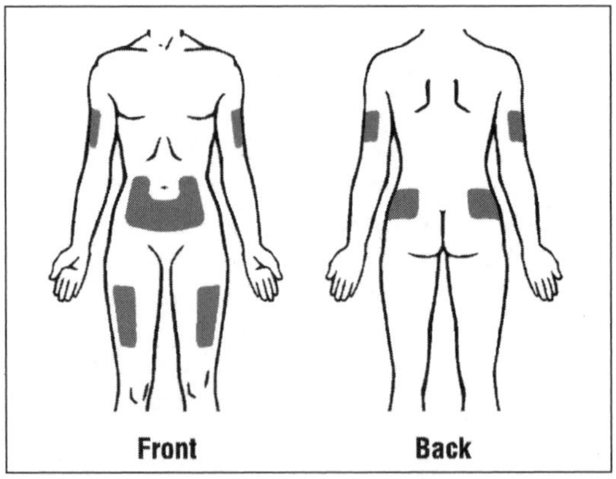

  - ❑ Rotate injections sites; do not inject into an area that is tender, red, bruised, hard or has scars or stretch marks.
  - ❑ Use each vial, syringe, pre-filled syringe and/or needle once only.
  - ❑ Throw away used needles and syringes in a puncture-proof container with a tight fitting lid. Keep this container out of the reach of children and pets. See the Medication Safety & Quality Improvement chapter for more information on disposal of injectable medications.

Aplastic Anemia

Aplastic anemia (AA) occurs when the bone marrow fails to make enough RBCs, WBCs and platelets. It can be caused by drugs, infectious diseases, autoimmune disorders or hereditary conditions, but in many cases, the cause is unknown. Patients with AA are at risk for developing life-threatening infections or bleeding. Treatment may include immunosuppressants, blood transfusions, or a stem cell transplant. Eltrombopag *(Promacta)*, a thrombopoietin nonpeptide agonist which increases platelet counts, was recently approved for the treatment of severe aplastic anemia in patients who are unresponsive to immunosuppressive therapy.

Hemolytic Anemia

Hemolytic anemia develops when RBCs are destroyed and removed from the bloodstream before their normal lifespan of 120 days. This type of anemia can be acquired (e.g., drug-induced, associated with an immune disorder) or inherited (e.g., sickle cell disease, G6PD deficiency). There is more than one mechanism of drug-induced hemolytic anemia, but most often the medication binds to the RBC surface and triggers the development of antibodies that attack the RBC. This autoimmune reaction can persist for several weeks despite the medication being discontinued. The direct Coombs test is used to detect antibodies that are stuck to the surface of RBCs. Medications that can cause acquired hemolytic anemia are listed in the box.

Glucose-6-phosphate dehydrogenase (G6PD) deficiency is an X-linked inherited disorder that most commonly affects persons of African, Asian, Mediterranean, or Middle Eastern descent. The G6PD enzyme protects RBCs from harmful substances (e.g., reactive oxygen species). Without sufficient levels of the enzyme, RBCs hemolyze (break apart) 24 – 72 hours after exposure to oxidative stress. Infections, certain foods (e.g., fava beans), severe stress, and certain drugs are factors that can increase the risk of hemolysis in a patient with G6PD deficiency. When hemolysis is severe, patients present with weakness, tachycardia, jaundice and hematuria, but these symptoms are self-limiting and usually resolve after 8 to 14 days. Most individuals do not need treatment but should be instructed to avoid certain high risk medications (see box) and foods, or other known triggers. Medications that can cause acquired, drug-induced, hemolysis are not prohibited in patients with G6PD deficiency but, if used, they should be monitored closely and discontinued if hemolysis develops.

SELECT DRUGS THAT CAN CAUSE HEMOLYTIC ANEMIA

Drug-Induced (Acquired)

Beta-lactamase inhibitors (e.g., clavulanate, sulbactam, tazobactam)

Cephalosporins (especially ceftriaxone and cefotetan)

Levodopa

Methyldopa

Penicillins (especially piperacillin)

Platinum-based chemotherapy agents (e.g., carboplatin, cisplatin, oxaliplatin)

Quinidine

Quinine

Rifampin

High Risk with G6PD Deficiency (Inherited)

Chloroquine

Dapsone

Methylene Blue

Nitrofurantoin

Primaquine

Probenecid

Sulfonamides

58

SICKLE CELL DISEASE

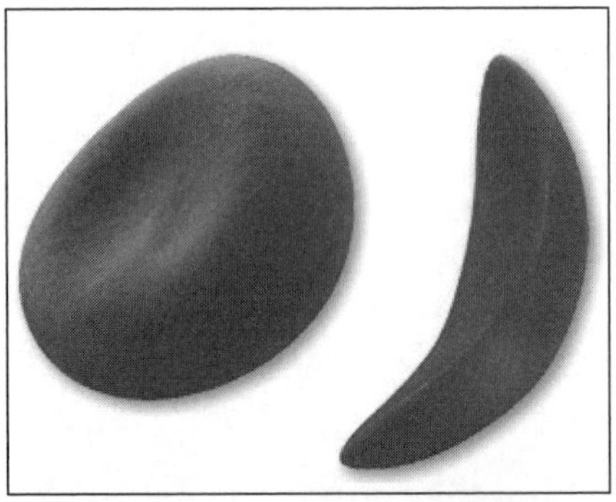

GUIDELINES/REFERENCES

National Heart, Lung, and Blood Institute. Evidence-based management of sickle cell disease. Expert panel report, 2014. http://www.nhlbi.nih.gov/sites/www.nhlbi.nih.gov/files/sickle-cell-disease-report.pdf (accessed 2016 Sep 27).

BACKGROUND

Normal red blood cells (RBCs), containing adult hemoglobin (HgbA), are shaped like a donut (without the hole). These normal RBCs have the flexibility to move through large and small blood vessels and deliver oxygen to the tissues. Sickle cell disease (SCD) is a group of inherited RBC disorders resulting from a genetic abnormality; it most commonly affects the African American population.

Patients with SCD have RBCs that contain abnormal hemoglobin, most commonly HgbS (sickle hemoglobin). This causes RBCs to be rigid with a concave "sickle" shape. It takes approximately 2 – 3 months after birth before symptoms of SCD develop. This is because the fetus, and young infants, have RBCs with fetal hemoglobin (HgbF), which blocks the sickling action of RBCs.

Unlike normal RBCs, which have a lifespan of 90 – 120 days, sickled RBCs burst (hemolyze) after 10 – 20 days, which causes anemia and fatigue. The irregularly shaped RBCs are unable to transport oxygen effectively and stick together, blocking smaller blood vessels and causing patients with SCD to experience a wide array of complications.

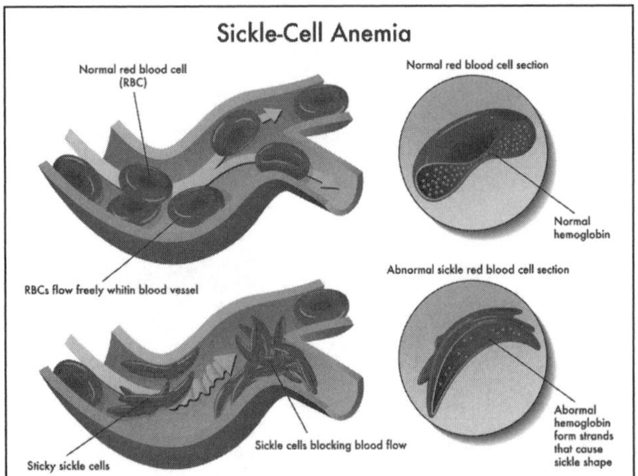

[Roberto Biasini]©123RF.COM

Acute and Chronic Complications

The hallmark of SCD is vascular occlusion, which causes tissues to become ischemic and oxygen-deprived. This can lead to various sickle cell crises, the most common of which is vasoocclusive crisis (VOC), or acute pain crisis. These occur most commonly in the lower back, legs, hips, abdomen and chest, and can last for days or weeks. If the pain is in the chest, and there is evidence of pulmonary infection, it is called acute chest syndrome. Acute chest syndrome is life-threatening and is the leading cause of death in SCD. After VOC and acute chest syndrome, the most common type of crisis is acute stroke. In light of this, preferred contraception methods for females includes progestin-only contraceptives, levonorgestrel intrauterine devices (IUDs) and barrier methods.

The most common chronic complications of SCD are chronic pain, avascular necrosis (bone death), pulmonary hypertension and renal impairment.

SICKLE CELL DISEASE COMPLICATIONS
Acute
Acute chest syndrome
Anemia
Cholecystitis (gallbladder infection)
Infection
Multiorgan failure (kidneys, liver, lung)
Priapism (painful and prolonged erection)
Spleen sequestration
Stroke
Vasoocclusive crisis (acute pain crisis)
Chronic
Avascular necrosis (bone death)
Gallstones
Leg ulcers
Pain
Pregnancy complications and loss
Pulmonary hypertension
Renal impairment
Retinopathy
Stuttering or recurrent priapism

Infection Risk

A healthy spleen has several physiologic roles, including the removal of old or damaged RBCs. It also aids in immune function, as it makes and stores white blood cells and clears some types of bacterial pathogens from the body, particularly the encapsulated organisms *Streptococcus pneumoniae*, *Haemophilus influenzae*, and *Neisseria meningitidis*. In SCD, the spleen becomes fibrotic and shrinks in size due to repetitive sickling and infarctions. This causes functional asplenia (decreased or absent spleen function), which typically manifests within the first year of life. Patients with functional asplenia are at increased risk for serious infections; they should receive immunizations, prophylactic antibiotics when indicated, and seek medical attention whenever temperature > 101.3°F occurs.

NON-DRUG TREATMENT

Blood transfusions protect against many of the life-threatening complications by providing RBCs with HgbA. Stroke, acute chest syndrome and severe anemia are acute complications that warrant blood transfusion. Chronic, monthly, blood transfusions can decrease the risk of stroke in adults and children. Regardless of the indication, the goal Hgb level is no higher than 10 g/dL post-infusion. One of the risks of blood transfusions is iron overload, which can lead to hemosiderosis (excess iron that impairs organ function). Chelation therapy to remove excess iron is discussed later in the chapter.

The only cure for SCD is bone marrow transplantation. Due to the high risks involved with such toxic therapy, as well as the substantial cost, it is not a widely used approach. Children are more likely to tolerate bone marrow transplantation than adults, who have accumulated organ damage. Gene therapy, by providing an antisickling gene and allowing for production of normal RBCs, is under investigation.

DRUG TREATMENT

The primary drug classes used in SCD are immunizations and antibiotics to reduce infection risk, analgesics to control pain, hydroxyurea to prevent or reduce the frequency of acute and chronic complications, and chelation therapy to manage iron overload from blood transfusions.

Immunizations and Antibiotics

Infections are a major cause of death, especially in children < 5 years of age. Sepsis and meningitis due to encapsulated bacteria *(S. pneumoniae, H. influenzae, N. meningitidis, Salmonella spp.)* can occur. Infections with atypical organisms *(Chlamydophila* and *Mycoplasma pneumoniae)* are also increased. Prophylactic penicillin, usually given orally, reduces the mortality associated with invasive pneumococcal infection in young children. Infants who screen positive for SCD at birth should be initiated on twice daily penicillin and treated until age 5 years. If a patient undergoes surgical removal of the spleen, or if invasive pneumococcal infection develops despite penicillin prophylaxis, it should be continued indefinitely. In addition to penicillin prophylaxis, vaccinations are essential to prevent infection.

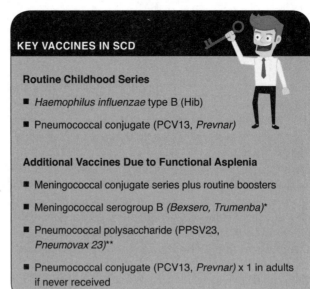

KEY VACCINES IN SCD

Routine Childhood Series

- *Haemophilus influenzae* type B (Hib)
- Pneumococcal conjugate (PCV13, *Prevnar)*

Additional Vaccines Due to Functional Asplenia

- Meningococcal conjugate series plus routine boosters
- Meningococcal serogroup B *(Bexsero, Trumenba)**
- Pneumococcal polysaccharide (PPSV23, *Pneumovax 23)***
- Pneumococcal conjugate (PCV13, *Prevnar)* x 1 in adults if never received

**At age ≥ 10 years*
***At age ≥ 2 years, booster 5 years later, and at age ≥ 65 years*

Analgesics

Mild to moderate pain can often be managed at home with rest, fluids, application of warm compresses to affected areas, and the use of NSAIDs or acetaminophen. For severe pain and VOC, management must be guided by the patient's self-reported pain severity. Outpatient analgesic use should be reviewed and a treatment plan initiated within 30 minutes of triage. Patients with severe pain and VOC will require IV administration of opioids or patient-controlled analgesia (PCA).

Hydroxyurea

Hydroxyurea is a disease-modifying agent that stimulates production of HgbF. Long-term use of hydroxyurea reduces the frequency of acute pain crises, episodes of acute chest syndrome, and the need for blood transfusions. It is indicated for adults with ≥ 3 moderate – severe pain crises in 1 year or patients with severe or recurrent acute chest syndrome, chronic symptomatic anemia, or disability. Use should be considered in all children > 9 months of age regardless of disease severity.

DRUG	DOSE	SAFETY/SIDE EFFECTS/MONITORING
Hydroxyurea *(Droxia, Hydrea)* Capsule	Start: 15 mg/kg daily as a single dose CrCl < 60 mL/min: start at 5-10 mg/kg daily Infants and children: start at 20 mg/kg daily Titrate by 5 mg/kg/day every 8 weeks to a goal absolute neutrophil count (ANC) of 2,000-4,000/mm^3 Max: 35 mg/kg daily Use IBW or TBW, whichever is less when calculating daily dose Round doses up to the nearest capsule	**BOXED WARNINGS** Myelosuppression (↓ WBCs and platelets), malignancy (leukemia, skin cancer). **WARNINGS** Embryo-fetal toxicity, skin ulcers, live vaccinations, macrocytosis, interactions with antiretroviral drugs. **SIDE EFFECTS** Alopecia, hyperpigmentation or atrophy of skin and nails, low sperm counts (males), anorexia, ↑ LFTs, uric acid, BUN and SCr. **MONITORING** CBC with differential every 4 weeks during initiation and titration, then every 2-3 months once stable dose achieved. If toxicity occurs (ANC < 2,000/mm^3, platelets < 80,000/mm^3), withhold hydroxyurea until bone marrow recovers, then restart at a dose 5 mg/kg/day lower. HgbF, uric acid, renal function, LFTs, baseline pregnancy test. **NOTES** Safety issue – see Pregnancy chapter. Contraception required during treatment and after discontinuation (6 months for females, 12 months for males). Hazardous agent – wear gloves when dispensing and wash hands before and after contact. Folic acid supplementation for macrocytosis. Clinical response can take 3-6 months.

Hydroxyurea Drug Interactions

Concurrent treatment with antiretrovirals (including didanosine and stavudine), has a higher risk for potentially fatal pancreatitis, hepatotoxicity, hepatic failure, and severe peripheral neuropathy. Use should be avoided in combination with other drugs that cause myelosuppression, including clozapine, leflunomide, natalizumab, pimecrolimus, tacrolimus (topical), and tofacitinib.

Hydroxyurea Patient Counseling

- Hydroxyurea can lower your body's ability to fight infection and make you more prone to illness or bleeding.
  - Call your healthcare provider immediately if you experience fever, chills, body aches, severe sore throat, mouth sores, cough, shortness of breath, painful or difficult urination, easy bruising/ bleeding, purple or red pinpoint spots under the skin, pale skin, rash, rapid heart rate, and/or confusion.
- Anyone handling the capsules (patient or caregiver) should wear disposable gloves to reduce the risk of exposure. Wash hands before and after handling. The capsules should not be opened.
- If you accidentally spill any of the contents, immediately wipe up with a damp cloth and throw cloth away in a sealed plastic bag, then clean the area three times with detergent solution followed by clean water.
- For males and females of reproductive age:
  - This medication can decrease sperm count in men.
  - Avoid getting pregnant while taking this medication as it can harm an unborn baby. Discuss effective birth control and family planning with your healthcare provider.
  - Effective contraception should be used during and even after stopping this medication (for males at least one year, females at least 6 months).
- Wear sun protection, as this medication can increase the risk of skin cancer.

Iron Chelation Treatment

Chronic blood transfusions cause iron overload, which damages the liver, heart and other organs. Chelation therapy is used to remove excess iron stores from the body. Historically, deferoxamine (the antidote for iron toxicity) was used, but it has significant toxicities, is not available in oral formulation, and requires slow, prolonged infusions over 8 – 12 hours when administered by IV or SC routes. In the last decade, the oral chelating agents, deferasirox *(Exjade, Jadenu)* and deferiprone *(Ferriprox)*, have become available and are more commonly used. Due to the side effect profile of both agents, treatment is typically prescribed, dispensed and monitored by specialty clinics and pharmacies.

59

DEPRESSION

GUIDELINES/REFERENCES

Institute for Clinical Systems Improvement (ICSI). Major depression in adults in primary care. Bloomington (MN): Institute for Clinical Systems Improvement (ICSI); March 2016.

Diagnostic and Statistical Manual of Mental Disorders (DSM-5).

Additional guidelines included with the online course.

We gratefully acknowledge the assistance of Jennifer Bean, PharmD, BCPS, BCPP, Clinical Pharmacist, VA Tennessee Valley Healthcare System, in preparing this chapter.

BACKGROUND

Major Depressive Disorder (MDD, or referred to here as "depression") is one of the most common health conditions in the world. The statistics are sobering. In 2015, approximately 16.1 million adults, 18 years or older, experienced a major depressive episode in the past year. Although approximately half of these people seek help for this condition, only 20 percent (10 percent of the total population with MDD) receive adequate treatment, and just 30 percent of those who receive adequate treatment reach the treatment goal of remission. People with depression suffer greatly with persistent feelings of hopelessness, dejection, constant worry, poor concentration, a lack of energy, an inability to sleep and, sometimes, suicidal tendencies.

Healthcare providers should remember that depression is usually a chronic illness that requires long-term treatment, much like diabetes or high blood pressure. Although some people experience only one episode, the majority have recurrent episodes. A significant treatment problem is patients who discontinue their medication, or, continue medication despite an inadequate response. This is discussed under "Treatment-Resistant Depression." Due to high rates of inadequate response, pharmacists should attempt to ensure adequate treatment trials: 6 – 8 weeks, at a therapeutic dose (the VA/DoD guideline recommends an 8 – 12 week trial).

CAUSES OF DEPRESSION

The causes of depression are poorly understood, but involve some combination of genetic, biologic and environmental factors. Neurotransmitters believed to be involved in depression include serotonin (5HT), glutamate, acetylcholine (ACh), dopamine (DA), norepinephrine (NE) and epinephrine (EPI). Serotonin (5HT) may be the most important neurotransmitter (NT) involved with feelings of well being. Recent research has focused on complex or completely novel pathways that may be involved in depression. Since it is not possible at this time to measure brain chemical imbalances, treatment for mood disorders, including depression, depends on a competent assessment and trial. If a drug does not work, after a suitable trial of at least 6 – 8 weeks, a trial of an alternative agent in the same class or a combination with an agent from a different class, targeting a different NT, is recommended. Patient history is critical in treating any mental illness; what worked in the past, or did not work, should help guide current and future therapy. Pharmacists should always counsel patients, family and caregivers that mood may worsen. The patient needs instructions on how to respond to worsened mood. This is critical for adolescents and young adults in particular, secondary to boxed warnings with regard to increased risk of suicidal thinking and behavior in this population.

DEPRESSION DIAGNOSIS

DSM-5 criteria requires the presence of at least 5 of the following symptoms (even if they are in response to a significant loss like bereavement or financial ruin) during the same two week period (must include depressed mood or diminished interest/pleasure):

Mood - depressed

Sleep - increased/decreased

Interest/pleasure - diminished

Guilt or feelings of worthlessness

Energy - decreased

Concentration - decreased

Appetite - increased/decreased

Psychomotor agitation or retardation

Suicidal ideation

Mnemonic: M SIG E CAPS

CONCURRENT BIPOLAR OR ANXIETY DISORDERS

It is necessary to rule-out bipolar disorder prior to initiating antidepressant therapy in order to treat the patient properly and avoid rapid-cycling (cycling rapidly from one phase to the other). This is why screening forms for MDD now include questions designed to identify mania symptoms such as "There are times when I get into moods where I feel very speeded up or irritable."

Benzodiazepine (BZD) therapy is often used adjunctively in depression with concurrent anxiety, although in many cases the BZD is the only "treatment" and the depression itself is left untreated. BZDs can cause and/or mask depression and put the patient at risk for physiological dependence and withdrawal symptoms when the dose is wearing off (tachycardia, anxiety, amongst others). Prescribers should also select BZDs carefully and monitor closely if patients have co-occurring substance use disorders. See Anxiety chapter for further discussion.

LAG EFFECT AND SUICIDE PREVENTION

Patients should be told that the medicine must be used daily, and will take time to work. It is important to inform the patient that physical symptoms such as low energy improve within a few weeks but psychological symptoms, such as low mood, may take a month or longer. It is imperative for clinicians to educate patients about the risk of suicidality and to screen for suicide risk. If a patient reports suicidal ideation, refer the patient to the ED, the suicide hotline, or elsewhere for help. If someone has a plan to commit suicide, it is more likely that the threat is real.

DRUG TREATMENT

The guidelines state that because the effectiveness of the different antidepressant classes is generally comparable, the initial choice of an agent should be based on the side effect profile, safety concerns and patient-specific symptoms. For most patients an SSRI, SNRI or (with specific concurrent conditions or considerations) mirtazapine or bupropion is preferred.

Due to safety concerns (drug-drug and drug-food interactions) the use of the oral nonselective monoamine oxidase inhibitors (MAO inhibitors) such as phenelzine, tranylcypromine and isocarboxazid is restricted to patients unresponsive to other treatments. Serotonin syndrome can occur with administration of one or more serotonergic medications (higher doses increase risk), but is most severe when an MAO inhibitor is administered with another serotonergic medication. Refer to the Drug Interactions chapter for additional information.

Psychotherapy or medication is acceptable for mild depression. Moderate to severe depression should be treated with medication in addition to the option of psychotherapy. If a drug is being discontinued, it should be tapered off over several weeks. An exception to this rule would be for a medication with a longer half-life such as fluoxetine which self-tapers given its long half-life. In some instances a drug with a longer half-life (e.g., fluoxetine) can be used to minimize withdrawal symptoms. Withdrawal symptoms (anxiety, agitation, insomnia, dizziness, flu-like symptoms) can be quite distressing to the patient. Paroxetine, venlafaxine, and some other agents carry a high risk of withdrawal symptoms and must be tapered upon discontinuation. It is imperative that pharmacists counsel patients on the risk of withdrawal symptoms with these medications and encourage the patient to not self-discontinue the medication without a discussion with their healthcare provider.

Treatment-Resistant Depression

Prescribers should supervise a trial of 6 – 8 weeks at an adequate (therapeutic) dose before concluding that the drug is not working well. Only about half of patients respond to the prescribed antidepressant and just about one-third will reach remission (the elimination of depressive symptoms). The goal of therapy is remission. An incomplete response can necessitate any of the following:

- A dosage increase.
- A combination of antidepressants utilizing different mechanism of actions.
- Augmentation with scheduled buspirone or a low dose of an atypical antipsychotic. Agents approved as augmentation therapy with antidepressants are aripiprazole *(Abilify)*, olanzapine + fluoxetine *(Symbyax)* and quetiapine extended release *(Seroquel XR)*.
- Other guideline recommendations (as there are several, with various recommendations) include augmentation with lithium, thyroid hormone, and in some cases, electroconvulsive therapy (ECT).
- In 2012, good trial results were reported with the use of ketamine, which suggests alternative mechanisms may be targeted for improved treatment response.

MEDICATIONS THAT CAN CAUSE OR WORSEN DEPRESSION

Beta-blockers (particularly propranolol)

Clonidine

Corticosteroids

Cyclosporine

Ethanol

Isotretinoin

Indomethacin

Interferons

Methadone, and possibly other chronic opioid use that can lower testosterone or estrogen levels

Oral contraceptives, anabolic steroids (medication-specific, patient specific)

Methyldopa

Methylphenidate/Other ADHD Stimulants/Atomoxetine: Monitor mood

Procainamide

Reserpine

Statins (patient specific, some cases)

Varenicline

Antidepressants require monitoring for worsening mood, especially among younger people

In addition to the medications listed, medical conditions such as stroke, Parkinson's disease, dementia, multiple sclerosis, thyroid disorders (particularly hypothyroidism), low vitamin D levels (possible link), metabolic conditions (e.g., hypercalcemia), malignancy, OAB and infectious diseases can be contributory.

Antidepressant Use in Pregnancy, Postpartum Depression

Untreated maternal depression, especially in the late second or early third trimesters, is associated with increased rates of adverse outcomes (e.g., premature birth, low birth weight, fetal growth restriction, postnatal complications). Depression in pregnant women often goes unrecognized and untreated. All drugs carry risk, and the risk/benefit must be considered individually.

If a woman is on antidepressants and wishes to become pregnant, it may be possible to taper the drug if the depression is mild and she has been symptom free for the previous six months. In more severe cases, medications may need to be continued or started. The ACOG guidelines for mild depression in pregnancy recommend psychotherapy first, followed by drug treatment if needed. The initiation of drug treatment for depression in pregnant patients is of concern because of the risks of adverse outcomes for both the mother and the unborn baby. Historically, SSRIs are often used initially, except for paroxetine, due to potential cardiac effects and the new formulation of paroxetine, *Brisdelle*, which is contraindicated. Although SSRIs have historically been preferred, in December of 2011 the FDA issued a warning regarding SSRI use during pregnancy and the potential risk of persistent pulmonary hypertension of the newborn (PPHN). Tricyclics are the second group of agents that are most commonly used. Refer to the Pregnancy chapter.

Postpartum depression is common but often unrecognized and under-treated, with adverse outcomes for the mother, baby, and family. Breastfeeding is helpful for most women for physical and emotional symptoms, and is considered beneficial for the baby. Drug safety in breastfeeding, therefore, is essential. SSRIs or tricyclics are generally preferred (with the exception of doxepin, per the ACOG recommendations).

NATURAL PRODUCTS

St. John's wort or SAMe (S-adenosyl-L-methionine) may be helpful. Both are classified as "likely effective" for treating depression in the *Natural Medicines Database*, but there is less evidence of efficacy than with standard treatments. Both agents cannot be used with other serotonergic agents. St. John's wort is a broad spectrum CYP450 enzyme inducer and has many significant drug interactions. It is a photosensitizer and is serotonergic; use caution with other 5HT drugs due to risk of serotonin syndrome.

SSRIs: Selective Serotonin Reuptake Inhibitors

<table>
<tr><th>DRUG</th><th>DOSING</th><th>SAFETY/SIDE EFFECTS/MONITORING</th></tr>
<tr><td>FLUoxetine
(PROzac, Sarafem, PROzac Weekly)

+ OLANZapine (Symbyax) – taken QHS, for resistant depression</td><td>10-60 mg/day (titrate to 60 mg/day for bulimia, max 80 mg/day for MDD, obsessive-compulsive disorder); 90 mg weekly

Premenstrual dysphoric disorder (PMDD): Sarafem 20 mg every day of menstrual cycle or 20 mg daily starting 14 days prior to menstruation through 1st full day of bleeding

Symbyax: initial 6/25 mg QHS</td><td rowspan="6">BOXED WARNING
Antidepressants increase the risk of suicidal thinking and behavior in children, adolescents, and young adults (18-24 years of age) with major depressive disorder (MDD) and other psychiatric disorders; consider risk prior to prescribing.

CONTRAINDICATIONS
Concurrent use with MAO inhibitors, linezolid, IV methylene blue, or pimozide; concurrent use with thioridazine (fluoxetine, paroxetine); concurrent use with alosetron, ramelteon, or tizanidine (fluvoxamine); concurrent use with disulfiram (sertraline); pregnancy (Brisdelle)

SIDE EFFECTS
Sexual side effects: include ↓ libido, ejaculation difficulties, anorgasmia

Somnolence, insomnia, nausea, dry mouth, diaphoresis (dose-related), weakness, tremor, dizziness, headache (but may help for migraines if taken continuously)

Fluoxetine can cause activation; take dose in AM, others AM (usually) or PM, if sedating

SIADH, hyponatremia (elderly at higher risk)

Restless leg syndrome (see if this began when treatment was started)

↑ fall risk; use extreme caution in frail patients, osteopenia/osteoporosis, use of CNS depressants

NOTES
All approved for depression and a variety of anxiety disorders except fluvoxamine, which is only approved for OCD.

FDA warning that olanzapine-containing products (Symbyax) can cause multiorgan hypersensitivity (DRESS) reactions.

FDA warning regarding QT risk and citalopram at > 40 mg/day or > 20 mg/day in elderly (60+ years), liver disease, with CYP 2C19 poor metabolizers or on 2C19 inhibitors. Similar, but lower risk for escitalopram at > 20 mg/day; do not exceed 10 mg/day in elderly. Bottom line: if cardiac risk is present, best to avoid citalopram. Sertraline is often the top choice for an SSRI in cardiac patients.

All available in solution except fluvoxamine.

Fluvoxamine has more drug interactions.

↑ bleeding risk with concurrent use of anticoagulants, antiplatelets, NSAIDs, gingko, thrombolytics.

Safety issue - see Pregnancy chapter.

To switch to fluoxetine 90 mg/weekly from fluoxetine daily, start 7 days after last daily dose.</td></tr>
<tr><td>PARoxetine
(Paxil, Pexeva, Paxil CR, Brisdelle)</td><td>IR: 10-60 mg/day

CR: 12.5-62.5 mg/day (max 75 mg/day for panic disorder)

Each 10 mg IR = 12.5 mg CR</td></tr>
<tr><td>FluvoxaMINE IR/ER (Luvox)</td><td>50-300 mg/day (daily doses > 100 mg/day should be divided BID)</td></tr>
<tr><td>Sertraline
(Zoloft)</td><td>50-200 mg/day

Premenstrual dysphoric disorder (PMDD): 50-150 mg every day of menstrual cycle or 50-150 mg daily starting 14 days prior to menstruation through 1st full day of bleeding</td></tr>
<tr><td>Citalopram
(CeleXA)</td><td>20-40 mg/day</td></tr>
<tr><td>Escitalopram
(Lexapro – S-enantiomer of citalopram)</td><td>10 mg/day (can ↑ 20 mg/day)</td></tr>
</table>

SSRI and Combined Mechanism

DRUG	DOSING	SAFETY/SIDE EFFECTS/MONITORING

SSRI and 5-HT1A Partial Agonist

DRUG	DOSING	SAFETY/SIDE EFFECTS/MONITORING
Vilazodone *(Viibryd)*	Start at 10 mg x 7 days, then 20 mg daily (dosing in patient starter kit); take with food	**BOXED WARNING** Antidepressants increase the risk of suicidal thinking and behavior in children, adolescents, and young adults (18-24 years of age) with major depressive disorder (MDD) and other psychiatric disorders; consider risk prior to prescribing. **CONTRAINDICATIONS** Potentially lethal drug interaction with MAO inhibitors; see washout information. Do not initiate in patients being treated with linezolid or methylene blue IV. **SIDE EFFECTS** N/V/D, insomnia, ↓ libido (less sexual SEs compared to SSRIs and SNRIs) **NOTES** ↑ bleeding risk with concurrent use of anticoagulants, anti-platelets, NSAIDs, gingko, thrombolytics.

SSRI, 5-HT Receptor Antagonist, 5-HT1A Agonist

DRUG	DOSING	SAFETY/SIDE EFFECTS/MONITORING
Vortioxetine *(Trintellix)*	10 mg/day, can ↑ 20 mg/day, with or without food (5 mg/day if higher doses not tolerated)	**BOXED WARNING** Antidepressants increase the risk of suicidal thinking and behavior in children, adolescents, and young adults (18-24 years of age) with major depressive disorder (MDD) and other psychiatric disorders; consider risk prior to prescribing. **CONTRAINDICATIONS** Potentially lethal drug interaction with MAO inhibitors; see washout information. Do not initiate in patients being treated with linezolid or methylene blue IV. **SIDE EFFECTS** Nausea, constipation, vomiting **NOTES** ↑ bleeding risk with concurrent use of anticoagulants, antiplatelets, NSAIDs, gingko, thrombolytics.

SSRI Drug Interactions

- MAO inhibitors and hypertensive crisis: allow 2 weeks either going to an MAO inhibitor or from an MAO inhibitor to an SSRI except fluoxetine which requires a 5 week washout period if going from fluoxetine to an MAO inhibitor (due to the long half-life of fluoxetine of at least 7 days).
- Fluoxetine: 2D6, 2C19 inhibitor. Fluvoxamine: 1A2, 2D6, 2C9, 2C19, 3A4 inhibitor. Paroxetine: 2D6 inhibitor. Note all three are 2D6 inhibitors and some other antipsychotics drugs are 2D6 substrates (e.g., aripiprazole, olanzapine). Antipsychotic drugs are sometimes used in combination and the dose of the antipsychotic may need to be lowered when given with these agents.

- Tamoxifen's effectiveness decreases with fluoxetine, paroxetine and sertraline (and duloxetine and bupropion).
- ↑ bleeding risk with concurrent use of anticoagulants, antiplatelets, NSAIDs, gingko, thrombolytics.
- Do not use with thioridazine or pimozide.
- Do not use with cimetidine.
- Do not initiate in patients receiving linezolid or methylene blue IV due to risk of serotonin syndrome.
- Caution with drugs that cause orthostasis or CNS depressants due to risk of falls.
- *Trintellix*: when a strong 2D6 inhibitor (e.g., bupropion, fluoxetine, paroxetine, or quinidine) is co-administered, reduce *Trintellix* dose by half. Consider increasing *Trintellix* dose when a strong CYP inducer (e.g., rifampin, carbamazepine, or phenytoin) is coadministered for more than 2 weeks.

SSRI Counseling

- Read the MedGuide that has been given to you. Especially in adolescents and young adults: counsel on risk of suicide – particularly during therapy initiation.
- Fluoxetine is taken in the morning; the others can be taken in the morning or at bedtime.
- To reduce your risk of side effects, your healthcare provider may start this drug at a low dose and gradually increase your dose.
- Take this medication exactly as prescribed. To help you remember, use it at the same time each day. Antidepressants do not work if they are taken as needed.
- It is important to continue taking this medication even if you feel well. Do not stop taking this medication without consulting your healthcare provider. Some conditions may become worse when the drug is suddenly stopped. Your dose may need to be gradually decreased.
- It may take 1 to 2 weeks to feel a benefit from this drug and 6 – 8 weeks to feel the full effect on your mood. Tell your healthcare provider if your condition persists or worsens. You can try a medication in a different class. One will work or it may take different tries to find the right medicine that will help you feel better.
- This medication increases the levels of a chemical in your blood called serotonin. If it is taken with other OTC or prescription medications that also increase serotonin, toxicity can occur. Seek urgent medical care if you have symptoms of toxicity: severe nausea, dizziness and headache, diarrhea, feeling very agitated, a racing heartbeat or hallucinations.
- Some patients, but not all, have sexual difficulties when using this medicine. If this happens, talk with your healthcare provider. They can change you to a medicine that does not cause these problems.
- Sertraline oral concentrate must be diluted before use. Immediately before administration, use the dropper provided to measure the required amount of concentrate; mix with 4 ounces (1/2 cup) of water, ginger ale, lemon/lime soda, lemonade, or orange juice only. Do not use with disulfiram.

SNRIs – Serotonin and Norepinephrine Reuptake Inhibitors

DRUG	DOSING	SAFETY/SIDE EFFECTS/MONITORING
Venlafaxine *(Effexor, Effexor XR)* Depression, GAD, Panic Disorder, Social Anxiety Disorder	75-375 mg/day (max 375 mg/day for IR and 225 mg/day for ER Can start low with 37.5 mg Different generics; check orange book	**BOXED WARNING** Antidepressants increase the risk of suicidal thinking and behavior in children, adolescents, and young adults (18-24 years of age) with major depressive disorder (MDD) and other psychiatric disorders; consider risk prior to prescribing. **CONTRAINDICATIONS** Potentially lethal DI: SNRIs and MAO inhibitors – see washout information. Do not initiate in a patient receiving linezolid or intravenous methylene blue. **SIDE EFFECTS** Similar to SSRIs (due to serotonin reuptake) and side effects due to ↑ NE uptake: ↑ pulse, dilated pupils (possibly leading to an episode of narrow angle glaucoma), dry mouth, excessive sweating and constipation. SNRIs can affect urethral resistance. Caution is advised when using SNRIs in patients prone to obstructive urinary disorders. All have warning for ↑ BP, but risk is greatest with venlafaxine when dosed > 150 mg/day; yet all have risk especially at higher doses. ↑ BP may respond to dose reduction, use of antihypertensive or change in therapy. **NOTES** The SNRI dose is ↓ in renal impairment. Do not use levomilnacipran with CrCl < 15 mL/min or duloxetine with CrCl < 30 mL/min. ↑ bleeding risk with concurrent use of anticoagulants, antiplatelets, NSAIDs, gingko, thrombolytics.
DULoxetine *(Cymbalta)* Depression, Peripheral Neuropathy (Pain), Fibromyalgia, GAD, Chronic Musculoskeletal Pain	40-60 mg/day (daily, or 20-30 BID); max dose 120 mg/day; doses > 60 mg/day not more effective Duloxetine is a good choice if the patient has both pain and depression	
Desvenlafaxine *(Pristiq, Khedezla)* Depression	50 mg/day, can ↑ 100 mg/day	
Levomilnacipran *(Fetzima)* Depression	40-120 mg/day Start at 20 mg/day x 2 days Do not open, chew or crush capsules; take whole. Do not take with alcohol.	

SNRI Drug Interactions

- MAO inhibitors and hypertensive crisis: 5 – 14 day (duloxetine) or 7 day (venlafaxine, desvenlafaxine, levomilnacipran) washout if going from SNRI to a MAO inhibitor, 14 day washout if going from MAO inhibitor to SNRI.
- Duloxetine is a moderate 2D6 inhibitor.
- Tamoxifen's effectiveness decreases with duloxetine.
- Do not initiate in patients receiving linezolid or methylene blue IV due to risk of serotonin syndrome.
- ↑ bleeding risk with concurrent use of anticoagulants, antiplatelets, NSAIDs, gingko, thrombolytics.
- If on antihypertensive medications, use caution and monitor (can ↑ BP), especially at higher doses.

SNRI Counseling

- Read the MedGuide that has been given to you. Especially in adolescents and young adults: counsel on risk of suicide – particularly during therapy initiation.
- This medication may cause nausea and stomach upset (if using venlafaxine IR, consider a change to XR).
- You may experience increased sweating; if so, discuss with your healthcare provider.
- This medication may increase your blood pressure. You should check your blood pressure regularly to make sure it stays in a safe range.
- Desvenlafaxine: When you take this medicine, you may see something in your stool that looks like a tablet. This is the empty shell from the tablet after the medicine has been absorbed by your body.
- Levomilnacipran: Take capsules whole. Do not open, chew or crush the capsules. Do not take with alcohol; this could cause the medicine to be released too quickly.
- To reduce your risk of side effects, your healthcare provider may start this drug at a low dose and gradually increase your dose.
- Do not crush or chew extended-release formulations.
- Take this medication exactly as directed. To help you remember, use it at the same time each day. Antidepressants do not work if they are taken as needed.
- It is important to continue taking this medication even if you feel well. Do not stop taking this medication without consulting your healthcare provider. Some conditions may become worse when the drug is suddenly stopped. Your dose may need to be gradually decreased.
- It can take 1 to 2 weeks to feel a benefit from this drug and 6 – 8 weeks to feel the full effect on your mood. Tell your healthcare provider if your condition persists or worsens. You can try a medication in a different class. One will work or it may take different tries to find the right medicine that will help you feel better.
- This medication increases the levels of a chemical in your blood called serotonin. If it is taken with other OTC or prescription medications that also increase serotonin, toxicity can occur. Seek urgent medical care if you have symptoms of toxicity: severe nausea, dizziness and headache, diarrhea, feeling very agitated, a racing heartbeat or hallucinations.
- Some patients, but not all, have sexual difficulties when using this medicine. If this happens, talk with your healthcare provider. They can change you to a medicine that does not cause these problems.

TRICYCLICS

NE and 5HT reuptake inhibitors primarily. They also block ACh and histamine receptors which contributes to the SE profile.

DRUG	DOSING	SAFETY/SIDE EFFECTS/MONITORING
TERTIARY AMINES **Amitriptyline** *(Elavil)* **Doxepin** – *Zonalon and Prudoxin* are creams for pruritus, *Silenor* is for insomnia ClomiPRAMINE *(Anafranil)* Imipramine *(Tofranil)* Trimipramine *(Surmontil)* **SECONDARY AMINES** Amoxapine Desipramine *(Norpramin)* Maprotiline **Nortriptyline** *(Pamelor)* Protriptyline (Secondary amines are relatively selective for NE – tertiary amines may be slightly more effective but have worse SE profile)	**AMITRIPTYLINE** Depression: 100-300 mg/day QHS or divided doses Neuropathic pain/migraine prophylaxis: 10-50 mg QHS **DOXEPIN** Depression: 100-300 mg/day **NORTRIPTYLINE** Depression: 25 mg TID-QID	**BOXED WARNING** Antidepressants increase the risk of suicidal thinking and behavior in children, adolescents, and young adults (18-24 years of age) with major depressive disorder (MDD) and other psychiatric disorders; consider risk prior to prescribing. **CONTRAINDICATIONS** Concurrent use with MAO inhibitors, linezolid, IV methylene blue; myocardial infarction, glaucoma (doxepin), urinary retention (doxepin) **SIDE EFFECTS** **Cardiotoxicity** QT prolongation with overdose (these agents can be used for suicide); obtain baseline ECG if cardiac risk factors or age > 50 years old Orthostasis, tachycardia **Anticholinergic** Dry mouth, blurred vision, urinary retention, constipation (taper off to avoid cholinergic rebound) Vivid dreams, weight gain (varies by agent and patient), sedation, sweating Myoclonus (muscle twitching – may be symptoms of drug toxicity) **NOTES** ↑ fall risk – especially in elderly due to combination of orthostasis and sedation Tertiary amines have increased anticholinergic properties, thus are more likely to cause sedation and weight gain

Tricyclic Drug Interactions

- MAO inhibitors and hypertensive crisis: 2 week washout if going to or from an MAO inhibitor.
- Additive QT prolongation risk; see Drug Interaction chapter for other high risk QT drugs to attempt to avoid additive risk.
- Metabolized by CYP 2D6 (up to 10% of Caucasians are slow metabolizers); check for drug interactions.

Tricyclic Counseling

- Read the MedGuide that has been given to you. Especially in adolescents and young adults: counsel on risk of suicide – particularly during therapy initiation. TCAs are dangerous if the patient wishes to commit suicide; a month's supply can be deadly. Counseling is critical.
- This medication dries you out. You may experience dry eyes and mouth, constipation, or difficulty urinating. You can use stool softeners or a laxative for constipation and an eye lubricant for dry eyes. Dry mouth can contribute to dental decay (cavities) and difficulty chewing food. It is important to use proper dental hygiene, including brushing and flossing, while taking this medication. Sugar free lozenges may be helpful.
- This drug can cause your blood pressure to fluctuate, which can cause dizziness and lightheadedness. This can cause falls. It is important to get up slowly from the lying position or from sitting, and to hold onto the bed, a bed rail or a strong table top until you feel steady.

- If you experience anxiety, or insomnia (sometimes with vivid dreams), these usually go away. If they do not, contact your healthcare provider.
- Take this medication exactly as prescribed. To help you remember, use it at the same time each day. Antidepressants do not work if they are taken as needed.
- It is important to continue taking this medication even if you feel well. Do not stop taking this medication without consulting your healthcare provider. Some conditions may become worse when the drug is suddenly stopped. Your dose may need to be gradually decreased.
- It can take 1 to 2 weeks to feel a benefit from this drug and 6 – 8 weeks to feel the full effect on your mood. Tell the healthcare provider if your condition persists or worsens. You can try a medication in a different class. It may take several tries to find the right medicine that will help you feel better.

Monoamine Oxidase Inhibitors

Monoamine oxidase inhibitors (MAOIs) inhibit the enzyme monoamine oxidase, which breaks down catecholamines, including 5-HT, NE, EPI, and DA. If these NTs ↑ dramatically, hypertensive crisis, and death can result.

<table>
<tr><th>DRUG</th><th>DOSING</th><th>SAFETY/SIDE EFFECTS/MONITORING/</th></tr>
<tr><td>Isocarboxazid (Marplan)</td><td>20 mg/day in divided doses, max 60 mg/day</td><td rowspan="3">BOXED WARNING
Antidepressants increase the risk of suicidal thinking and behavior in children, adolescents, and young adults (18-24 years of age) with major depressive disorder (MDD) and other psychiatric disorders; consider risk prior to prescribing.

CONTRAINDICATIONS
Cardiovascular disease, cerebrovascular defect, history of headache, history of hepatic disease, pheochromocytoma. Concurrent use of sympathomimetics and related compounds, CNS depressants, dextromethorphan, ethanol, meperidine, bupropion, or buspirone.
Severe renal disease (isocarboxazid, phenelzine).

WARNINGS
Not commonly used but watch for drug-drug and drug-food interactions – if missed could be fatal.
Hypertensive crisis (VERY high blood pressure) can occur when taken with TCAs, SSRIs, SNRIs, many other drugs and tyramine-rich foods (see interactions below).

SIDE EFFECTS
Anticholinergic effects (taper upon discontinuation to avoid cholinergic rebound)
Orthostasis
Sedation (except tranylcypromine causes stimulation)
Sexual dysfunction, weight gain, headache, insomnia</td></tr>
<tr><td>Phenelzine (Nardil)</td><td>15 mg TID, max 60-90 mg/day</td></tr>
<tr><td>Tranylcypromine (Parnate)</td><td>30 mg/day in divided doses, max 60 mg/day</td></tr>
<tr><td>Selegiline transdermal patch (EMSAM)
MAO-B Selective Inhibitor
Selegiline as Eldepryl and Zelapar (ODT) are oral drugs for Parkinson disease.</td><td>Start at 6 mg patch/day, can ↑ to 9 or 12 mg/day</td><td>CONTRAINDICATIONS
Discontinue at least 10 days prior to elective surgery requiring general anesthesia, do not use with local anesthesia containing sympathomimetic vasoconstrictors, foods high in tyramine, supplements containing tyrosine, phenylalanine, tryptophan, or caffeine. (No dietary issues with 6 mg patch.)

SIDE EFFECTS
Constipation, gas, dry mouth, loss of appetite, sexual problems</td></tr>
</table>

MAO Inhibitor Drug Interactions

- MAO inhibitors and hypertensive crisis: allow 2 week washout if going to or from an MAO inhibitor and an SSRI, SNRI or TCA antidepressant (exception: if going from fluoxetine back to an MAO inhibitor, need to wait 5 weeks).
- MAO inhibitors cannot be used with many other drugs. Significant DDIs can occur and result in hypertensive crisis, serotonin syndrome or psychosis. The interaction could be fatal. These include any drugs with effects on the concentrations of epinephrine, norepinephrine, serotonin or dopamine. This includes bupropion, carbamazepine, oxcarbazepine, ephedrine and analogs (pseudoephedrine, etc.), buspirone, levodopa, linezolid, lithium, meperidine, SSRIs, SNRIs, TCAs, tramadol, methadone, mirtazapine, dextromethorphan, cyclobenzaprine (and other skeletal muscle relaxants), OTC diet pills/herbal weight loss products and St. John's wort.
- Patients taking MAO inhibitors must avoid tyramine-rich foods, including aged cheese, pickled herring, yeast extract, air-dried meats, sauerkraut, soy sauce, fava beans and some red wines and beers (tap beer and any beer that has not been pasteurized – canned and bottled beers contain little or no tyramine). Foods can become high in tyramine when they have been aged, fermented, pickled or smoked.

MAO Inhibitor Counseling

- Read the MedGuide that has been given to you. Especially in adolescents and young adults: counsel on risk of suicide – particularly during therapy initiation.
- Warn patients regarding the need to avoid interacting foods and drugs. See list in above drug interaction section. Stay away from tyramine-rich containing foods.
- Seek immediate medical care if you experience any of these symptoms: sudden severe headache, nausea, stiff neck, vomiting, a fast or slow heartbeat or a change in the way your heart beats (palpitations), tight chest pain, a lot of sweating, confusion, dilated pupils, and sensitivity to light.
- Use this medication regularly in order to get the most benefit from it. Take this medication exactly as prescribed. To help you remember, use it at the same time each day. Antidepressants do not work if they are taken as needed.
- It is important to continue taking this medication even if you feel well. Do not stop taking this medication without consulting your healthcare provider. Some conditions may become worse when the drug is suddenly stopped. Your dose may need to be gradually decreased.
- It may take 1 to 2 weeks to feel a benefit from this drug and 6 – 8 weeks to feel the full effect on your mood. Tell the healthcare provider if your condition persists or worsens. You can try a medication in a different class. One will work or it may take different tries to find the right medicine that will help you feel better.
- *EMSAM* Patch Application: Change once daily. Pick a time of day you can remember. Apply to either upper chest or back (below the neck and above the waist), upper thigh, or to the outer surface of the upper arm. Rotate site and do not use same site 2 days in a row. Wash hands with soap after applying patch. Do not expose to heat. The washout period counseling above includes the patch.

Dopamine (DA) and Norepinephrine (NE) Reuptake Inhibitor

DRUG	DOSING	SAFETY/SIDE EFFECTS/MONITORING
BuPROPion *(Aplenzin, Wellbutrin SR, Wellbutrin XL, Forfivo XL)* + naltrexone *(Contrave)* – for weight management *Buproban, Zyban* – for smoking cessation *Wellbutrin XL* is approved for Seasonal Affective Disorder (SAD) – start in early fall, titrate to 300 mg/day, if desired can discontinue in late spring by cutting to 150 mg daily x 2 weeks	300-450 mg daily BuPROPion IR is TID *Wellbutrin SR* is BID (to 200 mg BID) *Wellbutrin XL* is daily Hydrobromide salt *(Aplenzin)*: Initial: 174 mg once daily in the morning; may increase as early as day 4 of dosing to 348 mg once daily (target dose); max dose: 522 mg daily. In patients receiving 348 mg once daily, taper dose down to 174 mg once daily prior to discontinuing. Do not exceed 450 mg/day due to seizure risk	**BOXED WARNING** Antidepressants increase the risk of suicidal thinking and behavior in children, adolescents, and young adults (18-24 years of age) with major depressive disorder (MDD) and other psychiatric disorders; consider risk prior to prescribing. **CONTRAINDICATIONS** Seizure disorder; history of anorexia/bulimia, abrupt discontinuation of ethanol or sedatives; concurrent use with MAO inhibitors, linezolid, IV methylene blue, or other forms of bupropion **SIDE EFFECTS** Dry mouth, insomnia, headache/migraine, nausea/vomiting, constipation, and tremors/seizures (dose-related), possible blood pressure changes (more hypertension than hypotension – monitor), weight loss No effects on 5HT and therefore no sexual dysfunction; may be used if issues with other antidepressants

Miscellaneous Antidepressants

DRUG	DOSING	SAFETY/SIDE EFFECTS/MONITORING
Mirtazapine ***(Remeron,*** *Remeron SolTab)* Used commonly in oncology and skilled nursing to help with sleep (dosed QHS) & to increase appetite (can help with weight gain in frail elderly)	Tetracyclic antidepressant that works by its central presynaptic alpha-2 adrenergic antagonist effects, which results in increased release of norepinephrine and serotonin 15-45 mg QHS	**BOXED WARNING** Antidepressants increase the risk of suicidal thinking and behavior in children, adolescents, and young adults (18-24 years of age) with major depressive disorder (MDD) and other psychiatric disorders; consider risk prior to prescribing. **WARNINGS** Anticholinergic effects, QT prolongation, blood dyscrasias, CNS depression **SIDE EFFECTS** Sedation and ↑ appetite, weight gain, dry mouth, dizziness Agranulocytosis (rare)
TraZODone Rarely used as an antidepressant due to sedation. Used primarily off-label for sleep (dosed 50-100 mg QHS) TraZODone ER *(Oleptro)* may be less sedating	Inhibits 5-HT reuptake, blocks H1 and alpha1-adrenergic receptors IR: 150-300 mg/day in divided doses ER: 150-375 mg QHS	**BOXED WARNING** Same as above **CONTRAINDICATIONS** Concurrent use with MAO inhibitors, linezolid, or IV methylene blue **SIDE EFFECTS** Sedation Orthostasis (risk in elderly for falls) Sexual dysfunction and risk of priapism (medical emergency – requires immediate medical attention if painful erection longer than 4 hrs)

Miscellaneous Antidepressants continued

DRUG	DOSING	SAFETY/SIDE EFFECTS/MONITORING
Nefazodone	200-600 mg/day divided BID	**BOXED WARNINGS** Antidepressants increase the risk of suicidal thinking and behavior in children, adolescents, and young adults (18-24 years of age) with major depressive disorder (MDD) and other psychiatric disorders; consider risk prior to prescribing, hepatotoxicity. **CONTRAINDICATIONS** Hepatic disease, concurrent use with MAO inhibitors, carbamazepine, cisapride, pimozide, or triazolam **SIDE EFFECTS** Similar to trazodone, but less sedating **NOTES** Rarely used due to hepatotoxicity: monitor LFTs, counsel on symptoms of liver damage

Bupropion Drug Interactions

- Do not use with *Buproban* or *Zyban* for smoking cessation; same drug.
- Do not use in patients with seizure history; drug ↓ seizure threshold. Do not exceed 450 mg daily in anyone.

Key Counseling Points For Above Agents

- Read the MedGuide that has been given to you. Especially in adolescents and young adults: counsel on risk of suicide – particularly during therapy initiation.
- Counsel on lag time, need to take daily as with other agents.
- Bupropion: Include not to exceed 450 mg daily, or 150 mg at each dose if using immediate-release formulations due to seizure risk. Avoid dosing at or near bedtime due to agent being activating. Avoid use in conjunction with eating disorders.
- Mirtazapine: Counsel to take at night, drug is sedating, and can increase appetite.

TREATMENT RESISTANT DEPRESSION

Rule out bipolar disorder, assess medication adherence and verify that the antidepressant is at an optimal dose, sometimes use a combination of standard antidepressants, or augment with various options. The antipsychotics in the following table are approved for treatment resistant depression as adjunctive agents (i.e., in addition to another agent).

All antipsychotics require MedGuides with this Warning:

Medicines like this one can raise the risk of death in elderly people who have lost touch with reality (psychosis) due to confusion and memory loss (dementia). This medicine is not approved for the treatment of patients with dementia-related psychosis.

And because it is being used to augment AD therapy:

Antidepressants have increased the risk of suicidal thoughts and actions in some children, teenagers, and young adults. See Schizophrenia/Psychosis chapter for more detail on the antipsychotics.

Antipsychotics for Adjunctive Therapy in Treatment Resistant Depression

<table>
<tr><th>DRUG</th><th>DOSING</th><th>SAFETY/SIDE EFFECTS/MONITORING</th></tr>
<tr><td>ARIPiprazole (Abilify, Abilify Maintena)
Abilify Maintena is only approved for schizophrenia</td><td>Start 2-5 mg/day (QAM), can ↑ to 15 mg/day</td><td rowspan="4">BOXED WARNINGS
Antidepressants increase the risk of suicidal thinking and behavior in children, adolescents, and young adults (18-24 years of age) with major depressive disorder (MDD) and other psychiatric disorders; consider risk prior to prescribing. Elderly patients with dementia-related psychosis treated with antipsychotic drugs are at ↑ risk of death.

WARNINGS
Risk of Neuroleptic Malignant Syndrome
Risk of Tardive Dyskinesia (TD)
Risk of leukopenia, neutropenia, agranulocytosis
Risk of multiorgan hypersensitivity (DRESS) reactions with OLANZapine/fluoxetine
Risk of pathological gaming and other compulsive behaviors with ARIPiprazole

CONTRAINDICATIONS
Symbyax: Do not use with pimozide, thioridazine & caution with other drugs/conditions that cause QT prolongation

SIDE EFFECTS
Each of these drugs can cause metabolic issues, including dyslipidemia, weight gain, diabetes (less with aripiprazole)
All can cause orthostasis/dizziness

Abilify
Anxiety, insomnia, constipation, agitation

Olanzapine
Sedation
Weight gain, ↑ lipids, ↑ glucose, EPS, QT prolongation (lower risk)

Quetiapine
Sedation, orthostasis
Weight gain, ↑ lipids, ↑ glucose
Little risk EPS

Brexpiprazole
Weight gain, dyspepsia, diarrhea, agitation</td></tr>
<tr><td>OLANZapine/fluoxetine (Symbyax)</td><td>Usually started at 6 mg/25 mg capsule QHS (fluoxetine is activating, but olanzapine is more sedating), can ↑ cautiously.</td></tr>
<tr><td>QUEtiapine extended release (SEROquel, SEROquel XR)</td><td>Start 50 mg QHS, ↑ nightly to 150-300 mg QHS</td></tr>
<tr><td>Brexpiprazole (Rexulti)</td><td>Start 0.5-1 mg/day, can ↑ 3 mg/day (titrate weekly)</td></tr>
</table>

PRACTICE CASE

SA is a 57 y/o male who appears thin and anxious. He is married with two children. His wife brought him to the clinic today due to constant worry, anxiety, and feelings of worthlessness. When he was in college, he had several bouts of depression and was successfully treated with doxepin at that time. He stopped taking the medication when he graduated and moved to California, because he felt the sunshine made him feel better. His wife reports that this is the third or fourth time in the past few years that her husband has felt so low that she became concerned he might harm himself. She reports that he stays up all night with constant worry and probably has not had a good night's sleep in months.

Per clinic records, SA was seen 2 months ago and started on Celexa 40 mg daily and lorazepam 1 mg 1-3 times daily as needed. SA has been using these medications, and states that they "help a little, but not much". He is taking the lorazepam 1 mg TID each day. He does not smoke, drink alcohol, or use illicit drugs.

Allergies: shellfish, contrast dye, latex

Medications:
Inderal LA 120 mg daily
Celexa 40 mg daily
Lorazepam 1 mg 1-3 times daily PRN
Fosinopril 20 mg daily

Vitals:
Height: 5'10" Weight: 155 lbs
BP: 158/102 mmHg HR: 80 BPM RR: 16 BPM Temp: 98.2°F Pain: 1/10

Labs: Na (mEq/L) = 140 (135 - 145)
K (mEq/L) = 4.1 (3.5 - 5)
Cl (mEq/L) = 99 (95 - 103)
HCO3 (mEq/L) = 26 (24 - 30)
BUN (mg/dL) = 12 (7 - 20)
SCr (mg/dL) = 0.7 (0.6 - 1.3)
Glucose (mg/dL) = 100 (100 - 125)
Ca (mg/dL) = 10.1 (8.5 - 10.5)
Mg (mEq/L) = 2.0 (1.3 - 2.1)
PO4 (mg/dL) = 4.1 (2.3 - 4.7)

AST (IU/L) = 27 (8 - 48)
ALT (IU/L) = 39 (7 - 55)
Albumin (g/dL) = 3.7 (3.5 - 5)

Patient reports minimal improvement of depression with current prescriptions.

Questions

1. SA has depression that has not responded to an adequate trial of fluoxetine or citalopram. Which of the following options represents the best alternative?
   a. Sertraline
   b. Venlafaxine
   c. Fluvoxamine
   d. Escitalopram
   e. Mirtazapine

2. If SA was started on *Effexor XR* (he won't be), which of the following parameters should be carefully monitored in this patient? (Select **ALL** that apply.)
   a. Blood pressure
   b. Thyroid parameters
   c. White blood cell count
   d. Metabolic acidosis
   e. Symptoms of depression

3. A pharmacist counseling a patient on the use of any antidepressant should include the following counseling points:
   a. Your energy level may pick up before your mood starts to feels better.
   b. Your mood should improve; this usually takes about a month.
   c. If this medicine does not work, the doctor will try a different agent, which may work better.
   d. This medication needs to be taken every day; it does not work if it is taken occasionally.
   e. All of the above.

4. What is the mechanism of action of venlafaxine?
   a. Selective serotonin reuptake inhibitor
   b. Serotonin and dopamine reuptake inhibitor
   c. Serotonin and norepinephrine reuptake inhibitor
   d. Norepinephrine and dopamine reuptake inhibitor
   e. Norepinephrine and acetylcholine reuptake inhibitor

5. The doctor takes a thorough medication history and decides that it would be worthwhile to try doxepin, since the patient had a good history of use with this agent. Which of the following statements is correct? (Select **ALL** that apply.)
   a. Doxepin is a monoamine oxidase inhibitor.
   b. Doxepin can cause excess salivation and has significant food interactions.
   c. He should be carefully evaluated for suicide risk.
   d. The brand name is *Sular*.
   e. The brand name is *Silenor.*

Questions 6-7 do not apply to the case.

6. A patient has been started on bupropion for depression. His other medications include *Lopid, Pravachol* and *Zyban*. Which of the following statement is correct?
   a. Bupropion will raise his triglycerides.
   b. Bupropion will raise his HDL cholesterol.
   c. Bupropion will lower his HDL cholesterol.
   d. Bupropion should not be used in this patient.
   e. *Lopid* is an inducer and will decrease the level of bupropion.

7. A patient has been started on bupropion 200 mg TID for depression. His medical conditions include partial seizures and obsessive compulsive disorder. His medications include fluvoxamine and phenytoin. Which of the following statements is correct? (Select **ALL** that apply.)
   a. Bupropion will induce the metabolism of phenytoin.
   b. The bupropion dose is too high.
   c. Bupropion should not be used in this patient.
   d. One of the brand formulation used for depression is called *Contrave.*
   e. Patients with sexual dysfunction should avoid the use of this drug.

Answers

1-e, 2-a,e, 3-e, 4-c, 5-c,e, 6-d, 7-b,c

SCHIZOPHRENIA/ PSYCHOSIS

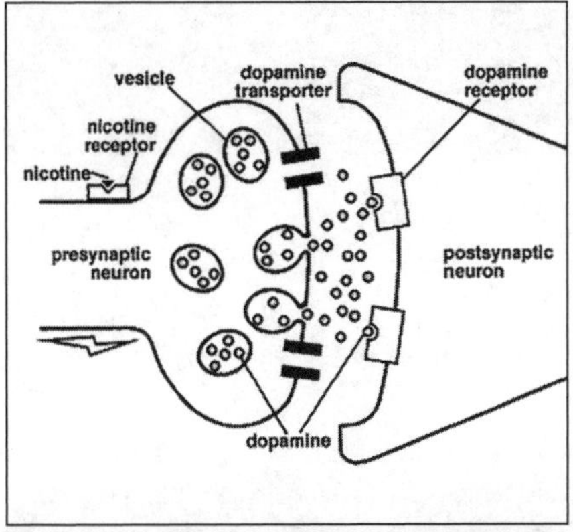

GUIDELINES/REFERENCES

American Psychiatric Association. (2013). Diagnostic and Statistical Manual of Mental Disorders: DSM-5. Washington, D.C: American Psychiatric Association

American Psychiatric Association Guideline Watch (September 2009): Practice Guideline for the Treatment of Patients with Schizophrenia http://psychiatryonline.org/pb/assets/raw/sitewide/practice_guidelines/guidelines/schizophrenia-watch.pdf (accessed 2016 Dec 15)

We gratefully acknowledge the assistance of Robin Wackernah, PharmD, BCPP, Regis University School of Pharmacy, Rueckert-Hartman College for Health Professions, in preparing this chapter.

BACKGROUND

Schizophrenia is a chronic, severe and disabling thought disorder that occurs in ~1% of all societies regardless of class, color, religion, or culture. The cause is multifactorial and includes altered brain structure and chemistry, primarily involving dopamine and glutamine. Genetics (inherited susceptibility) and environmental factors are important in disease development. Patients suffer from hallucinations, delusions (false beliefs), disorganized thinking and behavior. They can withdraw from the world around them and enter a world of psychosis, where they struggle to differentiate reality from altered perceptions. Schizophrenia ranges from relatively mild to severe. Some people may be able to function adequately in daily life, while others need specialized, intensive care. Treatment adherence is important and often difficult to obtain, primarily due to the patient's inability to recognize their illness. This is regrettable to the patient's family and to themselves as patients with schizophrenia typically live a life of torment where they may not be able to care for themselves. This condition has one of the highest suicide rates.

The onset of symptoms usually begins in young adulthood. A diagnosis is not based on lab tests, but on the patient's behavior, which should include both negative and positive signs and symptoms (described on the following page). The Diagnostic and Statistical Manual of Mental Disorders, 5th Edition (DSM-5) is the current tool used to diagnose schizophrenia and other psychiatric disorders.

PATHOPHYSIOLOGY

Schizophrenia is a thought disorder in which neurotransmitter abnormalities are central. Genetics, environment, stressors and some illicit drugs can be contributing factors. There is increased dopamine in the mesolimbic pathway. The older "dopaminergic model" is being supplemented with a more recent understanding of the role of the glutamatergic N-methyl-D-aspartate (NMDA) receptor and its role in the pathogenesis of schizophrenia. Antipsychotics primarily block dopamine receptors, although newer agents that block serotonin and additional receptors have benefit.

Antipsychotics target the positive symptoms, but the lack of motivation, cognitive and functional impairment remain challenges for many patients and often take longer to respond to antipsychotics, if at all. Researchers hope that a better understanding of glutamate receptors will improve functional levels. One problem with current treatment is that the drugs that target dopamine hyperactivity also target dopamine involved in focus and the ability to pay attention; dopamine and glutamine modulate each other. Glutamine synaptic dysfunction is a large area of current research. It is hoped that as the pathways are better understood, along with drug development, a "fine tuning" of treatment will improve results.

DSM-5 DIAGNOSTIC CRITERIA FOR SCHIZOPHRENIA Note: Delusions, hallucinations or disorganized speech must be present	
Negative signs and symptoms Loss of interest in everyday activities Lack of emotion (apathy) Inability to plan or carry out activities Poor hygiene Social withdrawal Loss of motivation (avolition) Poverty (lack) of speech (alogia)	**Positive signs and symptoms** Hallucinations; can be auditory (hearing voices), visual, or somatic Delusions: beliefs held by the patient that are without a basis in reality Disorganized thinking/behavior, incoherent speech, often on unrelated topics, purposeless behavior, or difficulty speaking and organizing thoughts, such as stopping in mid-sentence or jumbling together meaningless words Difficulty paying attention

NATURAL PRODUCTS

Fish oils are being used for psychosis, as well as other psychiatric disorders including ADHD and depression. The evidence is preliminary, but promising. Considering the debilitating nature of schizophrenia, natural products are not used in lieu of antipsychotics in patients that require them. Do not recommend cod liver oil due to risk of vitamin A toxicity. Keep in mind that natural products have dose-response relationships; check the *Natural Medicines Database* for dosing recommendations that appear to have benefit from clinical trials.

DRUG TREATMENT

Side-effect profiles play an important role in selecting initial treatment for schizophrenia. Second-generation antipsychotics (SGAs) may be used first-line due to a lower risk of extrapyramidal side effects (EPS); however, some patients respond better to a first-generation antipsychotic (FGA).

MEDICATIONS/ILLICIT DRUGS THAT CAN CAUSE PSYCHOTIC SYMPTOMS

KEY DRUGS

Anticholinergics (centrally-acting, high doses)

Cannabis

Dextromethorphan

Dopamine or dopamine agonists used for Parkinson disease (*Requip, Mirapex, Sinemet,* etc.)

Illicit substances:

- Bath salts (synthetic cathinones)
- Cocaine, esp. "crack" cocaine
- Lysergic acid diethylamide (LSD) and other hallucinogenics
- Methamphetamine, ice, crack
- MDPV (bath salts)
- Phencyclidine (PCP)

Interferons

Stimulants (especially if already at risk), including amphetamines used for ADHD

Systemic steroids (typically with lack of sleep – ICU psychosis)

First Generation Antipsychotics

High-potency FGAs such as haloperidol are associated with a high risk of EPS effects, a moderate risk of sedation and a lower risk of orthostatic hypotension, tachycardia, and anticholinergic effects compared to low-potency FGAs. In contrast, low-potency FGAs are associated with a lower risk of EPS, a high degree of sedation, and a high risk of cardiovascular effects (orthostatic hypotension, tachycardia), and anticholinergic effects. Although other side effects also vary with the specific medication, in general, the first-generation antipsychotic medications are associated with a moderate risk of weight gain, a low risk of metabolic effects, higher risk of EPS with the FGAs when compared with the SGAs, and a risk of sexual side effects. With certain agents (thioridazine particularly), QT risk is significant. Other possible side effects of FGAs include seizures, temperature dysregulation, allergic reactions, and dermatological, hepatic, ophthalmological, and hematological effects.

Second Generation Antipsychotics

SGAs have a variety of side effects. Metabolic side effects are a well known phenomenon with SGAs. These include weight gain, lipid abnormalities and hyperglycemia, which can sometimes lead to diabetes. Although at a lower incidence than FGAs, many SGAs exhibit dose-related EPS. Hormonal issues can be problematic with agents that increase prolactin levels, causing gynecomastia (painful, swollen breast tissue), galactorrhea (breastmilk production without pregnancy), sexual dysfunction and irregular or missed periods. Cardiovascular effects, including QT prolongation can be present with SGAs and ziprasidone has the highest risk. Adverse effects may limit the use of an agent; for example clozapine has superior efficacy, but has multiple boxed warnings and is particularly known for agranulocytosis, seizures and myocarditis – in addition to having high metabolic risk. Clozapine is not recommended for first-line use, but a trial should be considered for very ill patients who have had no or poor response to two trials of antipsychotic medication (at least one should be an SGA).

Due to the potential for significant metabolic side effects when initiating antipsychotics, the American Diabetes Association (ADA) recommends screening and monitoring for overweight and obesity, dyslipidemia, hyperglycemia, hypertension and personal or family history of risk. During treatment, the patient should be monitored for changes in weight, waist circumference, plasma lipid and glucose levels, and acute symptoms of diabetes.

Choosing an SGA

The SGAs are chosen based on several considerations, which should be identified when examining a patient case:

- Patient's past history: what drugs have helped control the symptoms (e.g., quieted the voices down), and drugs that did not help (if they were taken, and at a reasonable dose). Likely adherence to treatment should also be considered.
- Side effects: These can be acceptable in some patients but not in others, for example, if the patient is overweight, do not pick an agent which worsens metabolic issues. In patients with a history of tardive dyskinesia (TD), or any type of movement disorder, avoid risperidone, paliperidone and lurasidone, which can be associated with extrapyramidal symptoms. The table at the right lists the drugs most likely to cause major adverse effects – avoid using them in an at-risk patient.
- When assessing treatment resistance or evaluating the best option for a partial response, it is important to evaluate whether the patient has had an adequate trial (at least 4 – 6 weeks) of an antipsychotic, including whether the dose is adequate and whether the patient has been taking the medication as prescribed.
- Prescriber's familiarity with a drug, or formulary considerations, including costs will also factor in to treatment selection.

IMPORTANT ADVERSE EFFECTS OF SECOND GENERATION ANTIPSYCHOTICS

Metabolic side effects
Highest risk – Clozapine, olanzapine, quetiapine
Moderate risk – Risperidone, paliperidone
Lower risk – Aripiprazole, ziprasidone, lurasidone and asenapine

EPS
Lowest risk – Quetiapine (recommended in patients with Parkinson's who require antipsychotics)

Hematological effects
Highest risk – Clozapine (agranulocytosis)

QT prolongation
Highest risk – Ziprasidone

↑ Prolactin
Highest risk – Risperidone, paliperidone

Seizure
Highest risk – Clozapine (dose-dependent)

Formulations

Long-Acting Injections: Haloperidol is an older agent and comes in various formulations, including an IM injection for acute use, a long-acting decanoate, tablets and a solution. Long-acting injectables, including *Haldol* decanoate (every 4 weeks), *Risperdal Consta* (every 2 weeks), *Invega Sustenna* (every 4 weeks), *Invega Trinza* (every 3 months), *Abilify Maintena* (every 4 weeks), and a few others provide the benefit of increased adherence, or compliance, with the medication. They are also used in acute care settings prior to the release of patients without adequate resources (e.g., homelessness).

Orally Disintegrating Tablets (ODTs): Used to help solve the problem of "cheeking" where the patient avoids taking the medication by holding the dose in their cheek and then spitting it out. With ODTs the tablet dissolves rapidly in the mouth, without the need for water. Several of the SGAs are available as ODTs (clozapine, olanzapine, risperidone, aripiprazole and asenapine).

Acute IM Injections: Intramuscular (IM) injections provide "stat" relief to help calm down an acutely agitated, psychotic patient for their own safety and the safety of others. They are often mixed with other drugs, such as benzodiazepines for anxiolytic and sedative effects, and anticholinergics to reduce dystonic risk (for example the "*Haldol* cocktail", which contains haloperidol, lorazepam and diphenhydramine). In contrast, oral absorption could take up to an hour to calm the patient down. The patient will be sedated and hopefully sleep through the acute symptoms. Olanzapine and benzodiazepines should not be given together (IM) due to orthostasis risk.

Boxed Warning

Antipsychotics (APs) increase the risk of mortality in elderly patients with dementia-related psychosis, primarily due to an increased risk of stroke and infection. Note that APs are not particularly helpful to treat dementia-related anger/outbursts, but they are used and pharmacists are required to counsel on this risk. See the counseling section for wording suggestion. Additional drug-specific warnings are listed separately with the drugs.

NEUROLEPTIC MALIGNANT SYNDROME

Antipsychotics used to be called neuroleptics. Neuroleptic malignant syndrome (NMS) is rare but is highly lethal. It occurs most commonly with the FGAs and is due to D_2 blockade. NMS can occur, but is less common with SGAs and with other dopamine blocking agents, including metoclopramide (*Reglan*). The majority of cases occur within two weeks of starting treatment or immediately following high doses of injectables given alongside multiple oral doses. Occasionally, patients develop NMS even after years of antipsychotic use. NMS is a medical emergency as the intense muscle contractions can lead to acute renal injury (due to rhabdomyolysis from the destruction of muscle tissue), suffocation and death.

Signs Include

- Hyperthermia (high fever, with profuse sweating)
- Extreme muscle rigidity (called "lead pipe" rigidity), which can lead to respiratory failure
- Mental status changes
- Other signs can include tachycardia, tachypnea and blood pressure changes

Laboratory Results

- ↑ creatine phosphokinase and ↑ white blood cells

Treatment

- Taper off the antipsychotic quickly and consider another choice (quetiapine or clozapine).
- Provide supportive care: Cardiorespiratory and hemodynamic support and control of electrolyte balance.
- Cool the patient down: Cooling bed, antipyretics, cooled IV fluids.
- Muscle relaxation with benzodiazepines or dantrolene (*Ryanodex, Dantrium, Revonto*) is sometimes used, and some cases may require a dopamine agonist such as bromocriptine.

First-Generation Antipsychotics (FGAs) block D_2 receptors. Minimal $5HT_{2A}$ receptor blockade.

DRUG	DOSING
Low Potency	
ChlorproMAZINE	300-1,000 mg/day, divided
Thioridazine BOXED WARNING: QT prolongation	300-800 mg/day, divided
Mid potency	
Loxapine *(Loxitane, Adasuve* inhalation powder for acute agitation)	30-100 mg/day, divided
Perphenazine	8-64 mg/day, divided
High Potency	
FluPHENAZine Available in **2-wk decanoate** for IM use	6-12 mg/day, divided
Haloperidol *(Haldol)*, see formulations to right Class: butyrophenone (and DA-blocker) Haloperidol is also used for tics and vocal outbursts due to Tourette syndrome	Oral (tablet, solution): start 0.5-2 mg BID-TID, up to 30 mg/day IV: usually 5-10 mg Decanoate (monthly): IM only, for conversion from PO, use 10-20x the oral dose
Thiothixene *(Navane)*	15-60 mg/day, divided
Trifluoperazine	15-50 mg/day, divided

SAFETY/SIDE EFFECTS/MONITORING

BOXED WARNING (ALL APS)

Elderly patients with dementia-related psychosis treated with antipsychotics are at an increased risk of death compared to placebo. Most deaths appeared to be either cardiovascular (e.g., heart failure, sudden death) or infectious in nature. This drug is not approved for the treatment of dementia-related psychosis.

SIDE EFFECTS

All are sedating and all cause EPS, however the lower potency agents have ↑ sedation and ↓ incidence EPS (e.g., chlorpromazine), and the higher-potency agents (e.g., haloperidol) have ↓ sedation (but still sedating) with ↑ EPS.

Dystonias, which are prolonged contraction of muscles (including painful muscle spasms) can occur during initiation. May be life-threatening if airway is compromised. Higher risk with younger males. Centrally-acting anticholinergics (diphenhydramine, benztropine) may be used for prophylaxis during treatment initiation or for treatment if need arises.

Akathisia, which is restlessness with anxiety and an inability to remain still. May be treated with anticholinergics, benzodiazepines or propranolol.

Parkinsonism, which looks similar to Parkinson disease, with tremors, abnormal gait, bradykinesia, etc. Treat with anticholinergics or propranolol if tremor is the main symptom.

Tardive dyskinesias (TD), which are abnormal facial movements, primarily in the tongue or mouth. Risk is higher in elderly females. If TD occurs the drug should be stopped as soon as possible and replaced with an SGA with low EPS risk (quetiapine, clozapine). TD can be irreversible.

Dyskinesias, abnormal movements, are possible, however, this is more common with Parkinson drugs.

Seizures (phenothiazines, butyrophenones).

Cardiovascular Effects: orthostasis, tachycardia, QT prolongation; IV haloperidol has high risk.

Sexual dysfunction.

Adasuve: dysgeusia (bad, bitter, or metallic taste in mouth), sedation, bronchospasm risk, REMS drug.

Second-Generation Antipsychotics (SGAs) block D_2 and $5HT_{2A}$ receptors.
Aripiprazole and cariprazine are unique; act as a D_2 and $5HT_{1A}$ partial agonist.

DRUG	DOSING	SAFETY/SIDE EFFECTS/MONITORING
ARIPiprazole ***(Abilify, Abilify Discmelt ODT***, *Abilify Maintena* injection, *Aristada* injection) Tablet, ODT, IM solution, IM suspension	10-30 mg PO QAM Acute agitation: 9.75 mg IM soln x 1 (Q2H up to 30 mg/day) *Abilify Maintena*-IM suspension, give monthly *Aristada*-IM suspension, give every 4-6 weeks, dose-dependent (see notes at right)	**SIDE EFFECTS** Akathisia, anxiety, insomnia Constipation Less weight gain, some QT prolongation **NOTES** Also approved for irritability associated with autism *Aristada* 882 mg dose can be given Q6 weeks, all other strengths are given Q4 weeks
Asenapine *(Saphris)* Sublingual tablet	10-20 mg/day, divided BID No food/drink for 10 min after dose	**CONTRAINDICATIONS** Severe hepatic impairment **SIDE EFFECTS** Somnolence, tongue numbness; EPS (5% more than placebo), QT prolongation; aoid use with QT risk
Brexpiprazole (*Rexulti*) Also indicated for major depressive disorder (MDD)	2-4 mg daily	**SIDE EFFECTS** Weight gain, dyspepsia, diarrhea, akathisia
Cariprazine (*Vraylar*) Also indicated for bipolar disorder	1.5-6 mg daily	**SIDE EFFECTS** EPS, dystonias, headache, insomnia
CloZAPine *(Clozaril*, *FazaClo ODT*, *Versacloz* suspension) Only if failed to respond to treatment with 2 standard AP treatments, or had significant ADRs	300-900 mg/day, divided (start at 12.5 mg and titrate, also titrate off since abrupt discontinuation can cause seizures) Clozapine is very effective and has ↓ risk of EPS/TD, but used no sooner than 3rd line due to severe side effect potential (metabolic effects, agranulocytosis)	**BOXED WARNINGS, CLOZAPINE-SPECIFIC** Significant risk of potentially life-threatening agranulocytosis. Tachycardia, orthostatic hypotension, syncope, and cardiac arrest; risk is highest during the initial titration period especially with rapid dose increases. Titrate slowly. Myocarditis and cardiomyopathy; discontinue if suspect. Seizures, dose-correlated; start at no higher than 12.5 mg once or twice daily, titrate slowly, using divided doses. Use with caution in patients at seizure risk: seizure history, head trauma, alcoholism, or concurrent treatment with medications which lower seizure threshold. **SIDE EFFECTS** Orthostasis, syncope, weight gain, ↑ lipids, ↑ glucose, somnolence, dizziness, insomnia, GI upset, sialorrhea (hypersalivation), QT prolongation Risk of agranulocytosis, seizures, myocarditis **MONITORING** REMS: Prescribers and pharmacies must be certified and patients enrolled with the Clozapine REMS To start treatment, baseline ANC must be ≥ 1,500/mm³ Check ANC weekly x 6 months, then every 2 weeks x 6 months, then monthly Monitor for metabolic effects; see counseling section **NOTES** Smoking reduces drug levels

Second-Generation (SGA) Antipsychotics Continued

DRUG	DOSING	SAFETY/SIDE EFFECTS/MONITORING
Iloperidone (*Fanapt*)	12-24 mg/day, divided Titrate slowly due to orthostasis/dizziness	**SIDE EFFECTS** Dizziness, somnolence, orthostasis, tachycardia QT prolongation; avoid use with QT risk
Lurasidone (*Latuda*)	40-160 mg/day, divided	**CONTRAINDICATIONS** Use with strong CYP3A4 inducers and inhibitors **SIDE EFFECTS** Somnolence, EPS, dystonias, nausea, agitation, akathisia Nearly weight, lipid and blood glucose neutral **NOTES** Take with food ≥ 350 kcal
OLANZapine (***ZyPREXA***, *Zydis ODT*, *Relprevv* injection)	10-20 mg QHS IM Injection (acute agitation) *Relprevv* inj suspension lasts 2-4 weeks, restricted use, REMS drug	**BOXED WARNING, OLANZAPINE-SPECIFIC** *Zyprexa Relprevv* – patients should be monitored for 3 hr post-injection. Sedation (including coma) and delirium (including agitation, anxiety, confusion, disorientation) have been observed following use. **SIDE EFFECTS** Somnolence, weight gain, ↑ lipids, ↑ glucose EPS, QT prolongation (lower risk) **MONITORING** For metabolic effects; see counseling section **NOTES** Smoking reduces drug levels
Paliperidone (***Invega***, *Invega Sustenna* and ***Invega Trinza*** are long-acting injections) Active metabolite of risperidone; SEs similar	PO: 3-12 mg daily CrCl < 50 mL/min: 3 mg daily CrCl < 10 mL/min: Not recommended OROS delivery enables once daily dosing-do not break or crush *Invega Sustenna*, IM injection, give monthly *Invega Trinza*, IM injection, give every 3 months (start only after receiving *Invega Sustenna* x 4 months)	**SIDE EFFECTS** ↑ prolactin – sexual dysfunction, galactorrhea, irregular/missed periods EPS, especially at higher doses Tachycardia, headache, sedation, anxiety QT prolongation; avoid use with QT risk Weight gain, ↑ lipids, ↑ glucose **MONITORING** For metabolic effects; see counseling section
QUEtiapine (***SEROquel***, ***SEROquel XR***)	400-800 mg/day, divided BID or XR QHS	**SIDE EFFECTS** Somnolence, orthostasis Weight gain, ↑ lipids, ↑ glucose Low EPS risk – often used for psychosis in Parkinson disease, QT prolongation (lower risk) **MONITORING** For metabolic effects; see counseling section **NOTES** Take XR at night, without food or with a light meal (≤ 300 kcal)

Second-Generation (SGA) Antipsychotics Continued

DRUG	DOSING	SAFETY/SIDE EFFECTS/MONITORING
RisperiDONE (RisperDAL, RisperDAL M-TAB ODT), see injection at right Also approved for irritability associated with autism	4-16 mg/day, divided *Risperdal Consta*, Q 2 week injection, 25-50 mg	**SIDE EFFECTS** Somnolence EPS, especially at higher doses ↑ prolactin – sexual dysfunction, galactorrhea, irregular/ missed periods Orthostasis Weight gain, ↑ lipids, ↑ glucose QT prolongation **MONITORING** For metabolic effects; see counseling section **NOTES** > 6 mg ↑ prolactin and ↑ EPS
Ziprasidone *(Geodon)*, *Geodon* injection	40-160 mg/day, divided BID Acute injection: *Geodon IM* 10 mg Q2H or 20 mg Q4H Max: 40 mg/day IM	**CONTRAINDICATIONS** QT prolongation; contraindicated with QT risk **SIDE EFFECTS** Somnolence (some have insomnia), respiratory tract infection, headache, dizziness, nausea **NOTES** Take with food

Antipsychotic Drug Interactions

- All antipsychotics can prolong the QT interval – note that some are considered higher risk than others. The higher risk QT SGAs are noted. Thioridazine, an FGA, is high-risk for QT prolongation (boxed warning).
- Smoking can reduce plasma levels of olanzapine and clozapine, patients who smoke may require higher doses.
- High plasma levels of risperidone and paliperidone can ↑ prolactin and cause EPS. Caution when using risperidone concomitantly with CYP 2D6 inhibitors, including paroxetine and fluoxetine.
- With clozapine: avoid concurrent drugs that lower the seizure threshold.
- Some of the APs have CYP450 drug interactions which could require dosing adjustments.
- Monitoring is also required for an increased risk of respiratory depression and hypotension when administered with benzodiazepines.
- Caution with other dopamine blocking agents such as metoclopramide (*Reglan*) as EPS and TD risk may be increased.

ALL ANTIPSYCHOTIC COUNSELING

- Dispense MedGuide and instruct patient to read it. In addition to individual warnings, several of the agents have anti-depressive properties and these include a warning for suicidality, particularly among adolescents.
- This medication can decrease hallucinations (such as voices) and can quiet the noise. It can help you to think more clearly and feel positive about yourself, feel less nervous, and take a more active part in everyday life.
- There may be a slightly increased risk of serious, possibly fatal, side effects when this medication is used in older adults with dementia. This medication is not approved for the treatment of dementia-related behavior problems.
- Contact your healthcare provider right away if you experience uncontrollable movements of the mouth, tongue, cheeks, jaw, arms or legs.
- Contact your healthcare provider immediately and seek immediate medical attention if you experience fever, sweating, severe muscle stiffness (rigidity) and confusion.
- Use caution when driving, operating machinery, or performing other hazardous activities. This drug can cause dizziness, confusion and drowsiness.
- Dizziness may be more likely to occur when you rise from a sitting or lying position. Rise slowly to prevent dizziness and a possible fall.
- Avoid consuming alcohol during treatment with this drug. Alcohol will increase sleepiness and dizziness and can interfere with the drug's ability to work properly.
- Tell your healthcare provider if your condition persists or worsens.

Clozapine

- This medication can cause a serious immune system problem called agranulocytosis (low white blood cells). To make sure you have enough white blood cells, you will need to have a blood test before you begin taking clozapine and then have your blood tested regularly during your treatment.
- Clozapine can also cause seizures, especially with higher doses, or if it is increased too quickly when starting treatment. Let your healthcare provider know if you have ever had seizures. While taking this medication, avoid activities during which a sudden loss of consciousness could be dangerous (e.g., driving, operating machinery, swimming).
- This medication may rarely cause an inflammation of the heart muscle (myocarditis). Seek immediate medical attention if you have weakness, difficult/rapid breathing, chest pain, or swelling of the ankles/legs. The risk is highest during the first month of treatment.

Olanzapine, Clozapine, Risperidone, Paliperidone and Quetiapine

- This drug has a risk of weight gain, elevated cholesterol, elevated blood pressure and high blood glucose. These must be monitored, and treated if they occur. Talk to your healthcare provider if you experience any symptoms of high blood glucose, including excessive thirst, frequent urination, excessive hunger, or fatigue.
- Your healthcare provider will order blood tests during treatment to monitor for side effects.

Different Types of Oral Formulations

- *Saphris*: Place the sublingual tablet under the tongue and allow it to dissolve completely. The tablet will dissolve in saliva within seconds. Do not eat or drink for 10 minutes after taking this medication. Your tongue will feel numb afterwards.
- *FazaClo, Abilify Discmelt, Risperdal M-Tab, Zyprexa Zydis*: Immediately upon opening the foil blister, using dry hands, remove the tablet and place in your mouth. Do not push the tablet through the foil because it may crumble. The tablet dissolves quickly so it can be easily swallowed with or without liquid.
- Most ODTs contain phenylalanine. Do not dispense ODTs to patients with phenylketonuria (PKU).
- *Risperdal* oral solution can be administered directly from the calibrated pipette, or mixed with water, coffee, orange juice, and low-fat milk; it is not compatible with cola or tea.
- *Latuda* is taken with food, which must contain at least 350 kcal. *Geodon* is taken with food.
- Quetiapine immediate-release tablet may be taken without regard to meals. The extended-release tablet *(Seroquel XR)* should be taken without food or with a light meal (up to 300 kcal).
- Olanzapine is usually taken once daily at night (QHS), since it is long-acting and sedating.
- *Invega:* Part of the tablet may pass into your stool after your body has absorbed the medicine. If you see the tablet in your stool, it is nothing to worry about.

PRACTICE CASE

Ruby is a 24 year-old college student. Her parents have attempted to help Ruby over the past year. Her academic performance deteriorated and she began to look unkempt. About a month ago, her mom was sure she saw Ruby mumbling to herself. Ruby began to call her mother "evil" and told her mother that she was destroying her life. Later, Ruby accused her mother of trying to feed her poisoned food. Ruby has dropped her old high-school friendships, except for one girl who her mother feels is more troubled than Ruby. When the mother went to talk to one of Ruby's instructors, she found out that Ruby had accused the teacher of changing what Ruby had written on an exam, and that the teacher had seen Ruby mumbling to herself in class. The teacher also complained that Ruby lacks attention in class, and reported that her work is sloppy and disorganized. The teacher had assumed there was difficulty at home, since Ruby told her that her mother is dying from cancer. This report from Ruby was not truthful.

The crisis in the family came to a head recently when Ruby stole a bottle of vodka from the local convenience store and was caught. Fortunately, the store manager knew the family and declined to press charges. However, later that night Ruby took some unknown medication and attempted to drown herself in the bathtub. She was taken by ambulance to the hospital.

The psychiatric team, after a brief visit with Ruby and a history taken from her family, gave Ruby a tentative diagnosis of schizophrenia. She received an injection of haloperidol and lorazepam, and is sleeping soundly. The psychiatric resident has come to the family to discuss treatment options.

No current medications; no known medical history. Height 5'5", weight 125 lbs.

Questions

1. The physician gave the patient an injection of haloperidol. This medication comes in the following formulations. (Select **ALL** that apply.)
   a. Oral tablets
   b. IM injection
   c. Long-lasting (monthly) decanoate
   d. Oral solution
   e. Orally disintegrating tablet (ODT)

2. If Ruby were to experience neuroleptic malignant syndrome while receiving haloperidol, what therapies could be administered in this emergency situation? (Select **ALL** that apply.)
   a. Fluphenazine injection
   b. Cooled IV fluids, ice beds
   c. Heating blankets
   d. Muscle relaxants
   e. Airway support

Questions 3-7 do not apply to the case.

3. Choose the potential adverse reaction from haloperidol which can be irreversible (and, if it occurs, the medicine should be quickly tapered off):
   a. Dystonic reaction
   b. Tardive dyskinesia
   c. Akathisia
   d. Dizziness
   e. Orthostatic hypotension

4. A patient is started on olanzapine for psychotic symptoms. This agent puts the patient at high risk for the following adverse effects: (Select **ALL** that apply.)
   a. Weight loss
   b. Elevated blood glucose
   c. Increased risk lymphoma or other malignancies
   d. Elevated cholesterol
   e. Elevated creatine phosphokinase

5. A patient has been prescribed *Risperdal Consta*. Choose the correct statement:
   a. The medication lasts four weeks.
   b. The medication is given transdermally.
   c. *Risperdal Consta* is an orally-dissolving formulation for use with dysphagia.
   d. There remains a risk of EPS with this formulation.
   e. The benefit with the *Consta* formulation is little or no risk of elevated prolactin levels.

6. A patient has schizophrenia, with constant auditory hallucinations which have instructed the patient to harm himself and others. He has failed olanzapine and chlorpromazine. His other medications include sertraline for anxiety. His WBC is 3.4 cells/mm^3 with and ANC of 1400 and platelet count of 120,000. Which of the following statements is correct?
   a. He should begin clozapine treatment.
   b. Clozapine treatment is contraindicated due to his ANC.
   c. Clozapine treatment is contraindicated due to his platelet count.
   d. Clozapine treatment is not indicated since he has not tried haloperidol.
   e. He should begin treatment with *Zyprexa*.

7. A patient with psychotic symptoms takes the following medications for chronic conditions: metoprolol, warfarin, amiodarone, lisinopril and insulin. His physician wishes to begin an antipsychotic. Which of the following agents represents the best option for this patient?
   a. Thioridazine
   b. Haloperidol
   c. Ziprasidone
   d. Risperidone
   e. Aripiprazole

Answers

1-a,b,c,d, 2-b,d,e, 3-b, 4-b,d, 5-d, 6-b, 7-e

BIPOLAR DISORDER

GUIDELINES/REFERENCES

Diagnostic and Statistical Manual of Mental Disorders, Fifth Edition (DSM-5).

WFSBP: Update 2012 on the long-term treatment of bipolar disorder. *The World Journal of Biological Psychiatry.* 2013;14:154–219.

APA, Treatment of Patients with Bipolar Disorder. http://psychiatryonline.org/pb/assets/raw/sitewide/practice_guidelines/guidelines/bipolar.pdf (accessed 2016 Oct 30).

VA/DOD, Management of Bipolar Disorder in Adults, 2010. http://www.healthquality.va.gov/guidelines/MH/bd/bd_305_full.pdf (accessed 2016 Oct 30).

We gratefully acknowledge the assistance of Robin Wackernah, PharmD, BCPP, Regis University School of Pharmacy, Rueckert-Hartman College for Health Professions, in preparing this chapter.

BACKGROUND

Bipolar disorder is a mood disorder in which moods can fluctuate from an extremely sad or hopeless state of depression to abnormally elevated, overexcited or irritable mood called mania or hypomania. Each mood episode represents a drastic change from a person's usual mood and behavior. Sometimes, a mood episode includes symptoms of both mania and depression. This is called a mixed state.

Bipolar disorder is classified as bipolar I and bipolar II, which differ primarily by the severity of the mania. Another milder form not specifically addressed in this chapter is called "cyclothymic disorder" where the criteria for depression or mania are not fully met.

The prevalence of bipolar disorder is ~2.6% among U.S. adults. Bipolar disorder can lead to problems with relationships, employment, and disrupt lives. It can lead to anxiety disorders, drug abuse and suicide.

THE SEVERITY OF THE MANIA DETERMINES TYPE I OR TYPE II

BIPOLAR I
Severe mania (symptoms on next page), and usually, bouts of intense depression. The mania is severe enough that there's no doubt the person is manic.

May be psychotic/delusional & may require hospitalization.

BIPOLAR II
Hypomania, and usually, bouts of intense depression. Hypomania does not affect social/work functioning, does not cause psychosis or require hospitalization.

People feel better when they're manic; in the depressive phase, they may seek help & be misdiagnosed as having depression only.

Mania: abnormally, elevated or irritable mood for at least a week (or any duration if hospitalization needed),
3+ symptoms required for diagnosis (If mood is only irritable, 4+ symptoms

- Inflated self-esteem
- Sleeping less
- Talkative
- Jumping from one topic to the next
- Easily distracted
- Increase in goal-directed activity
- Involved with high-risk, pleasurable activities (buying sprees, sexual indiscretions, gambling)

+ Depression
(common, 1 in 5 commit suicide)

Diagnostic Criteria

Bipolar Mania or Illicit Drug Use?

A toxicology screen should be taken prior to the start of treatment, and as-needed, to rule-out mania due to illicit drug use.

DRUG TREATMENT

Patients with bipolar disorder usually cycle between both mania and depression. The goal of treatment is to stabilize the mood without inducing a depressive or manic state. Mood stabilizers, which include lithium, valproate, lamotrigine and carbamazepine, treat both mania and depression, without inducing either state. Antipsychotics are used when a patient with mania has psychosis, and are also indicated for monotherapy as mood stabilizers. Patients with bipolar disorder are more susceptible to drug-induced extrapyramidal symptoms (EPS); use antipsychotics cautiously, especially the first generation antipsychotics (FGAs) such as haloperidol, which have a high incidence of EPS. Second-generation antipsychotics (SGAs) are preferred.

Antidepressants can induce a manic episode and are not generally recommended unless the patient is on a mood stabilizer. The SGAs do not induce depression, and some have antidepressant effects. For example, lurasidone and olanzapine/fluoxetine *(Symbyax)* are indicated for bipolar depression and aripiprazole, brexpiprazole and quetiapine have FDA approvals for adjunctive therapy in major depressive disorder (MDD).

To select treatment, consider the following:

- The side effect profile of the drug.
- The patient's medication history, and first-degree family member's medication history; if the patient or family member responded well to a drug, it may be a reasonable option.
- The formulations available, and the cost.

First-line treatment for a patient in a manic state is valproate or lithium plus an antipsychotic. For bipolar depression, first-line treatment is lithium or lamotrigine. Lurasidone and olanzapine/fluoxetine *(Symbyax)* can also be used for bipolar depression. After treating an acute episode, maintenance treatment can help prevent a relapse.

Lamotrigine is used in bipolar depression and for maintenance treatment, but is not useful for acute mania due to the slow titration required, due to the risk of severe rash. Carbamazepine (as *Equetro)* and valproate are both used for bipolar mania.

Lithium is an old drug, but remains in common use for mania, depression and maintenance. Lithium is often paired with an SGA in severe cases.

MedGuides are required with all antidepressants (primarily due to suicide risk) and with all antipsychotics (primarily due to increased risk of death in elderly patients with dementia-related psychosis).

MOOD STABILIZERS & PREGNANCY

Lithium, valproate and carbamazepine have known fetal risk. Lamotrigine is a safer option, relative to the other agents. Lithium exposure in pregnancy is associated with an increase in congenital cardiac malformations.

- Valproate exposure in pregnancy is associated with increased risk of fetal anomalies, including neural tube defects, fetal valproate syndrome and long term adverse cognitive effects. It should be avoided in pregnancy, if possible, especially during the first trimester.
- Carbamazepine exposure in pregnancy is associated with fetal carbamazepine syndrome, which can cause facial abnormalities and other significant issues. It should be avoided in pregnancy, if possible, especially during the first trimester. Carbamazepine is a third-line agent for treating bipolar disorder but is occasionally used, and a formulation is approved for bipolar I *(Equetro)*.

ANTIEPILEPTIC DRUGS USED IN BIPOLAR DISORDER

See the Epilepsy/Seizures chapter for a detailed review of these medications, including drug interactions and patient counseling.

Lamotrigine *(Lamictal, Lamictal ODT, Lamictal XR, Lamictal Starter)*

Valproate/Valproic Acid Derivatives *(Depakene, Depakote, Depacon)*

Carbamazepine *(Equetro)* – Formulation approved for bipolar

SECOND-GENERATION ANTIPSYCHOTICS USED IN BIPOLAR DISORDER

SGAs are often used with or without lithium or valproate in patients with bipolar disorder. The agents listed are those with FDA approval for bipolar mania or bipolar depression; SGAs without FDA approval for these indications are also used clinically. For a more complete review of the SGAs, including drug interactions and counseling, refer to the See the Schizophrenia/Psychosis chapter for a detailed review of these medications, including drug interactions and patient counseling.

Aripiprazole *(Abilify, Abilify Maintena)*

Asenapine *(Saphris)*

Cariprazine *(Vraylar)*

Lurasidone *(Latuda)*

Olanzapine/Fluoxetine *(Symbyax)*

Olanzapine *(Zyprexa, Zydis ODT, Relprevv Inj.)*

Quetiapine *(Seroquel, Seroquel XR)*

Risperidone *(Risperdal, Risperdal Consta, Risperdal M-TAB)*

Ziprasidone *(Geodon)*

Lithium

Lithium has various proposed mechanisms, including influencing the reuptake of serotonin and/or norepinephrine and inhibiting postsynaptic D2 receptor supersensitivity. Lithium may be neuroprotective due to increased glutamate clearance and increasing brain-derived neurotropic factor (BDNF).

DRUG	DOSING	SAFETY/SIDE EFFECTS/MONITORING
Lithium *(Lithobid)* Tablet, capsule, solution	Start at 150-900 mg/day, divided TID, max 900-1,800 mg/day divided TID-QID Extended-release is taken BID **Therapeutic Range** 0.6-1.2 mEq/L (trough level) Acute mania may need up to 1.5 mEq initially	**BOXED WARNING** Serum lithium levels should be monitored to avoid toxicity **SIDE EFFECTS** GI upset (nausea, abdominal pain, anorexia, cognitive effects, cogwheel rigidity, fine hand tremor, weight gain, polyuria/polydipsia, hypothyroidism (see monitoring), hypercalcemia, cardiac abnormalities (inverted T waves), edema, worsening of psoriasis, blue-gray skin pigmentation, impotence **TOXICITY** > 1.5 mEq/L (coarse hand tremor, vomiting, persistent diarrhea, confusion, ataxia) > 2.5 mEq/L (CNS depression, arrhythmia, seizures, irreversible brain damage, coma) **MONITORING** Serum lithium levels, renal function, thyroid function (TSH, FT4), calcium, ECG (patients > 40 years old) **NOTES** Safety Issue - see previous text & pregnancy chapter Use cautiously in mild-moderate renal impairment, do not use if severe; lithium is 100% renally cleared Avoid use with other serotonergic agents

Lithium Drug Interactions

- These ↑ lithium: ↓ salt intake, NSAIDs, ACE inhibitors, ARBs, thiazide diuretics. Aspirin and sulindac are safer NSAID options.
- These ↓ lithium: ↑ salt intake, caffeine, and theophylline.
- These ↑ risk of serotonin syndrome if taken with lithium: SSRIs, SNRIs, triptans, linezolid and other serotonergic drugs.
- These ↑ risk of neurotoxicity (ataxia, tremors, nausea) if taken with lithium: verapamil, diltiazem, phenytoin and carbamazepine.

Lithium Counseling

- If you have worsened nausea or diarrhea, slurred speech, or feel shaky and confused, it is possible that the amount of lithium in your body has gone up. Contact your healthcare provider right away.

LITHIUM'S NOT EASY TO INITIATE

Common side effects

Nausea, anorexia, abdominal pain, dry mouth, thirst, sedation, confusion, tremor

Help out with suggestions

Titrate slowly, possibly shift more of the dose to QHS

Suggest taking dose at end of a meal; food in the stomach helps

Drink adequate fluids; avoid dehydration

Dose correctly

5 mL lithium citrate solution = 8 mEq

8 mEq = 300 mg lithium carbonate tabs/caps

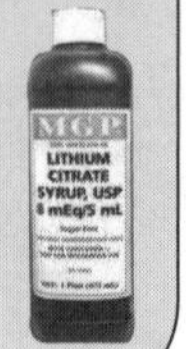

- You will need to have your blood checked occasionally during treatment.
- Do not crush, chew, or break any extended-release forms of lithium (*Lithobid*). The drug is specially formulated to release slowly in the body.
- Lithium can cause you to feel confused or "dizzy," especially when the dose is started or increased. Use caution when driving or performing other hazardous activities until you know how you feel taking this medication.
- Lithium is known to be harmful to an unborn baby. Do not take lithium without first talking to your healthcare provider if you are pregnant or are planning a pregnancy. Lithium can pass into breast milk. Discuss with your healthcare provider if you are breastfeeding.
- Drink 8 to 12 glasses of water or other fluids (not counting any caffeinated sodas, coffee or tea) every day while taking lithium. Heavy exercise, prolonged exposure to heat or sun, excessive sweating, diarrhea, or vomiting can cause dehydration and increased side effects from lithium. Do not let yourself get dehydrated, and limit time in the sun.
- Do not change the amount of salt you consume. This will increase or decrease the amount of lithium in your body. There is a lot of salt in many fast foods, luncheon meats, "TV dinners" and canned foods.
- Take the medication with food to help reduce nausea. It is often helpful to take the dose at the end of a meal, when the food is still in your stomach.
- Do not stop taking this medication, even if you are feeling better.

PRACTICE CASE

MH is a 65 y/o white female brought to the clinic today (11/1) by her sister. She has a long history of bipolar I that has been reasonably controlled on lithium therapy for many years. MH lives with her sister, who takes good care of her medical and social needs. Occasionally, her sister reports, MH gets "back to her old thing" and becomes convinced that she is on a mission to "change the world." MH can never explain what is involved with this mission. Her sister states that MH has always had a fine hand tremor, but today her hands are visibly shaking. She is nauseous and vomited the little she ate this morning. Her speech is slurred and confused. She appears to have difficulty walking into the examination room. She also has a cold with nasal congestion. Additional past medical history includes hypertension.

Allergies: NKDA

Medications:
Lithobid 450 mg BID
Oscal 500 mg BID with meals
B-complex tablet daily

9/9: Prescription provided for Diovan 80 mg daily for elevated blood pressure.

Vitals:
BP: 129/80 mmHg HR: 75 BPM RR: 15 BPM Temp: 38.1°C Pain: 2/10

Labs:

10/1/2013	11/1/2014
Na (mEq/L) = 136 (135 - 145)	Na (mEq/L) = 140 (135 - 145)
K (mEq/L) = 3.9 (3.5 - 5)	K (mEq/L) = 4.6 (3.5 - 5)
Cl (mEq/L) = 104 (95 - 103)	Cl (mEq/L) = 101 (95 - 103)
HCO3 (mEq/L) = 24 (24 - 30)	HCO3 (mEq/L) = 25 (24 - 30)
BUN (mg/dL) = 14 (7 - 20)	BUN (mg/dL) = 28 (7 - 20)
SCr (mg/dL) = 0.7 (0.6 - 1.3)	SCr (mg/dL) = 1.7 (0.6 - 1.3)
Glucose (mg/dL) = 120 (100 - 125)	Glucose (mg/dL) = 108 (100 - 125)
WBC (cells/mm3) = 8.2 (4 - 11 x 103)	WBC (cells/mm3) = 5.6 (4 - 11 x 103)
Hgb (g/dL) = 12.4 (13.5 - 18 male, 12 - 16 female)	Hgb (g/dL) = 14.3 (13.5 - 18 male, 12 - 16 female)
Hct (%) = 39.2 (38 - 50 male, 36 - 46 female)	Hct (%) = 42.1 (38 - 50 male, 36 - 46 female)
Plt (cells/mm3) = 201 (150 - 450 x 103)	Plt (cells/mm3) = 250 (150 - 450 x 103)
Lithium (mEq/L) = 0.9 (0.6 - 1.2)	Lithium (mEq/L) = 1.8 (0.6 - 1.2)

Questions

1. The following factors are likely contributing to the current symptoms of GI distress, coarse hand tremor, ataxia and confusion: (Select **ALL** that apply.)

   a. The use of a calcium supplement
   b. The patient's decline in renal function
   c. Lithium level of 1.8 mEq/L
   d. The use of a vitamin supplement (B-complex)
   e. The patient's ethnicity

2. MH is using *Lithobid*. Describe *Lithobid* clearance:

   a. 100% renal clearance; no hepatic metabolism.
   b. 50% metabolized by 3A4, 50% excreted unchanged in the urine.
   c. 75% metabolized by 2D6, 25% excreted unchanged in the urine.
   d. 100% metabolized by 2C9, 100% metabolites cleared renally.
   e. Metabolized by 2C19, metabolites cleared renally.

3. Select the correct statement regarding the medication added to the patient's regimen on September 9th:

   a. It will increase the risk of bradycardia.
   b. It will increase her blood pressure.
   c. It will contribute to rapid-cycling.
   d. It will increase appetite and could contribute to weight gain.
   e. It will increase lithium levels.

Questions 4-7 are NOT based on the above case.

4. A patient has a history of two myocardial infarctions. He has bipolar II which is moderately controlled with lithium monotherapy. He has been using lithium for many years. His physician wishes to use an antipsychotic as augmentation therapy. Which of the following antipsychotics can cause QT prolongation? (Select **ALL** that apply.)

   a. Seroquel
   b. Risperdal
   c. Geodon
   d. Mellaril
   e. Haldol

5. Patient counseling for lithium should include the following points: (Select **ALL** that apply.)

   a. Lithium could become unsafe if taken with over-the-counter ibuprofen or naproxen.
   b. You may notice that your hands develop a fine (light) tremor.
   c. If the tremor becomes worse and you feel nauseated, contact your healthcare provider at once.
   d. A safe level for this drug is 0.6-1.2 mg/L.
   e. You must keep the salt level in your diet around the same amount each day.

6. A patient is being treated with valproate therapy. Boxed warnings for this medication include: (Select **ALL** that apply.)

   a. Neuroleptic Malignant Syndrome
   b. Mitochondrial disease
   c. Hepatotoxicity
   d. Pancreatitis
   e. Teratogenicity

7. Which of the following statements regarding drug treatment of bipolar disorder are true: (Select **ALL** that apply.)

   a. Lithium, valproate/divalproex, lamotrigine, carbamazepine and asenapine are mood stabilizers.
   b. Antidepressants can induce a manic episode.
   c. Antidepressants should only be started if a mood stabilizer is also part of the regimen.
   d. FGAs are preferred in bipolar disease due to lower incidence of metabolic side effects.
   e. Lamotrigine is not useful in acute mania due to the slow titration that is required.

Answers

1-b,c, 2-a, 3-e, 4-a,b,c,d,e, 5-a,b,c,e, 6-b,c,d,e, 7-b, c, e

62

PARKINSON DISEASE

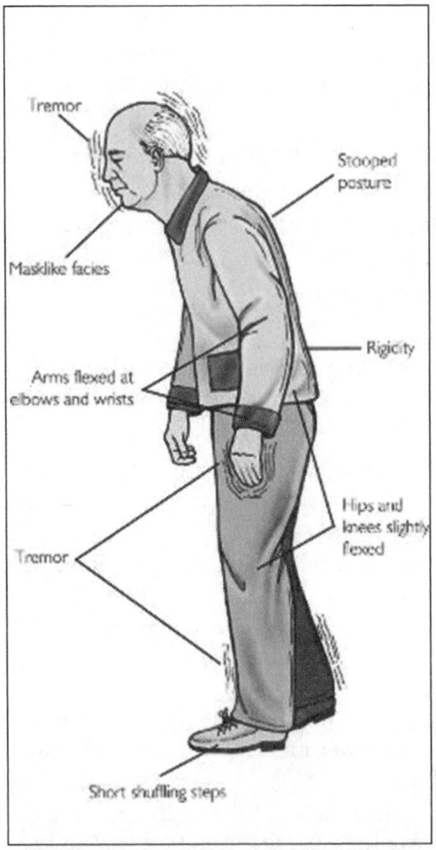

We gratefully acknowledge the assistance of George DeMaagd, PharmD, BCPS, Associate Dean of Academic Administration, Professor of Pharmacy, Union University School of Pharmacy, in preparing this chapter.

BACKGROUND

Parkinson disease (PD) is a brain disorder. It occurs when neurons in a part of the brain called the substantia nigra die or become impaired. The cause of neuronal death is not well understood, but is multi-factorial. Normally, these cells produce dopamine. (see Study Tip Box on the following page).

Dopamine allows smooth, coordinated function of the body's muscles and movement. When ~80% of the dopamine-producing cells are damaged, the motor symptoms of the disease appear. Biomarkers that can identify early disease, prior to visually noticeable symptoms, is a focus of research.

Motor symptoms include bradykinesia (slow movement), involuntary shaking and tremor, arm/leg/trunk rigidity (stiffness) and postural instability (trouble with balance, and falls). Non-motor symptoms can precede motor symptoms and may appear much earlier. These include loss of sense of smell (anosmia), constipation, sleep difficulties, low mood/depression and orthostasis. While this disease usually develops after the age of 65, 15% of those diagnosed are under 50. Initially (in what is called Stage I) the disease appears as tremor on one-side (unilateral) and eventually spreads bilaterally.

Even with high doses of PD drugs and various combinations, the disease will progress, including extended periods of "off time". This is when symptoms of the disease worsen before the next dose of medication is due. These are among the most frustrating and challenging aspects of disease management. An off episode, with muscle stiffness, slow movements and difficulty starting movement is one of the most frustrating aspects of living with the disease. Eventually, the patient will be unable to walk and have difficulty feeding themselves and swallowing.

GUIDELINES/REFERENCES

Diagnosis and prognosis of new onset Parkinson disease (an evidence-based review): Report of the Quality Standards Subcommittee of the American Academy of Neurology. *Neurology.* 2006 Apr 11;66(7):968-75.

Related Psychiatric Conditions

Patients with PD have a high incidence of depression. The agents with the highest efficacy for treatment in these patients are the tricyclic antidepressants, and preferably the secondary amines (such as desipramine and nortriptyline), due to less side effects than with the tertiary amines. The majority of PD patients, however, use SSRIs since many clinicians are familiar with this class and think that they are better tolerated. Although the SSRIs are commonly used, they may contribute to tremor or increase the risk of serotonin syndrome in patients who are taking other serotonergic drugs. The dopamine agonist pramipexole has been reported to provide antidepressant effect and is another option.

Psychosis can present with advanced disease. Quetiapine is the preferred antipsychotic, due to a low risk of movement disorders, causes metabolic complications, including increased blood glucose and cholesterol with lower doses. Clozapine has a low risk of aggravating movement disorders, but has risk of agranulocytosis, seizures and other complications. It requires weekly monitoring and reporting of white blood cells. Pimavanserin *(Nuplazid)*, a 5HT2A/2C receptor inverse agonist, is a recent new drug approved to treat hallucinations.

STUDY TIP: PARKINSON DISEASE: THE CAUSE, SYMPTOMS AND PRIMARY TREATMENT DRUGS

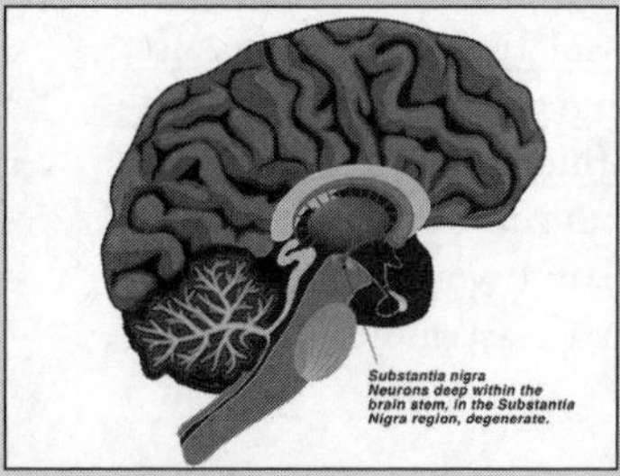
Substantia nigra
Neurons deep within the brain stem, in the Substantia Nigra region, degenerate.

Neurons deep within the brain stem, in the Substantia Nigra region, degenerate.
This part of the brain controls motor function, including movement and balance. These cells direct movement by releasing the neurotransmitter dopamine (DA), which transmits the movement instructions to other parts of the brain.

Parkinson's:
Less dopamine → Less instructions → movement problems, called the **TRAP major symptoms.**

TRAP major symptoms:	Additional Symptoms:
Tremor – when resting, worsened by anxiety	Small, cramped handwriting (micrographia)
Rigidity – in legs, arms, trunk, face (mask-like face)	Shuffling walk, bent over body
Akinesia/Bradykinesia – lack of/ slow start in movement	Muffled speech, drooling, dysphagia
Postural Instability – imbalance, falls	Depression, anxiety (psychosis in advanced disease)
	Constipation, incontinence

Primary Treatment: REPLACE DOPAMINE
✓ Give a precursor to dopamine that becomes dopamine in the brain (that's levodopa, in *Sinemet*).

✓ Give a drug that acts like dopamine (the dopamine agonists).

The other drugs help with symptoms (somewhat) or treat a specific symptom such as tremor.

Tremor is often the first noticeable symptom, and usually starts in one hand or foot (on just one side, unilateral) and eventually spreads to both sides (bilateral). It is a *resting* tremor because it appears when the hand is not moving, such as when a person's hand is resting in their lap. Initially, the tremor may be all that is treated in order to delay the need for the stronger *dopamin*-ergic drugs.

DRUG TREATMENT

Medications are used to help improve movement, and for the related issues, such as psychosis and constipation. Levodopa, a prodrug for dopamine, is in carbidopa-levodopa *(Sinemet)*, the most effective agent. Carbidopa is given with levodopa to prevent the peripheral (i.e., outside of the CNS) metabolism of levodopa, which would destroy most of the drug before it could cross the blood-brain barrier and provide efficacy. It is important to provide the right amount of carbidopa to block conversion of levodopa to dopamine, without causing excess side effects; see the drug table. Carbidopa-levodopa is sometimes better tolerated for initial treatment in the elderly than the dopamine agonists.

Initial treatment of tremor-predominant disease in younger patients can be treated with a centrally-acting anticholinergic. The considerable side effects of these drugs makes the drug difficult to use in elderly patients; the Beers criteria for potentially inappropriate medication use in older adults lists this group of drugs in the "Avoid" use category. Amantadine is sometimes used for initial treatment of tremor, usually in younger patients. A monoamine oxidase (MAO) inhibitor may also be used as the initial treatment and can provide a mild benefit. These are selective MAO inhibitors. The non-selective inhibitors are used for depression, and would be contraindicated with dopaminergic drugs because they would block drug metabolism.

The dopamine agonists are often given as the initial option in younger patients, and eventually in most patients. As the disease progresses, treatment will be directed at both reducing off periods and limiting dyskinesias (abnormal movement), and will require multiple therapies. Inhibitors of the enzyme catechol-o-methyltransferase (COMT) increase the effect of levodopa by blocking levodopa metabolism. Amantadine can be useful to help with tremor or dyskinesias. Apomorphine treats later stage severe freezing episodes, but it requires subcutaneous (SC) administration, has difficult side effects, and provides increased movement for just about an hour. Droxidopa *(Northera)* is a newer drug indicated for orthostatic hypotension, which (primarily) affects PD patients.

AVOID DOPAMINE BLOCKING DRUGS

KEY DRUGS: Avoid; will worsen PD

- Prochlorperazine and other phenothiazines, used for psychosis, nausea, agitation
- Butyrophenones used for psychosis, behavior disorders (haloperidol), nausea (droperidol)
- 2nd-generation antipsychotics risperidone (at higher doses), paliperidone
- Metoclopramide, do not overdose in elderly; renally-cleared drug

Dopamine Replacement Agents & Agonists

DRUG	DOSING	SAFETY/SIDE EFFECTS/MONITORING
COMT-INHIBITORS: Used only with levodopa to ↑ levodopa duration of action. Inhibits the enzyme Catechol-O-methyltransferase (COMT) to prevent peripheral and central conversion of levodopa		
Entacapone *(Comtan)* Levodopa/carbidopa + entacapone *(Stalevo)* Tolcapone *(Tasmar)* – not used much due to hepatotoxicity	200 mg with each dose of carbidopa/levodopa (max 1,600 mg/day) ***Stalevo***: carbidopa/levodopa in ratio of 1:4 with 200 mg entacapone, example: 12.5/50/200 mg	**SIDE EFFECTS** Similar to levodopa, due to extending levodopa: nausea, dyskinesias, dizziness, orthostasis, hypotension Can cause orange/brown urine, diarrhea **NOTES** ↓ in levodopa dose of 10-30% is usually necessary when adding on COMT inhibitor. Dyskinesias can occur earlier with COMT inhibitors.

Dopamine Replacement Agents & Agonists Continued

DRUG	DOSING	SAFETY/SIDE EFFECTS/MONITORING

Carbidopa/Levodopa: Levodopa is a precursor of dopamine. Carbidopa inhibits dopa decarboxylase enzyme, preventing peripheral metabolism of levodopa and nausea. Entacapone blocks peripheral conversion.

Carbidopa/Levodopa ***(Sinemet, Sinemet CR, Rytary ER, Duopa*** enteral suspension given via J-tube Levodopa and carbidopa available separately	Usual starting dose 25/100 TID IR: 10/100, 25/100, 25/250 mg tab CR: Usual starting dose 50/200 BID CR tab can be cut into half – do not crush or chew ER (*Rytary*): start at 23.75/95 mg TID if levodopa-naive 70-100 mg/day of carbidopa is required to inhibit dopa decarboxylase Titrate cautiously	**CONTRAINDICATION** Non-selective MAO inhibitors within 14 days, narrow angle glaucoma **SIDE EFFECTS** Nausea, dizziness, orthostasis, dry mouth, dyskinesias, dystonias (occasional, painful) ~1/3 of patients develop confusion, hallucinations, or psychosis Can cause brown, black or dark urine, saliva, sweat, discolor clothing, positive Coombs test: discontinue drug (hemolysis risk), unusual sexual urges, priapism, uric acid elevation (slight) **NOTES** Response fluctuations and dyskinesias after long term use Separate from iron, consider separating from protein. *Rytary*: take whole or sprinkle on small amount of applesauce; high-fat, high-kcal meal delays absorption.

DA-AGONISTS: Acts similar to dopamine at the dopamine receptor

Pramipexole ***(Mirapex, Mirapex ER)*** Both dopamine oral agonists IR formulations approved for restless legs syndrome (RLS), dosed QHS	Start 0.125 mg TID, titrate weekly to max 1.5 mg TID ER: Start 0.375 mg daily, titrate weekly to max 4.5 mg daily	**SIDE EFFECTS** Somnolence, including sudden daytime sleep attacks Nausea, dizziness, orthostasis, vomiting, dry mouth, peripheral edema, constipation Hallucinations, dyskinesias, impulse control disorders **NOTES** ↓ pramipexole dose if CrCl < 50 mL/min (90% renally-excreted). A slow titration (no more than weekly) is required due to orthostasis, dizziness, sleepiness. Ropinirole: CYP 450 1A2 substrate; caution with 1A2 inhibitors due to increased drug levels.
RoPINIRole ***(Requip, Requip XL)*** RLS: see above Bromocriptine (*Parlodel*) – no longer used for PD	Start 0.25 mg TID, titrate weekly to max 8 mg TID XL: Start 2 mg daily, can titrate to max 24 mg daily	
Rotigotine *(Neupro)* Patch formulation only Like the other dopamine agonists, approved for both PD and restless leg syndrome RLS: 1 mg/24 hours, can increase by 1 mg weekly	Patch: Start 2 mg/24 hrs (early PD) Max 8 mg/24 hours	**SIDE EFFECTS** Orthostasis, peripheral edema, somnolence, application site (skin) reactions, hyperhidrosis, dyskinesias, nausea, HA, fatigue, hallucinations, arthralgias **NOTES** Apply once daily, same time each day. Do not apply to same site for at least 14 days. Do not apply heat source over patch. Remove patch for MRI, avoid if sensitivity/allergy to sulfites.

Dopamine Replacement Agents & Agonists Continued

DRUG	DOSING	SAFETY/SIDE EFFECTS/MONITORING
DA-AGONIST injection for advanced disease; a "rescue" movement agent for off periods		
Apomorphine *(Apokyn)* SC inj: 10 mg/mL (3 mL) Lasts 45-90 minutes Used by patients for "off" periods; can be injected up to 5x/day. Taken in addition to other PD medications.	Start at 0.2 mL (2 mg) Max 0.6 mL (6 mg) Caution: dosed written in mL, not mg Must be started in a medical office	**CONTRAINDICATION** Do not use with 5HT3 antagonists (ondansetron, others) due to severe hypotension and loss of consciousness **SIDE EFFECTS** Severe N/V, hypotension, yawning, dyskinesias, somnolence, dizziness, QT **NOTES** Monitor supine and standing blood pressure. For emesis: trimethobenzamide *(Tigan)* 300 mg PO TID or similar antiemetic, started 3 days prior to initial dose

Carbidopa/Levodopa *(Sinemet)* Drug Interactions

- Contraindicated with non-selective MAO inhibitors (2 week separation).
- Do not use with dopamine blockers, which will worsen Parkinson's symptoms (see front section) this includes phenothiazines, metoclopramide, etc.
- Iron can ↓ absorption.
- Protein-rich foods can ↓ absorption.

Parkinson Drug Counseling (All)

- People with Parkinsons may be at a higher risk of getting a type of skin cancer called melanoma. It is important that you are monitored for this condition. Please discuss this with your healthcare provider.
- Call your healthcare provider right away if you have uncontrollable movements of the mouth, tongue, cheeks, jaw, arms, or legs, or if you have a fever and your body feels very hot.
- The medicines used for Parkinsons cannot be taken with a group of depression medicines called MAO inhibitors. Make sure the pharmacist knows about all the medicines you use, and any changes to your medicines.
- If you develop any urges, including unusual urges for sex, or uncontrollable activitites like buying sprees, let your healthcare provider know. Your mood can change; tell your provider if your mood becomes sad, or if you have thoughts of harming yourself.
- Do not stop taking this medicine suddenly. Stopping suddenly could make your condition much worse. Avoid drinking alcohol because it will make dizziness and sleepiness much worse, and could cause falls and injuries.
- If you miss a dose of any of your regular Parkinson medicines, take the dose as soon as you remember except if it is close to the time for the next dose, then skip the one you forgot, and just take the regular dose.

Carbidopa/Levodopa *(Sinemet)* Counseling

- Do not crush or chew any controlled-release forms of carbidopa and levodopa *(Sinemet CR)*. They are specially formulated to release slowly into your system. If necessary, the tablets can be split in half where they are scored, then swallowed without crushing or chewing.
- Use caution when driving, operating machinery, or performing other hazardous activities. Carbidopa and levodopa can cause dizziness or drowsiness, and can make you feel suddenly sleepy.
- This drug may cause the urine to become darker, even dark brown, and can stain clothing.

- Iron can decrease the amount of medicine that gets into your body; if you take iron pills they should be taken at a different time.
- Foods high in protein can reduce the amount of drug that gets into your body (however, protein intake is important and usually not reduced). *Rytary*: A high-fat or high-calorie meal can cause the drug to work slower.
- For males, in the unlikely event you have a painful or prolonged erection (lasting more than 4 hours), stop using this drug and seek immediate medical attention or permanent problems could result.

Ropinirole & Pramipexole *(Requip & Mirapex)* Counseling

- This medicine can be taken with or without food. Food will help if the medicine causes nausea.
- Nausea and drowsiness are the most common side effects. This medicine may cause you to fall asleep while you are doing daily activities such as driving, talking with other people, watching TV, or eating. If you experience increased drowsiness or dizziness, or episodes of falling asleep while performing daily activities, do not drive or participate in potentially dangerous activities.
- This drug can cause dizziness, which may be more likely to occur when you rise from a sitting or lying position. Rise slowly and use caution to prevent a fall.
- Alcohol, sleeping pills, antihistamines, antidepressants, pain medicine and other medicines that cause drowsiness can make the drowsiness worse, which could be dangerous. Do not use alcohol.
- Tell your healthcare provider if you experience thoughts which seem like they are paranoid, or excessive worry, or hearing voices. There is medicine that may help, or the dose may need to be changed.
- It is likely that the dose will be increased slowly, over time. This is normal since the dose has to start low due to dizziness and sleepiness.

Rotigotine *(Neupro)* Patch Counseling

- Side effects from the patch can include ankle swelling, headache, fatigue, nausea, changes in blood pressure, difficulty getting a good night's sleep, and unusual thoughts. If any of these occur and are troublesome, discuss with your healthcare provider.
- This medicine can cause you to become very sleepy. Do not drive a car or operate dangerous machinery until you are sure this can be done safely.
- You may find that you sweat more than usual. It is important to drink enough fluids and avoid direct sunlight.
- The patch contains aluminum, which can burn your skin if you have certain medical procedures. The patch must be removed prior to magnetic resonance imaging (MRI) or "cardioversion." Do not expose the patch to heat, such as heating pads.
- To apply the patch:
    - Choose the time of day that works best for you so it is easiest to remember.
    - Wear the patch for 24 hours. Remove before applying the next patch.
    - Do not apply to hairy skin, or skin that has cuts. Do not use moisturizer before applying the patch or it will not stick well.
    - After peeling off one side of the backing, apply to dry skin on the stomach, thigh, hip, side of the body, shoulder or upper arm. Press in place for 30 seconds.
    - Do not cut the patch. If the patch falls off, you can reapply with bandage tape.
    - The patch can irritate the skin. Report to your healthcare provider if you get a rash, swelling or itching that persists. Rotate the place where you place the patch. Wait at least 14 days before applying in the same location.
    - When the patch is removed, fold it in half (sticky sides together) and throw away the folded patch so that children and pets cannot reach it.

DRUG	DOSING	SAFETY/SIDE EFFECTS/MONITORING

Amantadine: blocks dopamine reuptake into presynaptic neurons, increases dopamine release from presynaptic fibers; Used for mild disease, or for dyskinesias in advanced disease

Amantadine	100 mg BID-TID ↓ dose in renal impairment	**SIDE EFFECTS** Dizziness (lightheadedness) and insomnia, abnormal dreams, hallucinations Toxic delirium (with renal impairment, ↓ dose) Cutaneous reaction called *livedo reticularis* (reddish skin mottling – requires drug discontinuation)

Selective MAO-B Inhibitors: used as adjunctive therapy with levodopa or as monotherapy (rasagiline has this indication)

Selegiline *(Eldepryl)* *Emsam* – patch for depression May need to reduce levodopa dose when beginning therapy w/selective MAO-B Inhibitor	5 mg BID, with breakfast & lunch Selegiline can be activating; do not dose at bedtime. If dosed twice, take 2nd dose at mid-day.	**CONTRAINDICATIONS** Concomitant use of cyclobenzaprine, dextromethorphan, methadone, propoxyphene, St John's wort, or tramadol; concomitant use of meperidine or an MAO inhibitor. **SIDE EFFECTS** Due to DA-excess, similar to levodopa Rasagiline, when taken as monotherapy, can cause headache, joint pain and indigestion. If taken with levodopa, any of the side effects from dopamine excess are possible. **NOTES** Selegiline is metabolized by several CYP450 enzymes to amphetamine metabolites. *Zelapar* ODT has greater liver bypass, with ↓ formation of amphetamine metabolites. Rasagiline is metabolized by CYP1A2 and has no amphetamine metabolites.
Selegiline *(Zelapar ODT)*	1.25-2.5 mg daily CrCl <30 mL/minute: Use is not recommended	
Rasagiline *(Azilect)*	0.5-1 mg daily	

Centrally-Acting Anticholinergics: used primarily for tremor in younger patients; decreases dystonic reactions

Benztropine *(Cogentin)*	0.5-2 mg TID (start QHS)	**SIDE EFFECTS** Dry mouth, constipation, urinary retention, blurred vision Somnolence, confusion, tachycardia, high incidence peripheral and central anticholinergic side effects **NOTES** Used primarily for tremor; avoid use in elderly.
Trihexyphenidyl	1-5 mg TID (start 1 mg QHS)	

Alpha/Beta Agonist: used for neurogenic orthostatic hypotension

Droxidopa *(Northera)*	Start at 100 mg TID, can titrate Q 24-48 hour to max 1800 mg/day Take with or without food, with last dose at least 3 hours prior to bedtime (to avoid supine hypertension during sleep)	**BOXED WARNING** Supine hypertension: monitor supine BP prior to and during treatment and more frequently when titrating. To reduce risk, elevate the head of the bed and measure BP in this position. If supine hypertension cannot be managed by elevation of the head of the bed, reduce dose or discontinue. **SIDE EFFECTS** Syncope, falls, HA, UTI **NOTES** Take capsule whole; do not open. Sound-alike drug name (levodopa, carbidopa, *Droxia).*

MAO-B Inhibitor Drug Interactions

- Selegiline and rasagiline should not be used with foods high in tyramine content: (aged or matured cheese, air-dried or cured meats including sausages and salamis; fava or broad bean pods, tap/draft beers, Marmite concentrate, sauerkraut, soy sauce, and other soybean condiments). Food's freshness is also an important concern; improperly stored or spoiled food can create an environment in which tyramine concentrations may increase. Avoid these foods during and for 2 weeks after discontinuation of medication. Avoid products containing dopamine, tyrosine, phenylalanine, tryptophan, or caffeine.
- Selegiline and rasagiline are MAO B inhibitors and at high doses become non-selective; use caution or avoid use with other serotonergic drugs.
- Rasagiline is a CYP 1A2 substrate and should not be dosed above 0.5 mg daily with ciprofloxacin or other CYP 1A2 inhibitors.

PRACTICE CASE

Patient Profile

Patient Name Benjamin Chen
Address 6401 Wisteria Drive
Age 70
Sex Male
Race Asian
Height 5'11"
Weight 185 lbs
Allergies none

DIAGNOSES

Sleepiness
Diziness

MEDICATIONS

Date	No.	Prescriber	Drug and Strength	Quantity	Sig
8/30	76525	Hayes	Carbidopa/Levodopa 25/250 mg	#90	TID
8/30	76526	Hayes	Ropinirole 1 mg	#90	TID (not using, per patient)
8/30	67527	Hayes	Ramipril 10 mg daily	#60	one capsule BID
8/30	76528	Hayes	Amlodipine 10 mg	#30	daily
8/30	76549	Hayes	Multivitamin	#100	daily

LAB/DIAGNOSTIC TESTS

Test	Reference Value	Results 9/15
Ca (mg/dL)	8.5 - 10.5	8.8
Cl (mEq/L)	95 - 103	99
Mg (mEq/L)	1.3 - 2.1	1.4
K (mEq/L)	3.5-5	4.1
P04 (mg/dL)	2.3 - 4.7	4.2
Na (mEq/L)	135 - 145	140
HC03 (mEq/L)	24 - 30	27
BUN (mg/dL)	7 - 20	16
SCr (mg/dL)	0.6 - 1.3	0.9
WBC (mm3)	4,000 - 11,000	5.3
RBC (106/-L)	4.5 - 5.5 male, 4 - 4.9 female	4.8
Hgb (g/dL)	13.5 - 18 male, 12 - 16 female	12.2
Hct (%)	38 - 50 male, 36 - 46 female	36
MCV (mm3)	80 - 96	82
MCHC (g/dL)	31 - 37	33
RDW (%)	11.5 - 14.5	12.1
BP		108/64
Temp		98.6°F
HR		84 BPM

01/11/2016 (today): Patient here for a follow-up due to worsening clinical state. Sinemet use x 3 years, he states it "worked fine" but is now "nearly useless." States he is choking swallowing his food and cannot move well.

Questions

1. Choose the correct statement concerning the patient's carbidopa/levodopa therapy:
   - *a.* The dose of carbidopa is too low.
   - *b.* The dose of carbidopa is too high.
   - *c.* The medication may make his urine turn brown.
   - *d.* The medication will worsen his hypertension.
   - *e.* The medication can cause severe rash.

2. When Benjamin started ropinirole, he found he could not tolerate the medicine due to excessive sleepiness. Choose the correct statement:
   - *a.* The starting dose of ropinirole was too high.
   - *b.* Pramipexole would be less sedating.
   - *c.* The brand name of ropinirole is *Mirapex.*
   - *d.* He should have been started on benztropine instead.
   - *e.* He should have been counseled to increase his caffeine intake during therapy initiation.

3. Choose the correct titration schedule for ropinirole or pramipexole:
   - *a.* Wait at least 2 days before increasing the dose.
   - *b.* Wait at least one week before increasing the dose.
   - *c.* Wait at least two weeks before increasing the dose.
   - *d.* Wait at least three weeks before increasing the dose.
   - *e.* Wait at least four weeks before increasing the dose.

4. Benjamin is using levodopa therapy. He is taking carbidopa concurrently, in the combination medicine *Sinemet*. Choose the correct statements concerning *Sinemet*. (Select **ALL** that apply.)
   - *a.* Carbidopa inhibits decarboxylase and prevents the breakdown of levodopa outside the CNS.
   - *b.* The dose of carbidopa should stay between 30-50 mg.
   - *c.* Using carbidopa with levodopa will decrease nausea.
   - *d.* A typical starting dose of *Sinemet* is 25/250 mg TID.
   - *e.* *Sinemet* is preferred for initial treatment in younger patients with tremor as the only presenting symptom.

5. Which of the following is a common side effect from ropinirole therapy?
   - *a.* Brown urine
   - *b.* Extreme hunger
   - *c.* Somnolence
   - *d.* Loss of consciousness
   - *e.* Hyperglycemia

Questions 6-8 do not apply to the case.

6. A patient has been started on selegiline. What is the mechanism of action of selegiline?
   - *a.* Selective inhibitor of monoamine oxidase A
   - *b.* Selective inhibitor of monoamine oxidase B
   - *c.* Dopamine reuptake inhibitor
   - *d.* Dopamine agonist
   - *e.* Anticholinergic

7. Which of the following medications will require a dose reduction with renal impairment?
   - *a.* Rasagiline
   - *b.* Pramipexole
   - *c.* Benztropine
   - *d.* Levodopa
   - *e.* *Stalevo*

Answers

1-c, 2-a, 3-b, 4-a,c, 5-c, 6-b, 7-b

63

ALZHEIMER'S DISEASE

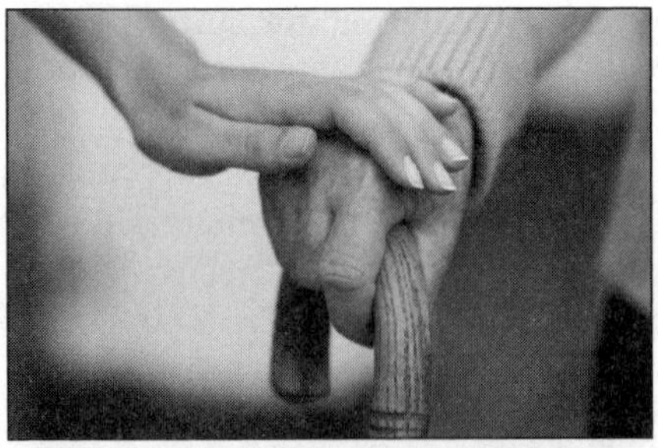

GUIDELINES

American Geriatrics Society. Guide to the management of psychotic disorders and neuropsychiatric symptoms of dementia in older adults. April 2011. https://www.nhqualitycampaign.org/files/AGS_Guidelines_for_Telligen.pdf (accessed 2016 Nov 29).

Qaseem, A, Snow, V, Cross JT Jr et al. Current pharmacologic treatment of dementia: a clinical practice guideline from the American College of Physicians and the American Academy of Family Physicians. *Ann Intern Med.* 2008;148(5):370-8.

We gratefully acknowledge the assistance of George DeMaagd, PharmD, BCPS, Associate Dean of Academic Administration, Professor of Pharmacy, Union University School of Pharmacy, in preparing this chapter.

BACKGROUND

Causes of Cognitive Decline

As people age, a mild age-associated cognitive decline can cause more bothersome than the significant symptoms, such as losing the car keys more often. Mild cognitive impairment (MCI) is a condition between the normal age-associated decline and the more serious decline due to dementia. With MCI, memory and mental function worsen, but not enough to significantly interfere with daily functioning.

With dementia, the prognosis is considerably more severe. Intellectual and social abilities progressively worsen, and functioning becomes impaired.

Initially, the most noticeable symptom of dementia is usually memory loss. As the dementia worsens, problems develop with judgment, attention, planning and personal grooming. Agitation, aggression and depression can be present, and pose difficult challenges for patients and caregivers.

Dementia Types and Diagnosis

There are different types of dementia, including Alzheimer's disease, vascular dementia and Lewy body dementia. The clinical findings in a patient can help the clinician characterize the dementia type. Alzheimer's is the most common type of dementia, and the one with well-defined treatment. Unfortunately, the treatments provide modest benefit.

At the present time, a definitive diagnosis of the actual cause and type of dementia cannot be made unless an autopsy is conducted post-mortem. Researchers are identifying markers and tests that can be used to identify dementia at an early stage. If the likely diagnosis is a dementia that will worsen over time, such as Alzheimer's disease, early diagnosis provides a person time to plan for the future while he or she can still participate in decision making.

Screening and Diagnostic Tools

Initial screening should attempt to rule out causes of memory impairment which could be reversible, such as vitamin B12 deficiency, depression and infection. In some patients, analgesics, benzodiazepines or other centrally-acting medications can cause or exacerbate memory loss. Exams used to identify or screen for dementia include the Folstein Mini-Mental State Exam (MMSE, a score < 24 indicates a memory disorder), Montreal Cognitive Assessment (MoCA), DSM-5 criteria, and the National Institute of Neurological and Communicative Disorders and Stroke and the Alzheimer's Disease and Related Diseases Association (NINCDS-ADRDA) criteria.

DRUGS THAT CAN WORSEN DEMENTIA

KEY DRUGS

- Peripheral anticholinergics (including incontinence & IBS drugs)
- Central anticholinergics (benztropine, etc.)
- Antihistamines & antiemetics
- Antipsychotics
- Barbiturates
- Benzodiazepines
- Skeletal muscle relaxants
- Other CNS depressants

ANTICHOLINERGICS & MEMORY IMPAIRMENT

Anticholinergics are used to treat incontinence (e.g., oxybutinin), allergies or insomnia (e.g., diphenhydramine), dystonic reactions (e.g., benztropine, diphenhydramine), and a few other conditions. A drug with strong central anticholinergic effects can cause acute cognitive impairment and, occasionally, psychosis and hallucinations. The effect depends on the patient's baseline cognitive function, the sensitivity to the drug, the clearance, and the number of drugs and dosing schedule. In elderly patients, centrally-acting anticholinergics are commonly avoided due to these risks. The anticholinergics used for overactive bladder (OAB) may affect cognition modestly. Incontinence is distressing to the patient, to the family, and can lead to nursing home placement; it is not a minor concern. When used, the reduction in symptoms should be evaluated at 6 weeks. If there is a lack of improvement, the drug should be discontinued.

ALZHEIMER'S SYMPTOMS

- Memory loss
- Difficulty communicating, repeating words
- Inability to learn or remember new information
- Difficulty with planning and organizing
- Poor coordination & motor functions
- Personality changes, getting lost
- Inappropriate behavior
- Paranoia, agitation, hallucinations

Pathophysiology

Neuritic plaques & tangles in brain tissue; neuron signaling is interrupted

Alteration of neurotransmitters (e.g., decreased acetylcholine)

NATURAL PRODUCTS USED FOR DEMENTIA

Vitamin E has been reported to benefit some patients with dementia, but the findings are inconsistent. Recent trial results suggest benefit in mild-to-moderate Alzheimer's. *Ginkgo biloba* is commonly used for memory, but the benefit is not well-defined. Ginkgo increases bleeding risk and should be discontinued with bleeding risk, and prior to elective surgical procedures. Other natural products include acetyl-L-carnitine and A-phosphatidylserine, both of which act as acetylcholine precursors, and may be helpful. Recent data suggests older adults with low vitamin D levels have an increased risk of developing cognitive decline, including memory loss. If vitamin D is low, it should be supplemented.

NON-DRUG TREATMENT

In all age groups, physical activity enhances the growth and survival of brain cells. The vascular health of the blood vessels in the brain is vital for cognitive function:

- Keep blood glucose, blood pressure and cholesterol controlled.
- Engage in "thinking" activities and regular physical activity.
- Eat a healthy diet, with fruits, vegetables, nuts, fish, and with a low intake of red meat and alcohol.

STUDY TIP

Dementia drugs help only a little & cause (primarily) nausea and bradycardia (AChE Is) and dizziness, confusion & headache (memantine).

Help the brain stay healthy (see bullets in text).

DRUG TREATMENT

Acetylcholinesterase inhibitors, such as donepezil, are the mainstay of therapy. These are used alone, or with memantine for more advanced disease. At best, one in twelve patients has improvement with these medications. However, for a family, this may mean that the patient who responds can feed themselves for a little while longer, or use the bathroom independently for several more months. Many others do not have noticeable improvement and likely experience side effects (nausea, diarrhea, dizziness). A key clinical pearl with the acetylcholinesterase inhibitors is that although patients may not improve clinically, they may have a slower clinical progression versus if they were not on therapy.

A higher dose of donepezil *(Aricept)* was released in 2010 for advanced disease, however the benefit is very mild (2-point improvement on a 100-point cognition scale). Patients receiving acetylcholinesterase inhibitors should be monitored for both improvement and side effects; if no improvement or intolerable side effects the drug can be discontinued. Discontinuation is also advisable if the dementia has advanced to the point where it lacks clinical benefit. However, discontinuation may not be acceptable to the family, and in some patients there will be noticeable deterioration when the medication is stopped. If nausea is present, evening administration can be helpful. Donepezil is administered QHS for this reason. If insomnia is a concern, the dose can be moved to the morning.

Memantine *(Namenda)* is approved for use alone or with donepezil for moderate-to-severe disease. It is common to add memantine to an acetylcholinesterase inhibitor when the condition moves beyond mild symptoms. *Namzaric* is a combination of donepezil with memantine. Patients stabilized on donepezil 10 mg can be switched to *Namzaric.*

Antidepressants (such as sertraline, citalopram and escitalopram) can be used to treat related depression and anxiety. Antipsychotics are used off-label to treat delusion/anger, but they provide little benefit in dementia, and increase the risk of death in elderly patients; see Boxed Warning in the Schizophrenia/Psychosis chapter.

DRUGS TO TREAT ALZHEIMER'S DISEASE

Acetylcholinesterase inhibitors inhibit centrally-active acetylcholinesterase, the enzyme responsible for hydrolysis (breakdown) of acetylcholine, which results in ↑ ACh. Used in mild-moderate disease, and in moderate-advanced disease in combination with memantine.

DRUG	DOSING	SAFETY/SIDE EFFECTS/MONITORING
Donepezil ***(Aricept, Aricept 23 mg)*** ODT, tablet + memantine (*Namzaric*) If stable on donepezil or memantine, can switch to *Namzaric*	Start 5 mg QHS 5-10 mg QHS for mild to moderate disease 23 mg QHS, for advanced disease, if stable on 10 mg dose x 3 mos memantine/donepezil 7/10, 14/10, 21/10, 28/10 mg, all taken Q daily	**SIDE EFFECTS** GI side effects: N/V/D Bradycardia, fainting, insomnia, tremors, weight loss QT (donepezil, galantamine) **NOTES** Start at lowest dose, and titrate over several weeks to the maximum tolerated dose, especially in patients weighing <50kg. *Donepezil* is dosed QHS to help ↓ nausea. *Aricept 23 mg* is used for advanced disease – minimal additional benefit with higher dose. *Namzaric*: can open and sprinkle on applesauce.
Rivastigmine *(Exelon, Exelon Patch)* Capsule, patch	Start 1.5 mg BID 1.5-6 mg BID w/breakfast & dinner patch: 4.6 (start), 9.5, 13.3 mg/24 hr Hepatic impairment: 4.6 mg patch max.	Recommend *Exelon* patch or *Aricept ODT* to decrease GI side effects – if cost acceptable. *Exelon* patch: titrate Q 4 weeks, apply first patch the day after last oral dose. Apply daily at same time of day. Rotate; do not use same spot for 14 days.
Galantamine *(Razadyne, Razadyne ER)* Tablet, solution	Start 4 mg BID 4-12 mg BID 4 mg/mL solution ER: start at 8 mg daily x 4 weeks, then ↑ to 16 - 24 mg Hepatic/renal impairment: 16 mg max, severe: do not use.	Galantamine IR taken BID without food or with breakfast and dinner (preferred). galantamine ER taken with breakfast. Solution: can mix with liquid, take within 4 hours.

Memantine blocks NMDA (N-methyl-D-aspartate), which inhibits glutamate from binding to NMDA receptors & ↓ abnormal activation. Used alone or in combination with donepezil for moderate-to severe disease.

Memantine *(Namenda, Namenda XR)* Oral solution 2 mg/mL memantine/donepezil (*Namzaric*) dosing- see donepezil	IR: 5-10 mg BID (start at 5 mg Q daily, titrate by 5 mg weekly to 10 mg BID) XR: 7, 14 or 28 mg daily (start at 7 mg daily and titrate not faster than weekly) Can switch IR 10 mg BID to 28 mg daily; begin XR the next XR day (not same day)	**SIDE EFFECTS** Dizziness, constipation, HA **NOTES** Mostly excreted unchanged in urine; do not exceed 5 mg BID or 14 mg XR daily if CrCl < 30 mL/min. XR caps: do not crush or chew, can be opened and sprinkled on applesauce. Oral solution: use provided dosing device, squirt slowly into corner of mouth.

Acetylcholinesterase Drug Interactions

- Use caution with concurrent use of drugs that can lower heart rate (beta blockers, diltiazem, verapamil, digoxin, etc.) and with drugs that cause dizziness (antipsychotics, antihypertensives, alpha blockers, skeletal muscle relaxants, hypnotics, opioids, etc.) due to the risk of dizziness and falls.
- Drugs that have anticholinergic effects can reduce efficacy (see previous table for drugs that can worsen symptoms). Discontinue incontinence drugs if there is no benefit.

- Use cautiously with NSAIDs due to risk GI bleeds. CYP 3A4/2D6 substrates; use caution with 3A4/2D6 inhibitors.

Acetylcholinesterase Counseling

- These medicines can cause nausea. Taking the medicine with food should help (or at bedtime with donepezil). If nausea remains a problem, talk to your doctor about changing to the longer acting formulations, or the *Exelon* patch, which has the least nausea.
- The dose of this medicine may be increased, but is started low due to the risk of dizziness, falls and nausea. Use caution when moving from a sitting to a standing position. It is best to avoid alcohol when using this medicine.
- Discuss with the pharmacist about all prescription and over-the-counter medicine you use since some of these can worsen memory problems. If you have nausea, weakness and dark, tarry-looking stools, let your prescriber know. Be extra careful to watch for this if you have had stomach bleeding.
- Donepezil is started at 5 mg, at bedtime. It is taken at night to help with nausea. If you experience sleep problems (insomnia), you can take the medicine in the morning. If you have trouble swallowing the medicine, there is a formulation that dissolves in your mouth that can be used instead.

Exelon patch application instructions

- Apply a new patch at the same time each day to the upper or lower back, upper arm, or chest; rotate applications site. Do not use the same site within 14 days. Do not apply to an area of the skin that is hairy, oily, irritated, broken, scarred, or calloused. Let your healthcare prescriber know if the skin gets a rash or becomes irritated from the patch.
- Do not apply to an area where cream, lotion or powder has recently been applied. Do not place the patch under tight clothing. Do not let the patch get hot from the sun or any other heat; this can cause too much medicine to get into your body.
- Remove the protective liner from one side of the patch. Place the sticky side of the patch on the application site, then remove the second side of the protective liner. Press the patch down firmly until the edges stick well.
- After 24 hours, remove the used patch. Do not touch the sticky side. Fold the patch in half with the sticky sides together and dispose of safely.

Memantine Counseling

- Take this medication by mouth, with or without food. When you first start taking this medicine, you will usually take it once daily. Once your dose increases to more than 5 mg daily, take this medication twice daily (5 mg twice daily, and then it usually increases to 10 mg twice daily). *Namenda XR*: Start 7 mg once daily.
- For the oral liquid: read the instruction sheet that comes with the bottle. Follow the directions exactly. Use the oral syringe that comes with the product to measure out your dose. Swallow the medicine directly from the syringe. Do not mix it with water or other liquids. For the capsule: If you have trouble swallowing, open the capsule and sprinkle on applesauce. Do not crush or chew the capsule.
- You may experience dizziness; use caution when moving from a sitting to a standing position. Try not to use with other drugs that can make you feel dizzy. It is best to avoid alcohol when using this medicine.
- If you become constipated from this medicine, please ask your pharmacist, who can recommend an over-the-counter medicine that will help relieve the constipation.
- The long acting form of the medicine comes in a capsule, which can be opened and sprinkled on a small spoonful of applesauce. This can be helpful if you have trouble swallowing the capsule. Do not chew the applesauce, and use it right away.

ATTENTION DEFICIT HYPERACTIVITY DISORDER (ADHD)

GUIDELINES/REFERENCES

Diagnostic and Statistical Manual of Mental Disorders, Fifth Edition (DSM-5).

Dobie C, Donald WB, Hanson M, et al. Institute for Clinical Systems Improvement's Diagnosis and Management of Attention Deficit Hyperactivity Disorder in Primary Care for School-Age Children and Adolescents. https://www.icsi.org/_asset/60nzr5/ADHD-Interactive0312.pdf (accessed 11 Oct 2016).

ADHD: Clinical Practice Guideline for the Diagnosis, Evaluation, and Treatment of Attention-Deficit/Hyperactivity Disorder in Children and Adolescents. *Pediatric Peds.* 2011; 2011-2654.

We gratefully acknowledge the assistance of Mary Soliman, PharmD, BCPPS, CPh, Assistant Professor, University of South Florida, in preparing this chapter.

BACKGROUND

ADHD is a chronic illness with primary symptoms of inattention, hyperactivity, and impulsivity. People with ADHD often have difficulty focusing, are easily distracted, have trouble staying still, and frequently are unable to control impulsive behavior. Primary symptoms vary; some patients are more inattentive, and others are more impulsive.

The primary treatments for ADHD are stimulant medications, primarily methylphenidate formulations *(Concerta, Ritalin,* others) and other amphetamine formulations, including lisdexamfetamine *(Vyvanse)* and dextroamphetamine/amphetamine *(Adderall)*. Stimulants raise dopamine and norepinephrine levels. In ADHD, it is thought there may be defects in the dopamine pathways that regulate reward anticipation and emotional self-regulation. Providing medications is challenging; similar to other psychiatric conditions, ADHD is marked by a wide variation in which drug a patient will respond to best, and at which dose. The patient variability in dose and response may be due to genetic factors. The primary focus of ADHD research is on the catecholamine system (dopamine is catalyzed to epinephrine and norepinephrine; refer to the Drug Mechanisms, Classes & Structures chapter).

Environment, as well as genetics, is a determinant in brain chemistry and both can affect behavior. In the popular book *Scattered* (Gabor Maté, MD), the author focuses on altering the environment to help control the condition. Cognitive behavioral therapy (using psychotherapy to identify and alter thoughts and feelings, which can change behavior), is first-line in managing ADHD. Even with strong support, some patients require medications.

ADHD is the most common neurodevelopmental disorder in children. Despite the stigma associated with giving stimulant medications to children, the decision to medicate should be weighed against the risk the child will face with the disorder, which can include impaired academic standing, poor social skills and risky behavior. Pharmacists can make sure that when medications are prescribed, they are used safely. Stimulants are common drugs of abuse and have a high street value; these should be dispensed with caution, and counseling must include instructions not to share with others and to store in a safe place.

About 10% of school-aged children are using ADHD medications, with boys outnumbering girls. ADHD should be considered a chronic illness; up to 80% of children will continue to exhibit symptoms into adolescence and up to 65% will continue to exhibit symptoms as adults. As the patient ages, inattention and impulsivity may remain, and hyperactivity can decrease.

DSM-5 DIAGNOSTIC CRITERIA

INATTENTION

6+ symptoms of inattention for children up to age 16, OR 5+ for ages 17 to adults; symptoms must have been present for at least 6 months, and are inappropriate for the developmental level. Symptoms:

- Fails to pay attention, has trouble holding attention, does not pay attention when someone is talking, does not follow through on instructions, fails to finish schoolwork, has difficulty organizing tasks, avoids or dislikes tasks which require mental effort, loses things, is easily distracted, and is forgetful.

HYPERACTIVITY & IMPULSIVITY

6+ symptoms of hyperactivity-impulsivity for children up to age 16, or 5+ for ages 17 to adults; symptoms have been present for at least 6 months and be disruptive and inappropriate for the person's developmental level:

- Often fidgets or squirms, leaves seat unexpectedly, runs about when not appropriate, unable to play quietly, is "on the go" as if "driven by a motor", talks excessively, blurts out answers, has trouble waiting his/her turn, and interrupts or intrudes on others.

THE FOLLOWING CONDITIONS MUST BE MET:

- Several inattentive or hyperactive-impulsive symptoms were present before age 12 years;
- Symptoms must have been present in 2 or more settings (at home, school, at work, with friends or relatives, babysitters, etc);
- Symptoms interfere with functioning, and are not caused by another disorder.

NATURAL PRODUCTS

Fish oils are a natural product increasingly used for a variety of psychiatric conditions, including ADHD. Fish oils have been shown to modestly improve cognitive function and behavior in children with ADHD.

DRUG TREATMENT

First-line drug therapy for ADHD are stimulants. When stimulants do not work well enough (after trials of 2 - 3 agents), atomoxetine *(Strattera)*, a non-stimulant medication, can be tried next, or will be used first-line by prescribers who are concerned about the possibility of abuse by the patient or family.

> **STUDY TIP**
>
> 
>
> Young children who cannot swallow capsules or tablets can take ADHD stimulants in a long-acting suspension *(Quillivant XR)*, chewable tablets *(Quillichew ER)* or for *Focalin XR, Ritalin LA, Metadate CD, Aptensio XR* and *Adderall XR*, the capsule contents can be sprinkled on a small amount of applesauce. Methylphenidate comes in a chewable and suspension, but they're not long-acting. Amphetamine comes in a new ODT and suspension.
>
> 
>
> When putting long-acting drugs in food, use a small amount of food to keep the child from chewing the beads.
>
> Don't warm the food and take right away.
>
> *Vyvanse* is different: the capsules contain a powder which can be mixed in water, orange juice or yogurt.

The stimulants, in methylphenidate and amphetamine formulations, come in formulations that are easier for children to swallow or more difficult to abuse. Methylphenidate formulations *(Concerta*, etc.) are used first line, mainly due to a better side effect profile. Amphetamines are also used, and include amphetamine/dextroamphetamine *(Adderall)*, and the drug lisdexamfetamine *(Vyvanse)*, which is the prodrug of dextroamphetamine. Longer-acting formulations are preferred for children who would otherwise need a dose during the day at school, and to help maintain more steady symptom control. Other stimulant classes can be tried. If stopped for a weekend or holiday, they do not require tapering off.

Guanfacine, approved in the extended-release (ER) formulation *(Intuniv)*, and clonidine (in the ER formulation *(Kapvay)* are used as adjunctive treatments, or alone. *Intuniv* or *Kapvay* can also be used to help with sleep in the evening as they are sedating. If discontinuing *Intuniv* or *Kapvay*, they must be tapered off. Diphenhydramine is used to help with sleep at night, however it is important to monitor for a paradoxical hyperactive reaction in some children. Another option to help with sleep is immediate-release (IR) clonidine, taken at bedtime. Do not substitute IR clonidine or guanfacine for the long-acting formulations.

1st-line drugs

Concerta (or ***Daytrana patch***, *Ritalin)*

Vyvanse

Adderall XR and ***IR*** (often older patients)

2nd line, or if abuse risk (non-stimulant, not controlled)

Strattera

Often added to stimulants, or used alone

Intuniv

Kapvay

Zzzzzzz….to help sleep, at night

Clonidine IR

Diphenhydramine (OTC, 25-50 mg)

Intuniv, Kapvay (less sedating than IR forms)

STIMULANTS FOR ADHD

CNS stimulants block the reuptake of norepinephrine and dopamine.

<table>
<tr><th>DRUG</th><th>DOSING</th><th>SAFETY/SIDE EFFECTS/MONITORING</th></tr>
<tr><td colspan="3">**Methylphenidate**</td></tr>
<tr><td>**Methylphenidate IR *(Ritalin, Methylin chewable***, oral susp)

All of the stimulants (including modafinil and armodafinil) and atomoxetine require a MedGuide. *Kapvay* and *Intuniv* do not.

All stimulants are C-II.</td><td>Start 5 mg BID
60 mg/day max, take 30 min before meals

Methylphenidate approved for 6+ yrs</td><td rowspan="7">**BOXED WARNINGS** (ALL STIMULANTS, WITH DIFFERENCES NOTED)
Potential for drug dependency; use caution if history alcohol/drug abuse. Avoid abrupt discontinuation.

Adderall: Misuse may cause sudden death and serious CV events.

CONTRAINDICATIONS
MAO inhibitor use within the past 14 days.

Marked anxiety, tension, and agitation, glaucoma, family history or diagnosis of Tourette's syndrome or tics (excluding *Aptensio XR*, *Quillivant XR*).

Metadate CD and *Metadate ER* only: Severe hypertension, heart failure, arrhythmia, hyperthyroidism, recent MI or angina; concomitant use of halogenated anesthetics. *Ritalin* and *Ritalin SR* only: Pheochromocytoma.

WARNINGS
Severe CV events, ↑ risk suicidal thoughts/behaviors, peripheral vasculopathy (Raynaud's Syndrome), priapism, blurry vision, seizures
Daytrana patch: loss of skin pigmentation at application site. Exacerbation of mixed/mania episodes if bipolar disorder, use caution with any pre-existing psychiatric condition, including depression, aggressive behavior or hostility.

SIDE EFFECTS
Nausea, loss of appetite, insomnia, dizziness, headache, lightheadedness, irritability, blurry vision, dry mouth, ↓ growth trajectory

↑ BP ~2-4 mmHg, ↑ HR ~3-8 BPM

MONITORING
Consider ECG prior to treatment, monitor BP and HR during treatment (all). Monitor height and weight (children).

Cardiac evaluation if symptoms such as chest pain, syncope.

Monitor for CNS effects, peripheral vasculopathy (e.g., digital changes), misuse/abuse/addiction.

NOTES
Focalin XR, Ritalin LA, Metadate CD, Aptensio XR and *Adderall XR* capsules open or sprinkled on applesauce (use right away, do not chew).

Concerta OROS delivery: The outer coat dissolves fast to give immediate action, and the rest is released slowly. May see ghost tablet in stool.

Dose most stimulants QAM (IRs and some others are divided), and *Daytrana* patch is QAM, applied to alternate hip 2 hours before desired effect (or as soon as the child awakens so it starts to deliver prior to school). Remove after 9 hours (at night, for sleep).

If overdosed, symptoms (anxiety, tachycardia) can be ↓ with a benzodiazepine.

For all: titrate up (increase dose) every 3-7 days, as-needed. Stimulants do not need to be tapered off. Some contain phenylalanine (avoid with PKU).

FDA-approved in children 3+ years: methylphenidate IR, amphetamine IR, amphetamine/dextroamphetamine IR, and dextroamphetamine IR.</td></tr>
<tr><td>Methylphenidate long-acting *(Ritalin LA)* ½ IR, ½ SR in one capsule</td><td>Start 20 mg QAM
10-40 mg LA caps</td></tr>
<tr><td>**Methylphenidate IR – ER *(Concerta)***

OROS system

Somewhat harder to abuse (harder to crush)</td><td>Start 18-36 mg QAM
18, 27, 36, 54 mg ER tabs

Swallow whole</td></tr>
<tr><td>Methylphenidate ER *(Methylin ER, Metadate ER)*</td><td>Start 20 mg QAM
10-60 mg ER tabs</td></tr>
<tr><td>Methylphenidate XR *(Aptensio XR)*

Quillichew ER chewable tablets
Quillivant XR oral suspension; reconstitute at pharmacy)</td><td>Start 10 mg QAM
10-60 mg caps

Suspension: 25 mg/5 mL</td></tr>
<tr><td>Methylphenidate IR – ER ***(Metadate CD)***
Beads that dissolve at different rates</td><td>Start 20 mg QAM
10-60 mg ER caps</td></tr>
<tr><td>**Methylphenidate transdermal patch *(Daytrana)***</td><td>1.1 mg/hr (10 mg/9 hr)-3.3 mg/hr (30 mg/9 hr)</td></tr>
</table>

Stimulants for ADHD Continued

DRUG	DOSING	SAFETY/SIDE EFFECTS/MONITORING

Dexmethylphenidate

Dexmethylphenidate IR *(Focalin)*	2.5-10 mg tabs QAM 20 mg max/day BID, 4+ hrs apart, with or without food	see Methylphenidate **NOTES** Active isomer of methylphenidate. To convert from methylphenidate to dexmethylphenidate: use one-half the dose of methylphenidate (racemic formulation).
Dexmethylphenidate ER *(Focalin XR)*	5-20 mg caps QAM 40 mg max/day	

Amphetamine, Dextroamphetamine/Amphetamine

Amphetamine *(Adzenys XR-ODT, Dyanavel XR* – suspension)	*Adzenys*: 3.1-18.8 mg QAM *Dyanavel:* 2.5-20 mg QAM *Evekeo*: 5-60 mg QAM (Higher doses of *Evekeo* shown here used for narcolepsy)	see Methylphenidate **NOTES** *Adzenys (long-acting ODT) and Dyanavel* (long-acting suspension) are 6+ years, alternatives that are easy to swallow. For each 5 mg of *Adderall* use ~3.1 mg *Adzenys.* Shake suspension prior to use. The American Academy of Pediatrics (2011) does not recommend use of dextroamphetamine in children ≤ 5 years due to insufficient evidence (although FDA-approved). Avoid use of acidic foods, juice or vitamin C; can decrease amphetamine level. Take with or without food.
Dextroamphetamine/ Amphetamine IR *(Adderall)*	5-30 mg scored tabs QAM or BID 2nd dose 4-6 h after 1st	
Dextroamphetamine/Amphetamine ER *(Adderall XR)*	5-30 mg ER caps QAM	
Dextroamphetamine IR *(Dexedrine, Zenzedi, ProCentra* – solution)	5-10 mg tabs QAM or BID Solution: 5 mg/5 m L	
Dextroamphetamine SR and IR *(Dexedrine Spansules)*	5-15 mg SR caps QAM	

Lisdexamfetamine (prodrug of dextroamphetamine)

Lisdexamfetamine *(Vyvanse)*	Start 20-30 mg QAM 10, 20, 30, 40, 50, 60, 70 mg caps Can mix contents with water, yogurt or orange juice; take right away	see Methylphenidate **NOTES** Lisdexamfetamine is a prodrug composed of l-lysine (amino acid) bonded to dextroamphetamine (d-amphetamine). It is hydrolyzed in the blood to active d-amphetamine. If injected or snorted, the fast effect (rush) would be muted. The design is to ↓ the abuse potential. Also approved for binge eating disorder.

Stimulant Drug Interactions

- 14-day wash out period after MAO inhibitor use.

Patient Counseling for Stimulants

- Please read the Medication Guide you are receiving. It contains important safety information atbout this medicine. This is a stimulant medicine. Stimulants should not be used in patients with heart problems or serious psychiatric conditions. Report at once if the child has chest pain, shortness of breath, or fainting. Report at once if the child is seeing or hearing things that are not real or believing things that are not real.
- The healthcare provider should check the child's blood pressure, heart rate, height and weight.

- Some children get nausea or headache when the dose is increased or can act "wired." This is why the dose is increased slowly at the beginning.
- This is a controlled medication and has potential to be abused. Do not share this medicine with anyone else and store in a safe place.
- Your child may not have much of an appetite. Children seem to be less hungry during the middle of the day, but they are often hungry by dinnertime as the medication wears off. Your child should eat a healthy breakfast. Pack healthy snacks for school, such as nuts, cheese and fruit.
- Certain food colorings and preservatives that are common in "junk" foods and candies can worsen hyperactive behavior in some children. If these foods affect your child, you can limit them.
- If the child has trouble sleeping, the formulation may be changed. Or, the prescriber may recommend OTC diphenhydramine or prescription clonidine to take before bedtime.
- Less commonly, a few children develop sudden, repetitive movements or sounds called tics. Changing the medication dosage may make tics go away. Some children also may appear to have a personality change, such as appearing "flat" or without emotion. Talk with your child's healthcare provider if you see any of these side effects.
- If your child develops an erection lasting longer than 4 hours he will need to get immediate medical help to prevent long-term damage to the penis.
- If using a capsule formulation that can be mixed with applesauce *(Focalin XR, Ritalin LA, Metadate CD, Adderall XR* and *Aptensio XR)* and your child has difficulty swallowing the capsules, they can be sprinkled on a small amount of applesauce (if not warm and used right away). Do not chew the applesauce; just swallow. A small amount only so it is not chewed. *Concerta:* may see a ghost tablet in stool; the medication has gotten into the body.
- *Vyvanse:* the capsule contents can be mixed in water, yogurt or orange juice. Take right away. It must be taken right after putting into the water.
- For *Adzenys XR-ODT*: Do not remove from blister until ready to administer. Using dry hands, peel backing off the blister; do not push tablet through foil. Remove tablet and immediately place on tongue and allow to disintegrate. Swallow with saliva. Do not chew or crush tablet.

Daytrana Patch Instruction

- Each morning put a new patch on the hip and alternate the side each day (left hip odd days, right hip even days). Do not apply where the waist of the pants could rub it off. Apply 2 hours before effect is needed.
- Hold patch on skin for 30 seconds and smooth down edges. It should stay on during swimming or bathing. Remove the patch after 9 hours so your child can sleep well at night.
- Wash your hands immediately after applying the patch. Patches should not be reapplied with bandages, tape, or other household adhesives. Do not use hair dryers, heating pads, electric blankets, or other heat sources directly on the patch. If you have to replace a patch that has fallen off, the total wear-time for the first and second patch should not be more than a total of 9 hours in 1 day. Do not reapply the same patch that fell off.
- When peeling off to discard, fold in half, put down the toilet or lidded trash can.

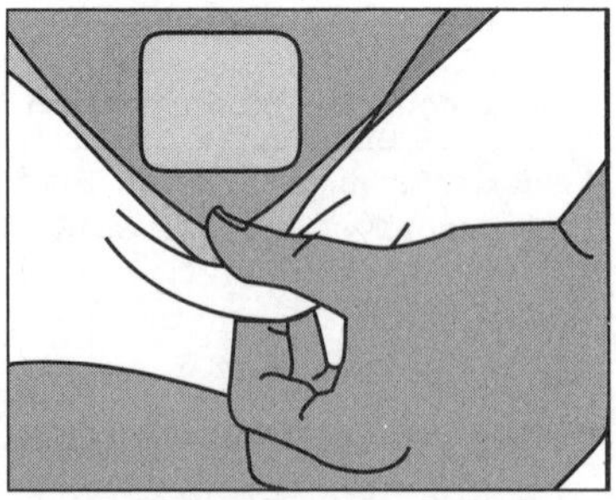

Place on hip each morning. Place firmly, hold down on skin for 30 secs, smooth edges. Alternate sides daily (left hip, then right hip....) Try to put on 2 hours before effect is needed, such as for school. Remove after 9 hours. Do not leave on at night or the child will not be able to sleep. Remove by peeling off slowly, fold down the edges so they stick to each other. Flush in toilet, or if septic tank, in lidded trash can.

Quillivant XR Suspension Instructions

- The bottle must contain liquid. Return to the pharmacist if it is powder.
- First, shake the bottle for at least 10 seconds. Use the dosing dispenser to measure the milliliters (mL) dose.
- Insert the tip of the dispenser into the upright bottle and push the plunger all the way down. Turn the bottle upside down and remove the correct amount; measure to the white end of the plunger. Use the oral dosing dispenser provided.
- Use the dosing dispenser to slowly squirt the medication into the child's mouth. Cap tightly and rinse the dispenser with tap water or in a dishwasher. Wash after each use.
- The medicine can be stored at room temperature for up to 4 months.

NON-STIMULANTS FOR ADHD – 2ND LINE AGENTS – NOT CONTROLLED

DRUG	DOSING	SAFETY/SIDE EFFECTS/MONITORING
Selective Norepinephrine Reuptake Inhibitor		
AtoMOXetine *(Strattera)*	Start at 40 mg/day, can Increase after 3+ days to 80 mg, max 100 mg/day, take daily or divide BID 80 mg max with CYP 2D6 inhibitors or if poor 2D6 metabolizer	**BOXED WARNING** Risk of suicidal ideation; monitor for suicidal thinking or behavior, worsening mood, or unusual behavior **CONTRAINDICATIONS** Glaucoma, pheochromocytoma, adrenal gland tumor, severe cardiovascular disorders, MAO inhibitor use within past 14 days **WARNINGS** Aggressive behavior, treatment-emergent psychotic or manic symptoms, orthostasis and syncope, allergic reactions, priapism Rare, but severe hepatotoxicity (most within 120 days of start of treatment) Risk of serious cardiovascular events; avoid use if known problems; conduct cardiac evaluation if needed. Use with caution if BP elevated **SIDE EFFECTS** Headache, insomnia (~10%), somnolence (~10%), dry mouth, nausea, abdominal pain, ↓ appetite, erectile dysfunction, ↓ libido, hyperhidrosis, fatigue, dizziness, hot flashes, dysmenorrhea, menstrual changes, paresthesia, urinary retention Orthostasis, use caution in patients at risk Psychiatric effects, including hallucinations and mania Priapism (more common than with methylphenidate) **MONITORING** HR, BP, ECG, height, weight, agitation **NOTES** Do not open capsule – irritant. Primarily a CYP450 2D6 substrate; 2D6 inducers or inhibitors may necessitate a change in atomoxetine dose.

Non-Stimulants for ADHD continued

DRUG	DOSING	SAFETY/SIDE EFFECTS/MONITORING
Central Alpha-2A Adrenergic Receptor Agonists Stimulate alpha adrenergic receptors in the brain. Both are (old) hypertension drugs which are now longer-acting formulations for ADHD (clonidine IR used off-label for sleep/benefit, taken QHS).		
GuanFACINE ER ***(Intuniv)*** With stimulants for additional benefit, or alone *Tenex* – for hypertension	1-4 mg, max 4 mg/day as adjunctive tx, 7 mg/day alone Start at 1 mg daily Do not take with high-fat meal (↑ absorption) With CYP 3A4 inducers, can increase dose With CYP 3A4 inhibitors, can decrease dose	**SIDE EFFECTS** Somnolence, dizziness, orthostasis, headache, fatigue, hypotension, nausea, constipation, abdominal pain, skin rash (rare, discontinue if occurs), bradycardia **NOTES** All cardiovascular effects (bradycardia, hypotension, orthostasis, syncope) are dose-dependent; titrate carefully. Sedation can impair physical and mental activities. Cases of skin rash with exfoliation; discontinue if rash develops. Do not interchange with other guanfacine formulations. Do not crush.
CloNIDine ER ***(Kapvay)*** With stimulants for additional benefit, or alone *Catapres* – for hypertension	0.1-0.4 mg daily Start at 0.1 mg at bedtime, ↑ 0.1 mg/day Q 7 days until desired response BID, if uneven, higher dose QHS	**SIDE EFFECTS** Headache, somnolence, abdominal pain, upper resp tract infections **NOTES** Rebound hypertension (with sweating/anxiety/tremors), if stopped abruptly – taper off by ↓ 0.1 mg Q 3-7 days. ER formulation has ↓ SEs. Do not crush.

Atomoxetine Drug Interactions

- Decrease dose if on strong CYP 2D6 inhibitors or if 2D6 poor metabolizer, up to max 80 mg/day.
- 14-day wash out period after MAO inhibitor use.

Patient Counseling for Atomoxetine

- Please read the Medication Guide you are receiving. It contains important safety information about possible depression/very low mood, and possible liver damage when using this medicine.
- Side effects can include headache, trouble sleeping or staying awake, dry mouth, nausea, lessened appetite, sweating and dizziness and fatigue. Girls and women can get hot flashes, ↓ sexual interest or menstrual changes.
- Watch for symptoms of depression, unusual behavior, or thoughts of hurting yourself. Your healthcare provider may need to check you at regular visits while you are taking this medication.
- The capsule cannot be opened. If the powder from inside gets into your eyes, rinse well with water and call your healthcare provider.
- Atomoxetine can cause side effects that may impair your thinking or reactions. Be careful if you drive or do anything that requires you to be awake and alert.
- Monitor for symptoms of liver damage: weakness, abdominal pain, yellowed skin, light colored stool or darkened urine.

Clonidine and Guanfacine Drug Interactions

- Both clonidine and guanfacine are sedating; use caution with other CNS depressants.
- Both clonidine and guanfacine lower blood pressure; use caution with other anti-hypertensives.
- Both clonidine and guanfacine come as other formulations; do not use concurrently.

ANXIETY DISORDERS

GUIDELINES/REFERENCES

Diagnostic and Statistical Manual of Mental Disorders, Fifth Edition (DSM-5). American Psychiatric Association. Arlington VA; 2013.

Baldwin DS, Waldman S, Allgulander C. Evidence-based pharmacological treatment of generalized anxiety disorder (DSM-IV-TR). *Int J Neuropsychopharmacol.* 2011 Jun;14(5):697-710.

We gratefully acknowledge the assistance of Jennifer Bean, PharmD, BCPS, BCPP, Clinical Pharmacist, VA Tennessee Valley Healthcare System, in preparing this chapter.

BACKGROUND

Anxiety exists to protect us from harm. For example, if an aggressive dog or bear comes along, fear (a symptom of anxiety) is important to avoid getting attacked and can help us escape from the situation. Occasional anxiety, which is normal, can occur in the general population when faced with challenging issues at work, home or school. The symptoms of occasional anxiety (fear, worry) should dissipate once the issue is gone. Any physical symptoms (tachycardia, palpitations, shortness of breath, stomach upset, chest pain or other pain, insomnia and fatigue) should also resolve. Medical conditions, including hyperthyroidism, can cause anxiety, and if present, will need to be treated.

When a person has an anxiety disorder, the symptoms are continuous and severe and cause great distress. The disorder can interfere with the ability to do well at school or work, and can harm relationships. The major types of anxiety disorders are generalized anxiety disorder (GAD), panic disorder (PD) and social anxiety disorder (SAD). Disorders that have symptoms of anxiety include obsessive compulsive disorder (OCD) and post-traumatic stress disorder (PTSD). Although OCD and PTSD have symptoms of anxiety, the Diagnostic and Statistical Manual of Mental Disorders, Fifth Edition (DSM-5) classifies these disorders differently. OCD has its own category called "obsessive-compulsive and related disorders" and PTSD is categorized under "trauma and stressor-related disorders."

Lifestyle changes can improve symptoms. Increasing physical activity, helping others, community involvement, yoga, meditation, and other methods can broaden the patient's outlook and reduce stress.

Cognitive Behavioral Therapy (CBT) is a type of mental health treatment in which a trained clinician helps the patient explore patterns of thinking that lead to self-destructive actions and behavior. CBT can be beneficial and, in some cases, provides adequate relief without the need for chronic medications.

NATURAL PRODUCTS

Kava is used as a relaxant but can damage the liver and should not be recommended. 5-HTP and L-tryptophan are used for both anxiety and depression, and may provide benefit, but the use has been associated with eosinophilia myalgia syndrome (EMS). St. John's wort is used for depression and anxiety; the primary concern is that St. John's wort is a strong inducer and the concentration of concurrent medications will be lowered. It is serotonergic, thus the risk of serotonin syndrome is present when used in combination with other serotonergic medications and causes photosensitivity. Valerian is used for anxiety and sleep, but some valerian products may have been contaminated with liver toxins; if this is being used, the liver should be monitored. Passionflower appears to be safe and is rated as "possibly effective" by the Natural Medicines Database.

SELECT DRUGS THAT CAN CAUSE ANXIETY
Theophylline
Levothyroxine
Acetazolamide
Albuterol (if used incorrectly-swallowed)
Aripiprazole, haloperidol
Caffeine, in high doses
Stimulants
Decongestants (pseudoephedrine and nasally inhaled agents)
Steroids
Bupropion
Illicit drugs, including cocaine, LSD, methamphetamine, others

DRUG TREATMENT

The primary first-line agents used to treat anxiety disorders are selective serotonin reuptake inhibitors (SSRIs) and serotonin norepinephrine reuptake inhibitors (SNRIs). Clomipramine, a tricyclic antidepressant, is indicated for OCD and is often used for this purpose. Although only some of the antidepressants (ADs) have specific anxiety indications, these agents are often chosen based on the healthcare provider's familiarity and/or the side effect profile. For example, although fluvoxamine was the first SSRI indicated for OCD, it is rarely used due to its drug interaction potential. SSRI and SNRI agents are often initiated at half the initial dose used for depression and are slowly titrated to minimize anxiousness and jitteriness that is common during the first couple of weeks of treatment; dose carefully to avoid worsening the anxiety. Clinicians may overlap SSRIs or SNRIs with a benzodiazepine for 2 – 4 weeks to help alleviate the initial stimulatory effects and regulate sleep. Benzodiazepines should be used with caution and closely monitored. Patients should be advised that immediate relief is not to be expected when initiating AD treatment for anxiety (or depression); it commonly takes 4 or more weeks for a noticeable benefit. Refer to the Depression chapter for specifics on antidepressants.

Buspirone is approved for GAD, and is an option with any of the following: a poor response to an antidepressant (including as adjunctive treatment), if at risk for benzodiazepine abuse, or if elderly. Buspirone is less sedating and has less cognitive effects than benzodiazepines, but it does cause some, and is known for causing dizziness. Buspirone does not work right away; it take 2 – 4 weeks to have a beneficial effect and should be dosed on a scheduled basis, not as needed.

Hydroxyzine *(Vistaril)* is FDA approved for anxiety and is considered second-line. It is occasionally used for short-term anxiety as an alternative to benzodiazepines. This is a sedating antihistamine, has anticholinergic activity, and works by sedating the patient, rather than treating any underlying condition. It should not be used long-term and is typically dosed on an as needed basis. It is used more commonly for pruritus. Refer to the Common Skin Conditions chapter.

Pregabalin *(Lyrica)* is not FDA approved for anxiety but does have literature to support its use, particularly in patients with anxiety and neuropathic pain. Pregabalin has immediate anxiolytic effects similar to benzodiazepines. It is a controlled substance (C-V) due to mild euphoric properties, which can have a calming effect.

Propranolol *(Inderal,* others) is used to reduce symptoms of stage fright or performance anxiety (e.g., tremor, tachycardia). It is dosed at 10 – 40 mg 1 hour prior to an event such as a public speech. Use caution with this approach due to CNS effects (e.g., confusion, dizziness). This is a non-selective beta blocker and should not be used in patients with asthma or COPD.

Benzodiazepines

Benzodiazepines are often used for anxiety. They provide fast relief for acute symptoms. Situations in which benzodiazepines are appropriate include short-term situations where anxiety is acute and can cause extreme stress, prevent proper sleep, and disrupt life. These symptoms can be the result of a recent death of a loved one, a natural disaster, or other stressful situations. In such cases, they should be used less than 1 – 2 weeks, and then discontinued. Benzodiazepines can cover-up anxiety symptoms, but do not treat the causes, and, in most cases, should not be used long-term.

When benzodiazepines are used in older adults, they pose significant risks for confusion, dizziness and falls – the risk increases with concurrent use of other CNS depressants. According to the Beers Criteria, benzodiazepines are potentially inappropriate for use in patients aged 65 and older (Quality of evidence – moderate; Strength of recommendation – strong). Additionally, older adults may have a "paradoxical" reaction to and respond to the drug with insomnia, agitation and excitement. The benzodiazepines are differentiated by their pharmacokinetic parameters, including the onset of action and the duration of action.

Benzodiazepines potentiate GABA, an inhibitory neurotransmitter, causing CNS depression and providing anxiolytic, anticonvulsant, sedative and/or muscle relaxant properties.

DRUG	DOSING	SAFETY/SIDE EFFECTS/MONITORING
LORazepam *(Ativan)* Tablet *LORazepam Intensol* is solution (sol for oral solution) LORazepam injection-used commonly for agitation, sedation	2-3 mg PO daily in divided doses	**BOXED WARNING** Use with opioids (including cough products containing opioids) can result in extreme sleepiness, respiratory depression, coma, and death. **CONTRAINDICATIONS** Varies among agents: acute narrow-angle glaucoma, sleep apnea, severe respiratory insufficiency, significant liver disease, use with ketoconazole or itraconazole (alprazolam), not for use in infants < 6 months of age (diazepam oral), myasthenia gravis (diazepam). **WARNINGS** Anterograde amnesia (after drug is taken some events may not be stored as memories), CNS depression, extravasation with IV use, paradoxical reactions (discontinue if hyperactive/aggressive behavior), potential for abuse, safety risks in patients aged 65 and older (impaired cognition, delirium falls/fractures), development of tolerance, withdrawal symptoms; taper off slowly Physiological dependence and tolerance develop with chronic use **SIDE EFFECTS** Somnolence, dizziness, weakness, ataxia, lightheadedness **NOTES** All C-IV All given PRN or scheduled, depending on condition Safety issue when used in pregnancy – see Pregnancy chapter. Diazepam: Lipophilic, fast onset, long half-life, high abuse potential. Alprazolam: Fast onset, often abused due to quick action. To avoid withdrawal symptoms (anxiety, shakiness, insomnia, tachycardia, muscle pain) taper off slowly. Withdrawal symptoms are likely if used > 10 days. Alcohol withdrawal: chlordiazepoxide, diazepam (fastest onset, comes as injection), lorazepam (has injection) or oxazepam (preferred if liver disease). Overdose causes respiratory depression. Antidote is flumazenil. Refer to the Emergency Preparedness, Toxicology & Antidotes chapter.
ALPRAZolam *(Xanax, Xanax XR)* Tablet, ODT *Alprazolam Intensol* (oral solution)	0.25-0.5 mg PO TID	
ChlordiazePOXIDE *(Librium)* Capsule	5-25 mg TID-QID	
ClonazePAM *(KlonoPIN)* Tablet, ODT	0.25-0.5 mg PO BID	
Clorazepate *(Tranxene-T)* Tablet	30 mg PO daily in divided doses	
Diazepam *(Valium)* Tablet ***Diazepam C-ject*** injection *Diazepam Intensol* (oral solution) *Diastat* (gel) – rectal, for acute seizure control	2-10 mg PO BID-QID	
Oxazepam Capsule	10-30 mg PO TID-QID	

Benzodiazepine Drug Interactions

- Additive effects with CNS depressants, including most pain medications, skeletal muscle relaxants, antihistamines, antipsychotics, anticonvulsants, mirtazapine, trazodone, alcohol, and others.
- Alprazolam is contraindicated with ketoconazole and itraconazole.
- Diazepam, clonazepam, chlordiazepoxide, alprazolam, clorazepate: ↑ levels with 3A4 inhibitors; caution/lower doses if used in combination.
- Caution if used with clozapine due to ↑ risk of delirium and sedation. Avoid use with methadone, olanzapine and sodium oxybate due to additive CNS depression. Valproate increases lorazepam concentration.

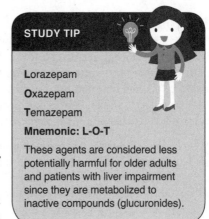

STUDY TIP

Lorazepam

Oxazepam

Temazepam

Mnemonic: L-O-T

These agents are considered less potentially harmful for older adults and patients with liver impairment since they are metabolized to inactive compounds (glucuronides).

Benzodiazepine Counseling

- Common side effects include drowsiness, dizziness, unsteadiness on your feet, slow reactions, lightheadedness and difficulty remembering what happened after taking the medicine. If any of these persist or worsen, contact your healthcare provider promptly.
- If you have been using the medication regularly on a daily basis (usually for more than 10 days), it cannot be stopped suddenly. The dose will have to be decreased slowly or you will experience withdrawal, which is uncomfortable and can be dangerous.
- This medication can cause drug-seeking behavior (addiction/habit forming). Do not increase your dose, take it more frequently or use it for a longer time than prescribed. Keep the bottle in a safe place to prevent others from taking it.
- When used for an extended time, this medication may not work as well and may require a higher dose. Talk with your healthcare provider if this medication stops working well. Do not increase the amount or take it more frequently than prescribed.
- Do not take with other medications that can make you sleepy, unless directed by your healthcare provider. Other sedating medications could cause a great deal of sedation and confusion if taken together with this medication. Do not use alcohol with this medication.
- Avoid driving and doing other tasks or actions that call for you to be alert until you see how this medication affects you.

Buspirone

The mechanism is unknown, but may be due to buspirone's affinity for 5-HT1A and 5-HT2 receptors.

DRUG	DOSING	SAFETY/SIDE EFFECTS/MONITORING
BusPIRone Tablet	Start 7.5 mg PO BID Can increase by 5 mg/day Q 2-3 days, max dose is 30 mg PO BID Take with or without food; be consistent. Avoid use if severe kidney or liver impairment.	**WARNINGS** Do not use with MAO inhibitors **SIDE EFFECTS** Nausea, dizziness, drowsiness, headache, lightheadedness, excitement **NOTES** No potential for abuse, tolerance or physiological dependence. When switching from a benzodiazepine to buspirone, the benzodiazepine should be tapered off slowly.

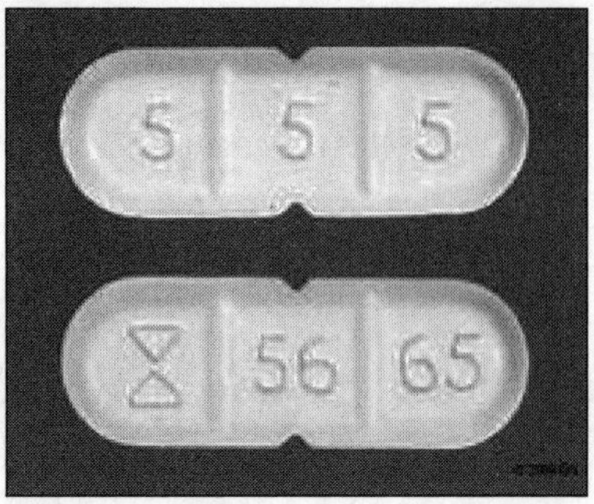

Buspirone Drug Interactions

- Do not use with MAO inhibitors.
- ↓ dose with erythromycin, diltiazem, itraconazole, verapamil; consider dose reduction with any 3A4 inhibitor.
- 3A4 inducers, including rifampin, may require an increase in the buspirone dose.
- Grapefruit increases the buspirone level; avoid concurrent use, or decrease buspirone dose.

Buspirone Counseling

- Common side effects can include dizziness, drowsiness, nausea, or headache.
- Buspirone 15 mg tablets come in a *Dividose* tablet that is designed to make dose adjustments easy. Each *Dividose* tablet is scored and can be broken accurately on the score lines into thirds. It snaps into pieces with finger pressure.
- Take this medication by mouth, usually 2 or 3 times a day, as directed by your healthcare provider. Take this medication with or without food, but it is important to choose one way and always take it the same way so that the amount of drug absorbed will stay the same. This medication does not have immediate effects, but takes 2 to 4 weeks to help reduce anxiety.
- Do not take with other medicines that can make you sleepy, unless directed by your healthcare provider. Do not use alcohol with this medicine.
- Grapefruit will increase the amount of buspirone in your bloodstream.
- Dosage is based on your medical condition and response to therapy. Use this medication scheduled in order to get the most benefit from it. To help you remember, use it at the same times each day. When this medication is started, symptoms of anxiety (e.g., restlessness) may sometimes get worse before they improve. It may take up to a month or more to get the full effect of this medication.

66

SLEEP DISORDERS: INSOMNIA, RESTLESS LEGS SYNDROME (RLS) & NARCOLEPSY

We gratefully acknowledge the assistance of Jennifer Bean, PharmD, BCPS, BCPP, Clinical Pharmacist, VA Tennessee Valley Healthcare System, in preparing this chapter.

BACKGROUND

There are several types of common sleep disorders. This chapter discusses the primary types for which common prescription drug treatments are available: insomnia, restless leg syndrome and narcolepsy. A lack of restful sleep contributes to poor health and is linked to the development of a number of chronic conditions, including cardiovascular disease and depression. Patients who are using chronic OTC sleep agents should be referred to a healthcare provider. Another common sleep disorder is sleep apnea, which is treated by non-drug measures, including continuous positive airway pressure (CPAP).

GUIDELINES/REFERENCES

American College of Physicians. Management of Chronic Insomnia Disorder in Adults: A Clinical Practice Guideline. *Ann Intern Med.* 2016; 165(2):125-133.

American Academy of Sleep Medicine: Practice Parameters for the Treatment of Insomnia. *Sleep.* 2007; 30:2:1415-1419.

Cappuccio FP, D'Elia L, Strazzullo P, Miller MA. Sleep duration and all-cause mortality: a systematic review and meta-analysis of prospective studies. *Sleep.* 2010; 33:585-92.

Insomnia

Insomnia is when a person wants to sleep but cannot. This is the most common sleep condition and occurs either when trying to fall asleep (sleep initiation), reduced sleep duration (sleep is normally 7-9 hours) or is due to poor sleep quality. A problem with either sleep initiation, duration or quality will contribute to daytime impairment with fatigue, somnolence, poor memory and concentration and, if long-term, chronic health conditions.

Primary treatments for insomnia include cognitive therapy and drug treatment. Cognitive Behavioral Therapy for Insomnia (CBT-I) is preferred and includes changes to sleep hygiene (these are called "lifestyle" changes, see the following box) that can reduce the need for drugs entirely. If a retired elderly person has a daily routine that includes watching television and napping for much of the day, they may be able to eliminate night-time sleep problems by reducing the naps and taking a brisk walk earlier in the day. In some cases, avoidance of caffeine later in the day is the answer. Other cognitive therapy that can be helpful includes biofeedback, where the patient is educated to monitor heart rate and muscle tension and record the daily patterns. They receive instruction on how to modify patterns to improve sleep.

DRUGS LIKELY TO CONTRIBUTE TO INSOMNIA
Bupropion
Stimulants (methylphenidate, etc.)
OTC appetite suppressants
Decongestants (pseudoephedrine, etc.)
MAO-B Inhibitors, if taken late in the day
Fluoxetine, if taken late in the day
Caffeine
Steroids
Alcohol (initially induces sleep, but prevents deeper stages of sleep and causes nocturia)
Any drug that causes urinary retention or nocturia, including antihistamines and diuretics taken later in the day.

SLEEP HYGIENE METHODS TO IMPROVE SLEEP (INCLUDE WITH COUNSELING)
Keep the bedroom dark, comfortable, and quiet
Keep a regular sleep schedule
Avoid daytime naps even after a poor night of sleep – or limit to 30 minutes
Reserve bedroom for only sleep and sex
Turn the face of clock aside to minimize anxiety about falling asleep
If unable to sleep, get up and do something to take your mind off sleeping
Establish a pre-bedtime ritual to condition your body for sleep
Relax before bedtime with soft music, mild stretching, yoga, or pleasurable reading
Avoid exercising right before bedtime
Do not eat heavy meals before bedtime
Do not take any caffeine in the afternoon

Medical conditions may contribute to insomnia. Heart failure or any condition that causes shortness of breath can worsen sleep. Anxiety and depression are known to cause insomnia; if the condition can be corrected with psychotherapy, a prescription agent, or both, treatment with a sedative-hypnotic may not be required.

When sleep hygiene issues or medical conditions cannot be corrected, or when the cause of insomnia has not been identified, sedative-hypnotics may be used to help provide a good night's rest. Sedative-hypnotics are over-prescribed and there is concern regarding increased mortality with the use of sedative-hypnotics, even with occasional use.

Natural Products used for Insomnia

If insomnia is due to depression, taking St. John's wort may be helpful but this will interact with many prescription drugs. St. John's wort induces CYP450, is a photosensitizer and is serotonergic. Chamomile tea taken in the evening helps many people feel calmer. Melatonin or valerian can be useful for some patients. There have been isolated reports of valerian causing liver toxicity; this risk is unclear at present. Check the Natural Medicines Database for doses and the current safety profile.

DRUG TREATMENT

The OTC first-generation antihistamines diphenhydramine and doxylamine are used for insomnia. Neither should be used chronically but can be helpful short-term for problems with sleep initiation and duration. Diphenhydramine has better evidence of efficacy and is available in many formulations and in less expensive generics. In patients using prescription agents long-term, the non-benzodiazepines are preferred over benzodiazepines due to a decreased risk of physical dependence and less daytime cognitive effects. The non-controlled prescription agents are not as effective in most patients but are useful in select cases. Most commonly non-benzodiazepines, such as zolpidem, are used chronically and are preferred over the benzodiazepines that are used as hypnotics. Although this is accurate, keep in mind that, if possible, drugs used chronically for sleep are now discouraged. Suvorexant *(Belsomra)* is a newer agent with a unique mechanism: it blocks the orexin neuropeptide signaling system, which is involved with promoting wakefulness. Non-24-Hour Sleep-Wake Disorder, or "Non-24", is a condition where patients have difficulty with obtaining restful sleep because their circadian rhythm is not synchronized with the 24-hour day-night cycle. This can be present in persons who are totally visually blind and non-blind. Tasimelteon *(Hetlioz)* is the first drug approved for this condition. It is a melatonin receptor agonist (similar to ramelteon).

<table>
<tr><th>DRUG</th><th>DOSING</th><th>SAFETY/SIDE EFFECTS/MONITORING</th></tr>
<tr><td colspan="3">Non-benzodiazepines: Acts selectively at the benzodiazepine receptors to increase GABA</td></tr>
<tr><td>Zolpidem (Ambien, Ambien CR)
Zolpimist – oral spray
Edluar SL tabs
Intermezzo SL – for night-time awakening
C-IV</td><td>Ambien 5-10 mg PO QHS, max 5 mg females and elderly
Ambien CR 6.25-12.5 mg PO QHS, max 6.25 mg females and elderly
Zolpimist 5 mg/spray (1-2 sprays) PO QHS
Edluar 5-10 mg PO QHS
Intermezzo SL 3.5 mg males, 1.75 mg females, and if using CNS depressants (decrease dose of these as well, if possible)</td><td rowspan="3">WARNINGS
↑ risk mortality (interferes with breathing at night, causes accidents/falls, confusion, and may ↑ risk infection and cancer), ↑ risk of next-day impairment with < 7-8 hours of sleep (especially with higher doses, coadministration of CNS depressants or alcohol)
Potential for abuse and dependence

SIDE EFFECTS
Somnolence
Dizziness, ataxia
Lightheadedness
"Pins and needles" feeling on skin
May cause parasomnias (unusual actions while sleeping – of which the patient may not be aware)
Withdrawal symptoms if used longer than 2 weeks

NOTES
Intermezzo SL
Do not take unless planning to sleep ≥ 4 more hours.
Lifestyle changes should be the primary method to improve sleep, not drugs.
Preferred over benzodiazepines for 1st line treatment of insomnia due to ↓ abuse, dependence and tolerance.
Do not take with fatty food, a heavy meal or alcohol.</td></tr>
<tr><td>Zaleplon (Sonata)
C-IV</td><td>5-10 mg PO QHS</td></tr>
<tr><td>Eszopiclone (Lunesta)
C-IV
Not limited to short-term use (officially, although all 3 used long-term commonly)</td><td>1-3 mg PO QHS
1 mg immediately before bed, can increase to 2 mg or 3 mg if necessary</td></tr>
<tr><td colspan="3">Orexin-receptor antagonist: The orexin neuropeptide signaling system promotes wakefulness.</td></tr>
<tr><td>Suvorexant (Belsomra)
C-IV</td><td>10 mg QHS if at least 7 hours sleep remaining, max 20 mg</td><td>CONTRAINDICATIONS
Narcolepsy

WARNINGS
Abnormal thinking and behavioral changes, worsening of depression/suicidal ideation, sleep paralysis, hypnagogic/hypnopompic hallucinations, cataplexy-like symptoms

SIDE EFFECTS
Somnolence, headache, dizziness, abnormal dreams, cough, upper respiratory tract infection

NOTES
Belsomra may cause sleep-driving and other complex behaviors while not being fully awake.
Use lower dose (5 mg) with moderate 3A4 inhibitors; avoid use with strong 3A4 inhibitors.</td></tr>
</table>

Insomnia Drugs Continued

DRUG	DOSING	SAFETY/SIDE EFFECTS/MONITORING
Melatonin Receptor Agonists		
Ramelteon *(Rozerem)* For insomnia Not limited to short-term use Not a controlled substance	8 mg PO QHS	**SIDE EFFECTS** Somnolence, dizziness **NOTES** Do not take with fatty food
Tasimelteon *(Hetlioz)* For Non-24-Hour Sleep-Wake Disorder Not a controlled substance	20 mg PO QHS	**WARNINGS** Use is not recommended in patients with severe hepatic impairment, may have significant drug interactions; check prior to dispensing ↑ ALT, URI **SIDE EFFECTS** Headache, abnormal dreams, ALT, URI **NOTES** Can take weeks to take effect. Take without food.
Antidepressants		
Doxepin extended-release *(Silenor)* Used for difficulty staying asleep (sleep maintenance) Generic doxepin, traZODone, mirtazapine used off-label for sleep	6 mg PO QHS 3 mg if ≥ 65 years	**CONTRAINDICATIONS** Requires 2 week washout for MAO inhibitors **SIDE EFFECTS** Somnolence, low incidence nausea and upper respiratory infections, possibility of anticholinergic SEs **NOTES** This is an antidepressant and requires MedGuide for unusual thoughts/suicide risk

Zolpidem, Sonata and *Lunesta* Drug Interactions

- Caution with the use of non-benzodiazepines with potent 3A4 inhibitors (e.g., ritonavir, indinavir, saquinavir, atazanavir, ketoconazole, itraconazole, erythromycin and clarithromycin).
- Additive effects with sedating drugs, including most pain medicines, muscle relaxants, antihistamines, the antidepressant mirtazapine *(Remeron)*, trazodone, alcohol and others.

Zolpidem, Sonata and *Lunesta* Counseling

- If using *Zolpimist*, spray directly into your mouth over your tongue (once for a 5 mg dose, twice for a 10 mg dose). Prime the bottle for first time use. If using *Edluar* SL tablets or *Intermezzo*: this drug is not swallowed, it dissolves under the tongue. Do not take *Intermezzo* unless you are planning to sleep 4 or more hours.
- You should not eat a heavy/high-fat meal within 2 hours of taking this medication; this may prevent the medicine from working properly.
- Call your healthcare provider if the insomnia worsens or is not better within 7 to 10 days. This may mean that there is another condition causing your sleep problem.

- Common side effects include sleepiness, lightheadedness, dizziness, "pins and needles" feeling on your skin and difficulty with coordination.
- You may still feel drowsy the next day after taking this medicine.
- This drug may (rarely) cause abnormal thoughts and behavior. Symptoms include more outgoing or aggressive behavior than normal, confusion, agitation, hallucinations, worsening of depression, and suicidal thoughts or actions. Some people have found that they get out of bed while not being fully awake and do an activity that they do not know they are doing.
- You may have withdrawal symptoms when you stop taking this medicine, if you have been taking it for more than a couple of weeks. Withdrawal symptoms include unpleasant feelings, stomach and muscle cramps, vomiting, sweating and shakiness. You may also have more trouble sleeping the first few nights after the medicine is stopped. The problem usually goes away on its own after 1 or 2 nights.
- Do not take with other medicines that can make you sleepy, unless directed by your healthcare provider. Do not use alcohol with any sleep medicine.
- After taking this medicine, you should not be driving a car or using any dangerous machinery.
- This medicine is a federally controlled substance (C-IV) because it can be abused or lead to dependence. Keep the bottle in a safe place to prevent misuse and abuse.

BENZODIAZEPINES

Potentiate GABA, an inhibitory neurotransmitter, causing CNS depression. According to the Beers Criteria, benzodiazepines (BZDs) are potentially inappropriate for use in patients aged 65 and older (Quality of evidence – moderate; Strength of recommendation – strong).

DRUG	DOSING	SAFETY/SIDE EFFECTS/MONITORING
LORazepam ***(Ativan)*** *LORazepam Intensol* is solution (sol for solution) Further information on the BZDs is in the Anxiety chapter. C-IV	0.5-2 mg PO QHS	See Anxiety chapter for a full discussion; these are important agents and cause risk of physical (physiological) dependence, abuse (addiction) and tolerance. Lorazepam, oxazepam, and temazepam (L-O-T): these are considered less potentially harmful for older patients (65 years and older) or those with liver impairment since they are metabolized to inactive compounds (glucuronides); choose L-O-T if a BZD is needed in an older patient for sleep.
Temazepam ***(Restoril)*** C-IV	7.5-30 mg PO QHS	**NOTES** Temazepam *(Restoril)* is approved for the short-term (generally 7-10 days) treatment of insomnia.
Estazolam C-IV		Cannot use with potent 3A4 inhibitors (i.e., ketoconazole, itraconazole)
Quazepam *(Doral)* C-IV		Caution when use in older adults due to its long half-life: confusion, risk of falls, fractures
Flurazepam C-IV		Caution when use in older adults due to its long half-life: confusion, risk of falls, fractures
Triazolam *(Halcion)* C-IV		Associated with higher rebound insomnia and daytime anxiety; Tapering upon discontinuation. Contraindicated with efavirenz *(Sustiva)*, delavirdine *(Rescriptor)*, azole antifungals, and protease inhibitors & all 3A4 Inhibitors

Benzodiazepine Drug Interactions: refer to Anxiety chapter for complete counseling.

Additional Counseling when Used for Sleep

- This medication should be taken before bedtime. Take the medicine immediately prior to sleep. Do not do anything dangerous, such as driving a car, after taking the medicine. Do not mix with alcohol.

ANTIHISTAMINES

Compete with (block) histamine H1 receptors. According to the Beers Criteria, first-generation antihistamines are potentially inappropriate for use in patients aged 65 and older (Quality of evidence – moderate; Strength of recommendation – strong).

DRUG	DOSING	SAFETY/SIDE EFFECTS/MONITORING
Diphenhydramine ***(Benadryl,*** *Sominex, Unisom SleepGels,* others, store brands)	50 mg PO QHS	**SIDE EFFECTS** Possible anticholinergic side effects: Sedation; tolerance to sedative effects can develop after 10 days of use Confusion (can exacerbate memory/cognition difficulty) Peripheral anticholinergic side effects: Dry mouth Urinary retention (will make it very difficult for males with BPH to urinate, can slow down/delay urination in females) Dry/blurry vision, risk increased IOP Constipation Best to avoid use in BPH (may worsen symptoms) and glaucoma (may elevate IOP). Beers Criteria drug; avoid use in older adults due to risk of confusion, dry mouth, constipation.
Doxylamine *(Unisom Nighttime,* store brands)	25 mg PO QHS	

Diphenhydramine *(Benadryl)* Counseling (for all indications – applies to other sedating antihistamines)

- Diphenhydramine is an antihistamine that is used to manage allergies, motion sickness, and occasionally Parkinson's disease. Diphenhydramine can also be used to help you relax and fall asleep.
- When using this medicine, you will become sleepy. It can also make you feel confused and make it difficult to concentrate.
- Do not take with other medicines that can make you sleepy, unless directed by your doctor. Do not use alcohol with any sleep medicine.
- This medicine can make it difficult to urinate (it will take longer for the urine to come out). You should not use this medicine if you have an enlarged prostate or BPH, unless directed by your doctor.
- If you have glaucoma, discuss use with your eye doctor. It may raise your the pressure in your eyes.
- If you have problems with constipation, this medicine will worsen the constipation.
- This medicine can cause your eyes to become dry and your vision to become blurry. It can also cause dry mouth.
- This medicine can make it difficult to urinate (it will take longer for the urine to come out).
- Although this drug is meant to be sedating, some children will experience excitability instead.
- After taking this medicine, you should not drive a car or use any dangerous machinery.
- Take the tablet, capsule, or liquid form by mouth, with or without food. Diphenhydramine may be taken with food or milk if stomach upset occurs. If you are taking the suspension, shake the bottle well before each dose. Measure liquid forms of this medication with a dose-measuring spoon or device, not a regular teaspoon, to make sure you have the correct dose.

- The rapidly-dissolving tablet or strip should be allowed to dissolve on the tongue and then swallowed, with or without water. A second strip may be taken after the first strip has dissolved. The chewable tablets should be chewed thoroughly before being swallowed.

RESTLESS LEGS SYNDROME

Restless legs syndrome (RLS) is an urge to move the lower legs which is sometimes described as a "creeping" sensation. RLS is worse at night and is relieved with movement. RLS is thought to be due to a dysfunction with dopamine in the brain's basal ganglia circuits. The primary treatment is dopamine agonists (most commonly) and the anticonvulsant gabapentin.

Drug Treatment

Pramipexole *(Mirapex)* and ropinirole *(Requip)* are dopamine agonists primarily used in longer-acting formulations for Parkinson disease (PD), or are taken TID. For RLS these are taken in the immediate-release (IR) formulations 1-3 hours before bedtime. Rotigotine *(Neupro)* is a dopamine agonist that comes in a patch formulation that is also used for PD and RLS. For both conditions the patch is applied once daily. Patients with PD usually start with the 2 mg patch and RLS treatment begins with the 1 mg patch. Patients must be told not to apply a heat source over the patch and to remove the patch if receiving an MRI procedure. The patch causes skin irritation; the same site cannot be used again for 14 days. The patch contains a sulfite (metabisulfite) and sulfite-sensitive patients will have an allergic reaction.

Dopamine agonists cause orthostasis, somnolence, and nausea that is dose-related. Even when used for RLS the dose is titrated upwards carefully (slowly). Patients should be monitored for psychiatric concerns (hallucinations, abnormal dreams) and movement disorders.

Gabapentin enacarbil (*Horizant*) is approved for postherpetic neuralgia (PHN) and RLS. With any indication gabapentin requires a reduced dose with renal impairment (CrCl < 60 mL/min) to avoid increased side effects (dizziness, somnolence, ataxia, peripheral edema, weight gain, diplopia, blurred vision, dry mouth). The tablet is taken with food and must be swallowed whole (it cannot be crushed or chewed). For RLS, it is taken at ~5:00 PM daily. The IR formulation of gabapentin is used off-label as a less expensive alternative. Refer to the Parkinson Disease chapter for additional information on the dopamine agonists, and the Epilepsy/Seizures chapter for additional information on gabapentin.

NARCOLEPSY

Narcolepsy is excessive daytime sleepiness with cataplexy (sudden loss of muscle tone) and sleep paralysis. Narcolepsy causes sudden daytime "sleep attacks" due to poor control of normal sleep-wake cycles, especially when the person is in a relaxed setting. The sleep attacks last a few seconds to several minutes. Patients have difficulty managing with narcolepsy; they can fall asleep while at work, school, or in the middle of a conversation. And, the sleep quality at night is poor.

Drug Treatment

Narcolepsy is treated with stimulants, such as modafinil or armodafinil or with sodium oxybate, which is derived from the inhibitory neurotransmitter gamma aminobutyric acid (GABA). Several of the stimulants used primarily for ADHD have narcolepsy indications, including dextroamphetamine, dextroamphetamine/amphetamine *(Adderall)* and various methylphenidate formulations *(Metadate ER, Methylin, Ritalin* and *Ritalin SR)*. Patients may be using drugs approved for other indications: selegiline can be useful for daytime sleepiness, and tricyclic antidepressants or fluoxetine can be useful for cataplexy.

These are drugs used to improve wakefulness in adult patients with excessive sleepiness associated with narcolepsy, obstructive sleep apnea/hypopnea syndrome, and shift work sleep disorder.

Stimulants for Wakefulness

DRUG	DOSING	SAFETY/SIDE EFFECTS/MONITORING
Modafinil *(Provigil)* C-IV	200 mg daily	**WARNINGS** Avoid use with pre-existing cardiac conditions. Use with caution with hepatic impairment, renal impairment, psychiatric disorders and Tourette's. **SIDE EFFECTS** Headache, dizziness, anxiety, agitation, nausea, diarrhea, insomnia, dry mouth, risk of severe rash. **NOTES** Both of these agents require a MedGuide due to risk of severe rash, which can be life-threatening.
Armodafanil *(Nuvigil)* R-isomer of modafinil; similar drug C-IV	150-250 mg daily	Similar side effects, similar drug to modafinil, including risk of severe rash – give MedGuide.

Note: Additional stimulants indicated for weight loss in Weight Loss chapter, and the ADHD stimulants are sometimes used for these conditions.

Sodium oxybate is derived from GABA. Indicated for narcolepsy with cataplexy (sudden loss of muscle strength). Helps with sleep at night, generally used with daytime stimulants.

DRUG	DOSING	SAFETY/SIDE EFFECTS/MONITORING
Sodium oxybate *(Xyrem)* C-III (narcolepsy) C-I (illicit use) REMS program: this is a "date rape" drug (sedative, called GHB) that requires strict measures to ensure it is going to narcolepsy with cataplexy patients only.	Start 2.25 g QHS and again 2.5-4 hours later after 1st dose; titrate to effect, dosing range ~6-9 g/night	**BOXED WARNINGS** Respiratory depression (strong CNS depressant). Sodium oxybate is a salt form of hydroxybutyrate (GHB), a drug of abuse. Danger is increased when taken with other CNS depressants; coma and death can result. Restricted access through the *Xyrem* REMS Program. **CONTRAINDICATIONS** Use with sedative-hypnotics or alcohol **WARNINGS** Depression and suicidality, confusion/anxiety, parasomnias (e.g., sleep walking) **SIDE EFFECTS** Dizziness, nausea, somnolence, enuresis (dose-related), daytime hangover effect **NOTES** Taken in ¼ cup water, usually in an empty pharmacy pill container. Patient should lie down immediately after taking and stay in bed. The second dose is taken 2.5-4 hours after the first. Will typically fall asleep within 5-15 minutes after taking 1st dose. Contains a high sodium content, monitor patients with heart failure, hypertension, or impaired renal function.

67

EPILEPSY/SEIZURES

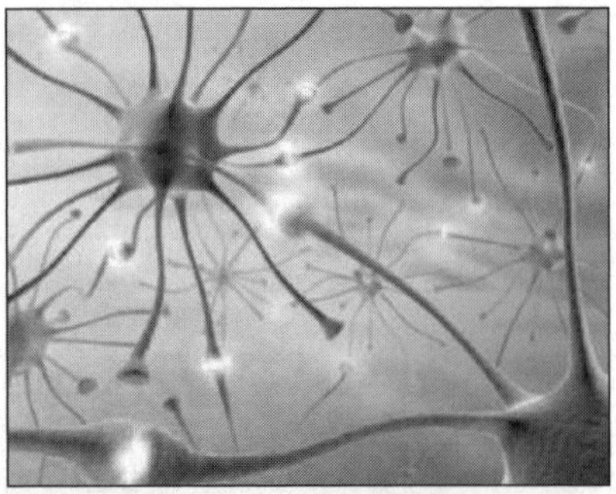

GUIDELINES/REFERENCES

Evidence-Based Guideline: Treatment of Convulsive Status Epilepticus in Children and Adults: Report of the Guideline Committee of the American Epilepsy Society. *Epilepsy Currents.* 2016;16(1):48-61.

Drugs for Epilepsy Treatment Guidelines, Medical Letter 2013;11(126): 9-18.

Operational Classification of Seizure Types by the International League Against Epilepsy. 2016 Update. http://www.ilae.org/visitors/centre/documents/ClassificationSeizureILAE-2016.pdf (accessed 2016 Dec 14).

Additional guidelines included with the online course.

We gratefully acknowledge the assistance of Jeannine M. Conway, PharmD, BCPS, Assistant Dean of the Professional Education Division at the University of Minnesota College of Pharmacy, in preparing this chapter.

BACKGROUND

Epilepsy is a disorder of the brain that causes seizures and affects 2.9 million adults and children in the United States. Seizures are the outward occurrence that result from abnormal, excessive and synchronous activity from a group of neurons. Seizures can vary widely from uncontrolled jerking movements (tonic-clonic seizure) to a subtle momentary loss of awareness (absence seizure). Unfortunately, many patients do not have complete seizure control, even with medications. Seizures can damage and destroy neurons, which can cause cognitive deficits and be life-threatening.

PATHOPHYSIOLOGY

Seizures can result from an imbalance between excitatory and inhibitory neurotransmitters. Excess excitatory neurotransmitters (norepinephrine, acetylcholine, histamine, corticotropin releasing factor, glutamate), altered receptor sensitivity to the neurotransmitters, or reduced function or deficiency of inhibitory neurotransmitters (gamma-aminobutyric acid, or GABA) can provoke seizures.

DIAGNOSIS

Many factors are evaluated for a diagnosis of epilepsy including age of onset, seizure type and frequency, description of witnessed seizure, identifiable causes or triggers and a thorough neurological exam. An electroencephalogram (EEG), the most common test used to diagnose epilepsy, records electrical activity of the brain, or brain waves. The EEG may show abnormal spike and wave patterns even when the patient is not having a seizure. Imaging of the brain (e.g., CT of the head, MRI) may also be done to detect causes of the seizures such as tumors, bleeding and cysts.

INTERNATIONAL CLASSIFICATION OF SEIZURE TYPES (UPDATED 2016)

Focal Seizures - start in one hemisphere of the brain, but can spread to the other hemisphere resulting in a "focal to bilateral tonic-clonic" seizure. If a focal seizure results in no loss of consciousness, and patient awareness, recall and responsiveness are all intact, it is called a focal aware seizure. If there is loss of consciousness, or the patient has impaired awareness, recall or responsiveness, it is termed a focal seizure with impaired awareness. In some cases, the seizure is classified as being with unknown awareness. Focal seizures are further classified by the presence of motor or non-motor signs and symptoms.

SEIZURE TYPE	SYMPTOMS
Focal Seizures (with motor signs and symptoms)	Tonic (sustained increase in muscle contraction lasting seconds to minutes) Atonic (sudden loss of muscle tone, limpness, of the head, trunk, jaw or limbs) Myoclonic (sudden, brief involuntary muscle contractions or jerking) Clonic (rhythmic jerking, either symmetric or asymmetric, involving the same muscle groups) Epileptic spasms (a sudden flexion, extension or mixed extension-flexion of proximal and truncal muscles; longer than a myoclonic movement but not as sustained as a tonic seizure) Hypermotor (bimanual or bipedal motor activity, such as kicking, thrashing, hugging, or clapping/rubbing or both hands)
Focal Seizures (with non-motor signs and symptoms)	Sensory [a perceptual experience (e.g., auditory, visual, olfactory) not caused by appropriate stimuli in the external world; usually a focally aware seizure] Cognitive (e.g., impairment in thinking, memory, language) Emotional (e.g., fear, laughing, crying, spontaneous joy, anger, paranoia) Autonomic (gastrointestinal sensations, sense of heat or cold, flushing, palpitations)

Generalized Seizures - begin in both hemispheres of the brain and usually result in impaired awareness. Generalized seizures are further classified as motor or absence seizures.

Motor Seizures	Includes tonic, atonic, myoclonic, clonic and epileptic spasm type seizures (see descriptions above) plus: Tonic-clonic (a sequence of a tonic phase followed by a clonic phase) Myoclonic-atonic (myoclonic jerking leading to an atonic drop) Clonic-tonic-clonic (one or a few jerks of the limbs bilaterally, similar to clonus or myoclonus, followed by a tonic-clonic seizure)
Absence Seizures	Typical (a sudden onset, interruption of ongoing activities, a blank stare with possibly a brief upward deviation of the eyes; duration of a few seconds to half a minute, during which the patient is unresponsive) Atypical (changes in tone that are more pronounced than a typical absence seizure or onset/cessation is not abrupt) Myoclonic (see description above) Eyelid myoclonia (eyelid jerking of about 3 per second, usually with upward eye deviation; usually lasts less than 10 seconds)

STATUS EPILEPTICUS

Seizures lasting longer than 5 minutes or 2 or more seizures between which the patient does not regain consciousness are called status epilepticus (SE), which is a medical emergency. Treatment consists of two phases outlined below:

- Phase 1 begins when the seizure exceeds 5 minutes and ends at 20 minutes or when the seizure is controlled. Choose one of the following equivalent first-line benzodiazepine options:
  - ❏ Midazolam IM x one dose (13 – 40 kg: give 5 mg; > 40 kg, give 10 mg)
  - ❏ Lorazepam *(Ativan)* IV, may repeat x 1 (0.1 mg/kg/dose, max of 0.4 mg/dose)
  - ❏ Diazepam *(Valium)* IV, may repeat x 1 (0.15 – 0.2 mg/kg/dose, max 10 mg/dose)

If none of these three options are available, choose phenobarbital IV, diazepam rectal gel *(Diastat AcuDial)*, intranasal or buccal midazolam. Diazepam rectal gel is dosed at 0.2 – 0.5 mg/kg (max 20 mg/dose). It is important to check that the dose has been dialed correctly and locked for both syringes prior to dispensing.

- Phase 2 begins at 20 minutes and concludes at 40 minutes. If the seizure was not controlled in phase 1, choose one of the following second-line options:
    - Fosphenytoin IV x 1 dose
    - Valproic acid IV x 1 dose
    - Levetiracetam IV x 1 dose

If none of these options are available, use phenobarbital IV (if not already given).

NON-DRUG TREATMENT

A ketogenic diet is often used in patients with refractory seizures (not responding to medications), primarily in children. The diet contains high fats, normal protein and low carbohydrates (usually a 4:1 ratio of fats to combined protein and carbohydrates), which forces the body to breakdown fatty acids into ketone bodies as an energy source. Ketone bodies pass into the brain and replace glucose. This elevated ketone state, ketosis, can lead to a reduction in seizure frequency.

MEDICAL MARIJUANA AND EPILEPSY

Presently, it is unknown if marijuana is a safe and effective treatment for epilepsy, including the impact on cognitive function. Safety concerns coupled with a lack of evidence of efficacy in clinical trials does not support the use of marijuana for the treatment of seizures at this time. Two phase III clinical trials are currently underway to evaluate the safety and efficacy of cannabidiol as adjunctive treatment in children and adults with inadequately controlled Dravet or Lennox-Gastaut syndromes. Pharmacists should keep in mind that there are parents who have seen improved seizure control in their child; these are select cases. In such situations, consider the impact of increased drug metabolism, which may require dose adjustments of other medications.

DRUG TREATMENT

An accurate diagnosis of seizure type, classification and frequency is critical to selecting an appropriate AED. Other factors are assessed such age, long-term side effect profile, comorbidities, insurance coverage and willingness to adhere to treatment. Monotherapy is preferred and 50 – 70% of patients are maintained on one drug. Many patients do not become seizure-free on monotherapy, and a second medication may be added. Treatment goals include seizure freedom or a reduction in seizure frequency while minimizing adverse effects of the medication. Roughly 30% of patients will have refractory seizures despite medication. Refer to the table of the most commonly used treatments per seizure type.

DRUGS/CONDITIONS THAT CAN LOWER THE SEIZURE THRESHOLD

Antipsychotics (e.g., clozapine, phenothiazines, butyrophenones)

Antivirals (e.g., amantadine, rimantadine, foscarnet, ganciclovir, valganciclovir, acyclovir IV)

Bupropion

Carbapenems (with higher doses/renal impairment – especially imipenem)

Cephalosporins

Lindane

Lithium and theophylline (in toxicity)

Mefloquine

Meperidine (chronic dosing with poor renal function)

Metoclopramide

Natural products such as dendrobium, evening primrose oil, gingko, melatonin

Penicillins

Quinolones

Sleep deprivation, alcohol intoxication, menstruation, infection and fever (especially in children) can worsen seizure.

Tramadol

Varenecline with alcohol

The most common side effects with AEDs are CNS-related, including somnolence, fatigue, cognitive impairment and coordination abnormalities such as ataxia and dizziness since these drugs have to penetrate the CNS to be effective. Side effects such as confusion and sedation can make it difficult for children to do well in school and for adults to perform well at work.

When AEDs are used in women of reproductive age, it is important to consider teratogenicity risk and provide proper counseling. Carbamazepine, clonazepam, phenobarbital/primidone, phenytoin/fosphenytoin, topiramate and valproic acid are known to increase the risk of fetal abnormalities in humans. Healthcare providers should always consider that untreated or inadequately treated epilepsy during pregnancy ↑ the risk of complications in both the pregnant mother and her developing baby. Valproic acid is thought to have the highest risk of fetal harm. As a result, using valproic acid for migraine prophylaxis in pregnancy is contraindicated. Use for seizures in this population must be carefully considered. Recently, the FDA issued a warning that valproic acid is associated with ↓ IQ scores in children following *in utero* exposure. All other AEDs are pregnancy category C. The metabolism of some of the AEDs increases during pregnancy (lamotrigine and others), resulting in breakthrough seizures. This can require a higher dose, which can ↑ risk to the fetus. Managing epilepsy during pregnancy is complex.

There are many drug interactions with most of the AEDs. Several of the AEDs are strong inducers and can ↓ the concentration of other drugs, including other AEDs the patient may be taking. AEDs that are inducers include carbamazepine, eslicarbazepine, oxcarbazepine, fosphenytoin, perampanel, phenytoin, phenobarbital, primidone and topiramate (≥ 200 mg/day).

Individuals with epilepsy may have ↑ fracture risk. Bone loss can occur as soon as two years after the start of AED therapy. Modifiable factors that affect bone density should be addressed (see Osteoporosis, Menopause & Testosterone Replacement chapter). The mechanism of AED-induced bone loss is not completely understood. Hepatic enzyme inducers ↓ vitamin D levels by ↑ metabolism, which ↓ calcium absorption. All patients on enzyme-inducing AEDs should supplement with vitamin D and calcium.

FIRST AID FOR SEIZURES

First aid for seizures involves responding in ways that can keep the person safe until the seizure stops by itself:

- Keep calm and reassure other people who may be nearby.
- Prevent injury by clearing the area around the person of anything hard or sharp.
- Ease the person to the floor and put something soft and flat, like a folded jacket, under the head. Turn the person gently onto one side. This will help keep the airway clear.
- Remove eyeglasses and loosen ties or anything around the neck that may make breathing difficult.
- Time the seizure with a watch. If the seizure continues for longer than five minutes without signs of slowing down or if the person has trouble breathing afterwards, appears to be injured, in pain, or has an unusual recovery, call 911.
- Do not hold people down or try to stop their movements.
- Contrary to popular belief, it is not true that people having a seizure can swallow their tongue. Do not put anything in the person's mouth. Efforts to hold the tongue down can injure the teeth or jaw.
- Do not attempt artificial respiration except in the unlikely event that a person does not start breathing again after the seizure has stopped.
- Stay with the person until the seizure ends naturally and the person is fully awake.
- Do not offer the person water or food until fully alert.
- Be friendly and reassuring as consciousness returns.
- Offer to call a taxi, friend or relative to help the person get home safely, particularly if the person seems confused or unable to get home without help.

All AEDs require a MedGuide due to the risk of suicidality. The MedGuide warning states: "Like other antiepileptic drugs, this medication may cause suicidal thoughts or actions in a very small number of people, about 1 in 500." This warning is not repeated in the drug tables.

Seizure drugs are titrated upwards when initiated to ↓ side effects and ↓ toxicity risk. Never discontinue abruptly. This will cause or worsen seizures. Taper the medication off slowly. Often, the new drug is being titrated up while the old drug is being titrated off (to continue providing seizure control), unless the patient is discontinuing treatment entirely.

Treatment of Choice

SEIZURE TYPE	1ST LINE TREATMENT
Focal, including Focal to Bilateral Tonic-Clonic	Carbamazepine Lamotrigine Levetiracetam Oxcarbazepine
Primary Generalized Tonic-Clonic	Lamotrigine Levetiracetam Valproic acid
Absence	Ethosuximide Valproic acid
Myoclonic, Atonic	Lamotrigine Levetiracetam Valproic acid

COMMONLY USED/IMPORTANT ANTICONVULSANTS

Levetiracetam

Mechanism of action is unknown; may inhibit voltage-dependent N-type calcium channels, facilitate GABA-ergic inhibitory transmission through displacement of negative modulators, reduce delayed rectifier potassium current and/or bind to synaptic proteins which modulate neurotransmitter release.

DRUG	DOSING	SAFETY/SIDE EFFECTS/MONITORING
LevETIRAcetam *(Keppra, Keppra XR, Spritam)* Tablet, solution, injection	Initial: 500 mg BID or 1,000 mg daily (XR) Maximum: 3,000 mg/d CrCl ≤ 80 mL/min: ↓ dose IV:PO ratio 1:1	**WARNINGS** Psychiatric reactions, including psychotic symptoms, somnolence, fatigue, coordination difficulties (ataxia, abnormal gait), severe skin reactions (SJS/TEN), hematologic abnormalities (mainly anemias) Loss of seizure control during pregnancy **SIDE EFFECTS** Irritability, dizziness, weakness, asthenia **MONITORING** Mental status and seizure frequency **NOTES** No significant drug interactions *Spritam* uses ZipDose technology with 3D printing to produce a porous tablet formulation that rapidly dissolves with a sip of liquid

Lamotrigine

Lamotrigine inhibits voltage-sensitive sodium channels, thereby stabilizing neuronal membranes and decreasing presynaptic transmitter release of glutamate (an excitatory amino acid).

DRUG	DOSING	SAFETY/SIDE EFFECTS/MONITORING
LamoTRIgine ***(LaMICtal, LaMICtal Starter, LaMICtal ODT, LaMICtal XR)*** Tablet, chewable, ODT	Starting Dose Week 1 and 2: 25 mg daily Week 3 and 4: 50 mg daily Week 5 and on: can ↑ by 50 mg daily every 1-2 weeks. Maintenance Dose: 300-400 mg daily Divide BID, unless using XR (daily) Higher doses (50 mg daily week 1 and 2) if taking hepatic inducers of glucuronidation (carbamazepine, phenytoin, phenobarbital, primidone, rifampin, and lopinavir/ritonavir); Lower doses if taking valproic acid (25 mg every other day week 1 and 2)	**BOXED WARNING** Serious skin reactions, including SJS/TEN (rate of rash is greater in pediatrics than adults); ↑ risk with higher than recommended starting doses, dose escalation, or co-administration of valproic acid. To ↓ risk of rash, use correct starting dose and follow the titration schedule – *Lamictal Starter Kit* and *Lamictal ODT Patient Titration Kits* provide the recommended dose/titration schedule for the first 5 weeks. Titration schedule is based on concomitant medications (see dosing). Discontinue at the first sign of rash and do not reinitiate. **WARNINGS** Risk of aseptic meningitis, blood dyscrasias, multiorgan hypersensitivity (DRESS) reactions **SIDE EFFECTS** N/V, somnolence, rash, tremor, ataxia, impaired coordination, dizziness, diplopia, blurred vision, alopecia (treat with a multivitamin with minerals as it needs to contain selenium and zinc) **MONITORING** Rash, seizure frequency **NOTES** Discontinue if any sign of hypersensitivity reaction or unspecified rash Comes in C-R (child-resistant) packaging. Starter kit packaging for those not taking interacting medications is orange; for those taking valproic acid is blue; for those taking an inducer is green.

Lamotrigine Drug Interactions

- Valproic acid ↑ lamotrigine concentrations more than 2-fold. Use the lower dose starter kit (blue box) upon initiation if currently taking valproic acid.
- Carbamazepine, phenytoin, phenobarbital, primidone and rifampin ↓ lamotrigine levels by 40%. Use the higher dose starter kit (green box) when using these drugs concurrently.
- Oral estrogen-containing contraceptives ↓ lamotrigine levels by 50%; monitor as a higher dose of lamotrigine may be needed.
- Lopinavir/ritonavir ↓ lamotrigine levels by 50%; atazanavir/ritonavir ↓ lamotrigine levels by 32%.
- Caution for additive CNS effects, including dizziness, somnolence, fatigue.

Carbamazepine

Fast sodium channel blocker; structurally similar to tricyclic antidepressants (TCAs); stimulates release of antidiuretic hormone (ADH), promoting reabsorption of water. In addition to anticonvulsant effects, carbamazepine has anticholinergic, antineuralgic, antidiuretic, muscle relaxant, antimanic, antidepressive and antiarrhythmic properties.

DRUG	DOSING	SAFETY/SIDE EFFECTS/MONITORING
CarBAMazepine *(TEGretol, TEGretol XR, Carbatrol, Epitol, Carnexiv)* Capsule, tablet, chewable, suspension, injection *Equetro* – for bipolar	Initial: 200 mg BID or divided QID (suspension) Maximum: 1,600 mg/day (some patients may require more) *Carnexiv* (IV): total daily dose is 70% of the oral carbamazepine dose; divide the total daily dose of *Carnexiv* equally into four infusions separated by 6 hours **Therapeutic Range** 4-12 mcg/mL Carbamazepine levels should be monitored within 3-5 days of initiation and again after 4 weeks due to autoinduction.	**BOXED WARNINGS** Serious skin reactions, including SJS/TEN: Patients of Asian descent should be tested for HLA-B*1502 allele prior to initiation; if positive for this allele, carbamazepine cannot be used (unless benefit clearly outweighs risk) Aplastic anemia and agranulocytosis; monitor CBC, platelets, and differential prior to and during therapy; discontinue if significant myelosuppression occurs **CONTRAINDICATIONS** Myelosuppression, hypersensitivity to TCAs, use of MAO inhibitors within past 14 days, concurrent use of nefazodone, concomitant use of delavirdine or other non-nucleoside reverse transcriptase inhibitors **WARNINGS** Risk of developing a hypersensitivity reaction may be ↑ in patients with the variant HLA-A*3101 allele Multiorgan hypersensitivity (DRESS) reactions Hyponatremia (SIADH), hypothyroidism Mild anticholinergic effects, cardiac conduction abnormalities Renal impairment/hepatic impairment: use with caution **SIDE EFFECTS** Dizziness, somnolence, N/V, ataxia, dry mouth, pruritus, photosensitivity, blurred vision, rash, vitamin D and calcium deficiency (bone loss), ↑ LFTs, alopecia (treat with a multivitamin with minerals as it needs to contain selenium and zinc) **MONITORING** CBC with differential, platelets, LFTs, s/sx of rash, ophthalmic exam, thyroid function tests, electrolytes (especially Na), renal function, mental status, seizure frequency, carbamazepine levels **NOTES** Safety issue – see Pregnancy chapter Potent CYP450 inducer and autoinducer – ↓ level of many other drugs and of itself Supplementation with calcium and vitamin D recommended

Carbamazepine Drug Interactions

- Carbamazepine is a strong inducer of many enzymes (1A2, 2C19, 2C8/9, 3A4), P-glycoprotein (P-gp) and is an autoinducer. It will ↓ the levels of many drugs, including hormonal contraceptives, other seizure medications, levothyroxine, warfarin and others. Use of an alternative, nonhormonal contraceptive is recommended.
- Carbamazepine is a major 3A4 substrate. 3A4 inhibitors will ↑ carbamazepine levels and 3A4 inducers will ↓ carbamazepine levels. Avoid use with nefazodone and non-nucleoside reverse transcriptase inhibitors.
- Caution for additive CNS effects, including dizziness, somnolence, fatigue.

Oxcarbazepine

Oxcarbazepine (OXC) is a prodrug that converts to active 10-monohydroxy derivative (MHD). Both OXC and MHD are voltage-sensitive sodium channel blockers, inhibiting repetitive firing and decreasing the propagation of synaptic impulses. Modulates activity at calcium channels.

DRUG	DOSING	SAFETY/SIDE EFFECTS/MONITORING
OXcarbazepine ***(Trileptal, Oxtellar XR)*** Tablet, suspension *(Trileptal)*, extended-release tablet *(Oxtellar XR)*	Initial: 300 mg BID *(Trileptal)*; 600 mg daily *(Oxtellar XR)* Maximum: 2,400 mg/day CrCl < 30 mL/min: start 300 mg daily Carbamazepine to oxcarbazepine dose conversion: 1.2 – 1.5x carbamazepine dose Extended release – take on empty stomach 1 hour before or 2 hours after meals	**WARNINGS** Hypersensitivity reactions to carbamazepine have 25-30% cross-sensitivity to oxcarbazepine ↑ risk for SJS/TEN, consider screening patients of Asian descent for HLA-B*1502 prior to initiating therapy Multiorgan hypersensitivity (DRESS) reactions Hyponatremia Hypothyroidism **SIDE EFFECTS** Somnolence, dizziness, N/V, abdominal pain, diplopia, visual disturbances, ataxia, tremor, vitamin D and calcium deficiency (bone loss) **MONITORING** Serum Na levels especially during first 3 months of therapy (hyponatremia more common than with carbamazepine), thyroid function, CBC, mental status, seizure frequency **NOTES** Supplementation with calcium and vitamin D recommended *Trileptal* oral suspension – once bottle is open use within 7 weeks

Oxcarbazepine Drug Interactions

- Oxcarbazepine is a weak 3A4 inducer and 2C19 inhibitor, but is not an auto-inducer. Strong 344 inducers can ↓ oxcarbazepine levels. Oxcarbazepine/MHD can ↑ levels of fosphenytoin, phenytoin and phenobarbital.
- Oxcarbazepine may ↓ hormonal contraceptive levels significantly. Use of an alternative, nonhormonal contraceptive is recommended.
- Caution for additive CNS effects, including dizziness, somnolence, fatigue.

Valproic Acid/Valproate

Valproic acid causes ↑ availability of gamma (γ)-aminobutyric acid (GABA), an inhibitory neurotransmitter. Divalproex sodium is a compound of sodium valproate and valproic acid. Divalproex dissociates to valproate in the GI tract.

DRUG	DOSING	SAFETY/SIDE EFFECTS/MONITORING
Valproate/Valproic acid *(Depakene, Depacon)* *Depakene* – capsule, syrup *Depacon* – IV **Divalproex *(Depakote, Depakote ER, Depakote Sprinkle)*** *Depakote* – delayed-release tablet *Depakote ER* – extended-release tablet *Depakote Sprinkle* – capsules can be opened and sprinkled on food Delayed-release divalproex ↓ GI upset Also used for bipolar and migraine prophylaxis	Initial: 10-15 mg/kg/day Maximum: 60 mg/kg/day **Therapeutic Range** 50-100 mcg/mL (some patients may need higher levels) ER tablets *(Depakote ER)* are not bioequivalent to delayed release tablets *(Depakote)*. For bioequivalence, increase total daily dose by 8-20% when converting to extended-release tablets. If the albumin is low (< 3.5 g/dL) the true valproic acid level will be higher than it appears – adjust with the same formula used for phenytoin.	**BOXED WARNINGS** Hepatic Failure: Occurs rarely in adults (1:50,000) usually during first 6 months of therapy. Children (1:600) under the age of two years and patients with mitochondrial disorders (mutations in mitochondrial DNA polymerase gamma (POLG) gene) are at ↑ risk. Monitor LFTs frequently during the first 6 months Teratogenicity: Including neural tube defects (e.g., spina bifida) and ↓ IQ scores following *in utero* exposure Pancreatitis: Can be fatal in children and adults **CONTRAINDICATIONS** Hepatic disease, urea cycle disorders, prophylaxis of migraine in pregnancy, known mitochondrial disorders caused by mutations in mitochondrial DNA POLG and suspected POLG-related disorder in children < 2 years of age **WARNINGS** Hyperammonemia (treat with carnitine in symptomatic adults only), hypothermia, dose-related thrombocytopenia (↑ bleeding risk), multiorgan hypersensitivity (DRESS) reactions **SIDE EFFECTS** N/V, anorexia, abdominal pain, dizziness, somnolence, tremor, alopecia (treat with a multivitamin with minerals as it needs to contain selenium and zinc), weight gain, edema, polycystic ovary syndrome (PCOS), vitamin D and calcium deficiency (bone loss), diplopia, blurred vision **MONITORING** LFTs (at baseline and frequently during first 6 months), CBC with differential, platelets, serum drug concentrations, mental status changes, seizures **NOTES** Safety issue – see Pregnancy chapter Supplementation with calcium and vitamin D recommended

Valproic Acid/Valproate Drug Interactions

- Valproic acid is an inhibitor of 2C9 (weak) and is a substrate of 2C19 (minor) and 2E1 (minor).
- Valproic acid can ↑ levels of lamotrigine, phenobarbital, phenytoin, warfarin and zidovudine.
- Use special caution with combination of valproic acid and lamotrigine due to risk of serious rash; use lower starting dose of lamotrigine and titrate slowly.
- Combination with topiramate can lead to hyperammonemia ± encephalopathy.
- Salicylates displace valproic acid from albumin and ↑ levels.
- Carbapenems (imipenem, meropenem etc.) can ↓ the levels of valproic acid.
- Caution for additive CNS effects, including dizziness, somnolence, fatigue.

Phenytoin/Fosphenytoin

Fast sodium channel blockers that stabilize neuronal membranes and reduce seizures by increasing efflux or decreasing influx of Na ions.

DRUG	DOSING	SAFETY/SIDE EFFECTS/MONITORING
Phenytoin *(Dilantin, Dilantin Infatabs, Phenytek)* Capsule, chewable, suspension, injection (IV only) **Fosphenytoin *(Cerebyx)*** Injection Prodrug of phenytoin (IV/IM)	Phenytoin: 15-20 mg/kg loading dose; up to 300-600 mg/day Fosphenytoin should always be dosed in phenytoin equivalents (PE): 1 mg PE = 1 mg phenytoin (fosphenytoin 1.5 mg = phenytoin 1 mg = 1 mg PE) **Therapeutic Range** Total PHT: 10-20 mcg/mL Free PHT: 1-2.5 mcg/mL (roughly 1/10th of the total PHT level) Exhibits saturable, or Michaelis-Menten, kinetics; a small change in dose can cause a large change in serum level If the albumin (alb) is low (< 3.5 g/dL), the true phenytoin level will be higher than it appears – adjust with formula below (if CrCl ≥ 10 mL/min) or measure a free phenytoin level. $\text{PHT correction} = \frac{\text{PHT measured}}{(0.2 \times \text{alb}) + 0.1}$ With CrCl < 10 mL/min and low albumin, use correction formula: $\text{PHT correction} = \frac{\text{PHT measured}}{(0.1 \times \text{alb}) + 0.1}$ IV:PO ratio 1:1 Enteral feedings ↓ phenytoin absorption; hold feedings 1-2 hours prior and 1-2 hours after phenytoin administration Phenytoin IV is compatible with NS only, requires a filter and is stable for 4 hours; do not refrigerate as may cause precipitation (which may dissolve upon warming). Fosphenytoin can be mixed with NS or D5W and is refrigerated (stable for 48 hrs at room temperature; 30 days if refrigerated).	**BOXED WARNINGS** Phenytoin IV administration should not exceed 50 mg/minute and fosphenytoin IV administration should not exceed 150 mg PE/minute in adults; if faster hypotension and cardiac arrhythmias can occur. **CONTRAINDICATIONS** Previous hepatoxicity due to phenytoin **WARNINGS** Extravasation: IV phenytoin is a vesicant; can cause venous irritation and "purple glove syndrome" (discoloration with edema and pain of distal limb); inject into a large vein slowly and follow with a saline flush With IV route (increased risk with rapid infusion): Hypotension, bradycardia, arrhythmias, cardiovascular collapse Serious skin reactions: ↑ risk of SJS/TEN, Asian patients should be screened for HLA-B*1502; ultiorgan hypersensitivity (DRESS) reactions May cause fetal harm when given to a pregnant woman Fraction of unbound (free) drug is higher with renal or hepatic failure or ↓ albumin; monitoring should be based on unbound phenytoin levels in these patients Blood dyscrasias, caution in cardiac disease patients, hepatic and renal impairment, hypothyroidism **SIDE EFFECTS** Dose-related (toxicity): Nystagmus, ataxia, slurred speech, dizziness, somnolence, lethargy, confusion, blurred vision and diplopia Chronic: Skin thickening (children), gingival hyperplasia, hair growth, vitamin D and calcium deficiency (bone loss), morbilliform rash (measles-like), rash, hepatotoxicity, peripheral neuropathy, hyperglycemia, metallic taste, connective tissue changes, enlargement of facial features (lips) **MONITORING** LFTs, CBC with differential, serum trough concentration, mental status, seizure frequency. For IV, continuous cardiac and respiratory monitoring (ECG, BP, HR) **NOTES** Safety issue – see Pregnancy chapter Supplementation with calcium and vitamin D, and possibly folic acid, is recommended Strong CYP450 enzyme inducer

Phenytoin/Fosphenytoin Drug Interactions

- Phenytoin and fosphenytoin are strong inducers of several CYP450 enzymes, including 2B6, 2C19, 2C8/9, 3A4, P-gp and UGT1A1; they are substrates of 2C19 (major), 2C9 (major) and 3A4 (minor). These 2 drugs can lower the concentration of many drugs including other anticonvulsants, contraceptives, warfarin, etc.
- Use of an alternative, non-hormonal contraceptive is recommended.
- Caution for additive CNS effects, including dizziness, somnolence, fatigue.
- These agents have high protein binding [fosphenytoin (95-99%)/phenytoin (90-95%)]; they can displace other highly-protein bound drugs. Other drugs can displace fosphenytoin/phenytoin, causing an ↑ in levels and potential toxicity.

Topiramate

Fast sodium channel blocker that enhances γ-aminobutyric activity (GABA), antagonizes the alpha-amino-3-hydroxy-5-methyl-4-isoxazolepropionic acid (AMPA)/kainate subtype of the glutamate receptors, and weakly inhibits carbonic anhydrase.

DRUG	DOSING	SAFETY/SIDE EFFECTS/MONITORING
Topiramate *(Topamax,* *Topiragen, Topamax* Sprinkle) Topiramate extended-release *(Qudexy XR, Trokendi XR)* Capsule, extended-release capsule, tablet Also used for migraine prophylaxis	Week 1: 25 mg BID (IR) or 50 mg daily (XR) Week 2: 50 mg BID (IR) or 100 mg daily (XR) Week 3: 75 mg BID (IR) or 150 mg daily (XR) Week 4: 100 mg BID (IR) or 200 mg daily (XR) ↑ by 100 mg weekly until max dose or therapeutic effect Maximum: 400 mg/day CrCl < 70 mL/min: ↓ dose by 50% *Topamax* Sprinkle Capsules: May be swallowed whole or opened to sprinkle the contents on a small amount (~1 teaspoon) of soft food (drug/food mixture should not be chewed; swallow immediately)	**CONTRAINDICATIONS** *Trokendi XR* only – recent alcohol use (within 6 hours prior to and 6 hours after dose), patients with metabolic acidosis and taking metformin **WARNINGS** Hyperchloremic nonanion gap metabolic acidosis due to inhibition of carbonic anhydrase and ↑ renal bicarbonate loss. Dose reduction or discontinuation (by tapering dose) should be considered in patients with persistent or severe metabolic acidosis. Oligohydrosis (reduced perspiration)/hyperthermia (mostly in children) – try to limit sun exposure and hydrate Nephrolithiasis (kidney stones) – keep hydrated; caution in those on a ketogenic diet Acute myopia and secondary angle closure glaucoma Hyperammonemia – alone and with co-administration of valproic acid Visual problems (reversible) – consider discontinuation Cognitive impairment **SIDE EFFECTS** Somnolence, dizziness, psychomotor slowing, cognitive problems (difficulty with memory/concentration/attention), weight loss, anorexia, paresthesia, ↓ sodium bicarbonate concentrations, vitamin D and calcium deficiency (bone loss) **MONITORING** Electrolytes (especially bicarbonate), renal function, hydration status, mental status, intraocular pressure, seizure frequency **NOTES** Safety issue – see Pregnancy chapter Supplementation with calcium and vitamin D recommended

Topiramate Drug Interactions

- Topiramate is an inhibitor of 2C19 (weak) and inducer of 3A4 (weak).
- Phenytoin, carbamazepine, valproic acid and lamotrigine can ↓ topiramate levels.
- Topiramate may ↓ oral contraceptive effectiveness, especially with higher doses (≥ 200 mg/day). Use of an alternative, non-hormonal contraceptive is recommended.
- Caution for additive CNS effects, including dizziness, somnolence, fatigue.

Pregabalin/Gabapentin

These agents bind to the alpha-2-delta subunit of voltage-dependent calcium channels within the CNS, inhibiting excitatory neurotransmitter release including glutamate, norepinephrine, serotonin, dopamine, substance P, and calcitonin gene-related peptide. Although structurally related to GABA, they do not bind GABA or benzodiazepine receptors.

DRUG	DOSING	SAFETY/SIDE EFFECTS/MONITORING
Pregabalin *(Lyrica)* C-V Capsule, solution Diabetic or spinal cord injury neuropathic pain, postherpetic neuralgia, fibromyalgia	Initial: 75 mg BID Maximum: 600 mg/day CrCl < 60 mL/min: ↓ dose and/or extend the interval	**WARNINGS** Angioedema, peripheral edema **SIDE EFFECTS** Dizziness, somnolence, peripheral edema, weight gain, ataxia, diplopia, blurred vision, dry mouth, mild euphoria **MONITORING** Edema/weight gain, somnolence, mental status, seizure frequency **NOTES** Often used for neuropathic pain treatment
Gabapentin *(Neurontin)* Capsule, tablet, solution, suspension *(Fanatrex* compounding kit) *Gralise* – postherpetic neuralgia *Horizant* (gabapentin enacarbil) – postherpetic neuralgia and restless legs syndrome	Initial: 300 mg TID Maximum: 3,600 mg/day CrCl < 60 mL/min: ↓ dose and/or extend the interval Immediate-release, extended-release and gabapentin enacarbil are not interchangeable	**WARNINGS** Multiorgan hypersensitivity (DRESS) reactions **SIDE EFFECTS** Dizziness, somnolence, ataxia, peripheral edema, weight gain, diplopia, blurred vision, dry mouth **MONITORING** Edema/weight gain, somnolence, mental status, seizure frequency **NOTES** More often used off-labeled for fibromyalgia, neuropathic pain, drug abuse, alcohol withdrawal

Pregabalin/Gabapentin Drug Interactions

- No significant drug-drug interactions; renally eliminated. Use caution with pregabalin and glitazones concurrently due to risk of additive edema.
- Caution for additive CNS effects, including dizziness, somnolence, fatigue.

Phenobarbital/Primidone

Barbiturate agents that enhance gamma (γ)-aminobutyric acid (GABA) to bind to GABA-A receptors and potentiate GABA-mediated chloride influx; shift in Cl ions results in hyperpolarization (a less excitable state) and membrane stabilization.

DRUG	DOSING	SAFETY/SIDE EFFECTS/MONITORING
PHENobarbital C-IV Tablet, solution, elixir, injection	Initial: 50-100 mg 2 or 3 times daily t½: ~100 hrs **Therapeutic Range** 20-40 mcg/mL in adults 15-40 mcg/mL in children	**CONTRAINDICATIONS** Severe hepatic impairment, dyspnea or airway obstruction, SC administration **WARNINGS** Do not discontinue abruptly as seizures can result (applies to all anticonvulsants); withdrawal symptoms will ↑ seizure risk Paradoxical reactions including hyperactive or aggressive behavior, particularly in acute pain and pediatric patients Hypotension especially when given IV Serious skin reactions (SJS/TEN) Respiratory depression
Primidone *(Mysoline)* Tablet Prodrug of phenobarbital and phenylethylmalonamide (PEMA) – both are active metabolites	Initial: 100-125 mg QHS Maximum: 2 grams/day	**SIDE EFFECTS** Somnolence, cognitive impairment, dizziness/ataxia, physiological dependence, tolerance, hangover effect, depression, vitamin D and calcium deficiency (bone loss), folate deficiency **MONITORING** LFTs, CBC with differential, mental status, serum drug concentration, seizure frequency **NOTES** Safety issue – see Pregnancy chapter Supplementation with calcium and vitamin D recommended Strong CYP450 enzyme inducers

Phenobarbital/Primidone Drug Interactions

- Phenobarbital (primidone is the prodrug) is a strong inducer of most CYP enzymes, including 1A2, 2C8/9, 3A4 and P-gp. These two drugs can ↓ the levels of many drugs metabolized by these enzymes.
- Use of an alternative, non-hormonal contraceptive is recommended.
- Caution for additive CNS effects, including dizziness, somnolence, fatigue.

Ethosuximide

T-type calcium channel blocker that ↑ seizure threshold and suppresses paroxysmal spike-and-wave pattern in absence seizures.

DRUG	DOSING	SAFETY/SIDE EFFECTS/MONITORING
Ethosuximide *(Zarontin)* Capsule, solution	Initial: 500 mg daily Maximum: 1,500 mg/day Therapeutic range: 40-100 mcg/mL	**WARNINGS** Serious skin rash (SJS/TEN) and blood dyscrasias **SIDE EFFECTS** N/V, abdominal pain, weight loss, hiccups, dizziness, somnolence **MONITORING** LFTs, CBC with differential, platelets, signs of rash, serum drug concentrations, seizure frequency.

Ethosuximide Drug Interactions

- Ethosuximide is a major 3A4 substrate; look for 3A4 inducers and inhibitors.
- Valproic acid can ↑ ethosuximide levels.
- Caution for additive CNS effects, including dizziness, somnolence, fatigue.

Lacosamide

Slow sodium channel blocker, thereby stabilizing hyperexcitable neuronal membranes.

DRUG	DOSING	SAFETY/SIDE EFFECTS/MONITORING
Lacosamide *(Vimpat)* C-V Tablet, solution, injection	Initial: 50-100 mg BID Maximum: 400 mg/day CrCl ≤ 30 mL/min: maximum dose is 300 mg/day	**WARNINGS** Lacosamide prolongs PR interval and ↑ risk of arrhythmias. Obtain an ECG prior to use and after titrated to steady state in patients with or at risk of cardiac conduction problems. Multiorgan hypersensitivity (DRESS) reactions Syncope, dizziness, ataxia **SIDE EFFECTS** Nausea, dizziness, headache, diplopia, blurred vision, ataxia, tremor, euphoria **MONITORING** ECG (baseline and at steady state) in at-risk patients, mental status, seizure frequency

Lacosamide Drug Interactions

- Lacosamide is a substrate of 2C19 (minor), 2C9 (minor), 3A4 (minor) and an inhibitor of 2C19 (weak). Caution with inhibitors of 2C19, 2C9 and 3A4 as they can ↑ lacosamide levels.
- Use caution with concomitant medications that prolong the PR interval (e.g., beta blockers, CCBs, digoxin) due to the risk of AV block or bradycardia.

OTHER ANTICONVULSANTS

DRUG	MOA	SAFETY/SIDE EFFECTS/MONITORING
Benzodiazepines, including: CloBAZam *(Onfi)* C-IV Tablet, suspension	Enhances GABA resulting in shift in Cl ions and hyperpolarization (a less excitable state)	**WARNINGS** Serious skin reactions (SJS/TEN) Paradoxical reactions including hyperactive or aggressive behavior Anterograde amnesia **NOTES** Causes physiological dependence, tolerance, drooling, pyrexia Supplementation with calcium and vitamin D recommended
Brivaracetam *(Briviact)*	Unknown; displays a high and selective affinity for synaptic vesicle protein 2A	**WARNINGS** Behavioral reactions including psychotic symptoms, irritability, depression, aggressive behavior and anxiety; bronchospasam and angioedema **MONITORING** Somnolence and fatigue, caution driving or operating machinery **NOTES** No added therapeutic benefit when used in combination with levetiracetam
Eslicarbazepine *(Aptiom)* Tablet Major active metabolite of oxcarbazepine	Fast Na channel blocker	**NOTES** Same warnings and side effects as oxcarbazepine including ↓ Na; monitor. Inducer of 3A4 (moderate); inhibitor of 2C19 (moderate) Supplementation with calcium and vitamin D recommended
Ezogabine *(Potiga)* C-V Tablet Due to limited usage, the manufacturer has announced that this product will no longer be available after June 30, 2017.	Binds the KCNQ voltage-gated K channels, enhancing the M-current and suppressing seizure activity	**BOXED WARNING** Retinal abnormalities that can progress to vision loss in ~33% of patients after 4 years of treatment **WARNINGS** Dose-related neuropsychiatric disorders, including confusion, psychosis, and hallucinations, generally within the first 8 weeks of treatment Skin discoloration (mostly blue) in ~ 10% of patients, generally after ≥ 2 years of treatment and at higher dosages (≥ 900 mg/day) Urinary retention, QT prolongation **MONITORING** Eye exam at baseline and every 6 months, monitor QT interval in at-risk patients, electrolytes, LFTs, renal function **NOTES** Urine discoloration (orange, red, brown)
Felbamate *(Felbatol)* Tablet, suspension	Enhances GABA, NMDA receptor blocker	**BOXED WARNINGS** Hepatic failure and aplastic anemia **MONITORING** LFT and CBC monitoring **NOTES** Informed consent needs to be signed by patient and prescriber prior to dispensing

Other Anticonvulsants Continued

DRUG	MOA	SAFETY/SIDE EFFECTS/MONITORING
Perampanel *(Fycompa)* C-III Tablet, suspension	Alpha-amino-3-hydroxy-5-methyl-4-isoxazolepropionic acid (AMPA) glutamate receptor blocker	**BOXED WARNING** Neuropsychiatric events (dose-related) including irritability, aggression, anger, paranoia and others mostly in the first 6 weeks **NOTES** Inducer of 3A4 (weak) Supplementation with calcium and vitamin D recommended
Rufinamide *(Banzel)* Tablet, suspension	Fast Na channel blocker	**CONTRAINDICATIONS** Patients with familial short QT syndrome due to QT shortening (dose-related) **NOTES** Take with food
TiaGABine *(Gabitril)* Tablet	Blocks GABA reuptake in the presynaptic neurons	**WARNINGS** Worsening of seizures/new onset seizures when used off-label for other indications, SJS/TEN **NOTES** Take with food
Vigabatrin *(Sabril)* Tablet, packet for solution	Irreversibly inhibits GABA transaminase, ↑ levels of GABA	**BOXED WARNING** Causes permanent vision loss (≥ 30% of patients) **MONITORING** Eye exam at baseline, every 3 months during therapy and 3-6 months after discontinuation of therapy **NOTES** Only available through SHARE distribution program (Support, Help And Resources for Epilepsy)
Zonisamide *(Zonegran)* Capsule	Fast Na channel blocker, T-type Ca channel blocker and weak carbonic anhydrase inhibitor	**CONTRAINDICATIONS** Hypersensitivity to sulfonamides **WARNINGS** Same as topiramate except: no hyperammonemia warning and there is a serious skin reaction risk (SJS/TEN); multiorgan hypersensitivity (DRESS) reactions **SIDE EFFECTS** Side effects similar to topiramate, including oligohydrosis (primarily in children) and risk of nephrolithiasis

Significant Toxicities

ADVERSE EFFECT	ASSOCIATED DRUGS	
Teratogenicity*	Carbamazepine Clonazepam Phenobarbital/Primidone	Phenytoin/Fosphenytoin Topiramate Valproic Acid
Hepatotoxicity	Carbamazepine Felbamate Phenobarbital/Primidone	Phenytoin Valproic Acid

Significant Toxicities continued

ADVERSE EFFECT	ASSOCIATED DRUGS	
Decreases efficacy of oral contraceptives	Carbamazepine Clobazam Eslicarbazepine Oxcarbazepine	Perampanel Phenobarbital/Primidone Phenytoin Topiramate (≥ 200 mg/day)
Fatal pancreatitis	Valproic Acid	
Aplastic anemia	Carbamazepine (and agranulocytosis)	Felbamate
Serious skin rash (SJS/TEN)	Carbamazepine Clobazam Ethosuximide Lamotrigine Levetiracetam	Oxcarbazepine Phenobarbital/Primidone Phenytoin/Fosphenytoin Tiagabine Zonisamide
Oligohydrosis – inability to sweat, risk of heat stroke – highest risk in children	Topiramate	Zonisamide
Nephrolithiasis (kidney stones)	Topiramate	Zonisamide
Weight gain	Valproic Acid Gabapentin	Pregabalin
Weight loss	Ethosuximide Felbamate	Topiramate Zonisamide
Hyponatremia	Carbamazepine Eslicarbazepine	Oxcarbazepine (more common)

* *Patients should be encouraged to enroll in the North American Antiepileptic Drug (NAAED) Pregnancy Registry if they become pregnant. This registry is collecting information about the safety of antiepileptic drugs during pregnancy (aed-pregnancyregistry.org).*

Patient Counseling for All Anticonvulsants

- Like other seizure medications, this drug can cause suicidal thoughts or actions in a very small number of people (about 1 in 500). Call your healthcare provider right away if you experience thoughts about suicide or dying, new or worsening depression or anxiety, panic attacks, irritability or other unusual behavior. Dispense MedGuide and instruct patient/family to read it.

- Do not stop taking this medication without consulting your healthcare provider. Seizures may become worse when the drug is suddenly stopped. When stopping therapy, the dose needs to be gradually decreased.

- Seizure medications can impair judgment, thinking and coordination. You may experience dizziness and drowsiness, especially when starting therapy. Do not drive, operate heavy machinery or do other dangerous activities until you know how this medication affects you.

- This medication can have additional drowsiness and dizziness with other drugs such as alcohol, barbiturates, benzodiazepines, hypnotics, opioids and skeletal muscle relaxants (any CNS depressant). Avoid use of other sedating drugs, if possible.

- Avoid drugs that can lower the seizure threshold (see chart at the beginning of the chapter). Avoid St. John's wort with all anticonvulsants.

- Use caution with different generic substitutions; try to stick to the same manufacturer. Small dosage variations can result in loss of seizure control.

Carbamazepine

- The most common side effects include sleepiness, dizziness, nausea, vomiting and problems with coordination. Take with food to decrease stomach upset.
- Carbamazepine can cause rare but very serious (possibly fatal) skin reactions. If you are of Asian descent, you should have a blood test prior to using this medicine to determine if you are at greater risk of developing a serious skin reaction. The serious skin reactions usually develop within the first few months of treatment. Seek immediate medical attention if you feel weak and feverish, develop a skin rash, hives, sores in your mouth or blistering or peeling of the skin.
- Carbamazepine can cause rare but serious blood problems (aplastic anemia or agranulocytosis). You will need to have your blood checked to make sure this is not occurring. Contact your healthcare provider right away if you develop fever, sore throat, other infections, easy bruising or bleeding, red or purple spots on your body or severe weakness and tiredness.
- Carbamazepine is FDA pregnancy category D. This means that the drug is known to be harmful to an unborn baby. Do not take this drug without first talking to your doctor if you are pregnant or are planning a pregnancy.
- This medication can lower the amount of vitamin D and calcium in your body; it is recommended to supplement with calcium and vitamin D while taking this medication.

Lamotrigine

- The most common side effects of this medication include sleepiness, dizziness, rash, nausea, vomiting, insomnia, lack of coordination or blurred or double vision.
- This medication can cause a serious skin rash. These serious skin reactions are more likely to happen in the first 2 to 8 weeks of treatment (but it can happen in people who have taken the medication for any period of time). Call your healthcare provider right away if you develop a fever, skin rash, hives, swollen lymph glands, sores in the mouth or around your eyes or unusual bleeding or bruising.
- This medication can rarely cause aseptic meningitis, which is a serious inflammation of the protective membrane of the brain. Call your healthcare provider right away if you develop a stiff neck, headache, fever, abnormal sensitivity to light, muscle pains, chills and/or confusion.
- Swallow tablets whole.
- The ODT formulation should be placed on the tongue and moved around the mouth to rapidly disintegrate.
- Chewable tablets can be swallowed whole, chewed, or mixed in water or diluted fruit juice. If mixed, take the whole amount right away.

Levetiracetam

- Take levetiracetam with or without food.
- Swallow the tablets whole. Do not chew, break or crush tablets. Ask your healthcare provider for levetiracetam oral solution or dissolvable tablet if you cannot swallow tablets.
- If taking levetiracetam oral solution, be sure to use a medicine dropper or medicine cup to help you measure the correct amount of levetiracetam oral solution. Do not use a household teaspoon or tablespoon.
- This medication can cause serious skin reactions, although this is rare. Seek immediate medical attention if you feel weak and feverish, develop a skin rash, hives, sores in your mouth or blistering or peeling of the skin.

Oxcarbazepine

- This medication can cause low sodium concentrations in the blood. Symptoms of low blood sodium include nausea, tiredness or lack of energy, headache, more frequent or more severe seizures and confusion.
- Take oxcarbazepine with or without food. Take oxcarbazepine extended release *(Oxtellar XR)* on an empty stomach at least 1 hour before or 2 hours after food. Swallow whole.
- Before taking oxcarbazepine oral suspension, shake the bottle for at least 10 seconds and use the oral dosing syringe to withdraw the amount of medicine needed. The dose may be taken directly from the oral syringe or may be mixed in a small glass of water immediately prior to swallowing. Rinse syringe with warm water after use and allow to dry thoroughly. Discard any unused portion after 7 weeks of first opening the bottle.
- This medication can lower the amount of vitamin D and calcium in your body; it is recommended to supplement with calcium and vitamin D while taking this medication.
- This medication can cause serious skin reactions, although this is rare. Seek immediate medical attention if you feel weak and feverish, develop a skin rash, hives, sores in your mouth or blistering or peeling of the skin.

Phenobarbital

- This medication can cause abuse and dependence and can slow your thinking and reflexes. Do not drive, operate heavy machinery, or do other dangerous activities until you know how this medication affects you.
- This medication can lower the amount of vitamin D and calcium in your body; it is recommended to supplement with calcium and vitamin D while taking this medication.

Phenytoin

- The most common side effects of this medication include sleepiness, dizziness, unsteady walking, confusion and slurred speech.
- This medication can lower the amount of folic acid, vitamin D and calcium in your body; it is recommended to supplement with calcium and vitamin D, and possibly folic acid, while taking this medication.
- This medication can cause a serious skin rash. Call your healthcare provider right away if you develop a skin rash, hives, fever, swollen lymph glands, sores in the mouth or unusual bleeding or bruising.
- This medicine can cause inflammation of your gums. Brush and floss regularly; do not miss dental cleanings or appointments.
- This medicine can cause birth defects if taken during pregnancy. Do not take phenytoin without first talking to your healthcare provider if you are pregnant or are planning a pregnancy.
- If using the suspension, shake the bottle well before each dose.
- Use this medication regularly in order to get the most benefit from it. It is important to take all doses on time to keep the amount of medicine in your body at a constant level.

Topiramate

- The most common side effects of this medication include sleepiness, dizziness, tingling of the arms and legs, weight loss and loss of appetite. This medication can cause confusion, problems with concentration, attention, memory, or speech.
- This medication may cause eye problems. Please contact your healthcare provider right away if you experience a sudden decrease in vision with or without eye pain and redness. Rarely, this medicine can increase the pressure in the eye. This can lead to permanent loss of vision if not treated.

- Topiramate may cause decreased sweating and increased body temperature. Children in particular should be watched for signs of decreased sweating and fever especially in hot weather. Keep your child out of direct sunlight and heat and have the child drink plenty of water when going outside when it is hot.
- Topiramate can increase the level of acid in your blood (metabolic acidosis). Contact your healthcare provider right away if you feel tired, have a loss of appetite, feel changes in heartbeat, or have trouble thinking clearly.
- Topiramate Sprinkle Capsules may be swallowed whole or may be opened and sprinkled on a teaspoon of soft food. Drink fluids right after eating the food and medicine mixture to make sure it is all swallowed. Do not chew the food and medicine mixture. Do not store any medicine and food mixture for later use.
- Drink plenty of fluids during the day. This helps prevent kidney stones while taking this medication.
- This medicine can cause birth defects if taken during pregnancy. Do not take without first talking to your healthcare provider if you are pregnant or are planning a pregnancy. An increased risk of oral clefts (cleft lip and/or palate) has been observed, particularly following first trimester exposure.
- This medication can lower the amount of vitamin D and calcium in your body; it is recommended to supplement with vitamin D and calcium while taking this medication.

Valproic Acid

- Common side effects with this medication include nausea, vomiting, sleepiness, weakness, increased appetite, weight gain, double or blurry vision and hair loss.
- This medication can rarely damage the liver. This is more likely to occur in the first 6 months of therapy. Call your healthcare provider right away if you develop severe fatigue, vomiting, loss of appetite, pain on the right side of your stomach, dark urine, light stools or yellowing of your skin or whites of your eyes.
- In rare cases, valproic acid has caused severe, sometimes fatal, cases of pancreatitis (inflammation of the pancreas). Call your healthcare provider right away if you have severe stomach pain that you may also feel in your back or have nausea or vomiting that does not go away. These symptoms may be early signs of pancreatitis.
- Do not crush, chew or break the capsules. Swallow them whole.
- Measure the liquid form of valproic acid with a special dose-measuring spoon or cup, not a regular teaspoon or tablespoon. If you do not have a dose-measuring device, ask your pharmacist for one.
- This medicine can cause birth defects if taken during pregnancy. Do not take without first talking to your healthcare provider if you are pregnant or are planning a pregnancy. Malformations of the face, head, brain and spinal cord have been reported (neural tube defects such as spina bifida). In addition, children born to mothers taking valproic acid products while pregnant may have impaired mental development.
- Take with food to help avoid stomach upset.
- You will need to have blood tests during treatment. It is important for your healthcare provider to know how much medication is in the blood and how well your liver is working.
- This medication can lower the amount of vitamin D and calcium in your body; it is recommended to supplement with vitamin D and calcium while taking this medication.

PRACTICE CASE

LK is a 35 y/o white female s/p MVA. She suffered a closed head injury, two broken ribs and a concussion. She had one seizure in the emergency room. During her hospital stay, she was initially treated with fosphenytoin then continued on phenytoin. She has no past medical history and does not smoke or drink alcohol. Her medications, vitals, and labs on the day of discharge are as follows:

Allergies: PCN, sulfa, "quinolones" and latex

Discharge Medications:
Phenytoin 100 mg PO TID
Norco 5/325 mg 1-2 tabs Q6 hours PRN pain #10
Patient states that she will continue her home medications, which include:
Loestrin 1 tab PO daily
Fish oil softgels 2 with dinner for "cholesterol"
Valerian root 3 capsules at bedtime for "calm sleep"
B complex tablet daily with lunch

Vitals:
BP: 138/76 mmHg HR: 85 BPM RR: 14 BPM Temp: 38°C Pain: 4/10

Labs:
Na (mEq/L) = 133 (135 - 145)
K (mEq/L) = 3.8 (3.5 - 5)
Cl (mEq/L) = 101 (95 - 103)
HCO_3 (mEq/L) = 26 (24 - 30)
BUN (mg/dL) = 10 (7 - 20)
SCr (mg/dL) = 0.7 (0.6 - 1.3)
Glucose (mg/dL) = 98 (100 - 125)
Ca (mg/dL) = 9.9 (8.5 - 10.5)
Mg (mEq/L) = 1.9 (1.3 - 2.1)
PO_4 (mg/dL) = 3.1 (2.3 - 4.7)
AST (IU/L) = 34 (8 - 48)
ALT (IU/L) = 42 (7 - 55)
Albumin (g/dL) = 2.2 (3.5 - 5)
Phenytoin (mcg/mL) = 7.7 (10 - 20)

Discharge patient with follow up in 1 week in the Internal Medicine clinic.

Questions

1. LK is receiving phenytoin for her seizure control. What is LK's true phenytoin level at this time?
   a. 4.8 mcg/mL
   b. 7.7 ng/mL
   c. 7.7 mcg/mL
   d. 10.8 mcg/mL
   e. 14.3 mcg/mL

2. The medical resident asks the pharmacist to explain why a total phenytoin level needs to be adjusted for the albumin level. The pharmacist should give this response:
   a. The total phenytoin level will appear artificially low if the albumin is low – and should be adjusted.
   b. The total phenytoin level will appear artificially high if the albumin is low – and should be adjusted.
   c. The total phenytoin level will appear artificially low if the albumin is high – and should be adjusted.
   d. The total phenytoin level will appear artificially high if the albumin is high – and should be adjusted.
   e. Albumin levels have no effect on total phenytoin levels.

3. LK will be counseled to recognize symptoms of acute phenytoin toxicity. Which of the following should be included? (Select **ALL** that apply.)
   a. Shakiness/walking unsteady
   b. Severe rash
   c. Double vision
   d. Nystagmus
   e. Osteomalacia

4. There is a serious drug interaction between LK's birth control pills and phenytoin. Choose the correct counseling statement(s):
   a. Phenytoin will lower the amount of contraceptive medicine in her body.
   b. She will need to use a different type of contraceptive method.
   c. Phenytoin will increase the amount of contraceptive medicine in her body.
   d. A and B
   e. B and C

5. If LK continues phenytoin long-term, which of the following medical condition(s) could result if she does not use proper supplementation? (Select **ALL** that apply.)
   a. Osteoporosis
   b. Vision loss
   c. Alopecia
   d. Arrhythmias
   e. Progressive multifocal leukoencephalopathy

Questions 6-13 do not apply to the case.

6. A patient is going to receive phenytoin via infusion. Which of the following statements are correct? (Select **ALL** that apply.)
   a. Phenytoin has saturable kinetics.
   b. The maximum infusion rate is 100 mg/minute.
   c. The therapeutic level of total phenytoin is 10-20 mcg/mL.
   d. Phenytoin should be mixed in dextrose only.
   e. The brand name of phenytoin is *Felbatol.*

7. A child has been receiving divalproex for seizure control. Unfortunately, the seizures are not well-controlled. The physician has ordered lamotrigine as adjunctive therapy, with a careful dose-titration. What is the reason that a slow titration is required when initiating lamotrigine?
   a. Risk of multiorgan hypersensitivity reaction
   b. Risk of cardiac myopathy
   c. Risk of fluid retention and heart failure
   d. Risk of severe, and potentially fatal, rash
   e. Risk of fulminant hepatic failure

8. What is the mechanism of action of phenobarbital?
   a. Enhances dopamine
   b. Enhances GABA
   c. Suppresses dopamine
   d. Suppresses GABA
   e. Fast sodium channel blocker

9. Which of the following drugs decrease sweating and can cause heat stroke in children, and requires counseling to parents to help children avoid the sun and keep hydrated? (Select **ALL** that apply.)

   a. Rufinamide
   b. Zonisamide
   c. Felbamate
   d. Topiramate
   e. Oxcarbazepine

10. Which of the following drugs can cause kidney stones and require counseling for adequate fluid intake?

   a. Topiramate
   b. Tiagabine
   c. Pregabalin
   d. Valproic Acid
   e. Carbamazepine

11. Which of the following drugs is a preferred agent for treating typical absence seizures?

   a. Ethosuximide
   b. Lamotrigine
   c. Felbamate
   d. Topiramate
   e. Zonisamide

12. You find a patient actively seizing and call 911. What steps should you take to ensure the patient is safe? (Select **ALL** that apply.)

   a. Turn the patient on their side
   b. Remove sharp or hard objects away from the patient seizing and support their head
   c. Insert a stick into the seizing patient's mouth to prevent them from swallowing their tongue
   d. Loosen the patient's clothes
   e. Time the seizure

13. Which of the following statements are true regarding status epilepticus? (Select **ALL** that apply.)

   a. It is a medical emergency.
   b. Benzodiazepines are preferred for the first phase of treatment.
   c. Clobazam is preferred for patients still having seizure activity after the first-line agent is given.
   d. It is defined as sub-clinical seizure activity on an EEG.
   e. Phenytoin is the drug that should be used first-line to break status epilepticus.

Answers

1-e, 2-a, 3-a,c,d, 4-d, 5-a, 6-a,c, 7-d, 8-b, 9-b,d, 10-a, 11-a, 12-a,b,d,e, 13-a,b

STROKE

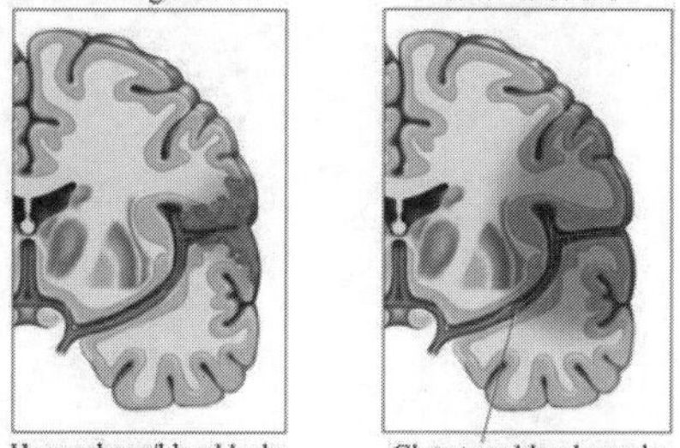
Hemorrhagic Stroke
Ischemic Stroke
Hemorrhage/blood leaks into brain tissue
Clot stops blood supply to an area of the brain

GUIDELINES/REFERENCES

Guidelines for the early management of patients with acute ischemic stroke. AHA/ASA. *Stroke.* 2013;44:870-947.

Guidelines for the prevention of stroke in patients with stroke and transient ischemic attack. AHA/ASA. *Stroke.* 2014;45:2160-2236.

Guidelines for the management of spontaneous intracerebral hemorrhage. AHA/ASA. *Stroke.* 2015;41:2108-2129.

Additional guidelines included with the online course.

BACKGROUND

A stroke, or cerebrovascular accident (CVA), occurs when blood flow to an area of the brain is interrupted. Acute ischemic stroke can be caused by a thrombus (e.g., from a cerebral atherosclerotic infarction) or an embolus (e.g., a clot from a cardiac source, known as a cardioembolic stroke). Intracerebral hemorrhage (ICH), subarachnoid hemorrhage (SAH) and subdural hematoma are all hemorrhagic strokes (bleeding in the brain due to a ruptured blood vessel). Approximately 85% of all strokes are ischemic and 15% are hemorrhagic.

When a stroke occurs, ischemia kills brain cells in the immediate area of injury. When brain cells die, they release chemicals that set off a chain reaction, endangering cells in the larger, surrounding area of brain tissue called the penumbra. Without prompt medical treatment, this larger area of brain cells can also die and the abilities controlled by that area of the brain can be lost or impaired.

Some people recover completely from less serious strokes (e.g., transient ischemic attacks, or TIAs), while others face chronic disability or loss of life. Stroke is the leading cause of disability and the 5th leading cause of death in the United States.

CLINICAL PRESENTATION AND DIAGNOSIS

The evaluation of a stroke patient should be done expeditiously. Early recognition of stroke signs and symptoms by the patient or bystander is the first link in the stroke chain of survival. The American Stroke Association (ASA) and the American Heart Association (AHA) have public education campaigns aimed to enhance this early recognition (see Signs and Symptoms of Stroke on the following page). Prompt response, by calling 9-1-1 and activating the emergency medical system, is essential as time is brain. Once in the care of healthcare professionals, a clinical assessment (e.g., history, physical exam, laboratory tests) and a neurological assessment, using stroke scales such as the National Institutes of Health Stroke Scale (NIHSS), help determine the severity of the stroke and provide prognostic information. Initial treatment includes supportive cardiac and respiratory care and quickly determining whether the stroke is ischemic or hemorrhagic via brain imaging. Brain imaging, either by computed tomography (CT) or, less commonly with magnetic resonance imaging (MRI), is essential to the diagnostic process and selection of appropriate treatment. This is especially important since agents used to treat ischemic stroke can increase the risk of bleeding and can be harmful, or even fatal, in cases of hemorrhagic stroke. Imaging should be interpreted, by a physician with expertise in reading these studies, within 45 minutes of the patient's arrival in the emergency department.

SIGNS AND SYMPTOMS OF STROKE

ACT F.A.S.T

Face: ask the person to smile. Does one side of the face droop or is it numb? Is the person's smile uneven?

Arms: ask the person to raise both arms. Does one arm drift downward?

Speech: ask the person to repeat a simple sentence. Are the words slurred? Is the sentence repeated correctly?

Time: If the person shows any of these symptoms, even if they go away, call 9-1-1 immediately!

THE 5 "SUDDENS"

SUDDEN numbness or weakness of the face, arm or leg, especially on one side of the body

SUDDEN confusion, trouble speaking or understanding

SUDDEN trouble seeing in one or both eyes

SUDDEN trouble walking, dizziness, loss of balance or coordination

SUDDEN severe headache with no known cause

DRUG TREATMENT FOR ISCHEMIC STROKE

Early Management of Acute Ischemic Stroke

The immediate goal of therapy is to restore blood flow to the ischemic area of the brain (to obtain complete neurological recovery), maintain normal intracranial pressure (ICP), control cerebral perfusion pressure (CPP), and manage blood pressure (BP). Restoring blood flow may require mechanical removal of a clot (e.g., with stent retrievers), or the clot can be dissolved with intravenous fibrinolytic therapy, if the patient presents to the hospital in a timely manner after symptom onset.

Alteplase

Alteplase is recombinant tissue plasminogen activator (tPA or rtPA). It binds to fibrin in a thrombus (clot) and converts entrapped plasminogen to plasmin resulting in fibrinolysis.

Alteplase is the only fibrinolytic agent that should be used in acute ischemic stroke. The principles of treatment with alteplase, for patients who are candidates for therapy (e.g., clot confirmed on brain imaging and the patient has no contraindications to use), include:

- Treatment within 3 hours of symptom onset (FDA approved time line).
- Treatment within 4.5 hours of symptom onset (not FDA approved; guideline extended window for select patients).
- Door-to-needle time (bolus administration) within 60 minutes of hospital arrival.
- If the only contraindication to treatment is BP > 185/110 mmHg, then BP should be safely lowered to ≤ 185/110 mmHg so alteplase can be administered.

DRUG	DOSING	SAFETY/SIDE EFFECTS/MONITORING
Alteplase *(Activase)* Must exclude intracranial hemorrhage before use	0.9 mg/kg (maximum dose 90 mg); give 10% of the dose as a bolus over 1 minute then infuse the remainder over 60 minutes Dosing is different for MI and pulmonary embolism indications	**CONTRAINDICATIONS** **Absolute (per package labeling)** Active bleed (including ICH, SAH, internal bleeding); recent (within past 3 months) serious head injury, intracranial surgery or intraspinal surgery; presence of intracranial conditions that may increase the risk of bleeding (e.g., intracranial neoplasms, AV malformations, or aneurysms); bleeding diathesis; current severe uncontrolled BP (> 185/110 mmHg) **Additional Exclusion Criteria (per AHA/ASA guidelines)** Stroke within past 3 months; previous ICH; INR > 1.7, platelet count < 100,000/mm^3, ↑ aPTT due to recent heparin use (within previous 48 hours), use of LMWH (prophylactic or treatment doses) within previous 24 hours, current use of direct thrombin inhibitors or direct factor Xa inhibitors with elevated anticoagulation tests (e.g., aPTT, PT/INR, factor Xa activity assays); blood glucose < 50 mg/dL; others **WARNINGS** Major bleeding (e.g., ICH), angioedema, cholesterol embolization (rare) **MONITORING** Neurological assessments and BP measurements every 15 minutes during the infusion and for 2 hours after, then every 30 minutes for the next 6 hours, then hourly until 24 hours after treatment Obtain follow-up brain imaging (e.g., head CT) 24 hrs after treatment, before starting anticoagulants or antiplatelets **NOTES** Must keep BP ≤ 185/110 mmHg If severe headache, acute hypertension, nausea, vomiting or worsening neurological function occurs, discontinue the infusion and obtain an emergency CT scan Contraindications for alteplase use in ACS may differ

Alteplase Drug Interactions

- Most drug interactions are due to additive effects with other agents that can ↑ bleeding risk. See Drug Interactions chapter for drugs that can increase bleeding risk.

Additional Therapies

Aspirin

Aspirin 325 mg PO within 24 – 48 hours after stroke onset is recommended in most patients to prevent early recurrent stroke. Aspirin should not be given within 24 hours of fibrinolytic therapy.

Hypertension Management

Antihypertensives should be used to lower BP to < 185/110 mmHg prior to giving alteplase. In patients who do not receive alteplase, BP should not be treated unless it becomes severely elevated (> 220/120 mmHg); in this case, the BP should be decreased by 15% during the first 24 hours after stroke onset. If neurologically stable, antihypertensive medications may be restarted after the first 24 hours in patients with preexisting hypertension.

Hyperglycemia Management

Maintain BG levels in the range of 140 – 180 mg/dL and closely monitor to prevent hypoglycemia.

Deep Vein Thrombosis (DVT) Prevention

DVT prophylaxis with SC anticoagulants is recommended for immobilized patients. However, these agents should not be used within 24 hours of receiving alteplase therapy.

Secondary Prevention of Ischemic Stroke

There are numerous risk factors for stroke (see box), many of which are modifiable. The recommendations below reflect secondary prevention measures after a first occurrence of stroke or TIA; many of the same recommendations are also presented in primary prevention of stroke guidelines.

RISK FACTORS FOR STROKE
Hypertension – most important risk factor
Atrial Fibrillation
Gender (females > males)
Ethnicity (highest risk in African Americans)
Age ≥ 55 years
Atherosclerosis
Diabetes
Prior stroke or TIA
Smoking
Dyslipidemia
Patent Foramen Ovale (PFO)
Sickle Cell Disease

Modifiable risk factors should be corrected:

- Hypertension – patients without preexisting hypertension should begin BP therapy after the first several days of stroke, especially if BP is ≥ 140/90 mmHg. The use of ACE inhibitors and thiazide-type diuretics have the best evidence for stroke risk reduction, even in patients without a history of hypertension or with BP < 140/90 mmHg at baseline. It is reasonable to target a BP goal < 140/90 mmHg; a goal SBP of < 130 mmHg is reasonable for patients with a lacunar stroke. Lifestyle modifications (see below) are an important part of BP management.
- Dyslipidemia – treat according to the 2013 ACC/AHA 2013 Guideline on the Treatment of Blood Cholesterol (see Dyslipidemia chapter).
- Diabetes – in patients with no established history, screening for diabetes should be performed in the post stroke period; A1C is the preferred test during this time. Manage according to the most recent ADA guidelines for glycemic control (see Diabetes chapter).
- Lifestyle modifications – after stroke, patients should be screened for obesity and counseled on lifestyle modifications for BP and CV risk reduction (e.g., smoking cessation, diet, exercise, weight loss).
    - Nutrition – it is reasonable to recommend sodium restriction to < 2.4 grams/day and further reduction to < 1.5 grams/day for greater BP reduction. Follow a Mediterranean-type diet emphasizing vegetables, fruits, whole grains, low-fat dairy products, poultry, legumes, and olive oil.
    - Physical activity – if capable, patients should engage in moderate-vigorous intensity exercise (at least 30 – 40 minutes most days of the week).
    - Weight reduction – recommended, if needed, to maintain a BMI 18.5 – 24.9 kg/m^2 and a waist circumference < 35 inches for women and < 40 inches for men.
    - Alcohol intake – limit to ≤ 2 drinks/day for males and ≤ 1 drink/day for females.
- Atrial fibrillation – patients with cardioembolic stroke due to atrial fibrillation should be placed on anticoagulant therapy to prevent future strokes (see Anticoagulation chapter).

Antiplatelet Therapy

For patients with noncardioembolic ischemic stroke or TIA, the use of antiplatelet agents, rather than oral anticoagulation, is recommended to reduce the risk of recurrent stroke, MI or death. Aspirin, aspirin plus extended-release dipyridamole, or clopidogrel are all acceptable options for initial therapy. For patients allergic to aspirin, clopidogrel should be used. The combination of aspirin and clopidogrel can be considered for initiation within 24 hours of a minor ischemic stroke or TIA and continued for 21 days. This combination should not be used long-term for secondary prevention of stroke or TIA as it increases the risk of hemorrhage. This is different than the recommendations for dual antiplatelet therapy in heart disease (see the Ischemic Heart Disease and Acute Coronary Syndromes chapters).

For patients who have an ischemic stroke or TIA while taking aspirin, there is no benefit to increasing the aspirin dose. Although alternative antiplatelet agents are often considered, no single agent or combination has been adequately studied in patients who have had an event while receiving aspirin.

Aspirin binds irreversibly to cyclooxygenase-1 and 2 (COX-1 and 2) enzymes, resulting in decreased prostaglandin (PG) and thromboxane A2 (TXA2) production; TXA2 is a potent vasoconstrictor and inducer of platelet aggregation. Aspirin has antiplatelet, antipyretic, analgesic, and anti-inflammatory properties. Dipyridamole inhibits the uptake of adenosine into platelets and increases cAMP levels, which inhibits platelet aggregation. Clopidogrel is a prodrug that irreversibly inhibits P2Y12 ADP-mediated platelet activation and aggregation. Ticlopidine, another P2Y12 ADP-receptor antagonist, is no longer used due to an undesirable side effect profile (e.g., life-threatening hematologic reactions).

DRUG	DOSING	SAFETY/SIDE EFFECTS/MONITORING
Aspirin *(Ascriptin, Bayer, Bufferin, Ecotrin,* *Durlaza,* others) **+ omeprazole *(Yosprala)*** OTC: tablet, chewable tablet, enteric-coated tablet, suppository Rx: ER capsule *(Durlaza)*, delayed-release tablet *(Yosprala)* See Pain chapter for more information	50-325 mg daily *Yosprala:* 81 mg/40 mg or 325 mg/40 mg daily Do not crush enteric-coated, delayed-release or ER products	**CONTRAINDICATIONS** NSAID or salicylate allergy; patients with asthma (due to risk of urticaria, angioedema, or bronchospasm), rhinitis, and nasal polyps; children and teenagers with viral infection (due to the risk of Reye's syndrome) **WARNINGS** Bleeding (including GI bleed/ulceration, others) – risk increased with heavy alcohol use or other drugs that ↑ bleeding risk (e.g., NSAIDs, anticoagulants, other antiplatelet agents) **SIDE EFFECTS** Dyspepsia, heartburn, nausea, tinnitus (in toxicity) **MONITORING** Bleeding, bruising **NOTES** *Yosprala* is indicated for patients who require aspirin but are at risk of developing aspirin-associated gastric ulcers; MedGuide required
Extended-release dipyridamole/ aspirin *(Aggrenox)* Capsule	200 mg/25 mg BID Intolerable headache: 200 mg/25 mg QHS (+ low-dose aspirin daily in the morning), then resume BID dosing within 1 week	As above for aspirin component plus: **WARNINGS** Chest pain (in patients with coronary artery disease), hypotension – both due to vasodilatory effects of dipyridamole **SIDE EFFECTS** Headache, diarrhea **NOTES** Not interchangeable with the individual components of aspirin and dipyridamole Amount of aspirin provided is not adequate for prevention of cardiac events (e.g., MI prevention)

Antiplatelet Therapy continued

DRUG	DOSING	SAFETY/SIDE EFFECTS/MONITORING
Clopidogrel ***(Plavix)*** Tablet	75 mg daily	**BOXED WARNING** Clopidogrel is a prodrug. Effectiveness depends on the conversion to an active metabolite, mainly by CYP450 2C19. Poor metabolizers of 2C19 exhibit higher cardiovascular events than patients with normal 2C19 function. Tests to check 2C19 genotype can be used as an aid in determining a therapeutic strategy. Consider alternative treatments in patients identified as 2C19 poor metabolizers. Refer to Pharmacogenomics chapter. **CONTRAINDICATIONS** Serious bleeding (e.g., GI bleed, intracranial hemorrhage) **WARNINGS** 2C19 inhibitors: avoid in combination with omeprazole or esomeprazole ↑ bleeding risk, stop 5 days prior to elective surgery (e.g., CABG) Thrombotic thrombocytopenic purpura (TTP) has been reported **SIDE EFFECTS** Gastrointestinal hemorrhage, hematoma, pruritus **MONITORING** Symptoms of bleeding, Hgb/Hct as necessary **NOTES** Used in stroke/TIA patients with a contraindication or allergy to aspirin; do not use in combination with aspirin long-term for stroke prevention MedGuide required

Antiplatelet Drug Interactions

- Most drug interactions are due to additive effects with other agents that can ↑ bleeding risk. See Drug Interactions chapter for drugs that can increase bleeding risk.
- Avoid using clopidogrel in combination with omeprazole and esomeprazole; use caution with other 2C19 inhibitors.

HEMORRHAGIC STROKE

Hemorrhagic strokes result in a significant amount of morbidity and mortality. Overall, treatment is largely supportive and includes airway management, establishing hemostasis, prevention or management of seizures, assessment for dysphagia, control of BP and blood glucose, and DVT prophylaxis. Hospitalized patients with hemorrhagic stroke should use intermittent pneumatic compression (devices for the legs to prevent DVT); anticoagulants should not be used while the patient is bleeding.

Drug Treatment of Intracerebral Hemorrhage (ICH)

There is a high risk for rapid neurological deterioration in the early hours of an ICH due to ongoing bleeding and enlargement of the hematoma in the brain. Patients with a severe coagulation factor deficiency or severe thrombocytopenia should receive appropriate factor replacement therapy or platelets, respectively. In patients with ICH who are anticoagulated, reversal of the anticoagulant effects should be considered (see Anticoagulation chapter for information on antidotes for the various anticoagulants). If there is clinical evidence of seizures, they should be treated, but prophylactic anticonvulsant medication should not be used.

One of the complications of ICH is increased intracranial pressure (ICP). Measures should be taken to lower the ICP; these include elevating the head of the bed by 30 degrees and using mannitol or hypertonic saline.

Mannitol

Mannitol produces an osmotic diuresis by increasing the osmotic pressure of glomerular filtrate, which inhibits tubular reabsorption of water and electrolytes and increases urinary output. Mannitol reduces ICP by withdrawing water from the brain parenchyma and excreting water in the urine.

DRUG	DOSING	SAFETY/SIDE EFFECTS/MONITORING
Mannitol *(Osmitrol)*	5%, 10%, 15%, 20%, 25% Mannitol 20%: 0.25-1 g/kg/dose IV Q6-8H PRN	**CONTRAINDICATIONS** Severe renal disease (anuria), severe dehydration, progressive heart failure, pulmonary edema or congestion **WARNINGS** May accumulate in the brain (causing rebound increases in ICP) if circulating for long periods of time as with continuous infusion; intermittent boluses preferred **SIDE EFFECTS** Fluid and electrolyte loss, dehydration, hyperosmolar-induced hyperkalemia, acidosis, ↑ osmolar gap, extravasation (vesicant) **MONITORING** Renal function, daily fluid intake and output, serum electrolytes, serum and urine osmolality, CPP, and ICP **NOTES** Maintain serum osmolality < 300-320 mOsm/kg

Drug Treatment of Acute Subarachnoid Hemorrhage (SAH)

SAH is bleeding that occurs in the space between the brain and the surrounding membrane (subarachnoid space). SAH usually results from rupture of a cerebral aneurysm and presents with severe headache, often described as the worst headache the patient has ever experienced. Surgical clipping or endovascular coiling, to completely obliterate the aneurysm, should be performed when feasible to prevent rebleeding. Vasospasm can occur 7 – 21 days after the bleed, causing delayed cerebral ischemia; oral nimodipine can be used to prevent vasospasm. The use of prophylactic anticonvulsants may be considered in the immediate post-hemorrhagic period to prevent seizures. The routine use of long-term anticonvulsants is not recommended, but may be considered for patients with known risk factors for delayed seizure disorder (e.g., prior seizure, intracerebral hematoma).

Nimodipine

Nimodipine is a dihydropyridine calcium channel blocker that is more selective for cerebral arteries due to increased lipophilicity.

DRUG	DOSING	SAFETY/SIDE EFFECTS/MONITORING
NiMODipine *(Nymalize)* Capsule, oral solution	60 mg PO Q4H for 21 days Start therapy within 96 hours of SAH onset Swallow capsules whole; administer on an empty stomach, at least 1 hour before or 2 hours after meals Patients with cirrhosis: 30 mg PO Q4H for 21 days (closely monitor)	**BOXED WARNING** Do not administer nimodipine IV or by other parenteral routes; death and serious life-threatening adverse events (including cardiac arrest, cardiovascular collapse, hypotension, and bradycardia) have occurred when the contents of nimodipine capsules have been inadvertently injected parenterally (see Notes) **CONTRAINDICATIONS** Use in combination with strong inhibitors of CYP 3A4 (see Drug Interactions below) – ↑ risk of significant hypotension **SIDE EFFECTS** Hypotension, bradycardia, headache, nausea, edema **MONITORING** CPP, ICP, BP, HR, neurological checks **NOTES** If capsules cannot be swallowed, contents may be withdrawn with a parenteral syringe, then transferred to an oral syringe that cannot accept a needle and that can only administer medication orally or via nasogastric tube; label oral syringes "For Oral Use Only" or "Not for IV Use"; pharmacy should draw up the medication to reduce medication errors

Nimodipine Drug Interactions

- Nimodipine is a major substrate of 3A4; strong 3A4 inhibitors (e.g., clarithromycin, some protease inhibitors, ketoconazole, nefazodone) are contraindicated. Strong 3A4 inducers (e.g., rifampin, carbamazepine, phenytoin, St. John's Wort) can decrease the levels of nimodipine and should be avoided. Avoid grapefruit juice.

GASTROESOPHAGEAL REFLUX DISEASE & PEPTIC ULCER DISEASE

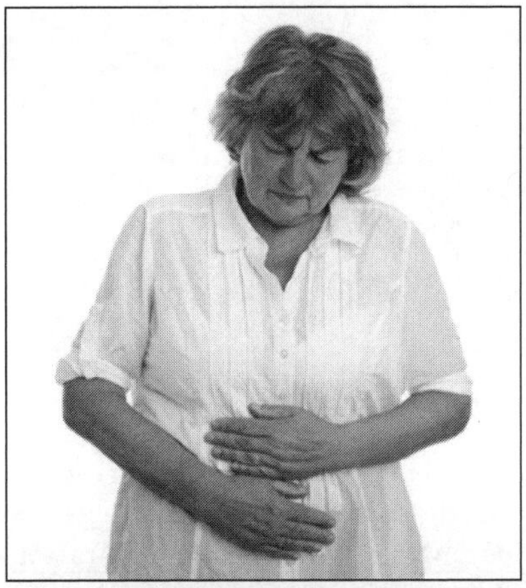

GUIDELINES/REFERENCES

Katz PO, Gerson LB, Vela MF. Guidelines for the diagnosis and management of gastroesophageal reflux disease. *Am J Gastroenterol.* 2013;108:308-28.

Fallone CA, Chiba N, Van Zanten et al. The Toronto Consensus for the Treatment of *Helicobacter pylori* Infection in Adults. *Gastroenterology.* 2016;151:51-69.

Additional guidelines included with the online course.

GASTROESOPHAGEAL REFLUX DISEASE

Background

Parietal cells in the epithelial lining of the stomach have receptors for histamine, acetylcholine, and gastrin. These substances stimulate secretion of hydrochloric acid (HCl) by acting on the H^+/K^+-adenosine triphosphatase (ATPase) pump, also known as the proton pump. Acidic gastric contents are normally prevented from backflow into the esophagus by a protective ring of muscle fibers called the lower esophageal sphincter (LES). Patients with gastroesophageal reflux disease (GERD) have reduced LES pressure (muscle tone); thus, gastric contents backflow into the esophagus.

Typical symptoms of GERD include heartburn (daytime or nocturnal), hypersalivation, and regurgitation of acidic contents into the mouth or throat. Less common symptoms include epigastric pain, nausea, cough, sore throat, hoarseness, and chest pain, which can be difficult to distinguish from cardiac pain. Diagnosis is based on patient-reported symptoms (duration, daytime and/or nocturnal occurrence), frequency (≥ 2 times per week), and risk factors (e.g., family history, diet and eating habits, sleep position); invasive testing is not required when typical symptoms are present.

GERD can decrease quality of life and lead to esophageal erosion, strictures, bleeding and Barrett's esophagus (abnormal cell growth of the esophageal lining which can lead to esophageal cancer).

Treatment Principles

The vast majority of patients self-treat with OTC products and do not seek medical attention unless this fails. It is common for a pharmacist to be the first healthcare encounter for a patient with GERD symptoms. Patients with alarm symptoms [odynophagia (painful swallowing), dysphagia, frequent nausea and vomiting, hematemesis, black bloody stools, unintentional weight loss] and those who do not respond to lifestyle modification and/or self-treatment with OTC products after 2 weeks should be referred for further evaluation.

Treatment should include lifestyle modifications and drugs. Infrequent heartburn (< 2 times per week) can be treated with OTC antacids, or PRN histamine-2 receptor antagonists (H2RAs). An 8-week course of a proton pump inhibitor (PPI) is the initial drug treatment of choice for GERD, and is used to heal any erosive esophagitis. There are no major efficacy differences between the various PPIs. After 8 weeks, therapy should be interrupted; if symptoms return, maintenance therapy is needed.

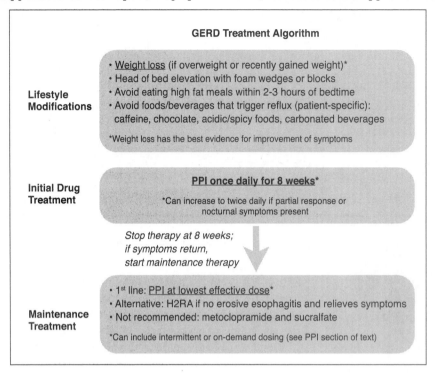

GERD Treatment Algorithm

Lifestyle Modifications

- Weight loss (if overweight or recently gained weight)*
- Head of bed elevation with foam wedges or blocks
- Avoid eating high fat meals within 2-3 hours of bedtime
- Avoid foods/beverages that trigger reflux (patient-specific): caffeine, chocolate, acidic/spicy foods, carbonated beverages

*Weight loss has the best evidence for improvement of symptoms

Initial Drug Treatment

PPI once daily for 8 weeks*

*Can increase to twice daily if partial response or nocturnal symptoms present

Stop therapy at 8 weeks; if symptoms return, start maintenance therapy

Maintenance Treatment

- 1st line: PPI at lowest effective dose*
- Alternative: H2RA if no erosive esophagitis and relieves symptoms
- Not recommended: metoclopramide and sucralfate

*Can include intermittent or on-demand dosing (see PPI section of text)

DRUG TREATMENT

Antacids

Antacids work by neutralizing gastric acid (producing salt and water), thus increasing gastric pH. Since antacids do not require systemic absorption, they provide relief within minutes but the duration of relief is short (30 – 60 minutes). This makes antacids most suitable for mild, infrequent symptoms. In 2016, the FDA issued a safety warning for consumers about the serious bleeding risk with antacids containing aspirin (e.g., *Alka-Seltzer Original*); see Patient Counseling section.

DRUG	DOSING	SAFETY/SIDE EFFECTS/MONITORING
Calcium carbonate *(Tums*, others) **Magnesium *[Phillips Milk of Magnesia (MOM)*,** others] **Magnesium + (aluminum or calcium) combo *(Mylanta Supreme*,** *Gaviscon, Rolaids*, others) **Magnesium + aluminum + simethicone (anti-gas) *(Maalox Advanced Max Strength, Mylanta Classic*,** others) Sodium bicarbonate + aspirin + citric acid *(Alka-Seltzer Original)*	Many formulations including suspensions, chewable tablets, capsules Dosing varies by product; many require administration 4-6 times per day	**WARNINGS** Aluminum and magnesium: can accumulate with severe renal dysfunction (not recommended if CrCl < 30 mL/min); risk of bleeding with aspirin-containing products (see Patient Counseling section) **SIDE EFFECTS** Unpleasant taste Calcium: constipation, bloating, belching Aluminum: constipation, hypophosphatemia Magnesium: loose stools (use with aluminum may counter-balance) **NOTES** Calcium-containing antacids may be preferred in pregnancy (see Drug Use in Pregnancy and Lactation chapter) *Alka-Seltzer Original* contains > 500 mg Na which can worsen edema in patients with heart failure or cirrhosis

Histamine-2 Receptor Antagonists

H2RAs reversibly inhibit H2 receptors on gastric parietal cells, which decreases gastric acid secretion. H2RAs are used PRN for infrequent or mild heartburn. They can be used as maintenance therapy for GERD in patients without esophageal erosions or for patients who complete 8 weeks of PPI therapy and are able to remain symptom-free on an H2RA. This could decrease side effects associated with long-term use of PPIs. If used for ulcer healing or hypersecretory conditions (e.g., Zollinger-Ellison syndrome), higher doses are needed.

DRUG	DOSING	SAFETY/SIDE EFFECTS/MONITORING
Famotidine ***(Pepcid, Pepcid AC, Pepcid AC Max Strength)*** Tablet, chewable tablet, suspension, injection **+ calcium carbonate and magnesium hydroxide** ***(Pepcid Complete)*** Chewable tablet + ibuprofen 800 mg *(Duexis)*	**OTC** 10-20 mg 1-2 times daily PRN **Rx** 20 mg BID	**WARNINGS** Confusion, usually reversible [risk factors: age > 50, severely ill, renal or hepatic impairment (see Notes)]; vitamin B12 deficiency with prolonged use (≥ 2 years) Famotidine: ECG changes (QT prolongation) with renal dysfunction Ranitidine: ↑ ALT **SIDE EFFECTS** Headache, agitation/vomiting in children < 1 year Cimetidine (high doses): gynecomastia, impotence **NOTES** Onset of relief: within 60 minutes Duration: 4-10 hours May be used in pregnancy when clinically indicated Decrease dose when CrCl < 50 mL/min (famotidine, ranitidine, nizatidine); CrCl < 30 mL/min (cimetidine) Cimetidine can ↑ SCr, without causing renal impairment Tachyphylaxis (tolerance to acid suppressing effects) can occur if used on a scheduled basis Avoid cimetidine entirely due to drug interactions and side effects To relieve symptoms, take PRN; to prevent symptoms, take PRN 30-60 minutes before food or beverages that cause heartburn
RaNITIdine ***(Zantac, Zantac Acid Reducer****, Deprizine FusePaq Compounding Kit)* Tablet, capsule, suspension, syrup, injection	**OTC** 75-150 mg 1-2 times daily PRN **Rx** 150 mg BID	
Nizatidine *(Axid)* Tablet (OTC), capsule, oral solution	**OTC** 75 mg 1-2 times daily PRN **Rx** 150 mg BID	
Cimetidine *(Tagamet)* Tablet, oral solution	**OTC** 200 mg 1-2 times daily PRN **Rx** 400 mg Q6H	

Proton Pump Inhibitors

PPIs irreversibly bind to the gastric H^+/K^+-ATPase pump in parietal cells. This shuts down the proton pump and blocks gastric acid secretion. PPIs are the most effective agents for GERD; an 8-week course of treatment is recommended for relief of symptoms and to heal erosions that may be present. All PPIs have similar efficacy, although an individual patient may respond better to one agent over another. If used for maintenance therapy long-term, the lowest effective dose should be used and the need for treatment should be assessed regularly. Intermittent use (PPI taken for a short period of time after relapse of GERD symptoms) and on-demand use (PPI taken only when symptoms occur) are additional options.

Recommended Administration of Oral PPIs

DRUG	TIMING
Dexlansoprazole *(Dexilant, Dexilant SoluTab)*	Capsule: without regard to meals (pre-meal if needed for symptoms) ODT: 30 minutes before meal
Esomeprazole magnesium *(Nexium)*	60 minutes before breakfast
Lansoprazole *(Prevacid, Prevacid SoluTab)*	Before breakfast (time not specified)
Omeprazole *(Prilosec)*	Before meal (time not specified)
Omeprazole + sodium bicarbonate *(Zegerid)*	60 minutes before breakfast (can control nocturnal symptoms if also given at bedtime)
Pantoprazole *(Protonix)*	30 minutes before breakfast
RABEprazole *(Aciphex, AcipHex Sprinkle)*	Capsule sprinkles: 30 minutes before meal Tablet: with or without food

DRUG	DOSING	SAFETY/SIDE EFFECTS/MONITORING
Omeprazole *(PriLOSEC, PriLOSEC OTC*; *First-Omeprazole, Omeprazole+Syrspend SF Alka suspension compounding kits)* Tablet (OTC), capsule, packet + sodium bicarbonate *(Zegerid, Zegerid OTC)* Capsule, packet **+ aspirin** 81 or 325 mg ***(Yosprala)*** Tablet	*Prilosec*: 20 mg daily *Zegerid:* dosing by omeprazole component (20 mg daily)	**WARNINGS** *C. difficile*-associated diarrhea (CDAD), osteoporosis-related fractures, hypomagnesemia, vitamin B12 deficiency with prolonged use (≥ 2 years), acute interstitial nephritis (hypersensitivity reaction), cutaneous and systemic lupus erythematosus **SIDE EFFECTS** Headache, nausea, diarrhea (all mild and infrequent) IV *Protonix*: thrombophlebitis, severe skin reactions (SJS/TEN)
Pantoprazole *(Protonix)* Tablet, injection, packet	40 mg daily	**NOTES** Onset in 1-3 hours, duration > 24 hrs for most PPIs
Lansoprazole *(Prevacid, Prevacid SoluTab, Prevacid 24H-OTC*, *First-Lansoprazole suspension compounding kit)* Capsule, ODT, suspension	15-30 mg daily	May be used in pregnancy when clinically indicated Pantoprazole and esomeprazole are the only PPIs available IV Do not crush, cut, or chew tablets or capsules
Dexlansoprazole *(Dexilant, Dexilant SoluTab)* Capsule, ODT	30-60 mg daily	Dexlansoprazole, esomeprazole, lansoprazole, omeprazole, and rabeprazole capsules can be opened (not crushed) and mixed in applesauce if patient cannot swallow pills
Esomeprazole magnesium *(NexIUM, NexIUM 24HR-OTC, NexIUM IV)* Capsule, injection, packet + naproxen 375 or 500 mg *(Vimovo)* Tablet	20-40 mg daily (esomeprazole base)	*Zegerid* 20 mg and 40 mg have the same Na bicarbonate content (300 mg); do not substitute two 20 mg capsules/packets for one 40 mg capsule/packet because the patient will recieve twice the amount of Na; caution in patients on Na restricted diet (e.g., heart failure, cirrhosis)
RABEprazole *(Aciphex, AcipHex Sprinkle)* Tablet, capsule sprinkle	20 mg daily	Suspension kits contain pre-measured powdered drug, suspension liquid (with flavoring) and mixing tools MedGuide required

Risks Associated with Acid-Suppression Therapy

Long-term use of PPIs causes chronic changes in gastric pH. This can promote growth of microorganisms and increase the risk of GI infections, including *C. difficile*, and possibly pneumonia (due to reflux of gastric contents beyond the oral cavity). PPIs also increase the risk of osteoporosis and fractures. For these reasons, the updated Beers Criteria recommend that PPIs not be used beyond 8 weeks in elderly patients unless there is a clear indication (e.g., high risk due to chronic NSAID use, demonstrated need for maintenance therapy). Since H2RAs can cause adverse CNS effects, the Beers Criteria recommend avoiding use in elderly patients with delirium (or high risk of), dementia or cognitive impairment.

Other Agents

Other agents historically used for GERD treatment include the cytoprotective agents, misoprostol and sucralfate, and the prokinetic agent, metoclopramide. There is currently no role for these agents in the management of GERD and they are not recommended by guidelines. Misoprostol and sucralfate can be used for peptic ulcer disease, which is discussed later in the chapter. Metoclopramide, and erythromycin, are most commonly used when patients have coexisting gastroparesis.

Metoclopramide

Metoclopramide is a dopamine antagonist. At higher doses, it blocks serotonin receptors in the chemoreceptor zone of the CNS (see Oncology I chapter). It also enhances the response to acetylcholine in the upper GI tract, causing enhanced motility and accelerated gastric emptying (peristaltic speed) and ↑ LES tone.

DRUG	DOSING	SAFETY/SIDE EFFECTS/MONITORING
Metoclopramide ***(Reglan**, Metozolv ODT)* Tablet, ODT, oral solution, injection	10-15 mg QID 30 min before meals and at bedtime Not recommended for use > 12 weeks	**BOXED WARNING** Can cause tardive dyskinesia (serious movement disorder, often irreversible); there is increased risk with high doses, long-term therapy (> 12 weeks) and in elderly patients **CONTRAINDICATIONS** GI obstruction, perforation or hemorrhage, history of seizures, pheochromocytoma, combination with other agents likely to increase extrapyramidal symptoms (EPS) **WARNINGS** Depression, EPS (including acute dystonia), parkinsonian-like symptoms, rare neuroleptic malignant syndrome (NMS) **SIDE EFFECTS** Drowsiness, restlessness, fatigue, cardiovascular (hypertension, pro-arrhythmic), diarrhea **NOTES** ↓ dose in patients with CrCl < 40 mL/min (use 50% of normal dose) CNS side effects are dose-related and more common in the elderly – use with caution and dose-adjust in renal impairment Avoid use in patients with Parkinson's disease Metoclopramide has a short duration of action (food must be present in gut) MedGuide required

DRUG INTERACTIONS

There are many types of interactions between acid-suppressing drugs and other medications. This section highlights the most important interactions for antacids, H2RAs and PPIs, but it is not all-inclusive. As appropriate, refer to other chapters (e.g., HIV, Hepatitis & Liver Disease, Infectious Diseases).

Antacids, H2RAs and PPIs

- Some drugs require an acidic gut for absorption, including enteric-coated or delayed-release products that can dissolve and release prematurely if the gastric pH is increased. Key drugs with decreased absorption when given concurrently with antacids, H2RAs and PPIs are listed in the table.
  - Due to the short duration of action of antacids, this type of interaction can often be alleviated by separating administration of the interacting drugs (see Antacids section below).
  - The following agents should be avoided completely when taking H2RAs or PPIs: delavirdine, dasatinib, pazopanib, and the delayed-release formulation of risedronate *(Atelvia)*. Erlotinib, rilpivirine and velpatasvir/sofosbuvir *(Epclusa)* are additional agents that should be avoided in combination with PPIs.

Antacids

- In addition to decreasing absorption of drugs that require an acidic pH, antacids can decrease absorption of some drugs by binding or adsorbing to them. It is necessary to separate administration of antacids from these agents. The specific window of separation can vary depending on the drug being used; for most products, avoiding antacids 2 – 4 hours before or 2 – 6 hours after is recommended.

KEY DRUGS WITH DECREASED ABSORPTION

Agents that require an acidic gut (absorption ↓ by antacids, H2RAs and PPIs)	Oral drugs/drug classes that antacids bind
■ Antiretrovirals: delavirdine (NNRTI), rilpivirine (NNRTI), atazanavir (PI)	■ Antiretrovirals (Integrase Inhibitors): dolutegravir, elvitegravir, raltegravir
■ Antivirals: ledipasvir, velpatasvir/sofosbuvir	■ Bisphosphonates
■ Azole antifungals: itraconazole, ketoconazole, posaconazole oral suspension*	■ Isoniazid
■ Cephalosporins (oral): cefditoren, cefpodoxime, cefuroxime	■ Mycophenolate
■ Iron products	■ Quinolones
■ Mesalamine	■ Sotalol
■ Risedronate delayed-release	■ Steroids (esp. budesonide)
■ Tyrosine kinase inhibitors: dasatanib, erlotinib, pazopanib, others	■ Tetracyclines (less of a concern with doxycycline and minocycline)
	■ Thyroid products

**Posaconazole oral suspension: absorption decreased by H2RAs and PPIs only*

H2RAs

- Use caution with CNS depressants due to the risk of additive delirium, dementia, and cognitive impairment, especially in the elderly. Use lower doses in elderly patients with renal impairment.
- Avoid using famotidine with highest risk QT-prolonging drugs.

- Cimetidine is a moderate inhibitor of CYP450 2C19 and a weak inhibitor of other enzymes (e.g., 3A4 and 1A2). Avoid use with dofetilide and use caution with many other drugs, including amiodarone, CCBs, clopidogrel, phenytoin, SSRIs, theophylline, and warfarin.

PPIs

- All PPIs inhibit 2C19; most are weak inhibitors but omeprazole and esomeprazole are moderate inhibitors. PPIs may ↑ levels of citalopram, phenytoin, tacrolimus, voriconazole and warfarin. Do not use PPIs with nelfinavir.
- PPIs may decrease the effectiveness of clopidogrel via 2C19 inhibition. If using these agents together, avoid omeprazole and esomeprazole.
- PPIs may inhibit renal elimination of methotrexate, leading to ↑ serum levels and risk of methotrexate toxicities.

Metoclopramide

- Avoid in patients receiving medications for Parkinson's disease (antagonistic effect). Avoid in combination with antipsychotic agents, droperidol, promethazine, tetrabenazine, and trimetazidine due to an increased risk of adverse effects. When used in combination with SSRIs, SNRIs or TCAs, monitor for possible EPS, NMS, and serotonin syndrome.

PEPTIC ULCER DISEASE

Background

Peptic ulcer disease (PUD) occurs from mucosal erosion within the gastrointestinal tract. Unlike gastritis, the ulcers in PUD extend deeper into the mucosa. Most ulcers occur in the duodenum but a small percentage also occur in the stomach. The three most common causes of PUD are *Helicobacter pylori (H. pylori)*-positive ulcers, nonsteroidal anti-inflammatory drug (NSAID)-induced ulcers and stress ulcers which occur in the presence of critical illness and in mechanically-ventilated patients (see Critical Care chapter). *H. pylori*, a spiral-shaped, pH sensitive, gram-negative bacterium that lives in the acidic environment of the stomach, is responsible for the majority of peptic ulcers (70 – 95%). Less common causes of PUD are hypersecretory states (e.g., ↑ gastric acid in Zollinger-Ellison syndrome), viral infections (e.g., cytomegalovirus), radiation therapy and infiltrative diseases (e.g., Crohn's Disease).

Under normal conditions, a physiologic balance exists between gastric acid secretion and the gut's mucosal defense and repair mechanisms, which include mucus and bicarbonate secretion, mucosal blood flow, prostaglandin synthesis, cellular regeneration, and epithelial cell renewal. These mechanisms protect the GI mucosa from damage caused by NSAIDs (including aspirin), *H. pylori*, acid, pepsin, and other GI irritants.

Symptoms

The primary symptom of PUD is dyspepsia, a gastric pain which can feel like a gnawing or burning sensation in the middle or upper stomach. The pain is usually most bothersome between meals or during the night. If the ulcer is duodenal (usually caused by *H. pylori*), eating generally lessens the pain. With gastric ulcers (primarily from NSAIDs), eating generally worsens the pain. Other symptoms include heartburn, belching, bloating, cramping, nausea and anorexia.

H. pylori Diagnostic Tests

H. pylori infection, if left untreated, can lead to gastric cancer. The infection should be treated if testing is positive. Common, non-invasive, diagnostic tests for *H. pylori* include the urea breath test (UBT), which identifies gas (CO_2) produced by the bacteria, and the fecal antigen test, which detects *H. pylori* in the stool. Discontinue PPIs, bismuth and antibiotics 2 weeks prior to these tests to avoid false negative results.

H. pylori Treatment

There are several combination regimens available to treat *H. pylori* (see table). The American College of Gastroenterology (ACG) guidelines recommend triple therapy with a PPI + two antibiotics (clarithromycin and amoxicillin) for 14 days. Due to recent failures with triple therapy (often due to clarithromycin resistance), quadruple therapy is now first-line in some countries outside of the U.S. and is used increasingly here. The ACG guidelines do not yet state this recommendation, however the more recent Toronto Consensus guidelines recommend against the use of triple therapy first-line unless clarithromycin resistance rates are low (< 15%) and local eradication rates are high (> 85%). They also recommend 14 days of treatment for all cases of *H. pylori*.

First-Line *H. pylori* Treatment Regimens

DRUG REGIMEN	NOTES
Triple Drug Therapy: Take for 14 days	
PPI BID (or esomeprazole 40 mg daily) + **Amoxicillin 1,000 mg BID +** **Clarithromycin 500 mg BID** (*Prevpac*, includes the PPI lansoprazole)	Penicillin or macrolide allergy: replace amoxicillin or clarithromycin with metronidazole 500 mg BID in this regimen or use alternative therapy below See GERD section for PPI side effects and Infectious Diseases I chapter for more information on the antibiotics *Prevpac* contains all medications on one blister card; take entire contents of one card each day for 14 days
Quadruple Therapy: Take for 10-14 days **(Use first-line if high local resistance rates to clarithromycin, triple therapy failed, or cannot tolerate amoxicillin and clarithromycin)**	
PPI BID (or esomeprazole 40 mg daily) + **Bismuth subsalicylate 525 mg QID +** **Metronidazole 250-500 mg QID +** **Tetracycline 500 mg QID** Or 3-in-1 combination product: Bismuth subcitrate potassium 420 mg QID + metronidazole 375 QID + tetracycline 375 mg QID (*Pylera*) + PPI	Tinidazole may be substituted for metronidazole If patient cannot tolerate a PPI, substitute H2RA (e.g., ranitidine 150 mg BID, famotidine 40 mg daily, nizatidine 150 mg BID) Swallow all capsules in the *Pylera* regimen (3 capsules per dose) **Alcohol use** Do not use metronidazole **Pregnancy/children** Do not use tetracycline during pregnancy or in children < 8 years of age **Salicylate allergy** Do not use bismuth subsalicylate

Other *H. pylori* Treatments

Sequential therapy is treatment with a PPI plus amoxicillin for 5 days, followed by triple therapy with a PPI, clarithromycin and metronidazole or tinidazole for the remaining 5 days. This therapy is not recommended by guidelines and is not well tested in the U.S.

Do not make drug substitutions in *H. pylori* eradication regimens. H2RAs should not be substituted for a PPI, unless the patient cannot tolerate a PPI. Likewise, other antibiotics within a class should not be substituted (for example, do not use ampicillin instead of amoxicillin). If the PPI is continued beyond 14 days, this is to help ulcer healing for a short period of time; it should not be continued indefinitely.

Drug Interactions

- Refer to previous sections for drug interactions with H2RAs and PPIs and Infectious Diseases I chapter for drug interactions with antibiotics.

Non-Steroidal Anti-Inflammatory Drug-Induced Ulcers

Background

Non-steroidal anti-inflammatory drugs (NSAIDs), including aspirin, can cause gastric mucosal damage by two mechanisms: direct irritation of the gastric epithelium and systemic inhibition of prostaglandin synthesis (by inhibiting COX-1). The chronic use of NSAIDs increases the risk for gastric (GI) ulcers. Patients are at high-risk if they have risk factors shown in the table.

RISK FACTORS FOR NSAID-INDUCED ULCERS
Age > 60 years
History of PUD (including *H. pylori*-induced)
High-dose NSAIDs
Using > 1 NSAID (e.g., NSAID plus aspirin)
Concomitant anticoagulant, steroids, or SSRIs

Prevention and Treatment

The choice of NSAID can be important when assessing the risk for GI ulcers and bleeding. NSAIDs with selective inhibition of COX-2 (e.g., celecoxib) have decreased GI risk but increased cardiovascular (CV) risk. Traditional NSAIDs that approach the selectivity of celecoxib are meloxicam, nabumetone, diclofenac and etodolac. Naproxen may be the preferred NSAID in patients with low-moderate GI risk and high CV risk.

Patients with high GI risk using non-selective NSAIDs can use concurrent PPI therapy to prevent or decrease the risk of ulcers and bleeding. The long-term risks of acid-suppression treatment need to be considered. The cytoprotective agent, misoprostol, is an alternative option to a PPI, but diarrhea, cramping and its four times per day dosing contribute to poor patient compliance. A COX-2 selective agent, with or without a PPI, can be used in patients who do not have CV risk factors. Since all NSAIDs elevate blood pressure and decrease renal blood flow, they should be used with caution in any person with cardiovascular or renal disease. If possible, both non-selective NSAIDs and COX-2 selective agents should be avoided in patients with both high GI and high CV risk.

If an ulcer develops, it should be treated with a PPI for 8-weeks and NSAIDs should be discontinued. If PPIs cannot be used, high dose H2RAs or sucralfate are other options. If NSAID therapy cannot be stopped, using a more selective COX-2 inhibitor and/or adding concurrent PPI or misoprostol to NSAID therapy should be considered. Combination products specifically marketed to reduce the risk of NSAID-induced ulcers include ibuprofen/famotidine *(Duexis)*, naproxen/esomeprazole *(Vimovo)* and diclofenac/misoprostol *(Arthrotec)*; these are indicated to relieve symptoms of osteoarthritis and rheumatoid arthritis in patients at risk of GI ulcers. *Yosprala*, a combination of aspirin and omeprazole, was approved in 2016 for secondary prevention of cardiovascular and cerebrovascular events in patients at risk for aspirin associated ulcers.

Cytoprotective Drugs

Misoprostol is a prostaglandin E1 analog that replaces the gastro-protective prostaglandins removed by NSAIDs. Sucralfate is in a sucrose-sulfate-aluminum complex and can interact with albumin and fibrinogen to form a physical barrier over an open ulcer. This protects the ulcer from further insult by HCl acid, pepsin, and bile and allows it to heal.

DRUG	DOSING	SAFETY/SIDE EFFECTS/MONITORING
MiSOPROStol *(Cytotec)* Tablet + diclofenac 50 mg *(Arthrotec)*	200 mcg QID with food; if not tolerated, may ↓ to 100 mcg QID; take with meals and at bedtime	**BOXED WARNING** Abortifacient – warn patients not to give this drug to others; do not use to ↓ NSAID-induced ulcers in women of childbearing potential unless capable of complying with effective contraceptive measures **SIDE EFFECTS** Diarrhea, abdominal pain **NOTES** Safety issue - see Pregnancy chapter Use of psyllium *(Metamucil)* may help decrease diarrhea
Sucralfate *(Carafate)* Tablet, suspension	1 g tablets QID before meals and at bedtime	**WARNING** Caution in renal impairment; sucralfate is in an aluminum complex and can accumulate **SIDE EFFECTS** Constipation **NOTES** Drink adequate fluids and use laxatives PRN for constipation Difficult to use due to binding interactions (separate antacids by 30 minutes and other drugs 2 hrs before and 4 hrs after)

PATIENT COUNSELING

Antacids, H2RAs, and PPIs

- Lifestyle counseling: refer to treatment algorithm.
- If you are self-treating your heartburn with medication for more than 14 days, or more than 2 times per week, you should discuss your symptoms with a healthcare provider.
- Seek urgent or emergent care if you have trouble or pain when swallowing food, bloody stools or vomit with blood or material that looks like coffee grounds.
- This medication can prevent other drugs from getting into the body. Check with a healthcare provider to see if you need to separate this medication from other drugs you are taking.

Antacids

- This medication provides immediate relief, but lasts only about 30 – 60 minutes. If you need a medication that lasts longer, please ask your healthcare provider.
- Do not use aluminum or magnesium products if you have kidney disease, or antacids with sodium if you require a sodium restricted diet (e.g., heart failure, high blood pressure, kidney disease).
- Magnesium-containing products can cause loose stools. Aluminum-containing products can cause constipation.
- Antacids with aspirin (e.g., *Alka-Seltzer Original)* have caused serious bleeding events and should be avoided. Your risk of bleeding is higher if you are > 60 years of age, have a history of stomach ulcers or bleeding problems, take blood-thinning medication, steroids, OTC pain relievers (e.g., *Motrin, Aleve)* or drink more than three alcoholic beverages per day.

H2RAs

- This medication provides heartburn relief in about 30 – 45 minutes and lasts 4 – 10 hours. If your symptoms remain bothersome, discuss with your healthcare provider.

- If elderly: this medication can cause you to be confused, dizzy or have memory problems. This can be more likely if you also have kidney disease. If you notice these symptoms, you should discuss them with your healthcare provider.

PPIs

- It is important to take this medication correctly to stop heartburn and other reflux symptoms. Some products work best when taken 30 – 60 minutes before a meal, often breakfast; others can be taken without regard to meals. Refer to the Recommended Administration of Oral PPIs chart and counsel according to the specific product.
- This medication does not work immediately; you need to take it everyday, as instructed, to get relief.
- Your risk of getting severe diarrhea, caused by an infection in your intestines, is increased with this medication. Call your healthcare provider if you have watery stool, stomach pain and a fever that does not go away.
- Using this medication for longer than a year can increase your risk of bone fractures. Make sure your calcium and vitamin D intake is optimal. Calcium citrate products may work best.
- You should not stop this medication abruptly as you may experience acid rebound. Discuss how to stop treatment with your healthcare provider.
- This medication can cause low levels of magnesium in your body. Tell your healthcare provider right away if you have dizziness, jitteriness, abnormal heartbeat, seizures, jerking movements or shaking, or weak, cramping or aching muscles.
- *Prevacid SoluTab* contains the sweetener aspartame. Do not use if you have phenylketonuria (PKU).
- Do not crush or chew any tablets or capsules. *Prevacid SoluTab* and *Dexilant SoluTab* should be placed on the tongue and allowed to dissolve; any small particles can be swallowed without water.

Metoclopramide

- Do not drive, operate machinery, or perform other dangerous tasks until you know how this drug affects you.
- Avoid drinking alcohol while taking this drug. Alcohol may increase drowsiness and dizziness.
- Contact your healthcare provider right away if you experience any unusual body movements, such as shakiness, stiffness, or uncontrollable movements of the mouth, tongue, cheeks, jaw, arms, or legs.

H. pylori Counseling

- For all *H. pylori* regimens: these medications are used together for stomach ulcers caused by an infection. It is very important that you take the medication as prescribed and complete the course of treatment.
- It is common to have some diarrhea while taking these medications. If it becomes severe or watery, contact your healthcare provider. Other side effects to watch for are headache, a bad taste in the mouth, or any sign of allergy, like a skin rash.
- A darkening of your tongue and stool may occur. It goes away when you stop taking this medication.
- *Prevpac:* each card has your dose (4 pills) for the morning and the evening. Take your dose before breakfast and before dinner.
- *Pylera:* to treat your stomach ulcers correctly, you will need two prescriptions, *Pylera* and a prescription for an acid reducing medication. You will take the acid reducing medication, as directed, for the same number of days as *Pylera*, but you should not continue taking it after that unless your healthcare provider has said to continue. You will take Pylera (3 capsules) 4 times each day (after breakfast, lunch, dinner and at bedtime), with a full glass of water. Swallow the capsules whole.
- You should avoid alcohol products during treatment and for at least 3 days after stopping *Pylera* as you may have headaches, flushing, cramps and an upset stomach.

PRACTICE CASE

PATIENT PROFILE

Patient Name	Benjamin Spector
Address	10 Pine Place
Age:	72 **Sex:** Male **Race:** Caucasian **Height:** 5'6" **Weight:** 160 lbs
Allergies	Aspirin (hives)

DIAGNOSES

Prostate enlargement	Seasonal allergies, occasional bronchodilator
Parkinson's disease	MI x 2 (last MI ~8 years ago)
Dyslipidemia	GERD

MEDICATIONS

Date	No.	Prescriber	Drug & Strength	Quantity	Sig	Refills
6/23	35421	Cooper	Clopidogrel 75 mg	#30	1 PO daily	6
6/23	35422	Cooper	Protonix 40 mg	#30	1 PO daily	6
6/23	35423	Cooper	Pravastatin 20 mg	#30	QHS	6
6/23	35424	Cooper	Sinemet 25/250	#90	1 PO TID	6
6/23	35425	Cooper	Lisinopril 40 mg	#30	1 PO daily	6
6/23	35426	Cooper	Metoprolol 50 mg	#60	1 PO BID	6
			Albuterol inhaler	#1	Occasional use	4
			Loratadine 10 mg		1 tablet PRN	
11/1	42877	Kreinfeldt	Metoclopramide 10 mg	#120	1 PO QID	

LAB/DIAGNOSTIC TESTS

Test	Normal Value	Results Date: 11/1	Date: 6/23	Date:
Protein, T	6.2-8.3 g/dL			
Albumin	3.6-5.1 g/dL			
Alk Phos	33-115 units/L			
AST	10-35 units/L	28		
ALT	10-35 units/L	22		
TC	125-200 g/dL			
TG	<150 g/dL			
Na	135-146 mEq/L		137	
K	3.5-5.3 mEq/L		4.8	
Cl	98-110 mEq/L		105	
C02	21-33 mmHg		24	
BUN	7-20 mg/dL	26	22	
Creatinine	0.6-1.2 mg/dL	1.9	1.2	
Glucose	65-99 mg/dL			
Calcium	8.6-10.2 mg/dL			
WBC	4-11 cells/mm^3			
RBC	3.8-5.1 mL/mm^3			
Hemoglobin	Male: 13.8-17.2 g/dL Female: 12.1-15.1 g/dL			
Hematocrit	Male: 40.4-50.3% Female: 36.1-44.3%			
MCHC	32-36 g/dL			
MCV	80-100 μm			
Platelet count	140-400 x 10^3/mm^3			
TSH	0.4-4.0 mIU/L			
FT4	4.5-11.2 mcg/dL			
Hgb A1c	4-6%			

ADDITIONAL INFORMATION

Date	Notes
11/1 (today)	PCP (Copper) on vacation. Reports bothersome heartburn and reflux after eating dinner and during sleep. Eats dinner at 8:30 pm, falls asleep 9:30-10 pm. Enjoys black tea with honey each night after dinner.

Questions

1. Mr. Spector is using *Protonix* once daily. Which of the following is an appropriate substitution?

   a. Omeprazole
   b. Esomeprazole
   c. Pantoprazole
   d. Rabeprazole
   e. Lansoprazole

2. Mr. Spector is still experiencing symptoms despite his current therapy. The physician decided to initiate metoclopramide to control the reflux symptoms. A better option would be:

   a. Increase *Protonix* to 60 mg daily.
   b. Add ranitidine 75 mg at bedtime.
   c. Add magnesium citrate PRN.
   d. Add misoprostol 200 mcg QID.
   e. Add sucralfate 1 gram at bedtime.

3. Why should metoclopramide 10 mg PO QID be avoided in Mr. Spector? (Select **ALL** that apply.)

   a. It can worsen Parkinson's disease symptoms.
   b. It can worsen prostate disease symptoms.
   c. It can cause drowsiness and sleepiness.
   d. He is at higher risk for side effects due to his age.
   e. He is at higher risk for side effects because of his kidney function.

4. Mr. Spector can make several lifestyle changes that can help with his symptoms. Which of the following are correct counseling points the pharmacist can provide? (Select **ALL** that apply.)

   a. Avoid high-fat foods at dinner.
   b. Eat dinner at an earlier time.
   c. Change evening drink to a carbonated beverage.
   d. Elevate the head of the bed 6-8 inches.
   e. Lose weight to reach a more ideal body weight.

5. Mr. Spector asks to try a different proton pump inhibitor for his GERD. Which of the following would be an appropriate alternative given his medication profile?

   a. *Prilosec*
   b. *Prevacid*
   c. *Dexilant*
   d. A or B
   e. B or C

Questions 6-14 are not based on the above case.

6. An elderly female presents to the pharmacy. She does not have health insurance coverage. Which of the following PPIs is available over-the-counter? (Select **ALL** that apply.)

   a. *Zegerid*
   b. *Prevacid*
   c. *Prilosec*
   d. *Protonix*
   e. *Nexium*

7. A patient has entered the pharmacy and asked the pharmacy technician to help her locate the store-brand version of *Pepcid*. Which of the following medications should the technician select?

   a. Famotidine
   b. Cimetidine
   c. Ranitidine
   d. Omeprazole
   e. Lansoprazole

8. Which of the following proton pump inhibitors is available in an IV formulation? (Select **ALL** that apply.)

   a. *Dexilant*
   b. *Nexium*
   c. *Protonix*
   d. *AcipHex*
   e. *Prilosec*

9. An elderly female patient has hypertension and heartburn. Her family states she has trouble swallowing large pills. She failed H2RA therapy and has been well-controlled on a PPI. She is currently using *Nexium* 40 mg daily. Which of the following would be a better option?

   a. *Gaviscon*
   b. *Alka-Seltzer Original*
   c. *Zegerid*
   d. *Prevacid SoluTab*
   e. *Maalox Advanced Maximum Strength*

10. A 46 year-old man has received a prescription for lansoprazole 15 mg daily, amoxicillin 500 mg BID and clarithromycin 500 mg BID for *H. pylori* treatment. Choose the correct statement:

    a. Contact the prescriber to correct the dose of lansoprazole.
    b. Contact the prescriber to correct the doses of lansoprazole and amoxicillin.
    c. Contact the prescriber to correct the doses of clarithromycin and amoxicillin.
    d. Contact the prescriber to correct the doses of lansoprazole and clarithromycin.
    e. Fill as written.

11. A 16 year-old patient has the following allergies noted on her patient profile: ciprofloxacin, aspirin and erythromycin. The allergic reaction is not listed, and the patient is not available by phone. You wish to fill the prescription for *H. pylori* therapy, which includes rabeprazole, amoxicillin and clarithromycin. Choose the correct statement:

    a. It is safe to fill; most allergies to erythromycin are gastrointestinal.
    b. It is safe to fill; there is no cross-reaction with these agents.
    c. It is not safe to fill due to the use of amoxicillin in a patient with ciprofloxacin allergy.
    d. It is not safe to fill due to the patient's age.
    e. It is not safe to fill until the erythromycin allergy is clarified.

12. Proton pump inhibitors can increase the risk of: (Select **ALL** that apply.)

    a. Bone fractures
    b. *C. difficile* infection
    c. Stroke
    d. Hypomagnesemia
    e. Dementia

13. A pharmacist is dispensing levofloxacin. Which of the following are correct counseling points? (Select **ALL** that apply.)

    a. Take this medication 2 hours before or 2 hours after taking any products containing magnesium, aluminum, or calcium, iron, zinc including vitamins, supplements and dairy products.
    b. Do not use sunlamps while using this therapy.
    c. You can stop taking this medication as soon as you feel better.
    d. You may experience stomach upset, including loose stools and nausea.
    e. Do not take if you are allergic to penicillin.

Answers

1-c, 2-b, 3-a,c,d,e, 4-a,b,d, 5-e, 6-a,b,c,e, 7-a, 8-b,c, 9-d, 10-b, 11-e, 12-a,b,d, 13-a,b,d

CONSTIPATION & DIARRHEA

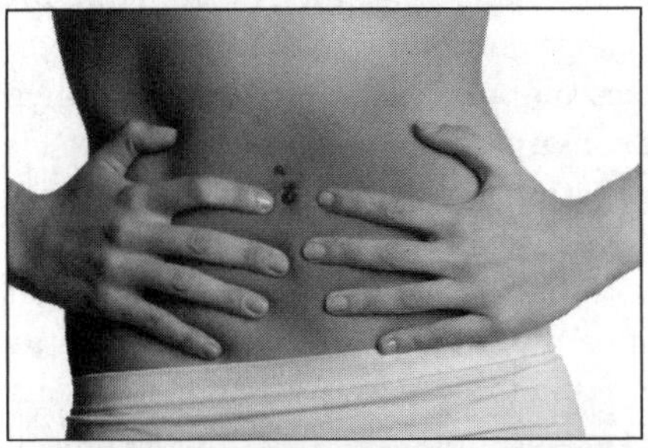

GUIDELINES/REFERENCES

American Gastroenterological Association, Bharucha AE, Dorn SD et al. American Gastroenterological Association Medical Position Statement on Constipation. *Gastroenterology.* 2013; 144:211–217.

CONSTIPATION

Background

Constipation is generally defined as infrequent stool passage (no bowel movements after 3 days) or difficulty in passing stools (e.g., straining, lumpy/hard stools, incomplete evacuation, pushing for more than 10 minutes, digital evacuation of stool, or sensation of incomplete evacuation). Constipation can be caused by lifestyle, drugs, GI disorders, pregnancy, and/or other medical conditions (see box that follows). If the cause of constipation is unknown, it is idiopathic. When constipation persists for several weeks or longer, it is chronic. Lifestyle measures to reduce constipation are preferred; however, if symptoms do not improve and/or if a constipating drug cannot be stopped, drug therapy for constipation can be used. When idiopathic constipation occurs frequently and is associated with chronic or recurrent abdominal discomfort, relieved by defecation, it is termed irritable bowel syndrome with constipation (IBS-C).

Drug Treatment

The AGA guidelines recommend gradually increasing fiber intake (dietary and as supplements) with the possibility of adding on a relatively inexpensive osmotic agent (milk of magnesia or polyethylene glycol). These are available OTC. Milk of magnesia contains magnesium and is not used with severe renal impairment. Polyethylene glycol is available OTC as *MiraLax* and by prescription in a larger container.

LIFESTYLE MEASURES TO REDUCE CONSTIPATION

- Correct fluid intake (64 oz – caution with CVD)
- Limit caffeine and alcohol (to avoid dehydration)
- Replace refined foods with whole grain products, bran, fruits & vegetables, beans
- Increase physical activity
- Do not delay going to the bathroom when the urge to defecate is present; may need to schedule time (important for young children)

If the patient needs to defecate, a suppository (bisacodyl or glycerol) will provide fast relief. Preferably, these should be administered 30 minutes after a meal when GI peristalsis has increased, but they can be used at any time of day. Oral stimulants (senna, bisacodyl) can be added on at bedtime, preferably at the lowest dose and for the shortest period of time. Senna is the usual first-line oral stimulant agent and is given as 2 tablets at bedtime. These agents take ~10 hours to work and the patient should have a bowel movement the following morning.

CONDITIONS/DRUGS THAT ARE CONSTIPATING

Medical conditions where constipation is common

Cerebrovascular events	Multiple sclerosis
Parkinson's disease	Irritable bowel syndrome (constipation-predominant)
Spinal cord tumors	Anal disorders (anal fissures, fistulae, rectal prolapse)
Diabetes	
Hypothyroidism	

Medications that are constipating

Opioids	Aluminum antacids (magnesium often in combination with aluminum to counteract effect)
Anticholinergic drugs	Aluminum complex in other drugs [sucralfate (*Carafate*)]
Antihistamines, phenothiazines, tricyclic antidepressants, antispasmodics, urge incontinence drugs [especially darifenacin *(Enablex)]*	Tramadol, tapentadol
Non-DHP calcium channel blockers, especially verapamil	Colesevelam
Clonidine	Milnacipran
Bismuth	Ranolazine
Iron (use docusate to avoid hard, compact stools)	Varenicline
NSAIDs	5-HT3 receptor antagonists (e.g., ondansetron)
	Phentermine/topiramate
	Aripiprazole

Fiber products (such as psyllium) are the first line treatment in most cases, and the treatment of choice in pregnancy. In addition to providing benefit for constipation, psyllium modestly improves cholesterol and blood glucose levels. Psyllium requires adequate fluids. An elderly female with incontinence would not likely be willing to increase fluid intake. Docusate, a commonly used stool softener, would be reasonable. Patients of any age using iron supplements will generally require docusate. Iron makes the stool hard and compact; it is difficult for fiber to mix in to soften the stool.

Patients using chronic opioids will often require a stimulant laxative because the opioids reduce the ability to push out the stool. Certain opioids are more constipating than others (e.g., morphine causes more constipation than fentanyl) but all are constipating, and some patients have more constipation than others. The stool softener docusate is given with the stimulant laxative if the stool is hard. If the stool is not hard but the patient cannot push it out ("moosh with no push"), a stimulant alone is the usual treatment. There are newer options for opioid-induced constipation (OIC) for patients who do not find relief with a stimulant + stool softener.

Laxative Agents Used for Bowel Prep

Laxatives can also be used for bowel prep before a colonoscopy. A successful colonoscopy requires a complete and thorough bowel prep. Several of the agents (the PEGs, and occasionally sodium phosphate) are used for both bowel prep and as laxatives. Sodium phosphate can cause fluid and electrolyte abnormalities, and is particularly risky in patients with renal or cardiac disease. Some PEG formulations are only used for bowel prep, such as *Golytely*. General counseling for bowel prep agents must include when to take the agent, what the patient can consume during the bowel cleansing process (i.e., after they have started using the bowel prep agent) and what must be avoided. Although usually safe and well-tolerated, in certain patients fluid and electrolyte loss could be critical. For this reason, some of the bowel prep agents require MedGuides. Use extra caution in patients with cardiovascular disease, renal insufficiency, and if taking diuretics (loops, due to additional fluid loss) and NSAIDs. Refer to the notes section on the Osmotics used for Whole Bowel Irrigation table for instructions on what is acceptable to consume with these agents.

Treatment for Constipation Associated with Irritable Bowel Syndrome

Many of the same modalities are used to treat IBS-C, including bulking agents and osmotic laxatives; additional agents may be needed to treat the pain/abdominal discomfort (e.g., dicyclomine). Lubiprostone and linaclotide are approved for both IBS-C and chronic idiopathic constipation (CIC). Due to cost considerations, polyethylene glycol is often used first and will provide relief in many cases.

Bulk-Forming Agents

Bulk-producing laxatives create a gel-like matrix in the stool, soaking up fluid in loose stool and adding bulk to the stool. This is first-line treatment (+/- an osmotic agent), and drug of choice in pregnancy.

DRUG	DOSING	SAFETY/SIDE EFFECTS/MONITORING
Psyllium *(Metamucil)* Capsule, powder Sugar-free options available	2.5-30 g/day in divided doses	**CONTRAINDICATIONS** Fecal impaction, GI obstruction (psyllium) **SIDE EFFECTS** Increased gas, bloating, bowel obstruction if strictures present, choking if powder forms are not taken with enough liquid. **NOTES** Onset of action 12 to 72 hours. Take 2 hours before/after other drugs (caution with other drugs that stick to fiber). Adequate fluids required. Inappropriate for patients who are on fluid restriction (e.g., heart failure), have difficulty swallowing (e.g., Parkinson's disease), or at risk for fecal impactment (e.g., intestinal ulcerations, stenosis).
Calcium polycarbophil *(FiberCon)* Caplet	1,250 mg 1-4 times/day	
Methylcellulose *(Citrucel)* Caplet, powder	Caplet: 1-6 g/day Powder: 2-6 g/day	

Osmotics

Osmotic laxatives cause fluid to be retained in the bowel lumen, with a net increase of fluid secretions in the small intestines. This distends the colon and increases peristalsis.

DRUG	DOSING	SAFETY/SIDE EFFECTS/MONITORING
Magnesium hydroxide *(Milk of Magnesia)*, magnesium citrate, magnesium sulfate	MgOH: 2.4-4.8 g QHS or in divided doses	**CONTRAINDICATIONS** Anuria (sorbitol), low galactose diet (lactulose), GI obstruction *(MiraLax)* **SIDE EFFECTS** Electrolyte imbalance, gas, dehydration Suppositories: rectal irritation **NOTES** Onset of action 30 minutes to 96 hours (oral), 15-30 minutes (rectal). Magnesium: caution with renal impairment. Suppository used commonly in children who need to defecate (soon).
Polyethylene glycol 3350 *(MiraLax,* *GaviLAX, GlycoLax, HealthyLax, PEGyLAX)*	17 g in 4-8 oz water daily	
Glycerin *(Pedia-Lax, Sani-Supp Fleet)* Suppository: adult & pediatric sizes	Insert 1 suppository PR	
Sorbitol Solution, enema	30-150 mL (70% solution) PO 120 mL (25-30% solution) PR	
Lactulose *(Constulose, Enulose, Generlac, Kristalose)*	10-20 g daily	

Stimulants

Stimulants/irritants work by reducing water and electrolyte absorption by stimulating colonic neurons and irritating the mucosal lining of the colon.

DRUG	DOSING	SAFETY/SIDE EFFECTS/MONITORING
Senna *(Ex-Lax, Senokot,* others)	17.2-50 mg PO daily-BID	**CONTRAINDICATIONS** Abdominal pain or obstruction (senna and bisacodyl); acute intestinal inflammation, colitis ulcerosa, appendicitis (senna); N/V (bisacodyl) **WARNINGS** Avoid use if stomach pain, N/V, or a sudden change in bowel movements which lasts > 2 weeks. **SIDE EFFECTS** Abdominal cramping, electrolyte imbalance, rectal irritation (supp) **NOTES** Onset of action 6-12 hours (oral), 15-60 minutes (rectal). Ideally, give 30 minutes after a meal (for ↑ peristalsis). Chronic opioid use often requires a stimulant laxative.
Bisacodyl *(Dulcolax,* others)	5-15 mg PO daily 10 mg PR daily; if too soft to insert, can cool in fridge or cold water first Do not crush or chew the enteric coated tablets, do not take within 1 hr of milk, dairy products or antacids.	

Emollients

Emollients soften fecal mass and make defecation easier. Emollients reduce the surface tension of the oil-water interface of the stool, allowing more water and fat to mix with the stool.

DRUG	DOSING	SAFETY/SIDE EFFECTS/MONITORING
Docusate sodium *(Colace)*, docusate calcium, docusate potassium	Docusate sodium: 50-360 mg PO daily or in divided doses 283 g/5 mL PR daily-TID	**CONTRAINDICATIONS** Abdominal pain, N/V, concomitant use with mineral oil **NOTES** Onset of action 12 to 72 hours (oral), 2-15 mins (rectal). Preferred when straining should be avoided (e.g., postpartum, post-MI, anal fissures, hemorrhoids). Use when stool is hard and/or dry.

Lubricants

Lubricants coat the bowel and the stool mass with a waterproof film. This keeps moisture in the stool and makes defecation easier.

DRUG	DOSING	SAFETY/SIDE EFFECTS/MONITORING
Mineral oil	Dose varies with product, take a multivitamin at a different time due to malabsorption of fat-soluble vitamins Do not take docusate and mineral oil together (absorption of mineral oil)	**CONTRAINDICATIONS** Age < 6 years, pregnancy, bedridden/aspiration risk, elderly, use > 1 week, difficulty swallowing **NOTES** Onset of action 6-8 hours (oral), 2-15 mins (rectal). Generally not recommended due to safety concerns; potential risk of aspiration (lipid pneumonitis).

Osmotics for Whole Bowel Irrigation

DRUG	DOSING	SAFETY/SIDE EFFECTS/MONITORING
Polyethylene glycol solution *(Colyte, GaviLyte-C, GaviLyte-G, Gavilyte-N, GoLYTELY, MoviPrep NuLYTELY, TriLyte)* *NuLytely, TriLyte* are sulfate-free; may taste better	Drink 240 mL every 10 minutes until 4 liters are consumed *MoviPrep:* Drink 240 mL every 15 minutes until 2 liters are consumed. Preferable to split the dose, such as half the night before, and half the morning of the procedure	**BOXED WARNING** Nephropathy *(OsmoPrep)* **CONTRAINDICATIONS** Ileus, gastrointestinal obstruction, gastric retention, bowel perforation, toxic colitis, toxic megacolon Acute phosphate nephropathy, gastric bypass or stapling surgery *(Prepopik)* Severe renal impairment, congestive heart failure, advanced liver disease *(OsmoPrep)* **SIDE EFFECTS** N/V, abdominal discomfort, bloating, arrhythmias, electrolyte abnormalities, seizures **NOTES** Onset of action within 1-6 hours. The following food items are acceptable to consume the day prior to colonoscopy: "Clear liquid diet," which can include water, clear broth (beef or chicken), juices without pulp (apple, white cranberry, white grape, lemonade), soda, coffee or tea (without milk or cream), clear gelatin (without fruit pieces), popsicles (without fruit pieces or cream). The following food items cannot be consumed prior to colonoscopy: Anything with red or blue/purple food coloring (including gelatin and popsicles), milk, cream, tomato, orange or grapefruit juice, alcoholic beverages, cream soups, and solid or semi-solid foods. MedGuide required for: *GoLYTELY, MoviPrep, NuLYTELY, Prepopik, OsmoPrep.*
Sodium picosulfate, magnesium oxide, and citric acid *(Prepopik)*	150 mL x 2 doses Combination stimulant laxative and osmotic, enables lower fluid intake	
Sodium phosphates *(OsmoPrep)*	32 tablets and 2 quarts of clear liquid	

Lubiprostone

Lubiprostone works by activating chloride channels in the gut, leading to increased fluid in the gut and peristalsis.

DRUG	DOSING	SAFETY/SIDE EFFECTS/MONITORING
Lubiprostone *(Amitiza)* Chronic idiopathic constipation (CIC) Opioid-induced constipation (OIC) with chronic non-cancer pain Irritable bowel syndrome with constipation (IBS-C) in adult women.	CIC & OIC: 24 mcg BID IBS-C: 8 mcg BID ↓ dose with mod-severe liver impairment	**CONTRAINDICATIONS** Mechanical bowel obstruction **SIDE EFFECTS** Nausea, diarrhea, headache, hypokalemia **NOTES** Take with food and water to decrease nausea. Swallow whole. Do not break, chew or crush. Consider alternative treatment in patients taking methadone (↓ lubiprostone effects).

Linaclotide

Linaclotide is an agonist of guanylate cyclase C, which increases chloride and bicarbonate secretion into the intestinal lumen, decreasing GI transit time. It is used for both chronic constipation, and for IBS with constipation.

DRUG	DOSING	SAFETY/SIDE EFFECTS/MONITORING
Linaclotide *(Linzess)* CIC in adults IBS-C in adults	CIC: 145 mcg PO daily IBS-C: 290 mcg PO daily Take at least 30 minutes before breakfast on an empty stomach.	**BOXED WARNING** Death due to dehydration in animal studies, avoid use in pediatric patients **CONTRAINDICATIONS** Age < 6 years, mechanical GI obstruction **SIDE EFFECTS** Diarrhea, abdominal distension, flatulence, headache **NOTES** Swallow whole; do not break, chew or crush. Keep in original container (contains desiccant). MedGuide required.

Peripherally-Acting Mu-Opioid Receptor Antagonist

Peripherally-acting mu-opioid receptor antagonists (PAMORAs) act on mu-opioid receptors found in the GI tract, decreasing constipation. Alvimopan is only for hospitalized patients and is given prior to surgery to reduce the risk of ileus that can occur post-op. Methylnaltrexone *(Relistor)* and naloxegol *(Movantik)* are only used in patients taking opioids who have opioid-induced constipation (OIC). Both of these agents are discussed in the Pain chapter.

DRUG	DOSING	SAFETY/SIDE EFFECTS/MONITORING
Alvimopan *(Entereg)* Post-surgical patients to ↓ risk of post-operative ileus REMS drug	12 mg PO, 30 min-5 hrs prior to surgery, and 12 mg BID for up to 7 days total (maximum 15 doses) Used inpatient only	**BOXED WARNING** Potential risk of MI with long-term use **CONTRAINDICATIONS** Patients who have taken therapeutic doses of opioids for more than 7 consecutive days prior to use **SIDE EFFECTS** ↓ K, dyspepsia, anemia, urinary retention, back pain

DIARRHEA

Background

Diarrhea occurs when there is an increase in the number of bowel movements or stools are more watery and loose than normal. When the intestines push stools through the bowel before the water in the stool can be reabsorbed, diarrhea occurs. Abdominal cramps, nausea, vomiting, or fever may occur along with the diarrhea. When idiopathic diarrhea is recurrent and associated with chronic or reoccurring abdominal discomfort, relieved by defecation, it is termed irritable bowel syndrome with diarrhea (IBS-D).

MEDICATIONS THAT CAN CAUSE DIARRHEA	
Antacids containing magnesium	Colchicine
Antibiotics, especially broad-spectrum antibiotics and clindamycin, erythromycin (due to prokinetic activity) – rule out *C. difficile* infection	Laxatives
Antineoplastics	Metoclopramide
	Misoprostol
	Quinidine
	Many drugs include diarrhea as a possible side effect

Most cases of diarrhea are viral, have a quick onset and usually resolve within a few days without treatment. Diarrhea can be idiopathic, caused by diseases, drugs, food poisoning or by consuming contaminated food/water (e.g., travelers diarrhea). *E. coli* is the most common bacterial cause. The treatment of diarrhea caused by a bacterial infection is discussed in the Infectious Diseases II chapter.

Patients who experience diarrhea after consuming milk or milk products could be lactose intolerant. Rule out lactose intolerance as the cause of the diarrhea by stopping the use of dairy products. Lactose intolerance can be confirmed through testing.

Non-Drug Treatment

Management of diarrhea includes fluid and electrolyte replacement; especially in moderate-severe cases and in the elderly, children, or adults with chronic medical conditions. For fluid and electrolyte loss, replace fluids with oral rehydration solutions (ORS), which are available at stores and pharmacies *(Pedialyte, Infalyte*, etc.) in developed countries. *Gatorade* or similar products can be used as alternatives.

Drug Treatment

Most patients with non-infectious diarrhea who require symptomatic relief, can use short-term bismuth subsalicylate *(Pepto-Bismol)* or loperamide if needed. Bismuth subsalicylate exhibits both antisecretory and antimicrobial effects when used as an antidiarrheal. Loperamide and diphenoxylate are antimotility agents that slow intestinal motility, prolonging water absorption.

Treatment for Diarrhea associated with Irritable Bowel Syndrome

In most cases, loperamide offers acceptable relief. Rifaximin *(Xifaxan)* is an antibiotic with approval for this condition. It is costly, and relapse often occurs within several months of treatment. Alosetron *(Lotronex)* is useful for women only, but has restricted use due to the risk of ischemic colitis. The pain/abdominal discomfort can be managed with additional agents, including antispasmodics (e.g., dicyclomine) and antidepressants in select patients.

Antidiarrheals

DRUG	DOSING	SAFETY/SIDE EFFECTS/MONITORING
Bismuth subsalicylate *(Pepto-Bismol,* others) Chewable tablet, suspension	525 mg Q 30-60 mins PRN or 1,050 mg Q 60 mins PRN Max 4,200 mg/day for 2 days	**CONTRAINDICATIONS** Salicylate allergy, concomitant use of salicylates, ulcer, coagulopathy, black/bloody stool **SIDE EFFECTS** Black tongue/stool, salicylate toxicity if used excessively (early s/sx include N/V, increased respiratory rate, tinnitus, diaphoresis) **NOTES** Caution in patients on aspirin therapy, anticoagulants, or those with renal insufficiency. Children and teenagers who are recovering from the flu, chickenpox, or other viral infections should not use this drug due to risk of Reye's syndrome.
Loperamide *(Imodium A-D, Loperamide A-D,* *Anti-Diarrheal, Diamode,* others)	4 mg PO after first loose stool, then 2 mg after each subsequent loose stool Max 16 mg/day Travelers diarrhea: max 8 mg/day	**CONTRAINDICATIONS** Abdominal pain without diarrhea, children < 2 years, acute dysentery (bloody diarrhea and high fever), acute ulcerative colitis, pseudomembranous colitis *(C. difficile)*, bacterial enterocolitis caused by invasive organisms (toxigenic *E. coli, Salmonella, Shigella*) **WARNINGS** QT prolongation, torsades de pointes, other ventricular arrhythmias, cardiac arrest, some resulting in death, with use of higher than recommended doses per day **SIDE EFFECTS** Abdominal cramping, constipation, nausea; potential serious heart problems from high doses with abuse/misuse **NOTES** Self-treatment should not be > 48 hours
Diphenoxylate/ atropine *(Lomotil)* Diphenoxylate 2.5 mg with atropine 0.025 mg C-V	Diphenoxylate 5 mg up to QID Max 20 mg/day	**CONTRAINDICATIONS** Diarrhea caused by enterotoxin-producing bacteria or pseudomembranous colitis, obstructive jaundice **SIDE EFFECTS** Sedation, constipation, urinary retention, tachycardia, blurred vision, dry mouth, depression **NOTES** Not recommended for use in children < 2 years. A subtherapeutic amount of atropine is include in the formulation to discourage abuse.

DRUG	DOSING	SAFETY/SIDE EFFECTS/MONITORING

Antispasmodic

DRUG	DOSING	SAFETY/SIDE EFFECTS/MONITORING
Dicyclomine ***(Bentyl)*** Tablet/capsule, solution	20 mg QID; max 80 mg/day for > 2 weeks (can use 40 mg QID for < 2 weeks if symptoms respond) Take 30-60 minutes before meals	**CONTRAINDICATIONS** GI obstruction, severe ulcerative colitis, reflux esophagitis, unstable cardiovascular status in acute hemorrhage, obstructive uropathy, breast feeding, narrow-angle glaucoma, myasthenia gravis, infants < 6 months of age **WARNINGS** Anticholinergic (use caution in patients 65 years and older, per Beer's Criteria), caution in mild-moderate ulcerative colitis (potential for toxic megacolon or paralytic ileus) **SIDE EFFECTS** Dizziness, dry mouth, nausea, blurred vision

Peripherally-Acting Mu-Opioid Receptor Agonist

Eluxadoline is a mu-opioid receptor agonist (in contrast to the PAMORAs, which are mu-receptor antagonists). While the PAMORAs compete and displace the binding of opioids to receptors in the periphery to reduce constipation, eluxadoline binds to the opioid receptors as an agonist to treat diarrhea. Patients who would use this drug would have IBS-D where the diarrhea is difficult to treat with usual measures. Patients without a gallbladder are at increased risk of sphincter of Oddi spasm. Signs and symptoms include right upper quadrant pain that may radiate to the back or shoulder and may be accompanied by N/V. This can lead to pancreatitis. The sphincter of Oddi is a muscular valve that controls the flow of digestive fluids/enzymes to the first part of the small intestine.

DRUG	DOSING	SAFETY/SIDE EFFECTS/MONITORING
Eluxadoline *(Viberzi)* C-IV REMS drug	100 mg PO BID (with gallbladder) 75 mg BID (without gallbladder) Take with food.	**CONTRAINDICATIONS** Biliary duct obstruction, sphincter of Oddi dysfunction/ disease, pancreatic disease, alcoholism, patients who drink > 3 alcoholic drinks/day, severe hepatic impairment (Child-Pugh class C), history severe constipation, known GI obstruction **WARNINGS** Potential risk of MI with long-term use. Sphincter of Oddi spasm, which can increase LFTs and cause pancreatitis. Increased risk of pancreatitis with > 3 alcoholic drinks/day. **SIDE EFFECTS** Constipation, nausea, abdominal pain, rash, dizziness LFTs, upper respiratory infections, nasopharyngitis **NOTES** Start with low dose and monitor for s/sx of sphincter of Oddi (e.g., abdominal pain, N/V) in patients without a gallbladder or consider alternative treatment.

Counseling for All Diarrhea Cases

- Contact your healthcare provider if you have a high fever (> 101°F), severe abdominal pain or blood in your stool that does not get better in 2 days. For female patients: contact your healthcare provider if you are pregnant.
- Drink fluids with electrolytes while you have diarrhea to prevent dehydration. *Pedialyte* and *Infalyte* are good options. *Gatorade* or similar products can also be used as an alternative.
- Additional counseling for parents of children with diarrhea:
  - If your child is less than 6 months you should have the infant seen by a healthcare provider.
  - If your child has diarrhea and fever/cold symptoms are present, aspirin should not be given. Aspirin rarely causes a serious condition called Reye's Syndrome in children. Aspirin should be avoided except under a healthcare providers care (it may rarely be used in a child with a heart condition, where benefit may outweigh risk). *Pepto-Bismol* should also be avoided. For the treatment of fever or mild pain, refer to the Pediatrics Conditions chapter.

Bismuth Subsalicylate Counseling

- Do not use if you have an allergy to bismuth, salicylates (including aspirin and NSAIDs, like ibuprofen).
- Tell your healthcare provider prior to starting this medicine if you are also taking a salicylate like aspirin.
- Do not give to children and teenagers who have flu signs, chickenpox, or other viral infections due to the chance of Reye's syndrome.
- Some products have phenylalanine. If you have PKU, do not use.
- This medicine may make your tongue and stool dark, this is normal. Contact your healthcare provider right away if you notice tarry or bloody stools or if you are throwing up blood or a substance that looks like coffee grounds.
- If you notice a ringing in the ears or a loss of hearing while taking this medicine, stop taking it and contact your healthcare provider.
- Do not take for longer than 7 days without the approval of your healthcare provider.

INFLAMMATORY BOWEL DISEASE

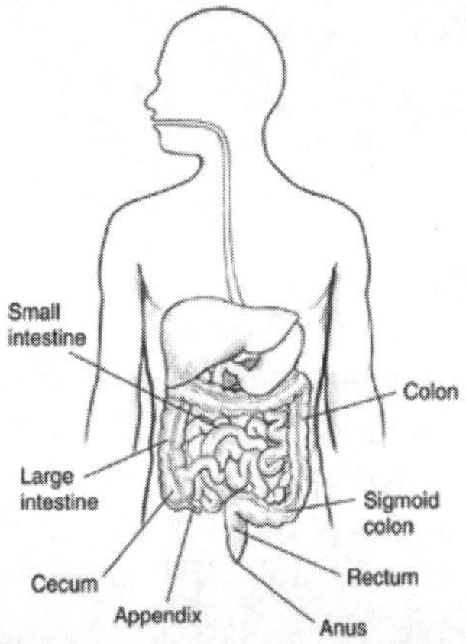

GUIDELINES/REFERENCES

Crohn's Disease Evaluation and Treatment: Clinical Decision Tool. *Gastroenterology* 2014;147:702-705. http://campaigns.gastro.org/algorithms/IBDCarePathway (accessed 2016 Nov 29).

Identification, Assessment, and Initial Medical Treatment of Ulcerative Colitis: Clinical Care Pathway. www.gastro.org/ucdecisiontool (accessed 2016 Nov 29).

World Gastroenterology Organization Global Guidelines: Inflammatory Bowel Disease. Updated August 2015. www.worldgastroenterology.org/global-guidelines/inflammatory-bowel-disease-ibd (accessed 2016 Nov 29).

BACKGROUND

Inflammatory bowel disease (IBD) is a group of inflammatory conditions of the colon and small intestine. The major types of IBD are ulcerative colitis and Crohn's disease. The classic symptom is bloody diarrhea. Other symptoms include rectal urgency, tenesmus (a feeling of having to pass stools, even if the colon is empty), abdominal pain, and in some cases, weight loss, night sweats, nausea, vomiting and constipation (e.g., ulcerative colitis limited to the rectum). IBD is a chronic, intermittent disease; symptoms may be mild to severe during flares (or exacerbations) and minimal or absent during periods of remission. Flares can occur at any time, and may be triggered by infections, use of NSAIDs, or certain foods. Food triggers are patient specific but can include fatty foods, and gas-producing foods (e.g., lentils, beans, legumes, cabbage, broccoli, onions). Food triggers can be avoided or food can be prepared in a way that improves tolerability.

IBD can be mistaken for irritable bowel syndrome (IBS), as they have similar symptoms (e.g., abdominal pain, bloating, gas, and either constipation or diarrhea). Unlike IBD, IBS does not cause inflammation and is not as serious of a condition. Drugs used to treat IBS primarily treat the constipation or diarrhea; refer to that chapter for drug specifics.

Ulcerative Colitis

Ulcerative colitis (UC) is characterized by mucosal inflammation confined to the rectum and colon with superficial ulcerations (in contrast to Crohn's disease, where the ulcers can be deep). When UC is limited to the descending colon and rectum, it is called distal disease and will be accessible with topical (rectal) treatment. Inflammation limited to the rectum is called proctitis. The larger the affected area (e.g., extensive UC), the worse the symptoms. When the disease flares, patients can have numerous stools per day, often with pain, which can significantly decrease quality of life. UC is classified as mild, moderate, severe or fulminant. Moderate disease is characterized by > 4 stools per day with minimal signs of toxicity and patients with severe disease have ≥ 6 bloody stools daily with evidence of toxicity [fever, tachycardia, anemia, or an elevated erythrocyte sedimentation rate (ESR)].

Crohn's Disease

Crohn's disease (CD) is characterized by deep, transmural (through the bowel wall) inflammation that can affect any part of the GI tract. The ileum and colon are most commonly affected. Damage to the bowel wall can cause strictures (narrowing of the bowel) and fistulas (abnormal connections or openings in the bowel). Symptoms of CD include chronic diarrhea (often nocturnal), abdominal pain, and weight loss. Perianal symptoms [e.g., bleeding, fissures (tears)] can be present before bowel symptoms.

CD and UC Comparison

CLINICAL FEATURES	CD	UC
Diarrhea	Bloody or non-bloody	Bloody
Smoking	Risk factor	Protective
Location	Entire GI tract (especially the ileum & colon)	Colon (especially the rectum)
Depth	Transmural	Superficial
Pattern	Non-continuous	Continuous
Fistulas/Strictures	Common	Uncommon

Lifestyle Measures, Supportive Care and Natural Products

As previously mentioned, patients with IBD should adapt their diet to avoid foods that are more likely to trigger flares. In general, eating smaller, more frequent meals that are low in fat and dairy products can be helpful. It is usually best to drink plenty of water, avoiding alcohol and caffeinated beverages, that can stimulate the GI tract, and carbonated beverages that can be gas-producing. The patient should watch for avoidable problems; both sorbitol and lactose are classified as excipients (or binders); they are present in various medications to help hold tablets together. Sorbitol is also used as a sweetener in some diet foods; it has laxative properties and can cause considerable GI distress in some patients. Lactose will worsen GI symptoms if the patient is lactose-intolerant.

Some patients may use antidiarrheals or antispasmodic agents [e.g., dicyclomine *(Bentyl)*] to help manage symptoms of diarrhea; these should be used cautiously, and under the supervision of a healthcare provider, as they may need to be avoided in select IBD patients (e.g., severe disease, acute exacerbations, post-bowel resection). See the Constipation & Diarrhea chapter for more information on these products. Vitamin supplements (e.g., B12, vitamin D, calcium, iron) can help prevent deficiencies related to malabsorption. Nicotine has been shown to worsen CD but can be protective in UC. Nicotine patches have been used as an adjunct therapy for UC; however, adverse effects (nausea, dizziness) limit the benefits.

The probiotics *Lactobacillus* or *Bifidobacterium infantis* can reduce abdominal pain, bloating, urgency, constipation or diarrhea in some patients. Fish oils with EPA and DHA (omega-3 fatty acids) can help fight inflammation, although the evidence for benefit is contradictory. Some natural products that may be useful include peppermint (in oils or teas), chamomile tea, green tea, and Indian frankincense gum resin.

DRUG TREATMENT

Treatments for IBD are used for induction of remission (they treat exacerbations or active disease) and/or maintenance of remission. Short courses of oral or IV steroids are commonly used to treat acute exacerbations in both UC and CD. Systemic steroids are not recommended for maintenance of remission and will usually be tapered over 8 – 12 weeks once remission is achieved.

In UC, aminosalicylates (active component is 5-aminosalicylic acid, or 5-ASA) are used for maintenance therapy in most patients with distal UC or mild extensive disease. For moderate-severe UC that extends beyond the colon and rectum, other immunosuppressive agents (e.g., thiopurines, anti-TNF agents, cyclosporine) can be used (see table on the following page).

For mild CD that is limited to the ileum and proximal colon, budesonide is preferred. In moderate-severe cases, immunosuppressive agents (e.g., thiopurines, anti-TNF agents, methotrexate) may be used; steroids may be needed for severe cases of CD. Integrin receptor antagonists (e.g., vedolizumab) are used in patients with IBD that is refractory to other therapies or that is steroid-dependent.

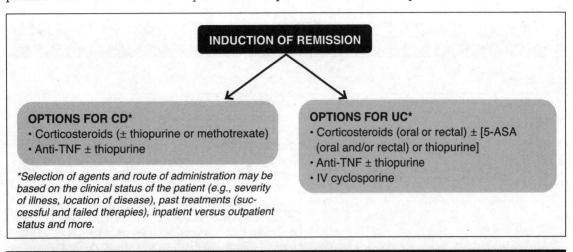

INDUCTION OF REMISSION

OPTIONS FOR CD*
- Corticosteroids (± thiopurine or methotrexate)
- Anti-TNF ± thiopurine

**Selection of agents and route of administration may be based on the clinical status of the patient (e.g., severity of illness, location of disease), past treatments (successful and failed therapies), inpatient versus outpatient status and more.*

OPTIONS FOR UC*
- Corticosteroids (oral or rectal) ± [5-ASA (oral and/or rectal) or thiopurine]
- Anti-TNF ± thiopurine
- IV cyclosporine

MAINTENANCE OF REMISSION: COMPARISON OF COMMON CD AND UC TREATMENTS

CROHN'S DISEASE	ULCERATIVE COLITIS
Mild disease of the ileum and/or right colon	**Mild disease**
■ Oral budesonide preferred	■ Mesalamine (5-ASA) rectal and/or oral preferred
Moderate-severe disease*	**Moderate-severe disease***
■ Anti-TNF agents**	■ Anti-TNF agents**
❑ Adalimumab *(Humira)*	❑ Adalimumab *(Humira)*
❑ Infliximab *(Remicade)*	❑ Infliximab *(Remicade)*
❑ Certolizumab *(Cimzia)*	❑ Golimumab *(Simponi)*
■ Thiopurine (azathioprine, mercaptopurine)	■ Thiopurine (azathioprine, mercaptopurine)
■ Methotrexate	■ Cyclosporine
Refractory to above treatments and/or corticosteroid dependent	**Refractory to above treatments and/or corticosteroid dependent**
■ Integrin receptor antagonists	■ Integrin receptor antagonists
❑ Natalizumab	❑ Vedolizumab
❑ Vedolizumab	

**Agents may be used as monotherapy or in combination*

***The biosimilars adalimumab-atto (Amjevita) and infliximab-dyyb (Inflectra) are also FDA approved for IBD*

Some of the more common drugs used to treat UC and CD are shown in the tables below. Additional agents [e.g., IV steroids, anti-TNF agents (infliximab, adalimumab, certolizumab), methotrexate] are discussed fully in the Systemic Steroids & Autoimmune Conditions chapter.

Corticosteroids

<table>
<tr><th>DRUG</th><th>DOSING</th><th>SAFETY/SIDE EFFECTS/MONITORING</th></tr>
<tr><td colspan="3">Oral Steroids</td></tr>
<tr><td>PredniSONE
Tablet (Deltasone)
Oral solution (PredniSONE Intensol)
Delayed-release tablet (Rayos)</td><td>5-60 mg daily</td><td rowspan="2">CONTRAINDICATIONS
Systemic fungal infections, live vaccines

SIDE EFFECTS
Short-term: ↑ appetite/weight gain, fluid retention, emotional instability (euphoria, mood swings, irritability), insomnia, GI upset, higher doses can cause an ↑ in BP and blood glucose
Long-term: adrenal suppression/Cushing's syndrome, immunosuppression/impaired wound healing, hypertension, hyperglycemia, cataracts, osteoporosis, others; refer to the Systemic Steroids & Autoimmune Conditions chapter

NOTES
All Steroids
For management of acute flares, avoid long-term use if possible
May use alternate day therapy (ADT) to ↓ adrenal suppression and other adverse effects
If used longer than 2 weeks, must taper to avoid withdrawal symptoms
If long-term use is required, assess bone density (optimize calcium and vitamin D intake and consider bisphosphonates if needed)

Budesonide
Undergoes extensive first-pass metabolism; ↓ systemic exposure than other oral steroids
Swallow whole – do not crush, chew or break</td></tr>
<tr><td>Budesonide (Entocort EC, Uceris)
Entocort EC: 3 mg extended release capsule (for CD only)
Uceris: 9 mg extended release tablet (for UC only)</td><td>Induction (CD and UC):
9 mg PO once daily in the morning for up to 8 weeks

Maintenance (CD only):
6 mg PO once daily for 3 months, then taper</td></tr>
<tr><td colspan="3">Rectal Steroids</td></tr>
<tr><td>Hydrocortisone (Cortifoam, Cortenema)</td><td>Induction and/or Maintenance
Cortenema: 1 enema (100 mg) QHS for 21 days or until remission, then taper
Cortifoam: 1 applicatorful (90 mg) 1-2 times daily for 2-3 weeks, then every other day thereafter; taper after long-term therapy</td><td rowspan="2">CONTRAINDICATIONS
Cortifoam: obstruction, abscess, perforation, peritonitis, fresh intestinal anastomoses, extensive fistulas and sinus tracts
Cortenema: ileocolostomy in immediate/early post-op period

NOTES
Rectal steroids are indicated for UC only; they have not been proven effective for maintenance of remission; maintenance use is limited to mild-moderate distal UC as an alternative to rectal and/or oral aminosalicylates
Budesonide rectal foam: propellant is flammable; avoid fire and smoking during and after use</td></tr>
<tr><td>Budesonide rectal foam (Uceris)</td><td>Induction
1 metered dose BID x 2 weeks, then 1 metered dose daily x 4 weeks
(1 metered dose = 2 mg budesonide)</td></tr>
</table>

Budesonide Drug Interactions

- Budesonide is a major substrate of CYP 3A4. Strong and moderate inhibitors of 3A4 should be avoided, including grapefruit juice and grapefruit products.
- Use of steroids with other immunosuppressants can increase the risk of serious adverse events.
- Antacids may cause enteric coated oral budesonide to dissolve prematurely due to ↑ gastric pH. Separate administration of antacids by two hours.

Aminosalicylates

Aminosalicylates are indicated for treatment of UC; the mechanism of action is unknown, but they appear to have a topical anti-inflammatory effect in the gastrointestinal tract. Mesalamine (5-ASA) is the primary aminosalicylate used in the U.S.; it is well tolerated and available in both oral and rectal formulations. The other aminosalicylates (sulfasalazine, balsalazide, olsalazine) are available in oral form only and must be converted to mesalamine to have an effect. Sulfasalazine is used less commonly due to the many side effects associated with the sulfapyridine component.

DRUG	DOSING	SAFETY/SIDE EFFECTS/MONITORING
Mesalamine ER ER capsules *(Apriso, Delzicol, Pentasa)* ER tablets *(Asacol HD, Lialda)* Enema *(Rowasa)* Suppository *(Canasa)*	**Induction** **(oral therapy for 6-8 weeks and/or rectal therapy for 3-6 weeks)** *Asacol HD:* 1.6 g PO TID *Delzicol:* 800 mg PO TID *Lialda:* 2.4-4.8 g PO daily *Pentasa:* 1 g PO QID Suppository: 1 g rectally QHS, retain for at least 1-3 hours Enema: 4 g rectally QHS, retain in the rectum overnight for approximately 8 hours **Maintenance** *Apriso:* 1.5 g PO daily *Delzicol*: 1.6 g PO in 2-4 divided doses *Lialda*: 2.4 g PO daily *Pentasa:* 1 g PO QID Enema: 2 g rectally QHS, or 4 g qHS every 2-3 days	**CONTRAINDICATIONS** Hypersensitivity to salicylates or aminosalicylates **WARNINGS** Acute intolerance syndrome (cramping, acute abdominal pain, bloody diarrhea); caution in patients with renal or hepatic impairment; delayed gastric retention (e.g., due to pyloric stenosis) may delay release of oral products in the colon; hypersensitivity reactions (including myocarditis, pericarditis, nephritis, hematologic abnormalities and other internal organ damage) – more likely with sulfasalazine than mesalamine; ↑ risk of blood dyscrasias in patients > 65 years of age *Apriso* contains phenylalanine; avoid in phenylketonuria (PKU) *Rowasa* enema contains potassium metabisulfite, a sulfite that may cause an allergic-type reaction **SIDE EFFECTS** Abdominal pain, nausea, headache, flatulence, eructation (belching), pharyngitis **MONITORING** Renal function, CBC, s/sx of IBD **NOTES** Mesalamine is better tolerated than other aminosalicylates Rectal mesalamine is more effective than oral mesalamine and rectal steroids for distal disease/proctitis in UC; can use oral and topical formulations together Swallow capsules and tablets whole; do not crush, chew, or break due to delayed-release coating *Apriso:* do not use with antacids (dissolution is pH-dependent)
SulfaSALAzine Tablets *(Azulfidine)* ER tablets *(Azulfidine EN-tabs)*	**Induction** 3-4 g PO divided TID or QID, titrate to 4-6 g PO QID **Maintenance** 2 g PO daily divided TID or QID	Refer to the Systemic Steroids & Autoimmune Conditions chapter **NOTES** Doses should be taken at ≤ 8 hour intervals May need to reduce dose if GI intolerance occurs

Aminosalicylates Continued

DRUG	DOSING	SAFETY/SIDE EFFECTS/MONITORING
Balsalazide Tablet *(Giazo)* Capsule *(Colazal)*	**Induction** *Colazal:* 2.25 g (three 750 mg capsules) PO TID for 8-12 weeks *Giazo* (approved in males only): 3.3 g (three 1.1 g tablets) PO BID for up to 8 weeks	**CONTRAINDICATION** Salicylate allergy **WARNINGS** Gastric retention (e.g., due to pyloric stenosis) may delay release of drug in the colon; acute intolerance syndrome; caution in patients with renal or hepatic impairment **SIDE EFFECTS** Headache, abdominal pain, N/V/D **MONITORING** Renal function, LFTs, s/sx of IBD **NOTES** *Colazal* capsule may be opened and sprinkled on applesauce; beads are not coated, so mixture can be chewed if needed; when used this way, it may cause staining of the teeth/tongue
Olsalazine *(Dipentum)* Capsule	**Maintenance** 500 mg PO BID Take with food	**CONTRAINDICATION** Salicylate allergy **SIDE EFFECTS** Diarrhea, abdominal pain **MONITORING** CBC, LFTs, renal function, symptoms of IBD

Thiopurines

The thiopurines, azathioprine and mercaptopurine, are immunosuppressive drugs, sometimes referred to as "immunomodulators". They do not have an FDA indication for IBD but are recommended as an option in guidelines for induction and maintenance of remission, often in combination with other drugs.

DRUG	DOSING	SAFETY/SIDE EFFECTS/MONITORING
AzaTHIOprine *(Azasan, Imuran)* Tablet, injection	1.5-3 mg/kg/day IV or PO Give 75% of dose if CrCl < 50 mL/min Give 50% of dose if CrCl < 10 mL/min PO: taking after meals or in divided doses may ↓ GI side effects	**BOXED WARNINGS** Chronic immunosuppression ↑ risk of malignancy in patients with IBD (especially lymphomas); mutagenic potential; risk for hematologic toxicities **WARNINGS** GI hypersensitivity reactions (severe N/V/D, rash, fever, ↑ LFTs); serious infections; hematologic toxicities (e.g., leukopenia, thrombocytopenia, anemia); patients with a genetic deficiency of thiopurine methyltransferase (TPMT) are at ↑ risk for myelosuppression; hepatotoxicity **SIDE EFFECTS** N/V/D, rash, ↑ LFTs **MONITORING** LFTs, CBC (weekly for 1st month), renal function, s/sx of malignancy **NOTES** Safety issue - see Pregnancy chapter Aminosalicylates inhibit TPMT; caution use in combination Allopurinol inhibits a pathway for inactivation of azathioprine; azathioprine dose reduction required if used in combination

Thiopurines Continued

DRUG	DOSING	SAFETY/SIDE EFFECTS/MONITORING
Mercaptopurine (*Purixan*) Tablet, oral suspension	1-1.5 mg/kg/day CrCl ≤ 50 mL/min: take Q48H	Same as azathioprine above (except no boxed warning) plus: **NOTES** Take on an empty stomach. Avoid old terms "6-mercaptopurine" and "6-MP"; they ↑ the risk of overdose due to administration of doses 6-fold higher than normal

Methotrexate and Cyclosporine

Methotrexate is an immunosuppressive drug with antiinflammatory properties. It does not have an FDA indication for IBD, but it is recommended by the guidelines for induction and maintenance of remission in moderate-severe CD in patients who cannot tolerate azathioprine. When used, it is dosed once weekly by IM or SC injection. See the Systemic Steroids & Autoimmune Conditions chapter for information on methotrexate. Cyclosporine is an immunosuppressive drug recommended for severe UC. It can be given orally or via IV continuous infusion. See the Transplant chapter for more information on cyclosporine.

Tumor Necrosis Factor Blocking (anti-TNF) Agents

The anti-TNF agents [infliximab, infliximab-dyyb (biosimilar), adalimumab, adalimumab-atto (biosimilar), certolizumab and golimumab] are monoclonal antibodies that bind to human tumor necrosis factor alpha, preventing induction of proinflammatory cytokines (e.g., interleukins). They are used in patients with moderate-severe UC or CD, often in combination with a thiopurine. These agents are discussed in the Systemic Steroids & Autoimmune Conditions chapter. See the Study Tips box earlier in the chapter for information on which specific anti-TNF agents are FDA approved for UC and CD.

Integrin Receptor Antagonists

Natalizumab and vedolizumab are monoclonal antibodies that bind to subunits of integrin molecules, blocking the ability of integrin to interact with adhesion molecules and preventing inflammatory cells from migrating into gastrointestinal tissue. They are indicated for induction and maintenance of remission in patients with IBD who have responded inadequately, or who cannot tolerate, conventional therapies or in patients who are steroid-dependent.

DRUG	DOSING	SAFETY/SIDE EFFECTS/MONITORING
Natalizumab (*Tysabri*) Injection Approved for Crohn's disease and multiple Sclerosis	300 mg IV over 1 hour every 4 weeks If taking steroids when initiating *Tysabri*, begin tapering when the onset of benefit is observed; stop *Tysabri* if patient cannot taper steroids within 6 months of initiation Discontinue if no response by 12 weeks	**BOXED WARNING** Progressive multifocal leukoencephalopathy (PML); PML is an opportunistic viral infection of the brain that leads to death or severe disability; monitor for mental status changes; risk factors include: anti-JCV antibodies, ↑ treatment duration and prior immunosuppressant use Only available through the REMS TOUCH Prescribing Program **WARNINGS** Herpes encephalitis and meningitis, hepatotoxicity, hypersensitivity (antibody formation), immunosuppression/infections **SIDE EFFECTS** Infusion reactions, headache, fatigue, arthralgia, nausea, rash, depression, gastroenteritis, abdominal/back pain **NOTES** Cannot be used with other immunosuppressants MedGuide required Stable in NS only; do not shake

Integrin Receptor Antagonists Continued

DRUG	DOSING	SAFETY/SIDE EFFECTS/MONITORING
Vedolizumab ***(Entyvio)*** Injection Approved for Crohn's disease and ulcerative colitis	300 mg IV at 0, 2, and 6 weeks, then every 8 weeks Discontinue if no benefit by week 14	**WARNINGS** Infusion reactions, hypersensitivity reactions, infections, liver injury, PML All immunizations must be up to date before starting therapy; should not receive live vaccines during therapy unless benefit outweighs risk **SIDE EFFECTS** Headache, nasopharyngitis, arthralgia, antibody development **MONITORING** LFTs, s/sx of infection, hypersensitivity, neurological symptoms (to monitor for PML), routine TB screening **NOTES** Refrigerate and store in original packaging Swirl during reconstitution, do not shake; after reconstitution, use immediately or refrigerate up to 4 hours (do not freeze) Infuse over 30 min Cannot be used with other immunosuppressants MedGuide required

PATIENT COUNSELING

Mesalamine

- Do not crush or chew long-acting formulations.
- *Asacol HD* and *Delzicol:* you may see a ghost tablet (empty shell) in the feces; the drug has been absorbed into your body and the tablet is empty.
- *Rowasa* enema: for best results, empty the bowel immediately before use.
    - *Rowasa* is an off-white suspension. Enema contents can darken over time when removed from the foil pouch. If the enema has dark brown contents, throw it away.
    - Remove the bottle from the pouch and shake well. Remove the protective sheath from the applicator tip. Hold the bottle at the neck to prevent any of the medication from being discharged.
    - Best results are obtained by lying on the left side with the left leg extended and the right leg flexed forward for balance. Gently insert the lubricated applicator tip into the rectum to prevent damage to the rectal wall, pointed slightly toward the navel.
    - Grasp the bottle firmly, and then tilt slightly so that the nozzle is aimed towards the back; squeeze slowly to instill the medication. Steady hand pressure will discharge most of the medicine. After administering, withdraw and discard the bottle.
    - Remain in position for at least 30 minutes, or preferably all night for maximum benefit.
    - *Rowasa* can cause staining of surfaces, including clothing and other fabrics, flooring, painted surfaces, marble, granite, vinyl and enamel. Take care in choosing a suitable location for administration of this product.
- *Canasa* suppository: for best results, empty your bowel immediately before use.
    - This medication should be used at bedtime. Detach one suppository from the strip. Remove the foil wrapper carefully while holding the suppository upright. Do not handle the suppository too much; it can melt from the heat from your hands and body.

- ❑ Insert the suppository, with the pointed end first, completely into your rectum, using gentle pressure. You may put a little bit of lubricating gel on the suppository if you have trouble.
- ❑ For best results, keep the suppository in your rectum for at least 1 – 3 hours.
- ❑ *Canasa* can cause staining of surfaces, including clothing and other fabrics, flooring, painted surfaces, marble, granite, vinyl and enamel. Keep *Canasa* away from these surfaces to prevent staining.

Hydrocortisone Rectal Foam *(Cortifoam)*

- Preparation: shake the foam container well for 5 – 10 seconds before each use. Hold the container upright on a level surface and place the tip of the applicator onto the nose of the container cap. Pull the plunger past the fill line on the applicator barrel. To fill the applicator barrel, press down firmly on the cap flanges, hold for 1 – 2 seconds and release. Wait 5 – 10 seconds for the foam to expand and fill the applicator barrel. Repeat until the foam reaches the fill line, then remove the applicator from the container.
- Use: hold the applicator firmly by the barrel (thumb and middle finger on the barrel "wings") and place the index finger on the plunger. Insert the tip gently into the anus and push the plunger to expel the foam. Withdraw the applicator. The foam container should never be inserted into the anus – only the applicator.
- After use, take apart and clean all parts with warm water for next use. Store at room temperature.
- Each aerosol container should deliver 14 doses.

Budesonide Rectal Foam *(Uceris)*

- This medication is for rectal use only. The *Uceris* rectal foam kit has 2 aerosol canisters and 28 lubricated applicators. Each canister contains 14 doses of foam.
- Empty your rectum completely before use. Attach a disposable applicator to the nozzle. Warm the canister in your hands and shake well for 10 – 15 seconds before using. Choose a position to administer – standing, lying or sitting on the toilet. The easiest way to use *Uceris* is to keep one foot on the floor and place the other foot onto a firm surface such as a stool or chair.
- Turn the canister upside down and place your forefinger on top of the pump dome. Insert the applicator into the rectum as far as it is comfortable. Push down with your forefinger on the pump dome one time and hold it for about 2 seconds. Release finger pressure on the pump dome and hold the applicator in place for 10 – 15 seconds. Remove the applicator from the anus, detach it from the canister and dispose of it in the plastic bag provided.
- Administer the evening dose before bedtime and try not to have a bowel movement until morning.
- Store at room temperature. The aerosol is flammable. Keep it away from fire, flames or smoking during and after use. Do not spray toward a flame. Do not puncture or burn the canisters.
- Do not use grapefruit or grapefruit juice while taking this medication. If you have been using grapefruit, do not change the amount without discussing first with your healthcare provider.

Oral Budesonide *(Entocort EC* and *Uceris)*

- Take this medication with a full glass of water before a meal. Do not crush, chew or break open the capsule.
- Tell your healthcare provider if you have changes in the shape or location of body fat (especially in your arms, legs, face, neck, breasts, and waist), high blood pressure, severe headache, fast or uneven heart rate, blurred vision, or a general ill feeling with headache, tiredness, nausea, and vomiting.
- You should have your blood pressure and blood sugar monitored on a regular basis.
- Do not use grapefruit or grapefruit juice products with this medication. If you have been using grapefruit, do not change the amount without discussing first with your healthcare provider.
- Avoid being near people who are sick or have infections.

PRACTICE CASE

Frank Clough: SOAP Note for 09/24
Age on DOS: 75 yrs, DOB: 01/14/1939

San Diego Medical Group
35 La Jolla Drive Suite 100 San Diego, CA 92130
(444) 444-4444

seen by: Alison James
seen on: Wednesday 24 September

Height:	Weight:	BMI:	Blood Pressure:	Temp:	Pulse:	Resp Rate:
65.0 in	148.0 lb	24.6	165 / 92 mmHg	98.9 F	97 bpm	16 rpm

Lots of diarrhea for the past few days and now there's blood in it

Mr. Clough presents with a 3 day history of 5-6 diarrhea episodes per day. He describes this as similar to his initial diagnosis of ulcerative colitis in Nevada about 5 months ago. He describes some cramping and bloating in the lower abdomen, but no other associated pain. He doesn't think the pain is worse or better with food, but he hasn't eaten much over the past few days. He has no nausea or vomiting. Today he noticed some streaks of blood in the diarrhea and his wife became concerned and made the appointment at the clinic. He states he is compliant with his mesalamine suppositories and they have worked well in controlling his UC over the past months until now. His usual diarrhea frequency is 1-2 episodes her day. Patient reports an allergy to penicillin which causes severe rash.

Past Medical History:
Ulcerative colitis (distal disease) and hypertension

Medications:
Canasa 1 gm suppository daily at HS x 5 months / Tenormin 100 mg daily x "many years"
Both prescribed by MD in Nevada and active. Patient states he is compliant.

Labs (reference range):
Na 139 mEq/L (135 - 145)
K 3.8 mEq/L (3.5 - 5)
Cl 100 mEq/L (95 - 103)
HCO3 26 mEq/L (24 - 30)
BUN 30 mg/dL (7 - 20)
SCr 1.4 mg/dL (0.6 - 1.3)
Glu 109 mg/dL (100 - 125)
WBC 8.6 cells/mm3 (4 - 11 x 10^3)
Hgb 16.8 g/dL (13.5 - 18 male, 12 - 16 female)
Hct 48 % (38 - 50 male, 36 - 46 female)
Plt 250 mm3 (150,000 - 450,000)

75 yo otherwise fairly healthy white gentleman here for an ulcerative colitis exacerbation.
(1) Ulcerative colitis (distal) exacerbation:
Patient has been well-controlled on mesalamine suppositories for his disease and finds this therapy acceptable. He has never required steroids of any kind. He is currently dehydrated as evidenced by objective data (HR and BUN/SCr ratio) and requires therapy to control the acute flare.
(2) Hypertension:
BP is not currently at goal. Since this is a new patient to our clinic, we may need to re-assess once he is more stable and rehydrated. Regardless, need to align therapy with JNC 8 guidelines.

Prednisone 10 mg daily for ulcerative colitis flare. Follow-up in clinic in 1 week.

Questions

1. The patient was originally prescribed mesalamine suppositories for distal disease classified as mild-moderate. Which of the following statements are correct? (Select **ALL** that apply.)
   a. Oral therapy is preferred for initial treatment.
   b. Mesalamine is available in oral and rectal (suppositories, enema) formulations.
   c. Sulfasalazine is preferred over mesalamine for distal disease.
   d. Mesalamine cannot be used in a sulfa allergy.
   e. Mesalamine is considered first-line therapy for distal disease.

2. Mesalamine rectal suppository counseling should include the following points: (Select **ALL** that apply.)
   a. Peel open the plastic and remove suppository prior to use.
   b. Handle unwrapped suppository as little as possible.
   c. Should be kept in the rectum for at least 1-3 hours.
   d. Lubricating gel may be used to ease application.
   e. Insert suppository just prior to a bowel movement.

3. The physician prescribed prednisone for the acute flare. Which of the following are short-term side effects that may occur and should be conveyed to the patient? (Select **ALL** that apply.)
   a. Elevated blood glucose
   b. Elevated blood pressure
   c. Osteoporosis
   d. Changes in mood
   e. Cataracts

4. Guidelines recommend against steroid treatment for long-term control of IBD symptoms; however, many patients use budesonide (or prednisone) daily. Which of the following are long-term side effects that may occur and should be conveyed to the patient? (Select **ALL** that apply.)
   a. Hepatotoxicity
   b. Poor wound healing
   c. Fat redistribution
   d. Adrenal suppression
   e. Peptic ulcers

Questions 5-6 are not based on the above case.

5. A female patient has failed her initial treatment for Crohn's disease, which included azathioprine and methotrexate. Her symptoms are described as severe. She is prescribed infliximab. Which of the following statements is correct?
   a. She can use *Enbrel* instead.
   b. She should have been prescribed *Tysabri* prior to use of infliximab.
   c. Infliximab suppositories are the preferred formulation.
   d. This medication comes in an IV formulation only.
   e. This medication can suppress TB activation.

6. A patient has been prescribed infliximab. Which of the following tests should be ordered prior to the start of therapy? (Select **ALL** that apply.)
   a. Pulmonary function
   b. TSH and FT4
   c. CBC
   d. TB
   e. HBV

Answers

1-b,e, 2-a,b,c,d, 3-a,b,d, 4-b,c,d,e, 5-d, 6-c,d,e

72

SEXUAL DYSFUNCTION

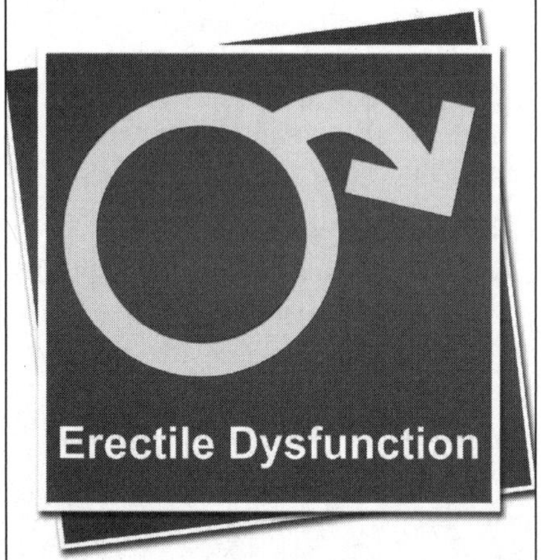

BACKGROUND

This chapter will focus on erectile dysfunction in males and hypoactive sexual desire disorder in females. Erectile dysfunction (impotence), refers to difficulty getting or sustaining an erection that is firm enough for sex. This is a common type of sexual dysfunction in men and can generally be treated with phosphodiesterase (PDE)-5 inhibitors. Males can experience other types of sexual dysfunction, including problems with ejaculation and low libido, which is sometimes treated with testosterone and is discussed in the chapter that covers hormone treatment.

In women, sexual dysfunction can be due to either an inability to reach orgasm (anorgasmia), painful intercourse, or hypoactive (i.e., lower than normal) sexual desire disorder (HSDD). Flibanserin (*Addyi*) is the sole drug for females with sexual dysfunction, and claims to treat HSDD. In clinical trials, 1 of every 11 females using flibanserin had an increase of one-half of a satisfying sexual event per month, compared to placebo. It is approved for premenopausal women only, and causes fainting, which can put the woman in a dangerous situation.

GUIDELINES/REFERENCES

Montague DK, Jarow JP, Broderick GA, et al. For The Erectile Dysfunction Guideline Update Panel. Chapter 1: The Management Of Erectile Dysfunction: An AUA Update. *J Urol.* 2005 July; 174(1): 230-239.

Bella JA, Lee JC, Carrier S, et al. CUA Practice Guidelines for Erectile Dysfunction. *Can Urol Assoc J.* 2015 Jan-Feb; 9(1-2): 23–29.

ERECTILE DYSFUNCTION

The most common cause of erectile dysfunction (ED) is reduced blood flow to the penis, which is commonly caused by diseases such as peripheral neuropathy, atherosclerosis, and hypertension. Drugs used to treat these conditions, such as blood pressure lowering drugs, can aggravate the condition. Since the arteries supplying blood to the penis are smaller than those supplying blood to the heart, they can become restricted sooner than the larger vessels. ED can be considered an early warning indicator of cardiovascular disease, and men with ED with risk factors should be referred for cardiac evaluation. Psychological issues (including depression and stress) and neurological illness (spinal cord injury, stroke) can be contributory. Low testosterone can be a factor, although the majority of men with low testosterone complain of low desire. Drugs that can contribute to erectile dysfunction are listed in the key drugs box on the following page.

NON-DRUG TREATMENT

Lifestyle changes, including losing weight, quitting tobacco use or reducing alcohol intake may be able to improve the condition. Underlying diseases that can contribute to ED should be properly managed and any offending agents should be discontinued, if possible.

Non-drug options that are beneficial in some men are vacuum erection devices, implants and surgery. Natural products used to treat ED include yohimbe, L-arginine, and panax ginseng. *The Natural Medicines Database* rates L-arginine (taken in high doses) and panax ginseng as "possibly effective" for this purpose. L-arginine can cause dizziness, headache and flushing. The same side effects are caused by PDE-5 inhibitors, and the additive effect should be avoided. Yohimbe is rated as "insufficient evidence to date." Yohimbe causes stomach upset, anxiety, and can cause more severe health concerns, including tachycardia and arrhythmias.

DRUG TREATMENT

PDE-5 inhibitors (sildenafil, vardenafil, tadalafil, avanafil) are the first-line treatment for ED. If a patient cannot tolerate or has a contraindication to PDE-5 inhibitors, alprostadil can be used instead. Alprostadil is either injected into the penis, or inserted into the penis with a urethral suppository. The treatment is invasive, painful, and short-acting.

Two of the PDE-5 inhibitors used for ED are indicated for other conditions. Sildenafil (*Viagra*) is indicated for ED and sildenafil (*Revatio*) is indicated for pulmonary arterial hypertension (PAH). Tadalafil (*Cialis*) is indicated for benign prostatic hypertrophy (BPH) and ED, and tadalafil (*Adcirca*) is indicated for PAH. A PDE-5 inhibitor used for ED should not be used concurrently with a PDE-5 inhibitor used for another condition.

DRUGS THAT CAN CAUSE ERECTILE DYSFUNCTION

KEY DRUGS

- Antidepressants – particularly SSRIs and SNRIs (mostly ↓ libido)
- Antihypertensives – beta blockers, clonidine, others
- Antipsychotics – first-generation (haloperidol, chlorpromazine) and prolactin-raising second generation (risperidone, paliperidone)
- BPH medications - finasteride, dutasteride, and silodosin (mostly retrograde ejaculation)

Others:

- Alcohol
- Anticancer drugs - leuprolide, flutamide, busulfan, cyclophosphamide
- Anticholinergics
- Atomoxetine
- Digoxin
- H2RAs – cimetidine, nizatidine, ranitidine
- Nicotine
- Opioids (chronic use) - methadone

The corpora cavernosa (plural) are the two spongy tubular vessels that run down the length of the penis. When the vessels are filled with blood, the penis is hard and erect.

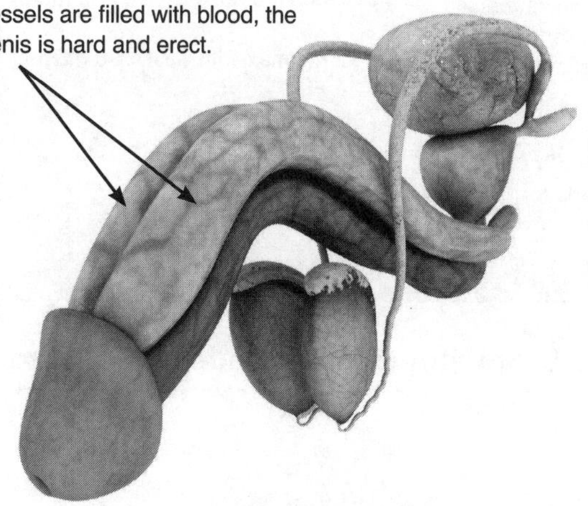

Nitric oxide (NO) → guanylate cyclase → ↑ cGMP → relaxes the smooth muscle in the arteries → blood flows into the vessels → erection.

Phosphodiesterase type 5 (PDE-5) degrades cGMP. PDE-5 inhibitors work for most men with ED. Use the right starting dose to avoid excess side effects; headache/flushing/dizziness can cause falls, especially in a frail, elderly man.

PDE-5 Inhibitors

Following sexual stimulation, PDE-5 inhibitors cause a local release of nitric oxide, which increases cGMP and smooth muscle relaxation. This causes the blood flow to the penis to increase, which results in an erection. PDE-5 inhibitors do not increase libido (sexual interest). Sexual interest must be present for the drugs to work.

DRUG	DOSING	SAFETY/SIDE EFFECTS/MONITORING
Sildenafil ***(Viagra)*** *Revatio* – PAH	25-100 mg daily Start at 50 mg, take ~1 hr before sexual activity Start at 25 mg w/conditions below	**CONTRAINDICATIONS** Concurrent use with nitrates. Do not use with riociguat. **WARNINGS** Impaired color discrimination, dose-related; patients with retinitis pigmentosa may have higher risk.
Vardenafil *(Levitra, Staxyn ODT)*	*Levitra* Start at 10 mg, take 1 hr before sexual activity *Staxyn ODT:* 10 mg dose only Take 10 mg, 1 hr before sexual activity If lower dose needed with conditions below, use *Levitra*	Hearing loss, with or without tinnitus/dizziness. Vision loss, rare, can be due to nonarteritic anterior ischemic optic neuropathy. Risk factors: low cup-to-disc ratio, CAD, diabetes, hypertension, hyperlipidemia, smoking > 50 yrs old. Avoid with retinal disorders. ↓ **BP**, due to vasodilation, higher risk if resting BP < 90/50 mmHg, fluid depletion, or autonomic dysfunction.
Tadalafil ***(Cialis)*** *Cialis* – ED and BPH *Adcirca* – PAH Known as the "weekend pill"- lasts longest	Daily dosing 2.5-5 mg daily Start at 2.5 mg; no daily dosing with severe renal or liver impairment As-needed dosing 5-20 mg Start at 10 mg, prior to sexual activity; start at 5 mg w/conditions below Renal Impairment 5 mg as-needed dose CrCl 30-50 mL/min 5 mg/72 hrs max with CrCl < 30 mL/min	Priapism, instruct to seek emergency medical care if erection lasts > 4 hrs. CVD, caution with low or very high BP, recent cardiac events. If chest pain, seek immediate medical help. **SIDE EFFECTS** Headache, flushing, dizziness, ↓ BP, dyspepsia, color vision changes, blurred vision, increased sensitivity to light, erythema, epistaxis, diarrhea, myalgia, muscle/back pain (tadalafil)
Avanafil ***(Stendra)***	50-200 mg Start at 100 mg, take 15-30 min prior to sexual activity' Start at 50 mg w/conditions below	**NOTES** If muscle/back pain w/tadalafil it usually lasts < 2 days. Take with or without food. For ED, no more than one dose/day is recommended. *Stendra* can be taken closest to sexual activity.

PDE-5 Inhibitor Dosing Guide - (V) *Viagra,* (C) *Cialis,* (L) *Levitra,* (S) *Stendra*

Typical starting dose

50 mg (V)
10 mg (L) (C)
100 mg (S)

With conditions below, use one-half of the typical starting dose.

25 mg (V)
5 mg (L) (C)
50 mg (S)

Know the starting dose (left circle above) for *Cialis* and *Viagra*, and the conditions that require half of the normal starting dose (right circle above). With slight variance, the conditions that require the lower dose for the 4 drugs are similar:

- **≥ 65 years**
- **Using an alpha-blocker**
- **Using a 3A4 Inhibitor**
- **Severe renal or liver impairment**

PDE-5 Inhibitor Drug Interactions

- Nitrates are an absolute contraindication for the use of PDE-5 inhibitors. Concurrent use of any prescription nitrates (including *Nitrostat, Nitrolingual,* and *BiDil*) or illicit alkyl nitrates ("poppers" such as amyl nitrate and butyl nitrate) increases the potential for severe hypotension.
- Caution with other agents that cause hypotension, including alpha blockers and antihypertensive drugs.
- If a patient with ED has taken a PDE-5 inhibitor and develops angina, nitroglycerin should not be used until after 12 hours for avanafil, after 24 hours for sildenafil or vardenafil and after 48 hours for tadalafil. Occasionally, if needed, nitrates are used in an acute emergency, with careful monitoring.
- Caution with PDE-5 inhibitor and concurrent alpha-1 blocker therapy: PDE-5 inhibitors can enhance the hypotensive effect of an alpha-1 blocker. The patient should be stable on the alpha-1 blocker (and be without excessive dizziness/hypotension) prior to starting the PDE-5 inhibitor. If *Cialis* is being used to treat BPH, do not use alpha-1 blockers concurrently.
- Moderate and strong 3A4 inhibitors increase the drug levels, and require lower starting doses and/or extended dosing intervals. Strong CYP450 3A4 inducers ↓ drug levels; monitor effectiveness.
- Grapefruit juice, a 3A4 inhibitor, can increase the PDE-5 inhibitor levels.

PDE-5 Inhibitor Patient Counseling.

- Take approximately 15 minutes (avanafil), 30 minutes (tadalafil, taken as-needed), or 1 hour (sildenafil and vardenafil) before sexual activity.
- Sildenafil, vardenafil, and avanafil last for 4-6 hours; tadalafil lasts for 36 hours.
- This medication can make you feel dizzy, cause headaches, flushing (red skin) and stomach indigestion. Your vision could be blurry and have color changes. If *Cialis,* counsel on muscle or back pain; occurs 12 to 24 hours after taking, and usually is gone within 2 days.
- Sexual activity can put an extra strain on your heart, especially if your heart is already weak from a heart attack or heart disease. Stop sexual activity and get medical help right away if you have chest pain, dizziness, or nausea during sex.
- This medication cause your blood pressure to drop suddenly to an unsafe level if it is taken with certain other medicines. Do not take this medication if you take medicines called "nitrates" (such as nitroglycerin) or street drugs called "poppers" (such as amyl nitrate and butyl nitrate). A sudden drop in blood pressure can cause you to feel dizzy, faint, or have a heart attack or stroke.
- This medication will not protect you or your partner from getting sexually transmitted diseases, including HIV.
- If you have an erection that lasts more than 4 hours or is painful, get medical help right away or the penis could be severely damaged.
- Sudden vision loss in one or both eyes can be a sign of a serious eye problem that can occur from the use of this medication. This is a rare occurrence, but if this happens, do not take any more and get medical help right away.
- Some people can have ringing in their ears (tinnitus) or loss of hearing in one or both ears. If you have any of these symptoms, stop taking the medication and contact your healthcare provider right away.

Alprostadil (Prostaglandin E1)

Alprostadil is prostaglandin E1, which causes vasodilation and allows blood flow into the cavernosal arteries, which enlarges the penis. The drug is either injected into the penis, or inserted into the penis through the urethra. The treatment is invasive, painful and does not last as long as the PDE-5 inhibitors. Alprostadil is used in some men who cannot tolerate or have contraindications to PDE-5 inhibitors.

DRUG	DOSING	SAFETY/SIDE EFFECTS/MONITORING
Alprostadil *(Caverject, Caverject Impulse, Edex)* Intracavernous injection Reconstitute prior to use	Inject 1.25-2.5 mg into the base of the penis, titrate until desired response is achieved. Appropriate dose should cause erection 5-10 min after injection, lasts ~1 hr. Max 1x/day, 3x/week Refrigerate	**CONTRAINDICATIONS** Sickle cell anemia, multiple myeloma, leukemia, anatomical deformation of fibrotic conditions of the penis, penile implants **SIDE EFFECTS** Penile pain, HA, dizziness, hematoma, priapism, scarring at injection site
Alprostadil *(Muse)* Urethral pellets	Insert 125-250 mcg pellet into urethra Urinate before administration Max 2x/day Refrigerate	**CONTRAINDICATIONS** Urethral stricture, balanitis, severe hypospadias and curvature, urethritis, venous thrombosis, sickle cell anemia, multiple myeloma, leukemia **SIDE EFFECTS** Penile pain, HA, dizziness, priapism, syncope

HYPOACTIVE SEXUAL DESIRE DISORDER

Hypoactive sexual desire disorder (HSDD) is characterized by a low sexual desire that causes marked distress or interpersonal difficulty. The low sexual desire is not due a health condition or drug.

5-HT1A Agonist and 5-HT2A Antagonist

Flibanserin exhibits agonist activity at 5-HT1A and antagonist activity at 5-HT2A, the exact mechanism of how this treats HSDD is unknown. Flibanserin does not enhance sexual performance. Premenopausal females only.

DRUG	DOSING	SAFETY/SIDE EFFECTS/MONITORING
Flibanserin *(Addyi)* REMS: Providers and pharmacies need to be certified. MedGuide required. Avoid use in pregnancy or breastfeeding.	100 mg QHS Discontinue if no benefit after 8 weeks	**BOXED WARNINGS** ↑ risk severe hypotension and syncope if taken with alcohol, moderate-to-strong 3A4 Inhibitors, or hepatic impairment **CONTRAINDICATIONS** Alcohol, concurrent use of moderate-to-strong 3A4 inhibitors, hepatic impairment **WARNINGS** Hypotension, syncope, CNS depression **SIDE EFFECTS** Dizziness, somnolence, nausea, fatigue, insomnia, dry mouth

Drug Interactions

- CNS depressants: ↑ risk of hypotension and syncope, Men who get back pain and muscle aches usually get it 12 to 24 hours after taking *Cialis*. Back pain and muscle aches usually go away within 2 days
- CYP3A4 inhibitors ↑ flibanserin; moderate-strong 3A4 inhibitors are contraindicated. CYP2C19 poor metabolizers: can increase the risk of hypotension and syncope, which can cause fainting.

PRACTICE CASE

JF is a 60 y/o black male who made an appointment at the Family Medicine clinic to be evaluated for impotence. He cannot sustain an erection. This has caused performance anxiety, which has worsened the situation. His medical conditions include hypertension, anxiety/low mood, obesity and prostate enlargement.

Allergies: NKDA

Medications:
Flomax 0.4 mg daily
Inderal LA 160 mg daily
Fosinopril 10 mg daily
Zoloft 100 mg daily
Vitamin D 200 IU daily
Aspirin 325 mg daily
Acetaminophen 325 mg 1-2 tablets PRN headache

Vitals:
Height: 5'9" Weight: 210 pounds
BP: 118/82 mmHg HR: 90 BPM RR: 16 BPM Temp: 98.6YF

Labs:
Na (mEq/L) = 140 (135 - 145)
K (mEq/L) = 5.1 (3.5 - 5)
Cl (mEq/L) = 100 (95 - 103)
HCO3 (mEq/L) = 25 (24 - 30)
BUN (mg/dL) = 16 (7 - 20)
SCr (mg/dL) = 1.0 (0.6 - 1.3)
Glucose (mg/dL) = 130 (100 - 125)
Ca (mg/dL) = 10.1 (8.5 - 10.5)
Mg (mEq/L) = 1.9 (1.3 - 2.1)
PO4 (mg/dL) = 4.5 (2.3 - 4.7)

Start sildenafil 50 mg - take 1 hour prior to sexual activity. Schedule follow-up appointment in 2 months. The cardiologist has written a new prescription for amiodarone 200 mg PO daily that AH would like to have filled.

Questions

1. Is sildenafil contraindicated in this patient? (Select **ALL** that apply.)

   a. Yes, the combination of *Flomax* and sildenafil is contraindicated.

   b. No, but he must be cautioned about dizziness, lightheadedness and fainting.

   c. No, but he has to begin sildenafil at 12.5 mg once daily.

   d. No, but the *Flomax* should be changed to doxazosin; this is a safer combination.

   e. No, but the dose of the alpha blocker should be stable (well-tolerated) prior to beginning the PDE-5 inhibitor.

2. Which of the following medications could be contributing to JF's problem with erectile dysfunction?

   a. *Inderal LA*

   b. OTC multivitamin

   c. Vitamin D

   d. Aspirin

   e. Acetaminophen

3. If JF begins sildenafil therapy, he should be counseled concerning the risk of priapism. Select the correct counseling statement:

   a. If you sustain an erection that lasts more than 4 hours, you should stop using the medicine. The erection will go away in about 24 hours.

   b. If you sustain an erection that lasts more than 4 hours, you should stop using the medicine and take 25 mg of over-the-counter diphenhydramine. The erection will go away in about 24 hours.

   c. If you sustain an erection that lasts more than 4 hours, you should stop using the medicine and rest in bed until the erection goes away, which takes about 4-6 hours.

   d. If you sustain an erection that lasts more than 2 hours, you will need to get medical help right away. Priapism must be treated as soon as possible or it can cause lasting damage to the penis.

   e. If you sustain an erection that lasts more than 4 hours, you will need to get medical help right away. Priapism must be treated as soon as possible or it can cause lasting damage to the penis.

4. The pharmacist should call the physician and recommend possible medication changes that could reduce or eliminate the ED problem. Reasonable suggestions could include: (Select **ALL** that apply.)

   a. Change the *Zoloft* to a medication that is not in the SSRI or SNRI class.

   b. Change the fosinopril to losartan.

   c. Change *Inderal LA* to a different class of medication, or try a trial with metoprolol.

   d. Change the fosinopril to amlodipine.

   e. Change the *Inderal LA* to furosemide.

Questions 5-6 do not apply to the above case.

5. A patient is using tadalafil three times weekly. He uses 10 mg, taken 1 hour before sexual intercourse. He has asked the physician to change him to the daily form of the medicine, since he uses it more than twice weekly. Choose the correct dosing range for daily tadalafil when used for ED:

   a. 0.125-2.5 mg daily

   b. 2.5-5 mg daily

   c. 5-10 mg daily

   d. 10-15 mg daily

   e. This medicine cannot be used daily

6. A 50 year old female is inquiring about *Addyi*. She has seen some advertisements on television and feels she is a prime candidate. Which of the following should be discussed during counseling:

   a. It is indicated for all female adult patients.

   b. The recommended starting dose is 50 mg daily increasing to 100 mg daily as tolerated.

   c. It may take time to see an effect so it is recommended to continue the medication for at least 90 days.

   d. Avoid drinking alcohol while using *Addyi*.

   e. You cannot use this drug if you have renal impairment.

Answers

1-b,e, 2-a, 3-e, 4-a,c, 5-b, 6-d

BENIGN PROSTATIC HYPERPLASIA (BPH)

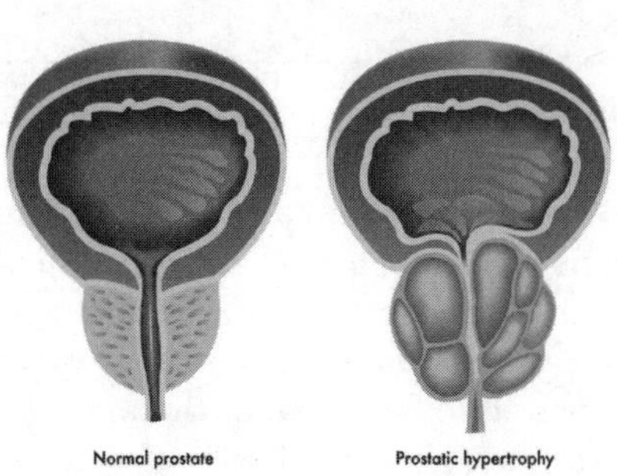

GUIDELINES/REFERENCES

Update on AUA Guideline on the Management of Benign Prostatic Hyperplasia. *The Journal of Urology*. 2011; 185:1793-1803.

American Urological Association Practice Guidelines Committee. AUA guidelines on management of benign prostatic hyperplasia 2003. Chapter 1: Diagnosis and treatment recommendations. *The Journal of Urology.* 2003; 170:530-547.

BACKGROUND

The prostate is a walnut-sized gland that surrounds the urethra at the base of the bladder. As part of the male reproductive system, the main function of the prostate is to secrete slightly alkaline fluid that becomes part of the seminal fluid carrying sperm.

The prostate is dependent on androgens (mainly testosterone) for development and maintenance of size and function. Testosterone is metabolized to dihydrotestosterone (DHT) by 5 alpha-reductase. DHT is responsible for normal and hyperplastic growth (increase in the number of cells). Benign prostatic hyperplasia (BPH) results from overgrowth of the stromal and epithelial cells of the prostate gland. The enlarged gland contributes to lower urinary tract symptoms (LUTS) via direct bladder outlet obstruction (BOO) and increased smooth muscle tone and resistance. As the prostate enlarges, the layer of tissue surrounding it stops it from expanding, causing the gland to press against the urethra like a clamp on a garden hose. The bladder wall becomes thicker and irritated. The bladder begins to contract even when it contains small amounts of urine, causing more frequent urination. Eventually, the bladder weakens and loses the ability to empty itself. Interestingly, there is not a direct linear correlation between prostate size and symptoms; some men are more bothered even with a smaller prostate size, while others with a larger prostate are not as symptomatic. The enlargement does not usually cause problems until later in life with a peak incidence around 65 years of age. When the prostate becomes larger, prostate specific antigen (PSA) levels can increase; yet, BPH does not increase the risk of prostate cancer.

SYMPTOMS/COMPLICATIONS

The signs and symptoms of BPH are mainly LUTS which include difficulty holding urine (storage) and emptying the bladder (voiding). These disturbances significantly impact the quality of life for the patient. LUTS can include:

- Hesitancy, intermittency, straining or weak stream of urine
- Urinary urgency and leaking or dribbling
- Incomplete emptying of the bladder (bladder always feels full)
- Urinary frequency, especially nocturia (urination at night)
- Bladder outlet obstruction (BOO)

BPH rarely causes more severe symptoms – but, if the blockage is severe, the urine could back up into the kidneys and result in acute renal failure. Urinary tract infections can also be present, but are uncommon in men.

DRUGS THAT CAN WORSEN BPH
Anticholinergics (e.g., benztropine)
Antihistamines (e.g., diphenhydramine, chlorpheniramine)
Caffeine (can worsen symptoms)
Decongestants (e.g., pseudoephedrine)
Diuretics (increase urination–be sure to take early in the day to limit nocturia)
SNRIs (affect urethral resistance)
TCAs, phenothiazines and other drugs with anticholinergic properties
Testosterone products

DIAGNOSIS

Prostate cancer symptoms can be similar to the symptoms of BPH. Diagnosis requires a careful patient medical history including surgeries and trauma, current medications including herbal and OTC drugs, focused physical exam including a digital rectal exam (DRE), and urinalysis and serum prostate specific antigen (PSA) to rule out conditions other than BPH (e.g., prostate or bladder cancer, neurogenic bladder, others). Patient may be asked to complete a voiding diary as well to better tailor therapy. PSA, a protein produced by prostate cells, is frequently ↑ in prostate cancer, however, it can also be increased in other conditions including BPH. Note that the recommendations for routine prostate cancer screening have changed (they will be done less frequently than in the past).

DRUG TREATMENT

The patient's perception of the severity of BPH symptoms guides selection of the treatment modality in a patient. Validated questionnaires, such as the AUA Symptom Score, are commonly used to quantify symptoms. The scoring system rates how bothersome the symptoms are to the patient, with higher scores indicating more severe or bothersome symptoms. Treatment options can include watchful waiting, pharmacologic therapy and surgical intervention. Choice of treatment is a shared decision-making process between the patient and the clinician. Mild disease is generally treated with watchful waiting, which entails having the patient return for reassessment yearly. Moderate/severe disease is generally treated with medications, a minimally invasive procedure, or surgery such as transurethral resection of the prostate (TURP). Medications include alpha blockers (selective and non-selective), alone or in combination with a 5 alpha-reductase inhibitor. The 5 alpha-reductase inhibitors should not be used in men with LUTS secondary to BPH without prostatic enlargement (as these medications work by decreasing prostate size). Peripheral-acting anticholinergic agents used for overactive bladder (such as tolterodine) are sometimes a reasonable option for men without an elevated post void residual (PRV) urine and when LUTS are predominately irritative. If anticholinergics are used, PVR should be < 250-300 mL (anticholinergics are discussed in the Overactive Bladder chapter). Another treatment option is using the phosphodiesterase-5 (PDE-5) inhibitor tadalafil. This can be used in men with BPH alone, and can be an attractive option for men with both BPH and erectile dysfunction (ED); the dose is sufficient for both indications. Tadalafil, in combination with an alpha blocker (especially a non-selective agent) would pose risk for additive hypotension and orthostasis in an elderly male.

Historically, alpha blockers have been considered the standard BPH drug treatment. They are used alone in mild symptoms, and often with a 5 alpha-reductase inhibitor with moderate symptoms. Recently, tamsulosin (the most popular alpha-blocker) has been associated with floppy iris syndrome, a condition that makes cataract surgery difficult to complete safely. Cataracts are common in elderly patients, and the use of alpha blockers increases the risk itself. The important thing is to let the ophthalmologist know if a patient has ever taken an alpha-blocker.

Natural Products

Saw palmetto is used for BPH, but it is rated as "possibly ineffective" by *The Natural Medicines Database* due to contradictory and inconsistent data. Pygeum is another natural product and it is rated as "likely effective". Do not recommend a pygeum product unless it has been harvested ethically; ripping the bark off the trees to extract pygeum is not sustainable. Beta-sitosterol (which is available as supplements, in margarine substitutes, in African wild potato extract products, in pumpkin seed and in soy and red clover) is rated as "likely effective" and rye grass pollen is rated as possibly effective. Lycopene is used for prostate cancer prevention, however, there is no good evidence for taking the supplement for this purpose. Pharmacists should not recommend natural products until the patient has seen a health care provider; it is not prudent to recommend a product that could be masking cancer symptoms. Although the symptoms will primarily be benign, the small risk of prostate cancer must be considered.

ALPHA BLOCKERS

These agents inhibit alpha-1 adrenergic receptors and relax the smooth muscle of the bladder neck reducing bladder outlet obstruction and improving urinary flow. There are 3 types of alpha receptors: 1A (prostate primarily has these receptors), 1B, and 1D; terazosin and doxazosin are non-selective and this results in more side effects (orthostasis, dizziness, fatigue, headache) than the selective agents (tamsulosin, alfuzosin, silodosin).

<table>
<tr><th>DRUG</th><th>DOSING</th><th>SAFETY/SIDE EFFECTS/MONITORING</th></tr>
<tr><td colspan="2">Non-Selective Alpha-1 Blockers</td><td rowspan="8">CONTRAINDICATIONS
Concurrent use silodosin or alfuzosin with strong 3A4 inhibitors, hepatic impairment (Child-Pugh class C for silodosin, class B/C for alfuzosin); severe renal impairment (silodosin)

WARNINGS
Orthostatic hypotension/syncope: typically with first dose, if therapy is interrupted for several days, dosage is increased too rapidly or another antihypertensive agent or PDE-5 inhibitor is started

Intraoperative floppy iris syndrome has occurred in cataract surgery patients who were on or were previously treated with an alpha-1 blocker

Priapism – seek medical attention if erection lasting > 4 hours

Angina – D/C if symptoms of angina begin or worsen

SIDE EFFECTS
Dizziness, fatigue, orthostatic hypotension, headache, fluid retention

Rhinitis (tamsulosin)

Abnormal ejaculation (esp. with tamsulosin and silodosin)

MONITORING
BP, PSA, urinary symptoms

NOTES
The non-selective agents are often given QHS to help minimize the initial "first dose" effect of orthostasis/dizziness. This requires careful counseling (see below) as the man likely has nocturia, where getting up at night to use the bathroom with dizziness and orthostasis can be dangerous.

Alpha blockers work right away, but 4-6 weeks may be required to assess whether beneficial effects have been achieved; they do not shrink the prostate and do not change PSA levels.

Take Cardura XL with breakfast. Cardura XL is an OROS formulation (see Drug Formulations chapter) and can leave a ghost tablet (empty shell) in the stool

Do not use alfuzosin in patients at risk for QT prolongation – prolongs QT interval

Silodosin can cause retrograde ejaculation (28%), reversible upon drug discontinuation

Alpha blockers – used for bladder outlet obstruction in women (off label)</td></tr>
<tr><td>Terazosin</td><td>Start at 1 mg at bedtime; titrate slowly to effect – generally 10 mg QHS (may ↑ to 20 mg QHS)</td></tr>
<tr><td>Doxazosin (Cardura, Cardura XL)</td><td>IR: Start at 1 mg; titrate slowly up to 4-8 mg daily, usually given at bedtime

XL: Start at 4 mg daily with breakfast; titrate to a max of 8 mg daily</td></tr>
<tr><td colspan="2">Selective Alpha-1A Blockers</td></tr>
<tr><td>Tamsulosin (Flomax)

+ dutasteride (Jalyn)</td><td>0.4 mg daily, 30 min after the same meal each day; max 0.8 mg daily</td></tr>
<tr><td>Alfuzosin (Uroxatral)</td><td>10 mg daily, immediately after same meal each day

CrCl < 30 mL/min: use with caution</td></tr>
<tr><td>Silodosin (Rapaflo)</td><td>8 mg daily with a meal

CrCl 30-50 mL/min: 4 mg daily

CrCl < 30 mL/min: do not use</td></tr>
</table>

Alpha Blocker Drug Interactions

- Use caution when co-administered with PDE-5 inhibitors *(Viagra/Revatio, Cialis/Adcirca, Levitra/Staxyn, Stendra)* due to additive hypotensive effects. Patients should be stable on alpha-blocker therapy before PDE-5 inhibitor therapy is initiated, using the lowest dose. Conversely, if a patient is already taking a PDE-5 inhibitor, the alpha blocker should be started at the lowest dose, and the selective agents will be preferred (over the non-selective agents).
- Use caution with other drugs that lower BP.
- Tamsulosin, alfuzosin and silodosin are major CYP 3A4 substrates; avoid use with strong 3A4 inhibitors.
- Silodosin cannot be used with strong P-gp inhibitors, such as cyclosporine.
- Alfuzosin: can cause QT prolongation; do not use with other QT prolonging agents. Use with caution in patients with known QT prolongation (congenital or acquired).

5 Alpha-Reductase Inhibitors

These agents inhibit the 5 alpha-reductase enzyme which blocks the conversion of testosterone to dihydrotestosterone (DHT). This class of medications is indicated for the treatment of symptomatic BPH in men with an enlarged prostate to improve symptoms, decrease the risk of acute urinary retention, and decrease the risk of need for surgery, including TURP or prostatectomy.

DRUG	DOSING	SAFETY/SIDE EFFECTS/MONITORING
Finasteride *(Proscar)* Affects 5α-receptors type 2 For hair loss (*Propecia* 1 mg daily)	5 mg daily	**CONTRAINDICATIONS** Women of child-bearing potential, pregnancy, children **WARNINGS** May ↑ risk of high-grade prostate cancer. **SIDE EFFECTS** Impotence, ↓ libido, ejaculation disturbances, breast enlargement and tenderness, rash – sexual SEs ↓ with time and approach placebo levels at one year of use in some men; in some men sexual issues persist **MONITORING** PSA, urinary symptoms
Dutasteride *(Avodart)* + tamsulosin (*Jalyn*) Affects both types of 5α-receptors (types 1 and 2)	0.5 mg daily	**NOTES** Safety issue – see Pregnancy chapter Pregnant women should not handle or take; can be absorbed through skin, can be detrimental to fetus, semen of male taking this drug may present a danger 6 months (or longer) of treatment may be required for maximal efficacy Usually used in men with larger prostate size (40+ grams) or more severe symptoms; due to the slow-onset, often given with α-blocker 5 alpha-reductase inhibitors shrink the prostate and ↓ PSA levels Swallow dutasteride whole. Do not chew or open as contents may cause oropharyngeal irritation. Take *Jalyn* 30 min after same meal each day.

5 Alpha-Reductase Inhibitor Drug Interactions

- Finasteride and dutasteride are minor CYP 3A4 substrates; strong CYP 3A4 inhibitors may ↑ levels.
- Do not use *Proscar* in a patient using *Propecia* for hair loss; refer to prescriber.

Phosphodiesterase-5 Inhibitor

Phosphodiesterase-5 mediated ↓ in smooth muscle and endothelial cell proliferation, ↓ nerve activity, and ↑ smooth muscle relaxation and tissue perfusion of the prostate and bladder.

DRUG	DOSING	SAFETY/SIDE EFFECTS/MONITORING
Tadalafil *Cialis* – for ED and Benign Prostatic Hypertrophy (BPH) *Adcirca* – for pulmonary arterial hypertension (PAH)	5 mg daily, same time each day CrCl 30-50 mL/min: 2.5 mg initially, max 5 mg daily CrCl < 30 mL/min: do not use Use 2.5 mg if using strong CYP 3A4 inhibitor	**CONTRAINDICATIONS** Concurrent use of nitrates or riociguat **WARNINGS** Impaired color discrimination, dose-related, caution in patients with retinitis pigmentosa Hearing loss, with our without tinnitus/dizziness Vision loss, rare, can be due to non-arteritic anterior ischemic optic neuropathy (NAION), Hypotension due to vasodilation Priapism – seek medical attention if erection lasting > 4 hours Concomitant use with alpha blockers is not recommended–discontinue alpha-blocker at least 1 day before initiating tadalafil. See Sexual Dysfunction chapter for complete review **SIDE EFFECTS** Headache, flushing, nausea, dyspepsia, myalgia, back pain, respiratory tract infection, nasopharyngitis **MONITORING** BP, PSA, urinary symptoms

For drug interactions/counseling for tadalafil, see Sexual Dysfunction chapter.

Patient Counseling

Alpha Blockers

- Especially for non-selective agents, such as doxazosin: This medicine can cause a sudden drop in blood pressure. You may feel dizzy, faint or "light-headed," especially after you stand up from a lying or sitting position. This is more likely to occur after you have taken the first few doses or if you increase your dose, but can occur at any time while you are taking the drug. It can also occur if you stop taking the drug and then restart treatment. When you get up from a sitting or lying position, go slowly and hold onto the bed rail or chair until you are steady on your feet.
- If you take the medicine at bedtime, but need to get up from bed to go to the bathroom, get up slowly and cautiously and hold onto the bed rail or chair until you are steady on your feet.
- You should not drive or do any hazardous tasks until you are used to the effects of the medicine. If you begin to feel dizzy, sit or lie down until you feel better.
- This medicine can cause side effects that may impair your thinking or reactions. Be careful if you drive or do anything that requires you to be awake and alert.
- Drinking alcohol can make the dizziness worse, and increase night-time urination if taken close to bedtime.
- Taking cold and allergy medications such as decongestants and antihistamines can make your symptoms worsen. Discuss what to use with your pharmacist if you need assistance.

- Tell your doctor (or ophthalmologist) about the use of this medication before cataract surgery. The doctor will want to know if you have ever taken this medication.
- Rarely, this medication can cause a painful erection which cannot be relieved by having sex. If this happens, get medical help right away. If it is not treated, you may not be able to get an erection in the future.

Tamsulosin
- The dose should be administered approximately half an hour following the same meal each day.

Alfuzosin
- Do not crush, chew, or break the alfuzosin tablets. Swallow them whole.
- Take after same meal each day (food increases absorption).

Silodosin
- The most common side effect seen with this medication is an orgasm with reduced or no semen (dry orgasm). This side effect does not pose a safety concern and is reversible with discontinuation of the drug (lower risk with tamsulosin).
- Take the same time each day with food.

5 Alpha-Reductase Inhibitor Counseling
- This medicine can take several months or longer to help reduce the BPH symptoms. It is effective, it just takes awhile to work because it shrinks the prostate slowly. If your doctor has given you another medicine called an alpha-blocker, that medicine works faster.
- Women who are or may become pregnant should not handle the tablets. (These drugs can cause birth defects to a developing male fetus – Pregnancy Category X). The semen of males using the medicine may also be harmful.
- Your doctor may perform blood tests or other forms of monitoring during treatment with finasteride. One of the tests that may be performed is called PSA (prostate-specific antigen). This drug can reduce the amount of PSA in the blood.
- Tell your doctor if you experience any of these side effects: decreased sex drive, decreased volume of ejaculate, impotence, breast tenderness or enlargement.
- Taking cold and allergy medications such as decongestants and antihistamines can make your symptoms worsen. Discuss what to use with your pharmacist if you need assistance.

OVERACTIVE BLADDER

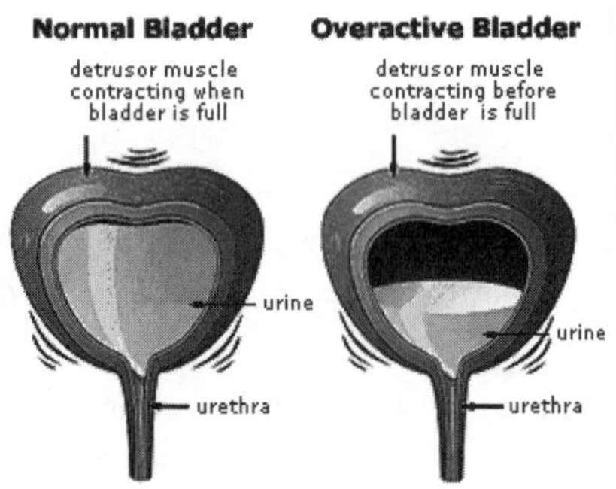

GUIDELINES/REFERENCES

Diagnosis and Treatment of Overactive Bladder (Non-Neurogenic) In Adults: AUA/SUFU Guideline. *J Urol.* 2012 Dec; 188(6):2455-63.

BACKGROUND

Overactive bladder (OAB) is a common, disabling urinary disorder that affects many people (1 in 6 people or over 33 million Americans). It is not a normal sign of aging. In overactive bladder, the detrusor muscle contracts frequently and before the bladder is full, leading to the classic symptoms of:

- Urinary urgency (a sudden, compelling desire to pass urine which is difficult to defer), and
- Urinary frequency (voiding ≥ 8 times in a 24 hour period), and
- Nocturia (≥ 2 awakenings to void per night)

Overactive bladder can lead to urinary urge incontinence. About 1/3 of patients have incontinent episodes (OAB wet) and the other 2/3 of patients do not have incontinence (OAB dry).

IMPLICATIONS OF OVERACTIVE BLADDER

Many comorbidities exist in patients with OAB including falls and fractures, skin breakdown and infections, UTIs, depression, and sexual dysfunction. Due to embarrassment of their condition, there are many social implications of OAB including low self-esteem, lack of sexual intimacy, social and physical isolation, sleep disturbances, limits on travel and dependence on caregivers; all leading to a reduced quality of life. Many patients become dehydrated because they limit their fluid intake. The cost of pads and adult diapers can be a huge financial burden.

PATHOPHYSIOLOGY

The bladder is commonly referred to as a "balloon" with an outer muscular layer known as the detrusor muscle. The detrusor muscle and the bladder outlet functions are neurologically coordinated to store and expel urine. The detrusor muscle is innervated mainly by the parasympathetic nervous system while the bladder neck is innervated by the sympathetic nervous system. The internal sphincter is also innervated by the sympathetic nervous system and the external sphincter is innervated by the somatic nervous system. Both voluntary and involuntary contractions of the detrusor muscle are mediated by activation of muscarinic receptors via acetylcholine. Of the five known muscarinic receptor subtypes, the human bladder is comprised of M2 and M3 receptors in a 3:1 ratio. It is the M3 receptor that is responsible for both emptying contractions as well as involuntary bladder contractions of incontinence. In overactive bladder, the detrusor muscle is hyperactive (overactive), causing the symptoms of frequent micturitions, urgency, nocturia, and/or incontinence.

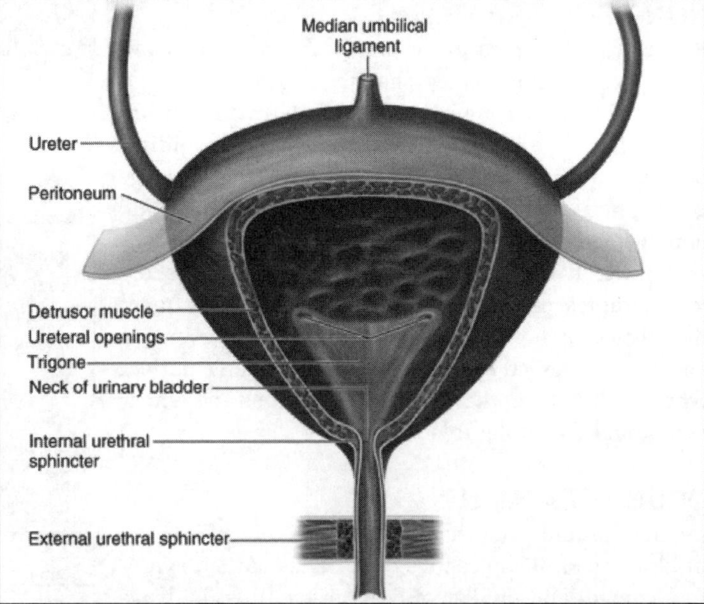

Risk Factors for Overactive Bladder

- Age > 40 years
- Diabetes
- Restricted mobility
- Obesity
- Prior vaginal delivery
- Neurologic conditions (e.g., stroke, Parkinson disease, dementia)
- Hysterectomy
- Drugs that can increase incontinence [e.g., ACE inhibitors (due to cough), alcohol, cholinesterase inhibitors, diuretics, sedatives, others]
- Pelvic injury

Diagnosis

Diagnosis requires a careful patient history intake including comorbid conditions, duration of symptoms, baseline symptoms, fluid intake and type of fluids (with and without caffeine), a physical exam and urinalysis. Validated questionnaires such as the Urinary Distress Inventory (UDI) or the Overactive Bladder Questionnaire (OAB-q) are used to quantify symptoms. Patients may be required to complete a bladder diary to accurately measure intake and voiding information. A urine culture and post-void residual assessment may be performed to rule out other causes.

FORMS OF URINARY INCONTINENCE

Functional
There is no abnormality in the bladder, but the patient may be cognitively, socially, or physically impaired thus hindering him or her from access to a toilet (e.g., patients in wheelchairs).

Overflow
Leakage that occurs when the quantity of urine stored in the bladder exceeds its capacity, often occurring without the urge to urinate (BPH is the most common cause).

Stress
Urine leaks out during any form of exertion (e.g., exercise, coughing, sneezing, laughing, etc.) as a result of pressure on the bladder.

Urge
Patient cannot hold in urine long enough to reach the toilet and is associated with neuropathy; often found in those who have diabetes, strokes, dementia, Parkinson disease, or multiple sclerosis (although people without comorbidities are also affected).

Mixed
Combination of urge and stress incontinence

Approximately 1/3 of incontinence is stress, 1/3 is urge and 1/3 is mixed.

NON-DRUG TREATMENT

Behavioral therapies are considered first-line to improve OAB symptoms by changing patient behavior and/or their environment. Behavioral treatments include bladder training, delayed or scheduled voiding, pelvic floor muscle exercises (Kegel exercises), urge control techniques (distraction, self-assertions), fluid management, dietary changes (avoiding bladder irritants), weight loss and other lifestyle changes. Behavior therapies can be combined with other treatment modalities such as medications. Surgical intervention should be reserved for the rare non-neurogenic patient who has failed all other therapeutic options and whose symptoms are intolerable.

PELVIC FLOOR MUSCLE EXERCISES

Pelvic Floor Muscle ("Kegel") Exercises
These exercises are done to strengthen the pelvic floor muscles and can diminish OAB symptoms.

Proper technique is key and this means finding the correct muscles. Instruct the patient to imagine that they are trying to stop urination midstream. Squeeze the muscles they would use. If they sense a "pulling" feeling, those are the correct muscles for pelvic exercise.

Pull in the pelvic muscles and hold for a count of 3. Then relax for a count of 3. Work up to 3 sets of 10 kegel exercises per day. Do these exercises 3 times a day to strengthen pelvic floor muscles and reduce wetting episodes.

DRUG TREATMENT

Behavioral and drug therapies are often used in combination in clinical practice to optimize patient symptom control and quality of life. Anticholinergic drugs are second-line therapy. These agents are antagonists of the muscarinic receptor and block acetylcholine, thus limiting contractions of the detrusor muscle. Patients with a post void residual (PVR) > 250 – 300 mL should not be started on an anticholinergic agent. Extended-release formulations are preferred over immediate-release formulations due to a lower rate of dry mouth. More selective (for the M3 receptor) anticholinergic agents (solifenacin, darifenacin, fesoterodine) have less CNS side effects over the nonselective, older agents such as oxybutynin. If a patient fails an antimuscarinic agent or develops an adverse effect, it is recommended to try at least one other anticholinergic agent or a dose adjustment before moving on to third-line recommendations, including onabotulinumtoxin A, nerve stimulation or surgical correction. In-dwelling catheters are used only as a last resort in select patients. Additive antimuscarinic drugs should be avoided, if possible.

CHOLINERGIC & ANTICHOLINERGIC PHARMACOLOGY

Cholinergic drugs act like acetylcholine at the acetylcholine receptors and cause the "SLUD" symptoms: Salivation, Lacrimation (tearing), Urination and Diarrhea. The classic cholinergic drug bethanechol is used occasionally to treat urinary retention by increasing urination, which occurs with neurogenic bladder. Another cholinergic agent is pilocarpine, which is sometimes used for dry mouth (to increase salivation).*

Anticholinergics have the opposite effect: they block acetylcholine, which is present in the periphery (outside of the CNS) and centrally (inside the CNS) and will cause the anti-SLUD peripheral symptoms of dry mouth, dry/blurry vision, urinary retention and constipation along with the central anticholinergic effects such as sedation, dizziness and cognitive impairment.

This is how diphenhydramine, which blocks acetylcholine in the CNS, works as a sedative. Diphenhydramine has to travel through the periphery (to get to the CNS) and will cause the peripheral side effects as well, including urinary retention. However, it is not an appropriate choice for an elderly patient due to the central effects which can increase fall risk and the peripheral effects that are not desired.

When incontinence drugs were first developed, the primary goal was to use agents with lower CNS penetration; therefore, exhibiting fewer central side effects. Oxybutynin is an older drug in this class and the prototype peripheral agent. Later on, drugs were designed to be specific for the M3 muscarinic receptor, the subtype present in high density on the bladder wall (the detrusor muscle). When this muscle contracts, there is a sudden urge to urinate; therefore blocking the M3 receptor can reduce the sudden urge to urinate. Darifenacin is an example of an M3-specific drug. Unfortunately, the M3 receptor is also found in high density on the salivary glands, causing dry mouth when this receptor is blocked. The pharmacist must help the patient to manage dry mouth, which is quite uncomfortable and increases the degree of dental decay. It is possible to reduce this side effect with the use of longer-acting agents (instead of IR formulations) and with drugs that bypass first-pass metabolism (patch and gel) since the drug metabolites contribute to the dry mouth. With the long-acting formulations, there are lower "peaks" and, thus, lower side effects. Although there is more drug to hit the "right" receptors (producing the desired effect) during peak concentrations, there will also be more drug to hit the "wrong" receptors (causing side effects).

* *Another mechanism to increase acetylcholine is to block the enzyme that breaks it down. These are the acetylcholinesterase inhibitors, which are used for dementia and to reverse neuromuscular blockade.*

Anticholinergic Drugs

These agents are competitive antagonists of the muscarinic receptors which inhibit binding of acetylcholine, thus limiting contractions of the detrusor muscle.

DRUG	DOSING	SAFETY/SIDE EFFECTS/MONITORING
Oxybutynin **Oxybutynin XL *(Ditropan XL)*** **Oxybutynin patch *(Oxytrol, Oxytrol for Women – OTC)*** Oxybutynin 10% topical gel *(Gelnique)* Oxybutynin 3% topical gel *(Gelnique 3%)*	5 mg PO BID-TID 5-30 mg PO daily 3.9 mg daily (Rx patch is changed every 3-4 days; OTC patch is changed every 4 days) Apply contents of 1 sachet to intact, dry skin daily 3 pumps daily	**CONTRAINDICATIONS** Urinary retention, gastric retention, decreased gastric motility and uncontrolled narrow angle glaucoma *Oxytrol for Women* OTC: Pain or burning when urinating, blood in urine, unexplained lower back or side pain, cloudy or foul-smelling urine, males, age < 18 years, urinary or gastric retention, glaucoma, accidental urine loss only due to coughing, sneezing, or laughing **WARNINGS** Anticholinergics may cause agitation, confusion, drowsiness, dizziness, hallucinations, headache, and/or blurred vision, which may impair physical or mental abilities; patients must be cautioned about performing tasks which require mental alertness (e.g., operating machinery or driving). Angioedema of the face, lips, tongue and/or larynx. **SIDE EFFECTS** Dizziness and drowsiness (greatest with oxybutynin and less with the newer, selective agents), xerostomia (dry mouth), constipation, dry eyes/blurred vision, urinary retention, application site reactions (with topicals and patch) **NOTES** ↓ dose in renal impairment (CrCl < 30 mL/min) with fesoterodine, solifenacin, tolterodine, and trospium (do not use trospium XR formulation in these patients). Extended-release formulations have less incidence of dry mouth than their IR counterparts. *Ditropan XL* is in an OROS formulation (see Drug Formulations chapter) and can leave a ghost shell (empty shell) in the stool. Oxybutynin patch and gel cause less dry mouth and constipation than oral forms. Darifenacin causes more constipation. *Oxytrol* patch should be placed on dry, intact skin on the abdomen, hips or buttocks. Avoid reapplication to the same site within 7 days. Available OTC for women ≥ 18 years. Men who are experiencing OAB symptoms should see their doctors to rule out other conditions. Antimuscarinic agents should be used with caution in patients using other medications with anticholinergic properties.
Tolterodine *(Detrol)* Tolterodine ER *(Detrol LA)*	1-2 mg PO BID 2-4 mg PO daily	
Trospium Trospium XR	20 mg BID 60 mg XR daily Take on an empty stomach	
Solifenacin *(VESIcare)*	5-10 mg PO daily	
Darifenacin *(Enablex)*	7.5-15 mg PO daily	
Fesoterodine *(Toviaz)*	4-8 mg PO daily	

Anticholinergic Drug Interactions

- All of the anticholinergics can have additive effects with other medications that have anticholinergic side effects.
- Acetylcholinesterase inhibitors used for dementia (e.g., donepezil) increase acetylcholine in the CNS, whereas the OAB agents primarily stay in the periphery (outside the CNS). However, some patients may experience some CNS side effects (e.g., memory impairment). The risk vs. benefit must be considered. If little to no improvement in OAB symptoms at 6 weeks, the anticholinergic drug should be discontinued.
- Tolterodine ER – do not exceed 2 mg/day when administered with strong 3A4 inhibitors.
- Solifenacin – do not exceed 5 mg/day when administered with strong 3A4 inhibitors.
- Darifenacin – do not exceed 7.5 mg/day when administered with strong 3A4 inhibitors.
- Fesoterodine – do not exceed 4 mg/day when administered with strong 3A4 inhibitors.

Beta-3 Agonist

Mirabegron relaxes the detrusor muscle during the storage phase of the fill-void cycle by activation of beta-3 receptors which increases bladder capacity.

DRUG	DOSING	SAFETY/SIDE EFFECTS/MONITORING
Mirabegron *(Myrbetriq)*	25-50 mg daily CrCl 15-29 mL/min: 25 mg CrCl < 15 mL/min: not recommended	**WARNINGS** Angioedema of the face, lips, tongue and/or larynx, ↑ BP, urinary retention in patients with BPH and when used with antimuscarinic drugs **SIDE EFFECTS** Hypertension, nasopharyngitis, UTI, headache **MONITORING** BP, HR, urinary symptoms **NOTES** Efficacy seen within 8 weeks

Mirabegron Drug Interactions

- Mirabegron is a moderate CYP2D6 inhibitor. Use caution with co-administration of narrow therapeutic window drugs metabolized by 2D6. Levels of metoproplol and desipramine are increased when co-administered with mirabegron. Use caution when administered concurrently with digoxin (use lowest digoxin dose and monitor levels).

Onabotulinum Toxin A *(Botox)*

Botox is a third-line treatment option for patients who are refractory to first- and second-line treatment options. It affects the efferent pathways of detrusor activity by inhibiting the release of acetylcholine.

DRUG	DOSING	SAFETY/SIDE EFFECTS/MONITORING
Onabotulinum toxin A *(Botox)*	100 units total dose, as 0.5 mL (5 units) injections, across 20 sites (given intradetrusor) – repeat therapy no sooner than 12 weeks from previous administration In adults treated with *Botox* for more than one indication, do not exceed a total dose of 360 units in a 3 month interval.	**BOXED WARNING** All botulinum toxin products may spread from the area of injection to produce symptoms consistent with botulinum toxin effects. Swallowing and breathing difficulties can be life-threatening. **CONTRAINDICATIONS** Infection at the proposed injection site, urinary tract infection and urinary retention **SIDE EFFECTS** Urinary tract infection, urinary retention, dysuria **MONITORING** Post-void residual volume, symptoms of OAB **NOTES** Potency units of *Botox* are not interchangeable with other preparations of botulinum toxin products. Prophylactic antimicrobial therapy (excluding aminoglycosides) should be administered 1-3 days prior to, on the day of, and for 1-3 days following *Botox* administration. MedGuide required.

Botox Drug Interactions

- Aminoglycosides and other agents affecting neuromuscular transmission can potentiate the effects of *Botox.*

Anticholinergic Patient Counseling

Ditropan XL

- Certain medications can interact with this medication. Tell your healthcare provider or pharmacist of the medications you are currently taking including any over the counter products, vitamins and herbal supplements.
- The tablet must be swallowed whole with liquid; do not crush, divide, or chew; take at approximately the same time each day.
- This medication can be taken without regards to meals (unlike trospium which needs to be taken on an empty stomach).
- If you miss a dose, skip it. Take at your next scheduled dose. Do not take 2 doses within the same day.
- Part of the tablet may pass into your stool after your body has absorbed the medicine. If you see the tablet in your stool, it is nothing to worry about.
- This medicine can cause dry mouth. Some formulations cause more dry mouth than others (the longer-lasting forms tend to cause less dry mouth). If dry mouth is bothersome, please discuss with your healthcare provider. Avoiding mouthwashes with alcohol, taking small sips of water, sucking on ice chips or sugar-free candy or chewing sugar-free gum can help with dry mouth symptoms. Take good care of your teeth since dry mouth contributes to tooth decay.

- Another possible side effect of this medicine is constipation. Some formulations cause more constipation than others with darifenacin *(Enablex)* causing the most. Maintain adequate water and dietary fiber, including vegetables and whole-grains. A stool softener, such as docusate, may be helpful. If not, a laxative such as senna may be helpful. You may need to discuss this with your healthcare provider. If you have any type of serious constipation or constipation for ≥ 3 days, or current stomach problems, you should let your healthcare provider know.
- This medication can make you feel dizzy or drowsy. Using alcohol can make this worse. Heat can make this worse. Do not operate any dangerous machinery (such as driving a car) until you know how this medicine affects your concentration and coordination.
- Doing pelvic floor muscle (Kegel) exercises in combination with this medicine will work better than taking the medicine alone. You should get instructions on how to do this correctly, and do them for a few minutes three times daily, so you can slowly build up these muscles.

Oxytrol Patch

- The patch causes less dry mouth than oral formulations.
- Open one pouch and apply immediately. Do not use if pouch is torn or opened.
- Apply one patch to clean, dry, intact skin on the abdomen, hips, or buttocks.
- Apply to an area of skin that is under clothing and protected from sunlight. Avoid applying the patch on your waistline, since tight clothing may rub the patch off.
- The Rx patch is changed every 3 to 4 days; the OTC patch is changed every 4 days.
- Select a new site for each new patch (avoid reapplication to same site within 7 days).
- Do not apply the patch to areas of skin that are irritated, oily, or to where lotions or powders have been applied.
- The patch must be removed prior to having an MRI procedure.
- Contact with water (e.g., swimming, bathing) will not change the way the drug works. Avoid rubbing the patch area during these activities.
- If the area around the patch becomes red, itchy, or irritated, try a new site. If irritation continues or becomes worse, notify your healthcare provider promptly.

Oxybutynin topical *(Gelnique)*

- For topical use only.
- This formulation causes less dry mouth and less constipation than other formulations.
- For *Gelnique* 10%, each packet is for one use only. For *Gelnique* 3%, use 3 pumps (must prime the pump prior to first use with 4 pumps).
- Apply to clean, dry, intact skin on abdomen, upper arm/shoulders, or thighs. Rub into skin until dry. Use a different site each day (cannot use the same site two days in a row).
- Do not apply to recently shaved skin.
- Do not bathe, swim or shower for 1 hour after application.
- Wash hands after use.
- Cover treated area with clothing after gel has dried to prevent transfer of medication to others.
- Oxybutynin gel is flammable. Avoid an open flame and do not smoke until the gel has completely dried on the skin.

GLAUCOMA, OPHTHALMICS & OTICS

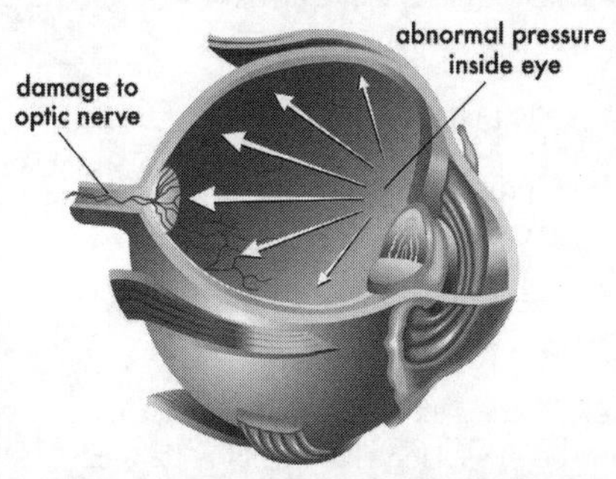

Eye & Ear Rx Interpretation

ABBREVIATION	MEANING	CAUTION
AD, AS, AU	Right Ear, Left Ear, Each Ear	These directions can be mistaken (interchanged) for each other and may mean other things; know how to interpret them but it is safer to write them out: use right eye, left eye, each eye, right ear, left ear, each ear.
OD, OS, OU	Right Eye, Left Eye, Each Eye	
Memory tip: A is from the Latin for ear (auris), O is from eye (oculus), D is from right (dextra) and S is from left (sinistra)		

GUIDELINE

American Academy of Ophthalmology Glaucoma Panel. Preferred Practice Pattern Guidelines. Primary Open-Angle Glaucoma Suspect. 2010. http://one.aao.org/preferred-practice-pattern/primary-openangle-glaucoma-ppp--october-2010 (accessed 2016 Dec 11).

EYE MEDICATION FORMULATIONS

- Solutions
- Suspensions – shake well or disperse prior to use.
- Ointments – apply to the conjunctival sac or over lid margins (for blepharitis). Ointments will make vision blurry and are not used with contact lenses.
- Gels – with cap on, invert and shake once to get medicine into the tip before instilling into the eye.

GLAUCOMA

Glaucoma is an eye disease caused by damage to the optic nerve and loss in the visual field (e.g., the vision straight ahead and the peripheral vision). In most cases, the intraocular pressure (IOP) is above the normal range of 12 – 22 mmHg. Whether the IOP is elevated, or with normal pressure glaucoma, the treatment goal is a reduction in IOP. If left untreated, glaucoma can result in damage to the optic nerve and a gradual loss of vision. There may be no symptoms felt by the patient, although some experience eye pain, headache and decreased vision.

There are two main forms of glaucoma. The more common type, open-angle glaucoma, is commonly treated with eye drops that lower IOP, or surgery. Angle-closure, or closed-angle glaucoma, is a sharp, sudden increase in IOP due to a blockage. This type of glaucoma is a medical emergency that is treated surgically.

RISK FACTORS

Risk factors for glaucoma include family history, increased age, African American ethnicity, and nearsightedness (myopia). A history of eye surgeries and diabetes can be contributory.

DRUG TREATMENT

Prostaglandin (PG) analogs and beta blockers are used most commonly as initial agents. PG analogs are the most effective drugs a decreasing IOP (~30%); they are safe and are used once daily. Beta blockers (e.g., timolol) are also used commonly as first-line drugs and decrease IOP ~22%. A beta blocker would be preferable if the pressure is high in one eye only, as the iris-darkening/eyelash thickening seen with PG analogs would not be desirable in one eye only. Brimonidine is most commonly used in addition when further IOP lowering is needed. The other classes of glaucoma medications are used less frequently.

KEY DRUGS THAT CAN INCREASE IOP

Cough/cold/motion sickness medications (antihistamines, including scopolamine)

Anticholinergics (e.g., oxybutynin, tolterodine, benztropine, trihexyphenidyl, tricyclic antidepressants)

Chronic steroids, especially eye drops such as prednisolone *(PredForte)*

Topiramate *(Topamax)*

Adherence & Technique: Improvement Is Needed

There are two common causes of persistently high IOP: 1) poor eye drop administration technique and 2) poor adherence. The correct way to administer eye drops is described later in this chapter. The asymptomatic presentation contributes to poor adherence. Counseling is critical for both administration technique and the need for therapy. The patient should understand the consequences of untreated glaucoma (e.g., loss of vision). Yet, even with counseling, adherence remains poor. For example, in one of the studies referenced in the glaucoma guidelines, less than 45% of the participants took < 75% of the daily doses. The patients had received counseling and the medication was provided at no charge and taken once daily.

GOAL: LOWER THE IOP

Options:

- Make less fluid (with beta blockers, like timolol)
- Move fluid out (with prostaglandin analogs, like latanoprost and travoprost)
- Or, do both: that's most often the result with the add-on brimonidine

All eye medications have something in common: the eyes sting and are blurry for a bit

DRUG	DOSING	SIDE EFFECTS/CLINICAL CONCERNS
Beta Blockers, Nonselective: reduce aqueous humor production		
Timolol 0.25% and 0.5% *(Timolol GFS, Timoptic, Timoptic-XE,* *Istalol, Betimol, Timoptic Ocudose)* + brimonidine *(Combigan)* + dorzolamide *(Cosopt, Cosopt PF)* + latanoprost *(Xalacom)* Levobunolol *(Betagan)* Carteolol *(Ocupress)* Metipranolol *(OptiPranolol)* Betaxolol *(Betoptic, Betoptic S)*	*Timolol:* 1 drop daily or BID *Timoptic-XE, Timolol GFS* (gels): daily Gels: shake once before use; wait 10 minutes after other eye drops before inserting gel	**CONTRAINDICATIONS** Sinus bradycardia; sinus node dysfunction; heart block > than first degree (except in patients with a pacemaker); cardiogenic shock; uncompensated cardiac failure; bronchospastic disease **SIDE EFFECTS** Slight burning, stinging, itching of the eyes or eyelids, changes in vision, increased sensitivity of the eyes to light, bradycardia, bronchospasm with non-selective agents, fatigue **NOTES** All are non-selective beta blockers except for betaxolol. Some contain the preservative benzalkonium chloride (BAK) which is absorbed by soft contact lenses. Use eye drops first, wait 15 minutes before inserting lenses (or remove prior to using eye drops). Occasionally patients have sensitivity to this preservative. The PF in *Cosopt PF* stands for "preservative free." Some contain sulfites, which can cause allergic reactions.

Glaucoma Medications Continued

Prostaglandin Analogs: increase aqueous outflow

DRUG	DOSING	SIDE EFFECTS/CLINICAL CONCERNS
Latanoprost *(Xalatan)* + timolol *(Xalacom)* **Travoprost** *(Travatan Z)* Bimatoprost *(Lumigan)* Unoprostone *(Rescula)* Tafluprost *(Zioptan)*	1 drop QHS, except *Rescula* is BID Cannot be administered with contact lenses (preservative BAK will absorb into lenses) – remove lenses and wait 15 min prior to re-insertion (most given QHS – instruct to remove contact lenses first)	**WARNINGS** Ocular effects: darkening of the iris, eyelid skin and eyelashes; eyelash length and number can increase; long-term consequences to the eye are not known; contamination of multiple-dose ophthalmic solutions can cause bacterial keratitis **SIDE EFFECTS** Blurred vision, stinging, foreign body sensation, increased pigmentation of the iris/eyelashes, eyelash growth/thickening **NOTES** Store unopened bottles of latanoprost in refrigerator. *Travatan Z* does not contain BAK, instead it has a different preservative. This may be helpful to some who have a reaction to BAK or dry eye, but most are fine with a less expensive generic. Bimatoprost *(Latisse)* is indicated for eyelash hypotrichosis (to ↑ eyelash growth) – do not use concurrently with drugs in the same class for glaucoma without MDs approval (using PG analogs more frequently ↓ effectiveness). *Zioptan* comes as 10 single-use containers in a foil pouch; store unopened pouches in the refrigerator. Once opened the contents are good for 28 days at room temperature. The single-use containers are sterile, but do not contain preservative. Discard each container after each single use, even if medicine is remaining.

Cholinergics (Miotics): increase aqueous outflow

DRUG	DOSING	SIDE EFFECTS/CLINICAL CONCERNS
Carbachol *(Isopto Carbachol, Miostat)*	1-2 drops up to TID	**SIDE EFFECTS** Corneal clouding, poor vision at night (due to pupil constriction), burning (transient), irritation, hypotension, bronchospasm, abdominal cramps/GI distress **NOTES** Use with caution in patients with a history of retinal detachment or corneal abrasion.
Pilocarpine *(Isopto Carpine, Pilopine HS)*	Solution: 1-2 drops up to 6x/day Gel: instill 0.5" ribbon into lower conjunctival sac once daily, at bedtime	

Glaucoma Medications Continued

DRUG	DOSING	SIDE EFFECTS/CLINICAL CONCERNS

Carbonic Anhydrase Inhibitors: reduce aqueous humor production

DRUG	DOSING	SIDE EFFECTS/CLINICAL CONCERNS
Dorzolamide *(Trusopt)* **+ timolol *(Cosopt, Cosopt PF)*** AcetaZOLAMIDE *(Diamox Sequels)* Brinzolamide *(Azopt)* + brimonidine *(Simbrinza)* Methazolamide *(Neptazane)*	*Trusopt:* 1 drop TID *Azopt:* 1 drop TID *Cosopt:* 1 drop BID Acetazolamide 250 mg PO 1-4x/day, or 500 mg ER PO BID	**WARNINGS** Sulfonamide allergy with the eye drops and oral acetazolamide: caution with allergy due to risk of systemic exposure **SIDE EFFECTS** Ocular agents: blurred vision, blepharitis, dry eye, discharge Oral agent (acetazolamide): CNS effects (ataxia, confusion), photosensitivity/skin rash (including risk of SJS and TEN), anorexia, nausea, risk of hematological toxicities **NOTES** Acetazolamide oral capsules are infrequently used for glaucoma. They are used for prevention and treatment of acute mountain (altitude) sickness. *Cosopt PF* comes in preservative-free (PF), single-use containers.

Adrenergic Alpha-2 Agonists: increase aqueous outflow, reduce aqueous humor production

DRUG	DOSING	SIDE EFFECTS/CLINICAL CONCERNS
Brimonidine *(Alphagan P)* + timolol *(Combigan)* + brinzolamide *(Simbrinza)* Dipivefrin *(Propine, Akpro)* Apraclonidine *(Iopidine)*	*Alphagan* and *Iopidine* are dosed TID	**WARNINGS** CNS depression: caution with heavy machinery, driving **SIDE EFFECTS** Sedation, burning/stinging/itchy eyes, dry mouth, dry nose

Patient Counseling (Eye Drops)

- Wash your hands.
- Before you open the bottle, shake it a few times. Gels need one shake prior to use (this helps the medication reach the tip).
- Bend your neck back a little so that you are looking up. Use one finger to pull down your lower eyelid. It is helpful, at least initially, to use a mirror.
- Without letting the tip of the bottle touch your eye or eyelid, squeeze one drop of the medication into the space between your eye and your lower eyelid. If you squeeze in more than one drop, you are wasting medication.
- After you squeeze the drop of medication into your eye, close your eye. Then press a finger between your eye and the top of your nose. Press for at least one full minute. This way, more of the medicine stays in your eye and you will be less likely to have side effects. Blot extra solution from the eyelid with a tissue.
- If your eye drop contains a preservative called benzalkonium chloride and you wear soft contact lenses, remove the lenses prior to administration (wait 15 minutes to reinsert).
- If you need to take more than one glaucoma medicine:
    - Put a drop of the first medication in your eye. If there are 2 drops of the same medication being given at the same time, wait 5 minutes between drops (do not administer two drops at once).
    - Wait at least 5 – 10 minutes to put a second medication in your eye. If administering a gel, wait 10 minutes after the other eye medication before use.

- ❑ If someone else puts your medications in your eye for you, remind that person to wait 5 – 10 minutes between each medication.

Prostaglandin Analog Counseling Specifics

- Remove contact lenses before using this medication because it contains a preservative that can be absorbed by the lenses, causing them to become discolored. Wait at least 15 minutes after using this medication before putting your lenses back in.
- You may experience an increase in brown coloring of the iris and gradual changes in eye color (for this reason, they are not usually given to patients with light eyes who have glaucoma in one eye only). Eyelash growth and darkening of eyelashes may increase (which is often pleasing to the patient). The skin on the eyelids and around the eyes may darken.
- This medication is well tolerated, but occasionally a patient can experience excessive tearing, eye pain, or lid crusting. If this occurs, please discuss with your optometrist or ophthalmologist.
- Latanoprost *(Xalatan)* unopened bottles should be stored in the refrigerator.
- Tafluprost *(Zioptan)* is kept refrigerated. Once opened the pouch of 10 single-use containers is good at room temperature for 28 days.
- Do not use this medication if you are also using Bimatoprost *(Latisse)*, to increase eyelash growth, without the approval of your optometrist or ophthalmologist. *Latisse* may reduce the effectiveness of the glaucoma medicine.

Timolol *(Timoptic)* Counseling Specifics

- Common side effects from beta blockers include burning/stinging or itching of the eyes, and possible light sensitivity.
- Timolol is a non-selective beta blocker, and although proper application should keep most of the medication in the eye, it is best to avoid use in patients with asthma, COPD, chronic bronchitis, emphysema, or advanced cardiac disease. The medication might exacerbate these disease symptoms. If you have any of these conditions, please discuss if this medication is safe to use with your healthcare provider.
- If dispensing drops using the *Ocudose* dispenser: to open the bottle, unscrew the cap by turning as indicated by the arrows on the top of the cap. Do not pull the cap directly up and away from the bottle. Pulling the cap directly up will prevent your dispenser from working properly.
- Invert the bottle, and press lightly with the thumb or index finger over the "Finger Push Area" until a single drop is dispensed into the eye.
- If dispensing the gel *(Timoptic XE, Timolol GFS)*: turn the container upside down once and shake the contents prior to use. The gel is used once daily. If using other eye drops beforehand, wait at least 10 minutes before using the gel.

OTHER OCULAR CONDITIONS

Medications can cause ocular adverse effects that disappear once the drug is discontinued (such as blurry vision from an anticholinergic). In other cases, the damage can be permanent (such as vision loss with a PDE5-inhibitor). Patients should be instructed to report visual changes immediately; in most cases the damage is reversible if the medication is stopped quickly.

Common Agents Known to Cause Vision Changes/Damage

- Alpha blockers (floppy iris syndrome-causes difficulty in cataract surgery)
- Amiodarone (corneal deposits, optic neuropathy)
- Bisphosphonates (ocular inflammation)
- Digoxin (yellow/green vision, blurriness, halos)

- Chloroquine *(Aralen)* (retinopathy, may cause permanent visual damage)
- Ethambutol *(Myambutol)*, linezolid *(Zyvox)* (optic neuropathy, especially with chronic use)
- Ezogabine *(Potiga)* (retinal changes, vision loss)
- Hydroxychloroquine *(Plaquenil)* (retinopathy)
- Isoniazid (optic neuritis)
- Isotretinoin (↓ night vision which may be permanent, dry eyes/irritation)
- Quinolones (retinal detachment)
- Sildenafil *(Viagra)* and other PDE5-inhibitors used for ED, PAH, BPH (greenish tinge around objects, possible permanent vision loss in one or both eyes)
- Tamoxifen *(Soltamox)* (corneal changes, decreased color perception)
- Voriconazole *(VFEND)* (abnormal vision, color vision change, photophobia)

Conjunctivitis: Allergic, Bacterial & Viral

Conjunctivitis or "pink eye" occurs in one or both eyes. Symptoms include swelling, itching, burning, and redness of the conjunctiva, the protective membrane that lines the eyelids and covers the white part of the eye (the sclera). Conjunctivitis can be due to a virus, a bacteria, an allergen or from some type of ocular irritant, such as chemicals or contact lenses. In most cases, conjunctivitis causes only mild discomfort, does not harm vision and will clear without medical treatment. Many times, treatment is given even if not clearly indicated. In some cases, treatment is required.

Viral and bacterial conjunctivitis occurs mostly in young children and is highly contagious. Until treatment is initiated, infected children should stay at home and should only be allowed to return to school once treatment has begun, unless there are systemic symptoms. Any patient with viral or bacterial conjunctivitis should be instructed to use proper hand hygiene:

- Don't touch your eyes with your hands.
- Wash your hands thoroughly and frequently.
- Change your towel and washcloth daily, and do not share towels with others.
- Discard eye cosmetics, particularly mascara.
- Do not use anyone else's eye cosmetics or personal eye care items.

For any type of conjunctivitis, compresses can help alleviate swelling and mild discomfort. To make a compress, soak a clean cloth in warm water (cool water for viral or allergic conjunctivitis), wring it out and apply gently to the closed eyelids. Artificial tears can be used to provide lubrication and help reduce a "gritty" feeling.

Chemical conjunctivitis has no specific drug treatment and is not described in the following table. The irritant should be flushed out of the eyes with saline and inflammation can be reduced with an NSAID or a steroid eye drop. If contact lenses have caused the irritation they should not be used until the condition has cleared. It may be helpful to change the type of contact lens or the brand of disinfectant solution. If the condition is severe, such as a burn, or the chemical is dangerous or unknown, the patient should be referred for emergency care.

Treatment Common to All Conjunctivitis Types

Most cases are mild and will resolve without treatment directed at the cause, such as an antibiotic for suspected bacterial conjunctivitis. However, these are often used, and in some cases are helpful in alleviating symptoms more quickly. Inflammation for any type of conjunctivitis can be reduced with NSAID (if mild) or steroid eye drops (if more severe). Artificial tears can help with a "gritty" feeling and will alleviate dryness. Instruct patients to return for follow-up if they do not recover within a few days (or longer with some types). If antibiotics are used, the course should be completed.

Conjunctivitis Types

VIRAL	BACTERIAL	ALLERGIC
Causes: adenovirus (most common), other viruses, most mild but some due to a more severe viral infection (e.g., zoster, HIV)	Causes: *Staph aureus, Strep pneumoniae, H. influenzae, Moraxella catarrhalis* More severe cases can be due to infection with *N. gonorrhoeae* or *Chlamydia*, which will require systemic treatment	Common allergens include pollen, dust mites, animal dander, molds
No topical treatment for common viral conjunctivitis; the infection will run its course, from several days to 2-3 weeks	Topical antibiotic eye drops or ointments, selected: **Azithromycin *(Azasite)*** – stored in refrigerator, 14 days at room temp Moxifloxacin *(Vigamox)* Besifloxacin *(Besivance)* Tobramycin/Dexamethasone *(TobraDex, TobraDex ST)* **Ciprofloxacin *(Ciloxan)*** **Ofloxacin *(Ocuflox)*** Gentamicin *(Garamycin)* Tobramycin *(Tobrex)* Erythromycin Sulfacetamide *(Bleph-10)* **Trimethoprim/Polymyxin B** *(Polytrim)* Neomycin/Bacitracin/Polymyxin B *(Neosporin)*	**MAST CELL STABILIZER EYE DROPS** Cromolyn Lodoxamide *(Alomide)* Nedocromil *(Alocril)* Pemirolast *(Alamast)* **ANTIHISTAMINE EYE DROPS** **Azelastine *(Optivar)*** Epinastine *(Elestat)* **Olopatadine *(Patanol)***

Eye Drops to Reduce Inflammation and Add Lubrication (Moisture)

DRUG	USAGE NOTES	EXAMPLES
Eye Drops to ↓ Inflammation	Steroid eye drops should be used short-term due to risk of ↑ IOP	**STEROIDS** Dexamethasone *(Maxidex, Ozurdex)* Loteprednol *(Alrex, Lotemax* suspension, ointment, gel) Fluorometholone *(Flarex, FML Forte, FML Liquifilm* suspension, ointment) **Prednisolone *(Pred Forte)*** **NSAIDs** **Ketorolac *(Acular, Acular LS, Acuvail)*** Flurbiprofen *(Ocufen)* Diclofenac Bromfenac
Artificial Tears to Moisturize Eyes	Common lubricants – mineral oil, glycerin, propylene glycol, dextran, hypromellose Administered multiple times daily, as needed	*Systane* *Refresh* *Clear Eyes* *Liquifilm* and others

Blepharitis (Eyelid Inflammation)

Blepharitis most commonly involves the part of the eyelid where the eyelashes come out of the skin. In many patients the condition is chronic and difficult to treat and in others, it is an acute, short-term condition. The primary symptoms are inflamed, irritated and itchy eyelids. The preferred treatment is gentle washing and application of compresses: apply a warm compress over the eye for a few minutes to loosen the crusty deposits, then use a warm moist washcloth (water plus a few drops of baby shampoo) to wipe away the debris. In some cases, antibiotic ointments, steroid eye drops and artificial tears are helpful.

OTICS

Background

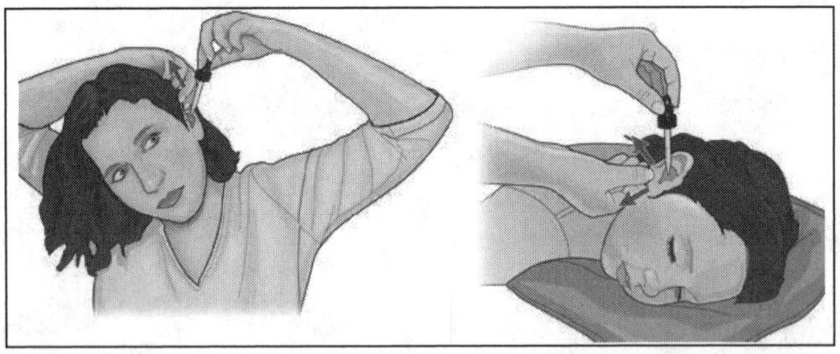

Common conditions treated in the ear include pain, such as from an otitis infection (these may be treated with topical antibiotics, although oral antibiotics are much more common), inflammation from swimmer's ear (otitis externa) and ear wax (cerumen) impaction. Otitis externa pain can be treated (preferentially) with systemic analgesics (e.g., ibuprofen, acetaminophen). During treatment, patients should stay out of the water, avoid flying due to the pressure changes, and avoid the use of headphones and ear plugs. Tinnitus (ringing or roaring or buzzing sounds) is caused by drug toxicity (primarily salicylates), noise exposure, or it can be idiopathic. There is no effective drug treatment for tinnitus. For any condition, eye drops may be used in the ear, but never use ear drops in the eyes; the ear drops may not have an appropriate pH, may not be isotonic, and may not be sterile.

Ear drops with antibiotics may also be used for outer ear infections. A few common products:

- Ciprofloxacin and hydrocortisone *(Cipro HC)*
- Ciprofloxacin and dexamethasone *(Ciprodex)*
- Neomycin, colistin, hydrocortisone, and thonzonium *(Cortisporin-TC)*

Ear Wax (Cerumen) Removal

Earwax blockage occurs when earwax (cerumen) accumulates in the ear or becomes too hard to wash away naturally. It is removed in a medical office. If the condition is chronic, ear-wax removal medication [carbamide peroxide *(Debrox)*, triethanolamine *(Cerumenex)*] is sometimes used every 4 – 8 weeks as a preventive measure. Instruct the patient to tilt the head sideways (see below) and instill 5 – 10 drops twice daily for up to four days.

Otic Medication Application

- If cold, gently shake the bottle or roll it in your hands for 1 or 2 minutes to warm the solution. Do not drop in cold medication. Ear drops that are too cold will be uncomfortable and can cause dizziness.
- Lie down or tilt the head so that the affected ear faces up.
- Gently pull the earlobe up and back for adults (down and back for children < 3 years) to straighten the ear canal.
- Administer the prescribed number of drops into the ear canal. Keep the ear facing up for about 5 minutes to allow the medication to coat the ear canal.
- Do not touch the dropper tip to any surface. To clean, wipe with a clean tissue.

MOTION SICKNESS

BACKGROUND

Motion sickness (kinetosis) is also called seasickness or airsickness. Symptoms are nausea, dizziness and fatigue. People can get motion sickness on a moving boat, train, airplane, car, or amusement park rides. This is a common condition.

NON-PHARMACOLOGIC TREATMENT

Some patients find benefit with a wrist band that presses on an acupuncture point located on the inside of the wrist, about the length of 2 fingernails up the arm from the center of the wrist crease. One popular brand is *Sea-Band* benefit. The best way to stop motion sickness, if possible, is to stop the motion.

Natural Products

Ginger, in teas or supplements, is used most commonly. Peppermint may be helpful.

DRUG TREATMENT

Medications for motion sickness are anticholinergics and may cause drowsiness and may impair judgment. Pilots, ship crew members, or anyone operating heavy equipment or driving a car should not take them. The military uses combinations of products (such as oral scopolamine to reduce nausea, taken with a stimulant, such as dextroamphetamine, to counteract the drowsiness from the scopolamine) but these combinations have significant risk and should not be routinely recommended.

Scopolamine *(Transderm-Scop)* is the most commonly prescribed medication for motion sickness. It is not more effective than generically-available OTC agents but is applied topically (behind the ear) and is taken less frequently (apply 4-6 hours prior to need, lasts three days, do not cut patch, alternate ears, do not get into eyes, wash hands afterwards). All of the antihistamines have anticholinergic effects similar to scopolamine. Make sure the oral agents are taken prior to travel (30-60 minutes prior) and ensure that the patient knows they will get tired. Instruct them not to consume alcohol or other CNS depressants.

Antihistamines used for motion sickness include cyclizine (*Marezine*), diphenhydramine *(Benadryl)*, dimenhydrinate *(Dramamine)* or meclizine *(Bonine)*. Dimenhydrinate, meclizine and cyclizine are long-acting piperazine antihistamines and are a little less sedating than other antihistamines, but they are still sedating. All of the antihistamines have anticholinergic effects similar to scopolamine. Make sure the oral agents are taken prior to travel (30-60 minutes prior) and ensure that the patient knows they will get tired. Instruct them not to consume alcohol or other CNS depressants.

Promethazine is used and is prescription only. Do not use promethazine in children. All promethazine products carry a boxed warning contraindicating use in children less than 2 years and strongly cautioning use in children age 2 and older. The FDA advises against the use of promethazine with codeine cough syrups in children less than 6 years of age, due to the risk of respiratory depression, cardiac arrest and neurological problems.

Anticholinergics

DRUG	DOSING	SAFETY/SIDE EFFECTS/MONITORING
Scopolamine 3-day patch ***(Transderm-Scop)*** Applied behind ear Q 72 hrs, rotate ears	1.5 mg, patch placed behind ear (hairless), 4-6 hours before needed, or 1 hour prior to cesarean section or evening before AM surgery – remove 24 hours after surgery Primarily for motion sickness, occasionally used inpatient. Do not use in children.	**WARNINGS** Hypersensitivity to belladonna alkaloids, narrow-angle glaucoma, paradoxical bradycardia, CNS depression, blurry vision/eye pain, withdrawal (high doses with abrupt d/c) **SIDE EFFECTS** Dry mouth, dizziness, stinging eyes (if touch eyes after handling patch), pupil dilation, ↑ risk IOP, confusion (can be significant in elderly, frail), hallucinations (rare), tachycardia (rare) **NOTES** Remove prior to MRI. Do not cut patch, wash hands before and after application.
Meclizine *(Dramamine Less Drowsy, Motion-Time, Medi-Meclizine, Travel Sickness)*	25-50 mg PO 1 hour before travel, can repeat Q 24 hrs if needed	**WARNINGS** CNS depression (may impair physical or mental abilities, caution in elderly), worsening of BPH symptoms, and can ↑ IOP (glaucoma) **SIDE EFFECTS** Sedation, dry mouth, dry/blurry vision, tachycardia
OTHER ANTIHISTAMINES USED Cyclizine, DiphenhydrAMINE, DimenhyDRINATE, Promethazine: Do not use in children due (primarily) to risk of respiratory depression. Do not give IV due to risk of severe tissue necrosis (vesicant). IM route is preferred for injection. Available in oral tablets, rectal suppository and injection.		

Transderm Scop Counseling

- Peel off the clear backing from the patch and apply it to a clean, dry, hairless area of the skin behind the ear. Press firmly for at least 30 seconds to make sure the patch sticks well, especially around the edges. The patch will slowly release the medication into your body over 3 days. Apply at least 4 hours before activity that will cause motion sickness. If getting an MRI procedure, remove patch before the MRI or it will burn your skin.
- Be sure to wash your hands thoroughly with soap and water before and immediately after handling the patch, so that any drug that might get on your hands will not come into contact with your eyes. Wash the area behind the ear where the patch was removed.
- No alcohol. Try to avoid other drugs that make you tired – this drug causes significant drowsiness.
- The most common side effect is dryness of the mouth. Other common side effects are drowsiness, blurry vision and widening of the pupils (especially if the drug is on your hands and you touch your eyes). Rarely, some people get disoriented, and others can get confusion, hallucinations or heart palpitations. If any of these occur remove the patch and contact your healthcare provider.

COMMON SKIN CONDITIONS

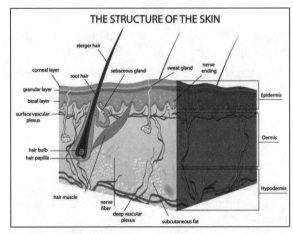

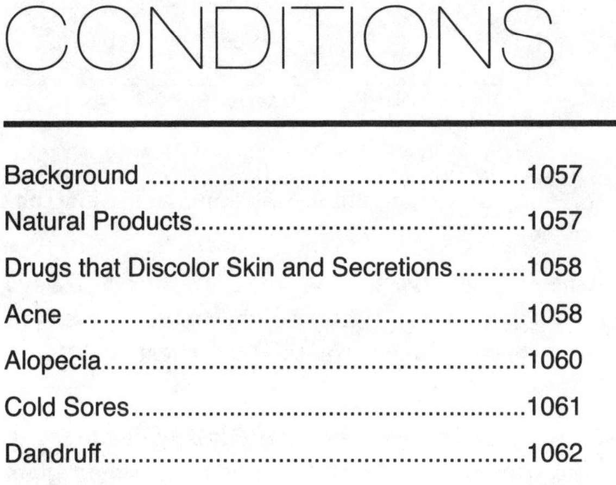

BACKGROUND

Patients in the community setting ask pharmacists for recommendations for a variety of skin conditions. Identifying the cause of a rash or sore can be simple, or challenging. *The Handbook of OTC Drugs* has pictures of common conditions, and many more are available at www.dermnet.com. If recommending OTC treatment, the patient should be counseled to seek further help if the condition does not improve or worsens. A pharmacist should be able to recognize a blemish that could be skin cancer; see the pictures and description in the Oncology I chapter.

Natural Products

Aloe is a natural product produced from the aloe vera plant that is used for many skin conditions, including sunburn and psoriasis. It has little proven efficacy but if used as a gel or lotion it may provide a soothing effect. Tea tree oil is used for a variety of skin conditions. It can be useful for treating acne. It may be helpful for onychomycosis symptoms (depending on the dose and application schedule), but is not useful in eradicating the infection in most patients. Lysine is used for cold sore (*herpes simplex labialis*) prevention and treatment. It is taken as a tablet, capsule or applied topically.

DRUGS THAT CAN DISCOLOR SKIN AND SECRETIONS			
Brown	**Brown/Black/Green**	**Yellow-Green**	**Red**
Levodopa, Entacapone	Methocarbamol	Propofol	Anthracyclines
Methyldopa		Flutamide	Deferasirox (urine)
	Purple/Ora/Red		
Brown/Yellow	Chlorzoxazone	**Red-Orange**	**Blue**
Metronidazole, Tinidazole		Phenazopyridine	Mitoxantrone
	Orange/Yellow		
Nitrofurantoin	Sulfasalazine	Rifapentine	Methylene blue
Riboflavin (B2)		Rifampin	
	Orange/Red/Brown		**Blue-Gray**
	Ezogabine		Chloroquine
			Amiodarone

Acne, Background & Treatment

- Most people develop acne, including infants, adults (and women, commonly, around the menstrual cycle) and, primarily, adolescents in puberty.
- Androgens (male sex hormones) are the primary determinant of acne (and is why boys often will have worse acne than girls) and the presence of the bacteria *P. acnes* and fatty acids (sebum) present in oil (sebaceous) glands. Where the glands are located is where acne occurs: the face, chest, shoulders and back.
- Emerging data suggest that diets with a high glycemic index will worsen acne. High glycemic foods cause higher insulin release, which increases sebum production. Dairy foods increase androgens and can worsen acne in some cases.
- Lesions are classified as whiteheads, blackheads, small bumps, cysts and nodules.
- Treatment is determined by severity: mild (few, occasional pimples), moderate (inflammatory papules), or severe (nodules and cysts).
- Acne is treated with four primary groups of agents: OTC (benzoyl peroxide and salicylic acid), retinoids, and topical or systemic (oral) antibiotics and systemic isotretinoin/
- Benzoyl peroxide (BPO) is the most effective OTC agent. It comes as Rx, including in combination with hydrocortisone, the retinoid adapalene or with the antibiotics erythromycin or clindamycin.
- Salicylic acid is a mildly useful OTC agent, and is primarily used in "medicated pads" for facial cleansing.
- Retinoids, primarily topical tretinoin and derivatives are the usual Rx drug of choice. [They are also used to reduce fine wrinkles.]
    - Retinoids are vitamin A derivatives. The mechanism is primarily to reduce adherence of the keratinocytes (outer skin cells) in the oil gland.
    - They are well-tolerated when used topically, with mild skin irritation (redness, drying) and photosensitivity possible. Start at night (or every other night) with the correct (pea sized) amount. Use moisturizer each morning, followed by sunscreen.
    - Retinoids take 4-12 weeks to work and acne may worsen initially. An antibiotic (often minocycline) taken concurrently can help.
    - They are not used in pregnancy or breastfeeding; some are pregnancy category C, others are X. Tazarotene often works better than tretinoin; it is used with difficult cases and is pregnancy category X.
    - Often a topical antibiotic is used concurrently – the retinoid allows the antibiotic to get into the pores to eradicate the bacteria.

  - ❑ The oral retinoid isotretinoin has many safety considerations, including severe teratogenicity, and is reserved for severe nodular acne only. Cholesterol and pregnancy tests are required, among other monitoring.

- Some women find benefit with birth control pills, especially if the acne is in combination with irregular periods or symptoms of androgenic excess.

- Azelaic acid *(Azelex, Finacea)* is a topical dicarboxylic acid cream or gel available OTC and Rx for acne and rosacea. It is well tolerated and can cause mild topical burning or "tingling."

DRUGS	NOTES	SAFETY/COUNSELING
Retinoid topicals are 1st line agents Tretinoin cream ***(Atralin, Renova, Retin-A, Retin-A Micro**, Avita, Refissa, Tretin-X)* Slower-release, less skin irritation with: ■ Microsphere gel ***(Retin-A Micro)*** ■ Polymerized cream or gel ***(Avita)*** **Adapalene *(Differin)*** cream, solution Adapalene + BPO *(Epiduo)* Tazarotene (*Tazorac*, Avage-creams, Fabior-foam) stronger, more irritating Dapsone gel *(Aczone)* Retinoids are popular and there are many other products, such as clindamycin + tretinoin gel *(Ziana)*, others	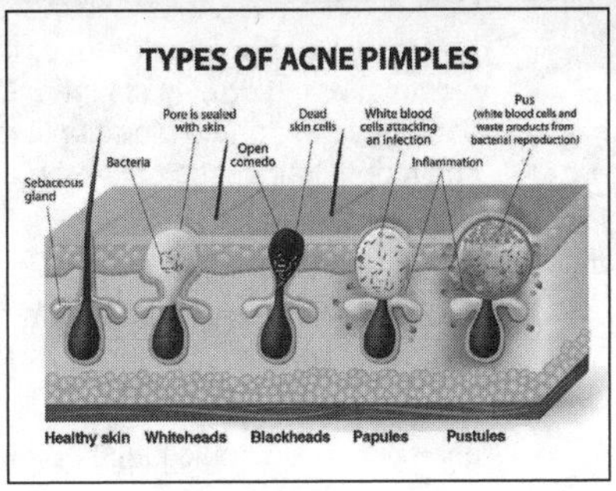	Apply daily, usually at bedtime, about 20 minutes after washing face. If irritation use lower strength, or every other night. May need to reduce contact initially (wash off if skin is irritated). A pea-sized amount is sufficient (for facial application); it should be divided into 4 equal parts and smoothed over the entire surface of the face – not just on acne. Avoid salicylic acid scrubs or astringents while starting a retinoid; this will worsen irritation. Wash only with mild soap twice daily. Takes 4-12 weeks to see response; may worsen acne initially. Limit sun exposure. Do not use dapsone gel if G6PD deficiency.
Benzoyl peroxide (BPO), OTC, Rx OTC (many products) including *Benoxyl, Benzac, Clearasil*, if needed with a retinoid Start with 2.5-5% BPO, which is generally adequate and less irritating than the higher strengths Erythromycin + BPO ***(Benzamycin)*** Clindamycin + BPO ***(Acanya, BenzaClin, Duac**, Neuac)* BPO+hydrocortisone *(Vanoxide-HC)* Azelaic acid *(Azelex, Finacea)*, OTC, Rx **Salicylic acid,** OTC, weaker efficacy	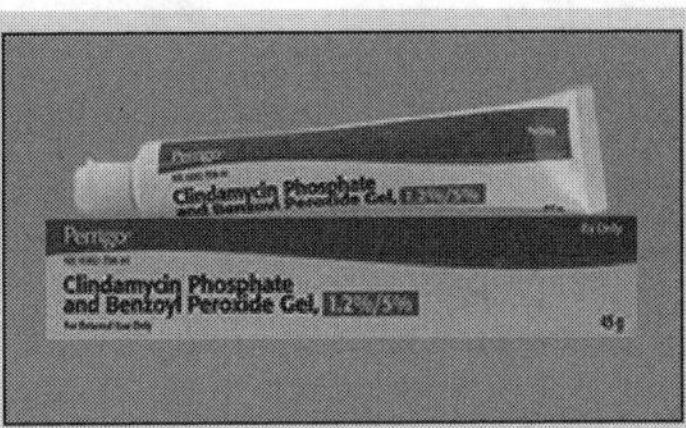 ***Duac*** Dispense with 60 day expiration. Apply QHS to affected areas. Can store at room temp, do not freeze. Limit sun exposure. **Clindamycin Topicals, usual instructions** Clean face, shake (if lotion), apply a thin layer once or twice daily. Avoid contact with eyes; if contact, rinse with cold water. Takes 2-6 weeks for effect and up to 12 weeks for full benefit.	BPO can bleach clothing, hair Limit sun exposure; skin will burn more easily. ***Benzamycin and BenzaClin*** Add indicated amount of purified water to the vial (70% ethyl alcohol for *Benzamycin)* and immediately shake to completely dissolve medication. If needed, add additional purified water to bring level up to the mark. Add the solution in the vial to the gel and stir until homogenous in appearance (1 to 1½ minutes). *Benzamycin* is kept refrigerated. *BenzaClin* is kept at room temp. Place a 3 month expiration date on the label following mixing.

Acne Background & Treatment Continued

DRUGS	NOTES	SAFETY/COUNSELING
Oral isotretinoin *(Amnesteem, Claravis, Myorisan, Absorica)* Only for the treatment of severe recalcitrant nodular acne 0.5–1.0 mg/kg/day, divided BID with food for 15-20 weeks. Comes as 10, 20, and 40 mg capsules. Counseling about contraception and behaviors associated with risk of pregnancy must be repeated on a monthly basis. Two forms of birth control are required while taking this medication (cannot use a progestin-only pill). Dryness: Carry bottled water, eye drops and lip balm.	Female patients must sign patient information/informed consent form about birth defects that contains warnings about the risk of potential birth defects if the fetus is exposed to isotretinoin. Must have had 2 negative pregnancy tests prior to starting treatment. Cannot get pregnant for one month before, while taking the drug, or for one month after the drug is stopped. Do not breastfeed or donate blood until at least one month has passed after the drug is stopped. Do not use with vitamin A supplements, tetracyclines, steroids, progestin-only contraceptives, or St. John's wort. Must swallow capsule whole, or puncture and sprinkle on applesauce or ice cream – this may irritate esophagus.	Pregnancy Category X: severe birth defects or miscarriage. Can only be dispensed by a pharmacy registered and activated with the pregnancy risk management iPLEDGE program. 1-month Rx at a time, fill within 7 days with yellow sticker attached. Teratogenicity, arthralgias, skeletal hyperostosis, osteoporosis, psychiatric issues (depression, psychosis, risk of suicide), decreased night vision (may be permanent), difficulty wearing contact lens (dry eyes/irritation), dry skin, chapped lips, elevated cholesterol and BG, transient chest pain and hearing loss, and photosensitivity.
ORAL ANTIBIOTICS USED COMMONLY FOR ACNE **Minocycline ext-rel** ***(Solodyn)*** 12 years and older, dosed by weight Doxycycline and minocycline are more effective than tetracycline in eradicating *P. acnes* Trimethoprim/Sulfamethoxazole is also used. Erythromycin used to be commonly used but is not currently due to resistance.	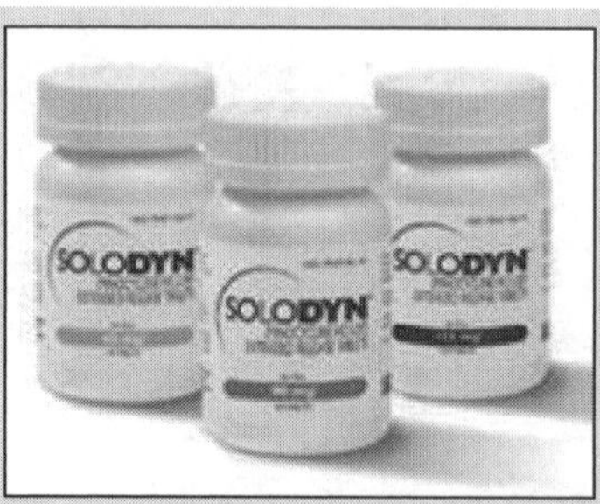	Photosensitivity, rash in susceptible patients, dizziness, diarrhea, somnolence Like other tetracyclines can cause fetal harm if administered during pregnancy. May cause permanent discoloration in teeth if used when teeth are forming (up to 8 years of age).

Alopecia (Hair Loss), Background & Treatment

- As people age, hair tends to gradually thin. Other causes of hair loss include hormonal factors, medical conditions and medications.
- The most common cause of hair loss is a hereditary condition called male-pattern baldness, and less commonly, female-pattern baldness.
- Hormonal changes in women that can result in hair loss are usually associated with pregnancy, childbirth or menopause.
- Medical conditions that cause hair loss include hypothyroidism, alopecia areata (an autoimmune condition), scalp infections and some other conditions, including lupus.
- Drugs that can contribute to alopecia include various chemotherapeutics (primarily because hair cells are rapidly dividing and therefore are targeted by the treatment) and infrequently with the following medications: clomiphene, heparin, hydroxychloroquine, interferons, lithium, some types of oral contraceptives, levonorgestrel, procainamide, valproate, spironolactone and warfarin.

- Zinc and vitamin D deficiency is thought to contribute to hair loss.
- Many people will seek surgical intervention for hair loss. The medications work modestly and are presented here. Bimatoprost in the *Latisse* formulation is for thinning eyelashes (hypotrichosis) and should not be used concurrently in patients using a prostaglandin analog for glaucoma (minimally, contact the optometrist or ophthalmologist to confirm because the IOP may increase if there is excessive use of prostaglandin analogs.)

DRUGS	NOTES	SAFETY/COUNSELING
Finasteride *(Propecia)* 5-alpha reductase type 2 inhibitor Do not dispense with someone on finasteride (*Proscar*) for BPH 1 mg daily, at least 3 months duration to begin to see effect	 Romic Eskandarian, PharmD *(God made a few good heads, and put hair on the rest of them.)*	Preg Categ X: females should not handle – can damage male fetus. Must be used indefinitely or condition reappears. **SIDE EFFECTS** Lower dose than *Proscar*; lower risk of sexual side effects; see overactive bladder chapter for further details
Minoxidil topical OTC 2% and 5% – 5% solution more effective, but more facial hair growth.	Rx tablets indicated for hypertension (very rarely used)	For men and women Must be used indefinitely or condition reappears.
Bimatoprost solution *(Latisse)* For thinning eyelashes (hypotrichosis)	Apply nightly to the skin at the base of the upper eyelashes only (do not apply to the lower lid). Use the applicator brush. Blot any excess. Repeat for other eye. Dispose of the applicator after one use.	May cause itchy eyes and/or eye redness. If discontinued, lashes eventually return to previous appearance. Eyelid skin darkening may occur, which may be reversible. Hair growth may occur in other skin areas that the solution frequently touches. Do not use concurrently with PG analogs used for glaucoma.

Cold Sores, Background & Treatment

- Cold sores (Herpes simplex labialis) are ubiquitous and are highly contagious. Children often pick up the infection from family members. Infection is usually due to herpes simplex virus type 1 (HSV-1) in children, but can be caused by HSV-2 when older due to oral/genital sex. Virus can be shed when asymptomatic but is most commonly spread with active lesions; the infectious exudate should not be transmitted (kissing, sharing drinks).
- Sore eruption is preceded by prodromal symptoms (tingling, itching, soreness). In most patients the sore appears in the same location repeatedly. The most common site is the junction between the upper and lower lip. Triggers that instigate sore outbreaks include fatigue/stress, stress to the skin (sun exposure, acid peels) and dental work. Patients should identify their own trigger/s and attempt to avoid them.

- The prodromal period is the optimal time to apply topical or take oral medication to reduce blister duration. If recurrences are frequent (> 4 times/year), chronic suppression, taken daily, can be used. OTC and Rx topicals shorten the duration by up to one day; oral (systemic) antivirals shorten the duration by up to two days.
- The natural product lysine is used commonly for cold sore prevention.

DRUGS	NOTES	SAFETY/COUNSELING
Docosanol *(Abreva)* – OTC **Rx** Acyclovir topical cream *(Zovirax)* Acyclovir buccal tablets *(Sitavig)* Penciclovir topical cream *(Denavir)*	Oral antivirals can be used, are more effective, and are discussed in the ID chapter. 	*Abreva* cream: Apply 5x daily at first sign of outbreak, continue until healed. *Zovirax* cream: Apply 5 times daily for 4 days (can be used on genital sores). *Sitavig* tablet: Apply one 50 mg tablet as a single dose to the upper gum region. *Denavir* cream: Apply every 2 hours during waking hours for 4 days.

Dandruff, Background & Treatment

- Dandruff occurs when the scalp is itchy and/or scaling with white oily flakes (dead skin) in the hair and on the shoulders, back or clothing.
- Dandruff can be due to either eczema or fungal (yeast) overgrowth, and worsened by hormones, the weather or shampoo. Seborrheic dermatitis is a common form of eczema that causes flaking, itchy skin on the face, back, chest or head. If it is on the scalp it is commonly referred to as dandruff.
- Patients are not likely to know the cause of the dandruff. A store-brand, inexpensive dandruff shampoo can be tried first, and if this is ineffective, the pricier ketoconazole antifungal shampoo can be used.

DRUGS	NOTES	SAFETY/COUNSELING
Selenium sulfide ((*Dandrex, Selsun, Tersi)*, zinc pyrithone (*Head & Shoulders*), coal tar shampoos, *Suave* or store brands "dandruff" shampoos Ketoconazole shampoo *(Nizoral A-D)* Ketoconazole topical comes in many formulations for dandruff or seborrheic dermatitis (see notes above): cream, foam, gel & shampoo	 There are many different dandruff shampoos. Shown here is the antifungal shampoo *Nizoral A-D*. It is prudent to have the patient try less expensive formulations first, since these may work as well, including store brands or *Suave* dandruff shampoo.	Rub shampoo in well and leave in for 5 minutes, then rinse out. Shampoo daily. If the shampoo stops working, switch products. Nizoral A-D Apply twice weekly, for up to 8 weeks. Do not use if open sores on scalp. Can cause skin irritation.

Diaper Rash, Background & Treatment

Diaper rash commonly occurs with nearly all babies. The skin is sensitive, and when exposed to the urine and stools, and a diaper moving back and forth, rash appears. Once the skin is damaged it is susceptible to bacteria and yeast overgrowth.

Prevention

- Change diapers frequently, do not cover diapers with plastic, use absorbent diapers.
- Wipe well with unscented wipes or plain water.
- Leave off the diaper, when possible, to let the skin air-dry. The baby can lie on a towel.
- Use a skin protectant:
  - Petrolatum ointment (*A & D Ointment*, store brands) – this is a good preventative every-day ointment, includes vitamins A and D.
  - Petrolatum with zinc oxide, such as in *Desitin* – is thicker and contains a dessicant (zinc oxide) to dry out the skin; may be preferable for babies more prone to rash.
- *"Butt Paste"* or *"Triple Paste"* – are other alternatives.
- Clotrimazole, miconazole, others – for stubborn rashes, if yeast thought to be involved.
- Hydrocortisone 0.5-1% cream – can be used BID, but not for more than several days at a time.
- Combinations of the above are used.

DRUGS	NOTES	SAFETY/COUNSELING
Desitin (petrolatum + zinc oxide, a dessicant to decrease moisture) *A&D Ointment*, or plain petrolatum, or store-brands. Miconazole+zinc oxide+petrolatum *(Vusion)* Or other products mentioned above.	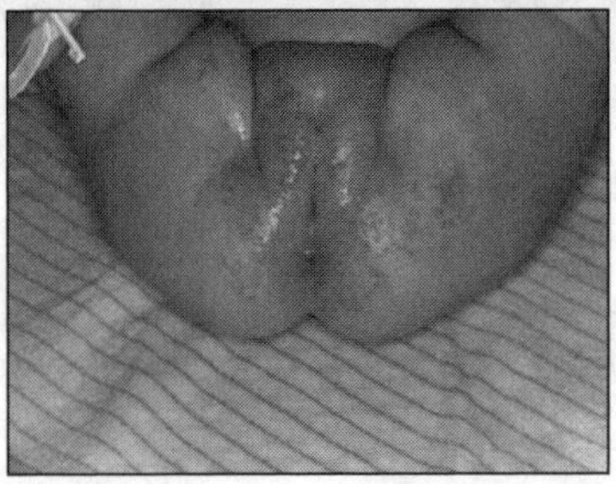	Review counseling tips above. Infants should be referred to the physician (especially if under 6 months) and older babies if condition appears serious or worsens. Topical antibiotics may be needed if bacterial involvement is suspected. Topical antifungals may be needed if fungal involvement is suspected. Topical steroids, low potency, may be used short-term. Diaper rashes can have more than one contributing organism.

Eczema (Atopic Dermatitis), Background & Treatment

- Eczema is a general term for many types of skin inflammation, and is used interchangeably with the term atopic dermatitis (which is sometimes used to refer to other conditions – this makes the term "atopic dermatitis" confusing).
- Eczema is most common in young children and infants, but can occur at any age.
- Eczema presents as skin rashes, which become crusty and scaly; blisters can develop. The rash is very itchy, red, dry and sore.
- Common locations are the insides of elbows, back of knees, face (often on the cheeks), behind the ears, buttocks, hands and feet.
- Outbreak "triggers" can be environmental irritants or allergens, including soaps, perfumes, pollution, stress or weather changes; patients should attempt to avoid triggers.
- Hydration is essential to reduce disease severity. Use moisturizers. Maintain humidity in the home.

- Treatment can include topical corticosteroids (and occasional oral courses, if-needed), antihistamines (for itching), or the immunosuppressant calcineurin inhibitors, if topical steroids with hydration are not adequate.
- In severe, refractive cases, oral immune-suppressants (cyclosporine, methotrexate, monoclonal antibody-type drugs such as etanercept and others) can be used. These are described in other chapters.

DRUGS	NOTES	SAFETY/COUNSELING
Tx: topical or oral steroids, antibiotics, antihistamines, keep skin well hydrated (moisturized with petrolatum, lanolin, products such as *Aquaphor, Eucerin, Keri* or store brands) Treat first with topical steroids, only use these agents if failed steroids: Tacrolimus (*Protopic*) **Pimecrolimus *(Elidel)*** Do not use in children younger than 2 years of age.	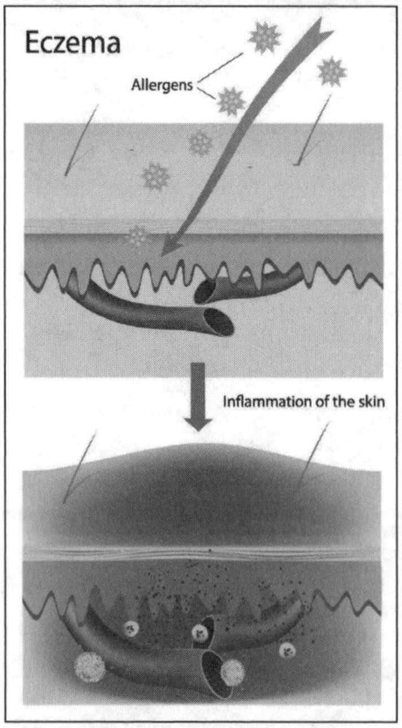	Dispense MedGuide for *Elidel* and *Protopic*: Associated with cases of lymphoma and skin cancer; use only as second-line agents for short-term and intermittent treatment of atopic dermatitis (eczema) in patients unresponsive to, or intolerant of other treatments. Apply a thin layer only to the affected skin areas, twice a day. Use the smallest amount needed to control symptoms. Takes weeks to work; continue to apply. Wash your hands after application. Limit sun exposure; photosensitizer. Side effects can include headache, skin burning, itching, cough, flu-like symptoms

Fungal Infections: Skin, Background & Treatment

Tinea pedis, cruris, corporis, and topical *Candida* infections (vaginal, onychomycosis, diaper rash see separate sections)

Athlete's foot (tinea pedis)

- A fungal infection of the foot caused by various fungi (commonly trichophyton rubrum).
- Symptoms are itching, peeling, redness, mild burning, and sometimes sores. This is a common infection, particularly among those using public pools, showers, and locker rooms. Diagnosis is usually by symptoms, but if unclear (psoriasis and other conditions can cause itchy skin), the skin can be scraped off and viewed under a microscope.
- It is treated topically with antifungals, except in severe cases.

Jock itch (tinea cruris)

- Affects the genitals, inner thighs and buttocks.
- The rash is red, itchy and can be ring-shaped.
- Jock itch is not very contagious, but can be spread person-to-person with close contact.
- Keep the skin dry (use a clean towel after showering) and treat with an antifungal topical. Creams work best.
- Change underwear at least daily.

Ringworm (tinea corporis)

- Not a worm, but a skin fungal infection.
- Ringworm can appear anywhere on the body and typically looks like circular, red, flat sores (one or more, may overlap), usually with dry, scaly skin. Occasionally the ring-like presentation is not present – just itchy red skin.
- The outer part of the sore can be raised while the skin in the middle appears normal. It can spread person-to-person or by contact with infected animals.
- Most cases are treated topically.
- Tinea capitis is "ringworm" on the scalp – this affects primarily young children, mostly in crowded, lower-income situations and requires systemic therapy, with the same drugs used for onychomycosis.

Cutaneous (skin) *Candida* infections

- Topical *Candida* infections cause red, itchy rashes, most commonly in the groin, armpits or anywhere the skin folds.
- These are more likely in obese persons because they will have more skin with folds; the infection can be in unusual places, such as under the breasts, if the skin is moist. Diabetes is another risk factor.
- Occasionally fungal infections appear in the corner of nails (on the skin, not in the nailbed). If this is a suspected bacterial infection, OTC antibiotic topicals or mupirocin (*Bactroban* – excellent gram positive coverage) can be used.
- *Candida* can cause diaper rash in infants (discussed under diaper rash).

DRUGS	NOTES	SAFETY/COUNSELING
Terbinafine and butenafine highly effective: Terbinafine (*Lamisil* AT cream and solution) Butenafine (*Lotrimin Ultra* cream) Clotrimazole (*Lotrimin* cream, lotion, solution, *Desenex*) Miconazole (*Monistat-Derm, Lotrimin* powder and spray) Miconazole+petrolatum (for moisture barrier, used in geriatrics) *(Baza)* *Monistat Derm* cream Tolnaftate (*Tinactin* powder, cream, spray) Undecylenic acid (*Cruex, Desenex*), others **Betamethasone/Clotrimazole *(Lotrisone)*** – popular for tinea with inflammation/itching **Rx** Ketoconazole (cream), ketoconazole foam *(Extina)* Note the same name in OTC products can refer to different active ingredients – do not instruct patient by brand name alone or there could be a product mix-up. The FDA will be attempting to eliminate this confusion by restricting name allocations.	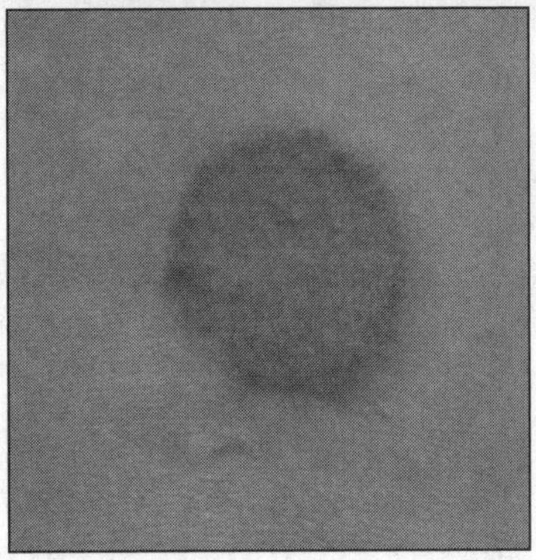 Tinea corporis (ringworm) – the name "ringworm" is a misnomer; this is a fungal infection. The rings can be single or overlap.	Topical antifungals come in creams, ointments, gels, solutions Creams work best and are used in most cases. Solutions can be easier to apply in hairy areas. Powders do not work well for treatment but may be used for prevention, such as in shoes after a gym workout. Use cotton socks. Apply medicine 1-2 inches beyond the rash. Use for at least 2-4 weeks, even if it appears healed. Reduce moisture to the infected area. If foot infection, do not walk barefoot (to avoid spreading it). Wear sandals in public showers (to avoid catching it).

Fungal Infections: Toenail & Fingernail, Background & Treatment

- Onychomycosis (tinea unguium) can cause pain, discomfort, and disfigurement and can lead to physical limitations, such as difficulty standing and walking. The discoloration and disfigurement can cause loss of self-esteem and psychological issues.
- Topical agents are limited to mild cases, patients who cannot tolerate systemic therapies, or are used concurrently with systemic treatment or as prophylaxis. They are not potent enough to cure most infections.
- Itraconazole and terbinafine are used most commonly and have FDA indications; fluconazole and posaconazole are used off-label. Griseofulvin is rarely used currently.
- It takes a long time for the nail bed to look better – sometimes up to a year in toenails. Toenails take longer to treat than fingernails, and are more commonly infected.
- Pulse therapy (intermittent) can be used to reduce costs and possibly toxicity, but may not be as effective.
- A 20% potassium hydroxide (KOH) smear is essential for diagnosis as other conditions can produce a similar presentation.

DRUGS	NOTES	SAFETY/COUNSELING
Itraconazole *(Sporanox)* Dose 200 mg Q daily x 12 weeks for 12 weeks, or "pulse-dosing" (fingernails only): 200 mg BID x 1 week, repeat 1-week course after 3 weeks off-time Terbinafine *(LamISIL, Terbinex)* – oral (topical is *LamISIL AT,* and is used for fungal skin infections) 250 mg PO daily for 6 weeks (fingernail) or 12 weeks (toenail) Ciclopirox *(Penlac, Loprox)* Apply evenly over entire nail plate QHS (or 8 hours before washing) to all affected nails with applicator brush Tavabarole *(Kerydin)* Efinaconazole *(Jublia)* *Kerydin* & *Jublia*: apply once daily for 48 weeks, both for toenails	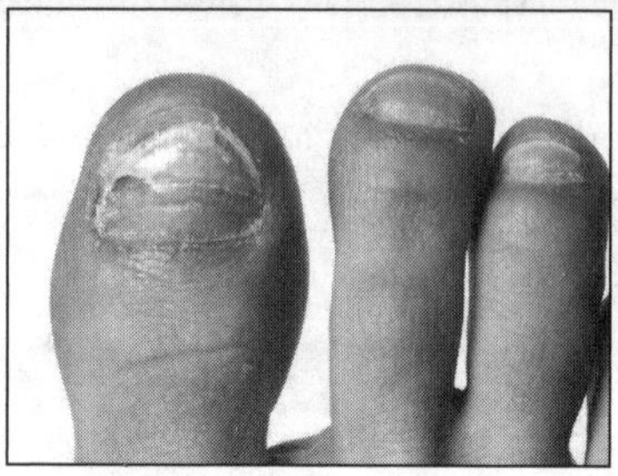 Ciclopirox (*Penlac, Loprox*) – used in combination with orals; poor efficacy when used alone. Occasionally used in patients who cannot tolerate systemic therapy, but generally cannot cure an infection when used alone. Occasionally used as prophylaxis. Tavaborole *(Kerydin)* – oxaborole antifungal, applied topically to toenails Q daily x 48 weeks to entire nail surface and under the nail tip. Efinaconazole *(Jublia)* – azole antifungal, applied topically to toenails Q daily x 48 weeks	For systemic azoles, refer to Infectious Disease chapter III. Systemic drugs used for nail fungal infections are hepatotoxic (monitor LFTs), QT prolongers (avoid in QT risk) and CYP 3A4 substrates & inhibitors (there are many drug interactions). Nausea and diarrhea are common. Itraconazole *(Sporanox)* Boxed warning to avoid use in heart failure. Requires gastric acid for absorption; cannot use strong acid suppressing agents concurrently. Terbinafine *(Lamisil, Terbinex)* – oral Primarily headache, rash, nausea, risk of hepatotoxicity. Recurrence is common. Practice proper foot care and keep the nails dry. Keep blood glucose controlled. Do not smoke.

Fungal Infections: Vaginal

This is a common infection; about 75% women will have at least one episode, and half of these women will have recurrence. In a small percentage of women the recurrence is chronic.

- The infection is uncommon before a girl begins menstruating, and occurs most commonly during the week prior to menstruation – this makes treatment decisions around the period important. The woman can begin treatment during menses, or wait until the bleeding stops. Tampons should not be used when medication is applied.

- Vaginal fungal infections are also common during pregnancy. Pregnant patients are hopefully seeing a physician, and require longer (7 - 10 day) treatment.
- Symptoms are primarily itching, with possible soreness and pain (burning) during urination or sex. Some women have a cottage-cheese like discharge (white, thick, clumpy).
- Diagnosis can be confirmed with either a vaginal culture to check for fungal growth or, via a pH test: a pH greater than 4.5 indicates the presence of either a *Candida* or trichomoniasis infection. OTC test kits such as the *Vagisil Screening Kit* test for vaginal pH. Generally, testing is not necessary if the woman has been seen by the physician for the initial infection and is able to recognize the symptoms.
- If the woman has had the infection before and is able to recognize the symptoms, she can self-treat with OTC products. If there are more than four infections in a year, or if symptoms recur within 2 months, refer to the physician to rule-out an underlying condition that could be causative (most likely diabetes, HIV, receiving steroids or other immune-suppressing agents, pregnancy, or irritation from repeated douching or use of lubricants). Women taking high-dose estrogen in birth control pills or in hormone replacement therapy are at elevated risk. Antibiotic use can be a risk factor; the antibiotic can wipe out the normal flora and lead to fungal overgrowth.
- Lactobacillus or yogurt with active cultures is thought to reduce infection occurrence; however, this is rated as "possibly ineffective" by the *Natural Medicines Database.*
- If self-treating, counsel that condoms and diaphragms may not provide adequate pregnancy protection; the oil in OTC antifungals weakens the latex.
- To avoid future infections, keep the vaginal area clean, wipe from the front to the back, use cotton underwear, avoid tight-fitting clothing, including pantyhose, change pads/tampons often, change out of wet swimsuits or clothing quickly, and recommend against use of vaginal douches, sprays and deodorant tampons; these can alter the vaginal pH and contribute to infection.

DRUGS	NOTES	SAFETY/COUNSELING
Mild-moderate, infrequent infection 1 or 3 day treatment, with vaginal cream, ointment or vaginal suppository/tab **OTC, topical** Butoconazole (*Gynazole-1*, others) Clotrimazole (*Gyne-Lotrimin*, others) Miconazole (*Monistat 3*, others) Terconazole (*Terazol 3*, others) Tioconazole (*Vagistat-1*) **Rx, oral** Fluconazole (*Diflucan*) 150 mg PO x 1 Complicated infections, pregnancy: 7-10 days treatment, or send for referral	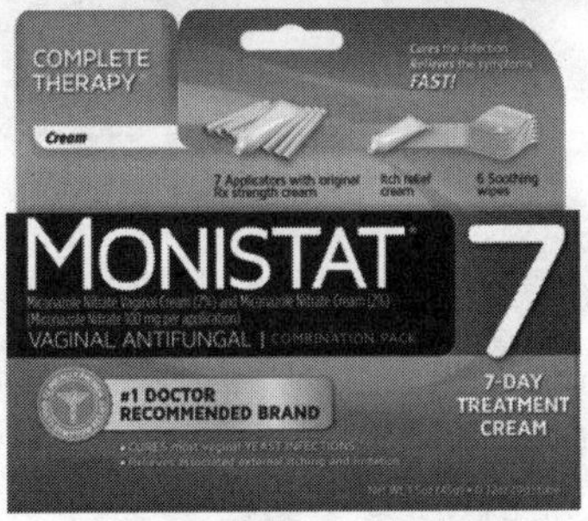 Always counsel on ways to avoid recurrence: avoid douching, wear cotton underwear, avoid tight-fitting pantyhose and pants, change out of wet swimsuits quickly. Some recommend avoiding hot tubs or very hot baths. The male sexual partner may be tested if the female's infections are recurrent; this is not commonly done	Counseling for OTC antifungals: Prior to using the product, wash the vagina with mild soap and water, and pat dry with a towel. Insert applicator, suppository, or vaginal tab at night before bed. Lying down immediately after insertion helps retain the medicine inside the vagina. It may be helpful to use a protective pad. The creams and suppositories are oil-based medications that can weaken latex condoms and diaphragms; avoid sexual intercourse. If you get your menstrual cycle during treatment, continue the treatment, otherwise a woman can wait until her menstrual cycle is over before starting treatment if she desires (this is not necessary). Do not use tampons during treatment. Complete entire course of treatment. Medical care is warranted if symptoms persist/recur within 2 months after using an OTC product, or if > 4/year.

Genital Warts, Background & Treatment

- Genital warts are caused by the human papillomavirus (HPV), a common sexually transmitted disease (STD), spread easily skin-to-skin. Consider recommending HPV vaccine, if series incomplete. *Gardasil* protects against the strains of HPV that cause most genital warts and reduces risk of cervical cancer. *Cervarix* protects against cervical cancer but not genital warts. Condoms reduce risk of STD transmission.
- Treatment may not be required if no symptoms, but if discomfort or emotional distress, treatment can reduce or remove the warts.
- Imiquimod (*Aldara, Zyclara*) will reduce warts. Avoid sexual contact while the cream is on your skin; weakens condoms, diaphragms and can irritate the partner's skin.

In addition to the treatments below, the warts may be removed by lasers, cryotherapy (with liquid nitrogen to freeze the warts, after which they come off), freezing, electrocautery (electrical current burns off warts) or surgical excision.

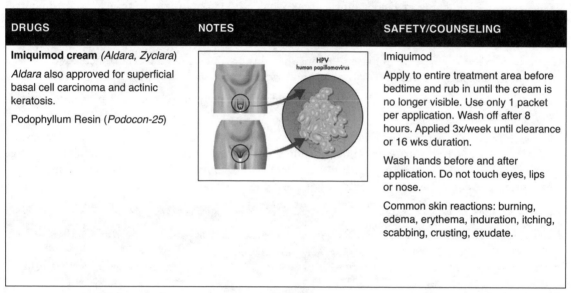

DRUGS	NOTES	SAFETY/COUNSELING
Imiquimod cream *(Aldara, Zyclara)* *Aldara* also approved for superficial basal cell carcinoma and actinic keratosis. Podophyllum Resin (*Podocon-25*)	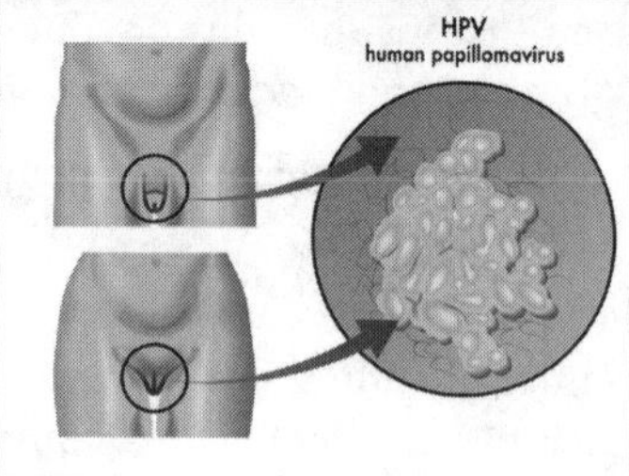	Imiquimod Apply to entire treatment area before bedtime and rub in until the cream is no longer visible. Use only 1 packet per application. Wash off after 8 hours. Applied 3x/week until clearance or 16 wks duration. Wash hands before and after application. Do not touch eyes, lips or nose. Common skin reactions: burning, edema, erythema, induration, itching, scabbing, crusting, exudate.

Hemorrhoids

- Hemorrhoids are swollen blood vessels in the lower rectum. They are in a sensitive location and have a rich blood vessel supply that can result in engorgement. Common symptoms are pruritus, burning and rectal bleeding. The blood is usually bright red.
- If dietary fiber is not optimum, increasing fiber intake can help reduce straining. Products such as psyllium will mix with the stool to make it spongier and easier to push out. A stool softener (such as docusate) will reduce straining.

- Phenylephrine (*Preparation H,* others) is a vasoconstrictor that shrinks the hemorrhoid and reduces burning and itching.
- Hydrocortisone (*Anusol-HC, Preparation H Hydrocortisone*, others) comes in anal suppositories and various topicals including creams and wipes. These reduce itching and inflammation.
- Witch hazel (*Tucks* pads) is a mild astringent that can relieve mild itching. Barriers (skin protectants) to reduce irritation from stool/urine are helpful in some cases (petrolatum, others – see Diaper Rash section).
- There are many combination products. Example: *Tucks* ointment contains mineral oil (skin protectant), zinc oxide (desiccant) and pramoxine (anesthetic).

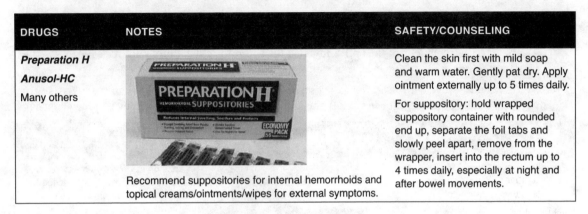

DRUGS	NOTES	SAFETY/COUNSELING
Preparation H ***Anusol-HC*** Many others	 Recommend suppositories for internal hemorrhoids and topical creams/ointments/wipes for external symptoms.	Clean the skin first with mild soap and warm water. Gently pat dry. Apply ointment externally up to 5 times daily. For suppository: hold wrapped suppository container with rounded end up, separate the foil tabs and slowly peel apart, remove from the wrapper, insert into the rectum up to 4 times daily, especially at night and after bowel movements.

Lice and Scabies, Background & Treatment

Note; this section largely discusses lice; scabies (mites) are treated with some of the same medications. Scabies are primarily spread through sexual contact. The primary treatment for scabies is permethrin in a cream formulation (*Elimite*) and the prescription drug ivermectin (*Stromectol*), two doses, taken one week apart. Ivermectin, when taken orally, can be difficult to tolerate due to lymph node enlargement, arthralgias, skin tenderness, pruritus and fever. Ivermectin was approved in 2012 in a topical formulation for lice called *Sklice*. Lindane (*Kwell*, others) used to be commonly used for scabies (and lice) but is not used commonly now due to neurotoxicity. Ivermectin in both topical and oral forms is not first-line for lice; these are options in difficult-to-treat cases. Oral ivermectin requires a body weight of at least 15 kg.

- Lice occurs most commonly in elementary school age children.
- Pyrethrins (permethrin) are the OTC drug of choice; can be used in infants as young as 2 months. Avoid with chrysanthemums or ragweed allergy.
- Malathion lotion 0.5% (*Ovide*) is an organophosphate. Only for use on persons 6 years of age and older. Can irritate the skin and is flammable; do not smoke or use electrical heat sources, including hair dryers, curlers, and curling or flat irons, when applying and while the hair is wet.
- Benzyl alcohol lotion (*Ulesfia* 5% lotion) kills live lice but not nits. Can irritate the skin and eyes; avoid eye contact.

- *Lindane* shampoo 1% is no longer recommended due to neurotoxicity and is reserved for refractive cases, and never in pregnancy, on irritated skin, or in infants, children, persons with small frames and the elderly.
- If the same medication has been used several times it may not be working.
- Repeating the procedure, and removing the nits from hair, bedding, and elsewhere is essential:
    - Wash clothes and bedding in hot water, followed by a hot dryer.
    - If something cannot be washed, seal it in an air-proof bag for 2 weeks or dry clean. Vacuum the carpet well. Soak combs and brushes in hot water for 10 minutes. Make sure to check other children in the household.
    - Do not use a combination shampoo/conditioner, or conditioner before using lice medicine. Do not re-wash the hair for 1 - 2 days after treatment.
    - After each treatment, check the hair and use a nit comb to remove nits and lice every 2 - 3 days. Continue to check for 2 - 3 weeks to be sure all lice and nits are gone.
    - Re-treatment is needed for OTC and prescription products (except *Sklice*) on days 7 - 10 (they vary; check the product) in order to kill any surviving hatched lice before they produce new eggs.

DRUGS	NOTES	SAFETY/COUNSELING
Permethrin, pyrethrins, OTC DOC for lice *(Nix, RID, Triple X)* 2 months+ (guideline says to retreat on day 9) Spinosad *(Natroba)* –works well, expensive. 4+ yrs Malathion *(Ovide)* – flammable, do not use near heat source, organophosphate Benzyl Alcohol Lotion *(Ulesfia)* 6+ months Ivermectin *(Sklice)* 6+ months Lindane (*Kwell*, others) is no longer routinely recommended; high risk neurotoxicity/seizures, requires MedGuide – more commonly used for scabies (mites)		In addition to OTC treatment, remove the live lice and nits by inspecting the hair in 1-inch segments and using a lice comb. Without removing live lice and nits, the OTC product will not work. Nits are "cemented" to the hair shaft and do not fall off after treatment. Nit removal requires multiple efforts, which should be continued for two weeks after treatment. See bulleted points above for additional counseling. Only in resistant/difficult cases use *Sklice* (topical ivermectin), or can use oral ivermectin (*Stromectol*) in those weighing at least 15 kg.

Minor Cuts, Abrasions and Burns, Background & Treatment

- The basic types of minor wounds are lacerations, abrasions, cuts, bites and burns.
- Some can be effectively treated through simple first aid and others, depending on the severity, may need more medical attention than first aid can provide.
- Anything that involves puncture wounds should be referred out.

- Make sure tetanus vaccine is current (Q 10 years, after series has been completed). If the wound is dirty a repeat tetanus vaccine may be required if it is >5 years since vaccination. The patient should be referred for medical care.
- If wound looks like abuse, contact authorities if able.
- Abrasions are minor injuries to the top layer of skin and are primarily treated with simple first aid.
- Abrasions such as a skinned knee can be cleaned thoroughly, antibiotic ointment applied and allowed to air heal.
- Lacerations are defined as irregular wounds with ragged edges, with the potential for deeper skin damage and bruising under the skin.
- If deep seek medical attention.
- A cut is different than a laceration because the edges will be more uniform or regular.
- After cleaning, if the bleeding does not stop, or it extends far below the surface layers of the skin, seek medical attention because it may require stitching to get the wound to close. If not, regular bandaging should get the edges of the wound to close over time.
- Antibiotic ointment can be applied prior to placing the bandage.
- Tissue adhesives *(Band-Aid Liquid Bandage, Nexcare Skin Crack Care*, others) create a polymer layer, which binds to the skin, keeping the wound clean and keeping moisture out. Some contain topical analgesics. *Seal-On* is a topical sponge (dressing) that can absorb blood and is used for nose-bleeds and other minor bleeds. There are other similar products.
- Bites (except minor insect bites) should never be treated with just simple first aid, because of the high risk of infection, especially with animal or human bites. Certain spider bites in the U.S. can be deadly: the brown recluse, the black widow and the hobo spiders. Spiders tend to stay hidden and are not aggressive. Bites can usually be avoided by inspecting and shaking out clothing or equipment prior to use, and wearing protective clothing. If bitten, stay calm, identify the type of spider if possible, wash with soap and cold water, apply cold compress with ice, elevate extremity, and get emergency medical care.
- Minor, harmless insect bites can be treated with a topical steroid or systemic antihistamine (such as diphenhydramine) to reduce itching.
- Burns are characterized as first degree (red/painful, minor swelling), second degree (thicker, very painful, produce blisters) and third degree (damage to all layers of skin, skin appears white or charred). Burns produced by chemical exposure, or in a person with underlying disease that reduces immunity should be referred for emergency medical care.
- If the burn is first or second degree OTC treatment is acceptable if the area is less than 2 inches in diameter and if the burn is not on the face, over a major joint or on the feet or genitals. In diabetes a burn on a foot, even mild, could lead to an amputation. Vigilance is required.
- Minor burns should be treated first by running the burn under cool running water or soaking in cool water for 5-20 minutes.
- Do not apply ice, which can further damage the injured skin. Bandages should be applied if the skin is broken, or if blisters pop. Burns heal best when kept moist (but not wet). Certain bandages designed for burns keep the environment moist, or ointments, such as antibiotic ointment, can be applied.

- Burned skin itches as it heals; the fingernails of children may need to be cut short and filed, or covered. The skin that has been burned will be more sensitive to the sun for up to a year.
- Ointments (80% oil/20% water, such as *Aquaphor*) should be used for skin protection over a minor burn to hold in moisture and reduce scarring risk.
- Silver sulfadiazene *(Silvadene; SSD; Thermazene)* may be used topically to reduce infection risk and promote healing, although it has not been shown to be very effective. If the skin is broken systemic toxicity could occur. Do not use if sulfa allergy or G6PD deficiency (due to hemolysis risk).

DRUGS	NOTES	SAFETY/COUNSELING
Triple antibiotic ointment (***Neosporin***, store brands) contains **polymyxin, bacitracin & neomycin**. If reaction to the neomycin component can use ***Polysporin*** (bacitracin and polymixin) or ***Bacitracin*** alone. Either of these is often sufficient. **Mupirocin *(Bactroban)*** is an Rx antibiotic cream or ointment; very good staph and strep coverage, including MRSA; can be used for nasal MRSA colonization. *(Bactroban nasal* is used for MRSA-nasal colonization) **Bacitracin, Neomycin, Polymyxin B**, and **Hydrocortisone *(Cortisporin*** ointment) is a popular Rx topical used for superficial skin infections. Tissue adhesives *(Band-Aid Liquid Bandage, Nexcare Skin Crack Care,* others) – "paint on" bandages to protect/keep moisture in skin via polymer layer. *Seal-On* is a sponge that is used to stop nosebleeds.	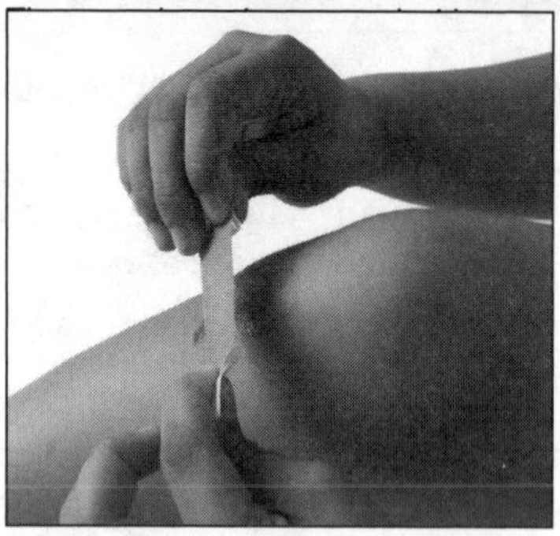 If the wound is not in an area that will get dirty or be rubbed by clothing, it does not need to be covered. Leaving a wound uncovered helps it stay dry and helps it heal.	To apply topical antibiotics: Clean the affected area and apply a small amount of medication (an amount equal to the surface area of the tip of a finger) to the affected area 1 to 3 times daily. If area can get dirty (such as a hand) or be irritated by clothing, cover with an adhesive strip (e.g., *Band-Aid*) or with sterile gauze and adhesive tape +/- antibiotic ointment. Change daily. Certain wounds, like large scrapes, should be kept moist and clean to help reduce scarring and speed healing. Bandages used for this purpose are called occlusive or semi-occlusive bandages. Burns require a moist (but not wet) environment by applying either ointment, or a bandage designed for burns.

Pinworm *(Vermicularis)* Infection

- Anthelmintics, such as mebendazole, pyrantel pamoate, and albendazole, are active against *Enterobius vermicularis.*
- Pinworm infection most commonly occurs in children and presents as anal itching. Pyrantel comes in several OTC products including the popular *Pin-X.* The pinworms can be resistant to treatment. Albendazole and mebendazole are prescription only.
- The "tape" test is used to identify eggs: stick a piece of tape around the anus in the morning prior to voiding/defecating. It can take up to 3 morning tape tests to identify the eggs. Reinfection after treatment is common.

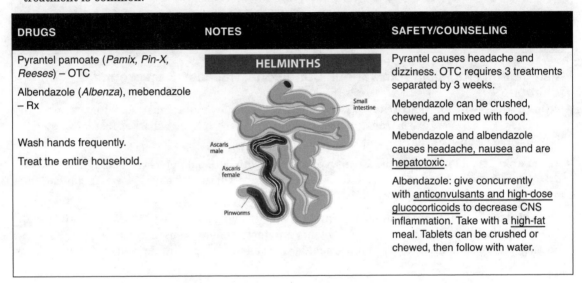

DRUGS	NOTES	SAFETY/COUNSELING
Pyrantel pamoate (*Pamix, Pin-X, Reeses*) – OTC Albendazole (*Albenza*), mebendazole – Rx Wash hands frequently. Treat the entire household.	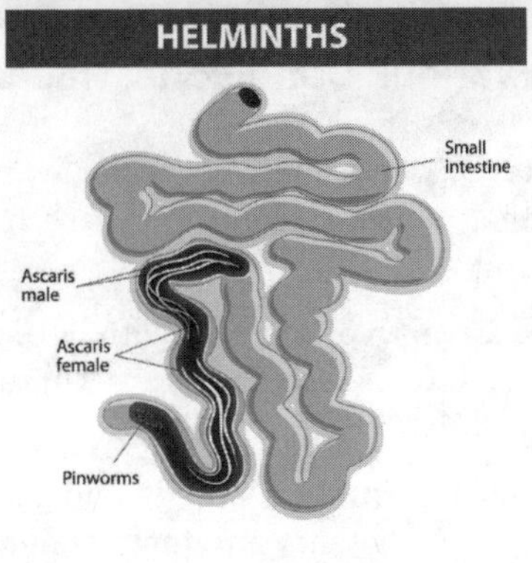	Pyrantel causes headache and dizziness. OTC requires 3 treatments separated by 3 weeks. Mebendazole can be crushed, chewed, and mixed with food. Mebendazole and albendazole causes headache, nausea and are hepatotoxic. Albendazole: give concurrently with anticonvulsants and high-dose glucocorticoids to decrease CNS inflammation. Take with a high-fat meal. Tablets can be crushed or chewed, then follow with water.

Poison Ivy, Oak and Sumac, Background & Treatment

- Poison ivy, oak or sumac poisoning is an allergic reaction that results from touching the sap of these plants, which contain the toxin uroshiol.
- The sap may be on the plant, in the ashes of burned plants, on an animal, or on other objects that came in contact with the plant, such as clothing, garden tools, and sports equipment.
- Small amounts of uroshiol can remain under a person's fingernails for several days unless it is deliberately removed with good cleaning.
- Poison ivy grows around lakes and streams in the midwest and east. Leaves are green in the summer and red in the fall.
- Poison oak grows in the west (along the Pacific coast) and in the east from New Jersey to Texas. The leaves look like oak, usually in clusters of three leaves. The plant has clusters of yellow berries.
- Poison sumac grows in boggy areas, especially in the southeast and west. The leaves have 7-13 smooth-edged leaflets, with pale yellow or cream-colored berries.

DRUGS	NOTES	SAFETY/COUNSELING
Aluminum acetate solution *(Burrow's)* Colloidal oatmeal *(Aveeno)* Calamine lotion – *Caladryl, IvaRest* are calamine + topical analgesics *Zanfel* is supposed to bind urushiol (this is the toxin) – low evidence for efficacy	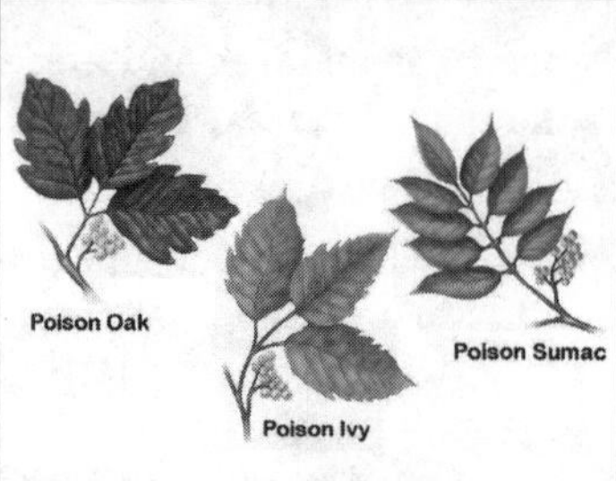 *"Leaves of three, Let it be."*	Wash the uroshiol off with soap and water carefully, including under fingernails and on clothing. Topical or oral steroids will help (oral needed in severe rash). Cold compresses can help.

Inflammation (Topical)(From Various Conditions, Rashes), Background & Treatment

- Primary treatment for skin irritation are topical steroids. Two strengths of hydrocortisone (HC) available OTC, 0.5% and 1%; all other topical steroids are prescription. A chart of Rx topical steroids is at the end of this chapter.
- The steroid vehicle influences the strength of the medication. Usual potency, from highest to weakest: ointment > creams > lotions > solutions > gels > sprays. Ointments have low water content; refer to the Compounding chapter for details.
- Parts of the body with thin skin, such as the face, eyelids and genitals, are highly susceptible to the side effects of topical steroids and low potency products should be used on these areas. Use low potency products on areas of the skin with folds, such as the armpits, groin, and under the breasts, where the absorption is higher.
- Local (skin) steroid side effects, if used long-term include skin thinning, pigment changes (lighter or darker), telangectasia (blood vessel) formation, rosacea, perioral dermatitis and acne, increased risk skin infections, delayed wound healing, irritation/burning/peeling, and possibly contact dermatitis from the steroid itself.

- For urticaria (hives) the second-generation antihistamines can be recommended (OTC) as the initial options due to better tolerability than first-generation antihistamines. Cetirizine is a common choice; see the Allergic Rhinitis, Cough & Cold chapter for a discussion of antihistamines. For hives, higher doses are used. The "non-sedating" antihistamines are more sedating with higher doses. First-generation antihistamines (diphenhydramine, others) can be given at bedtime if the sedative effects are desirable.
- H2-blockers (famotidine, others) are helpful in some patients for hives and urticaria. Hydroxyzine is often prescribed and is in the table below.

DRUGS	NOTES	SAFETY/COUNSELING
OTC steroids are low potency: Hydrocortisone 0.5% (infants) and 1% for mild conditions, thin skin (groin area, elderly) and for children. HC 1% lotion *(Aquanil)* See other steroids in chart at end of this section. Apply high potency Rx steroids once daily – Apply OTC/lower potency 1-2x daily. It is common to see a higher potency product, followed by a lower potency product, to treat acute inflammation. Severe rash likely to require oral steroids for 1-2 weeks.	Ointments often more potent than creams; use ointments for thick or dry skin. Ointments have low water content (reduced absorption) and form a skin barrier. Use lotions, gels and foams for hairy skin. No evidence for use of topical diphenhydramine – can use systemic but caution due to side effects. Skin should be lubricated (hydrated) with moisturizers for most conditions. The steroid vehicle can lubricate. Camphor, menthol, local anesthetics (often in combo creams with HC) can help relieve itching. Common topical steroids, ranked by potency, are included at the end of this chapter.	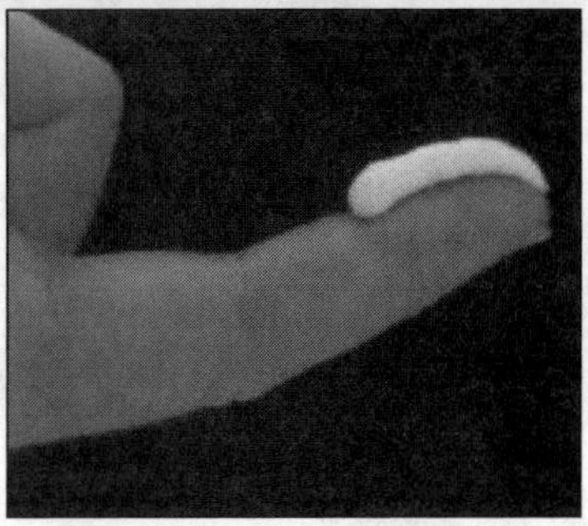 The "finger-tip" unit is used to estimate amount required: the amount that can be squeezed from the fingertip to the 1st joint covers one adult hand (about ½ g). Topical steroid over-use has risks; see top bullet points. Do not apply for longer than 2 weeks. Encourage patient not to use more than directed.
HydrOXYzine *(Vistaril)* 25 mg TID-QID	Used for general urticaria (hives) with severe itching	Anticholinergic; primarily sedation and dry mouth.

Sunscreens and Sun Protection, Background & Treatment

- Applying sunscreen is important due to the risk of sun damage and skin cancer. Keep in mind that sunscreen blocks vitamin D production in the skin and many Americans are vitamin-D deficient. This is a difficulty in current practice.
- It is advisable to stay out of the sun when it is strongest (between 10AM-4PM). The damaging ultraviolet (UV) rays penetrate clouds; this applies to overcast days as well.
- Another method to avoid the sun is to wear protective clothing.

- Where skin is exposed sunscreen can be applied that provides both UVA (A for aging – causes damage below the skin surface) and UVB (B for burning) protection. Both UVA and UVB contribute to skin cancer. A "broad spectrum" sunscreen should be chosen; it protects against both UVA and UVB. SPF stands for sun protection factor, which is a measure of how well the sunscreen deflects UVB rays.
- Some dermatologists recommend SPF 15 and others recommend SPF 30. The key is to apply liberally and at least every two hours. The American Academy of Pediatrics says to keep all babies less than 6 months old out of the sun.
- HOW SPF WORKS: If someone would normally burn in 10 minutes, an SPF of 5 would extend the time they would burn to 50 minutes (5 x 10 = 50.) However, it is not accurate to calculate that if one normally would burn in one hour, then a sunscreen with an SPF of 10 would permit the person to stay in the sun for 10 hours (10 times longer) without burning, since the intensity of the sun varies during the day, and the sunscreen would not last more than a couple of hours.
- Sunscreen labeling is no longer permitted to use "waterproof" or "sweatproof" since they all wash off, at least partially, in the water. They can claim to be "water-resistant" but only for 40-80 minutes. Always reapply after swimming, or sweating.
- The American Academy of Dermatology (AAD) recommends sunscreens with any of the following ingredients: avobenzone, cinoxate, ecamsule, menthyl anthranilate, octyl methoxycinnamate, octyl salicylate, oxybenzone or sulisobenzone.
- Oxybenzone irritates some people's skin; this is not common.

DRUGS	NOTES	SAFETY/COUNSELING
Many products, choose one with UVA and UVB coverage, SPF 15+. UVA: Blocks aging (A for aging – wrinkles). Ingredients that block UVA: ecamsule, avobenzone, oxybenzone, sulisobenzone, titanium dioxide, zinc oxide (zinc and titanium are common barrier agents). UVB: Blocks burning (B for burning). SPF (sun exposure factor) – measures how long it takes to burn versus not using sunscreen (measures UVB only). An SPF of 15 takes 15 times longer for skin to redden than without the sunscreen.	 Apply liberally, at least every two hours, prior to sun exposure, and after getting the skin wet from swimming or sweating.	All sunscreens wash off; reapply after going in the water and at least every 2 hours. Avoid peak sun (10AM-4PM), even if overcast. Wear protective clothing. Consider vitamin D deficiency-if avoiding sun or little sun exposure may need supplementation. UVA and UVB exposure increases risk of skin cancer, including most common type (squamous cell). "Broad spectrum" covers both UVA and UVB. Water resistant – means resistant for 40-80 minutes.

Potencies of Topical Steroids

TREATMENT	ACTIVE INGREDIENT
Very High Potency	
***Clobex* Lotion/Spray/Shampoo, 0.05%**	**Clobetasol propionate**
Cormax Cream/Solution, 0.05%	Clobetasol propionate
***Diprolene* Ointment, 0.05%**	**Betamethasone dipropionate**
***Olux* Foam, 0.05%**	**Clobetasol propionate**
***Temovate* Cream/Ointment/Solution, 0.05%**	**Clobetasol propionate**
***Ultravate* Cream/Ointment, 0.05%**	**Halobetasol propionate**
Vanos Cream, 0.1%	**Fluocinonide**
Psorcon Ointment, 0.05%	Diflorasone diacetate
Psorcon E Ointment, 0.05%	Diflorasone diacetate
High Potency	
***Diprolene* Cream AF, 0.05%**	**Betamethasone dipropionate**
***Elocon* Ointment, 0.1%**	**Mometasone furoate**
Florone Ointment, 0.05%	Diflorasone diacetate
Halog Ointment/Cream, 0.1%	Halcinonide
***Lidex* Cream/Gel/Ointment, 0.05%**	**Fluocinonide**
Psorcon Cream, 0.05%	Diflorasone diacetate
Topicort Cream/Ointment, 0.25%	Desoximetasone
Topicort Gel, 0.05%	Desoximetasone
High-Medium Potency	
Cutivate Ointment, 0.005%	Fluticasone propionate
***Lidex-E* Cream, 0.05%**	**Fluocinonide**
Luxiq Foam, 0.12%	Betamethasone valerate
Topicort LP Cream, 0.05%	Desoximetasone
Medium Potency	
Cordran Ointment, 0.05%	Flurandrenolide
***Elocon* Cream, 0.1%**	**Mometasone furoate**
***Kenalog* Cream/Spray, 0.1%**	**Triamcinolone acetonide**
Synalar Ointment, 0.03%	Fluocinolone acetonide
***Westcort* Ointment, 0.2%**	**Hydrocortisone valerate**

Potencies of Topical Steroids

TREATMENT	ACTIVE INGREDIENT
Lower Potency	
Capex Shampoo, 0.01%	Fluocinolone acetonide
Cordran Cream/Lotion/Tape, 0.05%	Flurandrenolide
Cutivate Cream/Lotion, 0.05%	Fluticasone propionate
DermAtop Cream, 0.1%	Prednicarbate
***DesOwen* Lotion, 0.05%**	**Desonide**
Locoid Cream/Lotion/Ointment/Solution, 0.1%	Hydrocortisone
Pandel Cream, 0.1%	Hydrocortisone
Synalar Cream, 0.03%/0.01%	Fluocinolone acetonide
***Westcort* Cream, 0.2%**	**Hydrocortisone valerate**
Mild Potency	
Aclovate Cream/Ointment, 0.05%	Alclometasone dipropionate
***Derma*-Smoothe/FS Oil, 0.01%**	**Fluocinolone acetonide**
Desonate Gel, 0.05%	Desonide
Synalar Cream/Solution, 0.01%	Fluocinolone acetonide
Verdeso Foam, 0.05%	Desonide
Lowest Potency	
Cetacort Lotion, 0.5%/1%	Hydrocortisone
Cortaid Cream/Spray/Ointment	**Hydrocortisone**
Hytone Cream/Lotion, 1%/2.5%	Hydrocortisone
Micort-HC Cream, 2%/2.5%	Hydrocortisone
Nutracort Lotion, 1%/2.5%	Hydrocortisone
Synacort Cream, 1%/2.5%	Hydrocortisone

WEIGHT LOSS

GUIDELINES/REFERENCES

2013 AHA/ACC/TOS Guideline for the Management of Overweight and Obesity in Adults: A Report of the American College of Cardiology/AHA Task Force on Practice Guidelines and The Obesity Society. *J Am Coll Cardiol.* 2014; 63:2985-3023.

Pharmacological Management of Obesity: An Endocrine Society Clinical Practice Guideline. *J Clin Endocrinol Metab.* 2015; 100(2):342-62.

US DHHS/DOA's 2015 - 2020 Dietary Guidelines for Americans, 8th Ed. available at https://health.gov/dietaryguidelines/2015/guidelines(accessed 2016 Oct 31).

We gratefully acknowledge the assistance of Elizabeth Pogge, PharmD, MPH, BCPS, FASCP, Associate Professor of Pharmacy Practice, Midwestern University College of Pharmacy-Glendale, in preparing this chapter.

BACKGROUND

Overweight and obesity are national health threats and a major public health challenge. Data from the CDC (2013 – 2014) estimates the percentage of U.S. adults who are overweight (BMI 25–29.9) or obese (BMI ≥ 30) at 70.7%, and in children and adolescents at 33.4%. A person who is overweight is at higher risk for coronary heart disease, hypertension, stroke, type 2 diabetes, certain types of cancer, and premature death. In addition to the health risks, being overweight reduces the quality of life and causes social stigmatization and discrimination.

Weight loss must involve an "energy deficit" – calories must be decreased in order to force the body to use fat as an energy source. If someone is hungry it is difficult not to eat. The weight loss drugs work primarily by increasing satiety (feeling full), which decreases appetite. There are many theories about the causes of overweight and obesity. Recent research has focused on how diets high in saturated fat and simple carbohydrates (the typical American diet) are thought to impair the regulation of the hormones leptin (which suppresses appetite) and ghrelin (which increases appetite). Consuming many calories from simple sugars and certain types of fats may damage the hypothalamus, which alters the function of leptin and ghrelin. This impairs the ability to control hunger and lose weight. This research is providing a better understanding of why the types of food a person eats is important. The 2015 – 2020 Dietary Guidelines for Americans issued by the US Department of Health and Human Services (DHHS) and Department of Agriculture (DOA) emphasize that a healthy eating pattern should include fruits, vegetables, protein, dairy, grains, and healthy fats while limiting saturated fats, trans fats, added sugars and sodium.

Fad diets may cause an acute weight loss, but are generally not recommended as they are difficult to maintain and can have harmful health consequences. Many people think they are heavier than they would like to be due to a low metabolism. If low metabolism is an issue it will show up on lab tests (i.e., as hypothyroidism) and can be treated.

SELECT DRUGS/CONDITIONS THAT CAN CAUSE WEIGHT GAIN

KEY DRUGS

Insulin, sulfonylureas, glitazones

Antipsychotics (including olanzapine, quetiapine, risperidone, paliperidone)

Steroids

Mirtazapine *(Remeron)*

Dronabinol *(Marinol)*, megestrol *(Megace)*

Conditions: Hypothyroidism

Others:

Divalproex/ valproic acid

Tricyclic antidepressants (more with tertiary amines)

MAO inhibitors

SSRIs (including paroxetine—*Paxil)*

Lithium (*Lithobid*)

Pregabalin *(Lyrica)*, Gabapentin *(Neurontin)*

GUIDELINE RECOMMENDATIONS

Prior to the release of the DHHS/DOA guidelines (discussed on the previous page), another set of guidelines that addressed the overweight/obesity epidemic was released in 2013 by the American College of Cardiology, the American Heart Association and The Obesity Society. These guidelines are notable because they focus on the importance of identifying overweight in patients and addressing it through a variety of approaches.

Often in practice, conditions resulting from excess weight are treated, but the overweight or obesity issue itself is not addressed. BMI and waist circumference should be assessed in all patients, at least annually. Overweight and obese patients should be warned of the health risks, and interventions by trained professionals should emphasize the benefits of lifestyle changes and offer a variety of diet plans to address patient preferences.

The high incidence of overweight and obesity in the U.S. is typically multi-factorial, with diet, environment, and genetics playing a role. Weight loss is successful when the patient is able to make permanent changes in diet and exercise habits. The guidelines support targeting interventions in multiple areas, including in the home, school, work, and in the community.

The guidelines state that a sustained weight loss of 3% – 5% will produce clinically meaningful health benefits (such as decreasing triglycerides, A1C, and the risk of developing type 2 diabetes). A greater percentage of weight loss will produce a greater benefit. Dietary strategies could consist of any of the following methods:

- Reducing food and calorie intake: 1,200–1,500 kcal/day for women and 1,500–1,800 kcal/day for men or using a 500–750 kcal/day energy deficit; a 500 kcal decrease per day equals 1 pound weight loss per week (3,500 kcal/pound).
- Using one of the evidence-based diets that restricts certain food types (such as restricting high-carbohydrate foods, low-fiber foods, or high-fat foods), in order to create an energy deficit by reduced food intake.
- In select patients, and only under medical monitoring, the use of a very low calorie diet (defined as < 800 kcal/day), can be recommended.

All patients who would benefit from weight loss should participate for ≥ 6 months in a comprehensive lifestyle program that includes weight loss support with a trained person. This person could be some type of healthcare professional, an exercise specialist or a trained lay person. The lifestyle program should include weight and diet monitoring and regular physical activity of 200 - 300 minutes/week.

The guidelines recommend bariatric surgery for adults with a BMI ≥ 40, or with a BMI ≥ 35 with an obesity-related condition. Using a surgical approach requires adjusting medications and providing nutrient support. Post-bariatric requirements are discussed in more detail later in this chapter.

Natural Products

OTC weight loss supplements commonly contain stimulants, such as bitter orange (which is either synephrine alone or with related compounds), and/or excessive amounts of caffeine. Caffeine is packaged under different names, including yerba mate, guarana and concentrated green tea powder. In general, OTC supplements for weight loss are ineffective and can potentially be harmful, especially in patients with cardiovascular disease; therefore, they should not be recommended.

KEY DRUGS

- Stimulants used for ADHD (including *Ritalin, Concerta, Adderall, Vyvanse)*
- Exenatide *(Byetta/ Bydureon)* and liraglutide *(Victoza,* & higher dose *Saxenda* approved for weight loss)
- Topiramate *(Topamax)*

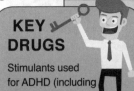

SELECT DRUGS/CONDITIONS THAT CAN CAUSE WEIGHT LOSS

Others:

- Antiepileptic Drugs (zonisamide, ethosuximide)
- Pramlintide (*Symlin*)
- Bupropion (*Wellbutrin, Zyban, others*)
- Interferons
- Acetylcholinesterase inhibitors (donepezil—*Aricept,* rivastigmine—*Exelon,* galantamine—*Razadyne*)
- Conditions: Hyperthyroidism, Lupus, Celiac Disease, Crohn's Disease, Cystic Fibrosis, Ulcerative Colitis, Tuberculosis (active disease)

Prescription agents are not appropriate for patients with small amounts of weight to lose. Prescription drugs are indicated in individuals with a BMI ≥ 30, or with a BMI ≥ 27 with at least one weight-related condition (such as dyslipidemia, hypertension or diabetes). They are only used in addition to a dietary plan and increased physical activity, per the FDA. Diabetes is common in overweight and obese adults. Weight loss can lower the requirement for medications; patients with diabetes who are using prescription weight loss drugs must monitor blood glucose carefully.

In the past, several drugs used to treat obesity have been pulled from the market due to safety concerns. In an effort to improve safety, the obesity drug market has become saturated with agents that are not systemically absorbed (*Xenical/Alli*) or agents that were previously FDA-approved for an indication other than weight management. Of the recent approvals for the long-term treatment of obesity, only one (*Belviq*) is a new compound. The four newer prescription drugs for weight loss are phentermine/topiramate ER (*Qsymia*), lorcaserin (*Belviq*), naltrexone/bupropion *(Contrave)* and liraglutide (*Saxenda*). The weight loss at one year, versus diet and lifestyle alone, is variable; *Qsymia* (~19 pounds), *Belviq* (~8 pounds), *Contrave* (~11 pounds) and *Saxenda* (~13 pounds).

The older stimulant agents are only used short-term to "jump start" a diet. The non-stimulant orlistat is available as an OTC *(Alli)* and as a prescription drug (*Xenical*); orlistat is a useful agent to reduce dietary fat absorption, but has GI tolerability issues and must be taken with a reduced fat diet in order to reduce flatulence and discharge. Too much dietary fat will cause a lot of "flat". Orlistat efficacy is modest with ~7 pound weight loss at one year, versus placebo.

The newer agents *Qsymia, Belviq, Contrave* and *Saxenda,* and the orlistat formulations, can be continued long-term for weight maintenance. Weight loss drugs should be discontinued if they are not producing a useful benefit of at least a 5% weight loss at 12 weeks.

Weight Loss Drugs

DRUG	DOSING	SAFETY/SIDE EFFECTS/MONITORING

Phentermine: Sympathomimetic (stimulant), with effects similar to amphetamines, causing an increase in norepinephrine.

Topiramate: Effects due to increased satiety and decreased appetite, possibly by enhancing GABA, blocking glutamate receptors and/or weak inhibition of carbonic anhydrase.

DRUG	DOSING	SAFETY/SIDE EFFECTS/MONITORING
Phentermine/Topiramate ER *(Qsymia)* C-IV REMS drug: only through certified pharmacy network. Teratogenic risk; obtain pregnancy test before treatment and monthly thereafter; use effective contraception.	Start at 3.75/23 mg PO QAM x 14 days, then titrate up based on weight loss Max 15/92 mg PO QAM CrCl < 50 mL/min the max dose is 7.5/46 mg/day	**CONTRAINDICATIONS** Hyperthyroidism, glaucoma, MAO inhibitor use within past 14 days, pregnancy, lactation **SIDE EFFECTS** Anxiety, depression, suicidal thoughts, tachycardia, headache, cognitive impairment, constipation, dry mouth, insomnia, paresthesias, ↓ HCO3, ↑ SCr, upper respiratory tract infection, pharyngitis **NOTES** Safety issue – see Pregnancy Chapter. Taper off due to seizure risk.

The naltrexone component ↓ food cravings and the bupropion component ↓ appetite.

DRUG	DOSING	SAFETY/SIDE EFFECTS/MONITORING
Naltrexone/Bupropion *(Contrave)*	ER tab 8 mg/90 mg Week 1: 1 tab QAM Week 2: 1 tab QAM, 1 tab QPM Week 3: 2 tabs QAM, 1 tab QPM Week 4+: 2 tabs QAM, 2 tabs QPM Do not cut, chew, or crush; swallow whole Fatty food increases drug levels; do not take with high-fat meal	**BOXED WARNING** Not approved for treatment of major depressive disorder (MDD) or psychiatric disorders. Antidepressants can increase the risk of suicidal thinking and behavior in children, adolescents, and young adults (18-24 years of age) with MDD and psychiatric disorders; consider risk prior to prescribing. **CONTRAINDICATIONS** Chronic opioid or opiate agonist or partial agonist use, or acute opiate withdrawal, abrupt discontinuation of alcohol, benzodiazepines, barbiturates, and antiepileptic drugs, uncontrolled hypertension, seizure disorder, use of other bupropion-containing products, bulimia/anorexia, concomitant use of MAO inhibitors, linezolid, methylene blue, pregnancy **WARNINGS** Use caution with psychiatric disorder, seizure risk, discontinue if s/sx hepatotoxicity **SIDE EFFECTS** N/V, constipation, headache, dizziness, dry mouth, sleep disorder (including abnormal dreams), can ↑ HR, ↑ BP, with higher risk during the first few months **NOTES** Safety issue – see Pregnancy Chapter. Naltrexone will block opioids and buprenorphine, which will block analgesia; do not use concurrently. Discontinue these drugs 7-10 days prior to use of *Contrave.*

Weight Loss Drugs Continued

DRUG	DOSING	SAFETY/SIDE EFFECTS/MONITORING

Serotonin 5-HT2C receptor agonist, ↑ satiety, resulting in weight loss.

Lorcaserin *(Belviq, Belviq XR)* C-IV	IR: 10 mg PO BID XR: 20 mg PO daily	**CONTRAINDICATIONS** Pregnancy **WARNINGS** Valvular heart disease, serotonin syndrome, CNS effects, ↓ WBC, ↓ RBC, ↑ prolactin, ↑ risk PAH, ↑ risk psychiatric disorders (including suicide risk), priapism **SIDE EFFECTS** Headache, dizziness, fatigue, nausea, dry mouth, constipation, hypoglycemia **NOTES** Safety issue – see Pregnancy Chapter.

GLP-1 receptor agonist, ↑ satiety, resulting in weight loss.

Liraglutide (*Saxenda*) *Victoza*– for diabetes	Start at 0.6 mg SC daily x 1 week, titrate up by 0.6 mg SC daily at weekly intervals Target dose: 3 mg SC daily	**CONTRAINDICATIONS** Patients with a personal or family history of medullary thyroid carcinoma (MTC) or patients with Multiple Endocrine Neoplasia syndrome type 2 (MEN 2), pregnancy **SIDE EFFECTS** Nausea (even with lower dose), tachycardia, hypogylcemia **NOTES** Safety issue – see Pregnancy Chapter. May need to ↓ insulin or sulfonylurea/meglitinide dose to ↓ risk of hypoglycemia; see Diabetes chapter. *Saxenda* REMS involves warning of risk MTC, pancreatitis.

Short term appetite suppressants – sympathomimetics (stimulants), with effects similar to amphetamines, causing increase in norepinephrine.

Phentermine *(Adipex-P,* *Suprenza-ODT, Lomaira)* C-IV	15-37.5 mg PO daily, before or after breakfast, or in divided doses	**CONTRAINDICATIONS** MAO inhibitors within the past 14 days Avoid use with hypertension, PAH, hyperthyroidism, glaucoma, abuse potential **SIDE EFFECTS** Tachycardia, agitation, ↑ BP, cardiovascular complications, insomnia, dizziness, tremor, risk of dependence, risk of psychotic symptoms **NOTES** Safety issue – see Pregnancy Chapter. Stimulants as single agents used up to 12 weeks to "jump-start" a diet. Monitor HR, BP. Taper off due to seizure risk. Stimulants taken later in the day contribute to insomnia.
Diethylpropion *(Tenuate)* C-IV	IR: 25 mg PO TID 1 hour before meals and mid-evening SR: 75 mg PO once in mid-morning	
Phendimetrazine C-III	IR: 35 mg PO BID-TID, 1 hr before meals ER: 105 mg PO Q daily, 30 - 60 minutes before morning meal	
Benzphetamine (*Regimex*) C-III	25-50 mg PO BID-TID	

Weight Loss Drugs Continued

DRUG	DOSING	SAFETY/SIDE EFFECTS/MONITORING
Long-term lipase inhibitor that decreases the absorption of dietary fats by ~30%.		
Orlistat Rx *(Xenical)*	120 mg PO w/each meal containing fat, take with meal or up to 1 hr after eating Indicated in ages > 12 years Both orlistat formulations must be used with a low-fat diet plan	**CONTRAINDICATIONS** Pregnancy, chronic malabsorption syndrome, cholestasis **WARNINGS** Liver damage (rare), cholelithiasis,↑ urinary oxalate/kidney stones, hypoglycemia (with diabetes) **SIDE EFFECTS** GI (flatus with discharge, fecal urgency, fatty stool) **NOTES** Take multivitamin with A, D, E, K and beta carotene at bedtime or separated by ≥ 2 hours. Do not use with cyclosporine or separate by ≥ 3 hours. Separate levothyroxine by ≥ 4 hours. Must stick to dietary plan for both weight improvement and to help lessen GI side effects (max 30% of kcals from fat).
Orlistat OTC (*Alli*)	60 mg PO w/each meal containing fat	Same as *Xenical* (above) for counseling, vitamin and diet/fat intake, and drug interactions.

Patient Counseling for all Weight Loss Agents

- This drug is used in adults who are obese, or who are overweight with at least one weight-related medical problem such as high blood pressure, high cholesterol, or type 2 diabetes.
- If you do not lose an expected amount of weight within the first three months, the medication is not effective for you and should be stopped; if you are not losing weight, let your healthcare provider know.
- You must be using a sensible eating plan and getting regular physical activity while taking this medication.
- If you have diabetes and you lose weight, you could get low blood glucose (hypoglycemia); you will need to monitor your blood glucose carefully, and your diabetes medicine) may need to be adjusted as you lose weight. (*Belviq*; warning for hypoglycemia.)
- Do not use this drug if you are pregnant or planning to become pregnant. Attempting to lose weight during pregnancy is not safe. (*Qsymia* has highest risk of causing harm to a baby and will make birth control pills not work as well.)

Orlistat *(Xenical and Alli)*

- Take one capsule with liquid at each main meal or up to one hour after a meal that contains fat, up to three times daily. You should be using a healthy eating plan that contains no more than 30% of calories that come from fat.
- You will need to take a daily multivitamin supplement that contains vitamins A, D, E, and K and beta carotene. Take the multivitamin once a day at least 2 hours before or after taking orlistat, such as at bedtime.
- If you take levothyroxine (for low thyroid), it should be separated from orlistat by at least 4 hours.
- If you take cyclosporine (a transplant medication) it must be separated from orlistat by at least 3 hours. Discuss using orlistat with your transplant team; it is important not to change the amount of transplant medication that your body is receiving.

Post-Bariatric Surgery; Pharmacists Role

The 2013 obesity guideline recommends advising adults with a BMI ≥ 40 or BMI ≥ 35 with an obesity-related condition who cannot successfully lose weight that bariatric surgery may be an appropriate option. These patients can be offered referral to a bariatric surgeon for evaluation. Traditional bariatric surgery restricts food intake, which leads to weight loss. Patients who have bariatric surgery must commit to a lifetime of healthy eating and regular exercise to sustain the weight loss.

Weight loss surgery requires changes to the drug regimen, and adjustments in nutrients with decreased absorption, depending on the surgery type. This summary will not distinguish between the needs with various surgeries, but rather provides a short review of the common problems.

Nutrient Deficiencies

One of the most common problems following bariatric surgery is nutrient deficiencies. Common deficiencies include:

- Calcium is mostly absorbed in the duodenum, which may be bypassed. Calcium citrate is preferred as it has non-acid-dependent absorption.
- Anemia may result from vitamin B12 and iron deficiency; both may require supplementation.
- Iron and calcium supplements should be taken 2 hours prior, or 4 hours after antacids.
- Patients may require life-long supplementation of the fat-soluble vitamins A, D, E and K, due to fat malabsorption.

Medications

- Medications may require dose-reduction, and may need to be crushed or put in liquid or transdermal form for up to two-months post-surgery. Pharmacists will need to assess which drugs can be safely crushed and provide alternatives to drugs that cannot be crushed (i.e., extended-release).
- Due to the risk of gallstones with rapid weight loss, patients may need ursodiol (*Actigall, Urso 250, Urso Forte*), which dissolves gallstones, unless the gallbladder has been removed. It cannot be administered with aluminum-based antacids (if used, give 2 hours after ursodiol). *Urso Forte* can be split into halves, but not crushed or chewed. *Urso* and *Urso Forte* should be taken with food. Ursodiol can be made into a sweetened suspension. The most common side effects are constipation or diarrhea (both about 26%) and nausea.
- Avoid drugs that are GI irritants – such as NSAIDs and bisphosphonates.

APPENDIX

PRESCRIPTION TOP-SELLERS

Brand names are provided as a study aid (generic may be top-seller).

RANK	DRUG	BRAND NAME
1	Lisinopril	*Prinivil, Zestril*
2	Hydrocodone/Acetaminophen	*Lortab, Norco, Vicodin, Vicodin ES, Vicodin HP, Lorcet Plus*
3	Levothyroxine	*Levoxyl, Synthroid, Unithroid*
4	Atorvastatin	*Lipitor*
5	Amlodipine	*Norvasc*
6	Omeprazole	*Prilosec*
7	Metformin	*Glucophage, Riomet*
8	Simvastatin	*Zocor*
9	Amoxicillin	*Moxatag*
10	Gabapentin	*Neurontin, Gralise*
11	Azithromycin	*Zithromax, Zithromax Z-Pak, Zmax*
12	Alprazolam	*Xanax, Alprazolam Intensol* (oral solution)
13	Hydrochlorothiazide	*Microzide*
14	Ibuprofen	*Advil, Advil Migraine, Childrens Advil, Motrin IB, Motrin Infants Drops*
15	Fluticasone Propionate (Nasal Inhaler)	*Flonase Allergy Relief, Flonase Sensimist*
16	Sertraline	*Zoloft*
17	Tramadol	*Ultram*
18	Losartan	*Cozaar*
19	Prednisone	*Deltasone, Prednisone Intensol* (oral solution)
20	Metoprolol Succinate	*Toprol XL*
21	Metoprolol Tartrate	*Lopressor*
22	Oxycodone/Acetaminophen	*Endocet, Percocet, Roxicet*
23	Furosemide	*Lasix*
24	Montelukast	*Singulair*
25	Zolpidem IR	*Ambien, Edluar, Intermezzo*
26	Citalopram	*Celexa*
27	Albuterol	*ProAir HFA, Proventil HFA, Ventolin HFA*
28	Pantoprazole	*Protonix*
29	Fluoxetine	*Prozac, Prozac Weekly, Sarafem*
30	Pravastatin	*Pravachol*
31	Cyclobenzaprine	*Amrix, Fexmid*
32	Escitalopram	*Lexapro*
33	Clonazepam	*Klonopin*
34	Meloxicam	*Mobic*
35	Lisinopril/HCTZ	*Zestoretic*
36	Trazodone	

Prescription Top-Sellers Continued

RANK	DRUG	BRAND NAME
37	Amoxicillin/Clavulanate	*Augmentin, Augmentin ES-600*
38	Atenolol	*Tenormin*
39	Lorazepam	*Ativan, Lorazepam Intensol* (oral solution)
40	Carvedilol	*Coreg*
41	Ciprofloxacin	*Cipro*
42	Cephalexin	*Keflex*
43	Clopidogrel	*Plavix*
44	Tamsulosin	*Flomax*
45	Sulfamethoxazole/ Trimethoprim	*Bactrim, Bactrim DS, Sulfatrim Pediatric* (oral suspension)
46	Duloxetine	*Cymbalta*
47	Warfarin	*Coumadin, Jantoven*
48	Potassium Chloride	*K-Sol, K-Tab, Klor-Con, Klor-Con 10, Klor-Con M10, Klor-Con M15, Klor-Con M20, Klor-Con Sprinkle, Micro-K*
49	Bupropion, extended release	*Wellbutrin XL, Forfivo XL, Aplenzin*
50	Oxycodone	*Roxicodone, Oxaydo*
51	Ranitidine	*Zantac, Zantac 75, Zantac 150*
52	Fluconazole	*Diflucan*
53	Rosuvastatin	*Crestor*
54	Naproxen	*Aleve, Anaprox DS, Naprosyn*
55	Venlafaxine ER	*Effexor XR*
56	Amphetamine Salts	*Adderall*
57	Methylprednisolone	*Medrol*
58	Acetaminophen/Codeine	*Tylenol with Codeine #3, Tylenol with Codeine #4*
59	Triamcinolone Acetonide	*Kenalog*
60	Losartan/HCTZ	*Hyzaar*
61	Allopurinol	*Zyloprim, Aloprim*
62	Diazepam	*Valium*
63	Metformin ER	*Glucophage XR, Fortamet, Glumetza*
64	Amitriptyline	*Elavil*
65	Clonidine	*Catapres* (HTN), *Kapvay* (ADHD)

RANK	DRUG	BRAND NAME
66	Paroxetine	*Paxil, Pexeva*
67	Spironolactone	*Aldactone*
68	Fenofibrate	*Antara, Fenoglide, Fibricor, Lipofen, Lofibra, Tricor, Triglide, Trilipix*
69	Valacyclovir	*Valtrex*
70	Quetiapine	*Seroquel*
71	Glimepiride	*Amaryl*
72	Doxycycline Hyclate	*Vibramycin, Morgidox*
73	Lamotrigine	*Lamictal, Lamictal ODT, Lamictal Starter*
74	Topiramate	*Topamax, Topamax Sprinkle*
75	Levofloxacin	*Levaquin*
76	Fluticasone/Salmeterol (Oral Inhaler)	*Advair Diskus, Advair HFA*
77	Lisdexamfetamine	*Vyvanse*
78	Triamterene/HCTZ	*Dyazide; Maxzide; Maxzide-25*
79	Ondansetron ODT	*Zofran ODT*
80	Metronidazole	*Flagyl*
81	Lovastatin	*Altoprev, Mevacor*
82	Folic acid, Vitamin B-9	
83	Latanoprost	*Xalatan*
84	Insulin Glargine (Pen-Injector)	*Lantus SoloStar*
85	Glipizide	*Glucotrol*
86	Alendronate	*Fosamax*
87	Clindamycin Phosphate (Topical)	*Cleocin cream, Clindagel*
88	Ondansetron	*Zofran*
89	Cefdinir	
90	Promethazine	*Phenergan*
91	Benzonatate	*Tessalon Perles*
92	Tizanidine	*Zanaflex*
93	Pregabalin	*Lyrica*
94	Propranolol	*Inderal LA, Inderal XL, InnoPran XL*

Prescription Top-Sellers Continued

RANK	DRUG	BRAND NAME
95	Amphetamine Salts XR	*Adderall XR*
96	Sumatriptan	*Imitrex, Imitrex STATdose*
97	Buspirone	
98	Mupirocin (Topical)	*Bactroban, Bactroban Nasal*
99	Morphine	*MS Contin, Kadian, Duramorph*
100	Methylphenidate ER	*Concerta, Metadate CD, Ritalin LA*
101	Diclofenac (Topical Gel)	*Voltaren Gel*
102	Formoterol/Budesonide	*Symbicort*
103	Finasteride	*Proscar:* BPH, *Propecia:* Alopecia
104	Polyethylene Glycol	*MiraLax (OTC version)*
105	Enalapril	*Vasotec*
106	Hydroxyzine	*Vistaril*
107	Bupropion, sustained release	*Wellbutrin SR:* depression, *Zyban:* smoking cessation
108	Esomeprazole	*Nexium*
109	Mirtazapine	*Remeron*
110	Phentermine	*Adipex-P*
111	Risperidone	*Risperdal*
112	Sitagliptin	*Januvia*
113	Tiotropium (Oral Inhaler)	*Spiriva HandiHaler*
114	Estradiol (Vaginal)	*Estrace, Estring, Vagifem*
115	Ergocalciferol	*Drisdol*
116	Acyclovir	*Zovirax*
117	Isosorbide Mononitrate	
118	Temazepam	*Restoril*
119	Nitrofurantoin	*Macrobid, Macrodantin*
120	Baclofen	*Lioresal*
121	Buprenorphine/Naloxone (SL Film)	*Suboxone*
122	Benazepril	*Lotensin*
123	Levetiracetam	*Keppra*
124	Valsartan/HCTZ	*Diovan HCT*

RANK	DRUG	BRAND NAME
125	Valsartan	*Diovan*
126	Inactivated Influenza Vaccine	*Fluvirin, Fluzone, Fluzone High Dose, Afluria, Fluarix*
127	Tadalafil	*Cialis*
128	Nystatin (Oral Suspension)	*Bio-Statin*
129	Famotidine	*Pepcid*
130	Insulin Glargine (Injection)	*Lantus*
131	Celecoxib	*Celebrex*
132	Donepezil	*Aricept*
133	Ketoconazole (Topical Cream, Shampoo, Foam, Gel)	*Nizoral, Nizoral A-D (OTC)*
134	Clobetasol (Topical Cream, Foam, Spray)	*Clobex, Clobex Spray, Cormax Scalp, Olux-E, Temovate*
135	Sildenafil	*Viagra:* ED, *Revatio:* PAH
136	Methocarbamol	*Robaxin, Robaxin-750*
137	Glipizide ER	*Glipizide XL, Glucotrol XL*
138	Amlodipine/Benazepril	*Lotrel*
139	Chlorhexidine (Topical)	*Betasept Surgical Scrub, Hibiclens, Peridex* oral rinse
140	Penicillin VK	
141	Rivaroxaban	*Xarelto, Xarelto Starter Pack*
142	Carisoprodol	*Soma*
143	Ethinyl Estradiol and Norgestimate	*MonoNessa, Ortho Tri-Cyclen Lo, Sprintec, Tri-Sprintec, TriNessa*
144	Butalbital/Acetaminophen/ Caffeine	*Fioricet*
145	Diltiazem	*Cartia XT, Tiazac*
146	Methotrexate (Tablet, Injection)	Tablet: *Rheumatrex, Trexall;* Auto-Injector: *Otrexup, Rasuvo*
147	Hydralazine	
148	Fluticasone (Oral Inhaler)	*Flovent Diskus, Flovent HFA, Arnuity Ellipta*
149	Ezetimibe	*Zetia*
150	Ramipril	*Altace*
151	Methylphenidate IR	*Methylin, Ritalin*
152	Nebivolol	*Bystolic*
153	Prednisolone Acetate (Ophthalmic)	*Omnipred, Pred Forte, Pred Mild*

Prescription Top-Sellers Continued

RANK	DRUG	BRAND NAME
154	Dicyclomine	*Bentyl*
155	Lansoprazole	*Prevacid, Prevacid 24HR, Prevacid SoluTab*
156	Hydroxychloroquine	*Plaquenil*
157	Meclizine	*Dramamine Less Drowsy, Motion-Time* (Both OTC)
158	Thyroid, Desiccated	*Armour Thyroid*
159	Fentanyl, Patch	*Duragesic*
160	Medroxyprogesterone	*Provera*
161	Beclomethasone (Oral Inhaler)	*QVAR*
162	Hydrocortisone (Topical Cream, Ointment, Foam)	*Dermasorb HC, Locoid, Westcort, Cortifoam*
163	Ropinirole	*Requip*
164	Pioglitazone	*Actos*
165	Oseltamivir	*Tamiflu*
166	Ethinyl Estradiol/Etonogestrel (Vaginal Ring)	*NuvaRing*
167	Codeine/Promethazine (Oral Solution)	
168	Nifedipine ER	*Adalat CC, Afeditab CR, Nifedical XL, Procardia XL*
169	Minocycline	*Minocin, Solodyn*
170	Clindamycin hydrochloride (oral)	*Cleocin* capsules
171	Verapamil SR	*Calan SR, Verelan*
172	Oxycodone ER	*Oxycontin*
173	Dextromethorphan/ Promethazine (Syrup)	
174	Mometasone (Nasal)	*Nasonex*
175	Cyanocobalamin, Vitamin B-12, Injection (Nasal Inhaler)	*Physicians EZ Use B-12, Nascobal*
176	Insulin Detemir (Pen-Injector)	*Levemir FlexTouch*
177	Levocetirizine	*Xyzal*
178	Aripiprazole	*Abilify*
179	Gemfibrozil	*Lopid*

RANK	DRUG	BRAND NAME
180	Dexlansoprazole	*Dexilant*
181	Doxazosin	*Cardura*
182	Canagliflozin	*Invokana*
183	Clotrimazole/Betamethasone (Topical)	*Lotrisone*
184	Nortriptyline	*Pamelor*
185	Glyburide	*Glynase*
186	Azelastine (Ophthalmic)	*Astepro*
187	Olanzapine	*Zyprexa, Zyprexa Zydis*
188	Chlorthalidone	
189	Ofloxacin	*Ocuflox*
190	Cetirizine	*Zyrtec*
191	Oxybutynin	*Oxytrol*
192	Insulin Aspart (Pen-Injector)	*Novolog FlexPen*
193	Prednisolone, Sodium Phosphate (Oral Solution, ODT)	*Millipred, Orapred, Pediapred, Veripred, Orapred ODT*
194	Oxybutynin ER	*Ditropan XL*
195	Lithium	*Lithobid*
196	Phenazopyridine	*Pyridium*
197	Olmesartan	*Benicar*
198	Divalproex ER	*Depakote ER*
199	Nitroglycerin (Sublingual)	*Nitrostat*
200	Timolol (Ophthalmic)	*Istalol, Timoptic, Timoptic Ocudose, Timoptic-XE*
201	Divalproex	*Depakote*
202	Ethinyl Estradiol/ Norethindrone/Ferrous Fumurate	*Gildess Fe, Junel Fe 1/20, Loestrin 24 Fe, Microgestin Fe 1/20, Minastrin 24 Fe*
203	Apixaban	*Eliquis*
204	Oxcarbazepine	*Trileptal*

Prescription Top-Sellers Continued

RANK	DRUG	BRAND NAME
205	Erythromycin	*E.E.S. 400, E.E.S. Granules, EryPed 200*
206	Brompheniramine/ Pseudoephedrine/ Dextromethorphan (Syrup)	*Bromfed DM*
207	Cefuroxime	*Ceftin*
208	Ketorolac (Ophthalmic)	*Acular, Acular LS, Acuvail*
209	Carbidopa/Levodopa	*Sinemet*
210	Metoclopramide	*Reglan*
211	Progesterone	*Prometrium*
212	Amiodarone	*Cordarone, Pacerone*
213	Hydromorphone	*Dilaudid, Exalgo*
214	Labetalol	
215	Digoxin	*Digitek, Digox, Lanoxin*
216	Insulin Lispro (Injection)	*Humalog*
217	Benztropine	*Cogentin*
218	Pramipexole	*Mirapex*
219	Irbesartan	*Avapro*
220	Terbinafine (Topical)	*Lamisil, Terbinex*
221	Terazosin	
222	Methadone	*Dolophine, Methadose*
223	Polymyxin B/Trimethoprim (Ophthalmic)	*Polytrim*
224	Zolpidem ER	*Ambien CR*
225	Tretinoin (Topical)	*Atralin, Renova, Retin-A*
226	Omega-3 Fatty Acids	*Lovaza, Vascepa*
227	Cyclosporine (Ophthalmic)	*Restasis*
228	Insulin Aspart (Injection)	*Novolog*
229	Neomycin/Polymyxin B/ Hydrocortisone (Topical)	*Cortisporin*
230	Testosterone (Topical Gel)	*AndroGel*
231	Doxycycline monohydrate	*Adoxa, Mondoxyine NL*
232	Insulin Lispro (Pen-Injector)	*Humalog KwikPen*
233	Lidocaine, Topical Solution (Viscous)	
234	Bimatoprost (Ophthalmic)	*Lumigan:* Glaucoma, *Latisse:* Eyelash Growth
235	Eszopiclone	*Lunesta*
236	Epinephrine (Injection)	*EpiPen, EpiPen Jr, Adrenaclick*
237	Olmesartan/HCTZ	*Benicar HCT*
238	Solifenacin	*VESIcare*
239	Albuterol/Ipratropium (Oral Inhaler)	*Combivent Respimat*
240	Indomethacin	*Indocin*
241	Olopatadine (Nasal Inhaler, Ophthalmic)	Nasal: *Patanase,* Ophthalmic: *Pataday, Patanol*
242	Estrogens, Conjugated	*Premarin*
243	Fluocinonide (Topical Cream, Gel, Ointment, Solution)	*Vanos*
244	Sitagliptin/Metformin	*Janumet*
245	Anastrozole	*Arimidex*
246	Sucralfate	*Carafate*
247	Bisoprolol/HCTZ	*Ziac*
248	Venlafaxine IR	*Effexor*
249	Prednisolone, base (Oral Tablet, Solution, Syrup)	*Millipred*
250	Dexamethasone	*DexPak*
251	Phenobarbital	
252	Ipratropium Bromide (Oral Inhaler)	*Atrovent HFA*

Prescription Top-Sellers Continued

RANK	DRUG	BRAND NAME
253	Quinapril	*Accupril*
254	Budesonide (Oral Inhaler)	*Pulmicort, Pulmicort Flexhaler*
255	Travoprost (Ophthalmic)	*Travatan Z*
256	Desvenlafaxine	*Pristiq*
257	Timolol/Dorzolamide (Ophthalmic)	*Cosopt, Cosopt PF*
258	Estradiol (Transdermal Patch)	*Alora, Climara, Menostar, Minivelle, Vivelle-Dot*
259	Mometasone/Formoterol (Oral Inhaler)	*Dulera*
260	Guanfacine	*Intuniv:* ADHD, *Tenex:* Hypertension
261	Phenytoin XR	
262	Doxepin	*Silenor*
263	Atomoxetine	*Strattera*
264	Ciprofloxacin/Dexamethasone (Otic)	*Ciprodex*

RANK	DRUG	BRAND NAME
265	Clarithromycin	*Biaxin*
266	Pneumococcal Conjugate Vaccine,13-Valent (Injection)	*Prevnar 13*
267	Sodium/Potassium/ Magnesium Sulfate	*Suprep Bowel Prep Kit*
268	Nabumetone	
269	Varenicline	*Chantix*
270	Diphenoxylate/Atropine	*Lomotil*
271	Bupropion IR	*Wellbutrin*
272	Buprenorphine (Buccal Film/ Patch)	Buccal Film: *Belbuca*, Patch: *Butrans*
273	Colchicine	*Colcrys*
274	Atenolol/Chlorthalidone	*Tenoretic*
275	Liraglutide (Injection)	*Victoza, Saxenda*

RxPrep thanks IMS Health and Mr. Robert Hunkler for providing this list to aid the students.

COMMON MEDICAL ABBREVIATIONS

ABBREVIATION	MEANING
AAA	Abdominal Aortic Aneurysm
A&O	Alert & Oriented
ABG	Arterial Blood Gas
ac	Before Meals
ACE	Angiotensin Converting Enzyme
ACIP	Advisory Committee on Immunization Practices
ACOG	American Congress of Obstetricians and Gynecologists
ACS	Acute Coronary Syndrome
ACTH	Adrenocorticotropic Hormone
ad	Right Ear
ADH	Anti-Diuretic Hormone
ADR	Adverse Drug Reaction
ADT	Alternate Day Therapy
AF	Atrial Fibrillation, or A.Fib.
AGEP	Acute Generalized Exanthematous Pustulosis

ABBREVIATION	MEANING
AIN	Acute Interstitial Nephritis
ALT	Alanine Aminotransferase
ANA	Antinuclear Antibody
ANC	Absolute Neutrophil Count
ANS	Autonomic Nervous System
APTT	Activated Partial Thromboplastin Time
ARB	Angiotensin Receptor Blocker
ARDS	Acute Respiratory Distress Syndrome
ARF	Acute Renal Failure
as	Left Ear
ASCVD	Atherosclerotic Cardiovascular Disease
AST	Aspartate Aminotransferase
ATC	Around the Clock
ATN	Acute Tubular Necrosis
au	Each Ear

Common Medical Abbreviations Continued

ABBREVIATION	MEANING
AVP	Arginine Vasopressin
BEE	Basal Energy Expenditure
BID	Twice a Day
BIW	Two Times Per Week
BM	Bowel Movement
BMI	Body Mass Index
BMP	Basic Metabolic Panel
BP	Blood Pressure
BPH	Benign Prostatic Hypertrophy
BPM	Beats Per Minute, Breaths Per Minute
BUN	Blood Urea Nitrogen
C or w/	With
C-I, C-II, C-III, C-IV, C-V	Refers to Controlled Drug Categories
C&S	Culture and Sensitivity
C/O	Complaining of
CA	Cancer
CABG	Coronary Artery Bypass Graft
CAD	Coronary Artery Disease
cAMP	Cyclic Adenosine Monophosphate
CA-MRSA	Community-Acquired MRSA
CAPES	*Citrobacter, Acinetobacter, Providencia, Enterobacter, Serratia*
CBC	Complete Blood Count
CC	Chief Complaint
CCB	Calcium Channel Blocker
CD	Crohn's Disease
CDI	C. *difficile* infection
CF	Cystic Fibrosis
CH	Cholesterol
CHF	Congestive Heart Failure
CI	Cardiac Index, Contraindicated
CMV	*Cytomegalovirus*
CNS	Central Nervous System
CO	Cardiac Output
COPD	Chronic Obstructive Pulmonary Disease
CP	Chest Pain or Cerebral Palsy
CPAP	Continuous Positive Airway Pressure
CPK	Creatine Phosphokinase
CPR	Cardiopulmonary Resuscitation
CrCl	Creatinine Clearance

ABBREVIATION	MEANING
CRE	Carbapenem-Resistant *Enterobacteriaceae*
CRF	Chronic Renal Failure
CRP	C-reactive Protein
CSF	Cerebrospinal Fluid
CT	Computerized Tomography
CV	Cardiovascular
CVA	Cerebrovascular Accident
CVP	Central Venous Pressure
CXR	Chest X-Ray
D1	Dopamine 1 Receptor
D2	Dopamine 2 Receptor
D/C	Discontinue or Discharge
D5W	5% Dextrose in Water
DDIs	Drug-Drug Interactions
DHP CCB	Dihydropyridine Calcium Channel Blockers
DJD	Degenerative Joint Disease (Osteoarthritis)
DKA	Diabetic Ketoacidosis
DM	Diabetes Mellitus
DOC	Drug of Choice
DOE	Dyspnea on Exertion
DPI	Dry Powder Inhaler
DRESS	Drug Reaction with Eosinophilia and Systemic Symptoms
dtd	Of Such Doses
DVT	Deep Venous Thrombosis
Dx	Diagnosis
EC	Enteric Coated
ECG	Electrocardiogram
EIAD	Extended-Interval Aminoglycoside Dosing (PK chapter)
ESBL	*Extended Spectrum Beta Lactamases*
ESR	Erythrocyte Sedimentation Rate
ESRD	End Stage Renal Disease
ETOH	Ethanol
F/U	Follow-Up
FBS	Fasting Blood Sugar
FDA	Food and Drug Administration
FEV1	Forced Expiratory Volume in 1 second
FT4	Free Thyroxine (T4)
GFR	Glomerular Filtration Rate

Common Medical Abbreviations Continued

ABBREVIATION	MEANING
GI	Gastrointestinal
GNR	Gram Negative Rod
gtt, gtts	Drop, Drops
GTT	Glucose Tolerance Test
H/O	History of
HA	Headache
HACEK	*Haemophilus, Actinobacillus, Cardiobacterium, Eikenella, Kingella*
HBV	Hepatitis B Virus
HCG	Human Chorionic Gonadotropin
HCT	Hematocrit
HCTZ, HCT	Hydrochlorothiazide
HCV	Hepatitis C Virus
HDL, HDL-C	High Density Lipoprotein
HF	Heart Failure
HFrEF	Heart Failure with Reduced Ejection Fraction
HFpEF	Heart Failure with Preserved Ejection Fraction
Hgb	Hemoglobin
HIV	Human Immunodeficiency Virus
HJR	Hepatojugular Reflex
HNPEK	*Haemophilus influenzae, Neisseria spp, Proteus mirabilis, E. coli, Klebsiella pneumonia*
HPI	History of Present Illness
HR	Heart Rate
HS	At Bedtime
HSV	Herpes Simplex Virus
HTN	Hypertension
HUS/TTP	Hemolytic-Uremic Syndrome and Thrombotic Thrombocytopenic Purpura
Hx	History
I&O	Intake and Output, Input and Output
IBD	Inflammatory Bowel Disease
IBS	Irritable Bowel Syndrome
IBW	Ideal Body Weight
ICU	Intensive Care Unit
ID	Intradermal
IE	Infective Endocarditis
IHD	Ischemic Heart Disease
IM	Intramuscular
Inj	Injection

ABBREVIATION	MEANING
INR	International Normalized Ratio
IV	Intravenous
IVP	Intravenous Push
IVPB	Intravenous Piggyback
LD	Loading Dose
LDH	Lactate Dehydrogenase
LDL, LDL-C	Low-Density Lipoprotein
LFTs	Liver Function Tests
LLSB	Left Lower Sternal Border
LVH	Left Ventricular Hypertrophy
M. ft.	Mix and Make
MAO	Monoamine Oxidase
MAO Inhibitor	Monoamine Oxidase Inhibitor
MAP	Mean Arterial Pressure
MCH	Mean Cell Hemoglobin
MCHC	Mean Cell Hemoglobin Concentration
MCV	Mean Corpuscular Volume
MD	Maintenance Dose
MDI	Metered-Dose Inhaler
MDR	Multidrug-Resistant
MI	Myocardial Infarction
MIC	Minimum Inhibitory Concentration
mL	Milliliter
mPAP	Mean Pulmonary Artery Pressure
MRI	Magnetic Resonance Imaging
MRSA	Methicillin-Resistant *Staphylococcus Aureus*
MS	Multiple Sclerosis (Do not use this abbreviation for Morphine Sulfate – potential med error)
MSSA	Methicillin-Sensitive *Staphylococcus Aureus*
MVA	Motor Vehicle Accident
MVI	Multivitamin Injection
NTE	Not to Exceed
N/V, N&V	Nausea and Vomiting
N/V/D	Nausea, Vomiting, Diarrhea
NG	Nasogastric
NKA	No Known Allergies
NKDA	No Known Drug Allergies

Common Medical Abbreviations Continued

ABBREVIATION	MEANING
NOAC	New Oral Anticoagulant
Non-DHP	Non-Dihydropyridine Calcium Channel Blockers
NPO	Nothing By Mouth
NR	No Refills
NRT	Nicotine Replacement Therapy
NSAIDs	Nonsteroidal Anti-Inflammatory Drugs
NSR	Normal Sinus Rhythm
NTG	Nitroglycerin
OD	Right Eye
ODT	Orally Disintegrating Tablet
OROS	Osmotic Release Delivery System
OS	Left Eye
OTC	Over-The-Counter
OU	Each Eye
P-gp	P-glycoprotein
PAP	Pulmonary Artery Pressure
pc	After Meals
PCC	Prothrombin Complex Concentrate
PCI	Percutaneous Coronary Intervention
PCN	Penicillin
PCOS	Polycystic Ovary Syndrome
PCV13	Pneumococcal conjugate vaccine (13-valent)
PCWP	Pulmonary Capillary Wedge Pressure
PE	Pulmonary Embolus or Physical Exam
PEK	*Proteus mirabilis, E. coli, Klebsiella pneumonia*
PKU	Phenylketonuria
PMH	Past Medical History
PO	By mouth, Oral
PPD	Purified Protein Derivative
PPI	Proton Pump Inhibitor
PPSV23	Pneumococcal Polysaccharide Valent (23-valent)
PRBC	Packed Red Blood Cells
PR	Per Rectum
PRN	As Needed
PT	Prothrombin Time or Physical Therapy

ABBREVIATION	MEANING
Pt	Patient
PTCA	Percutaneous Transluminal Coronary Angioplasty
PTH	Parathyroid Hormone
PUD	Peptic Ulcer Disease
PVC	Polyvinyl Chloride
Q	Every
QD	Every Day
QID	Four Times a Day
QOD	Every Other Day
QS	Sufficient Quantity
QS AD	A Sufficient Quantity to Make
R/O	Rule Out
RA	Rheumatoid Arthritis
RASS	Richmond Agitation and Sedation Scale
RBC	Red Blood Cell
RML	Right Middle Lobe
ROS	Review of Systems
RSI	Rapid Sequence Intubation
RSV	Respiratory Syncytial Virus
Rx	Prescription
rxn	Reaction
S or w/o	Without
S/P	Status Post
SCr	Serum Creatinine
SIADH	Syndrome of Inappropriate Antidiuretic Hormone
SIG	Write on Label
SJS	Stevens Johnson Syndrome
SL	Sublingual
SLE	Systemic Lupus Erythematous
SOAP	Subjective, Objective, Assessment, Plan
SOB	Shortness of Breath
SC, SQ, subc, subq	Subcutaneous
Spp.	Species

Common Medical Abbreviations Continued

ABBREVIATION	MEANING
ss	One-half
S/Sx	Signs and Symptoms
SSTI	Skin and Soft-Tissue Infection or Skin and Skin-Structure Infection
STAT	Immediately
STD	Sexually Transmitted Disease
STI	Sexually Transmitted Infection
Supp, sup	Suppository
SVR	Systemic Vascular Resistance
Sx	Symptoms
TB	Tuberculosis
TC	Total Cholesterol
TdP	Torsade de Pointes
TEG	Thromboelastography
TEN	Toxic Epidermal Necrolysis
TG	Triglycerides
TIA	Transient Ischemic Attack
TIBC	Total Iron Binding Capacity
TID	Three Times a Day
TIW	Three Times Per Week
TOP	Topically
TPN	Total Parenteral Nutrition
TSH	Thyroid Stimulating Hormone

ABBREVIATION	MEANING
TTP	Thrombotic Thrombocytopenic Purpura
TBW	Total Body Weight
Tx	Treatment
UA	Urinalysis
UC	Ulcerative Colitis
UFH	Unfractionated Heparin
ULN	Upper Limit of Normal
UNG	Ointment
URTI	Upper Respiratory Tract Infection
UTI	Urinary Tract Infection
V1	Vasopressin 1 Receptor
V2	Vasopressin 2 Receptor
VF	Ventricular Fibrillation
VRE	Vancomycin-Resistant Enterococcus
VT	Ventricular Tachycardia
WA	While Awake
WBC	White Blood Cells
WNL	Within Normal Limits
WPW	Wolff-Parkinson-White Syndrome
x	Times
y/o	Years Old
yr	Year

Meanings of abbreviations may vary. Not all of these abbreviations are considered safe, but all are used outpatient. In hospital settings, avoid unapproved abbreviations (See Medication Safety & Quality Improvement chapter).

80

INDEX

B

C

D

G

H

I

N

O

P

Q

R

U

V

W

X

Y

Z

NOTES

NOTES

NOTES

NOTES

NOTES

NOTES

NOTES